International Series in Operations Research & Management Science

Volume 315

The book series **International Series in Operations Research and Management Science** encompasses the various areas of operations research and management science. Both theoretical and applied books are included. It describes current advances anywhere in the world that are at the cutting edge of the field. The series is aimed especially at researchers, advanced graduate students, and sophisticated practitioners.

The series features three types of books:

- Advanced expository books that extend and unify our understanding of particular areas.
- Research monographs that make substantial contributions to knowledge.
- Handbooks that define the new state of the art in particular areas. Each handbook will be edited by a leading authority in the area who will organize a team of experts on various aspects of the topic to write individual chapters. A handbook may emphasize expository surveys or completely new advances (either research or applications) or a combination of both.

The series emphasizes the following four areas:

Mathematical Programming : Including linear programming, integer programming, nonlinear programming, interior point methods, game theory, network optimization models, combinatorics, equilibrium programming, complementarity theory, multiobjective optimization, dynamic programming, stochastic programming, complexity theory, etc.

Applied Probability: Including queuing theory, simulation, renewal theory, Brownian motion and diffusion processes, decision analysis, Markov decision processes, reliability theory, forecasting, other stochastic processes motivated by applications, etc.

Production and Operations Management: Including inventory theory, production scheduling, capacity planning, facility location, supply chain management, distribution systems, materials requirements planning, just-in-time systems, flexible manufacturing systems, design of production lines, logistical planning, strategic issues, etc.

Applications of Operations Research and Management Science: Including telecommunications, health care, capital budgeting and finance, economics, marketing, public policy, military operations research, humanitarian relief and disaster mitigation, service operations, transportation systems, etc.

This book series is indexed in Scopus.

More information about this series at https://link.springer.com/bookseries/6161

Jesús T. Pastor • Juan Aparicio • José L. Zofío

Benchmarking Economic Efficiency

Technical and Allocative Fundamentals

Springer

Jesús T. Pastor
Center of Operations Research (CIO)
Universidad Miguel Hernandez de Elche
Elche, Alicante, Spain

Juan Aparicio
Center of Operations Research (CIO)
Universidad Miguel Hernandez de Elche
Elche, Alicante, Spain

José L. Zofío
Department of Economics
Universidad Autónoma de Madrid
Madrid, Spain

ISSN 0884-8289 ISSN 2214-7934 (electronic)
International Series in Operations Research & Management Science
ISBN 978-3-030-84396-0 ISBN 978-3-030-84397-7 (eBook)
https://doi.org/10.1007/978-3-030-84397-7

This Springer imprint is published by the registered company Springer Nature Switzerland AG
The registered company address is: Gewerbestrasse 11, 6330 Cham, Switzerland

To Alberto, Irene, Dieguito, and Blanca,
Diego, Alba, and Teseo, and Mercedes.

To Julia, Aitana, Hugo, and Marta

To Irene, Silvia, and Paula

Preface

This book is the result of the theoretical and empirical research that the authors have undertaken throughout their careers on the topic of economic and productive efficiency measurement. This has been a recursive research topic since the last quarter of the twentieth century, which started with Michael Farrell's seminal work on decomposing economic efficiency according to technical and allocative criteria. Our text offers a comprehensive account of the microeconomic foundations of the decomposition of cost, revenue, profitability, and profit efficiency using a wide range of technical efficiency models that result in distinct multiplicative and additive approaches.

The guiding framework is that of duality theory, relating the equivalent representation of firms' behavior either through the production technology or the aforementioned economic functions. This theoretical construction relates a (dual) representation of the economic behavior of the firm in terms of a supporting function with a (primal) characterization on the production technology. Under the assumption of producers behaving as price takers, their technologies could be equivalently described by dual cost, revenue, profitability, or profit functions. This simply states that thanks to duality theory we can mathematically recover the primal and dual representations of firms' behavior from each other, provided that some axioms or assumptions are satisfied, that is, regularity conditions, for example, convexity. As firms produce multiple outputs using multiple inputs, the primal representation of the technology relies on the technical efficiency concept, or, more generally, the mathematical notion of distance function. In a production context, duality has witnessed a revival in business economics as it represents the essential cornerstone in the benchmarking of firms through frontier analysis. The idea can be summarized in a simple way. Economic efficiency is defined as the gap between a maximum attainable economic goal and that which is actually achieved by a firm under evaluation (e.g., maximum profit versus observed profit), and this difference can be attributed to technical inefficiencies related to engineering shortcomings (in the quantity space) and allocative inefficiency related to market mismanagement practices (including the price space). Duality theory allows to decompose economic inefficiency in these two mutually exclusive components and thereby identify the sources of a suboptimal economic behavior. In the benchmarking process, it provides guidance for understanding what is wrong within the firm when compared to its competitors. Moreover, the existence of many dual relationships between particular distance functions (input, output, generalized, directional, Hölder) and their supporting economic functions (cost, revenue, profit and profitability) offers the researcher the possibility of choosing which perspective of the firm is best suited for the analysis, depending on the specificities of the study at hand.

In this text, we are not only concerned about the theoretical underpinnings of economic efficiency, but we also pay attention to the practical side of efficiency measurement. With this aim in mind, we present, and introduce when necessary, the different formulations that allow implementing the different models through mathematical programming techniques known as data envelopment analysis (DEA). We present the optimization programs that solve both the classic and the new models. We illustrate the different models with straightforward examples and a real-life common dataset. This allows us to show that results vary depending on the specific model chosen by the analyst and that different answers to the benchmarking exercise may be obtained depending on the alternative characterizations of the economic goal and the technology. For example, whether the distance function can capture individual inefficiencies related to particular inputs or outputs (e.g., additive versus multiplicative models), how the reference efficient subset on the technological frontier is defined in terms of returns to scale, and the existence of strong or weak disposability. For each distance function definition and its associated economic efficiency DEA model, we discuss its relative pros and cons in terms of their economic interpretation, flexibility, and ability to capture all sources of (in)efficiency.

Moreover, the different examples and empirical applications are solved using a set of functions coded in the suitable and open environment represented by the Julia language. This set of functions is available to practitioners in the form of a self-contained package, allowing them to undertake research on their own without having to program the models by themselves. Practitioners can edit and change the specific functions, adapting the code according to their needs. The software is open source and is freely available at its dedicated site: www.benchmarkingeconomicefficiency.com. For most of the models it relies on linear optimization, but it also makes use of advanced computational methods of non-linear programming, including, among others, second-order cone programming (SOCP) and quadratic optimization methods linked to the use of special ordered sets (SOS). Using this toolbox and a collection of specific Jupiter notebooks associated with each chapter, we illustrate the practice of economic efficiency measurement following a step-by-step approach. This allows us to illustrate how different models lead to alternative decompositions of economic efficiency. Ultimately, our goal is to provide guidance on the best alternatives by taking into consideration the set of desirable properties that economic efficiency models should satisfy.

Most of the chapters draw from publications by the authors in field journals at the intersection of management science, economics, and operations research: *Omega-*

The International Journal of Management Science, *European Journal of Operational Research*, *Journal of Optimization Theory and Applications*, *Journal of Productivity Analysis*, *Economic Theory*, and *Journal of the Operational Research Society*, among others. In each of these chapters, we present a particular model of interest, including the details of the mathematical proofs and relevant examples that highlight its characteristics and how it compares to previous proposals in the literature. We are grateful to successive area editors that have promoted and managed the publications of relevant chapters in the field over the years, including Robert Dyson, Joe Zhu, William Greene, Robin Sickles, Knox Lovell, and many others. We have also benefited from regular conference meetings such as the *European Workshop on Efficiency and Productivity Analysis* and the *North American Productivity Workshop*, organized thanks to efforts of many members of its current partner society, the International Society for Efficiency and Productivity Analysis (ISEPA). We are grateful to participants at these conferences as well as to attendees at several workshops and seminars worldwide where we have presented the models included in the book.

We are intellectually indebted to the innovators whose contributions have been a constant guidance and source of inspiration to our research. Besides Farrell's original contribution, we have also been influenced by the work of Gérard Debreu, Tjalling Koopmans, and Ronald Shephard in the field of economics, and Abraham Charnes and William Cooper in the area of operations research. Authors whose studies encouraged later developments by many other scholars are intellectually responsible for the thriving state of the discipline. Our book is also intended to continue the path marked by both classic and authoritative texts on production economics, duality theory, and economic efficiency. In the 1970s, these were represented by the second volume of the series Frontiers of Quantitative Economics, edited by Michael Intriligator and David Kendrick—particularly the chapter by Erwin Diewert, as well as Daniel McFadden's book, along with Melvin Fuss, *Production Economics: A Dual Approach to Theory and Applications*. In the 1980s, the *Measurement of Efficiency of Production* by Rolf Färe, Shawna Grosskopf, and C. A. Knox Lovell, who quite surprisingly made no reference to duality theory, and the more accessible text *Applied Production Analysis: A Dual Approach*, by Robert Chambers. In the 1990s, the concise *Multi-Output Production and Duality* by Rolf Färe and Daniel Primont ably summarized the state of the art on economic efficiency measurement based on duality theory, while Bert Balk followed suit focusing on index number theory with his *Industrial Price*, *Quantity, and Productivity Indices*. These contributions constitute a clear timeline in the discipline of economic efficiency measurement, which we intend to bring up to date with the latest research in the field. The references included in the bibliography bear witness of the exponential growth of interest that these methods have drawn among scholars, researchers, and practitioners in the field.

Our work has benefited from these and other outstanding personalities in the area, some of which we mention again now as coauthors to whom we owe stimulus and motivation. It has been a pleasure to collaborate with them throughout the years. In particular Bert Balk, William Cooper, Knox Lovell, Subhash Ray, and Joe Zhu. The association with these authors has resulted in the edition of two relevant volumes, entitled *Advances in Efficiency and Productivity*, published in 2016 and 2020 by Springer Nature in its International Series in Operations Research & Management Science. Many ideas presented in the chapters of these books have a direct relation with our text, and we are grateful to the authors for their contributions.

On the Spanish side, it would not have been possible to complete the book without the constant support and understanding of our colleagues from the Center for Operations Research at Miguel Hernandez University of Elche (Alicante), and from the Economics Department at Universidad Autónoma de Madrid. Among former students, who are now outstanding colleagues, we would like to acknowledge Javier Barbero, currently economic analyst at the Directorate for Growth & Innovation in the European Commission-Joint Research Centre (JRC), for providing constant and invaluable support in the computational implementation of the models, as well as for compiling the set of functions in *Julia,* accompanying the book.

We thank Joe Zhu as area editor of Springer Nature's International Series in Operations Research & Management Science for his continuous support, patience, and understanding. We are also grateful to Matthew Amboy as the original senior editor for business and economics, as well as Maria David, the designated manager for this project. The authors thank the financial support from the Spanish Ministry of Science and Innovation and the State Research Agency under grant PID2019-105952GB-I00/ AEI / 10.13039/501100011033. J. L. Zofío also thanks the support from the Spanish Ministry of Science and Innovation and the State Research Agency under grant EIN2020-112260. Additionally, we acknowledge continuous support from the Spanish State Research Agency under several successive grants (MTM2013-43903-P, MTM2016-79765-P).

Last but not least, a few words of gratitude and encouragement to our readers interested in the measurement and decomposition of economic efficiency. At the time of writing the book, we intended it to be as accessible as possible for non-experts, so we included material covering the basics of the discipline. However, after the initial chapters devoted to this purpose, we delve into the most recent and advanced results offered in this active area of the efficiency and productivity literature. We also provide notebooks to solve the common examples aimed at facilitating the use of the accompanying software, so readers can undertake economic efficiency analysis on their own. In this respect, we thank you in anticipation for any comments or suggestions aimed at improving the text, the "hardware" of this project, as well as the software and learning material accompanying it.

Elche, Alicante, Spain — Jesús T. Pastor
Juan Aparicio
Madrid, Spain — José L. Zofío

Contents

List of Figures

List of Tables

About the Authors

Jesús T. Pastor is a professor of statistics and operations research at the Universidad Miguel Hernandez of Elche, Spain. He earned an MBA and a PhD in mathematical sciences from Valencia University, Spain. He has been visiting researcher at the Universities of Georgia (USA), Toronto (Canada), Queensland (Australia), and Warwick (UK). Prof. Pastor's research fields include location science, banking, and, for the last 25 years, efficiency analysis. He has served on the editorial review or advisory board of more than 20 international journals. He has been guest editor of one issue of European Journal of Operational Research (*EJOR*) and of two issues of Journal of Productivity Analysis (*JPA*). He has authored or co-authored 9 books in various fields of mathematics and has published over 150 research papers. His research has appeared in a wide variety of refereed top economic and operations research journals. In 2013, the Spanish Scientists Association accredited Prof. Pastor as one of the three distinguished scientists of the year. Lastly, in 2020, he was appointed by his University as Professor Emeritus.

Juan Aparicio is a professor in the Department of Statistics, Mathematics and Information Technology at the Miguel Hernandez University of Elche (UMH), Spain, and the head of the Center of Operations Research. He has been co-chair (with Prof. Knox Lovell) of the Santander Chair on Efficiency and Productivity. His research interest includes efficiency and productivity analysis combined with machine learning and data science. He has published and co-edited several books focusing on performance evaluation and benchmarking using data envelopment analysis, as well as publishing approximately 100 scientific articles in different international journals. He is associate editor of *Omega—The International Journal of Management Science*, *Journal of Productivity Analysis*, *Mathematics*, and *Advances in Operations Research*.

José Luis Zofío (www.joselzofio.net) is a professor of economics at the Universidad Autónoma de Madrid, and former chair of the Department of Economics. He is also visiting professor at Erasmus University and Wageningen University and Research, and visiting fellow to the Erasmus Research Institute of Management

ERIM, where he collaborates with several academics from the Rotterdam School of Management. His research interests are related to measurement theory in economics, in particular the use of index numbers for efficiency and productivity analysis, as well as spatial economics and trade theory. From an empirical perspective, he undertakes multidisciplinary research, publishing numerous articles in top fields journals and book chapters related to environmental economics, transportation, innovation, and regional science. Finally, he has made several contributions in the field computational economics, with several packages for Matlab and Julia that focus on data envelopment analysis and regression methods.

Chapter 1
Introduction

1.1 The Elements of Economic Efficiency Analysis: Markets, Management, and Production

It goes without saying that firms are for profit organizations whose main goal is to maximize the difference between the revenues they generate by selling goods and the cost they incur when acquiring their production factors. Firms' management is accountable to a wide range of stakeholders, both private and public, including shareowners, workers, customers, and governments. Although firms and other organizations might have alternative complementary goals, for example, by adopting corporate socially responsible practices, in market-oriented economies, the onus is on the managers to ensure that firms perform satisfactorily and, ultimately, can survive in competitive and ever-changing environments. Under the assumption of perfectly competitive markets, including many sellers and buyers, homogenous products, free entry and exit, and perfect information, firms do not have market power and take prices as exogenously given. Consequently, when aiming at profit maximization, their only decision variables are quantities, deciding on the amount of outputs to supply and inputs to demand.

Within this framework, the objective and scope of the book are to unify and extend the state of the art in the field of defining and measuring economic efficiency and its use as a real-life benchmarking technique for firms. We are convinced that Benchmarking Economic Efficiency in the way that it is presented in this book is a valuable tool for organizations in general. It represents a systematic way of evaluating their performance in comparison with those of their competitors and therefore contributes with relevant quantity and price indicators that can complement popular financial measures such as return on assets (ROA) and inform strategies aimed at identifying managerial strengths, weaknesses, opportunities, and threats (SWOT). It can be also used as a monitoring tool to raise awareness about internal and external processes. Internally, it provides objective information on the relative performance

J. T. Pastor et al., *Benchmarking Economic Efficiency*, International Series in Operations Research & Management Science 315,
https://doi.org/10.1007/978-3-030-84397-7_1

of individual units (branches, sales force, etc.) that allows a better allocation of incentives. Externally, it helps identify areas in which the firm lags its competitors, with the aim of taking action to improve its position (e.g., failing to adopt new technologies, growing market niches that may be overlooked).

A key feature of economic efficiency analysis is that it can be distinctly related to managerial and engineering practices, which can be incorporated to any workflow process aimed at improving performance. The optimal allocation of resources and production within firms is driven by input and output market characteristics. A profit-maximizing firm takes particular care in supplying the optimal amounts of outputs while demanding the corresponding amounts of the required inputs. This involves an efficient use of the available technology, with engineering competence preventing inefficiencies (avoiding sloth and slack), coupled with the right choice (mix) of input and output quantities given their relative prices, which ensures an allocative efficient behavior. Within the firm, managers must ensure that their accountancy and finance department can provide support and coordinate other areas such as sales, marketing, purchasing, human resources, and production, so they work in harmony and facilitate the achievement of maximum profit. Arguably, this organizational function is the characterizing feature of the members of an executive board, entrusted with the responsibility of supervising the activities of the firm and being accountable for its performance.

As economic efficiency analysis is based on both managerial and engineering dimensions, it should come as no surprise that it can be indistinctly addressed by academics, practitioners and consultants coming from the fields of business economics and technical sciences. While the former normally rely on economics and management science to guide their research questions and methods, the latter focus mainly on process measurement and improvement strategies, pertaining to the field of operations research. Indeed, when market decisions are involved, prices are key to the analysis, and we are in the realm of business and economics. Here, the sales and marketing department is key because they are knowledgeable on customer requirements, preferences, and needs. They can help translate customer demand into product specifications, which are key to production. Based on alternative market segmentations, these definitions may include different qualities, package sizes, color choices, feature modifications, and even shifts to new product lines. In this respect, the sales and marketing department is responsible for product definition and set production quotas. They can help estimate production capacity and guide the timing and quantity requirements of production. Ultimately, they are responsible for revenue maximization through optimal pricing strategies.

Conversely, if the optimization of production processes and physical operations is the main driver (e.g., production, logistics, supply chain), then engineering methods and practices prevail. For example, the production department is responsible for converting raw materials and other inputs into finished goods or services. In between the processes of production, the department works to improve the efficiency of the manufacturing plant or assembly line so that it can meet the output targets or quotas set by company management and ensure finished products offer consumers the best value and quality. Seamless production scheduling can save costs by reducing waste.

It is responsible for minimizing costs, ensuring product quality, and improving existing products and services.

In general, however, as previously argued, the managerial and engineering dimensions are intertwined within the firm. Profit maximization is achieved from both the revenue and cost dimensions, and therefore, market and engineering aspects must be jointly managed. This implies that the assessment of firms' performance must be undertaken not only from a technical perspective, by checking whether they can produce without incurring in input excesses or output shortfalls, but also from an allocative viewpoint, summarized by their capacity to supply and demand the profit-maximizing amounts of inputs and outputs. Eventually, it is the ability to consistently abide by the rationality underlying optimal economic behavior, what determines firms' long-term survival in the market.

This book relies on both approaches. On one hand, it resorts to economic theory to theoretically define the duality relationships that allow a consistent decomposition of economic efficiency into technical and allocative terms while resorting to Operations Research and Management Science (OR&MS) programing techniques, generically known as Data Envelopment Analysis (DEA), to illustrate its empirical implementation. The book stands in the middle ground between business economics and management science, with operations research constituting the tool that enables empirical analyses.

From a theoretical perspective, it relies on the economic theory of duality as the analytical guiding framework (Shephard, 1953, 1970). This framework relates a (dual) representation of the economic behavior of the firm in terms of cost, revenue, profit, and profitability functions, with a (primal) characterization of the production technology. As firms produce multiple outputs using multiple inputs, the primal representation of the technology relies on the mathematical concept of distance function, which is also interpreted as a measure of technical performance. Duality theory, which allows a firm's primal and dual representations to be recovered – provided several axioms or assumptions are satisfied – has witnessed a revival in economics and management science. The increasing number of publications bears witness of its importance as a cornerstone in the benchmarking of firms through frontier analysis. In fact, the existence of several dual relationships between the specific distance functions (e.g., input, output, generalized, or directional) and their supporting economic functions (cost, revenue, profitability, and profit) offers the researcher the possibility of choosing the perspective of the firm that is best suited for the analysis.

From an empirical perspective, the book shows how the alternative theoretical models can be implemented by way of DEA, first proposed by Boles (1967) and popularized by Charnes et al. (1978). It presents and introduces, when necessary, the mathematical programs that solve classical and new models. We illustrate the different models with simple examples and with a real-life dataset of financial institutions, showing that results vary depending on the specific model chosen by the analyst. Moreover, the different examples and empirical applications are solved using a set of functions coded in the Julia language (Bezanson et al., 2017). In parallel to writing the book, we have programmed these routines, and in each chapter, we show how to solve and interpret representative models. The package constitutes a self-contained set of functions that can be edited by the interested reader since Julia is open source. The package is called "BenchmarkingEconomicEfficiency.jl," shortened to "BEE" throughout the text. It is referenced in the general registry of Julia by complying with the general publication requirements (documentation, build, and coverage). The package is a compilation of all the models studied in this book. To replicate the measurement and decomposition of economic efficiency using alternative models, we have written a set of Jupyter Notebooks that can be used interactively for instruction and self-learning purposes. Moreover, all the supplementary material (data, examples, and source code) necessary to replicate all the results reported in the book is available for downloading in the following website: http://www.benchmarkingeconomicefficiency.com.

1.2 Benchmarking Economic Performance: Multiplicative and Additive Approaches

Our objective is to present the different alternatives that researchers have at their disposal when measuring the economic efficiency of organizations and decompose it according to the aforementioned technical and allocative criteria. We guide researchers when choosing a specific economic model and the underlying technical efficiency measure, taking into consideration the desirable properties that they satisfy. Nevertheless, before we proceed with the specific models presented in the remainder of the book, we devote the following chapter to present the necessary background concepts, pertaining to the economic theory of firms' behavior. These concepts constitute the building blocks upon which the measurement of economic efficiency lies. We review the formal representation of technologies producing multiple outputs from multiple inputs and how it is possible to measure technical efficiency from an input, output, or graph dimension. We measure technical efficiency in the standard way that considers the possibility or reducing inputs and increasing outputs, except in Chap. 13, where the introduction of new approaches for decomposing economic inefficiency opens the possibility of accounting for input and output variations, unrestricted in sign.

The choice of a particular approach depends on the economic goal of the firm. In business economics, these possibilities are related to distinct objectives. From a partial perspective, firms aim at minimizing cost or maximizing revenue, taking outputs or inputs as given, respectively. When both the input and output dimensions are considered, firms' economic performance is represented in terms of profitability or profit maximization. To cater for all the aforementioned possibilities, we present the duality between economic functions and their associated technical efficiency measures, which ultimately enables a consistent decomposition of economic efficiency into technical efficiency and allocative efficiency.

Making use of the same information, economic efficiency can be defined and subsequently decomposed in a multiplicative or additive way. For a firm operating within an industry, mathematically represented by the vector (x_o, y_o), if we choose a cost-minimizing viewpoint, the multiplicative definition of cost efficiency corresponds to an index number formulated as the ratio of the minimum cost of producing output-level $y_o \in \mathbb{R}^N_+$, denoted as $C(y_o, w) = w \cdot x^C$ to observed cost $C_o = w \cdot x_o$, i.e., $CE(x_o, y_o, w) = C(y_o, w)/C_o = w \cdot x^C/w \cdot x_o \leq 1$.[1] Alternatively, the additive version of economic performance is an indicator that defines the difference between observed cost and minimum cost as $CI(x_o, y_o, w) = C_o - C(y_o, w) \geq 0$.[2] From a revenue-maximizing perspective, the multiplicative version of revenue efficiency is an index number of observed revenue to the maximum revenue attainable with input quantities $x_o \in \mathbb{R}^M_+$, $RE(x_o, y_o, p) = R_o/R(x_o, p) = p \cdot y/p \cdot y^R \leq 1$, while its additive version is maximum revenue less observed revenue: $RI(x_o, y_o, p) = R(x_o, p) - R_o = p \cdot y^R - p \cdot y \geq 0$.[3]

The selection of multiplicative or additive versions of economic efficiency subsequently restricts, through duality, the nature of the associated technical efficiency measure that may be employed to decompose it. If cost and revenue efficiencies are defined as multiplicative functions of quantities and prices, then a dual relationship can be respectively established with the generalized distance function (*GDF*) introduced by Chavas and Cox (1999), as studied in Chap. 4. The generalized distance function, defined as $D_G(x, y; \alpha) = \min \{\delta : (\delta^{1-\alpha} x, y/\delta^{\alpha}) \in T\}, 0 \leq \alpha \leq 1$, measures the distance to the production frontier of the technology T by contracting inputs and expanding outputs according to the bearing parameter α. When $\alpha = 0$, we reduce inputs while keeping outputs constant and vice versa when $\alpha = 1$. This shows that the *GDF* nests the traditional multiplicative approach initiated by Farrell (1957) as particular cases.[4] Based on this characterization of the technology, the *GDF* can be considered as a measure of technical efficiency, limited to the input and output dimension under the two previous cases: $D_{G(I)}(x_o, y_o; \alpha = 0)$ and $D_{G(O)}(x_o, y_o; \alpha = 1)$. A key result throughout the book is that, thanks to duality theory, we are able to recover the following relationships: $CE(x_o, y_o, w) \leq D_{G(I)}(x_o, y_o; \alpha = 0)$ and

---

[1] Minimum cost $C(y_o, w) = w \cdot x^C$ corresponds to the inner product between the vector of input prices $w \in \mathbb{R}^M_+$ and the vector of optimal input quantities minimizing cost $x^C \in \mathbb{R}^M_+$. Although the formal definition of these economic and technological concepts is postponed to Chap. 2, we make use in this introduction of the general notation and terminology used throughout the book.

[2] We reserve the term *efficiency* for multiplicative measures of economic efficiency whose value is bounded by one from above and the term *in*efficiency for additive measures which are bounded by zero from below.

[3] Maximum revenue $R(x_o, p) = p \cdot y^R$ corresponds to the inner product between the vector of output prices $p \in \mathbb{R}^N_+$ and the vector of optimal output quantities maximizing revenue $y^R \in \mathbb{R}^N_+$.

[4] As shown in Chap. 3, the approach initiated by Farrell (1957) can be equivalently expressed in terms of the input and output distance functions proposed by Shephard (1953, 1970).

$RE(x_o, y_o, p) \leq D_{G(O)}(x_o, y_o; \alpha = 1)$.[5] Relying on these inequalities, excess costs or foregone revenues can be ascribed to technical failures (measured by the *GDF*) times a residual that is interpreted as allocative efficiency: $CE(x_o, y_o, w) = D_{G(I)}(x_o, y_o; \alpha) \times AE_{G(I)}(x_o, y_o, w) \leq 1$, and $RE(x, y, p) = D_{G(O)}(x, y; \alpha) \times AE_{G(O)}(x, y, p) \leq 1$.

On the contrary, if cost and revenue inefficiencies are defined additively, then a direct duality can be established with additive technical efficiency measures. For example, as discussed in Chap. 8, this duality can be obtained in terms of the shortage function introduced by Luenberger (1992a, b), later popularized under the name of directional distance function (*DDF*) by Chambers et al. (1996, 1998). The *DDF* defines as $D_T(x, y; g_x, g_y) = \max \{\beta : (x - \beta g_x, y + \beta g_y) \in T\}$, $g = (g_x, g_y) \in \mathbb{R}_+^{M+N}$, measuring once again the distance to the production frontier of the technology T in the direction represented by (g_x, g_y). From the perspective of cost inefficiency measurement, duality allows to recover the following inequality: $CI_{DDF(I)}(x_o, y_o, w) \geq D_{T(I)}(x_o, y_o; g_x, 0)(w \cdot g_x)$, where the distance is determined in the direction set by the input vector g_x. The reason is that since we are moving in the input space, inputs are reduced while outputs remain constant, so the output directional vector is assigned a zero value, resulting in $g = (g_x, 0)$. Alternatively, considering revenue inefficiency, we obtain $RI_{DDF(O)}(x_o, y_o, p) \geq D_{T(O)}(x_o, y_o; 0, g_y)\ (p \cdot g_y)$, with $g = (0, g_y)$. Now, cost or revenue inefficiency can be decomposed into the input- or output-oriented *DDF* and an additive residual that, once again, is interpreted as allocative inefficiency. For example, following the input orientation, $NCI_{DDF(I)}(x_o, y_o, \widetilde{w}) = D_T(x_o, y_o; g_x, 0) + AI_{DDF(I)}(x_o, y_o, \widetilde{w}) \geq 0$. Correspondingly, revenue inefficiency can be decomposed as $NRI_{DDF(O)}(x_o, y_o, \widetilde{p}) = D_T(x_o, y_o; g_x, g_y) + RI_{DDF(O)}(x_o, y_o, \widetilde{p}) \geq 0$. Note that in these last expressions, cost and revenue inefficiencies are qualified with the *DDF* subscript, while prices are modified with the tilde sign "~."[6] The identification of the underlying efficiency measure explicitly denotes the specific normalization that the directional distance function $D_T(x, y; g_x, g_y)$ entails to yield a consistent decomposition based on duality theory. In these decompositions, dividing cost and revenue inefficiencies and their associated allocative inefficiency terms by the normalization factors $(w \cdot g_x)$ and $(p \cdot g_y)$, respectively, results in the normalization of these expressions through their prices, which are denoted by $\widetilde{w}$ and $\widetilde{p}$ (see Chap. 8).[7] The need to explicitly normalize the economic efficiency is specific to the

[5]These relations, known in the literature as Fenchel-Mahler inequalities, are particular applications of Minkowski's theorem, i.e., a closed convex set is the intersection of the half-spaces that support it.

[6]For calculating any normalized inefficiency, expressed in monetary units, we divide it by a normalizing factor that is also expressed in monetary units, ending up with an equality between pure numbers. However, if the prices change, the normalized measure of economic inefficiency also changes. Consequently, $\widetilde{p}$ shows that prices influence the value of the decomposition.

[7]Moreover, regarding the additive decomposition of economic performance based on the directional distance function, Chambers et al. (1998) named these measures *Nerlovian* inefficiencies, in honor of Marc Nerlove, who first advocated their use as measures of economic performance (hence, the letter *N*, for Nerlovian or Normlized, preceding the abbreviation of cost and revenues inefficiencies).

additive approach, with each measure of technical efficiency having a particular normalizing factor. Additionally, normalizing economic inefficiency also leads to the compliance of a set of desirable properties discussed in Chap. 2, e.g., units invariance, but makes the numerical interpretation of the inefficiency scores difficult. Contrarily, in the multiplicative approach, efficiency scores have a straightforward interpretation in terms of proportionalities.

While based on duality cost and revenue efficiency can be defined through multiplicative or additive functions of quantities and prices, this is not the case for the profitability and profit functions. Arguably, these two functions convey all the available information by simultaneously considering the input and output dimensions of the production process and their market relations. While profitability is defined multiplicatively as revenue divided by cost, $\Gamma_o = R_o/C_o = p \cdot y_o/w \cdot x_o \geq 0$, profit represents the standard measure of economic performance in business economics, i.e., the difference between revenue and cost: $\Pi_o = R_o - C_o = p \cdot y_o - w \cdot x_o$. This initial representation of economic performance determines the subsequent characterization of profitability efficiency, defined multiplicatively as the ratio of observed profitability to maximum profitability, $\Gamma E(x_o, y_o, w, p) = \Gamma_o/\Gamma(w, p) = (p \cdot y_o/w \cdot x_o)/(p \cdot y^\Gamma/w \cdot x^\Gamma) \leq 1$, and profit inefficiency, defined additively as maximum profit less observed profit: $\Pi I(x_o, y_o, w, p) = \Pi(w, p) - \Pi_o = (p \cdot y^\Pi - w \cdot x^\Pi) - (p \cdot y_o - w \cdot x_o) \geq 0$.[8] Although several authors have proposed the decomposition of profit inefficiency in multiplicative terms (e.g., see Färe et al., 2019), a direct duality relationship cannot be obtained with multiplicative measures of technical efficiency. This implies that duality theory restricts the definition and decomposition of profitability to the multiplicative case and that of profit inefficiency to the additive case.

Profitability efficiency can be decomposed in terms of the generalized distance function for any value of α. Following Zofío and Prieto (2006), who prove the duality between the profitability function and the generalized distance function, the existing duality translates in the following inequality: $\Gamma E(x_o, y_o, w, p) \leq D_G^{CRS}(x_o, y_o; \alpha)$, where $D_G^{CRS}(x_o, y_o; \alpha)$ measures the distance to the *loci* of the production frontier characterized by constant returns to scale, T^{CRS}, since the optimal solution to the profitability maximization problem exhibits this characteristic. Again, the above inequality allows the multiplicative decomposition of profitability efficiency into the *GDF* and a residual capturing allocative efficiency: $\Gamma E(x_o, y_o, w, p) = D_G^{CRS}(x_o, y_o; \alpha) \times AE_G^{CRS}(x_o, y_o, w, p; \alpha) \leq 1$. This last result can be further qualified by decomposing productive efficiency, $D_G^{CRS}(x_o, y_o; \alpha)$, into technical efficiency with respect to the variable returns to scale technology, $D_G(x_o, y_o; \alpha)$, and scale efficiency, defined as $SE_G(x_o, y_o; \alpha) = D_G^{CRS}(x_o, y_o; \alpha) \,/\, D_G(x_o, y_o; \alpha)$. This results in the final expression for profitability efficiency decompositions: $\Gamma E(x_o, y_o, w, p) = D_G(x_o, y_o; \alpha) \times SE_G(x_o, y_o; \alpha) \times AE_G^{CRS}(x_o, y_o, w, p; \alpha) \leq 1$. Figure 1.1a illustrates the decomposition of profitability inefficiency for firm (x_o, y_o). First, from a technical perspective, this firm is projected on the frontier of the technology T through the

[8] Where (y^Γ, x^Γ) and (y^Π, x^Π) represent the optimal quantities maximizing profitability and maximizing profit, respectively.

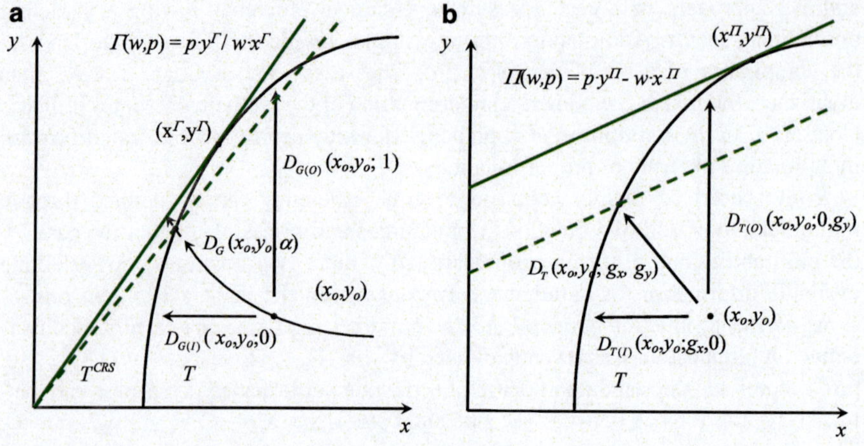

Fig. 1.1 (a–b). Profitability (**a**), profit (**b**), and technology

generalized distance function. Here, the projections in the input, output, and graph orientations are shown. Subsequently, focusing on the graph projection, the gap in economic performance due to a suboptimal scale is represented by the dashed arrows separating the variable returns to scale projections to the ray vector representing maximum profitability on the constant returns to scale technology T^{CRS}: $\Gamma(w,p) = p{\cdot}y^{\Gamma}/w{\cdot}x^{\Gamma}$. For the single input-single output case technology, no allocative inefficiencies are possible in the multiplicative approach.

Regarding the decomposition of profit inefficiency, many additive measures of technical efficiency can be employed. For convenience, we write the decomposition resorting to the already defined directional distance function, whose duality with the profit function was introduced by Chambers et al. (1998), implying that $\Pi I(x_o, y_o, w, p) \geq D_T(x_o, y_o; g_x, g_y)(p \cdot g_y + w \cdot g_x)$, where $(p \cdot g_y + w \cdot g_x)$ is the normalizing factor associated to the graph *DDF*. In this case, profit loss can be attributed to technical criteria in the amount given by the DDF plus a residual representing allocative inefficiency: $\Pi I(x_o, y_o, \widetilde{w}, \widetilde{p}) = D_T(x_o, y_o; g_x, g_y) + AI_{DDF}(x_o, y_o, \widetilde{w}, \widetilde{p}) \geq 0$.[9] Figure 1.1b illustrates the decomposition of profit inefficiency for firm (x_o, y_o). First, from a technical perspective, this firm is projected on the frontier of the technology T through the directional distance function. Again, the projections in the input, output, and graph orientations are shown. As before, considering the graph orientation, the gap in economic performance and maximum profit at (x^{Γ}, y^{Γ}) is the difference between the dashed isoprofit line passing through the frontier projection on the variable returns to scale T frontier and maximum isoprofit: $\Pi(p,w) = p{\cdot}y^{\Pi} - w{\cdot}x^{\Pi}$. Note that in this case, scale inefficiency plays no role in the evaluation of economic inefficiency.

[9]Where, once again, $(\widetilde{w}, \widetilde{p})$ denotes normalized market prices, resulting from diving profit inefficiency and its allocative component by the normalizing factor $(p \cdot g_y + w \cdot g_x)$

Figure 1.2 summarizes the analytical framework studied in this book, differentiating between the additive and multiplicative approaches. Starting from the top, we identify the key duality relationships between the functions representing the economic behavior of the firms, either cost minimization or revenue maximization, and their associated duality inequalities with the generalized distance function for the multiplicative approach and the directional distance function for the additive approach. In these partial orientations, the generalized and directional distance functions are respectively adjusted in the values of the bearing parameter α and the directional vector $g = (g_x, g_y)$, depending on the orientation. Following Farrell's tradition, closing the inequalities allows the decompositions in terms of the technical (in)efficiency measures and the corresponding allocative (in)efficiency residuals. The notation shows that in the additive approach, the values of the cost and revenue inefficiencies are normalized by $w \cdot g_x$ and $p \cdot g_y$, respectively, i.e., Normalized (or Nerlovian) Cost Inefficiency (*NCI*) and Normalized (or Nerlovian) Revenue Inefficiency (*NRI*) as presented above.

The lower part of Fig. 1.2 shows the decomposition of economic performance according to the profitability function (left side) and the profit function (right side) using their generalized and directional distance functions counterparts. Regarding profitability, the productive performance of firms in the direction set by the bearing parameter α is determined, considering both variable and constant returns to scale, which allows to differentiate between technical and scale efficiency. This distinction is relevant, because even if firms may be efficient by producing at the technological frontier, they cannot maximize profitability if they sustain scale inefficiencies because their productive scale is suboptimal; see Fig. 1.1a. These implies that, as studied in Chap. 4, if firms endure increasing or decreasing returns to scale, they cannot emerge as optimal benchmarks within the industry. Once this key feature of productive efficiency is taken into consideration, profitability efficiency can be decomposed into technical, scale, and allocative efficiencies. If profit inefficiency is the subject of study, it can be decomposed according to the value of the directional distance function in the direction set by the vector $g = (g_x, g_y)$ and the additive term representing allocative inefficiency. The decomposition of profit efficiency relying on the directional distance function is studied at length in Chap. 8, including different possibilities when choosing the directional vector g. We remark however that although we have considered the directional distance function to exemplify the additive decomposition of profit inefficiency, there are many other options available in the literature which allow a consistent decomposition based on duality theory. We comment on the alternatives we have reviewed in the following section, which outlines how the book is structured.

For about four decades, the measurement and decomposition of economic performance into technical and allocative criteria were restricted to the partial input and output dimensions. On the profitability side, although it is possible to indirectly obtain a dual relationship between the profitability function and the input and output distance functions, by minimizing cost for a given revenue or maximizing revenue for a given cost, a straightforward relationship would not be available until Zofío and Prieto (2006), relying on Chavas and Cox's (1999) generalized distance function,

Multiplicative approach (Generalized Distance Function, *GDF*)

Cost minimization (VRS)

$$CE(x_o, x_o, w) = \frac{C(y,w)}{w{\cdot}x_o} \leq D_G(x_o, y_o; 0)$$

$$\downarrow$$

$$\underbrace{\frac{C(y_o,w)}{w{\cdot}x_o}}_{CE(x_o,x_o,w)} = \underbrace{D_G(x_o, y_o; 0)}_{TE_{G(I)}(x_o,x_o)} \times AE_{G(I)}(x_o, y_o, w; 0)$$

Revenue maximization (VRS)

$$RE(x_o, x_o, p) = \frac{p{\cdot}y_o}{R(x,p)} \leq D_G(x_o, y_o; 1)$$

$$\downarrow$$

$$\underbrace{\frac{p{\cdot}y_o}{R(x_o,p)}}_{RE(x_o,x_o,p)} = \underbrace{D_G(x_o, y_o; 1)}_{TE_{G(O)}(x_o,x_o)} \times AE_{G(O)}(x_o, y_o, p; 1)$$

Profitability maximization (CRS)

$$\Gamma E(x_o, y_o, w, p) = \frac{p{\cdot}y_o / w{\cdot}x_o}{\Gamma(p,w)} \leq D_G^{CRS}(x, y; \alpha)$$

$$\downarrow$$

$$\underbrace{\frac{p{\cdot}y_o / w{\cdot}x_o}{\Gamma(p,w)}}_{\Gamma E(x_o,y_o,w,p)} \leq \underbrace{\underbrace{D_G(x,y;\alpha)}_{TE_G(x_o,y_o)} \times \underbrace{\frac{D_G^{CRS}(x,y;\alpha)}{D_G(x,y;\alpha)}}_{SE_G(x_o,y_o)}}_{TE_G^{CRS}(x_o,y_o)}$$

$$\downarrow$$

$$\underbrace{\frac{p{\cdot}y_o / w{\cdot}x_o}{\Gamma(p,w)}}_{\Gamma E(x_o,y_o,w,p)} = \underbrace{\underbrace{D_G(x,y;\alpha)}_{TE_G(x_o,y_o)} \times \underbrace{\frac{D_G^{CRS}(x,y;\alpha)}{D_G(x,y;\alpha)}}_{SE_G(x_o,y_o)}}_{TE_G^{CRS}(x_o,y_o)} \times AE_G(x_o, y_o, w, p; \alpha)$$

Additive approach (Directional Distance Function, *DDF*)

Cost minimization (VRS)

$$NCI = \frac{w{\cdot}x_o - C(y,w)}{w{\cdot}g_x} \geq D_T(x_o, y_o; g_x, 0)$$

$$\downarrow$$

$$\underbrace{\frac{w{\cdot}x_o - C(y,w)}{w{\cdot}g_x}}_{NCI(x_o,y_o,w)} = \underbrace{D_T(x, y; g_x, 0)}_{TI_{DDF(I)}(x_o,y_o;g_x,0)} + AI_{DDF(I)}(x_o, y_o, \tilde{w})$$

Revenue maximization (VRS)

$$NRI = \frac{R(x_o,p) - p{\cdot}y_o}{p{\cdot}g_y} \geq D_T(x_o, y_o; 0, g_y)$$

$$\downarrow$$

$$\underbrace{\frac{R(x_o,p) - p{\cdot}y_o}{p{\cdot}g_y}}_{NRI(x_o,y_o,p)} = \underbrace{D_T(x, y; 0, g_y)}_{TI_{DDF(O)}(x_o,y_o;0,g_y)} + AI_{DDF(O)}(x_o, y_o, \tilde{p})$$

Profit maximization (VRS)

$$N\Pi I_{DDF(G)} = \frac{\Pi(p,w) - (p{\cdot}y_o - w{\cdot}x_o)}{(p{\cdot}g_y + w{\cdot}g_x)} \geq D_T(x_o, y_o; g_x, g_y)$$

$$\downarrow$$

$$\underbrace{\frac{\Pi(p,w) - (p{\cdot}y_o - w{\cdot}x_o)}{p \cdot g_y + w \cdot g_x}}_{N\Pi I_{DDF(G)}(x_o,y_o,w,p)} = \underbrace{D_T(x, y; g_x, g_y)}_{TI_{DDF(G)}(x_o,y_o)} + AI_{DDF(G)}(x_o, y_o, \tilde{w}, \tilde{p})$$

Fig. 1.2 Duality and economic (in)efficiency: multiplicative and additive approaches

introduced the duality between these two functions. Regarding profit inefficiency, the radial distance functions do not verify the desired dual relationship with the profit function. This implies that an additive decomposition of profit inefficiency could not be consistently achieved while a suitable distance function counterpart was lacking. The analytical breakthrough represented by Luenberger's (1992a, b) shortage function, once reinterpreted as the directional distance function by Chambers et al. (1996, 1998), initiated the additive approach to economic inefficiency measurement.

Thanks to these advances, the duality between these representations of technology and profitability and profit functions, respectively, could be finally established, allowing to decompose the economic efficiency of organizations in a consistent way.[10] In this respect, although profitability is the function of choice by economists in long-term analysis of firms' performance given its index number characterization, which allows economic and productivity analyses to be linked, profit efficiency still represents the preferred option for managers and business analysts when it comes to benchmarking firms within an industry. This explains why in recent years there has been a fruitful amount of research on the decomposition of profit efficiency, based on different additive technical inefficiency measures.

1.3 Organization of the Book

Based on the distinction driven by duality theory between multiplicative and additive measures of economic performance, we structure the book according to this categorization. However, before presenting these two approaches, we devote Chap. 2 to review the necessary background material related to the technical (primal) and economic (dual) dimensions of measuring economic performance, including the definitions of the production technology and supporting economic functions; their characterization through Data Envelopment Analysis; and the notions of economic, technical, and allocative efficiency. More importantly, in this chapter, we not only present the desirable properties that the technical and economic efficiency measures should satisfy but also introduce new properties that a consistent decomposition of economic efficiency should verify, specifically the so-called essential property and extended essential property presented in Sect. 2.4.5 of Chap. 2. The essential property requires that the allocative efficiency of a firm projected to the optimizing economic benchmark is zero, while the extended essential property is more general, as it requires that the allocative efficiency should be equal to that of its projection on the production frontier (see Aparicio et al., 2021). We make use of these properties throughout the book and, particularly, in the last chapter where the main findings and conclusions are summarized, to guide practitioners in the choice of suitable

[10] Moreover, based on the input- and output-oriented directional distance functions, the additive definitions of cost and revenue inefficiency and their decomposition into technical and allocative terms were made possible at the same time.

economic decompositions and to know what the trade-offs are. For example, multiplicative decompositions in general and some additive decompositions (like that based on the DDF discussed above) may underestimate technical inefficiency because they do not comply with the notion of Pareto-Koopmans efficiency, and technical slacks may be present. On the contrary, while most additive measures do not present this shortcoming, they do not comply with the essential properties, relating the allocative efficiency of a firm under evaluation and that of its projection on the production frontier. This shortcoming arises from the use of firm-specific normalizing factors when defining economic efficiency decompositions that are units invariant. We also emphasize the introduction of the general direct approach in Chap. 13, due to Pastor, Zofío, Aparicio, and Pastor (2021b), that provides a straightforward profit, cost, and revenue decomposition for any additive measure. It decomposes the economic inefficiency of any firm as the sum of two terms, the first being related to its technical inefficiency and the second one related to the economic inefficiency of its technical frontier projection. Decomposing its first term as the product of the calculated technical inefficiency times a certain nonzero multiplicative factor, we derive the corresponding Nerlovian economic decomposition. The general direct approach has been key for introducing two types of specific reverse approaches, inspired by Pastor, Aparicio, Zofío, and Borrás (2021c) and Pastor, Zofío, Aparicio, and Alcaraz (2021d).

Part I of the book deals with the multiplicative approach. This part covers the classic definitions of cost and revenue efficiency in Chap. 3, which are decomposed in terms of Shephard's (1953, 1970) input and output distance functions. This presentation of the radial model is equivalent to Farrell's (1957) decomposition, measuring technical and allocative efficiency as described in Chap. 2, providing the latter with the theoretical underpinnings of duality theory. Subsequently, following the discussion in the previous section, we devote Chap. 4 to show how these early cost and revenue multiplicative approaches can be expanded to the notion of profitability efficiency, considering both the input and output dimension of the firm and relying on the generalized distance function introduced by Chavas and Cox (1999). The existing duality between the profitability function and the generalized distance function, presented by Zofío and Prieto (2006), allows profitability efficiency to be decomposed, as presented in Figure 1.2.

Part II of the book is devoted to the additive decompositions of profit inefficiency and, by extension, cost and revenue inefficiency. Here, we consider the most relevant measures of technical inefficiency proposed in the literature, which are covered from Chap. 5 to Chap. 12. Chapter 5 is devoted to the so-called Russell measures, which were introduced by Färe and Lovell (1978). A drawback of the original "graph" Russell measure is its nonlinearity, which certainly explains why it is not as popular as other measures of technical inefficiency, as well as its limited application in economic efficiency analysis. Nevertheless, recent advances allow its calculation through second-order cone programming (SOCP), which we incorporate in the Julia package "Benchmarking Economic Efficiency" accompanying this book. The current proposal to decompose profit inefficiency into a technical component represented by the Russell measure and a residual allocative term is due to Halická and Trnovská (2018).

Chapter 6 presents the decomposition of profit inefficiency based on the weighted additive distance function, *WADF*, introduced by Aparicio, Pastor, and Vidal (2016a), who endow additive-type models with a distance function structure. An appealing feature of the WADF is the flexibility offered when choosing the weights for the input and output slacks. In fact, different choices of weights lead to previous proposals of the additive model in the literature. Hence, the duality theory developed for the *WADF* encompasses a wide range of measures, enabling a consistent decomposition of profit inefficiency. This is the case, for example, of the normalized weighted additive model, Lovell and Pastor (1995); the measure of inefficiency proportions (*MIP*) introduced by Cooper et al. (1999); the range-adjusted measure (*RAM*) of inefficiency, Cooper et al. (1999); and the bounded adjusted measure (*BAM*) of inefficiency, Cooper et al. (2011). It is worth noting that all these models lead to different normalized values of profit inefficiency because the corresponding factors depend on the weights. Again, all these many options are available when measuring profit efficiency using the Julia software. Afterward, Chap. 7 revisits the enhanced Russell graph measure (*ERG*) introduced by Pastor et al. (1999), renamed as slack-based measure (*SBM*) by Tone (2001).[11] The difficulty for solving the nonlinear graph version of the Russell measure prompted these authors to propose a new formulation, which although initially corresponding to a fractional program, can be easily linearized following the methods proposed for the radially oriented models; see Charnes and Cooper (1962). In this chapter, we develop the duality that allows decomposing normalized profit inefficiency in the technical and allocative terms using the *ERG* or *SBM* measure. We also show how this model can be implemented using the package "Benchmarking Economic Efficiency."

Chapter 8 is devoted to the decomposition of profit inefficiency, relying on the duality between the profit function and the directional distance function as presented by Chambers et al. (1998). This approach is by far the most popular among researchers, so we discuss in detail different aspects related to the exogenous choice of the directional vector $g = (g_x, g_y)$. The consequences that choosing different vectors have on the value of the Nerlovian profit inefficiency through the normalizing factor are also considered. In fact, the interpretability of the profit inefficiency measure, as well as the possibility of comparing its numerical value across firms, hinges upon the choice of g. We consider three subfamilies of exogenous vectors and the proposal to endogenize it by Zofío et al. (2013). In the empirical section of this chapter, we show how to implement different models using the "Benchmarking Economic Efficiency" software. Users can pass their own directional vector g, but the most common options are readily available. These include the unit vector, the observed input and output quantities of the firm under evaluation – resulting in the

---

[11] A mathematically equivalent measure was proposed in an independent way in the same journal 2 years later by Tone (2001), who named it "slack-based measure (*SBM*)." In this book, we call it *ERG*=*SBM*.

so-called proportional *DDF*, and the average values of the inputs and outputs observed across the sample firms. We also implement the endogenous model which yields a distinct characterization of profit inefficiency as being either technical or allocative.

One feature of the additive measures of technical inefficiency, as in the case of the weighted additive distance function discussed in Chap. 6, is that, regardless of the advantage of projecting the firm to the strongly efficient frontier, they search for the maximum value of a certain combination of the input and output slacks. This implies that when searching for efficient benchmarks, the "farthest projection" from the firm under evaluation to the production frontier is sought. However, from a managerial perspective, it seems more appropriate to search for the shortest path to the production frontier when solving inefficiencies to minimize the effort of becoming, at least, weakly efficient. This is consistent with the "principle of least action" or "least distance" applied to input reduction and output expansion, which is associated with the calculation of the closest targets to the efficient frontier. With this goal in mind, but for a generic definition of distance, Briec (1998), Briec and Lesourd (1999), and Briec and Lemaire (1999) defined technical inefficiency using Hölder norms. These authors also stated the duality between the profit function and alternative norms, which is the content of Chap. 9, presenting the decomposition of profit inefficiency through this approach. In that chapter, we explore this decomposition considering the projection of the firms under evaluation to both the weakly and strongly efficient frontiers. This last possibility, due to Aparicio, Pastor, Sainz-Pardo, and Vidal (2020), is quite relevant because it ensures that the technical term complies with the notion of Pareto-Koopmans efficiency, so it cannot be underestimated when decomposing profit inefficiency. Moreover, the solution proposed by these authors also ensures that the profit inefficiency measure is units invariant. From an empirical perspective, we show in this chapter how to implement the decomposition of profit inefficiency based on the Hölder metrics using the "Benchmarking Economic Efficiency" Julia package. Users can choose between three predefined norms: ℓ_1, ℓ_∞, and the Euclidean norm ℓ_2, coupled with the unweighted and weighted versions of the model, with the latter being units invariant. Computationally, because the ℓ_1 and ℓ_∞ norms are equivalent to the directional distance function discussed in Chap. 8, under particular directional vectors $g = (g_x, g_y)$, they can be solved though linear programming. This is not the case for the Euclidean norm ℓ_2, whose resolution is based on quadratic optimization methods linked to the use of special ordered sets (SOS). The Julia function implementing this model resorts to the Gurobi Optimizer, which includes these techniques (Gurobi, 2021).

Chapter 10 extends the previous analytical framework by presenting the most general representation of an additive technical inefficiency measure complying with the definition of distance function. Pastor et al. (2012) introduced the notion of loss distance function, inspired by Debreu (1951), which measures the distance from the evaluated firm to the efficient DEA frontier using a set of normalization constraints for the input and output shadow prices. The most appealing feature of the loss distance function is that it can represent multiple technical inefficiency measures proposed in the literature, simply by changing the normalization constraints, i.e., it generalizes the existing definitions by relating them to specific restrictions on the shadow prices. Moreover, the loss distance function can be used to test whether new proposals of technical inefficiency measures (and their associated normalizing restrictions) comply with the basic properties characterizing a distance function. Subsequently, from an economic perspective, Aparicio, Borrás, Pastor, and Zofío (2016b) established the duality between the profit function and the general loss distance function, which is the cornerstone for decomposing profit inefficiency through any technical inefficiency measure. Because the notion of loss distance function is general, in the sense that it does not specify a particular way in which the technology is defined or estimated in practice, i.e., it is an axiomatic approach, this chapter does not include an empirical section. However, since different normalization sets result in specific technical inefficiency measures covered in this book, these can be solved using the Julia functions presented in each corresponding chapter.

The directional distance function presented in the previous section of this "Introduction" and studied in Chap. 8, $D_T(x, y; g_x, g_y) = \max\{\beta : (x - \beta g_x, y + \beta g_y) \in T\}$, $g = (g_x, g_y) \in \mathbb{R}_+^{M+N}$, contracts inputs and expands outputs according to the same value β when reaching the production frontier. Aparicio et al. (2013a, b) add flexibility to the standard model by allowing input contraction and output expansion in different proportions. This results in the so-called modified directional distance function (*MDDF*), which can be interpreted as technical inefficiency, i.e., $TI_{MDDF(G)}(x_o, y_o; g_x, g_y) = \max\{\beta_x + \beta_y : (x_o - \beta_x g_x, y_o + \beta_y g_y) \in T\}$, $\beta = (\beta_x, \beta_y) \in \mathbb{R}_+^{M+N}$, $g = (g_x, g_y) \in \mathbb{R}_+^{M+N}$. Chapter 11 presents the duality between the *MDFF* and the supporting profit, cost and revenue functions, and how economic inefficiency can be decomposed into technical and allocative terms. It also discusses the interpretation of these inefficiencies when the directional vector corresponds to the observed input and output quantities: $g = (x_o, y_o)$, resulting in normalizing constraints that correspond to either observed cost $C_o = w{\cdot}x_o$ (if observed profit is positive) or observed revenue $R_o = p{\cdot}y_o$ (if observed profit is negative). These results are then compared to those obtained with the directional distance function, whose normalization constraint, $R_o + C_o = p{\cdot}y_o + w{\cdot}x_o$, has a dubious economic interpretation. The "Benchmarking Economic Efficiency" software includes the set of functions that allow the *MDDF* to be calculated and decomposed under the above conditions.

Chapter 12 studies the reverse directional function, *RDDF*, proposed by Pastor et al. (2016). These authors offer an original methodology that allows representing any technical inefficiency measure as a directional distance function with equal value. Relevant to the conversion is that the inefficiency measure of interest yields a single inefficiency score for both inputs and outputs as well as a single projection. However, regarding the existence of two different efficiency scores, as with the modified directional distance function, this chapter shows how the *RDDF* can be modified to accommodate this case. As for the existence of multiple projections, the inclusion of a secondary goal related to economic efficiency, e.g., choosing the projection that is closer to maximum profit (or, equivalently, minimizes allocative inefficiency), will solve the problem. The relevance of the method is that given the good characteristics of the economic inefficiency model built upon the directional distance function, established through the number of properties that it satisfies (as summarized in the conclusions of the book), the *RDDF* provides a direct link between all efficiency measures presented in this book and the *DDF*. Once a reference benchmark for a firm under evaluation is identified on the production frontier, one can determine the directional vector that connects both units, consistent with the original efficiency score. Afterward, to decompose economic inefficiency, we just need to rely on the same duality results presented in Chap. 8 for the *DDF*, thereby decomposing economic efficiency according to technical and allocative criteria. In this chapter, we also show how to solve the economic inefficiency models based on the *RDDF*, using the package "Benchmarking Economic Efficiency."

The first chapter of Part III of the book (Chap. 13) presents new approaches to the measurement and decomposition of economic efficiency that do not rely on duality theory, which identifies allocative efficiency as a residual by closing the Fenchel-Mahler inequalities between economic efficiency and technical inefficiency, as shown in Figure 1.2. The first proposal, known as the *general direct approach*, departs from the previous *RDDF* as it requires information on the firm's technical inefficiency score, obtained through a specific model, and its associated projection on the frontier. However, rather than recovering the associated directional distance function, it measures the economic value of the technological gap between the firm under evaluation and its projection on the frontier, i.e., the foregone profit due to input excesses and output shortfalls. The difference between maximum profit and this value can be interpreted as allocative inefficiency, which is equivalent to the profit inefficiency of the projection. The original technical efficiency score can be multiplicatively related to the value of the technological gap through a normalization factor. Dividing profit inefficiency and allocative inefficiency by this factor results in a normalized decomposition of economic efficiency which satisfies desirable properties. Arguably, the general direct approach provides a unifying framework for decomposing economic inefficiency because it can be applied to any inefficiency model, but it is easier to develop and implement, i.e., it does not require obtaining the underlying duality with the profit function. The methodology can be reversed in the sense that rather that departing from a technical efficient projection, we may aim at projections that satisfy certain optimality with respect to the economic objective. In this respect, we propose two rather different reverse approaches, *the standard reverse approach* (Pastor, Aparicio, Zofío, and Borrás, 2021c) and *the flexible reverse approach* (Pastor, Zofío, Aparicio, and Alcaraz, 2021d). The first procedure is traditional and based on the general direct approach, while the second one is iconoclastic and incorporates the endogenous approach introduced by Zofío et al. (2013) for the *DDF*. The general direct approach is also available in the Julia software accompanying this book, and we illustrate how it can be used to decompose economic inefficiency.

We conclude the book with a separate chapter with some general remarks on the importance of Benchmarking Economic Efficiency for all business stakeholders and recalling the main conclusions obtained from many years of research on this topic. More importantly, given the numerous options that are available to decompose economic inefficiency, we systematically present the desirable properties that should be satisfied by the technical efficiency measures, the economic efficiency measures themselves, and their decomposition, i.e., in relation to the interpretation and value of the allocative efficiency term. Here, we show that no single decomposition satisfies all the desirable properties, yet we prioritize those related to the allocative efficiency term, in particular the essential property and its extended version presented in Sect. 2.4.5 of Chap. 2. These key properties, recently suggested by Aparicio et al. (2021), establish that allocative inefficiency must be zero when the technical benchmark corresponds to an optimal point from an economical perspective. Moreover, its extension states that the allocative inefficiency of a firm under evaluation must be equal to the allocative inefficiency of its projection at the production frontier. Although it may seem intuitive that this property should be verified, in this book, we exemplify that, quite frequently, firms that are projected to the optimal economic benchmark (e.g., firms maximizing profit), are allocatively inefficient with an associated score greater than zero. Judging the different proposals under these criteria, it turns out that the oriented multiplicative economic efficiency decompositions presented in this book satisfy both the essential property and its refinement, i.e., Shephard's (1953, 1970) input and output distance functions. This is not the case for the additive measures, where only those decompositions based on the directional distance function, under certain conditions, and its extensions (e.g., modified DDF, reverse DDF), as well as the general direct and reverse approaches, satisfy them. In this last chapter, we also refer to recent literature that extends the evaluation of economic efficiency to other models of productive efficiency, for example, those concerned with the evaluation of environmental efficiency that differentiate between desirable and undesirable outputs (see Aparicio, Kapelko, and Zofío, 2020) and those extending the cross-sectional analysis studied in this book, to multiple periods, thereby relating the changes in economic efficiency to productivity. In these approaches, considering the multiplicative approach represented by the generalized distance function, profitability change can be related to the Malmquist indices (Zofío and Prieto, 2006), while in the additive approach, in relation to the directional distance function, profit change can be related to the so-called Luenberger indicators (Juo et al., 2015, Balk 2018).

1.4 Objectives of the Book

We conclude this introduction by summarizing the goals of this book. In general, our main purpose is to establish a reference text for the measurement and decomposition of economic efficiency, implemented through Data Envelopment Analysis techniques. With this work, we intend to:

1. Provide a guide to the theory and practice of economic efficiency analysis within the multiplicative and additive approaches, particularly between the graph measures corresponding to either profitability efficiency or profit inefficiency.

2. Present an integrated framework and standardized notation for the different models that have been proposed over the last two decades to measure and decompose economic efficiency but departing form the seminal contributions by Debreu (1951), Shephard (1953, 1970), Farrell (1957), and Nerlove (1965), who inspired subsequent work.
3. Show the relationship between the alternative measures of economic efficiency, the underlying technology, and their decomposition into technical and allocative components, for example, the role that returns to scale and, therefore, scale efficiency play in economic inefficiency or the relevance of the strong and weak efficient frontiers when measuring technical efficiency through multiplicative and additive approaches.
4. Provide insights into the Data Envelopment Analysis models and optimization methods that are used throughout the book to implement the different approaches; for example, the use of nonlinear techniques when calculating graph multiplicative measures like the generalized distance function or quadratic programming with special order sets for the Hölder distance function based on the Euclidean norm. We also consider the introduction of the general direct approach as being particularly relevant as a unifying tool for decomposing economic inefficiency based on any of the additive measures, as well as for designing the reverse approaches.
5. Present and illustrate the use of the accompanying software package programmed in the Julia language. The code is freely available from www.benchmarkingeconomicefficiency.com and can be edited to suit the needs of specific researchers interested in implementing their own models.
6. Review, organize, and assess the increasing bibliography on the subject in a comprehensive way.
7. Serve as an educational textbook for those interested in training related to economic efficiency methods, by highlighting their potential uses though examples and comparing the different methods using the same dataset on real data.
8. Finally, provide a structured discussion of the different approaches in terms of their properties, so as to advise researchers on the choice of a specific economic efficiency model.

Chapter 2
Conceptual Background: Firms' Objectives, Decision Variables, and Economic Efficiency

2.1 Introduction

In this chapter, we summarize the analytical framework found in the book by presenting the main concepts in an intuitive and accessible way while relying on supporting graphical illustrations to ease comprehension. Arguably, the measurement of economic efficiency dates back to the seminal paper by Farrell (1957), who introduced the definition, decomposition, and measurement of *overall* (economic) efficiency, which he named productive efficiency. The model is based on the cost function and input-oriented technical efficiency, and we initiate our presentations with this approach to guide and illustrate the different concepts underlying the measurement of economic efficiency. Throughout the text, we use economic efficiency as a measure to compare best and actual economic performance reserving the term productive efficiency for the technical dimension of the analysis, which may include aspects related to alternative characterizations of returns to scale (e.g., constant or variable returns to scale resulting in scale efficiency), disposability (e.g., strong and weak disposability of inputs and outputs), etc.

In the first section of the chapter, we recall the definition of production technology and different measures of technical efficiency, the formal counterparts of which are the distance functions considered in subsequent chapters that constitute an alternative representation of technology. Next, in Sect. 2.2, we present the different economic goals of the firm to be considered and show how it is possible to define economic efficiency as the comparison between a best performing benchmark (e.g., minimum cost) and actual behavior (e.g., observed cost). Afterward, for economically inefficient firms and based on the duality introduced by Shephard (1953, 1970), we explain in Sect. 2.3 how it is possible to decompose the sources of inefficiency according to technological and allocative criteria. It is worth mentioning that Farrell (1957) deemed what is currently known as allocative efficiency as price efficiency since this source of inefficiency compares technically efficient production plans to

J. T. Pastor et al., *Benchmarking Economic Efficiency*, International Series in Operations Research & Management Science 315,
https://doi.org/10.1007/978-3-030-84397-7_2

those that maximize the economic goal of the firm, i.e., those consistent with optimal input demands and output supplies.

A formal presentation of duality results for measuring economic efficiency is postponed to subsequent chapters where alternative definitions of the technical component of economic efficiency are explored. Indeed, the duality framework serves as the backbone for newer decompositions of economic efficiency based on more flexible representations of production technology and therefore proves worth illustrating in detail from a conceptual perspective. Duality theory is aptly summarized by Diewert in an interview for *Econometric Theory* in the following way: "if producers or consumers behaved as price takers, then their technologies and preferences (with some regularity conditions) could be perfectly described by dual cost or profit functions (for producers) and dual expenditure or indirect utility functions (for consumers)" (Fox, 2018:513).

To render the analysis operational from an empirical perspective, we rely on Data Envelopment Analysis (DEA) methods, which are presented in Sect. 2.4 of the chapter. The precursor of DEA can be traced back to the activity analysis proposed by Koopmans (1951), which Farrell himself considered (Farrell, 1957:254). DEA was initially implemented in the field of agricultural economics by Boles (1967, 1971) but was later popularized by Charnes et al. (1978) in the field of operations research and management science, who coined the DEA denomination.[1] We also discuss the main characteristics of DEA models including the properties that ensure a consistent measurement of economic efficiency through duality and illustrate with simple examples the alternative definitions and decompositions of economic (in)-efficiency. Also, from an empirically oriented perspective, we have developed an accompanying software package programmed in Julia language (Bezanson et al., 2017). This package implements the different models presented in the book. In Sect. 2.5, we guide the reader through the different steps necessary to install this software and associated packages. We also illustrate its workings by calculating a simple example of economic efficiency measurement and decomposition. In each of the different chapters, we solve both ad hoc examples that can be illustrated graphically and apply the different models to a real dataset on quantities and prices of financial institutions.

The point of departure for any study of economic efficiency is the choice of function that best describes the economic behavior of the firm and the corresponding characterization of the production technology that is obtained through duality. Production technology can be characterized from a *graph* perspective that considers both the input and output dimensions. Alternatively, it can be represented either through an input correspondence that focuses on the input quantities required to produce a given level of output or through its output counterpart that considers the amount of outputs that can be produced with a given level of inputs. In economic efficiency analyses adopting duality as the guiding principle, the choice for a

[1] For the origins of Data Envelopment Analysis, we refer the reader to Førsund and Sarafoglou (2002).

technical (primal) dimension of the problem can be performed from a backward induction perspective, so as to determine a suitable representation of the technology in the first place. For example, if the economic objective of the firm is to minimize production costs because output levels are given or are exogenous, then an input radially oriented efficiency measure such as Shephard's (1953, 1970) input distance function is the right match in a multiplicative context (as presented in Chap. 3). Conversely, if what concerns our study is revenue maximization, then an output orientation should be chosen. Alternatively, if firms can change inputs and outputs at their own discretion and the economic goals is profitability or profit maximization, then more complete and flexible representations of the production technology such as the generalized distance function (dual to the profitability function, Chap. 4), the directional distance function, or other additive distance functions (dual to the profit function, as shown in the second part of the book) may be selected.

This simply shows that what drives the choice of orientation from a technological perspective is duality theory, which enables us to relate a technical (primal) representation of the technology (i.e., the distance function) with a supporting (dual) economic function, thereby providing a consistent decomposition of economic efficiency into a technical efficiency term and a (residual) counterpart corresponding to allocative efficiency. This residual emerges naturally from the application of Minkowski's (1911) theorem to economic theory: every closed convex set can be characterized as the intersection of its supporting half-spaces. Indeed, the cost, revenue, profitability, and profit functions are known as the support functions associated with their corresponding technology sets (see Rockafellar, 1972; p. 112).

Farrell (1957:254) cites Debreu (1951) as a source of inspiration when introducing his economic efficiency model, and therefore, we start out by presenting his overall setting, to which a given firm's performance can be related. Debreu (1951) introduced a well-known radial efficiency measure, which he named the *coefficient of resource utilization*. Farrell's technical efficiency—and therefore Shephard's radial distance functions on the technical side—has a direct parallel in Debreu's definition. This is the reason why several authors talk about Farrell-Debreu efficiency measures (e.g., starting with Färe & Lovell, 1978, and more recently Fried et al., 2008).[2] Debreu derived this scalar from the much less well-known *dead loss* function that characterizes the monetary value of several sources of inefficiencies and which has to be minimized: $\min_{z,p_z}\{p_z(z_0 - z)\}$, where z_0 is a vector representing the actual allocation of resources, z is a vector belonging to the set of optimal allocations, and p_z is a vector of the corresponding set of intrinsic or shadow price vectors for z. In this context, Debreu named the optimal value of this problem "the

[2] ten Raa (2008) compares the Farrell and Debreu concepts of economic efficiency at length, expressing disapproval given that he perceives both as being casually equated. He claims that Debreu's coefficient of resource allocation encompasses both Farrell's technical efficiency and his allocative efficiency measures while frees the latter from prices. Debreu's coefficient "calculates the resource costs not of a given consumption bundle, but of an (intelligently chosen) Pareto equivalent allocation. (And the prices are not given, but support the allocation)."

magnitude of the loss," and he pointed out that "p_z is affected by an arbitrary positive scalar." In order to eliminate the arbitrary multiplicative factor affecting all the prices that may drive the magnitude of the loss to zero, Debreu proposed dividing the objective function by a price index, reformulating the original problem as $\underset{z,p_z}{Min}\{p_z(z_0 - z)/p_z z\}$ or, equivalently, as $\underset{z,p_z}{Max}\{p_z z/p_z z_0\}$. Debreu obtained as a corollary that the optimal solution to these problems is $z^* = \rho \cdot z_0$, where the scalar ρ $(0 < \rho \leq 1)$ is the coefficient of resource utilization mentioned above (see Pastor et al., 2012).

We can recognize here a definition that, even if referring only to the cost side in a multiplicative setting, extends to all economic efficiency measures (a normalized ratio or difference between optimal and actual performance). Debreu formalized a system consisting of two activities, production and consumption, and identified three sources of economic loss: underemployment of resources, inefficiency in production, and imperfections of economic organization. The literature on economic efficiency analysis develops the productive side, which Debreu calls "the technical inefficiency of production units." In the above formulation, the optimal producers have an associated set of shadow prices, which could be replaced by market prices as in the Farrell setting (or even other imputed prices). We note that the different measures of economic efficiency studied throughout the book are different expressions of Debreu's coefficient of resource allocation with respect to producers, each one using a particular set of normalization restrictions on prices, resulting in a variety of normalization conditions. Moreover, Debreu's loss function represents a measure of overall economic efficiency. Therefore, the theoretical and computational developments that allow identifying the sources of inefficiency as related to technological or allocative (price) characteristics can be seen as qualifications of Debreu's definition. In particular, in Chap. 11, we present a general approach to measure economic efficiency based on Aparicio et al.'s (2016) loss distance function corresponding to Debreu's proposal.

2.2 The Technology: Input, Output, and Graph Technical Efficiency Measures

In this setting, from a production perspective, a firm selects a plan of action intended to maximize its utility, expressed in terms of an economic function, subject to the production technology. At the firm level, this results in their specific demand for inputs and supply of outputs. The engineering plan is constrained by the technology available to the firm:

$$T = \{(x, y) : x \in \mathbb{R}^M_+, y \in \mathbb{R}^N_+, \ x \text{ can produce } y\}, \tag{2.1}$$

where x is a vector of input quantities, y is a vector of output quantities, and M and N are the number of inputs and outputs. We assume that T is a subset of $\mathbb{R}_+^{M+N}$ that satisfies the following postulates (see, e.g., Färe et al., 1985):[3]

(T1) $T \neq \varnothing$.
(T2) $(0_N, y) \notin T$, i.e., output production, $y \neq 0_M$, requires the use of inputs (there is no free lunch).
(T3) $T(x) := \{(y', y) \in T : y' \leq y\}$ is bounded $\forall x \in \mathbb{R}_+^M$.
(T4) $(x, y) \in T$, $(x, -y) \leq (x', -y') \Rightarrow (x', y') \in T$; i.e., inputs and outputs are freely disposable.
(T5) T is a closed set.
(T6) T is a convex set.

Axiom T1 implies that the technology is non-empty. T2 postulates that a semi-positive output cannot be obtained from a null input vector. Moreover, any nonnegative input yields at least zero output. T3 states that finite input cannot produce infinite output. T4 implies that any input (output) vector whose elements are greater (smaller) than a reference vector belonging to the technology also belongs to it. This axiom is necessary in order to define the strongly efficient technology as a subset of the boundary of the production set. Axioms T5 and T6 are self-explanatory. They postulate that the technology is closed and convex and, along with non-emptiness T1, constitutes the basic requirements needed to develop the duality results presented in this book.

Equivalent representations of the technology that are useful in what follows are the partially oriented input requirement set $L(y) = \{x : (x, y) \in T\}$ and the output production possibility set $P(x) = \{y : (x, y) \in T\}$. If the technology exhibits (globally) constant returns to scale (CRS), then the corresponding set is denoted by $T^{CRS} = \{(\psi x, \psi y) : (x, y) \in T, \ \psi > 0\}$; i.e., T^{CRS} implies a mapping $x \to y$ that is homogeneous of degree one.[4] For the single output case, $N = 1$, the technology can be represented in what is termed as the primal approach by the production function f, $\mathbb{R}_+^M \to \mathbb{R}_+$, defined by: $f(x) = \max_y \{y : (x, y) \in T\}$, i.e., the maximum amount of output that can be obtained from any combination of inputs. The advantage of this interpretation is that it leaves room for technical inefficiency, since under the

---

[3] General notation: For a vector v of dimension D, $v \in \mathbb{R}_{++}^D$ means that each element of v is positive; $v \in \mathbb{R}_+^D$ means that each element of v is nonnegative; $v > 0_D$ means $v \geq 0_D$ but $v \neq 0_D$; and, finally, 0_D denotes a zero vector of dimension D. Given the two vectors v and u, $v \leq u \Leftrightarrow v_d \leq u_d$, $d \in \{1, \ldots, D\}$, $v < u \Leftrightarrow v_d < u_d$, $d \in \{1, \ldots, D\}$, and $v <^* u \Leftrightarrow v_d < u_d$ or $v_d = u_d = 0$, $d \in \{1, \ldots, D\}$. The inner product of two D dimensional vectors $v \equiv [v_1, \ldots, v_D]$ and $u \equiv [u_1, \ldots, u_D]$ is denoted as $v \cdot u \equiv \sum_{d=1}^D v_d u_d$.

[4] In empirical studies approximating the technology through DEA, a *global* CRS characterization is assumed for computational convenience when relevant definitions, such as the profitability efficiency index, require these returns to scale, and therefore, their associated distance functions are defined with respect to that benchmark technology. Nevertheless, as remarked in Sects. 2.3.3 and 2.4.3, this requirement requires only the existence of *local* CRS.

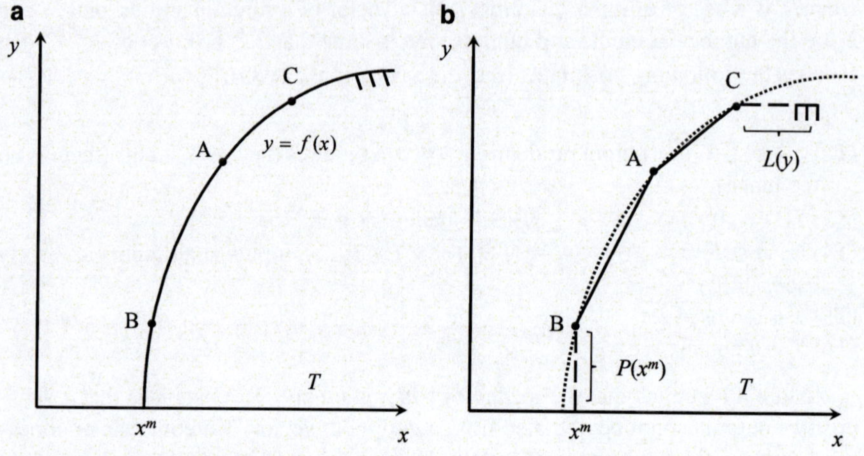

Fig. 2.1 (a–b) Technology sets

appropriate assumptions we can define a technology set departing from the production function as $T = \{(x, y) : f(x) \geq y, y \in \mathbb{R}_+\}$. In the general (and realistic) multiple output-multiple input case, Koopmans (1951:60) provides a practical definition of technical efficiency based on the notion of Pareto optimality: A producer is technically efficient if, given its actual production process, an increase in any output requires a reduction in at least one other output or an increase in at least one input and if a reduction in any input requires an increase in at least one other input or a reduction in at least one output. Consequently, an inefficient producer could produce the same outputs with less of at least one input or could use the same inputs to produce more of at least one output.

This definition suggests that the process of benchmarking requires the comparison of the actual performance of the firm with respect to a certain reference subset of the technology. The concept of the (strongly) efficient subset of T corresponds to the following reference subset[5]:

$$\partial^S(T) = \{(x, y) \in T : (x', -y') \leq (x, -y), (x', y') \neq (x, y) \Rightarrow (x', y') \notin T\}. \quad (2.2)$$

Intuitively, the strongly efficient subset includes all those feasible production plans which are not dominated. All these concepts are illustrated in the left panel of Fig. 2.1a for $M = N = 1$, where the variable returns to scale technology set, T, consists of all the input-output combinations below the production frontier $y = f(x)$—specifically, the technology exhibits decreasing returns to scale: $\lambda^\alpha y = f(\lambda x)$, $\alpha < 1$. We see that production requires a minimum amount of input, x^m, to produce a positive amount of output. In the case of the represented production function, the

[5]This notation, adopted from Briec (1998), differs from the one introduced by Färe et al. (1985), where $\partial^S(T)$ is denoted by $Eff(T)$.

strongly efficient subject of the technology corresponds to the production frontier itself.

From the nonparametric perspective of Data Envelopment Analysis (DEA) techniques presented in Sect. 2.4, the piecewise linear approximation of the production technology based on the principle of minimal extrapolation results in efficiency sets that are weakly efficient, i.e., by which firms belong to this set even if dominated in some input and output dimension. Formally, the latter corresponds to the following definition:

$$\partial^W(T) = \{(x, y) \in T : (x', -y') < (x, -y) \Rightarrow (x', y') \notin T\}. \tag{2.3}$$

Considering $j = 1, \ldots, J$ firms, DEA approximation of the technology set is presented in Fig. 2.1b, where the frontier corresponds to the linear combinations (segments) of the observed efficient firms, $\overline{\text{BAC}}$, and their vertical and horizontal projections. In this single input-single output case, these projections represent the output and input correspondences: $P(x)$ and $L(y)$, respectively. We can also see that the strongly efficient set $\partial^S(T)$ is given by the $\overline{\text{BAC}}$ frontier, with $\partial^S(T) \subset \partial^W(T)$.[6] Ultimately, the Pareto-Koopmans notion of efficiency is much more demanding than those associated with the standard DEA implementations of the radial Debreu-Farrell measures and the associated characterization of the technology.

Weak disposability constitutes a matter of concern in the empirical implementation of economic efficiency models through mathematical programming techniques such as DEA, because the existence of slacks is an additional source of technical inefficiency. The latter can be misattributed to allocative inefficiency if the efficiency measure fails to take into account these additional input excesses or output shortcomings. We tackle this problem later in the chapter when discussing the properties that a technical efficiency measure should satisfy. For this reason, since the most common approximation of the production technology by way of the standard DEA models, both under constant returns to scale (Charnes et al., 1978) and variable returns to scale (Banker et al., 1984), defines reference subsets characterized by weak disposability, throughout this book, we will emphasize whether a particular technical efficiency measure is capable of identifying benchmark peers that belong to the strongly efficient frontier (i.e., the so-called indication property). Nevertheless, we reconsider the characterization of the production technology through DEA methods and its relevance when measuring technical (in)efficiency in Sect. 2.4.

Efficiency measures can be broadly classified into multiplicative or additive, depending on whether the measurement of the distance or gap between a firm, represented by the production plan (x, y) and a reference benchmark on the production frontier, $(\widehat{x}, \widehat{y})$, entails projecting the former multiplicatively by a factor expanding outputs and/or reducing inputs or rather the addition of output quantities

---

[6] See Färe et al. (1985) for general conditions under which the two subsets coincide. Grosskopf (1986) discusses in a systematic way the role of the reference technology under different returns to scale and disposability assumptions when defining alternative efficiency subsets.

and/or subtraction of input quantities.[7] One of the characteristics of the multiplicative technical efficiency measures is that they are oriented, meaning that the projection follows a pre-specified path toward the frontier. On the contrary, additive measures are normally non-oriented, but there are exceptions such as the directional distance function, DDF, discussed by Chambers et al. (1996) and Chambers et al. (1988) that relies on a directional vector when projecting a firm to the production frontier.[8] As a general rule, we can anticipate that non-oriented additive efficiency measures based on the optimization of the sum of the input and/or output slacks identify benchmark peers on the strongly efficient frontier (2.2). On the contrary, radially oriented (input and output) multiplicative measures, other oriented graph measures, and additive measures based on directional vectors measure efficiency against the weakly efficient subset (2.3).[9]

This remark prompts the discussion on the set of properties that a technical efficiency measure should satisfy, where the reference set they identify, strong or weak, is just one of them. Once we present the most common alternative, multiplicative, and additive definitions of technical efficiency, we proceed to discuss the desirable set of properties that they should satisfy in order to be meaningful representations of firms' performance. In the following two sections, we present in a heuristic way a selection of the most relevant multiplicative and additive measures of technical and allocative efficiency, while a formal discussion based on production theory is presented in the following chapters.

2.2.1 *Input Technical (In)Efficiency Measures: Multiplicative and Additive Definitions*

2.2.1.1 The Multiplicative Approach

We can now introduce the two categories of technical efficiency measures to which existing definitions belong, namely, the multiplicative and additive approaches. To illustrate the multiplicative approach, we choose the classic radial input and output

---

[7] Russell and Schworm (2018:17) make an alternative distinction between "path-based" indices and "slack-based" indices. However, these categorizations are not equivalent to the multiplicative and additive definition of the technical efficiency measures.

[8] The DDF is adapted from the shortage function of Luenberger (1992a, 1992b) applied to the measurement of technical inefficiency by these authors.

[9] It is important to remark that whatever the approach for technical efficiency measurement, it is generally assumed that inputs are to be decreased and outputs increased. However, there are instances in economic efficiency measurement that taking advantage of the flexibility of some measures, it is possible to endogenize the direction so as to project inefficient observations directly onto the optimal economic benchmark by increasing inputs or reducing outputs; see Zofio et al. (2013) and Petersen (2018). This proposal questions the decomposition of economic efficiency into technical and allocative components, as the former is normally associated with a subjective choice of orientation. We discuss the possibility of endogenizing the orientation in subsequent chapters.

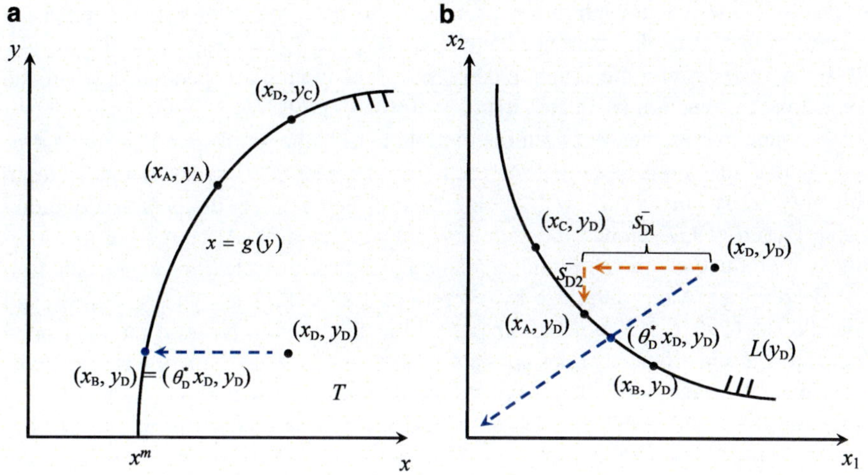

Fig. 2.2 **(a–b)** Input-oriented technical (in)efficiency

measures proposed by Farrell (1957). In this case, from the perspective of the production possibility set for a given level of outputs y, the radial input-oriented measure of technical efficiency corresponds to the maximum equiproportional contraction in all inputs that is feasible given the production technology, $L(y)$. A characteristic of radial measures is that the reduction in the input quantities is equiproportional (i.e., keeps the input mix fixed). In the single output case, if the production function $y = f(x)$ is invertible, $g(y) = f(x)^{-1}$ provides the minimum amount of inputs necessary for producing y. In the multiple output-multiple input case, the scalar-valued radial input measure of technical efficiency corresponds to the Euclidean length of the projected input vector $\widehat{x}$ that suffices to produce the reference output level y, divided by the length of the observed input vector x:[10]

$$TE_{R(I)}(x, y) = \|\widehat{x}\| / \|x\| = \theta^* \leq 1, \tag{2.4}$$

where θ^* denotes the optimal value obtained when applying empirical methods such as the Data Envelopment Analysis techniques to approximate the production technology and identify the reference benchmark. Therefore, the optimal benchmark on the efficient frontier corresponds to $\widehat{x} = \theta^* x$. If a firm j is technically efficient, then $\theta_j^* = 1$, while $\theta_j^* < 1$ signals technical inefficiency. We illustrate both situations in Fig. 2.2 using the graph representation of the technology T for $M = N = 1$ (left-hand side panel, (a) and the input correspondence $L(y_D)$ with two inputs (right-hand side panel, (b). On both cases, firms A, B, and C are technically efficient, while firm D is

[10] As shown in the remainder of the book, other projections that keep inputs' proportions (mix) fixed and associated with alternative aggregating functions different from the L_2 norm $\|\cdot\|$ (Euclidean length) are possible.

technically inefficient. While the projection on the production frontier precisely identifies firm B as the reference benchmark, i.e., $(\widehat{x}, y_{\mathrm{D}}) = (x_{\mathrm{B}}, y_{\mathrm{D}}) = (\theta_{\mathrm{D}}^{*} x_{\mathrm{D}}, y_{\mathrm{D}})$, this is not the case for the situation depicted for the input correspondence, where the benchmark projection is situated between firms A and B: $(\theta_{\mathrm{D}}^{*} x_{\mathrm{D}}, y_{\mathrm{D}})$.

We note that the nature of returns to scale in the input correspondence would be constant if the input quantities of each firm were divided by its (single) output quantity: x_{jm}/y_j, $m = 1,\ldots,M$ (i.e., in terms of technical coefficients and defining what Farrell (1957) named the—unitary—input isoquant). Although the measurement of productive efficiency and its relation to returns to scale (increasing, constant, or decreasing) was addressed by Farrell himself and later on by Farrell and Fieldhouse (1962), it is not further pursued in this section because the associated concept of scale efficiency does not play a role in the measurement of economic cost efficiency. The reason is that, given the input prices, the underlying (support) cost function from which the production technology can be recovered by duality (and vice versa) does not impose any restriction on the nature of returns to scale at the technological benchmarks (*loci*) minimizing production costs—as opposed to profitability and profit, which require constant and nonincreasing returns to scale, respectively, as shown in Sects. 2.2.3 and 2.2.4. Hence, in what follows, we allow for variable returns to scale and assume that, when calculating technical efficiency, the peer firms in the reference efficient set produce the same output quantity of the firm under evaluation, i.e., y_{D}; see, e.g., Kopp and Diewert (1982).[11] However, in the section below presenting graph efficiency from the multiplicative perspective, where scale effects are yet another source of inefficient behavior, we reintroduce this question.

The radial measure of input technical efficiency (2.4) is not the only possibility when defining efficiency considering the input correspondence $L(y)$. However, it is arguably the definition that provides the simplest interpretation of a firm's performance, i.e., the amount by which two inputs can be reduced equals one less the efficiency score. For example, if $\theta_j^{*}= 0.8$, the firm can reduce its inputs by 20% while producing the same amount of outputs. On the contrary, as a relevant drawback, being a radial measure, it does not comply with the property of measuring efficiency with respect to the strongly efficient subset, a property that is satisfied by additive measures.

2.2.1.2 The Additive Approach

Within the wide array of additive measures considered in the second part of the book, we choose the simplest one corresponding to the slack-based technical

[11] However, in the more general case that allows for non-homothetic technologies, Aparicio et al. (2015a, 2015b) and Aparicio and Zofío (2017) show that the standard radial measures a la Farrell would generally measure both technical *and* allocative efficiencies. We return to these qualifications in the following chapter.

inefficiency measure introduced by Charnes et al. (1985). In fact, this DEA model is known in the literature as *the additive model*, thereby representing a natural option to illustrate the additive approach. This measure is defined in terms of the additive reductions in the observed amounts of inputs (slacks) necessary to reach a reference benchmark $\widehat{x}$ on the production frontier subject to an optimization criterion, which in this case corresponds to the maximization of the aggregate value of the slacks:[12]

$$TI_{A(I)}(x,y) = \sum_{m=1}^{M} (x_m - \widehat{x}_m) = \sum_{m=1}^{m} s_m^{-*} \geq 0, \tag{2.5}$$

where the superscript "*" denotes the optimal values. Given this formulation, the optimal benchmark on the strongly efficient frontier corresponds to $\widehat{x} = x - s^{-*}$. If a firm j is technically efficient, then $s^{-*} = 0$, and $TI_{A(I)}(x_j, y_j) = 0$, while if $s^{-*} > 0$, $m = 1,\ldots,M$, the firm is technically inefficient because at least one input can be reduced maintaining the same level of output y_j, $TI_{A(I)}(x, y) > 0$. In Fig. 2.2a, the value of the slack corresponding to the graph representation of the technology T in the single input case is $s_{\mathrm{D}}^{-*} = x_{\mathrm{D}} - x_{\mathrm{B}}$ and therefore $TI_{A(I)}(x_{\mathrm{D}}, y_{\mathrm{D}}) = s_{\mathrm{D}}^{-*} = (x_{\mathrm{D}} - x_{\mathrm{B}}) > 0$. In the case of the input correspondence $L(y)$ with two inputs, Fig. 2.2b, technical inefficiency defines as in (2.5): $TI_{A(I)}(x_{\mathrm{D}}, y_{\mathrm{D}}) = \sum_{m=1}^{2} s_{\mathrm{D}m}^{-*} = s_{\mathrm{D}1}^{-*} + s_{\mathrm{D}2}^{-*}$. As before, in both panels, firms A, B, and C are technically efficient, while firm D is technically inefficient. Also, the projection on the production frontier corresponds once again to firm B, i.e., $(\widehat{x}, y_{\mathrm{D}}) = (x_{\mathrm{B}}, y_{\mathrm{B}}) = (x_{\mathrm{D}} - s_{\mathrm{D}}^{-*}, y_{\mathrm{D}})$. However, for the case of the input correspondence, the additive measure identifies as benchmark peer firm A, and therefore, $(\widehat{x}, y_{\mathrm{D}}) = (x_{\mathrm{A}}, y_{\mathrm{A}}) = (x_{\mathrm{D}} - s_{\mathrm{D}}^{-*}, y_{\mathrm{D}})$.

Comparing the first examples of multiplicative and additive measures (2.4) and (2.5) allows us to highlight the differences between both definitions of technical (in)efficiency. The most important one refers to the different values signaling (in)-efficiency, $TE_{R(I)}(x, y) = 1$ and $TI_{A(I)}(x, y) = 0$, as well as the monotonicity conditions for inefficient firms: the larger $TE_{R(I)}(x, y)$ is, the more efficient is the firm, while the larger $TI_{R(I)}(x, y)$ is, the more *in*efficient it is. Hence, this distinction in the denomination that we keep throughout the book for notational consistency.

The additive measure of Charnes et al. (1985), despite its main drawback,[13] opened the possibility of designing additive measures based on slacks. Following Lovell and Pastor (1995) and Ali et al. (1995), it is possible to define a family of

[12]This is rather counterintuitive since one would rather look for reference benchmarks that are closer to the evaluated firm. However, from an empirical perspective, minimizing the value of the input slacks involves solving substantially more complex programs than the textbook DEA models based on maximization; see Aparicio et al. (2007) and Aparicio et al. (2017c). We comment on this feature when evaluating the properties of technical (in)efficiency measures.

[13]The DEA additive model is not unit invariant, and consequently, the sum of slacks in the objective function, expressed in different units, has no apparent meaning. Additionally, the efficient projection of each firm depends on the units of measurement considered for each input and output.

well-defined inefficiency measures by multiplying (i.e., normalizing or weighting) the slacks by appropriate factors, giving rise to the input-oriented weighted additive measures:

$$TI_{WA(I)}(x, y, \rho^-) = \sum_{m=1}^{M} \rho_m^- s_m^{-*} \geq 0. \tag{2.6}$$

For example, if we choose the simplest factor $\rho_n^- = 1/x_n$, we encounter the measure of inefficiency proportions (*input MIP*)—originally termed weighted-quantity additive index by Cooper et al. (1999). Meanwhile, normalizing by the range of the input variables, $\rho_m^- = 1/R_m^- = 1/(\max\ (x_m) - \min\ (x_m))$, where max (x_m) and min (x_m) are, respectively, the maximum and minimum quantities observed in each input dimension, results in the range-adjusted inefficiency measure (*input RAM*). Other alternative relying on specific values yields the bound adjusted measure (*input* BAM).[14] Based on the additive decompositions of cost, revenue, and profit efficiency measures that we study in subsequent chapters, we resort to specific definitions that are particular variations of the above additive model. Hence, when studying a specific proposal, we will relate it to the above definition.

In passing, we note also that several authors have proposed to transform the additive measures of inefficiency so that they can be interpreted in the same way as their multiplicative counterparts, i.e., so they are bounded between zero and one as (2.4). For example, the simplest possibility is to transform technical inefficiency as defined in (2.6) as one less the average of the input slacks normalized by the observed input quantities, thereby obtaining the slack-based measure: $TE_{WA(I)}(x, y) = 1 - \frac{1}{M} \sum_{m=1}^{M} \frac{s_m^{-*}}{x_m} \leq 1$. Nevertheless, we remark that we do not endorse here such transformations because the duality relationships that allow the decomposition of normalized economic efficiency into a technical and allocative efficiency entail specific transformations.

2.2.2 *Output Technical (In)Efficiency Measures: Multiplicative and Additive Definitions*

2.2.2.1 The Multiplicative Approach

It is possible to measure technical efficiency considering a radial output orientation. In this case, the technical efficiency measure is defined as the maximum equiproportional expansion (increase) in all outputs that is feasible given the

[14]The main critic to the RAM, already contained in the original paper, is that it delivers small technical inefficiency values due to the large values of the normalization factors. To improve it, the BAM was proposed 12 years later by Cooper et al. (2011), relying on smaller normalization factors.

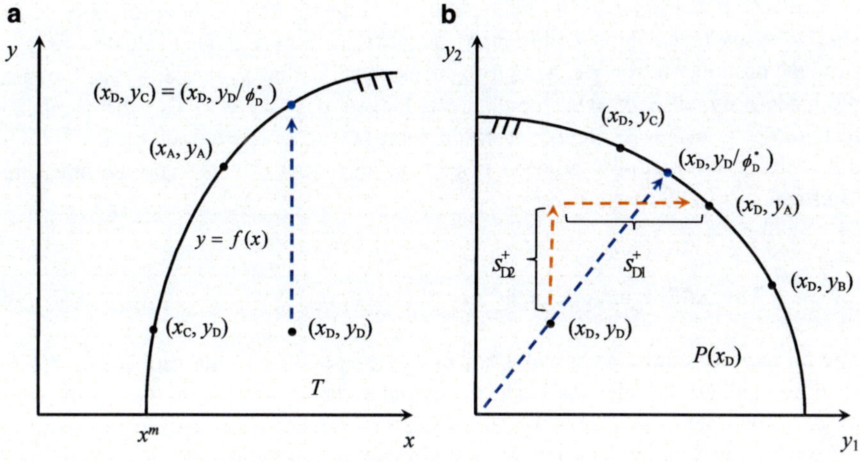

Fig. 2.3 (**a–b**) Output-oriented technical (in)efficiency

production technology and level of inputs, i.e., keeping the input mix fixed. In the single output case, the production function $y = f(x)$ provides the maximum amount of output that can be produced with inputs x, and the technical efficiency score is $TE_{R(O)} = y/f(x)$. In the multiple output-multiple input case, the scalar-valued radial output measure of technical efficiency corresponds to the Euclidean length of the observed output vector y divided by the optimal output vector $\widehat{y}$ given the input level x. Formally,

$$TE_{R(O)}(x, y) = \|y\|/\|\widehat{y}\| = \phi^* \leq 1, \tag{2.7}$$

where, once again, the superscript "*" denotes the optimal value once the production frontier has been approximated through empirical methods. Consequently, the benchmark on the efficient frontier corresponds to $\widehat{y} = y/\phi^*$. On this occasion, if a firm j is technically efficient, then $\phi_j^* = 1$, while $\phi_j^* < 1$ signals, once again, technical inefficiency.[15] In Fig. 2.3a, we illustrate output technical efficiency relying on the previous graph representation of the technology T for $M = N = 1$, while the output correspondence $P(x_D)$ with two outputs is presented in Fig. 2.3b. Regardless of the orientation, the same firms, A, B, and C, are technically efficient, while firm D is technically inefficient. On this occasion, the projection on the production frontier identifies firm C as the reference benchmark, i.e., $(x, \widehat{y}) = (x_D, y_C) = (x_D, y_D/\phi_D^*)$, while in the case of the output correspondence, the benchmark projection is situated between firms A and C: $(x_D, y_D/\phi_D^*)$.

[15] Some authors define the output-oriented technical efficiency measure as the ratio of optimal to observed output quantities (i.e., as its input-oriented counterpart (2.4)), and therefore, $TE_{R(O)}(x, y) = \|\widehat{y}\|/\|y\| \geq 1$. Here, we follow the convention of defining all multiplicative efficiency measures as being bounded by one from above, regardless of the orientation.

The radial measure of output technical efficiency (2.7) can be interpreted in similar terms to its input counterpart, quantifying how far the evaluated firm is from the production frontier. As before, let us consider that $\phi_{\mathrm{D}}^{*} = 0.8$, so that the firm produces only 80% of what could be achieved if it were to use the available technology at its best. Hence, it could increase observed output by 25% (=1/ 0.8 × 100). We can now proceed to present an output-oriented additive measure of efficiency counterpart to (2.7).

2.2.2.2 The Additive Approach

The measure of output technical efficiency corresponding to the additive model of Charnes et al. (1985), also known as the output additive measure, defines as the sum of the output increases (slacks) that are necessary to reach a reference benchmark on the production frontier $\widehat{y}$ subject to an optimization criterion—e.g., once again, the maximum aggregate value of the optimal slacks s^{+*}. This yields the following:

$$TI_{R(O)}(x, y) = \sum_{n=1}^{N} (\widehat{y}_n - y_n) = \sum_{n=1}^{N} s_n^{+*} \geq 0. \tag{2.8}$$

On this occasion, the optimal benchmark on the strongly efficient frontier corresponds to $\widehat{y} = y + s^{+*}$. If a firm j is technically efficient, $TI_{R(O)}(x_j, y_j) = 0$ implying that $s_n^{+*} = 0$, $n = 1, \ldots, N$. On the contrary, if $s_n^{+*} > 0$, for some n, $n = 1, \ldots, N$, the firm is technically inefficient because at least one output can be increased while using the same amount of inputs used by the firm under evaluation, x_j, and $TI_{R(O)}(x_j, y_j) > 0$. In Fig. 2.3a, the value of the slack corresponding to the graph representation of the technology T in the single output case (left-hand side panel, a) is $s_{\mathrm{D}}^{+*} = y_{\mathrm{C}} - y_{\mathrm{D}}$, and therefore, $TI_{R(O)}(x_{\mathrm{D}}, y_{\mathrm{D}}) = s_{\mathrm{D}}^{+*} = (y_C - y_{\mathrm{D}}) > 0$. In the case of the output correspondence $P(x)$ with two outputs, Fig. 2.3b, technical inefficiency defines as in (2.8): $TI_{R(O)}(x_{\mathrm{D}}, y_{\mathrm{D}}) = \sum_{n=1}^{2} s_{\mathrm{D}m}^{+*} = s_{\mathrm{D}2}^{+*} + s_{\mathrm{D}1}^{+*}$. As in the previous cases, firms A, B, and C are technically efficient, while firm D is technically inefficient. In the single input-single output case, the projection on the production frontier is also firm C as in the multiplicative case, i.e., $(x^{*}, y^{*}) = (x_{\mathrm{C}}, y_{\mathrm{C}}) = (x_{\mathrm{D}}, y_{\mathrm{D}} + s_{\mathrm{D}}^{+*})$. But for the case of the output correspondence, the additive measure identifies as benchmark peer firm A, and therefore, $(x_{\mathrm{D}}, \widehat{y}) = (x_{\mathrm{D}}, y_{\mathrm{A}}) = (x_{\mathrm{D}}, y_{\mathrm{D}} + s_{\mathrm{D}}^{+*})$.

Once more, we can compare the multiplicative and additive measures in order to highlight the numerical differences between both definitions of technical (in)-efficiency, (2.7) and (2.8), and their denomination. In the former case, a firm is technically efficient if $TE_{R(O)}(x, y) = 1$, while in the latter case, $TI_{A(O)}(x, y) = 0$. The monotonicity conditions for inefficient firms are also relevant as the larger $TE_{R(O)}(x, y)$ is, the more efficient is the firm, while the larger $TI_{A(O)}(x, y)$ is, the more *in*efficient it is. Again, following Cooper and Pastor (1995) and Lovell and Pastor (1995), we conclude our overview of the output orientation by considering the family of generalized efficiency measures corresponding to the multiplication of the slacks by a normalizing or weighting value:

$$TI_{A(O)}\left(x, y, \rho_n^+\right) = \sum_{n=1}^{N} \rho_n^+ s_n^{+*} \geq 0, \tag{2.9}$$

which can be particularized into the output MIP by choosing $\rho_n^+ = 1/y_n$, the output range-adjusted measure (RAM) with $\rho_n^+ = 1/R_n^+ = 1/(\max\ (y_n) - \min\ (y_n))$, or the output bound adjusted measure (BAM) with $\rho_n^+ = 1/B_n^+ = 1/(\max\ (y_n) - y_n)$. A transformation of additive technical inefficiency which can be interpreted in the same terms based on alternative weights is also possible: e.g., for the range-adjusted measure, we have $TE_{A(O)}\left(x, y, \rho_n^+\right) = 1 - \frac{1}{N} \sum_{n=1}^{N} \frac{s_n^{+*}}{R_n^+} \leq 1$. But, again, we do not pursue here these transformations because throughout the book we focus on the specific normalizations that duality theory requires for a consistent decomposition of economic efficiency.

2.2.3 *Graph Technical (In)Efficiency Measures: Multiplicative and Additive Definitions*

A characterization of the technical efficiency of firms in both the input and output dimensions, from either a multiplicative or an additive perspective, can be obtained by combining the previous partially oriented approaches.

2.2.3.1 The Multiplicative Approach

A natural way to extend Farrell's multiplicative approach to the input and output dimensions simultaneously is to propose a scalar measure that decreases inputs and increases outputs by the same proportion. A measure satisfying this property corresponds to the hyperbolic efficiency measure introduced by Färe et al. (1985, pp. 110–111).[16] With this measure, which can be reinterpreted in terms of a distance function, just as the Farrell measures represent the counterparts to Shephard's distance functions, these authors extended the partially oriented measures to a graph representation of the technology. Chavas and Cox (1999) further qualified this proposal by introducing the generalized distance function, which nests all previous multiplicative measures. We formally discuss this approach to measure technical efficiency within a profitability decomposition, defined as revenue to cost,

[16] They refer to this index as the "Farrell Graph Measure of Technical Efficiency". The measure inherits its name from the hyperbolic path it follows toward the production frontier.

in Chap. 4. Here, we present this concept heuristically as the scalar value that compares the input and output vectors of a firm against a reference benchmark on the frontier by way of the Hadamard product. Specifically, the value of this measure can be recovered from the component-wise (or pairwise) division of a reference benchmark $(\widehat{x}, \widehat{y})$ by the observed vector (x, y), where the former is consistent with the joint projection of inputs and outputs toward the production frontier: i.e., $(\widehat{x}, \widehat{y})./(x, y) = (\varphi^*, 1/\varphi^*)$. Once again, the superscript "*" indicates the specific optimal value consistent with the calculation of the reference benchmark through empirical methods. We can then define the graph (hyperbolic) technical efficiency measure as follows:

$$TE_{H(G)}(x, y) = (\varphi^*)^2 \leq 1. \tag{2.10}$$

This measure is defined as the square of φ^* for interpretative and duality reasons that become apparent in what follows.[17] It encompasses the partial approaches since φ^* reduces the input quantities similar to the input-oriented technical efficiency measure (2.4) while increasing the output quantities as for the output-oriented technical efficiency measure (2.7). On this occasion, the optimal benchmark corresponds to $(\widehat{x}, \widehat{y}) = (x\varphi^*, y/\varphi^*)$. If a firm j is inefficient, then $\varphi_j^* < 1$, while $\varphi_j^* = 1$ signals technical efficiency. This measure is illustrated once again using the graph representation of the technology for $N = M = 1$ in Fig. 2.4a. Now, the projection for firm D does not identify any of the efficient firms A, B, and C but a new one $(\widehat{x}, \widehat{y}) = (\varphi^* x_D, y_D/\varphi^*)$.

So far, the technical efficiency of firms has been evaluated with respect to the variable returns to scale technological frontier. However, within the graph approach to technical efficiency measurement, it is relevant to identify an additional source of inefficiency, resulting from firms operating at a suboptimal scale, which prevents them from attaining maximum productivity. We discuss here the concept of scale efficiency because it plays a critical role when explaining why firms fail to be economic efficient by maximizing profitability, defined as revenue to costs. The concept of scale efficiency can be related to that of productivity.[18] In multiple

[17] Moreover, as shown in Chap. 4 presenting the duality between the profitability function and the generalized distance function introduced by Chavas and Cox (1999), this latter measure corresponds to φ^*; i.e., the square root of $TE_{H(G)}(x, y)$. Actually, we could have developed the duality results presented below based on this measure, but it requires exponentiating φ^* to α and $(1-\alpha)$ for inputs and outputs, respectively. Hence, for simplicity, in this chapter, we stay with the (square of) hyperbolic efficiency measure.

[18] Chambers (1988), Morrison (1993), and Beattie et al. (2009) discuss the concepts of returns to scale and elasticity of scale within a standard (neoclassical) presentation of production theory, with emphasis on duality theory and its implications for empirical work. As a result, from a primal perspective, these books rely on (single output) functions rather than adopting a general axiomatic approach based on (multiple output-multiple input) distance functions like that initiated by Shephard (1953, 1970) and followed by Färe and Primont (1995). This is necessary since empirical production studies resort to regression analysis to estimate the technology, where production is the dependent variable. They also discuss duality issues within a parametric context since the definition and econometric estimation of cost, revenue, or profit functions represent a convenient framework for studying multi-output technologies and characterize their properties.

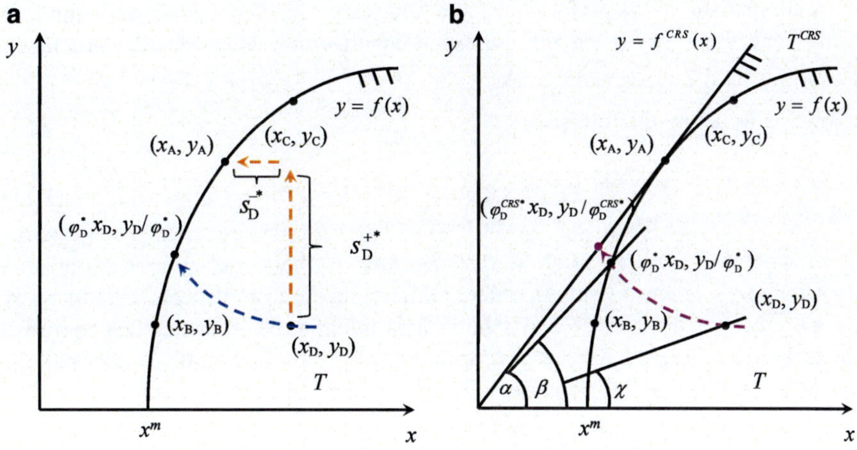

Fig. 2.4 (**a–b**) Graph (hyperbolic)-oriented technical (in)efficiency

output-multiple input technologies, the (total factor) productivity of a firm is a scalar measure corresponding to the ratio of aggregate outputs to aggregate inputs. Productivity in turn can be decomposed into several efficiency factors and can be linked to economic efficiency measurement as we show in subsequent chapters; e.g., see O'Donnell (2012) and Balk and Zofío (2018).[19] The reason is that profitability, defined as revenue to cost, is in itself a measure of productivity. In this measure, outputs in the numerator are aggregated using selling prices $p \in \mathbb{R}_+^N$, while inputs in the denominator are aggregated using buying prices $w \in \mathbb{R}_+^M$.

As maximum productivity is characterized by the existence of local constant returns to scale, we recall here the technology T^{CRS}, consisting of all input-output combinations below their corresponding production frontier, $y = f^{CRS}(x)$, as represented in Fig. 2.4b. We see that T^{CRS} is the convex cone spanned by T at firm A where local constant returns to scale hold, with $T \subset T^{CRS}$—i.e., constant returns to scale technology has a vertex at the origin. We remark that constant returns to scale virtual technology does not replace the actual variable returns technology. It is a construction that proves useful to convey the idea of benchmark production plans that exhibit the required (local) constant returns to scale necessary to maximize profitability. By spanning the technology at these *loci*, we can define the reference (total factor or aggregate) productivity values against which to calculate constant returns productive efficiency and, ultimately, profitability efficiency (given input and output prices).

[19]Distance functions represent specific aggregating functions for inputs and outputs. Data Envelopment Analysis techniques, in their dual (multiplier) formulations, aggregate inputs and outputs through shadow (optimizing) prices, while economic functions (i.e., cost, revenue, profitability, or profit) rely on observed market prices. Eventually, allocative efficiency can be seen as a disparity between vectors of aggregating weights (shadow and market prices) when evaluating technical efficiency (using shadow prices) and economic efficiency (using market prices).

A comparison of the performance of a firm with respect to the constant returns to scale benchmark results in the corresponding measure of productive efficiency. Resorting to the Hadamard product, $\left(\widehat{x}^{\mathrm{CRS}}, \widehat{y}^{\mathrm{CRS}}\right)./(x, y) = \left(\varphi^{\mathrm{CRS}*}, (\varphi^{\mathrm{CRS}*})^{-1}\right)$, allows us to define the following:

$$TE_{H(G)}^{CRS}(x, y) = (\varphi^{CRS*})^2 \leq 1. \tag{2.11}$$

In what follows, we refer to this measure as the constant returns to scale *productive efficiency* measure in order to differentiate it from its technical efficiency counterpart. It is then possible to define a measure of scale efficiency that compares the technical efficiency with respect to the variable returns to scale frontier with its constant returns to scale counterpart. This yields the following measure:

$$SE_{H(G)}(x, y) = \left(\frac{\varphi^{CRS*}}{\varphi^{*}}\right)^2 \leq 1. \tag{2.12}$$

$SE_{H(G)}(x, y)$ measures the inefficiency experienced by a firm that produces at a suboptimal scale (or size), thereby enduring either increasing or decreasing returns to scale, and therefore is unable to achieve the maximum productivity obtainable at an optimal scale, i.e., the highest ratio of aggregate output to aggregate input. In the multiple output-multiple input case, this ratio measure is known as total factor productivity, and depending on the aggregating functions and their associated weights, there can be several most productive scale sizes (MPSS, in the terminology of Banker et al., 1984).[20]

For the single input-single output case depicted in Fig. 2.4b, firm A maximizes average productivity, defined as the ratio of output to input, y/x, and whose value,

---

[20]Balk (1998:19) refers to these firms as those exhibiting a technically optimal scale. O'Donnell (2012:260) identifies them as *mix-invariant optimal scales*, because the radial projection of the firms to the efficient frontier keeps the input and output mixes constant. In the multiple output-multiple input case, the y and x axes in Figure 2.4 could be seen as aggregated outputs and inputs using specific aggregating functions. The comparison between an observed firm and its projections on the frontier associated with the radial efficiency measures (or Shephard's input or output distance functions) corresponds to particular aggregating functions of the input and output vectors:$X(x)$ and $Y(y)$—i.e., in these cases equivalent to the use of the L_2 norm $\|\cdot\|$ associated with the Euclidean length. O'Donnell (2012) shows that efficiency measurement can be performed considering alternative aggregating functions (e.g., linear, CES). Consequently, if an alternative aggregating function is selected (e.g., linear functions with specific weight vectors for inputs and outputs:$X(x) = w \cdot x$, $w \in \mathbb{R}_+^M$, and $Y(y) = p \cdot y$, $p \in \mathbb{R}_+^N$), then smaller (bigger) aggregate scalar input (output) quantities than those obtained with the radial efficient projections could be obtained. The scalar difference between the aggregate efficient output obtained by using the radial distance function and those obtained with alternative aggregating functions is termed *mix efficiency* by O'Donnell (2012), because the use of these alternative aggregating functions and associated weights results in changes in the input and output mixes. Later on, we recall that this interpretation is actually equivalent to the concept of allocative efficiency when the aggregating input and output functions correspond to the usual cost, revenue, profitability, or profit functions, i.e., those having a meaningful economic significance.

resorting to trigonometry, corresponds to the steepest slope of any ray vector joining the origin and the technology. Scale efficiency for firm D corresponds to the gap between average productivities; i.e., it defines as the ratio between the productivity level at the benchmark reference on the variable returns to scale frontier, $(\varphi_{\mathrm{D}}^{*}x_{D}, y_{\mathrm{D}}/\varphi_{\mathrm{D}}^{*})$, defined in turn as the observed output quantity divided by the optimal (projected) input amount, $((y_{\mathrm{D}}/\varphi_{\mathrm{D}}^{*})/\varphi_{\mathrm{D}}^{*}x_{\mathrm{D}}) = \left(y_{\mathrm{D}}/(\varphi_{\mathrm{D}}^{*})^{2}x_{D}\right)$, divided by the productivity at the optimal size given the technology, represented by firm A, $y_{\mathrm{A}}/x_{\mathrm{A}}$. Graphically, this corresponds to the productivity of the benchmark reference at the constant returns to scale frontier $y_{\mathrm{A}}/x_{\mathrm{A}} = ((y_{\mathrm{D}}/\varphi_{\mathrm{D}}^{CRS*})/\varphi_{\mathrm{D}}^{CRS*}x_{D}) = \left(y_{\mathrm{D}}/(\varphi_{\mathrm{D}}^{CRS*})^{2}x_{D}\right)$. Hence, scale efficiency as defined in (2.12) is $SE_{H(G)}(x_{\mathrm{D}}, y_{\mathrm{D}}) = \left(y_{\mathrm{D}}/(\varphi_{\mathrm{D}}^{*})^{2}x_{\mathrm{D}}\right)/\left(y_{\mathrm{D}}/(\varphi_{\mathrm{D}}^{CRS*})^{2}x_{\mathrm{D}}\right) = (\varphi_{\mathrm{D}}^{CRS*}/\varphi_{\mathrm{D}}^{*})^{2} \leq 1$.[21]

This demonstrates that technical efficiency comparisons can be interpreted in terms of differences in productivity levels between the firm under evaluation and alternative technological benchmarks. Indeed, the above definitions show that it is possible to multiplicatively decompose technical efficiency with respect to maximum productivity into a technical efficiency component under the variable returns to scale assumption times scale efficiency. This results in the following definition:

$$TE_{H(G)}^{CRS}(x,y) = TE_{H(G)}(x,y) \times SE_{H(G)}(x,y) = (\varphi^{CRS*})^{2} \leq 1, \tag{2.13}$$

and the productivity interpretation corresponds to the ratio of aggregate output to aggregate input. For unit D in Fig. 2.4b, $TE_{H(G)}^{CRS}(x,y) = (y_{\mathrm{D}}/x_{\mathrm{D}})/(y_{\mathrm{A}}/x_{\mathrm{A}}) = (\varphi_{\mathrm{D}}^{CRS*})^{2}$.[22]

The interpretation of the value of the hyperbolic measure of technical efficiency combines that of its input and output counterparts. Consequently, if $\varphi_j = 0.8$, then the amount of inputs can be reduced by 20% (=(1–0.8) × 100) while simultaneously increasing outputs by 25% (=(1/0.8–1) × 100). The combined effect of input contraction and output expansion results in a productivity increase of 56.25% (=(1/0.8^2–1) × 100). The triplet of measures can be related under the assumption that the technology exhibits constant returns to scale. Following Färe et al. (1985), if we calculate the input and output technical efficiencies under CRS, it can be shown that $\theta^{CRS*} = \phi^{CRS*} = (\varphi^{CRS*})^{2}$.[23]

---

[21] Resorting to trigonometry, scale efficiency defines equivalently as the ratio of the slope of the ray vector joining the origin and the efficient projection on the variable returns to scale technology to that of observation A, i.e., in Figure 2.4b, $SE_{G(H)}(x,y) = \tan\beta / \tan\alpha$.

[22] In trigonometric terms, productive efficiency defines as the ratio of the slope of the ray vector joining the origin and observation D to that of observation A, i.e., $TE_{H(G)}^{CRS}(x_{\mathrm{D}}, y_{\mathrm{D}})$ = slope 0D/slope 0A = $\tan\chi/\tan\alpha$.

[23] The relationship does not hold however for variable returns to scale despite what is stated in Färe et al. (1994, Chap. 8); see Zofio and Knox Lovell (2001).

2.2.3.2 The Additive Approach

Charnes et al. (1985) proposed the additive slack measure of efficiency in terms of both the input and output dimensions. Hence, the previous input- and output-oriented measures (2.5) and (2.8) are particular cases of a comprehensive technical efficiency measure defined on *T*. This measure defines as the sum of the input reductions and output increases necessary to reach a reference benchmark on the production frontier $(\widehat{x}, \widehat{y})$ subject to an optimization criterion—i.e., once again, maximizing the input and output slacks:

$$TI_{A(G)}(x, y) = \sum_{m=1}^{M} (x_m - \widehat{x}_m) + \sum_{n=1}^{N} (\widehat{y}_n - y_n) = \sum_{m=1}^{M} s_m^{-*} + \sum_{n=1}^{N} s_n^{+*} \geq 0, \quad (2.14)$$

where the subscript "*" denotes the optimal slack values that are obtained after approximating the production technology through empirical methods based on linear programming such as Data Envelopment Analysis. Again, the optimal benchmark on the strongly efficient frontier is $(\widehat{x}, \widehat{y}) = (x - s^{-*}, y + s^{+*})$. Therefore, if firm j is technically efficient, then $TI_{A(G)}(x_j, y_j) = 0$, while if any of the input slacks or output slacks are positive, the firm is technically inefficient because at least one input can be decreased or an output can be increased so as to reach the production frontier: $TI_{A(G)}(x_j, y_j) > 0$. In Fig. 2.4a, the value of the slacks corresponding to the graph representation of the technology is $\left(s_{\mathrm{D}}^{-*}, s_{\mathrm{D}}^{+*}\right) = (x_{\mathrm{D}} - x_A, y_{\mathrm{A}} - y_{\mathrm{D}})$ with $TI_{G(A)}(x_{\mathrm{D}}, y_{\mathrm{D}}) = s_{\mathrm{D}}^{-*} + s_{\mathrm{D}}^{+*} > 0$. Although the exemplified reference benchmark on the frontier maximizes productivity—firm A—and therefore firm D is scale-efficient at that projection, we do not present here measures of scale efficiency in the additive framework because, as discussed in Sect. 2.2.4, a natural duality between additive measures and profitability efficiency cannot be obtained, at least in their actual formulation. Hence, since the duality of these measures is restricted to profit inefficiency, which does not impose constant returns to scale on the technology, the definition of productive technical inefficiency in additive terms, including both technical and scale components, is unnecessary.

The numerical interpretation of the multiplicative and additive measures as for the value of (in)efficiency is equivalent to those commented for the partially oriented input and output approaches. Consequently, a firm is technically efficient in the multiplicative approach if $TE_{H(G)}(x, y) = 1$, while in the additive approach, $TI_{A(G)}(x, y) = 0$. Again, the monotonicity conditions imply that firms are more efficient the larger is $TE_{H(G)}(x, y)$, while the opposite holds for $TI_{A(G)}(x, y)$, since the larger this value, the more inefficient firms are. Finally, following Cooper and Pastor (1995) and Lovell and Pastor (1995), we can define a family of generalized efficiency measures corresponding to the multiplication of the input and output slack by a normalizing or weighting value:

$$TI_{WA(G)}\left(x, y, \rho_m^-, \rho_n^+\right) = \sum_{m=1}^{M} \rho_m^- s_m^{-*} + \sum_{n=1}^{N} \rho_n^+ s_n^{+*} \geq 0. \tag{2.15}$$

As before, if $\rho_m^- = 1/x_m$ and $\rho_n^+ = 1/y_n$, then technical inefficiency corresponds to the measure of inefficiency proportions (MIP), while the use of alternative weights, such as the range of the input and output variables or pre-specified bounds, results in the RAM and BAM measures. Finally, a transformation of the additive technical inefficiency which can be interpreted in the same terms as the multiplicative measures corresponds now to the following expression discussed by Pastor et al. (1999) and by Tone (2001): $TE_{A(G)}\left(x, y, \rho_m^-, \rho_n^+\right) = \left(1 - \frac{1}{M} \sum_{m=1}^{M} \frac{s_m^{-*}}{x_m}\right) / \left(1 + \frac{1}{N} \sum_{n=1}^{N} \frac{s_n^{+*}}{y_n}\right) \leq 1.$

2.2.4 *Properties of Technical (In)Efficiency Measures: Multiplicative and Additive*

So far, we have presented in a heuristic manner the framework for the measurement of multiplicative and additive technical efficiency measures. Here, we discuss some of the properties that these measures should satisfy to adequately measure the efficiency of the firms under evaluation from a technological perspective. Complying with these properties is critical to the analysis of economic efficiency. The reason is that the decomposition of economic efficiency into technical and allocative terms depends precisely on the value of the technical efficiency, i.e., the ability of the firm to exploit the existing technology to its full, which within the firm falls under the responsibility of the production department. To the extent that allocative efficiency is calculated as a residual, e.g., profit (in)efficiency that is not due to technical reasons, the actual measurement of technical efficiency is the key to a consistent decomposition.[24]

The most prominent example of this situation is multiplicative measures that fail to ensure that technical efficiency is measured against the strongly efficient technology set. For example, if non-radial sources of technical inefficiency (slacks) persist after solving radial inefficiencies, this will result in the overestimation of technical efficiency and the underestimation of allocative efficiency. Naturally, to the extent that both sources of inefficiency can be attributed to specific agents within the firm, a blame game on who is accountable and how to share the responsibility is likely to emerge. An example would be the production department being responsible for achieving the targeted quantities for specific products on schedule but based on the market projections submitted by the sales department. In this way, if the firm runs

[24] There is only one exception presented in Chap. 13 and related to the so-called reverse approaches, where technical inefficiency is a subsidiary of allocative inefficiency.

out of stock or endures unintended stock excesses as a result of misjudgments by the sales department, the firm will require an explanation from it. But if production falls short of the planned targets in the process of converting raw materials and other products into finished goods, the opposite takes place. Naturally, labor conflicts or delays in the supply chain would fall under the responsibility of the human resources and purchasing departments. How to anticipate the different sources of inefficiency that may emerge and how to solve them if they materialize are an everyday task for the ordinary firm, and the ability to quantify and identify these alternative sources through benchmarking can certainly assist in this process.

Over the years, a consensus has emerged in the literature about the properties or tests that technical efficiency measures should pass from an axiomatic perspective. Not surprisingly, the most important one, affecting oriented measures—mainly multiplicative—is their inability to characterize a firm as being efficient in terms of the Pareto-Koopmans definition. Färe and Lovell (1978) initiated a literature on the axiomatic approach to technical efficiency measurement by presenting three axioms that an input (or output)-based efficiency measure should satisfy. Later on, Pastor et al. (1999) and Russell and Schworm (2011) completed their presentation to those defined on the input and output spaces, i.e., graph measures of efficiency such as the hyperbolic or additive measures presented above. We highlight here the four most relevant properties that are identified in the literature as natural requirements for an (in)efficiency measure:

(E1a) *Indication*: Firm (x, y) should be deemed efficient if and only if it belongs to the strongly efficient subset, $\partial^S(T)$, in the above expression (2.2). Then, $TE(x, y) = 1$, and equivalently, $TI(x, y) = 0$. Consequently,

(E1b) Inefficient firms, $TE(x, y) < 1$ and $TI(x, y) > 0$, should be compared to reference benchmarks that belong to the strongly efficient subset, $\partial^S(T)$.

(E2) *Strong monotonicity*. For measures defined in the input space, an increase in any input, holding other inputs as well as all outputs constant, reduces the value of the measure and vice versa for the output measure; i.e., a decrease in any output, holding other outputs as well as all inputs constant, also reduces the value of the measure. For graph measures defined on the technology, both properties should be jointly verified. The weak version of the strong monotonicity axiom is simply called *monotonicity* and implies that the input and output measures cannot increase allowing the measure to remain invariant. This property is defined analogously for the additive approaches.

(E3) *Homogeneity*. For multiplicative measures defined in the input space, $TE_{R(I)}(x, y)$ should be homogenous of degree minus one in inputs; i.e., doubling all inputs and keeping outputs constant decreases the value of $TE_{R(I)}(x, y)$ by half. Equivalently, the output measure $TE_{R(O)}(x, y)$ should be homogenous of degree one in outputs; i.e., doubling all outputs and keeping inputs constant also double the value of $TE_{R(O)}(x, y)$. For graph measures, the relevant concept is that of almost homogeneity, implying that if inputs and outputs are, respectively, halved and doubled (a change in inverse proportions), then the measure also doubles—see Aczél 1966; Chaps. 5, 7) and Lau (1972).[25]

(E4) *Units invariance* (or *commensurability*) for multiplicative measures. This property implies that the values of the efficiency measure do not depend on the units of measurements of inputs and outputs. The radially oriented Farrell-type measures clearly verify this property since units of measurement are both in the numerator and denominator of $TE_{R(I)}(x, y)$ and $TE_{R(O)}(x, y)$. The graph measure also satisfies this property. For untransformed additive measures, it is also clear that the value of the slacks depends on the units of measurement, i.e., $TI_{A(I)}(x, y)$, $TI_{A(O)}(x, y)$, and $TI_{A(G)}(x, y)$. However, units invariance can be easily imposed adopting weighted additive measures of inefficiency, i.e., all $TI_{A(I)}\left(x, y, \rho_m^-\right)$, $TI_{A(O)}\left(x, y, \rho_n^+\right)$, and $TI_{A(G)}\left(x, y, \rho_m^-, \rho_n^+\right)$ satisfy it as long as the weights correspond to the (inverse) values expressed in the same units of measurement of inputs and outputs (Lovell & Pastor, 1995).

(E5) *Translation invariance.* This property ensures that additive measures are invariant to affine transformations of the variables (Lovell & Pastor, 1995).[26] This property is important for computational reasons when the data contain zero or negative values, i.e., if the data are not all strictly positive. However, its importance is limited when measuring and decomposing overall economic efficiency as we generally consider positive values for quantities and prices.

As anticipated, the most relevant property (E1) is intended to ensure that an (in)efficiency measure complies with Koopmans' definition of Pareto efficiency, given its implications in the decomposition of economic efficiency, while properties (E2) and (E3) address sensible regularities in the change of the (in)efficiency measures with respect to changes in inputs and outputs (either individual changes, *monotonicity*, or joint changes, *homogeneity*). In general, it can be proved that the multiplicative measures do not satisfy (E1a) and (E1b), while additive measures do, along with strong monotonicity (E2). On the contrary, multiplicative measures comply with homogeneity requirements, while additive measure requires specific transformations. Also, properties may be related with each other. For example, failure to satisfy (E1), as multiplicative and additively oriented measures do, implies that the efficiency measures exhibit weak monotonicity. But, on the other hand, while satisfying (E1), the standard additive measures search for the maximum distance to the strongly efficient frontier, which is rather counterintuitive since closer targets represent a more useful benchmark when advising managers on how to improve their production plans (Aparicio, 2016). Therefore, if we were to include

[25]From an empirical perspective, a key issue when calculating efficiency measures is to ensure that the chosen formulations satisfy the homogeneity conditions. In the case of the graph (hyperbolic) efficiency measure, Cuesta and Zofío (2005) show how the almost homogeneity condition can be imposed on the translog specification. Hence, although Russell and Schworm (2011) state that for graph measures, there is no obvious counterpart to the homogeneity properties of the partially oriented measures, there seems to be some guidance when exploring meaningful counterparts.

[26]For the use of negative data with DEA, see also Pastor (1996).

this criterion as an additional property, additive measures would fail it. More importantly, from the perspective of economic efficiency measurement, projecting inefficient firms to the farthest benchmark overvalues technical inefficiency and, complementarily, undervalues allocative efficiency. This has been a matter of concern in the literature. However, from an empirical perspective, minimizing the value of the input slacks, while feasible, requires the revision of the model and associated computational methods, because the DEA programs are more complex to solve, requiring, for example, bi-level linear programming; see Aparicio et al. (2007) and Aparicio et al. (2017c).

Hence, whether a particular technical efficiency measure contemplated in subsequent chapters satisfies some of these properties must be addressed on an individual basis. Since our guiding principle when choosing a specific measure is the existence of a dual relationship with a supporting economic function (either cost, revenue, profit, or profitability), the fact that a measure fails to satisfy some axioms should be acknowledged as a weakness, but does not necessarily lead to its rejection. As Bol (1986)—for the multiplicative case—and Russell and Schworm (2011) demonstrate, there exists no efficiency measure that satisfies indication, monotonicity, and homogeneity for all technologies satisfying minimal regularity conditions.

The only way out is either to weaken the above axioms or restrict the set of technologies to which the measure applies. In this latter case, Dmitruk and Koshevoy (1991) characterize the class of technologies for which there exists an efficiency index satisfying these three conditions. Compactness is a key property, which is satisfied under closedness (T5) and convexity (T6). Hence, the standard Data Envelopment Analysis characterizations of production technology through linear programming, satisfying T1–T6, imply the existence of a suitable efficiency measure. Unfortunately, as stated above, the multiplicative and additively oriented efficiency measures defined on these approximations of the technology do not comply with the necessary indication and strong monotonicity properties, while the non-oriented additive measures fail to meet homogeneity.

In the light of these possibilities, the axiomatic approach becomes a secondary criterion when choosing among different efficiency measures. This is particularly so since the existing literature on the decomposition of economic efficiency follows a path that has not been specially concerned with the number of desirable properties that efficiency measures should satisfy. Here, following Russell and Schworm (2009), we conclude that there is not a measure, or general class of measures, that satisfies all these properties, and therefore, a trade-off emerges when choosing from among the selected approaches, multiplicative or additive, and particular measures within each category; i.e., no particular efficiency measures dominate for all dimensions. Nevertheless, we anticipate that recent efforts have resulted in new measures that satisfy a wider range of properties, such as the additively "reversed directional distance function" introduced by Pastor et al. (2016) that measures the efficiency in the orientation set by a directional vector but ensures that the reference benchmark belongs to the strongly efficient subset.

2.3 Economic Behavior and Economic Efficiency

Within the market, firms aim at attaining the best possible economic outcome. In textbook characterizations of the market behavior of a representative firm, it is assumed that it intends to maximize profit, defined as revenue less cost. It is possible however that the firm faces constraints on the output or input sides that prevent the maximization of profit by choosing what would be optimal output and input quantities. For example, a regulated industry may result in firm-level production quotas that leave little room of maneuver, and therefore, with sales practically fixed, the only way a firm can achieve better economic performance is by focusing on the minimization of costs. In this way, the production and purchase departments will take the lead in identifying opportunities for cost reduction. Conversely, institutional arrangements can result in limited control over the amount of labor, capital, or intermediate inputs, so the firm sees little margin to reduce production costs. In this situation, the sales and marketing departments gain relevance in increasing the revenue of the firm through improvements in the portfolio of products and price revenue management practices (if output markets are not competitive). Hence, it is relevant to study the economic behavior of the firm from these three complementary perspectives: cost, revenue, and profit, complemented with the possibility of reinterpreting the economic behavior of the firm in terms of the ratio of revenue to costs, rather than their difference, corresponding to the concept of profitability. Profitability can be easily related to standard measures of productivity which, given the variation of input and output prices over short periods of time, is critical to the competitiveness and survival of the firm in the long run.

These economic objectives are recalled throughout the book, and therefore, it is relevant to present them in this initial chapter for future reference. Particularly, in this section, we present the properties of the cost, revenue, profitability, and profit functions and illustrate the optimal choice of input and output quantities that ensure that the firm reaches these goals. We assume that there exist market prices for inputs and outputs, denoted by the following vectors: $w \in \mathbb{R}^M_{++}$ and $p \in \mathbb{R}^N_{++}$. In the following section, we illustrate the decomposition of firms' economic (in)efficiency thanks to the duality between these functions and the previously selected measures. Mirroring the presentation of the latter in the previous section starting with the input space, we begin with the cost function, followed by the revenue, profitability, and profit functions.

2.3.1 *Cost Minimization and Cost (In)Efficiency*

The cost function represents the minimum cost of producing a fixed amount of outputs given input prices. Assuming the necessary derivative properties—including continuity and differentiability—it is possible to determine the input demand functions by applying Shephard's lemma. Following different authors, e.g., McFadden (1978) and Färe and Primont (1995), the cost function defines as follows[27]:

$$C(y, w) = \min_{x} \{w \cdot x : x \in L(y)\}, \quad w \in \mathbb{R}^{M}_{++}, y \geq 0_N. \tag{2.16}$$

Under the minimal regularity conditions on the production possibility sets T1–T6, inherited by the input correspondence $L(y)$, it can be shown that:

(C1) $C(y, w)$ is a nonnegative function and nondecreasing in w.
(C2) $C(y, w)$ is linearly homogeneous of degree one in w.
(C3) $C(y, w)$ is concave and continuous in w.

Additionally, if we impose stronger regularity conditions, such as the existence of constant returns to scale, implying homotheticity, so the technology is the closed convex cone T^{CRS} previously defined, then $C(y, w)$ will be a linearly homogeneous, convex, and nondecreasing function of y for fixed w and $C(y, w) = yC(1, w)$. However, cost minimization does not impose a priori restrictions on the scale or homotheticity characteristics of technology in order to be defined in a meaningful way (as opposed to the profitability or profit functions presented in what follows), so that we stay within the weaker non-homothetic context. This, however, has relevant implications in the measurement of input-oriented economic efficiency as shown by Aparicio et al. (2015a, 2015b) in the nonparametric DEA context and Aparicio and Zofío (2017) in a parametric framework that revisits Kopp and Diewert (1982). Regardless of the (non)homotheticity assumption, we follow the literature for now and assume that firms target a fixed level of output y in their production plans (even if, from the perspective of researchers, it is unknown whether the output level y was that originally intended by the firm or not). Hence, if the firm is capable of producing this output level incurring the minimum cost given input prices w, then it demands the optimal input quantities $x^C(y,w)$.[28] This locus corresponds to $x^C(y, w)$ in Fig. 2.5a where $C(y, w) = w_1 x_1^C + w_2 x_2^C$ is represented by the solid isocost line tangent to the

[27]Notice that $L(y)$ is closed since we are supposing that T is closed. However, it is not enough to assure that "inf" can be substituted by "min" in $\inf_{x} \{w \cdot x | x \in L(y)\}$. So, hereafter, we assume that the optimization problem associated with the calculation of the cost function $C(y, w)$ always attains its minimum in the set $L(y)$. There exist several sufficient conditions in the literature which ensure such result. For example, Shephard (1970, p. 223) assumed that the subset of Pareto-efficient points of $L(y)$ are bounded. Another case is when the technology is a polyhedral set (see Mangasarian, 1994, p. 130).

[28]Shephard's lemma allows us to recover the system of demand equations defined by the partial derivatives of the cost function with respect to input prices: $x^C(y, w) = \nabla_w C(y, w)$. The result requires that the multiple output-multiple input transformation function characterizing the technology is (i) well behaved satisfying all desirable neoclassical properties and regularity conditions, particularly quasi-concavity, which ensures that the associated input production possibility sets are convex, e.g., Madden (1986), and (ii) continuous and twice differentiable. In textbooks, where the technology is represented by the single output production function $y = f(x)$, for any two inputs k and l with associated market prices w_k and w_l, the first-order conditions also imply that the marginal rate of technical substitution of factor k for factor l must be equal to their price ratio: $MRS_l^k = -dl/dk = f_k(x)/f_l(x) = w_k/w_l$, where $f_k(x) = \partial f(x)/\partial x_k$ and $f_l(x) = \partial f(x)/\partial x_l$ are marginal productivities. It is assumed that given our assumptions about the production function, the second-order conditions are verified, and therefore, the sign of the bordered Hessian determinant is negative.

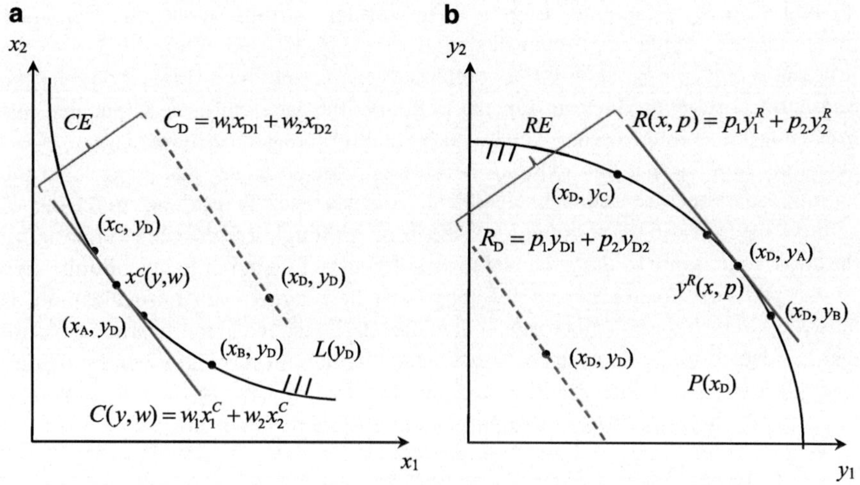

Fig. 2.5 (**a–b**) Cost minimization, revenue maximization, and economic (in)efficiency

isoquant of the production possibility set $L(y)$. The isocost line represents the set of input vectors that, given input prices, entail the same cost for the firm. It is easy to see that any alternative input combination different from $x^C(y, w)$ cannot produce output level y incurring lower costs given the technology. We also see that the technical inefficient firm (x_D, y_D) is also economically inefficient because it incurs higher production costs, as represented by the dashed isocost line passing through it: $C_D = w_1x_{D1} + w_2x_{D2}$, i.e., $C_D > C(y_D, w)$. Regarding the technically efficient firms A, B, and C, they are also cost-inefficient. As presented in the following section, since the source of this inefficiency is not technical (i.e., these firms belong to the production frontier), it becomes apparent that this is the result of demanding a suboptimal mix of inputs given their prices, i.e., allocative inefficiency.

Following Farrell (1957), cost efficiency is defined multiplicatively as the ratio of minimum cost to observed cost:

$$CE(x, y, w) = \frac{C(y, w)}{w \cdot x} = \frac{w \cdot x^C(y, w)}{w \cdot x} \leq 1. \tag{2.17}$$

Therefore, unless the firm under evaluation demands optimal input quantities, it incurs cost inefficiency. For cost-efficient firms, $CE(x, y, w) = 1$, while $CE(x, y, w) < 1$ signals cost inefficiency. One may define cost inefficiency in an additive framework as observed cost less optimal cost, i.e.,

$$CI(x, y, w) = w \cdot x - C(y, w) \geq 0. \tag{2.18}$$

In this case, $CI(x, y, w) = 0$ implies cost efficiency, with $CI(x, y, w) > 0$ measuring the cost excess in monetary (currency) units. Therefore, the interpretation of $CE(x, y,$

w) and $CI(x, y, w)$ is quite different. The former informs about the proportion representing minimum cost over observed cost; e.g., if $CE(x, y, w) = 0.5$, then the firm could reduce its cost by 50%, or alternatively, taking the inverse, it doubles the minimum cost of production. On the contrary, the latter informs about the cost excess in dollars, euros, etc., which can be readily interpreted by managers. However, this implies that the additive measure of cost efficiency, as opposed to the multiplicative one, is not unit-independent. This is a result that extends to the rest of additive measures in the following subsections. Although it is possible to normalize the additive measure so that it can be interpreted in terms similar to its multiplicative counterpart, we do not pursue this approach here since such normalization, as presented in the subsequent chapters, depends on the technical inefficiency measure that is selected to decompose cost inefficiency, which, in turn, is driven by duality theory. Finally, the cost excess corresponding to firm (x_D, y_D) is represented in Fig. 2.5a by the gap between the optimal and observed isocost lines.

2.3.2 *Revenue Maximization and Revenue (In)Efficiency*

From an output perspective, the revenue function represents the maximum revenue of selling output quantities given (fixed) amounts of input and output prices. Assuming the necessary derivative properties, again including continuity and differentiability, we can recover the output supply functions by applying Shephard's lemma. Following, once again, the previous authors, the revenue function defines as follows[29]:

$$R(x, p) = \max_{y} \{p \cdot y : y \in P(x)\}, \quad p \in \mathbb{R}^N_{++}, x \geq 0_N. \tag{2.19}$$

As before, under the minimal regularity conditions on the technologies T1–T6, inherited by the output correspondence $P(x)$, the properties of the revenue function are the following:

(R1) $R(x, p)$ is a nonnegative function and nondecreasing in p.
(R2) $R(x, p)$ is linearly homogeneous of degree one in p.
(R3) $R(x, p)$ is convex and continuous in p.

As in the input case, stronger regularity conditions such as the existence of constant returns to scale, T^{CRS}, which in turn implies homotheticity, can be imposed. This results in $R(x, p)$ being linearly homogeneous, convex, and nondecreasing in x for fixed p—with $R(x, p) = xR(1, p)$. However, revenue maximization does not impose scale or homotheticity restrictions on the technology in order to be meaningfully defined, so we can contemplate the general case. Thus, if the firm raises

[29]Equivalent remarks to those previously made for the cost function as to whether $R(x, p)$ attains a maximum in the set $P(x)$ can be recalled here.

maximum revenue given the level of inputs x and output prices p, then it supplies the optimal amount of output y^R.[30] We represent this optimal situation in Fig. 2.5b through the production plan $y^R(x,p)$, where $R(x,p) = p_1 y_1^R + p_2 y_2^R$ corresponds to the solid isorevenue line tangent to the isoquant of the output production possibility set $P(x)$. Again, an isorevenue line represents the set of input and output vectors that, given the output prices, yield the same revenue for the firm. Any other alternative output production different from y^R cannot yield higher revenue given output prices and the existing technology. We also see that the technical inefficient firm (x_D, y_D) is also economically inefficient because it falls short from maximizing revenue, as represented by the dashed isorevenue line passing through it: $R_D = p_1 y_{D1} + p_2 y_{D2}$, i.e., $R_D < R(x_D, p)$. As before, the remaining technically efficient firms A, B, and C are also revenue-inefficient, and since the source of this inefficiency is not technical, it corresponds to a suboptimal mix of supplied outputs given their prices, i.e., allocative inefficiency.

As its input counterpart (2.17), Farrell's measure of revenue efficiency is defined multiplicatively as the ratio of observed revenue to maximum revenue:

$$RE(x,y,p) = \frac{p \cdot y}{R(x,p)} = \frac{p \cdot y}{p \cdot y^R(x,p)} \leq 1. \tag{2.20}$$

Therefore, if the firm supplies the optimal output quantities, then $RE(x,y,p) = 1$, while if it fails to produce these amounts, it incurs revenue losses, $RE(x,y,p) < 1$. The revenue loss corresponding to the revenue inefficient firm (x_D, y_D) is represented in Fig. 2.5b by the gap between the observed and optimal isorevenue lines. Again, as in the previous case, revenue inefficiency can be easily defined in the additive framework as optimal revenue less observed revenue:

$$RI(x,y,p) = R(x,p) - p \cdot y \geq 0, \tag{2.21}$$

whose interpretation is equivalent to that of its cost inefficiency counterpart. Thus, if the firm maximizes revenue, then $RI(x,y,p) = 0$, while $RI(x,y,p) > 0$ informs about foregone revenue in monetary (currency) terms. As before, the multiplicative and additive terms inform of the magnitude of revenue inefficiency in proportional and absolute terms, respectively.

[30] On this occasion, under the conditions previously stated, Shephard's lemma allows us to recover the system of supply equations defined by the partial derivatives of the revenue function with respect to output prices: $y^R(x,p) = \nabla_p R(x,p)$. Then, for any two outputs k and l with associated market prices p_k and p_l, the first-order conditions also imply that the marginal rate of technical transformation of output k for output l, defined on a general transformation function $g(y)$, must be equal to the price ratios: $MRT_l^k = -dl/dk = g_k(y)/g_l(y) = p_k/p_l$, where $g_k(y) = \partial g(y)/\partial y_k$ and $g_l(y) = \partial g(y)/\partial y_l$. Again, given the necessary assumptions about the transformation function, the second-order conditions are also verified.

2.3.3 Profitability Maximization and Profitability Efficiency

Our first economic efficiency measure jointly defined in the input and output space corresponds to the profitability function.[31] This function represents the maximum revenue to cost given the technology and input and output prices. Following Zofio and Prieto (2006), the profitability function defines in the following terms[32]:

$$\Gamma(w,p) = \max_{x,y} \{p \cdot y / w \cdot x : (x,y) \in T\}, \ \ w \in \mathbb{R}^M_{++}, \ \ p \in \mathbb{R}^N_{++}, \ \ x \geq 0_N, \ \ y \geq 0_M. \tag{2.22}$$

Given the regularity conditions T1–T6 of the production possibility set, the profitability function is characterized by the following properties:

(P1) $\Gamma(w,p)$ is nonnegative, nonincreasing in w, and nondecreasing in p.
(P2) $\Gamma(w,p)$ is homogeneous of degree minus one in w, homogeneous of degree one in p, and homogenous of degree zero in w and p.
(P3) $\Gamma(w,p)$ is convex and continuous in p and w.

An additional property of the profitability function, which characterizes the definition and decomposition of profitability efficiency below, is that the technology exhibits local constant returns to scale at the optimal solution. This can be shown by examining the first-order conditions of the maximization problem (2.22). Expressing profitability equivalently as $\Gamma(w,p) = \max_{y} \{p \cdot y / C(y,w) : (x,y) \in T^{CRS}\}$, where $C(y,w)$ is the cost function previously defined in (2.16), from the first-order conditions of the optimization problem, $p/p \cdot y = \nabla_y C(y,w)/C(y,w)$, we observe that cost elasticity $\varepsilon_C(y,w) = 1$; see Balk (1998:66). In turn, this implies that the scale elasticity is $\varepsilon(x,y) = 1$, and therefore, local constant returns to scale prevail.[33]

If a firm is capable of producing the output and input quantities that maximize profitability, then it also maximizes productivity defined as aggregated output divided by aggregated input, where their respective prices constitute the aggregating weights. The optimal production plan is denoted by $(x^\Gamma(w,p), y^\Gamma(w,p))$ in Fig. 2.6a, where $\Gamma(w,p) = p \cdot y^\Gamma / w \cdot x^\Gamma$ is once again illustrated by the solid line tangent to the

[31] Diewert (2014:59) credits Balk (2003:9–10) for introducing the term "profitability." Georgescu-Roegen (1951:103) also proposed this function to characterize economic behavior and termed it "return-to-dollar." This function is the inverse of the so-called efficiency ratio, representing one of the most important financial key performance indicators. Grifell-Tatjé and Knox Lovell (2015: Chap. 2) discuss the origins of profitability as an indicator of economic performance.

[32] Again, we assume that the optimization problem associated with the calculation of $\Gamma(w,p)$ always attains its maximum in T.

[33] In the standard, single output-multiple input production function, $y = f(x)$, scale elasticity is defined as follows: $\varepsilon(x,y) = (\partial \ln f(\psi x)/\partial \ln \psi)|_{\psi=1} = \sum_{m=1}^{M} (\partial f(x)/\partial x_m) \cdot (x_m/y) = \sum_{m=1}^{M} \varepsilon_m$. The definition implies proportional changes in the inputs quantities; i.e., the input mix (relative input quantities) remains unchanged.

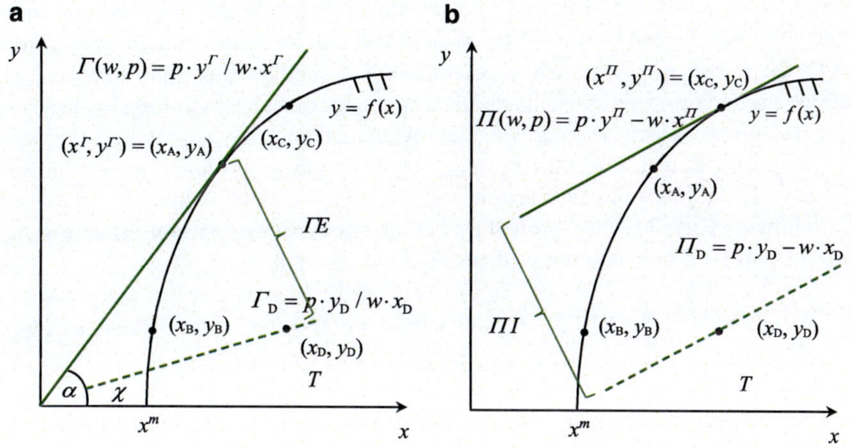

Fig. 2.6 (**a–b**) Profitability maximization, profit maximization, and economic (in)efficiency

graph representation of the technology. This isoprofitability line represents the set of input and output vectors that, given their prices, are capable of achieving the maximum revenue to cost or, equivalently, in this single input-single output representation, average productivity, defined as y/x. On this occasion, as anticipated in Fig. 2.4b, maximum profitability coincides with firm (x_A, y_A), precisely because it operates at the optimal scale. In the single input-single output case represented in Fig. 2.6a, no other firm maximizes (average) productivity. Any production plan different from $(x_A, y_A) = (x^\Gamma(w,p), y^\Gamma(w,p))$ achieves lower profitability. This is the case of the technical inefficient firm (x_D, y_D), whose profitability is lower than that achieved at the most productive scale. Its profitability corresponds to the dashed isoprofitability line passing though the firm and the origin: $\Gamma_D = p \cdot y_D / w \cdot x_D$, i.e., $\Gamma_D < \Gamma(w,p)$. In this case, we observe that the remaining technically efficient firms B and C are also profitability inefficient. As we present in the following section and recalling the decomposition of graph technical efficiency into scale and technical efficiencies in Sect. 2.1.3, expression (2.13), $TE_H^{CRS}(x,y) = TE_H(x,y) \times SE_H(x,y)$, we see that the difference between observed and maximum profitability can be fully attributed to technical and scale inefficiencies. For the single input-single output case, there cannot be, by definition, allocative inefficiencies. In this case, if the firm was to reduce its inputs and increase its outputs along the graph (hyperbolic) path to remove technical inefficiency while exhausting any possible increasing returns to scale and avoiding decreasing returns to scale (i.e., removing scale inefficiencies), it would produce under constant returns to scale and maximize profitability. In the multiple output-multiple input case, several firms can produce under local constant returns to scale, thereby satisfying this necessary condition for profitability maximization. However, for different input and output price vectors, only a subset of these firms maximize revenue to cost. The reason is that observed revenue and cost are (scalar) linear aggregating functions that rely on prices to weight quantities.

Consequently, although there may be several firms producing at alternative most productive scale sizes, only a subset of them will maximize profitability subject to a particular vector of prices, while others will fall short of this goal. In that case, despite producing in a technically efficient way under local constant returns to scale, the firm incurs allocative inefficiencies by demanding and supplying input and output quantities that, given their prices, do not maximize profitability. We discuss this situation in the following section.

Following Farrell (1957), profitability efficiency is defined multiplicatively as the ratio of observed to maximum profitability:

$$\Gamma E(x, y, w, p) = \frac{p \cdot y / w \cdot x}{\Gamma(p, w)} = \frac{p \cdot y / w \cdot x}{p \cdot y^{\Gamma} / w \cdot x^{\Gamma}} \leq 1. \tag{2.23}$$

Therefore, unless the firm under evaluation demands and supplies optimal input and output quantities, it incurs profitability inefficiency. As in previous cases, for profitability-efficient firms, $\Gamma E(x, y, w, p) = 1$, while $\Gamma E(x, y, w, p) < 1$ quantifies the magnitude of economic inefficiency. In this case, the profitability loss of firm (x_D, y_D) is represented in Fig. 2.6a by the gap between the optimal and observed isoprofitability ray vectors.[34] Finally, we note that the parallel concept to profitability efficiency in the additive framework corresponds to the concept of profit inefficiency that we present next.

2.3.4 *Profit Maximization and Profit Inefficiency*

The most representative measure of economic efficiency is based on the profit function, defined as maximum difference between revenue and cost given the technology and input and output prices. The reason is that profit maximization is the actual operating goal for firms and constitutes the economic benchmark for stakeholders. For example, wage (re)negotiations through individual and collective bargaining, dividends paid to shareholders (which represent a distribution of non-reinvested profits), or taxes due to fiscal authorities are calculated based on this operating income.[35]

On this occasion, assuming the necessary derivative properties, including continuity and differentiability, we can recover both the input demand and output supply functions applying Hotellings's lemma: $x^{\Pi}(w, p)$ and $y^{\Pi}(w, p)$. Following McFadden

[34] We can relate this result to the comparison of productivities in Sect. 2.1. Resorting once again to trigonometry, profitability efficiency defines equivalently as the ratio of the slope of the ray vector joining the origin and firm under evaluation to that of firm A maximizing profitability, i.e., in Figure 2.5a, $\Gamma E(x,y,w,p) = \tan \chi / \tan \alpha$.

[35] "Operating income" is a standard accounting figure that measures the amount of profit realized from a firm's operations, after deducting from the sales revenue all operating expenses such as wages and the cost of other inputs (e.g., materials, rent and utilities), known as cost of goods sold (COGS), and depreciation. Another relevant measure of a company's operating performance widely used by analysts is earnings before interest, tax, depreciation, and amortization (EBITDA). This measure allows evaluating a firm's performance without having to factor in financing decisions, accounting decisions, or tax environments.

(1978) or Färe and Primont (1995), the profit function defines in the following terms[36]:

$$\Pi(w,p) = \max_{x,y} \{p \cdot y - w \cdot x : (x,y) \in T\}, \ w \in \mathbb{R}^M_{++}, \ p \in \mathbb{R}^N_{++}, \ x \geq 0_M, \ y \geq 0_N. \tag{2.24}$$

Given the regularity conditions T1–T6 of the production possibility set, the profitability function is characterized by the following properties:

(Π1) $\Pi(w,p)$ is nonnegative, nonincreasing in w, and nondecreasing in p.
(Π2) $\Pi(w,p)$ is homogeneous of degree one in w and p.
(Π3) $\Pi(w,p)$ is convex and continuous in p and w.

As with profitability $\Gamma(w,p)$, it is relevant from a technological perspective to characterize the value of the profit function given the nature of returns to scale. If the technology exhibits increasing returns to scale, then $\Pi(w,p) = +\infty$, while if constant returns to scale hold, $\Pi(w,p) = +\infty$, or $\Pi(w,p) = 0$ depending on the value of the input and output prices relative to the technology T. In the latter case, $\Pi(w,p) = 0$ is consistent with the assumption of long-run perfectly competitive markets in economic theory. Finally, the profit function is well defined for positive input and output prices when the technology is characterized by decreasing returns to scale. This result has relevant implications in the definition and decomposition of profit inefficiency. In particular, since local constant returns to scale do not hold at the profit-maximizing benchmark, scale inefficiency cannot be a source of profit inefficiency. Moreover, an economic efficient firm subject to decreasing returns to scale demands and supplies the optimal amounts of input and outputs that maximize profit, yet it would not maximize productivity and, given prices, profitability. This suggests that there is a trade-off between both measures of economic performance, profitability and profit, and that both economic objectives are generally incompatible.

This can be easily shown in Fig. 2.6 by comparing the optimal firms maximizing each economic function. Given the common technology and input and output prices, Fig. 2.6b presents the optimal firm maximizing profit, which on this occasion corresponds to $(x_C, y_C) = (x^{\Pi}(w,p), y^{\Pi}(w,p))$. Note that for this particular example, the technology is characterized by diminishing returns. Hence, while (x_C, y_C) maximizes profit, if its economic goal was profitability maximization, it would need to reduce both input and output quantities so as to increase the amount of output per unit of input, i.e., its productivity defined as y/x, as discussed in the previous version. In Fig. 2.6b, the solid isoprofit line tangent to the technology represents the set of input and output vectors that are capable of achieving the maximum profit. Consequently, any other firm, regardless of its technical (in)efficiency, falls short from

[36] Again, we assume that the optimization problem associated with the calculation of $\Pi(w,p)$ always attains its maximum in T.

profit maximization. This is the case of the technical inefficient firm (x_D, y_D), whose profit fails to reach the maximum value. Its actual profit value is represented by the dashed isoprofit line passing through it: $\Pi_D = py_D - wx_D$, i.e., $\Pi_D < \Pi(w,p)$. Notice that both isoprofits are parallel (as opposed to the isoprofitability case), because, graphically, the slope of both functions is the same: $y = \Pi/p - (w/p)x$. Compared to the profitability case, firm $(x_A, y_A) = (x^{\Gamma}(w,p), y^{\Gamma}(w,p))$ turns out to be profit-inefficient, and since the firm is technically efficient, all profit loss can be attributed to allocative inefficiency, i.e., the inability of the firm to demand and supply the optimal amounts of inputs and outputs. This is the same case for firm B, whose profit inefficiency is more severe than that of firm A. But, what about firm D whose economic loss is represented by the gap between its observed profit and maximum profit? Can profit inefficiency be explained on technical and allocative grounds? As previously explained, the answer to this question depends on the definition of technical efficiency that is chosen, and based on duality grounds, we explore this issue in detail in the following section.

We formally define profit inefficiency in an additive way as the difference between maximum and observed profit:

$$\begin{aligned} \Pi I(x,y,w,p) &= \Pi(w,p) - (p \cdot y - w \cdot x) \\ &= p \cdot y^{\Pi} - w \cdot x^{\Pi} - (p \cdot y - w \cdot x) \geq 0. \end{aligned} \tag{2.25}$$

Correspondingly, if a firm maximizes profit, $\Pi I(x,y,w,p) = 0$, while failing to use and produce the optimal amounts of inputs and outputs results in $\Pi I(x,y,w,p) > 0$. Again, note that in contrast to the Farrell-type measures of cost, revenue, and profitability efficiency, whose properties correspond to those of their corresponding functions, profit inefficiency does not satisfy units invariance (commensurability) by being dependent on the units of measurement. Indeed, inefficiency is measured in monetary (currency) values. While it is possible to redefine these measures in relative terms so as to bound inefficiency and make it unit-independent, it is better to postpone these normalizations to the following section and chapters since they ultimately depend on the technical inefficiency measure that is chosen. This in turn has an effect on the values of the technical and allocative terms in which profit inefficiency decomposes through duality.

2.3.5 *Properties of Economic (In)Efficiency Measures: Multiplicative and Additive*

Related to the desirable properties that an economic efficiency measure should satisfy, various researchers have adopted, explicitly or implicitly, desirable properties of the profit efficiency measure, e.g., Asmild et al. (2007) and, more recently, Färe et al. (2019). Here, we follow Aparicio, Pastor, Sainz-Pardo, and Vidal (2020) and summarize several such desirable properties in relation to both profitability efficiency and profit inefficiency, although equivalent counterparts can be stated for the cost and revenue based (in)efficiencies:

(P1) *Boundness*: (a) $\Gamma E(x, y, w, p) \leq 1$, and (b) $\Pi I(x, y, w, p) \geq 0$.
(P2) *Indication*: (a) $\Gamma E(x, y, w, p) = 1 \Leftrightarrow (x, y) \in \arg \max \{p \cdot y/w \cdot x : (x, y) \in T\}$, and (b) $\Pi I(x, y, w, p) = 0 \Leftrightarrow (x, y) \in \arg \max \{p \cdot y - w \cdot x : (x, y) \in T\}$.

These two properties state that the economic (in)efficiency measures are well-defined functions for all finite maximal and observed profitability and profit levels and for all firms belonging to the technology. Also, when the maximum profitability and profit are a finite value, the economic (in)efficiency values are also finite:

(P3) $\Gamma E(x, y, w, p)$ and $\Pi I(x, y, w, p)$ are well defined in the case that production costs are greater or equal than revenues, e.g., in the additive case, for nonpositive profits.
(P4) *Homogeneity in prices*: (a) $\Gamma E(x, y, w, p)$ is homogenous of degree zero in prices, and (b) $\Pi I(x, y, w, p)$ is homogenous of degree one in prices.
(P5) *Homogeneity in quantities:* (a) $\Gamma E(x, y, w, p)$ is homogenous of degree zero in quantities, and (b) $\Pi I(x, y, w, p)$ is homogenous of degree one in quantities.
(P6) *Units invariance* (or *commensurability*): $\Gamma E(x, y, w, p)$ is independent of units of measurement, while $\Pi I(x, y, w, p)$ depends on them.

The importance of these properties is self-evident. In this way, the economic (in)efficiency measures are always less or equal to one (P1a) and nonnegative (P1b), with unitary (P2a) and nil (P2b) (in)efficiencies signaling that the firm is efficient. Indeed, $\Gamma E(x, y, w, p)$ and $\Pi I(x, y, w, p)$ satisfy these conditions if and only if the firm archives maximum profitability and maximum profit, respectively (indication). (P3) is also relevant because profit inefficiency is well defined even in the case that nonpositive profits are observed, as opposed to ratio-form definitions of profit inefficiency dividing observed profit by maximum profit: $(p \cdot y - w \cdot x)/\Pi(w, p)$, e.g., Cooper et al. (2007). In general, the different profitability and profit inefficiency measures presented in the following chapters satisfy these properties. An exception concerning the homogeneity and commensurability properties of the additive profit inefficiency measure, resulting from the duality relationships presented in the following section, is that by using *normalized* prices $(\widetilde{w}, \widetilde{p})$, i.e., dividing $N\Pi I(x, y, w, p)$ by way of suitable factors, the resulting profit inefficiency measure $N\Pi I(x, y, \widetilde{w}, \widetilde{p})$ is both homogenous of degree zero in prices (P4b) and quantities (P5b), while it turns independent of units of measurement: (P6b). This is a desirable result that matches the homogeneity properties of the profitability efficiency measure. The different duality results presented in this book that allow a consistent decomposition of profit inefficiency into technical and allocative terms resort to alternative normalizations depending on the underlying technical inefficiency measure, but all of them result in the stated zero degree of homogeneity in prices and quantities.

2.4 Duality and the Decomposition of Economic Efficiency into Technical and Allocative Components: The Essential Properties of Allocative Efficiency

This section constitutes the core of economic efficiency analysis by relating the characteristics of the production technology with the economic objectives of the firm. Duality refers to the possibility of recovering technology T (or its associated input, $L(y)$, and output, $P(x)$, sets) from supporting economic functions and vice versa. Therefore, duality allows to relate the primal (quantity) space with the dual (price) space that characterizes the technological and economic behavior of the firm in a consistent way, so both representations of the firm contain the same information. Sometimes, in the literature, one of these representations is preferred in order to prove a specific result. Mathematically, the different duality relationships considered in this book are economic particularizations of Minkowski's (1911) theorem, stating that every closed convex set can be characterized as the intersection of its supporting half-spaces.[37] In this chapter, we present duality theory in a heuristic way, resorting to its geometrical illustration, while its formal representation, based on the properties of the distance functions, is reserved to subsequent chapters.

Following the structure of the previous sections, we show that the cost, revenue, profitability, and profit functions constitute the relevant support functions associated with their corresponding characterizations of the production technology. While Shephard (1953, 1970) introduced duality theory, Diewert (1974) and McFadden (1978) represent classic formalizations of the subject. More recently, Chambers (1988) provides descriptions based on its geometrical interpretation for the case of the input correspondence $L(y)$ and the cost function $C(y, w)$ and the technology T and the profit function, $\Pi(w, p)$. However, the former authors do not allow for technical (in)efficiency in their exposition. Contrarily, Färe and Primont (1995) are the reference contribution of duality theory allowing for technical efficiency measures defined in terms of distance functions. Finally, regarding the decomposition of economic efficiency in this section and given the duality results presented for each economic function of interest and corresponding to subsequent chapters in the book, we restrict our exposition to the multiplicative approach and simply outline the duality results corresponding to its additive counterpart. However, these results can be found in the chapters dealing with the additive decompositions of economic inefficiency.

[37] See Rockafellar (1972:112) or Chambers (1998:306) for a general exposition of Minkowski's theorem. On the relevance of the convexity assumption for duality theory, we refer the reader to Kuosmanen (2003), who concludes its necessity for the decomposition of economic efficiency. For a recent overview of non-convexity in production and economic (cost) functions, see Briec et al. (2021).

2.4.1 Decomposing Cost (In)Efficiency

The standard presentation of duality starts out from the definition of the cost function $C(y, w)$ and shows that the input production possibility set $L(y)$ can be recovered by way of the supporting half-spaces that $C(y, w)$ generate for alternative input prices. Assuming that the cost function is defined by (2.16), we invoke Minkowski's theorem and define $L(y)$ in the following terms:

$$L(y) = \{x : w \cdot x \geq C(y, w),\ \ \forall\ w \in \mathbb{R}^M_{++}, y \geq 0_N\}. \tag{2.26}$$

This expression reveals that for a given output level y and a particular input vector w, the cost function supports a half-space of the form $H(w, c) = \{x : w \cdot x \geq c = C(y, w), w \in \mathbb{R}^M_{++}, y \geq 0_N\}$. Since, by definition, $C(y, w)$ is the minimum cost of producing y, there is no feasible combination of inputs $x \in H(w, c)$ that can produce that output quantity in a less expensive way. Equivalently, if the cost-minimizing input combination belongs to $H(w, c)$, then it lies on the hyperplane $w \cdot x = C(y, w)$.

This situation is geometrically depicted in Fig. 2.7a, where the price vector w^1 defines the half-space above the hyperplane (line) consistent with $w_1^1 x_1 + w_2^1 x_2 = C(y, w^1)$ and passing through $x^C(y, w^1)$, i.e., the optimal amount of inputs presented in Sect. 2.2.1. Following the above argument, the cost-minimizing bundle cannot be below this line, and therefore, the half-space above it, $H(w^1, C(y, w^1))$, must contain $L(y)$. If there was an alternative bundle $x \in L(y)$ below the isocost line, it could produce y with less cost, but then, we incur in the contradiction that $x^C(y, w^1)$ would not minimize cost. Nevertheless, since at least one input bundle in the isocost $w^1 \cdot x = C(y, w^1)$ must be able to produce y, then $w^1 \cdot x$ and $L(y)$ must share at least one x in the quantity (primal) space.

By repetition, consider an alternative price vector $w^2 \neq w^1$ that supports a second half-space above the hyperplane (line) consistent, on this occasion, with $w_1^2 x_1 + w_2^2 x_2 = C(y, w^2)$ and passing through $x^C(y, w^2)$. Then, no elements of the associated half-space $x \in H(w^2, C(y, w^2))$ could produce y any strictly cheaper than the value of the cost function $C(y, w^2)$. Also, the isocost $w_1^2 x_1 + w_2^2 x_2 = C(y, w^2)$ must contain $L(y)$, and once again, $w^2 \cdot x$ and $L(y)$ share at least one x. But then, combining the half-spaces $H(w^1, C(y, w^1))$ and $H(w^2, C(y, w^2))$, the input production possibility set $L(y)$ must belong to the intersection between both supporting hyperplanes. We can continue with this sequence for every price combination until all price vectors have been considered, as defined in (2.26). In Fig. 2.7a, we consider one last (third) vector w^3, to which the associated isocost line $w_1^3 x_1 + w_2^3 x_2 = C(y, w^3)$ characterizes the corresponding half-space $H(w^3, C(y, w^3))$, now passing through $x^C(y, w^3)$. It is possible to see that the input set $L(y)$ and its boundary start resembling the shape of the standard convex set and isoquant defined in microeconomic textbooks. Given the properties of the cost function (2.16), $L(y)$ is a non-empty, closed, convex set in $\mathbb{R}^M_+$, satisfying strong disposability of inputs.

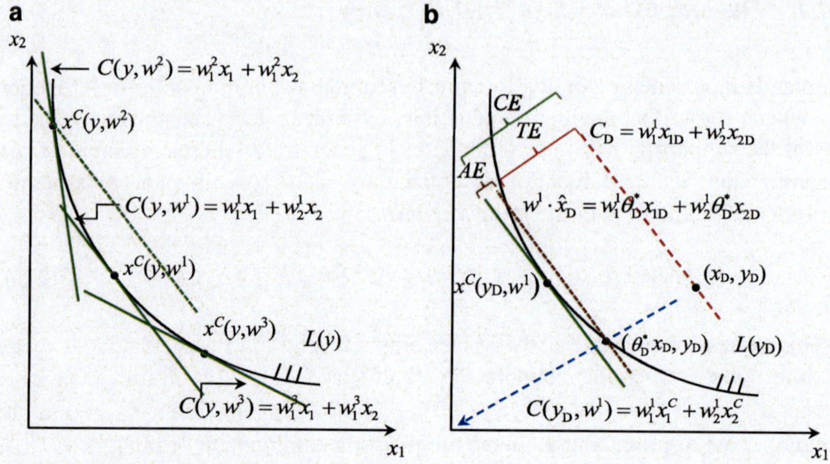

Fig. 2.7 **(a–b)** Duality between the input technical efficiency measure and the cost function

Alternatively, once we have recovered $L(y)$, we can in turn define the cost function in terms of the supporting half-spaces corresponding to different isocosts, representing minimum cost for alternative prices, i.e.,

$$C(y, w) = \min_x \{w \cdot x : x \in L(y)\}. \tag{2.27}$$

In Fig. 2.7a, this expression corresponds to each isocost line that, minimizing cost for each price vector, is tangent to the isoquant of the input set $L(y)$. Here, for each vector of optimal input demands, the first-order conditions for cost minimization subject to the technology are satisfied; i.e., the marginal rate of substitution among inputs (slope of the isoquant) must be equal to their relative prices (slope of the isocost line).[38]

The results presented in (2.26) and (2.27), showing that the technology can be recovered from the cost function and vice versa, summarize the duality between the input set and the cost function. Formally, duality theory is concerned with the regularity conditions that both the technology and the cost function should satisfy so as to ensure that, for each output quantity y and price vector w, the minimum cost exists and is unique; i.e., it is possible to define input demand functions $x^C(y, w)$ that

[38]Expression (2.27) corresponds to the standard cost-minimizing program presented in every microeconomics textbook, where the technological restriction $x \in L(y)$ is substituted by single output production function $y = f(x)$.

can be recovered through Shephard's lemma by differentiating the cost function with respect to the input prices.[39]

A relevant concept related to the first-order conditions, which we recall later in this section when decomposing cost efficiency, is that of *shadow prices*. This refers to the vector of prices that would satisfy the first-order conditions for cost minimization if a given combination of input quantities was considered as optimal. Rather than reading Fig. 2.7a as the input combinations that minimize the cost of producing an output quantity y given input prices w, one looks for the price vector that minimizes cost given an (would be) optimal input combination capable of producing y. Let us denote this vector of shadow prices by $\nu \in \mathbb{R}_{+}^{M}$. Then, if a firm fails to minimize cost, it is because it does not demand the optimal input quantities given the observed market prices w; i.e., it incurs allocative inefficiency. But this can be reinterpreted as a divergence between its associated shadow prices, ν, for which it would be cost-efficient, i.e., $\nu \cdot x = \nu \cdot x^C(y, v) = C(y, v)$, and actual market prices. In this case, $v \neq w$, and therefore, $w \cdot x > w \cdot x^C(y, w) = C(y, w)$.[40]

In Fig. 2.7a, this situation is represented for firm $x^C(y, w^2)$, which minimizes cost for prices w^2, implying that its associated shadow prices are $v = w^2$. But when actual market prices are w^1, this firm exceeds minimum cost since $v \cdot x = w^2 \cdot x^C(y, w^2) > w^1 \cdot x^C(y, w^1)$. This is illustrated in Fig. 2.7a through the dashed isocost line parallel to $w^1 \cdot x^C(y, w^1)$ and passing through $x^C(y, w^2)$, i.e., $w^1 \cdot x^C(y, w^2)$.

2.4.1.1 The Multiplicative Approach

The above duality relationship between the input set and the cost function must be qualified to include the concept of technical efficiency if we intend to decompose economic efficiency into our two components of interest, technical and allocative.

[39] From a parametric perspective, duality theory assumes that (i) the production function is well behaved satisfying all desirable neoclassical properties and regularity conditions, particularly quasi-concavity, which ensures that the associated input production possibility sets are convex, e.g., Madden (1986), and (ii) it is continuous and twice differentiable. In the case of single output production functions, $y = f(x)$, the quasi-concavity assumption, ensuring that the input isoquants are convex, is satisfied by the most common functional forms—e.g., Cobb-Douglas and CES. Although, in this book, we do not consider the parametric approach to measure and decompose economic efficiency (given the existing difficulties to impose the desired properties on the system of demand equations that characterize the optima and the challenges it poses for econometric estimation), the regularity and differentiability conditions of the production function pass on the distance functions defined in subsequent chapters—see Blackorby and Diewert (1979).

[40] Considering the single output cost function $C(y, v)$, v_k and v_l are the (shadow) prices that, applying Shephard's lemma, precisely correspond to minus the ratio of the given input combination that, in consequence, is optimal by minimizing the cost of producing output amount y: i.e., $C_k(y, v)/C_l(y, v) = -\left(x_k^C(y, v)/x_l^C(y, v)\right)$, where$C_k(y, v) = \partial C(y, v)/\partial v_k$ and $C_l(y, v) = \partial C(y, v)/\partial v_l$ are the marginal costs associated with the input prices. Correspondingly, given the shadow prices, $x_k^C(y, v)$ and $x_k^C(y, v)$ are the optimal input quantities whose marginal rate of technical substitution equals their ratio: $MRS_l^k = -dl/dk = f_k\left(x_k^C(y, v)\right)/f_l\left(x_l^C(y, v)\right) = v_k/v_l$.

First, let us recall Farrell's radial definition of input technical efficiency, $TE_{R(I)}(x, y) = \|\widehat{x}\|/\|x\| = \theta^*$, presented in (2.4) and where the superscript "*" denotes the optimal value for a firm under evaluation that is obtained through empirical methods. This measure is capable of characterizing the input correspondence, $L(y) = \{x : \theta^* \leq 1\}$, or equivalently, it satisfies the representation property: $\theta^* \leq 1 \Leftrightarrow x \in L(y)$. Then, as shown in Fig. 2.7a, it is clear that a technically inefficient input bundle cannot minimize production cost for any input price vector, because it is dominated in the sense of Pareto-Koopmans efficiency. Therefore, one may reduce input quantities while producing the same output amount. This suggests that we can redefine (2.26) in the following way:

$$L(y) = \left\{x : w \cdot \theta^* x = w \cdot \widehat{x} \geq C(y, w),\ \ \theta^* \leq 1, \forall\ w \in \mathbb{R}^M_{++}, y \geq 0_N\right\}. \tag{2.28}$$

This expression rewrites the input set in terms of the supporting half-spaces defined by the cost function but qualifying it to include technical efficiency.[41] By proceeding this way, we have enhanced Minkowski's theorem to allow for technical inefficiency, where the input vectors belonging to the intersecting half-spaces can be expressed in terms of their projections to the different supporting hyperplanes. We can now recover the cost function from the input possibility set including technical efficiency as follows:

$$C(y, w) = \min_x \{w \cdot \theta^* x = w \cdot \widehat{x} :\ \ \theta^* \leq 1\}. \tag{2.29}$$

Departing from (2.28), we obtain that $C(y, w) \leq w \cdot \theta^* x$, or equivalently, recalling the definition of cost efficiency presented in (2.17) and thanks to the homogeneity of degree one of production cost in input quantities, $w \cdot \widehat{x} = w \cdot \theta^* x = \theta^*(w \cdot x)$, $\theta^* \leq 1$ (i.e., radially contracting the input amounts by the scalar θ^* reduces production cost in the exact same proportion), we achieve our key result:

$$CE(x, y, w) = C(y, w)/w \cdot x \leq \theta^*. \tag{2.30}$$

Hence, cost efficiency, defined as the ratio of minimum cost to observed cost, is not larger than Farrell's radial technical efficiency measure. This result, known in the literature as a Fenchel-Mahler inequality (Mahler, 1939), along with the previous developments, is the basis for the following duality:[42]

---

[41] Since Farrell radial input measure (2.4) can be expressed as $TE_{R(I)}(x, y) = \{\theta^* : \theta^* x \in L(y)\}$ $\Rightarrow w \cdot \theta^* x = w \cdot \widehat{x} \geq C(y, w)$

[42] This duality can be expressed equivalently as $C(y, w) = \min_x \{w \cdot x : \theta^* \leq 1\}$, if and only if $\theta^* = 1/\left(\min_w \{w \cdot x : C(y, w) \geq 1\}\right)$. Here, we follow Färe and Primont (1995) who present this result in terms of Shephard's (1953, 1970) input distance function rather than its inverse, corresponding to Farrell's input technical efficiency measure. Chapter 3 revisits the decomposition of cost efficiency based on the input distance function.

$$C(y,w) = \min_{x} \ \{w \cdot \theta^* x\}, \text{if and only if } \theta^* = \max_{w} \{C(y,w)/w \cdot x\}. \tag{2.31}$$

Therefore, if the cost function is derived from the radial input efficiency measure by minimizing cost over all feasible input vectors, then the radial input efficiency measure can be recovered from the cost function by finding the maximum of the ratio of minimum cost to actual cost over all feasible input price vectors. In the latter case, the solution to this problem corresponds to the aforementioned shadow prices.

We are now in a position to decompose cost efficiency by closing the inequality in (2.30) as follows:

$$CE(x,y,w) = \frac{C(y,w)}{w \cdot x} = \frac{w \cdot \widehat{x}}{w \cdot x} \times \frac{C(y,w)}{w \cdot \widehat{x}} = \frac{\theta^*(w \cdot x)}{w \cdot x} \times \frac{C(y,w)}{w \cdot \theta^* x}$$
$$= \theta^* \times \frac{w \cdot x^C(y,w)}{w \cdot \theta^* x} \leq 1. \tag{2.32}$$

In this expression, the second factor in the last equality captures the gap between minimum cost and the radial projection of the firm to the production frontier. To the extent that $TE_{R(I)}(x,y) = \theta^*$ measures technical efficiency, the remainder is a residual that captures allocative efficiency, i.e., the cost excess that can be attributed to the fact that the technically projected benchmark $\widehat{x}$ does not demand the optimal input quantities minimizing cost, $x^C(y,w)$. Consequently, this results in the following decomposition:

$$CE(x,y,w) = \frac{C(y,w)}{w \cdot x} = \theta^* \times \frac{w \cdot x^C(y,w)}{w \cdot \widehat{x}} = TE_{R(I)}(x,y) \times AE_{R(I)}(x,y,w) \leq 1, \tag{2.33}$$

where $AE_{R(I)}(x,y,w) = CE(x,y,w)/TE_{R(I)}(x,y)$ is calculated as the multiplicative residual between cost and technical efficiencies.

We can now recall the concept of shadow pricing previously introduced to illustrate the notion of allocative inefficiency as the discrepancy between shadow prices and market prices (i.e., between supporting hyperplanes). Particularly, in Fig. 2.7b, let us consider v as the price vector that would render the efficient projection of (x_D, y_D) cost-efficient, i.e., $v \cdot \widehat{x}_D = v_1\theta^*_D x_{1D} + v_2\theta^*_D x_{2D} = C(y,v)$; then, allocative inefficiency can be reinterpreted as $AE_{R(I)}(x_D, y_D, w^1) = C(y_D, w^1)/w^1 \cdot \widehat{x}_D = w^1 \cdot x^C(y_D, w^1)/w^1 \cdot x^C(y_D, v)$. As a result, if market prices w coincided with the shadow prices v of firm (x_D, y_D), $v = w$, it would be allocative efficient: $AE_{R(I)}(x_D, y_D, w^1) = 1$. This result is formalized in the following chapter for a multiple output-multiple input technology where technical efficiency is represented by Shepard's input distance function. From an empirical perspective, as shown in Sect. 2.4, we highlight that since the nonparametric DEA methods aggregate input (and output) quantities using multipliers that can be interpreted as shadow prices (in the so-called dual or multiplier approach that defines the reference hyperplanes), the discrepancy between cost at the optimal (technological) prices and market prices determines the magnitude of the allocative efficiency.

The decomposition of cost efficiency into its technical and allocative components is depicted in Fig. 2.7b. For firm (x_D, y_D), given the output quantity y_D and input prices w^1, cost efficiency defines as the ratio of minimum cost, $C(y_D, w^1) = w_1^1 x_1^C + w_2^1 x_2^C$, to observed cost, $C_D = w_1^1 x_{1D} + w_2^1 x_{2D}$; i.e., $CE(x_D, y_D, w^1) = C(y_D, w^1)/C_D$. Cost efficiency can then be decomposed into its technical and allocative components: $CE(x_D, y_D, w^1) = \theta_D^* \times C(y_D, w^1)/w^1 \cdot \widehat{x}_D = TE_{R(I)}(x_D, y_D) \times AE_{R(I)}(x_D, y_D, w^1)$, where $w^1 \cdot \widehat{x}_D = w_1^1 \theta_D^* x_{1D} + w_2^1 \theta_D^* x_{2D}$. In Fig. 2.7b, cost efficiency, technical efficiency, and allocative efficiency are identified by the corresponding gaps between the parallel isocost lines.

As previously remarked, a relevant issue when decomposing cost efficiency based on Farrell's radially oriented measure is that it does not ensure that efficient projections $\widehat{x}$, whose efficiency scores are equal to one, belong to the strongly efficient subset of the technology. All that can be ensured is that they belong to the weakly efficient subset: $\partial^W L(y) = \{x \in L(y) : x' < x \Rightarrow x' \notin L(y)\}$. Therefore, as there might be individual input excesses (slacks), the extra cost associated with these technical inefficiencies is identified in (2.33) as allocative inefficiency. We see then the relevance of the indication property from a duality perspective, i.e., the trade-off between technological assumptions for specific technologies and particular measures of technical efficiency in terms of the values of the technical and allocative efficiencies. In general, the guiding principle that we adopt in this book in order to correctly define and interpret technical efficiency is that the projected firms must belong to the strongly efficient frontier, and therefore, all means to improve a firm's performance from an engineering perspective have been exhausted (i.e., no Pareto inefficiency remains). Complementarily, the remaining cost inefficiency is interpreted as allocative inefficiency.

From an empirical perspective, in approximations of the production technology where the strongly and weakly efficient sets coincide, as it is generally the case in the parametric approach to efficiency measurement, the above trade-off does not arise. Indeed, while the parametric approach requires choosing a specific functional form, it does not have to deal with the problems associated with weakly efficient projections that are dominated in terms of Pareto efficiency. Consequently, radial measures can be regarded as valid definitions of technical efficiency, because additional (individual) reductions in input quantities are impossible. Moreover, combined with the homotheticity properties of the technology, Aparicio et al. (2015a, 2015b) and Aparicio and Zofío (2017) show that in such a case, allocative efficiency can be distinctly related to those changes in the input mix that are necessary to match the cost-minimizing input quantities once the firm has been radially projected to the efficient frontier. That is, since radial measures proportionally reduce input quantities leaving the input mix unchanged (as opposed to the additive measures), they can be rightly interpreted as reducing technical inefficiency only, while subsequent changes in the input mix along the production frontier solve allocative inefficiency. Hence, in those cases in which the strongly and weakly efficient sets coincide and the technology is homothetic, whether the input mix changes or not becomes the criterion to categorize radial measures as valid definitions of technical efficiency and the remaining changes that adjust the input mix, as allocative efficiency.

2.4.1.2 The Additive Approach

Departing from the duality relationships presented in (2.26) and (2.27), it is possible to obtain similar results by expressing the production possibility set in terms of additive projections on the supporting hyperplanes and then recover the cost function, so as to decompose (2.18). A departing point, based on Cooper et al. (1999), would be the following inequality $C(y,w) \leq w \cdot \widehat{x} = w \cdot (x - s^{-*}) = w \cdot x - w \cdot s^{-*}$, or equivalently, recalling the definition of cost inefficiency presented in (2.18), we achieve that:

$$CI(y,w) = w \cdot x - C(y,w) \geq \ (w \cdot x - w \cdot \widehat{x}) = \sum_{m=1}^{M} w_m s_m^{-*}. \tag{2.34}$$

It would then be possible to close the inequality and decompose cost inefficiency into the following terms:

$$CI(x,y,w) = w \cdot x - C(y,w) = \sum_{m=1}^{M} w_m s_m^{-*} + (w \cdot \widehat{x} - C(y,w)) \geq 0, \tag{2.35}$$

where the value of the allocative inefficiency could be calculated as the difference between cost inefficiency less the monetary value of technical inefficiency: $TI_{A(I)}(x, y, w) = CI(x,y,w) - \sum_{m=1}^{M} w_m s_m^{-*}$. Unfortunately, one drawback of the above proposal is that the additional cost associated with the inputs excesses (slacks) cannot be interpreted as a technical efficiency measure as it depends on prices—as opposed to (2.33). Also, the above expression is homogeneous of degree one in prices and quantities and dependent on the units of measurement (i.e., it does not satisfy the commensurability property).

Following Nerlove (1965), this suggests that both the cost inefficiency measure and the resulting technical and allocative components should be normalized, so that they exhibit a zero degree of homogeneity and are not measured in nominal monetary units. This prompts the development of the additive decompositions presented in subsequent chapters, where economic inefficiencies comply with these desirable properties, i.e., (P4b), (P5b), and (P6b) in Sect. 2.3.5, by being normalized with factors that, depending on the underlying definition of technical inefficiency measures, are consistent with duality theory. In general, these deflators correspond to the value of a reference bundle of input and output quantities and/or prices depending on the dimensions considered in the analysis.

Here, we recall the results presented in Aparicio et al. (2016a, 2016b), who introduced the duality between the profit function and the weighted additive distance function, but particularize their results for the case of cost inefficiency and assuming that the slack weights are equal to 1_M. This results in the following normalized decomposition:[43]

$$\begin{aligned} NCI(x, y, \widetilde{w}) &= \frac{w \cdot x - C(y, \widetilde{w})}{\min\{w_1, \ldots, w_M\}} = \widetilde{w} \cdot x - C(y, \widetilde{w}) = (\widetilde{w} \cdot x - \widetilde{w} \cdot \widehat{x}) + (\widetilde{w} \cdot \widehat{x} - C(y, \widetilde{w})) \\ &= \sum_{m=1}^{M} s_m^{-*} + AI_{A(I)}(x, y, \widetilde{w}) = TI_{A(I)}(x, y) + AI_{A(I)}(x, y, \widetilde{w}) \geq 0, \end{aligned} \tag{2.36}$$

where $\widetilde{w} = w/\min\{w_1, \ldots, w_m\}$ is the vector of normalized input prices, $TI_{A(I)}(x, y) = \sum_{m=1}^{M} s_m^{-*} \geq 0$ can be rightly interpreted as a measure of technical inefficiency that captures the (normalized) cost excess resulting from the existence of input slacks, and the difference between cost at the technically efficient projection, $\widehat{x}$, and minimum cost, $C(y, \widetilde{w})$, reflects the extra cost in which the firm incurs by not demanding the optional amount of inputs; i.e., $\widehat{x} \neq x^C(y, \widetilde{w})$, i.e., allocative inefficiency. We stress that the interpretation of allocative inefficiency as the difference in cost as a result of normalized shadow prices, $\widetilde{\nu}$, being different from normalized market prices, $\widetilde{w}$, holds in the exact same way as presented above.

2.4.2 *Decomposing Revenue (In)Efficiency*

It is possible to present the revenue-efficient counterpart to the above duality departing from the revenue function $R(x, p)$ and show that, resorting to Minkowski's theorem, we can recover the output production possibility set $P(x)$ from the supporting half-spaces that the revenue function generates for alternative output prices. Departing from the revenue function (2.19), we have the following:

$$P(x) = \{y : p \cdot x \leq R(x, p), \ \forall \ p \in \mathbb{R}^N_{++}, x \geq 0_M\}. \tag{2.37}$$

Therefore, for each output price vector p, the revenue function supports a half-space of the form $H(p, c) = \{y : p \cdot y \leq c = R(x, p), p \in \mathbb{R}^N_{++}, x \geq 0_M\}$. Again, given that $R(x, p)$ is the maximum revenue that can be obtained from x, there is no feasible combination of outputs $y \in H(p, c)$ producible with that input quantity that can yield greater revenue. Consequently, if the revenue-maximizing output belongs to $H(p, c)$, then it lies on the hyperplane $p \cdot y = R(x, p)$.

[43]The decomposition of the profit inefficiency based on its duality with the weighted additive distance function is presented in Chap. 7. Also, in Sect. 2.4.4, we develop this result for the general case corresponding to the profit inefficiency decomposition.

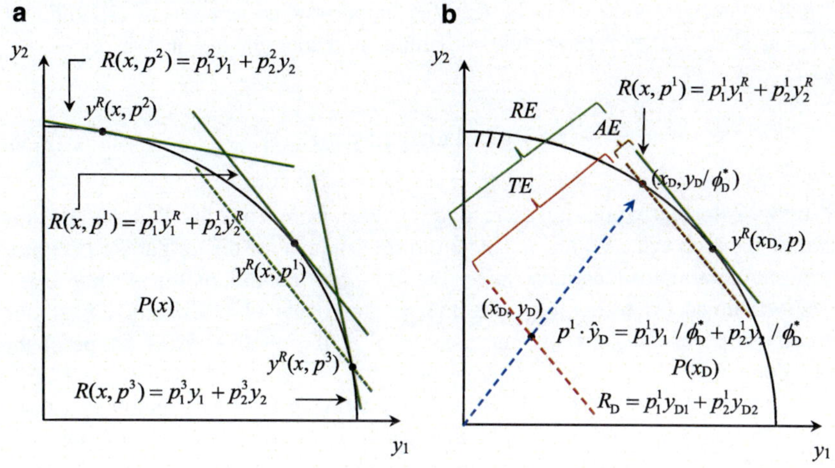

Fig. 2.8 (**a–b**) Duality between the output technical efficiency and the revenue function

This situation is geometrically depicted in Fig. 2.8a where the price vector p^1 defines the half-space below the hyperplane (line) consistent with $p_1^1 y_1 + p_2^1 y_2 = R(y, p^1)$ and passing through $y^R(x, p^1)$, i.e., the optimal amount of outputs presented in the previous section. Therefore, no revenue-maximizing output bundle can be above this line, and accordingly, the half-space below it must contain $P(x)$. If there was an alternative bundle $y \in P(x)$ above the isorevenue line, it could use x generating greater revenue, but then, we incur in the contradiction that $y^R(x, p^1)$ would not maximize revenue. Nevertheless, since at least one output bundle in the isorevenue $p^1 \cdot y = R(x, p^1)$ must be able to produce y, then $p^1 \cdot y$ and $P(x)$ must share at least one y in the quantity (primal) space.

We do not replicate the above exposition for the cost function, but by repetition, we can consider two alternative price vectors $p^2 \neq p^1$ and $p^3 \neq p^2 \neq p^1$ that support two additional half-spaces below the hyperplanes (lines) consistent with $p_1^2 y_1 + p_2^2 y_2 = R(x, p^2)$ and $p_1^3 y_1 + p_2^3 y_2 = R(x, p^3)$—passing through $y^R(x, p^2)$ and $y^R(x, p^3)$, respectively. Then, by definition, no elements of the associated half-spaces, $y \in H(p^2, R(x, p^2))$ and $y \in H(p^3, R(x, p^3))$, could raise greater revenue than the associated revenue functions $R(x, p^2)$ and $R(x, p^3)$. Therefore both maximizing isorevenues for this pair of prices must each share at least one y with $P(x)$. Then, combining all half-spaces $H(p^1, R(x, p^1))$, $H(p^2, R(x, p^2))$, and $H(p^3, R(x, p^3))$, the output production possibility set $P(x)$ belongs to the intersection between both supporting hyperplanes. Considering all possible price combinations, as defined in (2.37), allows us to recover the output set $P(x)$ and its boundary, which once again takes the shape of a standard concave output isoquant. Given the properties of the revenue function (2.19), $P(x)$ is a non-empty, closed, convex set in $\mathbb{R}^N$, satisfying strong disposability of outputs.

Conversely, once we have recovered $P(x)$ from the revenue function, it is possible to retrace our way back and express the revenue function in terms of the output correspondence from the intersection of the supporting half-spaces corresponding to different isorevenues, representing maximum revenues for alternative prices, i.e., (2.37):

$$R(x,p) = \max_{y} \{p \cdot y : y \in P(x)\}. \tag{2.38}$$

In Fig. 2.8a, this expression corresponds to each isorevenue line that, maximizing revenue for each price vector, is tangent to the isoquant of the output set $P(x)$; i.e., these optimal output quantities satisfy the first-order conditions for revenue maximization subject to technology; i.e. the marginal rate of transformation among outputs (slope of the isoquant) must be equal to the relative prices (slope of the isorevenue line).

The results presented in (2.37) and (2.38) showing that the technology can be recovered from the revenue function and vice versa summarize the duality between the output set and the revenue function. Assuming that the necessary regularity conditions hold, it is possible to define output supply functions $y^R(x,p)$ that can be recovered through Shephard's lemma by differentiating the revenue function with respect to the output prices.

We can now present the concept of output shadow prices. As before, these correspond to the vector of prices that satisfy the first-order conditions for revenue maximization in the case that a combination of output quantities was taken as optimal. If Fig. 2.8a illustrates the output combinations that maximize revenue given the amount of inputs x and output prices p, we are now interested in the problem of finding the price vector that maximizes revenue given an (optimal) output bundle producible with x. Let us denote this vector of shadow prices by $\mu \in \mathbb{R}^N_+$. Then, if a firm fails to maximize revenue, it is because it does not supply the optimal output quantities given the observed market prices p; i.e., it incurs allocative inefficiency. But this can be reinterpreted as a divergence between its associated shadow prices, μ, for which it would be revenue-efficient, i.e., $\mu \cdot y = \mu \cdot y^R(x,\mu) = R(x,\mu)$, and actual market prices. Now, $\mu \neq p$, and therefore, $p \cdot y < p \cdot y^R(x,p) = R(x, p)$.[44]

In Fig. 2.8a, this situation is represented for firm $y^R(x,p^3)$, which maximizes revenue for p^3, implying that its associated shadow prices are $\mu = p^3$. But when actual market prices are p^1, this firm falls short from maximum revenue $\mu \cdot y = p^3 \cdot y^R(x,p^3) < p^1 \cdot y^R(x,p^1)$. This is illustrated in Fig. 2.8a through the discontinuous isocost line parallel to $p^1 \cdot y^R(x,p^1)$ and passing through $y^R(x,p^3)$, i.e., $p^1 \cdot y^R(x,p^3)$.

[44]Considering the single input revenue function $R(x,\mu)$, μ_k and μ_l are the (shadow) prices that, applying Shephard's lemma, precisely correspond to minus the ratio of the given output combination that, in consequence, is optimal by maximizing the revenue using input amount x: i.e., $R_k(y,\mu)/R_l(y,\mu) = -\left(y_k^R(x,\mu)/y_l^R(x,\mu)\right)$, where $R_k(y,\mu) = \partial R(y,\mu)/\partial\mu_k$ and $R_l(y,\mu) = \partial R(y,\mu)/\partial\mu_l$ are the marginal revenues corresponding to each output price. Correspondingly, given the shadow prices, $y_k^R(x,\mu)$ and $y_l^R(x,\mu)$ are the optimal output quantities whose marginal rate of technical transformation equals their ratio: $MRT_l^k = -dl/dk = g_k(y)/g_l(y) = \mu_k/\mu_l$.

2.4.2.1 The Multiplicative Approach

As before, the duality relationship between the output set and the revenue function can be expanded to include the concept of technical efficiency, allowing us to decompose revenue efficiency into technical and allocative efficiencies. We now rely on Farrell's definition of radial output technical efficiency, $TE_{R(O)}(x, y) = \|y\|/\|\widehat{y}\| = \phi^* \leq 1$, presented in (2.7). This measure characterizes the output correspondence, $P(x) = \{y : \phi^* \leq 1\}$, satisfying the representation property: $\phi^* \leq 1 \Leftrightarrow y \in P(x)$. In this case, a technically inefficient output bundle cannot maximize revenue for any output price vector, because it is dominated in the sense of Pareto-Koopmans efficiency, as illustrated in Fig. 2.8a. This suggests that we can redefine (2.37) in the following way:

$$P(x) = \left\{y : p \cdot \widehat{y} = p \cdot y/\phi^* \leq R(x, p),\ \ \phi^* \leq 1, \forall\ p \in \mathbb{R}^N_{++}, x \geq 0_M\right\}. \tag{2.39}$$

Consequently, the supporting half-spaces defined by the revenue function can be modified to include technical efficiency.[45] Once the output set is expressed in terms of the output efficiency measure, we are in a position to recover the associated revenue function including it; i.e.,

$$R(x, p) = \max_y \{y : p \cdot \widehat{y} = p \cdot y/\phi^* : \quad \phi^* \leq 1\}. \tag{2.40}$$

Departing from (2.40), we obtain that $R(x,p) \geq p \cdot y/\phi^*$. Equivalently, recalling the definition of revenue efficiency presented in (2.20) and thanks to the homogeneity of degree one of revenue in output quantities $p \cdot \widehat{y} = p \cdot y/\phi^* = (p \cdot y)/\phi^*$, $\phi^* < 1$ (i.e., a radial expansion of the output amounts by the scalar ϕ increases revenue in the same proportion), we obtain the following Fenchel-Mahler inequality:

$$RE(x, y, p) = p \cdot y/R(x, p) \leq \phi^*. \tag{2.41}$$

Thus, revenue efficiency, defined as the ratio of observed revenue to maximum revenue, is not larger than Farrell's radial technical efficiency measure. It is now possible to state the corresponding duality as follows:[46]

$$R(x, p) = \max_y \ \{p \cdot y/\phi^*\}, \text{if and only if } \phi^* = \max_p \{p \cdot y/R(x, p)\}. \tag{2.42}$$

---

[45] The Farrell radial output measure (2.4) can be expressed as $TE_{R(O)}(x, y) = \min\{\phi^* : y/\phi^* \in P(x)\} \Rightarrow p \cdot y/\phi^* = p \cdot \widehat{y} \leq R(x, p)$.

[46] This duality can be expressed equivalently as $R(x, p) = \max_y \ \{p \cdot y : \phi^* \leq 1\} \ \Leftrightarrow \phi^* = \max_p \{p \cdot y : R(x, p) \leq 1\}$—see Färe and Primont (1995).

Then, if the revenue function is derived from the radial output efficiency measure by maximizing revenue over all feasible output vectors, then the radial output efficiency measure can be recovered from the revenue function by finding the maximum over all feasible output price vectors. Again, in the latter case, the solution to this problem corresponds to the shadow prices previously commented.

We are now in a position to decompose cost efficiency by closing (2.41):

$$RE(x,y,p) = \frac{p\cdot y}{R(x,p)} = \frac{p\cdot y}{p\cdot \widehat{y}} \times \frac{p\cdot \widehat{y}}{R(x,p)} = \frac{p\cdot y}{(p\cdot y)/\phi^*} \times \frac{p\cdot y/\phi^*}{R(x,p)} =$$
$$= \phi^* \times \frac{p\cdot y/\phi^*}{p\cdot y^R(x,p)} \leq 1. \tag{2.43}$$

The second factor in the last equality captures the gap between the radial projection of the firm to the production frontier and maximum revenue. To the extent that $TE_{R(O)}(x, y) = \phi^*$ measures technical efficiency, the remainder is a residual that captures allocative efficiency, i.e., the revenue loss that can be attributed to the fact that the technically projected production plan $\widehat{y}$ does not match the one maximizing revenue $y^R(x, p)$. This results in the following decomposition:

$$RE(x,y,p) = \frac{p\cdot y}{R(x,p)} = \phi^* \times \frac{p\cdot \widehat{y}}{p\cdot y^R(x,p)} = TE_{R(O)}(x,y) \times AE_{R(O)}(x,y,p) \leq 1, \tag{2.44}$$

where $AE_{R(O)}(x, y, p) = RE(x, y, p)/TE_{R(O)}(x, y)$ is calculated as the multiplicative residual between revenue and technical efficiency.

The decomposition of revenue efficiency (2.44) is illustrated in Fig. 2.8b. For firm (x_D, y_D), given the input quantity x_D and output prices p^1, revenue efficiency defines as the ratio of observed revenue, $R_D = p_1^1 y_{D1} + p_2^1 y_{D2}$, to maximum revenue, $R(x_D, p) = p_1^1 y_1^R + p_2^1 y_2^R$; i.e., $RE(x_D, y_D, p) = R_D/R(x_D, p)$. Revenue efficiency can then be decomposed into its technical and allocative components: $RE(x_D, y_D, p) = \phi_D^* \times p^1 \cdot \widehat{y}_D/R(x_D, p^1) = TE_{R(O)}(x_D, y_D) \times AE_{R(O)}(x_D, y_D, p)$, where $p^1 \cdot \widehat{y}_D = p_1^1 y_1/\phi_D^* + p_2^1 y_2/\phi_D^*$. In Fig. 2.8b, revenue efficiency, technical efficiency, and allocative efficiency are identified by the corresponding gaps between the parallel isorevenues. We can now recall the concept of shadow pricing previously introduced to illustrate the concept of allocative inefficiency as the discrepancy between shadow prices, μ, and market prices, p^1 (i.e., between supporting hyperplanes). Specifically, let us consider μ as the price vector that would render the efficient projection of (x_D, y_D) revenue-efficient, i.e., $\mu \cdot \widehat{y}_D = \mu_1 y_{1D}/\phi_D^* + \mu_2 y_{2D}/\phi_D^* = R(x, \mu)$; then, allocative inefficiency can be reinterpreted as $AE_{R(O)}(x_D, y_D, p^1) = p^1 \cdot \widehat{y}_D/R(x_D, p^1) = p^1 \cdot y^R(x_D, \mu)/p^1 \cdot y^R(x_D, p^1)$. As a result, if market prices coincided with the shadow prices of firm (x_D, y_D), $\mu = p$, it would be allocative efficient: $AE_{R(O)}(x_D, y_D, p^1) = 1$. Therefore, allocative inefficiency corresponds to the difference in revenue at the optimal (technological) shadow prices and market prices. This result is formalized in the following chapter for a multiple output-multiple input technology where technical efficiency is represented by Shepard's output distance function.

Again, from an empirical perspective, we stress that when using DEA methods based on the dual approach, which aggregate output (and input) quantities using multipliers that can be interpreted as shadow prices (thereby defining the different reference hyperplanes), the discrepancy between these optimal (technological) prices and market prices determines the magnitude of the allocative inefficiency.

Finally, we highlight that the same trade-off between the value of technical and allocative efficiencies depending on whether the technically efficient projection belongs to the strong or weak disposability frontier also emerges on this occasion. The discussion is symmetric to the exposition made for the case of cost efficiency, so that we do not reproduce it here.

2.4.2.2 The Additive Approach

As before, departing now from the duality relationships presented in (2.39) and (2.40), we can present comparable results by rewriting the production possibility set in terms of additive projections on the supporting hyperplanes. Then, relying on Cooper et al. (1999) and starting from the following inequality, $R(x,p) \geq p \cdot \widehat{y} = p \cdot (y + s^{+*}) = p \cdot y + p \cdot s^{+*}$, we obtain that:

$$RI(x,y,p) = R(x,p) - p \cdot y \geq (p \cdot \widehat{y} - p \cdot y) = \sum_{n=1}^{N} p_n s_n^{+*}. \tag{2.45}$$

By closing the inequality, it is possible to decompose revenue inefficiency (2.21):

$$RI(x,y,p) = R(x,p) - p \cdot y = \sum_{n=1}^{N} p_n s_n^{+*} + (R(x,p) - p \cdot \widehat{y}) \geq 0, \tag{2.46}$$

where allocative inefficiency is calculated as the difference between revenue inefficiency less the monetary value of technical inefficiency: $AI_{A(O)}(x,y,p) = RI(x,y,p) - \sum_{n=1}^{N} p_n s_n^{+*}$. But, once more, this decomposition exhibits the drawbacks already mentioned for the cost case; i.e., the revenue loss associated with outputs deficits (slacks) cannot be interpreted as technical efficiency because it depends on prices—as opposed to (2.43). Also, the above expression is homogeneous of degree one in prices and quantities and, by not satisfying the commensurability property, dependent on the units of measurement.

Therefore, we can mirror the developments made in Sect. 2.3.1.1 and normalize the revenue inefficiency by a suitable factor, so that it exhibits a zero degree of homogeneity in prices and quantities while being independent of monetary units.

Recalling, once again, Aparicio et al. (2016a, 2016b), this results in the following normalized decomposition:[47]

$$NRI(x,y,\widetilde{p}) = \frac{R(x,p) - p \cdot y}{\min\{p_1,\ldots,p_N\}} = R(x,\widetilde{p}) - \widetilde{p} \cdot y = (\widetilde{p} \cdot \widehat{y} - \widetilde{p} \cdot y) + (R(x,\widetilde{p}) - \widetilde{p} \cdot \widehat{y}) = \\ = \sum_{n=1}^{N} s_m^{+*} + AI_{A(O)}(x,y,\widetilde{p}) = TI_{A(O)}(x,y) + AI_{A(O)}(x,y,\widetilde{p}) \geq 0, \tag{2.47}$$

where $\widetilde{p} = p/\min\{p_1,\ldots,p_N\}$ is the vector of normalized output prices, $TI_{A(O)}(x,y) = \sum_{n=1}^{N} s_n^{+*} \geq 0$ can be rightly interpreted as a measure of technical inefficiency that captures the (normalized) cost excess resulting from the existence of output slacks, and the difference between revenue at the technically efficient projection, $\widehat{y}$, and maximum revenue, $R(x,\widetilde{p})$, reflects the additional revenue loss in which the firm incurs by not supplying the optimal amount of outputs; i.e. $\widehat{y} \neq y^R(x,\widetilde{p})$, i.e., allocative inefficiency. Finally, as previously mentioned in the case of cost inefficiency, note that the interpretation of allocative inefficiency as the revenue difference between shadow prices, $\widetilde{\mu}$, and market prices, $\widetilde{p}$, can be presented in the exact same terms as above.

2.4.3 *Decomposing Profitability Efficiency*

The decomposition of profitability efficiency into technical, scale, and allocative components follows comparable steps. Departing from the profitability function defined in (2.22), we can recover the optimal production plan that is characterized by *local* constant returns to scale (CRS); i.e., firms cannot exhibit increasing or decreasing returns to scale as this is incompatible with profitability maximization. Hence, we highlight this property by adopting the notation presented in Sect. 2.2, but we refer to the *loci* where these returns hold. Hence, in this case, Minkowski's theorem allows us to define the technology in the following terms:

$$T^{CRS} = \{(x,y) : p \cdot y / w \cdot x \leq \Gamma(w,p),\ \forall\ w \in \mathbb{R}^M_{++}, \forall\ p \in \mathbb{R}^N_{++},\ x \geq 0_M, y \geq 0_N\}. \tag{2.48}$$

This expression reveals that for a particular price vector (w,p), the profitability function supports a half-space of the form $H(w,p,c) = \{(x,y) : p \cdot y / w \cdot x \leq c = \Gamma(w,p), w \in \mathbb{R}^M_{++},\ p \in \mathbb{R}^N_{++},\ x \geq 0_M, y \geq 0_N\}$. Since,

[47] The decomposition of the profit inefficiency based on its duality with the weighted additive distance function is presented in Chap. 6. Also, in Sect. 2.3.4, we develop this result for the general case corresponding to the profit inefficiency decomposition.

by definition, $\Gamma(w,p)$ is the maximum profitability given prices and technology, there is no feasible firm $(x,y) \in H(w,p,c)$ that yields higher profitability. Correspondingly, if the production plan maximizing profitability belongs to $H(w,p,c)$, then it lies on the hyperplane $p \cdot y/w \cdot x = \Gamma(w,p)$.

This situation is geometrically depicted in Fig. 2.9a further on, where the price vector (w^1,p^1) defines the half-space below the hyperplane (line) consistent with $p^1 \cdot y/w^1 \cdot x = \Gamma(w^1,p^1)$ and tangent to the technology T at $(x^\Gamma(w^1,p^1), y^\Gamma(w^1,p^1)) \in T^{CRS}$. Note that this is a three-dimensional representation of a quasi-concave production function using two inputs (x_1,x_2) to produce one output y. The actual technology T is subject to decreasing returns to scale, and a minimum amount of both inputs is necessary to produce a positive amount of output. Also, note that the supporting profitability hyperplane represents the convex cone spanned at T and, therefore, passing through the origin, is characterized by constant returns to scale (CRS) as presented in Sect. 2.2.3. Following the above argument, the profitability-maximizing bundle cannot be above this hyperplane (plane), and therefore, the half-space below it must contain T^{CRS}. If there was an alternative firm $(x,y) \in T^{CRS}$ above that hyperplane, it could attain higher profitability given the technology, but then, we incur in the contradiction that $(x^\Gamma(w^1,p^1), y^\Gamma(w^1,p^1))$ would not maximize profitability. Again, since at least one firm in the isoprofitability $p^1 \cdot y/w^1 \cdot x = \Gamma(w^1,p^1)$ must be able to produce with the existing technology T^{CRS}, then $p^1 \cdot y/w^1 \cdot x$, and T^{CRS} must share at least one (x,y) in the quantity (primal) space.

Consider as before two alternative price vectors $(w^2,p^2) \neq (w^1,p^1)$ and $(w^3,p^3) \neq (w^2,p^2) \neq (w^1,p^1)$ that support their corresponding half-spaces above the (hyper)-planes corresponding to $p^2 \cdot y/w^2 \cdot x = \Gamma(w^2,p^2)$ and $p^3 \cdot y/w^3 \cdot x = \Gamma(w^3,p^3)$, passing through $(x^\Gamma(w^2,p^2), y^\Gamma(w^2,p^2))$ and $(x^\Gamma(w^3,p^3), y^\Gamma(w^3,p^3))$, respectively. Then, no elements of the associated half-spaces $(x,y) \in H(w^2,p^2,\Gamma(w^2,p^2))$ and $(x,y) \in H(w^3,p^3,\Gamma(w^3,p^3))$ could yield higher profitability given the technology T^{CRS} than $\Gamma(w^2,p^2)$ and $\Gamma(w^3,p^3)$. Hence, the isoprofitabilities $p^2 \cdot y/w^2 \cdot x = \Gamma(w^2,p^2)$ and $p^3 \cdot y/w^3 \cdot x = \Gamma(w^3,p^3)$ must contain also T^{CRS}, which implies that, once again, these hyperplanes and the technology must share at least one (x,y), different from each other. Now, combining all three half-spaces $H(w^1,p^1,\Gamma(w^1,p^1))$, $H(w^2,p^2,\Gamma(w^2,p^2))$, and $H(w^3,p^3,\Gamma(w^3,p^3))$, the technology T^{CRS} is approximated by the intersection between both supporting hyperplanes. Continuing with every price combination until all price vectors are exhausted results in expression (2.48).

From the above, we conclude that the relevant benchmark technology defined by the intersection of the supporting hyperplanes for different price vectors represents an outer approximation of the benchmark technology T^{CRS} consisting of the *loci* where CRS hold. In this particular representation, the CRS subset of the technology corresponds to a specific isoquant, comparable to that depicted in Fig. 2.7, but is characterized by CRS. In Fig. 2.9a, this isoquant is depicted by the arc joining all the optimal firms for different price vectors. As a result, it follows that the *loci* of the technology characterized by CRS are a subset of the actual technology, i.e., $T^{CRS} \subseteq T$.[48] This notation stresses that if the technology exhibits *global* constant

[48]This constitutes McFadden's (1978, p. 22) *envelopment technology* but, on this occasion, is defined on the constant returns to scale subset of the technology, relevant for profitability maximization (rather than for the case of the cost function and its dual input set developed by McFadden). Hence, it follows that since $T^{CRS} \subseteq T \Rightarrow \partial^S(T^{CRS}) \subseteq \partial^S(T)$.

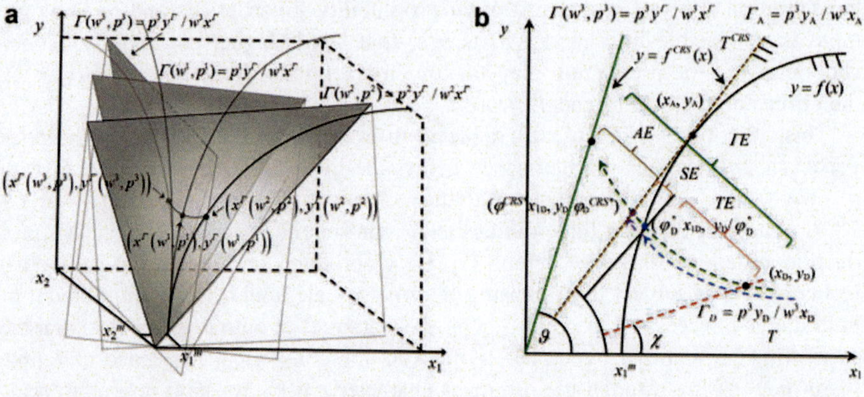

Fig. 2.9 (**a–b**) Duality between the graph technical efficiency and the profitability function

returns to scale, the benchmark and actual technologies coincide.[49] In Fig. 2.9a, the 3D representation is necessary to show that several firms exist that, satisfying the local constant returns to scale condition, are candidates to maximizing profitability depending on a given vector of prices. Notice also that the 3D representation of the technology resembles the standard (homothetic) Cobb-Douglas production function $y = f(x)$, presented in microeconomic textbooks. Formally, the elasticity of scale is equal to one, $\varepsilon(x, y) = 1$, and constant returns to scale hold locally at the optimal input quantities (i.e., in the neighborhood of these inputs): $f(\psi x^{\Gamma}(w^k, p^k)) = \psi f(x^{\Gamma}(w^k, p^k))$, $\psi \geq 1$, $k = 1$, 2, and 3. In this figure, the set of firms that generate T^{CRS} correspond to the isoquant including the previous cases: $(x^{\Gamma}(w^k, p^k), y^{\Gamma}(w^k, p^k))$, $k = 1$, 2, and 3, and therefore, the output quantities are equal. Graphically, the supporting hyperplanes pivot at the origin as the price vector changes and are tangent to the technology T at each optimal vector of quantities characterized by CRS.

Consequently, as before, once the benchmark technology has been recovered from the profitability function, we can in turn define the profitability function by the intersection of the supporting half-spaces corresponding to different isoprofitabilities, representing maximum revenue to cost, as in (2.48):

[49]This is in contrast to the nonparametric Data Envelopment Analysis (DEA) techniques discussed in Sect. 2.4 and used in the empirical applications throughout the book, where, for convenience, the benchmark technology is characterized through global constant returns to scale, rather than allowing for variables returns to scale, which nevertheless allows identifying the reference hyperplanes (faces) consistent with local CRS.

$$\Gamma(w,p) = \max_{x,y} \left\{ p \cdot y / w \cdot x : (x,y) \in T^{CRS} \right\}. \tag{2.49}$$

Again, in Fig. 2.9a, this expression corresponds to each isoprofitability plane that, maximizing profitability for each price vector, is tangent to the technology T^{CRS} and therefore satisfies the first-order conditions for profitability maximization subject to the technology.[50]

The results presented in (2.48) and (2.49) showing that the technology can be recovered from the profitability function and vice versa summarize their duality. It is now possible to comment on the concept of shadow prices in the profitability case. Here, we refer to the vector of prices that satisfy the first-order conditions for profitability maximization if a given firm (combination of input and output quantities) was optimal. Rather than reading Fig. 2.9a as the input and output combinations that maximize profitability, we focus on the input and output price vectors that maximize profitability given a (would be optimal) production plan. Let us denote again these vectors of shadow prices as $\nu \in \mathbb{R}_+^M$ and $\mu \in \mathbb{R}_+^N$. Then, a firm incurs allocative inefficiency if it does not maximize profitability by failing to demand the optimal input and output quantities given the observed market prices (w,p). But, as before, this can be reinterpreted as a divergence between its associated shadow prices, (ν,μ), for which it would be profitability-efficient, i.e., $\mu \cdot y / \nu \cdot x = \mu \cdot y^{\Gamma}(\nu,\mu)/\nu \cdot x^{\Gamma}(\nu,\mu) = \Gamma(\nu,\mu)$, and actual market prices. In this case, $(\nu,\mu) \neq (w,p)$, and therefore, $p \cdot y^{\Gamma}(\nu,\mu)/w \cdot x^{\Gamma}(\nu,\mu) < p \cdot y^{\Gamma}(w,p)/w \cdot x^{\Gamma}(w,p) = \Gamma(w,p)$.[51] In Fig. 2.9b, this situation is represented by firm $(x_A, y_A) = (x^{\Gamma}(w^2,p^2), x^{\Gamma}(w^2,p^2))$, which maximizes profitability for prices (w^2,p^2), implying that its associated shadow prices are $(\nu,\mu) = (w^2,p^2)$. But if market prices were (w^3,p^3), then this firm would experience a profitability loss because $p^3 \cdot y^{\Gamma}(w^2,p^2)/w^3 \cdot x^{\Gamma}(w^2,p^2) < p^3 \cdot y^{\Gamma}(w^3,p^3)/w^3 \cdot x^{\Gamma}(w^3,p^3) = \Gamma(w^3,p^3)$. This is illustrated through the two isoprofitabilities corresponding to $p^3 \cdot y_A/w^3 \cdot x_A$ and $p^3 \cdot y^{\Gamma}(w^3,p^3)/w^3 \cdot x^{\Gamma}(w^3,p^3)$. We see that the slope of the latter is steeper, consistent with the profitability differential in its favor.

We can now proceed to include the measure of graph (hyperbolic) technical efficiency in the duality relationship. The relevant notion is that of productive efficiency with respect to the constant returns to scale technological benchmark as previously shown and represented by $TE_{H(G)}^{CRS}(x,y) = (\varphi^{CRS*})^2 \leq 1$; see expression (2.11). Then, as shown in Fig. 2.9a, it is clear that a productively inefficient firm cannot maximize profitability for any price vector. The reason is that it can be technically inefficient, and therefore, input reductions and output increases are

[50] It is assumed once again that the profitability function is continuous and twice differentiable.

[51] Similar considerations to those made for the cost and revenue shadow prices can be made with respect to their profitability counterparts. The link between these functions and their first-order conditions is straightforward since the profitability function can be equivalently expressed either as $\Gamma(w,p) = \max_{y} \left\{ p \cdot y / C(y,w) : (x,y) \in T^{CRS} \right\}$ or $\Gamma(w,p) = \max_{x} \left\{ R(x,p)/w \cdot x : (x,y) \in T^{CRS} \right\}$. However, relevant to duality theory, it has been shown that the first-order conditions characterize local constant returns to scale.

feasible given the technology T, but it can also be scale-inefficient, incurring in increasing or decreasing returns to scale. For example, focusing on the case that holds the second input constant at its minimum required amount, x_2^m, i.e., $y = f(x_1 | x_2^m)$, as shown by the slice parallel to x_1 in Fig. 2.9b, firm (x_D, y_D) is productively inefficient. On the one hand, it could reach the actual variable returns to scale technology T by projecting itself along the path described by $TE_{H(G)}(x, y) = (\varphi^*)^2 \leq 1$, decreasing inputs and increasing outputs and reaching its technical efficient projection: $(\varphi_D^* x_{1D}, x_2^m, y_D/\varphi_D^*) = (\widehat{x}_{1D}, x_2^m, \widehat{y}_D)$. On the other hand, there remains an additional source of inefficiency related to a suboptimal scale by which the size of the projected firm $(\widehat{x}, \widehat{y})$ does not maximize productivity, defined as the ratio of aggregate output to aggregate input. In Fig. 2.9b, it is firm (x_{1A}, x_2^m, y_A) the one maximizing productivity by reaching a scale for which neither increasing nor decreasing returns to scale exist, and therefore, local constant returns to scale hold. In this single output-two input case (keeping the second input constant at x_2^m), the plane maximizing productivity is $\mu y^{CRS} / (\nu_1 x_{1A}^{CRS} + \nu_2 x_2^m) = \mu \cdot \widehat{y}_D^{CRS} / \left(\nu_1 \widehat{x}_{1D}^{CRS} + \nu_2 x_2^m\right) > \mu \cdot \widehat{y}_D / (\nu_1 \widehat{x}_{1D} + \nu_2 x_2^m) > \mu \cdot y_D / (\nu_1 x_{1D} + \nu_2 x_2^m)$, where (ν, μ) is a vector of input and output multipliers (aggregating weights) that we intentionally denote as the shadow prices, to convey the idea that if market prices were equal to them, $(\nu, \mu) = (w^2, p^2)$ —as previously discussed—firm (x_D, y_D) would be profitability-efficient, which is not the case in the graphical example since market prizes are assumed to be (w^3, p^3). Hence, we can recall the notion of scale efficiency capturing the productivity difference between maximum productivity given the weights (ν, μ) and the technical efficiency projections. Consequently, for the general multiple output-multiple input case, one can decompose constant returns to scale productive efficiency into technical and scale efficiency as shown in (2.11): $TE_{H(G)}^{CRS}(x, y) = (\varphi^{CRS*})^2 = (\varphi \times (\varphi^{CRS*}/\varphi))^2 = (\varphi^*)^2 \times SE_{H(G)}(x, y) \leq 1$—see (2.12).

From this discussion, it is evident that the productive efficiency measure $TE_{H(G)}^{CRS}(x, y)$characterizes the set of relevant hyperplanes that maximize productivity consistent with benchmarks exhibiting local constant returns to scale—thereby satisfying the necessary (but not sufficient) condition for profitability maximization: i.e., $(\varphi^{CRS})^2 \leq 1 \Leftrightarrow (x, y) \in T^{CRS}$. Hence, relying on Minkowski's theorem, we can define (2.48) as follows:

$$T^{CRS} = \left\{ (x, y) : \frac{p \cdot (y/\varphi^{CRS*})}{w \cdot (\varphi^{CRS*} x)} = \frac{p \cdot \widehat{y}^{CRS}}{w \cdot \widehat{x}^{CRS}} \leq \Gamma(w, p),\ \varphi^{CRS*} \leq 1, \forall\ w \in \mathbb{R}_{++}^M, \forall\ p \in \mathbb{R}_{++}^N,\ x \geq 0_M, y \geq 0_N \right\}. \tag{2.50}$$

This expression shows that the supporting half-spaces defined by the profitability function can be qualified to include productive efficiency. As before, we can recover the profitability function from the technology:

$$\Gamma(w,p) = \max_{x,y}\left\{\frac{p\cdot(y/\varphi^{CRS*})}{w\cdot(\varphi^{CRS*}x)} = \frac{p\cdot\widehat{y}^{CRS}}{w\cdot\widehat{x}^{CRS}}:\ \varphi^{CRS*}\leq 1\right\}. \tag{2.51}$$

Following Zofio and Prieto (2006) and departing from expression (2.50), we obtain that $\Gamma(w,p) \geq p\cdot(y/\varphi^{CRS*})/w\cdot(\varphi^{CRS*}x) = p\cdot\widehat{y}^{CRS}/w\cdot\widehat{x}^{CRS}$. Equivalently, recalling the definition of profitability inefficiency presented in (2.23) and the following homogeneity property of profitability in input and output quantities, $p\cdot\widehat{y}^{CRS}/w\cdot\widehat{x}^{CRS} = p\cdot(y/\varphi^{CRS*})/w\cdot(\varphi^{CRS*}x) = (p\cdot y/w\cdot x)\ \times\ (\varphi^{CRS*})^{-2}$, we achieve the following Fenchel-Mahler inequality:

$$\begin{aligned}\Gamma E(x,y,w,p) = (p\cdot y/w\cdot x)/\Gamma(p,w) \leq\ & (\phi^{CRS*})^2\\ = (\phi^{*})^2 \times SE_{H(G)}(x,y),&\end{aligned} \tag{2.52}$$

where the last equality follows from the decomposition of the constant returns to scale productive efficiency into technical efficiency and scale efficiency, (2.12). In this case, profitability efficiency defined as the ratio of observed profitability to maximum profitability is not larger than the (square of) the constant returns to scale graph (hyperbolic) technical efficiency measure.[52] The above and previous results allow us to obtain the following relationship:[53]

$$\begin{aligned}\Gamma(w,p) = \max_{x,y}\ &\left\{\frac{p\cdot(y/\varphi^{CRS*})}{w\cdot(\varphi^{CRS*}x)}\right\}, \text{if and only if}\left(\varphi^{CRS*}\right)^2\\ = \max_{w,p}\ &\{(p\cdot y/w\cdot x)/\Gamma(w,p)\}.\end{aligned} \tag{2.53}$$

Consequently, if profitability is derived from the graph technical efficiency measure by maximizing profitability over all feasible quantity vectors, then the efficiency measure can be recovered from the profitability function by finding the maximum of profitability over all feasible price vectors.

Departing from (2.52), it is possible to decompose profitability efficiency as follows:

---

[52] As previously remarked, in Chap. 4, we show that it is possible to do away with the square of the technical efficiency measure by developing these duality relationships in terms of the generalized distance function introduced by Chavas and Cox (1999).

[53] This duality can be expressed equivalently as $\Gamma(w,p) = \max_{x,y}\left\{\Gamma(w,p) : (\varphi^{CRS*})^2 \leq 1\right\}$, if and only if $(\varphi^{CRS*})^2 = \max_{w,p}\{(p\cdot y/w\cdot x) : \Gamma(w,p) \leq 1\}$.

$$
\begin{aligned}
\Gamma E(x,y,w,p) &= (p\cdot y/w\cdot x)/\Gamma(p,w) = \\
&= \left(\phi^{CRS*}\right)^2 \times \left(\left(p\cdot\widehat{y}^{CRS}/w\cdot\widehat{x}^{CRS}\right)/\Gamma(p,w)\right) = \\
&= TE_{H(G)}^{CRS}(x,y) \times AE_{H(G)}(x,y,w,p) = \\
&= (\phi^*)^2 \times \left(\phi^{CRS*}/\phi^*\right)^2 \times AE_{H(G)}(x,y,w,p) = \\
&= TE_{H(G)}(x,y) \times SE_{H(G)}(x,y) \times AE_{H(G)}(x,y,w,p) \leq 1 \ ,
\end{aligned}
\tag{2.54}
$$

where the second multiplicative factor in the second row measures the gap between profitability at the constant returns to scale benchmark and maximum profitability, i.e., allocative efficiency. As the factor $TE_{H(G)}^{CRS}(x,y) = (\varphi^{CRS*})^2$ measures constant returns productive efficiency, the remainder is a residual that captures the profit loss resulting from demanding and supplying suboptimal quantities of inputs and outputs, $\left(\widehat{x}^{CRS},\ \widehat{y}^{CRS}\right)$, when compared to the optimal amounts maximizing profitability: $(x^{\Gamma}(w,p), y^{\Gamma}(w,p))$. Consequently, allocative efficiency can be recovered as follows:

$$
AE_{H(G)}(x,y,w,p) = \Gamma E(x,y,w,p)/TE_{H(G)}^{CRS}(x,y) \leq 1 \ . \tag{2.55}
$$

Finally, as shown in the last two rows of expression (2.54), it is possible to recall the decomposition of constant returns productive efficiency into technical and scale efficiencies presented in (2.13). This allows us to learn whether the firm is producing at a suboptimal scale, as well as quantifying the loss that would be entailed in the form of lower profitability.

The decomposition of profitability inefficiency into its technical and allocative components is depicted in Fig. 2.9b. Assuming that market prices are (w^3, p^3), profitability efficiency for firm (x_D, y_D) defines as the ratio of observed profitability to maximum profitability, i.e., $\Gamma E(x_D, y_D, w^3, p^3) = p^3 \cdot y_D/w^3 \cdot x_D \,/\, \Gamma(w^3, p^3)$. Profitability efficiency can then be decomposed into constant returns productive efficiency (and, successively, into its technical and scale efficiency components) and allocative efficiency. Technical efficiency is $TE_{H(G)}(x_D, y_D) = \left(\varphi_D^*\right)^2 = p^3 \cdot y_D/ w^3 \cdot x_D \,/\, \left(p^3 \cdot \left(y_D/\varphi_D^*\right)/w^3 \cdot \left(\varphi_D^* x_D\right)\right)$. This measure however is net of scale effects because it does not evaluate the profitability of the firm with respect to a constant returns to scale benchmark that complies with the necessary (but insufficient) scale condition for profitability maximization. This is achieved when evaluating the constant returns to scale productive efficiency: $TE_{H(G)}^{CRS}(x_D, y_D) = \left(\varphi_D^{CRS*}\right)^2 = (p^3 \cdot y_D/w^3 \cdot x_D) \,/\, \left(p^3 \cdot \left(y_D/\varphi_D^{CRS*}\right)/w^3 \cdot \left(\varphi_D^{CRS*} x_D\right)\right)$. Subsequently, the mismatch between the profitability evaluated at the constant returns to scale benchmark and maximum profitability represents allocative efficiency: $AE_{H(G)}(x_D, y_D, w^3, p^3) = \left(p^3\left(y_D/\varphi_D^{CRS*}\right)/w^3\left(\varphi_D^{CRS*} x_D\right)\right) \,/\, \Gamma E(x_D, y_D, w^3, p^3)$.

In this graphical example, it is worth noticing that if market prices were (w^2, p^2), the aggregation of inputs and outputs through the corresponding shadow prices

(ν, μ), corresponding to the reference hyperplane defined by them, i.e., $(\nu, \mu) = (w^2, p^2)$, $\mu \cdot \widehat{y}_{\mathrm{D}}^{CRS} / \left(\nu_1 \widehat{x}_{1\mathrm{D}}^{CRS} + \nu_2 x_2^m \right)$, would maximize profitability. As a result, the constant returns to scale benchmark for firm $(x_{\mathrm{D}}, y_{\mathrm{D}})$ would be profitability-efficient because $\Gamma(w^2, p^2) = \left(p^2 \cdot y_{\mathrm{D}} / \varphi_{\mathrm{D}}^{CRS*}\right) / \left(w_1^2 \varphi_{\mathrm{D}}^{CRS*} x_{1\mathrm{D}} + w_2^2 x_2^m\right) = (p^2 \cdot y^{\Gamma}(w^2, p^2) / w^2 \cdot x^{\Gamma}(w^2, p^2))$. In this case, there would not be allocative inefficiency, and all profitability loss would be due to technical and scale reasons. Thus, if the aggregation of the input and output mixes through the shadow prices (ν, μ) associated with the graph (hyperbolic) constant returns to scale productive efficiency measure is not equal to the market prices, then allocative inefficiency emerges because of the discrepancy between both sets of prices.

From the above, we see that, although a firm can indeed maximize productivity by producing at a constant returns to scale technically efficient *locus*—where neither increasing nor decreasing returns to scale exist—the resulting aggregation may not match maximum profitability, which is precisely associated with the use of market prices as aggregating weights. Accordingly, profitability corresponds to a specific productivity definition. Indeed, following O'Donnell (2012), we consider that the constant returns to scale projections associated with the graph (hyperbolic) productive efficiency measure under constant returns to scale preserve the relative input and output mixes within their respective bundles; i.e., $TE_{H(G)}^{CRS}(x, y)$ identifies mix-invariant optimal scales *within* inputs and *within* outputs (but not *between* them). Since this measure implies a specific aggregating function of the input and output vectors using the multipliers (ν, μ) as weights, we can express the associated maximum productivity with respect to the reference constant returns to scale benchmark hyperplane as the ratio: $Y\left(\widehat{y}^{CRS}, \mu\right) / X\left(\widehat{x}^{CRS}, \nu\right) = \mu \cdot \widehat{y}^{CRS} / \nu \cdot \widehat{x}^{CRS}$.[54] However, if the multipliers are interpreted as shadow prices, it is then clear that $\Gamma(\nu, \mu) = Y\left(\widehat{y}^{CRS}, \mu\right) / X\left(\widehat{x}^{CRS}, \nu\right) = \mu \cdot \widehat{y}^{CRS} / \nu \cdot \widehat{x}^{CRS} = \mu \cdot y^{\Gamma}(\nu, \mu) / \nu \cdot x^{\Gamma}(\nu, \mu)$. Finally, if shadow prices coincide with market prices $(\nu, \mu) = (w, p)$, then maximum productivity coincides with maximum profitability: $\Gamma(\nu, \mu) = \Gamma(w, p) = Y\left(\widehat{y}^{CRS}, p\right) / X\left(\widehat{x}^{CRS}, w\right) = Y(y^{\Gamma}(w, p)) / X(x^{\Gamma}(w, p)) = p \cdot \widehat{y}^{CRS} / w \cdot \widehat{x}^{CRS} = p \cdot y^{\Gamma}(w, p) / w \cdot x^{\Gamma}(w, p)$. This implies that the difference between profitability under shadow prices and under market prices can be interpreted as allocative efficiency, rather than *mix technical efficiency* in O'Donnell's (2012) and Balk and Zofío's (2018) productivity context. That is, the profitability loss resulting from demanding and supplying the wrong mix of inputs and outputs given their market prices implies that $\Gamma(\nu, \mu) < \Gamma(w, p)$. We elaborate this result in detail in Chap. 4 which deals with the measurement and decomposition of profitability efficiency.

Finally, it is relevant to recall that the graph (hyperbolic) measure of technical efficiency, being multiplicative, projects inefficient firms to the weakly efficiency

[54] Here, $X(x,\nu)$ and $Y(y,\mu)$ are aggregator functions that are nonnegative, nondecreasing, and linearly homogeneous, i.e., satisfy constant returns to scale.

subset of technology (2.3), both in terms of constant and variable returns to scale. As a result, it may understate technical (and productive) efficiency by not complying with the criterion of Pareto-Koopmans efficiency (indication property, E1), and therefore, individual input reductions and output increases may prove feasible in order to reach the strongly efficient frontier. This implies that the decomposition of profitability efficiency (2.54) could understate allocative efficiency because the remaining economic inefficiency between the technical efficiency projections and the optimal economic benchmarks may not be solely attributable to a wrong mix of inputs and outputs at the strongly efficient frontier. The existence of individual input and output slacks under the standard Data Envelopment Analysis (DEA) approximation of the technology makes the decomposition of profitability inefficiency using nonparametric methods prone to this drawback.

2.4.4 Decomposing Profit Inefficiency

We now present the decomposition of profit efficiency into technical and allocative components. Following previous developments but departing from the profit function defined in (2.24), we can recover the technology by resorting to Minkowski's theorem:

$$T = \left\{(x,y) : p\cdot y - w\cdot x \leq \Pi(w,p),\ \ \forall\ w\in \mathbb{R}^M_{++}, \forall\ p\in \mathbb{R}^N_{++},\ \ x\geq 0_M, y\geq 0_N\right\}. \tag{2.56}$$

This expression reveals that, on this occasion and for a given price vector (w,p), the profit function supports a half-space of the form $H(w,p,c) = \left\{(x,y) : p\cdot y - w\cdot x \leq c = \Pi(w,p), w\in \mathbb{R}^M_{++},\ p\in \mathbb{R}^N_{++},\ x\geq 0_M, y\geq 0_N\right\}$. As before, since, by definition, $\Pi(w,p)$ is the maximum profit given the prices and technology, there is no feasible firm $(x,y) \in H(w,p,c)$ yielding higher profits. Correspondingly, if the profit-maximizing production plan belongs to $H(w,p,c)$, then it lies on the hyperplane $p\cdot y - w\cdot x = \Pi(w,p)$.

This situation is geometrically depicted in Fig. 2.10a where the price vector (w^1, p^1) defines the half-space below the hyperplane (line) given by $p^1\cdot y - w^1\cdot x = \Pi(w^1,p^1)$ and passing through $(x^\Pi(w^1,p^1), y^\Pi(w^1,p^1))$, i.e., the optimal amounts of inputs and outputs presented in Sect. 2.2.4. Following the above argument, the profit-maximizing bundle cannot be above this isoprofit line, and therefore, the half-space below it must contain T. If there was an alternative production plan $(x,y)\in T$ above the isoprofit, it could attain higher profit given the technology, but then, we incur in the contradiction that $(x^\Pi(w^1,p^1), y^\Pi(w^1,p^1))$ would not maximize profit. Again, since at least one firm in the isoprofit $p^1\cdot y - w^1\cdot x = \Pi(w^1,p^1)$ must be able to produce with the existing technology T, then $p^1\cdot y - w^1\cdot x$ and T must share at least one (x,y) in the quantity (primal) space.

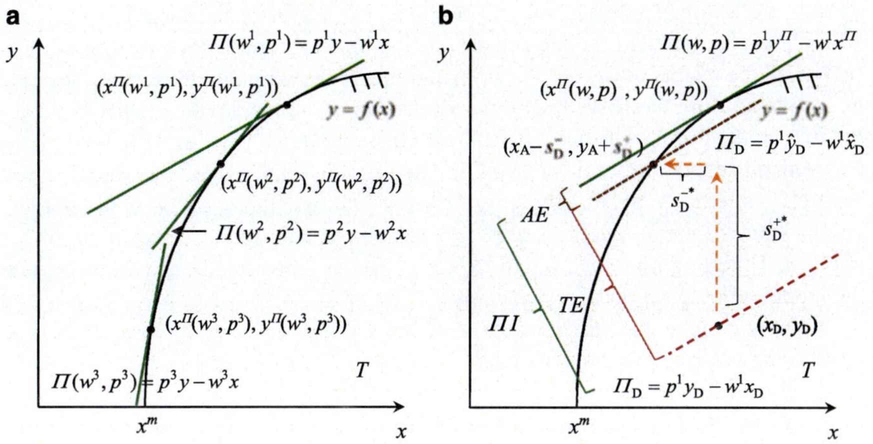

Fig. 2.10 **(a–b)** Duality between slack-based technical inefficiency and the profit function

Consider as before two alternative price vectors $(w^2,p^2) \neq (w^1,p^1)$ and $(w^3,p^3) \neq (w^2,p^2) \neq (w^1,p^1)$ that support their corresponding half-spaces above the hyperplanes (lines), associated with $p^2 \cdot y - w^2 \cdot x = \Pi(w^2,p^2)$ and $p^3 \cdot y - w^3 \cdot x = \Pi(w^3, p^3)$—and passing through $(x^\Pi(w^2,p^2), y^\Pi(w^2,p^2))$ and $(x^\Pi(w^3,p^3), y^\Pi(w^3,p^3))$. Then, no elements of the associated half-spaces $(x,y) \in H(w^2,p^2,\Pi(w^2,p^2))$ and $(x,y) \in H(w^3,p^3,\Pi(w^3,p^3))$ could yield higher profit given the technology T than $\Pi(w^2,p^2)$ and $\Pi(w^3,p^3)$. Hence, the isoprofits $p^2 \cdot y - w^2 \cdot x = \Pi(w^2,p^2)$ and $p^3 \cdot y - w^3 \cdot x = \Pi(w^3,p^3)$ must contain also T, which implies that, once again, these hyperplanes and the technology must share at least one (x,y), different from each other. Now, combining all three half-spaces $H(w^1,p^1,\Pi(w^1,p^1))$, $H(w^2,p^2,\Pi(w^2,p^2))$, and $H(w^3,p^3,\Pi(w^3,p^3))$, the technology T is approximated by the intersection between both supporting (enveloping) hyperplanes. Continuing with every price combination until all price vectors are exhausted results in expression (2.56). In Fig. 2.10a, the different supporting hyperplanes, the technology, and its corresponding boundary are presented, resembling the standard, single output, concave production function $y = f(x)$, presented in microeconomics textbooks.

Then, once again, as the technology can be recovered from the profit function, it is possible to retrace our steps back and define the profit function as the intersection of the supporting half-spaces corresponding to different isoprofits, representing maximum revenue less cost for alternative prices, i.e.,

$$\Pi(w,p) = \max_{x,y} \{p \cdot y - w \cdot x : (x,y) \in T\}. \tag{2.57}$$

In Fig. 2.10a, this expression corresponds to each isoprofit line that, maximizing profit for each price vector, is tangent to the technology T, satisfying the first-order conditions for profit maximization subject to the technology; i.e., when inputs and outputs are optimally demanded and supplied, the marginal productivity of inputs with respect to outputs is equal to their relative prices (slope of the isoprofit line).[55]

Again, the results presented in (2.56) and (2.57) showing that the technology can be recovered from the profit function and vice versa summarize the duality between the two. In the profit case, duality theory is concerned with the regularity conditions that both the technology and the profit function should satisfy so as to ensure that, for each price vector (w, p), maximum profit exists and is unique; i.e., it is possible to obtain input demand equations $x^{\Pi}(w, p)$ and output supply equations $y^{\Pi}(w, p)$ by applying Hotelling's lemma, i.e., differentiating the profit function with respect to the input and output prices, respectively.

We now comment on the concept of shadow prices in the profit case. Here, we refer to the vector of prices that satisfy the first-order conditions for profit maximization if a firm was optimal. Now, instead of reading Fig. 2.10a as the input and output combinations that maximize profit, we focus on the input and output price vectors that maximize profit given a (would be optimal) production plan (as in the previous cost and revenue cases, this can be recovered from Hotelling's lemma). As before, we denote these vectors of input and output shadow prices by $\nu \in \mathbb{R}^M_+$ and $\mu \in \mathbb{R}^N_+$. Then, a firm incurs allocative inefficiency if it does not maximize profit by failing to demand the optimal input and output quantities given the observed market prices (w, p). But, once again, this can be reinterpreted as a divergence between its associated shadow prices, (ν, μ), for which it would be profit-efficient, i.e., $\mu \cdot y - \nu \cdot x = \mu \cdot y^{\Pi}(\nu, \mu) - \nu \cdot x^{\Pi}(\nu, \mu) = \Pi(\nu, \mu)$, and actual market prices. In this case, $(\nu, \mu) \neq (w, p)$, and therefore, $p \cdot y^{\Pi}(\nu, \mu) - w \cdot x^{\Pi}(\nu, \mu) < p \cdot y^{\Pi}(w, p) - w \cdot x^{\Pi}(w, p) = \Pi(w, p)$. In Fig. 2.10b, this situation is represented by the benchmark projection of firm D, $(\widehat{x}_{\mathrm{D}}, \widehat{y}_{\mathrm{D}}) = \left(x_{\mathrm{D}} - s_{\mathrm{D}}^{-*}, \widehat{y}_{\mathrm{D}} + s_{\mathrm{D}}^{+*}\right)$, which maximizes profit for prices (w^2, p^2) as shown in Fig. 2.10a, implying that its associated shadow prices are $(\nu, \mu) = (w^2, p^2)$, i.e., $\Pi(w^2, p^2) = p^2 \cdot y^{\Pi}(w^2, p^2) - w^2 \cdot x^{\Pi}(w^2, p^2) = p^2 \cdot (y_{\mathrm{D}} + s_{\mathrm{D}}^{+*}) - w^2 \cdot \left(x_{\mathrm{D}} - s_{\mathrm{D}}^{-*}\right)$. But if market prices are (w^1, p^1) , then this firm experiences a profit loss because $p^1 \cdot y^{\Pi}(w^2, p^2) - w^1 \cdot x^{\Pi}(w^2, p^2) < p^1 \cdot y^{\Pi}(w^1, p^1) - w^1 \cdot x^{\Pi}(w^1, p^1) = \Pi(w^1, p^1)$. This is illustrated through the two isoprofits corresponding to $\Pi(w, p) = p^1 \cdot y^{\Pi} - w^1 \cdot x^{\Pi}$ and $p^1 \cdot y^{\Pi}(w^2, p^2) - w^1 \cdot x^{\Pi}(w^2, p^2)$.

Regarding the decomposition of profit inefficiency, we do not pursue the multiplicative approach because a natural duality between the technology and the profit function, based on the possibility of defining a Fenchel-Mahler inequality that, in turn, allows the decomposition of profit inefficiency into a technical term and (a residual) allocative term, cannot be obtained (unless one is willing to resort to the partial input (cost) or output (revenue) frameworks already considered).[56] Additionally, in the additive approach, we want to exploit the fact that additive technical measures of inefficiency satisfy the indication property (E1) and therefore fulfill the

[55] It is once again assumed that a maximum is achieved and that the profit function is continuous and twice differentiable.

[56] For example, the hyperbolic measure (2.10) cannot be recovered from the profit function in the form of a Fenchel-Mahler inequality.

criteria for Pareto-Koopmans efficiency; i.e., they identify the strongly efficient subset of the technology. This ensures that technical inefficiency is not undervalued when decomposing profit inefficiency. Hence, the remaining inefficiency can be solely attributed to the allocative inefficiency resulting from wrongly demanded and supplied combinations (mixes) of inputs and outputs (x, y), when compared to their optimal counterparts $(x^{\Pi}(w,p), y^{\Pi}(w,p))$. Since the Farrell-type input, output, or graph (hyperbolic) measures of technical efficiency do not ensure strongly efficient projections, such criteria cannot be met. At the end of this section, we further revisit this question considering recent contributions that attempt to define multiplicative decompositions of profit inefficiency.

The above duality relationship summarized in (2.56) and (2.57) between the technology and the profit function can be qualified to include the concept of additive technical inefficiency. This represents a necessary step if we are to decompose economic efficiency into our two components of interest. First, let us recall the additive definition of graph technical inefficiency, $TI_{A(G)}(x,y) = \sum_{m=1}^{M}(x_m - \widehat{x}_m) + \sum_{n=1}^{N}(\widehat{y}_n - y_n) = \sum_{m=1}^{M} s_m^{-*} + \sum_{n=1}^{N} s_n^{+*} \geq 0$, as presented in (2.14). As before, this measure is capable of characterizing the technology, $T = \left\{(x,y) : \sum_{m=1}^{M} s_m^{-*} + \sum_{n=1}^{N} s_n^{+*} \geq 0\right\}$, or equivalently, it satisfies the representation property: $\sum_{m=1}^{M} s_m^{-*} + \sum_{n=1}^{N} s_n^{+*} \geq 0 \Leftrightarrow (x,y) \in T$.[57] Then, as shown in Fig. 2.10a, it is clear that a technically inefficient firm cannot maximize profit for any price vector, since it is dominated in terms of Pareto-Koopmans efficiency and input reductions and output increases are feasible given the technology. As before, this suggests that we can redefine (2.56) in the following way:

$$T = \left\{ \begin{array}{l} (x,y) : p\cdot(y+s^{+*}) - w\cdot(x-s^{-*}) = p\cdot\widehat{y} - w\cdot\widehat{x} \leq \Pi(w,p),\ \sum_{m=1}^{M} s_m^{-*} + \sum_{n=1}^{N} s_n^{+*} \geq 0, \\ \forall\ w \in \mathbb{R}_{++}^{M}, \forall\ p \in \mathbb{R}_{++}^{N},\ x \geq 0_M, y \geq 0_N \end{array} \right\} \tag{2.58}$$

This expression shows that the supporting half-spaces defined by the profit function can be qualified to include technical inefficiency. Once Minkowski's theorem has been enhanced to allow for technical inefficiency, we can recover the profit function from the technology:

[57] For $(x,y) \notin T$, we define $\sum_{m=1}^{M} s_m^{-*} + \sum_{n=1}^{N} s_n^{+*} = -\infty$, since the associated optimization problem is unfeasible.

$$\Pi(w,p) = \max_{x,y}\left\{p\cdot(y+s^{+*}) - w\cdot(x-s^{-*}) = p\cdot\widehat{y} - w\cdot\widehat{x}:\ \sum_{m=1}^{M} s_m^{-*} + \sum_{n=1}^{N} s_n^{+*} \geq 0\right\}. \tag{2.59}$$

Now, following Cooper et al. (1999) and expression (2.58), we obtain that $\Pi(w, p) \geq p\cdot(y+s^{+*}) - w\cdot(x-s^{-*}) = p\cdot y - w\cdot x + p\cdot s^{+*} + w\cdot s^{-*}$, or equivalently, recalling the definition of profit inefficiency presented in (2.25), we achieve that:

$$\Pi I(x,y,w,p) = \Pi(p,w) - (p\cdot y - w\cdot x) \geq \sum_{m=1}^{M} w_m s_m^{-*} + \sum_{n=1}^{N} p_n s_n^{+*}. \tag{2.60}$$

In this case, profit inefficiency defined as the difference between maximum profit and observed profit is greater than the monetary value of the technical inefficiency: $\sum_{m=1}^{M} w_m s_m^{-*} + \sum_{n=1}^{N} p_n s_n^{+*}$. It is immediate that the value of the allocative inefficiency could be calculated by closing the inequality in (2.60), i.e., as the difference between profit inefficiency less the value of technical inefficiency: $\Pi I(x,y,w,p) - \sum_{m=1}^{M} w_m s_m^{-*} + \sum_{n=1}^{N} p_n s_n^{+*}$. Unfortunately, this exposition does not correspond to a dual result between the quantity (primal) and price (dual) spaces; i.e., the right-hand side of (2.60) should depend on quantities only.

To achieve this result, we follow Aparicio et al. (2016a, 2016b), who show that it can be obtained by relying on the normalization of profit inefficiency using the minimum of the input or output prices. Adopting this approach allows us to obtain the following Fenchel-Mahler inequality[58]:

$$\begin{aligned} N\Pi I(x,y,\widetilde{w},\widetilde{p}) = \Pi(\widetilde{p},\widetilde{w}) - (\widetilde{p}\cdot y - \widetilde{w}\cdot x) &= \frac{\Pi(p,w) - (p\cdot y - w\cdot x)}{\min\{w_1,\ \ldots, w_m, p_1,\ \ldots, p_n\}} \\ &\geq \sum_{m=1}^{M} s_m^{-*} + \sum_{n=1}^{N} s_n^{+*}, \end{aligned} \tag{2.61}$$

where $(\widetilde{w},\widetilde{p}) = (w/\min\{w_1,\ \ldots, w_m, p_1,\ \ldots, p_n\}, p/\min\{w_1,\ \ldots, w_m, p_1,\ \ldots,\ p_n\})$ is the vector of normalized prices. Thanks to this normalization, the profit inefficiency satisfies desirable properties. In particular, it is homogeneous of degree zero in prices—as opposed to (2.60), which makes the measure invariant to currency units for input and output prices.

Based on the above result, we can present the following duality result:

[58] This is a particular case of the weighted additive duality presented in Chap. 6, where the weights are set equal to one and, therefore, the slacks are measured in the units of the original observed data.

$$\Pi(\widetilde{w},\widetilde{p}) = \max_{x,y} \left\{ (p \cdot y - w \cdot x) + \left(\sum_{m=1}^{M} s_m^{-*} + \sum_{n=1}^{N} s_n^{+*} \right) \times \min\{w_1, \ldots, w_m, p_1, \ldots, p_n\} \right\}, \quad \text{iff}$$
$$\sum_{m=1}^{M} s_m^- + \sum_{n=1}^{N} s_n^+ = \min_{\widetilde{w},\widetilde{p}} \{\Pi(\widetilde{p},\widetilde{w}) - (\widetilde{p} \cdot y - \widetilde{w} \cdot x)\}. \tag{2.62}$$

Thus, if the (price normalized) profit function is derived from the additive technical inefficiency measure by maximizing profit over all feasible quantity vectors, then the inefficiency measure can be recovered from the profit function by finding the minimum profit over all feasible (normalized) price vectors.

We may now decompose normalized profit efficiency departing from (2.61) as follows:

$$\begin{aligned} N\Pi I(x,y,\widetilde{w},\widetilde{p}) &= \Pi(\widetilde{p},\widetilde{w}) - (\widetilde{p} \cdot y - \widetilde{w} \cdot x) = \\ &= \sum_{m=1}^{M} s_m^{-*} + \sum_{n=1}^{N} s_n^{+*} + AI_{A(G)}(x,y,\widetilde{w},\widetilde{p}) = \\ &= TI_{A(G)}(x,y) + AI_{A(G)}(x,y,\widetilde{w},\widetilde{p}) \geq 0. \end{aligned} \tag{2.63}$$

In this expression, the second factor in the last equality captures the gap between maximum profit and the additive projection of the firm to the production frontier. To the extent that $TI_{A(G)}(x,y) = \sum_{m=1}^{M} s_m^{-*} + \sum_{n=1}^{N} s_n^{+*}$ measures technical inefficiency, the remainder is a residual that captures allocative inefficiency, i.e., the profit loss resulting from demanding and supplying (technically efficient) quantities of inputs and outputs $(\widehat{x}, \widehat{y})$ that do not correspond to the optimal amounts that maximize profit $(x^{\Pi}(w,p), y^{\Pi}(w,p))$. Hence, allocative inefficiency is calculated as the difference between profit and technical inefficiencies:

$$AI_{A(G)}(x,y,\widetilde{w},\widetilde{p}) = N\Pi I(x,y,\widetilde{w},\widetilde{p}) - \left(\sum_{m=1}^{M} s_m^{-*} + \sum_{n=1}^{N} s_n^{+*} \right) \geq 0. \tag{2.64}$$

The decomposition of profit inefficiency into its technical and allocative components for firm (x_D, y_D) is illustrated in Fig. 2.10b, considering that the market prices correspond to (w^1, p^1). Here, profit inefficiency defines as the difference between maximum profit, $\Pi(w^1,p^1) = p^1 \cdot y^{\Pi} - w^1 \cdot x^{\Pi}$, and observed profit, $\Pi_D = p^1 \cdot y_D - w^1 \cdot x_D$. In terms of normalized prices, $(\widetilde{w}^1,\widetilde{p}^1)$, $N\Pi I_D(x,y,\widetilde{w}^1,\widetilde{p}^1) = \Pi(\widetilde{w}^1,\widetilde{p}^1) - (\widetilde{p}^1 \cdot y_D - \widetilde{w}^1 \cdot x_D)$. Profit inefficiency can be then decomposed into its technical and allocative components: $N\Pi I(x_D,y_D,\widetilde{w}^1,\widetilde{p}^1) = s_D^{-*} + s_D^{+*} + (\Pi(\widetilde{p}^1,\widetilde{w}^1) - (\widetilde{p}^1 \cdot \widehat{y}_D - \widetilde{w}^1 \cdot \widehat{x}_D)) = TI_{A(G)}(x_D,y_D) + AI_{A(G)}(x_D,y_D,\widetilde{w}^1,\widetilde{p}^1)$, where $(\widetilde{p}^1 \cdot \widehat{y} - \widetilde{w}^1 \cdot \widehat{x}) = (\widetilde{p}^1 \cdot (y_D + s_D^{+*}) - \widetilde{w}^1 \cdot (x_D - s_D^{-*}))$. In Fig. 2.10b, profit inefficiency, technical inefficiency, and allocative inefficiency are identified by the corresponding gaps between the parallel isoprofit lines.

We can now recall the concept of shadow price previously introduced to illustrate the concept of allocative inefficiency as the discrepancy between shadow prices, (ν, μ), and market prices, (w^1, p^1) (i.e., between supporting hyperplanes). Specifically, let us consider (ν, μ) as the price vector that would render the efficient projection of (x_D, y_D) profit-efficient, i.e., $\mu \cdot \widehat{y}_D - \nu \cdot \widehat{x}_D = \mu \cdot (y_D + s_D^{*+}) - \nu \cdot (x_D - s_D^{*-}) = \Pi(\nu, \mu)$; then, allocative inefficiency can be reinterpreted as $AI_{A(G)}(x_D, y_D, w^1, p^1) = \Pi(w^1, p^1) - (p^1 \cdot \widehat{y}_D - w^1 \cdot \widehat{x}_D) = (p^1 \cdot y^{\Pi}(w^1, p^1) - w^1 \cdot x^{\Pi}(w^1, p^1)) - (p^1 \cdot y^{\Pi}(\nu, \mu) - w^1 \cdot x^{\Pi}(\nu, \mu))$. As a result, if market prices coincided with the shadow prices of firm (x_D, y_D) at its benchmark projection, $(\nu, \mu) = (w^1, p^1)$, it would be allocative efficient: $AI_{A(G)}(x_D, y_D, w^1, p^1) = 0$. Therefore, allocative inefficiency corresponds to the difference in profit at the optimal (technological) shadow prices and market prices.

Since the (slack-based) additive measures of technical inefficiency project the inefficient firms to the strongly efficient subset of the technology $\partial^S(T)$, (2.2), this measure complies with the Pareto-Koopmans efficiency criterion, and therefore, the remaining allocative inefficiency can be solely attributed to a wrong mix of inputs and outputs when compared to the optimal ones (i.e., no technical improvements reducing inputs or increasing outputs are feasible). From an empirical perspective, this property of the additive measures is verified under a Data Envelopment Analysis (DEA) approximation of the technology, and therefore, the decomposition of profit inefficiency does not suffer from the drawbacks discussed for multiplicative Farrell-type measures. Nevertheless, since alternative definitions of additive technical inefficiency can be chosen for projecting the evaluated firm toward the strongly efficient subset, as shown in the second part of this book, the relative values of technical and allocative inefficiencies may change. A relevant discussion on the upper and lower bounds for technical and allocative inefficiencies when decomposing profit inefficiency, relying on slack-based technical efficiency measures as above, is given by Ruiz and Sirvent (2011).

We conclude this section commenting on a recent proposal by Färe et al. (2019) who, despite this shortcoming, develop the multiplicative approach for profit inefficiency decomposition based on Farrell-type measures. However, the changes to the profit inefficiency definition that are required to make it compatible with a multiplicative approach result in expressions whose interpretation lacks the consistency required for economic efficiency measurement. For example, despite profit inefficiency being defined additively as in (2.24), these authors propose the following profit efficiency measure that normalizes (divides) profit inefficiency by the revenue attained by the firm, i.e., $\Pi E_{R(O)}(x, y, w, p) = 1 + [\Pi I(x, y, w, p)]/p \cdot y = 1 + [\Pi(w, p) - (p \cdot y - w \cdot x)]/p \cdot y$, with $\Pi E_{R(O)}(x, y, w, p) \geq 1$, since $\Pi I(x, y, w, p) \geq 0$.[59] This results in an expression that corresponds to a measure consisting of two factors:

[59] Following these authors, we comment on the output-revenue decomposition, and for clarity in the exposition, adopt our notation.

(i) the realized cost-revenue ratio (i.e., the inverse of profitability as defined in (2.23)), plus (ii) "the best possible profit margin for the firm," which is actually defined as profit inefficiency over revenue: $\Pi E_{R(O)}(x, y, w, p) = [w \cdot x/p \cdot y] + [\Pi(w, p) - (p \cdot y - w \cdot x)] / p \cdot y = [C/R] + [\Pi I(x, y, w, p)] / R$, where C and R are observed cost and revenue.[60] Although this expression allows these authors to link profit inefficiency to Farrell's radial output measure, we see that the profit efficiency measure requires modifications that, ultimately, combine several measures of firm performance such as the (inverse of) attained profitability and revenue, which give rise to their own decompositions, naturally based on their supporting functions, as shown in previous sections.

Besides the undesirable definition of firms' performance combining several economic measures of economic efficiency, the use of partially oriented measures in an additive context results in a decomposition of profit efficiency that requires differentiating between a technical inefficiency term corresponding to the inverse of the output-oriented technical efficiency measure (2.7), $TE_{R(O)}(x, y)$, and two allocative residuals: a first one resulting from the wrong output or input mix (depending on the chosen orientation) with respect to the optimal quantities maximizing revenue (or minimizing cost), i.e., the inverse of $AE^{R}_{R(O)}(x, y, w, p)$ in expression (2.44), and a second one accounting for the remaining input (or output) dimension. In the output case, this results in $\Pi E_{R(O)}(x, y, w, p) = TE_{R(O)}(x, y)^{-1} \times AE_{R(O)}(x, y, p)^{-1} \times AE^{R}_{R(O)}(x, y, w, p)^{-1}$, where $AE^{R}_{R(O)}(x, y, w, p)^{-1} = \Pi E_{R(O)}(x, y, w, p) \times RE(x, y, p)$, and the latter term corresponds to revenue efficiency, as defined in expression (2.20).

Therefore, combining the additive and radial approaches results in an additional term, whose interpretation involves the multiplication of profit efficiency—the magnitude to be decomposed—and revenue efficiency. This result proves both undesirable given its circularity and being problematic because of its partial (one-sided) interpretation. Indeed, $AI^{R}_{R(O)}(x, y, w, p)$ shows the improvement of profits once maximum revenue has been achieved for a given input vector. This means that when eliminating output-oriented technical inefficiency and allocative inefficiency, inputs are kept constant. This implies that only output mixes are supposed to change. But to eliminate the final inefficiency gap between maximum profit and profit at the revenue-efficient projection, changes in input quantities are also needed, but these cannot be identified from the solution to the model and are also dependent on the initially chosen orientation.

We conclude that rather than pursuing this type of decompositions based on partial orientations, it is worth relying on the principle of parsimony and aim at definitions of technical efficiency that can be recovered in a simple and concise way through duality and therefore allow for an unambiguous and consistent

[60] Alternatively, normalizing profit inefficiency by observed cost yields the alternative decomposition $\Pi E(x, y, w, p) = [R/C] + [\Pi I(x, y, w, p)]/C$, which can be related to Farrell's radial input measure. Also, combining observed revenue and cost, $\Pi E(x, y, w, p) = [R(x, p)/R] + [C - C(y, w)]/C$, where the first summand is the inverse of revenue efficiency in (2.20).

decomposition of profit inefficiency into technical and allocative terms. This can be achieved through slack-based additive measures that (i) measure the additional profit gains available from both individual changes in the input and output mixes necessary to achieve maximum profit (allocative inefficiency) and (ii) are not forcing radial projections, identifying as reference benchmarks firms on the strongly efficient subset of the technology (technical inefficiency).

2.4.5 *An Essential Property for the Decomposition of Economic (In)Efficiency: Multiplicative and Additive*

In Sects. 2.2.4 and 2.3.5, we showed the properties that a technical efficiency index and an economic efficiency index must satisfy, following the previous literature. However, so far, only a few authors have discussed the properties that the own decomposition of the economic efficiency index into technical and allocative components should meet. Next, in this subsection, we focus our attention on a particular property that, from our viewpoint, is essential for a correct interpretation of the terms of the decomposition: technical efficiency and allocative efficiency. All the definitions and results linked to the new essential property that appear in the book were previously discussed by Aparicio et al. (2021), who also review the scarce literature on the properties of economic efficiency decompositions. Additionally, we will also focus our attention on an extended version of the essential property, which endows the decomposition with a meaningful allocative component.

Before introducing the definition of the essential property for the decomposition of economic efficiency, we recall that our classification of efficiency measures is either multiplicative or additive, depending on whether the measurement of the distance or gap between firm (x, y) and a reference benchmark on the production frontier, $(\widehat{x}, \widehat{y})$, entails projecting the former multiplicatively by a factor expanding outputs and/or reducing inputs or rather the addition of output quantities and/or subtraction of input quantities. Next, given input and output market prices (w, p), we introduce the formal definition of the new property:

(D1) (a) If $(\widehat{x}, \widehat{y})$ is such that $p \cdot \widehat{y} / w \cdot \widehat{x} = \Gamma(w, p)$, then $AE(x, y, w, p) = 1$, and (b) if $(\widehat{x}, \widehat{y})$ is such that $p \cdot \widehat{y} - w \cdot \widehat{x} = \Pi(w, p)$, then $AI(x, y, w, p) = 0$.

In other words, in the graph case and under the multiplicative approach, if the measure used to gauge technical efficiency projects the assessed firm onto a benchmark that maximizes profitability, then it should be allocative efficient. This means that the term $AE(x, y, w, p)$ should be necessarily one. On the other hand, when the additive approach is applied, if the technical efficiency measure identified a benchmark firm that maximizes profit, then allocative inefficiency $AI(x, y, w, p)$ should be nil.

Obviously, we are assuming above that the projection point that is generated by the measure of technical efficiency is unique. Property D1 could be modified to fit well to the more general framework, which considers the existence of alternative solutions. In this sense, let $\widehat{F}$ be the set of all benchmark projections yielded by the (in)efficiency model for firm (x, y). Then, D1 may be adapted as follows:

(D1') (a) If $\exists(\widehat{x}, \widehat{y}) \in \widehat{F}$ such that $p \cdot \widehat{y}/w \cdot \widehat{x} = \Gamma(w, p)$, then $AE(x, y, w, p) = 1$, and (b) if $\exists(\widehat{x}, \widehat{y}) \in \widehat{F}$ such that $p \cdot \widehat{y} - w \cdot \widehat{x} = \Pi(w, p)$, then $AI(x, y, w, p) = 0$.

It is worth mentioning that it is possible to define similar properties for the oriented cases. Under the input orientation, if the projection point $\widehat{x} \in L(y)$ is such that it minimizes cost, then the allocative efficiency (inefficiency) term in the corresponding decomposition should value one (zero). In the same vein, under the output orientation, if the projection point $\widehat{y} \in P(x)$ maximizes revenue, then the allocative efficiency (inefficiency) component should be equal to one (zero).

This essential property is rather sensible and has been neglected in the literature so far. The main reason is that the first efficiency measures used for decomposing economic efficiency, that is, the input and output radial efficiency measures proposed by Farrell (1957) or their alternative representation through Shephard's (1953, 1970) distance functions, meet this property for the decomposition in a natural way, although it was never proven. We will show this proof in Chap. 3.

The subsequent developments in the literature with the objective of introducing and decomposing economic efficiency, as the hyperbolic measure and the directional distance functions, assumed the satisfaction of the essential property. Fortunately, as we show in the book, both cases meet the property, and therefore, the terms in their decomposition may be correctly interpreted. Unfortunately, more modern approaches for measuring and decomposing overall efficiency do not satisfy the essential property, except the measures based upon the Hölder metrics (see Chap. 9). Consequently, some evaluated firms can exhibit an overestimation of the actual value of price (allocative) inefficiency. As shown above, in the additive approach, it should take a value of zero when the corresponding projection firm maximizes profit at market prices, but instead, it takes a strictly positive value. Something similar happens with the multiplicative approach. In this case, allocative efficiency is underestimated since it should take value one, and yet, the corresponding component in the decomposition takes a value strictly less than one.

The fundamental cause for the above drawback is the practice followed in the research literature to decompose economic efficiency. The first authors concerned with the empirical implementation of economic efficiency (Farrell, 1957; Färe & Primont, 1995; Chambers et al., 1996; Chambers et al., 1988) never mentioned the essential property or similar ones. Instead, they took the fulfillment of the property for granted. In the Farrell (1957) tradition, the allocative efficiency term in the decomposition of economic efficiency is defined as the residual derived from closing the Fenchel-Mahler inequalities previously established between an overall economic efficiency measure and certain technical efficiency measure—see the above decompositions of cost, revenue, profitability, and profit efficiency. This equality can then be stated by including a new term multiplying the technical efficiency component, interpreted as allocative efficiency since, in the standard framework, no other reason exists which can cause economic inefficiency. As shown in Chap. 8, authors like

Chambers et al. (1988) resorted to the same argument for deriving an allocative inefficiency term for the decomposition of the so-called Nerlovian efficiency, after establishing an inequality between economic inefficiency and technical inefficiency (represented by the directional distance function in this case):

> Finally, allocative efficiency is defined as the gap in inequality (17), namely, AE.... (Chambers et al., 1988, pp. 360–361)

The same happens, for example, in the paper by Färe et al. (2002) on the hyperbolic measure and its relationship with economic efficiency. The authors claimed the following:

> Following the tradition of Farrell (1957) we may define allocative efficiency AE as a residual (Färe et al., 2002, p. 673)

Subsequent authors exploited an identical argument for decomposing overall (in)-efficiency into technical and price (in)efficiency, without questioning whether such decomposition was sensible or not. Unfortunately, most of the approaches in the literature devoted to the measurement of economic efficiency do not meet the essential property, as shown in this book.

Another interesting property that, in our opinion, the components of the decomposition of economic efficiency should fulfill is introduced next (see Aparicio et al., 2021), as an extended version of the essential property:

(D2) (a) $AE(x, y, w, p) = AE(\widehat{x}, \widehat{y}, w, p)$, and (b) $AI(x, y, w, p) = AI(\widehat{x}, \widehat{y}, w, p)$.

The extended essential property of the decomposition of economic efficiency means that for any evaluated firm (x, y), its allocative efficiency, under the multiplicative approach, always coincides with the price efficiency gauged at its corresponding benchmark firm $(\widehat{x}, \widehat{y})$. In the case of considering the additive perspective, then, allocative inefficiency of (x, y) is equivalent to allocative inefficiency calculated at its benchmark projection $(\widehat{x}, \widehat{y})$.

Certain results are worth mentioning here. First, if a decomposition satisfies the extended essential property, then it also meets the essential property. To see that, observe that if $(\widehat{x}, \widehat{y})$ is such that $p \cdot \widehat{y}/w \cdot \widehat{x} = \Gamma(w, p)$, then, for this benchmark $(\widehat{x}, \widehat{y})$, the measure of profitability efficiency would be one and the component of technical efficiency would also take a value of one because $(\widehat{x}, \widehat{y})$ belongs to the frontier. Consequently, $AE(\widehat{x}, \widehat{y}, w, p) = 1/1 = 1$, which implies that $AE(x, y, w, p) = 1$ by the satisfaction of the extended essential property. Additionally and because of this previous result, we observe that if a measure does not satisfy the essential property, then said measure results in a decomposition that cannot meet the extended essential property since, otherwise, it would satisfy the essential property, in complete contradiction with the starting hypothesis.

The two properties already introduced in this subsection are defined for the graph framework. In the same way, it is possible to define analogous properties for the cost and revenue decompositions. Let us formally establish these definitions next:

(CD1) If $\widehat{x}$ is such that $w \cdot \widehat{x} = C(y, w)$, then $AE_{M(I)}(x, y, w) = 1$ and $AI_{M(I)}(x, y, w) = 0$, depending on the nature of the input-oriented measure (denoted, in general, as M): multiplicative or additive, respectively.
(RD1) If $\widehat{y}$ is such that $p \cdot \widehat{y} = R(x, p)$, then $AE_{M(O)}(x, y, p) = 1$ and $AI_{M(O)}(x, y, p) = 0$, depending on the nature of the output-oriented measure: multiplicative or additive, respectively.

Now, let $\widehat{F}_{M(I)}$ be the set of all the projection firms yielded by the model associated with the input-oriented measure $M(I)$. Then, CD1 may be adapted as follows:

(CD1') If $\exists \widehat{x} \in \widehat{F}_{M(I)}$ such that $w \cdot \widehat{x} = C(y, w)$, then $AE_{M(I)}(x, y, w) = 1$ and $AI_{M(I)}(x, y, w) = 0$, depending on the nature of the input-oriented measure: multiplicative or additive, respectively.

Let now $\widehat{F}_{M(O)}$ be the set of all the projection points yielded by the model associated with the output-oriented measure $M(O)$. Then, RD1 may be adapted as follows:

(RD1') If $\exists \widehat{y} \in \widehat{F}_{M(O)}$ such that $p \cdot \widehat{y} = R(x, p)$, then $AE_{M(O)}(x, y, p) = 1$ and $AI_{M(O)}(x, y, p) = 0$, depending on the nature of the output-oriented measure: multiplicative or additive, respectively.

As for the extended version of the essential property, we state the following adaptations for the contexts where minimizing cost or maximizing revenue are the main objectives:

(CD2) (a) $AE_{M(I)}(x, y, w) = AE_{M(I)}(\widehat{x}, y, w)$, and (b) $AI_{M(I)}(x, y, w) = AI_{M(I)}(\widehat{x}, y, w)$
(RD2) (a) $AE_{M(O)}(x, y, p) = AE_{M(O)}(x, \widehat{y}, p)$, and (b) $AI_{M(O)}(x, y, p) = AI_{M(O)}(x, \widehat{y}, p)$

It is one of the objectives of this book to check the satisfaction of these two essential properties for a wide list of considered technical (in)efficiency measures. In each case, we will provide either proofs of the fulfillment of the properties or, at least, a numerical example where the existence of problems with the interpretability of the terms in the decomposition is illustrated. Additionally, alternative general solutions to overcome these weaknesses will be introduced, specifically in Chaps. 12 and 13.

2.5 Data Envelopment Analysis Methods

To render the economic efficiency analysis operational, it is necessary to approximate the production technology and economic behavior from observed data. This requires consideration of the empirical methods that allow the measurement of firms' efficiency using both production (primal) and economic (dual) approaches. More precisely, since both the true technology and economic behavior of the firms are unknown, they are often approximated by using either nonparametric mathematical programming or econometric techniques (regression analysis).[61] The two most popular approaches rely either on the activity analysis introduced by Koopmans (1951) and popularized by Charnes et al. (1978), resulting in what is known as Data Envelopment Analysis (DEA), and the parametric approach introduced by Aigner et al. (1977), based on the specification of a functional form and known as Stochastic Frontier Analysis (SFA).[62] The main advantages of DEA compared to SFA are that, from the perspective of the primal approach, it can accommodate multiple outputs, and it does not require a specific functional form, which may impose undesirable restrictions on the technology (e.g., substitutability, homotheticity). On the other hand, the main disadvantages of DEA versus SFA are that, in general, they characterize linear technologies and are deterministic; i.e., results are prone to noise and measurement errors.

From the perspective of DEA, its deterministic nature has been qualified thanks to the extension of statistical methods to mathematical programming. This is the case of chance constrained DEA and bootstrapping techniques based on data resampling (see Simar & Wilson, 2007; Daraio & Simar, 2007). These techniques allow testing different hypotheses regarding the significance of the efficiency scores and the characteristics of the technology (e.g., returns to scale, strong or weak disposability) and can be customarily found in several software packages thanks to the increase in processing capacity.[63] As for the need to adopt a specific functional form in SFA that may satisfy the desired regularity conditions locally, the introduction of flexible functional forms, such as the quadratic or translog formulations, makes possible the estimation of distance functions. This is quite relevant since these functional forms are amenable to the imposition of the necessary homogeneity conditions in inputs and outputs and therefore constitute an alternative to the dual approach based on cost or profit functions when characterizing multiple output technologies. Also, regarding likely misspecification biases, the availability of semi-parametric and Bayesian techniques is opening new opportunities—e.g., Kumbhakar et al. (2007). Finally, the divide between the two approaches is closing thanks to new proposals based on convex nonparametric least squares (CNLS) and the so-called Stochastic Nonparametric Envelopment of Data (StoNED), which aim at bridging the gap between both methods—see Johnson and Kuosmanen (2015).

Nevertheless, the final choice of a particular approach normally hinges upon the availability and reliability of methods. DEA methods, based on mathematical programming, pertain to the domain of management science and operations research

[61] It is rather curious that the first DEA radial models due to Charnes et al. (1978) were designed based on engineering reasoning.

[62] For a comprehensive survey of the Stochastic Frontier Analysis literature, see Kumbhakar and Lovell (2000) and Fried et al. (2008).

[63] A recent review of the available general purpose and dedicated software options for efficiency and productivity analysis can be found in Daraio et al. (2019).

and have witnessed numerous applications of economic efficiency analysis. Alternatively, SFA methods relying on regression analysis, which constitutes the main empirical method of applied economic analysis, are not as popular. The reason is that, arguably, the development of parametric techniques to measure and decompose economic efficiency presents relevant econometric challenges that are still being addressed in the literature; e.g., see Parmeter and Kumbhakar (2014) or Atkinson and Tsionas (2016). Unfortunately, as stated by Greene (2008) and despite the encouraging progress witnessed in recent years, no method is yet available in the mainstream literature that permits a convenient analysis of economic efficiency in the context of a fully integrated econometric frontier model.[64] On the contrary, nonparametric DEA techniques have been used over the years to calculate and decompose economic efficiency under different orientations, technological assumptions, and efficiency measures, as the literature mentioned in each one of the following chapters bears witness. Given the flexibility that these methods offer, once the early models based on radial projections were evolved, we can assert that, currently, the DEA methods are dominant in the empirical implementation of economic efficiency analysis.

We follow this approach here and render all the models operational though a DEA characterization of the production technology. Also, as mentioned in the introduction to this chapter, we have developed a software package in the Julia language that implements the main models presented in the book.

2.5.1 The Production Technology

Following Koopmans (1951), DEA approximates the production technology from observed historical, cross-sectional data, relying on the activity analysis approach and mathematical programming. Based on the principle of minimum extrapolation,

[64] An early example of these difficulties when decomposing economic efficiency into technical and allocative factors was the so-called Greene problem. Formal analysis of economic, technical, and allocative inefficiencies requires estimation of both a cost (revenue) and profit function along with its corresponding system of demand and supply share equations. This model complies with the neoclassical assumptions by which the latter system is consistent with Shephard's lemma in the case of the cost (revenue) functions and Hotelling's lemma for the profit function. Therefore, deviations from the optimality conditions in any input or output dimension translate into higher costs or lower profits. The difficulties emerge because the error terms capturing technical and allocative inefficiencies in the different equations of the model are not independently distributed, resulting in biased and inconsistent estimators. Moreover, it is necessary to disentangle technical and allocative efficiencies from the error terms in the cost or profit functions and their share equations because they interact among themselves. These errors present complex and nonlinear specifications, and under the usual distributional assumptions, the likelihood function necessary for estimation does not have a closed-form expression. See Kumbhakar et al. (2015) for recent single and multiple equations cross-sectional models of profit efficiency based on the primal approaches, overcoming some of these difficulties and using seemingly unrelated regression (SUR) and maximum-likelihood estimation methods.

DEA yields the smallest subset of the input-output space $\mathbb{R}_{+}^{M+N}$ as an inner approximation containing all observations and satisfying certain technological assumptions, which can be compared on a one-to-one basis with the technological axioms T1–T6 previously introduced in Sect. 2.1.[65]

DEA generates convex polyhedral technologies (i.e., intersections of finite numbers of half-spaces), consisting of piecewise linear combinations of the observed $j = 1,\ldots,J$ firms, thereby allowing for multiple inputs and outputs.[66] The DEA approximation of the technology T is given by the following:

$$T = \left\{ (x,y) : \sum_{j=1}^{J} \lambda_j x_{jm} \leq x_m, \; m = 1, \ldots, M; \; \sum_{j=1}^{J} \lambda_j y_{jn} \geq y_n, \; n = 1, \ldots, N; \right.$$
$$\left. \sum_{j=1}^{J} \lambda_j = 1 \;\; \lambda_j \geq 0 \;\; j = 1 \ldots J \right\}, \tag{2.65}$$

where λ is an intensity vector whose values determine the (convex) linear combinations of *facets*, which define the production frontier of the DEA polyhedral technology.[67] Hence, DEA makes use of individual intensity (activity) variables λ_j for each firm. These are nonnegative variables whose solution value may be interpreted as the extent to which a firm is involved in frontier production. Also, alternative restrictions on their joint value allow considering different returns to scale; i.e., in (2.65), variable returns to scale are imposed through the restriction $\sum_{j=1}^{J} \lambda_j = 1$. Finally, the inequalities associated with the input and output combinations characterize their strong disposability. Therefore, among the technology axioms incorporated into the reference DEA model (2.65), we highlight *convexity*, *strong disposability of inputs and outputs*, and *variable returns to scale*. Fig. 2.1b in Sect. 2.1 shows how DEA approximates the technology T according to (2.65) in the single input-single output case. Fig. 2.11(a–b) represents equivalent approximations of the input and output production possibility sets under strong or weak disposability. Regarding the input set, all firms produce the same output level y, while in the case of the output set, all firms use the same amount of inputs x.

Regarding *convexity*, it implies that any weighted average (convex linear combination) of feasible production plans by way of the intensity vector λ is feasible as well. There are alternative DEA models dropping this assumption, most notable the free disposal hull (FDH) (where $\lambda_j \in \{0,1\}$) or the free replicability hull (FRH)

---

[65] Färe and Grosskopf (1996; Chap. 2) prove that the DEA technology satisfies the usual axioms.

[66] See Färe et al. (1994) and Cooper et al. (2007) for an introduction to the activity analysis DEA within a production theory context.

[67] A facet can be full dimensional, in which case it corresponds to a face, or not. For instance, in a three-dimensional space, under VRS, the full-dimensional facet corresponds to a subset of a plane defined by three extreme efficient points, while a non-full-dimensional facet corresponds to a subset of a line defined by two extreme efficient points.

(where $\lambda_j \in \mathbb{N}_0$); see Deprins et al. (1984). However, these are inconsistent with duality theory (i.e., Minkowski's theorem), since convexity is key when recovering the technology from supporting economic functions and vice versa. Hence, in accordance with axiom T6 and proper duality requirements, in what follows, we consider DEA approximations of the technology that satisfy the convexity assumption.[68]

As for *strong (or free) disposability*, this implies that it is feasible to discard unnecessary inputs and increase outputs without incurring in technological opportunity costs. It is a rather flexible assumption that, nevertheless, has its drawbacks when combined with particular efficiency measures such as those based on radial (Farrell) or other preassigned orientations. Particularly, when measuring technical efficiency through DEA and considering an input- and output-oriented radial perspectives, (2.4) and (2.7), unitary values of the efficiency scores are capable of reflecting whether the firm belongs to the weakly efficient subsets of the technology, i.e., $\partial^W L(y) = \{x \in L(y) : x' < x, x' \neq x \Rightarrow x' \notin L(y)\}$ and $\partial^W P(x) = \{y \in P(x) : y' > y, y' \neq y \Rightarrow y' \notin P(x)\}$, but not if it belongs to the strongly efficient frontier associated with the Pareto-Koopmans notion of efficiency, as required by the indication property (E1) consistent with the Pareto-Koopmans notion of efficiency, i.e., $\partial^S L(y) = \{x \in L(y) : x' \leq x, x' \neq x \Rightarrow x' \notin L(y)\}$ and $\partial^S P(x) = \{y \in P(x) : y' \geq y, y' \neq y \Rightarrow y' \notin P(x)\}$.[69] In Fig. 2.11, from right to left, the weakly efficient subsets correspond to the DEA segments joining firms B, A, and C, as well as their vertical and horizontal extensions (i.e., $\overline{BAC}$ and discontinuous lines), while the strongly efficient subsets are given by $\overline{BAC}$.

Alternatively, one could also rely on the so-called isoquant subsets to determine technical efficiency: i.e., $\partial^{Isoq} L(y) = \{x : x \in L(y),\ \gamma x \notin L(y),\ \gamma < 1\}$ and $\partial^{Isoq} P(x) = \{y : y \in P(x),\ \gamma y \notin P(x),\ \gamma > 1\}$. These isoquants can be recovered from the technology (2.65) and graphically correspond to the boundaries of the DEA production possibility sets characterized by the weak disposability of inputs or outputs, i.e., $L^W(y)$ and $P^W(x)$. These sets can be recovered from (2.65) by changing the corresponding input and output inequalities to equalities. In particular, $\partial^{Isoq} L(y)$ corresponds to the connected line segments $\overline{BACE}$ and the horizontal extension from B, while $\partial^{Isoq} P(x)$ is given by $\overline{BACE}$ and the ray vector extensions from B and E passing through the origin. Notice that the weakly efficient subsets $\partial^W L(y)$ and $\partial^W P(x)$, generated under the DEA assumption of strong disposability of inputs and outputs, are not to be confused with the production possibility sets $L^W(y)$ and $P^W(x)$, defined under the assumption of weakly disposable inputs and outputs. Arguably,

[68] Duality theory assumes that prices are exogenous and therefore independent of output quantities. For the economic meaning of FDH, see Thrall (1999) and Cherchye et al. (2000). More generally, Kuosmanen (2003) discusses duality theory of non-convex technologies.

[69] This is the also the case for the multiplicative approach based on the Farrell graph measure (2.10), identifying whether the firm belongs to the weakly efficient set (2.3). For a dedicated discussion on radial measures based on Shephard's (1953, 1970) input and output distance functions; see Chap. 3. Chapter 4 is devoted to the case of the generalized distance function, extending the Farrell graph approach corresponding to the hyperbolic efficiency measure.

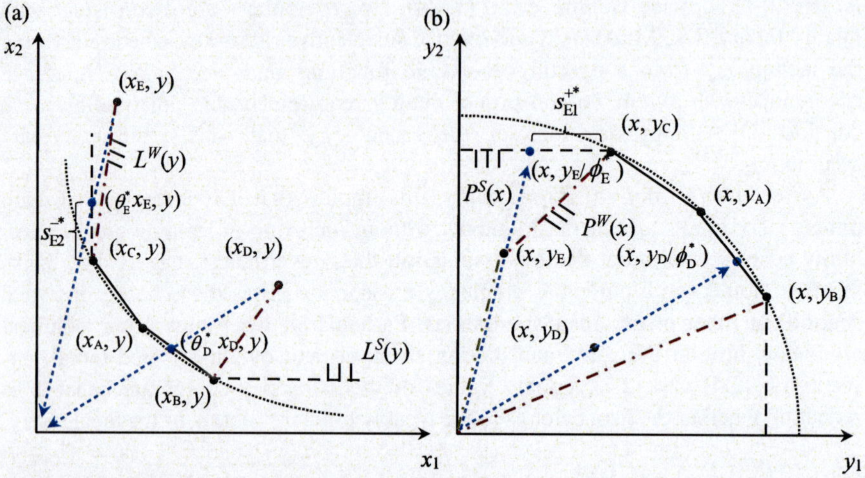

Fig. 2.11 **(a–b)** DEA approximation of the production technology and technical efficiency

the terms weak efficiency and weak disposability may create some confusion among readers, as they do not relate to each other. Indeed, the isoquant subsets $\partial^{Isoq}L(y)$ and $\partial^{Isoq}P(x)$ correspond to an even weaker notion of efficiency than those represented by the weakly efficient subsets $\partial^{W}L(y)$ and $\partial^{W}P(x)$, and these, in turn, as their names imply, represent a less stringent notion of efficiency than the Pareto-Koopmans definition characterized through the strongly efficient subsets $\partial^{S}L(y)$ and $\partial^{S}P(x)$. Indeed the alternative definitions yield the following relations: $\partial^{S}L(y) \subseteq \partial^{W}L(y) \subseteq \partial^{Isoq}L(y)$, and $\partial^{S}P(x) \subseteq \partial^{W}P(x) \subseteq \partial^{Isoq}P(x)$.

This discussion shows the importance of delimiting the relationship between the alternative definitions of efficiency and the DEA methods used to approximate the production technology, with its alternative efficiency sets, and associated efficiency scores. In the case of the standard DEA techniques, one can solve for the radial input and output measures of efficiency that measure efficiency against the weakly efficient production possibility sets associated with strong disposability of inputs and outputs and, then, in a subsequent step, recover non-radial slacks to identify benchmarks on the strongly efficient frontiers. This can be achieved either through a single-run formulation including non-Archimedean measures or relying on a two-stage process to avoid computational difficulties (Ali & Seiford, 1993; MirHassani & Alirezaee, 2005).

Hence, relying on the guiding notion of Pareto-Koopmans efficiency already discussed, we remark once again the importance of efficiency measures satisfying the *indication* property (E1), by which efficiency is measured against the strongly efficient subset of the production possibility set, $\partial^{S}(T)$, in expression (2.2). As discussed in Sect. 2.1 in regard to the properties of the technical (in)efficiency measures, much research effort has been devoted to propose DEA-based models that measure (in)efficiency against this subset or incorporate the slacks associated with the weak (non-Pareto-Koopmans) definition of the efficiency set, $\partial^{W}(T)$, in expression (2.3). The reason is that, as shown in what follows, DEA combines the characterization of the technology with the measurement of performance in relation to that specific technology. It thereby solves simultaneously the two basic problems of defining a performance standard, i.e., the reference technology with their associated efficiency sets and how the firm performs against such standard. Consequently, both objectives are interrelated, and ultimately, one can modify the DEA technology, so the associated measure satisfies relevant properties.

In this case, from a DEA perspective, there is a trade-off between the axiom of strong disposability of inputs and outputs and the existence of weakly efficient subsets, against which radial and other preassigned directions cannot account for possible slacks in their efficiency scores.[70] This is illustrated in Fig. 2.11a, b, where firms (x_D, y_D) and (x_E, y_E) are radially projected toward the strongly and weakly efficient subsets of the technology, respectively. From an input-oriented perspective in Fig. 2.11a, firm (x_E, y_E) could further reduce the second input individually from its technically efficient projection ($\theta_E^* x_E$, y_E) on the weakly efficient frontier, so as to reach the strongly efficient counterpart, i.e., $s_{E2}^{-*} > 0$. From an output perspective, Fig. 2.11b, a similar situation is represented, and firm (x_E, y_E) could increase the first output in the amount $s_{E1}^{+*} > 0$, from the efficient projection (x_E, y_E/ϕ_E^*).

Alternatively, as an example of the relationship between alternative technological definitions and the value of particular efficiency measures, let us assume a DEA technology under *weak* (*or costly*) disposability by changing in program (2.65) the inequalities associated with the feasible input and output linear combinations to equalities. Then, the production frontiers correspond to the boundaries of $L^W(y)$ and $P^W(x)$ in Fig. 2.11(a–b), and now, firm (x_E, y_E) is technically efficient, so that the Farrell input and output measures, $TE_{R(I)}(x, y)$ in (2.4) and $TE_{R(O)}(x, y)$ in (2.7), are equal to one. This is an undesirable result since it is inconsistent with the notion of Pareto-Koopmans efficiency that guides efficiency measurement. It shows that weak disposability would be enough for radial and other preassigned distance functions (constituting the formal mathematical definition of efficiency measures), to wrongly characterize efficient subsets—in this case $\partial^{Isoq}L(y)$ and $\partial^{Isoq}L(y)$, since (x_E, y_E) is dominated. However, rather than pairing technological axioms with specific efficiency measures, we contend that the DEA technology satisfying the basic postulates T1–T6, as presented in expression (2.65), constitutes the less restrictive

[70]This trade-off has prompted research on the general problem of transforming any weak DEA (in)efficiency measure into a strong DEA (in)efficiency, e.g., Fukuyama and Weber (2009) and Pastor and Aparicio (2010). Pastor et al. (2016) show that any DEA model that projects inefficiency observations onto the weakly efficient frontier, rather than onto the strongly efficient frontier, can be related to a reversed directional distance function, RDDF. They propose a two-stage process that combines a given efficiency measure (e.g., radial), which offers a first-stage projection for each observation on the weakly efficient frontier, with a second stage based on the additive model that projects each first-stage projection onto the strongly efficient frontier, ending up with a strongly efficient benchmark. Relating each inefficient observation with that final second-stage benchmark through the corresponding RDDF results in a comprehensive DDF (in)efficiency measure that combines radial and non-radial inefficiencies into a single scalar. In Chap. 11, we present the decomposition of economic efficiency based on the RDDF.

characterization of the technology compatible with duality theory and therefore represents a fixed point in economic efficiency analysis. In addition, since it is capable of identifying the strongly efficient subset of the technology in accordance with the notion of Pareto-Koopmans efficiency, one can rely on DEA programs that would ensure efficiency measurement against this subset. As anticipated in Sect. 2.1, this is the case of the standard additive models or the two-stage process previously mentioned, despite the strongly disposable characterization of the production technology—but at the expense of maximizing the sum of the slacks. This means that checking the desirable properties of the alternative technical efficiency measures should be generally performed against the background of a common characterization of the production technology, even if changing some of its characteristics (e.g., the disposability assumptions) may result in differences both within and between specific efficiency measures.

Finally, alternative *returns to scale* can be postulated in (2.65) through the vector of intensity variables λ. The variable returns to scale assumption can be dropped in favor of constant returns to scale by removing $\sum_{j=1}^{J}\lambda_j = 1$, and nonincreasing and nondecreasing returns to scale correspond to $\sum_{j=1}^{J}\lambda_j \leq 1$ and $\sum_{j=1}^{J}\lambda_j \geq 1$, respectively. As commented in Sect. 2.2, the measurement of economic efficiency from a cost and revenue perspective does not impose restrictions on returns to scale, while profitability maximization requires local constant returns to scale and profit maximization decreasing returns to scale. This means that one must consider the characterization of returns to scale along with the economic model that is chosen.

2.5.2 *Calculating Technical (In)Efficiency Measures*

Once the technology is approximated empirically through activity analysis, we present the mathematical programs that solve the multiplicative and additive efficiency measures considered in this chapter. In the next section, we illustrate how to calculate them resorting to a simple example and using a dedicated software package developed for the Julia language environment (Bezanson et al., 2017). Here, we restrict the presentation to the definitions of economic efficiency considering both input and output dimensions. Consequently, we focus on profitability and profit, $\Gamma(w,p)$ and $\Pi(w,p)$, as defined in (2.22) and (2.24), and show the different steps required to calculate and decompose these measures into their technical and allocative components. This is also consistent with the fact that the cost and revenue efficiency analyses based on either the input or output measures of technical (in)-efficiency can be considered as particular cases of the profitability and profit analyses. Moreover, the next chapter is devoted to the cost and revenue approaches, and therefore, we refer the reader to it.

Taking duality theory as the guiding analytical framework, it has been shown in Sect. 2.3 that the dual measure of profitability considered in this chapter corresponds to the hyperbolic technical efficiency measure, $TE_{H(G)}^{CRS}(x,y)$ in (2.11), while for the profit inefficiency, we have considered the (unweighted) additive measure $TI_{A(G)}(x, y)$ in (2.14). Hence, the first step is to calculate these technical (in)efficiencies accounting for the scale properties that the maximization of profitability and profit impose on the technology. In particular, for a specific firm under evaluation (x_o, y_o), calculating its hyperbolic and additive efficiencies requires solving the following programs:

Multiplicative hyperbolic efficiency (Envelopment formulation)

$$\begin{aligned} \left(TE_{H(G)}^{CRS}(x_o, y_o)\right)^{1/2} &= \min_{\varphi^{CRS},\lambda^{CRS}} \varphi^{CRS} \\ \text{s.t.} \quad & \sum_{j=1}^{J} \lambda_j^{CRS} x_{jm} \leq \varphi^{CRS} x_{om}, \quad m = 1, \ldots, M, \\ & \sum_{j=1}^{J} \lambda_j^{CRS} y_{jn} \geq y_{on}/\varphi^{CRS}, \quad n = 1, \ldots, N, \\ & \lambda^{CRS} \geq 0. \end{aligned} \tag{2.66}$$

Additive slack inefficiency (Envelopment formulation)

$$\begin{aligned} TI_{A(G)}(x_o, y_o) &= \max_{s^-,s^+,\lambda} \sum_{m=1}^{M} s_m^- + \sum_{n=1}^{N} s_n^+ \\ \text{s.t.} \quad & \sum_{j=1}^{J} \lambda_j x_{jn} + s_m^- = x_{om}, \quad m = 1, \ldots, M, \\ & \sum_{j=1}^{J} \lambda_j y_{jn} - s_n^+ = y_{on}, \quad n = 1, \ldots, N, \\ & \sum_{j=1}^{J} \lambda_j = 1, \\ & \lambda_j \geq 0, \;\; s^- \geq 0, \;\; s^+ \geq 0. \end{aligned} \tag{2.67}$$

Note that these programs incorporate the DEA technology set presented in (2.65). Besides the values of the technical (in)efficiency scores, relevant information can be obtained both from the above "envelopment" formulations of the technology and from their "multiplier" duals. As identified in (2.66) and (2.67), an advantage of DEA is that it yields explicit, real-life benchmarks. A firm can indeed study the technical and economic behavior of its peers—those firms with optimal $\lambda_j^{CRS*} > 0$

and $\lambda_j^* > 0$, so as to improve its own efficiency and productivity, and the value corresponds to the relevance of the benchmark firm in the linear combination.

For the hyperbolic efficiency measure, program (2.66) calculates the constant returns to scale efficiency score φ^{CRS}. However, to decompose productive efficiency into its variable returns and scale efficiency components according to (2.13), $TE_{H(G)}^{CRS}(x,y) = TE_{H(G)}(x,y) \times SE_{H(G)}(x,y)$, we need to calculate the former value. This can be achieved by including the associated restriction, $\sum_{j=1}^{J}\lambda_j = 1$, in (2.66). We note that the hyperbolic envelopment formulation (2.66) corresponds to a nonlinear program, which requires the use of advanced solvers searching for a global solution. Developments in the field of nonlinear programming have greatly improved the algorithms available to solve these models with confidence. Arguably, the fact that inefficiency is bounded simplifies the problem by restricting the range of feasible solutions, which combined with the inclusion of starting seeds results in an easier convergence to the global optimum.[71] In the accompanying dedicated software using the Julia language, we rely on the "JuMP" package developed by Dunning et al. (2017), combined with the "Ipopt" solver, initially introduced by Wächter and Biegler (2006).[72]

Resorting to the dual formulations of the above programs, several technological relationships between inputs and outputs can be discerned, in the form of shadow prices involving their vector of multipliers, (ν^{CRS}, μ^{CRS}) and (ν, μ), defining the supporting (reference) hyperplanes against which technical efficiency is measured. In this case, the firm is efficient if it belongs to one of the supporting hyperplanes (forming the faces of the envelopment surface) for which all firms (x_j, y_j) lie on or beneath it. The duals corresponding to the hyperbolic and additive distance functions are the following[73]:

Multiplicative hyperbolic efficiency (Dual formulation)

[71] Some alternatives to approximate the value of the hyperbolic efficiency measures have been recently proposed in the literature. Färe et al. (2016) devise a method that relates its value to that of the additive directional distance function. This results in an algorithm that, relying on the dual (multiplier) formulation of the DDF and the quadratic formula, allows for the estimation of the HDF through linear programming techniques. Recently, Halická and Trnovská (2019) reformulate the hyperbolic model into a semidefinite programming framework, opening the way to solving it with reliable and efficient interior point algorithms, as well as establishing the primal-dual correspondence.

[72] Ipopt, short for "Interior Point Optimizer," is a software library for large-scale nonlinear optimization of continuous systems. At the time of writing, the latest stable release is 3.14.4, from Sep. 20, 2021. See https://github.com/coin-or/Ipopt. A list of commercial and free solvers compatible with the Julia (JuMP) environment can be found in http://www.juliaopt.org/JuMP.jl/stable/installation/

[73] Relying on semidefinite programming Halická and Trnovská (2019: 415) introduce the dual counterpart of the hyperbolic envelopment formulation under CRS and VRS.

$$
\begin{aligned}
TE^{CRS}_{H(G)}(x_o, y_o)^{1/2} = & \max_{\nu^{CRS}, \mu^{CRS}} 1 - \sum_{m=1}^{M} \nu^{CRS}_m x_{om} + \sum_{n=1}^{N} \mu^{CRS}_n y_{on} \\
& - \left(\sqrt{1 - \sum_{m=1}^{M} \nu^{CRS}_m x_{om}} - \sqrt{\sum_{n=1}^{N} \mu^{CRS}_n y_{on}} \right)^2 \\
\text{s.t.} \quad & \sum_{m=1}^{M} \nu^{CRS}_m x_{jm} - \sum_{n=1}^{N} \mu^{CRS}_n y_{jn} \geq 0, \quad j = 1, \ldots, J, \\
& \sum_{m=1}^{M} \nu^{CRS}_m x_{jm} \leq 1, \\
& \sum_{n=1}^{N} \mu^{CRS}_n y_{on} \geq 0, \\
& \nu^{CRS} \geq 0, \quad \mu^{CRS} \geq 0.
\end{aligned} \tag{2.68}
$$

Additive slack inefficiency (Dual formulation)

$$
\begin{aligned}
TI_{A(G)}(x, y) = & \min_{\nu, \mu} \sum_{m=1}^{M} \nu_m x_{om} - \sum_{n=1}^{N} \mu_n y_{on} + \omega \\
\text{s.t.} \quad & \sum_{m=1}^{M} \nu_m x_{jm} - \sum_{n=1}^{N} \mu_n y_{jn} + \omega \geq 0, \; j = 1, \ldots, J, \\
& \nu \geq 1, \quad \mu \geq 1.
\end{aligned} \tag{2.69}
$$

The choice of the primal "envelopment" formulations (2.66)–(2.67) or their "multiplier" duals (2.68)–(2.69) depends on the analytical objective of researchers and the specific characteristics of the study. We note that the simplex method for solving the envelopment form also produces the optimal values of the dual variables (and vice versa), and all existing optimization software provide both sets of results readily, so there is no any computational burden on a particular choice of model.[74] For peer evaluation and determination of the nature of returns to scale, the envelopment formulations are normally used, while the duals are required if one wants to compare shadow prices with market prices. Indeed, recall that, from an applied perspective, it is the comparison between the optimal shadow prices recovered through DEA, either (ν^{CRS*}, $\mu^{CRS\,*}$) or (ν^{*}, μ^{*}), and the observed market prices,

[74]Nevertheless, the computational effort of solving the envelopment problems grows in proportion to powers of the number DMUs, J. As the number of firms is considerably larger than the number of inputs and outputs ($N + M$), it takes longer and requires more memory to solve the envelopment problems. We contend that except for simulation analyses and the use of recursive statistical methods such as bootstrapping, nowadays processing power allows calculation of either method without computational burdens.

(w, p), that determines the existence of allocative (in)efficiency, as shown in the previous section. Also, the dual formulations are amenable to the introduction of assurance regions through weight restrictions, rather than adhering to the "most favorable weights" that DEA yields by default (Thompson et al., 1986; Podinovski 2015). Finally, as optimal weights are not unique, one can define secondary goals in comparative analyses that, using cross-efficiency methods, help to rank efficient observations that are assigned the same (unitary) score in the standard (first stage) DEA (Sexton et al., 1986; Aparicio & Zofío, 2020a; Aparicio & Zofío, 2020b; Balk et al., 2021).

2.5.3 *Calculating and Decomposing Economic (In)Efficiency*

Once the technical (in)efficiency measures have been calculated, in order to calculate economic efficiency, it is first necessary to determine the optimal economic values. Considering the input and output dimensions jointly, these values correspond to the maximum profitability $\Gamma(w,p)$ and maximum profit $\Pi(w,p)$, while similar programs can be formulated for minimum cost and maximum revenue. The programs that allow calculating these magnitudes are the following:

Maximum profitability

$$\begin{aligned} \Gamma(w,p) = \max_{x,y,\lambda} \quad & p \cdot y / w \cdot x \\ \text{s.t.} \quad & \sum_{j=1}^{J} \lambda_j^{CRS} x_{jm} \leq x_m, \quad m = 1, \ldots, M, \\ & \sum_{j=1}^{J} \lambda_j^{CRS} y_{jn} \geq y_n, \quad n = 1, \ldots, N, \\ & \lambda^{CRS} \geq 0. \end{aligned} \tag{2.70}$$

Maximum profit

$$\Pi(w,p) = \max_{x,y,\lambda} \quad p \cdot y - w \cdot x$$

$$\begin{aligned} \text{s.t.} \quad & \sum_{j=1}^{J} \lambda_j x_{jm} \leq x_m, \quad m = 1, \ldots, M, \\ & \sum_{j=1}^{J} \lambda_j y_{jn} \geq y_n, \quad n = 1, \ldots, N, \\ & \sum_{j=1}^{J} \lambda_j = 1, \\ & \lambda \geq 0. \end{aligned} \tag{2.71}$$

After these values have been calculated, we can easily evaluate profitability efficiency, $\Gamma E(x, y, w, p)$, and profit inefficiency, $\Pi I(x, y, w, p)$, by applying expressions (2.23) and (2.25). Afterward, these overall values of economic efficiency can be decomposed by combining them with their technical (in)efficiency counterparts, closing the expressions (2.52) and (2.61), and thereby recovering the residuals representing allocative (in)efficiency, i.e., $AE_{H(G)}(x, y, w, p)$ in expressions (2.55) and $AI_{A(G)}(x, y, \widetilde{w}, \widetilde{p})$ in expression (2.64). In the profit inefficiency case, the decomposition requires using normalized prices $(\widetilde{w}, \widetilde{p}) = (w/\min\{w_1, \ldots, w_m, p_1, \ldots, p_n\}, p/\min\{w_1, \ldots, w_m, p_1, \ldots, p_n\})$. We also note that the returns to scale characterization of the additive technical inefficiency measure and profit inefficiency, in expressions (2.67) and (2.71), corresponds to variable returns to scale rather than nonincreasing returns: $\sum_{j=1}^{J} \lambda_j \leq 1$. We follow standard practice here since the above program normally finds a suitable solution where the returns to scale restriction is binding and therefore verified as an equality. However, we remark that the decomposition into technical and allocative components may differ depending on the nature of returns to scale.

2.6 Introducing a Free "Julia" Package to Calculate and Decompose Economic Efficiency Using DEA

The models presented in this chapter can be implemented empirically through a set of newly developed functions coded in the Julia language (Bezanson et al., 2017).[75] Although there are by now both free and commercial software packages that solve the basic economic efficiency models, we find it useful to have a set of routines that consistently implement all the models presented in this book under a common language. Julia is a high-level open-source language for numerical and scientific computing. The language is designed for high performance and easy parallelism.

[75] Julia is available for download with accompanying documentation from 'The Julia Programming Language' at https://julialang.org

The JuMP package for Julia contains an algebraic modeling language for linear and nonlinear optimization problems (Dunning et al., 2017). JuMP supports a wide number of open-source and commercial solvers such as GLPK, Ipopt, CPLEX, and Gurobi. This makes Julia and the JuMP package a suitable combination for solving Data Envelopment Analysis problems.

Basic economic efficiency methods are included in some standard software packages used by econometricians (e.g., LIMDEP, Econometric Software, Inc., 2009), available in dedicated noncommercial software accompanying academic handbooks: Cooper et al. (2007), Wilson (2008), and Bogetoft and Otto (2011) (these latter two implemented in R); commercial software including trial versions: Emrouznejad and Cabanda (2014); freeware programs: Sheel (2000) and Aparicio et al. (2018) (using Shiny); and even tutorials for spreadsheets: Sherman and Zhu (2006) and Zhu (2014). Álvarez et al. (2020) also offer the basic multiplicative and additive DEA economic efficiency models in the MATLAB environment. Daraio et al. (2019) provide a comprehensive survey of the available options. Their eligibility criteria include only software that are distributed as self-contained programs or packages and toolboxes for general computing environments.

While these software packages implement the main economic efficiency models, there is a lack of a full set of functions for Julia, including the recent theoretical contributions included in this book, many of which are missing in the existing software. In parallel to writing the book, we have programmed these routines so that in each chapter, we show how to solve and interpret representative models using simple examples for visualization and real datasets that help us to illustrate general implementations. The package represents a specific and self-contained set of functions related to the topic of economic efficiency measurement. The package is called "BenchmarkingEconomicEfficiency.jl," shortened to "BEE" throughout the text. It draws the basic DEA routines from a more general Data Envelopment Analysis package "DataEnvelopmentAnalysis.jl," which includes additional efficiency measures (e.g., environmental, cross-efficiency) and productivity change indices (e.g., quantity-only and price-based measures).[76] Both packages are referenced in the general registry of Julia by complying with the general publication requirements (documentation, build, and coverage; see https://github.com/JuliaRegistries/General).[77] Thus, besides including the classic and most popular models in the Julia environment, the package implements the new ones presented in the first and second parts of the book devoted to the multiplicative and additive approaches, for example, those models decomposing economic efficiency based on the generalized, directional, and weighted additive measures, which allow for a greater degree of flexibility in the orientations; i.e., users can supply their preferred directional and weight vectors.

---

[76] See https://github.com/javierbarbero/DataEnvelopmentAnalysis.jl.

[77] In particular, visit https://github.com/JuliaRegistries/General/tree/master/D/DataEnvelopmentAnalysis and https://github.com/JuliaRegistries/General/tree/master/B/BenchmarkingEconomicEfficiency

The Julia package for Benchmarking Economic Efficiency is available as free software, under the MIT License, and can be downloaded from http://www.benchmarkingeconomicefficiency.com, with accompanying Jupyter Notebooks that can be used interactively for instruction and self-learning purposes and all the supplementary material (data, examples, and source code) to replicate all the results reported in the book. The package is also hosted on the GitHub open-source repository from which it can be downloaded: https://github.com/joselzofio/BenchmarkingEconomicEfficiency.jl.

2.6.1 *Installing the Benchmarking Economic (In)Efficiency Julia Package*

Step 1: Users can download Julia from the official website (https://www.julialang.org) and follow the standard installation procedure for their operating system (Windows, macOS, or Linux). We recommend installing the 64-bit version.

Step 2: Once Julia is installed, launch the Julia executable, and you will see the Julia read-eval-print loop (REPL), where you can evaluate Julia statements—Fig. 2.12:

Step 3: To install the necessary packages for the economic efficiency measures presented in this book type:

```
julia> using Pkg
julia> Pkg.add("DataEnvelopmentAnalysis")
julia> Pkg.add("BechmarkingEconomicEfficiency")
```

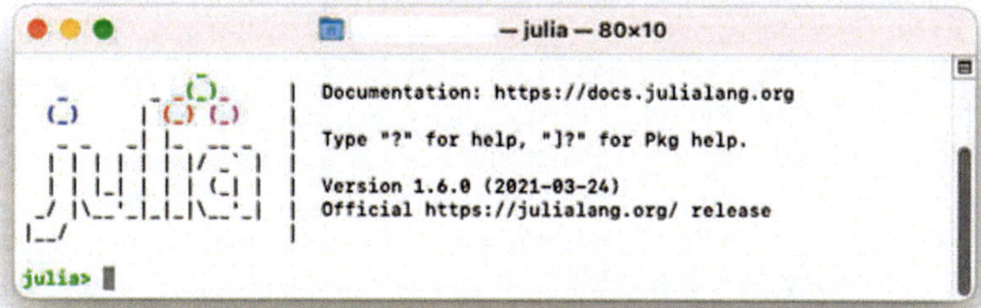

Fig. 2.12 The Julia REPL

This will install the "DataEnvelopmentAnalysis" package for basic DEA functions and this book's "BenchmarkingEconomicEfficiency" package, together with the JuMP algebraic modeling language package and the GLPK and Ipopt solvers.

Step 4: Although the reader can work directly in the Julia REPL, it is more convenient to use a Jupyter Notebook or an integrated development environment (IDE) to write the code. To install the Jupyter notebook within Julia type:

```
julia> using Pkg
julia> Pkg.add("IJulia")
```

And launch the notebook by typing the following:

```
julia> using IJulia
julia> notebook()
```

If the reader prefers to work with an integrated development environment, we recommend installing Visual Studio Code (https://code.visualstudio.com) with the Julia Language Support.[78]

2.6.2 *Examples and Empirical Data*

Throughout the book, we illustrate the different multiplicative and additive economic efficiency measures through three simple examples, each corresponding to the input, output, and graph dimensions, and a real dataset on financial institutions previously used in the literature.

Table 2.1 presents the different input-output vectors for eight firms and their corresponding market prices. The example dataset allows for a variety of production situations, including technical efficient and inefficient firms, belonging to the strong and weak efficiency subsets (i.e., there exist slacks at the optimal solution), as well as allocative (in)efficiencies. In these examples, prices are assumed to be common to all firms, while for the empirical dataset on financial institutions, observed prices are different for each firm. Note that, for simplicity and following the literature (e.g., Färe et al., 1985), in the input-oriented example, all firms are assumed to produce the same unit amount of output, while in the output orientation, they use the same unit amount of input. This effectively corresponds to the unitary input and output isoquants considered by Farrell (1957). It also presents a couple of computational

[78]To install the Julia Language Support for Visual Studio Code visit: https://marketplace.visualstudio.com/items?itemName=julialang.language-julia

Table 2.1 Example data illustrating the economic (in)efficiency models

	Model							
	Input orientation Cost model			Output orientation Revenue model			Graph Profitability and profit models	
Firm	x_1	x_2	y	x	y_1	y_2	x	y
A	2	2	1	1	7	7	2	1
B	1	4	1	1	4	8	4	5
C	4	1	1	1	8	4	8	8
D	4	3	1	1	3	5	12	9
E	5	5	1	1	3	3	6	3
F	6	1	1	1	8	2	14	7
G	2	5	1	1	6	4	14	9
H	1.6	8	1	1	1.5	5	9.412	2.353
Prices	$w_1 = 1$	$w_2 = 1$			$p_1 = 1$	$p_2 = 1$	$w = 1$	$p = 2$

and interpretative advantages when illustrating the models. In these cases, the solution to the envelopment or multiplier models is the same regardless of the returns to scale assumption, either constant or variable. For example, under constant returns to scale, it is verified that $\sum_{j=1}^{8} \lambda_j^* = 1$ at the optimal solution, thereby matching the solution to the variable returns to scale model that includes this restriction explicitly. Also, for the same reason, the efficiency scores under strong or weak disposability of outputs (for the input-oriented model) or inputs (for the output-oriented model) are the same; i.e., whether the input and output constraints are included as inequalities or equalities makes no difference. This is a convenient result that ensures that when evaluating technical and economic efficiency, the optimal output and input levels are kept constant to those of the firm under evaluation, as required by the definitions of minimum cost, $C(y, w)$, and maximum revenue, $R(x, p)$, respectively. As for the single input-single output graph example, we also include a diversity of situations with respect to alternative efficiency subsets and technical and allocative (in)efficiencies. The particularities associated with the solutions corresponding to each example will be commented when solving the different economic models.

Regarding the real-life empirical dataset that is used to compare the alternative economic efficiency models, it corresponds to a set of 31 Taiwanese banks observed in 2010, previously studied by Juo et al. (2015).[79] Table 2.2 presents descriptive statistics for these variables. A complete discussion of the statistical sources and

[79] We are grateful to these authors for sharing the data. The same dataset has been used to illustrate the decompositions of total factor productivity change using quantities-only and price-based indices by Balk and Zofío (2018), as well as symmetric decompositions of cost variation by Balk and Zofío (2020).

Table 2.2 Descriptive statistics. Taiwanese banks, 2010

	Inputs						Outputs			
	x_1	x_2	x_3	w_1	w_2	w_3	y_1	y_2	p_1	p_2
Average	795,536	3,826	13,393	0.0064	1.2586	0.3141	146,808	609,489	0.0349	0.0211
Median	428,995	3,146	8,721	0.0061	1.2168	0.3014	147,870	328,574	0.0147	0.0140
Max.	3,141,493	9,538	76,576	0.0186	2.2963	0.7625	904,580	2,091,100	0.3044	0.0687
Min.	25,014	202	505	0.0025	0.7140	0.0730	1,681	66,947	0.0059	0.0125
Stand. Dev.	768,008	2,729	14,185	0.0026	0.3963	0.1697	214,063	582,854	0.0668	0.0095

Source: Juo et al. (2014)

variable specification can be found there. Regarding the technology and interrelations between inputs and outputs, the variables reflect the so-called intermediation approach suggested by Sealey and Lindley (1977), whereby financial institutions, through labor and capital, collect deposits from savers to produce loans and other earning assets for borrowers. Inputs are financial funds (x_1), labor (x_2), and physical capital (x_3). The output vector includes financial investments (y_1) and loans (y_2). The unit prices of outputs correspond to average interest earned per New Taiwan Dollar (TWD) of investment (p_1) and average interest earned per TWD of loan (p_2). The unit prices of inputs include average interest paid per TWD of financial funds (w_1), the ratio of personnel expenses to the number of employees (w_2), and the nonlabor operational cost (operational expenses net of personnel expenses) per TWD of fixed assets (w_3). Firm-specific prices are calculated as unit values, that is, individual revenues and costs divided by quantities. The models presented in this book assume that there exist common prices for all firms operating within the industry, implying competitive markets for inputs and outputs. However, the dataset that we use offers different prices for each bank. Here, rather than calculating average input and output industry prices common to all firms in order to meet the assumption of singles prices, we have decided to implement the different models allowing for price variability. In this respect, although there is a recent strand of literature dealing with the decomposition of economic efficiency applying different prices, here, we follow the standard approach that finds the economic optima (e.g., maximum profitability or maximum profit) for the firm under evaluation using its observed prices. For other alternatives, see Camanho and Dyson (2008) and Portela and Thanassoulis (2014).

In the rest of the book, we use this dataset to illustrate the different economic efficiency models and their decomposition according to technical and allocative criteria. In this chapter, we demonstrate the use of the Benchmarking Economic Efficiency package for Julia with the example dataset presented in Table 2.1.

2.6.3 *Data Structures: Reading and Reporting Results*

We rely on the open (web-based) Jupyter Notebook interface to illustrate these economic models.[80] All economic efficiency models can be computed in three easy steps:

Step 1: To import the packages for the algebraic modeling language, the optimizers and the DEA functions, type the following code in the input window "`In[]:`" and execute it:

```
In[]:   using DataEnvelopmentAnalysis
        using BenchmarkingEconomicEfficiency
```

Step 2: Load the data as matrices. Elements in different columns are separated by a blank space, while a semicolon separates each row, containing the data of one of the firms. A vector with the names of the firms can be included. Otherwise, observations are numbered by default.

Here, we calculate and decompose the cost and profitability efficiency models presented in Sects 2.3.1 and 2.3.3, respectively, using the example data in Table 2.1. The quantity and price vectors of the cost model are as follows:

```
In[]:   X = [2 2; 1 4; 4 1; 4 3; 5 5; 6 1; 2 5; 1.6 8];
        Y = [1; 1; 1; 1; 1; 1; 1; 1];
        W = [1 1; 1 1; 1 1; 1 1; 1 1; 1 1; 1 1; 1 1];
        FIRMS = ["A", "B", "C", "D", "E", "F", "G", "H"]
```

while those corresponding to the profitability model are:

```
In[]:   X = [2; 4; 8; 12; 6; 14; 14; 9.412];
        Y = [1; 5; 8; 9; 3; 7; 9; 2.353];
        W = [1; 1; 1; 1; 1; 1; 1; 1];
        P = [2; 2; 2; 2; 2; 2; 2; 2];
        FIRMS = ["A", "B", "C", "D", "E", "F", "G", "H"]
```

Step 3: Use the corresponding package function to compute the specific economic efficiency measure. Results will be reported after the command is executed.

For the cost efficiency model:

```
In[]:   deacost(X, Y, W, names = FIRMS)
```

[80] All Jupyter Notebooks implementing the different economic models in this book can be downloaded from the reference site: http://www.benchmarkingeconomicefficiency.com

Table 2.3 Illustration of the cost efficiency model using BEE for Julia

In[]:

```
using DataEnvelopmentAnalysis
using BenchmarkingEconomicEfficiency

X = [2 2; 1 4; 4 1; 4 3; 5 5; 6 1; 2 5; 1.6 8];
Y = [1; 1; 1; 1; 1; 1; 1; 1];
W = [1 1; 1 1; 1 1; 1 1; 1 1; 1 1; 1 1; 1 1];
FIRMS = ["A", "B", "C", "D", "E", "F", "G", "H"]

deacost(X, Y, W, names = FIRMS)
```

Out[]:

```
Cost DEA Model
DMUs = 8; Inputs = 2; Outputs = 1
Orientation = Input; Returns to Scale = VRS
```

	Cost	Technical	Allocative
A	1.0	1.0	1.0
B	0.8	1.0	0.8
C	0.8	1.0	0.8
D	0.571	0.6	0.952
E	0.4	0.4	1.0
F	0.571	1.0	0.571
G	0.571	0.667	0.857
H	0.417	0.625	0.667

For the profitability efficiency model:

In[]:

```
deaprofitability(X, Y, W, P, names=FIRMS)
```

Combining all the information in a single run, simply type the following code, and execute it to compute your first cost efficiency measure and its decomposition according to (2.33). The corresponding results are shown in the "`Out[]:`" window of Table 2.3:

Figure 2.13 presents a screenshot of the notebook window with the calculation and decomposition of cost efficiency.

For the profitability model, the corresponding technical efficiency corresponds to the hyperbolic measure, which is calculated using the generalized distance function command since the hyperbolic measure is equivalent to the generalized distance function when its associated parameter is $\alpha = 0.5$, as presented in Chap. 4. Consequently, this package function solves the hyperbolic measure under constant and variable returns to scale, i.e., expressions (2.10) and (2.11). To compute profitability efficiency and its decomposition according to (2.54), type the following code in the "`In[ ]:`" window, and execute it. Results are shown in the "`Out[]:`" window of Table 2.4.

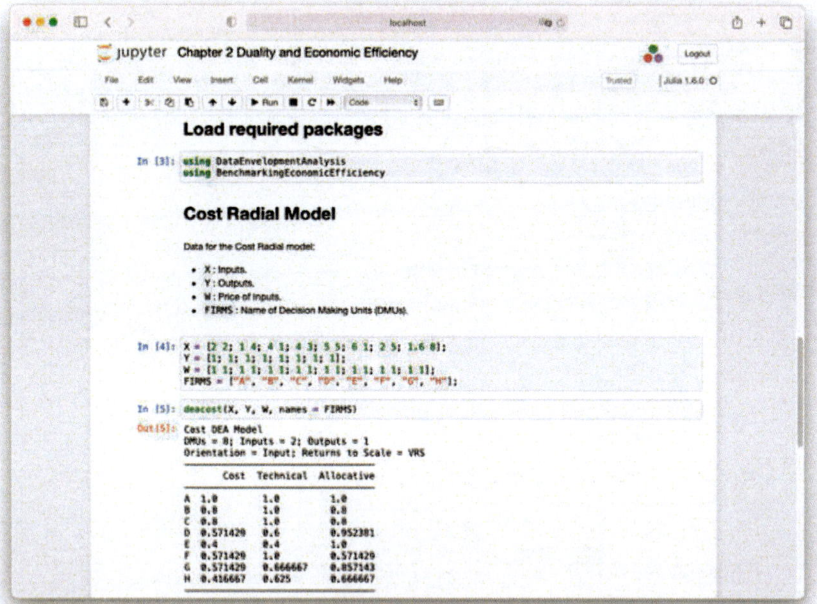

Fig. 2.13 Jupyter Notebook for the cost model using BEE for Julia

Table 2.4 Illustration of the profitability model using BEE for Julia

In[]:

```
using JuMP, GLPK, Ipopt
using DataEnvelopmentAnalysis
using BenchmarkingEconomicEfficiency

X = [2; 4; 8; 12; 6; 14; 14; 9.412];
Y = [1; 5; 8; 9; 3; 7; 9; 2.353];
W = [1; 1; 1; 1; 1; 1; 1; 1];
P = [2; 2; 2; 2; 2; 2; 2; 2];
FIRMS = ["A", "B", "C", "D", "E", "F", "G", "H"]

deaprofitability(X, Y, W, P, names=FIRMS)
```

Out[]:

```
Profitability DEA Model
DMUs = 8; Inputs = 1; Outputs = 1
alpha = 0.5; Returns to Scale = VRS
```

	Profitability	CRS	VRS	Scale	Allocative
A	0.4	0.4	1.0	0.4	1.0
B	1.0	1.0	1.0	1.0	1.0
C	0.8	0.8	1.0	0.8	1.0
D	0.6	0.6	1.0	0.6	1.0
E	0.4	0.4	0.410	0.975	1.0
F	0.4	0.4	0.634	0.630	1.0
G	0.514	0.514	1.0	0.514	1.0
H	0.2	0.2	0.205	0.975	1.0

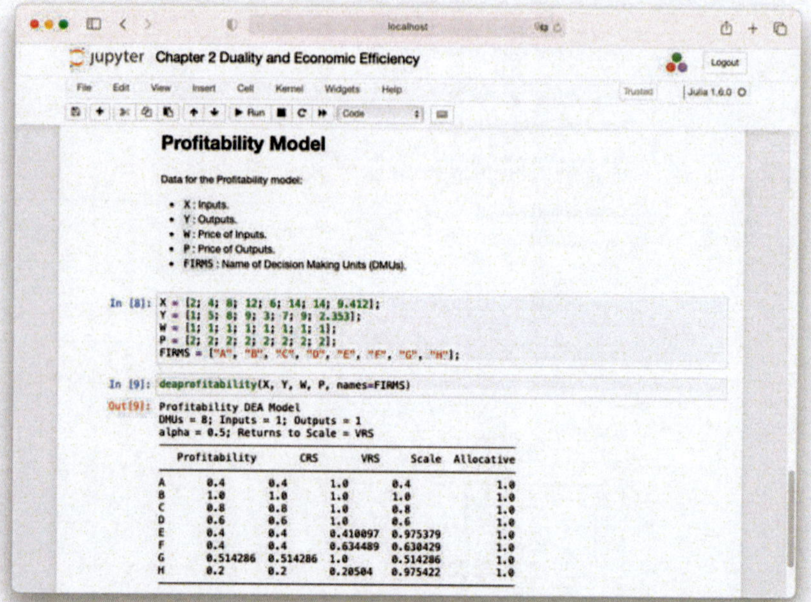

Fig. 2.14 Jupyter Notebook for the profitability model using BEE for Julia

Again, Fig. 2.14 presents a screenshot of the notebook window with the calculation and decomposition of profitability efficiency.

Finally, ancillary information on the economic or technical side (i.e., slacks, peers) can be obtained using additional functions.

Step 4: Use the corresponding package function to compute the corresponding technical efficiency model. This provides additional information, such as the slacks of the variables. The package solves for the slacks through a two-stage process, by calculating the efficiency scores and, subsequently, once the firms are projected to the efficient frontiers, also solves the standard additive model. This provides all the information necessary to determine whether the firms belong to the strongly efficient subset consistent with the notion of Pareto-Koopmans efficiency.

For the cost model, the corresponding technical efficiency is the input-oriented radial model under variable returns to scale (Table 2.5).

For the profitability model, the hyperbolic measure corresponds to the generalized distance function with the α parameter set to 0.5. Slacks can be computed for both the constant and variable returns to scale projections. The existence of slacks results in the overestimation of technical efficiency and the underestimation of allocative and scale efficiencies. Here, we show how to calculate the slacks under

Table 2.5 Illustration of the radial efficiency measure model using BEE for Julia

In:

```
dea(X, Y, orient = :Input, rts = :VRS, names = FIRMS)
```

Out:

```
Radial DEA Model
DMUs = 8; Inputs = 2; Outputs = 1
Orientation = Input; Returns to Scale = VRS
```

	efficiency	slackX1	slackX2	slackY1
A	1.0	0.0	0.0	0.0
B	1.0	0.0	0.0	0.0
C	1.0	0.0	0.0	0.0
D	0.6	0.0	0.0	0.0
E	0.4	0.0	0.0	0.0
F	1.0	2.0	0.0	0.0
G	0.667	0.0	0.0	0.0
H	0.625	0.0	1.0	0.0

Table 2.6 Illustration of the hyperbolic efficiency measure model using BEE for Julia

In[]:

```
deagdf(X, Y, alpha = 0.5, rts = :VRS, names = FIRMS)
```

Out[]:

```
Generalized DF DEA Model
DMUs = 8; Inputs = 1; Outputs = 1
alpha = 0.5; Returns to Scale = VRS
```

	efficiency	slackX1	slackY1
A	1.0	0.0	0.0
B	1.0	0.0	0.0
C	1.0	0.0	0.0
D	1.0	0.0	0.0
E	0.410	0.0	0.0
F	0.634	0.0	0.0
G	1.0	2.0	0.0
H	0.205	0.0	0.0

variable returns to scale (Table 2.6), while the constant returns to scale case can be computed by excluding "`rts = :VRS`" from the syntax.[81]

[81] Also, we note that in the second stage of the profitability model calculating the slacks, the optimizer may flag infeasibility results before stopping at the last iteration. The reason is that for this model, nonlinear optimizers are called upon to solve the generalized distance function (or hyperbolic efficiency measure). The precision of the solution will depend on the level of tolerance. Since, for the calculation of slacks, firms are projected to the efficient frontier, small deviations would result, effectively, in a super efficiency model, for which the standard additive formulation cannot find a solution, as some slacks would adopt infinitesimal negative values, thereby violating the nonnegativity constraints on the slacks.

Table 2.7 Information on the reference peers of the cost efficiency model using BEE for Julia

In[]:

```
peersmatrix(dea(X, Y, orient = :Input, rts = :VRS, names =
FIRMS))
```

Out[]:

```
1.0    .      .    .    .    .    .    .
 .    1.0     .    .    .    .    .    .
 .     .     1.0   .    .    .    .    .
 .     .     0.2   .    .    .    .    .
1.0    .      .    .    .    .    .    .
 .     .      .    .    .   1.0   .    .
0.333 0.667   .    .    .    .    .    .
 .    1.0     .    .    .    .    .    .
```

Step 5: To obtain information on the reference peers of the firms, use the "peersmatrix" function with the corresponding economic or technical model, e.g., the radial cost efficiency model in Table 2.7.

Electronic Supplementary Material
A series of Jupyter Notebooks containing the installation process and all the examples presented in this book by chapter, starting with those above, can be downloaded from http://www.benchmarkingeconomicefficiency.com.

2.7 Summary and Conclusions

The measurement and decomposition of economic efficiency are one of the main goals of any market-oriented organization. In today's competitive world, benchmarking is an indispensable tool to assess one's position within the business environment. Arguably, economic benchmarking is mandatory if the firm aims at surviving in the market, particularly when economic downturns are experienced with firms struggling to maintain a competitive edge. The benchmarking process forces the firm to reflect on the best standard of performance seen within the company, when the evaluation is done internally or within the industry, when it has an external scope.

This chapter presents the theory of economic benchmarking based on duality and how to render it operational through operations research methods, in particular relying on mathematical programming techniques known as Data Envelopment Analysis, DEA. The process of benchmarking illustrated through the different models surveyed in this introductory chapter delineates the process of economic efficiency analysis, which can be summarized in the following steps:

- Firstly, it implies determining the set of relevant units within the company or competitors within the industry, collecting data regarding both their quantities and prices. This allows quantifying the performance of each observation by characterizing the production technology and optimal economic benchmark. From a practical perspective, it identifies those units that perform best by optimizing a suitable economic objective, e.g., maximize profitability or profits. Subsequently, one may compare the performance of every firm with the optimal benchmark. An efficiency scalar measure, comparing observed and optimal values, can be easily calculated and interpreted.

- Secondly, thanks to duality theory, it is possible to quantify the areas in which the organization is falling behind, resulting in potential economic losses, and thereby isolate actionable insights aimed at each of them. In particular, from an operational or engineering perspective, we refer to those involving production, supply chain, and quality processes. In the analysis, this dimension is captured by the specific technical efficiency measure that is adopted (e.g., radial or additive). Alternatively, from a marketing and sales perspective, reference is made to those areas related with product pricing and revenue management, which correspond to the concept of allocative efficiency.
- Thirdly, once these results are obtained, the organization studies the gaps between their actual performance and that of the reference benchmark, in each of the above two dimensions. For example, benchmarking provides organizations with valuable data on the frontier technology and processes followed in the business environment. These are aimed at increasing productivity while reducing cost. Also, product diversification, along with improvements in the quality of the products and services, will result in greater revenue. Overall, organizations observe their current standard and try to surpass it by learning from their peer benchmarks. In this regard, the graph efficiency measure suits this kind of analysis by considering both the input and output dimension of the production process. On their part, the use of the additive models (as well as knowledge on individual slacks in the radial models) allows individual analyses for each input and output dimension, e.g., exploiting the substitutability across inputs and outputs to reduce cost and increase revenue. This can also be related to key performance indicators concerning different aspects of the company.

The methods included in this book enable firms to recognize areas of improvement, specifically those where technical or allocative efficiency is lower and therefore the gap with the frontrunners is largest. This also helps organizations to prioritize the strategies that they need to work on to improve their results. Finally, benchmarking can also help firms to identify those areas where they perform better than what is observed in the market, for example, by defining the reference economic and/or technological frontier. Ultimately, having all this information helps organizations to determine their weaknesses and strengths within their markets. Once firms have internalized the need for benchmarking, they should benefit from better performance, as they strive to achieve and set higher standards, to overcome complacency and to stay relevant in the market.

Part I
Benchmarking Economic Efficiency: The Multiplicative Approach

Chapter 3
Shephard's Input and Output Distance Functions: Cost and Revenue Efficiency Decompositions

3.1 Introduction

In this chapter, we present the classic approach to calculate and decompose cost and revenue efficiency based on Shephard's radial input and output distance functions. These decompositions follow closely the presentation done in Chap. 2 where both economic efficiency measures can be separated into technical and allocative components, i.e., expressions (2.33) and (2.44). However, rather than resorting to Farrell's input and output technical efficiency measures, the decomposition is formalized in terms of the distance function and duality theory. At the time of publishing his seminal paper in 1957, Farrell did not seem to be aware of the work by Shephard, printed initially in his 1953 book titled *Theory of Cost and Production Functions*. There, he formalized the duality between the cost function and the input distance function, constituting the theoretical base for the decomposition of economic efficiency.[1] Farrell cites Debreu's (1951) "coefficient of resource utilization" as a source of inspiration, although, had he been aware of it, he could have relied equally on Shephard's contribution, which is specific to production theory. Nevertheless, Shephard never introduced the concept of overall economic efficiency nor that of allocative efficiency, being one step short of proposing this decomposition explicitly.

Indeed, as we recall in what follows and for the cost efficiency case, the only difference between both approaches is that Farrell's radial input-oriented measure (2.4) is equivalent to the inverse of Shephard's input distance function. As for the revenue case, it is customary to associate Farrell's output measure to the inverse of ϕ^* in (2.7). This is because, within a Data Envelopment Analysis (DEA) approach, solving directly for ϕ^* results in a nonlinear program. While it is trivial to solve for

[1] Interestingly, a precursor of the input distance function was also introduced independently by Malmquist in the same year but in a consumer context (Malmquist, 1953).

J. T. Pastor et al., *Benchmarking Economic Efficiency*, International Series in Operations Research & Management Science 315,
https://doi.org/10.1007/978-3-030-84397-7_3

the inverse of (2.7), as shown in what follows, measuring economic and technical efficiency with efficiency scores greater than one does not allow to numerically compare the results pertaining to the input, output, and graph dimensions. In this book, we follow the convention that multiplicative efficiency measures should be equal or smaller than one regardless of the orientation: $TE(x, y) \leq 1$, i.e., corresponding to property (E1b) presented in Sect. 2.2 of Chap. 2. For this reason, even if for historical fidelity this chapter presents the definition and measurement of overall cost efficiency in terms of Shephard's input distance functions, whose values he defined as greater or equal to one, we shall take its inverse for measurement consistency.

Neither Farrell nor Shephard explicitly explored the possibility of decomposing cost or revenue efficiency resorting to Fenchel-Mahler inequalities, which constitute the standard approach to study overall economic efficiency based on duality. This approach allows the identification of the technical efficiency measures with distance functions depending only on quantities, which measure how far a firm is from the technological frontier. Subsequently, the economic allocative component is recovered as a residual.[2] Interestingly enough, the text that popularized the measurement of efficiency of production, written by Färe, Grosskopf, and Lovell in 1985, relied on Farrell efficiency measures and operations research methods to decompose economic efficiency (i.e., the equality approach), rather than Shephard's distance functions. Indeed, the term duality is missing from the subject index. This decision removed from consideration the role played by duality and, consequently, the fact that allocative inefficiency derives from the disparity between shadow and market prices and, ultimately, between the projected technically efficient input and output bundles and those corresponding to the optimal amounts of inputs demanded and outputs supplied—as discussed in Sect. 2.4 of the previous chapter. This was resolved a decade later by Färe and Primont (1995), who appraised the value of duality theory and associated shadow pricing when studying cost and revenue efficiency through Fenchel-Mahler inequalities. Balk (1998) also represents an authoritative contribution presenting the measurement of economic efficiency based on duality and index number theory.

In the following section, we rely on the definition of the production technology presented in Sect. 2.2 of the preceding chapter and its equivalent representation through Shephard's input and output distance functions. Precisely, this characteristic of the distance functions is referred to in the literature as the representation property, which is considered below. Next, in Sect. 3.2, we recall the economic goals of the firm that will be considered and how it is possible to define economic efficiency as the comparison between a best performing benchmark, either minimum cost or maximum revenue, and actual performance, i.e., observed cost or revenue. Afterward, for economically inefficient firms and based on the duality introduced by

[2]For a discussion on the relevance of considering either the equality approach or that based on duality recovering Fenchel-Mahler inequalities, we refer the reader to Sect. 2.4.5 of Chap. 2 and Chap. 13 related to the so-called essential property.

Shephard (1953, 1970), we show in Sect. 3.3 how to decompose its sources according to technological and allocative criteria. Throughout these sections, we present the alternative Data Envelopment Analysis programs that enable the empirical implementation of economic efficiency measurement. Finally, Sect. 3.4 illustrates the calculation of these measures using the accompanying benchmarking economic efficiency package for Julia. For this purpose, we solve the cost and revenue efficiency models for the input- and output-oriented examples presented in Sect. 2.6 of the previous chapter, as well as for the empirical dataset on financial institutions.

3.2 The Input and Output Correspondences: Shephard's Radial Distance Functions

We recall the characterization of the production technology in expression (2.1) of the preceding chapter: $T = \{(x, y) : x \in \mathbb{R}_+^M, y \in \mathbb{R}_+^N, \ x \text{ can produce } y\}$, where x is a vector of input quantities, y is a vector of output quantities, and M and N are the number of inputs and outputs. For convenience, it is possible to represent the technology through the input and output correspondences. The input correspondence characterizes the set of input vectors capable of producing a given level of output y, while the output correspondence characterizes the set of output vectors that can be produced with a given amount of inputs x. Formally, we define these multiple input-multiple output production possibility sets as follows:

$$L(y) = \{x : (x, y) \in T\}, \tag{3.1}$$

and

$$P(x) = \{y : (x, y) \in T\}. \tag{3.2}$$

These primal representations of the technology satisfy axioms comparable to those presented for the technology in Sect. 2.2 of the previous chapter. Färe et al. (1985: 23–26), Färe and Primont (1995: 27), and Balk (1998: 12) discuss these axioms. Here, we recall those concerning the so-called strong (or free) and weak (or costly) disposability of inputs and outputs because they are critical when defining alternative efficiency subsets of the technology, i.e., the reference benchmarks considered when evaluating technical efficiency. The definitions of these subsets, combined with the value of the input and output distance functions, serve to identify whether a firm is efficient with respect to these subsets, specifically when the value of these functions (interpreted as efficiency score) is equal to one. Also, as shown below, these disposability assumptions must be taken into consideration from the empirical perspective when approximating the production technology through DEA techniques. A precautionary note discussed below is that the radial nature of the input and output distance functions, defined under either disposability assumption, does not guarantee that unitary scores indicate that the firm under evaluation is efficient with respect to the only subset of the technology compatible with the Pareto-Koopmans definitions of efficiency, i.e., the so-called strongly efficient subset, defined in expression (2.2) of the preceding chapter. Notably, it is possible that the value of the radial distance functions is equal to one, yet individual input and output slacks exist, and the evaluated firm is dominated. Therefore, the same output can be produced using less inputs (input orientation), or more outputs can be produced with a given amount of inputs (output orientation).

Starting with the input set (3.1), strong and weak disposability of inputs is verified when:[3]

$$\text{L.S.D. If } x \in L^S(y) \text{ and } x' \geq x, \text{ then } x' \in L^S(y). \tag{3.3}$$

$$\text{L.W.D. If } x \in L^W(y), \psi x \in L^W(y) \text{ for } \psi \geq 1. \tag{3.4}$$

As for the output set (3.2), strong and weak disposability of outputs is defined in equivalent terms:

$$\text{P.S.D. If } y \in P^S(x) \text{ and } y' \leq y, \text{ then } y' \in P^S(x). \tag{3.5}$$

$$\text{P.W.D. If } y \in P^W(x), \ \psi y \in P^W(x) \text{ for } 0 \leq \psi \leq 1. \tag{3.6}$$

Note that we identify the disposability characteristics of the input and output sets using the corresponding superscript. We make use of this notation when discussing the suitability of Shephard's radial distance functions as measures of technical efficiency. A graphical representation of the efficiency sets generated under these alternative disposability assumptions, in combination with DEA methods, is provided in Fig. 3.2.

Shephard (1953, 1970) introduced equivalent representations of the input and output sets (3.1) and (3.2) by way of the input and output distance functions. The input distance function is given by

$$D_I(x, y) = \max\{\lambda : (x/\lambda, y) \in T\} = \max\{\lambda : (x/\lambda) \in L(y)\}, \tag{3.7}$$

while its output counterpart is as follows:

[3] General notation: For a vector v of dimension D, $v \in \mathbb{R}^D_{++}$ means that each element of v is positive; $v \in \mathbb{R}^D_+$ means that each element of v is nonnegative; $v > 0_D$ means $v \geq 0_D$ but $v \neq 0_D$; and, finally, 0_D denotes a zero vector of dimension D. Given two vectors v and u, $v \leq u \Leftrightarrow v_d \leq u_d$, $d \in \{1, \ldots, D\}$, $v < u \Leftrightarrow v_d < u_d$, $d \in \{1, \ldots, D\}$, and $v <^* u \Leftrightarrow v_d < u_d$ or $v_d = u_d = 0$ and $d \in \{1, \ldots, D\}$. The inner—or scalar—product of two D dimensional vectors $v \equiv [v_1, \ldots, v_D]$ and $u \equiv [u_1, \ldots, u_D]$ is denoted as $v \cdot u \equiv \sum_{d=1}^{D} v_d u_d$.

$$D_O(x, y) = \min\{\phi : (x, y/\phi) \in T\} = \min\{\phi : (y/\phi) \in P(x)\}. \tag{3.8}$$

The above definitions are valid under the assumptions of either strong or weak disposability. When needed, in what follows, we will denote them adding the corresponding superscripts to the distance functions. The input-oriented distance function (3.7) corresponds to the inverse of the radial Farrell efficiency measure (2.4) in Chap. 2, i.e., $D_I(x, y) \equiv 1/TE_{R(I)}(x, y) = 1/\theta$. It is homogeneous of degree one in inputs and nonincreasing in outputs. As for the output-oriented distance function (3.8), it is equivalent to the Farrell efficiency measure presented in (2.7), and therefore, we deliberately denote it by the same scalar, $D_O(x, y) \equiv TE_{R(O)}(x, y) = \phi$. The output distance function is homogenous of degree one in outputs and nonincreasing in inputs. A complete discussion on the properties of both functions can be consulted in Russell (1988).

If the technology satisfies the customary axioms, including either strong or weak disposability, the input distance function has the range $D_I(x, y) \geq 1$, while the value of the output distance function is $D_O(x, y) \leq 1$. From the perspective of technical efficiency measurement, the relevance of these values is summarized in the capability of the input and output distance functions to characterize the production technology and, alongside with it, whether a firm is technically efficient or not. The so-called representation property is expressed as follows:

$$x \in L(y) \text{ if and only if } D_I(x, y) \geq 1, \tag{3.9}$$

and

$$y \in P(x) \text{ if and only if } D_O(x, y) \leq 1. \tag{3.10}$$

Consequently, relying on the representation property, a firm is deemed technically inefficient from an input perspective if $D_I(x, y) > 1$ or, inversely, $1/D_I(x, y) \equiv TE_{R(I)}(x, y) = \theta < 1$, thereby complying with the convention that multiplicative technical efficiency scores should be smaller than one (see the indication property (E1b) in Sect. 2.2.4 of the previous chapter). Alternatively, from an output perspective, a firm is technically inefficient if $D_O(x, y) \equiv TE_{R(O)}(x, y) = \phi < 1$. Interestingly, based on definitions (3.7) and (3.8), the input and output distance functions—and therefore their associated technical efficiency measures—are related with each other in the following way:

$$D_I(x, y) = \max\{\lambda : D_O(x/\lambda, y) \leq 1\}, \tag{3.11}$$

and

$$D_O(x, y) = \min\{\phi : D_I(x, y/\phi) \geq 1\}. \tag{3.12}$$

Under standard regularity conditions on the production technology, i.e., not intersecting efficiency sets (isoquants), and regardless of the nature of returns to the scale, Färe (1988; Lemma 2.3.10) proves that $D_O(x, y) = 1$ if and only if $D_I(x, y) = 1$. Moreover, if constant returns to scale hold, $T^{CRS} = \{(\psi x, \psi y) : (x, y) \in T,\ \ \psi > 0\}$, the input distance function is the reciprocal (inverse) of the output distance function: $D_I^{CRS}(x, y) = 1/D_O^{CRS}(x, y)$, e.g., Färe and Primont (1995: 24). Consequently, the input-oriented and output-oriented technical efficiency scores are equal: $TE_{R(I)}^{CRS}(x, y) = TE_{R(O)}^{CRS}(x, y)$. Boussemart et al. (2009) generalized this result to alternative degrees of homogeneity, corresponding to either increasing or decreasing returns to scale. In particular, these authors show that for a technology exhibiting returns to scale of degree, α, $D_I(x, y) = 1/D_O(x, y)^{1/\alpha}$, where $\alpha > 1$ and $0 < \alpha < 1$ characterize technologies satisfying strictly increasing and strictly decreasing returns to scale, respectively. Nevertheless, in this chapter, we do not consider productive efficiency with respect to constant returns to scale benchmark, which allows studying both technical and scale inefficiencies—see equation (2.13) and related discussion in the previous chapter. The reason is that the (minimum) cost and (maximum) revenue functions do not require technological benchmarks characterized by constant returns to scale, as opposed to maximum profitability—as discuss in the next Chap. 4. This implies that throughout this chapter, the underlying reference technology is as general as possible with respect to the nature of returns to scale, thereby allowing for variable returns to scale.

Recalling the illustrations of the Farrell efficiency measures in Figs. 2.2b and 2.3b of the previous chapter, the input and output distance functions are represented in Fig. 3.1 for the three-dimensional case including two inputs or two outputs. Taking as reference the firm (x_D, y_D), we present the input correspondence $L(y_D)$ in the left-hand side panel (a). In the right-hand side panel (b), we have the output

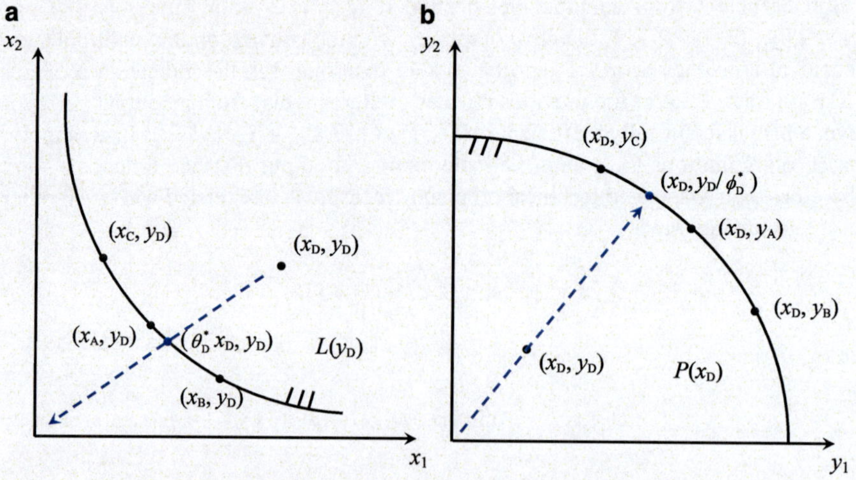

Fig. 3.1 (**a**, **b**) Input and output distance functions and technical efficiency

correspondence $P(x_D)$. In both cases, firm (x_D, y_D) is inefficient, laying in the interior of the input and output production possibility sets. Both the inverse of the input distance function and the output distance function project firm D to the production frontiers—or the boundaries of each production possibility set, i.e., $(\widehat{x}_D, y_D) = (\theta_D^* x_D, y_D)$ and $(x, \widehat{y}_D) = (x_D, y_D/\phi_D^*)$. Figure 3.1 also illustrates the case of the technically efficient firms A, B, and C, with $1/D_I(x, y) \equiv TE_{R(I)}(x, y) = \theta = 1$ or, alternatively, $D_O(x, y) \equiv TE_{R(O)}(x, y) = \phi = 1$.

3.2.1 Pareto-Koopmans Efficiency and Input and Output Disposability

Here, a comprehensive discussion on the capabilities of Shephard's distance functions to characterize technical efficiency in terms of the notion of Pareto-Koopmans efficiency and under the assumption of strong or weak disposability is needed. As discussed in Sect. 2.2 of the previous chapter, the family of radial measures to which the input and output distance functions belong does not comply with the *indication* property (E1a). This means that they fail to signal if the firm belongs to the strongly efficient frontiers:[4]

$$\partial^S L(y) = \{x \in L(y) : \ x' \leq x, x' \neq x \Rightarrow x' \notin L(y)\}, \tag{3.13}$$

and

$$\partial^S P(x) = \{y \in P(x) : y' \geq y, y' \neq y \Rightarrow y' \notin P(x)\}. \tag{3.14}$$

This shortcoming emerges empirically when the technology is approximated through standard DEA techniques, generating piecewise linear approximations of the production frontier (alternative efficiency subsets) that, combined with unitary values of these radial measures, do not preclude the existence of individual slacks—under strong disposability: (3.3) and (3.5)—or even signal as efficient firms that may be dominated by other observations in all input or output dimensions, under weak disposability: (3.4) and (3.6). This latter case is quite undesirable from the standpoint of efficiency measurement, and therefore, weak disposability is generally discarded as a suitable technological assumption when characterizing production technologies empirically.[5] Notice that it also distorts the subsequent decomposition of economic

[4] In these definitions, at least one element of the comparison vectors, x' and y', could be equal or, respectively, smaller or greater than those in the strongly efficient reference vectors x and y.

[5] This is one of the regularity conditions imposed on the production function or, more generally, the transformation function, so they are *well behaved*, i.e., they are characterized by a decreasing (increasing) marginal of substitution (transformation) between inputs (outputs) resulting from strictly convex (concave) isoquants.

efficiency into technical and allocative factors as commented below. Therefore, although Shephard's distance functions may deem firms as efficient when resorting to DEA methods, to determine if it complies with the definition of Pareto efficiency, it is necessary to check if non-radial improvements in the form of individual input reductions or output increases are still feasible.

In particular, the standard representations of the production technology relying on DEA methods under the assumption of strong disposability of inputs and outputs, (3.3) and (3.5), result in the identification of firms belonging (or being projected) to the weakly efficient sets, i.e.,[6]

$$\partial^W L^S(y) = \{x \in L^S(y) : \ x' < x \Rightarrow x' \notin L^S(y)\} = \{x : D_I^S(x, y) = 1\}, \qquad (3.15)$$

and

$$\partial^W P^S(x) = \{y \in P^S(x) : y' > y \Rightarrow y' \notin P^S(x)\} = \{y : D_O^S(x, y) = 1\}, \qquad (3.16)$$

where, following the notation introduced above, the superscript S indicates the strong disposability assumption. The above shows that the input and output distance functions can successfully identify if radial input reductions or output increases are feasible. If not, firms belong to (and empirically define) the weakly efficient boundary of the production technology, i.e., $\partial^W L^S(y) = \{x : D_I^S(x, y) = 1\}$ and $\partial^W P^S(x) = \{y : D_O^S(x, y) = 1\}$, as shown in the last equalities of (3.15) and (3.16).

Additionally, the assumption of weak disposability in conjunction with DEA methods results in input and output distance functions identifying firms as technically efficient with respect to an even weaker notion of efficiency, i.e., those corresponding to the input and output isoquants of the technology. Hence, whether the firms belong (or, again, are projected) to the following boundary sets,

$$\partial^{Isoq} L^W(y) = \{x : x \in L^W(y), \ \gamma x \notin L^W(y), \ \gamma < 1\} = \{x : D_I^W(x, y) = 1\}, \quad (3.17)$$

and

$$\partial^{Isoq} P^W(x) = \{y : y \in P^W(x), \ \gamma y \notin P^W(x), \ \gamma > 1\} = \{y : D_O^W(x, y) = 1\}. \quad (3.18)$$

However, as shown in what follows, these definitions of efficiency, as the previous ones corresponding to $\partial^W L^S(y)$ and $\partial^W P^S(x)$, are incompatible with the Pareto-Koopmans notion of efficiency corresponding to the strongly efficient subsets, as required by the *indication* property (E1a) presented in Sect. 2.2 of the previous chapter. Consequently, to prevent that firms are categorized as efficient using DEA by belonging to either $\partial^{Isoq} L^W(y)$ or $\partial^{Isoq} P^W(x)$, weak disposability is

[6] In these definitions, all the elements of the comparison vectors, x' and y', are, respectively, smaller or greater than those in the weakly efficient reference vectors x and y.

disregarded when characterizing the production technology.[7] In any case, despite the specific disposability assumption and given that the alternative reference sets are nested, $\partial^S L(y) \subseteq \partial^W L(y) \subseteq \partial^{Isoq} L(y)$ and $\partial^S P(x) \subseteq \partial^W P(x) \subseteq \partial^{Isoq} P(x)$, it is immediate that while $D_I(x, y) = 1$ and $D_O(x, y) = 1$ cannot identify whether a firm belongs to their corresponding strongly efficient sets, $\partial^S L(y)$ and $\partial^S P(x)$, if a firm is technically efficient with respect to the weakly efficient sets, $\partial^W L(y)$ and $\partial^W P(x)$, it is also technically efficient with respect to the isoquant sets $\partial^{Isoq} L(y)$ and $\partial^{Isoq} P(x)$.

In Fig. 3.1, these relevant sets are depicted so they coincide, i.e., $\partial^S L(y) = \partial^W L(y) = \partial^{Isoq} L(y)$ and $\partial^S P(x) = \partial^W P(x) = \partial^{Isoq} P(x)$. However, as previously remarked, the use of standard DEA techniques gives rise to technologies where these efficiency sets differ, due to its piecewise linear nature, and empirically depend on the assumption of either strong or weak disposability: e.g., see Färe et al. (1985: 28–30).[8] In what follows, we discuss these alternative definitions of the efficiency sets from the empirical DEA perspective.

3.2.2 *Calculating Radial Technical Efficiency Using Data Envelopment Analysis*

We now render the technical efficiency analysis operational by approximating the input and output correspondences through Data Envelopment Analysis (DEA) methods. In particular, given a set of $j=1,\ldots,J$ firms, it is possible to characterize the input and output production possibility sets in the following way; e.g., Färe et al. (1985: 74–77):

$$L^S(y) = \left\{ x : \sum_{j=1}^{J} \lambda_j x_{jm} \leq x_m,\ m = 1, \ldots, M;\ \sum_{j=1}^{J} \lambda_j y_{jn} \geq y_n,\ n = 1, \ldots, N;\ \sum_{j=1}^{J} \lambda_j = 1,\ \lambda_j \geq 0,\ j = 1, \ldots, J \right\}, \tag{3.19}$$

and

$$P^S(x) = \left\{ y : \sum_{j=1}^{J} \lambda_j x_{jm} \leq x_m, m = 1, \ldots, M : \sum_{j=1}^{J} \lambda_j y_{jn} \geq y_n, n = 1, \ldots N; \sum_{j=1}^{J} \lambda_j = 1, \lambda_j \geq 0, j = 1, \ldots, J \right\}. \tag{3.20}$$

---

[7] An exception can be found in the field of environmental economics, where the technological trade-off between desirable and undesirable outputs, including the null-jointness axiom, is usually modelled through their weak disposability; see Färe et al. (1989) and Zofío and Prieto (2001).

[8] Again, this issue is not of concern in the parametric approach based on *well-behaved* production functions satisfying the desirable regularity conditions. The usual functional forms present equal strong, weak, and isoquant efficiency subsets. An example is the Cobb-Douglas function, whose input set corresponds to $L(y) = \left\{ \prod_{m=1}^{M} x_m^{\alpha_m} \geq y,\ \alpha_m > 0 \right\}$.

Recalling the presentation of DEA methods in Sect. 2.5 of the previous chapter, these sets are characterized by convexity, strong disposability of inputs and outputs, and variable returns to scale. Empirically, the assumption of strong disposability, associated with the input and output inequalities, anticipates the need for a two-stage process to measure technical efficiency. In the first stage, the radial measures associated with Shephard's radial distance function are calculated, followed by a subsequent additive model that checks if further individual (non-radial) input reduction or output increases are still feasible in the form of slacks. As for variable returns to scale, $\sum_{j=1}^{J} \lambda_j = 1$, this basic assumption is consistent with the postulates of cost minimization and revenue maximization that do not impose restrictions on the nature of returns to scale at the economic optima, e.g., as constant returns to scale are required for profitability maximization—see also Sect. 2.3 of the previous chapter.

Figure 3.2 illustrates the DEA approximations of the input and output production possibility sets according to (3.19) and (3.20). Note that, from the perspective of the input correspondence, the output level y is assumed equal for all firms. This is also the case for the input vector x associated with the output correspondence, which is common to all firms.

As previously discussed, strong disposability implies that it is feasible to discard unnecessary inputs and that it is possible to produce additional outputs, without incurring in technological opportunity costs. Empirically, this implies that technical efficiency is measured against the weakly efficient sets, (3.15) and (3.16), rather than the strongly efficient sets (3.13) and (3.14). In Fig. 3.2, from the right to left, the weakly efficient subsets correspond to the hyperplanes joining firms B, A, and C, as well as their vertical and horizontal extensions (i.e., $\overline{\text{BAC}}$ and discontinuous lines), while the strongly efficient subsets are given by $\overline{\text{BAC}}$. The different characterization of the efficiency sets shows that, from the perspective of DEA methods, there is a trade-off between the axiom of strong disposability and the existence of weakly

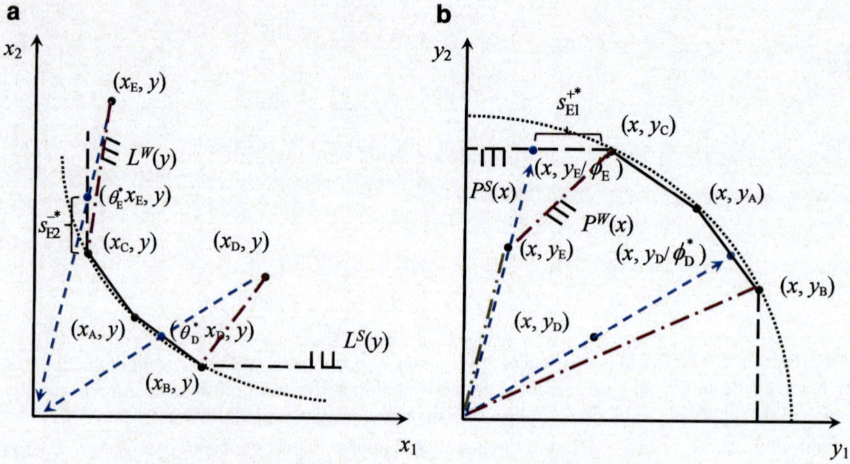

Fig. 3.2 (**a, b**) DEA approximation of the input and output production sets

efficient subsets, against which radial and other preassigned directions cannot account for possible slacks in their efficiency scores. Again, this is illustrated in Fig. 3.2, where firms (x_D, y) and (x_E, y) are radially projected toward the strongly and weakly efficient subsets of the technology, respectively. From the input-oriented perspective in Fig. 3.2a, firm (x_E, y) could further reduce the second input individually from its technically efficient projection (θ_E^* x_E, y) on the weakly efficient frontier, so as to reach the strongly efficient counterpart, i.e., $s_{2E}^{-*} > 0$. From the output perspective, in Fig. 3.2b, a similar situation is represented, and firm (x, y_E) could increase the first output in the amount $s_{1E}^{+*} > 0$, from the efficient projection (x, $y_E/\,\phi_E^*$). Therefore, for the case of the radial input and output distance functions, although technical performance should be measured against the strongly efficient sets $\partial^S L(y)$ and $\partial^S P(x)$ to comply with the notion of Pareto-Koopmans efficiency (i.e., the *indication* property, E1a), this cannot be achieved empirically relying on radial measures of technical efficiency within standard DEA techniques. This is because DEA simultaneously solves the characterization of the technology and the calculation of the efficiency measure. In the case of radial projections, technical efficiency is measured against the weakly efficient production possibility sets associated with strong disposability of inputs and outputs.

As previously shown, this problem is further aggravated if we were to consider that inputs and outputs as weakly disposable, resulting in reference frontiers that match the isoquant subsets of the input and output correspondences: i.e., (3.17) and (3.18). These particular isoquants correspond to the boundaries of the DEA production possibility sets as characterized in (3.19) and (3.20) but changing the input and output constraints from inequalities to equalities, i.e.,

$$L^W(y) = \left\{ \begin{array}{l} x : \sum_{j=1}^{J} \lambda_j \psi x_{jm} = x_m, \quad \psi \in [1, \infty), m = 1, \ldots, M; \quad \sum_{j=1}^{J} \lambda_j y_{jn} \geq y_n, \quad n = 1, \ldots, N; \\ \sum_{j=1}^{J} \lambda_j = 1, \ \lambda_j \geq 0, \ j = 1, \ldots, J \end{array} \right\} \tag{3.21}$$

and

$$P^W(x) = \left\{ \begin{array}{l} y : \sum_{j=1}^{J} \lambda_j x_{jm} \leq x_m, \quad m = 1, \ldots, M; \quad \sum_{j=1}^{J} \lambda_j \psi y_{jn} = y_n, \quad \psi \in [0, 1], n = 1, \ldots, N; \\ \sum_{j=1}^{J} \lambda_j = 1, \ \lambda_j \geq 0, \ j = 1, \ldots, J \end{array} \right\} \tag{3.22}$$

In Fig. 3.2, the isoquant sets $L^W(y)$ and $P^W(x)$ are depicted through the dashed dotted lines—as opposed to the input sets defined under the standard assumption of strong disposability. The associated efficiency subset $\partial^{Isoq} L^W(y)$ corresponds to the connected line segments $\overline{\text{BACE}}$ and the horizontal extension from B, while that for

$\partial^{Isoq}P^W(x)$ is given by $\overline{\text{BACE}}$ and the ray vector extensions from B and E passing through the origin.[9] Regarding efficiency measurement, it can be seen that adopting weak disposability generates reference subsets that are wrongly characterized as efficient by the input and output distance functions because these peers are dominated in the sense of Pareto-Koopmans efficiency; e.g., firm E in Fig. 3.2 is assigned a score of one.

For all these reasons, the functions that allow calculating and decomposing cost and revenue efficiency using the package "Benchmarking Economic Efficiency" are implemented under the default assumptions of convexity, strongly disposable inputs and outputs, and variable returns to scale. As for the measurement of the underlying distance functions, to check if individual input reductions or output increases are still feasible, a second stage is applied to recover non-radial slacks, thereby identifying the final benchmarks on the strongly efficient frontiers. Although this could be achieved through a single run formulation including non-Archimedean measures, the two-stage approach is preferred to avoid computational difficulties (Ali & Seiford, 1993; MirHassani & Alirezaee, 2005). Nevertheless, following the literature on duality based on the input and output distance functions introduced by Shephard, who did not account for specific empirical methods, in this chapter the standard decomposition of economic efficiency using DEA is performed. Consequently, the measurement of technical efficiency through these distance functions corresponds to radial projections on the weakly efficient frontier, i.e., gross of input or output individual slacks. As discussed in Sect. 2.4 of the preceding chapter, when decomposing cost and revenue efficiency, unaccounted slacks result in technical efficiency overestimation (actual technical efficiency is lower than the value of the radial input or output efficiency measure) and, correspondingly, allocative efficiency underestimation.

We now show the specific DEA linear programs that allow calculating the input and output distance functions for a specific firm under evaluation, denoted by (x_o, y_o). Specifically, for the input dimension, the conventional DEA program (3.23) calculates the inverse of Shephard's input distance function, corresponding to Farrell's radial input measure of technical efficiency: $1/\ D_I(x_o, y_o) \equiv TE_{R(I)}(x_o, y_o) = \theta$. This program corresponds to the "envelopment" formulation proposed by Banker et al. (1984)—the so-called BCC model in the DEA literature, see Banker et al. (1984).[10] The optimal solution θ^* yields the efficiency score against the weakly efficient subset, which, once duality is introduced, will measure cost inefficiency due to technological reasons. Subsequently, a second stage is solved through program

[9] It is relevant to recall that the weakly efficient subsets $\partial^W L^S(y)$ and $\partial^W P^S(x)$, generated under the DEA assumption of strong disposability of inputs and outputs, are not to be confused with the production possibility sets $L^W(y)$ and $P^W(x)$, defined under the assumption of weakly disposable inputs and outputs.

[10] DEA started with the seminal paper of Charnes et al. (1978) where the CRS versions of the input-oriented and output-oriented radial models where proposed. Having been formulated as linear programs, they had, from the beginning on, two alternative dual formulations: the envelopment form, or primal linear program, and the multiplier form, or dual linear program.

(3.24), to capture any feasible non-radial input reductions in the form of additive slacks that would project the evaluated firm to the strongly efficient frontier. Again, note that these values are merely informative, as they are not used explicitly in the measurement of cost inefficiency based on the radial approach. The standard two-stage programs, necessary to implement the radial input approach for technical efficiency measurement, are the following:[11]

First stage Radial input technical efficiency (Envelopment formulation)		Second stage Additive slacks inefficiency (Envelopment formulation)	
$TE_{R(I)}(x_o, y_o) = \min_{\theta,\lambda} \theta$ s.t. $\sum_{j=1}^{J} \lambda_j x_{jm} \leq \theta\ x_{om},\ m = 1, \ldots, M,$ $\sum_{j=1}^{J} \lambda_j y_{jn} \geq y_{on},\ n = 1, \ldots, N,$ $\sum_{j=1}^{J} \lambda_j = 1.\ \lambda \geq 0.$	(3.23)	$TI_{A(G)}(\theta^* x_o, y_o) = \max_{s^-, s^+, \lambda} \sum_{m=1}^{M} s_m^- + \sum_{n=1}^{N} s_n^+$ s.t. $\sum_{j=1}^{J} \lambda_j x_{mj} + s_m^- = \theta^* x_{mo},\ m = 1, \ldots, M,$ $\sum_{j=1}^{J} \lambda_j y_{nj} - s_n^+ = y_{no},\ n = 1, \ldots, N,$ $\sum_{j=1}^{J} \lambda_j = 1,\ \lambda_j \geq 0,\ s^- \geq 0,\ s^+ \geq 0.$	(3.24)

It can be seen that program (3.23) incorporates the DEA input correspondence presented in (3.19), while (3.24) captures any existing slacks from the projected benchmark to the strongly efficient frontier within the same technology, i.e., once inputs have been contracted by multiplying them by the optimal solution to (3.23), i.e., $(\theta^* x_o, y_o)$.[12] Besides the technical efficiency score, relevant information can be obtained from the optimal benchmarks in both programs. In this case, those firms whose associated multipliers are positive, $\lambda_j^* > 0$, constitute reference peers for (x_o, y_o), which can improve its technical efficiency by learning from them.[13] In these programs, the larger the value of the multiplier, the more relevant is an actual firm in the optimal reference benchmark, constructed as a linear combination of efficient observations.

[11]The second-stage additive model is a particular case of the third oldest DEA model (Charnes et al., 1985). It corresponds to its primal or envelopment form where the original right-hand side term of the first M restrictions, x_{mo}, $m = 1, \ldots, M$, have been replaced by $\theta^* x_{mo}$, $m = 1, \ldots, M$, being θ^* the optimal value of the first-stage model (3.23). It can be refined searching for the strong efficient projection that minimizes the same objective function, at the expense of solving a more complex nonlinear program (see Aparicio et al., 2007).

[12]Program (3.24) can be refined and substituted by a more complex nonlinear program that has the advantage of identifying the closest projection (minimizing the objective function) instead of the "farthest" projection, which means that the new optimal slacks can be much smaller; see Aparicio et al. (2007, 2017c).

[13]This procedure can also be refined, by reducing the set of possible peers from the subset of strong efficient firms to the subset of extreme strong efficient firms, those that cannot be deleted without modifying its frontier facet. For VRS technologies, the last subset guarantees that any projection accepts a single representation as convex linear combination of extreme strong efficient firms.

From an output orientation, Shephard's output distance function is equivalent to Farrell's radial output measure of technical efficiency, $D_O(x_o, y_o) \equiv TE_{R(O)}(x_o, y_o) = \phi$. This value corresponds to the inverse of the solution to the following DEA program (3.25), which is the output formulation of the BCC model. As before, once the radial technical efficiency projecting (x_o, y_o) to the weakly efficient frontier has been calculated, it is possible to account for individual slacks resorting to the associated additive model (3.26):

First stage Radial output technical efficiency (Envelopment formulation)		Second stage Additive slacks inefficiency (Envelopment formulation)	
$TE_{R(O)}(x_o, y_o)^{-1} = \max_{\xi, \lambda} \ \xi$ s.t. $\sum_{j=1}^{J} \lambda_j x_{jm} \leq x_{om}, \ m = 1, \ldots, M,$ $\sum_{j=1}^{J} \lambda_j y_{jn} \geq \xi y_{on}, \ n = 1, \ldots, N,$ $\sum_{j=1}^{J} \lambda_j = 1.$ $\lambda \geq 0.$	(3.25)	$TI_{A(G)}(x_o, \xi^* y_o) = \max_{s^-, s^+, \lambda} \sum_{m=1}^{M} s_m^- + \sum_{n=1}^{N} s_n^+$ s.t. $\sum_{j=1}^{J} \lambda_j x_{jm} + s_m^- = x_{om}, \ m = 1, \ldots, M,$ $\sum_{j=1}^{J} \lambda_j y_{jn} - s_n^+ = \xi^* y_{on}, \ n = 1, \ldots, N,$ $\sum_{j=1}^{J} \lambda_j = 1,$ $\lambda_j \geq 0, \ s^- \geq 0, \ s^+ \geq 0.$	(3.26)

Again, program (3.25) incorporates the DEA output correspondence presented in (3.20), while (3.26) identifies any remaining slacks from the projected benchmark to the strongly efficient frontier, i.e., once outputs have been expanded by multiplying them by the optimal solution to (3.25): $(x_o, \xi^* y_o)$, $\xi^* \geq 1$. And since $\phi^{* - 1} = \xi^*$, the optimal projection is $(x_o, y_o/\phi^*)$ as defined in (3.8) and represented in Fig. 3.2b. As for the optimal multipliers, their values identify once again the intensity of the different peers on the frontier constructed as linear combination of the existing observations, $\lambda_j^* > 0$. The comparison between programs (3.23) and (3.25) reveals that, when evaluating the technical efficiency of firm (x_o, y_o), the DEA input and output correspondences presented in (3.19) and (3.20), stemming from the same technology, provide complementary visions of performance. This difference is due to the nature of the returns to scale, since under constant returns they are equivalent. The disparity resides in the way the efficient subset is reached, through either input contractions or output expansions, plus any existing slacks in both dimensions.

The linear duals to programs (3.23) and (3.25) provide relevant information concerning the multipliers that define the reference hyperplanes for the measurement of technical efficiency. These correspond to the following "multiplier" formulations:

Radial input technical efficiency (Multiplier formulation)		Radial output technical efficiency (Multiplier formulation)	
$TE_{R(I)}(x_o, y_o) = \max\limits_{\nu,\mu,\omega} \sum\limits_{N=1}^{N} \mu_n y_{on} + \omega$ s.t. $\sum\limits_{M=1}^{M} \nu_m x_{jm} - \sum\limits_{n=1}^{N} \mu_n y_{jn} - \omega \geq 0,$ $j = 1, \ldots, J,$ $\sum\limits_{m=1}^{M} \nu_m x_{om} = 1,$ $\nu \geq 0, \mu \geq 0.$	(3.27)	$TE_{R(O)}(x_o, y_o) = \min\limits_{\nu,\mu,\omega} \sum\limits_{M=1}^{M} \nu_m x_{om} + \omega$ s.t. $\sum\limits_{M=1}^{M} \nu_m x_{jm} - \sum\limits_{n=1}^{N} \mu_n y_{jn} - \omega \geq 0,$ $j = 1, \ldots, J,$ $\sum\limits_{N=1}^{N} \mu_n y_{on} = 1,$ $\nu \geq 0, \mu \geq 0.$	(3.28)

The optimal solutions yield the vector of decision variables (ν^*, μ^*, ω^*) associated with the reference hyperplane defined by a certain subset of efficient peers, whose individual optimal constraints are equal to zero: $\sum\limits_{M=1}^{M} \nu_m^* x_{jm} - \sum\limits_{n=1}^{N} \mu_n^* y_{jn} - \omega^* = 0.$[14] As discussed in Sect. 2.4 of Chap. 2 presenting duality theory, the multipliers (ν^*, μ^*) represent the empirical approximation of the *shadow prices* of each input and output, constituting their weights on the reference hyperplane. If any of the optimal multipliers ν_m^* or μ_n^* is zero, then the corresponding input or output is irrelevant for defining the benchmark frontier. The importance of the shadow prices emerges in full when assessing economic performance, since their comparison with the market prices determines whether the efficient projection of the firm under evaluation is allocative efficient or not, by demanding and supplying the optimal amounts of inputs and outputs that minimize cost or maximize revenue. See Figs. 2.6 and 2.7 of the preceding chapter for an illustration of the duality relationships behind this result. It is also relevant to highlight that there may exist multiple optimal solutions to problem (3.27). As for the parameter ω, it informs us about the scale properties of the reference hyperplane. Following Banker and Thrall (1992), if $\omega^* < 0$, then increasing returns to scale (IRS) prevails at the efficient projection of (x_o, y_o) and increasing inputs in a given proportion increases outputs to a larger extent, while if $\omega^* = 0$, constant returns to scale (CRS) hold. Finally, if $\omega^* > 0$, the technology exhibits decreasing returns to scale (DRS). In this chapter, we do not elaborate further on the scale characteristics of the frontier since, as previously remarked, and extensively addressed in Sect. 2.3 of Chap. 2, scale efficiency does not play any role in explaining cost and revenue inefficiency—contrary to the case of profitability efficiency discussed on the following chapter. This implies that failure to produce at a most productive scale size, characterized by CRS—in the terminology of Banker

[14] The subset of efficient peers are all the efficient firms that belong to the mentioned optimal hyperplane. For large problems, it is interesting to consider as peers only the subset of "extreme efficient firms," that is, firms that cannot be expressed as a convex linear combination of other efficient firms.

et al. (1984), does not result in larger cost or revenue inefficiency, since economic optimality does not require such technological property.

3.3 Economic Behavior and Cost and Revenue Efficiencies

We now recover the partially oriented economic objectives of the firm corresponding to either cost minimization or revenue maximization. Following different authors, e.g., McFadden (1978) or Färe and Primont (1995), the cost and revenue functions are defined by the following:

$$C(y, w) = \min_x \{w \cdot x : x \in L(y)\}, \quad w \in \mathbb{R}^M_{++}, y \geq 0_N, \tag{3.29}$$

and

$$R(x, p) = \max_y \{p \cdot y : y \in P(x)\}, \quad p \in \mathbb{R}^N_{++}, x \geq 0_N, \tag{3.30}$$

whose properties under minimal regularity conditions are discussed in Sect. 2.3 of the preceding chapter. From an input perspective, the cost function represents the minimum expenditure of producing a given (fixed) amount of outputs y given input prices w. From an output perspective, the revenue function represents the maximum value of selling output quantities given the (fixed) amounts of inputs x and output prices p. Here, we recall that the cost and revenue functions do not impose strong regularity conditions on the technology such as constant returns to scale (as already anticipated) or, more generally, homotheticity. For example, the existence of constant returns to scale imposes further restrictions on the technology that, under this assumption, corresponds to a closed convex cone that is homogeneous of degree one: $T^{CRS} = \{(\psi x, \psi y) : (x, y) \in T, \ \psi > 0\}$. This results in $C(y, w)$ being a linearly homogeneous, convex, and nondecreasing function of y for fixed w. Additionally, input homotheticity implies that $C(y, w) = yC(1, w)$. Regarding the revenue function, under CRS, $R(x, p)$ is linearly homogeneous, convex, and nondecreasing in x for fixed p—with homotheticity implying that $R(x, p) = xR(1, p)$.

Therefore, as cost minimization and revenue maximization do not impose restrictions a priori on the homotheticity characteristics of the input and output sets (3.1) and (3.2), all forthcoming results related to the definition and decomposition of cost and revenue efficiency are valid for non-homothetic representations of the production technology. As shown by Aparicio et al. (2015b; Proposition 3), this is indeed the case of multiple input-multiple output technologies approximated through DEA methods, which are non-homothetic even under the assumption of CRS. We discuss the implications of non-homotheticity when decomposing economic efficiency in Sect. 3.3. Again, we remark that one relevant consequence of this assumption is that the associated measures of technical performance exclude scale efficiency, as defined in expression (2.12) of the preceding chapter, which does not play a meaningful role in the measurement of cost and revenue efficiency. This implies that, from an applied perspective, constant returns to scale should not be imposed on the technology when assessing economic performance.

3.3.1 Cost Minimization and Cost Efficiency

Assuming that firms target a fixed level of output y in their production plans, if they are capable of producing this output level incurring in the minimum cost given input prices w, this implies that they are cost efficient by demanding optimal input quantities: $x^C(y, w)$. Shephard's lemma allows us to recover the system of demand equations defined by the partial derivatives of the cost function with respect to input prices: $x^C(y, w) = \nabla_w C(y, w)$.[15] This result requires that the multiple output-multiple input transformation function characterizing the technology is (i) well behaved satisfying all desirable neoclassical properties and regularity conditions, particularly quasi-concavity, which ensures that the associated input production possibility sets are convex, e.g., Madden (1986), and (ii) continuous and twice differentiable. In textbooks, where the technology is represented by the single-output production function $y = f(x)$, for any two inputs k and l with associated market prices w_k and w_l, the first-order conditions for cost minimization also imply that the marginal rate of technical substitution of factor k for factor l must be equal to their price ratio: $MRS_l^k = -dl/dk = f_k(x)/f_l(x) = w_k/w_l$, where $f_k(x) = \partial f(x)/\partial x_k$ and $f_l(x) = \partial f(x)/\partial x_l$ are marginal productivities. It is assumed that given the properties satisfied by the production function, the second-order conditions are verified, and therefore, the sign of the bordered Hessian determinant is negative.

Unfortunately, due to the piecewise linear nature of the DEA technologies, which prevents differentiability, it is not generally possible to recover input demand functions making use of these results based on continuous calculus. In return, as shown in what follows, it is rather easy to identify the input demand quantities minimizing production cost and without relying on specific functional forms. Recalling Fig. 2.4 of the previous chapter, this locus corresponds to $x^C(y, w)$ in Fig. 3.3a, where $C(y, w) = w_1 x_1^C + w_2 x_2^C$ is depicted by the solid isocost line tangent to the isoquant of the production possibility set $L(y)$. The isocost line represents the set of input vectors that, given the input prices, entail the same cost to the firm. Consequently, if a firm attains output level y using an amount of inputs different from $x^C(y, w)$, it incurs higher production cost than the minimum given the technology. For firm (x_D, y_D), this is represented by the distance between the isocost lines separating minimum and observed cost, the latter represented by the dashed line passing through (x_D, y_D): $C_D = w_1 x_{D1} + w_2 x_{D2}$, i.e., $C_D > C(y_D, w)$. Based on Shephard's input distance function, firm D is technically inefficient because $1/D_I(x_D, y_D) \equiv TE_{R(I)}(x_D, y_D) = \theta^* < 1$, and therefore, it does not belong to the weakly

[15]This results was named after Shephard by Diewert; see Fox (2018: 514).

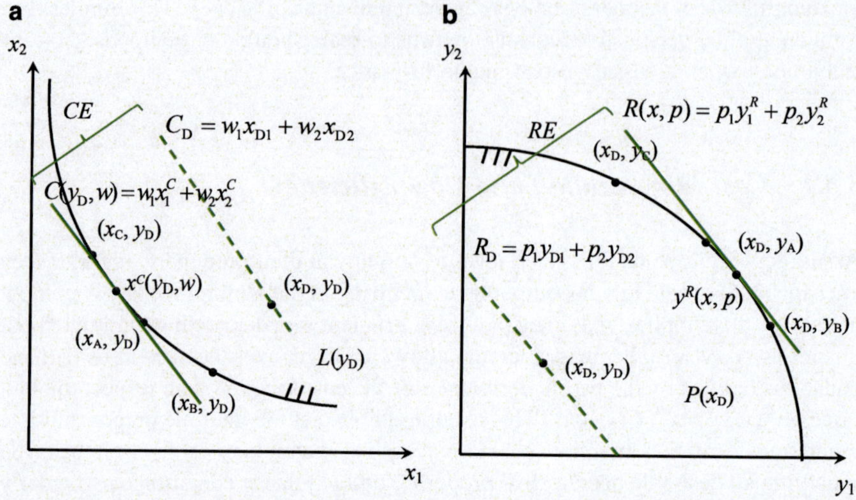

Fig. 3.3 (**a**, **b**) Cost minimization, revenue maximization, and economic efficiency

efficient frontier; see expression (3.15). But recall that firms A, B, and C are also cost-inefficient, despite being technically efficient. As presented in the following section, since the source of this inefficiency is not technical, it becomes apparent that it is the result of demanding a suboptimal mix of inputs given their prices, i.e., allocative inefficiency.

Following Farrell (1957), the cost efficiency measure is defined multiplicatively as the ratio of minimum cost to observed cost:

$$CE(x, y, w) = \frac{C(y, w)}{w \cdot x} = \frac{w \cdot x^C(y, w)}{w \cdot x} \leq 1. \tag{3.31}$$

Therefore, unless the firm under evaluation demands optimal input quantities, it incurs cost inefficiency. Clearly, for cost-efficient firms, $CE(x, y, w) = 1$.

3.3.2 *Revenue Maximization and Revenue Efficiency*

From the output side of the firm, if the value of its sales corresponds to the maximum feasible revenue given the level of inputs and output prices p, then it supplies the optimal amount of outputs: $y^R(x, p)$. Now, under the conditions previously stated, Shephard's lemma allows us to recover the system of supply equations defined by the partial derivatives of the revenue function with respect to output prices: $y^R(x, p) = \nabla_w R(x, p)$. Then, for any two outputs k and l with associated market prices p_k and p_l, the first-order conditions also imply that the marginal rate of technical transformation of output k for output l, defined on a general transformation function

$g(y)$, must be equal to the price ratios: $MRT_l^k = -dl/dk = g_k(y)/g_l(y) = p_k/p_l$, where $g_k(y) = \partial g(y)/\partial y_k$ and $g_l(y) = \partial g(y)/\partial y_l$. Again, given the regularity assumptions about the transformation function, the second-order conditions are also verified. As before, DEA methods characterizing the technology through linear faces lack differentiability and therefore do not allow recovering supply functions in terms of the above first-order conditions for revenue maximization. Nevertheless, as shown below, it is straightforward to obtain the optimal output supply amounts through linear programs.

We represent this optimal situation in Fig. 3.3b through firm $y^R(x,p)$, where $R(x,p) = p_1 y_1^R + p_2 y_2^R$ corresponds to the solid isorevenue line tangent to the isoquant of the output production possibility set $P(x)$. In this case, an isorevenue line represents the set of output vectors that, given their prices, would yield the same revenue for the firm. Any other alternative output production different from $y^R(x,p)$ cannot yield higher revenue given the output prices and the existing technology. Firm (x_D, y_D) is technically inefficient since $D_O(x_D, y_D) \equiv TE_{R(O)}(x_D, y_D) = \phi < 1$. We also see that it is also economically inefficient because it falls short from maximizing revenue, as represented by the dashed isorevenue line passing through it: $R_D = p_1 y_{D1} + p_2 y_{D2}$, i.e., $R_D < R(x_D, p)$. As before, the remaining technically efficient firms A, B, and C are also revenue-inefficient, and since the source of this inefficiency is not technical, it corresponds to a suboptimal mix of supplied outputs given their prices, i.e., allocative inefficiency.

As its input counterpart (3.31), Farrell's revenue efficiency measure is defined multiplicatively as the ratio of observed revenue to maximum revenue:

$$RE(x,y,p) = \frac{p \cdot y}{R(x,p)} = \frac{p \cdot y}{p \cdot y^R(x,p)} \leq 1. \tag{3.32}$$

Therefore, if the firm supplies the optimal output quantities, then $RE(x,y,p) = 1$, while if it fails to produce these amounts, it incurs revenue losses, $RE(x,y,p) < 1$. The revenue loss corresponding for the inefficient firm (x_D, y_D) is represented in Fig. 3.3b by the gap between the observed (dashed) and optimal (solid) isorevenue lines.

3.3.3 Calculating Minimum Cost and Maximum Revenue Using Data Envelopment Analysis

From an empirical perspective, calculating cost and revenue efficiency for a set of observed firms requires information on their input and output quantities (x, y), as well as their corresponding prices (w, p). Based on this dataset and for firm (x_o, y_o), calculating minimum cost $C(y_o, w)$ and maximum revenue $R(x_o, p)$ require approximating the technology to account for the particular output and input levels (isoquants). To prevent inconsistencies in the decomposition of cost and revenue efficiencies, the technology must coincide with that employed to calculate the input and output technical efficiencies, (3.23) and (3.24), respectively. Therefore, relying on the DEA production possibility sets (3.19) and (3.20), the following programs allow calculating the minimum cost and maximum revenue.

Minimum cost (Envelopment formulation)		Maximum revenue (Envelopment formulation)	
$C(y_o, w) = \min\limits_{x,\lambda} \sum\limits_{m=1}^{M} w_m x_m$ s.t. $\sum\limits_{j=1}^{J} \lambda_j x_{jm} \leq x_m,\ m = 1, \ldots, M,$ $\sum\limits_{j=1}^{J} \lambda_j y_{jn} \geq y_{on},\ n = 1, \ldots, N,$ $\sum\limits_{j=1}^{J} \lambda_j = 1,$ $\lambda \geq 0,\ x \geq 0.$	(3.33)	$R(x_o, p) = \max\limits_{y,\lambda} \sum\limits_{n=1}^{N} p_n y_n$ s.t. $\sum\limits_{j=1}^{J} \lambda_j x_{jm} \leq x_{om},\ m = 1, \ldots, M,$ $\sum\limits_{j=1}^{J} \lambda_j y_{jn} \geq y_n,\ n = 1, \ldots, N,$ $\sum\limits_{j=1}^{J} \lambda_j = 1,$ $\lambda \geq 0, y \geq 0.$	(3.34)

The solution to programs (3.33) and (3.34) yields the optimal input demands $x^C(y_o, w)$ and output supplies $y^R(x_o, p)$, as well as the specific j=1,. . .,J reference economic benchmarks minimizing cost or maximizing revenue and whose associated intensity variables are positive $\lambda_j > 0$. When markets are competitive resulting in a common price for each input and output, it is rather unusual that more than a single firm sets the optimal economic benchmark. Otherwise, for different observed prices across firms, this reference can change for each firm under evaluation, depending on the prices considered in (3.33) and (3.34). For these alternatives, see, for example, Camanho and Dyson (2008) and Portela and Thanassoulis (2014).

Once minimum cost or maximum revenue has been calculated, it is straightforward to substitute the optimal solutions in the definitions of cost efficiency (3.31) and revenue efficiency (3.32), so as to obtain $CE(x_o, y_o, w)$ and $RE(x_o, y_o, p)$.

3.4 Duality and the Decomposition of Economic Efficiency as the Product of Technical and Allocative Efficiencies

It is now possible to present the decomposition of cost and revenue efficiency based on the duality between the cost function and the input distance function and the revenue function and the output distance function. Generally speaking, duality refers to the possibility of recovering the technology T (or its associated input $L(y)$ and output $P(x)$ sets) from supporting economic functions and vice versa. Therefore, duality allows to relate the primal (quantity) space with the dual (price) space that characterizes the technological and economic behavior of the firm in a consistent way, so both representations of the firm contain the same information. As discussed in Sect. 2.4 of the previous chapter, duality theory constitutes a particularization to the field of economic theory of Minkowski's theorem. This theorem states that every closed convex set can be characterized as the intersection of its supporting half-spaces. Shephard (1953, 1970) introduced duality theory, while Diewert (1971) and McFadden (1978) represent classic formalizations of the subject. However, relevant to the goal of this book focused on the decomposition of economic efficiency according to technical and allocative criteria, we remark that it was Shephard (1953, 1970; Chap. 8) who, for the first time, presented the duality between a primal representation of the technology based on distance functions and the cost and revenue functions. As previously remarked, Färe et al. (1985), arguably the first book popularizing the measurement of efficiency of production, ignored the economic approach based on duality and focused on operations research methods. Subsequently, Färe and Primont (1995) took stock of the economic theory approach and further elaborated Shephard's results to explicitly decompose overall economic efficiency into technical and allocative components a la Farrell (1957), by resorting to Fenchel-Mahler inequalities.[16] We present here the approach that allows the composition of cost and revenue efficiency as defined in the previous section.[17]

3.4.1 Decomposing Cost Efficiency

3.4.1.1 Duality Between the Input Set and the Cost Function

The standard presentation of duality starts from the definition of the cost function $C(y, w)$ and shows that the input production possibility set $L(y)$ can be recovered by way of the supporting half-spaces that it generates for alternative input prices. Assuming that the cost function is defined by (3.29) and the input set is convex and satisfies strong disposability of inputs as in (3.3) (for convenience, the superscript S is omitted in what follows), this result is formalized through the following proposition characterizing the input correspondence.

Proposition 3.1 If the cost function is defined by (3.29), then

$$L(y) = \left\{x : w \cdot x \geq C(y, w),\ \ \forall w \in \ \mathbb{R}^M_{++}, y \geq 0_M\right\}. \tag{3.35}$$

Proof The proof resorts to Minkowski's theorem; i.e., a closed, convex set is the intersection of the half-spaces that support it. See McFadden (1978: 23).

This expression reveals that for a given output level y and a particular input price vector w, the cost function supports a half-space of the form $H(w, c) = \left\{x : w \cdot x \geq c = C(y, w), w \in \mathbb{R}^M_{++}, y \geq 0_M\right\}$. Since, by definition, $C(y, w)$ is the minimum cost of producing y, there is no feasible combination of inputs $x \in H(w, c)$ that can produce that output quantity in a less expensive way. Equivalently, if the

[16] Shephard himself did not introduce the concept of cost or revenue efficiency, neither proposed their decompositions.

[17] The proofs of the propositions included in this chapter can be found in these references.

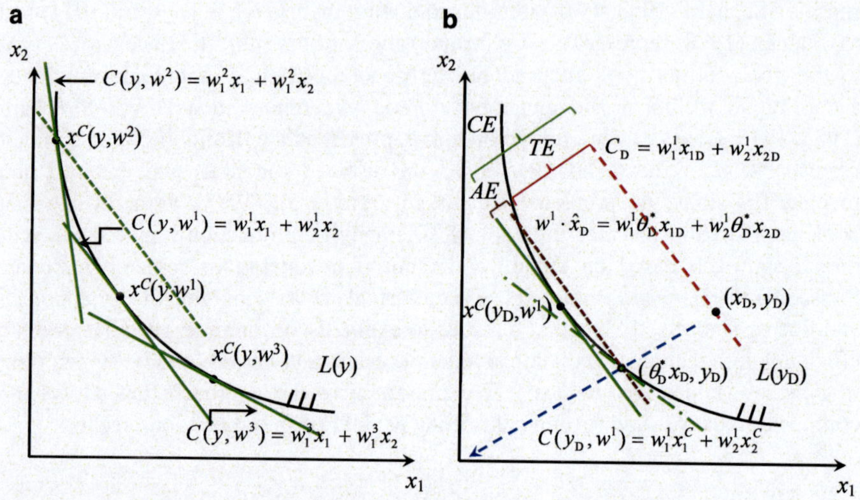

Fig. 3.4 (**a**, **b**) Duality between the input distance function and the cost function

cost-minimizing input combination belongs to $H(w, c)$, then it lies on the hyperplane $w \cdot x = C(y, w)$.

We recall here Fig. 2.6 of the preceding chapter where a detailed graphical exposition of duality is offered. Based on Proposition 3.1, we observe in Fig. 3.4a that the price vector denoted as w^1 defines the half-space $H(w^1, C(y, w^1))$, supported by the hyperplane (line) consistent with $w_1^1 x_1 + w_2^1 x_2 = C(y, w^1)$ and passing through $x^C(y, w^1)$, i.e., the optimal amount of inputs presented in Sect. 3.2.1. Following the above argument, the cost-minimizing bundle cannot be below this line, and therefore, the half-space above it must contain $L(y)$. Consequently, since at least one input bundle in the isocost $w^1 \cdot x = C(y, w^1)$ must be able to produce y, then $w^1 \cdot x$ and $L(y)$ must share at least one x in the quantity (primal) space.

Proceeding in the same way for two additional price vectors, $w^2 \neq w^3$ ($\neq w^1$), their corresponding half-spaces $H(w^2, C(y, w^2))$ and $H(w^3, C(y, w^3))$ are generated. These half-spaces are supported by the isocosts $w_1^2 x_1 + w_2^2 x_2 = C(y, w^2)$ and $w_1^3 x_1 + w_2^3 x_2 = C(y, w^3)$—passing through $x^C(y, w^2)$ and $x^C(y, w^3)$, respectively. The latter isocosts must contain also $L(y)$, sharing at least one x. Consequently, combining the different half-spaces $H(w^1, C(y, w^1))$, $H(w^2, C(y, w^2))$, and $H(w^3, C(y, w^3))$, the input production possibility set $L(y)$ emerges as the intersection between the supporting hyperplanes. Continuing with this sequence for every price combination until all price vectors have been exhausted, as defined in Proposition 3.1, we observe that the input set $L(y)$, and its boundary, materializes as a conventional convex isoquant.

Therefore, applying Minkowski's theorem, we see that we can recover the technology $L(y)$ as the non-empty, closed, convex set in $\mathbb{R}_+^M$, (3.3), characterized by the intersection of the supporting half-spaces corresponding to different isocosts, representing minimum cost for alternative prices, as presented in (3.35). Departing from this expression, Minkowski's theorem allows us to recover the cost function through the following:

Proposition 3.2 If $L(y) = \{x : w \cdot x \geq C(y, w),\ \forall\ w \in \mathbb{R}^M_{++}, y \geq 0_M\}$, then

$$C(y, w) = \underset{x}{\text{Min}}\{w \cdot x : x \in L(y)\}. \tag{3.36}$$

Proof See McFadden (1978: 23).

In Fig. 3.4a, this expression corresponds to each isocost line that, minimizing cost for each price vector, is tangent to the isoquant of the input set $L(y)$. Here, for each vector of optimal input demands, the first-order conditions for cost minimization subject to the technology are satisfied; i.e., the marginal rate of substitution among inputs (slope of the isoquant) must be equal to their relative prices (slope of the isocost line).

3.4.1.2 Duality Between the Input Distance Function and the Cost Function

The above duality relationship between the input set and the cost function must be qualified to include the concept of technical efficiency if we intend to decompose economic efficiency into technical and allocative factors. This is accomplished by relying on the input distance function as an equivalent representation of the input set $L(y)$. Indeed, from the representation property (3.9), we can define the input set as follows:

$$L(y) = \{x : D_I(x, y) \geq 1\}. \tag{3.37}$$

Then, as shown in Fig. 3.4b and recalling that the inverse of the input distance function is equal to the Farrell input technical efficiency measure, $D_I(x, y) \equiv 1/TE_{R(I)}(x, y) = 1/\theta$, it is clear that if a firm is technically inefficient with $D_I(x, y) > 1$, it cannot minimize production cost for any input price vector, because it is dominated in the sense of Pareto-Koopmans efficiency. Therefore, it is possible to reduce input quantities while producing the same output amount. Combining (3.35) and (3.37), we obtain the following:

$$L(y) = \{x : w \cdot x/D_I(x, y) = w \cdot \widehat{x} \geq C(y, w),\ D_I(x, y) \geq 1, \forall\ w \in \mathbb{R}^M_{++}, y \geq 0_M\}. \tag{3.38}$$

So the input set can be defined in terms of the supporting half-spaces defined by the cost function but embedding the input distance function $D_I(x, y)$. This enhances Minkowski's theorem to allow for a measure of technical inefficiency, where the input vectors belonging to the intersecting half-spaces are expressed in terms of their projections to the different supporting hyperplanes, i.e., $\widehat{x} = x/D_I(x, y)$.

Then, it is possible to recover the cost function from the input correspondence including the input distance function in the following way:

$$C(y, w) = \min_x \{w \cdot x/D_I(x, y) = w \cdot \widehat{x}, D_I(x, y) \geq 1\}. \tag{3.39}$$

This expression constitutes the core of the duality relationship introduced by Färe and Primont (1995) allowing the decomposition of cost efficiency. Here, for the sake of completeness, we summarize their duality results characterizing the relationship between the primal and dual representation of the firm. Namely,

Proposition 3.3 Assuming Propositions 3.1 and 3.2 hold, as well as expression (3.37), then

$$\begin{aligned} C(y, w) &= \min_x \ \{w \cdot x : D_I(x, y) \geq 1\}, \text{ if and only if} \\ D_I(x, y) &= \min_w \{w \cdot x : C(y, w) \geq 1\} \end{aligned} \tag{3.40}$$

or, alternatively,

$$\begin{aligned} C(y, w) &= \min_x \ \{w \cdot x/D_I(x, y)\}, \text{ if and only if} \\ D_I(x, y) &= \min_w \{w \cdot x/C(y, w)\}. \end{aligned} \tag{3.41}$$

Proof See Färe and Primont (1995: 47–48).

The last expression (3.41) states that under the required assumptions, the cost function can be derived from the input distance function by minimizing cost over all feasible input vectors, just as the input distance function can be recovered from the cost function by finding the minimum of the ratio of actual cost to minimum cost over all feasible input price vectors. Note that this last expression precisely corresponds to the inverse of the definition of cost efficiency (3.31) for the optimal (shadow) prices, w^*, rather than market prices, w. We make use of this result below when interpreting the meaning of allocative efficiency.

Hence, from (3.38) or (3.41), we obtain that $C(y, w) \leq w \cdot x/D_I(x, y)$ or, equivalently, recalling the definition of cost efficiency presented in (3.31):

$$CE(x, y, w) = C(y, w)/w \cdot x \leq 1/D_I(x, y), \tag{3.42}$$

where cost efficiency can be expressed in terms of (inverse of) the input distance function thanks to the homogeneity of degree one of production cost in input quantities, i.e., $w \cdot \widehat{x} = w \cdot x/D_I(x, y) = (w \cdot x)/D_I(x, y),\ D_I(x, y) \geq 1$, implying that radial contractions of the input quantities bring a reduction in production cost in the exact same proportion.

Expression (3.42) is known in the literature as the Fenchel-Mahler inequality (Fenchel, 1949; Mahler, 1939). Closing the inequality results in the decomposition of cost efficiency based on the radial input distance function:

$$CE(x,y,w) = \frac{C(y,w)}{w\cdot x} = \frac{w\cdot \widehat{x}}{w\cdot x}\times\frac{C(y,w)}{w\cdot\widehat{x}} = \frac{(w\cdot x)/D_I(x,y)}{w\cdot x}\times\frac{C(y,w)}{w\cdot x/D_I(x,y)} = \\ = \frac{1}{D_I(x,y)}\times\frac{w\cdot x^C(y,w)}{w\cdot x/D_I(x,y)}\leq 1. \tag{3.43}$$

In this expression, the second factor in the last equality captures the gap between minimum cost and cost at the radial projection of the firm to the production frontier. Since $TE_{R(I)}(x,y) = \theta = 1/D_I(x,y)$ measures technical efficiency, the remainder measures the cost excess that can be attributed to the fact that the technically projected benchmark $\widehat{x}$ does not employ the optimal input demand quantities $x^C(y, w)$ that minimize cost, i.e., a residual capturing allocative efficiency. Therefore, the decomposition of cost efficiency is as follows:

$$CE(x,y,w) = \frac{C(y,w)}{w\cdot x} = \frac{1}{D_I(x,y)}\times\frac{w\cdot x^C(y,w)}{w\cdot\widehat{x}} \\ = TE_{R(I)}(x,y)\times AE_{R(I)}(x,y,w)\leq 1, \tag{3.44}$$

where the radial allocative measure of cost efficiency, $AE_{R(I)}(x,y,w) = CE(x,y,w)/TE_{R(I)}(x,y)$, is calculated as the multiplicative residual between cost and technical efficiencies.

Allocative efficiency can be interpreted in terms of the disparity between the inputs' shadow prices and market prices resorting to Proposition 3.3. Recalling the last expression in (3.41), the shadow prices correspond to the solution to $D_I(x,y) = \min_{w}\{w\cdot x/C(y,w)\}$, which we denote as $w^* = \nu$ to connect the following results to the discussion on shadow prices presented in Sect. 2.4.1 of the previous chapter, as well as their empirical calculation through the DEA multiplier formulation of the Farrell technical efficiency measure (3.27). Then, at the optimum, it is verified that:

$$D_I(x,y) = \nu\cdot x/C(y,\nu). \tag{3.45}$$

Therefore, vector ν corresponds to the (shadow) input prices that make the optimal projection of the firm $\widehat{x} = x/D_I(x,y)$ cost-efficient. It is now possible to normalize or rescale any vector of shadow prices satisfying (3.45), so it is verified that $\overline{\nu}\cdot x = w\cdot x$, $\overline{\nu} = \psi\nu$, $\psi > 0$. Because the cost function is linearly homogeneous in the input prices, this transformation does not affect the value of the distance function in (3.45). Then, substituting (3.45) into the definition of allocative efficiency in (3.44) yields the following:

$$AE_{R(I)}(x,y,w) = \frac{C(y,w)}{w \cdot x / D_I(x,y)} = \frac{\nu \cdot x}{w \cdot x} \times \frac{C(y,w)}{C(y,\nu)} = \frac{C(y,w)}{C(y,\overline{\nu})} \leq 1. \tag{3.46}$$

Consequently, allocative efficiency corresponds to the cost excess in which a technically efficient firm incurs by not demanding the optimal input amounts at the existing market prices, which is equivalent to the cost ratio of minimum cost at the market prices to minimum cost at the shadow prices. It follows immediately that if the shadow prices coincide with the market prices $\nu = w$, the firm is allocative efficient: $AE_{R(I)}(x,y,w) = 1$. This also means that the Shephard input distance function meets the essential property associated with the decomposition of economic efficiency, in this case cost efficiency, which allows a correct interpretation of the terms technical efficiency and allocative efficiency, in the decomposition. The proof of the satisfaction of this property can also be seen through the expression: $AE_{R(I)}(x,y,w) = \frac{C(y,w)}{w \cdot x / D_I(x,y)} = \frac{C(y,w)}{w \cdot \widehat{x}}$. Then, if $\widehat{x}$ is such that $w \cdot \widehat{x} = C(y,w)$, we immediately get that $AE_{R(I)}(x,y,w) = 1$. Consequently, although Farrell (1957) and the remaining subsequent researchers on economic efficiency in production neglected the satisfaction of the so-called essential property, his definition and decomposition of cost efficiency do really meet this necessary condition for representing a consistent decomposition. Probably, Farrell did not focus his attention on this issue because the satisfaction of the property is trivial in the case of radial projections for measuring technical efficiency, as a component of the natural cost efficiency term defined as the ratio between minimum cost and actual cost. However, this is not true for most of the measures introduced in the last 25 years in the Data Envelopment Analysis literature, as we show throughout the book. Additionally, given $AE_{R(I)}(x,y,w) = \frac{C(y,w)}{w \cdot x / D_I(x,y)} = \frac{C(y,w)}{w \cdot \widehat{x}}$, since the benchmark for (x_o, y_o) onto the isoquant $L(y)$ is precisely $\widehat{x}$, we have that $AE_{R(I)}(\widehat{x},y,w) = \frac{C(y,w)}{w \cdot \widehat{x}}$, which coincides with $AE_{R(I)}(x,y,w)$. This means that the Shephard input distance function also satisfies the extended version of the essential property, defined in Chap. 2.

The decomposition of cost efficiency is illustrated in Fig. 3.4b. For firm (x_D, y_D), producing output quantity y_D and facing market prices w^1, economic efficiency defines as the ratio of minimum cost to observed cost, i.e., $CE(x_D, y_D, w^1) = (w_1^1 x_1^C + w_2^1 x_2^C)/(w_1^1 x_{D1} + w_2^1 x_{D2}) = C(y_D, w^1)/C_D$. Subsequently, following (3.44), cost efficiency can be decomposed into Farrell's technical efficiency measure, corresponding to the inverse of Shephard's input distance function, and allocative efficiency: $CE(x_D, y_D, w^1) = \theta_D^* \times C(y_D, w^1)/w^1 \cdot \widehat{x}_D = TE_{R(I)}(x_D, y_D) \times AE_{R(I)}(x_D, y_D, w^1)$, where $w^1 \cdot \widehat{x}_D = w_1^1 \theta_D^* x_{D1} + w_2^1 \theta_D^* x_{D2}$. Graphically, cost efficiency, technical efficiency, and allocative efficiency are identified by the corresponding distances between the parallel isocost lines at the cost-minimizing, technically efficient, and observed production plans. The interpretation of allocative efficiency as the ratio between cost at market prices and shadow prices, (3.46), is also graphically represented. This entails comparing the two isocost lines representing minimum cost for the two vectors of prices, w and v. Particularly, let us consider $\overline{v}$ as the (normalized) shadow price vector that would render the efficient projection of $(x_{\mathrm{D}}, y_{\mathrm{D}})$ cost-efficient, i.e., $\overline{v} \cdot \widehat{x}_{\mathrm{D}} = \overline{v}_1 \theta^*_{\mathrm{D}} x_{\mathrm{D}1} + \overline{v}_2 \theta^*_{\mathrm{D}} x_{\mathrm{D}2} = C(y, \overline{v})$, which corresponds to the dashed-dotted line tangent to the input set $L(y)$. Then, relying on expression (3.46), allocative inefficiency can be reinterpreted as $AE_{R(I)}(x_{\mathrm{D}}, y_{\mathrm{D}}, w^1) = C(y_{\mathrm{D}}, w^1)/w^1 \cdot \widehat{x}_{\mathrm{D}} = w^1 \cdot x^C(y_{\mathrm{D}}, w)^1/w^1 \cdot x^C(y_{\mathrm{D}}, \overline{v})$. As a result, if market prices w coincide with the shadow prices $\overline{v}$ of firm $(x_{\mathrm{D}}, y_{\mathrm{D}})$, it would be allocative efficient.

3.4.1.3 Calculating and Decomposing Cost Efficiency

From an empirical perspective based on Data Envelopment Analysis (DEA) methods, computing (3.44) for firm (x_o, y_o) is straightforward. It requires solving program (3.23), corresponding to Farrell's technical efficiency, θ^*, and program (3.33) solving for the minimum cost, $C(y_o, w)$. Then, the ratio of minimum cost to observed cost can be easily calculated and, subsequently, the residual allocative efficiency. Additionally, one can recover the associated shadow prices ν^* from the multiplier (dual) formulation of the technical efficiency model (3.27), which define the supporting hyperplanes or faces that characterize the (weakly) efficient input subset (3.15). However, comparing the actual shadow prices with the market prices, either in absolute or in relative terms, is not as illustrative as it may seem, because the piecewise linear nature of DEA allows quite frequently for multiple optimal solutions.

3.4.2 Decomposing Revenue Efficiency

3.4.2.1 Duality Between the Output Set and the Revenue Function

We now discuss the output side of the production process concerned with the maximization of revenue and its associated optimal supplied amounts of goods and services. Here, revenue efficiency, comparing maximum and observed revenues, can be also decomposed into technical and allocative components. To achieve this goal, we present first the existing duality between the revenue function $R(x, p)$ and the production technology, represented on this occasion by the output production possibility set $P(x)$. Assuming that the revenue function corresponds to (3.30) and the output set is convex and satisfies strong disposability of outputs, (3.5), then $P(x)$ (omitting the superscript S for convenience) can be defined in terms of $R(x, p)$.

Proposition 3.4 If the revenue function is defined by (3.30), then

$$P(x) = \{y : p \cdot y \leq R(x, p), \ \forall \ p \in \mathbb{R}^N_{++}, x \geq 0_M\}. \tag{3.47}$$

Proof The proof mirrors that of Proposition 3.1 (McFadden, 1978: 23).

Then, for a given quantity of inputs x and a particular output price vector p, the revenue function supports a half-space of the form $H(p,c) = \{y : p \cdot y \leq c = R(x,p), p \in \mathbb{R}^N_{++}, x \geq 0_M\}$. Therefore, as $R(x,p)$ represents the maximum attainable revenue y, there is no other alternative combination of outputs $y \in H(p,c)$ that, using input quantities x, can yield greater revenue. Therefore, if the revenue-maximizing output belongs to $H(p,c)$, then it lies on the hyperplane $p \cdot y = R(x,p)$.

Replicating Fig. 2.7 of the preceding chapter, where duality results were presented in an intuitive way, we illustrate Proposition 3.4 in Fig. 3.5a. Here, the price vector p^1 defines the half-space $H(p^1, R(x,p^1))$ below the hyperplane (isorevenue line) consistent with $p_1^1 y_1 + p_2^1 y_2 = R(x,p^1)$ and passing through $y^R(x, p^1)$, i.e., the optimal amount of outputs presented in the previous Sect. 3.2.2. Following the argument, no alternative revenue-maximizing output bundle can be above this line, and accordingly, the half-space below it contains $P(x)$.

We can proceed in the same way for two alternative price vectors $p^2 \neq p^1$ and $p^3 \neq p^2 \neq p^1$, whose corresponding half-spaces spaces are denoted by $H(p^2, R(x,p^2))$ and $H(p^3, R(x,p^3))$. These half-spaces are supported by the hyperplanes (isorevenue lines) $p_1^2 y_1 + p_2^2 y_2 = R(x,p^2)$ and $p_1^3 y_1 + p_2^3 y_2 = R(x,p^3)$, passing through $y^R(x,p^2)$ and $y^R(x,p^3)$, respectively. As these isorevenues share at least one y with $P(x)$, combining all three different half-spaces $H(p^1, R(x,p^1))$, $H(p^2, R(x,p^2))$, and $H(p^3, R(x,p^3))$, the output production possibility set $P(x)$ is recovered as the intersection between the supporting hyperplanes. Considering all possible price vectors, as defined in Proposition 3.4, allows us to recover the output set $P(x)$ and its boundary, which takes the shape of a standard concave output isoquant.

Consequently, relying on Minkowski's theorem, we can recover the technology $P(x)$ as the non-empty, closed, convex set in $\mathbb{R}^N_+$, (3.5), characterized by the intersection of the supporting half-spaces corresponding to different revenues, representing maximum revenues for alternative prices, i.e., Proposition 3.4. Considering this result, the relevance of duality lies in the possibility of recovering the revenue function.

Proposition 3.5 If $P(x) = \{y : p \cdot x \leq R(x,p),\ \forall\ p \in \mathbb{R}^N_{++}, x \geq 0_M\}$, then

$$R(x,p) = \max_y \{p \cdot y : y \in P(x)\}. \tag{3.48}$$

Proof Again, the proof mirrors that of Proposition 3.2 (McFadden, 1978: 23).

In Fig. 3.5a, this expression corresponds to the isorevenue lines that, maximizing revenue for each price vector, are tangent to the isoquant of the output set $P(x)$. For each vector of optimal output supplies, the first-order conditions for revenue maximization subject to the technology are satisfied; i.e., the marginal rate of technical transformation among outputs (slope of the isoquant) must be equal to their relative prices (slope of the isorevenue line).

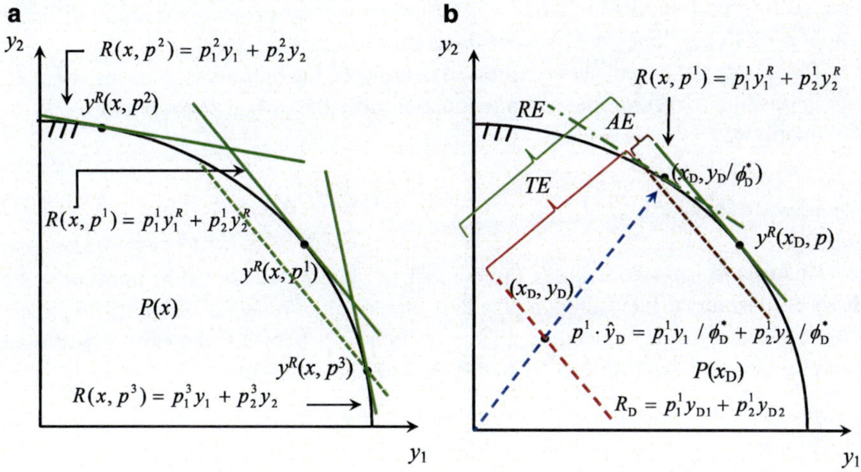

Fig. 3.5 (**a**, **b**) Duality between the output distance function and the revenue function

3.4.2.2 Duality Between the Output Distance Function and the Revenue Function

We can proceed now to extend the above duality between the output set and the revenue function to enable the decomposition of revenue efficiency into technical and allocative factors and where the former is represented by the output distance function. Since the output distance function constitutes an equivalent representation of the output set $P(x)$, as established in (3.10), it is possible to express it as follows:

$$P(x) = \{y : D_O(x, y) \leq 1\}. \tag{3.49}$$

As shown in Fig. 3.5b and recalling that the output distance function is equal to the Farrell output technical efficiency measure, $D_O(x, y) \equiv TE_{R(O)}(x, y) = \phi$, if a firm is technically inefficient $D_O(x, y) < 1$, then it cannot maximize revenue for any input price vector, because it is dominated in the sense of Pareto-Koopmans efficiency. As a result, it is possible to increase output quantities while using the same input amounts. Combining (3.47) and (3.49) results in the following output set:

$$P(x) = \left\{y : p \cdot \hat{y} = p \cdot y / D_O(x, y) \leq R(x, p), D_O(x, y) \leq 1, \forall\ p \in \mathbb{R}^N_{++}, x \geq 0_M\right\}. \tag{3.50}$$

Accordingly, the output set can be defined in terms of the supporting half-spaces defined by the revenue function but qualified with the inclusion of the output distance function $D_O(x, y)$. Again, this extends Minkowski's theorem to allow for a measure of technical inefficiency, where the output vectors belonging to the intersecting half-spaces are expressed in terms of their projections to the different supporting hyperplanes, i.e., $\widehat{y} = y/D_O(x, y)$.

Then, once the output set is expressed in terms of the output distance function, we are in position to recover the revenue function from the output correspondence in the following way:

$$R(x,p) = \max_y \{y : p \cdot \widehat{y} = p \cdot y/D_O(x, y),\ D_O(x, y) \leq 1\}. \tag{3.51}$$

This relationship constitutes the core of the duality relationship introduced by Färe and Primont (1995) allowing the decomposition of revenue efficiency. As in the cost case, the result characterizing the relationship between the primal and dual representation of the firm can be stated through the following.

Proposition 3.6 Assuming Propositions 3.4 and 3.5 hold, as well as expression (3.49), then

$$\begin{aligned} R(x,p) &= \max_y \{p \cdot y :\ D_O(x, y) \leq 1\}, \text{ if and only if} \\ D_O(x, y) &= \max_p \{p \cdot y : R(x,p) \leq 1\} \end{aligned} \tag{3.52}$$

or, alternatively,

$$\begin{aligned} R(x,p) &= \max_y \{p \cdot y/\ D_O(x, y)\}, \text{if and only if} \\ D_O(x, y) &= \max_p \{p \cdot y/R(x,p)\}. \end{aligned} \tag{3.53}$$

Proof See Färe and Primont (1995: 50).

Expression (3.53) states that under the required assumptions, the revenue function can be derived from the output distance function by maximizing revenue over all feasible output vectors, while the output distance function can be recovered from the revenue function by finding the maximum of the ratio of actual revenue to maximum revenue over all feasible output price vectors. We underline that this last expression precisely corresponds to the inverse of the definition of revenue efficiency (3.32) for the optimal (shadow) prices p^* rather than market prices, p. We retake this result below when interpreting allocative efficiency.

We can now recover the definition of revenue efficiency (3.32) either from (3.50) or (3.53). From these expressions, we obtain that $R(x,p) \geq p \cdot y/D_O(x, y)$ and, therefore, rearranging:

$$RE(x, y, p) = p \cdot y/R(x,p) \leq D_O(x, y). \tag{3.54}$$

Here, revenue efficiency is expressed in terms of the output distance function thanks to the homogeneity of degree one of the revenue function in output quantities, i.e., $p \cdot \hat{y} = p \cdot y/D_O(x,y) = (p \cdot y)/D_O(x,y),\ D_O(x,y) \leq 1$, implying that radially expanding output quantities increases revenue in the exact same proportion.

Expression (3.54) is the Fenchel-Mahler inequality associated with the revenue efficiency model. Consequently, closing the inequality results in the decomposition of revenue efficiency in terms of the radial output distance function:

$$RE(x,y,p) = \frac{p \cdot y}{R(x,p)} = \frac{p \cdot y}{p \cdot \hat{y}} \times \frac{p \cdot \hat{y}}{R(x,p)} = \frac{p \cdot y}{(p \cdot y)/D_O(x,y)} \times \frac{p \cdot y/D_O(x,y)}{R(x,p)} = \\ = D_O(x,y) \times \frac{p \cdot y/D_O(x,y)}{p \cdot y^R(x,p)} \leq 1. \tag{3.55}$$

We can now interpret the residual corresponding to the second factor capturing the difference between maximum revenue and revenue at the radial projection of the firm to the production frontier. Hence, since $TE_{R(O)}(x,y) = \phi \equiv D_O(x,y)$ measures technical efficiency, the remainder measures the loss in revenue that can be attributed to the fact that the technically projected production plan $\hat{y}$ does not correspond to the optimal output supply quantities $y^R(x,p)$ that maximize revenue, i.e., allocative efficiency. Therefore, the decomposition of revenue efficiency is as follows:

$$RE(x,y,p) = \frac{p \cdot y}{R(x,p)} = D_O(x,y) \times \frac{p \cdot \hat{y}}{p \cdot y^R(x,p)} \\ = TE_{R(O)}(x,y) \times AE_{R(O)}(x,y,p) \leq 1, \tag{3.56}$$

where the radial allocative measure of revenue efficiency, $AE_{R(O)}(x,y,p) = RE(x,y,p)/TE_{R(O)}(x,y)$, is calculated as the multiplicative residual between revenue and technical efficiency.

Allocative efficiency can be interpreted in terms of the disparity between the output's shadow prices and market prices resorting to Proposition 3.6. Recalling the last expression in (3.53), the shadow prices correspond to the solution to $D_O(x,y) = \max_p \{p \cdot y/R(x,p)\}$, which we denote as $p^* = \mu$ to link the following results to the discussion on shadow prices presented in Sect. 2.4.2 of the preceding chapter, as well as their empirical calculation through the DEA multiplier formulation of the output distance function (3.28). Then, at the optimum, it is verified that:

$$D_O(x,y) = \mu \cdot y/R(x,\mu). \tag{3.57}$$

Therefore, μ corresponds to the (shadow) output prices that make the optimal projection of the firm, $\hat{y} = y/D_O(x,y)$, revenue-efficient. It is now possible to normalize or rescale any vector of shadow prices satisfying (3.57), so it is verified that $\bar{\mu} \cdot y = p \cdot y$, $\bar{\mu} = \psi\mu$, $\psi > 0$. Given that the revenue function is linearly homogeneous in the output prices, this transformation does not affect the value of the distance function in (3.57). Then, substituting (3.57) into the definition of allocative efficiency in (3.56) yields the following:

$$AE_{R(O)}(x,y,p) = \frac{p \cdot y / D_O(x,y)}{R(x,p)} = \frac{p \cdot y}{\mu \cdot y} \times \frac{R(x,\mu)}{R(x,p)} = \frac{R(x,\overline{\mu})}{R(x,p)} \leq 1. \tag{3.58}$$

Hence, allocative efficiency corresponds to the revenue loss in which a technically efficient firm incurs by not supplying the optimal output amounts at the existing market prices, which is equivalent to the ratio of maximum revenue under shadow prices to maximum revenue under market prices. From (3.58), it follows that if the shadow prices coincide with the market prices $\mu = p$, then the firm is allocative efficient: $AE_{R(O)}(x,y,p) = 1$. As in the input-oriented case, this also means that the Shephard output distance function satisfies the essential property linked to the correct decomposition of economic efficiency, in this particular case revenue efficiency. The same can be claimed regarding the satisfaction of the extended essential property, which states that allocative efficiency of a firm coincides with the allocative efficiency corresponding to its technical projection onto the isoquant of the technology.

The decomposition of revenue efficiency is illustrated in Fig. 3.5b. For firm (x_D, y_D), employing the input amounts x_D and facing market prices p^1, economic efficiency defines as the ratio of observed revenue to maximum revenue, i.e., $RE_D(x_D, y_D, p) = (p_1^1 y_{1D} + p_2^1 y_{2D}) / (p_1^1 y_1^R + p_2^1 y_2^R) = R_D / R(x_D, p^1)$. Subsequently, following (3.56), revenue efficiency can be decomposed into Shephard's output distance function—equivalent to Farrell's technical efficiency measure, and allocative efficiency: $RE(x_D, y_D, p) = \phi_D^* \times p^1 \cdot \widehat{y}_D / R(x_D, p^1) = TE_{R(O)}(x_D, y_D) \times AE_{R(O)}(x_D, y_D, p)$, where $p^1 \cdot \widehat{y}_D = p_1^1 y_1 / \phi_D^* + p_2^1 y_2 / \phi_D^*$. Graphically, the revenue efficiency, technical efficiency, and allocative efficiency are identified by the corresponding distances between the parallel isorevenues at the revenue-maximizing, technically efficient, and observed production plans. The interpretation of allocative efficiency as the ratio between revenues under shadow prices and market prices, (3.58), is illustrated comparing the two isorevenue lines representing maximum revenue for the two vector of prices. Particularly, let us consider $\overline{\mu}$ as the (rescaled) shadow price vector that would render the efficient projection of (x_D, y_D) revenue-efficient, i.e., $\overline{\mu} \cdot \widehat{y}_D = \overline{\mu}_1 y_{1D} / \phi_D^* + \overline{\mu}_2 y_{2D} / \phi_D^* = R(x, \overline{\mu})$, which corresponds to the dashed-dotted line tangent to the output set $P(x)$; then, relying on expression (3.58), allocative efficiency can be interpreted as $AE_{R(O)}(x_D, y_D, p^1) = p^1 \cdot \widehat{y}_D / R(x_D, p^1) = p^1 \cdot y^R(x_D, \overline{\mu}) / p^1 \cdot y^R(x_D, p^1)$. As a result, if for firm (x_D, y_D) its shadow prices μ coincided with the market prices p, then it would be allocative efficient.

3.4.2.3 Calculating and Decomposing Revenue Efficiency

In applied studies, it is possible to compute (3.56) for firm (x_o, y_o) solving the Data Envelopment Analysis programs previously presented in Sects. 3.1.1 and 3.2.2. Shephard's output distance function, representing technical efficiency ϕ^*, corresponds to the inverse of the solution to (3.25), while maximum revenue $R(x_o, p)$ can be determined by solving program (3.34). Subsequently, the ratio of observed revenue to maximum revenue can be calculated, and finally, it is possible to recover the residual allocative efficiency as the difference between technical efficiency and revenue efficiency. Additionally, a vector of optimal shadow prices μ^* can be obtained from the multiplier (dual) formulation of the technical efficiency model (3.28). This vector defines the supporting hyperplane or facet that characterizes the (weakly) efficient output subset (3.28). However, as in the input case, comparing the shadow prices with the market prices, either in absolute or in relative terms, is not as useful as it may seem in a first instance, because the piecewise linear nature of DEA allows for multiple solutions.

We conclude this section emphasizing, once again, two caveats related to the measurement and decomposition of cost and revenue inefficiency based on the standard DEA approach calculating Shephard's radial distance functions—i.e., the so-called BCC models introduced by Banker et al. (1984), which corresponds to the input and output radial models under VRS. Firstly, the likely existence of slacks that signal the possibility of individual increases in outputs amounts. Indeed, this is one well-known shortcoming of the conventional DEA program (3.25), related to the definition of a weakly efficient production frontier. Secondly, if the production technology under the variable returns to scale is non-homothetic, the interpretation of the radial input distance function as a measure of technical efficiency does not hold. Aparicio et al. (2015a, b: Proposition 3) prove that even under the assumption of constant returns to scale, the conventional DEA technology is only homothetic in the case of one single output (and, correspondingly, one single input for the output case). These authors show that in the general case of non-homothetic DEA technologies, the radial contraction (expansion) of the input (output) vector resulting in efficiency gains does not maintain allocative efficiency constant along the firm's projection to the production frontier. This result invalidates the residual nature of allocative efficiency. Again, as for the first drawback, this implies that the interpretation of the distance function as a measure of technical efficiency is not as direct as presumed in the standard theoretical literature. While the existence of slack has been previously addressed in detail, we have not discussed the consequences of non-homotheticity when decomposing economic efficiency. We comment on this matter in the following section.

3.4.3 Decomposing Cost and Revenue Efficiency Under Non-homothetic Technologies

So far, in this section, we have assumed that the technology is characterized by variable returns to scale, but no specific reference has been made to the underlying non-homotheticity assumption and the role that it plays in the decomposition and interpretation of the technical and allocative factors. This discussion is relevant because the standard DEA characterization of the input and output sets, $L(y)$ and $P(x)$, corresponding to programs (3.23) and (3.24), is in general non-homothetic. For example, for the input set $L(y)$ and even under the assumption of constant returns to scale, Aparicio et al. (2015a, b: Proposition 3) prove that this set is input homothetic only in the case of one single output. An equivalent result can be proved for the output set.

Focusing initially on the input side, if the technology was homothetic, Aparicio et al. (2015a, b) confirm that resorting to radial distance functions to characterize technical efficiency a la *Farrell* and subsequently decompose economic efficiency is appropriate. The reason is that allocative efficiency is independent of the output level and, therefore, radial input shifts leave it unchanged.[18] However, for non-homothetic technologies, they show that the use of radial measures is inadequate because the input demand functions $x^C(y, w)$ depend on the output targeted by the firm, as does the inequality between marginal rates of substitution and market prices—i.e., allocative inefficiency: $AE_{R(I)}(x, y, w)$. To restore a consistent measure of technical efficiency in the non-homothetic case, they introduce a method that takes as reference for the economic efficiency decomposition the preservation of the allocative efficiency of firms producing in the interior of the technology. This builds upon the so-called reversed approach introduced by Bogetoft et al. (2006), who propose calculating allocative efficiency without presuming that technical efficiency has already been accomplished; i.e., rather than considering allocative efficiency as a residual, it is calculated initially at the efficient output isoquant of the firm. Hence, the starting point is that it considers that the firm is inefficient from an output perspective. This implies that it might be indeed demanding the intended bundle of inputs that minimize the cost of producing the targeted output and, yet, fall short from achieving it. The reverse approach is considered in Chap. 13, represented by two rather different models in the additive framework, being the so-called standard reverse approach the one that fits better to Bogetoft et al.'s (2006) proposal. Moreover, in the last-mentioned chapter, we introduce a new way of decomposing

[18]This is a standard assumption in the parametric approach to economic efficiency measurement where the preferred functional forms impose homotheticity, for example, the case of the Cobb-Douglas specification. Even when relying on flexible functional forms such as the translog or the quadratic specifications, homotheticity is routinely imposed by restricting the value of the associated parameters, normally without testing whether this restriction holds empirically or not. For a discussion on how to decompose cost efficiency relying on the parametric approach under non-homotheticity, we refer the reader to Aparicio and Zofío (2017).

economic efficiency resorting to the general direct decomposition approach that allows us to identify the normalizing factor associated with any inefficient firm by relating the so-called price technological gap with the technical inefficiency of the mentioned firm. Consequently, the new normalizing factors do not rely on the Fenchel-Mahler inequalities derived from duality theory. Although our two reverse approaches give rise to additive decompositions, the idea of the mentioned authors can also be applied to the corresponding multiplicative decomposition, as we are going to show immediately.

Aparicio et al. (2015a, b) demonstrate that a correct definition of technical efficiency corresponds to the directional distance function, because its flexibility ensures that allocative efficiency is kept constant along the input reductions through the production possibility set when measuring technical inefficiency. Consequently, the associated cost reductions can be solely—and rightly—ascribed to technical improvements, and the decomposition is consistent.[19] From the point of view of decomposing cost efficiency, this result invalidates the residual nature of allocative efficiency and requires the use of more flexible characterizations of the technology like the directional distance function studied in Chap. 8.

The relevance of the homotheticity property when resorting to the radial input distance function to decompose economic efficiency can be illustrated by comparing the standard definition of allocative efficiency in expression (3.43), $AE_{R(I)}(x, y, w)$, taking as reference the output level y, and the allocative efficiency that would exhibit the firm at the output level that it would have produced if it had been efficient. That is, at the efficient output projection, $\widehat{y} = y/D_O(x, y)$, $D_O(x, y) \leq 1$. For this purpose, we define the following input set $L(\widehat{y} = y/D_O(x, y))$, with its corresponding strong, weak, and isoquant efficiency subsets: $\partial^S L(\widehat{y}) \subseteq \partial^W L(\widehat{y}) \subseteq \partial^{Isoq} L(\widehat{y})$. Let us consider the case of strong disposability of inputs that, using DEA methods, generates as reference benchmark the weakly efficient set: $\partial^W L(\widehat{y})$—as discussed in the preceding Sect. 3.1. Then, it is clear that $D_O(x, \widehat{y}) = 1$, because the firm is technically efficient at $\partial^W L(\widehat{y})$, and making use of the relationship (3.11), $D_O(x, \widehat{y}) = D_I(x, \widehat{y}) = 1$. Therefore, cost efficiency with respect to the output-efficient isoquant coincides with allocative efficiency:[20]

$$\begin{aligned} CE(x, \widehat{y}, w) &= \frac{C(\widehat{y}, w)}{w \cdot x} = \frac{1}{D_I(x, \widehat{y})} \times \frac{C(\widehat{y}, w)}{w \cdot x / D_I(x, \widehat{y})} = \frac{w \cdot x^C(\widehat{y}, w)}{w \cdot x} \\ &= AE^R_{R(I)}(x, \widehat{y}, w) \leq 1. \end{aligned} \tag{3.59}$$

The *reverse* (*R*) approach combines the projection of the cost-minimizing input bundle $x^C(\widehat{y}, w)$ to the efficient set of the observed output level, $\partial^W L(y)$, i.e.,

[19] Färe et al. (2019) rely on this property in their proposal to decompose profit efficiency in a multiplicative way.

[20] The allocative efficiency term corresponding to the reverse approach, $AE^R_{R(I)}(x, \widehat{y}, w)$, can be expressed in terms of the disparity between shadow prices and market prices at $\partial^W L(\widehat{y})$, as in (3.46).

$D_I(x^C(\widehat{y}, w), y)$, and the allocative efficiency of the firm with respect to $\partial^W L(\widehat{y})$, (3.59). Then,

$$CE^R(x, y, \widehat{y}, w) = \frac{1}{D_I(x^C(\widehat{y}, w), y)} \times \frac{w \cdot x^C(\widehat{y}, w)}{w \cdot x}$$
$$= TE^R_{R(I)}(x, y, \widehat{y}, w) \times AE^R_{R(I)}(x, \widehat{y}, w) \leq 1. \quad (3.60)$$

Bogetoft et al. (2006: Proposition 1) show that if the technology is input homothetic, then both the allocative efficiencies and the technical efficiencies are pairwise equal; i.e., $AE_{R(I)}(x, y, w) = AE^R_{R(I)}(x, \widehat{y}, w)$ and $TE_{R(I)}(x, y) = TE^R_{R(I)}(x, y, \widehat{y}, w)$. This latter result stems from the fact that two firms belonging to a given isoquant have the same distance to a different isoquant. In this case, $x^C(\widehat{y}, w)$ and $(x, \widehat{y})$ belong to $\partial^W L(\widehat{y})$, and therefore, their distances to $\partial^W L(y)$ are equal: $D_I(x^C(\widehat{y}, w), y) = D_I(x, y)$. Altogether, these results imply that the cost efficiencies under the standard and reversed approaches coincide: $CE(x, y, w) = CE^R(x, y, \widehat{y}, w)$.

Then, it makes no difference whether allocative efficiency is measured at the efficient input set for either the observed output level, y, or the efficient output, $\widehat{y}$. However, if the technology is non-homothetic, radially projecting the firm from the cost-efficient input bundle $x^C(\widehat{y}, w)$ to the efficient frontier of $L(y)$ (i.e., once allocative inefficiency has been solved) will not coincide with the cost-minimizing quantities $x^C(y, w)$, serving as reference for the standard Farrell approach, and therefore, both approaches differ. In general, since researchers do not know whether the firm is using inputs in excess or falling short from a targeted output, choosing the efficient set at which allocative efficiency is evaluated, either $\partial^W L(y)$ or $\partial^W L(\widehat{y})$, is not neutral.

However, as previously anticipated and despite non-homotheticity, Aparicio et al. (2015a, b) show that it is possible to keep both approaches equivalent by resorting to the input directional distance function: $\vec{D}_{DDF(I)}(x, y; g_x) = \max_{\beta} \{\beta : x - \beta g_x \in L(y)\}$, where g_x is a quantity directional vector for the inputs—we refer the reader to Chap. 8 where the additive decomposition of cost inefficiency relying on the directional distance function is presented. Then, it can be proved that the difference between the standard and reverse cost efficiencies is equal to the value of the directional distance function, as long as the directional vector g is chosen in a way that allocative efficiency is kept constant at both reference sets: $\partial^W L(y)$ and $\partial^W L(\widehat{y})$. This result relies on the flexibility of the directional distance function and an additive decomposition of cost inefficiency.

The decomposition of cost efficiency following the standard and reverse approaches for a non-homothetic technology is illustrated in Fig. 3.6a. Here, the input isoquants representing the efficient input sets for each level of output, y and $\widehat{y}$, are not parallel expansions along ray vectors departing from the origin, as would be the case for homothetic technologies, and where the marginal rate of substitution is constant—graphically corresponding to the slope of the successive isoquants.

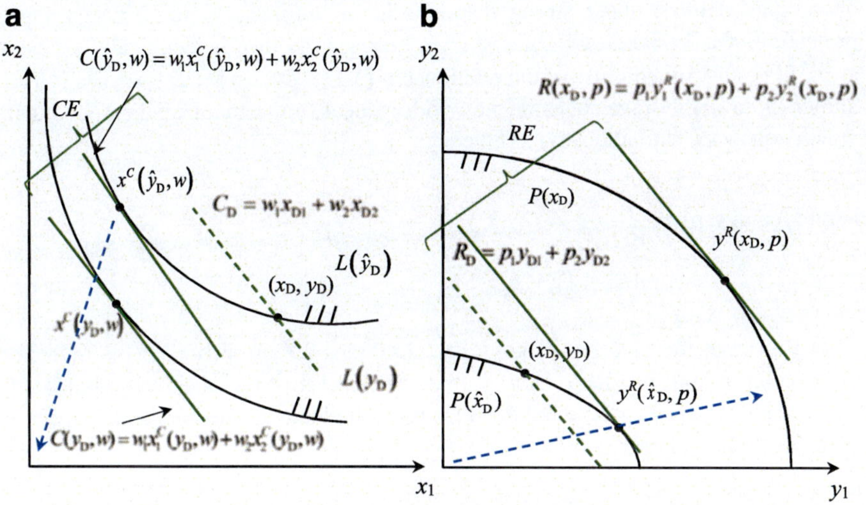

Fig. 3.6 (**a**, **b**) Cost and revenue efficiency under non-homotheticity

Consequently, for each output level y, the optimal input bundle $x^C(y, w)$ presents different proportions. This implies that allocative efficiency, measured with respect to $\partial^W L(y)$ and $\partial^W L(\widehat{y})$, is not equal, and the standard and reversed decompositions yield different results. For example, for firm (x_D, y_D), the standard definition of allocative efficiency illustrated in Fig. 3.5a is $AE_{R(I)}(x, y, w) = w \cdot x^C(y_D, w) / w \cdot \widehat{x}_D$, which now differs from the reverse approach $AE^R_{R(I)}(x, \widehat{y}, w) = w \cdot x^C(\widehat{y}_D, w) / w \cdot x_D$, while in the case of homothetic technologies, they coincide. Moreover, it can be seen that in the reverse approach, once (x_D, y_D) achieves allocative efficiency by adopting the optimal input quantities $x^C(\widehat{y}_D, w)$, projecting it radially to the reference input amounts that allow producing the observed output level y_D efficiently results in a different benchmark from the cost-minimizing input quantities: $x^C(\widehat{y}_D, w)/D_I(x^C(\widehat{y}_D, w), y_D) \neq x^C(y_D, w)$. The difference between the two corresponds to an additional allocative term that was named "second order" allocative efficiency by Bogetoft et al. (2006), i.e. $AAE_{R(I)}(x_D, y_D, \widehat{y}_D, w) = w \cdot x^C(y_D, w) / w \cdot x^C(\widehat{y}_D, w)/D_I(x^C(\widehat{y}_D, w), y_D)$. This implies that the input distance function does not measure the cost gap between minimum cost at both output levels and, subsequently, between $CE(x_D, y_D, w)$ and $CE^R(x_D, \widehat{y}_D, w)$.

The comparison between the standard and reverse decompositions of revenue efficiency mirrors the one presented above. In this case, we presume that the firm intends to produce with the observed amount of inputs x but ends up using a larger amount than necessary to produce the observed output level y, i.e., $\widehat{x} = x/D_I(x, y)$, $D_I(x, y) \leq 1$. Then, we can compare the standard allocative efficiency term as defined in (3.55), $AE_{R(O)}(x, y, p)$, and the allocative efficiency of $(\widehat{x}, y)$ at the efficient output subset $\partial^W P(\widehat{x})$ of the corresponding production possibility set $P(\widehat{x} = x/D_I(x, y))$, once again defined under strong disposability of outputs. At the efficient input projection, it is verified that $D_I(\widehat{x}, y) = 1$, because the firm is technically efficient at $\partial^W P(\widehat{x})$, and, making use of the relationship (3.12), $D_I(\widehat{x}, y) = D_O(\widehat{x}, y) = 1$. This allows us to define revenue efficiency with respect to the input efficient isoquant, which coincides with allocative efficiency:[21]

$$\begin{aligned} RE(\widehat{x}, y, p) &= \frac{p \cdot y}{R(\widehat{x}, p)} = D_O(\widehat{x}, y) \times \frac{p \cdot y / D_O(\widehat{x}, y)}{R(\widehat{x}, p)} = \frac{p \cdot y}{p \cdot y^R(\widehat{x}, p)} \\ &= AE^R_{R(O)}(\widehat{x}, y, p) \leq 1. \end{aligned} \tag{3.61}$$

In this case, the *reverse* (*R*) approach combines the projection of the revenue-maximizing output bundle $y^R(\widehat{x}, p)$ to the efficient set of the observed input level, $\partial^W P(x)$, i.e., $D_O(x, y^R(\widehat{x}, p))$, and the allocative efficiency of the firm with respect to $\partial^W P(\widehat{x})$, (3.61). Then,

$$\begin{aligned} RE^R(x, \widehat{x}, y, p) &= D_O(x, y^R(\widehat{x}, p)) \times \frac{p \cdot y^R(\widehat{x}, p)}{R(\widehat{x}, p)} \\ &= TE^R_{R(O)}(x, \widehat{x}, y, p) \times AE^R_{R(O)}(\widehat{x}, y, p) \leq 1. \end{aligned} \tag{3.62}$$

As before, mirroring Bogetoft et al. (2006: Proposition 1) for the output case, if the technology is output homothetic, then both the allocative efficiencies and the technical efficiencies are pairwise equal, i.e., $AE_{R(O)}(x, y, p) = AE^R_{R(O)}(\widehat{x}, y, p)$ and $TE_{R(O)}(x, y) = TE^R_{R(O)}(x, \widehat{x}, y, p)$. Again, the latter result holds because two firms belonging to the same isoquant have the same distance to a different isoquant. Here, $y^R(\widehat{x}, p)$ and $(\widehat{x}, p)$ belong to $\partial^W P(\widehat{x})$, and therefore, their distances to $\partial^W P(x)$ are the same: $D_O(x, y^R(\widehat{x}, p)) = D_O(x, y)$. These results imply the equivalence between the revenue efficiencies corresponding to the standard and reversed approaches.

Therefore, under output homotheticity, it does not matter what particular isoquant, x or $\widehat{x}$, is considered as reference when decomposing revenue efficiency. However, in the general non-homothetic case, the radial projection of the firm from its revenue-efficient output bundle $y^R(\widehat{x}, p)$ to the efficient frontier of $P(x)$ (after allocative inefficiency has been solved) will not coincide with the revenue-maximizing quantities $y^R(x, p)$, and both approaches differ. As already remarked, since researchers ignore if the firm is falling short from its potential output or is overusing the amount of input it had initially planned, choosing the efficient set at which allocative efficiency is evaluated, either $\partial^W P(x)$ or $\partial^W P(\widehat{x})$, yields different results.

The model proposed by Aparicio et al. (2015a, b) to account for non-homotheticity can be easily adapted to the output case. Now, relying on the

[21] Now, the reverse allocative efficiency term corresponding $AE^R_{R(O)}(\widehat{x}, y, p)$ can be expressed in terms of the disparity between shadow prices and market prices at $\partial^W P(\widehat{x})$, as in (3.58).

output directional distance function, $D_{DDF(O)}\left(x,y;g_y\right) = \max_{\beta}\left\{\beta : y+\beta g_y \in P(x)\right\}$—where g_y is now a quantity directional vector for the outputs, it is possible to keep the equality between both approaches by endogenizing the directional vector g_y, so the value of the reverse allocative efficiency, when measured on $\partial^W P(\widehat{x})$, is kept constant when projecting the observation to $\partial^W P(x)$. Then, the difference between the standard and reverse revenue efficiencies, $RE(x,y,p)$ and $RE(\widehat{x},y,p)$, is equal to the value of the directional distance function.

The decomposition of revenue efficiency following the standard and reverse approaches is illustrated in Fig. 3.6b for a non-homothetic technology. In this occasion, the output isoquants representing the efficient output sets for each level of input x are not parallel contractions along ray vectors departing from the origin and where the marginal rates of output transformation are equal. Therefore, for each input level x, the optimal output bundle $y^R(x,p)$ consists of different output mixes. This implies that allocative efficiency, measured at $\partial^W P(x)$ and $\partial^W P(\widehat{x})$, will likely yield different values, and the standard and reversed decompositions differ. For example, the standard definition of allocative efficiency for firm (x_D, y_D), as presented in Fig. 3.5b, is $AE_{R(O)}(x,y,p) = p\cdot\widehat{y}_D \,/\, p\cdot y^R(x_D,p)$, which differs from the reverse approach $AE^R_{R(O)}(\widehat{x},y,p) = p\cdot y_D \,/\, p\cdot y^R(\widehat{x}_D,p)$, while for homothetic technologies, they are equal. Finally, it can be seen that in the reverse approach, once (x_D, y_D) achieves allocative efficiency by adopting the optimal output quantities $y^R(\widehat{x},p)$, projecting it radially by expanding the output amounts that can be produced employing efficiently the observed input level x_D results in a benchmark that differs from the revenue-maximizing output quantities: $y^R(\widehat{x}_D,p) \,/\, D_O(x_D, y^R(\widehat{x}_D,p)) \neq y^R(x_D,p)$. As before, to account for the disparity, it is necessary to define a residual "second-order" allocative efficiency, i.e. $AAE^R_{R(O)}(x_D,\widehat{x}_D,y_D,p) = p\cdot y^R(\widehat{x}_D,p) \,/\, D_O(x_D, y^R(\widehat{x}_D,p)) \,/\, p\cdot y^R(x_D,p)$, which implies that the output distance function does not measure the revenue gap separating maximum revenue at both input levels and, consequently, between $RE(x_D,y_D,p)$ and $RE^R(\widehat{x}_D,y_D,p)$.

3.5 Empirical Illustration of the Radial Cost and Revenue Efficiency Models

In this section, we illustrate the calculation and decomposition of the cost and revenue efficiency measures using their corresponding Shephard's radial distance functions. Table 3.1 replicates the input and output production possibility sets presented in Sect. 2.6 of Chap. 2. The particularities of this dataset can be consulted there. A graphical representation is depicted in Figs. 3.7 and 3.8.

The functions included in the Benchmarking Economic Efficiency package for the Julia language that compute these measures, including their decompositions into technical and allocative efficiencies, are the following: "`deacost(X, Y, W, names=FIRMS)` and `dearevenue(X, Y, P, names=FIRMS)`".

Table 3.1 Example data illustrating the cost and revenue efficiency models

	Model					
	Input orientation Cost			Output orientation Revenue		
Firm	x_1	x_2	y	x	y_1	y_2
A	2	2	1	1	7	7
B	1	4	1	1	4	8
C	4	1	1	1	8	4
D	4	3	1	1	3	5
E	5	5	1	1	3	3
F	6	1	1	1	8	2
G	2	5	1	1	6	4
H	1.6	8	1	1	1.5	5
Prices	$w_1 = 1$	$w_2 = 1$			$p_1 = 1$	$p_2 = 1$

On a first stage, these functions solve problems (3.23) and (3.25) to calculate the corresponding technical efficiency measures: either $\theta^* = TE_{R(I)}(x, y) \equiv 1/D_I(x, y)$ or $\xi^* = 1/\, D_O(x, y) \equiv 1/\, TE_{R(O)}(x, y) = 1/\phi^*$. As previously justified in Sect. 3.2.1, these calculations are carried out under the default assumptions of (a) variable returns to scale and (b) strong disposability of input and outputs.[22] Subsequently, they solve problem (3.33) for minimum cost and problem (3.34) for maximum revenue. The last step calculates allocative efficiencies as residuals. Economic, technical, and allocative efficiencies are displayed once the calculations have been completed.

3.5.1 *The Radial Cost Efficiency Model*

We rely on the open (web-based) Jupyter Notebook interface to illustrate these economic models.[23] However, it can be implemented in any integrated development environment (IDE) of preference. To calculate and decompose the cost efficiency model based on Shephard's input distance function according to (3.44), type the following code in the input window "`In[]:`," and execute it. The corresponding results are shown in the output window, "`Out[]:`," of Table 3.2.

We can identify reference peers for each firm using the "peersmatrix" function with the corresponding economic or technical model. For the economic model,

[22] Both options can be easily changed to constant returns and weak disposability. The syntax necessary to calculate both options simultaneously is the following: `deacost(X, Y, W, rts = :CRS, dispos = :Weak, names=FIRMS)`, and `dearevenue(X, Y, W, rts = :CRS, dispos = :Weak, names=FIRMS)`.

[23] We refer the reader to Sect. 2.6.1 in Chap. 2 for the installation of the "Benchmarking Economic Efficiency" package. All Jupyter Notebooks implementing the different economic models in this book can be downloaded from the reference site: http://www.benchmarkingeconomicefficiency.com.

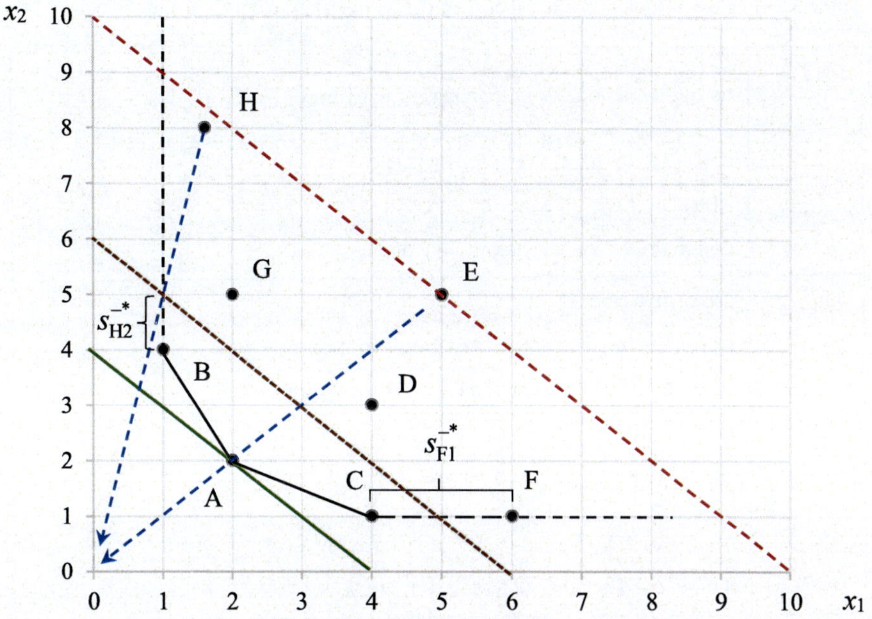

Fig. 3.7 Example of the radial cost efficiency model using BEE for Julia

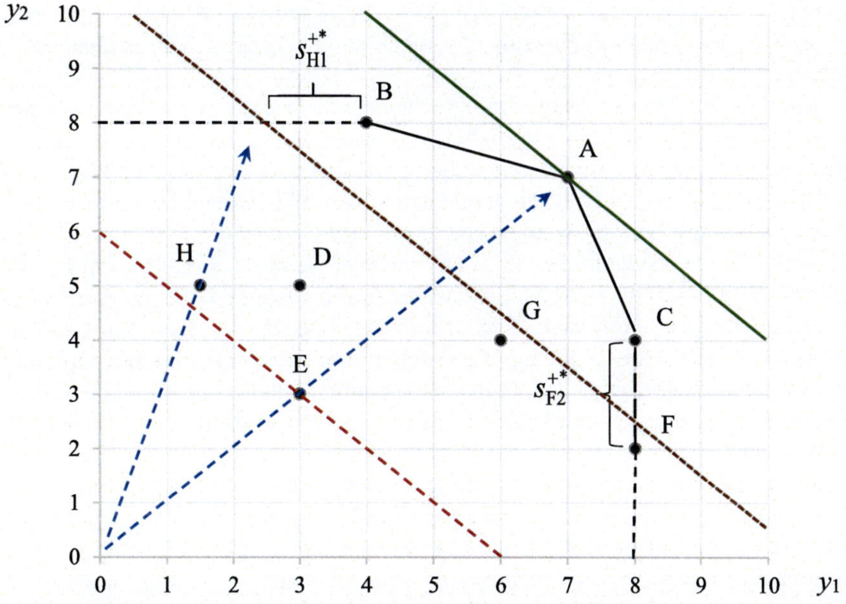

Fig. 3.8 Example of the radial revenue efficiency model using BEE for Julia

Table 3.2 Implementation of the radial cost efficiency model using BEE for Julia

In[]:

```
using DataEnvelopmentAnalysis
using BenchmarkingEconomicEfficiency

X = [2 2; 1 4; 4 1; 4 3; 5 5; 6 1; 2 5; 1.6 8];
Y = [1; 1; 1; 1; 1; 1; 1; 1];
W = [1 1; 1 1; 1 1; 1 1; 1 1; 1 1; 1 1; 1 1];
FIRMS = ["A", "B", "C", "D", "E", "F", "G", "H"];

deacost(X, Y, W, names = FIRMS)
```

Out[]:

```
Cost DEA Model
DMUs = 8; Inputs = 2; Outputs = 1
Orientation = Input; Returns to Scale = VRS
```

	Cost	Technical	Allocative
A	1.0	1.0	1.0
B	0.8	1.0	0.8
C	0.8	1.0	0.8
D	0.571	0.6	0.952
E	0.4	0.4	1.0
F	0.571	1.0	0.571
G	0.571	0.667	0.857
H	0.417	0.625	0.667

executing "`peersmatrix(deacost(X, Y, W, names = FIRMS))`" returns firm A as the benchmark minimizing cost for all remaining firms. This is illustrated, once again, in Fig. 3.7.

Regarding the internal calculation of technical efficiency, it is possible to obtain all the information concerning the efficiency scores and accompanying input and output slacks by solving the corresponding BEE function, as shown in Table 3.3. Note that we need to specify the input orientation, as well as variable returns to scale; see the code in the "`In[]:`" window.

Looking at the results in the "`Out[]:`" window, we observe that four firms, A, B, C, and F, conform the weakly efficient subset of the input production possibility set, corresponding to expression (3.15). Moreover, since the first three firms do not present any slacks in any of the input and output dimensions, they comply with the Pareto-Koopmans efficiency definition corresponding to the strongly efficient input production possibility set, (3.13). In this regard, firm F uses the first input in excess by two units.

As before, it is also of interest to identify the reference technological benchmarks of the radial input measure. A matrix of the peers conforming the weakly efficient subset of the input production possibility set can be obtained using the following syntax: "`peersmatrix(dea(X, Y, orient = :Input, rts = :VRS, names = FIRMS))`". The output is shown in Table 3.4. The four firms, A, B, C, and F, present unit values in the main diagonal of the square ($J \times J$) matrix containing their own

Table 3.3 Calculating the radial input efficiency measure using BEE for Julia

In[]:

```
dea(X, Y, orient = :Input, rts = :VRS, names = FIRMS)
```

Out[]:

```
Radial DEA Model
DMUs = 8; Inputs = 2; Outputs = 1
Orientation = Input; Returns to Scale = VRS
```

	efficiency	slackX1	slackX2	slackY1
A	1.0	0.0	0.0	0.0
B	1.0	0.0	0.0	0.0
C	1.0	0.0	0.0	0.0
D	0.6	0.0	0.0	0.0
E	0.4	0.0	0.0	0.0
F	1.0	2.0	0.0	0.0
G	0.667	0.0	0.0	0.0
H	0.625	0.0	1.0	0.0

Table 3.4 Reference peers of the radial input efficiency measure model using BEE for Julia

In[]:

```
peersmatrix(dea(X, Y, orient = :Input, rts = :VRS, names =
FIRMS))
```

Out[]:

1.0	.	.	.	.	.	.	.
.	1.0	.	.	.	.	.	.
.	.	1.0	.	.	.	.	.
0.8	.	0.2	.	.	.	.	.
1.0	.	.	.	.	.	.	.
.	.	.	.	.	1.0	.	.
0.333333	0.666667	.	.	.	.	.	.
.	1.0	.	.	.	.	.	.

intensity variables λ_j=1, while firms E, G, and H are projected to other firms whose $\lambda_j >$ 0.

Figure 3.7 illustrates the results for the cost efficiency model. Regarding the weakly and strongly efficient subsets of the input set, it can be easily seen that firm F, presenting a slack in the first input, does not belong to the strong frontier defined by firms A, B, and C. Commenting now on firm E, we see that its cost inefficiency is equal to 0.4=4/10 (graphically represented by the distance between the isocost lines passing through firm E and firm A minimizing cost) and is solely due to technical reasons, since its relative input mix is exactly the same as that of the cost-minimizing firm A. Graphically, this implies that the radial efficient projection of firm E is firm A. The rest of either the technically efficient or inefficient firms are allocative inefficient. For the first group, firms B and C, despite the fact that they lay on the strongly efficient frontier, fail to minimize cost given the market prices. For the rest of the firms, their efficient projections on the weakly efficient frontier do not minimize cost either. If we consider firm H, whose cost efficiency is 0.417=4/9.6, we see that its projection on the vertical extension of the strongly efficient frontier—departing from B—leaves room for a slack amount of one unit in the second input. This implies that the observed cost at the projection is equal to 6, and hence, its technical efficiency is 0.625=6/9.6, and therefore, its allocative inefficiency is 0.667=4/6 (graphically represented by the distance between the isocost lines passing through its projection on the weakly efficient frontier and firm A).

The case of firm H illustrates that technical efficiency may be overestimated when using radial efficiency measures, thereby resulting in allocative inefficiency underestimation. This is the consequence of adhering to the notion of Pareto-Koopmans efficiency represented by the strongly efficient set. Indeed, if the slack in the second input was taken into account by considering firm B as the actual (strongly) efficiency projection, technical efficiency would be 0.521=5/9.6 and allocative efficiency 0.8=4/5. This situation is even clearer for firm F, whose technical efficiency would be 0.714=5/7 if firm C was considered as reference benchmark (by eliminating the slack in the first input), while its allocative efficiency would be 0.8=4/5. Compare these values to 1 and 0.571, which are the scores reported by the standard implementation of the cost efficiency model. This has led to further research on how to measure efficiency considering only strongly efficient benchmarks, resulting in new proposals such as the Russell efficiency measure presented in Chap. 5. Alternatively, one may rely on some additive technical efficiency measures, also presented in the second part of this book, which do not suffer from this drawback. A suitable candidate is the weakly additive efficiency measure discussed in Chap. 7. There is still another interesting alternative based on reverse directional distance functions, RDDFs; see Chap. 12. According to Pastor et al. (2016), each weak efficiency measure can be transformed into a strong RDDF just by projecting their benchmarks onto the strong efficient subset by means of an appropriate DEA program, such as the program associated with each DEA strong efficiency measure. Particularly, we prefer to use the nonlinear program developed by Aparicio et al. (2007) to find the closest strong efficient projection, which allows us to define a new strong RDDF. Last, but not least, firms D and G in Fig. 3.7, whose efficient projections do not result in individual slacks, exhibit a combination of both technical and allocative inefficiencies.

Table 3.5 Implementation of the radial revenue efficiency model using BEE for Julia

In[]:

```
using DataEnvelopmentAnalysis
using BenchmarkingEconomicEfficiency

X = [1; 1; 1; 1; 1; 1; 1; 1];
Y = [7 7; 4 8; 8 4; 3 5; 3 3; 8 2; 6 4; 1.5 5];
P = [1 1; 1 1; 1 1; 1 1; 1 1; 1 1; 1 1; 1 1];
FIRMS = ["A", "B", "C", "D", "E", "F", "G", "H"];

dearevenue(X, Y, P, names = FIRMS)
```

Out[]:

```
Revenue DEA Model
DMUs = 8; Inputs = 1; Outputs = 2
Orientation = Output; Returns to Scale = VRS
```

	Revenue	Technical	Allocative
A	1.0	1.0	1.0
B	0.857	1.0	0.857
C	0.857	1.0	0.857
D	0.571	0.643	0.889
E	0.429	0.429	1.0
F	0.714	1.0	0.714
G	0.714	0.786	0.909
H	0.464	0.625	0.743

3.5.2 The Radial Revenue Efficiency Model

The second radial model is concerned with the measurement of revenue efficiency based on Shephard's output distance function, equivalent to Farrell's radial output measure of technical efficiency. In this case, to calculate and decompose revenue efficiency following expression (3.56), we rely on the syntax presented in the input window "`In[]:`," of Table 3.5. The corresponding results are shown in the output window, "`Out[]:`," reporting the revenue, technical, and allocative efficiencies.

Again, to know the reference set for the evaluation of revenue inefficiency, we rely on the "peers" function. For this model, we execute "`peersmatrix(dearevenue(X, Y, P, names = FIRMS))`". The output identifies firm A as the benchmark maximizing revenue for the rest of the firms (see Fig. 3.8).

To gain insight on the underlying two-stage technical model, solving the efficiency scores in the first stage, along with any possible slacks in the second stage, one runs the corresponding BEE function as presented in Table 3.6; see the "`In[]:`" window. As for the technical efficiency scores, the function `dea(X, Y, orient = :Output, rts=:VRS, names = FIRMS)` returns values greater than one, corresponding to the solution of problem (3.25), i.e., the inverse

Table 3.6 Calculating the radial output efficiency measure using BEE for Julia

In[]:

```
dea(X, Y, orient = :Output, rts = :VRS, names = FIRMS)
```

Out[]:

```
Radial DEA Model
DMUs = 8; Inputs = 1; Outputs = 2
Orientation = Output; Returns to Scale = VRS
```

	efficiency	slackX1	slackY1	slackY2
A	1.0	0.0	0.0	0.0
B	1.0	0.0	0.0	0.0
C	1.0	0.0	0.0	0.0
D	1.556	0.0	0.0	0.0
E	2.333	0.0	0.0	0.0
F	1.0	0.0	0.0	2.0
G	1.272	0.0	0.0	0.0
H	1.6	0.0	1.6	0.0

of Shephard's output distance function: $D_O(x, y)^{-1} \equiv TE_{R(O)}(x, y)^{-1} = \phi^{-1} = \xi$.[24] Besides these scores, the function solves problem (3.26), calculating the values of the input and output slacks. Again, in the syntax of the function, notice the explicit consideration of the output orientation as well as the choice of variable returns to scale, consistent with the assumptions of the model. In this example, firms A, B, C, and F define the weakly efficient subset of the output correspondence, given by expression (3.16). This is signaled by their unitary technical efficiency scores. However, based on the information provided by the slacks, only the first three firms define the strongly efficient frontier (3.14), presenting null slack values. In this regard, firm F falls short by two units of achieving the efficient amount of the second output, thereby belonging to the weakly efficient frontier.

The reference benchmarks for the output-oriented technical inefficiency model can be recovered using the "peers" function, i.e., "`peersmatrix(dea(X, Y, orient = :Output, rts = :VRS, names = FIRMS))`". The output, shown in matrix form in Table 3.7, confirms that the reference benchmark for firm F is firm C.

Figure 3.8 illustrates the results for the revenue efficiency model. For firm E, we observe that given the maximum observed revenue at firm A, its revenue efficiency is equal to 0.429=6/14. This value is graphically represented by the Euclidean distance between the isorevenue lines passing through both firms. We also observe that its radial projection keeping the output bundle constant corresponds to firm A precisely, indicating that firm E is allocative efficient. Consequently, the only source of economic inefficiency is technological. All other firms are allocative inefficient. Particularly, while firms B, C, and F are technically efficient, they fail to supply the optimal amounts of outputs that maximize revenue given the market prices. The rest

[24] When calculating the decomposition of revenue efficiency as presented in Table 3.5, the function `dearevenue(X, Y, P, names = FIRMS)` reports the inverse of these efficiency scores.

Table 3.7 Reference peers of the radial output efficiency measure model using BEE for Julia

In[]:

```
peersmatrix(dea(X, Y, orient = :Output, rts = :VRS, names =
FIRMS))
```

Out[]:

```
1.0     .       .       .   .   .   .   .
 .      1.0     .       .   .   .   .   .
 .       .      1.0     .   .   .   .   .
0.222   0.778   .       .   .   .   .   .
1.0      .      .       .   .   .   .   .
 .       .      1.0     .   .   .   .   .
0.364    .      0.636   .   .   .   .   .
 .      1.0     .       .   .   .   .   .
```

of the firms are both technical and allocative inefficient. The case of firms F and H is worth commenting since, as in the cost case, they show that using the radial output measure results in the overestimation of technical efficiencies and the underestimation of allocative inefficiencies. The reason is once again the existence of slacks in the second and first output, respectively. For firm F, whose revenue inefficiency is 0.714=10/14, it is attributed in full to the allocative component using the standard radial decomposition. However, if we were to consider firm C as its reference peer—i.e., its technically efficient projection net of individual slacks, the foregone revenue due to technical reasons would be equal to 2 (since prices are unitary), resulting in a revenue efficiency score due to technical inefficiencies of 0.833=10/12 and, consequently, an associated allocative inefficiency score of 0.857=12/14. The same situation is observed for firm H, whose technical projection on the horizontal extension from firm B, representing part of the weakly efficient subset of the output correspondence, results in a slack in the first output equal to 1.6. Hence, the revenue inefficiency associated with the technical measure, equal to 0.625=6.5/10.4, differs from the one accounting for the slacks that would be 0.542=6.5/12, with the allocative inefficiencies adjusting accordingly from 0.743=10.4/14 to 0.857=12/14. The former is graphically represented by the distance between the isorevenue lines passing through its projection on the weakly efficient frontier and firm A maximizing revenue. Nevertheless, as previously commented for the cost efficiency case, other additive models addressing this issue and based on alternatives definitions of technical efficiency are reviewed in this book.

3.5.3 An Application: Taiwanese Banking Industry

We close this empirical section calculating and decomposing cost and revenue efficiency using a dataset of 31 Taiwanese banks observed in 2010, compiled by Juo et al. (2015). A brief presentation of the data, including descriptive statistics, can be found in Sect. 2.6.2 of Chap. 2. We remark that we are using these data to illustrate the different models and therefore do not aim at analyzing the economic performance of the Taiwanese banking industry or any individual bank. In this dataset, each bank presents its own prices, (w_o, p_o), which are taken as reference in the objective functions of programs (3.33) and (3.34), when calculating minimum cost and maximum revenue using the BEE functions "`deacost(X, Y, W, names=FIRMS)`" and "`dearevenue(X, Y, P, names=FIRMS)`."

Table 3.8 presents the cost and revenue efficiency scores along with their corresponding technical and allocative factors. Both models are solved under the assumptions of variable returns to scale and strong disposability of inputs and outputs, respectively. Descriptive statistics for each efficiency score are provided at the bottom. Results show that, on average, the industry could reduce cost by 32.9%=(1−0.672)×100 and increase revenue by 35.7%=1/0.737×100. As many as six banks are cost-efficient, while five banks are revenue-efficient. Interestingly, although both dimensions are independent when calculating economic efficiency, four banks are both cost- and revenue-efficient: no. 1, no. 2, no. 5, and no. 10. This suggests that successful managers are capable of achieving high levels of economic performance on both sides of the production process (operations and sales). Indeed, as shown in the following chapters, this is the case since these banks tend to exhibit larger values of profitability efficiency and profit efficiency. Overall, the Spearman rank correlation between both measures is rather high, $\rho(CE(x, y, w), RE(x, y, p)) = 0.923$, showing their agreement. In this respect, the largest difference in performance is found for bank no. 26 that is cost-efficient, while its revenue efficiency is 0.898.

As for the technical and allocative sources of inefficiency, descriptive statistics show that both are equally relevant on average. Average radial input technical efficiency stands at 0.799, while cost allocative efficiency is 0.815. On the revenue side, average radial output technical efficiency is 0.845, while revenue allocative efficiency is 0.840. Also, the fact that the radial input and output technical efficiencies measures are highly correlated, with a Spearman coefficient of $\rho(TE_{R(I)}(x, y), TE_{R(O)}(x, y)) = 0.995$, suggests that the industry is characterized by relatively mild variable returns to scale—as both scores are equivalent under CRS. The disparity in the rankings for the allocative component is relatively higher with $\rho(AE_{R(I)}(x, y, w), AE_{R(O)}(x, y, p)) = 0.678$.

Finally, to establish whether individual input reductions or output increases are still feasible beyond the radial contractions or expansions, we report in Table 3.9 the magnitude of the input and output slacks. Their values are recovered using the corresponding BEE functions as presented above. The presence of inputs slacks is pervasive. Most banks present a clear excess in labor (x_2) from both the input and the output perspectives. In the input-oriented model, its average quantity amounts to 486.8 million TWD. While it is not the largest quantity in absolute value, it represents the highest percentage of the average quantities across inputs, reaching 12.7%. Indeed, in the input model, the largest slack amount corresponds to financial funds (x_1), with an average value of 3175.5 million TWD. However, this quantity represents just 0.4% of the average amount of this input. Alternatively, in the output-oriented model, the largest output slack amount in percentage terms is observed in

Table 3.8 Decomposition of cost and revenue efficiency based on Shephard's radial distance functions

Bank	Cost efficiency, eq. (3.44)			Revenue efficiency, eq. (3.56)		
	Cost Eff. $CE(x,y,w)$	Technical Eff. $TE_{R(I)}(x,y)$	Allocative Effi. $AE_{R(I)}(x,y,w)$	Revenue Eff. $RE(x,y,p)$	Technical Eff. $TE_{R(O)}(x,y)$	Allocative Eff. $AE_{R(O)}(x,y,p)$
1	1.000	1.000	1.000	1.000	1.000	1.000
2	1.000	1.000	1.000	1.000	1.000	1.000
3	0.922	1.000	0.922	0.919	1.000	0.919
4	0.597	0.647	0.922	0.508	0.734	0.691
5	1.000	1.000	1.000	1.000	1.000	1.000
6	0.960	1.000	0.960	1.000	1.000	1.000
7	0.990	1.000	0.990	0.965	1.000	0.965
8	0.811	0.944	0.860	0.945	0.948	0.996
9	0.704	0.935	0.753	0.928	0.942	0.985
10	1.000	1.000	1.000	1.000	1.000	1.000
11	0.544	0.710	0.767	0.571	0.722	0.791
12	0.788	0.887	0.888	0.836	0.901	0.928
13	0.315	0.499	0.632	0.104	0.592	0.176
14	1.000	1.000	1.000	0.995	1.000	0.995
15	0.779	0.842	0.925	0.859	0.891	0.965
16	0.127	0.228	0.559	0.128	0.446	0.288
17	0.467	0.824	0.567	0.823	0.837	0.982
18	0.641	0.856	0.749	0.861	0.880	0.979
19	0.324	0.482	0.673	0.450	0.614	0.733
20	0.539	0.811	0.665	0.682	0.838	0.814
21	0.744	1.000	0.744	0.947	1.000	0.947
22	0.388	0.601	0.646	0.443	0.696	0.636
23	0.250	0.373	0.668	0.350	0.573	0.612
24	0.806	0.967	0.833	0.951	0.968	0.982
25	0.610	0.725	0.841	0.724	0.772	0.937
26	1.000	1.000	1.000	0.898	1.000	0.898
27	0.301	0.346	0.870	0.567	0.578	0.982
28	0.282	0.488	0.579	0.402	0.610	0.659
29	0.646	1.000	0.646	0.785	1.000	0.785
30	0.789	0.893	0.884	0.896	0.900	0.996
31	0.512	0.702	0.729	0.299	0.743	0.403
Average	0.672	0.799	0.815	0.737	0.845	0.840
Median	0.704	0.887	0.841	0.859	0.900	0.947
Maximum	1.000	1.000	1.000	1.000	1.000	1.000
Minimum	0.127	0.228	0.559	0.104	0.446	0.176
Std. Dev.	0.270	0.232	0.149	0.275	0.169	0.222

Table 3.9 Input and output slacks in the cost and revenue efficiency models

Bank	Slacks in the cost efficiency model, eq. (3.24)					Slacks in the revenue efficiency model, eq. (3.26)				
	Funds (x_1) s_1^-	Labor (x_2) s_2^-	Ph. Capital (x_3) s_3^-	Investments (y_1) s_1^+	Loans (y_2) s_2^+	Funds (x_1) s_1^-	Labor (x_2) s_2^-	Ph. Capital (x_3) s_3^-	Investments (y_1) s_1^+	Loans (y_2) s_2^+
1	0.0	0.0	0.0	0.0	0.0	0.0	0.0	0.0	0.0	0.0
2	0.0	0.0	0.0	0.0	0.0	0.0	0.0	0.0	0.0	0.0
3	0.0	0.0	0.0	0.0	0.0	0.0	0.0	0.0	0.0	0.0
4	0.0	90.5	0.0	4,418.7	0.0	0.0	210.0	0.0	7,113.7	0.0
5	0.0	0.0	0.0	0.0	0.0	0.0	0.0	0.0	0.0	0.0
6	0.0	0.0	0.0	0.0	0.0	0.0	0.0	0.0	0.0	0.0
7	0.0	0.0	0.0	0.0	0.0	0.0	0.0	0.0	0.0	0.0
8	0.0	711.5	3,446.0	0.0	0.0	0.0	739.0	3,347.3	0.0	0.0
9	0.0	1,740.6	8,277.1	0.0	0.0	0.0	1,840.9	8,492.1	0.0	0.0
10	0.0	0.0	0.0	0.0	0.0	0.0	0.0	0.0	0.0	0.0
11	0.0	1,050.3	6,377.9	0.0	0.0	0.0	1,551.4	9,045.5	0.0	0.0
12	0.0	0.0	1,876.2	0.0	0.0	0.0	0.0	1,929.4	0.0	0.0
13	0.0	911.0	2,025.5	4,312.3	0.0	0.0	1,951.9	4,260.5	12,936.6	0.0
14	0.0	0.0	0.0	0.0	0.0	0.0	0.0	0.0	0.0	0.0
15	0.0	0.0	2,448.5	0.0	0.0	0.0	337.5	0.0	0.0	13,700.0
16	0.0	182.2	900.0	1,444.0	11,774.0	0.0	1,225.8	4,627.6	9,770.8	0.0
17	0.0	2,534.2	7,394.4	0.0	0.0	0.0	3,122.8	8,994.7	0.0	0.0
18	0.0	1,464.3	0.0	0.0	0.0	0.0	1,745.7	0.0	0.0	0.0
19	0.0	267.1	871.7	0.0	0.0	0.0	747.7	1,952.1	0.0	0.0
20	72,067.1	927.8	0.0	3,252.0	0.0	80,613.5	1,148.0	0.0	7,617.6	0.0
21	0.0	0.0	0.0	0.0	0.0	0.0	0.0	0.0	0.0	0.0
22	0.0	560.9	3,721.4	10,260.9	0.0	0.0	1,017.0	6,326.2	18,303.6	0.0
23	0.0	185.8	1,918.2	4,355.8	0.0	0.0	708.9	5,474.0	13,701.7	0.0
24	0.0	1,507.8	1,557.5	0.0	0.0	0.0	1,565.8	1,616.4	0.0	0.0
25	0.0	501.9	0.0	28,836.1	0.0	0.0	740.8	0.0	39,044.5	0.0
26	0.0	0.0	0.0	0.0	0.0	0.0	0.0	0.0	0.0	0.0
27	2,910.0	67.7	0.0	1,896.6	0.0	0.0	409.1	182.1	7,639.0	0.0
28	23,463.3	309.6	0.0	399.5	0.0	10,850.5	651.1	0.0	12,956.4	0.0
29	0.0	0.0	0.0	0.0	0.0	0.0	0.0	0.0	0.0	0.0
30	0.0	909.1	0.0	0.0	0.0	0.0	1,042.4	0.0	0.0	0.0
31	0.0	1,168.8	1,140.6	19,737.6	0.0	0.0	1,717.2	1,708.9	29,414.5	0.0
Average	3,175.5	486.8	1,353.4	2,545.6	379.8	2,950.5	724.9	1,869.6	5,112.9	441.9
Median	0.0	182.2	0.0	0.0	0.0	0.0	651.1	0.0	0.0	0.0
Maximum	72,067.1	2,534.2	8,277.1	28,836.1	11,774.0	80,613.5	3,122.8	9,045.5	39,044.5	13,700.0
Minimum	0.0	0.0	0.0	0.0	0.0	0.0	0.0	0.0	0.0	0.0
Std. Dev.	13,466.1	654.0	2,276.0	6,321.9	2,114.7	14,544.7	803.4	2,945.9	9,486.4	2,460.6

the first output, investments (y_1). With an average value of 5,112.9 million TWD, it represents about 2.6% of the average amount. We conclude that the highest percentage values are observed in the input dimensions.

These results illustrate that measuring technical efficiency against the weakly efficient subset results in unaccounted technical inefficiencies in the form of input and output slacks. Since the values are non-negligible, they cannot be simply ignored, and practitioners should be aware of their importance when decomposing cost and revenue efficiencies into their technical and allocative factors.

3.6 Summary and Conclusions

In this chapter, we have revised the early approaches to economic efficiency measurement based on duality theory and corresponding to the partially oriented input or output dimensions. These developments were introduced by Shephard (1953, 1970) relying on the definition of distance function, at the same time that Farrell (1957) developed his seminal approach based on efficiency scores. Both approaches nicely complement each other, with Shephard's work providing solid theoretical background, based on economic theory, to Farrell's approach. On the one hand, Shephard discusses the axioms necessary to equivalently represent the production technology by way of the input or output distance functions or their supporting cost and revenue functions. On the other hand, Farrell explicitly introduced the decomposition of economic efficiency into technical and allocative (price) factors. To the extent that distance functions can be considered as measures of technical efficiency, both approaches return a complementary and unifying framework to benchmark economic efficiency. Unsurprisingly, the approach has withstood the test of time and is still quite popular in empirical research. The reason being the interpretational ease of the economic, technical, and allocative efficiency scores.

While the measurement of technical efficiency immediately caught up in the nonparametric and parametric fields, with the emergence of the Data Envelopment Analysis techniques introduced by Boles (1967, 1971) and Charnes et al. (1978) and the Stochastic Frontier Analysis (SFA) introduced by Aigner et al. (1977), the former has proved more popular in empirical applications, with a larger number of studies adopting it. The reason is that, as discussed in Sect. 2.6 of the preceding chapter, the development of parametric techniques to measure and decompose economic efficiency presents relevant econometric challenges that are still being addressed; e.g., see Parmeter and Kumbhakar (2014) or Atkinson and Tsionas (2016). Unfortunately, as stated by Greene (2008) and despite the encouraging progress witnessed in recent years, no method is yet in the mainstream that allows convenient analysis of economic efficiency in the context of a fully integrated econometric frontier model. On the contrary, nonparametric DEA techniques have been used over the years to calculate and decompose economic efficiency under different orientations, technological assumptions, and efficiency measures, as the literature mentioned in each one of the following chapters bears witness. Given the flexibility that these methods offer and once the early models based on radial projections were evolved, we can assert that, as of today, the DEA approach is dominant in the empirical implementation of economic efficiency analysis. An example is the SFA module of a representative software such as LIMDEP, which does not include economic efficiency measurement, while its DEA counterpart includes the standard models presented in this chapter, Econometric Software, Inc. (2014). Nevertheless, the Stata packages presented in Kumbhakar et al. (2015), who implement single and multiple equations' cross-sectional models of profit efficiency based on the primal approaches, overcome some of the above stated difficulties by way of seemingly unrelated regressions and maximum-likelihood estimation methods.

The above does not imply that the DEA techniques are free from methodological weaknesses. In this chapter, we have identified as one of the most relevant for the correct identification and measurement of technical and allocative efficiencies the fact that the standard DEA models assuming strong disposability of inputs and outputs, combined with a radial definition of technical efficiency, result in the characterization of a weakly efficient subset of the technology. This implies that individual input reductions and output increases may still be feasible once the firm under evaluation is projected to the weakly efficient frontier. If the values of the input and output slacks are relevant (as in the above empirical application on the Taiwanese banking sector), then, from a managerial perceptive, technical efficiency is overestimated while allocative efficiency is underestimated. Consequently, this may lead to erroneous managerial advice about the sources of economic efficiency. In this respect, the adoption of additive measures of inefficiency that project the firms under evaluation to the strongly efficient frontier represents an interesting alternative to the radial measures. The second part of this book is devoted to these measures, which nevertheless have their own drawbacks as presented in Sect. 2.4.5 of Chap. 2, discussing the so-called essential property to be satisfied by the decompositions of economic efficiency.

Chapter 4
The Generalized Distance Function (GDF): Profitability Efficiency Decomposition

4.1 Introduction

This chapter is concerned with the measurement of profitability efficiency, defined as the ratio of revenue to cost, and its multiplicative decomposition into a productive efficiency measure—including technical and scale efficiencies, corresponding to the generalized distance function introduced by Chavas and Cox (1999), and allocative efficiency. The generalized distance function, GDF, received such name by these authors because it generalizes Shepard's radial distance functions and the graph (hyperbolic) efficiency measure introduced by Färe et al. (1985:110–111).[1] Building upon this measure, which can be reinterpreted in terms of a distance function, these authors extended the input- and output-oriented measures to a graph representation of the technology including both dimensions of the production technology. In contrast to the partial dimensions represented by input and output orientations, the hyperbolic technical efficiency measure, presented in Sect 2.1.3 of Chap. 2, is a scalar value function that projects the firm under evaluation to the production frontier by simultaneously reducing its inputs and increasing its outputs. As we show below, Chavas and Cox (1999) qualified this definition by making these changes dependent on an exponent that weights the outputs and inputs differently. Therefore, setting the value of such bearing (or directional) parameter to a specific value, it is possible to recover, among others, the hyperbolic efficiency measure as well as Farrell's input and output radial counterparts. Since the latter corresponds to Shepard's input and output distance functions, as shown in Chap. 3, the generalized distance function represents an improvement over the previous definitions, by adding flexibility to the orientation and as we show below providing a dual counterpart to the profitability function.

[1] They refer to this index as the "Farrell Graph Measure of Technical Efficiency." The measure inherits its name from the hyperbolic path it follows toward the production frontier.

J. T. Pastor et al., *Benchmarking Economic Efficiency*, International Series
in Operations Research & Management Science 315,
https://doi.org/10.1007/978-3-030-84397-7_4

Therefore, the generalized distance function nests previous efficiency measures. This quality is shared by other distance functions, most notably the directional distance function introduced by Chambers et al. (1996, 1998) based on Luenberger's (1992) shortage function. However, while this function is additive and presents a natural duality with the profit function, defined as revenue minus cost, the generalized distance function retains the multiplicative definition of its partially oriented input and output cases. This makes the interpretation of the generalized distance function straightforward, as the percentage (proportional) reduction in the observed amount of inputs and percentage increase in the observed amount of outputs necessary to reach the production frontier, Also, the multiplicative definition results in the satisfaction of desirable homogeneity properties with respect to input and output variation. These properties ease the interpretation of the generalized distance function as a measure of relative (total factor) productivity, as we show in Sect. 4.2. Combined with duality theory, the GDF becomes a natural candidate for the technical efficiency component in the decomposition of profitability efficiency into technical and allocative factors.[2]

The measurement of technical efficiency based on the hyperbolic technical efficiency measure has proved quite popular among researchers and practitioners. This function has been employed in cross-sectional and time series studies. Examples are the Malmquist productivity indices introduced by Zofío and Lovell (2001), and the superefficiency models by Johnson and McGinnis (2009), who study the infeasibility of some solutions, as it is the case with the intertemporal comparisons of efficiency required by the Malmquist indices. Also, Yu and Lee (2009) apply the hyperbolic distance function to Network Data Envelopment Analysis (DEA) models, while Wheelock and Wilson (2009) propose an estimator of the hyperbolic efficiency measure based on bootstrapping techniques.

However, it is the field of environmental economics where the hyperbolic distance function has proved crucial when evaluating the productive efficiency of firms by allowing the simultaneous reduction of undesirable (or bad) outputs and increase of desirable (or marketable) outputs. Färe et al. (1989) introduced the possibility of treating both sets of outputs asymmetrically. Since then, many theoretical and empirical applications qualifying the characterization of the environmental technology have followed, e.g., Zofío and Prieto (2001), Hailu and Veeman (2001), Seiford and Zhu (2002), and Cherchye et al. (2015). Dakpo et al. (2016) account for the

[2] These characteristics are not satisfied by the additive directional distance functions, whose numeric interpretation as measure of productivity change, based on the so-called Luenberger indicator, cannot be directly related to conventional index number theory. Index numbers define as ratios, while productivity indicators define as differences. Therefore, the interpretation of the latter is not straightforward. See Diewert (2005), Balk et al. (2008), and Briec et al. (2012) for a discussion of the differences between the two approaches. A recent application of productivity analysis based on the Luenberger indicator is carried out by Juo et al. (2015), whose data is used in this book to illustrate the different models—see Balk (2018) for relevant qualifications.

different alternatives when modeling the by-production technologies, as well as pros and cons of the different approaches.[3]

However, although most of this literature was published after the introduction of the generalized distance function by Chavas and Cox (1999), the added flexibility that this function offers has remained largely unexploited. The reason is that the bearing parameter is exogenously chosen by the researcher, just as the directional vector in the case of the additive directional distance function. For this reason, absent prior information regarding specific weights for input reductions and output increases, treating them equally, results in the generalized distance function being equivalent to the square root of the graph (hyperbolic) efficiency measure. Consequently, rather than using the generalized distance function formulation, researchers have relied on the hyperbolic efficiency measure. Exceptions are from Jiménez-Sáez et al. (2011), who study the technical efficiency of research groups within national R&D programs employing Data Envelopment Analysis techniques, and Jiménez-Sáez et al. (2013) who extend the previous analysis by calculating Malmquist productivity indices based on the generalized distance function. These authors suggest that the bearing parameter establishing the relative weight between the input and output adjustments should be agreed with relevant stakeholders, as there might be a principal-agent conflict where those evaluating performance are not the subjects of the evaluation. In this case, the principal maybe interested in cost savings, while the agent aims at revenue increases. Besides its flexibility, an additional advantage of employing the generalized distance function rather than its particular hyperbolic case is that the former does not require to square the Malmquist index and the different factors in which it decomposes to obtain correct measures of productivity change, i.e., technological change and efficiency change, along with any scale and mixed-effect components.

From an economic perspective, the dual relationship between the hyperbolic distance function and the profitability (or "return-to-dollar") measure of economic performance was suggested by Färe et al. (2002). Subsequently, Zofío and Prieto (2006) formalized it for the generalized distance function, showing that profitability efficiency can be decomposed multiplicatively into the usual technical and allocative terms. These authors highlight that the reference technology exhibits local constant returns to scale at the profitability-maximizing benchmark, implying the need to account for scale efficiency as one of the sources of profitability inefficiency from a technological perspective. They also extend these definitions to a dynamic context, showing that profitability change can be decomposed into the Malmquist productivity index, defined in terms of the generalized distance function, and allocative efficiency change. In this chapter, we rely on these duality results to present the

[3]Cuesta and Zofío (2005) introduce the parametric methods allowing the calculation of the hyperbolic distance function using Stochastic Frontier Analysis. These authors show that the almost homogeneity condition can be easily imposed on a translog specification of the distance function. Subsequently, Cuesta et al. (2009) extend the model to the field of environmental economics including the production of undesirable outputs as by-product.

multiplicative decomposition of profitability efficiency into a technical term represented by the generalized distance function and allocative efficiency.

In the following section, we recall the definition of the production technology presented in Sect. 2.1 of Chap. 2 and its equivalent representation by way of the generalized distance function. Again, this property is crucial when proving the duality results between the profitability function and the generalized distance function. Next, in Sect. 4.3, we recall the properties of the profitability function and the scale properties that it imposes on the technology and define profitability efficiency as the ratio between observed profitability to maximum profitability. Afterward, for economically inefficient firms and based on the duality introduced by Zofío and Prieto (2006), we present in Sect. 4.4 the decomposition of profitability efficiency according to technical, scale, and allocative criteria. Throughout these sections, we present the Data Envelopment Analysis programs that enable the empirical implementation of profitability efficiency measurement. As the DEA program for calculating the generalized distance function is nonlinear, we comment on recent alternatives by Färe et al. (2016) and Halická and Trnovská (2019) to calculate its value by resorting to different approximations, namely, an approximate procedure for identifying the VRS hyperbolic projection based on the CRS projection and its associated directional distance function, and the possibility of reformulating the hyperbolic model into a semidefinite programming framework. Finally, Section 4.5 illustrates the calculation of these measures using the accompanying Benchmarking Economic Efficiency package for Julia. For this purpose, we solve the profitability efficiency model for the simple one input-one output example presented in Sect. 2.6 of Chap. 2, as well as for the empirical dataset on Taiwanese banks. Section 4.6 summarizes the main results and concludes.

4.2 The Generalized Distance Function: Productive, Technical, and Scale Efficiencies

We recall the characterization of technology in terms of the production possibility set presented in Sect. 2.2 of Chap. 2:

$$T = \{(x, y) : x \in \mathbb{R}_{+}^{M}, y \in \mathbb{R}_{+}^{N},\ x \text{ can produce } y\}, \tag{4.1}$$

where x is a vector of input quantities, y is a vector of output quantities, and M and N are the number of inputs and outputs. It is assumed that the technology satisfies the axioms (T1)–(T5) discussed in that chapter—see also, among others, Färe et al. (1985:46–47). A relevant property for the decomposition of profitability efficiency is whether the technology exhibits constant returns to scale (CRS). Since we recall this property in what follows, if the technology satisfies constant returns to scale globally, we denote it by $T^{CRS} = \{(\psi x, \psi y) : (x, y) \in T,\ \psi > 0\}$. T^{CRS} implies a mapping $x \to y$ that is homogeneous of degree one. When relying on Data Envelopment

Analysis (DEA) methods to calculate and decompose profitability efficiency, as it is the case in this book, it is important to note that there is no underlying reason to impose global returns to scale. However, for operational convenience, the computational process approximates the technology both under the variable and constant returns to scale assumptions. The reason is that to calculate technical efficiency against the *loci* that represent suitable candidates for profitability maximization, satisfying local constant returns to scale, it is simpler to rely on the global CRS characterization. Afterward, solving the generalized distance function under variable returns to scale, VRS, yields the actual technical efficiency of the firm. Calculating the ratio of the former to the latter, as presented in expression (2.12) of Chap. 2, allows to recover the scale efficiency of the firm, which is an integral element of its technological performance when aiming at maximizing profitability. Hence, it is important to remark that while the actual reference technology is characterized by variable returns, its *global* constant returns counterpart is recalled only for computational convenience, which simplifies the calculation of the scale inefficiency.

As in the previous chapter focused on Shephard's input and output distance functions, a second characteristic that is critical for the assessment of technical and allocative efficiency is whether one assumes weak or strong disposability of inputs and outputs. The reason is that, depending on the assumption, the efficiency subsets serving as benchmark for technical efficiency measurement are different. In turn, these sets, combined with the value of the generalized distance function, signal if the firm under evaluation is efficient or not. From an operational perspective, this shows the relevance of the disposability assumptions when defining the production possibility set using DEA methods, whose consideration materializes in alternative restrictions. Additionally, as the generalized distance function is multiplicative, it endures the same drawback as the input and output distance functions that it nests. In particular, the fact that it does not comply with the indication property (E1a) presented in Sect. 2.2. of Chap. 2, ensuring that the firm is evaluated against the strongly efficient subset of the technology, which includes production plans that satisfy the Pareto-Koopmans definition of efficiency. This definition implies that no additional output can be produced given the observed amount of inputs or that the observed output amount cannot be produced using less inputs.

Strong and weak disposability of inputs and outputs with respect to the technology set T is defined in the following way:

$$\text{T.S.D.If } (x,y) \in T^S, (x,-y) \leq (x',-y') \Rightarrow (x',y') \in T^S, \tag{4.2}$$

$$\text{T.W.D.If } (x,y) \in T^W, (\lambda x, y/\lambda) \in T^W, \;\; \lambda \geq 1. \tag{4.3}$$

As in the discussion laid out in Chap. 3, strong and weak disposability is denoted by the corresponding superscript, and we will recall it when interpreting the value of the generalized distance function as a measure of technical efficiency in terms of the Pareto-Koopmans definition. Note that these definitions hold regardless of (global) constant or variable returns to scale.

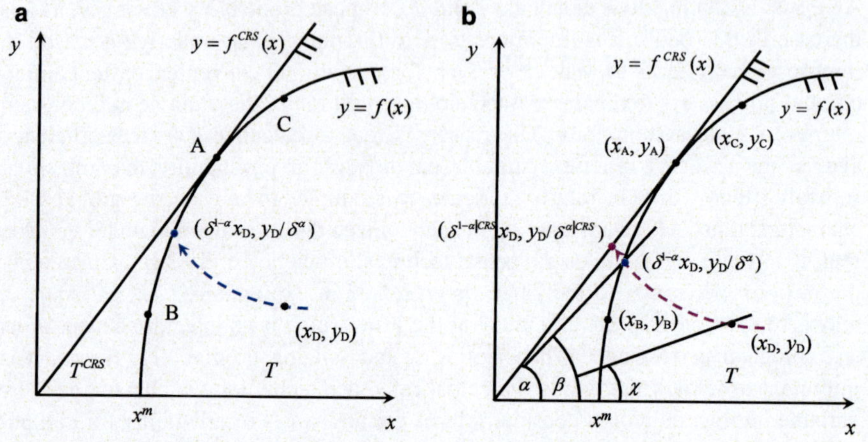

Fig. 4.1 (**a–b**) Technology sets, GDF, and technical and scale efficiencies

For the single output case, $N = 1$, the technology is normally represented by the production function f, $\mathbb{R}_+^M \to \mathbb{R}_+$, defined by $f(x) = \max_y \{y : (x, y) \in T\}$, i.e., the maximum amount of output that can be obtained from any combination of inputs. As already noted in Chap. 2, the advantage of this is that it allows for technical inefficiency, since under the appropriate assumptions we can define the technology set (4.1) from the production function as $T = \{(x, y) : f(x) \geq y, y \in \mathbb{R}_+\}$. We illustrate the production function recalling Fig. 2.3 of Chap. 2 for $M = N = 1$. Here, in Fig. 4.1, the variable returns to scale technology set, T, consists of all input-output combinations below the production frontier $y = f(x)$; specifically, the technology exhibits decreasing returns to scale: $\lambda^{\alpha} y = f(\lambda x)$, $\alpha < 1$. We see that production requires a minimum amount of input, x^m, to produce a positive amount of outputs. Regarding constant returns to scale, we observe in Fig. 4.1a that the corresponding production function corresponds to $y = f^{CRS}(x)$. We see that the global T^{CRS} coincides with the convex cone spanned by T at firm A where local constant returns to scale hold, with $T^{CRS} \subseteq T$. The spanned technology has vertex at the origin and, graphically, is equivalent to the technology satisfying global CRS. Regarding disposability, the continuous production function represents a technology characterized by strongly disposable inputs and outputs.

Following Chavas and Cox (1999), it is possible to represent the technology T through the generalized distance function:

$$D_G(x, y; \alpha) = \min \left\{ \delta > 0 : \left(\delta^{1-\alpha} x, \delta^{-\alpha} y \right) \in T \right\}, \quad \alpha \in [0, 1] \tag{4.4}$$

If the technology satisfies the customary axioms, the GDF verifies the following properties: (i) it is almost homogenous—Aczél (1966, Chap.7)—of degree one, and (α–1) and α in x and y, $D_G(\lambda^{\alpha-1} x, \lambda^{\alpha} y; \alpha) = \lambda D_G(x, y; \alpha)$, $\lambda > 0$; (ii) it is nonincreasing in x, $D_G(x, y; \alpha) \leq D_G(\lambda x, y; \alpha)$, $\lambda \geq 1$; (iii) it is nondecreasing in

y, $D_G(x, \lambda y; \alpha) \leq D_G(x, y; \alpha)$, $\lambda \in [0,1]$; (iv) it is lower semicontinuous in x and y; and (v) it is independent of α under constant returns to scale, CRS, and decreasing (increasing) in α under increasing RTS (decreasing RTS). The above definition holds regardless the nature of return to scale and strong or weak disposability of inputs and outputs. Finally, given these properties, the generalized distance function can be interpreted as a measure of technical efficiency: $D_G(x, y; \alpha) = TE_G(x, y; \alpha)$. In case that constant returns to scale hold, it captures productive efficiency with respect to a technological benchmark characterized by CRS, $D_G^{CRS}(x, y; \alpha) = TE_G^{CRS}(x, y; \alpha)$, comprising both technical and scale efficiency. We discuss the efficiency interpretation of the generalized distance functions in the next section.

It is immediately clear that $D_G(x, y; \alpha)$ generalizes the input and output distance functions presented in (3.11) and (3.12) of the previous chapter. Particularly, for $\alpha = 0$, $D_G(x, y; 0) = 1/D_I(x, y)$, while for $\alpha = 1$, $D_G(x, y; 1) = D_O(x, y)$. It also nests the graph (hyperbolic) efficiency technical measure presented in expression (2.10) of the second chapter. If $\alpha = 0.5$, $D_G(x, y; 0.5) = TE_{H(G)}(x, y) = (\varphi^*)^2$—note that φ^* corresponds to the actual definition introduced by Färe et al. (1985:110). In passing, Chavas and Cox (1999) remark that the GDF can be related to the "Farrell equiproportionate distance" measure introduced by Briec (1997), based on Luenberger's shortage function, and coinciding with the directional distance function defined by Chambers et al. (1998). It is also related to the "generalized Farrell graph measure" presented by Färe et al. (1985:126). These latter results suggest that the duality theory underlying the relationship between the GDF and the profitability function may be extended to alternative definitions of technical efficiency. Nevertheless, the straightforward definition of the GDF eases its interpretation and results in a natural multiplicative decomposition of profitability efficiency. Under the assumption of CRS and regardless the bearing parameter α, the generalized and the input and output distance functions are numerically equivalent in the following way: $D_G^{CRS}(x, y; \alpha) = D_O^{CRS}(x, y) = 1/ D_I^{CRS}(x, y)$, $\alpha \in [0, 1]$.[4] This implies that from an operational perspective, it is possible to calculate the technical efficiency against the reference CRS frontier relying on any of these definitions, which eases the computation as one does not need to resort to nonlinear optimization. This is the case of productive efficiency with respect to CRS frontier (comprising VRS and scale efficiency; see expression (4.6)). Nevertheless, when assessing technical efficiency with respect to the variable returns to scale frontier, nonlinear optimization is necessary. We return to this question in Sect. 4.2.3.

We can now consider the *representation* property that constitutes the cornerstone for the measurement of technical efficiency. In this case, it indicates that the technology T can be represented equivalently as follows:

$$(x, y) \in T \text{ if and only if } D_G(x, y; \alpha) \leq 1. \tag{4.5}$$

[4] The relationship does not hold however for variable returns to scale despite what is stated in Färe et al. (1994, Chap. 8); see Zofío and Lovell (2001).

Therefore, a firm is deemed efficient if $D_G(x, y; \alpha) = 1$, while it is inefficient if $D_G(x, y; \alpha) < 1$. The GDF is illustrated in Fig. 4.1. Firms A, B, and C are efficient, while firm D, (x_D, y_D), lays in the interior of the technology, and therefore, $D_G(x_D, y_D; \alpha) < 1$. In this case, its projection on the VRS frontier constitutes the reference benchmark $(\widehat{x}, \widehat{y}) = (\delta^{1-\alpha} x_D, \delta^{-\alpha} y_D)$. The equivalence with the graph (hyperbolic) efficiency measure of technical efficiency expression (2.10) considered in Chap. 2 is clear, with $\delta^{0.5} = \varphi^*$.

4.2.1 *Defining Productive, Technical, and Scale Efficiencies*

Following Chavas and Cox (1999:301), the generalized distance function can be interpreted as a measure of technical efficiency: $D_G(x, y; \alpha) = TE_G(x, y; \alpha)$, indicating the proportional rescaling of inputs and outputs that brings the firm to the production frontier. At this projection, increasing, constant, or decreasing constant returns to scale may hold. If we assume that *constant returns to scale hold*, the corresponding distance function captures *productive efficiency*, a concept that can be interpreted in terms of the productivity differential between the firm under evaluation and that of a most productive scale size that serves as benchmark. In this case, productive efficiency corresponds to $D_G^{CRS}(x, y; \alpha) = TE_G^{CRS}(x, y; \alpha)$, *comprising both technical and scale efficiencies* as we show in what follows.

The nature of returns to scale and the associated inefficiency is critical when measuring productive efficiency because it represents a sizeable source of economic loss for the firm, when failing to attain maximum profitability. As shown in the following section, *profit maximization is characterized by the existence of local constant returns to scale*, *implying that* the *scale elasticity is equal to one*. In principle, one can rely on the generalized distance function to determine whether a technically efficient firm exhibits increasing, constant, or decreasing returns to scale. Assuming that the GDF is *differentiable*, it is possible to calculate the elasticity of scale parametrically following Cuesta and Zofío (2005:38). These authors obtain the specific formulation for a translog specification of the hyperbolic distance function (i.e., with $\alpha = 0.5$). When relying on nonparametric techniques like DEA methods, it is also possible to determine the nature of returns to scale by examining the aggregate value of the intensity variables λ_j and whether it is greater, equal, or smaller than one; see Cooper et al. (2007: Chap. 5). However, it is straightforward and actually simpler to measure the economic loss resulting from producing at a suboptimal scale by resorting to the concept of scale efficiency, which compares technical efficiency against the actual variable returns to scale technology, with the virtual constant returns to scale benchmark, serving as technological reference for profitability maximization.

Recalling the concept of scale efficiency presented in Sect. 2.2.3 of the second chapter—expression (2.12), it defines as follows in the case of the generalized distance function:

$$SE_G(x,y;\alpha) = \frac{TE_G^{CRS}(x,y;\alpha)}{TE_G(x,y;\alpha)} = \frac{D_G^{CRS}(x,y;\alpha)}{D_G(x,y;\alpha)} \leq 1. \tag{4.6}$$

$SE_G(x, y; \alpha) < 1$ measures the inefficiency experienced by a firm that produces at a suboptimal scale (or size), thereby enduring either increasing or decreasing returns to scale, which prevents it to attain maximum productivity at one of the optimal scales, i.e., the highest ratio of aggregate output to aggregate input. In the multiple output-multiple input case, this ratio measure is known as *total factor productivity*, and depending on the aggregating functions and their associated weights, there can be several most productive scale sizes (MPSS, in the terminology of Banker et al., 1984). Balk (2008; 19) refers to these firms as those exhibiting a technically optimal scale. O'Donnell (2012; 260) identifies them as *mix-invariant optimal scales*, because the radial projection of the firms to the efficient frontier keeps the input and output mixes constant. It can be seen immediately that this analysis can be generalized to the GDF since this function keeps inputs and outputs mixes fixed within themselves.

For the single output-single input case depicted in Fig. 4.1b, firm A maximizes average productivity, defined as the ratio of output to input, y/x, and whose value, resorting to trigonometry, corresponds to the steepest slope of any *ray vector* joining the origin and the technology. Scale efficiency for firm D corresponds to the gap between average productivities; i.e., it defines as the ratio between the productivity level at the benchmark reference on the variable returns to scale frontier, $(\delta^{1-\alpha}x_D, y_D/\delta^{\alpha})$—defined in turn as the observed output quantity divided by the optimal (projected) input amount, $((y_D/\delta^{\alpha})/\delta^{1-\alpha}x_D) = (y_D/\delta x_D)$, divided by the productivity at the optimal size given the technology, represented by firm A, y_A/x_A. Graphically, this corresponds to the productivity of the benchmark reference at the constant returns to scale frontier $y_A/x_A = ((y_D/\delta^{\alpha|CRS})/\delta^{1-\alpha|CRS}x_D) = (y_D/\delta^{CRS}x_D)$. Hence, scale efficiency as defined in (4.6) is $SE_G(x_D, y_D; \alpha) = (y_D/\delta x_D)/(y_D/\delta^{CRS}x_D) = \delta^{CRS}/\delta \leq 1$.[5]

In the multiple output-multiple input case, the y and x axes in Fig. 4.1 could be seen as aggregated outputs and inputs using specific aggregating functions. The comparison between a firm and its projection on the frontier associated with the radial efficiency measures (or Shephard's input or output distance functions as presented in Chap. 3) corresponds to particular aggregating functions of the input and output vectors: $X(x)$ and $Y(y)$—i.e., in these cases equivalent to the use of the L_2 norm $\|\cdot\|$ associated with the Euclidean length. O'Donnell (2012) shows that efficiency measurement can be performed considering alternative aggregating functions (e.g., linear, CES). Consequently, if an alternative aggregating function is selected (e.g., linear functions with specific weight vectors for inputs and outputs: $X(x, \nu) = \nu \cdot x, \nu \in \mathbb{R}^M_+$, and $Y(y, \mu) = \mu \cdot y, \mu \in \mathbb{R}^N_+$), then smaller (bigger) aggregate

[5] Resorting to trigonometry, scale efficiency defines equivalently as the ratio of the slope of the ray vector joining the origin and the efficient projection on the variable returns to scale technology to that of observation A, i.e., in Fig. 2.3b, $SE_G(x, y; \alpha) = \tan\beta/\tan\alpha$.

scalar input (output) quantities than those obtained with the distance function may be obtained. The scalar difference between the aggregate efficient output obtained by using the generalized distance function and those obtained with alternative aggregating functions is termed *mix efficiency* by O'Donnell (2012), because the use of these alternative aggregating functions and associated weights results in changes in the input and output mixes. Later on, we recall that this interpretation is actually *equivalent to the concept of allocative efficiency when the aggregation of the inputs and outputs uses market prices* ($w \in \mathbb{R}_+^M$ and $p \in \mathbb{R}_+^N$), resulting in *the profitability function*, i.e., an objective function with a meaningful economic significance.

This demonstrates that technical efficiency comparisons based on the generalized distance function can be interpreted in terms of differences in productivity levels between the firm under evaluation and alternative technological benchmarks. Indeed, the above definitions show that it is possible to multiplicatively decompose technical efficiency with respect to maximum productivity—termed *productive efficiency* by Farrell (1957)—into a technical efficiency component under the variable returns to scale assumption times scale efficiency. This results in the following definition:

$$D_G^{CRS}(x, y; \alpha) = D_G(x, y; \alpha) \times SE_G(x, y; \alpha) = \delta^{CRS} \leq 1, \tag{4.7}$$

whose productivity interpretation corresponds to the ratio of aggregate productivities. In particular, for unit D in Fig. 4.1a, $D_G^{CRS}(x_D, y_D; \alpha) = (y_D/x_D)/(y_A/x_A) = \delta^{CRS}$. In trigonometric terms, productive efficiency defines as the ratio of the slope of the ray vector joining the origin and observation D, to that of observation A, i.e., $D_G^{CRS}(x_D, y_D; \alpha) =$ slope 0D/slope 0A $= \tan \chi/\tan \alpha$.

The interpretation of the value of the generalized distance function as a measure of technical efficiency combines that of its input and output counterparts. Consequently, if $\delta = 0.64$ and $\alpha = 0.5$, then the amount of inputs can be reduced by 20% (=(1–0.64$^{0.5}$) × 100) while increasing outputs by 25% (=(1/0.64$^{0.5}$–1) × 100). Jointly, productivity can be increased by 56.25% (=(1/0.64–1) × 100). Again, in the case of productive efficiency, since constant returns to scale hold, the input, output, and generalized distance functions are related: $D_G^{CRS}(x, y; \alpha) = D_O^{CRS}(x, y) = 1/D_I^{CRS}(x, y)$.

4.2.2 *Pareto-Koopmans Efficiency and Input and Output Disposability*

As in Chap. 3 discussing the notion of efficiency for the input and output distance functions, it is relevant to stress that under a DEA characterization of the production technology, a unitary value of the GDF does not ensure that the firm is efficient from a Pareto-Koopmans perspective (Koopmans, 1951). Consequently, the GDF does not comply with the *indication property* (E1a), presented in Sect. 2.2 of Chap. 2. In particular, the GDF, interpreted as efficiency measure, is incapable of indicating if the firm belongs to the strongly efficient production possibility set:

$$\partial^S(T) = \{(x,y) \in T : (x', -y') \leq (x, -y), (x', y') \neq (x, y) \Rightarrow (x', y') \notin T\}. \quad (4.8)$$

This drawback is the result of two related facts: in the first place, the piecewise linear approximation of the production frontier that DEA generates, which results in the likely existence of inputs and outputs slacks, and, in the second place, the definition of the GDF, based on T but without imposing that the corresponding projection belongs to the strong efficient subset of T. This is observed regardless of inputs and outputs being considered as strongly or weakly disposable according to (4.2) and (4.3). For this reason, when relying on DEA methods, it is necessary to adopt a two-stage approach in case we are interested in identifying the strong efficient projection of each firm. While in the first stage the GDF function is calculated, in the second stage, an additive problem is solved searching for individual slacks. We present this method below when discussing the DEA methods relevant for the calculation of the GDF.

Specifically, in the case of the standard approximation of the production technology T through DEA methods under the assumption of strong disposability of inputs and outputs, (4.2), the GDF is only capable of identifying if a firm (or its projection) belongs to the weakly efficient set of the technology, i.e.,

$$\begin{aligned} \partial^W\left(T^S\right) &= \left\{(x,y) \in T^S : (x', -y') < (x, -y) \Rightarrow (x', y') \notin T^S\right\} \\ &= \left\{(x,y) : D_G^S(x,y;\alpha) = 1\right\}, \quad \alpha \in [0,1], \end{aligned} \quad (4.9)$$

where, following the notation introduced above, the superscript S indicates the strong disposability assumption. The above shows that the generalized distance function can successfully identify if simultaneous radial input reductions and output expansions are feasible when $D_G^S(x,y;\alpha) < 1$. If not, firms belong to (and empirically define) *the weakly efficient boundary of the production technology*, i.e., $\partial^W\left(T^S\right) = \left\{(x,y) : D_G^S(x,y;\alpha) = 1\right\}$, as shown in the last equality of (4.9).

In the case of weakly disposable inputs and outputs, (4.3), the use of DEA methods results in the GDF identifying firms as technically efficient with respect to a weaker notion of efficiency, i.e., that corresponding to the graph "isoquant" subset of the technology; see Färe et al. (1985:46). That is, whether the firms (or, again, their projections) belong to the following subset:

$$\begin{aligned} \partial^{Isoq}\left(T^W\right) &= \left\{(x,y) \in T^W : \left(\gamma x, \gamma^{-1} y\right) \notin T^W, \ 0 < \gamma < 1\right\} \\ &= \left\{(x,y) : D_G^W(x,y;\alpha) = 1\right\}. \end{aligned} \quad (4.10)$$

However, as anticipated, this definition of efficiency suffers from the same problem that $\partial^W(T^S)$ concerning its inability to satisfy the indication property (E1a). The situation is worse, because, in this case, a unitary value of the GDF approximated through DEA methods may deem as efficient firms that are dominated in all input or output dimensions. This possibility is undesirable from the perspective of technical efficiency measurement because it aggravates the wrong characterization of technical efficiency, resulting in misleading decompositions of economic efficiency, since allocative efficiency is recovered as a residual. Hence, weak disposability of inputs and outputs is normally disregarded when characterizing the production technology.[6,7] Nevertheless, despite the specific disposability assumption and given that the alternative reference sets are nested, $\partial^S(T) \subseteq \partial^W(T) \subseteq \partial^{Isoq}(T)$, it is immediate that while $D_G(x, y; \alpha) = 1$ cannot identify whether a firm belongs to strongly efficient set, $\partial^S(T)$, if a firm is technically efficient with respect to the weakly efficient set, $\partial^W(T)$, it is also technically efficient with respect to the isoquant set $\partial^{Isoq}(T)$.

In Fig. 4.1a, all three efficiency sets coincide for the variable returns to scale production frontier $y = f(x)$. However, as already remarked, the use of DEA techniques gives rise to technologies where these sets differ, due to its piecewise linear nature, and empirically depend on the assumption of either strong or weak disposability: e.g., see Färe et al. (1985:28–30).[8] In what follows, we discuss these alternative definitions of the efficiency sets from the empirical DEA perspective.

4.2.3 *Calculating the Generalized Distance Function Using Data Envelopment Analysis*

Recalling Sect. 2.5 of the second chapter, the empirical approximation of the production technology through Data Envelopment Analysis methods generates convex polyhedral technologies (i.e., intersections of finite numbers of half-spaces), consisting of piecewise linear combinations of the observed $j = 1,\ldots,J$ firms.[9] The DEA approximation of the technology T is given by the following:

[6] This is one of the regularity conditions imposed on the production function or, more generally, the transformation function, so they are *well-behaved*; i.e., they are characterized by a decreasing (increasing) marginal rates of substitution (transformation) between inputs (outputs) resulting from strictly convex (concave) isoquants.

[7] An exception can be found in the field of environmental economics, where the technological trade-off between desirable and undesirable outputs, including the null-jointness axiom, is usually modelled through their weak disposability. Färe et al. (1989) develop the environmental efficiency model based on the hyperbolic distance function where inputs and undesirable outputs are reduced, while desirable outputs are increased. See Zaim and Taskin (2000) for a later application of this model.

[8] Again, this issue is not of concern in the parametric approach based on *well-behaved* production functions satisfying the desirable regularity conditions. The usual functional forms present equal strong, weak, and isoquant efficiency subsets. An example is the Cobb-Douglas function, whose input set corresponds to $L(y) = \left\{\prod_{m=1}^{M} x_m^{\alpha_m} \geq y,\ \alpha_m > 0\right\}$.

[9] See Färe et al. (1994) and Cooper et al. (2007) for an introduction to the activity analysis-DEA within a production theory context.

$$T^S = \left\{ \begin{array}{l} (x, y) : \sum_{j=1}^{J} \lambda_j x_{jm} \leq x_m, \;\; m = 1, \ldots, M; \;\; \sum_{j=1}^{J} \lambda_j y_{jn} \geq y_n, \;\; n = 1, \ldots, N; \\ \sum_{j=1}^{J} \lambda_j = 1, \;\; \lambda_j \geq 0, \;\; j = 1, \ldots, J \end{array} \right\}, \tag{4.11}$$

where λ is an intensity vector whose nonzero values determine the (convex) linear combinations of facets or of subsets of horizontal or vertical supporting hyperplanes of T which define the production frontier of the DEA polyhedral technology.[10] Hence, DEA makes use of individual intensity (activity) variables λ_j for each firm. These are nonnegative variables whose optimal value is interpreted as the extent to which a firm is involved in frontier production. Also, alternative restrictions on their joint value allow imposing different returns to scale. In (4.11), variable returns to scale are allowed through the restriction $\sum_{j=1}^{J} \lambda_j = 1$. Finally, the inequalities associated with the input and output combinations characterize their strong disposability. Therefore, among the technological axioms incorporated into the reference DEA model (4.11), we highlight *convexity*, *strong disposability of inputs and outputs*, and *variable returns to scale*. Next, Fig. 4.2 shows the DEA approximation of the production technology represented by $y \leq f(x)$ in the single output-single input case. Here, the production frontier $y = f(x)$ is constructed through the linear combinations of firms A, B, and C, along with the vertical and horizontal extensions.

Strong disposability implies that it is feasible to discard unnecessary inputs and that it is possible to produce additional outputs, without incurring in technological opportunity costs. Empirically, this implies that technical efficiency is measured against the weakly efficient set (4.9), $\partial^W(T^S)$, rather than the strongly efficient set (4.8), $\partial^S(T^S)$. In Fig. 4.2, from left to right, the weakly efficient subsets correspond to the hyperplanes joining firms B, A, and C, as well as their vertical and horizontal extensions (i.e., $\overline{\text{BAC}}$ and discontinuous lines), while the strongly efficient subset corresponds to the two $\overline{\text{BAC}}$ segments. The different characterization of the efficiency sets shows that, from the perspective of DEA methods, there is a trade-off between the axiom of strong disposability and the existence of weakly efficient subsets, against which the generalized distance function projects the firms under evaluation, but cannot account for individual slacks in their efficiency scores. This is illustrated in Fig. 4.2, where firms (x_D, y_D) and (x_E, y_E) are projected toward the strongly and weakly efficient subsets of the technology, respectively. In the latter case, firm (x_E, y_E) could further reduce the input quantity from its technically efficient projection $(\delta^{1-\alpha}|^{T^S} x_E, y_E / \delta^{\alpha}|^{T^S})$ on the weakly efficient frontier, so as to reach the strongly efficient counterpart, i.e., $s_E^{-*} > 0$. A similar example could be presented resulting in a slack in the output quantity. Therefore, for the case of the generalized distance function, although technical performance should be measured against the strongly efficient set $\partial^S(T)$ to comply with the notion of Pareto-Koopmans efficiency, this cannot be achieved empirically relying on a single DEA

[10] A facet is a subset of a T supporting hyperplane satisfying that each of its points can be expressed as a convex linear combination of a finite subset of strong efficient firms belonging to the facet.

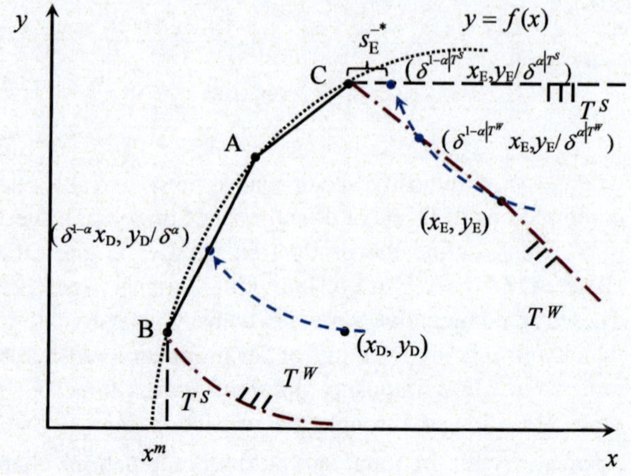

Fig. 4.2 DEA approximation or the technology set

model. As noted in the preceding chapters, this result is due to the fact that DEA simultaneously solves the characterization of the technology and the calculation of the efficiency measure. In the case of radial projections or of any projection associated with any GDF, technical efficiency is measured against the weakly efficient production possibility sets associated with strong disposability of inputs and outputs.

As previously remarked, this problem worsens in the case of weak disposability of inputs and outputs, resulting in reference frontiers that match the isoquant subset of the technology, (4.10). This set corresponds to the DEA characterization of the technology (4.11) but changing the input and output constraints to equalities. Generalizing the definition of the input and output production possibility sets under weak disposability—presented in expressions (3.21) and (3.22) of the previous chapter—to the graph case including both dimensions, we obtain the corresponding technology set:

$$T^W = \left\{ \begin{array}{l} (x,y) : \sum_{j=1}^{J} \lambda_j \psi x_{jm} = x_m, \;\; m = 1, \ldots, M; \;\; \sum_{j=1}^{J} \lambda_j \psi^{-1} y_{jn} = y_n, \;\; n = 1, \ldots, N; \psi \in [1, \infty); \\ \sum_{j=1}^{J} \lambda_j = 1, \;\; \lambda_j \geq 0, \;\; j = 1, \ldots, J. \end{array} \right\} \tag{4.12}$$

In Fig. 4.2, the isoquant set T^W is shaped through the dashed-dotted curve and line extensions. The associated efficiency subset $\partial^{Isoq}(T^W)$ corresponds to the connected line segments $\overline{\text{BACE}}$, plus the curved extension departing from B and the line extension departing from E, projecting $\partial^{Isoq}(T^W)$ to the x-axis.[11] Regarding

---

[11] Again, it is relevant to remark that the weakly efficient subset $\partial^W(T^S)$, generated under the DEA assumption of strong disposability of inputs and outputs, must not be confused with the production set under the assumption of weakly disposable inputs and outputs, T^W.

efficiency measurement, it can be seen that adopting weak disposability generates reference subsets that are wrongly characterized as efficient by the input and output distance functions because these peers (or their projections) are dominated in the sense of Pareto-Koopmans efficiency: for example, given a particular choice of α, firm E is projected through $D_G^W(x, y; \alpha)$ to the dash-dotted line segment of the isoquant $\partial^{Isoq}(T^W)$ connecting firms C and E: ($\delta^{1-\alpha}|^{T^W}$ x_E, y_E/ $\delta^{\alpha}|^{T^W}$). A segment that is clearly inefficient by using more input to produce less output than the dominating firm C. This result also represents an awkward situation in which the efficient projection of a firm is given by a linear combination that includes itself. Also, we could imagine a result in which a different choice of α would render firm E efficient.

The previous exposition of the role that returns to scale and disposability play in the measurement of technical efficiency through the GDF justifies that the functions that allow calculating and decomposing profitability efficiency using the package "Benchmarking Economic Efficiency" are implemented under the default assumptions of convexity, strongly disposable inputs and outputs, and both variable and constant returns to scale, to account for scale efficiency. Consequently, the most relevant characteristics of the standard DEA measurement of technical efficiency relying on the generalized distance function are that it corresponds to graph projections on the weakly efficient frontier, i.e., gross of input and output individual slacks. As discussed in Sect. 2.4 of Chap. 2, when decomposing profitability efficiency, *unaccounted slacks result in technical efficiency being overstated* (actual technical efficiency is lower than the value of the generalized distance function) and, correspondingly, *allocative efficiency being understated.* As for the measurement of individual input reductions or output increases that may be still feasible, a second stage is applied to recover the individual slacks, thereby identifying the final benchmarks on the strongly efficient frontiers. Although this could be achieved through a single run formulation including non-Archimedean measures, the two-stage approach is preferred to avoid computational difficulties (Ali & Seiford, 1993; MirHassani & Alirezaee, 2005).

The DEA model that allows calculating the generalized distance function for a specific firm under evaluation, denoted by (x_o, y_o), is presented in program (4.13). As discussed above, this program returns the optimal value δ^* of the generalized distance function against the weakly efficient frontier, $\partial^W(T)$, which is subsequently employed in the second stage to solve the additive model (4.14), searching for individual input and output slacks. This allows identifying the firm's ultimate benchmark on the strongly efficient frontier $\partial^S(T)$. However, we remark that based on general duality results presented in the following section, which are unconcerned with the particular empirical methods used to implement economic efficiency analysis—subject to specific pros and cons, these slacks are only informative, as they are not taken into consideration when measuring technical efficiency in the standard decomposition of profitability efficiency:

First stage
Generalized distance function (Envelopment formulation)

$$D_G(x_o, y_o; \alpha) = \min_{\delta, \lambda} \delta$$

$$\begin{aligned} \text{s.t.} \quad & \sum_{j=1}^{J} \lambda_j x_{jm} \leq \delta^{1-\alpha} x_{om}, \quad m = 1, \ldots, M, \\ & \sum_{j=1}^{J} \lambda_j y_{jn} \geq y_{on} / \delta^{\alpha}, \quad n = 1, \ldots, N, \\ & \sum_{j=1}^{J} \lambda_j = 1, \\ & \lambda_j \geq 0. \end{aligned} \tag{4.13}$$

Second stage
Additive slack inefficiency (Envelopment formulation)

$$TI_{A(G)}(x_o, y_o; \delta^*, \alpha) = \max_{s^-, s^+, \lambda} \sum_{m=1}^{M} s_m^- + \sum_{n=1}^{N} s_n^+$$

$$\begin{aligned} \text{s.t.} \quad & \sum_{j=1}^{J} \lambda_j x_{mj} + s_m^- = \delta^{*1-\alpha} x_{mo}, \quad m = 1, \ldots, M, \\ & \sum_{j=1}^{J} \lambda_j y_{nj} - s_n^+ = y_{no} / \delta^{*\alpha}, \quad n = 1, \ldots, N, \\ & \sum_{j=1}^{J} \lambda_j = 1, \\ & \lambda_j \geq 0, \quad s_m^- \geq 0, \quad s_n^+ \geq 0. \end{aligned} \tag{4.14}$$

Note that the strongly disposable technology (4.11) is incorporated in program (4.13)—the superscript S is omitted for simplicity in the generalized distance function. The optimal value δ^*, corresponding to the GDF, measures the profitability loss due to technical efficiency against the variable returns to scale, as signaled by the associated restriction, $\sum_{j=1}^{J} \lambda_j = 1$. Hence, to calculate productive efficiency against the constant returns to scale benchmark, δ^{CRS*}—expression (4.7), and subsequently recover the scale efficiency of the firm, it is necessary to solve the same program but dropping the variable returns constraint. Once both programs have been solved, we can calculate scale efficiency: $SE_G(x_o, y_o; \alpha) = \delta^{CRS*}/\delta^*$.[12] The nature of the returns to scale responsible of the scale inefficiency of the firm can

[12] In passing, we note that a second-stage evaluation of the CRS model, searching for input and output slacks, can be performed to shed light on these sources of inefficiency.

be determined by examining the value of the sum of the optimal lambdas in the CRS model—Cooper et al. (2007: Chap. 5):

(i) Decreasing returns to scale (DRS) prevails for $(x_o, y_o) \Leftrightarrow \sum_j \lambda_j^{CRS*} > 1$ for all optimal solutions.
(ii) Increasing returns to scale (IRS) prevails for $(x_o, y_o) \Leftrightarrow \sum_j \lambda_j^{CRS*} < 1$ for all optimal solutions.
(iii) Constant returns to scale (CRS) prevail for $(x_o, y_o) \Leftrightarrow \sum_j \lambda_j^{CRS*} = 1$ for some optimal solutions.

Therefore, by solving the CRS counterpart of program (4.13), we can determine what type of returns to scale locally hold for (x_o, y_o)—which, in turn, implies that a suboptimal scale is observed if the firm is inefficient with $D_G^{CRS}(x_o, y_o; \alpha) < 1$.

We can now explore the productivity interpretation of the generalized distance function, in terms of the index number formula that constitutes the objective function in the dual DEA formulations. The dual of program (4.13) under constant returns to scale, CRS, i.e., without the VRS constraint, $\sum_{j=1}^{J} \lambda_j = 1$, can be directly related to the seminal model introduced by Charnes et al. (1978). This result holds thanks to the equivalence between the generalized distance function and the inverse of the input distance function: $D_G^{CRS}(x, y; \alpha) = 1/\, D_I^{CRS}(x, y) = TE_{R(I)}(x, y)$, which, in turn, is equal to the input technical efficiency measure; see expression (2.4) of Chap. 2.[13] The DEA model corresponding to this measure is presented in program (3.27) of the preceding chapter. Here, we recall this program in its original fractional programming formulation as presented by Charnes et al. (1978):

Generalized distance function, α =0, CRS (Multiplier formulation, fractional programming)

$$
\begin{aligned}
D_G^{CRS}(x_o, y_o; 0) = \max_{\mu^{CRS}, \nu^{CRS}} \; & \frac{\sum_{n=1}^{N} \mu_n^{CRS} y_{no}}{\sum_{m=1}^{M} \nu_m^{CRS} x_{mo}} \\
\text{s.t.} \; & \frac{\sum_{n=1}^{N} \mu_n^{CRS} y_{nj}}{\sum_{m=1}^{M} \nu_m^{CRS} x_{mj}} \leq 1, \quad j = 1, \ldots, J, \\
& \mu^{CRS} \geq 0, \;\; \nu^{CRS} \geq 0.
\end{aligned}
\tag{4.15}
$$

[13] The relationship between the hyperbolic and input technical efficiency measures is explored in detail by Halická and Trnovská (2019:415).

Generalized distance function, $\alpha = 0$, CRS (Multiplier formulation, linear programming)

$$D_G^{CRS}(x_o, y_o; 0) = \max_{\nu^{CRS}, \mu^{CRS}} \sum_{N=1}^{N} \mu_n^{CRS} y_{no}$$

$$\begin{aligned} \text{s.t.} \quad & \sum_{M=1}^{M} \nu_m^{CRS} x_{mj} - \sum_{n=1}^{N} \mu_n^{CRS} y_{nj} \geq 0, \ j = 1, \ldots, J, \\ & \sum_{m=1}^{M} \nu_m^{CRS} x_{mo} = 1, \\ & \nu^{CRS} \geq 0, \ \mu^{CRS} \geq 0. \end{aligned} \tag{4.16}$$

Examining (4.15), we confirm that the DEA implementation of the generalized distance function corresponds to a total factor productivity index where inputs and outputs are aggregated through the optimal multipliers ν^{CRS*} and μ^{CRS*}. In program (4.15), maximum productivity is normalized to 1, and ν^{CRS*} and μ^{CRS*} can be interpreted as the weights or shadow prices that render the firm under evaluation productively efficient. For each evaluated firm, DEA searches for the most favorable weights when comparing its productivity level to that of all $j = 1, \ldots, J$ firms, including itself. Consequently, depending on the optimal weights, several firms can be identified as most productive scale sizes. If a firm belongs to the production frontier represented by the weakly efficient subset $\partial^W(T)$, it implies that the associated weights for inputs and outputs, $X(x, \nu^{CRS}) = \nu^{CRS*} \cdot x$ and $Y(y, \mu^{CRS}) = \mu^{CRS*} \cdot y$, maximize the productivity index, i.e., $D_G^{CRS}(x_o, y_o; \alpha) = Y(y, \mu^{CRS}) \, / \, X(x, \nu^{CRS}) = \mu^{CRS*} \cdot y \, / \, \nu^{CRS*} \cdot x = 1$.[14] As we remark in what follows, profitability represents a measure of total factor productivity where the observed input and output prices are used as aggregators, i.e., $X(x, w) = w \cdot x$ and $Y(y, p) = p \cdot y$. Hence, while a firm may maximize productivity by representing a most productive scale size given its associated multipliers, it may fall short from maximizing profitability, defined as $\Gamma(w, p) = \max_{x,y} \{p \cdot y / w \cdot x : (x, y) \in T^{CRS}\}$—see expression (4.17). This reflects the disparity between the optimal multipliers (ν^{CRS*}, μ^{CRS*}) and market prices (w, p). We return to this question in the following section, as *this difference between*

[14] We also note that there may exist multiple solutions to problem (4.15), which results in different total factor productivity values depending on the specific vector of multipliers that is obtained (μ^{CRS*}, ν^{CRS*}). This lack of uniqueness is especially important in interpreting the multipliers and slacks. Note that the existence of output and input slacks, associated with zero multipliers, implies that the attained productivity would be larger if the aggregate output and aggregate input are larger or smaller, respectively.

the productivity under shadow prices and market prices (profitability) *can be interpreted as allocative inefficiency.*

Program (4.15) corresponds to a fractional (ratio form) formulation, which after some transformations can be expressed as the equivalent linear program (4.16). Specifically, applying the transformation proposed by Charnes et al. (1978) to (4.15), which normalized the sum of optimal inputs to one, $\sum_{m=1}^{M} \nu_m^{CRS} x_{mo} = 1$, one obtains program (4.16). Program (4.16) represents the standard multiplier formulation of the CRS technical efficiency measure from an input orientation. Its objective function is linearly homogeneous of degree one, thereby defining a production frontier characterized by constant returns to scale (CRS) (Cooper et al.) (2007: Chap. 2). The variable returns to scale formulation is presented in program (3.27) of Chap. 3. We refer the reader to Sect. 3.2 for a complete description of that model, including the interpretation of the scale parameter ω^* that also allows identifying the nature of returns to scale: increasing, decreasing, and constant. In the case of variable returns to scale, the objective function and the J restrictions in program (4.15) correspond to $\left(\sum_{N=1}^{N} \mu_n y_{no} + \omega\right) / \sum_{m=1}^{M} \nu_m x_{mo}$. The output technical efficiency measure with $\alpha = 1$ is also discussed in Chap. 3. The specific fractional formulation corresponds to the inverse of program (4.15), whose objective function is minimized and whose linear programing counterpart is presented in model (3.28).

Once we have discussed the productivity interpretation of the generalized distance function under CRS, which results in a program than can be solved through linear programming techniques, we return to its VRS definition in (4.13) and the optimizing methods that allow its calculation. Since the envelopment formulation (4.13) corresponds to a nonlinear program, its computation requires the use of advanced solvers searching for global solutions. Several authors have explored other computational alternatives to calculate the hyperbolic technical efficiency measure (i.e., for $\alpha = 0.5$), which could be extended to the generalized distance function. For example, Färe et al. (2016) devise *an approximate method* that considers the solution of the CRS hyperbolic model and resorts to the directional distance function vector associated with it, so as to progress toward the VRS hyperbolic solution. This results in an algorithm that, relying on the dual (multiplier) formulation of the DDF and the quadratic formula, allows for the calculation of the hyperbolic distance function through linear programming techniques. Recently, Halická and Trnovská (2019) reformulate the hyperbolic model within a semidefinite programming framework—see program (2.68) in Chap. 2—opening the way to solve it through efficient interior point algorithms, as well as to establish simple primal-dual correspondences. Despite these proposals, current developments in the field of nonlinear programming are greatly improving the algorithms available to solve these models with confidence. Arguably, the fact that inefficiency is bounded simplifies the problem by restricting the range of feasible solutions, which, combined with the inclusion of seeds, results in an easier convergence to the global optimum. For this reason, in the accompanying dedicated software using the Julia language, we calculate the generalized distance function relying on the "JuMP" package developed by Dunning et al. (2017), combined with the "Ipopt" solver, initially introduced by Wächter and Biegler (2006).[15]

4.3 Economic Behavior and Profitability Efficiency

We now focus our analysis on a specific economic objective of the firm, defined as *the ratio of revenue to cost*, which simultaneously accounts for its input and output dimensions. This function is currently known as *profitability*, although in the economics literature it was initially termed as 'return-to-dollar" by Georgescu-Roegen (1951:103), a denomination that was maintained by Färe et al. (2002) and Zofío and Prieto (2006), among others. Diewert (2014:59) credits Balk (2003:9–10) for introducing the term "profitability." However, much earlier, Georgescu-Roegen (1951:103) argued in favor of this function to characterize the economic behavior of the firm. Recently, Grifell-Tatjé and Lovell (2015: Chap. 2) discuss the concept of profitability as an indicator of economic performance in the business literature. This function is the inverse of the so-called efficiency ratio, representing one of the most important financial key performance indicators. They also survey the origins of a variety of measures involving alternative definitions of revenue and cost, resulting in a family of profitability indicators.

The profitability function represents the maximum revenue to cost given the technology and input and output prices. It defines as follows:[16]

$$\Gamma(w,p) = \max_{x,y} \{p \cdot y / w \cdot x : (x,y) \in T\}, \quad w \in \mathbb{R}^M_{++}, \quad p \in \mathbb{R}^N_{++}, \quad x \geq 0_N, \quad y \geq 0_M, \tag{4.17}$$

and whose properties, under minimal regularity conditions, are discussed in Sect. 2.3 of Chap. 2. As already noted, a relevant property of the profitability function, which characterizes the definition and decomposition of profitability efficiency, is that the technology exhibits *local constant returns to scale* at the optimal solution. This can be shown by examining the first-order conditions of the maximization problem (4.17). Expressing profitability equivalently as $\Gamma(w,p) = \max_y \left\{p \cdot y / C(y,w) : (x,y) \in T^{CRS}\right\}$, where $C(y,w) = \min_x \{w \cdot x : x \in L(y)\}$, is

[15] Ipopt, short for "Interior Point Optimizer," is a software library for large-scale nonlinear optimization of continuous systems. At the time of writing, the latest stable is 3.14.4, from Sep. 20, 2021. See https://github.com/coin-or/Ipopt. A list of commercial and free solvers compatible with the Julia (JuMP) environment can be found in http://www.juliaopt.org/JuMP.jl/v0.20.0/installation/

[16] It is assumed that the optimization problem associated with the calculation of $\Gamma(w,p)$ always attains its maximum in T.

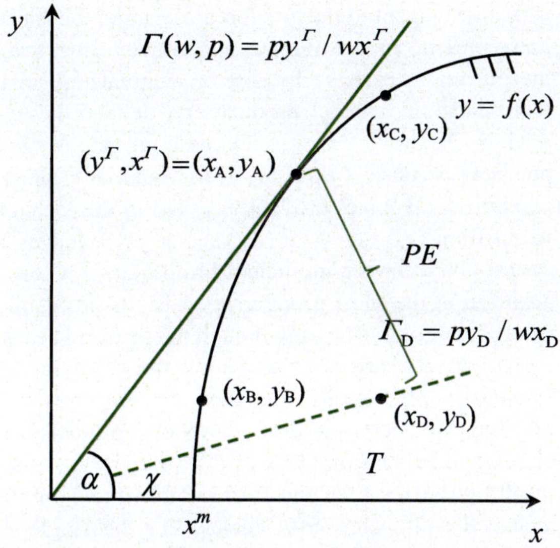

Fig. 4.3 Profitability maximization and profitability efficiency

the usual cost function defined in (2.16) of Chap. 2; the first-order conditions are $p/p \cdot y = \nabla_y C(y, w)/C(y, w)$ and, therefore, cost elasticity $\varepsilon_C(y, w) = 1$; see Balk (2008:66).[17] In turn, this implies that the scale elasticity is $\varepsilon(x, y) = 1$, showing that local constant returns to scale prevail at the profitability-maximizing benchmark, a property that was emphasized by Georgescu-Roegen (1951). This author advocated the use of the profitability function as "…an *economic* criterion on which to base the choice between two linear processes…," which "*must be independent of the scale of production*, whereas $p{\cdot}y$, $w{\cdot}x$, and $p{\cdot}y$—$w{\cdot}x$ are not"—his italics and our notation.

The choice for a measure of economic performance independent of returns to scale is also desirable when relating the generalized distance function to productivity indices, which in principle should satisfy a proportionality property, which is met under a constant returns to scale technological specification; see, e.g., Balk and Zofío (2018). Indeed, as anticipated in the previous section, if a firm is capable of producing the output and input quantities that maximize profitability, then it also maximizes productivity defined as aggregated output divided by aggregated input, where their respective prices constitute the aggregating weights: $\Gamma(w, p) = p \cdot y^\Gamma / w \cdot x^\Gamma$. Recalling Fig. 2.5, the optimal production plan is denoted by $(x^\Gamma(w, p), y^\Gamma(w, p))$ in Fig. 4.3, where $\Gamma(w, p) = p \cdot y^\Gamma / w \cdot x^\Gamma$ is once again illustrated by the green

[17] In the standard, single output-multiple input production function, $y = f(x)$, scale elasticity defines as follows: $\varepsilon(x, y) = (\partial \ln f(\psi x)/\partial \ln \psi)|_{\psi=1} = \sum_{m=1}^{M} (\partial f(x)/\partial x_m) \cdot (x_m/y) = \sum_{m=1}^{M} \varepsilon_m$. The definition implies proportional changes in the inputs quantities; i.e., the input mix (relative input quantities) remains unchanged.

solid line tangent to the graph representation of the technology. This isoprofitability line represents the set of input and output vectors that, given their prices, can achieve the maximum revenue to cost or, equivalently in this single output-single input representation, average productivity, defined as *y*/*x*—or its economic counterpart $p{\cdot}y/w{\cdot}x$. On this occasion, maximum profitability is attained by firm (x_A, y_A) only, precisely because it operates at the optimal scale. In this example, no other firm maximizes (average) productivity. Given the technology, any production plan different from $(x_A, y_A) = (x^\Gamma(w,p), y^\Gamma(w,p))$ achieves lower profitability. This is the case of the technical inefficient firm (x_D, y_D), whose profitability is lower than that achieved at the most productive scale. Its profitability corresponds by the dashed isoprofitability line passing though the firm and the origin: $\Gamma_D = py_D/wx_D$, i.e., $\Gamma_D < \Gamma(w,p)$. In this case, we observe that the remaining technically efficient firms B and C are also profitability inefficient. As we present in the following section and recalling the decomposition of productive efficiency into technical and scale efficiencies in expression (4.7), $D_G^{CRS}(x,y;\alpha) = D_G(x,y;\alpha) \times SE_G(x,y;\alpha)$, we see that the difference between observed and maximum profitability can be fully attributed to technical and scale inefficiencies. For the single output-single input case, there cannot be, by definition, allocative inefficiencies. In this case, if the firm was to reduce its inputs and increase its outputs along the path defined by the generalized distance function to remove technical inefficiency, while exhausting any possible increasing returns to scale and avoiding decreasing returns to scale (i.e., removing scale inefficiencies), it would produce under constant returns to scale and maximize profitability. In the multiple output-multiple input case, several firms can produce under local constant returns to scale, thereby satisfying this necessary condition for profitability maximization. However, for a given input and output market price vectors, only a subset of these firms maximize revenue to cost. The reason is that, as previously anticipated, observed revenue and cost are (scalar) linear aggregating functions that use prices to weight quantities. Consequently, although there may be several firms producing at alternative most productive scale sizes, only a subset of them will maximize profitability subject to a particular vector of market prices, while others fall short from this goal. In that case, despite producing in a technically efficient way under local constant returns to scale, the firm incurs allocative inefficiencies by demanding and supplying input and output suboptimal quantities that, given market prices, do not maximize profitability. We present this possibility in the following section.

It is now possible *to define profitability efficiency* as the ratio of observed to maximum profitability:

$$\Gamma E(x,y,w,p) = \frac{p \cdot y/w \cdot x}{\Gamma(p,w)} = \frac{p \cdot y/w \cdot x}{p \cdot y^\Gamma/w \cdot x^\Gamma} \leq 1. \tag{4.18}$$

Therefore, unless the firm under evaluation demands inputs and supplies outputs in optimal quantities, it incurs profitability inefficiency. As in previous cases, for profitability-efficient firms, $\Gamma E(x,y,w,p) = 1$, while $\Gamma E(x,y,w,p) < 1$ quantifies the magnitude of economic inefficiency. In our graphical example, the profitability loss of firm (x_D, y_D) is represented in Fig. 4.3 by the gap between the optimal and observed isoprofitability ray vectors. We can relate this result to the comparison of productivities that we discussed in Sect. 4.2.1. On this occasion, resorting once again to trigonometry, profitability efficiency defines equivalently as the ratio of the slope of the ray vector joining the origin and firm under evaluation to that of firm A maximizing profitability, i.e., in Fig. 4.3, $\Gamma E(x,y,w,p) = \tan\chi/\tan\alpha$.

4.3.1 Calculating Maximum Profitability Using Data Envelopment Analysis

Once the generalized distance functions representing technical and productive efficiency have been respectively calculated solving program (4.13) with and without the variable returns constraint $\sum_{j=1}^{J}\lambda_j = 1$, to calculate economic efficiency, it is first necessary to determine the vector of optimal input demand and output supply quantities: $(x^{\Gamma}(w,p), y^{\Gamma}(w,p))$. These optimal amounts are obtained by solving the DEA program that calculates maximum profitability $\Gamma(w,p)$, whose formulation corresponds to the following:

$$
\begin{aligned}
\Gamma(w,p) = \max_{x,\,y,\,\lambda^{CRS}} \quad & p\cdot y/w\cdot x \\
\text{s.t.} \quad & \sum_{j=1}^{J}\lambda_j^{CRS}x_{jn} \le x_n, \quad n = 1,\ldots,N, \\
& \sum_{j=1}^{J}\lambda_j^{CRS}y_{jm} \ge y_m, \quad m = 1,\ldots,M, \\
& \lambda^{CRS} \ge 0.
\end{aligned}
\tag{4.19}
$$

Note that, for consistency, the technology set corresponds to the DEA approximation of the production technology presented in (4.11), under constant returns to scale. This shows that the reference technology must be the same when calculating the productive efficiency measure corresponding to the generalized distance function, $D_G^{CRS}(x,y;\alpha)$—see program (4.13)—and maximum profitability. The solution to (4.19) allows identifying the specific $j = 1,\ldots,J$ reference economic benchmarks that maximize profitability and whose associated intensity variables are positive $\lambda_j^{CRS} > 0$. Also, as program (4.13), the DEA profitability program is nonlinear, so it must be solved through nonlinear optimizers. Therefore, as in the previous case, in the accompanying dedicated software using the Julia language and illustrated in Sect. 4.5, we calculate maximum profitability relying on the "JuMP" package, combined with the "Ipopt" nonlinear solver.

Under perfectly competitive input and output markets, profitability $\Gamma(w, p)$ equals 1 in the long run—a result consistent with null maximum profit: $\Pi(w, p) = 0$, which also results in a single price for each input and output. However, in the short run, this result may not hold, and firms may be inefficient from the technical, scale, and allocative perspectives, while prices may also differ across firms because of individual market power. In this case, when different market prices are observed across observations, (w_o, p_o), we assume that they hold for the firm under evaluation when solving (4.19). For other alternatives, see, for example, Camanho and Dyson (2008) and Portela and Thanassoulis (2014). Finally, once maximum profitability has been calculated, it is straightforward to calculate profitability efficiency $\Gamma E(x, y, w, p)$ through expression (4.18). How profitability efficiency can be decomposed based on duality theory and according technical, scale, and allocative criteria is presented in the following section.

4.4 Duality and the Decomposition of Profitability Efficiency as the Product of Technical, Scale, and Allocative Efficiencies

This section presents the decomposition of profitability efficiency based on the *duality* between the generalized distance function and the profitability function. In this case, duality refers to the possibility of recovering the technology T from the profitability function serving as support function and vice versa. In this case, the relevant technology is characterized by *constant returns to scale*, as required by profitability maximization and discussed in the previous section. As in the case of other measures of economic efficiency, duality allows to relate the primal (quantity or engineering) space with the dual (price or market) space that characterizes the technological and economic behavior of the firm in a consistent way, so both representations contain the same information. As discussed in Sect. 2.4 of Chap. 2, duality theory constitutes a particularization to the field of economic theory of *Minkowski's theorem*. This theorem states that every closed convex set can be characterized as the intersection of its supporting half-spaces. Here, the elements are the technology, represented by either the production possibility set or the generalized distance function, and the profitability function. Regarding their duality, Zofío and Prieto (2006) showed that it could be formalized by extending the results previously obtained in the literature by Färe and Primont (1995), for the case of the cost function and the input distance function, as presented in Chap. 3. Ultimately, following Farrell's (1957) approach, this allows the multiplicative decomposition of profitability efficiency into technical, scale, and allocative components.

4.4.1 Duality Between the Technology Set and the Profitability Function

The duality between the profitability function $\Gamma(w,p)$ and the technology set is characterized by the existence of local constant returns to scale at the optimal input and output production plans that attain maximum profitability, as defined in (4.17). Consequently, since the profitability function can only support half-spaces characterized by CRS, we adopt this notation but emphasize that the actual technology T may exhibit variable returns to scale. However, it is clear that T cannot be recovered from the profitability function but only the convex cone spanned by T at the *loci* where local constant returns to scale hold and corresponding to $T^{CRS} = \{(\psi x, \psi y) : (x,y) \in T,\ \psi > 0\}$.

Then, duality analysis shows that the technology set T^{CRS}, satisfying the axioms considered in Sect. 2.2 of Chap. 2, can be recovered from the profitability function, as follows.

Proposition 4.1 If the profitability function is defined by (4.17), then

$$T^{CRS} = \left\{(x,y) : p \cdot y / w \cdot x \leq \Gamma(w,p),\ \ \forall\ w \in \mathbb{R}^M_{++}, \forall\ p \in \mathbb{R}^N_{++},\ \ x \geq 0_M, y \geq 0_N\right\}. \tag{4.20}$$

Proof Following existing results, e.g., McFadden (1978:23) for the input set and the cost function, the proof replicates the structure found therein which resorts to Minkowski's theorem; i.e., a closed, convex set is the intersection of the half-spaces that support it.

This expression reveals that given a price vector (w,p), the profitability function supports a half-space of the form $H(w,p,c) = \left\{(x,y) : p \cdot y / w \cdot x \leq c = \Gamma(w,p), w \in \mathbb{R}^M_{++},\ p \in \mathbb{R}^N_{++},\ x \geq 0_M, y \geq 0_N\right\}$. Since, by definition, $\Gamma(w,p)$ is the maximum profitability given prices and technology, there is no feasible firm $(x,y) \in H(w,p,c)$ that yields higher profitability. Correspondingly, if the production plan maximizing profitability belongs to $H(w,p,c)$, then it lies on the hyperplane $p \cdot y/w \cdot x = \Gamma(w,p)$.

We can illustrate this result in Fig. 4.4a—replicating Fig. 2.8a of Chap. 2, where a detailed graphical exposition of duality is presented. Here, we consider three different price vectors: (w^1,p^1), (w^2,p^2), and (w^3,p^3), each one defining its corresponding half-space below the (hyper)plane consistent with their corresponding maximum profitabilities: $p^k \cdot y/w^k \cdot x = \Gamma(w^k,p^k)$, $k = 1$, 2, and 3, thereby tangent to the technology T at $(x^\Gamma(w^k,p^k), y^\Gamma(w^k,p^k)) \in T^{CRS}$, $k = 1$, 2, and 3. Note that this is a three-dimensional representation of a quasi-concave production function that is subject to decreasing returns to scale, with two inputs (x_1,x_2) producing one output y. Also, note that each supporting profitability hyperplane represents the convex

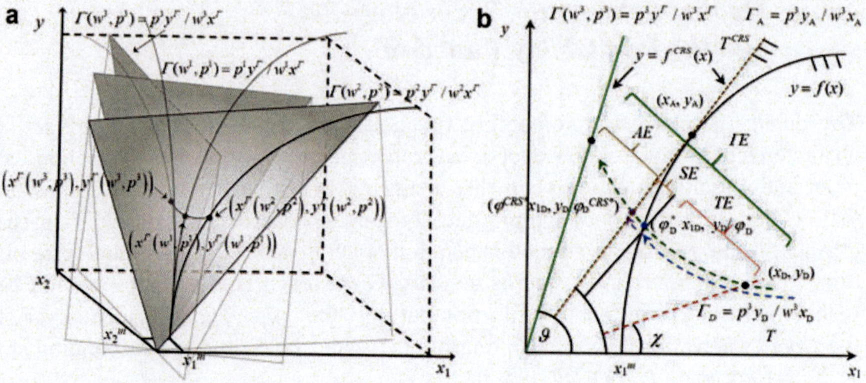

Fig. 4.4 **(a–b)** Duality between the technology and the profitability function

cone spanned at T and, therefore, passing through the origin and characterized by constant returns to scale (CRS) as presented in Sect. 4.2. According to Proposition 4.1, each profitability-maximizing bundle cannot be above this (hyper)plane, and therefore, the half-space below it must contain T^{CRS}. If, for each price vector, there were an alternative firm $(x, y) \in T^{CRS}$ above the corresponding hyperplane, it could attain higher profitability given the technology, but then, we incur in the contradiction that $(x^{\Gamma}(w^k, p^k), y^{\Gamma}(w^k, p^k))$, $k = 1$, 2, and 3, would not maximize profitability. That is, no elements of the associated half-spaces $(x, y) \in H(w^k, p^k, \Gamma(w^k, p^k))$, $k = 1$, 2, and 3, could yield higher profitabilities given the technology T^{CRS} than $\Gamma(w^k, p^k)$, $k = 1$, 2, and 3. This implies that since at least one firm in each isoprofitability plane $p^k \cdot y / w^k \cdot x = \Gamma(w^k, p^k)$, $k = 1$, 2, and 3, must be able to produce with the existing technology T^{CRS}, then each $p^k \cdot y / w^k \cdot x$, $k = 1$, 2, and 3, and T^{CRS} must share at least one (x, y) in the quantity (primal) space. Combining all three half-spaces $H(w^1, p^1, \Gamma(w^1, p^1))$, $H(w^2, p^2, \Gamma(w^2, p^2))$, and $H(w^3, p^3, \Gamma(w^3, p^3))$, the technology T^{CRS} is approximated by the intersection between the three supporting hyperplanes. Continuing with every price combination until all price vectors are exhausted results in expression (4.20).

Graphically, the technology T^{CRS} jointly defined by the profitability-maximizing firms as stated in (4.20) corresponds to the isoquant including the previous cases: $(x^{\Gamma}(w^k, p^k), y^{\Gamma}(w^k, p^k))$, $k = 1$, 2, and 3, and therefore, the output quantities are equal. In this example, the supporting hyperplanes pivot at the origin as the price vector changes and are tangent to the technology T at each optimal vector of quantities characterized by CRS. Notice also that in Fig. 4.4a, the 3D representation of the technology resembles the standard (homothetic) Cobb-Douglas production function $y = f(x)$. Formally, the elasticity of scale is equal to one, $\varepsilon(x, y) = 1$, and constant returns to scale hold locally at the optimal input quantities (i.e., in the neighborhood of these inputs): $f(\psi x^{\Gamma}(w^k, p^k)) = \psi f(x^{\Gamma}(w^k, p^k))$, $\psi \geq 1$, $k = 1$, 2, and 3.

From the discussion above, we conclude that the relevant benchmark technology defined by the intersection of the supporting hyperplanes for different price vectors represents an outer approximation of the benchmark technology T^{CRS} consisting of the *loci* where CRS hold. This constitutes McFadden's (1978, p. 22) *envelopment technology* but, on this occasion, defined on the constant returns to scale subset of the technology, relevant for profitability maximization (rather than for the case of the cost function and its dual input set developed by McFadden). Then, it follows that the *loci* of the technology characterized by CRS are a subset of the actual technology, i.e., $T^{CRS} \subseteq T$ and, consequently, $\partial^S(T^{CRS}) \subseteq \partial^S(T)$.[18] In Fig. 4.4a, the 3D representation is necessary to show that there exist several firms that, satisfying the local constant returns to scale condition, are candidates to maximize profitability, although only one emerges as optimum for a specific vector of prices.

Once the benchmark technology has been recovered from the profitability function as stated by Proposition 4.1, we can in turn define the profitability function by the intersection of the supporting half-spaces corresponding to different isoprofitabilities, representing maximum revenue to cost for each price vector, as follows:

Proposition 4.2
If $T^{CRS} = \{(x,y) : p \cdot y/w \cdot x \leq \Gamma(w,p), \forall\ w \in \mathbb{R}^M_{++}, \forall p \in \mathbb{R}^N_{++}, x \geq 0_M,\ y \geq 0_N\}$, then

$$\Gamma(w,p) = \max_{x,y} \{p \cdot y/w \cdot x : (x,y) \in T^{CRS}\}. \tag{4.21}$$

Proof Again, the proof requires extending duality results like those presented, e.g., in McFadden (1978:23) for the cost function and the input set: $C(y,w) = \min_x \{w \cdot x : x \in L(y)\}$. Specifically, the proof relies on the equivalent definition of profitability as $\Gamma(w,p) = \max_y \{p \cdot y/C(y,w) : (x,y) \in T^{CRS}\}$; see our remarks in Sect. 4.1.

In Fig. 4.4a, this expression corresponds to each isoprofitability plane that, maximizing profitability for each price vector, is tangent to the technology T^{CRS}, thereby satisfying the first-order conditions for profitability maximization subject to the technology.[19] Before showing the duality results between the generalized distance function and the profitability function allowing for technical and scale efficiency, we comment on the concept of shadow prices. Here, we refer to the vector of

[18]This notation stresses that if the technology exhibits *global* constant returns to scale, the benchmark and actual technologies coincide. Despite the fact that the actual technology exhibits variable returns to scale, when using the nonparametric Data Envelopment Analysis (DEA) methods discussed in Sect. 4.2.3, researchers approximate the benchmark technology from observed data both under global CRS and VRS and then recover scale efficiency through (4.6). The global CRS characterization allows identifying the reference hyperplanes (faces) consistent with local CRS, i.e., the outer approximation of T^{CRS}.

[19]In this case, it is assumed once again that the profitability function is continuous and twice differentiable.

prices that satisfy the first-order conditions for profitability maximization if a given production plan (combination of input and output quantities) is optimal. In this case, rather than reading Fig. 4.4a as the input and output combinations that maximize profitability, we focus on the input and output price vectors that maximize profitability given a (would be optimal) production plan. Let us denote again these vectors of shadow prices as $\nu^{CRS} \in \mathbb{R}^M_+$ and $\mu^{CRS} \in \mathbb{R}^N_+$. Then, a firm incurs allocative inefficiency if it does not maximize profitability by failing to demand the optimal input and output quantities given observed market prices (w, p). But, as before, this can be reinterpreted as a divergence between its associated shadow prices, (ν^{CRS}, μ^{CRS}), for which it would be profitability-efficient, i.e., $\mu^{CRS} \cdot y/\nu^{CRS} \cdot x = \mu \cdot y^{\Gamma}(\nu^{CRS}, \mu^{CRS})/\nu \cdot x^{\Gamma}(\nu^{CRS}, \mu^{CRS}) = \Gamma(\nu^{CRS}, \mu^{CRS})$, and actual market prices. In this case, $(\nu^{CRS}, \mu^{CRS}) \neq (w, p)$, and therefore, $p \cdot y^{\Gamma}(\nu^{CRS}, \mu^{CRS})/w \cdot x^{\Gamma}(\nu^{CRS}, \mu^{CRS}) < p \cdot y^{\Gamma}(w, p)/w \cdot x^{\Gamma}(w, p) = \Gamma(w, p)$. In Fig. 4.4b, this situation is represented by firm $(x_A, y_A) = (x^{\Gamma}(w^2, p^2), x^{\Gamma}(w^2, p^2))$, which maximizes profitability for prices (w^2, p^2), implying that its associated shadow prices are $(\nu^{CRS}, \mu^{CRS}) = (w^2, p^2)$. But if market prices are (w^3, p^3), then this firm experiences a profitability loss because $p^3 \cdot y^{\Gamma}(w^2, p^2)/w^3 \cdot x^{\Gamma}(w^2, p^2) < p^3 \cdot y^{\Gamma}(w^3, p^3)/w^3 \cdot x^{\Gamma}(w^3, p^3) = \Gamma(w^3, p^3)$. This is illustrated through the two isoprofitabilities corresponding to $p^3 \cdot y_A/w^3 \cdot x_A$ and $p^3 \cdot y^{\Gamma}(w^3, p^3)/w^3 \cdot x^{\Gamma}(w^3, p^3)$. We see that the slope of the latter is steeper, consistent with the profitability differential in its favor. In the following section, we show that the difference between profitability under shadow prices and market prices precisely measures the extent of allocative inefficiency of the firm.

4.4.2 Duality Between the Generalized Distance Function and the Profitability Function

We can now present the equivalent duality results between the production possibility set and the profitability function but relying on the generalized distance function as an equivalent representation of the technology. This allows to explicitly account for (in)efficiency in duality theory. As already justified, we consider productive efficiency with respect to the constant returns to scale technological benchmark. Then, relying on the representation property (4.5), we can define the constant returns technology as follows:

$$T^{CRS} = \{(x, y) : D_G^{CRS}(x, y; \alpha) \leq 1\}. \tag{4.22}$$

Consequently, as shown in Fig. 4.4a, a productively inefficient firm cannot maximize profitability for any price vector. The reason is that it can be (i) technically inefficient and, therefore, input reductions and output increases are feasible given the technology T and/or (ii) scale-inefficient, thereby subject to increasing or decreasing returns to scale. This situation is shown in Fig. 4.4b for firm (x_D, y_D). Here, the production technology is represented for the particular case that holds the second input constant at its minimum required amount, x_2^m—i.e., $y = f\left(x_1 \middle| x_2^m\right)$. This is visualized through the slice parallel to x_1. Firm $(x_\mathrm{D}, y_\mathrm{D})$ is productively inefficient because it could reach the actual variable returns to scale technology by projecting itself along the path described by $D_G(x, y; \alpha) = \delta < 1$, decreasing inputs and increasing outputs to reach its technical efficient projection: $\left(\delta^{1-\alpha}x_{1\mathrm{D}}, x_2^m, y_\mathrm{D}/\delta^\alpha\right) = \left(\widehat{x}_{1\mathrm{D}}, x_2^m,\ \widehat{y}_\mathrm{D}\right)$. But there remains an additional source of inefficiency related to a suboptimal scale by which the size of the projected firm $(\widehat{x}_\mathrm{D},\ \widehat{y}_\mathrm{D})$ does not maximize productivity, defined as the ratio of aggregate output to aggregate input. In Fig. 4.4b, it is firm $\left(x_{1\mathrm{A}}, x_2^m, y_\mathrm{A}\right)$ the one maximizing productivity by reaching a scale for which neither increasing nor decreasing returns to scale exist, and therefore, local constant returns to scale hold. In this single output-two inputs case (keeping the second input constant at x_2^m), the plane maximizing productivity is $\mu^{CRS} y_\mathrm{A}^{CRS} / \left(v_1^{CRS} x_{1\mathrm{A}}^{CRS} + v_2^{CRS} x_2^m\right) = \mu^{CRS} \cdot \widehat{y}_\mathrm{D}^{CRS} / \left(v_1^{CRS} \widehat{x}_{1\mathrm{D}}^{CRS} + v_2^{CRS} x_2^m\right) > \mu \cdot \widehat{y}_\mathrm{D} / \left(v_1 \widehat{x}_{1\mathrm{D}} + v_2 x_2^m\right) > \mu \cdot y_\mathrm{D} / \left(v_1 x_{1\mathrm{D}} + v_2 x_2^m\right)$, where (ν^{CRS}, μ^{CRS}) and (ν, μ) are the vectors of input and output multipliers (aggregating weights) that we intentionally denote as the shadow prices, to convey the idea that if market prices were equal to them, $(\nu^{CRS}, \mu^{CRS}) = (w^2, p^2)$ —as previously discussed, firm $(x_\mathrm{D}, y_\mathrm{D})$ would be profitability-efficient, which is not the case in the graphical example since market prizes are assumed to be (w^3, p^3). Hence, we can recall the notion of scale efficiency capturing the productivity difference between maximum productivity given the weights (ν^{CRS}, μ^{CRS}) and the technical efficiency projections with (ν, μ). Consequently, for the general multiple output-multiple input case, one can decompose constant returns to scale productive efficiency into technical and scale efficiency as shown in (4.7): $D_G^{CRS}(x, y; \alpha) = D_G(x, y; \alpha) \times SE_G(x, y; \alpha) = \delta \times \left(\delta^{CRS}/\delta\right) \leq 1$.

From this discussion, it is evident that the productive efficiency measure $D_G^{CRS}(x, y; \alpha)$ characterizes the set of relevant hyperplanes that maximize productivity consistent with benchmarks satisfying local constant returns to scale—thereby complying with the necessary (but not sufficient) condition for profitability maximization: i.e., $\delta^{CRS} \leq 1 \Leftrightarrow (x, y) \in T^{CRS}$. Hence, relying on Minkowski's theorem and combining (4.20) and (4.22), we obtain the following:

$$T^{CRS} = \left\{ \begin{array}{l} (x, y) : \dfrac{p \cdot \left(y / D_G^{CRS}(x, y; \alpha)^\alpha\right)}{w \cdot \left(D_G^{CRS}(x, y; \alpha)^{1-\alpha} x\right)} = \dfrac{p \cdot \widehat{y}^{CRS}}{w \cdot \widehat{x}^{CRS}} \leq \Gamma(w, p),\ \ D_G^{CRS}(x, y; \alpha) \leq 1, \\ \alpha \in [0, 1], \forall\ w \in \mathbb{R}_{++}^M, \forall\ p \in \mathbb{R}_{++}^N,\ \ x \geq 0_M, y \geq 0_N. \end{array} \right\} \tag{4.23}$$

Therefore, the relevant constant returns to scale technology consisting of the supporting half-spaces defined by the profitability function can be qualified to include productive efficiency. In turn, the above characterization of T^{CRS} allows us to recover the profitability function from the generalized distance function as follows:

$$\Gamma(w,p) = \max_{x,y}\left\{\frac{p\cdot\left(y/D_G^{CRS}(x,y;\alpha)^{\alpha}\right)}{w\cdot\left(D_G^{CRS}(x,y;\alpha)^{1-\alpha}x\right)} = \frac{p\cdot\widehat{y}^{CRS}}{w\cdot\widehat{x}^{CRS}}, D_G^{CRS}(x,y;\alpha)\leq 1\right\}. \quad (4.24)$$

This expression contains the information needed to characterize the duality between the economic and technological characteristics of the firm, which following Zofío and Prieto (2006) is summarized as follows:

Proposition 4.3 Assuming Propositions 4.1 and 4.2 hold, as well as expression (4.22), then

$$\begin{aligned}\Gamma(w,p) &= \max_{x,y}\left\{\frac{p\cdot\left(y/D_G^{CRS}(x,y;\alpha)^{\alpha}\right)}{w\cdot\left(D_G^{CRS}(x,y;\alpha)^{1-\alpha}x\right)}\right\}, \text{if and only if}\\ D_G^{CRS}(x,y;\alpha) &= \max_{w,p}\{(p\cdot y/w\cdot x)/\Gamma(w,p)\},\end{aligned} \quad (4.25)$$

or, alternatively,

$$\begin{aligned}\Gamma(w,p) &= \max_{x,y}\ \{\Gamma(w,p) : D_G^{CRS}(x,y;\alpha)\leq 1\ \}, \text{if and only if}\\ D_G^{CRS}(x,y;\alpha) &= \max_{w,p}\{(p\cdot y/w\cdot x) : \Gamma(w,p)\leq 1\}.\end{aligned} \quad (4.26)$$

Proof The proof mirrors the duality results presented by Färe and Primont (1995: 47–48) for the cost function and the input distance function. Again, it builds upon the equivalent definition of profitability given by $\Gamma(w,p) = \max_{y}\left\{p\cdot y/D_G^{CRS}(x,y;\alpha)^{\alpha}/D_G^{CRS}(x,y;\alpha)^{1-\alpha}C(y,w) : (x,y)\in T^{CRS}\right\}$, where the cost function defines as in (2.16) of Chap. 2; see Balk (2008:66). Once more, this notation reflects that the reference technology is characterized by local constant returns to scale as presented in Sect. 4.3.

Proposition 4.3 states that under the required assumptions, if profitability is derived from the generalized distance function by maximizing profitability over all feasible quantity vectors, then the generalized distance function can be recovered from the profitability function by finding the maximum of revenue to cost over all feasible price vectors. Note that the second part of expression (4.25) corresponds to the definition of profitability efficiency (4.18) for the optimal prices (w^*, p^*). Indeed, these prices exactly correspond to the concept of shadow prices previously discussed and denoted by (ν^{CRS}, μ^{CRS}), which are now the result of the optimization problem in (4.25). We make use of these concepts below when interpreting the meaning of allocative efficiency.

Therefore, from (4.23) or (4.26), we obtain that $\Gamma(w,p)\geq p\cdot\left(y/D_G^{CRS}(x,y;\alpha)^{\alpha}\right)/w\cdot\left(D_G^{CRS}(x,y;\alpha)^{1-\alpha}x\right) = p\cdot\widehat{y}^{CRS}/w\cdot\widehat{x}^{CRS}$. Equivalently, recalling the definition of profitability inefficiency presented in (4.18) and the following homogeneity property of profitability in input and output quantities, $p \cdot \widehat{y}^{CRS}/w \cdot \widehat{x}^{CRS} = p \cdot \left(y/D_G^{CRS}(x,y;\alpha)^{\alpha}\right)/w \cdot \left(D_G^{CRS}(x,y;\alpha)^{1-\alpha}x\right) = (p \cdot y/w \cdot x)\ /D_G^{CRS}(x,y;\alpha)$, we achieve the following Fenchel-Mahler inequality:

$$\begin{aligned}\Gamma E(x,y,w,p) = (p \cdot y/w \cdot x)/\Gamma(p,w) \le \\ D_G^{CRS}(x,y;\alpha) = D_G(x,y;\alpha) \times SE_G(x,y;\alpha),\end{aligned} \tag{4.27}$$

where the last equality follows from the decomposition of the constant returns to scale productive efficiency into technical efficiency and scale efficiency, (4.6). In this case, profitability efficiency, defined as the ratio of observed profitability to maximum profitability, is not larger than the generalized distance function.

Closing the inequality in (4.27) allows us to achieve the decompensation of profitability into technical, scale, and allocative efficiencies:

$$\begin{aligned}\Gamma E(x,y,w,p) &= (p \cdot y/w \cdot x)/\Gamma(p,w) = D_G^{CRS}(x,y;\alpha) \times \left(\left(p \cdot \widehat{y}^{CRS}/w \cdot \widehat{x}^{CRS}\right)/\Gamma(p,w)\right) = \\ &= TE_G^{CRS}(x,y;\alpha) \times AE_G(x,y,w,p;\alpha) = \\ &= \delta \times \left(\delta^{CRS}/\delta\right) \times AE_G(x,y,w,p;\alpha) = \\ &= TE_G(x,y;\alpha) \times SE_G(x,y;\alpha) \times AE_G(x,y,w,p;\alpha) \le 1,\end{aligned} \tag{4.28}$$

where the second multiplicative factor in the first row measures the gap between profitability at the constant returns to scale benchmark and maximum profitability, i.e., the generalized allocative measure of profitability efficiency. Before we discuss the interpretation of allocative efficiency, we remark that since the scalar $D_G^{CRS}(x,y;\alpha) = \delta^{CRS} = TE_G^{CRS}(x,y;\alpha)$ measures productive efficiency at an optimal scale size characterized by CRS, it is possible to recall its decomposition into technical and scale efficiencies as presented in (4.7). This is shown in the last two rows of expression (4.28). Consequently, if $SE_G(x,y;\alpha) < 1$, the firm is producing at a suboptimal scale, and these factors measure the proportional monetary loss that it brings in the form of lower profitability.

We focus now on the residual allocative efficiency factor that captures the profit loss resulting from demanding and supplying suboptimal quantities of inputs and outputs, $\left(\widehat{x}^{CRS}, \widehat{y}^{CRS}\right)$, when compared to the optimal amounts that maximize profitability: $(x^{\Gamma}(w,p), y^{\Gamma}(w,p))$. Then, from (4.28), allocative efficiency is recovered as follows:

$$AE_G(x,y,w,p;\alpha) = \Gamma E(x,y,w,p)/TE_G^{CRS}(x,y;\alpha) \le 1\ . \tag{4.29}$$

This term of allocative efficiency can be interpreted in that way, i.e., as price efficiency, because the expression shown in (4.28) satisfies the essential property for the decomposition of economic efficiency defined in Chap. 2. The property says that if $(\widehat{x},\widehat{y})$ is such that $p\cdot\widehat{y}/w\cdot\widehat{x}=\Gamma(w,p)$, then the allocative component should be equal to one. In the case of the generalized distance function, this means that if $\left(\widehat{x}^{CRS},\widehat{y}^{CRS}\right):=\left(\left(\delta^*\right)^{1-\alpha}x_1,\ldots,\left(\delta^*\right)^{1-\alpha}x_N,y_1/\left(\delta^*\right)^{\alpha},\ldots,y_M/\left(\delta^*\right)^{\alpha}\right)$ meets $p\cdot\widehat{y}^{CRS}/w\cdot\widehat{x}^{CRS}=\Gamma(w,p)$, where $\delta^*=TE_G^{CRS}(x,y;\alpha)$, then $AE_G(x,y,w,p;\alpha)$ should value one. By definition, $AE_G(x,y,w,p;\alpha)=\Gamma E(x,y,w,p)/TE_G^{CRS}(x,y;\alpha)$, which is equivalent to $AE_G(x,y,w,p;\alpha)=[(p\cdot y/w\cdot x)/\Gamma(w,p)]/\delta^*=\left(\sum_{m=1}^{M}p\left(\frac{y_m}{(\delta^*)^{\alpha}}\right)/\sum_{n=1}^{N}w\left(\delta^*\right)^{1-\alpha}x\right)/\Gamma(w,p)=\left(p\cdot\widehat{y}^{CRS}/w\cdot\widehat{x}^{CRS}\right)/\Gamma(w,p)$. Therefore, if $\left(\widehat{x}^{CRS},\widehat{y}^{CRS}\right)$ is such that $p\cdot\widehat{y}^{CRS}/w\cdot\widehat{x}^{CRS}=\Gamma(w,p)$, then $AE_G(x,y,w,p;\alpha)=1$, and the essential property is satisfied by the generalized distance function. The same happens with respect to the satisfaction of the extended essential property (see Chap. 2) since $AE_G\left(\widehat{x}^{CRS},\widehat{y}^{CRS},w,p;\alpha\right)=\left(p\cdot\widehat{y}^{CRS}/w\cdot\widehat{x}^{CRS}\right)/\Gamma(p,w)=AE_G(x,y,w,p;\alpha)$.

Allocative efficiency can be interpreted in terms of the disparity between shadow prices and market prices resorting to Proposition 4.3. Recalling the last expression in (4.25), the shadow prices correspond to the solution to $D_G^{CRS}(x,y;\alpha)=\max_{w,p}\{(p\cdot y/w\cdot x)/\Gamma(w,p)\}$, which we denote as $(w^*,p^*)=(\nu^{CRS},\mu^{CRS})$ to connect the following results to the discussion on shadow prices presented above, as well as to their empirical calculation through the DEA multiplier formulations of the generalized distance function, either (4.15) or (4.16). Then, at the optimum, it is verified that:

$$D_G^{CRS}(x,y;\alpha)=\left(\mu^{CRS}\cdot y/\nu^{CRS}\cdot x\right)/\Gamma\left(\nu^{CRS},\mu^{CRS}\right). \tag{4.30}$$

Therefore, (ν^{CRS},μ^{CRS}) represent the (shadow) prices that render the optimal projection of the firm $\left(\widehat{x}^{CRS},\ \widehat{y}^{CRS}\right)$ profitability-efficient. We can then normalize or rescale any vector of shadow prices satisfying (4.30), so it is verified that $\left(\overline{\mu}^{CRS}\cdot y/\overline{\nu}^{CRS}\cdot x\right)=p\cdot y/w\cdot x$ and $\left(\overline{\nu}^{CRS},\overline{\mu}^{CRS}\right)=\left(\psi\nu^{CRS},\xi\mu^{CRS}\right)$, $\psi>0$ and $\xi>0$. Because the profitability function is homogeneous of degree ξ/ψ in prices, $(\xi/\psi)\Gamma(\nu^{CRS},\mu^{CRS})=\Gamma(\psi\nu^{CRS},\xi\mu^{CRS})$, this transformation does not affect the value of the distance function in (4.30). Then, substituting (4.30) into the definition of allocative efficiency in (4.28) yields the following:

$$\begin{aligned}AE_G(x,y,w,p;\alpha)&=\frac{\left(p\cdot y/D_G^{CRS}(x,y;\alpha)^{\alpha}/w\cdot D_G^{CRS}(x,y;\alpha)^{1-\alpha}x\right)}{\Gamma(p,w)}=\frac{\left(p\cdot y/w\cdot D_G^{CRS}(x,y;\alpha)x\right)}{\Gamma(p,w)}=\\&=\frac{(p\cdot y/w\cdot x)}{\Gamma(p,w)}\times\frac{1}{D_G^{CRS}(x,y;\alpha)}=\frac{(p\cdot y/w\cdot x)}{\left(\mu^{CRS}\cdot y/\nu^{CRS}\cdot x\right)}\times\frac{\Gamma\left(\nu^{CRS},\mu^{CRS}\right)}{\Gamma(p,w)}=\\&=\frac{\Gamma\left(\overline{\nu}^{CRS},\overline{\mu}^{CRS}\right)}{\Gamma(p,w)}\leq 1.\end{aligned} \tag{4.31}$$

This expression reveals that allocative efficiency represents the profitability loss endured by a technically efficient firm that does not demand and supply the optimal input and output amounts at the existing market prices, which is equivalent to the profitability ratio of maximum profitability at the shadow prices to maximum profitability at the market prices. It immediately follows that if the shadow prices coincide with the market prices, $(\nu^{CRS}, \mu^{CRS}) = (w, p)$, the firm is allocative efficient: $AE_{R(I)}(x, y, w) = 1$.

The decomposition of profitability inefficiency into its technical and allocative components is depicted in Fig. 4.4b. Assuming that market prices are (w^3, p^3), profitability efficiency for firm (x_D, y_D) defines as the ratio of observed profitability to maximum profitability, i.e., $\Gamma E(x, y, w^3, p^3) = p^3 \cdot y_D/w^3 \cdot x_D \,/\, \Gamma(w^3, p^3)$. Profitability efficiency can be then decomposed into the constant returns to scale productive efficiency (and, subsequently, into its technical and scale efficiency components) and allocative efficiency. Technical efficiency is $TE_G(x, y; \alpha) = \delta = p^3 \cdot y_D/w^3 \cdot x_D \,/\, \left(p^3 \cdot \left(y_D/\delta_D^{\alpha}\right)/w^3 \cdot \left(\delta_D^{1-\alpha} x_D\right)\right)$. This measure however is net of scale effects because it does not evaluate the profitability of the firm with respect to one of the constant returns to scale benchmarks that complies with the necessary (but insufficient) scale condition for profitability maximization. This is achieved when evaluating the constant returns to scale productive efficiency: $TE_G^{CRS}(x, y; \alpha) = \delta^{CRS} = (p^3 \cdot y_D/w^3 \cdot x_D) \,/\, \left(p^3 \cdot \left(y_D/\delta_D^{\alpha|CRS}\right)/w^3 \cdot \left(\delta_D^{1-\alpha|CRS} x_D\right)\right)$. Subsequently, the mismatch between profitability evaluated at the constant returns to scale benchmark and maximum profitability represents allocative efficiency: $AE_G(x_D, y_D, w^3, p^3; \alpha) = \left(p^3 \left(y_D/\delta_D^{\alpha|CRS}\right)/w^3 \left(\delta_D^{1-\alpha|CRS} x_D\right)\right) \,/\, \Gamma E(x_D, y_D, w^3, p^3)$.

In this graphical example, it is relevant to notice that if market prices were (w^2, p^2), the aggregation of inputs and outputs through the corresponding shadow prices (ν^{CRS}, μ^{CRS}) would maximize profitability. In this case, the reference hyperplane would be that defined under these prices, i.e., $(\nu^{CRS}, \mu^{CRS}) = (w^2, p^2)$: $\mu^{CRS} \cdot \widehat{y}_D^{CRS} / \left(\nu_1^{CRS} \widehat{x}_{1D}^{CRS} + \nu_2^{CRS} x_2^m\right)$. As a result, the constant returns to scale benchmark for firm (x_D, y_D) would be profitability-efficient because $\Gamma(w^2, p^2) = \left(p^2 \cdot y_D/\delta_D^{\alpha|CRS}\right)/\left(w_1^2 \delta_D^{1-\alpha|CRS} x_{1D} + w_2^2 x_2^m\right) = (p^2 \cdot y^{\Gamma}(w^2, p^2)/w^2 \cdot x^{\Gamma}(w^2, p^2))$. Then, the firm would be allocative efficient, and all profitability loss would be solely due to technical and scale reasons. Thus, if the aggregation of the input and output mixes through the shadow prices (ν^{CRS}, μ^{CRS}) associated with the generalized distance function is not equal to that corresponding to the market prices, then allocative inefficiency emerges as a result of the discrepancy between both sets of prices.

From the above, we see that, although a firm can indeed maximize productivity by producing at a constant returns to scale technically efficient *locus*—where neither increasing nor decreasing returns to scale exist, the resulting aggregation may not match maximum profitability, which is precisely associated with the use of market prices as aggregating weights. Accordingly, profitability corresponds to a specific productivity definition. Indeed, following O'Donnell (2012), we consider that the constant returns to scale projections associated with the generalized distance function under constant returns to scale preserve the relative input and output mixes within their respective bundles; i.e., $TE_G^{CRS}(x, y; \alpha)$ identifies mix-invariant optimal scales *within* inputs and *within* outputs (but not *between* them). Since this measure implies a specific aggregating function for the input and output vectors using the vector of multipliers (ν^{CRS}, μ^{CRS}) as weights, we can express the associated maximum productivity with respect the benchmark hyperplane as the ratio: $Y\left(\widehat{y}^{CRS}, \mu^{CRS}\right) / X\left(\widehat{x}^{CRS}, \nu^{CRS}\right) = \mu^{CRS} \cdot \widehat{y}^{CRS} / \nu^{CRS} \cdot \widehat{x}^{CRS}$.[20] When these multipliers are interpreted as shadow prices through duality theory, then $\Gamma(\nu^{CRS}, \mu^{CRS}) = Y\left(\widehat{y}^{CRS}, \mu^{CRS}\right) / X\left(\widehat{x}^{CRS}, \nu^{CRS}\right) = \mu^{CRS} \cdot y^{\Gamma}(\nu^{CRS}, \mu^{CRS}) / \nu^{CRS} \cdot x^{\Gamma}(\nu^{CRS}, \mu^{CRS})$. Finally, if shadow prices coincide with market prices $(\nu^{CRS}, \mu^{CRS}) = (w, p)$, then maximum productivity coincides with maximum profitability: $\Gamma(\nu^{CRS}, \mu^{CRS}) = \Gamma(w, p) = Y\left(\widehat{y}^{CRS}, \mu^{CRS}\right) / X\left(\widehat{x}^{CRS}, \nu^{CRS}\right) = Y(y^{\Gamma}(w, p)) / X(x^{\Gamma}(w, p)) = p \cdot \widehat{y}^{CRS} / w \cdot \widehat{x}^{CRS} = p \cdot y^{\Gamma}(w, p) / w \cdot x^{\Gamma}(w, p)$.

We conclude then that the productivity ratio of efficient aggregated output quantities to aggregated input quantities using shadow prices and defining shadow profitability is smaller than the productivity ratio obtained with the optimal quantities corresponding to maximum profitability at market prices. The gap between both ratios is interpreted as *mix technical efficiency* in O'Donnell's (2012) and Balk and Zofío's (2018) productivity context, because the input and output mixes attained at the constant returns to scale benchmarks (as those between inputs and outputs) are different from those corresponding to maximum profitability. But we have shown that since this difference can be attributed to the discrepancy between aggregating the input and output quantities according to their specific shadow prices rather than market prices, this implies that the firm would have to change its production plan so as to match the optimal input and output amounts that maximize profitability. Hence, as suggested by O'Donnell (2008) and presented in (4.31), we have shown that in an economic context formalized trough duality theory, the mix technical efficiency measure with respect to a reference vector of aggregating weights is equivalent to the allocative efficiency.

4.4.3 Calculating and Decomposing Profitability Efficiency

Measuring and decomposing profitability efficiency can be performed relying on the previous Data Envelopment Analysis programs. Given a firm (x_o, y_o) under evaluation, it requires solving program (4.13) under both variable and constant returns to scale, calculating technical efficiency δ^* and productive efficiency δ^{CRS*}, respectively. This allows recovering scale efficiency in a subsequent step: $SE_G(x, y; \alpha) = \delta^{CRS*} / \delta^*$, as shown in expression (4.6). This completes the measurement of the productive efficiency of the firm in terms of its technical and scale performance:

[20] Here, $X(x,\nu)$ and $Y(y,\mu)$ are aggregator functions that are nonnegative, nondecreasing, and linearly homogeneous, i.e., satisfy constant returns to scale.

$TE_G^{CRS}(x,y;\alpha) = TE_G(x,y;\alpha) \times SE_G(x,y;\alpha)$. The nature of the constant returns to scale can be determined from the sum of the optimal lambdas λ_j^{CRS*} when solving program (4.13) under CRS. The optimal shadow prices (ν^{CRS*}, μ^{CRS*}) that define the corresponding CRS supporting hyperplane can be obtained from the dual (4.16). If solved under VRS, we obtain the reference hyperplane defined by (ν^*, μ^*, ω^*) serving as reference benchmark for technical efficiency. Subsequently, we solve for maximum profitability $\Gamma(w,p)$ relying on program (4.19). Finally, profitability efficiency $\Gamma E(x,y,w,p)$ can be obtained by dividing $\Gamma(w,p)$ by the observed profitability as in (4.18). Based on duality theory, this allows recovering allocative efficiency as the ratio between profitability efficiency and productive efficiency: $AE_G(x,y,w,p;\alpha) = \Gamma E(x,y,w,p)/TE_G^{CRS}(x,y;\alpha)$. Combining all these elements results in the decomposition of profitability efficiency according to (4.28).

4.5 Empirical Illustration of the Profitability Efficiency Model

We illustrate the calculation of profitability efficiency and its decomposition according to the generalized distance function using the one input-one output example presented in Table 2.1 of Chap. 2. The data is replicated in Table 4.1, while a graphical representation of the technology is depicted in Fig. 4.5.

The function included in the Benchmarking Economic Efficiency package for the Julia language that computes the profitability model, including the decomposition into technical, scale, and allocative efficiencies, is `deaprofitability(X, Y, W, P, names=FIRMS)`. Following the steps given in previous section, this function solves problem (4.13) to calculate the corresponding productive technical efficiency measure under constant returns to scale: $\delta^{CRS*} = TE_G^{CRS}(x,y;\alpha)$. The value of the bearing parameter is preset by default to $\alpha = 0.5$, which makes the generalized distance function equivalent to the graph (hyperbolic)

Table 4.1 Example data illustrating the profitability efficiency model

	Model	
	Graph profitability model	
Firm	x	y
A	2	1
B	4	5
C	8	8
D	12	9
E	6	3
F	14	7
G	14	9
H	9.412	2.353
Prices	$w = 1$	$p = 2$

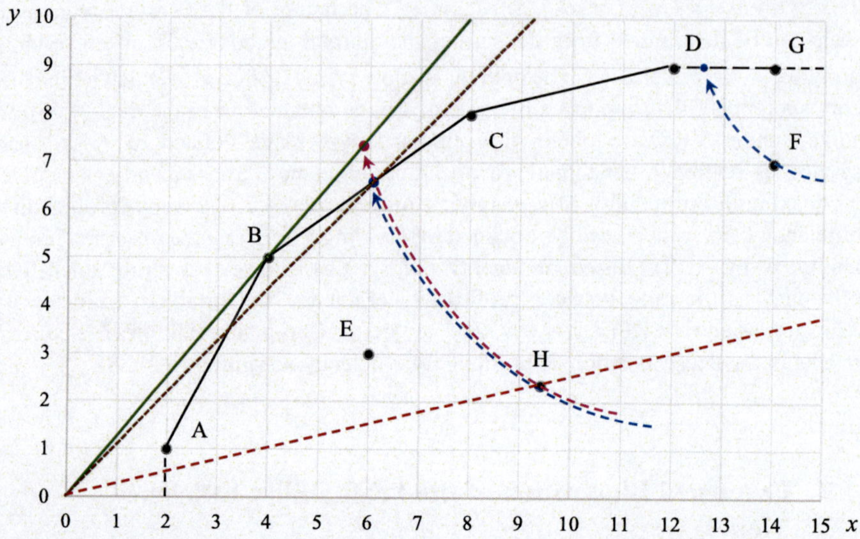

Fig. 4.5 Example of the GDF profitability efficiency model using BEE for Julia

distance function, either under variable or constant returns to scale: $\delta^* = TE_G(x, y; 0.5) = (\varphi^*)^2 = TE_{H(G)}(x, y)$. However, this can be changed by introducing the value of alpha as one of the arguments of the function. For example, weighting output expansions to a larger extent than input contractions can be done by setting $\alpha = 0.7$. In this case, the syntax is as follows: `deaprofitability(X, Y, W, P, alpha=0.7, names=FIRMS)`.[21] Since the decomposition of profitability efficiency according to (4.28) into productive efficiency and allocative efficiency requires constant returns to scale, these are initially assumed. Later on, this assumption is relaxed to calculate technical efficiency under variable returns to scale, as shown in program (4.13), and from the two solutions, scale efficiency is recovered as $SE_G(x, y; \alpha) = \delta^{CRS*}/\delta^*$. Also, as previously justified in Sect. 4.2.2, all previous calculations are carried out under the default assumptions of strong disposability of input and outputs. The final step calculates maximum profitability $\Gamma(w, p)$ by solving program (4.19), which allows calculating allocative efficiency: $AE_G(x, y, w, p; \alpha) = \Gamma E(x, y, w, p)/TE_G^{CRS}(x, y; \alpha)$. Both DEA programs solving for the VRS generalized distance function and profitability are nonlinear. The accompanying Julia software resorts to the "JuMP"

[21] For the first-level decomposition of profitability efficiency, involving CRS, the value of the bearing parameter α is irrelevant, and the function takes advantage of the known relationship $D_G^{CRS}(x, y; \alpha) = D_O^{CRS}(x, y)$, $\forall \alpha \in [0, 1]$, Then, the function internally solves the equivalent model corresponding to the output distance function, whose inverse, in turn, can be easily computed with a linear DEA program; see program (3.25) of the preceding chapter.

Table 4.2 Implementation of the profitability efficiency model using BEE for Julia

In[]:

```
using DataEnvelopmentAnalysis
using BenchmarkingEconomicEfficiency

X = [2; 4; 8; 12; 6; 14; 14; 9.412];
Y = [1; 5; 8; 9; 3; 7; 9; 2.353];
W = [1; 1; 1; 1; 1; 1; 1; 1];
P = [2; 2; 2; 2; 2; 2; 2; 2];
FIRMS = ["A", "B", "C", "D", "E", "F", "G", "H"];

deaprofitability(X, Y, W, P, alpha = 0.7, names=FIRMS)
```

Out[]:

```
Profitability DEA Model
DMUs = 8; Inputs = 1; Outputs = 1
alpha= 0.7; Returns to Scale = VRS
```

	Profitability	CRS	VRS	Scale	Allocative
A	0.4	0.4	1.0	0.4	1.0
B	1.0	1.0	1.0	1.0	1.0
C	0.8	0.8	1.0	0.8	1.0
D	0.6	0.6	1.0	0.6	1.0
E	0.4	0.4	0.423	0.945	1.0
F	0.4	0.4	0.698	0.573	1.0
G	0.514	0.514	1.0	0.514	1.0
H	0.2	0.2	0.232	0.864	1.0

package developed by Dunning et al. (2017), combined with the "Ipopt" solver, initially introduced by Wächter and Biegler (2006).

To illustrate the package, we rely on the open (web-based) Jupyter Notebook interface.[22] However, it can be implemented in any integrated development environment (IDE) of preference. To calculate and decompose the profitability efficiency model according to (4.28), type the code presented in the input window "`In[]:`" of Table 4.2, and execute it. As previously suggested, in this illustration, we choose as bearing parameter $\alpha = 0.7$, since setting $\alpha = 0.5$ would result in the exact same results reported in the empirical section of Chap. 2, where the graph (hyperbolic) distance function is illustrated. Once run, the function reports the calculations for profitability efficiency, constant, variable, and scale efficiencies and, finally, allocative efficiency. The corresponding results are shown in the output window, "`Out[]:`".

We can identify reference peers for each firm maximizing profitability using the "peersmatrix" function with the corresponding economic or technical model. This requires

[22]We refer the reader to Sect. 2.6.1 in Chap. 2 for the installation of the "Benchmarking Economic Efficiency" Julia package. All Jupyter Notebooks implementing the different economic models in this book can be downloaded from the reference site: https://www.benchmarkingeconomicefficiency.com

Table 4.3 Calculating the generalized distance function with BEE for Julia

```
In[]:   deagdf(X, Y, alpha=0.7, rts = :VRS, names=FIRMS)
```

```
Out[]:  Generalized DF DEA Model
        DMUs = 8; Inputs = 1; Outputs = 1
        alpha = 0.7; Returns to Scale = VRS
        ________________________________
             efficiency  slackX1    slackY1
        ____________________________________
        A    1.0         0.0        0.0
        B    1.0         0.0        0.0
        C    1.0         0.0        0.0
        D    1.0         0.0        0.0
        E    0.423       0.0        0.0
        F    0.698       0.570      0.0
        G    1.0         2.0        0.0
        H    0.232       0.0        0.0
        ____________________________________
```

executing "`peersmatrix(deaprofitability(X, Y, W, P, alpha = 0.7, names=FIRMS))`," which returns firm B as the benchmark maximizing profitability for all remaining firms. This is illustrated, once again, in Fig. 4.5.[23]

Regarding the internal calculation of the general distance function, it is possible to obtain all the information concerning the efficiency scores and accompanying input and output slacks by solving the corresponding BEE function, as shown in Table 4.3. The syntax depends on whether we consider the constant or the variable returns to scale specification. In the first case, the syntax is as `deagdf(X, Y, alpha=0.7, rts = :CRS, names=FIRMS)`, while in the second case, we need to substitute "`rts=:VRS`" for "`rts= :CRS`". Here, we illustrate the VRS case; see the code in the "`In[]:`" window.

Looking at the results in the "`Out[]:`" window, we observe that five firms, A, B, C, D, and G, create the weakly efficient subset of the technology, corresponding to expression (4.9). Also, since the first four firms do not present any slacks in the input and the output dimensions, they comply with the Pareto-Koopmans efficiency definition corresponding to the strongly efficient input production possibility set, (4.8). In this regard, firm G uses the input in excess by two units.

It is also of interest to identify the set of reference technological benchmarks of the generalized distance function measure. In this case, a matrix of the peers conforming the weakly efficient subset of the input production possibility set, for either constant or variable returns to scale, can be obtained using the following syntax: "`peersmatrix(deagdf(X, Y, alpha = 0.7, rts = :VRS, names=FIRMS))`".

[23]To prevent that the reported set of peers include observations with infinitesimal intensity variables, it is possible to adjust the tolerance of the solver in the "peers" function, for example, `peers(deaprofitability(X, Y, W, P, alpha=0.7, names=FIRMS), atol=1e-7)`.

Table 4.4 Reference peers of the GDF efficiency measure using BEE for Julia

In[]:
```
peersmatrix(deagdf(X, Y, alpha=0.7, rts = :VRS,
names=FIRMS))
```

Out[]:
```
1.0    .      .      .      .  .  .      .
 .    1.0     .      .      .  .  .      .
 .     .     1.0     .      .  .  .      .
 .     .      .     1.0     .  .  .      .
 .   0.841  0.159    .      .  .  .      .
 .     .      .    0.902    .  .  0.098  .
 .     .      .    0.691    .  .  0.309  .
 .   0.483  0.517    .      .  .  .      .
```

The output is shown in Table 4.4. The five firms, A, B, C, D, and G, present unit values in the main diagonal of the square ($J \times J$) matrix containing their own intensity variables $\lambda_j = 1$, while firms E, F, and H are projected to other firms whose $\lambda_j > 0$.

Figure 4.5 illustrates the results of the profitability model. There, for firm H, we identify that its profitability efficiency (4.18) is equal to 0.2 = 0.5/2.5, with firm B determining maximum profitability at 2.5—as shown by the ray vector with the highest slope joining the origin and firm B. The hypothetical CRS benchmark projection for firm H in the convex cone spanned by firm B is the input-output vector (9.412 × 0.2^0.3, 2.353/0.2^0.7) = (5.807, 7.259)—along the path marked by the purple dashed line and whose profitability coincides with that of firm B. In the single output-single input case, profitability efficiency coincides with productive efficiency because allocative inefficiency cannot exist by definition; i.e., firms cannot demand or supply the wrong mix of inputs and outputs, as there is only one of each. Therefore, profitability efficiency can be decomposed according to its technical and scale efficiencies: 0.2 = 0.232 × 0.864. For firm H, its VRS projection is given by the input-output vector (9.412 × 0.232^0.3, 2.353/0.232^0.7) = (6.071, 6.543), now represented by the blue dashed line. Scale efficiency is then equal to 0.864 = 0.2/0.232. It can be seen that scale inefficiency is the result of decreasing returns to scale at the technical efficient projection of firm H. Similar remarks can be made for firms E and F that are both technical and scale-inefficient—with firm F presenting a slack input amount of $s_{\mathrm{F}}^{-} = 0.57$—while the rest of firms are only scale-inefficient by belonging to the weakly efficient subset and therefore having a technical efficiency score of one.[24] Nevertheless, as for firm F, the scale efficiency of firm G is underestimated because there exists an input slack of two units, $s_{\mathrm{E}}^{-} = 2$, resulting in the overestimation of technical efficiency.

[24] In Table 4.4, firm F has as peers firms D and G, being the last one a weak efficient firm. In case we deleted G, F would have as peer only firm D plus the slack input amount s_{F}^{-} =0.57, determining the new weak efficient point (12,9.57).

4.5.1 An Application to the Taiwanese Banking Industry

In this section, we calculate and decompose profitability efficiency using the dataset of the 31 Taiwanese banks observed in 2010, compiled by Juo et al. (2015). A brief description of the data, including summary statistics, can be found in Sect. 2.6.2 of Chap. 2. We remark that we rely on these data to illustrate the different models, but do not aim at analyzing the economic performance of the Taiwanese financial sector or any individual bank. In this dataset, each bank presents it is own prices, (w_o, p_o), which are taken as reference when evaluating maximum profitability in program (4.19). As opposed to the simple example presented in the previous section, in this case, we weight inputs and outputs equally by choosing $\alpha = 0.5$. Therefore, our results are equivalent to those that would be obtained with the graph (hyperbolic) efficiency measure considered in Chap. 2.

Table 4.5 presents the profitability efficiency scores $\Gamma E(x, y, w, p)$, along with their corresponding productive and allocative factor, $TE_G^{CRS}(x, y;\ 0.5)$ and $AE_G(x, y, w, p; 0.5)$. The former is coupled with its technical $TE_G(x, y;\ 0.5)$ and scale efficiency $SE_G(x, y;\ 0.5)$ scores (reported in columns 3 and 4). Descriptive statistics for each efficiency component are provided at the bottom. Results show that, on average, the industry could reduce production costs by 39.8% $(=1\text{–}0.362^{0.5}) \times 100$ while increasing the revenue by 66.2% $(=(1/0.362^{0.5}–1) \times 100$. From a profitability perspective, this implies that, on average, it could be increased by 176.24% $(=(1/0.362–1) \times 100$. These results are driven by the first bank maximizing profitability, $\Gamma E(x, y, w, p) = 1$, whose economic performance exceeds by 69.2% $(=1/0.591 \times 100)$ the profitability of the second bank in the ranking (bank no. 10)—or, alternatively, bank no. 10 achieves just 59.1% of the profitability of the first bank. Since the difference between the first bank and the rest of observations depends on both quantities (i.e., productive, technical, and scale efficiencies) and prices (i.e., allocative efficiency), this result suggest that the first bank is performing substantially better than its competitors when both dimensions are jointly considered. Indeed, only three banks reach profitability efficiency scores larger than 0.5, i.e., about half the profitability of the leading bank. This result is quite robust since all banks present different market prices, and yet, bank no. 1 always emerges as the most profitable, demanding and supplying the optimal amounts of inputs and outputs that maximize profitability.

The analysis of productive efficiency, including its technical and scale components, as well as allocative efficiency sheds light on the sources of profitability inefficiency. On average, while VRS technical efficiency is relatively high at 0.827, scale inefficiency represents a more relevant source of inefficiency with a score of 0.677. Looking at the data, the input and output amounts of the first bank are well below the average, representing one of the smallest sizes in the sample. This suggests that most of the banks endure decreasing returns to scale. In total, there are four banks that are efficient with respect to the constant returns to scale benchmark: $TE_G^{CRS}(x, y; 0.5) = 1$, thereby representing a most productive scale size. However, given the observed market prices, only the first bank is profitability-efficient. Bank

Table 4.5 Decomposition of profitability efficiency based on the generalized distance function

Bank	Profitability efficiency, eq. (4.28)				
	Profitability Eff. $\Gamma E(x,y,w,p)$	Technical Eff. (CRS) $TE_G^{CRS}(x,y;0.5)$	Technical Eff. (VRS) $TE_G(x,y;0.5)$	Scale Eff. $SE_G(x,y;0.5)$	Allocative Effi. $AE_G(x,y,w,p;0.5)$
1	1.000	1.000	1.000	1.000	1.000
2	0.393	1.000	1.000	1.000	0.393
3	0.445	0.614	1.000	0.614	0.724
4	0.400	0.481	0.701	0.687	0.832
5	0.502	0.830	1.000	0.830	0.604
6	0.393	0.672	1.000	0.672	0.585
7	0.417	0.667	1.000	0.667	0.626
8	0.412	0.602	0.946	0.636	0.684
9	0.385	0.523	0.939	0.557	0.736
10	0.591	0.855	1.000	0.855	0.691
11	0.228	0.435	0.717	0.607	0.523
12	0.387	0.755	0.895	0.844	0.513
13	0.048	0.209	0.557	0.375	0.229
14	0.425	1.000	1.000	1.000	0.425
15	0.370	0.578	0.860	0.672	0.641
16	0.055	0.195	0.354	0.551	0.282
17	0.264	0.343	0.831	0.413	0.770
18	0.363	0.657	0.869	0.755	0.553
19	0.242	0.276	0.567	0.488	0.877
20	0.331	0.631	0.826	0.765	0.525
21	0.290	0.417	1.000	0.417	0.697
22	0.216	0.249	0.660	0.377	0.866
23	0.181	0.229	0.508	0.451	0.790
24	0.411	0.545	0.968	0.563	0.755
25	0.336	0.478	0.753	0.635	0.703
26	0.523	1.000	1.000	1.000	0.523
27	0.272	0.329	0.497	0.661	0.828
28	0.268	0.476	0.566	0.841	0.564
29	0.449	0.948	1.000	0.948	0.474
30	0.461	0.648	0.897	0.722	0.712
31	0.156	0.287	0.726	0.396	0.543
Average	0.362	0.578	0.827	0.677	0.634
Median	0.385	0.578	0.895	0.667	0.641
Maximum	1.000	1.000	1.000	1.000	1.000
Minimum	0.048	0.195	0.354	0.375	0.229
Std. Dev.	0.173	0.254	0.192	0.196	0.174

no. 2 represents an interesting case, because while it maximizes productivity given its associated shadow prices, once its market prices are considered to aggregate inputs and outputs, bank no. 1 significantly outperforms it, leaving its profitability efficiency at a mere 0.393. Banks no. 14 and no. 26 are the only two additional banks whose profitability inefficiency is due only to allocative inefficiency. For all banks, once technical and scale efficiencies are combined into productive efficiency, the overall efficiency score is 0.578 on average, which is lower than of allocative efficiency, 0.634. Nevertheless, a diversity of cases, with productive and allocative efficiencies being either greater or smaller than each other, is observed. However, we conclude that they are quite balanced in this dataset.

Finally, we present in Table 4.6 the input and output slacks corresponding to productive efficiency $TE_G^{CRS}(x, y; 0.5)$ and technical efficiency $TE_G(x, y; 0.5)$, which are unaccounted for in the standard decomposition of profitability efficiency. These represent individual input reductions and output increases that would place the projected firm on the strongly efficient subset of the technology (4.8)—either under constant or variable returns to scale, rather than the weakly efficient subset. The slack values are recovered using the corresponding BEE functions as presented in the example above.

The presence of inputs slacks regarding individual projections to the strongly efficient frontier under constant returns to scale is pervasive, resulting in allocative efficiency underestimation and productive efficiency overestimation. In particular, most banks present a clear excess in financial funds (x_1) with respect to the constant return to scale benchmark. Its average quantity amounts to 140.3 billion TWD, which represents 17.6% of the average input quantity for all banks. It is also the largest percentage by far, since the average slack in physical capital (x_3) represents 3.9% and that of labor (x_2) 3.9%. The output slack amounts are rather small, and quite remarkably, there are no slacks concerning loans (y_2). Hence, we conclude that the highest percentage slack values are observed in the input dimensions.

Regarding the existence of individual slacks with respect to the strongly efficient frontier under variable returns to scale, which in this case results in scale efficiency underestimation and technical efficiency overestimation, their values tend to be in the same order of magnitude. The only exception is financial funds (x_1), whose average values are now 3.0 billion TWD, much lower than the 140.3 billion calculated in the previous case. Now, the largest number of banks (18) with a positive amount in any input slack concerns labor (x_2), with an average value of 601.8 million TWD. This is followed by physical capital (x_3), with 14 slack inefficient banks and a larger average amount to the tune of 1.6 billion TWD. Completing the input side and as previously remarked, although the largest average amount corresponds to financial funds (x_1) with 3.0 billion TWD, the slack corresponds to just two banks (no. 21 and no. 27). Also, contrary to the previous case under constant returns to scale, slack amounts in the first output, investments (y_1), are quite significant, reaching 3.9 billion TWD on average. Regarding loans (y_2), on this occasion, there is one single bank with a positive amount (no. 15).

Table 4.6 Input and output slacks in the profitability efficiency model

Bank	Slacks in the profitability model, technical efficiency under CRS, eq. (4.14)					Slacks in the profitability model, technical efficiency under VRS, eq. (4.14)				
	Funds (x_1)	Labor (x_2)	Ph. Capital (x_3)	Investments (y_1)	Loans (y_2)	Funds (x_1)	Labor (x_2)	Ph. Capital (x_3)	Investments (y_1)	Loans (y_2)
	s_1^-	s_2^-	s_3^-	s_1^+	s_2^+	s_1^-	s_2^-	s_3^-	s_1^+	s_2^+
1	0.0	0.0	0.0	0.0	0.0	0.0	0.0	0.0	0.0	0.0
2	5.7	0.0	0.2	0.0	0.0	0.1	0.0	0.0	0.0	0.0
3	275,814.0	0.0	0.0	0.0	0.0	0.2	0.0	0.0	0.0	0.0
4	51,656.3	0.0	0.0	0.0	0.0	0.0	154.8	0.0	5,868.5	0.0
5	734,791.0	0.0	0.0	0.0	0.0	0.0	0.0	0.0	0.1	0.0
6	507,390.0	0.0	0.3	0.0	0.0	0.1	0.0	0.0	0.0	0.0
7	367,286.0	0.0	0.1	0.0	0.0	0.0	0.0	0.0	0.1	0.0
8	293,912.0	0.0	0.2	0.0	0.0	0.0	725.6	3,395.1	0.2	0.0
9	98,034.2	0.0	0.1	0.0	0.0	0.0	1,792	8,389.0	0.1	0.0
10	819,355.0	0.0	0.0	0.0	0.0	0.1	0.0	0.0	0.0	0.0
11	124,847.0	0.0	0.2	0.0	0.0	0.0	1,286	7,636.2	0.2	0.0
12	81,700.8	0.0	0.0	0.0	0.0	0.1	0.0	1,904.0	0.0	0.0
13	0.0	276.8	997.7	0.0	0.0	0.0	1,424	3,127.3	8,564.1	0.0
14	0.0	0.0	0.0	0.0	0.0	0.0	0.0	0.0	0.0	0.0
15	147,684.0	0.0	0.0	0.0	0.0	0.0	0.0	886.1	0.0	0.1
16	0.0	353.1	1,744.2	2,252.3	0.0	0.0	678.7	2,673.5	5,258.0	0.0
17	0.0	302.2	2,298.5	0.0	0.0	0.0	2,827	8,192.9	0.1	0.0
18	44,047.2	1,025.2	0.0	0.0	0.0	0.0	1,613	0.0	0.1	0.0
19	0.0	51.3	420.2	0.0	0.0	0.0	518.4	1,436.6	0.0	0.0
20	132,106.0	741.3	0.0	0.0	0.0	76,494.5	1,041	0.0	5,513.8	0.0
21	19.2	0.0	5,385.3	0.0	0.0	0.0	0.0	0.0	0.0	0.1
22	0.0	34.9	2,403.5	2,195.9	0.0	0.0	802.5	5,101.1	14,520.9	0.0
23	0.0	54.2	2,163.9	3,808.6	0.0	0.0	468.9	3,842.4	9,413.1	0.0
24	240,281.0	0.0	0.0	0.0	0.0	0.0	1,537	1,587.6	0.2	0.0
25	100,311.0	335.3	0.0	0.0	0.0	0.0	625.6	0.0	34,121.2	0.0
26	0.0	0.0	0.0	0.0	0.0	0.0	0.0	0.0	0.0	0.0
27	13,222.8	108.4	0.0	467.5	0.0	0.0	251.2	69.1	4,781.5	0.0
28	36,459.2	433.6	0.0	0.0	0.0	16,949.5	486.0	0.0	6,884.2	0.0
29	0.0	0.0	856.7	0.0	0.0	0.9	0.0	0.0	0.0	0.0
30	246,382.0	0.0	0.0	0.0	0.0	0.0	976.2	0.0	0.2	0.0
31	34,280.1	119.4	0.0	0.0	0.0	0.0	1,444	1,425.8	24,594.6	0.0
Average	140,309.2	123.7	524.9	281.4	0.0	3,014.4	601.8	1,602.1	3,855.5	0.0
Median	44,047.2	0.0	0.0	0.0	0.0	0.0	468.9	0.0	0.1	0.0
Maximum	819,355.0	1,025.2	5,385.3	3,808.6	0.0	76,494.5	2,827	8,389.0	34,121.2	0.1
Minimum	0.0	0.0	0.0	0.0	0.0	0.0	0.0	0.0	0.0	0.0
Std. Dev.	213,127.5	241.6	1,171.2	859.5	0.0	13,972.6	720.9	2,559.3	7,839.8	0.0

As in the case of cost or revenue efficiency presented in the preceding chapter, these results illustrate that measuring efficiency against the weakly efficient subsets overlooks relevant sources of technical inefficiency in the form of input and output slacks. When ignored and depending on whether constant or variable returns to scale are assumed, these values mask the actual levels of productive or technical inefficiency, resulting in the overestimation of allocative or scale inefficiency, respectively. Therefore, it is important to keep these values in mind when prescribing efficiency-improving strategies that aim at achieving the optimal input and output benchmarks that maximize profitability, including the correction of the scale of production to benefit from increasing returns or to prevent incurring in decreasing returns. Ultimately, the consideration of inputs slacks may change substantially the relative attention that each one of these elements receive under the standard approach.

4.6 Summary and Conclusions

Measuring the economic performance of the firm in terms of profitability efficiency is not as popular as its cost, revenue, or profit counterparts are. This situation may be due to a number of reasons. The first one is that managers and stakeholders are concerned about the economic outcome of the firm in terms of absolute monetary units. Profits valued in actual currencies are of interest for the financial planning of the firm at all levels, as well as the firm employees and other stakeholders such as lenders and tax agencies. Nevertheless, we have shown in this paper that profitability efficiency is linked to an economic optimum that is characterized by an optimal production scale, which is of interest from an engineering perspective and allows the firm to exploit the existence of increasing returns or to avoid incurring in decreasing returns. Studying profitability efficiency allows stakeholders to compare the productivity of the firm, where inputs and outputs are aggregated through shadow prices, with its economic counterpart represented by profitability, where they are aggregated through market prices. Performing well in productivity terms is critical for the subsistence of the firm in the long run, since profit and prices are affected by short run market variations because of changes in supply and demand. Therefore, a steadier picture of the economic sustainability of the firm can be drawn from the analysis of profitability efficiency and the underlying productivity. As put forward by Kendrick (1984:52), *over the long run, probably the most important factor influencing profit margins is the relative rate of productivity advance... In the short run, the effects of productivity trends may be obscured.* Earlier, Smith (1973:53–55) remarked that *the existence of a relationship between the productivity of the firm and profits cannot be denied but there can be no certainty that they will move in the same direction at all times and under all circumstances*. In this respect, the profitability analysis covered in this chapter complements those presented in the preceding chapters related to cost and revenue efficiency, as well as those that follow, focused on profit efficiency and its decomposition. A relevant contribution is Grifell-Tatjé and Lovell (2015), who, citing the above quotes, survey the literature relating the productivity and the financial performance of the firm. They also discuss how the financial benefits of productivity growth are distributed across stakeholders and present alternative decompositions of profitability change into quantity and price indices. Indeed, as shown in this chapter, this simply reflects the fact that the definition of profitability coincides with that of a productivity index, and therefore, it can be consistently studied through index number theory; see Balk and Zofío (2018).

The second reason is that no one has explored the flexibility that the bearing (power) parameter offers when evaluating the technical performance of the firm. The existing literature is mainly focused on the particular case corresponding to the hyperbolic measure, which is equivalent to the generalized model for $\alpha = 0.5$. However, several scenarios immediately come to mind where the analyst may choose to give a larger weight to output expansions than input contractions and vice versa. Indeed, any efficiency analysis involves two parties: that responsible for evaluating and that subject to evaluation. In this regard, the objective of both parties may not be aligned. For example, top management in headquarters may be interested in reducing cost by saving resources, while departments, branches, or subsidiaries may be interested in increasing revenues by expanding output production. This suggests that a principal-agent situation exists with conflicting efficiency improvement strategies, where the value of α would represent a compromise between both sides of the benchmarking problem. Jiménez-Sáez et al. (2011) suggested this interpretation for the choice of this parameter in the context of the evaluation of individual research groups within national R&D&I programs. In this situation, financing bodies may be forced to cut back on funding due to financial restrictions, while researchers would like to keep their resources intact and be judged on their output achievements. All these possibilities are open, and the generalized distance function offers the option of incorporating the outcome of this bargaining process within the model.

Yet, another reason that has withheld the application of the generalized model is that, on the one hand, the calculation of the efficiency score under variable returns to scale requires solving a nonlinear problem and, on the other hand, no software package is currently available to the public. As for the need to rely on nonlinear methods, a couple of alternatives have been recently offered in the literature, proposing suitable transformations of the original problem. In this regard, Färe et al. (2016) devise an iterative method that approximates the value of the VRS hyperbolic measure resorting to the additive directional distance function. This results in an algorithm that, relying on the dual (multiplier) formulation of the DDF and the quadratic formula, allows for the calculation of the hyperbolic distance function through linear programming techniques. A different approach is followed by Halická and Trnovská (2019), who reformulate the hyperbolic model within a semidefinite programming framework, opening the way to solve it through efficient interior point algorithms, as well as to establish simple primal-dual correspondences. Again, these alternatives require either programming algorithms with several steps until convergence is reached or resorting to semidefinite optimization. Arguably, recent developments in the computational field of nonlinear optimization have shown the validity of these methods when calculating the efficiency scores of the generalized model. We resort to these optimizers to solve both our simple example and the empirical application using a real-life dataset of financial institutions. The obtained results are reliable, including the calculation of the slacks associated with the weakly efficient frontiers. The optimization process is simplified by the fact that the efficiency scores are bounded by one, which restricts the range of valid solutions. In addition, any errors are flagged by the solver's diagnostics. The output messages tag their origin, which can be corrected by changing some of the default options (e.g., algorithm, tolerance) and resorting to alternative seeds for the initial values, which normally eases convergence. For this reason, we implement this approach in the Benchmarking Economic Efficiency package accompanying this book. This software is programmed in the Julia language and relies on the "JuMP" package developed by Dunning et al. (2017), along with the "Ipopt" solver introduced by Wächter and Biegler (2006). We are confident that the new software, which introduces the possibility of solving the generalized distance function for any α defined by the user, as well as the profitability efficiency model, will encourage analysts to adopt this evaluation model.

In summary, we believe that this chapter serves to bring the profitability model to the forefront of economic efficiency analysis. The underlying duality with the generalized distance function provides it with a solid foundation on economic theory, justifying the decomposition of profitability inefficiency into its technical, scale, and allocative sources. This decomposition provides managers and stakeholders with relevant information upon which undertake educated decision-making. It also allows them to act by targeting specific domains where the firm may be performing poorly, such as the failure to attain an optimal technical scale (maximizing productivity) or the inability to demand and supply the optimal amounts of inputs and outputs that maximize profitability. Ultimately, the model is a relevant tool in helping them to devise strategies aimed at improving both the productive and economic efficiency of the firm.

Part II
Benchmarking Economic Efficiency: The Additive Approach

Chapter 5
The Russell Measures: Economic Inefficiency Decompositions

5.1 Introduction

Over past decades, one of the aspects related to the measurement of technical efficiency that has attracted the attention of Data Envelopment Analysis (DEA) researchers has been the development of the generalized efficiency measures (GEMs), also called graph measures. The initial motivation for these measures was the design of indicators that would satisfy the indication property, denoted as (E1a) in Sect. 2.2.4 of Chap. 2, thereby including all kinds of inefficiencies (both radial and non-radial) when evaluating a firm against the strongly efficient subset of technology. In addition, it was intended that these measures satisfied additional desirable properties, such as units invariance (E4), translation invariance (E5), and even monotonicity (E2).

As previously mentioned, the measurement of technical efficiency using frontiers began with the work of Debreu (1951), Shephard (1953), and Farrell (1957). Subsequently, some of the limitations of the Farrell approach such as the need to consider more complex scenarios motivated further progress in this area. One of these research lines consisted in generalizing Farrell's measure to allow it to take into account non-equiproportional reductions in inputs or increases in outputs, that is, for the development of non-radial-type efficiency measures. This generalization was originally due to Färe and Lovell (1978), who proposed an axiomatic approach to the problem suggesting that an ideal measure of efficiency should satisfy certain desirable properties – see Sect. 2.2.4 in Chap. 2. For an input-oriented measure, these were the following: (1) an input vector that should be evaluated as technically efficient if, and only if, it belongs to the strongly efficient frontier (E1); (2) inefficient input vectors that should be compared with vectors of the Pareto-efficient set of the frontier; (3) homogeneity of degree minus one (E3); and 4) strong monotonicity (E2). In line with these ideas, they defined what was called the Russell measure of input efficiency, which supposedly satisfied all these properties. However, Färe et al.

J. T. Pastor et al., *Benchmarking Economic Efficiency*, International Series in Operations Research & Management Science 315,
https://doi.org/10.1007/978-3-030-84397-7_5

(1985) remarked that this measure did not verify the property of homogeneity of degree minus one in inputs. In this book, the authors also proposed an extension of the input-oriented Russell measure to the output-oriented case, working with multiple outputs.

Other suggestions of efficiency measures were introduced by, for example, Zieschang (1984). In particular, this last measure is defined as a combination of the Farrell measure and the Russell measure by Färe and Lovell to bring together the best features of each approach.

In the context of Data Envelopment Analysis, as remarked in Sect. 2.1.4 of Chap. 2, no measure satisfies all desirable properties for measuring technical efficiency (see Russell & Schworm, 2009). Consequently, one must choose between several "imperfect" alternatives to measure technical efficiency. In particular, Bol (1986) and Russell (1988) showed that no measure of technical efficiency can simultaneously meet the four requirements proposed by Färe and Lovell (1978) in a wide class of production technologies. Despite this, non-radial measures have an advantage over radial ones since they comply with the Pareto-Koopmans definition of technical efficiency. However, it would be difficult to even choose between non-radial measures attending only to theoretical arguments because none of them meet all the requirements for an ideal measure at the same time. In this way, the debate on what is the best technical efficiency measure to use remains open, which may partly explain why in practice radial measures are still utilized for the evaluation of efficiency, neglecting a possible analysis for the definition of a more appropriate and complex alternative measure.

In 1985, in their path-breaking book, Färe, Grosskopf, and Lovell introduced the hyperbolic measure (see Sect. 2.2.3.1 of Chap. 2), a graph (non-oriented) extension of the Farrell input- or output-oriented measures. Its graph character implies that this measure captures simultaneously input and output inefficiencies. Other contributions in this line are, for example, the graph extension of the Farrell measure due to Briec (1997), the directional distance function by Chambers et al. (1996, 1998), and the weighted additive models (Lovell & Pastor, 1995) or the slacks-based measure (Pastor et al., 1999; Tone, 2001).

Färe et al. (1985) also defined a Russell graph measure of technical efficiency, to which we dedicate the first part of this chapter. This measure extended the two oriented versions in the sense that it simultaneously considered inefficiency (radial and non-radial) in both inputs and outputs. Clearly, the Russell input measure of technical efficiency and the Russell output measure of technical efficiency, on which we focus in the second part of the chapter, are particular cases of the unoriented version.

It is worth mentioning that the result for duality relating the oriented and unoriented Russell measures to a support function (either a cost, revenue, or profit function) is very recent in the literature on production. So far, duality was only established for a few measures in DEA, such as the radial measures and the directional distance function. However, the interest on this issue has grown in recent times. Note that, as we pointed out above, no measure satisfies all the desirable properties for measuring technical efficiency. Therefore, the DEA researchers and practitioners must select between a list of imperfect alternatives for measuring technical efficiency. Nevertheless, this fact is true if the focus is placed on treating the technical efficiency measures as being completely independent from market prices and economic efficiency. Russell (1985) showed that if the existence of a dual relationship with the cost or revenue function is required as a desirable property, then Shephard's distance functions are the adequate selection between all the options since they are the natural dual to the usual measures of economic efficiency (as presented in Chap. 3), allowing the decomposition of the economic efficiency index. In this case, Russell's reasoning is based upon assuming that the (oriented) Russell measures do not have a dual relationship with the cost or revenue functions. And the same is claimed by other authors like Kopp (1981) and Färe et al. (1985, p. 142).

In contrast to this established knowledge, recent contributions show that the Russell measures of technical efficiency are also natural dual precursors of the cost, revenue, and profit functions. In this respect, a previous attempt to solve this problem was made by Färe et al. (2007), where the original notion is modified in order to define a "multiplicative" version of the Russell measure. To do that, they resorted to the geometrical mean as the objective function instead of the usual arithmetic mean. In this way, they were able to obtain a decomposition of cost efficiency in terms of the redefined Russell measure, a residual allocative efficiency component and yet an unusual third component called "the Debreu-Farrell deviation." In this chapter, we revise the model and duality results related to the traditional versions of the Russell measures.

The rest of the chapter is organized as follows: Sect. 5.2 introduces the Russell (graph) measure of technical efficiency in the framework of DEA. Section 5.3 is devoted to introducing the Russell measure of input efficiency, while in Sect. 5.4, we show the main results associated with the Russell measure of output efficiency. Section 5.5 shows several numerical examples. Finally, Sect. 5.6 concludes.

5.2 The Russell Graph Measure of Technical Efficiency and the Decomposition of Profit Inefficiency

In this section, we restrict our attention to the non-radial and unoriented efficiency measures defined in the context of Data Envelopment Analysis under VRS.

Following Färe et al. (1985), the value of the Russell measure of technical efficiency—here denoted by RM—for the firm (x_o, y_o) should be determined through the next nonlinear optimization program:

$$
\begin{aligned}
TE_{RM(G)}(x_o, y_o) = & \min_{\substack{\theta_1,\ldots,\theta_M \\ \phi_1,\ldots,\phi_N \\ \lambda_1,\ldots,\lambda_J}} \frac{1}{M+N}\left(\sum_{m=1}^{M}\theta_m + \sum_{n=1}^{N}\frac{1}{\phi_n}\right) \\
& s.t. \\
& \sum_{j=1}^{J}\lambda_j x_{jm} = \theta_m x_{om}, \quad m = 1, \ldots, M \\
& \sum_{j=1}^{J}\lambda_j y_{jn} = \phi_n y_{on}, \quad n = 1, \ldots, N \\
& \sum_{j=1}^{J}\lambda_j = 1, \\
& \theta_m \leq 1, \quad m = 1, \ldots, M \\
& \phi_n \geq 1, \quad n = 1, \ldots, N \\
& \lambda_j \geq 0, \quad j = 1, \ldots, J
\end{aligned}
\tag{5.1}
$$

As mentioned before, non-radial measures have the advantage that they satisfy the indication property, thereby meeting the Pareto-Koopmans definition of efficiency, constituting an advantage over their radial counterparts. Specifically, the efficiency measures obtained from the radial DEA models suffer from the main drawback that any associated efficiency scores do not account for non-radial inefficiencies (the slacks). In this way, the classical (radial) efficiency scores would underestimate the technical inefficiency of a unit when slacks are present and, consequently, overestimate allocative inefficiency. On the other hand, it is also essential that the efficiency measures provide values that can be used to evaluate each assessed unit, something that is not always possible. For example, the traditional additive model, which sums input and output slacks directly at the objective function, identifies the sources and magnitude of all types of inefficiencies, but it does not provide values that can be used as efficiency measures since it directly aggregates inefficiencies measured in noncomparable units (i.e., for this, normalizing weights are required). In this context, the Russell measure obtained in (5.1) could represent a solution in this line. However, although the optimal value of this problem exists, its resolution is more complicated than standard DEA models because it is nonlinear.

From a theoretical point of view, (5.1) is an optimization problem with good properties. First, it achieves a global optimum via the Weierstrass theorem, since the objective function is continuous and the constraints define a compact set. Additionally, (5.1) is a convex problem, since both the objective function and the restrictions are convex. This fact implies that any Karush-Kuhn-Tucker (KKT) point is a global optimum. Equally, every global optimum of (5.1) is also a KKT point since the constraints are linear. In summary, the set of global optima of (5.1) coincide with the set of KKT points, and this set is not empty in terms of the Weierstrass theorem.

Therefore, the set of global optima of (5.1) coincide with the set of solutions of the system of nonlinear equations associated with the KKT conditions. This system is as follows:

$$
\begin{aligned}
&\frac{1}{M+N}-\alpha_m x_{om}+\delta_m=0, && m=1,\ldots,M\\
&-\frac{1}{(M+N)\phi_n^2}+\beta_n y_{on}-\varepsilon_n=0, && n=1,\ldots,N\\
&\sum_{m=1}^{M}\alpha_m x_{jm}-\sum_{n=1}^{N}\beta_n y_{jn}+\gamma=0, && j=1,\ldots,J\\
&\delta_m(\theta_m-1)=0, && m=1,\ldots,M\\
&\varepsilon_n(1-\phi_n)=0, && n=1,\ldots,N\\
&\delta_m,\varepsilon_n\geq 0, && \forall m,n\\
&\alpha_m,\beta_n,\gamma \text{ free}\\
&\sum_{j=1}^{J}\lambda_j x_{jm}=\theta_m x_{om}, && m=1,\ldots,M\\
&\sum_{j=1}^{J}\lambda_j y_{jn}=\phi_r y_{on}, && n=1,\ldots,N\\
&\sum_{j=1}^{J}\lambda_j=1,\\
&\theta_m\leq 1, && m=1,\ldots,M\\
&\phi_r\geq 1, && n=1,\ldots,N\\
&\lambda_j\geq 0, && j=1,\ldots,J
\end{aligned}
\tag{5.2}
$$

In view of (5.2), the conclusion is that it is practically impossible to give an analytical solution to the system. Therefore, in order to obtain a solution for the Russell efficiency measure, it seems a priori necessary to resort to algorithms for the resolution of nonlinear equation systems or to algorithms for solving nonlinear programming problems. Probably, this is the reason why some authors had paid attention to introducing approximation methods for solving (5.1). Next, we show two of them.

The first approximation is rather involved requiring two stages. It is based on the use of another model, for example, the additive one, and the use of its projection point $(\widehat{x},\widehat{y})$ as a way of evaluating the objective function of (5.1), to obtain $\frac{1}{M+N}\times\left(\sum_{m=1}^{M}\frac{\widehat{x_m}}{x_{om}}+\sum_{n=1}^{N}\frac{y_{on}}{\widehat{y_n}}\right)$. Then, this value is considered as an approximation of the actual Russell measure of technical efficiency. See, for example, Ševčovič et al. (2001). The second approach comprises a linear approximation of the nonlinear terms in the objective function in (5.1). If $s_{om}^{-}=(1-\theta_m)x_{om}$, $m=1,\ldots,M$, and $s_{on}^{+}=$

$(\phi_n - 1)y_{on}$, $n = 1, \ldots, N$, then $\frac{1}{M+N}\left(\sum_{m=1}^{M}\theta_m + \sum_{n=1}^{N}\frac{1}{\phi_n}\right) = \frac{1}{M+N} \times \left(\sum_{m=1}^{M}\left(1 - \frac{s_{om}^-}{x_{om}}\right) + \sum_{n=1}^{N}\frac{y_{on}}{y_{on}+s_{on}^+}\right) \approx \frac{1}{M+N}\left(\sum_{m=1}^{M}\left(1 - \frac{s_{om}^-}{x_{om}}\right) + \sum_{n=1}^{N}\left(1 - \frac{s_{on}^+}{y_{on}}\right)\right)$ (see Cooper et al., 1999).

However, it is possible to obtain the exact value of the Russell measure of technical efficiency by reformulating model (5.1) as a second-order cone programming (SOCP) model (see Sueyoshi & Sekitani, 2007a). Resorting to the change of variables $\psi_n = \frac{1}{\phi_n}$, we obtain the following model:

$$\begin{aligned}
&\min_{\substack{\theta_1,\ldots,\theta_M \\ \psi_1,\ldots,\psi_N \\ \lambda_1,\ldots,\lambda_J}} && \frac{1}{M+N}\left(\sum_{m=1}^{M}\theta_m + \sum_{n=1}^{N}\psi_n\right) && (5.3.0)\\
&s.t. && && \\
&\sum_{j=1}^{J}\lambda_j x_{jm} = \theta_m x_{om}, && m = 1,\ldots,M && (5.3.1)\\
&\sum_{j=1}^{J}\lambda_j y_{jn} = y_{on}/\psi_n, && n = 1,\ldots,N && (5.3.2)\\
&\sum_{j=1}^{J}\lambda_j = 1, && && (5.3.3)\\
&\theta_m \le 1, && m = 1,\ldots,M && (5.3.4)\\
&\psi_n \le 1, && n = 1,\ldots,N && (5.3.5)\\
&\lambda_j \ge 0, && j = 1,\ldots,J && (5.3.6)
\end{aligned} \qquad (5.3)$$

Thus, the nonlinearity has passed from the objective function to the constraints. The method consists in substituting constraints (5.3.2) with the second-order cone ones:

$$\left(\frac{\sum_{j=1}^{J}\lambda_j y_{jn} + \psi_n}{2}\right)^2 \ge \left(\frac{\sum_{j=1}^{J}\lambda_j y_{jn} - \psi_n}{2}\right)^2 + \left(\sqrt{y_{on}}\right)^2 \quad n = 1,\ldots,N. \qquad (5.4)$$

Finally, the model can be solved by any SOCP solver.

Recently, Halická and Trnovská (2018) introduced a second method along similar lines, where the graph Russell measure is solved in an exact way. In particular, they show how to reformulate the original nonlinear model (5.1) as a semidefinite programming (SDP) model while describing how to derive the corresponding dual program. On the one hand, the SDP reformulation of the Russell measure can be solved efficiently using standard SDP solvers. On the other hand, the dual program allows establishing, for the first time, a specific relationship between the profit function and the Russell measure.

Following Halická and Trnovská (2018), the semidefinite programming formulation of (5.1) is as follows:

$$
\begin{aligned}
TE_{RM(G)}(x_o, y_o) = \quad & \min_{\substack{\theta_1,\ldots,\theta_M\\ \phi_1,\ldots,\phi_N\\ \psi_1,\ldots,\psi_N\\ \lambda_1,\ldots,\lambda_J}} \quad \frac{1}{M+N}\left(\sum_{m=1}^{M}\theta_m + \sum_{n=1}^{N}\psi_n\right) \\
& \sum_{j=1}^{J}\lambda_j x_{jm} = \theta_m x_{om}, \qquad m = 1, \ldots, M \\
& s.t. \sum_{j=1}^{J}\lambda_j y_{jn} = \phi_n y_{on}, \qquad n = 1, \ldots, N \\
& \sum_{j=1}^{J}\lambda_j = 1, \\
& \theta_m \leq 1, \qquad m = 1, \ldots, M \\
& \phi_n \geq 1, \qquad n = 1, \ldots, N \\
& \lambda_j \geq 0, \qquad j = 1, \ldots, J \\
& \begin{pmatrix} \psi_n & 0 \\ 0 & \phi_n \end{pmatrix} \succ 0, \qquad n = 1, \ldots, N,
\end{aligned}
\tag{5.5}
$$

where $A \succ 0$ means that the matrix A is positive semidefinite. In this case, for a matrix $A = \begin{pmatrix} a_1 & a_3 \\ a_3 & a_2 \end{pmatrix}$, this means that $a_1, a_2 \geq 0$ and $\det(A) = a_1a_2 - a_3^2 \geq 0$.

Its dual is the following program:

$$
\begin{aligned}
& \max_{\substack{\sigma, u_1,\ldots,u_N\\ v_1,\ldots,v_M\\ z_{1n}, z_{2n}, z_{3n}}} \quad -\sigma + \sum_{n=1}^{N} u_n y_{on} - \sum_{m=1}^{M} v_m x_{om} + 1 - \sum_{n=1}^{N}(z_{1n} + z_{2n} + 2z_{3n}) \\
& s.t. \\
& \sum_{n=1}^{N} u_n y_{jn} - \sum_{m=1}^{M} v_m x_{jm} \leq \sigma, \qquad j = 1, \ldots, J \\
& v_m \geq \frac{1}{M+N}\frac{1}{x_{om}}, \qquad m = 1, \ldots, M \\
& u_n \geq \frac{z_{2n}}{y_{on}}, \qquad n = 1, \ldots, N \\
& z_{1n} = \frac{1}{M+N}, \\
& \begin{pmatrix} z_{1n} & z_{3n} \\ z_{3n} & z_{2n} \end{pmatrix} \succ 0, \qquad n = 1, \ldots, N
\end{aligned}
\tag{5.6}
$$

Regarding the duality results associated with the profit function, Halická and Trnovská (2018) prove that the Russell measure of technical efficiency can be reinterpreted as a gauge function that minimizes shadow profit minus shadow actual profit given a set of normalization conditions defined over the space of prices. Additionally, the objective function of the measure is affected by a term interpreted as a penalty function. Specifically, these authors show that one minus the Russell measure of technical efficiency is equivalent to the following:

$$1 - TE_{RM(G)}(x_o, y_o) = \min_{\substack{u_1,\ldots,u_N \\ v_1,\ldots,v_M \\ t_1,\ldots,t_N}} \Pi(v,u) - \left(\sum_{n=1}^{N} u_n y_{on} - \sum_{m=1}^{M} v_m x_{om} \right) + \frac{1}{M+N} \sum_{n=1}^{N} F(t_n)$$

$$\begin{aligned}
& s.t. \\
& v_m \geq \frac{1}{M+N} \frac{1}{x_{om}}, \quad m = 1, \ldots, M \\
& u_n \geq \frac{1}{M+N} \frac{t_n}{y_{on}}, \quad n = 1, \ldots, N \\
& t_n \geq 0, \quad n = 1, \ldots, N.
\end{aligned} \tag{5.7}$$

where $F(t_n) = (1 - \sqrt{t_n})^2$.

It can be proved that $t_n \leq 1$, $n = 1, \ldots, N$, at the optimum. This means, by the constraints of model (5.7), that u_n can take values even smaller than $\frac{1}{M+N} \frac{1}{y_{on}}$, depending on the value of t_n. Note also that $F(t_n)$ is a decreasing function in t_n that appears with positive sign in the objective function of model (5.7), which is minimized. So, at optimum, some t_n could be smaller than one if it is worth giving a wider range of values for the output shadow prices u_n, so that the value of $\Pi(v,u) - \left(\sum_{n=1}^{N} u_n y_{on} - \sum_{m=1}^{M} v_m x_{om} \right)$ compensates for the value of the term $\frac{1}{M+N} \times \sum_{n=1}^{N} F(t_n)$.

Moreover, given the market prices (w,p), we have that $\frac{(w,p)}{(M+N) \min\{w_1 x_{o1}, \ldots, w_M x_{oM}, p_1 y_{o1}, \ldots, p_N y_{oN}\}}$ with $t_n = 1$ for all $n = 1, \ldots, N$ is a feasible solution of model (5.7), with a value in the objective function equal to the Russell profit inefficiency measure: $\frac{\Pi(w,p) - \left(\sum_{n=1}^{N} p_n y_{on} - \sum_{m=1}^{M} w_m x_{om} \right)}{(M+N) \min\{w_1 x_{o1}, \ldots, w_M x_{oM}, p_1 y_{o1}, \ldots, p_N y_{oN}\}}$, thanks to the homogeneity of degree one of the profit function. Given that this is only a feasible solution of model (5.7) that can be suboptimal, we trivially obtain the following inequality:

$$\frac{\Pi(w,p) - \left(\sum_{n=1}^{N} p_n y_{on} - \sum_{m=1}^{M} w_m x_{om} \right)}{(M+N) \min\{w_1 x_{o1}, \ldots, w_M x_{oM}, p_1 y_{o1}, \ldots, p_N y_{oN}\}} \geq 1 - TE_{RM(G)}(x_o, y_o). \tag{5.8}$$

Finally, following Farrell's tradition, one could close the inequality in (5.8) including a term that will be interpreted as the Russell allocative measure of profit inefficiency (*AI*):

$$N\Pi I_{RM(G)}(x_o, y_o, \widetilde{w}, \widetilde{p}) = \underbrace{\frac{\Pi(w,p) - \left(\sum_{n=1}^{N} p_n y_{on} - \sum_{m=1}^{M} w_m x_{om}\right)}{(M+N)\min\{w_1 x_{o1}, \ldots, w_M x_{oM}, p_1 y_{o1}, \ldots, p_N y_{oN}\}}}_{\text{(Normalized) Profit Inefficiency}} = \underbrace{\left[1 - TE_{RM(G)}(x_o, y_o)\right]}_{\text{Technical Inefficiency}} + AI_{RM(G)}(x_o, y_o, \widetilde{w}, \widetilde{p}). \tag{5.9}$$

Note that if we multiple the profit inefficiency measure in (5.9) and its components by the normalization factor $(M + N)\min\{w_1 x_{o1}, \ldots, w_M x_{oM}, p_1 y_{o1}, \ldots, p_N y_{oN}\}$, then all these measures would be expressed in monetary terms. This operation allows the comparison between different profit inefficiency measures.

Furthermore, Halická and Trnovská (2018) establish a second duality result regarding the profit function and the Russell measure of technical efficiency, where the penalty term appears explicitly. To achieve such a, they need to resort to a different normalization of the profit loss in (5.9) by including part of the optimal solution of model (5.7). In particular, they show that:

$$\underbrace{\frac{\Pi(w,p) - \left(\sum_{n=1}^{N} p_n y_{on} - \sum_{m=1}^{M} w_m x_{om}\right)}{(M+N)\min\left\{w_1 x_{o1}, \ldots, w_M x_{oM}, \frac{p_1 y_{o1}}{t_1^*}, \ldots, \frac{p_N y_{oN}}{t_N^*}\right\}}}_{\text{(Normalized) Profit Inefficiency}} = \underbrace{\left[1 - TE_{RM(G)}(x_o, y_o)\right]}_{\text{Technical Inefficiency}} + AI'_{RM(G)}(x_o, y_o, \widetilde{w}, \widetilde{p}) - \frac{1}{M+N}\sum_{n=1}^{N} F\left(t_n^*\right). \tag{5.10}$$

These authors prove that (5.10) results in a smaller allocative inefficiency residual than in (5.9), i.e., $AI'_{RM(G)}(x_o, y_o, \widetilde{w}, \widetilde{p}) \le AI_{RM(G)}(x_o, y_o, \widetilde{w}, \widetilde{p})$. However, it is not clear how to interpret the final term in the decomposition of the normalized loss profit in (5.10), and additionally, both this term and the profit inefficiency measure, i.e., the left-hand side in (5.10), can take different values if there are alternative optimal solutions for model (5.7).

5.3 The Russell Input Measure of Technical Efficiency and the Decomposition of Cost Inefficiency

In this section, we turn our attention to the partially oriented input version of the Russell measure of technical efficiency. In the most general framework, a company is technically inefficient if it is possible to either expand its output mix without requiring any increase in its inputs or contract its input mix without requiring a reduction in its outputs. It was the case studied in the previous section. On the other hand, the potential for reducing the input bundle reflects input-oriented inefficiency. Indeed, in most empirical applications, technical efficiency is measured either by input or in output orientation instead of by its graph version. When the outputs are fixed (e.g., like the number of different types of patients to be treated at a hospital), managing the use of inputs to reduce costs is the aim. In this case, when measuring technical efficiency is the objective, attaining input-oriented targets on the frontier of the production possibility set by scaling down the input mix to the maximum extent possible is the logical approach to be adopted. To achieve full cost efficiency, it is usually necessary to modify the input bundle in the light of the relative market prices of inputs. Potential for cost reduction through input substitution is associated with the allocative efficiency of the evaluated unit.

This section is devoted to reviewing the result on duality related to the Russell measure of input efficiency that has been recently published in the literature. As we will show, it is very different from the results related to the graph Russell measure of technical efficiency presented above, in the sense that its input-oriented version does not need a penalty term in its multiplier form. The nature of the oriented version, allows it to be written as a linear programming problem.

As we previously mentioned in Chap. 2, the most popular approach for measuring and decomposing cost efficiency is that attributable to Farrell (1957). Under this approach, cost efficiency, the ratio between optimal and actual cost, can be decomposed into components exploiting Shephard's input distance function (Shephard, 1953). In particular, technical efficiency is calculated as the reciprocal of Shephard's input distance function, whereas allocative efficiency is retrieved as a residual (see Sect. 3.2.2 of Chap. 3). In the case of DEA, the inverse of Shephard's input distance function is computed through the well-known radial measure, projecting the assessed firm to the efficient frontier of technology through equiproportional changes in inputs and, consequently, preserving the input mix. This last feature, the conservation of the mix, has been criticized in the DEA literature for not being flexible enough. As previously mentioned, another well-known drawback of Shephard's input distance function, which is the tool used for determining the technical efficiency component in the Farrell decomposition of cost efficiency, is that it neglects slacks. This means that the assessed firm is projected onto the weakly efficient frontier in the input space and, specifically, input slacks could play an important role in the evaluation of technical efficiency if they are detected. This fact has implications on the interpretation of the allocative component in the traditional Farrell approach given that if input slacks are present, then a certain amount of technical inefficiency is accounted for in the value of the allocative inefficiency term (i.e., this term is overestimated). Some researchers think erroneous since this component would then reflect not only the savings in cost that could be accomplished by substitutions along the efficient frontier, but it would also include some type of technical inefficiency (the slacks).

In this section, we show a possible solution for addressing these problems that is based on the input-oriented Russell measure (Färe & Lovell, 1978; Färe et al., 1985). The results, published by Aparicio et al. (2015a), are derived from a novel Fenchel-Mahler inequality that shows the existence of a new dual correspondence between the cost function and the Russell measure of input efficiency. One clear benefit of this approach, in contrast to previous approaches, is that the technical efficiency component in the decomposition of cost efficiency is the input-oriented Russell measure. This fact guarantees that all sources of technical inefficiency in the corresponding input space will be considered, since the Russell measure of input efficiency satisfies the indication property, thereby complying with the Pareto-Koopmans definition of technical efficiency.

The Russell input measure of technical efficiency is defined through the following linear optimization program:

$$
\begin{aligned}
TE_{RM(I)}(x_o, y_o) = \quad & \min_{\substack{\theta_1,\ldots,\theta_M \\ \lambda_1,\ldots,\lambda_J}} \quad \frac{1}{M}\sum_{m=1}^{M}\theta_m \\
s.t. \quad & \\
& \sum_{j=1}^{J}\lambda_j x_{jm} = \theta_m x_{om}, \quad m = 1, \ldots, M \\
& \sum_{j=1}^{J}\lambda_j y_{jn} \geq y_{on}, \quad n = 1, \ldots, N \\
& \sum_{j=1}^{J}\lambda_j = 1, \\
& \theta_m \leq 1, \quad m = 1, \ldots, M \\
& \lambda_j \geq 0, \quad j = 1, \ldots, J
\end{aligned}
\tag{5.11}
$$

Since the graph version of the Russell measure (5.1) nests its input counterpart, (5.11) can be easily derived from it by deleting the decision variables related to the output dimension and averaging over the input reductions. In model (5.11), θ_m evaluates the relative proportional reduction of input m, $m = 1, \ldots, M$, whereas the objective function averages these proportional rates of input contraction. Also, in the above formulation, the constraints $\theta_m \leq 1$ are the requirements for dominance.

Regarding the properties of the Russell measure of input efficiency, let us show the following ones taken from Aparicio et al. (2015a) and considered in Sect. 2.2.4 of Chap. 2:

1. $TE_{RM(I)}(x_o, y_o) = 1$ if and only if $(x_o, y_o) \in \partial^s(L(y_o))$, i.e., indication (E1a).
2. $0 < TE_{RM(I)}(x_o, y_o) \leq 1$, (E1b).
3. $TE_{RM(I)}(x_o, y_o)$ is strongly monotonic in inputs, (E2).
4. $TE_{RM(I)}(x_o, y_o)$ is units invariant (E4).

Additionally, and once the properties of this measure are met, it is possible to define its technical inefficiency counterpart, i.e., the Russell input measure of technical inefficiency: $TI_{RM(I)}(x_o, y_o) = 1 - TE_{RM(I)}(x_o, y_o)$.

The linear dual program of (5.11) is as follows:

$$TE_{RM(I)}(x_o, y_o) = \max_{\substack{\alpha, v_1, \ldots, v_M \\ u_1, \ldots, u_N \\ \xi_1, \ldots, \xi_M}} -\alpha + \sum_{n=1}^{N} u_n y_{on} - \sum_{m=1}^{M} \xi_m \tag{5.12.0}$$

s.t.

$$\alpha - \sum_{n=1}^{N} u_n y_{jn} + \sum_{m=1}^{M} v_m x_{jm} \geq 0, \quad j = 1, \ldots, J \tag{5.12.1}$$

$$v_m x_{om} - \xi_m = \frac{1}{M}, \quad m = 1, \ldots, M \tag{5.12.2}$$

$$v_m \geq 0, \quad m = 1, \ldots, M \tag{5.12.3}$$

$$u_n \geq 0, \quad n = 1, \ldots, N \tag{5.12.4}$$

$$\xi_m \geq 0 \quad m = 1, \ldots, M \tag{5.12.5}$$

By (5.12.2), $\xi_m = v_m x_{om} - \frac{1}{M}$, $m = 1, \ldots, M$. Therefore, $\sum_{m=1}^{M} \xi_m = \sum_{m=1}^{M} \left(v_m x_{om} - \frac{1}{M}\right) = \sum_{m=1}^{M} v_m x_{om} - 1$. Additionally, ξ_m works like a slack in constraint (5.12.2). In this way, we can equivalently rewrite model (5.12) in the following way:

$$TE_{RM(I)}(x_o, y_o) = \max_{\substack{\alpha, v_1, \ldots, v_M \\ u_1, \ldots, u_N}} -\alpha + \sum_{n=1}^{N} u_n y_{on} - \sum_{m=1}^{M} v_m x_{om} + 1$$

s.t.

$$\alpha - \sum_{n=1}^{N} u_n y_{jn} + \sum_{m=1}^{M} v_m x_{jm} \geq 0, \quad j = 1, \ldots, J, \tag{5.13}$$

$$v_m \geq \frac{1}{M x_{om}}, \quad m = 1, \ldots, M$$

$$v_m \geq 0, \quad m = 1, \ldots, M$$

$$u_n \geq 0, \quad n = 1, \ldots, N$$

which may be rewritten as follows:

$$TE_{RM(I)}(x_o, y_o) = \max_{\substack{\alpha, v_1, \ldots, v_M \\ u_1, \ldots, u_N}} 1 - \left(\alpha - \left(\sum_{n=1}^{N} u_n y_{on} - \sum_{m=1}^{M} v_m x_{om}\right)\right)$$

$s.t.$

$$\begin{aligned} &\alpha - \sum_{n=1}^{N} u_n y_{jn} + \sum_{m=1}^{M} v_m x_{jm} \geq 0, && j = 1, \ldots, J \\ &v_m \geq \frac{1}{M x_{om}}, && m = 1, \ldots, M \\ &v_m \geq 0, && m = 1, \ldots, M \\ &u_n \geq 0, && n = 1, \ldots, N \end{aligned} \tag{5.14}$$

But then, the Russell measure of input efficiency is equal to the following:

$$TE_{RM(I)}(x_o, y_o) = 1 - \min_{\substack{\alpha, v_1, \ldots, v_M \\ u_1, \ldots, u_N}} \alpha - \left(\sum_{n=1}^{N} u_n y_{on} - \sum_{m=1}^{M} v_m x_{om}\right) \tag{5.15.0}$$

$s.t.$

$$\alpha \geq \sum_{n=1}^{N} u_n y_{jn} - \sum_{m=1}^{M} v_m x_{jm}, \quad j = 1, \ldots, J \tag{5.15.1}$$

$$v_m \geq \frac{1}{M x_{om}}, \quad m = 1, \ldots, M \tag{5.15.2}$$

$$v_m \geq 0, \quad m = 1, \ldots, M \tag{5.15.3}$$

$$u_n \geq 0, \quad n = 1, \ldots, N \tag{5.15.4}$$

Now, we are going to prove the most important result necessary for establishing the Fenchel-Mahler inequality that relates the cost function to the Russell measure of input inefficiency. This result states that the decision variable α in model (5.15) at the optimum must be interpreted as a (shadow) optimal profit.

Proposition 5.1 Let (v^*, u^*, α^*) be an optimal solution of (5.15). Then, $\alpha^* = \Pi(v^*, u^*)$.

Proof First, let us assume that $\alpha^* > \Pi(v^*, u^*)$. On the one hand, we have that $\Pi(v^*, u^*) = \max_{x,y} \left\{ \sum_{n=1}^{N} u_n^* y_n - \sum_{m=1}^{M} v_m^* x_m : (x, y) \in T \right\} \geq \sum_{n=1}^{N} u_n^* y_{jn} - \sum_{m=1}^{M} v_m^* x_{jm}$, $\forall j = 1, \ldots, J$, since $(x_j, y_j) \in T$, $\forall j = 1, \ldots, J$. Then, $(v^*, u^*, \Pi(v^*, u^*))$ is a feasible solution of (5.15). On the other hand, $\Pi(v^*, u^*) - \left(\sum_{n=1}^{N} u_n^* y_n - \sum_{m=1}^{M} v_m^* x_m \right) < \alpha^* - \left(\sum_{n=1}^{N} u_n^* y_n - \sum_{m=1}^{M} v_m^* x_m \right)$, which is a contradiction given the fact that (v^*, u^*, α^*) is an optimal solution of (5.15) by hypothesis. Second, let us now assume that $\alpha^* < \Pi(v^*, u^*)$.

By (5.15.1), we have that $\alpha^* \geq \sum_{n=1}^{N} u_n^* y_{jn} - \sum_{m=1}^{M} v_m^* x_{jm}, \forall j = 1, \ldots, J$. By the definition of the technology T in DEA under VRS, we have that for any $(x, y) \in T$, there exists a vector $(\lambda_1, \ldots, \lambda_J) \in R_+^J$ with $\sum_{j=1}^{J} \lambda_j = 1$ such that $\sum_{n=1}^{N} u_n^* y_{jn} - \sum_{m=1}^{M} v_m^* x_{jm} \leq \sum_{n=1}^{N} u_n^* \left(\sum_{j=1}^{J} \lambda_j y_{jn} \right) - \sum_{m=1}^{M} v_m^* \left(\sum_{j=1}^{J} \lambda_j x_{jm} \right) = \sum_{j=1}^{J} \lambda_j \left(\sum_{n=1}^{N} u_n^* y_{jn} - \sum_{m=1}^{M} v_m^* x_{jm} \right) \leq \alpha^* < \Pi(v^*, u^*)$. Therefore, the maximum profit at prices (v^*, u^*) is not achieved at any point in T, which is clearly a contradiction. ■

By Proposition 5.1, we have that the Russell measure of input efficiency can be computed through the following model since (5.15.1) is then trivially satisfied:

$$
\begin{aligned}
TE_{RM(I)}(x_o, y_o) = 1 - \min_{\substack{v_1, \ldots, v_M \\ u_1, \ldots, u_N}} \quad & \Pi(v, u) - \left(\sum_{n=1}^{N} u_n y_{on} - \sum_{m=1}^{M} v_m x_{om} \right) \\
s.t. \quad & \\
v_m \geq \frac{1}{M x_{om}}, \quad & m = 1, \ldots, M \\
v_m \geq 0, \quad & m = 1, \ldots, M \\
u_n \geq 0, \quad & n = 1, \ldots, N
\end{aligned}
\tag{5.16}
$$

From (5.16), it is not difficult to obtain an inequality between profit inefficiency and the Russell measure of input inefficiency. But, in this case, it is not the inequality that we are seeking.

Proposition 5.2 The Russell input measure of technical inefficiency, $TI_{RM(I)}(x_o, y_o)$, is greater or equal than the optimal value of model (5.17):

$$
\begin{aligned}
\min_{v_1, \ldots, v_M} \quad & \sum_{m=1}^{M} v_m x_{om} - C(y_o, v) \\
s.t. \quad & \\
v_m \geq \frac{1}{M x_{om}}, \quad & m = 1, \ldots, M \\
v_m \geq 0, \quad & m = 1, \ldots, M
\end{aligned}
\tag{5.17}
$$

Proof Färe and Primont (1995) established that $\Pi(v, u) = \sup_y \left\{ \sum_{n=1}^{N} u_n y_n - C(y, v) \right\}$. So, considering $y = y_o$, $\Pi(v, u) = \sup_y \left\{ \sum_{n=1}^{N} u_n y_n - C(y, v) \right\} \geq \sum_{n=1}^{N} u_n y_{no} - C(y_o, v)$, which implies that $\Pi(v, u) - \left(\sum_{n=1}^{N} u_n y_{on} - \sum_{m=1}^{M} v_m x_{om} \right) \geq \sum_{m=1}^{M} v_m x_{om} - C(y_o, v)$.

Thus, the minimum calculated in (5.16) is greater or equal to (5.17). And, consequently, $1 - TE_{RM(I)}(x_o, y_o) = TI_{RM(I)}(x_o, y_o)$ is lower bounded by the optimal value of model (5.17).■

Now, we want to derive the other inequality, upper bounding the Russell measure of input inefficiency $TI_{RM(I)}(x_o, y_o)$ by the optimal value of model (5.17). It should necessarily lead us to the equality between $TI_{RM(I)}(x_o, y_o)$ and the optimal value of (5.17). From this inequality, it is easy to obtain the desired Fenchel-Mahler inequality.

To achieve that result, we first need to demonstrate the linear optimization program that is used in DEA to calculate minimum cost given the input market prices w and an output level y_o together with the formulation of its dual linear program:

$$\begin{aligned} C(y_o, w) = \min_{\substack{x_1,\ldots,x_N \\ \lambda_1,\ldots,\lambda_J}} \quad & \sum_{m=1}^{M} w_m x_m \\ \text{s.t.} \quad & \\ & \sum_{j=1}^{J} \lambda_j x_{jm} \leq x_m, \qquad m = 1, \ldots, M \\ & \sum_{j=1}^{J} \lambda_j y_{jn} \geq y_{on}, \qquad n = 1, \ldots, N \\ & \sum_{j=1}^{J} \lambda_j = 1, \\ & \lambda_j \geq 0, \qquad j = 1, \ldots, J \\ & x_n \geq 0, \qquad n = 1, \ldots, N \end{aligned} \tag{5.18}$$

and

$$C(y_o, w) = \max_{\substack{\alpha, v_1,\ldots,v_M \\ u_1,\ldots,u_N}} \quad \sum_{n=1}^{N} u_n y_{on} - \alpha \tag{5.19.0}$$

s.t.

$$\alpha \geq \sum_{n=1}^{N} u_n y_{jn} - \sum_{m=1}^{M} v_m x_{jm}, \quad j = 1, \ldots, J \tag{5.19.1}$$

$$v_m \leq w_m, \quad m = 1, \ldots, M \tag{5.19.2}$$

$$v_m \geq 0, \quad m = 1, \ldots, M \tag{5.19.3}$$

$$u_n \geq 0, \quad n = 1, \ldots, N \tag{5.19.4}$$

Now, we operate with both models in order to prove that the Russell measure of input inefficiency is also a lower bound of the optimal value of model (5.17).

Proposition 5.3 The Russell input measure of technical inefficiency, $TI_{RM(I)}(x_o, y_o)$, is less or equal than the optimal value of model (5.17).

Proof Let (v^*, u^*, α^*) be an optimal solution of model (5.19). Then, by linear duality, we have that the optimal value of (5.19), i.e., $\sum_{n=1}^{N} u_n^* y_{on} - \alpha^*$, equals the optimal value of model (5.18), which is $C(y_o, w)$. Therefore, $C(y_o, w) = \sum_{n=1}^{N} u_n^* y_{on} - \alpha^*$, which is equivalent to $\alpha^* - \left(\sum_{n=1}^{N} u_n^* y_{no} - \sum_{m=1}^{M} w_m x_m\right) = \sum_{m=1}^{M} w_m x_m - C(y_o, w)$ (Result A). On the other hand, by (5.19.2) and (5.19.1), we have that $\alpha^* - \left(\sum_{n=1}^{N} u_n^* y_{jn} - \sum_{m=1}^{M} w_m x_{jm}\right) \geq \alpha^* - \left(\sum_{n=1}^{N} u_n^* y_{jn} - \sum_{m=1}^{M} v_m^* x_{jm}\right) \geq 0$, for all $j = 1, \ldots, J$ (Result B). Finally, for all $w \in R_{++}^M$ such that $w_m \geq \frac{1}{Mx_{om}}$, $m = 1, \ldots,$ M, we have at least an optimal solution of model (5.19), says $(v^*(w), u^*(w), \alpha^*(w))$. We are going to prove that $(w, u^*(w), \alpha^*(w))$ is a feasible solution of model (5.15). By Result B, it satisfies (5.15.1), whereas (5.15.2) is trivially satisfied by the hypothesis. Consequently, $TE_{RM(I)}(x_o, y_o) \geq 1 - \left[\alpha^*(w) - \left(\sum_{n=1}^{N} u_n^*(w) y_{on} - \sum_{m=1}^{M} w_m x_{om}\right)\right]$, which implies that $1 - TE_{RM(I)}(x_o, y_o) \leq \alpha^*(w) - \left(\sum_{n=1}^{N} u_n^*(w) y_{on} - \sum_{m=1}^{M} w_m x_{om}\right)$. Thus, $TI_{RM(I)}(x_o, y_o) \leq \inf_w \left\{\alpha^*(w) - \left(\sum_{n=1}^{N} u_n^*(w) y_{on} - \sum_{m=1}^{M} w_m x_{om}\right) : w_m \geq \frac{1}{Mx_{om}}, m = 1, \ldots, M\right\}$. By Result A, $TI_{RM(I)}(x_o, y_o) \leq \inf_w \left\{\sum_{m=1}^{M} w_m x_m - C(y_o, w) : w_m \geq \frac{1}{Mx_{om}}, m = 1, \ldots, M\right\}$. Consequently, the Russell measure of input inefficiency is less or equal than the optimal value of model (5.17) since inf can be changed by min in the case of DEA. ■

Using the last two propositions, we are able to prove the following result.

Theorem 5.1 The following result holds:

$$
\begin{aligned}
TI_{RM(I)}(x_o, y_o) = \; & \min_{v_1, \ldots, v_M} \sum_{m=1}^{M} v_m x_{om} - C(y_o, v) \\
s.t. \; & \\
& v_m \geq \frac{1}{Mx_{om}}, \quad m = 1, \ldots, M \\
& v_m \geq 0, \quad m = 1, \ldots, M
\end{aligned} \tag{5.20}
$$

Given the input market prices w, Theorem 5.1 may be invoked for deriving the desired Fenchel-Mahler inequality between cost inefficiency and the Russell measure of input inefficiency. It is enough to note that, given any input price vector $w \in R^M_{++}$, $w/\min\{Mx_{o1}w_1, \ldots, Mx_{oM}w_M\}$ satisfies the constraints of model (5.20). In this way, $w/\min\{Mx_{o1}w_1, \ldots, Mx_{oM}w_M\}$ is a feasible solution of that model, and therefore, the objective function evaluated at this "normalized" vector is greater or equal than the Russell input measure of technical inefficiency. In particular, we get the following inequality between the Russell cost inefficiency measure and technical inefficiency thanks to the cost function being homogeneous of degree plus one:

$$\frac{\sum_{m=1}^{M} w_m x_{om} - C(y_o, w)}{\min\{Mx_{o1}w_1, \ldots, Mx_{oM}w_M\}} \geq TI_{RM(I)}(x_o, y_o). \tag{5.21}$$

Following Farrell's tradition, the normalized cost loss may be decomposed into a technical inefficiency component and the Russell allocative measure of cost inefficiency measure (AI):

$$\begin{aligned} NCI(x_o, y_o, \widetilde{w}) &= \underbrace{\frac{\sum_{m=1}^{M} w_m x_{om} - C(y_o, w)}{M \min\{x_{o1}w_1, \ldots, x_{oM}w_M\}}}_{\text{(Normalized) Cost Inefficiency}} \\ &= \underbrace{TI_{RM(I)}(x_o, y_o)}_{\text{Technical Inefficiency}} + AI_{RM(I)}(x_o, y_o, \widetilde{w}) \end{aligned} \tag{5.22}$$

Finally, we would like to highlight that if we multiple the cost inefficiency measure in (5.22) and its components by the normalization factor $M \min\{x_{o1}w_1, \ldots, x_{oM}w_M\}$, then all would be measured in monetary terms.

5.4 The Russell Output Measure of Technical Efficiency and the Decomposition of Revenue Inefficiency

Once we have introduced the main results regarding the Russell measure of input efficiency, deriving the results associated with its output-oriented version is straightforward by pure analogy.

The Russell output measure of technical efficiency can be computed through the following linear model:

$$
\begin{aligned}
TE_{RM(O)}(x_o, y_o) = \max_{\substack{\phi_1, \ldots, \phi_N \\ \lambda_1, \ldots, \lambda_J}} \quad & \frac{1}{N}\sum_{n=1}^{N}\phi_n \\
s.t. \quad & \\
& \sum_{j=1}^{J}\lambda_j x_{jm} \leq x_{om}, \qquad m = 1, \ldots, M \\
& \sum_{j=1}^{J}\lambda_j y_{jn} = \phi_n y_{on}, \qquad n = 1, \ldots, N \\
& \sum_{j=1}^{J}\lambda_j = 1, \\
& \phi_n \geq 1, \qquad n = 1, \ldots, N \\
& \lambda_j \geq 0, \qquad j = 1, \ldots, J
\end{aligned}
\tag{5.23}
$$

This measure takes values greater or equal to one, with one signaling Pareto-Koopmans efficiency in the output space. Additionally, as in the case of the Russell measure of input efficiency, it is possible to define a Russell output measure of technical inefficiency: $TI_{RM(O)}(x_o, y_o) = TE_{RM(O)}(x_o, y_o) - 1$.

Regarding the measurement of economic inefficiency and its decomposition into technical and allocative components, Aparicio et al. (2015a) propose the following Russell revenue inefficiency measure, which can be decomposed into the technical inefficiency measure and the Russell allocative measure of revenue inefficiency:

$$
\begin{aligned}
NRI(x_o, y_o, \widetilde{p}) &= \underbrace{\frac{R(x_o, p) - \sum_{n=1}^{N} p_n y_{on}}{N \min\{y_{o1}p_1, \ldots, y_{oN}p_N\}}}_{\text{(Normalized) Revenue Inefficiency}} \\
&= \underbrace{TI_{RM(O)}(x_o, y_o)}_{\text{Technical Inefficiency}} + AI_{RM(O)}(x_o, y_o, \widetilde{p})
\end{aligned}
\tag{5.24}
$$

Finally, to conclude the methodological part of this chapter, we would like to pinpoint that if we multiply revenue inefficiency, technical inefficiency, and allocative inefficiency in (5.24) by the normalization factor N min $\{y_{o1}p_1, \ldots, y_{oN}p_N\}$, then all the components would be gauged in monetary terms.

5.5 Empirical Illustration of the Russell Profit, Cost, and Revenue Inefficiency Models

In this section, we illustrate the calculation of the three economic inefficiency measures and their decompositions based on their corresponding Russell technical inefficiency scores and using the example data presented in Sect. 2.6.2 of Chap. 2. Table 5.1 replicates the data.

The package functions computing these measures and their decompositions into technical and allocative inefficiencies are the following:

```
deaprofitrussell(X, Y, W, P, names=FIRMS)
```

```
deacostrussell(X, Y, W, names=FIRMS)
```

```
dearevenuerussell(X, Y, P, names=FIRMS)
```

5.5.1 *The Russell Profit Inefficiency Model*

We rely on the open (web-based) Jupyter Notebook interface to illustrate our first economic model. However, it can be implemented in any integrated development environment (IDE) of preference.[1] To calculate the Russell profit inefficiency model,

Table 5.1 Example data illustrating the economic inefficiency models

	Model							
	Graph profit model		Input orientation Cost model			Output orientation Revenue model		
Firm	x	y	x_1	x_2	y	x	y_1	y_2
A	2	1	2	2	1	1	7	7
B	4	5	1	4	1	1	4	8
C	8	8	4	1	1	1	8	4
D	12	9	4	3	1	1	3	5
E	6	3	5	5	1	1	3	3
F	14	7	6	1	1	1	8	2
G	14	9	2	5	1	1	6	4
H	9.412	2.353	1.6	8	1	1	1.5	5
Prices	$w = 1$	$p = 2$	$w_1 = 1$	$w_2 = 1$			$p_1 = 1$	$p_2 = 1$

[1] We refer the reader to Sect. 2.6.1 in Chap. 2 for the installation of the "Benchmarking Economic Efficiency" Julia package. All Jupyter Notebooks implementing the different economic models in this book can be downloaded from the reference site: http://www.benchmarkingeconomicefficiency.com

Table 5.2 Implementation of the Russell profit inefficiency model using BEE for Julia

In[]:

```
using DataEnvelopmentAnalysis
using BechmarkingEconomicEfficiency

X = [2; 4; 8; 12; 6; 14; 14; 9.412];
Y = [1; 5; 8; 9; 3; 7; 9; 2.353];
W = [1; 1; 1; 1; 1; 1; 1; 1];
P = [2; 2; 2; 2; 2; 2; 2; 2];
FIRMS = ["A"; "B"; "C"; "D"; "E"; "F"; "G"; "H"];

deaprofitrussell(X, Y, W, P, names = FIRMS)
```

Out[]:

```
Russell Profit DEA Model
DMUs = 8; Inputs = 1; Outputs = 1
Orientation = Graph; Returns to Scale = VRS
```

	Profit	Technical	Allocative
A	2.0	0.000	2.0
B	0.25	0.000	0.25
C	0.0	0.000	0.000
D	0.083	0.000	0.083
E	0.667	0.367	0.3
F	0.286	0.277	0.009
G	0.143	0.071	0.071
H	1.350	0.552	0.798

enter the following code in the "`In[]:`" panel, and run it. Since the DEA program solving the Russell technical efficiency measure (5.1) is nonlinear, the accompanying Julia software resorts to the "JuMP" package developed by Dunning et al. (2017), combined with the "Ipopt" solver, initially introduced by Wächter and Biegler (2006). Given the good properties of the program as indicated in Sect. 5.2, a suitable solution is found for all firms in both this example and the empirical application that follows below. The corresponding results are shown in the "`Out[]:`" panel in Table 5.2.

We can learn about the reference peers for each firm using the "peers" function with the corresponding economic or technical model. For the economic model, executing "`peersmatrix(deaprofitrussell(X, Y, W, P, names = FIRMS))`" identifies firm C as the reference benchmark maximizing profit for the rest of the firms (see Fig. 5.1).

As for the underlying Russell technical efficiency model, we can obtain all the information by running the corresponding function, as shown in Table 5.3.

It is also of interest to identify the reference benchmarks of the Russell graph technical efficiency measure corresponding to program (5.1). We make use once again of the "peersmatrix" function, i.e., "`peersmatrix (dearussell(X, Y, rts = :VRS, orient = :Graph, names = FIRMS))`." The output results shown in Table 5.4 ("`Out[]:`") identify firms A, B, C, and D as those conforming the strongly efficient production possibility set, i.e., those with unit

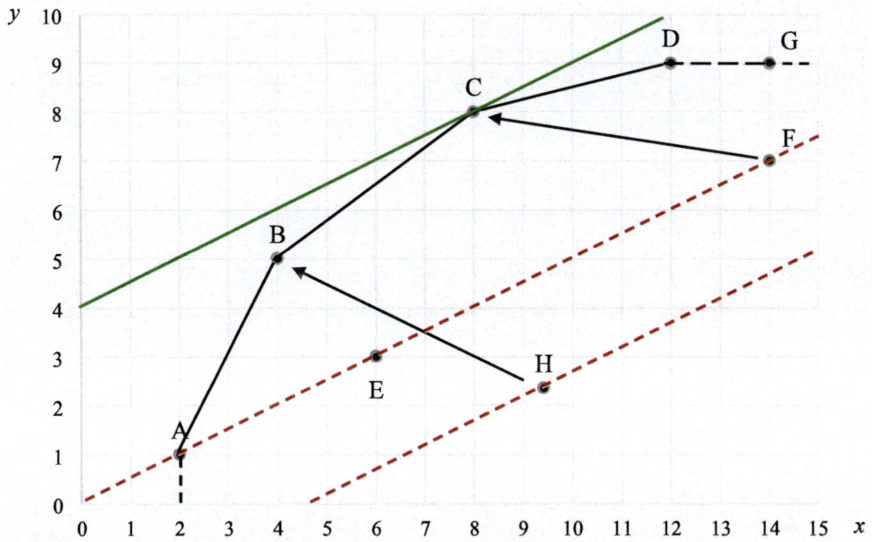

Fig. 5.1 Example of the Russell profit inefficiency model using BEE for Julia

Table 5.3 Implementation of the Russell graph efficiency measure using BEE for Julia

In[]:	`dearussell(X, Y, rts = :VRS, orient = :Graph, names = FIRMS)`
Out[]:	Russell DEA Model DMUs = 8; Inputs = 1; Outputs = 1 Orientation = Graph; Returns to Scale = VRS

	efficiency	effX1	effY1
A	1.0	1.0	1.0
B	1.0	1.0	1.0
C	1.0	1.0	1.0
D	1.0	1.0	1.0
E	0.633	0.667	1.667
F	0.723	0.571	1.143
G	0.929	0.857	1.0
H	0.448	0.425	2.125

values in the main diagonal of the square ($J \times J$) matrix containing their own intensity variables λ (note the matrix syntax in "`In[]:`").

Figure 5.1 illustrates the results for the Russell profit inefficiency model. There, for firm H, we identify that its normalized profit inefficiency with respect to firm C, according to (5.9), is equal to 1.350=[8 − (−4.706)]/(2 × 4.076), which can be decomposed into the Russell measure of technical inefficiency and the residual allocative inefficiency. As for technical inefficiency, this value is equal to one

Table 5.4 Reference peers of the Russell graph efficiency measure using BEE for Julia

In[]:	`peersmatrix(dearussell(X, Y, rts = :VRS, orient = :Graph, names = FIRMS))`
Out[]:	see output below

```
1.   .    .    .    .  .  .  .
.   1.0   .    .    .  .  .  .
.    .   1.0   .    .  .  .  .
.    .    .   1.0   .  .  .  .
.   1.0   .    .    .  .  .  .
.    .   1.0   .    .  .  .  .
.    .    .   1.0   .  .  .  .
.   1.0   .    .    .  .  .  .
```

minus the Russell technical efficiency score: $0.552 = TI_{RM(G)}(x_H, y_H) = 1 - 0.448 = 1 - TE_{RM(G)}(x_H, y_H)$, with the latter value being that reported in Table 5.3. The difference between the profit and technical inefficiencies yields 0.798 as allocative inefficiency: $0.798 = 1.350 - 0.552$. An interesting case is firm F identifying firm C as the economic and technological benchmark and whose allocative inefficiency should be zero. This illustrates that the Russell model fails to satisfy the essential property introduced in Sect. 2.4.5. Indeed, while this firm exhibits a profit inefficiency equal to 0.286, its technical inefficiency is 0.277, yielding a residual allocative inefficiency of 0.009. This justifies the adoption of methods such as those proposed in Chaps. 12 and 13 in order to adjust the economic decomposition. It is also worth mentioning that the Russell model does not satisfy the extended version of the essential property either because, otherwise, it would also fulfill the essential property, which is not true.

5.5.2 *The Russell Cost Inefficiency Model*

We now solve the example for the Russell cost inefficiency model according to expression (5.22). To calculate this model, enter the code included in the "`In[]:`" panel in the notebook, and execute it. The corresponding results are shown in the "`Out[]:`" panel of Table 5.5.

As aforementioned, we can learn about the reference benchmarks using the "peers" function with the corresponding economic or technical model. For the cost model, we run "`peersmatrix(deacostrussell(X, Y, W, names = FIRMS))`." In this case, firm A is identified as the only firm minimizing cost (see Fig. 5.2).

The function "deacostrussell" calls internally the Russell input-oriented technical efficiency measure (5.11), $TE_{RM(I)}(x_o, y_o)$, from which we recover the technical inefficiency presented in Table 5.5: $TI_{RM(I)}(x_o, y_o) = 1 - TE_{RM(I)}(x_o, y_o)$ To obtain all the information related to technical efficiency, the user may run the following code in the "`In[]:`" panel. Note that this function returns zero-valued slacks for the outputs, while there cannot be any in the input dimension (Table 5.6).

Table 5.5 Implementation of the Russell cost inefficiency model using BEE for Julia

In[]:

```
using DataEnvelopmentAnalysis
using BenchmarkingEconomicEfficiency

X = [2 2; 1 4; 4 1; 4 3; 5 5; 6 1; 2 5; 1.6 8];
Y = [1; 1; 1; 1; 1; 1; 1; 1];
W = [1 1; 1 1; 1 1; 1 1; 1 1; 1 1; 1 1; 1 1];
FIRMS = ["A"; "B"; "C"; "D"; "E"; "F"; "G"; "H"];

deacostrussell(X, Y, W, names = FIRMS)
```

Out[]:

```
Russell Cost DEA Model
DMUs = 8; Inputs = 2; Outputs = 1
Orientation = Input; Returns to Scale = VRS
```

	Cost	Technical	Allocative
A	0.0	0.0	0.0
B	0.5	0.0	0.5
C	0.5	0.0	0.5
D	0.5	0.417	0.083
E	0.6	0.6	0.0
F	1.5	0.167	1.333
G	0.75	0.35	0.4
H	1.75	0.438	1.312

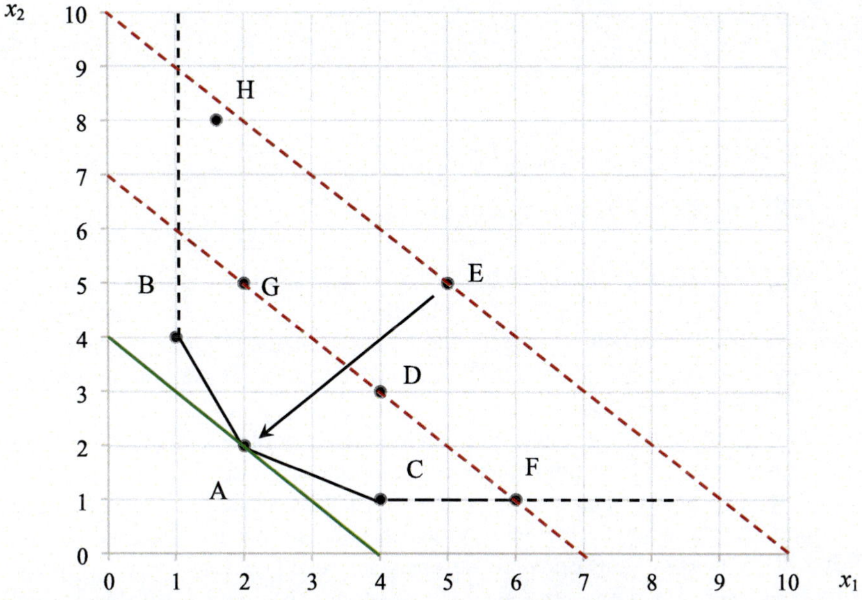

Fig. 5.2 Example of the Russell cost inefficiency model using BEE for Julia

Table 5.6 Implementation of the Russell input efficiency measure using BEE for Julia

In[]:
```
dearussell(X, Y, orient = :Input, rts = :VRS, names =
FIRMS)
```

Out[]:
```
Russell DEA Model
DMUs = 8; Inputs = 2; Outputs = 1
Orientation = Input; Returns to Scale = VRS
```

	efficiency	effX1	effX2	slackY1
A	1.0	1.0	1.0	0.0
B	1.0	1.0	1.0	0.0
C	1.0	1.0	1.0	0.0
D	0.583	0.5	0.667	0.0
E	0.4	0.4	0.4	0.0
F	0.833	0.667	1.0	0.0
G	0.65	0.5	0.8	0.0
H	0.562	0.625	0.5	0.0

Table 5.7 Reference peers of the Russell input efficiency measure using BEE for Julia

In[]:
```
peersmatrix(dearussell(X, Y, orient = :Input, rts = :VRS,
names = FIRMS))
```

Out[]:
```
1.0  .    .    .    .    .    .    .
.    1.0  .    .    .    .    .    .
.    .    1.0  .    .    .    .    .
1.0  .    .    .    .    .    .    .
1.0  .    .    .    .    .    .    .
.    .    1.0  .    .    .    .    .
.    1.0  .    .    .    .    .    .
.    1.0  .    .    .    .    .    .
```

Again, the reference benchmarks of the technical model can be recovered using the "peers" function, i.e., "`peersmatrix(dearussell(X, Y, orient = :Input, rts = :VRS, names = FIRMS))`." The output shown in Table 5.7 identifies firms A, B, and C as those conforming the production frontier (see "`Out[]:`").

Figure 5.2 illustrates the results for the Russell cost inefficiency model. Here, for firm E, we learn that its normalized cost inefficiency with respect to firm A, according to (5.22), is equal to 0.6 = (10 − 4)/10. This overall inefficiency can be decomposed into technical inefficiency, which is equal to one minus the Russell technical efficiency measure – expression (5.11): $0.6 = TI_{RM(I)}(x_E, y_E) = 1 - 0.4 = 1 - TE_{RM(I)}(x_E, y_E)$ – the latter value is reported in Table 5.6 and the residual allocative inefficiency, which is null, $0 = 0.6 - 0.6$. Note that since the economic and technical peer for firm E is the same (i.e., firm A), allocative efficiency is null (satisfying the essential property on this occasion). This is not observed for firm D, whose allocative efficiency is positive: $AI_{RM(I)}(x_D, y_D, \widetilde{w}) = 0.083 = NCI_{RM(I)}(x_D, y_D, \widetilde{w}) - TI_{RM(I)}(x_D, y_D) = 0.5 - 0.417$, showing that the essential property is not satisfied in general. For the last three firms, their economic benchmark, firm A, differs from their technological targets: firm C (for firm F) or firm B (for firms G and H).

5.5.3 *The Russell Revenue Inefficiency Model*

We now proceed to illustrate the revenue inefficiency model based on the Russell measure. To calculate this model, we type the code presented in "`In[]:`", Table 5.8. The corresponding results are shown in the "`Out[]:`" panel.

We can identify the reference set for the evaluation of economic and technical inefficiency using the function "peers" with the corresponding model. For the revenue model, we execute "`peersmatrix(dearevenuerussell(X, Y, P, names = FIRMS))`". The output identifies firm A as the benchmark maximizing revenue for the rest of the firms (see Fig. 5.3).

As for the underlying technical efficiency measure, corresponding to the Russell output-oriented measure (see program (5.23)), it is possible to identify the efficiency

Table 5.8 Implementation of the Russell revenue inefficiency model using BEE for Julia

In[]:

```
using DataEnvelopmentAnalysis
using BenchmarkingEconomicEfficiency

X = [1; 1; 1; 1; 1; 1; 1; 1];
Y = [7 7; 4 8; 8 4; 3 5; 3 3; 8 2; 6 4; 1.5 5];
P = [1 1; 1 1; 1 1; 1 1; 1 1; 1 1; 1 1; 1 1];
FIRMS = ["A"; "B"; "C"; "D"; "E"; "F"; "G"; "H"];

dearevenuerussell(X, Y, P, names = FIRMS)
```

Out[]:

```
Russell Cost DEA Model
DMUs = 8; Inputs = 1; Outputs = 2
Orientation = Output; Returns to Scale = VRS
```

	Revenue	Technical	Allocative
A	0.0	0.0	0.0
B	0.25	0.0	0.25
C	0.25	0.0	0.25
D	1.0	0.867	0.133
E	1.333	1.333	0.000
F	1.0	0.5	0.5
G	0.5	0.458	0.042
H	2.5	2.056	0.444

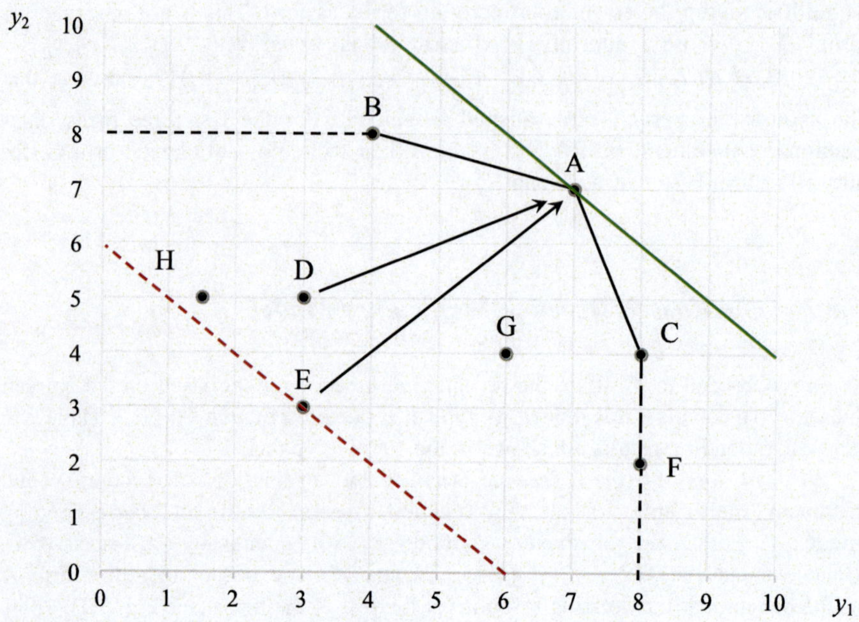

Fig. 5.3 Example of the Russell revenue inefficiency model using BEE for Julia

Table 5.9 Implementation of the Russell output efficiency measure using BEE for Julia

In[]:	`dearussell(X, Y, orient = :Output, rts = :VRS, names = FIRMS)`
Out[]:	See output below

```
Russell DEA Model
DMUs = 8; Inputs = 1; Outputs = 2
Orientation = Output; Returns to Scale = VRS
```

	efficiency	effY1	effY2	slackX1
A	1.0	1.0	1.0	0.0
B	1.0	1.0	1.0	0.0
C	1.0	1.0	1.0	0.0
D	1.867	2.333	1.4	0.0
E	2.333	2.333	2.333	0.0
F	1.5	1.0	2.0	0.0
G	1.458	1.167	1.75	0.0
H	3.056	5.111	1.0	0.0

scores running the code shown in Table 5.9. Again, the function returns the technical efficiency values. Subtracting one from these values yields the technical inefficiency scores that can be related to the revenue inefficiency measure: $TI_{RM(O)}(x_o, y_o) = TE_{RM(O)}(x_o, y_o) - 1$.

Table 5.10 Reference peers of the Russell output efficiency measure using BEE for Julia

In[]:
```
peersmatrix(dearussell(X, Y, orient = :Output, rts  = :VRS,
names = FIRMS))
```

Out[]:
```
1.0     .     .     .   .   .   .   .
 .     1.0    .     .   .   .   .   .
 .      .    1.0    .   .   .   .   .
1.0     .     .     .   .   .   .   .
1.0     .     .     .   .   .   .   .
 .      .    1.0    .   .   .   .   .
1.0     .     .     .   .   .   .   .
0.333   .    0.667  .   .   .   .   .
```

The reference benchmarks of the Russell technical inefficiency model can be recovered using the "peers" function, i.e., "`peersmatrix(dearussell(X, Y, orient = :Output, rts  = :VRS, names = FIRMS))`." The output shown in Table 5.10 identifies firms A, B, and C as those defining the strongly efficient production possibility set ("`Out[]:`").

Figure 5.3 illustrates the results for the Russell revenue inefficiency model. For firm E, its economic and technological benchmarks correspond to firm A. The value of its normalized economic inefficiency according to (5.24) is equal to $1.333 = (14 - 6)/(2 \times 3)$, which can be decomposed into the Russell technical inefficiency measure, $1.333 = TI_{RM(O)}(x_E, y_E) = TE_{RM(O)}(x_E, y_E) - 1 = 2.333 - 1$, and the residual allocative inefficiency equals to zero: $0 = 1.333 - 1.333$. For firm E, the essential property is verified. However, this is not the case for firm D, whose peer is also firm A from an economic and technological perspective, yet it presents a positive allocative inefficiency equal to $0.133 = NRI_{RM(O)}(x_D, y_D, \widetilde{p}) - TI_{RM(O)}(x_D, y_D) = 1 - 0.867$.

5.5.4 An Application to the Taiwanese Banking Industry

We conclude this empirical section solving the economic decomposition of profit inefficiency based on the Russell technical efficiency measure for the panel of 31 Taiwanese banks observed in 2010; see Juo et al. (2015). A brief presentation of the data, including descriptive statistics, can be found in Sect. 2.6.2 of Chap. 2. We highlight the fact that the use of these data is only as an example, and therefore we do not propose analyzing the economic results of the Taiwanese banking industry or any individual bank. The dataset includes individual prices for each firm. Here, we follow the standard approach that finds the maximum profit for the firm under evaluation using its observed prices. Hence, a firm can be profit-inefficient under its own prices yet maximize profit under other firm's prices, serving as the reference peer (and vice versa).

Table 5.11 presents the values of the profit inefficiency in the second column, including its descriptive statistics at the bottom. In this model, profit inefficiency is

Table 5.11 Decomposition of profit inefficiency based on Russell inefficiency measure

Bank	Economic inefficiency, eq. (5.9)			Technical Efficiency, eq. (5.1)					
	Profit Ineff. $N\Pi I_{RM(G)}(x_o, y_o, \tilde{w}, \tilde{p})$	Technical Ineff. $TI_{RM(G)}(x_o, y_o)$	Allocative Ineff. $AI_{RM(G)}(x_o, y_o; \tilde{w}, \tilde{p})$	Technical Eff. $TE_{RM(G)}(x_o, y_o)$	Funds (x_1) θ_1	Labor (x_2) θ_2	Ph. Capital (x_3) θ_3	Investments (y_1) ϕ_1	Loans (y_2) ϕ_2
1	0.000	0.000	0.000	1.000	1.000	1.000	1.000	1.000	1.000
2	0.180	0.000	0.180	1.000	1.000	1.000	1.000	1.000	1.000
3	0.220	0.000	0.220	1.000	1.000	1.000	1.000	1.000	1.000
4	4.957	0.320	4.638	0.680	0.715	0.624	0.654	2.439	1.000
5	0.000	0.000	0.000	1.000	1.000	1.000	1.000	1.000	1.000
6	0.285	0.000	0.285	1.000	1.000	1.000	1.000	1.000	1.000
7	0.239	0.000	0.239	1.000	1.000	1.000	1.000	1.000	1.000
8	0.240	0.125	0.116	0.875	0.961	0.776	0.640	1.000	1.000
9	0.445	0.211	0.234	0.789	1.000	0.648	0.458	1.194	1.000
10	0.000	0.000	0.000	1.000	1.000	1.000	1.000	1.000	1.000
11	0.815	0.335	0.480	0.665	0.800	0.633	0.366	1.896	1.000
12	1.345	0.154	1.192	0.846	0.845	0.960	0.428	1.000	1.000
13	25.115	0.540	24.575	0.460	0.597	0.241	0.228	4.254	1.000
14	0.377	0.000	0.377	1.000	1.000	1.000	1.000	1.000	1.000
15	0.458	0.130	0.328	0.870	0.839	0.851	0.658	1.000	1.000
16	146.250	0.701	145.549	0.299	0.276	0.142	0.094	8.522	1.154
17	1.121	0.316	0.805	0.684	0.924	0.498	0.335	1.505	1.000
18	1.529	0.207	1.322	0.793	0.940	0.489	0.840	1.434	1.000
19	5.356	0.458	4.898	0.542	0.606	0.357	0.313	2.298	1.000
20	6.539	0.323	6.217	0.677	0.629	0.452	0.859	2.242	1.000
21	0.495	0.000	0.495	1.000	1.000	1.000	1.000	1.000	1.000
22	47.149	0.536	46.613	0.464	0.667	0.319	0.164	5.782	1.000
23	125.035	0.615	124.420	0.385	0.425	0.256	0.111	7.568	1.000
24	0.663	0.140	0.524	0.860	1.000	0.694	0.801	1.240	1.000
25	23.775	0.362	23.413	0.638	0.743	0.462	0.691	3.405	1.000
26	2.864	0.000	2.864	1.000	1.000	1.000	1.000	1.000	1.000
27	136.010	0.544	135.466	0.456	0.372	0.309	0.389	4.826	1.000
28	43.613	0.529	43.084	0.471	0.329	0.256	0.539	4.285	1.000
29	1.564	0.000	1.564	1.000	1.000	1.000	1.000	1.000	1.000
30	0.422	0.125	0.297	0.875	0.928	0.749	0.845	1.175	1.000
31	9.672	0.435	9.237	0.565	0.778	0.368	0.433	4.090	1.000
Average	18.927	0.229	18.698	0.771	0.819	0.680	0.672	2.328	1.005
Median	1.121	0.154	0.805	0.846	0.928	0.694	0.691	1.194	1.000
Maximum	146.250	0.701	145.549	1.000	1.000	1.000	1.000	8.522	1.154
Minimum	0.000	0.000	0.000	0.299	0.276	0.142	0.094	1.000	1.000
Std. Dev.	40.803	0.225	40.638	0.225	0.227	0.302	0.316	2.049	0.028

normalized by the minimum observed value across individual input cost and output revenue using firms' specific prices and quantities, i.e., the denominator in Eq. (5.9) corresponds to $(M + N)$ min $\{w_{o1}x_{o1}, \ldots, w_{oM}x_{oM}, p_{o1}y_{o1}, \ldots, p_{oN}y_{oN}\}$. This means that the industry does not face exogenously determined market prices, but they differ across firms. Three banks are profit-efficient given their observed prices (no. 1, no. 5, and no. 10), constituting the most frequent benchmarks for the remaining banks. From a technical perspective, eleven banks are efficient, while the remaining twenty banks are both technical and allocative inefficient. Technical and allocative inefficiencies are reported in the third and fourth columns of Table 5.11. In this case, average normalized profit inefficiency equals 18.927, while average technical and allocative inefficiencies are 0.229 and 18.698, respectively. Consequently, most of the normalized profit loss is attributed to allocative inefficiency, whose proportion is 98.8% versus that corresponding to technical inefficiency, 1.2%.

In the last five columns of Table 5.11, we present the individual efficiency scores for the three inputs and two outputs that are obtained when solving Eq. (5.1). Note that the input scores are smaller or equal to one, while the output scores are greater or equal to one. The resulting Russell (graph) technical efficiency measure, corresponding to the objective function of (5.1), is reported in the fifth column. This measure is calculated as the average of the sum of the input and (inverse) of the output efficiency scores: $1/\phi_n$. Looking at the three inputs, we observe that the largest inefficiency corresponds to physical capital (x_3), whose average score is 0.672, while the largest average score, corresponding to less inefficiency, is observed for financial funds (x_1), with an average value of 0.819. On the output side, financial investments (y_1) exhibit the largest inefficiency with a score equal to 2.238, while there is practically no inefficiency in the form of unrealized loans (y_2), whose average score is 1.005.

Finally, it is worth mentioning that, in this real dataset, the violation of the so-called essential property is not detected.

5.6 Summary and Conclusions

In this chapter, we discussed the traditional Russell measure of technical efficiency, both in its graph version and its oriented forms. In the first case, we showed the standard well-known expression of the nonlinear optimization program needed to determine the "graph" Russell measure of technical efficiency (Färe et al., 1985). Probably, its nonlinearity has been the reason why this measure has not been customarily used in practice for measuring technical efficiency. However, recently, some contributions have been published related to the computation of the "graph" Russell measure of technical efficiency. One option to obtain the exact value of the Russell measure consists in reformulating the original model into a second-order cone programming (SOCP) model (see Sueyoshi & Sekitani, 2007a). Another possibility is associated with the reformulation of the original nonlinear model as a semidefinite programming (SDP) model (Halická & Trnovská, 2018). In this last case, the authors also presented a dual relationship between a measure of (normalized) profit inefficiency and the value of the Russell measure of technical efficiency, which was decomposed into technical and price inefficiency, as usual. In the second case, i.e., when certain orientation is imposed, the Russell measure of input efficiency and the Russell measure of output efficiency were introduced. The optimization models to be solved for these two oriented measures are, in contrast to the graph version, linear. Indeed, it can be proved that the Russell-oriented versions are mathematically equivalent to a particular weighted additive model. This part of the chapter draws especially from Aparicio et al. (2015a), where an economic efficiency measure was introduced related to the Russell-oriented versions, being the allocative efficiency component derived as a residual.

As we also showed in this chapter, through several numerical instances, the Russell measures do not satisfy the essential property of the decomposition of economic efficiency (see Sect. 2.4.5 of Chap. 2). This has implication for the correct interpretability of the components: both technical inefficiency and allocative inefficiency. The same can be said regarding the satisfaction of the extended version of the essential property. The Russell model does not fulfill this property. Certain solutions to overcome this type of drawbacks will be introduced in the final part of this book.

Chapter 6
The Weighted Additive Distance Function (WADF): Economic Inefficiency Decompositions

6.1 Introduction

After the introduction in the Data Envelopment Analysis literature of the radial measures, other approaches and ways of measuring the distance from a firm to the efficient frontier were defined, with the aim of solving certain drawbacks of the radial ones. On the one hand, radial measures are too restrictive in the sense that each assessed unit is evaluated keeping the input or the output mix constant, depending on the selected orientation. However, as Chambers and Mitchell (2001) pointed out, firms routinely consider changes in outputs that are not "radial" in nature. Indeed, the firm's very reason to change its output vector may be to change its mix. For example, the firm may want to partially phase out a product while increasing the production of another output. Therefore, it seems interesting to identify non-radial changes as a way of reducing technical inefficiency since this type of movements could be more realistic than those implied by the radial approach. Additionally, standard radial models are subject to the input or the output orientation, neglecting a global consideration of all the decision variables (resources and products). Again, the introduction of a more flexible framework became necessary. On the other hand, the classical Pareto-Koopmans definition of technical efficiency (Koopmans, 1951) is not taken into account by the radial measures, meaning that certain inefficiency that comes from the slacks of the optimization model is overlooked.

In this context, the additive model by Charnes et al. (1985) was the first graph linear model that guaranteed that firms were compared exclusively with respect to the set of Pareto-efficient benchmarks in the input-output space. The Russell graph measure (Färe et al., 1985) presented in the previous chapter also complies with the definition of technical efficiency by Koopmans, but the objective function in the optimization model that must be solved is not linear. Departing from Charnes et al. (1985), other researchers have introduced some modifications to the original additive model, weighting the slacks that appear in the objective function (see, e.g., Lovell &

J. T. Pastor et al., *Benchmarking Economic Efficiency*, International Series in Operations Research & Management Science 315,
https://doi.org/10.1007/978-3-030-84397-7_6

Pastor, 1995; Cooper et al., 1999, 2011a; and Pastor et al., 2015), also relying on the strongly efficient frontier to measure inefficiency. Additionally, input- and output-oriented versions of the weighted additive (WA) model may be traced in the literature to Lovell et al. (1995), Grifell-Tatjé et al. (1998), Prieto and Zofío (2001), and Cook and Hababou (2001). In all these cases, the objective function of the optimization program is restricted in a way that only input or output slacks are maximized, depending on the orientation, generating the oriented versions of the additive-type models.

Regarding the measurement of overall economic efficiency, which is the main objective of this book, so far, there have been three attempts at defining and decomposing overall inefficiency through additive-type models using Data Envelopment Analysis methods. In the appendix of Cooper et al. (1999), we can find the first attempt. Cooper et al. (1999) directly define profit inefficiency as the difference between optimal profit minus actual profit at market prices. However, as it was very well known in the economic literature (see Nerlove, 1965), such a measure is homogeneous of degree one in prices, i.e., it depends on the currency. Moreover, Cooper et al. (1999) decompose profit inefficiency into a technical component that consists of the sum of the optimal slacks from the additive model weighted by the market prices used (see the remarks regarding expression (2.60) in Sect. 2.4.4 of Chap. 2). Therefore, the value of the technical inefficiency component is not independent of alternative optimal solutions of the additive model. A second attempt to define and decompose profit inefficiency can be found in Cooper et al. (2011b), where the difference-form measure of economic inefficiency is normalized dividing optimal profit minus actual profit by a factor that relates market prices and the input and output weights of the corresponding weighted additive model. Moreover, Cooper et al. (2011b) decompose this normalized measure of profit inefficiency into a technical inefficiency component that coincides with the optimal value of the weighted additive model, and consequently, it is independent on alternative solutions. Finally, the allocative or price component is residually retrieved, as usual. The third attempt to measure overall inefficiency in the context of DEA is due to Aparicio et al. (2016a). These authors do not introduce a new definition of profit inefficiency for the additive model, but they endow the additive-type models with a distance function structure, introducing the weighted additive distance function (WADF), stating its main properties.

Distance functions in production theory are mathematical apparatus that characterize the belonging to the reference technology through a numerical value (i.e., the so-called representation property), can be interpreted and behave as technical efficiency or inefficiency measures when an observation is evaluated, and have a dual relationship with respect to the profit function, the cost function, the revenue function, or another money metric function. As shown in Sect. 2.4 of Chap. 2, most of the results and applications in the literature associated with the measurement and decomposition of economic efficiency are grounded on the concept of distance function and duality. The same can be said in the case of measuring and decomposing productivity change over time from panel data, which are also based on the notion of distance function. This last scenario is possible because the distance functions characterize the belonging or not belonging to the technology by means of a sign, as happens with the directional distance function, or by being greater or lesser than one, as in the case of Shephard's distance functions. This property allows measuring productivity change over time even in the case of cross-period evaluation. In that case, a firm observed, for example, in period t+1 could be outside the technology corresponding to period t, and the distance function for firm in period t +1 is capable of indicating whether this cross-period situation is observed.

As we show in this book, there are many technical efficiency or inefficiency measures in the nonparametric framework of Data Envelopment Analysis, DEA. However, only a few present the mathematical structure of a distance function: the Shephard's radial distance functions, the generalized (hyperbolic) distance function, the directional distance function, and the Hölder distance function. Actually, in the case of DEA, these distance functions were inherited from the parametric world for measuring efficiency in microeconomics. All these functions present duality relationships with respect to classical economic functions, when it is assumed that the reference production possibility set fulfills general axioms (e.g., convexity). This implies that these general duality results work well in the DEA context, where the production possibility set is polyhedral. Additionally, we also show in this book that most of the DEA measures, even those that are not defined as a distance function, may be used for decomposing overall inefficiency. However, these approaches neglect the notion of distance function, a circumstance that contrasts meaningfully with the traditional view of production theory in economics, where both this concept and duality are the cornerstones of the literature (see Sect. 2.4 in Chap. 2). For these reasons, in this chapter, revisiting Aparicio et al. (2016a), we show how the weighted additive model in DEA can be encompassed within a more general distance function notion: the weighted additive distance function (WADF). Of course, we also show how economic inefficiency can be decomposed into technical and allocative components, where the technical term is, in particular, the optimal value of the weighted additive model in DEA. Note that the WADF was only defined for polyhedral technologies like in the DEA framework. This structure was not introduced for the general context where the production possibility set satisfies general conditions. This implies that the WADF cannot be directly adapted for measuring technical and economic efficiency in the parametric approach. Anyway, it is not clear if it would be really necessary since the Pareto-Koopmans notion of efficiency and dealing with slacks seem not to be key concepts for the parametric world, where the production functions are not piecewise linear but smooth functional forms.

Finally, it is worth mentioning that so far, there are not too many empirical applications that consider the additive-type approach for measuring and decomposing economic efficiency. We can mention one due to Aparicio et al. (2013b), where it is shown that DEA can be used to measure and decompose revenue inefficiency considering all sources of technical waste. In particular, the empirical application has as a goal the evaluation of the Spanish quality wine sector. In this sense, Aparicio et al. (2013b), following Cooper et al. (2011b), try to go beyond the standard approaches, like the Shephard distance functions or directional distance functions, to provide a decomposition that incorporates slacks as a source of technical inefficiency, something that is a novelty in the literature and contrasts with the rest of distance functions. Probably, this is the main feature of the additive approach for determining overall inefficiency: the technical inefficiency component encompasses radial and non-radial technical inefficiencies.

The remainder of the chapter is organized as follows: In Sect. 6.2, we introduce the weighted additive distance function in the graph case, how it can be calculated, and the way of using it to measure and decompose profit inefficiency. Section 6.3 is devoted to the introduction of an input-oriented WADF, showing additionally the main duality results for decomposing cost inefficiency. In Sect. 6.4, the dual relationship between the output-oriented WADF and the revenue function is shown. Section 6.5 illustrates the implementation of the WADF using the Julia package for Benchmarking Economic Efficiency. In Sect. 6.6, we present the conclusions.

6.2 The Weighted Additive Distance Function and the Decomposition of Profit Inefficiency

In this section, we review Aparicio et al. (2016a) and its main results, where the weighted additive distance function (WADF) is introduced. Additionally, we show how to measure and decompose profit inefficiency into technical efficiency, the optimal value of the weighted additive model in DEA, and a residual term representing allocative inefficiency. In particular, we remark that the profit inefficiency measure coincides with the classical difference-form formulae but normalized with a specific factor, which mixes the input and output weights of the weighted additive model and the observed market prices. Nevertheless, before doing that, we need to introduce the origin of the WADF, i.e., the weighted additive model in Data Envelopment Analysis introduced by Lovell and Pastor (1995).[1] As discussed in Chap. 2, throughout the chapter, we assume variable returns to scale (VRS).

To estimate the technical inefficiency for firm (x_o, y_o) under the definition of efficiency due to Pareto-Koopmans, one possibility is to solve the following linear program, whose optimal value defines the well-known weighted additive inefficiency measure (Lovell & Pastor, 1995) (see also the additive approach to measure technical inefficiency in Sect. 2.2.3.2 of Chap. 2):

[1] Ali et al. (1995) introduced the same model in a parallel way.

$$
\begin{aligned}
TI_{WA(G)}(x_o, y_o, \rho^-, \rho^+) = & \max_{\substack{\lambda_1,\ldots,\lambda_J \\ s_1^-,\ldots,s_M^- \\ s_1^+,\ldots,s_N^+}} \sum_{m=1}^{M} \rho_m^- s_m^- + \sum_{n=1}^{N} \rho_n^+ s_n^+ \\
s.t. & \\
& \sum_{j=1}^{J} \lambda_j x_{jm} + s_m^- \leq x_{om}, \qquad m = 1, \ldots, M \\
& -\sum_{j=1}^{J} \lambda_j y_{jr} + s_n^+ \leq -y_{on}, \qquad n = 1, \ldots, N \\
& \sum_{j=1}^{J} \lambda_j = 1, \\
& s_m^- \geq 0, \qquad m = 1, \ldots, M \\
& s_n^+ \geq 0, \qquad n = 1, \ldots, N \\
& \lambda_j \geq 0, \qquad j = 1, \ldots, J
\end{aligned} \tag{6.1}
$$

The vectors $\rho^- = (\rho_1^-, \ldots, \rho_M^-) \in R_{++}^M$ and $\rho^+ = (\rho_1^+, \ldots, \rho_N^+) \in R_{++}^N$ contain, respectively, input and output weights representing the relative importance of unit inputs and unit outputs from a technical point of view. Different routes have been established for defining such weights in practice. If we fix $\rho^- = 1_M$ and $\rho^+ = 1_N$, we then get the additive model (Charnes et al., 1985). However, the most popular option chooses the set of weights based upon the observations. In this way, it is possible to define a dimensionless optimal value in (6.1), what is reasonable from the point of view of the satisfaction of interesting properties. This line has been followed by the next authors and measures:

1. The measure of inefficiency proportions (MIP) (see Cooper et al., 1999) considering $(\rho^-, \rho^+) = (1/x_o, 1/y_o)$, where $1/x_o = (1/x_{o1}, \ldots, 1/x_{oM})$ and $1/y_o = (1/y_{o1}, \ldots, 1/y_{oN})$
2. The range-adjusted measure of inefficiency (RAM) (see Cooper et al., 1999) considering $(\rho^-, \rho^+) = (1/(M + N)R^-, 1/(M + N)R^+)$ where $R^- = (R_1^-, \ldots, R_M^-)$ with $R_m^- = \max_{1 \leq j \leq J}\{x_{jm}\} - \min_{1 \leq j \leq J}\{x_{jm}\}$, $m = 1, \ldots, M$, and $R^+ = (R_1^+, \ldots, R_N^+)$ with $R_n^+ = \max_{1 \leq j \leq J}\{y_{jn}\} - \min_{1 \leq j \leq J}\{y_{jn}\}$
3. The bounded adjusted measure of inefficiency (BAM) (see Cooper et al., 2011a) considering $\rho^- = 1/[(M + N)(x_o - \underline{x})]$, where $\underline{x} = (\underline{x}_1, \ldots, \underline{x}_M)$ with $\underline{x}_m = \min_{1 \leq j \leq J}\{x_{jm}\}$, $m = 1, \ldots, M$, and $\rho^+ = 1/[(M + N)(\overline{y} - y_o)]$, where $\overline{y} = (\overline{y}_1, \ldots, \overline{y}_N)$ with $\overline{y}_n = \max_{1 \leq j \leq J}\{y_{jn}\}$, $n = 1, \ldots, N$

4. The normalized weighted additive model (see Lovell & Pastor, 1995) considering $(\rho^-, \rho^+) = (1/\sigma^-, 1/\sigma^+)$ where $\sigma^- = (\sigma_1^-, \ldots, \sigma_M^-)$ is the vector of sample standard deviations of inputs and $\sigma^+ = (\sigma_1^+, \ldots, \sigma_N^+)$ is the vector of sample standard deviations of outputs

The optimal value of (6.1) represents a score of the technical inefficiency of firm (x_o, y_o). Notice that the idea behind the WA model in DEA to measure technical inefficiency is maximizing a weighted ℓ_1 distance from the assessed unit to the frontier of the production possibility set, by simultaneously increasing outputs and reducing inputs. This feature contrasts with the Hölder distance functions (Briec, 1998), which have as an objective to determine the "least" distance from (x_o, y_o) to the frontier of the technology. Note also that, given the nonnegativity constraints linked to the slacks, $TI_{WA(G)}(x_o, y_o, \rho^-, \rho^+) \geq 0$. Moreover, constraint $\sum_{j=1}^{J} \lambda_j x_{jm} + s_m^- \leq x_{om}$ can be transformed into an equality since, at optimum, s_m^- will be as large as possible. The same happens with respect to constraint $-\sum_{j=1}^{J} \lambda_j y_{jr} + s_n^+ \leq -y_{on}$. Other interesting properties that the WA model meet are that $(x_o, y_o) \in \partial^S(T)$ if and only if $TI_{WA(G)}(x_o, y_o, \rho^-, \rho^+) = 0$. In other words, the WA model is able to characterize the strongly efficient frontier and therefore satisfies the indication property (E1a) (see Sect. 2.2.4 of Chap. 2). Consequently, let $(\lambda^*, s^{-*}, s^{+*})$ be an optimal solution of (6.1); then, the target (x_o^*, y_o^*), defined as $x_{om}^* = \sum_{j=1}^{J} \lambda_j^* x_{jm}$, $m = 1, \ldots, M$, and $y_{on}^* = \sum_{j=1}^{J} \lambda_j^* y_{jn}$, $n = 1, \ldots, N$, belongs to the strongly efficient frontier. Overall, the WA model, in contrast to the radial models, the directional distance function, and others, deals with the notion of Pareto-Koopmans efficiency considering all the sources of technical inefficiency, radial and non-radial.

The dual of the linear program (6.1) is as follows:

$$
\begin{aligned}
\min_{\substack{\alpha, v_1, \ldots, v_M \\ u_1, \ldots, u_N}} \quad & \sum_{m=1}^{M} v_m x_{om} - \sum_{n=1}^{N} u_n y_{on} + \alpha \\
s.t. \quad & \sum_{m=1}^{M} v_m x_{jm} - \sum_{n=1}^{N} u_n y_{jn} + \alpha \geq 0, \quad j = 1, \ldots, J \\
& v_m \geq \rho_m^-, \qquad m = 1, \ldots, M \\
& u_n \geq \rho_n^+, \qquad n = 1, \ldots, N
\end{aligned}
\tag{6.2}
$$

Proposition 6.1 Let (v^*, u^*, α^*) be an optimal solution of (6.2). Then, $\alpha^* = \Pi(v^*, u^*)$.

Proof First, let us assume that $\alpha^* > \Pi(v^*, u^*)$. On the one hand, we have that $\Pi(v^*, u^*) = \max_{x,y}\left\{\sum_{n=1}^{N} u_n^* y_n - \sum_{m=1}^{M} v_m^* x_m : (x,y) \in T\right\} \geq \sum_{n=1}^{N} u_n^* y_{jn} - \sum_{m=1}^{M} v_m^* x_{jm}$, $\forall j = 1, \ldots, J$, since $(x_j, y_j) \in T$, $\forall j = 1, \ldots, J$. Then, $(v^*, u^*, \Pi(v^*, u^*))$ is a feasible solution of (6.2) since $v_m^* \geq \rho_m^-$, $m = 1, \ldots, M$, and $u_n^* \geq \rho_n^+$, $n = 1, \ldots, N$. On the other hand, $\Pi(v^*,u^*) - \left(\sum_{n=1}^{N} u_n^* y_{on} - \sum_{m=1}^{M} v_m^* x_{om}\right) < \alpha^* - \left(\sum_{n=1}^{N} u_n^* y_{on} - \sum_{m=1}^{M} v_m^* x_{om}\right) = \sum_{m=1}^{M} v_m^* x_{om} - \sum_{n=1}^{N} u_n^* y_{on} + \alpha^*$, which is a contradiction with the fact that (v^*,u^*,α^*) is an optimal solution of (6.2) by hypothesis. Second, let us now assume that $\alpha^* < \Pi(v^*,u^*)$. By the first constraint in (6.2), we have that $\alpha^* \geq \sum_{n=1}^{N} u_n^* y_{jn} - \sum_{m=1}^{M} v_m^* x_{jm}$, $\forall j = 1, \ldots, J$. By the definition of the technology T in DEA under VRS, we have that for any $(x,y) \in T$, there exists a vector $(\lambda_1, \ldots, \lambda_J) \in R_+^J$ with $\sum_{j=1}^{J} \lambda_j = 1$ such that $\sum_{n=1}^{N} u_n^* y_n - \sum_{m=1}^{M} v_m^* x_m \leq \sum_{n=1}^{N} u_n^* \left(\sum_{j=1}^{J} \lambda_j y_{jn}\right) - \sum_{m=1}^{M} v_m^* \left(\sum_{j=1}^{n} \lambda_j x_{jm}\right) = \sum_{j=1}^{J} \lambda_j \left(\sum_{n=1}^{N} u_n^* y_{jn} - \sum_{m=1}^{M} v_m^* x_{jm}\right) \leq \alpha^* < \Pi(v^*, u^*)$. Therefore, the maximum profit at prices (v^*, u^*) is not achieved at any point in T, which is clearly a contradiction.

As a consequence of Proposition 6.1, we have that, given (v^*, u^*, α^*) an optimal solution of (6.2), v^* can be interpreted as shadow input prices, u^* as shadow output prices, and α^* as shadow profit at prices (v^*, u^*).

The WA model was defined as a tool for measuring technical inefficiency. However, it is not a distance function since, for example, it cannot determine a value for firms outside the reference technology. Indeed, if $(x_o, y_o) \notin T$, then (6.1) is infeasible ($TI_{WA(G)}(x_o, y_o, \rho^-, \rho^+) := -\infty$), and its dual is not bounded (the optimal value of model (6.2) equals $-\infty$). For this reason, Aparicio et al. (2016a) endowed the WA model with a distance function structure, raising the weighted additive measure in DEA to the category of distance function.

Such new distance function, called weighted additive distance function (WADF), is obviously based fundamentally on the WA model. Indeed, when the WADF is used for assessing firm (x_o, y_o) efficiency with respect to its contemporaneous technology as a reference, the distance is determined regarding the strongly efficient frontier, as opposed to the standard distance functions that use the weakly efficient frontier. In this sense, it seems reasonable to conclude that in DEA, where the technology is piecewise linear, the projection of a set of firms using standard radial distance functions will result in frequent slacks, and therefore, the WADF is the most suitable distance function among those existing nowadays if the indication property is taken as reference.

The WADF graph measure of technical inefficiency for assessing a non-necessarily observed input-output vector $(x, y) \in R_+^{M+N}$ with respect to the

DEA technology under variable returns to scale generated from the observed dataset $\{(x_j, y_j)\}_{j=1,\ldots,J}$ is defined as follows:

$$TI_{WADF(G)}(x,y,\rho^-,\rho^+) = \max\left\{TI_{WA(G)}(x,y,\rho^-,\rho^+), TI'_{WA(G)}(x,y,\rho^-,\rho^+)\right\}, \tag{6.3}$$

where $TI'_{WA(G)}(x,y,\rho^-,\rho^+)$ is the optimal value of the following linear program:

$$\begin{aligned}
TI'_{WA(G)}(x,y,\rho^-,\rho^+) = \max_{\substack{\lambda_1,\ldots,\lambda_J \\ s_1^-,\ldots,s_M^- \\ s_1^+,\ldots,s_N^+}} \quad & \sum_{m=1}^{M}\rho_m^- s_m^- + \sum_{n=1}^{N}\rho_n^+ s_n^+ \\
s.t. \quad & \\
\sum_{j=1}^{J}\lambda_j x_{jm} + s_m^- \le x_m, \quad & m = 1,\ldots,M \\
-\sum_{j=1}^{J}\lambda_j y_{jn} + s_n^+ \le -y_n, \quad & n = 1,\ldots,N \\
\sum_{j=1}^{J}\lambda_j = 1, \quad & \\
s_m^- \le 0, \quad & m = 1,\ldots,M \\
s_n^+ \le 0, \quad & n = 1,\ldots,N \\
\lambda_j \ge 0, \quad & j = 1,\ldots,J
\end{aligned} \tag{6.4}$$

The main difference between models (6.1) and (6.4) is that the slacks are nonnegative in (6.1), while the slacks must be nonpositive in (6.4). In the last program, this feature allows projecting the possible exterior point (x, y) onto the frontier of T. Obviously, in that case, $TI'_{WA(G)}(x,y,\rho^-,\rho^+) < 0$. Let us now illustrate how programs (6.1) and (6.4) work through a simple numerical example with one single input and output (Fig. 6.1). In this example, firms A, B, and C are used for generating the DEA technology. Let us also assume that $\rho_1^- = \rho_1^+ = 1$. Now, we are going to evaluate firm C, which is located in the interior of the production possibility set, by means of programs (6.1) and (6.4). Resorting to (6.1), we get that the optimal value is 6 and the projection point is firm B. Any other firm belonging to the efficient frontier is closer to firm C than firm B. Even more, we can claim that any other point of the strongly efficient frontier, which corresponds to the bold solid line consisting of the segment between A and B, is closer to firm C than unit B. On the other hand, if we use model (6.4) for evaluating firm C, we get that this program has an optimal value of zero. It is due to the fact that, in model (6.4), we are maximizing $\sum_{m=1}^{M}\rho_m^- s_m^- + \sum_{n=1}^{N}\rho_n^+ s_n^+$, which is negative or equal to zero since $s_m^- \le 0$, $m = 1, \ldots,$

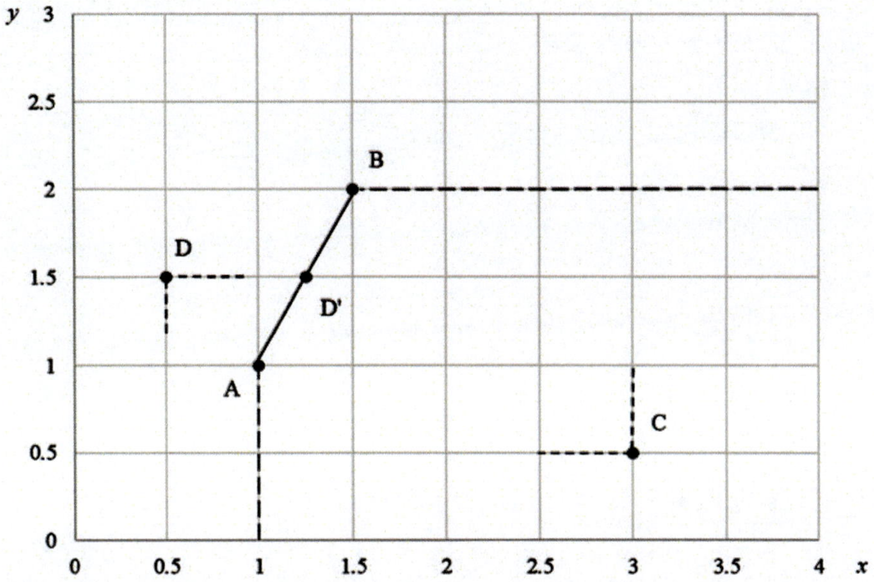

Fig. 6.1 Illustration of the weighted additive distance function (WADF)

M, and $s_n^+ \leq 0$, $n = 1, \ldots, N$. Additionally, $\lambda_A = \lambda_B = 0$ and $\lambda_C = 1$ with $s_1^- = s_1^+ = 0$ are a feasible solution of program (6.4), which has an associated objective function of zero. Thus, it is in fact an optimal solution of the model. As for the exterior firm D, again, we are going to apply programs (6.1) and (6.4). If we use model (6.4), we obtain an optimal value of -1.5. The projection benchmark in this case is D, which coincides with the frontier firm closest to the evaluated unit D′. On the other hand, if we apply model (6.1) for assessing firm D, we get that the model is infeasible (with a value previously defined of $-\infty$). Overall, we highlight that for units that are in the reference technology, the traditional WA model maximizes slacks, generating the furthest targets. In contrast, program (6.4) minimizes slacks and yields closest targets for units that are outside the reference technology. In this sense, the firms located below and above the frontier follow opposite rationales. The general idea is that the more a firm moves northwest, the better it is in the sense of efficiency (see Fig. 6.1). It corresponds to less input and more output. Therefore, the WADF for firms located inside the technology tries to project the unit following this path as closely as possible. Regarding the firms located above the frontier, they are really "good" units if we use as reference the actual technology since they are beyond the efficient frontier. Consequently, if we have to determine a projection point on T for this exterior firm, it seems natural to take that located as close as possible from the evaluated firm.

Regarding the implementation of the WADF, we have two possibilities. The first one is based upon solving two linear programs, (6.1) and (6.4). However, this task can be carried out in one step by solving a mixed-integer linear programming model.

It exploits the similarities between models (6.1) and (6.4) since both are identical except in the sign of the slacks:

$$
\begin{aligned}
TI_{WADF(G)}(x_o, y_o, \rho^-, \rho^+) = \quad & \max_{\substack{b, \lambda_1, \ldots, \lambda_J \\ s_1^-, \ldots, s_M^- \\ s_1^+, \ldots, s_N^+}} \sum_{m=1}^{M} \rho_m^- s_m^- + \sum_{n=1}^{N} \rho_n^+ s_n^+ \\
s.t. \quad & \\
& \sum_{j=1}^{J} \lambda_j x_{jm} + s_m^- \leq x_{om}, \qquad m = 1, \ldots, M \\
& -\sum_{j=1}^{J} \lambda_j y_{jn} + s_n^+ \leq -y_{on}, \qquad n = 1, \ldots, N \\
& \sum_{j=1}^{J} \lambda_j = 1, \\
& s_m^- \leq Qb, \qquad m = 1, \ldots, M \\
& s_m^- \geq Q(b-1), \qquad m = 1, \ldots, M \\
& s_n^+ \leq Qb, \qquad n = 1, \ldots, N \\
& s_n^+ \geq Q(b-1), \qquad n = 1, \ldots, N \\
& b \in \{0, 1\}, \\
& \lambda_j \geq 0, \qquad j = 1, \ldots, J,
\end{aligned}
\tag{6.5}
$$

where Q is a sufficiently large positive number.

Program (6.5) uses the same constraints as models (6.1) and (6.4) and an additional binary decision variable, b, which determines the sign of the slacks. If $b = 1$, then the slacks are nonnegative, and model (6.5) is equivalent to solving model (6.1). Otherwise, if $b = 0$, then the slacks are nonpositive, and (6.5) is equivalent to solving model (6.4).

As for the properties that the WADF meets, the sign of WADF characterizes the production plans of T, as can be trivially deduced from the sign of the slacks in models (6.1) and (6.4). That is to say, $TI_{WADF(G)}(x, y, \rho^-, \rho^+) \geq 0$ if and only if $(x, y) \in T$. This means that the WADF indicates whether the evaluated firm is inside or outside the production possibility set used for the corresponding assessment. This result is relevant in contexts where the estimation of productivity change is the focus since, in this case, the determination of the so-called mixed-period distance functions, which reflect the distance of a data point in time period t relative to the technology of period t+1 and vice versa, is a must. In this respect, another interesting feature of the WADF is feasibility. It always takes a real value. This characteristic is very important for intertemporal analysis since other options, like Shephard's radial distance functions, can be infeasible, producing a problem of indetermination of the productivity index value.

Additionally, in the case that $(x, y) \in T$, we showed that $TI_{WADF(G)}(x, y, \rho^-, \rho^+)$ is equivalent to directly determine the WA model (program (6.1)). Therefore, the WADF inherits the property of the WA model that characterized the strongly efficient frontier of T: $(x, y) \in \partial^S(T)$ if and only if $TI_{WADF(G)}(x, y, \rho^-, \rho^+) = 0$ (indication property (E1a)).

As far as profit inefficiency is concerned, we are going to prove that the WADF and, of course, the WA model in DEA can be used for decomposing a normalized difference form of overall inefficiency. The following theorem formalizes the decomposition of profit inefficiency resorting to the WADF profit inefficiency measure.

Theorem 6.1 Let $(w, p) \in R^{M+N}_{++}$ be a vector of input and output market prices. Let $(x_o, y_o) \in T$. Then,

$$\frac{\Pi(w,p) - \left(\sum_{n=1}^{N} p_n y_{on} - \sum_{m=1}^{M} w_m x_{om}\right)}{\min\left\{\frac{w_1}{\rho_1^-}, \ldots, \frac{w_M}{\rho_M^-}, \frac{p_1}{\rho_1^+}, \ldots, \frac{p_N}{\rho_N^+}\right\}} \geq TI_{WADF(G)}(x_o, y_o, \rho^-, \rho^+)$$
$$= TI_{WA(G)}(x_o, y_o, \rho^-, \rho^+). \qquad (6.6)$$

Proof The equality is trivially true because $(x_o, y_o) \in T$. Therefore, $TI_{WADF(G)}(x_o, y_o, \rho^-, \rho^+) = TI_{WA(G)}(x_o, y_o, \rho^-, \rho^+)$. Now, we are going to prove the inequality. Given $(w, p) \in R^{M+N}_{++}$, $(\widetilde{w}, \widetilde{p})$, defined as $\widetilde{w} = \frac{w}{\min\left\{\frac{w_1}{\rho_1^-}, \ldots, \frac{w_M}{\rho_M^-}, \frac{p_1}{\rho_1^+}, \ldots, \frac{p_N}{\rho_N^+}\right\}}$ and $\widetilde{p} = \frac{p}{\min\left\{\frac{w_1}{\rho_1^-}, \ldots, \frac{w_M}{\rho_M^-}, \frac{p_1}{\rho_1^+}, \ldots, \frac{p_N}{\rho_N^+}\right\}}$, satisfies all the constraints in program (6.2) with $\widetilde{\alpha} = \Pi(\widetilde{w}, \widetilde{p})$.

Therefore, the optimal value of model (6.2) is less than or equal to $\sum_{m=1}^{M} \widetilde{w}_m x_{mo} - \sum_{n=1}^{N} \widetilde{p}_n y_{no} + \widetilde{\alpha}$. By duality in linear programming, we know that the optimal value of model (6.2) coincides with $TI_{WA(G)}(x_o, y_o, \rho^-, \rho^+)$. Finally, by homogeneity of degree +1 of the profit function, we have that $\frac{\Pi(w,p) - \left(\sum_{n=1}^{N} p_n y_{on} - \sum_{m=1}^{M} w_m x_{om}\right)}{\min\left\{\frac{w_1}{\rho_1^-}, \ldots, \frac{w_M}{\rho_M^-}, \frac{p_1}{\rho_1^+}, \ldots, \frac{p_N}{\rho_N^+}\right\}} \geq TI_{WA(G)}(x_o, y_o, \rho^-, \rho^+)$.■

Following Farrell's tradition, the normalized profit inefficiency can be decomposed into the technical inefficiency component and a WADF allocative measure of profit inefficiency (AI):

$$N\Pi I(x_o, y_o, \rho^-, \rho^+, \widetilde{w}, \widetilde{p}) = \underbrace{\frac{\Pi(w,p) - \left(\sum_{n=1}^{N} p_n y_{on} - \sum_{m=1}^{M} w_m x_{om}\right)}{\min\left\{\frac{w_1}{\rho_1^-}, \ldots, \frac{w_M}{\rho_M^-}, \frac{p_1}{\rho_1^+}, \ldots, \frac{p_N}{\rho_N^+}\right\}}}_{\text{(Normalized) Profit Inefficiency}} = \tag{6.7}$$
$$= \underbrace{TI_{WADF(G)}(x_o, y_o, \rho^-, \rho^+)}_{\text{Technical Inefficiency}} + \underbrace{AI_{WADF(G)}(x_o, y_o, \rho^-, \rho^+, \widetilde{w}, \widetilde{p})}_{\text{Allocative Inefficiency}}.$$

Expression (6.7) is a Fenchel-Mahler inequality (Färe & Primont, 1995). Note that the technical inefficiency component is really the optimal value of the weighted additive model since the WADF and the WA model coincides when the assessed point belongs to the reference production possibility set.

In (6.7), if we multiply the left- and right-hand sides of the expression by the normalization factor $\min\left\{\frac{w_1}{\rho_1^-}, \ldots, \frac{w_M}{\rho_M^-}, \frac{p_1}{\rho_1^+}, \ldots, \frac{p_N}{\rho_N^+}\right\}$, then we get a measure of profit inefficiency and a corresponding decomposition expressed in monetary terms, what makes easer the comparison with other alternative decomposition linked to other measures of technical efficiency.

As we showed in Chap. 3, Shephard's input and output distance functions are associated through duality theory with the cost function and the revenue function, respectively. These relationships make them (technical) components in the decomposition of the cost and revenue measures of overall efficiency. Precisely, cost efficiency may be multiplicatively decomposed into the Shephard input distance function and an input allocative term. A similar breakdown holds for the revenue efficiency measure. However, until the nineties, there was no known simple natural dual relationship between distance functions and the profit function. Profit is the difference between revenue and cost, and consequently, it has a natural additive structure that does not fit well with the "multiplicative" Shephard's distance functions (see the efforts by Färe et al., 2019). In this regard, the missing link between the profit function and duality in production theory was the shortage function (Luenberger, 1992a, b), later reinterpreted as the directional distance function by Chambers et al. (1998). These functions present the necessary structure to provide the dual to the profit function and are the basis for a suitable and natural decomposition of economic inefficiency into technical inefficiency plus allocative inefficiencies. However, the directional distance function is not the only distance function having a dual relationship with the profit function, at least in the context of Data Envelopment Analysis. Particularly in this chapter, we have shown that the weighted additive distance function also allows decomposing a normalized measure of profit inefficiency into its usual drivers.

6.3 The Input-Oriented WADF and the Decomposition of Cost Inefficiency

In this section, we turn on the input-oriented version of the weighted additive distance function in Data Envelopment Analysis. The potential for reducing the input bundle reflects input-oriented inefficiency. When the outputs are prefixed, managing the use of inputs to reduce costs is the main objective in an efficiency analysis. So, achieving input-oriented targets on the efficient frontier by reducing the input bundle to the extent possible is the usual approach, when measuring technical efficiency. To get full cost efficiency, it is usually necessary to adjust the input bundle (mix) considering the relative input market prices. Potential for cost reduction through input substitution is associated with the allocative or price efficiency of the assessed firm.

Although it is more usual in practice to apply the weighted additive model following its graph version, there are some contributions in the literature where it was deemed necessary to restrict the standard model for measuring technical efficiency to an input-oriented or output-oriented framework. Examples are the aforementioned studies by Lovell et al. (1995), Grifell-Tatjé et al. (1998), Prieto and Zofio (2001), and Cook and Hababou (2001). In all these cases, the objective function of the optimization program linked to the WA model is restricted in such a way that only input or output slacks are maximized, depending on the orientation, generating the oriented versions of the (weighted) additive-type models.

This section is devoted to introducing the WADF input measure of technical inefficiency and shows its main duality results, principally the Fenchel-Mahler inequality that exists between this distance function and the cost function. This inequality will allow us to decompose a normalized measure of cost inefficiency into technical inefficiency and price inefficiency.

We start by presenting the input-oriented WA model in DEA, assuming variable returns to scale, which is a model that is directly linked to the input-oriented version of the WADF (see also the additive approach to measuring technical inefficiency in Sect. 2.2.1.2 of Chap. 2):

$$
\begin{aligned}
TI_{WA(I)}(x_o, y_o, \rho^-) = \quad & \max_{\substack{\lambda_1, \dots, \lambda_J \\ s_1^-, \dots, s_M^-}} \quad \sum_{m=1}^{M} \rho_m^- s_m^- \\
s.t. \quad & \\
& \sum_{j=1}^{J} \lambda_j x_{mj} + s_m^- \leq x_{om}, \quad m = 1, \dots, M \\
& -\sum_{j=1}^{J} \lambda_j y_{rj} \leq -y_{on}, \quad n = 1, \dots, N \\
& \sum_{j=1}^{J} \lambda_j = 1, \\
& s_m^- \geq 0, \quad m = 1, \dots, M \\
& \lambda_j \geq 0, \quad j = 1, \dots, J
\end{aligned}
\tag{6.8}
$$

The components of the vector $\rho^- = (\rho_1^-, \ldots, \rho_M^-) \in R_{++}^M$ represent the relative importance of unit inputs and are called "input weights".

As in its graph version, the input-oriented WA model satisfies the following properties. The optimal value of (6.8) represents a score of the input technical inefficiency of firm (x_o, y_o) and $TI_{WA(I)}(x_o, y_o, \rho^-) \geq 0$. The input-oriented WA model maximizes a weighted ℓ_1 distance from x_o to the frontier of the input set $L(y_o)$ by reducing inputs. In particular, it is well known that $x_o \in \partial^S(L(y_o))$ if and only if $TI_{WA(I)}(x_o, y_o, \rho^-) = 0$, characterizing the strongly efficient frontier and satisfying the indication property (E1a). Furthermore, let (λ^*, s^{-*}) be an optimal solution of (6.8); then, the target x_o^*, defined as $x_{om}^* = \sum_{j=1}^{J} \lambda_j^* x_{jm}$, $m = 1, \ldots, M$, belongs to the strongly efficient frontier of the input set $L(y_o)$. Therefore, the input-oriented WA model contrasts with the Shephard input distance function and the input-oriented radial model in DEA since these last two measures can yield projection points that belong to the weakly efficient frontier, neglecting individual (i.e., non-equiproportional) sources of technical inefficiency.

The dual of the linear program (6.8) is as follows:

$$\min_{\substack{\alpha, v_1, \ldots, v_M \\ u_1, \ldots, u_N}} \sum_{m=1}^{M} v_m x_{om} - \sum_{n=1}^{N} u_n y_{on} + \alpha \tag{6.9.0}$$

$$s.t. \quad \sum_{m=1}^{M} v_m x_{jm} - \sum_{n=1}^{N} u_n y_{jn} + \alpha \geq 0, \quad j = 1, \ldots, J \tag{6.9.1}$$

$$v_m \geq \rho_m^-, \qquad m = 1, \ldots, M \tag{6.9.2}$$

$$u_n \geq 0, \qquad n = 1, \ldots, N \tag{6.9.3}$$

Next, we establish that the decision variable α in model (6.9) can be interpreted as (shadow) profit at (shadow) prices at optimum. This result will be particularly useful later for determining the Fenchel-Mahler inequality.

Proposition 6.2 Let (v^*, u^*, α^*) be an optimal solution of (6.9). Then, $\alpha^* = \Pi(v^*, u^*)$.

Proof The proof is like that corresponding to Proposition 6.1. ■

Once we have introduced the input-oriented WA model, we next introduce the input-oriented version of the WADF.

The WADF input measure of technical inefficiency for assessing a non-necessarily observed input-output vector $(x, y) \in R_+^{M+N}$ with respect to the DEA technology under variable returns to scale generated from the observed dataset $\{(x_j, y_j)\}_{j=1,\ldots,J}$ is defined as follows:

$$TI_{WADF(I)}(x, y, \rho^-) = \max\left\{TI_{WA(I)}(x, y, \rho^-), TI'_{WA(I)}(x, y, \rho^-)\right\}, \tag{6.10}$$

where $TI'_{WA(I)}(x, y, \rho^-)$ is the optimal value of the following linear program:

$$
\begin{aligned}
TI'_{WA(I)}(x, y_o, \rho^-) = \quad & \max_{\substack{\lambda_1, \ldots, \lambda_J \\ s_1^-, \ldots, s_M^-}} \sum_{m=1}^{M} \rho_m^- s_m^- \\
s.t. \quad & \\
& \sum_{j=1}^{J} \lambda_j x_{jm} + s_m^- \leq x_m, \quad m = 1, \ldots, M \\
& -\sum_{j=1}^{J} \lambda_j y_{jn} \leq -y_n, \quad n = 1, \ldots, N \\
& \sum_{j=1}^{J} \lambda_j = 1, \\
& s_m^- \leq 0, \quad m = 1, \ldots, M \\
& \lambda_j \geq 0, \quad j = 1, \ldots, J
\end{aligned}
\tag{6.11}
$$

Note that the slacks are nonnegative in (6.8) and they are nonpositive in (6.11). Therefore, $TI'_{WA(I)}(x, y, \rho^-) < 0$ when the evaluated point x is located outside the reference input set $L(y)$.

In order to implement the input-oriented WADF, one can solve two models, (6.8) and (6.11), or equivalently resort to the following mixed-integer linear programming model:

$$
\begin{aligned}
TI_{WADF(I)}(x, y, \rho^-) = \quad & \max_{\substack{b, \lambda_1, \ldots, \lambda_J \\ s_1^-, \ldots, s_M^-}} \sum_{m=1}^{M} \rho_m^- s_m^- \\
s.t. \quad & \\
& \sum_{j=1}^{J} \lambda_j x_{jm} + s_m^- \leq x_m, \quad m = 1, \ldots, M \\
& -\sum_{j=1}^{J} \lambda_j y_{jn} \leq -y_n, \quad n = 1, \ldots, N \\
& \sum_{j=1}^{J} \lambda_j = 1, \\
& s_m^- \leq Qb, \quad m = 1, \ldots, M \\
& s_m^- \geq Q(b-1), \quad m = 1, \ldots, M \\
& b \in \{0, 1\}, \\
& \lambda_j \geq 0, \quad j = 1, \ldots, J
\end{aligned}
\tag{6.12}
$$

It is worth highlighting that if $x \in L(y)$, then $TI_{WADF(I)}(x, y, \rho^-) = TI_{WA(I)}(x, y, \rho^-)$. Otherwise, $TI_{WADF(I)}(x, y, \rho^-) = TI'_{WA(I)}(x, y, \rho^-)$.

Finally, in this section, we want to derive the corresponding Fenchel-Mahler inequality between cost inefficiency and the input-oriented weighted additive distance function in Data Envelopment Analysis. To do that, we will work on the dual program of the input-oriented weighted additive model.

By Proposition 6.2, we have that the dual of the input-oriented WA model can be computed through the following linear program:

$$\begin{aligned} \min_{\substack{v_1,\ldots,v_M \\ u_1,\ldots,u_N}} \quad & \Pi(v,u) - \left(\sum_{n=1}^{N} u_n y_{on} - \sum_{m=1}^{M} v_m x_{om} \right) \\ s.t. \quad & \\ v_m \geq \rho_m^-, \quad & m = 1, \ldots, M \\ u_n \geq 0, \quad & n = 1, \ldots, N \end{aligned} \tag{6.13}$$

Proposition 6.3 The optimal value of the input-oriented WA model when $(x_o, y_o) \in T$ is assessed, $TI_{WA(I)}(x_o, y_o, \rho^-)$, coincides with the optimal value of program (6.13).

Proof By Proposition 6.2, at optimum, we know that $\alpha = \Pi(v, u)$. By the definition of profit function at prices (v, u), we have that $\Pi(v, u) \geq \sum_{n=1}^{N} u_n y_{jn} - \sum_{m=1}^{M} v_m x_{jm}$, for all $j = 1, \ldots, J$, since $(x_j, y_j) \in T$, for all $j = 1, \ldots, J$. This is equivalent to $\sum_{m=1}^{M} v_m x_{jm} - \sum_{n=1}^{N} u_n y_{jn} + \Pi(v, u) \geq 0, j = 1, \ldots, J$, which implies that these conditions in model (6.9) are trivially satisfied when we invoke Proposition 6.2. Thus, the optimal value of program (6.13) coincides with the optimal value of program (6.9). Consequently, we get the desired result since, by duality in linear programming, $TI_{WA(I)}(x_o, y_o, \rho^-)$ equals the optimal value of model (6.9). ■

From (6.13), it is not difficult to get an inequality between profit inefficiency and the input-oriented WA model. However, it is not the inequality that we are seeking since the relationship should be stated with respect to the cost function. For this reason, we prove the next two connected propositions to establish the desired relationship between the WA model and the cost function.

Proposition 6.4 The input-oriented weighted additive model when $(x_o, y_o) \in T$ is assessed, $TI_{WA(I)}(x_o, y_o, \rho^-)$, is greater or equal than the optimal value of the following optimization model:

$$\begin{aligned} &\min_{v_1,\ldots,v_M} \quad \sum_{m=1}^{M} v_m x_{om} - C(y_o, v) \\ &s.t. \\ &v_m \geq \rho_m^-, \quad m = 1, \ldots, M \end{aligned} \tag{6.14}$$

Proof $\Pi(v,u) = \sup_y \left\{ \sum_{n=1}^{N} u_n y_n - C(y,v) \right\}$ (see Färe & Primont, 1995). Therefore, considering $y = y_o$, $\Pi(v,u) = \sup_y \left\{ \sum_{n=1}^{N} u_n y_n - C(y,v) \right\} \geq \sum_{n=1}^{N} u_n y_{on} - C(y_o,v)$, which implies operating that $\Pi(v,u) - \left(\sum_{n=1}^{N} u_n y_{on} - \sum_{m=1}^{M} v_m x_{om} \right) \geq \sum_{m=1}^{M} v_m x_{om} - C(y_o,v)$. So, the minimum calculated in (6.13) is greater or equal to (6.14). And, consequently, $TI_{WA(I)}(x_o, y_o, \rho^-)$ is lower bounded by the optimal value of model (6.14).■

Next, we state the other inequality, upper bounding the input-oriented weighted additive model by the optimal value of model (6.14).

To get such result, we first need to show the linear optimization program that is used in DEA to calculate minimum cost given the input market prices w and an output level y_o and the formulation of its dual linear program:

$$\begin{aligned} C(y_o, w) = \quad & \min_{\substack{x_1,\ldots,x_N \\ \lambda_1,\ldots,\lambda_J}} \sum_{m=1}^{M} w_m x_m \\ s.t. \quad & \\ & \sum_{j=1}^{J} \lambda_j x_{jm} \leq x_m, \quad m = 1, \ldots, M \\ & \sum_{j=1}^{J} \lambda_j y_{jn} \geq y_{on}, \quad n = 1, \ldots, N \\ & \sum_{j=1}^{J} \lambda_j = 1, \\ & \lambda_j \geq 0, \quad j = 1, \ldots, J \\ & x_n \geq 0, \quad n = 1, \ldots, N \end{aligned} \tag{6.15}$$

$$C(y_o, w) = \max_{\substack{\alpha, v_1, \ldots, v_M \\ u_1, \ldots, u_N}} \sum_{n=1}^{N} u_n y_{on} - \alpha \tag{6.16.0}$$

s.t.

$$\alpha \geq \sum_{n=1}^{N} u_n y_{jn} - \sum_{m=1}^{M} v_m x_{jm}, \quad j = 1, \ldots, J \tag{6.16.1}$$

$$v_m \leq w_m, \quad m = 1, \ldots, M \tag{6.16.2}$$

$$v_m \geq 0, \quad m = 1, \ldots, M \tag{6.16.3}$$

$$u_n \geq 0, \quad n = 1, \ldots, N \tag{6.16.4}$$

In Proposition 6.5, we prove that the WA model of input inefficiency is also a lower bound of the optimal value of model (6.14).

Proposition 6.5 The input-oriented weighted additive model when $(x_o, y_o) \in T$ is assessed, $TI_{WA(I)}(x_o, y_o, \rho^-)$, is less or equal than the optimal value of model (6.14).

Proof Let (v^*, u^*, α^*) be an optimal solution of model (6.16). Then, by linear duality, we have that the optimal value of (6.16), i.e., $\sum_{n=1}^{N} u_n^* y_{on} - \alpha^*$, equals the optimal value of model (6.15), which is $C(y_o, w)$. Therefore, $C(y_o, w) = \sum_{n=1}^{N} u_n^* y_{on} - \alpha^*$, which is equivalent to $\alpha^* - \left(\sum_{n=1}^{N} u_n^* y_{on} - \sum_{m=1}^{M} w_m x_{om} \right) = \sum_{m=1}^{M} w_m x_m - C(y_o, w)$ (Result A). On the other hand, by (6.16.2) and (6.16.1), we have that $\alpha^* - \left(\sum_{n=1}^{N} u_n^* y_{jn} - \sum_{m=1}^{M} w_m x_{jm} \right) \geq \alpha^* - \left(\sum_{n=1}^{N} u_n^* y_{jn} - \sum_{m=1}^{M} v_m^* x_{jm} \right) \geq 0$, for all $j = 1, \ldots, J$ (Result B). Finally, for all $w \in R_{++}^M$ such that $w_m \geq \rho_m^-$, $m = 1, \ldots, M$, we have at least an optimal solution of model (6.16), say $(v^*(w), u^*(w), \alpha^*(w))$. We are going to prove that $(w, u^*(w), \alpha^*(w))$ is a feasible solution of model (6.9). By Result B, it satisfies (6.9.1), whereas (6.9.2) is trivially satisfied by the hypothesis. Consequently, $TI_{WA(I)}(x_o, y_o, \rho^-) \leq \alpha^*(w) - \left(\sum_{n=1}^{N} u_n^*(w) y_{on} - \sum_{m=1}^{M} w_m x_{om} \right)$. Thus, $TI_{WA(I)}(x_o, y_o, \rho^-) \leq \inf_w \left\{ \alpha^*(w) - \left(\sum_{n=1}^{N} u_n^*(w) y_{on} - \sum_{m=1}^{M} w_m x_{om} \right) : w_m \geq \rho_m^-, m = 1, \ldots, M \right\}$. By Result A, $TI_{WA(I)}(x_o, y_o, \rho^-) \leq \inf_w \left\{ \sum_{m=1}^{M} w_m x_m - C(y_o, w) : w_m \geq \rho_m^-, m = 1, \ldots, M \right\}$. Consequently, the input-oriented WA model is less or equal than the optimal value of model (6.14). ■

Combining the last two propositions, we get that the input-oriented WA model can be equivalently determined by solving model (6.14). This is formally established in Theorem 6.2.

Theorem 6.2 The following result holds:

$$\begin{aligned} TI_{WA(I)}(x_o, y_o, \rho^-) = \quad & \min_{v_1, \ldots, v_M} \quad \sum_{m=1}^{M} v_m x_{om} - C(y_o, v) \\ s.t. \quad & \\ v_m \geq \rho_m^-, \quad & m = 1, \ldots, M \end{aligned} \tag{6.17}$$

From Theorem 6.2, it is trivial to derive a Fenchel-Mahler inequality between cost inefficiency and the input-oriented weighted additive distance function since this distance function coincides with the weighted additive model of input inefficiency when the assessed unit belongs to the reference technology. Given input market prices $w \in R_{++}^M$, $w / \min\{w_1/\rho_1^-, \ldots, w_M/\rho_M^-\}$ satisfies the constraints of model (6.17). Consequently, $\widetilde{w} = \min\{w_1/\rho_1^-, \ldots, w_M/\rho_M^-\}$ is a feasible solution of that model, and hence, the objective function evaluated at this "normalized" vector is greater or equal than the input-oriented WA model, which coincides with the input-oriented WADF if $(x_o, y_o) \in T$. In particular, due to the homogeneity of degree +1 of the cost function, we get the following inequality between the WADF cost inefficiency measure and its associated technical inefficiency:

$$\frac{\sum_{m=1}^{M} w_m x_{om} - C(y_o, w)}{\min\{w_1/\rho_1^-, \ldots, w_M/\rho_M^-\}} \geq TI_{WADF(I)}(x_o, y_o, \rho^-). \tag{6.18}$$

Following Farrell's tradition, the normalized cost loss that appears in the left-hand side of (6.18) can be decomposed into the technical inefficiency component and a WADF allocative measure of cost inefficiency (AI) (corresponding to the additive decomposition of cost inefficiency presented in Sect. 2.4.1.2 of Chap. 2):

$$\begin{aligned} NCI_{WADF(I)}(x_o, y_o, \widetilde{w}) = \underbrace{\frac{\sum_{m=1}^{M} w_m x_{om} - C(y_o, w)}{\min\{w_1/\rho_1^-, \ldots, w_M/\rho_M^-\}}}_{\text{(Normalized) Cost Inefficiency}} = \\ \underbrace{TI_{WADF(I)}(x_o, y_o, \rho^-)}_{\text{Technical Inefficiency}} + AI_{WADF(I)}(x_o, y_o, \rho^-, \widetilde{w}) \end{aligned} \tag{6.19}$$

In particular, the technical inefficiency component is really the value of the input-oriented weighted additive model when $(x_o, y_o) \in T$ is evaluated.

Additionally, if we multiply the left- and right-hand sides in (6.19) by the normalization factor $\min\{w_1/\rho_1^-, \ldots, w_M/\rho_M^-\}$, then we get measures of cost, technical and allocative inefficiency expressed in monetary terms.

6.4 The Output-Oriented WADF and the Decomposition of Revenue Inefficiency

This section is devoted to introducing the WADF output measure of technical inefficiency in Data Envelopment Analysis. Additionally, we show the main results regarding duality, relating revenue inefficiency to a (weighted) additive-type inefficiency measure.

The output-oriented WA model in DEA, assuming variable returns to scale, can be computed as follows (see also the additive approach to measure technical inefficiency in Sect. 2.2.1.2 of Chapter 2):

$$\begin{aligned} TI_{WA(O)}(x_o, y_o, \rho^+) = & \max_{\substack{\lambda_1,\ldots,\lambda_J \\ s_1^+,\ldots,s_N^+}} \sum_{n=1}^{N} \rho_n^+ s_n^+ \\ s.t. & \\ \sum_{j=1}^{J} \lambda_j x_{jm} \leq x_{om}, & \quad m = 1, \ldots, M \\ -\sum_{j=1}^{J} \lambda_j y_{jn} + s_n^+ \leq -y_{on}, & \quad n = 1, \ldots, N \\ \sum_{j=1}^{J} \lambda_j = 1, & \\ s_n^+ \geq 0, & \quad n = 1, \ldots, N \\ \lambda_j \geq 0, & \quad j = 1, \ldots, J \end{aligned} \tag{6.20}$$

The components of the vector $\rho^+ = \left(\rho_1^+, \ldots, \rho_N^+\right) \in R_{++}^N$ represent the relative importance of unit outputs and are the so-called output weights of the weighted additive model.

Regarding the output-oriented weighted additive distance function for assessing a non-necessarily observed input-output vector $(x, y) \in R_+^{M+N}$ with respect to the DEA technology under variable returns to scale generated from the observed dataset $\{(x_j, y_j)\}_{j=1,\ldots,J}$, it can be defined as follows:

$$TI_{WADF(O)}(x, y, \rho^+) = \max\left\{TI_{WA(O)}(x, y, \rho^+), TI'_{WA(O)}(x, y, \rho^+)\right\}, \tag{6.21}$$

where $TI'_{WA(O)}(x, y, \rho^+)$ is the optimal value of the following linear program:

$$
\begin{aligned}
TI'_{WA(O)}(x, y, \rho^{+}) = \quad & \max_{\substack{\lambda_1, \ldots, \lambda_J \\ s_1^{+}, \ldots, s_N^{+}}} \sum_{n=1}^{N} \rho_n^{+} s_n^{+} \\
s.t. \quad & \\
& \sum_{j=1}^{J} \lambda_j x_{jm} \leq x_m, \qquad m = 1, \ldots, M \\
& -\sum_{j=1}^{J} \lambda_j y_{jn} + s_n^{+} \leq -y_n, \quad n = 1, \ldots, N \\
& \sum_{j=1}^{J} \lambda_j = 1, \\
& s_n^{+} \leq 0, \qquad n = 1, \ldots, N \\
& \lambda_j \geq 0, \qquad j = 1, \ldots, J
\end{aligned}
\tag{6.22}
$$

To solve the output-oriented WADF, it is also possible to resort to a unique optimization model, where a binary decision variable is included. That model is as follows:

$$
\begin{aligned}
TI_{WADF(O)}(x, y, \rho^{+}) = \quad & \max_{\substack{b, \lambda_1, \ldots, \lambda_J \\ s_1^{+}, \ldots, s_N^{+}}} \sum_{n=1}^{N} \rho_n^{+} s_n^{+} \\
s.t. \quad & \\
& \sum_{j=1}^{J} \lambda_j x_{jm} \leq x_m, \qquad m = 1, \ldots, M \\
& -\sum_{j=1}^{J} \lambda_j y_{jn} + s_n^{+} \leq -y_n, \quad n = 1, \ldots, N \\
& \sum_{j=1}^{J} \lambda_j = 1, \\
& s_n^{+} \leq Qb, \qquad n = 1, \ldots, N \\
& s_n^{+} \geq Q(b-1), \qquad n = 1, \ldots, N \\
& b \in \{0, 1\}, \\
& \lambda_j \geq 0, \qquad j = 1, \ldots, J
\end{aligned}
\tag{6.23}
$$

It is worth highlighting that if $y \in P(x)$, then $TI_{WADF(O)}(x, y, \rho^{+}) = TI_{WA(O)}(x, y, \rho^{+})$. Otherwise, $TI_{WADF(O)}(x, y, \rho^{+}) = TI'_{WA(O)}(x, y, \rho^{+})$.

Finally, as for the definition of the WADF revenue inefficiency measure, given the output market prices $p \in R_{++}^{N}$, the following inequality holds for firm $(x_o, y_o) \in T$:

$$\frac{R(x_o,p)-\sum_{n=1}^{N}p_n y_{on}}{\min\left\{p_1/\rho_1^+,\ldots,p_N/\rho_N^+\right\}}\geq TI_{WADF(O)}(x_o,y_o,\rho^+). \tag{6.24}$$

Following Farrell's tradition, the normalized revenue inefficiency measure in (6.24) may be decomposed into the technical inefficiency component and a WADF allocative measure of revenue inefficiency (*AI*) (corresponding to the additive decomposition of revenue inefficiency presented in Sect. 2.4.2.2 of Chap. 2):

$$NRI_{WADF(O)}(x_o,y_o,\widetilde{p})=\underbrace{\frac{R(x_o,p)-\sum_{n=1}^{N}p_n y_{on}}{\min\left\{p_1/\rho_1^+,\ldots,p_N/\rho_N^+\right\}}}_{\text{(Normalized) Revenue Inefficiency}}= \\ \underbrace{TI_{WADF(O)}(x_o,y_o,\rho^+)}_{\text{Technical Inefficiency}}+AI_{WADF(O)}(x_o,y_o,,\rho^+,\widetilde{p}) \tag{6.25}$$

The technical inefficiency component in (6.25) is really the value of the output-oriented weighted additive model when $(x_o, y_o) \in T$ is evaluated. Moreover, if we multiply the left- and right-hand sides in (6.25) by the normalization factor $\min\left\{p_1/\rho_1^+,\ldots,p_N/\rho_N^+\right\}$, then we get a measure of revenue inefficiency and its corresponding decomposition expressed in monetary terms.

6.5 Empirical Illustration of the Weighted Additive Profit, Cost, and Revenue Inefficiency Models

In this section, we illustrate the calculation of the three economic inefficiency measures and their decomposition based on their corresponding weighted additive distance functions for the example data presented in Sect. 2.6.2 of Chap. 2. Table 6.1 replicates the data.

The functions within the Benchmarking Economic Efficiency package for the Julia language that compute these measures, as well as their decompositions into technical and allocative inefficiencies, are the following:

```
deaprofitadd(X, Y, W, P, :Ones, names = FIRMS)
```

```
deacostadd(X, Y, W, :Ones, names = FIRMS)
```

```
dearevenueadd(X, Y, P, :Ones, names = FIRMS)
```

Table 6.1 Example data illustrating the economic efficiency models

	Model							
	Graph profit model		Input orientation Cost model			Output orientation Revenue model		
Firm	x	y	x_1	x_2	y	x	y_1	y_2
A	2	1	2	2	1	1	7	7
B	4	5	1	4	1	1	4	8
C	8	8	4	1	1	1	8	4
D	12	9	4	3	1	1	3	5
E	6	3	5	5	1	1	3	3
F	14	7	6	1	1	1	8	2
G	14	9	2	5	1	1	6	4
H	9.412	2.353	1.6	8	1	1	1.5	5
Prices	$w = 1$	$p = 2$	$w_1 = 1$	$w_2 = 1$			$p_1 = 1$	$p_2 = 1$

The above syntax, including "`:Ones`," indicates that the weights corresponding to the inputs are set to one, and therefore, the unweighted additive model introduced by Charnes et al. (1985) is calculated. This may be replaced with the following options to calculate alternative measures:

- "`:MIP`." Calculates the measure of inefficiency proportions (MIP) (see Cooper et al., 1999) considering $(\rho^-, \rho^+) = (1/x_o, 1/y_o)$, where $1/x_o = (1/x_{o1}, \ldots, 1/x_{oM})$ and $1/y_o = (1/y_{o1}, \ldots, 1/y_{oN})$.
- "`:RAM`." Calculates the range-adjusted measure of inefficiency (RAM) (see Cooper et al., 1999) considering $(\rho^-, \rho^+) = (1/(M + N)R^-, 1/(M + N)R^+)$ where $R^- = \left(R_1^-, \ldots, R_M^-\right)$ with $R_m^- = \max\limits_{1 \le j \le J}\{x_{jm}\} - \min\limits_{1 \le j \le J}\{x_{jm}\}$, $m = 1, \ldots, M$, and $R^+ = \left(R_1^+, \ldots, R_N^+\right)$ with $R_n^+ = \max\limits_{1 \le j \le J}\{y_{jn}\} - \min\limits_{1 \le j \le J}\{y_{jn}\}$.
- "`:BAM`." Calculates the bounded adjusted measure of inefficiency (BAM) (see Cooper et al., 2011a) considering $\rho^- = 1/[(M + N)(x_o - \underline{x})]$, where $\underline{x} = (\underline{x}_1, \ldots, \underline{x}_M)$ with $\underline{x}_m = \min\limits_{1 \le j \le J}\{x_{jm}\}$, $m = 1, \ldots, M$, and $\rho^+ = 1/[(M + N)(\overline{y} - y_o)]$, where $\overline{y} = (\overline{y}_1, \ldots, \overline{y}_N)$ with $\overline{y}_n = \max\limits_{1 \le j \le J}\{y_{jn}\}$, $n = 1, \ldots, N$.
- "`:Normalized`." Calculates the normalized weighted additive model (see Lovell & Pastor, 1995) considering $(\rho^-, \rho^+) = (1/\sigma^-, 1/\sigma^+)$ where $\sigma^- = \left(\sigma_1^-, \ldots, \sigma_M^-\right)$ is the vector of sample standard deviations of inputs and $\sigma^+ = \left(\sigma_1^+, \ldots, \sigma_N^+\right)$ is the vector of sample standard deviations of outputs.

To illustrate the different possibilities, we implement in the following examples the unweighted model ("`:Ones`") to measure and decompose profit inefficiency (6.7), the MIP model for cost inefficiency (6.19), and the RAM model for revenue inefficiency (6.25).

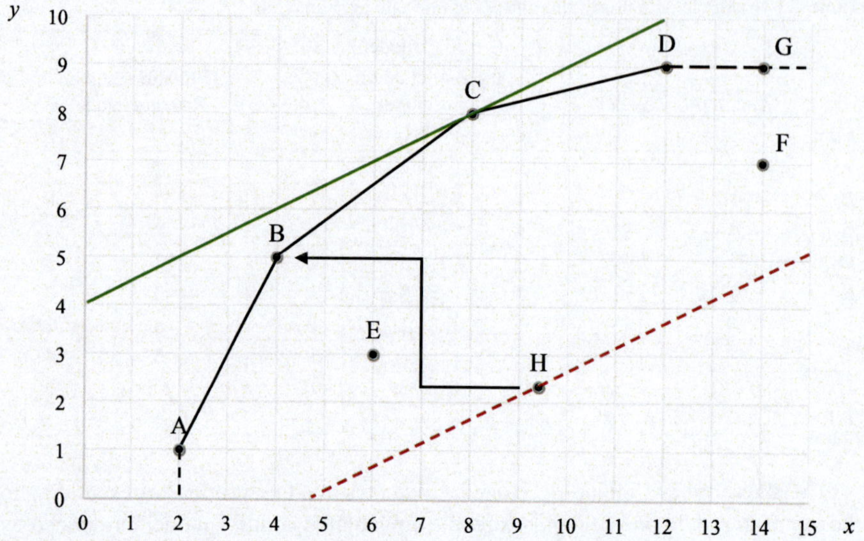

Fig. 6.2 Example of the WADF profit inefficiency model using BEE for Julia

6.5.1 *The WADF Profit Inefficiency Model*

We rely on the open (web-based) Jupyter Notebook interface to illustrate our economic models. Nevertheless, they can be implemented in any integrated development environment (IDE) of preference.[2] To calculate the weighted additive profit inefficiency model, enter the following code in the "`In[]:`" panel, and run it. In this first case, we choose unit weights to ease the illustration of the WADF through Fig. 6.2. Note that the syntax for the unweighted model allows the omission of ("`:Ones`"), as this is the default option in the function. The corresponding results are shown in the "`Out[]:`" panel in Table 6.2.

We can learn about the reference peers for each firm using the "peersmatrix" function with the corresponding economic or technical model. For the economic model, executing "`peersmatrix(deaprofitadd(X, Y, W, P, names = FIRMS))`" identifies firm C as the reference benchmark maximizing profit for the rest of the firms (see Fig. 6.2).

As for the underlying (un)weighted additive (graph) technical efficiency model, we can obtain all the information running the corresponding function, as shown in Table 6.3.

It is also of interest to identify the reference benchmarks of the weighted additive graph distance function. Once again, this information can be recovered through the

[2] We refer the reader to Sect. 2.6.1 in Chapter 2 for the installation of the "Benchmarking Economic Efficiency" Julia package. All Jupyter Notebooks implementing the different economic models in this book can be downloaded from the reference site: http://www.benchmarkingeconomicefficiency.com

Table 6.2 Implementation of the WADF profit inefficiency model using BEE for Julia

In[]:

```
using DataEnvelopmentAnalysis
using BenchmarkingEconomicEfficiency

X = [2; 4; 8; 12; 6; 14; 14; 9.412];
Y = [1; 5; 8; 9; 3; 7; 9; 2.353];
W = [1; 1; 1; 1; 1; 1; 1; 1];
P = [2; 2; 2; 2; 2; 2; 2; 2];
FIRMS = ["A"; "B"; "C"; "D"; "E"; "F"; "G"; "H"];

deaprofitadd(X, Y, W, P, names = FIRMS)
```

Out[]:

```
Profit Additive DEA Model
DMUs = 8; Inputs = 1; Outputs = 1
Weights = Ones; Returns to Scale = VRS
```

	Profit	Technical	Allocative
A	8.0	0.0	8.0
B	2.0	0.0	2.0
C	0.0	0.0	0.0
D	2.0	0.0	2.0
E	8.0	4.0	4.0
F	8.0	7.333	0.667
G	4.0	2.0	2.0
H	12.706	8.059	4.647

Table 6.3 Implementation of the WADF graph inefficiency measure using BEE for Julia

In[]:

```
deaadd(X, Y, names = FIRMS)
```

Out[]:

```
Weighted Additive DEA Model
DMUs = 8; Inputs = 1; Outputs = 1
Orientation = Graph; Returns to Scale = VRS
Weights = Ones
```

	efficiency	slackX1	slackY1
A	0.0	0.0	0.0
B	0.0	0.0	0.0
C	0.0	0.0	0.0
D	0.0	0.0	0.0
E	4.0	2.0	2.0
F	7.333	7.333	0.0
G	2.0	2.0	0.0
H	8.059	5.412	2.647

Table 6.4 Reference peers of the WADF graph inefficiency measure using BEE for Julia

In[]:	`peersmatrix(deaadd(X, Y, names = FIRMS))`
Out[]:	(see output below)

```
1.0  .    .    .    .  .  .  .
 .  1.0   .    .    .  .  .  .
 .   .   1.0   .    .  .  .  .
 .   .    .   1.0   .  .  .  .
 .  1.0   .    .    .  .  .  .
 .  0.333 0.667 .   .  .  .  .
 .   .    .   1.0   .  .  .  .
 .  1.0   .    .    .  .  .  .
```

"peers" function, i.e., "`peersmatrix(deaadd(X, Y, names = FIRMS))`". The output results shown in Table 6.4 ("`Out[]:`") identify firms A, B, C, and D as those conforming the strongly efficient production possibility set, i.e., those with unit values in the main diagonal of the square ($J \times J$) matrix containing their own intensity variables λ (note the matrix syntax in "`In[]:`").

Figure 6.2 illustrates the results for the weighted additive profit inefficiency model. There, for firm H, we identify that its normalized profit inefficiency with respect to firm C, according to (6.7), is equal to $12.706 = 8 - (-4.706)$, which can be decomposed into the weighted additive distance function representing technical inefficiency, whose value is $8.059 = 5.412 + 2.647$, and allocative inefficiency, whose value is $4.647 = 12.706 - 8.059$. Note that, for this example and contrary to the cost and revenue inefficiency examples that follow, none of the firms identify the same economic and technological benchmark, i.e., firm C.

6.5.2 The WADF Cost Inefficiency Model

We now solve the example for the weighted additive cost inefficiency model using the measure of inefficiency proportions (MIP) option. To calculate this model, type the code included in the "`In[]:`" panel in the notebook, and execute it. The corresponding results are shown in the "`Out[]:`" panel of Table 6.5.

As before, we can learn about the reference benchmarks using the "peers" function with the corresponding economic or technical model. For the cost model, we run "`peersmatrix(deacostadd(X, Y, W, :MIP, names = FIRMS))`". In this case, firm A is identified as the only firm minimizing cost (see Fig. 6.3).

As for the underlying weighted additive (input oriented) technical inefficiency model, we obtain all the information running the corresponding function, as shown

Table 6.5 Implementation of the WADF cost inefficiency model using BEE for Julia

In[]:

```
using DataEnvelopmentAnalysis
using BenchmarkingEconomicEfficiency

X = [2 2; 1 4; 4 1; 4 3; 5 5; 6 1; 2 5; 1.6 8];
Y = [1; 1; 1; 1; 1; 1; 1; 1];
W = [1 1; 1 1; 1 1; 1 1; 1 1; 1 1; 1 1; 1 1];
FIRMS = ["A"; "B"; "C"; "D"; "E"; "F"; "G"; "H"];

deacostadd(X, Y, W, :MIP, names = FIRMS)
```

Out[]:

```
Cost Additive DEA Model
DMUs = 8; Inputs = 2; Outputs = 1
Orientation = Input; Returns to Scale = VRS
Weights = MIP
```

	Cost	Technical	Allocative
A	0.0	0.0	0.0
B	1.0	0.0	1.0
C	1.0	0.0	1.0
D	1.0	0.833	0.167
E	1.2	1.2	0.000
F	3.0	0.333	2.667
G	1.5	0.7	0.8
H	3.5	0.875	2.625

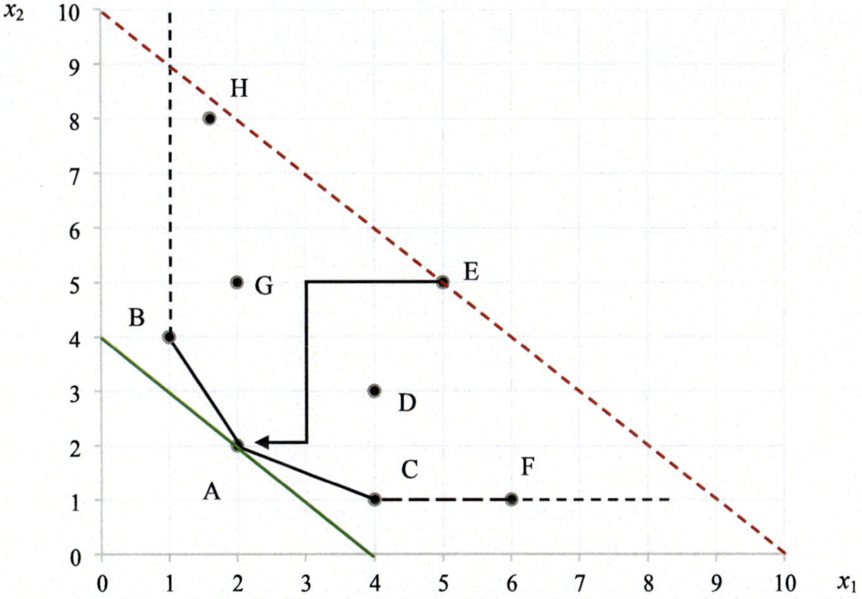

Fig. 6.3 Example of the WADF cost inefficiency model using BEE for Julia

Table 6.6 Implementation of the WADF input inefficiency measure using BEE for Julia

```
In[]:   deaadd(X, Y, orient = :Input, :MIP, names = FIRMS)

Out[]:  Weighted Additive DEA Model
        DMUs = 8; Inputs = 2; Outputs = 1
        Orientation = Input; Returns to Scale = VRS
        Weights = MIP
        ──────────────────────────────────────────────
             efficiency   slackX1   slackX2    slackY1
        ──────────────────────────────────────────────
        A    0.0          0.0       0.0        0.0
        B    0.0          0.0       0.0        0.0
        C    0.0          0.0       0.0        0.0
        D    0.833        2.0       1.0        0.0
        E    1.2          3.0       3.0        0.0
        F    0.333        2.0       0.000      0.0
        G    0.7          1.0       1.0        0.0
        H    0.875        0.6       4.0        0.0
        ──────────────────────────────────────────────
```

Table 6.7 Reference peers of the WADF cost inefficiency measure using BEE for Julia

```
In[]:   peersmatrix(deaadd(X, Y, orient = :Input, :MIP, names =
        FIRMS))

Out[]:  1.0  .    .    .    .    .    .    .
        .    1.0  .    .    .    .    .    .
        .    .    1.0  .    .    .    .    .
        1.0  .    .    .    .    .    .    .
        1.0  .    .    .    .    .    .    .
        .    .    1.0  .    .    .    .    .
        .    1.0  .    .    .    .    .    .
        .    1.0  .    .    .    .    .    .
```

in Table 6.6. Note that despite the input orientation, this function returns the slack values for both inputs and outputs.

Again, the reference benchmarks of the technical model can be recovered using the "peers" function, i.e., "`peersmatrix(deaadd (X, Y, orient = :Input, :MIP, names = FIRMS))`". The output shown in Table 6.7 identifies firms A, B, and C as those conforming the production frontier (see "`Out[]:`").

Figure 6.3 illustrates the results for the weighted additive cost inefficiency model. There, for firm E, we learn that its normalized cost efficiency with respect to firm A, according to (6.19), is equal to 1.2 = (10 – 4)/5, which can be decomposed into the weighted additive distance function, whose value is 1.2 = 3/5 + 3/5, and the residual allocative inefficiency, which is null, 0 = 1.2 – 1.2. Note that while the economic and technical reference peer for firm E is the same (i.e., firm A) and therefore its allocative inefficiency is zero, this is not the case for the last three firms, whose economic benchmark is also firm A, but their technical peers are either firm C (for firm F) or firm B (for firms G and H). Additionally, firm D illustrates that the cost inefficiency model based on the WADF does not satisfy the essential property. This means (see Chap. 2) that the decomposition associated with this measure does not satisfy the extended version of the essential property either. As for firm E, the economic and technological benchmark for firm D is firm A, yet its allocative inefficiency is positive: 0.167 = 1.0 – 0.833. This justifies the proposal of the methods proposed in Chaps. 12 and 13 to adjust the economic decomposition.

6.5.3 The WADF Revenue Inefficiency Model

We now proceed to illustrate the revenue inefficiency model based on the weighted additive distance function. On this occasion, the weights correspond to those of the range-adjusted measure, RAM. To calculate the RAM revenue model, we type the code presented in "`In[]:`" (Table 6.8). The corresponding results are shown in the "`Out[]:`" panel.

Again, to know the reference set for the evaluation of economic and technical inefficiency, we rely on the "peers" function with the corresponding model. For the revenue model, we execute "`peersmatrix (dearevenueadd(X, Y, P, :RAM, names = FIRMS))`". The output identifies firm A as the benchmark maximizing revenue for the rest of the firms (see Fig. 6.4).

As for the underlying weighted additive distance function, corresponding to the output oriented measure, it is possible to identify its slacks running the code shown in Table 6.9. Again, it returns the (unweighted) slack values for both inputs and outputs.

Again, the reference benchmarks of the additive technical inefficiency model can be recovered using the "peers" function, i.e., "`peersmatrix (deadd(X, Y, W, names = FIRMS))`". The output shown in Table 6.10 identifies firms A, B, and C as those defining the strongly efficient production possibility set ("`Out[]:`").

Figure 6.4 illustrates the results for the weighted additive revenue inefficiency model. There, for firm E, we identify that adopting the RAM model, the normalized economic inefficiency with respect to firm A, according with (6.25), is equal to 0.667 = (14 – 6)/12, which can be decomposed into the weighted additive distance function, whose value is 0.641 = (4/13.5 + 4/12), and the residual allocative inefficiency, whose value is 0.026 = 0.667 – 0.641. The fact that the allocative inefficiency of firm E is positive, even though it is projected to the same economic and technological benchmark, illustrates that the WADF model fails to satisfy the

Table 6.8 Implementation of the WADF revenue inefficiency model using BEE for Julia

In[]:

```
using DataEnvelopmentAnalysis
using BenchmarkingEconomicEfficiency

X = [1; 1; 1; 1; 1; 1; 1; 1];
Y = [7 7; 4 8; 8 4; 3 5; 3 3; 8 2; 6 4; 1.5 5];
P = [1 1; 1 1; 1 1; 1 1; 1 1; 1 1; 1 1; 1 1];
FIRMS = ["A"; "B"; "C"; "D"; "E"; "F"; "G"; "H"];

dearevenueadd(X, Y, P, :RAM, names = FIRMS)
```

Out[]:

```
Revenue Additive DEA Model
DMUs = 8; Inputs = 1; Outputs = 2
Orientation = Output; Returns to Scale = VRS
Weights = RAM
```

	Revenue	Technical	Allocative
A	0.0	0.0	0.0
B	0.167	0.0	0.167
C	0.167	0.0	0.167
D	0.5	0.474	0.027
E	0.667	0.641	0.026
F	0.333	0.167	0.167
G	0.333	0.327	0.006
H	0.625	0.590	0.035

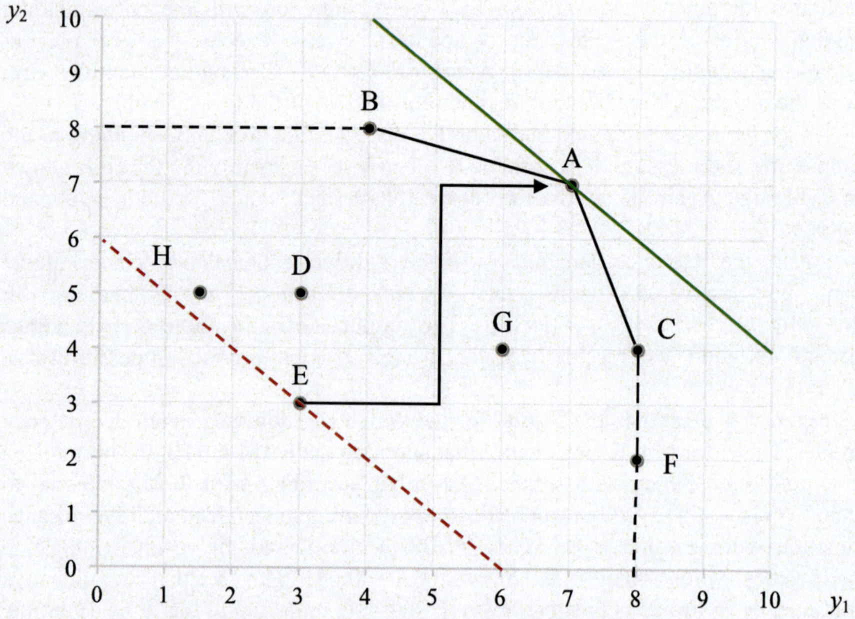

Fig. 6.4 Example of the WADF revenue inefficiency model using BEE for Julia

Table 6.9 Implementation of the WADF output inefficiency measure using BEE for Julia

In[]:	`deaadd(X, Y, orient = :Output, :RAM, names = FIRMS)`
Out[]:	(see output below)

```
Weighted Additive DEA Model
DMUs = 8; Inputs = 1; Outputs = 2
Orientation = Output; Returns to Scale = VRS
Weights = RAM
```

	efficiency	slackX1	slackY1	slackY2
A	0.0	0.0	0.0	0.0
B	0.0	0.0	0.0	0.0
C	0.0	0.0	0.0	0.0
D	0.474	0.0	4.0	2.0
E	0.641	0.0	4.0	4.0
F	0.167	0.0	0.0	2.0
G	0.327	0.0	1.0	3.0
H	0.590	0.0	5.5	2.0

Table 6.10 Reference peers of the WADF output inefficiency measure using BEE for Julia

In[]:	`peersmatrix(deaadd(X, Y, orient = :Output, :RAM, names = FIRMS))`
Out[]:	(see output below)

1.0	.	.	.	.	.	.	.
.	1.0	.	.	.	.	.	.
.	.	1.0	.	.	.	.	.
1.0	.	.	.	.	.	.	.
1.0	.	.	.	.	.	.	.
.	.	1.0	.	.	.	.	.
1.0	.	.	.	.	.	.	.
1.0	.	.	.	.	.	.	.

essential property and the extended essential property, both presented in Sect. 2.4.5 of Chap. 2. Moreover, the same happens for inefficient firms D, G, and H. Only for firm F, whose economic benchmark is firm A, presents a different technological target, firm C.

6.5.4 An Application to the Taiwanese Banking Industry

As in previous chapters, we close this empirical section solving the economic decomposition of profit inefficiency based on the weighted additive distance function for the panel of 31 Taiwanese banks observed in 2010; see Juo et al. (2015). A brief presentation of the data, including descriptive statistics, can be found in Sect. 2.6.2 of Chap. 2. We remark that we are using these data only as an example and therefore do not aim at analyzing the economic results of the Taiwanese banking industry or any individual bank. The dataset includes individual prices for each firm. Here, we follow the standard approach that finds the maximum profit for the firm under evaluation using its observed prices. Hence, a firm can be profit-inefficient under its own prices yet maximize profit under other firm's prices, serving as reference target (or vice versa).

For the implementation, we choose the unweighted additive model that assigns unit values to the vector of weights; see Eq. (6.7). Table 6.11 presents the values of profit inefficiency in the second column, including its descriptive statistics at the bottom. In this model, profit inefficiency is normalized by the minimum observed value of the input and output prices for each bank; i.e., the denominator in (6.7) is $\min\left\{\frac{w_{o1}}{\rho_1^-}, \ldots, \frac{w_{oM}}{\rho_M^-}, \frac{p_{o1}}{\rho_1^+}, \ldots, \frac{p_{oN}}{\rho_N^+}\right\}$. Consequently, the industry does not face exogenously determined market prices, but they differ across firms. Three banks are profit-efficient given their observed prices (no. 1, no. 5, and no. 10), constituting the most frequent benchmarks for the remaining banks. From a technical perspective, eleven banks are efficient, while the remaining twenty banks are both technical and allocative inefficient. Technical and allocative inefficiencies are reported in the third and fourth columns of Table 6.11. In this case, average normalized profit inefficiency equals to 4,158,402.4, while average technical and allocative inefficiencies are 110,508.7 and 4,407,893.7, respectively. Consequently, most of the normalized profit loss is attributed to allocative inefficiency, whose proportion is 97.6% versus that corresponding to technical inefficiency, 2.4%.

In the last five columns of Table 6.11, we present the optimal slacks obtained when solving equation (6.1), whose sum yields the value of the WADF in the unweighted case. Looking at the three inputs, we observe that the largest average slack amount corresponds to financial funds (x_1), whose value is 20,092.5 million TWD, while the smallest slack is observed for labor (x_2), with an average of 414.8 employees. This result exemplifies why it is advisable to resort to a weighted measure (e.g., MIP, RAM, BAM, or normalized), whose efficiency value is dimensionless, when the variables are expressed in different units of measurement. Otherwise, the additive model by Charnes et al. (1985) yields meaningless aggregations. Again, the normalized weighted additive model of Lovell and Pastor (1995) was the first proposal to make the additive model units invariant. In the output dimension, financial investments (y_1) present the largest slack, to the tune of 85,975.8 million TWD, while the value of unrealized loans (y_2) is rather reduced in comparison, 1,814.5 million TWD. Finally, it is worth mentioning that, in this real dataset, the violation of the so-called essential property was not detected.

Table 6.11 Decomposition of profit inefficiency based on the weighted additive distance function (WADF)

Bank	Economic inefficiency, eq. (6.7)			Slacks, eq. (6.1)				
	Profit Ineff. $NI\Pi I_{WADF(G)}(x_o, y_o; \tilde{w}, \tilde{p})$	Technical Ineff. $TI_{WADF(G)}(x_o, y_o; 1, 1)$	Allocative Ineff. $AI_{WADF(G)}(x_o, y_o; 1, 1; \tilde{w}, \tilde{p})$	Funds (x_1) s_1^-	Labor (x_2) s_2^-	Ph. Capital (x_3) s_3^-	Investments (y_1) s_1^+	Loans (y_2) s_2^+
1	0.0	0.0	0.0	0.0	0.0	0.0	0.0	0.0
2	652,948.4	0.0	652,948.4	0.0	0.0	0.0	0.0	0.0
3	1,141,717.9	0.0	1,141,717.9	0.0	0.0	0.0	0.0	0.0
4	1,844,604.0	120,158.8	1,724,445.2	5,474.2	0.0	0.0	114,685.0	0.0
5	0.0	0.0	0.0	0.0	0.0	0.0	0.0	0.0
6	761,896.0	0.0	761,896.0	0.0	0.0	0.0	0.0	0.0
7	1,148,242.1	0.0	1,148,242.1	0.0	0.0	0.0	0.0	0.0
8	1,138,825.5	112,051.2	1,026,774.3	0.0	131.3	2,231.7	109,688.0	0.0
9	1,687,612.8	109,081.8	1,578,531.0	0.0	1,259.2	7,424.2	100,398.0	0.0
10	0.0	0.0	0.0	0.0	0.0	0.0	0.0	0.0
11	5,498,651.6	478,809.8	5,019,841.8	201,645.0	701.5	9,664.8	266,798.0	0.0
12	2,718,193.6	105,603.9	2,612,589.7	100,302.0	0.0	5,302.2	0.0	0.0
13	33,639,620.0	268,921.8	33,370,698.2	0.0	929.8	5,496.6	244,552.0	17,943.8
14	547,933.6	0.0	547,933.6	0.0	0.0	0.0	0.0	0.0
15	1,931,006.5	159,820.9	1,771,185.6	144,604.0	544.1	4,231.0	10,441.6	0.0
16	35,007,191.0	162,323.9	34,844,867.0	0.0	897.9	4,744.1	134,202.0	22,480.2
17	4,156,612.4	190,283.7	3,966,328.7	27,861.0	2,486.5	8,552.9	151,383.0	0.0
18	1,591,837.4	97,202.3	1,494,635.1	0.0	1,303.5	107.1	95,791.7	0.0
19	3,117,004.4	167,939.0	2,949,065.5	0.0	250.6	2,376.3	157,043.0	8,269.5
20	2,611,504.0	202,288.6	2,409,215.4	58,873.3	401.0	0.0	143,014.0	0.0
21	3,301,280.6	0.0	3,301,280.6	0.0	0.0	0.0	0.0	0.0
22	5,175,806.8	176,338.2	4,999,468.6	0.0	307.1	7,218.2	168,813.0	0.0
23	6,601,607.2	168,124.0	6,433,483.1	0.0	255.6	5,792.8	155,747.0	6,328.6
24	1,047,511.7	67,909.9	979,601.8	0.0	1,277.0	1,983.4	64,649.4	0.0
25	3,762,964.3	201,626.8	3,561,337.5	0.0	0.0	62.8	201,564.0	0.0
26	1,106,139.8	0.0	1,106,139.8	0.0	0.0	0.0	0.0	0.0
27	2,956,882.8	131,672.1	2,825,210.7	0.0	96.4	274.1	130,075.0	1,226.8
28	3,993,341.9	119,799.3	3,873,542.6	29,993.2	504.4	0.0	89,301.6	0.0
29	335,918.3	0.0	335,918.3	0.0	0.0	0.0	0.0	0.0
30	1,518,202.3	124,070.5	1,394,131.8	54,114.4	876.6	0.0	69,079.5	0.0
31	11,075,418.7	261,743.3	10,813,675.3	0.0	636.8	3,081.9	258,025.0	0.0
Average	4,518,402.4	110,508.7	4,407,893.7	20,092.5	414.8	2,211.1	85,975.8	1,814.5
Median	1,844,604.0	112,051.2	1,724,445.2	0.0	131.3	62.8	89,301.6	0.0
Maximum	35,007,191.0	478,809.8	34,844,867.0	201,645.0	2,486.5	9,664.8	266,798.0	22,480.2
Minimum	0.0	0.0	0.0	0.0	0.0	0.0	0.0	0.0
Std. Dev.	8,288,407.2	109,534.7	8,241,475.5	47,334.6	579.1	3,047.8	86,840.2	5,276.4

6.6 Summary and Conclusions

In this chapter, we have revised the well-known weighted additive (WA) model in Data Envelopment Analysis and the less known weighted additive distance function (WADF), which endows the WA model with a structure of distance function. The sign of the WADF characterizes the belonging to the technology, what allows using the distance function for measuring productivity change over time. Regarding technical efficiency, the WADF collapses to the WA model when an observation is assessed. And, as for overall inefficiency, the WADF is related to the profit function and allows decomposing a normalized difference-form measure of profit loss in terms of technical inefficiency and price inefficiency. The technical inefficiency component coincides with the value of the WA model.

We have revised the most usual form of the WA model where inputs and outputs are simultaneously changed, i.e., the graph version of this measure, as well as its corresponding input- and output-oriented versions. In these last cases, we showed that both the WADF and the WA model are associated, by duality, with the cost and revenue functions, respectively.

Regarding the implications of the results of this chapter, we have shown that the WADF coincides with the WA model when the assessed unit belongs to the reference production possibility set, which means that technical inefficiency is measured following the Pareto-Koopmans definition of efficiency. This contrasts with the standard and more known distance functions, which yield projections on the weakly efficient frontier. Additionally and from an economic evaluation of the firms, we have shown that the directional distance function is not the only natural link between the profit function and a distance function, at least in a DEA context, since the WADF also presents a similar relationship with the profit function.

Finally, we would like to point out that the WA model and the WADF suffer the problem derived from not satisfying the essential properties of the decomposition of economic efficiency, as we showed through several numerical examples. How to modify these approaches in order to meet these interesting properties from the point of view of interpretability will be shown in the last chapters of this book.

Chapter 7
The Enhanced Russell Graph Measure (*ERG=SBM*): Economic Inefficiency Decompositions

7.1 Introduction

The enhanced Russell graph measure, *ERG*, (Pastor et al., 1999) was designed as a new global efficiency measure to overcome the computational difficulties of the Russell graph measure of technical efficiency, *RG* (Färe et al., 1985). Historically, Farrell (1957) implemented the first measure of technical efficiency, while Färe and Lovell (1978), after suggesting some desirable properties that an ideal technical efficiency measure should satisfy, proposed the so-called Russell input measure of technical efficiency.[1] An output version and a graph version were presented in the first book by Färe et al. (1985). These three initial Russell measures have been already presented in Chap. 5. The difficulty in solving the graph version motivated, in the last 1990s, the search for a new formulation easier to handle and to solve, and the proposed solution was the *ERG* measure. In the literature, two papers can be found, the first one by Pastor et al. (1999) and the second one by Tone (2001). Both proposed exactly the same linear fractional programming model for solving the Russell graph measure through the same reformulation. Hence, the *ERG* model was consecutively published twice with a gap of 2 years, which is something that occurs quite seldom in research. Pastor et al. (1999) published it first in the European Journal of Operational Research, and Tone (2001) published exactly the same models in the same journal under a different name, *SBM*, and related them also to the *RG* measure. It shows that two groups of researchers, without any interaction, may developed the same idea in a quasi-contemporary way without being aware of it. This is the reason why we refer to both measures, which are the same, as *ERG=SBM* and call it the "enhanced Russell graph slack-based measure."

[1] Actually, according to Russell and Schworm (2009), the "Russell measure" corresponds to the Färe-Lovell index introduced by Färe and Lovell (1978), who named it after the first author in recognition of his teaching activity.

J. T. Pastor et al., *Benchmarking Economic Efficiency*, International Series in Operations Research & Management Science 315,
https://doi.org/10.1007/978-3-030-84397-7_7

More recently, two other papers have appeared, due to Sueyoshi and Sekitani (2007a) and Halická and Trnovská (2018), using the original formulation and solving the original Russell graph measure by means of more complex nonlinear programs. The very last one has the advantage of providing, for the first time, a dual relationship between the profit function and the Russell graph measure (for a detailed description of the last two contributions, see Chap. 5). In the case of the *ERG* measure, things become easier than with the *RG* measure after the proposal of the new formulation, which corresponds to a fractional linear programming that can be easily linearized, as happened with the first proposed DEA radial oriented models (Charnes et al., 1978). The novelty in Pastor et al. (1999) was to propose a new non-radial non-oriented DEA model. Curiously enough, they formulated the *ERG* measure resorting to the same variables as the *RG* measure, the "lambdas" for combining the units, the "thetas" for the proportional individual reduction of each of the M inputs, and the "phys" for the proportional individual output increment of each of the N outputs (model (7.1) is the VRS version of model (2) formulated under CRS on the last-mentioned paper). Moreover, Pastor et al. (1999) proposed a change of variables for expressing the *ERG* measure as a "slack-based model" providing its formulation as model (4) of the last-mentioned paper, and transformed it resorting to the change of variables proposed by Charnes and Cooper (1962), to a linear program, which originally appeared as model (6). In this chapter, to decompose the corresponding economic inefficiencies, we are going to consider, as usual, the VRS version of both models (see (7.1) and (7.3)), whose translation invariance version appeared later on in the literature (Sharp et al., 2007).

If we revise the DEA literature during the last two decades, we realize that the *ERG=SBM* has had a great impact, being used in most of the recent developed research avenues, such as productivity change measurement (Tone, 2004), network DEA models (Tone & Tsutsui, 2009), dynamic DEA (Tone & Tsutsui, 2010), efficiency and abatement Costs (Choi et al., 2012), dynamic DEA and network structure (Tone & Tsutsui, 2014), and negative data and SBM (Tone et al., 2020).

A few years ago, part of our research group at the Miguel Hernandez University (Elche, Spain) published two decompositions of profit inefficiency for the ERG=SBM graph measure of technical efficiency (Aparicio et al., 2017a). The first one was inspired in the decomposition corresponding to the weighted additive model (Cooper et al., 2011b). In this chapter, we develop the graph version of the *ERG=SBM*. Its two oriented versions will be presented briefly afterward, because they are identical to the original Russell-oriented models, already developed in Chap. 5.[2]

[2] With respect to the output-oriented measure, we only want to point out that, in Chap. 5 and for reasons of simplicity, instead of minimizing $1/\frac{1}{N}\sum_{n=1}^{N}\phi_n$, we proposed directly to maximize its inverse $\frac{1}{N}\sum_{n=1}^{N}\phi_n$.

7.2 Formulation, Solution, and Properties of the Graph ERG=SBM

7.2.1 *Formulating the* ERG=SBM *as a Linear Fractional Model*

Since our final goal is to evaluate and decompose profit inefficiency, we are going to formulate directly the VRS version of our model.[3]

$$
\begin{aligned}
& TE_{ERG=SBM(G)}(x_o, y_o) = \min_{\theta,\phi,\lambda} \frac{\frac{1}{M}\sum_{m=1}^{M}\theta_m}{\frac{1}{N}\sum_{n=1}^{N}\phi_n} \\
& s.t. \\
& \sum_{j=1}^{J}\lambda_j x_{mj} = \theta_m x_{om}, \qquad m = 1, \ldots, M \\
& \sum_{j=1}^{J}\lambda_j y_{nj} = \phi_n y_{on}, \qquad n = 1, \ldots, N \\
& \sum_{j=1}^{J}\lambda_j = 1, \\
& \theta_m \le 1, \qquad m = 1, \ldots, M \\
& \phi_n \ge 1, \qquad n = 1, \ldots, N \\
& \lambda_j \ge 0, \qquad j = 1, \ldots, J.
\end{aligned}
\tag{7.1}
$$

Comparing model (7.1) with the model that defines the Russell graph measure, program (5.1) in Chap. 5, we realize that the only difference is the objective function, originally formulated as $\frac{1}{M+N}\left(\sum_{m=1}^{M}\theta_m + \sum_{n=1}^{N}\frac{1}{\phi_n}\right)$. From the perspective of finding the solution of model (7.1), the difference is relevant because we have replaced the original nonlinear objective function with a linear fractional objective function, i.e., a fraction of two linear expressions that is much easier to solve. As we will see later on, the difference is also notable in favor of the new formulation for dealing with economic efficiencies.

---

[3] As usual, just by modifying the equality in the convexity constraint, $\sum_{j=1}^{J}\lambda_j = 1$, we get the NIRS ($\le$) and the NDRS ($\ge$). If we want to get the CRS version, as originally formulated by Pastor et al. (1999), we just need to delete the convexity constraint. Model (7.1) was the only one not considered by Tone (2001).

Pastor et al. (1999) also proposed an alternative equivalent formulation of model (7.1) that considers slack variables instead of the individual proportional reductions of each input and augmentations of each output. In fact, if slacks are defined in the usual way as $s_m^- = x_{om} - \theta_m x_{om}, s_m^- \geq 0$ for $m = 1, \ldots, M$ and $s_n^+ = \phi_n y_{on} - y_{on}, s_n^+ \geq 0$, for $n = 1, \ldots, N$, we can derive the next set of equalities:

$$\begin{aligned} \theta_m &= \frac{x_{om} - s_m^-}{x_{mo}} = 1 - \frac{s_m^-}{x_{om}}, s_m^- \geq 0, m = 1, \ldots, M, \\ \phi_n &= \frac{y_{no} + s_{on}^+}{y_{on}} = 1 + \frac{s_n^+}{y_{on}}, s_n^+ \geq 0, n = 1, \ldots, N. \end{aligned} \tag{7.2}$$

Hence, model (7.1) can be reformulated in terms of slacks as follows:[4]

$$\begin{aligned} TE_{ERG=SBM(G)}(x_o, y_o) = \; & \min_{s^-, s^+, \lambda} \frac{1 - \frac{1}{M}\sum_{m=1}^{M} \frac{s_m^-}{x_{om}}}{1 + \frac{1}{N}\sum_{n=1}^{N} \frac{s_n^+}{y_{on}}} \\ s.t. \; & \\ & \sum_{j=1}^{J} \lambda_j x_{jm} = x_{om} - s_m^-, \quad m = 1, \ldots, M \\ & \sum_{j=1}^{J} \lambda_j y_{jn} = y_{on} + s_n^+, \quad n = 1, \ldots, N \\ & \sum_{j=1}^{J} \lambda_j = 1, \\ & s_m^- \geq 0, \quad m = 1, \ldots, M \\ & s_n^+ \geq 0, \quad n = 1, \ldots, N \\ & \lambda_j \geq 0, \quad j = 1, \ldots, J. \end{aligned} \tag{7.3}$$

For solving it, we follow the method proposed by Charnes and Cooper (1962), who were the first to show how to solve a linear fractional program through the introduction of a new variable used to transform all the slacks giving rise to an equivalent linear program.[5] After computing an optimal solution of the linear program, we can immediately generate a solution of the original fractional program (7.3). In case the linear program has multiple alternative solutions, the same happens

---

[4]Equalities (7.2) and the CRS version of model (7.3) appeared in Pastor et al. (1999) referenced as (3) and (4). Moreover, the CRS version of model (7.3) appeared in Tone (2001) referenced as (7). It should be clear that from the beginning we must assume that all input and output values are positive.

[5]The new variable is equal to the inverse of the denominator of the objective function; see next section.

with the fractional program. Model (7.3) is preferred to model (7.1) not only because DEA researchers are more used to handle slacks than to handle individual input contractions and output expansions but also because the economic efficiency part is easier to develop.

7.2.2 *Solving the* ERG=SBM

According to Charnes and Cooper (1962), the new variables to be considered for solving model (7.3) are obtained by multiplying all the slack and lambda variables by a new variable, "beta," that, as already mentioned, is exactly the inverse of the denominator of the objective function and whose definition must be incorporated as a new restriction in the transformed model. The definition of the new variables $\beta, t_{mo}^{-}, \forall m, t_{no}^{+}, \forall n, \mu_j, \forall j$ follows:

$$\begin{aligned} \beta &= \left(1 + \frac{1}{N}\sum_{n=1}^{N}\frac{s_n^+}{y_{on}}\right)^{-1}, \\ t_m^- &= \beta s_m^-, m = 1, \ldots, M, \\ t_n^+ &= \beta s_n^+, n = 1, \ldots, N, \\ \mu_j &= \beta\lambda_j, j = 1, \ldots, J. \end{aligned} \tag{7.4}$$

Let us observe that β is a positive number that is always greater or equal to zero and also that the first equality of (7.4) can be written as follows:[6]

$$\beta\left(1 + \frac{1}{N}\sum_{n=1}^{N}\frac{s_n^+}{y_{on}}\right) = \beta + \frac{1}{N}\sum_{n=1}^{N}\frac{t_n^+}{y_{on}} = 1.$$

Moreover, the objective function is reformulated as $\frac{1-\frac{1}{M}\sum_{m=1}^{M}\frac{s_o^-}{x_{om}}}{1+\frac{1}{N}\sum_{n=1}^{N}\frac{s_n^+}{y_{on}}} = \beta\left(1 - \frac{1}{M}\sum_{m=1}^{M}\frac{s_m^-}{x_{om}}\right) = \beta - \frac{1}{M}\sum_{m=1}^{M}\frac{t_{mo}^-}{x_{mo}}$. Hence, the linear program equivalent to (7.3) is formulated as follows:

[6]The inequality $\beta \geq 0$ is a must for having a well-defined linear program as (7.5), although we know that, due to its definition, β is always a positive number.

$$
\begin{aligned}
TE_{ERG=SBM(G)}(x_o, y_o) = \quad & \min_{t^-, t^+, \mu, \beta} \ \beta - \frac{1}{M}\sum_{m=1}^{M}\frac{t_m^-}{x_{om}} \\
s.t. \quad & \\
& \beta + \frac{1}{N}\sum_{n=1}^{N}\frac{t_n^+}{y_{on}} = 1 \\
& \sum_{j=1}^{J}\mu_j x_{jm} = \beta x_{om} - t_m^-, \quad m = 1, \ldots, M \\
& \sum_{j=1}^{J}\mu_j y_{jn} = \beta y_{on} + t_n^+, \quad n = 1, \ldots, N \\
& \sum_{j=1}^{J}\mu_j = \beta, \\
& \beta \geq 0, \\
& t_m^- \geq 0, t_n^+ \geq 0, \quad \forall m, n, \\
& \mu_j \geq 0, \quad j = 1, \ldots, J.
\end{aligned}
\tag{7.5}
$$

Notes

1. Usually, within the restrictions of the last model, the equations of the second and third blocks, associated respectively with inputs and outputs, are written with all their three terms, related to variables of the program, on the left-hand side, and with a zero on the other side. In fact, the first restriction is already written in this way, but the rest of the restrictions are not. If we perform these movements, all the last *M*+*N*+1 restrictions will have on its right-hand side a zero. Program (7.5) is linear and can be solved by any computer optimizer and, particularly, with our DEA Julia package, where the *ERG=SBM* is already available (see Sect. 2.5 and the applications below for more details).
2. If we want to deal with the same measure under different returns to scale conditions, the reader can verify that model (7.5) only changes its last equality $\sum_{j=1}^{J}\mu_j = \beta$ that will consider a $\leq$ inequality under NIRS (non-increasing returns to scale) or a $\geq$ under NDRS (non-decreasing returns to scale). In case a CRS model is needed, just delete the mentioned last equality from model (7.5).

7.2.3 *Basic Properties of the* ERG=SBM

Let us enunciate and prove the most relevant properties of the *ERG=SBM* in terms of Chap. 2.

E1a. *Indication*: only the strong efficient points are deemed as efficient, or equivalently, the efficient projection of any unit under scrutiny belongs to the strong efficient frontier.

E2. *Strong monotonicity*: considering a firm (x_o, y_o) and a second related firm $(x_1, y_1) = (x_o - h_1, y_o + k_1)$, where $h_1 \geq 0_M$, $k_1 \geq 0_N$ and at least one of the components of (h_1, k_1) is strictly greater than zero, it always happens that $TE_{ERG\ =\ SBM(G)}(x_o, y_o) > TE_{ERG\ =\ SBM(G)}(x_1, y_1)$.

E3. $0 < TE_{ERG\ =\ SBM(G)}(x_o, y_o) \leq 1$.

E4. *Units invariant* (*or commensurability*): a change of the units of measurement of inputs and outputs does not alter the value of *ERG=SBM(G)*.

E5. *Translation invariance*: the *ERG=SBM(G)* is not translation invariant. However, Sharp et al. (2007) proposed a translation invariant version of the *ERG=SBM(G)*, which requires, according to Lovell and Pastor (1995), a VRS technology.

Proofs

E1a. *Indication*: it is a direct consequence of the formulation of the objective function, which maximizes at the same time all the input and output slacks. Hence, the projection of any inefficient unit always belongs to the strong efficient frontier.

E2. *Strong monotonicity*: Let us start by considering two firms, (x_o, y_o) and (x_1, y_1), which only differ in one of its components, let's say its first input $(x_1, y_1) = (x_{o1} - h_1, x_{o2}, \ldots, x_{oM}, y_o)$, $h_1 > 0$. Intuitively, (x_1, y_1) is strictly closer to the frontier than (x_o, y_o).[7] We are going to prove that $TE_{ERG\ =\ SBM(G)}(x_1, y_1) < TE_{ERG\ =\ SBM(G)}(x_o, y_o)$. The proof starts by considering the optimal *ERG=SBM(G)* slacks $\left(s_o^{-*}, s_o^{+*}\right)$ associated to (x_o, y_o) and realizing that $\left(s_{o1}^{-*} - h_1, \ldots, s_{oM}^{-*}, s_o^{+*}\right)$ is a feasible solution for (x_1, y_1). As a consequence, the optimal *ERG=SBM(G)* slacks $\left(s_1^{-*}, s_1^{+*}\right)$ for (x_1, y_1) satisfy $\left(s_1^{-*}, s_1^{+*}\right) \leq \left(s_{o1}^{-*} - h_1, \ldots, s_{oM}^{-*}, s_o^{+*}\right)$ and particularly $s_{11}^{-*} \leq s_{o1}^{-*} - h_1 < s_{o1}^{-*}$. Since all the fractions associated to the *ERG=SBM(G)* but the first one satisfy $\frac{s_{1m}^{-*}}{x_{1m}} = \frac{s_{om}^{-*}}{x_{om}}, m \geq 2$, $\frac{s_{1n}^{+*}}{y_{1n}} = \frac{s_{on}^{+*}}{y_{on}}, n \geq 1$, the possible difference in the *ERG=SBM(G)* values will be due exclusively to their first components. Hence, we are going to compare the fractions that appear in the objective function associated with the first input of both firms, namely, $\frac{s_{o1}^{-*}}{x_{o1}}$ for $TE_{ERG\ =\ SBM(G)}(x_o, y_o)$ and $\frac{s_{11}^{-*}}{x_{11}} = \frac{s_{11}^{-*}}{x_{o1} - h_1}$ for the optimal projection of (x_1, y_1). Being $s_{11}^{-*} \leq s_{o1}^{-*} - h_1 < s_{o1}^{-*}$, we deduce that $\frac{s_{11}^{-*}}{x_{11}} \leq \frac{s_{o1}^{-*} - h_1}{x_{o1} - h_1}$. Let us finally show that $\frac{s_{11}^{-*}}{x_{11}}$ is strictly smaller than $\frac{s_{o1}^{-*}}{x_{o1}}$, which will conclude the proof. In fact, since $\frac{s_{11}^{-*}}{x_{11}} \leq \frac{s_{o1}^{-*} - h_1}{x_{o1} - h_1}$, it is sufficient to prove that $\frac{s_{o1}^{-*} - h_1}{x_{o1} - h_1} < \frac{s_{o1}^{-*}}{x_{o1}}$ or,

[7] Geometrically, the intuition is confirmed: when using any type of slack-based model, the distance to the frontier can be measured along the L_1 path defined by the corresponding slacks.

equivalently, that $x_{o1}\left(s_{o1}^{-*} - h_1\right) < s_{o1}^{-*}(x_{o1} - h_1)$. Hence, cancelling out the product $x_{o1}s_{o1}^{-*}$ from both sides, we obtain $-x_{o1}h_1 < -s_{o1}^{-*}h_1$ or $x_{o1}h_1 > s_{o1}^{-*}h_1$. Since we have assumed that $h_1 > 0$, we can cancel it out in the last strict inequality obtaining the desired result $x_{o1} > s_{o1}^{-*}$.

E3. Since each slack has the same units as its corresponding input or output, the associated fractions in the objective function are invariant to the units of measurement. Hence, *ERG=SBM(G)* is just a number, which means that it is dimensionless.

E4. It is trivial.

E5. Under VRS, if we translate all the units, the optimal slacks for reaching the strong efficient frontier will not change, but its denominators in the objective function will. Hence, the measure is not translation invariant.

Note Pastor et al. (1999: 600) listed and proved other five properties of minor relevance. The first three are a type of *quasi-homogeneity*, based on inequalities rather than on equalities (see Property (E5) in Sect. 2.2.4). The last two compare the *ERG=SBM(G)* with the input and output radial efficiency scores. Although the original proofs were made for the CRS model, they are also extensible to the VRS model.

7.3 The Graph *ERG=SBM* and the Decomposition of Profit Inefficiency

Program (7.3) is an efficiency model that, at point (x_o, y_o), calculates a technical efficiency measure $TE_{ERG\ =\ SBM(G)}(x_o, y_o)$ equal to the minimum value of its objective function $\frac{1-\frac{1}{M}\sum_{m=1}^{M}\frac{s_m^{-*}}{x_{om}}}{1+\frac{1}{N}\sum_{n=1}^{N}\frac{s_n^{+*}}{y_{on}}}$. Its associated *technical inefficiency measure* (the ERG=SBM graph measure of technical inefficiency) is derived easily as follows:

$$TI_{ERG=SBM(G)}(x_o, y_o) = 1 - TE_{ERG=SBM(G)}(x_o, y_o) = 1 - \frac{1 - \frac{1}{M}\sum\limits_{m=1}^{M}\frac{s_m^{-*}}{x_{om}}}{1 + \frac{1}{N}\sum\limits_{n=1}^{N}\frac{s_n^{+*}}{y_{on}}}$$

$$= \frac{\frac{1}{N}\sum\limits_{n=1}^{N}\frac{s_n^{+*}}{y_{on}} + \frac{1}{M}\sum\limits_{m=1}^{M}\frac{s_m^{-*}}{x_{om}}}{1 + \frac{1}{N}\sum\limits_{n=1}^{N}\frac{s_n^{+*}}{y_{no}}}. \tag{7.6}$$

According to Property (E3), the technical inefficiency is also a number in the interval (0,1), taking the lowest value when (x_o, y_o) is a strongly efficient point and taking a value close to 1 when the mentioned firm is very inefficient. Property (E4) shows that $TI_{ERG\ =\ SBM(G)}(x_o, y_o)$ is also units invariant, which means that it is a dimensionless number.

Let us derive directly the normalized profit inefficiency at the generic point (x_o, y_o), whose *ERG=SBM* projection $(\widehat{x}_o, \widehat{y}_o)$ is precisely $(\widehat{x}_o, \widehat{y}_o) = (x_o - s^{-*}, y_o + s^{+*}) \in T$, where the optimal slacks are obtained through model (7.3).[8] Then, the profit inefficiency $\Pi I(x_o, y_o, p, w)$, defined as usual, satisfies the following:

$$\begin{aligned}\Pi I(x_o, y_o, p, w) &= \Pi(w, p) - (p \cdot y_o - w \cdot x_o) \geq (p \cdot \widehat{y}_o - w \cdot \widehat{x}_o) - (p \cdot y_o - w \cdot x_o) = \\ &= p \cdot (\widehat{y}_o - y_o) - w \cdot (\widehat{x}_o - x_o) = p \cdot s^{+*} + w \cdot s^{-*} = \sum_{n=1}^{N} p_n s_n^{+*} + \sum_{m=1}^{M} w_m s_m^{-*} \\ &= \frac{1}{N} \sum_{n=1}^{N} N p_n y_{no} \frac{s_n^{+*}}{y_{no}} + \frac{1}{M} \sum_{m=1}^{M} M w_m x_{mo} \frac{s_m^{-*}}{x_{mo}},\end{aligned} \tag{7.7}$$

where, in the expression $\sum_{n=1}^{N} p_n s_n^{+*} + \sum_{m=1}^{M} w_m s_m^{-*}$, we have multiplied and divided each output component n by $N y_{on}$ and each input component m by $M x_{om}$.[9]

If we now substitute each of the N+M expressions $N p_n y_{on}$, $n = 1, \ldots, N$ and $M w_m x_{om}$, $m = 1, \ldots, M$, expressed in prices, by its minimum:

$$\delta_{(x_o, y_o, p, w)} = \min \{N p_n y_{on}, n = 1, \ldots, N, M w_m x_{om}, m = 1, \ldots, M\},$$

which is a fixed value also expressed in prices, the above inequality continues to hold, and we get the following:

$$\begin{aligned}\Pi I(x_o, y_o, p, w) &\geq \frac{1}{N} \sum_{n=1}^{N} N p_n y_{no} \frac{s_n^{+*}}{y_{no}} + \frac{1}{M} \sum_{m=1}^{M} M w_m x_{mo} \frac{s_m^{-*}}{x_{mo}} \\ &\geq \delta_{(x_o, y_o, p, w)} \left(\frac{1}{N} \sum_{n=1}^{N} \frac{s_n^{+*}}{y_{no}} + \frac{1}{M} \sum_{m=1}^{M} \frac{s_m^{-*}}{x_{mo}} \right).\end{aligned} \tag{7.8}$$

[8] In Aparicio et al. (2017a), the normalization procedure was not derived directly, as explained later on. Moreover, until now, the usual way of relating profit inefficiency with technical inefficiency has been obtaining a suitable Fenchel-Mahler inequality based on duality results. Here, we are proposing a more direct approach taking advantage of the final inequality obtained in the last-mentioned paper. However, developing this process has inspired us for proposing an alternative way of getting a profit inefficiency decomposition, as proposed later on in Chap. 13 based on Pastor et al. (2021b).

[9] The inequality is an equality if, and only if, the projection $(\widehat{x}_o, \widehat{y}_o)$ achieves maximum profit.

Since we want to accommodate on the right-hand side $TI_{ERG\ =\ SBM(G)}(x_o, y_o)$, we have to multiply and divide the last right-hand side expression by $\left(1 + \frac{1}{N}\sum_{n=1}^{N}\frac{s_n^{+*}}{y_{no}}\right)$, which gives rise to the next inequality: $\Pi I(x_o, y_o, p, w) \geq$

$$\left(\delta_{(x_o,y_o,p,w)}\left(1 + \frac{1}{N}\sum_{n=1}^{N}\frac{s_n^{+*}}{y_{on}}\right)\right)\left(\frac{\frac{1}{N}\sum_{n=1}^{N}\frac{s_n^{+*}}{y_{on}} + \frac{1}{M}\sum_{m=1}^{M}\frac{s_m^{-*}}{x_{om}}}{\left(1+\frac{1}{N}\sum_{n=1}^{N}\frac{s_n^{+*}}{y_{on}}\right)}\right).$$

If we transform the last inequality into an equality by adding to the right-hand side a residual term, we find that profit inefficiency can be expressed as the sum of the expression on the right plus the mentioned residual term:

$$\Pi I(x_o, y_o, p, w) = \left(\delta_{(x_o,y_o,p,w)}\left(1 + \frac{1}{N}\sum_{n=1}^{N}\frac{s_n^{+*}}{y_{on}}\right)\right) TI_{ERG=SBM(G)}(x_o, y_o)$$
$$+ A\Pi I_{ERG=SBM(G)}(x_o, y_o, p, w), \tag{7.9}$$

or $\Pi I(x_o, y_o, p, w) = T\Pi I_{ERG\ =\ SBM(G)}(x_o, y_o, p, w) + A\Pi I_{ERG\ =\ SBM(G)}(x_o, y_o, p, w)$.

This last decomposition qualifies as a *profit inefficiency decomposition*. Since its first component, the technical profit inefficiency, only depends on the point (x_o, y_o) and the optimal output slacks, we can compare all the firms of our sample through the values of $\Pi I(x_o, y_o, p, w)$ and of $T\Pi I_{ERG\ =\ SBM(G)}(x_o, y_o, p, w)$. Moreover, since $A\Pi I_{ERG\ =\ SBM(G)} = \Pi I - T\Pi I_{ERG\ =\ SBM(G)}$ is the difference of two comparable quantities, all expressed in monetary units, it is also comparable between firms. This constitutes the most distinguished feature of the *profit inefficiency decomposition*, and we say that it satisfies *the comparison property*.

It is easy to derive the *normalized profit inefficiency decomposition* from (7.9). Since our aim is to isolate the technical inefficiency, all we have to do is to *divide all three terms by* the multiplicative factor accompanying precisely the mentioned technical inefficiency, which is called *the normalizing factor*. For the *ERG=SBM*, the mentioned factor is not unique, because it depends on $\delta_{(x_o,y_o,p,w)}$ and on the optimal output slacks associated to each firm, with the only exception of the efficient firms, for which the mentioned factor is reduced to $\delta_{(x_o,y_o,p,w)}$. Nonetheless, we can maintain the general expression for the normalizing factor deriving the next *normalized profit inefficiency decomposition*:

$$\Pi I_{ERG=SBM(G)}(x_o, y_o, \widetilde{w}, \widetilde{p}) = \frac{\Pi I_{ERG=SBM(G)}(x_o, y_o, p, w)}{\delta_{(x_o, y_o, p, w)}\left(1 + \frac{1}{N}\sum_{n=1}^{N}\frac{s_n^{+*}}{y_{on}}\right)} = \\ = TI_{ERG=SBM(G)}(x_o, y_o) + \frac{A\Pi I_{ERG=SBM(G)}(x_o, y_o, p, w)}{\delta_{(x_o, y_o, p, w)}\left(1 + \frac{1}{N}\sum_{n=1}^{N}\frac{s_n^{+*}}{y_{on}}\right)}. \tag{7.10}$$

The last normalized decomposition splits the value of the *normalized profit inefficiency* in two parts, all of which are dimensionless numbers. Basically, it compares a normalized $\Pi I(x_o, y_o, w, p)$, denoted as $\Pi I_{ERG=SBM}(x_o, y_o, \widetilde{w}, \widetilde{p})$, with $TI_{ERG=SBM}(x_o, y_o)$.[10] As usual, the normalization eliminates in this case the prices in the numerator through the presence of $\delta_{(x_o, y_o, p, w)}$ in the denominator, obtaining a dimensionless number that is comparable to $TI_{ERG=SBM(G)}(x_o, y_o)$. The corresponding *allocative inefficiency*, $AI_{ERG=SBM(G)}(x_o, y_o)$, is equal to the *normalized allocative profit inefficiency*, as shown in (7.10). Finally, we get the decomposition of the ERG=SBM profit inefficiency measure into the ERG=SBM graph measure of technical inefficiency plus the ERG=SBM allocative measure of profit inefficiency:

$$\Pi I_{ERG=SBM(G)}(x_o, y_o, \widetilde{w}, \widetilde{p}) = TI_{ERG=SBM(G)}(x_o, y_o) \\ + AI_{ERG=SBM(G)}(x_o, y_o, \widetilde{w}, \widetilde{p}). \tag{7.11}$$

Decomposition (7.10) using (7.9) corresponds to the best decomposition proposed in Aparicio et al. (2017a), in the sense that the value of the allocative inefficiency was the smallest that could be found.[11]

Going back to inequality (7.9) and knowing that the *ERG=SBM* can deliver multiple optimal solutions, it is clear that the "best" optimal solution offering a lower allocative inefficiency is the one that maximizes the term $\left(1 + \frac{1}{N}\sum_{n=1}^{N}\frac{s_n^{+*}}{y_{on}}\right)$; see (7.10). According to (7.11), it generates the lowest normalized profit inefficiency. The search for the best alternative optimal solution, if it exists, is solved by means of

[10] The normalized profit inefficiency was originally called by Chambers et al. (1998) the Nerlovian profit inefficiency in honor of the economist Marc Nerlove, who was the first to suggest that profit inefficiency must be normalized in order to obtain a dimensionless number that is comparable to technical inefficiency, which, as already shown, is also a pure number.

[11] According to Proposition 1 in Aparicio et al. (2017a), the other decomposition was achieved realizing that the numerator of $TI_{ERG=SBM}(x_o, y_o)$, $\sum_{n=1}^{N}\frac{1}{Ny_{on}}s_n^+ + \sum_{m=1}^{M}\frac{1}{Mx_{om}}s_m^-$, is a weighted additive function. The inequality obtained was similar to (7.9) but less tightened since the normalizing denominator was simply $\delta_{(x_o, y_o, p, w)}$. In the last-mentioned paper, this first decomposition was used for deriving the second decomposition (7.9) that we have derived here directly.

the next linear program as proposed by Aparicio et al. (2017a), where ν^* corresponds to the optimal objective function value associated to the first optimal solution found:[12]

$$
\begin{aligned}
& \max_{s^-, s^+, \lambda} \left(1 + \frac{1}{N} \sum_{n=1}^{N} \frac{s_n^+}{y_{on}}\right) \\
& s.t. \\
& \sum_{j=1}^{J} \lambda_j x_{jm} = x_{om} - s_m^-, && m = 1, \ldots, M \\
& \sum_{j=1}^{J} \lambda_j y_{jn} = y_{on} + s_n^+, && n = 1, \ldots, N \\
& \sum_{j=1}^{J} \lambda_j = 1, \\
& 1 - \frac{1}{M} \sum_{m=1}^{M} \frac{s_m^-}{x_{om}} = \nu^* \left(1 + \frac{1}{N} \sum_{n=1}^{N} \frac{s_n^+}{y_{on}}\right) \\
& s_m^- \geq 0, \forall m, && s_n^+ \geq 0, \forall n, \\
& \lambda_j \geq 0, && j = 1, \ldots, J.
\end{aligned}
\tag{7.12}
$$

Note

In this particular case associated with the *ERG=SBM*, it is remarkable that, due to the last equality restriction of model (7.12), the fact that we are maximizing the "output component" of the mentioned measure implies also that we are, at the same time, maximizing its input component, something that is necessary for getting the same technical inefficiency; see (7.5). Moreover, maximizing the output component can only be achieved by increasing certain output slacks, and similarly, maximizing the input component can only be achieved by decreasing certain input slacks. Hence, the new projection will get a better profit than the previous one, which is directly connected with getting a lower allocative inefficiency, as we will make even clearer in Chap. 13 when proposing a new unified way of making profit decompositions, through a method called "the general direct approach."

Additionally, the above decompositions can be interpreted in monetary terms if one multiplies each component by the normalization factor. Something similar happens in the case of the oriented versions of these decompositions that will be shown in the next sections of the chapter.

[12] Not all the firms generate multiple optimal solutions, as our next example shows.

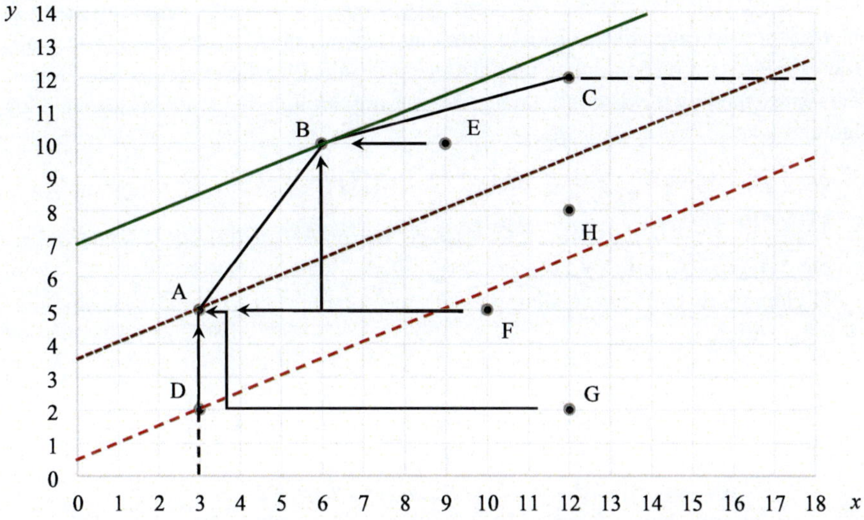

Fig. 7.1 Example of the *ERG=SBM* profit inefficiency decomposition, $(p, w) = (2, 1)$

Example 7.1

Let us consider an easy numerical example with a single input and a single output. The sample of nine units is A=(3,5), B=(6,10), C=(12,12), D=(3,2), E=(9,10), F=(10,5), G=(12,2), H=(12,8), and I=(24,4). Under VRS, we get that the first three units are strongly efficient and that the last six units are inefficient. Moreover, there are only two efficient facets: the segment connecting points (3,5) and (6,10) and the segment connecting points (6,10) and (12,12). Let us further assume that the vector of prices (per unit) is $(p, w) = (2, 1)$. Hence, at each efficient point, (3,5), (6,10) and (12,12), the profit is equal to 10−3=7, 20−6=14, and 24−12=12, which means that the only profit-maximizing efficiency is unit C (6,10).[13] Figure 7.1 illustrates the dataset, omitting the last unit for graphical convenience, as well as maximum isoprofit line.

Let us now calculate the technical inefficiency through the *ERG=SBM* for each of the inefficient units (3,2), (9,10), (10,5), (12,2), (12,8), and (24,4). After getting its first optimal projection, let us check if we can find another one with a better profit value. We do not know beforehand if it will influence or not the profit inefficiency decomposition. In any case, it is a good exercise to know better the *ERG=SBM* and to appreciate that it is a multivalue function.

Unit D (3,2) Its projection is point (3,5), and its technical inefficiency is, according to (7.6),$TI_{ERG=SBM(G)}(3,2) = \frac{0+\frac{5-2}{2}}{1+\frac{3}{2}} = \frac{\frac{3}{2}}{\frac{5}{2}} = \frac{3}{5}$.

[13] It is well known that the profit-maximizing point(s) must be located close to the NW corner of the sample, which intuitively means "less inputs and more outputs." As a consequence, a non-efficient point can never be a profit maximizing point.

Since (3,2) has no alternative optimal projection, let us start calculating its profit inefficiency decomposition (7.9). Its profit inefficiency is $14-(2\times2-1\times3)=13_\$$ (the isoprofits corresponding to unit D and its technically efficient projection, unit A, are represented by the discontinuous lines passing through them) and its normalizing factor

$\delta_{(x_o,y_o,p,w)}\left(1+\frac{1}{N}\sum_{n=1}^{N}\frac{s_{no}^{+*}}{y_{no}}\right)=\min\{2\cdot2,1\cdot3\}\left(1+\frac{3}{2}\right)=\frac{15_\$}{2}$. Hence, we obtain

$13_\$=\frac{15_\$}{2}\frac{3}{5}+A\Pi I_{ERG=SBM(G)}(x_o,y_o,p,w)=\frac{9_\$}{2}+A\Pi I_{ERG=SBM(G)}(x_o,y_o,p,w)$,
where $A\Pi I_{ERG=SBM(G)}(x_o,y_o,p,w)=13_\$-\frac{9_\$}{2}=\frac{17_\$}{2}$.

Dividing now by the normalizing factor, we obtain the corresponding normalized decomposition:

$$\Pi I_{ERG=SBM(G)}(x_o,y_o,\widetilde{p},\widetilde{w})=\frac{13_\$}{\frac{15_\$}{2}}=\frac{26}{15}=\frac{3}{5}+\frac{17}{2}\frac{2}{15}=\frac{3}{5}+\frac{17}{15}=$$
$$TI_{ERG=SBM(G)}(x_o,y_o)+AI_{ERG=SBM(G)}(x_o,y_o,\widetilde{p},\widetilde{w}).$$

Unit E (9,10) Its projection is point (6,10), and its technical inefficiency is, according to (7.6),

$$TI_{ERG=SBM(G)}(9,10)=\frac{\frac{9-6}{9}+\frac{10-10}{10}}{1+0}=\frac{\frac{3}{9}}{1}=\frac{1}{3}.$$

Since its actual projection is a profit-maximizing firm, we cannot improve it. Let us now calculate the corresponding normalizing factor value: $\delta_{(x_o,y_o,p,w)}\left(1+\frac{1}{N}\sum_{n=1}^{N}\frac{s_{no}^{+*}}{y_{no}}\right)=\min\{2\cdot10,1\cdot9\}\left(1+\frac{10-10}{10}\right)=9_\$$. Knowing that the profit inefficiency equals to $14-(2\cdot10-1\cdot9)=14-11=3_\$$, we calculate $\Pi I_{ERG=SBM(G)}(x_o,y_o,\widetilde{p},\widetilde{w})=\frac{3_\$}{9_\$}=\frac{1}{3}$, and consequently, its allocative component equals to $AI_{ERG=SBM(G)}(x_o,y_o,\widetilde{p},\widetilde{w})=\frac{1}{3}-\frac{1}{3}=0$. The corresponding profit inefficiency decomposition is as follows: $\Pi I=3_\$=9_\$\frac{1}{3}=T\Pi I+0_\$$.

Unit F (10,5) Its projection is point (3,5), and its technical inefficiency $TI_{ERG=SBM(G)}(x_o,y_o)=\frac{7}{10}$. The normalization factor associated to this projection is equal to $\min\{2\cdot5,1\cdot10\}\left(1+\frac{0}{5}\right)=10\cdot1=10_\$$. However, resorting to linear program (7.12), we find that there exists an alternative optimal solution with an improved profit, namely, point (6,10). The normalizing denominator associated to the latter projection is equal to $\min\{2\cdot5,1\cdot10\}\left(1+\frac{10-5}{5}\right)=10\cdot2=20_\$$. The profit inefficiency associated to unit (10,5) equals to $\Pi I_{ERG=SBM(G)}(x_o,y_o,p,w)=14-(2\cdot5-1\cdot10)=14-0=14_\$$, and consequently, the $\Pi I_{ERG=SBM(G)}(x_o,y_o,\widetilde{p},\widetilde{w})=\frac{14_\$}{20_\$}=\frac{7}{10}$. As a consequence, its allocative component equals to $AI_{ERG=SBM(G)}(x_o,y_o,\widetilde{p},\widetilde{w})=\frac{7}{10}-\frac{7}{10}=0$. Let us point out that if we would have keep the initial projection, then the normalized profit inefficiency would have been $\frac{14_\$}{10_\$} = \frac{7}{5}$, i.e., twice as much as with the second best projection, and with the same technical inefficiency. Consequently, the allocative inefficiency would have been $\frac{7}{5} - \frac{7}{10} = \frac{7}{10}$ instead of 0.

Unit G (12,2) Its projection is point (3,5), with $TI_{ERG=SBM(G)}(12, 2) = \frac{9}{10}$. Again, by solving (7.11), we find a "better profit projection," exactly point (6,10). Its profit inefficiency equals to $\Pi I_{ERG=SBM(G)}(x_o, y_o, p, w) = 14 - (2 \cdot 2 - 1 \cdot 12) = 14 + 8 = 22_\$$, and the corresponding normalizing factor value for the second projection is equal to $\min\{2 \cdot 2, 1 \cdot 12\} \cdot \left(1 + \frac{10-2}{2}\right) = 4 \cdot 5 = 20_\$$. Hence, the $\Pi I_{ERG=SBM(G)}(x_o, y_o, \widetilde{p}, \widetilde{w}) = \frac{22_\$}{20_\$} = \frac{11}{10}$, and consequently, its allocative component equals to $AI_{ERG=SBM(G)}(x_o, y_o, \widetilde{p}, \widetilde{w}) = \frac{11}{10} - \frac{9}{10} = \frac{1}{5}$.

Unit H (12,8) Its first projection is point $\left(\frac{24}{5}, 8\right)$, with an associated profit of $2 \cdot 8 - \frac{24}{5} = \frac{80-24}{5} = \frac{66}{5} = 13\frac{1}{5}$, quite close to 14, the maximum profit. Nonetheless, we search, by solving (7.12), for a better alternative solution and find that it corresponds to the maximal profit point (6,10). Now, the corresponding normalizing denominator is $\min\{2 \cdot 8, 1 \cdot 12\} \cdot \left(1 + \frac{10-8}{8}\right) = 12\frac{5}{4} = 15_\$$, and the associated $\Pi I_{ERG=SBM(G)}(x_o, y_o, \widetilde{p}, \widetilde{w}) = \frac{1}{15}(14 - (2 \cdot 8 - 1 \cdot 12)) = \frac{14-4}{15} = \frac{10_\$}{15_\$} = \frac{2}{3}$. Since $TI_{ERG=SBM(G)}(12, 8) = \frac{6}{10} = \frac{3}{5}$, we obtain that $AI_{ERG=SBM(G)}(x_o, y_o, \widetilde{p}, \widetilde{w}) = \frac{2}{3} - \frac{3}{5} = \frac{1}{15}$.

Unit I (24,4) Its projection is point (3,5), with $TI_{ERG=SBM(G)}(24, 4) = \frac{9}{10}$. Following the same procedure as before, we try to find a "better" alternative optimal projection, getting point (6,10), which, as already said, is the best alternative optimal projection. Its normalization factor is $\min\{2 \cdot 4, 1 \cdot 24\} \cdot \left(1 + \frac{10-4}{4}\right) = 8\frac{10}{4} = 20_\$$, and being its profit inefficiency equal to $\Pi I_{ERG=SBM(G)}(x_o, y_o, p, w) = 14 - (2 \cdot 4 - 1 \cdot 24) = 14 + 16 = 30_\$$, we get the corresponding normalized profit inefficiency $\Pi I_{ERG=SBM(G)}(x_o, y_o, \widetilde{p}, \widetilde{w}) = \frac{30_\$}{20_\$} = \frac{3}{2}$. Therefore, $AI_{ERG=SBM(G)}(x_o, y_o, \widetilde{p}, \widetilde{w}) = \frac{3}{2} - \frac{9}{10} = \frac{6}{10} = \frac{3}{5}$.

Let us finally revise what happens with the three efficient units: (3,5), (6,10), and (12,12). Obviously, its technical inefficiency equals to zero, and consequently, all its normalized profit inefficiency is equal to its allocative component. Moreover their normalizing denominator, $\delta_{(x_o,y_o,p,w)}\left(1 + \frac{1}{N}\sum_{n=1}^{N}\frac{s_{no}^{+*}}{y_{no}}\right)$, is equal to $\delta_{(x_o,y_o,2,1)} = \min\{2y_o, x_o\}$, because all the slacks are zero. Hence, in each case, we get the following:

Unit (3,5) $\rightarrow \Pi I_{ERG=SBM(G)}(x_o, y_o, p, w) = 14 - (2 \cdot 5 - 1 \cdot 3) = 14 - 7 = 7_\$$, $\delta_{(3,5,2,1)} = \min\{10, 3\} = 3_\$$, and consequently,

$$\Pi I_{ERG=SBM(G)}(x_o, y_o, \widetilde{p}, \widetilde{w}) = \frac{\Pi I_{ERG=SBM(G)}(x_o, y_o, p, w)_\$}{\delta_{(3,5,2,1)\$}} = \frac{7}{3}$$
$$= AI_{ERG=SBM(G)}(x_o, y_o, \widetilde{p}, \widetilde{w}).$$

Unit (6,10) $\rightarrow \Pi I_{ERG=SBM(G)}(x_o, y_o, p, w) = 14 - (2 \cdot 10 - 1 \cdot 6) = 14 - 14 = 0_\$$, $\delta_{(6,10,2,1)} = \min\{20, 6\} = 6_\$$, and consequently,

$$\Pi I_{ERG=SBM(G)}(x_o, y_o, \widetilde{p}, \widetilde{w}) = \frac{\Pi I_{ERG=SBM(G)}(x_o, y_o, p, w)_\$}{\delta_{(6,10,2,1)}} = \frac{0_\$}{6_\$} = 0$$
$$= AI_{ERG=SBM(G)}(x_o, y_o, \widetilde{p}, \widetilde{w}).$$

Unit (12,12) $\rightarrow \Pi I_{ERG=SBM(G)}(x_o, y_o, p, w) = 14 - (2 \cdot 12 - 1 \cdot 12) = 14 - 12 = 2_\$$, $\delta_{(12,12,2,1)} = \min\{24, 12\} = 12_\$$, and consequently,

$$\Pi I_{ERG=SBM(G)}(x_o, y_o, \widetilde{p}, \widetilde{w}) = \frac{\Pi I_{ERG=SBM(G)}(x_o, y_o, p, w)_\$}{\delta_{(12,12,2,1)}} = \frac{2_\$}{12_\$} = \frac{1}{6}$$
$$= AI_{ERG=SBM(G)}(x_o, y_o, \widetilde{p}, \widetilde{w}).$$

Next, Table 7.1 summarizes the numerical results of Example 7.1. We start incorporating to the table column 1 that identifies the firms being analyzed, starting with the three efficient units. Next columns 2, 3, and 4 show the best projection, the technical inefficiency, and the profit inefficiency associated to each firm. The value of the normalizing factor follows in column 5, where we can appreciate how different they are. Columns 6 and 7 provide the two components of the profit inefficiency decomposition, the technical profit inefficiency, and the allocative profit inefficiency, which are related to columns 3 and 4. Finally, the last two columns provide two components of the normalized profit inefficiency decomposition, which appears in column 8, and the allocative inefficiency in column 9. On the other hand, in row 2, we have entered the number of each column in brackets, as well as the arithmetic relationship of the values of each column with the previous ones.

As we have point out when analyzing firm (10,5), if we had maintained the initial projection, its associated allocative inefficiency would not have been zero but positive. The reader can easily verify that, for the rest of the firms that have changed their initial projection—firms (10,5), (12,2), (12,8), and (24,4)—the allocative inefficiency would also have been higher, which is quite reasonable.

As a final comment, we would like to point out that only half of the firms that are projected on (6,10), the unique profit-maximizing unit that has obviously an allocative inefficiency equal to zero, get the same allocative inefficiency value, while the other half—firms (12,2), (12,8), and (24,4)—get a positive allocative inefficiency. This unexpected result shows that the ERG=SBM does not comply with the essential property introduced in Sect. 2.4.5 of Chap. 2, and consequently, it does not satisfy its extended version either. The solution to this question will be offered and explained later on in Chap. 13. It certainly justifies the development of

Table 7.1 Results based on the decomposition of Aparicio et al. (2017a, b, c), $(p, w) = (2,1)$

Firm	Best projection	TI	ΠI	NF	TΠI= TI × NF	AΠI= ΠI − TΠI	ΠI/NF	AI
(1)	(2)	(3)	(4)	(5)	(6)=(3)× (5)	(7)=(4)− (6)	(8)=(4)/ (5)	(9)=(7)/ (5)
A=(3,5), eff.	(3,5)	0	7	3	0	7	7/3	7/3
B=(6,10), eff.	(6,10)	0	0	6	0	6	0	0
C=(12,12), eff.	(12,12)	0	2	12	0	2	1/6	1/6
D=(3,2)	(3,5)	3/5	13	15/2	9/2	17/2	26/15	17/15
E=(9,10)	(6,10)	1/3	3	9	3	0	1/3	0
F=(10,5)	(6,10)	7/10	14	20	14	0	7/10	0
G=(12,2)	(6,10)	9/10	22	20	18	4	11/10	2/10
H=(12,8)	(6,10)	3/5	10	15	9	1	2/3	1/15
I=(24,4)	(6,10)	9/10	30	20	18	12	3/2	3/5

an alternative and more accurate normalized profit inefficiency decomposition, presented at the mentioned chapter.

7.4 The Input-Oriented *ERG=SBM* and the Decomposition of Cost Inefficiency

Model (7.1) defines the graph *ERG=SBM(G)*. Similarly, the ERG=SBM input measure of technical efficiency, denoted as $ERG = SBM(I)$, is formulated as follows:

$$
\begin{aligned}
& TE_{ERG=SBM(I)}(x_o, y_o) = \min_{\theta,\lambda} \frac{1}{M}\sum_{m=1}^{M}\theta_m \\
& s.t. \\
& \sum_{j=1}^{J}\lambda_j x_{jm} = \theta_m x_{om}, \qquad m = 1, \ldots, M \\
& \sum_{j=1}^{J}\lambda_j y_{jn} \geq y_{on}, \qquad n = 1, \ldots, N \\
& \sum_{j=1}^{J}\lambda_j = 1, \\
& \theta_m \leq 1, \qquad m = 1, \ldots, M \\
& \lambda_j \geq 0, \qquad j = 1, \ldots, J.
\end{aligned}
\tag{7.13}
$$

The input efficiency measure $ERG = SBM(I)$ overlaps with the Russell measure of input efficiency, as originally defined by Färe et al. (1985). In fact, model (7.13) is exactly the same as model (5.11). Consequently, since the properties of model (7.13) appear already listed in Chap. 5, we are not going to repeat them.

We may even consider the slack version of the $ERG = SBM(I)$, obtained by considering the change of variables proposed in (7.2) limited to the input variables, that is $\theta_m = \frac{x_{om} - s_m^-}{x_{om}} = 1 - \frac{s_m^-}{x_{om}}, s_m^- \geq 0, m = 1, \ldots, M$. Hence, the alternative slack formulation to (7.13) is the next one:

$$\begin{aligned}
TE_{ERG=SBM(I)}(x_o, y_o) = & \min_{s^-, \lambda} 1 - \frac{1}{M} \sum_{m=1}^{M} \frac{s_m^-}{x_{mo}} \\
s.t. & \\
\sum_{j=1}^{J} \lambda_j x_{jm} = x_{om} - s_m^-, & \quad m = 1, \ldots, M \\
\sum_{j=1}^{J} \lambda_j y_{jn} \geq y_{on}, & \quad n = 1, \ldots, N \\
\sum_{j=1}^{J} \lambda_j = 1, & \\
s_m^- \geq 0, & \quad m = 1, \ldots, M \\
\lambda_j \geq 0, & \quad j = 1, \ldots, J.
\end{aligned} \tag{7.14}$$

This input-oriented measure does not generate any slack on the input side since each input is reduced as much as possible, but it may generate slacks on the output side. Hence, in principle, the projection of any non-efficient point may be an output-weak efficient point.[14] However, for analyzing the cost inefficiency of a specific firm (x_o, y_o), we do not consider the entire production possibility set under variable returns to scale, T, but the so-called input set, defined as $L(y_o) := \{x : (x, y_o) \in T\}$; see Chap. 2. Consequently, the projection we want to identify by means of (7.13) must belong to $L(y_o)$ and is expressed as $(\widehat{x}_o, y_o) = \left(\theta_1^* x_{o1}, \ldots, \theta_M^* x_{oM}, y_o\right)$. The same happens with model (7.14), where the projection of firm (x_o, y_o) is expressed as $(\widehat{x}_o, y_o) = \left(x_{o1} - s_1^{-*}, \ldots, x_{oM} - s_M^{-*}, y_o\right)$.[15]

[14] An output-weak efficient point is a point whose projection on the strong efficient frontier by means of the additive model only identifies nonzero output slacks.

[15] It may happen that the projection identified by either of the last two models gets an optimal projection with an output value $\sum_{j=1}^{J} \lambda_j^* y_j \geq y_o$ but different from y_o. But since $\left(\widehat{x}_o, \sum_{j=1}^{J} \lambda_j^* y_j\right) \geq (\widehat{x}_o, y_o)$ and we are sure that the obtained projection belongs to T, the properties of T guarantee that $(\widehat{x}_o, y_o)$ also belongs to T, and consequently, it belongs to $L(y_o)$.

The corresponding input inefficiency measure associated with models (7.13) or (7.14) is $TI_{ERG=SBM(I)}(x_o, y_o) = 1 - \frac{1}{M}\sum_{m=1}^{M}\theta_m^* = \frac{1}{M}\sum_{m=1}^{M}\frac{s_m^{-*}}{x_{om}}$, a value greater than or equal to zero and less than one. In case it is equal to zero, it signals that the point being rated belongs to the strong frontier of the corresponding input set.

Example 7.2
Let us now consider the next "two input-one output example" with nine firms, where all firms have the same output value y_o. This decision simplifies our calculus, because $L(y_o)$ and $C(y_o, w)$ are a common subset and a common value for all the firms of this example. Hence, since we are going to use an input-oriented measure, it is sufficient to consider for each firm its two inputs. Here is the sample of nine firms: A = (2,10), B = (4,6), C = (6,3), D = (8,2), E = (10,2), F = (12,6), G = (16,12), H = (8,12), and I = (6,16). Figure 7.2 illustrates the example, including the minimum isocost line.

Under VRS, we get that the first four firms are strongly efficient and that the last five firms are inefficient.[16] Graphically, we appreciate that the strong efficient frontier has three facets, respectively defined by the pair of firms {(8,2),(6,3)}, {(6,3),(4,6)}, and {(4,6),(2,10)}. We will see later on that the rest of the firms are inefficient, being only one of them, firm (10,2), weakly efficient. Let us further assume that the market input costs (per firm) are $w = (w_1, w_2) = (2, 1)$. Hence, at

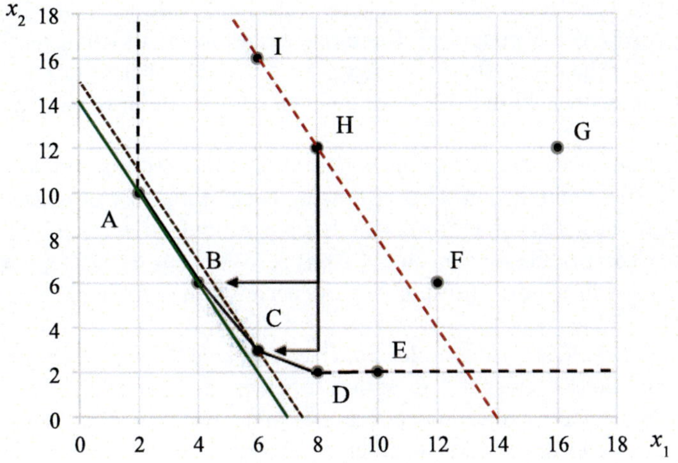

Fig. 7.2 Example of the *ERG=SBM* (*I*) cost inefficiency decomposition, $w = (2, 1)$

[16] Since the measure we are using is a strong efficient measure, we can use to classify the firms the—simplest—additive model or, alternatively, draw a picture in the two-input plane to see geometrically the position of the firms; see Fig. 7.2.

Table 7.2 Results based on the input-oriented *ERG=SBM (I)*, $w = (2, 1)$

Firm	Project RM(I)	*TI*	*CI*	*NF*	*TCI=TI*×NF	*ACI=CI−TCI*	*CI/NF*	*AI=ACI/NF*
(1)	(2)	(3)	(4)	(5)	(6)=(3)×(5)	(7)=(4)−(6)	(8)=(4)/(5)	(9)=(7)/(5)
A=(2,10)	(2,10)	0	0	8	0	0	0	0
B=(4,6)	(4,6)	0	0	12	0	0	0	0
C=(6,3)	(6,3)	0	15−14=1	6	0	1	1/6	1/6
D=(8,2)	(8,2)	0	4	4	0	4	1	1
E=(10,2)	(8,2)	1/10	8	4	2/5	38/5	8/4=2	19/10
F=(12,6)	(6,3)	1/2	16	12	6	10	16/12=4/3	5/6
G=(16,12)	(6,3)	11/16	30	24	33/2	27/2	30/24=5/4	27/48
H=(8,12)	(4,6)	1/2	14	24	12	2	7/12	1/12
I=(6,16)	(2,10)	25/48	14	24	25/2	3/2	7/12	1/16

each efficient firm, (8,2), (6,3), (4,6), and (2,10), the cost is equal to 16+2=18, 15, 14, and 14, which means that the two *cost-minimizing efficient firms* are (4,6) and (2,10), and consequently, all the points that belong to its facet are also cost-minimizing points. The technical inefficiency for firm (x_o, y_o) is equal to $\frac{1}{2} \times \left(\frac{s_{o1}^{-*}}{x_{o1}} + \frac{s_{o2}^{-*}}{x_{o2}}\right)$, and the general normalizing factor, according to Chap. 6, is equal to $M \cdot \min\{x_{o1}w_1, \ldots, x_{oM}w_M\}$, which simplifies when dealing with two inputs to $2 \cdot \min\{x_{o1}w_1, x_{o2}w_2\}$.[17] Let us analyze Table 7.2, indicating that two of our inefficient firms get a couple of alternative projections, which means that the input-Russell technical inefficiency associated to each inefficient firm is the same for its two projections. Firm F(12,6) has the option to choose between efficient firms (8,2) and (6,3), while firm H(8,12) has (6,3) and (4,6) as options. Since any of the two projections in the two cases gives rise to different decompositions, we have selected the "best" projection. Hence, looking back at the cost associated to each efficient firm calculated before, we conclude that we should prefer as projection for F (12,6) firm C(6,3), while for firm H(8,12), our best choice is firm B(4,6), which is a cost-minimizing firm—the corresponding isocost lines for (4,6), (6,3), and (8,12) are shown in Fig. 7.2.

Some particularities of the results contained in Table 7.2 are worth mentioning. All the projections correspond to strong efficient firms of $L(y_o)$. The last two inefficient firms whose projection corresponds to the two cost-minimizing firms do not achieve an allocative inefficiency equal to zero; see last column. Hence, the input-oriented Russell measure or, equivalently, the input-oriented $ERG = SBM(I)$ does not satisfy the *essential property* introduced in Sect. 2.4.5 of Chap. 2.

[17] Let us point out that the normalizing factor of the traditional approach does only depend on the input components of the firm being rated and on their market costs, which shows that in case of multiple projections, any of them will give rise to the same normalized cost decomposition.

Consequently, this measure does not meet the extended version of the essential property either. From the point of view of the cost inefficiency, we appreciate certain regularity between columns 3 and 4 of Table 7.2: a bigger technical inefficiency almost corresponds to a bigger cost inefficiency. It can be better explained looking at the *cost inefficiency decomposition*, where its technical part is much bigger than its allocative part, at least for the last four firms; see columns 4, 6, and 7. A final comment: suppose for a moment that we choose as projection of firm (12,6) the other possibility, firm (8,2). If we revise in Table 7.2 the row associated to (12,6), with the exception of the second column, the rest of the data will not vary: the technical inefficiency, in column 3, is just the same, by definition. The cost inefficiency, in column 4, is the same because it depends only on the firm (12,6) and on the minimum cost, independent of the projection used. The normalization factor, in the next column, only depends on the firm and on the costs; see its expression above. And, finally, the rest of the columns, being derived from the former five, only depend on the firm being rated and on its technical inefficiency and not on its projection. As a matter of fact, the normalized cost inefficiency decomposition relates column 8, the normalized cost inefficiency with column 3, the technical inefficiency, through the corresponding Fenchel-Mahler inequality, deriving the allocative inefficiency in column 9 as a residual value. The conclusion is surprising: on the one hand, the cost inefficiency decomposition and the normalized cost inefficiency decomposition are the same, independent of the projections considered for the firms with more than one projection, as is the case with firms F and H in Example 7.2, which gives rise to two opposite conclusions. The positive one is that the uniqueness of the cost inefficiency decompositions is guaranteed, independent of the projection used for calculating them. The negative one is that a "better" projection does not modify the allocative cost inefficiency nor the allocative inefficiency.[18]

7.5 The Output-Oriented ERG=SBM and the Decomposition of Revenue Inefficiency

Going back to graph *ERG=SBM(G)* model defined in (7.1), we could derive its output-oriented version just as we did with its input-oriented version, in which case we would obtain as new objective function to be minimized the expression $\left(\frac{1}{N}\sum_{n=1}^{N}\phi_n\right)^{-1}$, with the corresponding linear restrictions. Since minimizing the last expression is equivalent to maximizing its inverse, the ERG=SBM output measure of technical efficiency, denoted as $ERG = SBM(O)$, is formulated next:

[18] Obviously, when dealing with single-value inefficiency measures, the negative conclusion cannot be formulated.

$$TE_{ERG=SBM(O)}(x_o, y_o) = \max_{\phi,\lambda} \frac{1}{N}\sum_{n=1}^{N}\phi_n$$

$$\begin{aligned}
&s.t. \\
&\sum_{j=1}^{J}\lambda_j x_{jm} \le x_{om}, && m = 1, \ldots, M \\
&\sum_{j=1}^{J}\lambda_j y_{jn} = \phi_n y_{on}, && n = 1, \ldots, N \\
&\sum_{j=1}^{J}\lambda_j = 1, \\
&\lambda_j \ge 0, && j = 1, \ldots, J \\
&\phi_n \ge 1, && n = 1, \ldots, N.
\end{aligned} \tag{7.15}$$

This formulation corresponds exactly with the output-oriented Russell measure; see Chap. 5. We can also rewrite it by considering only the change of output variables proposed in (7.2), $\phi_n = \frac{y_{on}+s_n^+}{y_{on}} = 1 + \frac{s_n^+}{y_{on}}, s_n^+ \ge 0, n = 1, \ldots, N$, obtaining the next equivalent formulation:

$$TE_{ERG=SBM(O)}(x_o, y_o) = \max_{s^+,\lambda} 1 + \frac{1}{N}\sum_{n=1}^{N}\frac{s_n^+}{y_{on}}$$

$$\begin{aligned}
&s.t. \\
&\sum_{j=1}^{J}\lambda_j x_{jm} \le x_{om}, && m = 1, \ldots, M \\
&\sum_{j=1}^{J}\lambda_j y_{jn} = y_{on} + s_n^+, && n = 1, \ldots, N \\
&\sum_{j=1}^{J}\lambda_j = 1, \\
&\lambda_j \ge 0, && j = 1, \ldots, J \\
&s_n^+ \ge 0, && n = 1, \ldots, N.
\end{aligned} \tag{7.16}$$

It is clear that this output-oriented measure does not generate any slack on the output side since each input is increased as much as possible, but it may generate slacks on the input side. Hence, in principle, the projection of any non-efficient point may be an input-weak efficient point.[19] However, for analyzing the revenue inefficiency of a specific firm (x_o, y_o), we do not consider the entire production possibility

[19] An input-weak efficient point is a point whose projection on the strong efficient frontier by means of the additive model only identifies nonzero input slacks.

set under variable returns to scale, T, but the so-called output set, defined as $P(x_o) := \{y : (x_o, y) \in T\}$; see Chap. 2. Consequently, the projection we want to identify by means of either of the two equivalent last models must belong to $P(x_o)$ and can be expressed in two ways, according to the model used, that is $(x_o, \widehat{y}_o) = (x_o, \phi_1^* y_{o1}, \ldots, \phi_N^* y_{oN}) = (x_o, y_{o1} + s_1^{+*}, \ldots, y_{oN} + s_N^{+*})$.[20]

The corresponding output inefficiency measure associated to models (7.15) or (7.16) is $TI_{ERG=SBM(O)}(x_o, y_o) = \frac{1}{N}\sum_{n=1}^{N}\phi_n = \frac{1}{N}\sum_{n=1}^{N}\frac{s_n^+}{y_{on}}$, a value greater or equal to zero.[21] In case it is equal to zero, the point being rated belongs to the strong frontier of the corresponding output set.

Example 7.3

Let us once again remind the reader that *the output-oriented ERG=SBM* coincides with the Russell output measure presented in Chap. 5. Let us now consider the next "one input-two output example" with nine firms, where all the inputs take the same value; let's say x'. Hence, $P(x')$ and $R(x', p)$ are a common subset and a common value for all the firms of this example. Moreover, since we are going to use an output-oriented measure, it is sufficient to consider for each firm its two outputs. Here are the output values for all the firms of our finite sample: A = (4,8), B = (8,6), C = (12,2), D = (2,1), E = (2,4), F = (4,2), G = (4,6), H = (6,4), and I = (10,2). Figure 7.3 illustrates the example, including the maximum isorevenue line.

The first three firms are strongly efficient, and the last six firms are output-inefficient.[22] Graphically, we appreciate that the strong efficient frontier has two facets, respectively defined by the pair of firms {(4,8), (8,6)} and {(8,6), (12,2)}. Let us further assume that the market output prices are $p = (p_1, p_2) = (1, 2)$. Hence, at each efficient firm, (4,8), (8,6), and (12,2), the revenue is equal to 20, 20, and 16, which means that the two *revenue-maximizing efficient firms* are (4,8) and (8,6); consequently, all the points that belong to this facet are also revenue-maximizing points. The *output-oriented ERG=SBM* technical inefficiency for firm (x_o, y_o) is equal to $\frac{1}{2}\left(\frac{s_{o1}^{++}}{y_{o1}} + \frac{s_{o2}^{++}}{y_{o2}}\right)$, and the corresponding normalizing factor, according to Aparicio et al. (2015a) (see Chap. 5), is equal to $N \cdot \min\{p_1 y_{o1}, \ldots, p_N y_{oN}\}$, which simplifies in our case to $2 \cdot \min\{y_{o1}, 2y_{o2}\}$. Before revising the results gathered in

[20] It may happen that the projection identified by model (7.13) gets an optimal projection with an input value $\sum_{j=1}^{J}\lambda_j^* x_j \leq x_o$ but different from x_o. But since $\left(\sum_{j=1}^{J}\lambda_j^* x_j, \widehat{y}_o\right) \leq (x_o, \widehat{y}_o)$ and the obtained projection belong to T, the properties of T guarantee that $(x_o, \widehat{y}_o)$ also belongs to T, and consequently, it belongs to $P(x_o)$.

[21] Since we are assuming a VRS technology, each optimal slack is upper bounded. Being more precise, for firm (x_o, y_o), its vector of optimal output slack s^{++} is upper bounded by $Y - y_o$, where Y is the vector of maximum output values over the sample of firms.

[22] Since the measure we are using is a strong efficient measure, we can use to classify the firms the additive model or even draw a picture, like Fig. 7.3, in the two output planes to see geometrically the location of the firms.

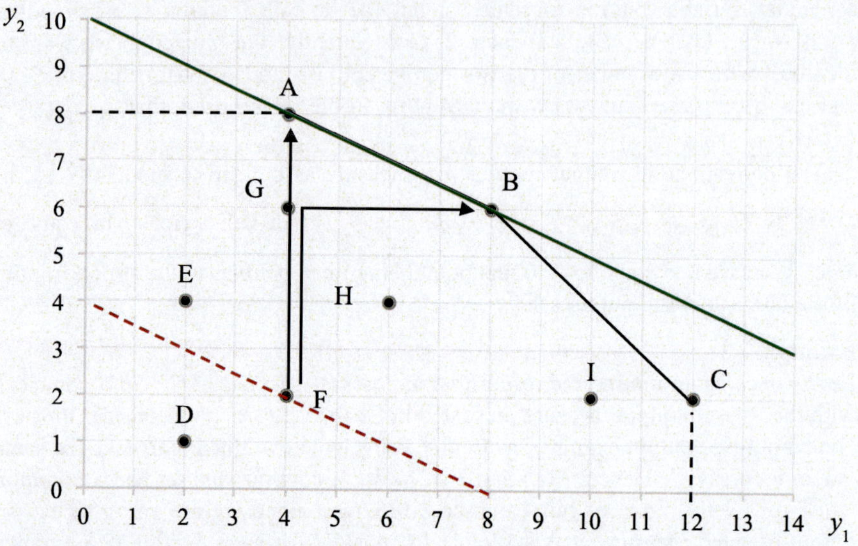

Fig. 7.3 Example of the $ERG = SBM(O)$ revenue inefficiency decomposition, $p = (1, 2)$

Table 7.3 Results based on the output-oriented *ERG=SBM* (*O*), $p = (1, 2)$

Firm	Project.	*TI*	*RI*	*NF*	*TRI=NF×TI*	*ARI=RI−TRI*	*RI/NF*	*AI=ARI/NF*
(1)	(2)	(3)	(4)	(5)	(6)=(3)×(5)	(7)=(4)−(6)	(8)= (4)/(5)	(9)= (7)/(5)
A=(4,8)	(4,8)	0	0	8	0	0	0	0
B=(8,6)	(8,6)	0	0	16	0	0	0	0
C=(12,2)	(12,2)	0	4	8	0	4	1/2	1/2
D=(2,1)	(8,6)*	4	16	4	16	0	4	0
E=(2,4)	(8,6)	7/4	10	4	7	3	5/2	3/4
F=(4,2)	(8,6)*	3/2	12	8	12	0	3/2	0
G=(4,6)	(4,8)	1/2	4	8	4	0	1/2	0
H=(6,4)	(8,6)	5/12	6	12	5	1	1/2	1/12
I=(10,2)	(10,4)	1/2	6	8	4	2	3/4	1/4

Table 7.3, let us remind the reader that the Russell output-oriented measure may produce multiple projections. In our case, there are two of our inefficient firms that get a couple of alternative projections, which means that the technical inefficiency associated to these inefficient firm is the same for its two projections. Firms (2,1) and (4,2) have the same double option between efficient firms (8,6) and (4,8)—as shown by the projecting lines for the latter. The choice is initially easy because we are involved in a revenue-maximizing process: we should take as projection the one that has maximum revenue, but in this particular case, both projections are revenue-maximizing firms. Considering that the actual production plan of each firms is more

similar to (8,6), we decided to select it as the projection of both firms[23]. Let us consider the next table and make some comments on it.

First of all, let us comment that the projection of the last firm, (10,2), is a point that without belonging to our sample of nine firms is obtained as the convex combination of two of the efficient firms, $\frac{1}{2}(8,6)+\frac{1}{2}(12,2)$. We will use it very soon when analyzing the allocative inefficiency. The first two columns are devoted, as usual, to identify each firm and its output-oriented *ERG=SBM* projection. The next three columns report the items that integrate the Fenchel-Mahler inequality: column 3 reports the output-oriented *ERG=SBM technical inefficiency* scores, column 4 the *revenue inefficiency*, and Column 5 the *normalization factor*. With respect to *the revenue inefficiency decomposition*, we have to consider columns 4, 6, and 7. Column 6, *the technical revenue inefficiency*, is just the product of columns 3 and 5, row by row. Moreover, column 7, *the allocative revenue inefficiency*, is retrieved as a residual from columns 4 and 6. It is curious that all the firms that have the same projection do not get the same value in column 7.[24] The third column, together with the two last columns, reports the values of *the normalized revenue inefficiency decomposition*. The story is similar to the one explained for the non-normalized decomposition, and the five firms of the sample that get a zero value as allocative revenue inefficiency get the same numerical value, 0, for *the allocative inefficiency. The essential property*, discussed in Sect. 2.4.5 of Chap. 2, does not hold—violated by firms (2,4) and (6,4)—and since the normalizing factors are different, the three terms of the normalized revenue inefficiency cannot be compared between firms. If the essential property does not hold, then its extended version does not hold either. However, *the revenue inefficiency decomposition* allows always comparing firms, and this is one of his virtues. At the firm level, two efficient firms—A and B—are revenue maximizers, with their three normalized components at level 0. The third efficient firm, (12,2), has obviously zero as technical inefficiency, which means that its normalized revenue inefficiency, 1/2, is all allocative. Moreover, the first five inefficient firms have all the same projection, firm (8,6). Three of them show an allocative inefficiency equal to zero, just as their common projection, but the other two have nonzero allocative values. However, the last firm has to this respect a nice behavior. The same convex combination that applies for locating it in the facet determined by (8,6) and (12,2) is useful for relating their allocative inefficiencies: $\frac{1}{4}=\frac{1}{2}\times 0+\frac{1}{2}\times\frac{1}{2}$. We can see clearly in column 4 that there are three highly *revenue-inefficient firms*, with values in the interval (10,16), and other three moderately inefficient, with values in the interval (4,6). On the other hand, the *technical revenue inefficiencies* are quite similar to the revenue

[23] Since the normalizing factor is independent of the projection, we can choose any of them for the two mentioned firms with double projections. Hence, the uniqueness of the revenue inefficiency decompositions is guaranteed in this case, being independent of the assigned projection. We have add an asterisk to the projection of each of this two units in Table 7.3 to indicate that a second projection is possible.

[24] This property is always satisfied by the general direct approach, as we are going to show very soon.

inefficiencies but follow a slightly different pattern, with just two highly inefficient firms with values in the interval (12,16) and another four moderately inefficient, with values in the range (4,7). As a consequence, the *allocative revenue inefficiency* is mostly equal to zero, and the remaining four firms present moderate values in the range (1,4). With respect to the *normalized revenue decomposition*, three firms—D, E, and F—have their revenue inefficiency bigger than one. The same three units are the ones that have also their *technical inefficiency* bigger than one, while all the units have their *allocative inefficiency* below one.

7.6 Empirical Illustration of the ERG=SBM Profit Inefficiency Model

Beyond the particular examples presented in the previous section to illustrate different particularities of the *ERG*=*SBM* model, in this section, we resort to the common examples that we solve in each chapter to show the implementation of the different economic measures and their decompositions in the "Benchmarking Economic Efficiency" package programmed in the Julia language. Since the *ERG*=*SBM* model coincides with its Russell precursor in the case of the partial input and output orientations, both the cost and revenue inefficiency decompositions correspond to those already presented in Chap. 5. Therefore, here, we present only the calculation of the profit inefficiency measure using the data in Table 7.4 see below, which are commented in Sect. 2.5 of Chap. 2.

The package function computing the *ERG*=*SBM(G)* measure of profit inefficiency is `deaprofiterg(X, Y, W, P, names = FIRMS)`. We rely on the open (web-based) Jupyter Notebook interface to illustrate the profit inefficiency model. However, it can be implemented in any integrated development environment (IDE)

Table 7.4 Example data illustrating the economic inefficiency models

	Model	
	Graph profit model	
Firm	x	y
A	2	1
B	4	5
C	8	8
D	12	9
E	6	3
F	14	7
G	14	9
H	9.412	2.353
Prices	w=1	p=2

Table 7.5 Implementation of the *ERG=SBM(G)* profit inefficiency model using BEE for Julia

In[]:

```
using DataEnvelopmentAnalysis
using BechmarkingEconomicEfficiency

X = [2; 4; 8; 12; 6; 14; 14; 9.412];
Y = [1; 5; 8; 9; 3; 7; 9; 2.353];
W = [1; 1; 1; 1; 1; 1; 1; 1];
P = [2; 2; 2; 2; 2; 2; 2; 2];
FIRMS = ["A";"B";"C";"D";"E";"F";"G";"H"];

deaprofiterg(X, Y, W, P, names = FIRMS)
```

Out[]:

```
Enhanced Russell Graph Slack Based Measure Profit DEA Model
DMUs = 8; Inputs = 1; Outputs = 1
Returns to Scale = VRS
```

	Profit	Technical	Allocative
A	4.0	0.0	4.0
B	0.5	0.0	0.5
C	0.0	0.0	0.0
D	0.167	0.0	0.167
E	0.8	0.6	0.2
F	0.571	0.524	0.048
G	0.286	0.143	0.143
H	1.270	0.8	0.471

of preference.[25] To calculate the *ERG=SBM* profit inefficiency model (7.11), enter the following code in the "`In[]:`" panel, and run it. The corresponding results are shown in the "`Out[]:`" panel in last Table 7.5 above.

We can learn about the reference peers for each firm using the "peersmatrix" function with the corresponding economic or technical model. For the profit model, executing "`peersmatrix(deaprofiterg(X, Y, W, P, names = FIRMS))`" identifies firm C as the reference benchmark maximizing profit for the rest of the firms (see Fig. 7.4).

As for the underlying *ERG=SBM(G)* graph technical efficiency model (7.5), we can obtain all the information running the corresponding function, as shown in Table 7.6 below.

Besides the technical inefficiency scores, the result window reports the value of β (beta) in (7.5). From this program, we can recover the values of the slacks s_{mo}^- and s_{no}^+ reported above, relying on the ancillary variables t_m^- and t_n^+ and expression (7.4)—note that if $\beta = 1$, then $s_m^- = t_m^-$ and $s_n^+ = t_n^+$. It is also of interest to identify the reference benchmarks of the *ERG=SBM* graph technical efficiency measure corresponding to

[25]We refer the reader to Sect. 2.6.1 in Chap. 2 for the installation of the "Benchmarking Economic Efficiency" Julia package. All Jupyter Notebooks implementing the different economic models in this book can be downloaded from the reference site: http://www.benchmarkingeconomicefficiency.com.

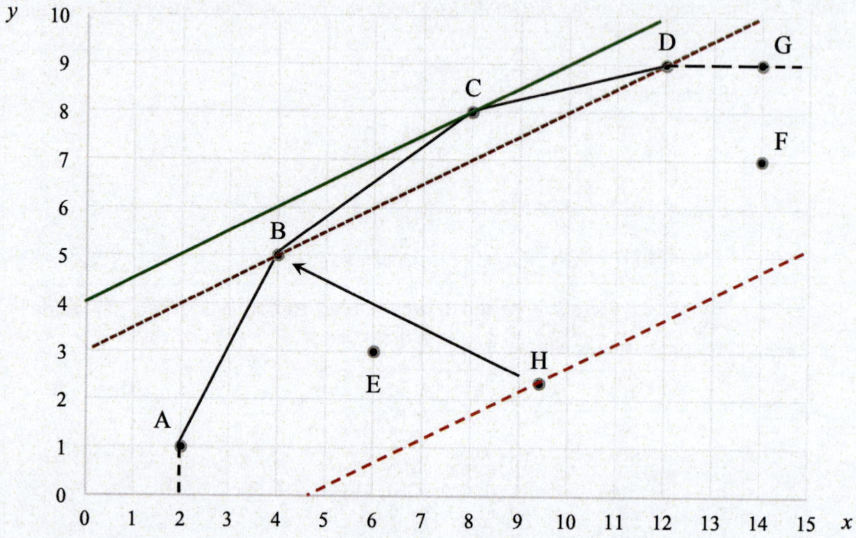

Fig. 7.4 Example of the *ERG=SBM* profit inefficiency model using BEE for Julia

Table 7.6 Implementation of the *ERG=SBM* graph inefficiency measure using BEE for Julia

```
In[]:   deaerg(X, Y, rts  = :VRS, names = FIRMS)

Out[]:  Enhanced Russell Graph (or Slack Based Measure) DEA Model
        DMUs = 8; Inputs = 1; Outputs = 1
        Orientation = Input; Returns to Scale = VRS
        ──────────────────────────────────────────────
             efficiency   beta   slackX1   slackY1
        ──────────────────────────────────────────────
        A    1.0          1.0    0.0       0.0
        B    1.0          1.0    0.0       0.0
        C    1.0          1.0    0.0       0.0
        D    1.0          1.0    0.0       0.0
        E    0.4          0.6    2.0       2.0
        F    0.476        1.0    7.333     0.0
        G    0.857        1.0    2.0       0.0
        H    0.2          0.471  5.412     2.647
        ──────────────────────────────────────────────
```

program (7.5). We make use once again of the "peers" function, i.e., "`peersmatrix(deaerg(X, Y, rts  = :VRS, names = FIRMS))`". The output results shown in Table 7.7 below ("`Out[]:`") identify firms A, B, C, and D as those conforming the strongly efficient production possibility set, i.e., those with unit values in the main diagonal of the square ($J \times J$) matrix containing their own intensity variables λ (note the matrix syntax in "`In[]:`").

Table 7.7 Reference peers of the *ERG=SBM* graph inefficiency measure using BEE for Julia

```
In[]:    peersmatrix(deaerg(X, Y, rts  = :VRS, names = FIRMS))

Out[]:   1.0   .      .      .    .    .    .    .
          .   1.0     .      .    .    .    .    .
          .    .     1.0     .    .    .    .    .
          .    .      .     1.0   .    .    .    .
          .   1.0     .      .    .    .    .    .
          .   0.333  0.667   .    .    .    .    .
          .    .      .     1.0   .    .    .    .
          .   1.0     .      .    .    .    .    .
```

Figure 7.4 illustrates the results for the Russell profit inefficiency model. There, for firm H, we identify that its normalized profit inefficiency with respect to firm C, according (7.10), is equal to 1.271=[8−(−4.706)]/[2×2.353×(1+2.647/2.353)]. Profit inefficiency can be decomposed into the *ERG=SBM* measure of technical inefficiency and the residual allocative inefficiency. As for technical inefficiency, this value is equal to one minus the *ERG=SBM(G)* technical efficiency score: $0.8 = TI_{ERG\,=\,SBM(G)}(x_H, y_H) = 1 - 0.2 = 1 - TE_{ERG\,=\,SBM(G)}(x_H, y_H)$, with the latter value being that reported in Table 7.6. The difference between the profit and technical inefficiencies yields 0.471 as allocative inefficiency: 0.471 = 1.271 − 0.8.

7.6.1 An Application to the Taiwanese Banking Industry

We conclude this empirical section solving the economic decomposition of profit inefficiency based on the Russell technical efficiency measure for the panel of 31 Taiwanese banks observed in 2010; see Juo et al. (2015). A brief presentation of the data, including descriptive statistics, can be found in Sect. 2.5.2 of Chap. 2. We remark that we are using these data only as an example and therefore do not aim at analyzing the economic results of the Taiwanese banking industry or any individual bank. The dataset includes individual prices for each firm. Here, we follow the standard approach that finds the maximum profit for the firm under evaluation using its observed prices. Hence, a firm can be profit-inefficient under its own prices yet maximize profit under other firm's prices, serving as reference peer (and vice versa).

Table 7.8 below presents the values of the profit inefficiency in the second column, including its descriptive statistics at the bottom. In this model, profit inefficiency is normalized by the denominator in equation (7.10), including firm-specific prices w_{om} and p_{on}, i.e., corresponding to $\delta_{(x_o,y_o,p,w)}\left(1+\frac{1}{N}\sum_{n=1}^{N}\frac{s_n^{+*}}{y_{on}}\right)$, where $\delta_{(x_o,y_o,p,w)} = \min\{Np_{on}y_{on}, n = 1, \ldots, N, Mw_{om}x_{om}, m = 1, \ldots, M\}$. This means that the industry does not face exogenously determined market prices, but they

Table 7.8 Decomposition of profit inefficiency based on the *ERG=SBM(G)* efficiency measure

Bank	Economic inefficiency, eq. (7.10)			Technical Efficiency, eqs. (7.5) and (7.4)						
	Profit Ineff. $N\Pi I\,(x_o, y_o, \tilde{w}, \tilde{p})$	Technical Ineff. $TI\,(x_o, y_o)$	Allocative Ineff. $AI\,(x_o, y_o; \tilde{w}, \tilde{p})$	Technical Eff. $TE\,(x_o, y_o)$	Beta β	Funds (x_1) s_1^-	Labor (x_2) s_2^-	Ph. Capital (x_3) s_3^-	Investments (y_1) s_1^+	Loans (y_2) s_2^+
1	0.000	0.000	0.000	1.000	1.000	0.0	0.0	0.0	0.0	0.0
2	0.300	0.000	0.300	1.000	1.000	0.0	0.0	0.0	0.0	0.0
3	0.550	0.000	0.550	1.000	1.000	0.0	0.0	0.0	0.0	0.0
4	2.751	0.783	1.968	0.217	0.222	1,680.2	0.0	129.2	117,345.0	0.0
5	0.000	0.000	0.000	1.000	1.000	0.0	0.0	0.0	0.0	0.0
6	0.712	0.000	0.712	1.000	1.000	0.0	0.0	0.0	0.0	0.0
7	0.565	0.000	0.565	1.000	1.000	0.0	0.0	0.0	0.0	0.0
8	0.558	0.208	0.351	0.792	1.000	62,264.6	1,594.1	8,968.7	0.0	0.0
9	0.987	0.364	0.623	0.636	0.887	0.0	2,071.2	12,530.9	65,394.4	0.0
10	0.000	0.000	0.000	1.000	1.000	0.0	0.0	0.0	0.0	0.0
11	1.219	0.593	0.626	0.407	0.669	262,932.0	2,101.0	16,042.7	160,570.0	0.0
12	2.669	0.257	2.412	0.743	0.977	84,708.6	0.0	5,833.0	10,933.0	0.0
13	4.581	0.934	3.647	0.066	0.109	28,607.9	1,123.7	5,671.8	225,670.0	0.0
14	0.942	0.000	0.942	1.000	1.000	0.0	0.0	0.0	0.0	0.0
15	0.925	0.217	0.708	0.783	1.000	150,628.0	681.6	4,857.9	0.0	0.0
16	10.581	0.988	9.593	0.012	0.029	32,486.0	1,118.0	4,943.0	112,761.0	2,104.0
17	2.105	0.532	1.573	0.468	0.798	56,043.9	3,130.1	11,485.8	102,533.0	0.0
18	2.744	0.416	2.328	0.584	0.718	0.0	1,395.0	402.8	86,299.5	0.0
19	3.543	0.813	2.731	0.187	0.265	13,184.2	339.9	2,457.0	148,341.0	0.0
20	4.999	0.735	4.264	0.265	0.306	58,873.3	401.0	0.0	143,014.0	0.0
21	1.210	0.000	1.210	1.000	1.000	0.0	0.0	0.0	0.0	0.0
22	7.383	0.959	6.424	0.041	0.063	0.0	515.9	6,735.0	165,582.0	0.0
23	9.245	0.981	8.264	0.019	0.030	10,089.7	324.0	5,854.6	149,088.0	0.0
24	1.377	0.279	1.098	0.721	0.830	0.0	1,277.0	1,983.4	64,649.4	0.0
25	7.711	0.877	6.835	0.123	0.130	0.0	0.0	481.7	194,898.0	0.0
26	4.773	0.000	4.773	1.000	1.000	0.0	0.0	0.0	0.0	0.0
27	15.719	0.959	14.760	0.041	0.046	1,955.9	109.7	286.0	128,784.0	0.0
28	8.362	0.942	7.420	0.058	0.077	29,993.2	504.4	0.0	89,301.6	0.0
29	3.911	0.000	3.911	1.000	1.000	0.0	0.0	0.0	0.0	0.0
30	0.763	0.227	0.537	0.773	0.920	67,084.9	1,172.7	1,349.8	46,597.5	0.0
31	2.870	0.906	1.963	0.094	0.119	0.0	636.8	3,081.9	258,025.0	0.0
Average	3.357	0.418	2.938	0.582	0.651	27,759.1	596.6	3,003.1	73,218.9	67.9
Median	2.105	0.279	1.573	0.721	0.887	0.0	324.0	402.8	64,649.4	0.0
Maximum	15.719	0.988	14.760	1.000	1.000	262,932.0	3,130.1	16,042.7	258,025.0	2,104.0
Minimum	0.000	0.000	0.000	0.012	0.029	0.0	0.0	0.0	0.0	0.0
Std. Dev.	3.743	0.398	3.457	0.398	0.408	55,722.5	801.2	4,331.4	78,937.9	377.9

differ across firms. Three banks are profit-efficient given their observed prices (no. 1, no. 5, and no. 10) and constituting the most frequent benchmarks for the remaining banks. From a technical perspective, 11 banks are efficient, while the remaining 20 banks are both technical and allocative inefficient. Technical and allocative inefficiencies are reported in the third and fourth columns of Table 7.8. In this case, average normalized profit inefficiency equals 3.357, while average technical and allocative inefficiencies are 0.418 and 2.938, respectively. Consequently, most of the normalized profit loss is attributed to allocative inefficiency, whose proportion is 87.5% versus that corresponding to technical inefficiency, 12.5%.

Finally, in the last six columns of Table 7.8, we present value of the beta parameter and the individual slacks for the three inputs and two outputs, which are obtained when solving equations (7.5) and (7.4). The resulting *ERG=SBM(G)* technical efficiency measure corresponding to the objective function of (7.5) is reported in the fifth column. Looking at the three inputs, we observe that the largest inefficiency corresponds by large to financial funds (x_1), whose average slack is 27,759.1 million TWD, followed by labor (x_2) and physical capital (x_3), whose average slacks are 596.6 employees and 3,003.1 million TWD, respectively. On the output side, financial investments (y_1) exhibit the largest inefficiency with an average slack equal to 73,218.9 million TWD, while practically, there is no inefficiency in the form of unrealized loans (y_2). Indeed, only bank (no. 16) presents a positive value of 2,104.0 million TWD. It is worth mentioning that, in this real dataset, the violation of the so-called essential property was not detected.

7.7 Summary and Conclusions

The *ERG* = *SBM* is a graph efficiency measure that admits two alternative and equivalent formulations. First, it can be formulated in terms of proportional input reductions and output expansions; see Pastor et al. (1999), which relates it conceptually with the *proportional directional distance function*, *DDF*, that uses as directional vector the observed quantities of inputs and outputs (see Sect. 8.2.1 of Chap. 8), although the different formulations of their respective objective functions give rise to rather different efficiency measures. In fact, we have seen that the *ERG* = *SBM* is a multivalue function, since more than one projection may be identified for some firms, while the *proportional DDF* is a single-value function, like any *DDF*. The *ERG* = *SBM* is conceptually closer to the *graph Russell* measure, see Färe et al. (1985), and this is the reason for calling it the enhanced *R*ussell *g*raph measure. When it was published, the *graph Russell* measure was still unsolved, and it took 22 years until Sueyoshi and Sekitani (2007a), resorting to a nonlinear program with a linear objective function, proposed a way for getting an approximate solution and 11 more years until Halická and Trnovská (2018) proposed an alternative way based on semidefinite programming for getting an exact solution. (see, to this respect, Chap. 5). The package "Benchmarking Economic Efficiency," coded in the Julia language, implements all economic models based on these measures using this last programming techniques. We illustrate their implementation in the last empirical section.

The $ERG = SBM$ can also be formulated in terms of slacks (see Pastor et al., 1999, and Tone, 2001), which relates it conceptually with the family of weighted additive models (see Chap. 6), which are likely to obtain also multiple projections. In any case, we have shown how to calculate the $ERG = SBM$ by means of a linear program, as well as to find the projection that offers the highest profit value. Unfortunately, the profit inefficiency decomposition based on the corresponding Fenchel-Mahler inequality is independent of the mentioned projection, which has as advantage the unicity of the decomposition. However, we are going to introduce in Chap. 13 a new more direct and easy way of deriving the profit inefficiency decomposition, due to Pastor et al. (2021a), that takes into account not only the technical inefficiency but also the associated efficiency projection. In some sense, we should expect that the new proposed decomposition is more accurate than the traditional one, as shown in Chap. 13.

The two derived input- and output-oriented cases, identified as $ERG = SBM(I)$ and $ERG = SBM(O)$, present a similar behavior and are also able to generate multiple projections. However, they are easier to solve than the graph case, since their formulations are directly linear programs. The corresponding cost inefficiency and revenue inefficiency decompositions present the same characteristics as the graph case. One the one hand, the good news is that the decompositions are unique, and as counterpart, the bad news is that they are unable to incorporate the knowledge of the cost or revenue conditions associated to the corresponding projection. Just as for the profit case, we recommend the reader to consider the alternative decomposition proposal, developed in Chap. 13 and identified as the *general direct approach*, which incorporates the characteristics of the corresponding projection.

Chapter 8
The Directional Distance Function (DDF): Economic Inefficiency Decompositions

8.1 Introduction

The birth of the directional distance function as an inefficiency measure was linked to the consumer theory work developed by Luenberger in the early 1990s. Luenberger (1992a) introduced the concept of the *benefit function in consumer theory* in order to develop group welfare relations and, particularly, considered the *Shephard's input distance function*, claiming that it would be useful in developing relations between individuals. Chambers et al. (1996) redefined Luenberger's benefit function as an inefficiency measure and called it *the directional input distance function*. Although mathematically related, the last two distance functions are conceptual opposites: while Shephard's distance function is *multiplicative* by nature, the directional distance function is *additive* by nature. The same happens with the *Shephard's output distance function* and *the directional output distance function*, first studied by Chung (1996) in his Ph.D. dissertation, where he also considered *undesirable outputs*, which have experienced since then a great diffusion, boosting the analysis of environmental issues. Luenberger (1992b), transposing the benefit function into a production context, defined the so-called shortage function, which basically measures the distance, in the direction of a vector g, from a production plan toward the boundary of the production possibility set. However, Luenberger interprets the distance as a shortage of the production plan to reach the frontier of T, while Chambers et al.'s (1998) interpretation was that of an inefficiency measure, giving rise to the general definition of a *directional distance function*, *DDF*, and analyzing its properties.[1,2] In the aforementioned paper, they considered three specific DDFs: the two mentioned oriented distance functions and the graph inefficiency measure of

[1] Chambers et al. interpretation was "by how much output can be expanded and input contracted remaining the production plan feasible."

[2] Initially, the *DDF* was called *the directional technology distance function*.

J. T. Pastor et al., *Benchmarking Economic Efficiency*, International Series in Operations Research & Management Science 315,
https://doi.org/10.1007/978-3-030-84397-7_8

Briec (1997) presently known as *the proportional DDF* (see Boussemart et al., 2003).

In our opinion, the conceptual and computational simplicity and flexibility of the *DDF* has facilitated its rapid dissemination and use, having promoted the development of specific tools for additive measures. For instance, the comparative measurement of economic efficiency considering ratios resorting to the multiplicative Shephard's distance functions and other multiplicative efficiency measures[3] has evolved into the comparative measurement of economic inefficiency considering addition and subtraction resorting to *DDFs.*[4] However, flexibility is a double-edged sword, and when a single directional vector is used in the same inefficiency analysis, we need to be aware that we may not be able to find the projection of firms located outside of the production possibility. In such cases, we always have the alternative option of considering a specific directional vector for each firm, but then we must worry about guaranteeing the interpretation and numerical comparability of the *DDF* inefficiencies.

Recently, the additive world has been significantly expanded with the introduction of the *reverse DDF* (*RDDF*) (Pastor et al., 2016). An improved version of the original *RDDF* is presented in Chap. 12. As a summary, efficiency measurement has partly moved from the initial multiplicative world to the rather new additive world. Very recently, a new link has been established in the opposite direction by Pastor et al. (2020): assuming *CRS*, they have *reformulated* the *proportional DDF*, an additive measure, *as an output-oriented radial measure*—a multiplicative measure—providing the first example of a *total factor productivity Malmquist index*, something that was considered a chimera for a long time.

There are other relevant contributions of Chambers et al.'s (1998) paper: the *dual relationship* between a *graph DDF and profit inefficiency*, the introduction of a new related concept, *the Nerlovian inefficiency*, and its decomposition into technical and allocative inefficiencies based on the definition of a Fenchel-Mahler inequality for the directional distance function. With respect to the dual relationship, we will also show that a parallel relation holds between an *input-oriented DDF* and *cost inefficiency* as well as between an *output-oriented DDF* and *revenue inefficiency. The Nerlovian inefficiency* concept is related to *the decomposition of economic inefficiency* associated with any firm and calculated by means of a *graph DDF*, as an extension of the previous proposal of Nerlove (1965) for radial multiplicative measures. The *Nerlovian inefficiency* is basically a *normalized economic inefficiency*, i.e., a number without any unit of measurement that *allows us to compare*

[3] In DEA, researchers have devised many efficiency measures, accounting for input and output slacks that replicate the properties of the earlier radial measures. They have also been used as multiplicative measures to determine the economic efficiency, resorting to all the tools that were devised for radial measures—see Chap. 2—or even to measure productivity, such as the Malmquist indexes (Caves et al., 1982). A collection of most of the initial measures dated before the start of the actual millennium can be found in Cooper et al. (1999).

[4] See Chap. 2 for a comparison between the original multiplicative approach to measure economic efficiencies and the more recent additive proposals—cost, revenue, or profit.

the normalized profit at each firm with its technical DDF inefficiency, which is also a pure number. It is also interesting to compare Nerlovian inefficiencies between firms, which is only possible if all the firms have the same normalization factor. We will show that this is precisely the case for a directional distance function when we make a proper choice of the sample of directional vectors.

The typical Fenchel-Mahler inequality—developed for each of the efficiency measures presented in the rest of the chapters of this book—establishes that the normalized economic inefficiency is greater or equal than the technical inefficiency. The gap between the two is precisely the so-called allocative inefficiency. Until the introduction of the so-called *essential* property and its extended version in Sect. 2.4.5 of Chap. 2, presenting the desirable characteristics that a decomposition of economic efficiency should satisfy, nobody had studied whether the gap quantifying allocative inefficiency, based on an inequality, was "too wide." To address this problem of the additive models, and following Pastor et al. (2021b), in Chap. 13 we develop a new profit decomposition that compared to the standard one benefits from the advantage that it is not based on an inequality but on an equality, which determines exactly the size of the gap. Additionally, we can relate the allocative inefficiency of the firms being rated with the profit inefficiency of its technical benchmark on the frontier. Interestingly, the *DDF* is one of the efficiency measures for which the two profit decompositions are equal, complying with the aforementioned *essential property* of economic efficiency decompositions. Moreover, the *DDF* allows the numerical comparison of the normalized profit inefficiencies of different firms as well as their allocative inefficiencies, provided the different directional vectors used give rise to the same market value.[5]

There are two issues that we deem of interest for the definition of the *DDF* and the measurement of economic inefficiency based on it. The first issue is how to select *directional vectors*, *DVs*, that provide comparable inefficiency scores between firms, which are relevant for comparing their associated economic inefficiency decompositions.[6] The second issue is a relatively recent one: what are the advantages and disadvantages of choosing nonstandard directional vectors?[7] This question was first considered by Zofío et al. (2013), who endogenized the *DV* with respect to optimal economic benchmarks, and very recently by Pastor et al. (2021b, c) in two different scenarios. All three issues are related with the choice of appropriate directional vectors showing its influence in the *DDF's* ability to properly analyze and compare firms. Clearly, to the extent that the value of the *DDF* represents the technical inefficiency, the decomposition of economic inefficiency into the technical and allocative components depends on the choice of *DVs*.

[5]The market value of the directional vector (g_x, g_y), representing the normalization factor of the DDF, is equal to $p \cdot g_y + w \cdot g_x$, where p is the vector of output prices and w the vector of input prices, common to the firms.

[6]It is also highly relevant for productivity measurement, a topic that exceeds the limits of this book.

[7]A standard directional vector finds a $\partial^W(T)$ projection by not increasing inputs and not reducing outputs.

The chapter unfolds as follows. Section 8.2 presents the definition of the *DDF*, its interpretation as measure of technical inefficiency, how it can be calculated through Data Envelopment Analysis methods, and, finally, its more relevant properties. Section 8.3 discusses the different choices for *DVs* and classifies them as *endogenous* or *exogenous*. The last three sections, Sects. 8.4, 8.5, and 8.6, study the *profit*, *cost*, and *revenue inefficiencies*, through the corresponding *DDFs* and, assuming that *market prices are known*, provide the corresponding *Nerlovian inefficiency decompositions* into technical and allocative inefficiencies. Section 8.7 illustrates the measurement and decomposition of economic inefficiency based on the *DDF* using the common examples presented in all chapters as well as the real dataset on Taiwanese banks. Last section concludes.

8.2 The Directional Distance Functions: Orientation, Calculation, and Properties

In this section, we define the directional distance function, *DDF*, which is an additive efficiency measure. Since for obtaining an *economic inefficiency decomposition* for a *finite sample of firms* based on a *DDF* we need to determine the *DDF technical inefficiency of each firm*, the next subsection will provide its definition for firms belonging to the production possibility set *T* generated by the mentioned sample. As happens with other inefficiency measures considered in this book, the *DDF* is a non-negative number that satisfies *the representation property*, i.e., a firm belongs to the production technology *T* if and only if its value is non-negative. In particular, it takes the value 0 only for the firms that belong to its frontier, or, in other words, only for the firms that are weakly efficient, i.e., belong to $\partial^W(T)$ (see Sect. 2.2 in Chap. 2). For positive values, the firm is technically inefficient. As usual, calculating the *DDF inefficiency* identifies a relevant benchmark (projection in geometrical terms) onto the production frontier. The second subsection discusses the most relevant properties of the *DDF* as a technical inefficiency measure.

8.2.1 Graph, Input, and Output Directional Distance Functions

The definition of a *DDF* for the firms of the production possibility set *T* was first published in 1996 by Chambers et al. (1996b).[8] Intuitively, we assign to each firm a certain directional vector, *DV*, that may identify a $\partial^W(T)$ projection by reducing

[8] As in the rest of the book, we denote by *T* the production possibility set under variable returns to scale. When considering constant, nonincreasing or nondecreasing returns to scale, we write T^{CRS}, T^{NIRS}, T^{NDRS}, respectively.

inputs and/or increasing outputs. Moreover, the detected technical inefficiency is closely related to the mentioned *DV*. Prior to offering the precise definition of the projection and the corresponding *DDF inefficiency score*, we stress that the *DDF* is the most flexible known efficiency measure, thanks to the different alternatives that exist when choosing the *DVs*. The *DDF assigns for each firm* $(x_o, y_o) \in T \subset \mathbb{R}_+^{M+N}$ *a specific directional vector*, $g = (g_x, g_y) \in \mathbb{R}_+^{M+N}$ with $(g_x, g_y) \neq (0_M, 0_N)$, which constitutes the essence of this efficiency measure. The ray starting at (x_o, y_o) and with directional vector $(-g_x, g_y)$, reducing inputs and/or increasing outputs, identifies a frontier point of T which is written as $(\widehat{x}_o, \widehat{y}_o)$ and is called the projection of (x_o, y_o). Based on these elements, we are ready to define *the DDF technical inefficiency*, denoted as β^*, *associated with firm* (x_o, y_o) *and with its directional vector g*.

Definition 8.1 *The directional technology distance function DDF,* $\vec{D}_T(x_o, y_o, g_x, g_y)$, *defines as the non-negative number* β^* *that multiplied by vector g defines a linear segment connecting firm* $(x_o, y_o) \in T$ *and the frontier of the technology in the direction defined by g*[9]:

$$\beta^* \equiv \vec{D}_T(x_o, y_o, g_x, g_y) = \max\{\beta \in \mathbb{R}^+ : (x_o - \beta g_x, y_o + \beta g_y) \in T\}. \quad (8.1)$$

The characteristics of T (see Chap. 2) guarantee that the maximum is achieved.[10] Moreover, the projection $(\widehat{x}_o, \widehat{y}_o) = (x_o - \beta^* g_x, y_o + \beta^* g_y)$ satisfies that it belongs to the weakly efficient frontier $\partial^W(T) = \{(x, y) \in T : (x', -y') < (x, -y) \Rightarrow (x', y') \notin T\}$ (see expression (2.3) in Chap. 2).[11] As a consequence, β^* is a non-negative real number. When (x_o, y_o) belongs to $\partial^W(T)$, it happens that $(\widehat{x}_o, \widehat{y}_o) = (x_o, y_o)$ or, equivalently, that $\beta^* = 0$, provided the two input and output components of the directional vector are different from 0. We will show later on how to calculate β^* through a linear program. Expression (8.1) is exactly the same as the one published in 1996, and is valid for *graph DVs*, for which $g_y \neq 0_N$, $g_x \neq 0_M$. If the direction is set to zero in the output dimension, resulting in *input-oriented DVs* with $g_y = 0_N$, then we qualify Definition 8.1 by defining *input-oriented DDFs*. Conversely, if the directional input vector is zero, representing *output-oriented DVs* with $g_x = 0_M$, then we define *output-oriented DDFs*. Therefore, with a *graph DV*, we try to reduce inputs and to increase outputs of $(x_o, y_o) \in T$ for identifying its DDF projection; with an *input-oriented DV*, we only try to reduce inputs keeping its output values constant; and finally, with an *output-oriented DV*, we only try to increase outputs

[9] Being precise, the L_2 distance between $(x_o, y_o) \in T$ and the frontier of T is given by the L_2 length of the vector $\beta^*(-g_x, g_y)$.

[10] When we "maximize"—or "minimize"—a variable like β_o that takes real values, we are sure that the biggest, or smallest, value is a real number. If we are not, we search for the "supreme"—or the "infimum"—in which case it can be equal to $+\infty$ or to $-\infty$.

[11] The production frontier contains always strong-efficient firms, also called Pareto-Koopmans efficient firms, and may also contain weakly efficient points, i.e., points that are dominated by at least one strongly efficient firm.

maintaining its input values. In each particular case, we do not need to reduce all the inputs and/or to increase all the outputs, which gives an interesting added flexibility to the *DDF*. For instance, the *DDF* allows us to easily solve problems where certain variables are nondiscretionary, such as inputs in a problem that we do not want to alter, others that are considered good outputs that we want to increase, and finally undesirable outputs, which we want to reduce.

Additionally, we can relate the input-oriented and output-oriented directional distance functions to the radial input and output distance functions proposed by Shephard (1953, 1970), to which Chap. 3 is devoted. Indeed, since the first published paper on *DDFs*, researchers have been interested in connecting them with previous proposed distance functions. Chambers et al. (1996) revealed, in their first *DDF* paper, how to formulate Shephard's input distance function, $D_I(x_o, y_o)$ (see expression (3.7) in Chap. 3), as an *input-oriented DDF*, and 2 years later, Chambers et al. (1998) formulated Shephard's output distance function, $D_O(x_o, y_o)$—expression (3.8) in Chap. 3—as an *output-oriented DDF*, giving rise to the following equalities:

$$D_I(x_o, y_o) = \frac{1}{1 - \vec{D}_T(x_o, y_o; x_o, 0_N)}, \tag{8.2}$$

$$D_O(x_o, y_o) = \frac{1}{1 + \vec{D}_T(x_o, y_o; 0_M, y_o)}. \tag{8.3}$$

In fact, $\vec{D}_T(x_o, y_o, x_o, 0_N)$ was baptized as the directional input distance function (input DDF) and $\vec{D}_T(x_o, y_o, 0_M, y_o)$ as the directional input distance function (output DDF). The relation with the input- and output-radial inefficiency scores, θ^*, ξ^*, is even easier to remember knowing that $\theta^* = \frac{1}{D_I(x_o, y_o)}, \xi^* = \frac{1}{D_O(x_o, y_o)}$ (see programs (3.23) and (3.25) in Chap. 3), and, consequently, each radial inefficiency score is equal to the corresponding denominator of (8.2) and (8.3).

In the aforementioned paper, the authors also comment upon the "graph type extension of Farrell measure" proposed by Briec (1997), which corresponds to *a graph DDF* with $g_o = (x_o, y_o)$, known today as *the proportional directional distance function (proportional DDF)*, given the interpretation of the function as the proportional reduction in outputs and increase in outputs necessary to reach the production frontier, with respect to the observed amounts.

Let us assume in what follows a *CRS technology*, T^{CRS}. It is well known that in this case, the Farrell or Shephard input- and output-oriented measures are numerically related, since one is the inverse of the other: $D_I^{CRS}(x, y) = 1/D_O^{CRS}(x, y)$, e.g., Färe and Primont (1995, p. 24). What has been discovered very recently (see Pastor et al. 2020) is the relation between any of the oriented inefficiencies and the proportional inefficiency, which extends the use of the reformulated *proportional DDF* as a multiplicative efficiency measure, able to resort to Malmquist indexes. Under CRS, this is the newly found relationship:

$$D_O(x_o, y_o) = \frac{1 - \vec{D}_T(x_o, y_o, x_o, y_o)}{1 + \vec{D}_T(x_o, y_o, x_o, y_o)}. \tag{8.4}$$

8.2.2 *Calculating the Directional Distance Functions Using Data Envelopment Analysis*

Considering the representation of the VRS production technology based on Data Envelopment Analysis (DEA):

$$T = \left\{ (x, y) : \sum_{j=1}^{J} \lambda_j x_{jm} \leq x_m,\ m = 1, \ldots, M;\ \sum_{j=1}^{J} \lambda_j y_{jn} \geq y_n,\ n = 1, \ldots, N; \right.$$
$$\left. \sum_{j=1}^{J} \lambda_j = 1,\ \lambda_j \geq 0,\ j = 1, \ldots, J \right\} \tag{8.5}$$

we write the linear dual forms that allow calculating the directional technology distance function measure of technical inefficiency- or directional graph distance function measure of technical inefficiency- for firm (x_o, y_o), with $g_o = (g_x, g_y) \in R_+^{M+N}$ as the pre-specified non-null directional vector, as:

Envelopment form

$$\max_{\beta, \lambda} \beta \tag{8.6}$$

s.t.

$$\sum_{j \in J} \lambda_j x_{jm} \leq x_{om} - \beta g_{x_m},$$
$$m = 1, \ldots, M$$
$$\sum_{j \in J} \lambda_j y_{jn} \geq y_{on} + \beta g_{y_n},$$
$$n = 1, \ldots, N$$
$$\sum_{j \in J} \lambda_j = 1$$
$$\lambda_j \geq 0, j \in J.$$

Multiplier form

$$\min_{\omega, \mu, \nu} \quad -\sum_{n=1}^{N} \mu_n y_{on} + \sum_{m=1}^{M} \nu_m x_{om} + \omega \tag{8.7}$$

s.t.

$$\sum_{n=1}^{N} \mu_n y_{on} - \sum_{m=1}^{M} \nu_m x_{om} - \omega \leq 0, \quad j \in J$$
$$\sum_{n=1}^{N} \mu_n g_{y_n} + \sum_{m=1}^{M} \nu_m g_{x_m} = 1,$$
$$\nu \geq 0_M, \mu \geq 0_N.$$

Whenever we are considering a firm (x_o, y_o) that belongs to the VRS production possibility set T (8.5) generated by the finite sample of firms $\{(x_j, y_j), j \in J\}$, we know that β^*, the optimal value of linear program (8.6) for firm (x_o, y_o), is a finite and non-negative real number that equals the objective function value of its linear dual

(8.7).[12] Being more precise, $\beta^* \in \mathbb{R}_+$ is a positive number unless (x_o, y_o) is located onto $\partial^W(T)$ with $\beta^* = 0$. Generally speaking, the *DDF projection* of (x_o, y_o) onto $\partial^W(T)$ is $(x_o - \beta^* g_x, y_o + \beta^* g_y)$, which requires that the components of any *directional vector*, (g_x, g_y), are expressed in exactly the same units of measurement as the components of (x_o, y_o). When evaluating the technical performance of firm (x_o, y_o), *the inefficiency gap* represented by the *DDF* is the straight segment that connects it to its $\partial^W(T)$ *projection*. The mentioned segment can be represented as the vector that starts at the firm and ends at its projection, corresponding to the scalar $\beta^* \in \mathbb{R}_{+}$, obtained by solving program (8.6), times the directional vector (g_x, g_y). Since adding to the vector representing (x_o, y_o) the vector associated with the inefficiency gap generates the vector associated with the projection, we say that *the DDF is an additive distance function*. The *DDF inefficiency* or *inefficiency score* is the number β^* that is positive for inner firms and 0 for strong and sometimes weakly efficient frontier firms.

8.2.3 Characterizing the Technical Inefficiency of Firms Through the DDF

We may be interested in knowing if the projection is a weak efficient benchmark, belonging to the weakly efficient subset of the technology $\partial^W(T)$, or a strongly efficient point, belonging to $\partial^S(T) = \{(x, y) \in T : (x', -y') \leq (x, -y), (x', y') \neq (x, y) \Rightarrow (x', y') \notin T\}$, see expression (2.2) in Chap. 2. For this purpose, we can reduce the set of efficient points to a much smaller subset, the subset of extreme efficient points. To this end, we propose to identify first the subset of strongly efficient firms among the firms belonging to our finite sample of *J* firms by means of the next linear program, which corresponds to a particular version of the additive model, which we call the *improved additive model*. This model provides a complete classification of the four different types of firms of our production possibility set.

$$\begin{aligned} &\max_{s^-, s^+, \lambda} \sum_{m=1}^{M} s_m^- + \sum_{n=1}^{N} s_n^+ - \lambda \\ &s.t. \\ &\sum_{j \in J} \lambda_j x_{jm} + s_m^- = x_{om}, \ m = 1, \ldots, M \\ &\sum_{j \in J} \lambda_j y_{jn} - s_n^+ = y_{on}, n = 1, \ldots, N \\ &\sum_{j \in J} \lambda_j = 1 \\ &\lambda_j \geq 0, j \in J. \end{aligned} \tag{8.8}$$

[12] As usual, both dual linear models can be defined under any returns to scale by modifying or deleting the lambda restriction in the primal problem and modifying accordingly the dual model.

Proposition 8.1 Let (x_o, y_o) represent any firm of our finite sample and let us solve model (8.8) for each of them. The firms of our sample are classified into four disjoint subsets, as follows:

(S.1) The subset of *extreme efficient firms*, the ones that can only be projected onto themselves, identified through model (8.8) as the only ones with an optimal objective function value equal to -1, with all the optimal slacks at level 0.
(S.2) The subset of *non-extreme efficient firms*, the subset of efficient firms that can be projected onto a convex linear combination of other efficient firms and that are identified through model (8.8) as the only firms that achieve an optimal objective value equal to 0 with all the optimal slacks equal to 0.
(S.3) The subset of *weak efficient firms*. Each of these firms gets at least one optimal slack equal to 0 and at least one optimal slack positive, achieving a positive optimal objective value.
(S.4) The subset of *non-frontier firms*. Each of these firms gets all their optimal slacks positive, and, consequently, its optimal objective value is also positive.

Proof Linear program (8.8) is an *improved additive model* because the original objective function has been modified to include the additional last term $-\lambda$. Therefore, model (8.8), seeking to maximize its objective function, tries to avoid that $\lambda \neq 0$, thereby preventing that the firm being evaluated appears as part of its projection. Consequently, the four proposed characterizations are easy to prove as we show next. It is obvious that the projection of any (strongly) efficient firm will get all their optimal slacks at level 0 since they already belong to $\partial^S(T)$.

1. Only the extreme efficient firms, that by definition are the firms that can only be projected onto themselves, cannot avoid that the optimal value of model (8.8) is negative and equals -1. The reverse statement holds trivially since any firm that obtains an optimal value of -1 is necessarily an extreme efficient firm.
2. The subset of non-extreme efficient firms contains, by definition, the firms that can be projected into a convex linear combination of other efficient firms, and this is exactly what model (8.8) does, since its objective is to maximize its objective function, avoiding the presence of the firm being evaluated. Hence, the optimal value of (8.8) is equal to 0.
3. Each weak efficient firm is, by definition, dominated by a convex linear combination of efficient firms. The second characteristic that identifies a weak efficient firm is that at least one of its optimal slacks must necessarily be equal to 0, which guarantees that it belongs to $\partial^W(T)$, and that at least another one of its optimal slacks is positive, since it is dominated by a convex linear combination of efficient firms. Hence, the optimal value is positive in this case and equal to the sum of the positive optimal slacks.
4. Finally, the subset of non-frontier firms cannot have any optimal slack equal to 0 since then it would be a weakly efficient firm. Consequently, all the optimal slacks must be positive, and therefore its optimal objective function value is also positive and equal to the sum of all the optimal slacks. □

After identifying the subset of extreme efficient firms by means of linear program (8.8), we can reformulate the dual linear programs (8.6) and (8.7) in terms of the subset of extreme efficient firms, which we denote as E. We leave it as a simple exercise for the reader, since formally the only change is to consider $j \in E$ instead of $j \in J$. The computational initial effort of identifying the subset E can be rewarded in terms of savings in computational time when analyzing a large set of firms, as long as the size of the subset E is considerably smaller than that of set J. Moreover, with our new version, we are able to know directly if the mentioned *DDF projection*, $(x_o - \beta^* g_x, y_o + \beta^* g_y)$, is an efficient point or a weakly efficient point, simply comparing it with $\left(\sum_{j \in E} \lambda_j^* x_j, \sum_{j \in E} \lambda_j^* y_j\right)$: if they are equal, then the projection is an efficient point, and, if not, then the projection is a weakly efficient point. Identifying the subset of weak efficient points can be interesting, since eventually they can also be considered as desirable peers since their L_1 distance to the firm being evaluated is shorter than the distance associated with efficient peers.

8.2.4 Properties of the Directional Distance Function

We now revise the basic properties of the *DDF* interpreted as a technical inefficiency measure.

Proposition 8.2

1. $\vec{D}_T(x_o, y_o, g_x, g_y)$ completely characterizes the technology T, i.e., $\vec{D}_T(x_o, y_o, g_x, g_y) \geq 0$ if $(x_o, y_o) \in T$ and $\vec{D}_T(x_o, y_o, g_x, g_y) < 0$ if $(x_o, y_o) \notin T$.
2. $\vec{D}_T(x_o, y_o, \mu g_x, \mu g_y) = \frac{1}{\mu} \vec{D}_T(x_o, y_o, g_x, g_y), \mu > 0$.
3. $y_o' > y_o \Rightarrow \vec{D}_T(x_o, y_o', g_x, g_y) \leq \vec{D}_T(x_o, y_o, g_x, g_y)$.
4. $x_o' > x_o \Rightarrow \vec{D}_T(x_o', y_o, g_x, g_y) \geq \vec{D}_T(x_o, y_o, g_x, g_y)$.
5. If g is a constant vector, or, alternatively, if $g_{x_m} = f_m(x_{om}), m = 1, \ldots, M$, $g_{y_n} = f_{M+n}(y_{on}), n = 1, \ldots, N$, and each f_k, $k = 1, \ldots, M + N$ is homogeneous of degree 1, then $\vec{D}_T(x_o, y_o, g_x, g_y)$ is units invariant.
6. If T exhibits *CRS*, then $\vec{D}_T(\mu x_o, \mu y_o, g_x, g_y) = \mu \vec{D}_T(x_o, y_o, g_x, g_y)$ for $\mu > 0$.

Proof

1. We have already explained how a *DDF* works when considering an inner firm and an outer firm.
2. We have also explained that if an initial *DV* is multiplied by a positive constant, the value of the initial efficiency score is automatically divided by the same quantity.

3. This property establishes that $\vec{D}_T(x_o, y_o, g_x, g_y)$ is weakly monotonic in outputs. We provide a proof for inner firms and leave to the reader the proof for outer firms. Since we are assuming that $y'_o > y_o$, we can write $y'_o = (y_{o1} + h_1, y_{o2} + h_2, \ldots, y_{oN} + h_N) > y_o$, where $h_n \geq 0$, $n = 1, \ldots, N$, and at least one of them is positive. Let us assume that $h_1 > 0$. Then $y'^1_o = (y_{o1} + h_1, y_{o2}, \ldots, y_{oN}) > y_o$, and the optimal inefficiency score associated with point (x_o, y'^1_o), denoted as β'^{1*}, generates a projection $(x_o, y'^1_o) + \beta'^{1*} \cdot g$ that clearly dominates firm $(x_o, y_o) + \beta'^{1*} \cdot g$ through its first output component. If this last firm belongs to $\partial^W(T)$, it must be a weak efficient point with β^*, the inefficiency score associated with (x_o, y_o) satisfying $\beta^* = \beta'^{1*}$. Otherwise, it is not a frontier point and clearly $\beta^* > \beta'^{1*}$. Last reasoning can be repeated $N - 1$ times, generating intermediate points until (x_o, y'_o) has been reached getting the desired result.
4. This property establishes that $\vec{D}_T(x_o, y_o, g_x, g_y)$ is weakly monotonic in inputs. We omit its proof, which follows the previous one.
5. Let us first assume that g is a constant vector. By definition, the units of measurement of each of the $M + N$ components of g are the same as those corresponding to any firm (x_o, y_o). Hence, if any units associated with an input or an output changes, the same change must be applied to the corresponding g component, and the result follows. Let us now assume that each component of g is a homogeneous function of degree 1 in inputs and outputs. Any change of units in one input (or output), let us say input m, will change the corresponding component of g as follows: $\mu_m g_{x_m} = \widehat{g}_{x_m} = f_m(\widehat{x}_{om}) = f_m(\mu_m x_{om}) = \mu_m f_m(x_{om})$, and being $\mu_m > 0$ the result follows.
6. For a *CRS* technology, $\vec{D}_T(\mu x_o, \mu y_o, g_x, g_y) = \mu \vec{D}_T(x_o, y_o, g_x, g_y)$ for $\mu > 0$ is a direct consequence of the ancient Thales theorem: the two rays starting at the origin of coordinates and passing each through (x_o, y_o) and through its projection $(x_o, y_o) + \vec{D}_T(x_o, y_o, g_x, g_y) g$ also contain the points $(\mu x_o, \mu y_o)$, $\mu > 0$ and its projection $(\mu x_o, \mu y_o) + \vec{D}_T(\mu x_o, \mu y_o, g_x, g_y) g$. Moreover, since $\vec{D}_T(\mu x_o, \mu y_o, g_x, g_y) == \mu \vec{D}_T(x_o, y_o, g_x, g_y)$, according to (5), we end up realizing that the two segments that connect each point and its projection are parallel, as established by Thales theorem. □

Notes

In relation to the six properties, some comments are pertinent.

1. We have maintained the traditional formulation of this property, although, being more precise we should say additionally, "... and $\beta(x_o, y_o; g) < 0$ if $(x_o, y_o) \notin T$ whenever the projection exists and belongs to T."
2. Alternatively, this property can be formulated as "$\vec{D}_T(x_o, y_o, g_x, g_y)$ is homogeneous of degree -1 in g."

3. This property shows that "$\vec{D}_T(x_o, y_o, g_x, g_y)$ *is weakly decreasing in outputs.*"
4. Similarly, this property shows that "$\vec{D}_T(x_o, y_o, g_x, g_y)$ is weakly increasing in inputs."
5. Property (5) establishes two alternative conditions that a directional vector must satisfy to get a units invariant *DDF*. It is easy to consider *DDFs that are not units invariant.* For instance, if in the one input-one output space we consider $g = (x_o^2, y_o^3)$ and the respective units of measurement are changed by the scalars 3 and 2 in inputs and outputs, *the value of the new DV will be 72 times the old DV.*
6. This property shows that *under CRS,* $\vec{D}_T(x_o, y_o, g_x, g_y)$ *is homogeneous of degree 1 in* (x_o, y_o).

8.3 Exogenous and Endogenous Directional Vectors, DVs

Many different types of *DVs* have been proposed and used since the *DDF* was introduced, which is not at all surprising: the *DV* is the building block on which the definition of any *DDF* is based, and it influences all the efficiency and productivity related measures, such as technical inefficiency, scale inefficiency, and, finally, the economic inefficiency measures. In this section, we do not intend to be exhaustive but to present the main types of *DVs* that are useful for our purposes, and particularly, for studying *economic inefficiency.* To get a wider perspective, and, particularly, for analyzing environmental issues, we recommend the recent paper by Wang et al. (2019). Our first subsection will be devoted to *exogenous DVs*, while the second one will deal with *endogenous DVs*. As usual we will resort exclusively to DEA models and assume *VRS*, which is the reference technology in profit and revenue maximization, as well as cost minimization (see Sect. 2.3 in Chap. 2). As previously said, we take for granted that the components of the considered *DV* have the same units of measurement as those corresponding to the firms being analyzed, which is a must in order to guarantee that the corresponding *DDF inefficiency* is a well-defined number.

8.3.1 *The Family of Exogenous DVs*

This type of *directional vectors* depends exclusively on the personal decision of the researcher, without considering any endogenous characteristics related to the problem being solved, that could help to achieve specific objectives or that considers certain features of the sample of firms. We are going to differentiate within this family three subfamilies: *the subfamily of constant DVs, the subfamily of self-evaluating DVs*, and *the subfamily of sample driven DVs.*

The first subfamily offers different possibilities. The standard one assigns the same constant directional vector to all the firms being analyzed. The great advantage of using a single constant directional vector is that all companies are evaluated in the same way, projecting them in the same direction and obtaining inefficiencies that can be compared numerically in terms of the length of the *DV*. As usual, we always have the three standard options when dealing with a *DDF*: to use a *constant graph DV*, a *constant input DV*, or a *constant output DV*. It is a fair comparison that produces fair results, whenever the sample does not include firms, or yield projections, on the weakly efficient frontier, i.e., slacks do not emerge. Since we are not using any endogenous information relative to the data associated with the firms being analyzed, the typical constant vector used is *the vector of 1's, oriented or not*. In case of dealing with a sample of firms where *weak efficient firms are present*, we must be aware that the inefficiency detected by our *graph DDF* will be underestimated with respect to their strongly efficient benchmarks, i.e., those complying with the notion of Pareto-Koopmans efficiency (see Chap. 2). For *oriented DDFs*, the firms that are *input weak efficient*, meaning that they have to reduce certain inputs in order to become efficient, may get an efficient projection when dealing with *output DDFs*, and a symmetric statement is valid for *output weak efficient* firms. We must be also aware that firms belonging to the interior of the production possibility set may obtain as a projection a weak efficient point. Consequently, anytime we want our *DDF* to capture all types of inefficiencies, we must be prepared to modify the chosen *DVs*. Since we are currently dealing with the simplest *DV*, let us show in this case which path we must follow to achieve our objective. Fortunately, the path is the same for any type of *DV* we are considering. In this method, we can keep the choice of our initial constant *DV for the efficient and most of the inefficient firms*, and *to calculate specific new constant vectors for each of the weakly efficient firms and for any inefficient firm whose projection is a weak efficient firm.* Hence, instead of using a single constant *DV*, we end up using the mentioned *constant DV for many firms of our sample, and a specific constant DV for each of the weak efficient firms and also for each of the inefficient firms whose projection depends on at least one weak efficient firm.* In other words, we end up considering a *mixed set of constant DVs.*[13] In order to obtain comparable inefficiencies when resorting to different constant directional vectors, an easy requirement is that all of them have the same *Euclidean length*. Let us show the next numerical example.

Example 8.1
Let us consider, in the one input-one output space, the next sample of ordered firms illustrated in Fig. 8.1: A = (4,4), B = (8,12), C = (4,3), D = (5,2), E = (6,4), F = (8,8), G = (9,11), H = (10,12), and I = (12,11). As previously mentioned, let us choose the *constant graph DV* (1,1). The first two units are the only efficient units, and, consequently, the (strongly) efficient frontier is the segment that connects them.

[13] Generally speaking, a *mixed set of constant DVs* is used when we want to account for all types of inefficiencies, which means that all the non-efficient firms, which includes all the inefficient and all the weak efficient firms, are projected onto the strongly efficient frontier.

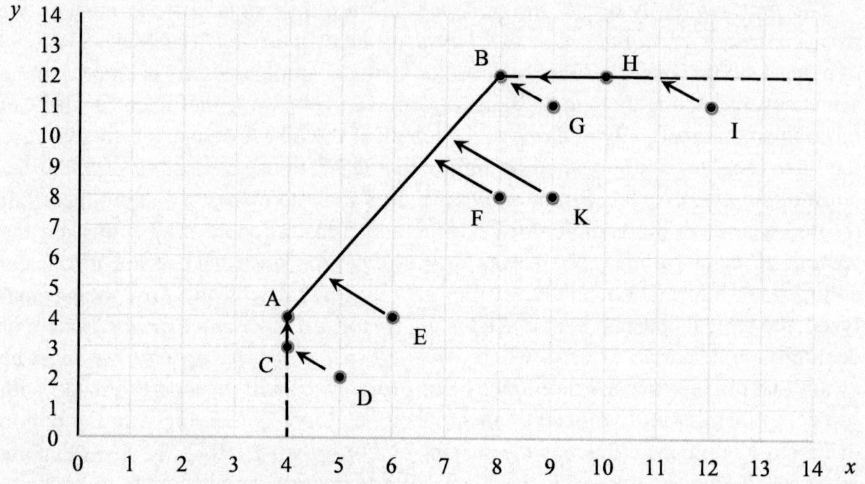

Fig. 8.1 Strongly efficient projections and *DVs*

The calculated *DDF inefficiencies* β^*, are, in the same order, 0, 0, 0, 1, 4/3, 4/3, 1, 0, 1, and 1, while their projections are (4,4), (8,12), (4,3), (4,3), (14/3,16/3), (20/3,28/3), (8,12), (10,12), and (11,12). Since firm A = (4,4) dominates firm C = (4,3) and firm B = (8,12) dominates both firms H = (10,12) and I = (11,12), the three dominated firms are weak efficient. Since firm (4,3) cannot increase its output, it belongs to the output weak frontier, and, similarly, since (10,12) and (11,12)—the projection of (12,11)—cannot reduce its inputs, they belong to the input weak frontier. Moreover, there is another firm that is projected onto the input weak efficient firm (4,3), namely, firm D = (5,2). If we want our *DDF* to account for all types of inefficiencies, we shall project any unit onto the strongly efficient frontier, in this case onto the segment limited by (4,4) and (8,12). Therefore, (4,3) and (5,2) should be projected onto the strong efficient firm (4,4), while the projection of (10,12) and (12,11) should be the strong efficient firm (8,12). Hence, each of the four mentioned firms *needs to change their original constant DV by a new one that guarantees its new strong efficient projection*. Let us show how to do it if we want to obtain *comparable DDF inefficiencies*. Firm C = (4,3) must be projected onto firm A = (4,4) = (4,3) + (0,1), which means that its new inefficiency score must be calculated after adjusting the Euclidean length of the new constant *DV* (0,1) to the length of the original constant vector (1,1), which is equal to $\sqrt{2}$. Hence, instead of (0,1), we need to consider $\left(0, \sqrt{2}\right)$ as the *new DV*, and, consequently, the new inefficiency score under the Euclidean norm (L2) is $\beta^*_{L2}(4,3) = \frac{1}{\sqrt{2}}$, so that the last equality is satisfied: $(4,4) = (4,3) + \frac{1}{\sqrt{2}}\left(0, \sqrt{2}\right)$. Similarly, for firm D = (5,2), we have A = (4,4) = (5,2) + (−1,2), and adjusting $\sqrt{5}$, the actual Euclidean length of *DV* (1,2), to $\sqrt{2}$ we get $(4,4) = (5,2) + \frac{\sqrt{5}}{\sqrt{2}}\left(-\frac{\sqrt{2}}{\sqrt{5}}, \frac{2\sqrt{2}}{\sqrt{5}}\right)$. For the other two firms, the reader can verify that the new DVs and corresponding $\beta^*_{o,L2}$ are as follows: for firm H = (10,12), firm $B = (8,12) = (10,12) + (-2,0) = (10,12) + \sqrt{2}\left(-\sqrt{2}, 0\right)$; and for firm I = (12,11), again firm B = $(8, 12) = (12, 11) + (-4, 1) = (12, 11) + \frac{\sqrt{17}}{\sqrt{2}}\left(\frac{-4\sqrt{2}}{\sqrt{17}}, \frac{\sqrt{2}}{\sqrt{17}}\right)$. Hence, *the initial set of DDF inefficiencies*, 0, 0, 0, 1, 4/3, 4/3, 1, 0, 1, and 1, *associated with DV* (1,1), that corresponds to the initial sample of ordered firms and that *did not account for non-DDF inefficiencies*, have been modified, considering new *DVs* for firms at positions 3, 4, 7, and 9, and accounting now for all types of inefficiencies, obtaining $0, 0, \frac{1}{\sqrt{2}} \simeq 0.71, \frac{\sqrt{5}}{\sqrt{2}} \simeq 1.58, \sqrt{2} \simeq 1.41, \frac{4}{3} \simeq 1.33, 0, 1, \frac{\sqrt{17}}{\sqrt{2}} \simeq 2.92$. The new derived *DVs* associated with firms that have changed are as follows: for firm C = (4,3), $\left(0, \sqrt{2}\right) \simeq (0, 1.41)$; for firm E = (5,2), $\left(-\frac{\sqrt{2}}{\sqrt{5}}, \frac{2\sqrt{2}}{\sqrt{5}}\right) \simeq (-0.63, 1.26)$; for firm H = (10,12), $\left(-\sqrt{2}, 0\right) \simeq (-1.41, 0)$; and finally, for firm I = (12,11), $\left(\frac{-4\sqrt{2}}{\sqrt{17}}, \frac{\sqrt{2}}{\sqrt{17}}\right) \simeq (-1.37, 0.34)$.

The second type of *exogenous DVs* are known as *the subfamily of self-evaluating directions*, inspired by the origins of efficiency analysis. In contrast with the first subfamily, *this second subfamily requires a specific DV for each firm* that is based exclusively on itself. Therefore, the *DVs* used are not of equal length, meaning that the *DDF inefficiencies* are not directly comparable. The three basic options, *graph DVs*, *input DVs*, or *output DVs*, correspond to the three differentiated *DDFs* introduced in Sect. 8.2.1. Therefore, for firm (x_o, y_o), the *graph DV* is (x_o, y_o), the *input DV* is $(x_o, 0_N)$, and the *output DV* is $(0_M, y_o)$, what additionally justifies the name of this subfamily. Let us briefly revise the *input DV* $(x_o, 0_N)$. The projection obtained by the *input DDF* is $(\widehat{x}_o, \widehat{y}_o) = (x_o, y_o) - \beta^*(x_o, 0_N) = ((1 - \beta^*)x_o, y_o)$, which shows that the input vector is *reduced proportionally* while the output vector is maintained. It is well known that, in this case, $0 \leq \beta^* < 1$, and as shown in Sect. 8.2.1, $(1 - \beta^*) = \theta^*$, the technical efficiency score of the DEA radial input-oriented model (see Sect. 3.2.2 of Chap. 3). Hence, the comparison between firms is in terms of *proportional reductions of inputs for each firm* which completely departs from comparing absolute values as in the first revised subfamily. These types of *DVs* are easy to assume when working under homothetic technologies (e.g., CRS): in this case, the firms that belong to the same ray starting at the origin of coordinates reduce the same proportion of inputs; and in case they belong to different rays, the firm that obtains a bigger reduction belongs to a ray that is located further from the frontier. Hence, *this second subfamily allows comparing in terms of proportions*, which is a relative concept linked to each firm. It is well known that this type of comparison has been widely used in the past and that the projections can be weakly efficient points. The only attempt to achieve strongly efficient projections maintaining the spirit of the proportional reductions was proposed by Coelli (1998), although it has been seldom used. Similar comments apply for the other two options belonging to this subfamily.

The last subfamily corresponds to the *sample driven DVs*. The typical example is to consider the *graph DV* whose components are the average of the corresponding inputs and outputs of the firms of the sample. It has been justified, when data represent all industries in a specific sector, that this *DV* corresponds to the average behavior of the mentioned industrial sector (see, e.g., Aparicio et al., 2013a). Another *DV* used is based on the zenith point of the sample of firms, first proposed by Portela et al. (2004) to define their range directional model. A different and more specific proposal was previously published by Bogetoft and Hougaard (1999), based on the definition of a different ideal point for each firm. Both models may generate projections that belong to the weakly efficient frontier, which means that these measures do not account for all types of inefficiencies. Asmild and Pastor (2010) studied both measures and proposed how to generate the corresponding strong efficient projections.

8.3.2 The Family of Endogenous DVs

This type of directional vector does not depend at all on the personal decision of the researchers, since their choice is based on certain endogenous characteristics related to the problem being solved. There are *basically two subfamilies of DVs: the geometric-based subfamily and the market-based subfamily.*

With respect to the first subfamily, we are going to show three possibilities, the first two related to the technical inefficiency measurement and the last one taking advantage of the relationship between the dual linear programs (8.6) and (8.7). *The first one seeks the projection of each firm toward the frontier point that offers the biggest technical improvement*, while *the second one does just the opposite.* The best way to comply with the first option is to resort to *the improved additive model* (8.8), which corresponds to the usual additive model where the role firms have been restricted to the subset of extreme efficient firms.[14] The next step is to transform the obtained "maximal inefficiency" expressed as a sum of slacks, into a *DDF inefficiency* which corresponds exactly with the corresponding *reverse DDF* explained in Chap. 12. With respect to the second subfamily, we apply first the method developed by Aparicio et al. (2007), based on a mixed integer linear program, that also delivers the minimal distance toward the frontier based on slacks. Its transformation into the corresponding *DDF* follows the same steps as mentioned for the first subfamily. The third proposal we comment on is the "virtual profit efficiency model" proposed by Petersen (2018). This model is based on the relation between the projection found by model (8.6) when determining the *DDF* inefficiency β_o^* associated with firm (x_o, y_o) and the dual shadow prices—*virtual multipliers*—(ν^*, μ^*) of model (8.7), which are associated with the supporting hyperplane to which the projection belongs. Inspired by Zofio et al. (2013), Petersen (2018) proposes to find the minimum Euclidean distance between the firm and $\partial^S(T)$ in order to identify its projection, which gives rise to the corresponding *endogenous graph DV*, and showed that it corresponds to the minimal difference between

[14] To see how to build the *improved additive model*, see Sect. 8.3.1, model (8.8).

maximal profit and profit, evaluated both at shadow prices—associated with model (8.7)—and normalized to a unit vector (see Sect. 2.4.4 in Chap. 2). The same result is valid for an *input DV* and *virtual cost* or an *output DV* and *virtual revenue*. The solution implies certain mathematical complexity and requires the solution of a combinatorial linear optimization problem in the primal space or an equivalent non-convex DEA model in the multiplier space with the vector of multipliers with Euclidean length equal to 1. A weakness of this first proposal is that the models are not units invariant. Two years later, the same author published a new paper, Petersen (2020), proposing an improved solution at the expense of an increase in computational complexity.

With respect to the *market-dependent subfamily*, there are many options. For instance, following Zofío et al. (2013), when market prices are observed, we can consider three different objectives: to maximize profit, to maximize revenue, or to minimize cost. Let us focus on maximizing profit, which can be accomplished by choosing a standard directional vector that also assesses technical inefficiency, or, alternatively, we can choose a free directional vector that points toward the maximum profit-efficient benchmark. In the former case, the corresponding profit inefficiency decomposition can be accomplished, while in the latter one, only allocative inefficiency will be detected by certain firms. For a detailed presentation of these two alternatives, see Zofío et al. (2013). In case our objective is to minimize costs or to maximize revenues, we obtain similar results. We may also be primarily interested in minimizing allocative inefficiency in the first place, as proposed by Bogetoft et al. (2006). In that case, we need to follow a different strategy that cannot be accomplished by resorting to traditional distance functions, as explained in Chap. 13 through the so-called Standard and Flexible Reverse Approaches.

8.4 The Graph DDFs and the Decomposition of Profit Inefficiency

In this section, we assume that market prices are known and valid for all the firms under scrutiny. As usual we denote as w the vector of M *positive input prices*, $w \in \mathbb{R}^M_{++}$, and as p the vector of N *positive output prices*, $p \in \mathbb{R}^N_{++}$. We consider a finite sample of $j = 1,\ldots, J$ firms and variable returns to scale (VRS).

The profit generated by firm (x_o, y_o) is defined as $py_o - wx_o$, which can take any unrestricted in sign value, including 0, while the *profit function* $\Pi(w,p)$ is defined as $\Pi(w,p) = \max\{(p \cdot y - w \cdot x) : (x,y) \in T\}$, and is achieved in at least one firm denoted as $(x^\Pi, y^\Pi) \in T$, i.e., $\Pi(w,p) = p \cdot y^\Pi - w \cdot x^\Pi$ (see Sect. 2.3.4 in Chap. 2). From an empirical perspective, recalling program (2.71) in Sect. 2.5.1 of Chap. 2, we calculate maximum profit for the sample of firms by solving the following DEA linear program:

$$
\begin{aligned}
\Pi(w,p) = \max_{x,\,y,\,\lambda} \quad & \sum_{n=1}^{N} p_m y_m - \sum_{m=1}^{M} w_m x_m \\
\text{s.t.} \quad & \sum_{j=1}^{J} \lambda_j x_{jm} \le x_m, \quad m = 1, \ldots, M, \\
& \sum_{j=1}^{J} \lambda_j y_{jn} \ge y_n, \quad n = 1, \ldots, N, \\
& \sum_{j=1}^{J} \lambda_j = 1, \\
& \lambda \ge 0.
\end{aligned} \tag{8.9}
$$

It is usually faster to use an Excel sheet to calculate the profits generated by each of the firms, obtaining their maximum value, and then calculate the profit inefficiency for each firm, as we will do in the Example 8.2 that follow.

Historically, it is interesting to know that Chambers et al. (1998, p. 358) were the first to establish a *dual relationship between the DDF and the profit function*. Within a DEA framework, the mentioned duality is expressed as follows (see Färe & Grosskopf, 2000):

$$
\Pi(w,p) = \max\left\{ (p\cdot y - w\cdot x) + \vec{D}_T\left(x, y, g_x, g_y\right)\left(p\cdot g_y + w\cdot g_x\right) : (x,y) \ge 0_{M+N} \right\},
$$

$$
\vec{D}_T(x, y, g^-, g^+) = \min\left\{ \frac{\Pi(w,p) - (p\cdot y - w\cdot x)}{(p\cdot g_y + w\cdot g_x)} : (p,w) \ge 0 \right\}. \tag{8.10}
$$

The penultimate equality allows us to write, for any firm $(x, y) \in T$, the next inequality:

$$
\Pi(w,p) - (p\cdot y - w\cdot x) \ge \vec{D}_T\left(x, y; g_x, g_y\right)\left(p\cdot g_y + w\cdot g_x\right). \tag{8.11}
$$

Its left-hand side term is known as *the profit inefficiency of* (x, y), $\Pi I(x, y, w, p)$, which is a non-negative number expressed in monetary units. Since $(p \cdot g_y + w \cdot g_x)$ is a positive number expressed in the same monetary units, we can divide by it and obtain the so-called Nerlovian profit inefficiency or DDF profit inefficiency measure, which is a pure number and therefore comparable with the DDF technical inefficiency, $\vec{D}_T\left(x, y; g_x, g_y\right)$. The inequality is closed by adding an allocative term:

$$
\begin{aligned}
N\Pi I_{DDF(G)}(x, y, \widetilde{w}, \widetilde{p}) &= \frac{\Pi I(x, y, w, p)}{(p\cdot g_y + w\cdot g_x)} \\
&= \vec{D}_T\left(x, y; g_x, g_y\right) + AI_{DDF(G)}(x, y, \widetilde{w}, \widetilde{p}),
\end{aligned} \tag{8.12}
$$

where $(\widetilde{w}, \widetilde{p})$ denotes normalized prices. Last expression is known as *the Nerlovian profit inefficiency decomposition into technical* (i.e., *the directional graph distance function measure of technical inefficiency) and allocative* (i.e., *the DDF allocative measure of profit inefficiency) components*, also due to Chambers et al. (1998).

As shown in Chap. 13, *the allocative inefficiency* associated with (x, y) is directly related to the profit inefficiency associated with its *DDF projection* $(\widehat{x}, \widehat{y})$, given the associated *graph DV* (g_x, g_y). In fact, we prove in the mentioned chapter that the *allocative inefficiency of* (x, y) is equal to the *Nerlovian profit inefficiency of its projection*, or, equivalently, equal to *the normalized profit inefficiency of its projection.* Additionally, since $(\widehat{x}, \widehat{y})$ *belongs to* $\partial^W(T)$, its technical *DDF* inefficiency is equal to 0, or, equivalently, its *Nerlovian profit inefficiency is equal to its allocative inefficiency*. In this regard, we can state the next proposition.

Proposition 8.3
Given input and output market prices (w, p), let (g_x, g_y) be a graph directional vector belonging to the subfamily of constant market valued *DV*s, i.e., $p \cdot g_y + w \cdot g_x = k_\$ > 0_\$$. Then, the directional output distance function approach satisfies the essential, the extended essential, and the comparison properties. In particular, the last proposition holds when (g_x, g_y) is a constant graph vector.

Proof Aparicio et al. (2021) proved that $AI_{DDF(G)}(x, y, \widetilde{w}, \widetilde{p}) = \frac{\Pi(w,p) - \left(p \cdot \left(y + \vec{D}_T(x, y; g_x, g_y) g_y\right) + w \cdot \left(x - \vec{D}_T(x, y; g_x, g_y) g_x\right)\right)}{(p \cdot g_y + w \cdot g_x)}$, which is equivalent to $\frac{\Pi(w,p) - \left(p \cdot \widehat{y} + w \cdot \widehat{x}\right)}{(p \cdot g_y + w \cdot g_x)}$. This is enough to show that the essential, the extended essential, and the comparison properties are satisfied for this specific type of DDF (see Chap. 13). □

This result clearly shows that for *graph DDFs*, the profit inefficiency decomposition establishes an economical relationship between the firm being rated, (x, y), and its technical projection $(\widehat{x}, \widehat{y})$.

It is easy to show that, regardless of the format of the directional vector, the DDF satisfies the essential property. However, it is not true in the case of the extended version of that property (see Chap. 2). It is not hard to show how, in the case of, for example, the usual directional vector $(g_x, g_y) = (x, y)$, the allocative inefficiency component could not coincide with the allocative inefficiency term associated with its projection point $(\widehat{x}, \widehat{y})$ as a consequence of using different normalization factors.

Example 8.2
Let us consider in the one input-one output space the sample of firms A = (3,5), B = (6,10), C = (12,12), D = (3,2), E = (8,8), F = (9,11), G = (10,10), and H = (14,11). Let as further assume a *VRS* technology, market prices $(p, w) = (3, 2)$, and the common *graph DV* (1,1). Considering the *modified additive model* (8.8), defined as an additive model with a slightly modified objective function, in this case

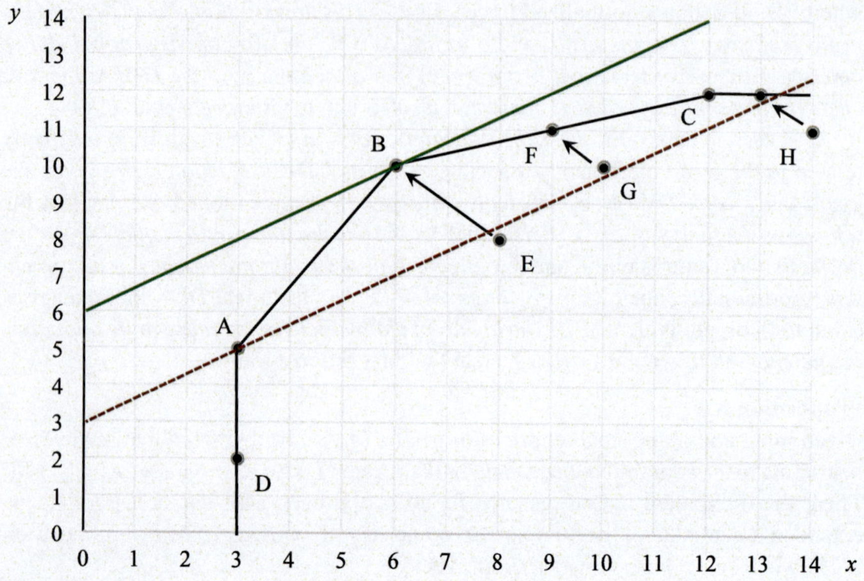

Fig. 8.2 Profit inefficiency decomposition based on the *graph DDF*

equal to $s^{-} + s^{+} - \lambda$, we identify the subset of *extreme efficient firms*: A = (3,5), B = (6,10), and C = (12,12), which are the only ones for which the optimal value of the last modified objective function equals (−1) (see Fig. 8.2).[15] Hence, we can *reformulate the corresponding DDF model* (8.6) taking as reference just the three extreme efficient firms and solve it for the rest of the non-efficient firms, since the efficient ones will get $\beta^* = 0$. The *DDF projections* obtained for the rest of the firms are $(\widehat{x}_{\mathrm{D}}, \widehat{y}_{\mathrm{D}}) = (3, 5)$, $(\widehat{x}_{\mathrm{E}}, \widehat{y}_{\mathrm{E}}) = (6, 10)$, $(\widehat{x}_{\mathrm{F}}, \widehat{y}_{\mathrm{F}}) = (9, 11) = 0.5(6, 10) + 0.5(12, 12)$, $(\widehat{x}_{\mathrm{G}}, \widehat{y}_{\mathrm{G}}) = (9, 11)$, and $(\widehat{x}_{\mathrm{H}}, \widehat{y}_{\mathrm{H}}) = (13, 12)$, with associated inefficiency scores equal to 0, 2, 0, 1, and 1. Since firms D = (3,2) and F = (9,11) get $\beta^* = 0$, they must necessarily be frontier firms, with (3,2) being a weakly efficient firm dominated by (3,5) and (9,11) a non-extreme efficient firm. The projection of firm H = (14,11) is (13, 12), which is also a weakly efficient point dominated by the extreme efficient firm C = (12,12). The profit values for each of the firms of the sample, maintaining the initial ordering, are $3 \cdot 5 - 2 \cdot 3 = \$9$ for A = (3,5), \$18 for B = (6,10), \$12 for C = (12,12), \$0 for D = (3,2), \$8 for E = (8,8), \$15 for F = (9,11), \$10 for G = (10,10), and \$5 for H = (14,11). Hence, the only profit-maximizing firm is B = (6,10), with $\Pi(3, 2) = \$18$, represented by the isoprofit line in Fig. 8.2. It is easy to calculate *the Nerlovian profit inefficiency decomposition* for each of the firms.

[15] *Extreme-efficient firms* cannot be represented as a convex linear combination of the rest of efficient firms, which are obviously classified as *non-extreme efficiency firms*. In our example, only (9,11) corresponds to this second type. In addition, working with extreme-efficient firms allows us to identify weakly efficient firms through the presence of inequality gaps in the optimal solution of a modified *DDF* model.

Since $(p \cdot g_y + w \cdot g_x) = 3 \cdot 1 + 2 \cdot 1 = \$5$, we have for firm A = (3,5), $\frac{\Pi(p,w)-(p \cdot y_{\mathrm{A}} - w \cdot x_{\mathrm{A}})}{\left(p \cdot g_{\mathrm{A}}^{+} + w \cdot g_{\mathrm{A}}^{-}\right)} = \frac{18-9}{5} = \frac{9}{5} = \vec{D}_T\left(x_{\mathrm{A}}, y_{\mathrm{A}}, g_{\mathrm{A}}^{-}, g_{\mathrm{A}}^{+}\right) + AI(x_{\mathrm{A}}, y_{\mathrm{A}}, \widetilde{w}, \widetilde{p}) = 0 + \frac{9}{5}$, where the allocative inefficiency has been retrieved as a residual (geometrically equal to the gap between the maximum isoprofit line and that passing through firm A).

8.5 The Input-Oriented DDFs and the Decomposition of Cost Inefficiency

We want to analyze a finite sample of firms by means of an *input-oriented DDF*, which means that for each firm (x, y_o) we need to determine which *input DV* $(g_x, 0_N)$ we are going to use in order *to calculate its projection* $(\widehat{x}, y_o) \in \partial^W(T)$ *as well as its DDF technical inefficiency* $\beta^* \geq 0$. Since we want to maintain the firm's output, we no longer consider the whole production possibility set under variable returns to scale, T, but focus on the subset consisting of all the observations that produce y_o as its output vector, known as *the input set* $L(y_o) \coloneqq \{x : (x, y_o) \in T\}$, introduced in Sect 2.1 of Chap. 2. $L(y_o)$ has its own frontier, which is a subset of $\partial^W(T)$. Let us assume, as usual, that T is generated by a finite sample of production firms (x_j, y_o), $j \in J$. Given market input prices $w \in \mathbb{R}^M_{++}$, the *minimum cost for points* (x, y_o) *satisfying* $x \in L(y_o)$ is represented by the cost function denoted as $C(y_o, w)$, which is empirically obtained through DEA methods by solving the next linear program:

$$
\begin{aligned}
C(y, w) = \quad & \min_{x, \lambda} \sum_{m=1}^{M} w_m x_m \\
& s.t. \\
& \sum_{j=1}^{J} \lambda_j x_{jm} \leq x_m, \quad m = 1, \ldots, M, \\
& \sum_{j=1}^{J} \lambda_j y_{jn} \geq y_{on}, \quad n = 1, \ldots, N, \\
& \sum_{j=1}^{J} \lambda_j = 1, \\
& \lambda_j \geq 0, \quad j = 1, \ldots, J, \\
& x_m \geq 0, \quad m = 1, \ldots, M.
\end{aligned}
\tag{8.13}
$$

Any quasi-optimal solution of the last program, (x^C, y_o), where $x^C = \sum_{j=1}^{J} \lambda_j^* x_j$, is a *cost-minimizing firm.*[16] For any firm (x, y_o), its *cost inefficiency* is defined as $CI(x, y_o, w) = w \cdot x - C(y_o, w) \geq 0$, that is, the difference between the input cost at (x, y_o), $w \cdot x$, and the minimum cost $C(y_o, w) = w \cdot x^C$. The optimal solution of the last linear program must belong to $\partial^W(T)$, by contradiction.[17]

For decomposing the cost inefficiency $CI(x, y_o, w)$ at firm (x, y_o), we need to develop *an inequality that relates it with* β^* *times a certain quantity* so that the two members of the inequality are expressed in the same units. To this end, let us consider the technical projection $(\widehat{x}, y_o) \in \partial^W(T)$ of the mentioned firm that satisfies the next equality $(\widehat{x}, y_o) = (x, y_o) + \beta^*(g_x, 0_N)$. By multiplying its input components by the input cost vector w, we obtain the next equality $w \cdot \widehat{x} = w(x - \beta^* g_x) = w \cdot x - \beta^*(w \cdot g_x)$. Transposing the last term, we deduce that $w \cdot x = \beta^*(w \cdot g_x) + w \cdot \widehat{x}$. Subtracting $C(y_o, w)$ from the left- and right-hand side of the last equality allows us to obtain the *cost inefficiency*:

$$CI_{DDF(I)}(x, y_o, w) = \beta^*(w \cdot g_x) + CI(\widehat{x}, y_o, w) \tag{8.14}$$

The last equality between quantities expressed in monetary units shows, as a sub-product, that the cost inefficiency $CI_{DDF(I)}(x, y_o, w)$ of firm (x, y_o) is greater or equal than the product of a certain positive factor $w \cdot g_x > 0_\$$ times its *DDF technical inefficiency* β^*, taking into account that for any projection $(\widehat{x}, y_o) \in \partial^W(T)$, *we know that* $CI(\widehat{x}, y_o, w) \geq 0$, being 0 only in the case that $(\widehat{x}, y_o)$ is a cost-minimizing point:

$$CI_{DDF(I)}(x, y_o, w) \geq \beta^*(w \cdot g_x). \tag{8.15}$$

The mentioned factor $w \cdot g_x$ is called the *normalization factor*, since, dividing the last inequality by it, we obtain an inequality between numbers.[18] The left normalized term is called the Nerlovian *DDF cost inefficiency measure*, while the right normalized term is simply β^* (i.e., the directional input distance function of technical inefficiency). Finally, *allocative inefficiency* (the DDF allocative contribution to the normalized cost inefficiency) is defined as the gap in the mentioned normalized inequality, which is obtained as a residual giving rise to the next equality:

---

[16] The optimal solution $\left(\sum_{j=1}^{J} \lambda_j^* x_j, \sum_{j=1}^{J} \lambda_j^* y_j\right)$ of program (8.13) may not belong to $L(y_o)$, but the quasi-optimal solution does, and it is easy to verify that it belongs to the frontier of $L(y_o)$. A more direct alternative procedure is shown below in Example 8.3.

[17] If it does not, we can always find a frontier point with at least one of its inputs reduced, and the rest remaining at the same level.

[18] Each firm (x, y_o) *may have a different normalization factor* $w \cdot g_x$. In case all the *input DVs satisfy that all of them have the same* $w \cdot g_x$, then the corresponding DDF satisfies the extended essential property as well as the comparison property (see Chaps. 2 and 13).

$$NCI_{DDF(I)}(x, y_o, \widetilde{w}) = \frac{CI(x, y_o, w)}{w \cdot g_x} = \beta^* + AI_{DDF(I)}(x, y_o, \widetilde{w}), \tag{8.16}$$

where $\widetilde{w}$ denotes the influence of input prices. Firm (x, y_o) is Nerlovian efficient if, and only if, it is technical efficient and allocative efficient. In other words, the three terms of (8.16) must be equal to 0. Otherwise, it is Nerlovian inefficient, as a consequence of being technical inefficient, or allocative inefficient or both. One easy deduction is that any Nerlovian efficient firm must necessarily belong to $\partial^S(L(y_o))$.

Going back to the equality Eq. (8.14), dividing it by the normalization factor, and comparing it with (8.16), we can provide the next interesting interpretation of the allocative inefficiency:

$$AI_{DDF(I)}(x, y_o, \widetilde{w}) = \frac{CI_{DDF(I)}(\widehat{x}, y_o, w)}{w \cdot g_x}. \tag{8.17}$$

In words, the *allocative inefficiency of* (x, y_o) is *the normalized cost inefficiency of its projection*. Hence, we enounce the next proposition without proof (it is really analogous to the graph case).

Proposition 8.4 Given input market prices w, let g_x be a directional input vector belonging to the subfamily of constant market valued DVs, i.e., $w \cdot g_x = k_\$ > 0_\$$. Then, the directional input distance function approach satisfies the essential, the extended essential, and the comparison properties. In particular, the last proposition holds when g_x is a constant input vector.

This result clearly shows that for input-oriented DDFs, the cost inefficiency decomposition establishes an economical relationship between the firm being rated, (x, y_o), and its technical strongly efficient projection $(\widehat{x}, y_o)$. Additionally, it is easy to show that, regardless of the format of the directional vector, the *input DDF* satisfies the essential property. However, it is not true in the case of the extended version of that property. It is not hard to show how, in the case of, for example, the usual directional vector $g_x = x$, the allocative inefficiency component may not coincide with the allocative inefficiency term associated with its projection point $(\widehat{x}, y_o)$ because of using different normalization factors. This fact contrasts with the decomposition of cost efficiency based on the input Shephard's distance function, which does meet the extended essential property. Although in the literature, erroneously, it is assumed that the input Shephard's distance function approach is a particular case of the input-oriented directional distance function approach, this statement is only true for the technical component. Hence, it is false in the case of the cost inefficiency measure and its corresponding allocative or price component (see Aparicio et al., 2017a).

Example 8.3
Let us consider in the two input-one output space the ordered sample of firms A = (2,4,10), B = (4,2,10), C = (5,6,10), D = (6,4,10), E = (8,10,10),

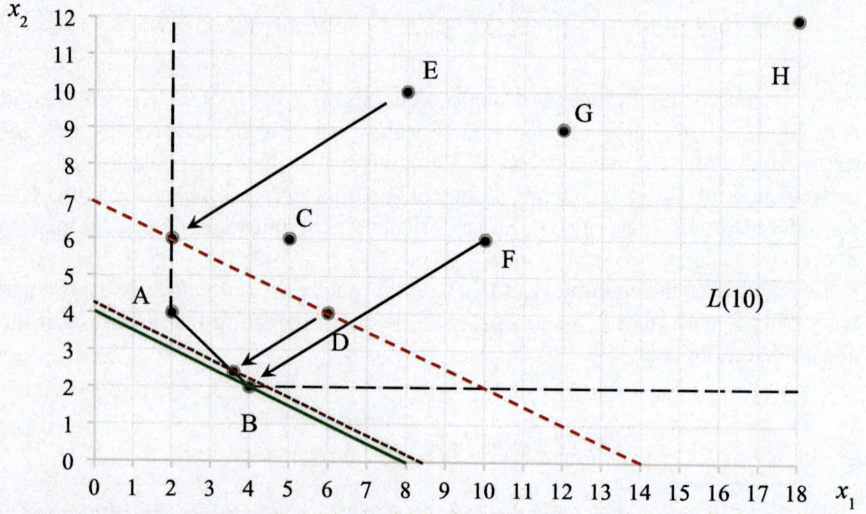

Fig. 8.3 Cost inefficiency decomposition based on the *input-oriented DDF*

F = (10,6,10), G = (12,9,10), and H = (18,12,10). Assume that the *input DDF* is defined in terms of a constant *input DV* (3,2,0), and that *the cost vector* is $w = (1, 2)$. Resorting to *the modified additive model* (8.8), it is easy to verify that the only two efficient firms of *the input requirement set L*(10) are A = (2,4,10) and B = (4,2,10). The *DDF projections* of each of the eight firms are, in the same order, (2,4,10), (4,2,10), (2,4,10), $\left(\frac{18}{5}, \frac{12}{5}, 10\right)$, (2, 6, 10), (4,2,10), (3,3,10), and $\left(\frac{18}{5}, \frac{12}{5}, 10\right)$, where the projection of firms D = (6,4,10) and H = (18,12,10) is the same efficient benchmark $\left(\frac{18}{5}, \frac{12}{5}, 10\right) = \frac{1}{5}(2, 4, 10) + \frac{4}{5}(4, 2, 10)$, the projection of firm G = (12,9,10) is the efficient firm $(3, 3, 10) = \frac{1}{2}(2, 4, 10) + \frac{1}{2}(4, 2, 10)$, and only the projection of firm E = (8,10,10) is a weakly efficient benchmark: (2,6,10). The *DDF technical inefficiencies* of the eight considered firms are $0, 0, 1, \frac{4}{5} = 0.8, 2, 2, 3$ and $\frac{24}{5} = 4.8$. Since the *cost vector* is $w = (1, 2)$, *the input costs* associated with each firm are 10, 8, 17, 14, 28, 22, 30, and 42. Hence, the unique *cost-minimizing firm* is (4,2,10), whose cost is equal to 8—the corresponding isocost line is depicted in Fig. 8.3 (see also Sect. 2.4.1 of Chap. 2).[19] The difference between the cost of each firm and the minimum cost is its *cost inefficiency* that can be easily calculated for our sample of firms, obtaining 10-8 = 2, 8-8 = 0, 9, 6, 20, 14, 22, and 34. Additionally, *the unique normalization factor* associated with the *unique DV* is $w \cdot g_o^- = (1, 2) \cdot (3, 2) = 3 + 4 = 7$. Now we are ready to calculate the *DDF Nerlovian cost inefficiency* for our sample of firms. We will show them for three firms of the sample and leave the rest to the reader. *Efficient firm* B = (4,2,10), which is also the unique *cost-minimizing firm*, has *cost inefficiency* equal to 0, as well as its *Nerlovian cost inefficiency*. Therefore, its technical and allocative inefficiencies must both be

[19]There could be more than one cost-minimizing firm, which depends on the cost vector used.

0. Firm D = (6,4,10) has $\beta_{\mathrm{D}}^{*} = 4/5$, a cost inefficiency equal to 6, and an allocative inefficiency equal to 1/17.5. Hence, its *Nerlovian cost inefficiency* is equal to 6/7. Firm F = (10,6,10) has $\beta_{\mathrm{F}}^{*} = 2$ and a cost inefficiency equal to 14. Hence, its *Nerlovian cost inefficiency* is equal to 2, which means that its *allocative inefficiency* is equal to 0, as corresponds to any firm whose projection is a cost-minimizing firm.

8.6 The Output-Oriented DDFs and the Decomposition of Revenue Inefficiency

We now analyze a finite sample of firms by means of an *output-oriented DDF*. For each firm (x_o, y), we need to choose an *output DV* $(0_M, g_y)$ to calculate its projection $(x_o, \hat{y}) \in \partial^W(T)$, as well as its DDF technical inefficiency $\beta^* \geq 0$. Since we want to maintain the firm's input, we no longer consider the whole production possibility set under variable returns to scale, T, but focus on the subset consisting of all the observations that maintain x_o as its fix input vector, known as the output set $P(x_o) := \{y : (x_o, y) \in T\}$, introduced in Sect. 2.1 of Chap 2. $P(x_o)$ has its own frontier, embedded in $\partial^W(T)$. Given market output prices $p > 0_N$, the maximum revenue for points (x_o, y) satisfying $y \in P(x_o)$, denoted as $R(x_o, p)$, can be obtained by solving the next linear program:

$$
\begin{aligned}
R(x_o, p) = \quad & \max_{y,\lambda} \sum_{n=1}^{N} p_n y_n \\
\text{s.t.} \quad & \\
& \sum_{j=1}^{J} \lambda_j x_{jm} \leq x_{om}, \quad m = 1, \ldots, M, \\
& \sum_{j=1}^{J} \lambda_j y_{jn} \geq y_n, \quad n = 1, \ldots, N, \\
& \sum_{j=1}^{J} \lambda_j = 1, \\
& \lambda_j \geq 0, \quad j = 1, \ldots, J, \\
& y_n \geq 0, \quad n = 1, \ldots, N.
\end{aligned}
\tag{8.18}
$$

Any quasi-optimal solution of the last program, (x_o, y^R), where $y^R = \sum_{j=1}^{J} \lambda_j^* y_{nj}$, is a *revenue-maximizing point*. For any firm, its *revenue inefficiency* $RI(x_o, y, p)$ is defined as $RI(x_o, y, p) = R(x_o, p) - p \cdot y \geq 0$, that is, the difference between the maximum revenue $R(x_o, p)$ and the revenue at (x_o, y), $p \cdot y$. Again, the optimal solution of the last linear program must surely belong to $\partial^W(T)$, by contradiction.[20]

For decomposing the revenue inefficiency $RI(x_o, y, p)$, we need to develop *an inequality that relates it to β^* times a certain quantity* so that the two members of the inequality are expressed in the same monetary units. To this end, let us consider the technical *output DDF projection* of the mentioned firm, $(x_o, \widehat{y}) \in \partial^W(T)$, that satisfies the equality $(x_o, \widehat{y}) = (x_o, y) + \beta^*(0_M, g_y)$. By multiplying all their output components by the output price vector p, we finally obtain the equality $p \cdot \widehat{y} = p \cdot y + \beta^*(p \cdot g_y)$. Finally, transposing the last term, we obtain $p \cdot y = p \cdot \widehat{y} - \beta^*(p \cdot g_y)$. Subtracting from $R(x_o, p)$ the left- and right-hand sides of last equality, we obtain $R(x_o, p) - p \cdot y = R(x_o, p) - (p \cdot \widehat{y} - \beta^*(p \cdot g_y)) = \beta^*(p \cdot g_y) + (R(x_o, p) - p\widehat{y})$, which allows us to decompose the *revenue inefficiency* $RI_{DDF(O)}(x_o, y, p) = R(x_o, p) - p \cdot y$ as follows:

$$RI_{DDF(O)}(x_o, y, p) = \beta^*(p \cdot g_y) + (R(x_o, p) - p\widehat{y}). \tag{8.19}$$

The last equality between quantities expressed in monetary units shows, as a subproduct, that the revenue inefficiency of firm (x_o, y) is greater than or equal to the product of a certain monetary factor, $p \cdot g_y > 0$, times its *output DDF technical inefficiency*, β^*, taking into account that for any projection $(x_o, \widehat{y}) \in \partial^W(T)$, *we know that* $(R(x_o, p) - p\widehat{y}) \geq \$0$, being \$0 only in the case that $(x_o, \widehat{y}) \in \partial^W(T)$ is a revenue-maximizing point:

$$RI_{DDF(O)}(x_o, y, p) \geq \beta^*(p \cdot g_y). \tag{8.20}$$

The mentioned factor $p \cdot g_y > 0$ is called the *normalization factor*, since, dividing the last inequality by it, we obtain an inequality between numbers. In expression (8.19), the left normalized term is called the Nerlovian revenue inefficiency of firm (x_o, y), while the first right normalized term is simply β^* (i.e., the directional output distance function of technical inefficiency), while the second right normalized term is called the *allocative inefficiency* (i.e., the DDF allocative measure of normalized revenue inefficiency associated with (x_o, y)), giving rise to the next equality.

$$NRI(x_o, y, \widetilde{p}) = \frac{RI(x_o, y, p)}{p \cdot g_y} = \beta^* + AI_{DDF(O)}(x_o, y, \widetilde{p}), \tag{8.21}$$

where $\widetilde{p}$ denote the influence of input prices. Firm (x_o, y) is Nerlovian efficient if, and only if, it is technical efficient and allocative efficient. In other words, the three terms of (8.21) must be equal to 0. Otherwise, it is Nerlovian inefficient, because of being technical inefficient, or allocative inefficient, or both.

[20] If it does not, we can always find a frontier benchmark with at least one of its outputs increased and the rest remaining at the same level.

Going back to equality (8.19), dividing it by the normalization factor, and comparing it with (8.21), we can provide the next interesting interpretation of the allocative inefficiency:

$$AI_{DDF(O)}(x_o, y, \widetilde{p}) = \frac{RI(x_o, \widehat{y}, p)}{p \cdot g_y}. \tag{8.22}$$

In words, the *allocative inefficiency of* (x_o, y) is *the revenue inefficiency of its projection divided by its own normalization factor*. Hence, we can establish the next proposition without proof (it is analogous to the graph case).

Proposition 8.5 Given output market prices p, let g_y be an output directional vector belonging to the subfamily of constant market value DVs, i.e., $p \cdot g_y = k_{\$} > 0_{\$}$. Then, the directional output distance function approach satisfies the essential, the extended essential, and the comparison properties. In particular, the last proposition holds when g_y is a constant output vector.

It is easy to show that, regardless of the format of the directional vector, the *output-oriented DDF* satisfies the essential property. However, it is not true in the case of the extended version of that property. It is not hard to show how, in the case of considering, for example, the directional vector $g_y = y$, the allocative inefficiency component could not coincide with the allocative inefficiency term associated with its projection, point $(x_o, \widehat{y})$ because of using different normalization factors. This fact contrasts with the decomposition of revenue efficiency based on the output Shephard's distance function, which does meet the extended essential property. Although in the literature, erroneously, it is assumed that the output Shephard's distance function approach is a particular case of the output-oriented directional distance function approach, this statement is only true for the technical component. Therefore, it is false in the case of the revenue inefficiency measure and its corresponding allocative component (see Aparicio et al., 2017a).

Example 8.4

Let us consider in the one input-two output space the sample of firms A = (1,2,6), B = (1,2,3), C = (1,4,6), D = (1,4,12), E = (1,5,5), F = (1,8,12), and G = (1,12,8). For this example, we choose as *output DDF* that corresponding to the *proportional DDF*, i.e., $g_o = (0, y_1, y_2)$, and assume that *the output price vector* is $p = (4,4)$. Solving *the improved additive model* (8.8), we obtain that the only two efficient firms of *the output requirement set* $P(1)$ are firms F = (1,8,12) and G = (1,12,8) (see Fig. 8.4). The *DDF projections* of each of the other five firms are, keeping the initial ordering, (1,4,12), (1,8,12), (1,8,12), (1,4,12), and $(1, 10, 10) = 0.5(1, 8, 12) + 0.5$ $(1, 12, 8)$. It is clear that firm D = (1,4,12) is a weakly efficient firm, dominated by firm F = (1,8,12). The associated *DDF inefficiencies* for these five units are 1, 3, 1, 0, and 1. The revenues associated with each of the seven firms are, in the same initial order, 32, 20, 40, 64, 40, 80, and 80, which means that the last two efficient firms are *revenue-maximizing firms* (in this case, the maximum isorevenue line $4y_1 + 4y_2 = 80$ contains the efficient segment $[(8, 12), (12, 8)]$ in the plane $x = 1$). Hence, the

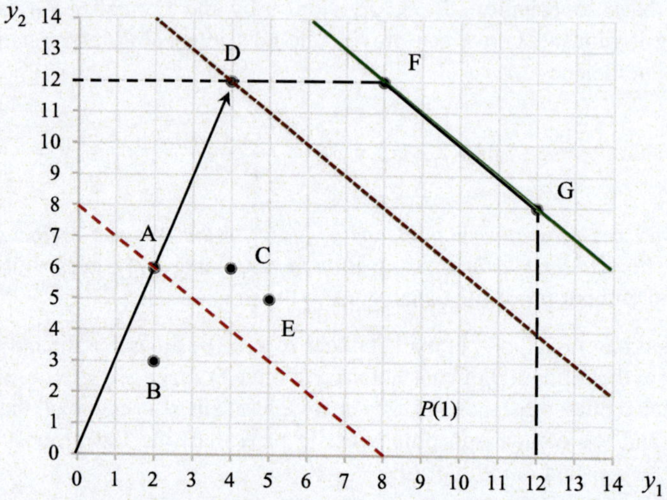

Fig. 8.4 Revenue inefficiency decomposition based on an *output-oriented DDF*

revenue inefficiencies associated with them are 80-32 = 48, 60, 40, 16, 40, 0, and 0. The respective normalizing factors, $p \cdot g_y > 0$, are, in this case, equal to the revenue associated with each firm already listed above. Hence, the Nerlovian revenue inefficiencies, equal in each case to the revenue inefficiency divided by $p \cdot g_y$, are $\frac{48}{32} = \frac{3}{2}$, $\frac{60}{20} = 3$, $\frac{40}{40} = 1$, $\frac{16}{64} = \frac{1}{4}$, $\frac{40}{40} = 1$, $\frac{0}{80} = 0$ *and* $\frac{0}{80} = 0$. The revenue inefficiency decomposition for the first five firms are $\frac{3}{2} = 1 + \frac{1}{2}$, $3 = 3 + 0$, $1 = 1 + 0$, $\frac{1}{4} = 0 + \frac{1}{4}$, $1 = 1 + 0$, while the last two revenue-maximizing firms are Nerlovian revenue efficient, with the same decomposition, $0 = 0 + 0$.

8.7 A Price-Based Method for Comparing DDF Inefficiencies based on the Normalization of the DVs

We provide an interpretation of the technical inefficiency in monetary terms based on *the normalization factor* associated with each of the three Nerlovian economic inefficiency formulations. We focus our attention on the case of *the (Nerlovian) DDF profit inefficiency measure* since it can be easily remade for the cost and revenue cases. Just as a reminder, the equality (8.12), $\frac{\Pi(w,p)-(p \cdot y - w \cdot x)}{(p \cdot g_y + w \cdot g_x)} = \vec{D}_T(x, y; g_x, g_y) + AI(x, y, \widetilde{w}, \widetilde{p})$, is equivalent to $\frac{\Pi(w,p)-(p \cdot y - w \cdot x)}{(p \cdot g_y + w \cdot g_x)} = \vec{D}_T(x, y; g_x, g_y) + \frac{\Pi(w,p)-(\widehat{p \cdot y - w \cdot x})}{(p \cdot g_y + w \cdot g_x)}$, or to $\Pi(w,p) - (p \cdot y - w \cdot x) = \vec{D}_T(x, y; g_x, g_y)(p \cdot g_y + w \cdot g_x) +$

$\Pi(w,p) - (p \cdot \widehat{y} - w \cdot \widehat{x})$. Finally, by deleting $\Pi(w,p)$ and transposing the negative terms, we obtain

$$(p \cdot \widehat{y} - w \cdot \widehat{x}) = \vec{D}_T(x, y; g_x, g_y)(p \cdot g_y + w \cdot g_x) + (p \cdot g_y + w \cdot g_x) \tag{8.23}$$

(see also Chap. 13). Hence, knowing that $\beta^* = \vec{D}_T(x, y; g_x, g_y) > 0$, *the product* $\beta^*(p \cdot g_y + w \cdot g_x)$ is *the monetary profit increase that must be applied to the profit of firm* (x, y) *to reach the profit of its projection*, or, equivalently, the term $(p \cdot g_y + w \cdot g_x)$ is equal to *the monetary profit gap divided by the scalar* $\beta^* > 0$. This interpretation of $(p \cdot g_y + w \cdot g_x)$ in terms of *profit gains per unit of DDF inefficiency* has gone unnoticed to date.

What we are interested in is the possibility of normalizing the different *DVs* in such a way that they all generate the same amount of profit gains, in which case the associated $\beta^* > 0$ *will be comparable*, according to *Proposition 8.3*. Here follows our new proposal.

8.7.1 A Procedure for Normalizing the DVs

For the sample of firms (x_j, y_j), $j = 1, \ldots, J$, being analyzed through a specific *graph DDF*, let us consider the subsample for which $\beta_j^* > 0, j = 1, \ldots, K < J$, and define a *new constant DV* $\left(\underline{g}_x, \underline{g}_y\right)$ as follows: $p \cdot \underline{g}_y + w \cdot \underline{g}_x = \min_{g_{jx}, g_{jy}} \{p \cdot g_{jy} + w \cdot g_{jx}, j = 1, \ldots, K\} > 0$. Defining $\sigma_j \geq 1$ as $\sigma_j = \frac{p \cdot g_{jy} + w \cdot g_{jx}}{p \cdot \underline{g}_y + w \cdot \underline{g}_x}, j = 1, \ldots, K$, it is straightforward to verify that we can use a proportional *graph DV*, $\frac{1}{\sigma_j}(g_{jx}, g_{jy})$, for each of the non-frontier firms of our original sample, being its new DDF inefficiency equal to $\underline{\beta}_j^* = \sigma_j \beta_j^*, j = 1, \ldots, K$. The last equality can be extended to include the frontier firms and since $\beta_j^* = 0, j = K + 1, \ldots, J$ we deduce that also $\underline{\beta}_j^* = 0, j = K + 1, \ldots, J$. Moreover, the original technical profit gap can be rewritten as $\beta_j^*(p \cdot g_{jy} + w \cdot g_{jx}) = \underline{\beta}_j^*\left(\frac{p \cdot g_{jy} + w \cdot g_{jx}}{\sigma_j}\right) = \underline{\beta}_j^*\left(p \cdot \underline{g}_y + w \cdot \underline{g}_x\right)$, we are resorting to *a new set of modified DVs* $\left(\frac{g_j^-}{\sigma_j}, \frac{g_j^+}{\sigma_j}\right)$ for each of the non-frontier firms that verify the last equality. Therefore, *the new DDF inefficiencies* $\underline{\beta}_j^*, j = 1, \ldots, J$ *are comparable in terms of profit gaps, which are equal to* $\underline{\beta}_j^*\left(p \cdot \underline{g}_y + w \cdot \underline{g}_x\right), j = 1, \ldots, J$.[21]

[21] In case we want to analyze a panel dataset, e.g., in the vein of the Profit-Luenberger indicator discussed by Juo et al. (2015) and Balk (2018), we must make sure that the prices for the different time periods are referred to the same base period.

Example 8.5

Let us consider the same data of Example 8.2 in the one input-one output space, already depicted in Fig. 8.2 of Sect. 8.4 and consisting of firms A = (3,5), B = (6,10), C = (12,12), D = (3,2), E = (8,8), F = (9,11), G = (10,10), and H = (14,11). There we have proved that, under VRS, the subset of extreme efficient firms are the three initial firms. Let us also consider the same market prices $(p, w) = (3, 2)$ and let us take a different *graph DV* for each firm. Assume that for firm (x_j, y_j), $j = 1, \ldots, 8$, we choose the *proportional (graph) DV* (x_j, y_j). As with any efficiency measure, the *DDF projection* of each extreme efficient firm is the firm itself. The *DDF projections* obtained for the rest of the firms are $(\widehat{x}_{\mathrm{D}}, \widehat{y}_{\mathrm{D}}) = (3, 2)$, $(\widehat{x}_{\mathrm{E}}, \widehat{y}_{\mathrm{E}}) = (6, 10)$, $(\widehat{x}_{\mathrm{F}}, \widehat{y}_{\mathrm{F}}) = (9, 11) = 0.5(6, 10) + 0.5(12, 12)$, $(\widehat{x}_{\mathrm{G}}, \widehat{y}_{\mathrm{G}})$ $(9, 11)$, and $(\widehat{x}_{\mathrm{H}}, \widehat{y}_{\mathrm{H}}) = \left(\frac{140}{11}, 12\right) = (12, 12) + \left(\frac{8}{11}, 0\right)$, representing a weakly efficient point. Their respective inefficiency scores are equal to 0, 1/4, 0, 1/10, and 1/11. Since firm D = (3,2) gets $\beta^*_{\mathrm{D}} = 0$, it must necessarily be a weakly efficient firm.[22] The same happens for firm H = (14,11), whose projection $(\widehat{x}_{\mathrm{H}}, \widehat{y}_{\mathrm{H}}) = \left(12\frac{8}{11}, 12\right)$ is dominated by efficient firm C = (12,12), and is therefore also a weakly efficient benchmark. On the other hand, firm F = (9,11) is a convex combination of the two extreme efficient firms, with $\lambda = 0.5 = 1 - \lambda$, which means that it is also an efficient firm, although a non-extreme one. Summarizing, five firms obtain $\beta^* = 0$, which means that the value gap $\beta^*\left(p \cdot g_y + w \cdot g_x\right)$, between each of them and their projections, is 0. Consequently, modifying their original *DVs* makes no sense because the value gain will always be equal to 0. Therefore, the only firms that need adjusting their *DV* to get comparable *DDF inefficiencies* are the non-frontier firms E = (8,8), G = (10,10), and H = (14,11). The market values of their respective directional vectors are $3 \cdot 8 + 2 \cdot 8 = 40$, $3 \cdot 10 + 2 \cdot 10 = 50$, and $3 \cdot 11 + 2 \cdot 14 = 33 + 28 = 61$. In order to establish the smallest value, 40, as the common reference for all *DVs*, we need to firstly reduce *DV* (10,10) multiplying it by 40/50 = 4/5, the reciprocal of the associated $\sigma_j = \frac{5}{4} \geq 1$, and secondly reduce *DV* (14,11), multiplying it by 40/61. Consequently, the corresponding *comparable DDF inefficiencies* must be multiplied by the inverse of these fractions, yielding 0.125 instead of 0.1 for firm G = (10,10), and 0.139 instead of 0.091 for firm H = (14,11). For firm G = (10,10), the comparable inefficiency increases by 2.5% with respect to the proportional inefficiency, while for firm H = (14,11), the rise is close to 5.3%. The latter percentages are, in our opinion, rather moderate indicating that the *DVs* of the firms of our sample have similar sizes which give rise to similar profit gains although, strictlly speaking, non comparable.

[22] It is impossible to write firm (3,2) as a convex linear combination of any pair of extreme-efficient points.

8.8 Empirical Illustration of the DDF Profit, Cost, and Revenue Inefficiency Models

In this section, we illustrate the calculation of the three economic inefficiency measures, profit, cost, and revenue, and their decomposition based on their corresponding directional distance functions, graph, input, and output, using the example data presented in Sect. 2.5 of Chap. 2. Table 8.1 replicates the data. Also, in Sect. 8.8.4, we illustrate the calculation and decomposition of profit inefficiency using the dataset on Taiwanese banks studied by Juo et al. (2015).

As previously remarked, when implementing economic inefficiency models based on the *DDF*, it is necessary to choose a *graph DV*, $g_o = (g_x, g_y) \neq 0_{M+N}$. In the literature, the most usual choice corresponds to the observed input and output amounts, i.e., $g = (x, y)$, characterizing the so-called proportional DDF, since inputs are proportionally reduced and outputs are proportionally increased. The functions included in the "Benchmarking Economic Efficiency" package for the Julia language solve this particular DDF, but researchers can choose from among different alternatives as shown next, i.e., we consider the three subfamilies of exogenous *DVs* presented in Sect. 8.3.1. Specifically, the functions that compute these measures, as well as their decompositions into technical and allocative inefficiencies, are the following:

```
deaprofit(X, Y, W, P, Gx = :Observed, Gy = :Observed, names = FIRMS)
deacostddf(X, Y, W, Gx = :Observed, names = FIRMS)
dearevenueddf(X, Y, P, Gy = :Observed, names = FIRMS)
```

In the above syntax, it is possible to substitute "`:Observed`" with the following options of directional vectors:

Table 8.1 Example data illustrating the economic inefficiency models

	Model							
	Graph profit model		Input orientation Cost model			Output orientation Revenue model		
Firm	x	y	x_1	x_2	y	x	y_1	y_2
A	2	1	2	2	1	1	7	7
B	4	5	1	4	1	1	4	8
C	8	8	4	1	1	1	8	4
D	12	9	4	3	1	1	3	5
E	6	3	5	5	1	1	3	3
F	14	7	6	1	1	1	8	2
G	14	9	2	5	1	1	6	4
H	9.412	2.353	1.6	8	1	1	1.5	5
Prices	$w = 1$	$p = 2$	$w_1 = 1$	$w_2 = 1$			$p_1 = 1$	$p_2 = 1$

- "`:Ones`." Sets the *graph DV* to $g = (1_M, 1_N)$.
- "`:Mean`." Sets the *graph DV* to $g = (\bar{x}_M, \bar{y}_N)$, where each common *m*-th and *n*-th element corresponds to the arithmetic mean of each input and output: $\bar{x}_m = \sum_{j=1}^{J} x_{mj}$ and $\bar{y}_n = \sum_{j=1}^{J} y_{nj}$, respectively.
- "`:Zeros`." Sets the output or input direction to zero. Combining with the previous options allows calculating *input-oriented DDFs*, e.g., $g = (x, 0_N)$, $g = (1_M, 0_N)$, or $g = (\bar{x}_M, 0_N)$, and *output-oriented DDFs*, e.g., $g = (0_M, y)$, $g = (0_M, 1_N)$, or $g = (0_M, \bar{y}_N)$.
- "`:Monetary`." Following Zofío et al. (2013, p. 263), this option returns profit inefficiency, including its technical and allocative components, whose values are equivalent to monetary unitary units (e.g., dollars). To this end, profit inefficiency (8.12) is calculated under the condition that the normalizing factor satisfies $p \cdot g_y + w \cdot g_x = \$1$, implying that technical inefficiency $\beta^* > 0$ can be interpreted as the profit difference between (x, y) and its technical projection and, subsequently, allocative inefficiency can be interpreted as the profit difference between the latter and maximum profit. The condition $p \cdot g_y + w \cdot g_x = \$1$ can be implemented by considering a neutral directional vector that assigns to each input and output element of the *DV* the same value. In this case, the common individual directions are calculated as $g_{x_m} = 1_{q_{xm}} \cdot \$ / \left(\sum_{m=1}^{M} w_{m_{\$/q_{xm}}} 1_{q_{xm}} + \sum_{n=1}^{N} p_{n_{\$/q_{yn}}} 1_{q_{yn}} \right)_{\$}$ and $g_y = 1_{q_{y_n}} \cdot \$ / \left(\sum_{m=1}^{M} w_{m_{\$/q_{xm}}} 1_{q_{xm}} + \sum_{n=1}^{N} p_{n_{\$/q_{yn}}} 1_{q_{yn}} \right)_{\$}$. In the denominator of these expressions, we explicitly denote that each individual w_m and p_n corresponds to unit prices ($\$/q_{x_m}$ and $\$/q_{y_n}$), which once multiplied by one unit of the input and output variables, result in an aggregate monetary amount ($). Finally, assuming that the numerator corresponds to a value of one, whose unit of measurement is quantity times the monetary unit, $q_{x_m} \cdot \$$ and $q_{y_n} \cdot \$$, we ensure that each element of the input and output directional vector is expressed in the original unit of measurement of the input and output variables. Finally, profit inefficiency, being normalized by $p \cdot g_y + w \cdot g_x = \$1$, is a pure number that, quite conveniently, coincides with the value of economic inefficiency in monetary terms (as its technical and allocative components).

Researchers can also pass their own values for the exogenous directional vectors by defining the corresponding variables in advance. For example, using "`Gx = X, Gy = Y`" is equivalent to using "`Gx = :Observed, Gy = :Observed`." They may also implement other alternatives discussed in this chapter, such as the *modified DVs* $\left(\frac{g_j^-}{\sigma_j}, \frac{g_j^+}{\sigma_j}\right)$ presented in Sect. 8.7.1, making the *DDF* inefficiencies comparable in terms of proportional profit gains.

To illustrate the different possibilities, we implement the three economic inefficiency models choosing alternative directional vectors. We use the "`:Monetary`" option to calculate and decompose the example of profit inefficiency—expression (8.12). The "`:Ones`" option is used to calculate and decompose the examples for the cost inefficiency and the revenue inefficiency models: (8.16) and (8.19) (the

Table 8.2 Implementation of the *DDF* profit inefficiency model using BEE for Julia

In[]:

```
using DataEnvelopmentAnalysis
using BenchmarkingEconomicEfficiency

X = [2; 4; 8; 12; 6; 14; 14; 9.412];
Y = [1; 5; 8; 9; 3; 7; 9; 2.353];
W = [1; 1; 1; 1; 1; 1; 1; 1];
P = [2; 2; 2; 2; 2; 2; 2; 2];
FIRMS = ["A", "B", "C", "D", "E", "F", "G", "H"];

deaprofit(X, Y, W, P, Gx = :Monetary, Gy = :Monetary, names
= FIRMS)
```

Out[]:

```
Profit DEA Model
DMUs = 8; Inputs = 1; Outputs = 1
Returns to Scale = VRS
Gx = Monetary; Gy = Monetary
```

	Profit	Technical	Allocative
A	8.0	0.0	8.0
B	2.0	0.0	2.0
C	0.0	0.0	0.0
D	2.0	0.0	2.0
E	8.0	6.0	2.0
F	8.0	6.0	2.0
G	4.0	0.0	4.0
H	12.706	11.496	1.210

corresponding functions assigns the "`:Zeros`" option internally for the output and output dimensions, respectively). Finally, in Sect. 8.8.4, we calculate the profit inefficiency using the dataset of Taiwanese banks using *the proportional DDF*, whose directional vector corresponds to the "`:Observed`" quantities of inputs and outputs.

8.8.1 The Graph DDF Profit Inefficiency Model

We rely on the open (web-based) Jupyter notebook interface to illustrate our economic models. Nevertheless, they can be implemented in any integrated development environment (IDE) of preference.[23] To calculate the profit inefficiency model (8.12), run the following code in the "`In[]:`" window. The results are shown in the "`Out[]:`" panel in Table 8.2.

[23]We refer the reader to Sect. 2.6.1 in Chap. 2 for the installation of the "Benchmarking Economic Efficiency" Julia package. All Jupyter notebooks implementing the different economic models in this book can be downloaded from the reference site: http://www.benchmarkingeconomicefficiency.com

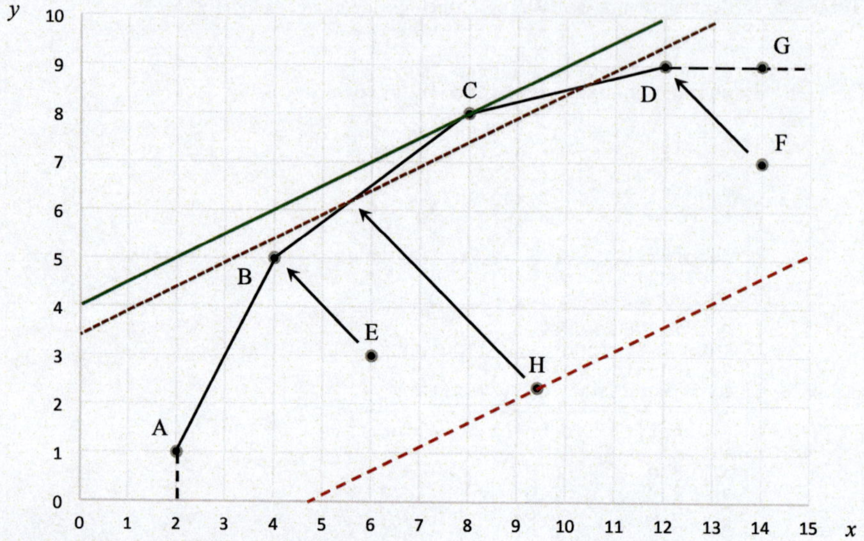

Fig. 8.5 Example of the *graph DDF* profit inefficiency model using BEE for Julia

Table 8.3 Implementation of the graph DDF inefficiency measure using BEE for Julia

In[]:
```
deaddf(X, Y, rts = :VRS, Gx = repeat(G, 1, m), Gy = repeat(G,
1, n), names = FIRMS)
```

Out[]:
```
Directional DF DEA Model
DMUs = 8; Inputs = 1; Outputs = 1
Returns to Scale = VRS
Gx = Custom; Gy = Custom
```

	efficiency	slackX1	slackY1
A	0.0	0.0	0.0
B	0.0	0.0	0.0
C	0.0	0.0	0.0
D	0.0	0.0	0.0
E	6.0	0.0	0.0
F	6.0	0.0	0.0
G	0.0	2.0	0.0
H	11.496	0.0	0.0

We can learn about the reference benchmarks for each firm using the "peersmatrix" function with the corresponding economic or technical model. For the economic model, executing "`peersmatrix(deaprofit(X, Y, W, P, Gx = :Monetary, Gy = :Monetary, names = FIRMS))`" identifies firm C as the reference benchmark-maximizing profit for the rest of the firms (see Fig. 8.5).

As for the underlying graph DDF technical inefficiency model, we obtain all the information running the corresponding function, as shown in Table 8.3. As previously mentioned, these technical inefficiencies are obtained by solving program (8.6) considering a neutral direction that assigns the same value to all input and output elements of the directional vector: $g_{x_m} = 1_{q_{x_m}} \cdot \$ / \left(\sum_{m=1}^{M} w_{m_{\$/q_{x_m}}} 1_{q_{x_m}} + \sum_{n=1}^{N} p_{n_{\$/q_{y_n}}} 1_{q_{y_n}} \right)_{\$}$ and $g_y = 1_{q_{y_n}} \cdot \$ / \left(\sum_{m=1}^{M} w_{m_{\$/}} q_{x_m} 1_{q_{x_m}} + \sum_{n=1}^{N} p_{n_{\$/q_{y_n}}} 1_{q_{y_n}} \right)_{\$}$. This common value g is calculated through the following syntax: "`G = 1 ./ (sum(W, dims = 2) + sum(P, dims =2)); m=size(X,2); n=size(Y,2);`", which is later used in the calculation of the graph DFF measures—in this example G = 0.333.[24] Finally, since the graph DDF identifies weakly efficient benchmarks, the improved additive model (8.8) is solved at a second stage in order to calculate individual input reductions and output increases. In this case, Table 8.6 shows that firm G has an input slack of two units.

The identification of the reference benchmarks corresponding to the graph DDF distance function also proves of interest. Once again, these benchmarks can be recovered through the "peersmatrix" function, i.e., "`peersmatrix(deaddf(X, Y, rts = :VRS, Gx = repeat(G, 1, m), Gy = repeat(G, 1, n), names = FIRMS))`". The output results shown in Table 8.7 ("`Out[]:`") identify firms A, B, C, and D as those conforming the weakly efficient production possibility set, i.e., those with unit values in the main diagonal of the square ($J \times J$) matrix containing their own intensity variables λ. Note that the benchmark for firm G is firm D, despite firm G having an efficiency score $\beta_G^* = 0$. The reason is that when solving program (8.6), the input constraint is verified as an inequality, with the corresponding input slack, later quantified through (8.8), being equal to two (Table 8.3).

Table 8.4 Reference peers of the graph DDF inefficiency measure using BEE for Julia

In[]:
```
peersmatrix(deaddf(X, Y, rts = :VRS, Gx = repeat(G, 1, m),
 Gy = repeat(G, 1, n), names = FIRMS))
```

Out[]:
```
1.0    .      .      .    .  .  .  .
 .    1.0     .      .    .  .  .  .
 .     .     1.0     .    .  .  .  .
 .     .      .     1.0   .  .  .  .
 .    1.0     .      .    .  .  .  .
 .     .      .     1.0   .  .  .  .
 .     .      .     1.0   .  .  .  .
 .    0.605  0.395   .    .  .  .  .
```

[24]The syntax in Table 8.3 is adapted for the case of multiple inputs (m) and multiple outputs (n), where the common value G is applied to all the elements of the matrix containing the column values for inputs and outputs, i.e., "`Gx = repeat(G, 1, m); Gy = repeat(G, 1, n);`."

Figure 8.5 illustrates the results for the graph DDF profit inefficiency whose results can be interpreted in monetary terms. Here, for firm H, we identify that the profit inefficiency with respect to firm C, according to (8.12), is equal to $N\Pi I_{DDF(G)}(x_{\mathrm{H}}, y_{\mathrm{H}}, w, p) = \Pi(w, p) - (p \cdot y_{\mathrm{H}} - w \cdot x_{\mathrm{H}}) = 12.706 = 8-(-4.703)$. The latter can be decomposed into the graph DDF distance function representing technical inefficiency, whose value is $\vec{D}_T(x_{\mathrm{H}}, y_{\mathrm{H}}, g_x, g_y) = \beta^*_{\mathrm{H}} = 11.496$, and also allocative inefficiency, $AI_{DDF(G)}(x_H, y_H, w, p) = 12.706 - 11.496 = 1.210$. Note that, for this example, and contrary to the cost and revenue inefficiency examples that follow, none of the firms identify the same economic and technological benchmark, i.e., firm C.

8.8.2 The Input-Oriented DDF Cost Inefficiency Model

We now solve the example for the cost inefficiency model whose technical inefficiency corresponds to the input-oriented DDF. In this case, we choose the unit value directional vector $g = (1_M, 0_N)$, while the software function internally assigns a zero value to the output dimension g_y. To calculate this model, run the code included in the "`In[]:`" window of the notebook. The corresponding results are shown in the "`Out[]:`" panel of Table 8.5.

It is possible to determine the reference benchmarks resorting to the "peersmatrix" function with the corresponding economic or technical model. For the cost model,

Table 8.5 Implementation of the *DDF* cost inefficiency model using BEE for Julia

In[]:

```
using DataEnvelopmentAnalysis
using BenchmarkingEconomicEfficiency

X = [2 2; 1 4; 4 1; 4 3; 5 5; 6 1; 2 5; 1.6 8];
Y = [1; 1; 1; 1; 1; 1; 1; 1];
W = [1 1; 1 1; 1 1; 1 1; 1 1; 1 1; 1 1; 1 1];
FIRMS = ["A", "B", "C", "D", "E", "F", "G", "H"];

deacostddf(X, Y, W, Gx = :Ones, names=FIRMS)
```

Out[]:

```
Cost DDF DEA Model
DMUs = 8; Inputs = 2; Outputs = 1
Orientation = Input; Returns to Scale = VRS
Gx = Ones
```

	Cost	Technical	Allocative
A	0.0	0.0	0.0
B	0.5	0.0	0.5
C	0.5	0.0	0.5
D	1.5	1.333	0.167
E	3.0	3.0	0.0
F	1.5	0.0	1.5
G	1.5	1.0	0.5
H	2.8	0.6	2.2

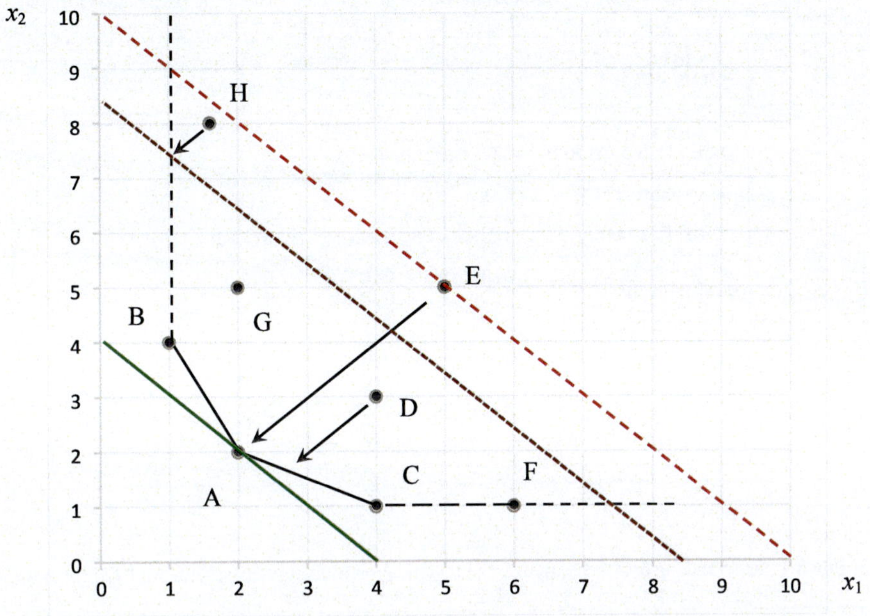

Fig. 8.6 Example of the input-oriented DDF cost inefficiency model using BEE for Julia

we run "`peersmatrix(deacostddf(X, Y, W, Gx=:Ones, names=FIRMS))`". In this case, firm A is identified as the only firm-minimizing cost (see Fig. 8.6).

We can learn about firms' technical inefficiencies by running the function that calculates the input-oriented DDF model, as shown in Table 8.6. Besides providing the efficiency score, $\beta^* \geq 0$, this function solves the improved additive model (8.8) at a second stage in order to determine the existence of slacks, once the firms under evaluation are projected to their benchmark. In this example, two inefficient firms, F and H, either belong or are projected to the weakly efficient production possibility set, and therefore endure the existence of input slacks. With firm C as reference benchmark, firm F presents a slack of two units in the first input. On its part, firm H is projected to the weakly frontier defined by firm B, with a slack of 3.4 units in the second input.

The reference benchmarks of the technical model can be recovered using the "peersmatrix" function, i.e., "`peersmatrix(deaddf(X, Y, rts = :VRS, Gx=:Ones, Gy=:Zeros, names = FIRMS))`". The output shown in Table 8.7 identifies firms A, B, and C as those conforming the production frontier (see "`Out[]:`").

Figure 8.6 illustrates the results for the input-oriented DDF cost inefficiency model with a unitary directional vector. Here, for firm E, we learn that its normalized cost efficiency with respect to firm A, according to (8.16), is equal to $NCI_{DDF(I)}(x_{\text{E}}, y_{\text{E}}, \widetilde{w}) = 3 = (10 - 4)/2$, which can be decomposed into the input-oriented DDF, whose value is $\beta^*_{\text{E}} = 3$, and the residual allocative inefficiency, which in this case is equal to zero, $AI_{DDF(I)}(x_{\text{E}}, y_{\text{E}}, \widetilde{w}) = 0$. This shows that decomposing

Table 8.6 Implementation of the input DDF technical inefficiency measure using BEE for Julia

In[]:

```
deaddf(X, Y, rts = :VRS, Gx=:Ones, Gy=:Zeros, names =
FIRMS)
```

Out[]:

```
Directional DF DEA Model
DMUs = 8; Inputs = 2; Outputs = 1
Orientation = Input; Returns to Scale = VRS
Gx = Ones; Gy = Zeros
```

	efficiency	slackX1	slackX2	slackY1
A	0.0	0.0	0.0	0.0
B	0.0	0.0	0.0	0.0
C	0.0	0.0	0.0	0.0
D	1.333	0.0	0.0	0.0
E	3.0	0.0	0.0	0.0
F	0.0	2.0	0.0	0.0
G	1.0	0.0	0.0	0.0
H	0.6	0.0	3.4	0.0

Table 8.7 Reference peers of the input DDF technical inefficiency measure using BEE for Julia

In[]:

```
peersmatrix(deaddf(X, Y, rts = :VRS, Gx=:Ones, Gy=:Zeros,
names = FIRMS))
```

Out[]:

1.0	.	.	.	.	.	.	.
.	1.0	.	.	.	.	.	.
.	.	1.0	.	.	.	.	.
0.667	.	0.333	.	.	.	.	.
1.0	.	.	.	.	.	.	.
.	.	1.0	.	.	.	.	.
.	1.0	.	.	.	.	.	.
.	1.0	.	.	.	.	.	.

economic efficiency based on the directional distance function satisfies the essential property discussed in Sect. 2.4.5 of Chap. 2. As for firm H, its cost, technical, and allocative inefficiencies are $NCI_{DDF(I)}(x_{\mathrm{H}}, y_{\mathrm{H}}, \widetilde{w}) = 2.8 = (9.6 - 4)/2$, $\beta^*_{\mathrm{H}} = 0.6$, and $AI_{DDF(I)}(x_{\mathrm{H}}, y_{\mathrm{H}}, \widetilde{w}) = 2.8 - 0.6 = 2.2$.

8.8.3 The Output-Oriented Revenue Inefficiency Model

We proceed to illustrate the revenue inefficiency model based on the output-oriented directional distance function. We consider the same choice of directional vector as in the previous model but from an output dimension: $g = (0_M, 1_N)$. Again, the software

Table 8.8 Implementation of the DDF revenue inefficiency model using BEE for Julia

In[]:

```
using DataEnvelopmentAnalysis
using BenchmarkingEconomicEfficiency

X = [1; 1; 1; 1; 1; 1; 1; 1];
Y = [7 7; 4 8; 8 4; 3 5; 3 3; 8 2; 6 4; 1.5 5];
P = [1 1; 1 1; 1 1; 1 1; 1 1; 1 1; 1 1; 1 1];
FIRMS = ["A", "B", "C", "D", "E", "F", "G", "H"];

dearevenueddf(X, Y, P, Gy = :Ones, names = FIRMS)
```

Out[]:

```
Revenue DDF DEA Model
DMUs = 8; Inputs = 1; Outputs = 2
Orientation = Output; Returns to Scale = VRS
Gy = Ones
```

	Revenue	Technical	Allocative
A	0.0	0.0	0.0
B	1.0	0.0	1.0
C	1.0	0.0	1.0
D	3.0	2.5	0.5
E	4.0	4.0	0.0
F	2.0	0.0	2.0
G	2.0	1.5	0.5
H	3.75	2.875	0.875

function internally assigns a zero value to the input dimension g_y. To calculate the model, we type the code presented in "`In[]:`", Table 8.8. The corresponding results are shown in the "`Out[]:`" panel.

To know the reference set for the evaluation of economic and technical inefficiency, we use the "peersmatrix" function with the corresponding model. For the revenue model, we run "`peersmatrix(dearevenueddf (X, Y, P, Gy=:Ones, names=FIRMS))`". The output identifies firm A as the benchmark-maximizing revenue for the rest of the firms (see Fig. 8.7).

As for the technical inefficiency corresponding to the output-oriented distance function, we identify its value along with any remaining slacks running the code shown in Table 8.9. The slacks are calculated by solving an additive model for the efficient benchmarks on the weakly efficient frontier.

The information on the reference benchmarks for the output technical efficiency model can be recovered using the "peersmatrix" function, i.e., "`peersmatrix (deaddf(X, Y, rts =:VRS, Gx=:Zeros, Gy=:Ones, names = FIRMS))`". The output shown in Table 8.10 identifies firms A, B, and C as those defining the strongly efficient production possibility set ("`Out[]:`"), while firm F defines the weakly efficient frontier as shown by its null efficiency score in Table 8.9, accompanied by a positive slack value.

Figure 8.7 illustrates the results for the revenue inefficiency model based on the output-oriented DDF. Here, for firm E, we see that normalized economic inefficiency with respect to firm A, as defined in (8.21), is equal to $NRI_{DDF(O)}(x_E, y_E, \widetilde{p}) = 4 = (14 - 6)/2$. Revenue inefficiency can be decomposed into the output-oriented

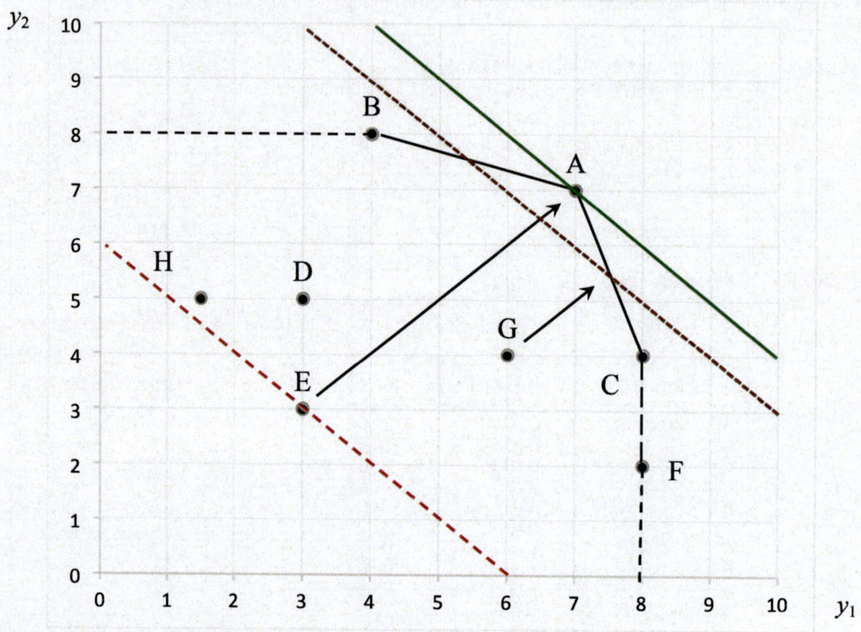

Fig. 8.7 Example of the output-oriented DDF revenue inefficiency model using BEE for Julia

Table 8.9 Implementation of the output DDF inefficiency measure using BEE for Julia

In[]:	`deaddf(X, Y, rts = :VRS, Gx=:Zeros, Gy=:Ones, names = FIRMS)`
Out[]:	Directional DDF DEA Model DMUs = 8; Inputs = 1; Outputs = 2 Orientation = Output; Returns to Scale = VRS Gx = Zeros; Gy = Ones

	efficiency	slackX1	slackY1	slackY2
A	0.0	0.0	0.0	0.0
B	0.0	0.0	0.0	0.0
C	0.0	0.0	0.0	0.0
D	2.5	0.0	0.0	0.0
E	4.0	0.0	0.0	0.0
F	0.0	0.0	0.0	2.0
G	1.5	0.0	0.0	0.0
H	2.875	0.0	0.0	0.0

DDF, whose value is $\beta_{\mathrm{E}}^{*} = 4$, and the residual allocative inefficiency, which is null, $AI_{DDF(O)}(x_{\mathrm{E}}, y_{\mathrm{E}}, \widetilde{p}) = 0$. The case of firm E further illustrates once again that this economic efficiency model under the output-oriented DDF satisfies the essential property presented in Sect. 2.4.5 of Chap. 2. For firm G, its cost, technical, and

Table 8.10 Reference peers of the output DDF inefficiency measure using BEE for Julia

```
In[]:   peersmatrix(deaddf(X, Y, rts = :VRS, Gx=:Zeros, Gy=:Ones,
        names = FIRMS))

Out[]:  1.0     .      .     .  .  .  .  .
        .       1.0    .     .  .  .  .  .
        .       .      1.0   .  .  .  .  .
        0.5     0.5    .     .  .  .  .  .
        1.0     .      .     .  .  .  .  .
        .       .      1.0   .  .  .  .  .
        0.5     .      0.5   .  .  .  .  .
        0.125   0.875  .     .  .  .  .  .
```

allocative inefficiencies are $NRI_{DDF(O)}(x_G, y_G, \widetilde{p}) = 2 = (14 - 10)/2$, $\beta^*_H = 1.5$, and $AI_{DDF(O)}(x_G, y_G, \widetilde{p}) = 2 - 1.5 = 0.5$.

8.8.4 An Application to the Taiwanese Banking Industry

As in previous chapters, we calculate the Nerlovian profit inefficiency model using a real dataset of 31 Taiwanese banks observed in 2010 (see Juo et al., 2015). A brief presentation of the data, including descriptive statistics, can be found in Sect. 2.5.2 of Chap. 2. In this dataset, individual firm prices for each input and output are observed. We adopt the standard approach in the literature and solve for the reference maximum profit of firm (x_o, y_o) including its vector of prices (w_o, p_o) in the objective function of program (8.9). The variation of prices makes the results specific for each firm, and therefore bilateral comparisons of profit inefficiency are price dependent. For instance, it is possible that a technically efficient firm is profit inefficient under its own prices by not demanding the optimal input and output mix (allocative inefficiency), yet it may maximize profit under other firm's prices, serving as reference target. Of course, the opposite situation may be observed.

In order to calculate and decompose Nerlovian profit inefficiency, we chose the *proportional DDF* model that uses the observed vector of inputs and outputs, $g = (x, y)$. Following expression (8.12), Table 8.11 presents the values of profit inefficiency in the second column, including its descriptive statistics at the bottom. In this model, profit inefficiency is normalized by $(p_o \cdot y + w_o \cdot x)$, including the prices observed for each firm. Three banks are profit efficient under their own prices (no. 1, no. 5, and no. 10), with $N\Pi I_{DDF(G)}(x, y, \widetilde{w}, \widetilde{p}) = 0$ and constituting the most frequent benchmarks for the remaining banks. From a technical perspective, as in the rest of the chapters, 11 banks are efficient, while the remaining 20 banks are both technical and allocative inefficient. Technical and allocative inefficiencies are reported in the third

Table 8.11 Decomposition of profit inefficiency based on the proportional directional distance function.

Bank	Economic inefficiency, eq. (8.12)			Slacks, eq. (8.8)				
	Profit Ineff. $N\Pi I_{DDF(G)}(x_o, y_o, \tilde{w}, \tilde{p})$	Technical Ineff. $\vec{D}_T(x_o, y_o; x_o, y_o)$	Allocative Ineff. $AI_{DDF(G)}(x_o, y_o, \tilde{w}, \tilde{p})$	Funds (x_1) s_1^-	Labor (x_2) s_2^-	Ph. Capital (x_3) s_3^-	Investments (y_1) s_1^+	Loans (y_2) s_2^+
1	0.000	0.000	0.000	0.0	0.0	0.0	0.0	0.0
2	0.061	0.000	0.061	0.0	0.0	0.0	0.0	0.0
3	0.146	0.000	0.146	0.0	0.0	0.0	0.0	0.0
4	1.730	0.179	1.551	0.0	149.5	0.0	5,748.9	0.0
5	0.000	0.000	0.000	0.0	0.0	0.0	0.0	0.0
6	0.076	0.000	0.076	0.0	0.0	0.0	0.0	0.0
7	0.115	0.000	0.115	0.0	0.0	0.0	0.0	0.0
8	0.124	0.028	0.096	0.0	725.5	3,395.8	0.0	0.0
9	0.211	0.032	0.180	0.0	1,792.0	8,387.3	0.0	0.0
10	0.000	0.000	0.000	0.0	0.0	0.0	0.0	0.0
11	0.625	0.165	0.459	0.0	1,266.0	7,526.3	0.0	0.0
12	0.721	0.056	0.665	0.0	0.0	1,903.2	0.0	0.0
13	17.056	0.290	16.766	0.0	1,348.6	2,965.1	7,938.2	0.0
14	0.234	0.000	0.234	0.0	0.0	0.0	0.0	0.0
15	0.323	0.076	0.247	0.0	0.0	979.5	0.0	0.0
16	31.301	0.520	30.781	0.0	523.4	2,118.7	3,976.7	0.0
17	0.639	0.092	0.547	0.0	2,814.3	8,155.9	0.0	0.0
18	0.682	0.070	0.611	0.0	1,608.4	0.0	0.0	0.0
19	2.388	0.284	2.104	0.0	484.3	1,360.0	0.0	0.0
20	1.628	0.096	1.533	76,290.5	1,036.6	0.0	5,409.4	0.0
21	0.297	0.000	0.297	0.0	0.0	0.0	0.0	0.0
22	4.546	0.208	4.338	0.0	778.8	4,965.9	14,103.4	0.0
23	8.162	0.340	7.822	0.0	424.6	3,541.7	8,622.9	0.0
24	0.188	0.016	0.172	0.0	1,537.2	1,587.3	0.0	0.0
25	1.811	0.142	1.668	0.0	617.1	0.0	33,758.7	0.0
26	0.724	0.000	0.724	0.0	0.0	0.0	0.0	0.0
27	4.693	0.355	4.338	0.0	219.2	46.1	4,201.1	0.0
28	6.150	0.284	5.866	17,845.0	461.8	0.0	5,992.9	0.0
29	0.871	0.000	0.871	0.0	0.0	0.0	0.0	0.0
30	0.236	0.054	0.181	0.0	974.4	0.0	0.0	0.0
31	3.695	0.160	3.535	0.0	1,422.1	1,403.1	24,207.2	0.0
Average	2.885	0.111	2.774	3,036.6	586.6	1,559.2	3,676.1	0.0
Median	0.639	0.056	0.547	0.0	424.6	0.0	0.0	0.0
Maximum	31.301	0.520	30.781	76,290.5	2,814.3	8,387.3	33,758.7	0.0
Minimum	0.000	0.000	0.000	0.0	0.0	0.0	0.0	0.0
Std. Dev.	6.302	0.137	6.193	13,967.6	715.8	2,523.8	7,691.3	0.0

and fourth columns of Table 8.11. Average normalized profit inefficiency amounts to 2.885. Out of this overall amount, just 3.9% corresponds to technical inefficiency, whose average value is 0.111, while the remaining 96.1% is due to allocative inefficiency, with an average value equal to 2.774. Therefore, as in other additive decompositions of profit inefficiency, most of the normalized profit loss is due to errors in the amount of inputs demanded and the amount of outputs supplied given their market prices.

In the last five columns of Table 8.11, we present the optimal slacks obtained when solving, at a second stage, the standard additive program (8.8) for the optimal projections obtained by the graph DDF. Regarding the inputs' dimension, we observed that the largest average slack associated with the proportional DDF corresponds to financial funds (x_1), whose value is 3,036.6 million TWD, followed by capital (x_3) with an average value of 1,559.2, and, finally, labor (x_2), which amounts to 857.5 employees on average. On the output side, financial investments (y_1) present the only positive slack in this dimension, with an average value of 3,676.1 million TWD. It is worth mentioning that no bank is projected to the weakly efficient frontier defined by loans (y_2), since there are no slacks in this output.

8.9 Summary and Conclusions

We start this chapter by providing a historical overview of the directional distance function since its introduction as an efficiency measure in 1996 and 1998, highlighting the different topics that we consider relevant in the measurement of economic inefficiency and its decomposition into technical and allocative terms.

The first topic we study in detail is the definition of the *DDF* and its use when the characterization of the technical efficiency of a sample of firms with respect to the weakly and strongly efficient production possibility sets is the focus, i.e., in terms of the notion of Pareto-Koopmans efficiency. For this purpose, we propose solving an improved additive model to identify the subset of extreme efficient points from which we can characterize the strongly efficient frontier. This information is later used to propose a method that changes the directional vectors in such way that all firms are projected to the strongly efficient frontier.

The second topic presents an overview of the different types of directional vectors that can be considered, classified into two exclusive families: the family of *exogenous DVs* and the family of *endogenous DVs*. For the first family, we distinguish three subfamilies that are among the most widely used *DVs*: *the subfamily of constant DVs, the subfamily of self-evaluating DVs*, and *the subfamily of sample driven DVs*. We revise the most popular *DVs* for each of the subfamilies and incorporate the latest proposals in the literature.

We then proceed to the core of the chapter dealing with the measurement of *profit, cost, and revenue inefficiency*, associated with each firm of a finite sample when market prices are known. We also show how these inefficiencies can be decomposed according to technological and allocative criteria, the former being represented by the directional distance function. Within a DEA framework, we provide the methods for calculating the *maximum profit*, the *maximum revenue*, and the *minimum cost*, as well as an easy deduction of the *Nerlovian inefficiency decomposition associated with each firm* in each of the three cases. We provide, as usual, numerical examples. We also introduce a new procedure for deriving *comparable inefficiency scores* related to *DDFs* with *nonconstant DVs*, based on the value associated with each *DV* that relates the economic inefficiency of each firm to the economic inefficiency of its projection.

We conclude the chapter presenting the "Benchmarking Economic Efficiency" software that implements all these economic models based on the directional distance function. This should popularize these methods among academics and researchers interested in implementing the measurement of economic performance in empirical analysis. We provide examples for all the functions and, using a dataset of Taiwanese banks, show how these models can be applied to real-life analyses.

Chapter 9
The Hölder Distance Functions: Economic Inefficiency Decompositions

9.1 Introduction

Data Envelopment Analysis can determine both a technical efficiency score and benchmarking information on how to change inputs and outputs to reach the efficient frontier if the firm under evaluation is technically inefficient. All measures studied in this book resort to the determination of benchmarking information through the calculation of the farthest targets for the evaluated DMU—"farthest" in the sense that the measure corresponds to the maximum value of the sum of slacks of the corresponding model or some variation. In the case of the (weighted) additive model discussed in Chap. 6, for example, this is clearly shown in the objective function of program (6.1). The objective function of this mathematical model consists of the weighted sum of the slack in each dimension (input and output), i.e., the difference between the target located on the strongly efficient frontier and the evaluated unit. In the case of the radial measures, i.e., the Farrell measure of technical efficiency, the situation is not so evident. In DEA, it is not strange to apply a second stage when the radial model is utilized in order to determine Pareto-efficient targets from the projection point. This second stage exploits the additive model. Consequently, we are also maximizing slacks. This means that most of the traditional measures in DEA generate the farthest targets. In other words, they yield the targets that are the most difficult ones to be achieved for the firm/organization in the short run.

In contrast, it is more natural to assume that inefficient units apply a principle of least action (PLA) with the goal of being technically efficient, reaching the frontier (see Aparicio et al., 2014). Otherwise, inefficient DMUs would need to make extra efforts: decreasing inputs and/or increasing outputs in larger quantities than required under the PLA to reach the frontier. The application of the PLA is associated with the calculation of the closest targets on the efficient frontier.

The calculation of the closest targets is directly linked to the determination of the "least distance" from the assessed DMU to the frontier of the production possibility

J. T. Pastor et al., *Benchmarking Economic Efficiency*, International Series in Operations Research & Management Science 315,
https://doi.org/10.1007/978-3-030-84397-7_9

set. Indeed, the closest targets are determined by solving certain mathematical programming model related to minimizing some (mathematical) distance (e.g., the Euclidean distance). Historically speaking, probably the first contribution to this field was that by Charnes et al. (1996), in this case, for assessing sensitivity in efficiency classification in DEA. Coelli (1998) recommended an adaptation of the second stage for radial models with the purpose of looking for targets as similar as possible to the assessed DMU. Briec (1998), Briec and Lesourd (1999), and Briec and Lemaire (1999) defined technical inefficiency using Hölder norms. Frei and Harker (1999) and Cooper et al. (2000, p. 60–61) also recommended in the literature applying Hölder norms to measure efficiency in a DEA context: the Euclidean distance in the case of Frei and Harker (1999) and a weighted ℓ_∞ distance in the case of Cooper et al. (2000). However, the papers by Briec are defined in a general production context, assuming convexity and other traditional axioms, being DEA a particular case. Other interesting papers are Cherchye and Van Puyenbroeck (2001), who worked in an input-oriented space framework; Gonzalez and Alvarez (2001), who maximized the input-oriented Russell efficiency measure, while the traditional input-oriented Russell efficiency measure is really minimized; Portela et al. (2003), who dealt with the computation problems associated with the determination of the least distance; Lozano and Villa (2005), who introduced an approach that, step-by-step, determines a sequence of targets to be achieved in successive stages; and Aparicio et al. (2007), who suggested the mathematical model that allows to determine the Pareto-efficient closest targets without previously calculating all the efficient faces of the DEA production possibility set. Additionally, other authors have paid attention on the Euclidean distance, such as Baek and Lee (2009), Suzuki et al. (2010), Amirteimoori and Kordrostami (2010), and Aparicio and Pastor (2014a). Fukuyama et al. (2014b) focused on ratio-form efficiency measures, and Fukuyama et al. (2016) applied the principle of least action on FDH (Free Disposal Hull) technologies. For more details, see the survey by Aparicio (2016).

Nevertheless, probably the main contribution in the literature of least distance, from a theoretical perspective, is due to Walter Briec and his coauthors, who formally defined technical inefficiency to the "weakly" efficient frontier through mathematical distances. Additionally, these authors stated several results regarding duality, which we analyze in this chapter.

The remainder of the chapter is organized as follows: In Sect. 9.2, we introduce the (graph) Hölder distance function and their weighted version, showing how they may be exploited for decomposing profit inefficiency based on the weakly efficient frontier. In Sect. 9.3, we briefly revise the recent contribution by Aparicio et al. (2020), where a new measure of profit inefficiency is introduced and decomposed through a particular weighted Hölder distance function defined on the strongly efficient frontier. Section 9.4 is devoted to introducing the input-oriented Hölder distance functions and their corresponding duality results with respect to the cost function. In Sect. 9.5, the results for the input-oriented framework are mirrored for the output-oriented Hölder distance functions and their duality with the revenue function. Finally, in Sect. 9.6, an empirical illustration of the introduced methodology based on the examples and the empirical dataset on banks used throughout the book is carried out. In Sect. 9.7, we present the conclusions.

9.2 The Weakly and Strongly Efficient Graph Hölder Distance Functions

In this section, we introduce the necessary notation and review the literature on least distance and the estimation and decomposition of profit inefficiency in DEA. As far as we are aware, there are only two papers that relate the notion of least distance and the profit function. We are referring to Briec and Lesourd (1999) and, more recently, Aparicio et al. (2020a). In the case of Briec and Lesourd (1999), these authors resort to Hölder norms for measuring technical inefficiency but using as a reference set the weakly efficient frontier instead of the strongly efficient one. In contrast, Aparicio et al. (2020a) focus on the strongly efficient frontier and, therefore, comply with the indication property of Pareto efficiency (as discussed in Sect. 2.2.4 of Chap. 2).

Hölder distance functions, in their graph version, were firstly introduced with the goal of relating the notions of technical efficiency and metric distances (Briec, 1998). Russell (1985) suggested the introduction of an index defined in terms of some notion of metric distance for comparing production units. A distance is said to be "metric" if it is defined with respect of a given norm on a linear vector space (e.g., the well-known Euclidean distance is a metric distance). However, the relation between the way efficiency is measured in production economics and the concept of distance in topology was mis-studied until the paper by Briec (1998).

The Hölder norms ℓ_h ($h \in [1, \infty]$) are defined over a g-dimensional real normed space as follows:

$$\|.\|_h : z \to \|z\|_h = \begin{cases} \left(\sum_{j=1}^{g} |z_j|^h \right)^{1/h} & \text{if } h \in [1, \infty[\\ \max\limits_{j=1,\ldots,g} \{|z_j|\} & \text{if } h = \infty \end{cases} \tag{9.1}$$

where $z = (z_1, \ldots, z_g) \in R^g$. From (9.1), Briec (1998) defined the Hölder distance function for the firm under evaluation (x_o, y_o), as follows:

Fig. 9.1 An example of the weakly efficient Hölder distance functions for $h = \infty$

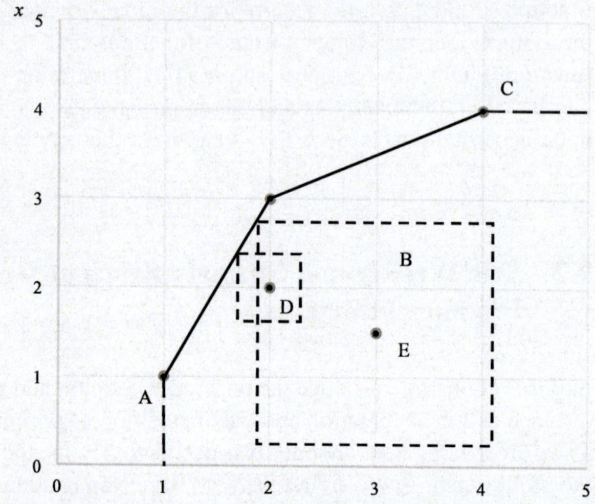

$$TI_{WH\ddot{o}lder(G)}(x_o, y_o; h) = \inf_{u,v} \left\{ \|(x_o, y_o) - (u, v)\|_h : (u, v) \in \partial^W(T) \right\} \tag{9.2}$$

The optimization model that appears in (9.2) minimizes the distance from (x_o, y_o) to the weakly efficient frontier of the technology and is interpreted as the weakly Hölder graph measure of technical inefficiency. Briec and Lesourd (1999), Briec and Lemaire (1999), and Briec and Leleu (2003) are also other studies where the Hölder distance functions have been developed from a theoretical perspective. Hereinafter, we will call *weakly* efficient Hölder distance function to $TI_{WH\ddot{o}lder(G)}(x_o, y_o; h)$ in order to differentiate this notion from one where $\partial^W(T)$ is substituted with $\partial^S(T)$ in its definition.

In Fig. 9.1, we show an example of the weakly efficient Hölder distance function for $h = \infty$. In the figure, the balls associated with this distance are graphically represented for units D and E.

Regarding the computational point of view, the Hölder distance functions are related to nonlinear optimization programs. However, in two particular cases, it is possible to determine these measures of technical inefficiency through linear programming models when the technology is approximated through Data Envelopment Analysis. We are referring to the cases $h = 1$ and $h = \infty$, where the topological balls associated with these norms define polyhedral sets. In particular, $TI_{WH\ddot{o}lder(G)}(x_o, y_o; 1)$ is calculated as the minimum of the values $TI_{DDF(G)}\left(x_o, y_o; \left(0, \ldots, 1_{(m')}, \ldots 0\right)\right)$, $m' = 1, \ldots, M$, and the values $TI_{DDF(G)}\left(x_o, y_o; \left(0, \ldots, 1_{(n')}, \ldots 0\right)\right)$, $n' = 1, \ldots, N$, where

$$\begin{aligned}
& TI_{DDF(G)}\left(x_o, y_o; \left(0, \ldots, 1_{(m')}, \ldots 0\right)\right) = \max_{\beta, \lambda} \beta \\
& s.t. \sum_{j=1}^{J} \lambda_j x_{jm} \leq x_{om}, \; m = 1, \ldots, M, m \neq m' \\
& \sum_{j=1}^{J} \lambda_j x_{jm'} \leq x_{om'} - \beta, \\
& \sum_{j=1}^{J} \lambda_j y_{jn} \geq y_{on}, \; n = 1, \ldots, N \\
& \sum_{j=1}^{J} \lambda_j = 1, \\
& \lambda_j \geq 0, \qquad j = 1, \ldots, J \\
& \beta \geq 0
\end{aligned} \tag{9.3}$$

$$\begin{aligned}
& TI_{DDF(G)}\left(x_o, y_o; \left(0, \ldots, 1_{(n')}, \ldots 0\right)\right) = \max_{\beta, \lambda} \beta \\
& s.t. \sum_{j=1}^{J} \lambda_j x_{jm} \leq x_{om}, \; m = 1, \ldots, M \\
& \sum_{j=1}^{J} \lambda_j y_{jn} \geq y_{on} + \beta, \; n = 1, \ldots, N, n \neq n' \\
& \sum_{j=1}^{J} \lambda_j y_{jn'} \geq y_{on'}, \\
& \sum_{j=1}^{J} \lambda_j = 1, \\
& \lambda_j \geq 0, \; j = 1, \ldots, J \\
& \beta \geq 0
\end{aligned} \tag{9.4}$$

and $\left(0, \ldots, 1_{(m')}, \ldots 0\right)$ is a vector with $M + N$ components where all components are zero except for the m'-th input and $\left(0, \ldots, 1_{(n')}, \ldots 0\right)$ is a vector with $M + N$ components where all components are zero except for the n'-th output. Notice that the above models correspond to the directional distance function discussed in Chap. 8.

In the case of $h = \infty$, the optimization program to be solved is as follows:

$$
\begin{aligned}
& TI_{WH\ddot{o}lder(G)}(x_o, y_o; \infty) = \max_{\beta,\lambda} \beta \\
& s.t. \sum_{j=1}^{J} \lambda_j x_{jm} \leq x_{om} - \beta, \quad m = 1, \ldots, M \\
& \sum_{j=1}^{J} \lambda_j y_{jn} \geq y_{on} + \beta, \quad n = 1, \ldots, N \\
& \sum_{j=1}^{J} \lambda_j = 1, \\
& \lambda_j \geq 0, \qquad j = 1, \ldots, J \\
& \beta \geq 0
\end{aligned}
\tag{9.5}
$$

It is worth mentioning that the above model is identical to the directional distance function when the directional vector is fixed at $g = (1_M, 1_N)$.

Another significant norm to be considered is the Euclidean one. In this case, it is not easy to resort to the envelopment formulation of the DEA model to solve this particular Hölder distance function, with $h = 2$. It is because the determination of the least distance is a hard task from a computational perspective. This difficulty comes from the complexity of determining the least distance to the frontier of a DEA technology from an interior point, as this problem is equivalent to minimizing a convex function on the complement of a convex set. Instead, we resort to a quadratic optimization problem linked to the use of special ordered sets (SOS), which is a special computational strategy for dealing with complementarity conditions. The first step to do that consists in writing the Euclidean distance from firm (x_o, y_o) to the weakly efficient frontier as a bi-level linear program (see, for example, Colson et al., 2007), which is a linear program that includes another linear program among its constraints:

$$TI_{WHölder(G)}(x_o, y_o; 2) = \min_{x,y,\lambda,\beta,\gamma} \sqrt{\sum_{m=1}^{M} (x_{om} - x_m)^2 + \sum_{n=1}^{N} (y_n - y_{on})^2} \quad (9.6.0)$$

$$s.t. \sum_{j=1}^{J} \lambda_j x_{jm} \leq x_m, \; m = 1, \ldots, M \quad (9.6.1)$$

$$\sum_{j=1}^{J} \lambda_j y_{jn} \geq y_n, \; n = 1, \ldots, N \quad (9.6.2)$$

$$\sum_{j=1}^{J} \lambda_j = 1, \quad (9.6.3)$$

$$\beta = 0, \quad (9.6.4)$$

$$\max_{\beta, \gamma_1, \ldots, \gamma_J} \beta \quad (9.6.5)$$

$$s.t. \sum_{j=1}^{J} \gamma_j x_{jm} \leq x_m - \beta, \; m = 1, \ldots, M \quad (9.6.6)$$

$$\sum_{j=1}^{J} \gamma_j y_{jn} \geq y_n + \beta, \; n = 1, \ldots, N \quad (9.6.7)$$

$$\sum_{j=1}^{J} \gamma_j = 1, \quad (9.6.8)$$

$$\lambda_j, \gamma_j \geq 0, \; j = 1, \ldots, J \quad (9.6.9)$$

$$x_m \geq 0, \; m = 1, \ldots, M \quad (9.6.10)$$

$$y_n \geq 0, \; n = 1, \ldots, N \quad (9.6.11)$$

By bi-level programming, we are seeking a point (x, y) in T such that when it is evaluated through a directional distance function with reference vector $(1_M, 1_N)$, the optimal value is zero, i.e., it is a (weakly) efficient point. Notice that in DEA, when the reference vector is strictly positive in each of its components, then the directional distance function is zero for any firm if and only if the evaluated unit belongs to the weakly efficient frontier. Additionally, at the objective function, we are minimizing the Euclidean distance from the firm (x_o, y_o) to the generic benchmark $(x, y) \in \partial^w(T)$. It is worth mentioning that we do not need to force the projection point to dominate the assessed firm (x_o, y_o) since, by Lemma 1 in Briec (1998), it always happens in a natural way when we consider the Hölder norms.

Many different ways of solving bi-level programming models have been introduced in the literature, from exact methods to heuristics and metaheuristics. In our case, we suggest to use the Karush-Kuhn-Tucker conditions of the linear program that appears as a constraint in model (9.6). Therefore, we should substitute linear programs (9.6.5)–(9.6.8) by the following set of constraints:

$$\sum_{j=1}^{J} \gamma_j x_{jm} = x_m - \beta - s_m^-, \qquad m = 1, \ldots, M \quad (9.7.1)$$

$$\sum_{j=1}^{J} \gamma_j y_{jn} = y_n + \beta + s_n^+, \qquad n = 1, \ldots, N \quad (9.7.2)$$

$$\sum_{j=1}^{J} \gamma_j = 1, \quad (9.7.3)$$

$$\sum_{m=1}^{M} \nu_m + \sum_{n=1}^{N} \mu_n = 1, \quad (9.7.4)$$

$$\sum_{m=1}^{M} \nu_m x_{jm} - \sum_{n=1}^{N} \mu_n y_{jn} + \psi - \tau_j = 1, \quad j = 1, \ldots, J \quad (9.7.5)$$

$$\tau_j \gamma_j = 0, \qquad j = 1, \ldots, J \quad (9.7.6)$$

$$\nu_m s_m^- = 0, \qquad m = 1, \ldots, M \quad (9.7.7)$$

$$\mu_n s_n^+ = 0, \qquad n = 1, \ldots, N \quad (9.7.8)$$

$$\gamma_j, \tau_j \geq 0, \qquad j = 1, \ldots, J \quad (9.7.9)$$

$$\nu_m, s_m^- \geq 0, \qquad m = 1, \ldots, M \quad (9.7.10)$$

$$\mu_n, s_n^+ \geq 0, \qquad n = 1, \ldots, N \quad (9.7.11)$$

Constraints (9.7.6)–(9.7.8) are the complementarity constraints that can be implemented in the solver through SOS. Additionally, the square root can be deleted in the objective function of (9.6). So, the final model to be solved is a quadratic programming problem with SOS conditions. The package "Benchmarking Economic Efficiency" programmed in the Julia language solves model (9.6) with constraints (9.7) using the Gurobi Optimizer—see Sect. 9.6.

In many recent papers, Hölder norms are used to estimate technical inefficiency. Examples are Baek and Lee (2009), Amirteimoori and Kordrostami (2011), Ando et al. (2012), Aparicio and Pastor (2014a, 2014b), Fukuyama et al. (2014a, 2014b), Fukuyama et al. (2015), Ando et al. (2017), and Aparicio et al. (2020a). However, in all these cases, the authors resort to the notion of Pareto-Koopmans efficiency, substituting the weakly efficient frontier by the strongly efficient frontier as the reference set.

The strongly efficient Hölder distance function is defined as follows:

$$TI_{SHölder(G)}(x_o, y_o; h) = \inf_{u,v} \left\{ \|(x_o, y_o) - (u, v)\|_h : (u, v) \in \partial^S(T) \right\} \quad (9.8)$$

9.3 The Hölder Distance Functions and the Decomposition of Profit Inefficiency

9.3.1 *Decomposing Profit Inefficiency Based on the Weakly Efficient Hölder Distance Functions*

Now, we are going to show how a difference-form measure of profit inefficiency may be derived from the following duality result proven in Briec and Lesourd (1999):

Proposition 9.1 [Briec & Lesourd, 1999] Let (x_o, y_o) an input-output vector in T. Let ℓ_q be the dual norm[1] of ℓ_h with $1/h + 1/q = 1$. Then,

$$TI_{WHölder(G)}(x_o, y_o; h) = \inf_{d,e\geq 0}\left\{\Pi(d,e) - \left(\sum_{n=1}^{N} e_n y_{on} - \sum_{m=1}^{M} d_m x_{om}\right) : \|(d,e)\|_q \geq 1\right\}. \tag{9.9}$$

Invoking Proposition 9.1, if the input-output market prices, (w, p), are such that $\|(w,p)\|_q \geq 1$, then $\Pi(w,p) - \left(\sum_{n=1}^{N} p_n y_{on} - \sum_{m=1}^{M} w_m x_{om}\right) = \Pi(w,p) - \Pi_o \geq TI_{WHölder}(x_o, y_o; h)$, where Π_o is the observed profit. So, we obtain a difference-form measure of profit inefficiency in the left-hand side of the inequality and the weakly efficient Hölder distance function in the right-hand side, showing that it is possible to decompose profit inefficiency through the Hölder distance functions. However, the term $\Pi(w,p) - \Pi_o$ should be normalized in order to obtain an appropriate (units invariant) measure of profit inefficiency (Nerlove, 1965). A possible solution, resulting in the Hölder profit inefficiency measure, is to normalize the term as follows:

Proposition 9.2 Let (x_o, y_o) an input-output vector in T. Let ℓ_q be the dual norm of ℓ_h with $1/h + 1/q = 1$. Let $(w,p) \in R_{++}^{M+N}$. Then,

$$\frac{\Pi(w,p) - \left(\sum_{n=1}^{N} p_n y_{on} - \sum_{m=1}^{M} w_m x_{om}\right)}{\|(w,p)\|_q} \geq TI_{WHölder(G)}(x_o, y_o; h). \tag{9.10}$$

[1] For the norm $\|.\|_h$ on R^g, the dual norm $\|.\|_q$ on R^g is defined as $\|z\|_q = \max_{\|w\|_h=1}\left\{\sum_{j=1}^{g} z_j w_j\right\}$ (see, for example, Mangasarian, 1999).

Proof $(w', p') := \frac{(w,p)}{\|(w,p)\|_q} \in R^{M+N}_{++}$ and satisfies $\left\| \frac{(w,p)}{\|(w,p)\|_q} \right\|_q = 1$. Therefore, (w', p') is a feasible solution of the program in (9.9). Thus, $\Pi(w',p') - \left(\sum_{n=1}^{N} p'_n y_{on} - \sum_{m=1}^{M} w'_m x_{om} \right) \geq TI_{WHölder(G)}(x_o, y_o; h)$. Finally, $\frac{\Pi(w,p) - \left(\sum_{n=1}^{N} p_n y_{on} - \sum_{m=1}^{M} w_m x_{om} \right)}{\|(w,p)\|_q} \geq TI_{WHölder(G)}(x_o, y_o; h)$ since the profit function is homogeneous of degree +1 in prices. ■

By (9.9), profit inefficiency may be measured and decomposed into the term representing technical inefficiency and the Hölder allocative measure of profit inefficiency (AI), as follows:

$$N\Pi I_{WHölder(G)}(x_o, y_o, \widetilde{w}, \widetilde{p}; h) = \underbrace{\frac{\Pi(w,p) - \left(\sum_{n=1}^{N} p_n y_{on} - \sum_{m=1}^{M} w_m x_{om} \right)}{\|(w,p)\|_q}}_{\text{(Normalized) Profit Inefficiency}} = \underbrace{TI_{WHölder(G)}(x_o, y_o; h)}_{\text{Technnical Inefficiency}} + AI_{WHölder(G)}(x_o, y_o, \widetilde{w}, \widetilde{p}; h). \tag{9.11}$$

We would like to remind that profit efficiency and its components in (9.11) could be interpreted in monetary units if we multiply everything by the normalization factor $\|(w,p)\|_q$.

Throughout the text, we have highlighted the so-called essential property for getting a consistent decomposition of economic efficiency (see Sect. 2.4.5 of Chap. 2). Not all the technical efficiency measures are associated with a decomposition satisfying such property, as we have shown in this book. Regarding the weakly efficient Hölder distance function, we are going to prove that these measures always meet the essential property.

Proposition 9.3 The weakly Hölder distance functions satisfy the essential property.

Proof See Aparicio et al. (2021), who use results from Briec (1998) and Mangasarian (1999). ■

However and as this point is very striking, the Hölder distance functions satisfy the essential property linked to their economic decomposition but does not meet the extended version of that property, as we show next. This means that allocative inefficiency of an interior point could not coincide with the allocative inefficiency assigned to its technical projection point onto the efficient frontier, which may seem somehow incongruous. To illustrate that the extended essential property does not hold, it is enough to consider the following data set for one input and one output: A = (4,4), B = (5,3), C = (3,3), and D = (5,5). Let us assume that $(w, p) = (1, 4)$. If we evaluate unit B using the Euclidean distance, we get that its allocative inefficiency equals 0.526, being A the corresponding technical projection point. On the other hand, if we assess unit A, we get an allocative inefficiency term equal to 0.728, which does not coincide with 0.526.

From the point of view of the satisfaction of properties, a critique associated with the Hölder distance functions is that they do not satisfy units invariance. The Hölder distance functions are dependent on the units of measurement of inputs and outputs. This means that the comparison between two observations through this measure of technical inefficiency can be altered by the units of measurement chosen by the analyst. In order to solve this problem, Briec (1998, p. 125) introduced the weighted weakly efficient Hölder distance function:

$$TI_{WWH\ddot{o}lder(G)}(x_o, y_o; h) = \inf_{u,v}\left\{\left\|\left(\frac{x_{o1}-u_1}{x_{o1}},\ldots,\frac{x_{oM}-u_M}{x_{oM}},\frac{y_{o1}-v_1}{y_{o1}},\ldots,\frac{y_{oN}-v_N}{y_{oN}}\right)\right\|_h : (u,v)\in\partial^w(T)\right\}. \quad (9.12)$$

Next, we state that it is possible to establish an inequality like in Proposition 9.2 but with respect to the weighted weakly efficient Hölder distance function.

Proposition 9.4 Let (x_o, y_o) an input-output vector in T such that $(x_o, y_o) \in R^{M+N}_{++}$. Let ℓ_q be the dual norm of ℓ_h with $1/h + 1/q = 1$. Let $(w, p) \in R^{M+N}_{++}$. Then,

$$\frac{\Pi(w,p) - \left(\sum_{n=1}^{N} p_n y_{on} - \sum_{m=1}^{M} w_m x_{om}\right)}{\left\|(w_1 x_{o1}, \ldots, w_M x_{oM}, p_1 y_{o1}, \ldots, p_N y_{oN})\right\|_q} \geq TI_{WWH\ddot{o}lder(G)}(x_o, y_o; h). \quad (9.13)$$

Proof The DEA technology under VRS can be rewritten as $\left\{(x,y)\in R^{M+N}_{+} : \sum_{n=1}^{N} a_n^f y_n - \sum_{m=1}^{M} b_m^f x_m \leq \Pi(b^f, a^f), f = 1,\ldots,F\right\}$, where $(b^f, a^f) \in R^{M+N}_{+}$ for all $f = 1, \ldots, F$ since T is a polyhedral set (Proposition 1 in Briec & Leleu, 2003). In words, the production possibility set can be expressed as the intersection of a finite number of half-spaces. Then, the weighted weakly efficient Hölder distance function for (x_o, y_o) can be computed by the minimum of the distances from this point to each hyperplane $\sum_{n=1}^{N} a_n^f y_n - \sum_{m=1}^{M} b_m^f x_m = \Pi(b^f, a^f)$, $f = 1, \ldots, F$. Applying the Ascoli's formula, $TI_{WWH\ddot{o}lder}(x_o, y_o; h) = \min_{f=1,\ldots,F}\left\{\frac{\Pi(b^f,a^f) - \left(\sum_{n=1}^{N} a_n^f y_{on} - \sum_{m=1}^{M} b_m^f x_{om}\right)}{\left\|(b_1 x_{o1},\ldots,b_M x_{oM}, a_1 y_{o1},\ldots,a_N y_{oN})\right\|_q}\right\}$. Additionally, for the definition of the profit function, $\left\{(x,y)\in R^{M+N}_{+} : \sum_{n=1}^{N} a_n^f y_n - \sum_{m=1}^{M} b_m^f x_m \leq \Pi(b^f, a^f), f = 1,\ldots,F, \sum_{n=1}^{N}\right.$

$p_n y_{on} - \sum_{m=1}^{M} w_m x_{om} \leq \Pi(w,p)\}$. Now, following the same steps than before, we have that $TI_{WWH\ddot{o}lder(G)}(x_o,y_o;h) = \min\left\{ \min_{f=1,\ldots,F} \left\{ \frac{\Pi(b^f,a^f) - \left(\sum_{n=1}^{N} a_n^f y_{on} - \sum_{m=1}^{M} b_m^f x_{om} \right)}{\|(b_1 x_{o1},\ldots,b_M x_{oM}, a_1 y_{o1},\ldots,a_N y_{oN})\|_q} \right\}, \frac{\Pi(w,p) - \left(\sum_{n=1}^{N} p_n y_{on} - \sum_{m=1}^{M} w_m x_{om} \right)}{\|(w_1 x_{o1},\ldots,w_M x_{oM}, p_1 y_{o1},\ldots,p_N y_{oN})\|_q} \right\}$. This finally implies that $\frac{\Pi(w,p) - \left(\sum_{n=1}^{N} p_n y_{on} - \sum_{m=1}^{M} w_m x_{om} \right)}{\|(w_1 x_{o1},\ldots,w_M x_{oM}, p_1 y_{o1},\ldots,p_N y_{oN})\|_q} \geq TI_{WWH\ddot{o}lder(G)}(x_o,y_o;h)$. ■.

Again, from Proposition 9.4, we can decompose the (Normalized) Hölder profit inefficiency measure as follows:

$$N\Pi I_{WWH\ddot{o}lder(G)}(x_o, y_o, \tilde{w}, \tilde{p}; h) = \underbrace{\frac{\Pi(w,p) - \left(\sum_{n=1}^{N} p_n y_{on} - \sum_{m=1}^{M} w_m x_{om} \right)}{\|(w_1 x_{o1}, \ldots, w_M x_{oM}, p_1 y_{o1}, \ldots, p_N y_{oN})\|_q}}_{\text{(Normalized) Profit Inefficiency}} = \underbrace{TI_{WWH\ddot{o}lder(G)}(x_o, y_o; h)}_{\text{Technical Inefficiency}} + AI_{WWH\ddot{o}lder(G)}(x_o, y_o, \tilde{w}, \tilde{p}; h). \tag{9.14}$$

The left-hand side in (9.13) is a normalized measure of profit inefficiency, while the right-hand side represents the sum of technical inefficiency and allocative inefficiency. In particular, (9.13) can be rendered an equality by introducing a residual allocative inefficiency component, defined as profit inefficiency minus technical inefficiency. In (9.14), each term may be expressed in monetary units if it is multiplied by $\|(w_1 x_{o1}, \ldots, w_M x_{oM}, p_1 y_{o1}, \ldots, p_N y_{oN})\|_q$.

Regarding how to calculate the value of $TI_{WWH\ddot{o}lder(G)}(x_o, y_o; h)$ for $h = 1, 2, \infty$, we should use the same programs than before but slightly changing the expression of the objective function or modifying the directional vectors to be utilized. For $h = 1$, we should substitute the directional vectors $g_x = \left(0, \ldots, 1_{(m')}, \ldots 0\right)$, $m' = 1, \ldots, M$, and $g_y = \left(0, \ldots, 1_{(n')}, \ldots 0\right)$, $n' = 1, \ldots, N$, by the vectors $g_x = \left(0, \ldots, x_{(om')}, \ldots 0\right)$, $m' = 1, \ldots, M$, and $g_y = \left(0, \ldots, y_{(on')}, \ldots 0\right)$, $n' = 1, \ldots, N$. For $h = \infty$, we should resort to the directional vector $g = (g_x, g_y) = (x_o, y_o)$. Finally, in the case of the Euclidean norm, we should substitute the objective function in (9.6) by $\min \sum_{m=1}^{M} \left(\frac{1}{x_{om}}\right)^2 (x_{om} - x_m)^2 + \sum_{n=1}^{N} \left(\frac{1}{y_{on}}\right)^2 (y_n - y_{on})^2$.

9.3.2 *Decomposing Profit Inefficiency Based on the Strongly Efficient Hölder Distance Functions*

The results of duality related to the strongly efficient Hölder distance functions are very recent and due to Aparicio et al. (2020a). These authors introduce a measure of profit inefficiency that is related to both Pareto efficiency and least distance when technical inefficiency is determined. We address this issue in the next paragraphs.

The existing approaches for operationalizing the idea of profit inefficiency differ in the manner they implement the distance between the point that maximizes profit and the point associated with the firm to be evaluated. Aparicio et al. (2017a, b, c) define profit inefficiency for the firm characterized by (x_o, y_o) as a measure that explicitly considers this distance:

$$\mathrm{N\Pi}I_h(x_o, y_o, \tilde{w}, \tilde{p}) = \frac{\left(\sum_{n=1}^{N} \left| p_n \left(y_n^{\Pi} - y_{on} \right) \right|^h + \sum_{m=1}^{M} \left| w_m \left(x_{om} - x_m^{\Pi} \right) \right|^h \right)^{1/h}}{\left\| \left(w_1 x_{o1}, \ldots, w_M x_{oM}, p_1 y_{o1}, \ldots, p_N y_{oN} \right) \right\|_q} \tag{9.15}$$

This program measures profit inefficiency by calculating the distance between the firm-maximizing profit, (x^{Π}, y^{Π}), and the firm under evaluation, (x_o, y_o), normalized by a specific scheme of weights related to the observed inputs and outputs. In particular, (9.15) uses the same deflator (denominator) than that utilized by (9.13).

Hereinafter, we will assume that if there are more than one profit-maximizing benchmark given market prices (w, p), then (x^{Π}, y^{Π}) will represent the closest point to the evaluated(x_o, y_o), among all the alternatives that generate optimal profit.

Additionally, $\mathrm{N\Pi}I_h(x_o, y_o, \tilde{w}, \tilde{p})$ meets a list of well-known and interesting properties like (see Aparicio et al. 2017a, b, c) the following:

$$\mathrm{N\Pi}I_h(x_o, y_o, \tilde{w}, \tilde{p}) \geq 0.$$

$$\mathrm{N\Pi}I_h(x_o, y_o, \tilde{w}, \tilde{p}) = 0 \Leftrightarrow (x_o, y_o) \in \arg\max \left\{ \sum_{n=1}^{N} p_n y_n - \sum_{m=1}^{M} w_m x_m : (x, y) \in T \right\}.$$

(i) $\mathrm{N\Pi}I_h(x_o, y_o, \tilde{w}, \tilde{p})$ is well-defined for non-positive profits.
(ii) $\mathrm{N\Pi}I_h(x_o, y_o, \tilde{w}, \tilde{p})$ is homogeneous of degree zero in prices.
(iii) $\mathrm{N\Pi}I_h(x_o, y_o, \tilde{w}, \tilde{p})$ is homogeneous of degree zero in quantities.

Therefore, $\mathrm{N\Pi}I_h(x_o, y_o, \tilde{w}, \tilde{p})$ is always non-negative and takes value zero if and only if there is not profit inefficiency. Moreover, $\mathrm{N\Pi}I_h(x_o, y_o, \tilde{w}, \tilde{p})$ is units' invariant for prices and quantities. So, it is possible to work with any currency, e.g., dollars or euros, and get the same value of profit inefficiency. In the same way, it is possible to consider different measurement units, e.g., labor hours or labor days, because we will get the same overall inefficiency values. Finally, the measure is also well-defined even for negative profits, something problematic for ratio-form profit inefficiency measures.

However, the decomposition of the above profit inefficiency measure needs the introduction of a *weighted* version of the strongly efficient Hölder distance function where, additionally, the market prices are present. The weighted strongly efficient Hölder distance function defines as follows:

$$TI_{WSHölder(G)}(x_o, y_o; h) = \min_{u,v}\left\{\frac{\|(w_1(x_{o1}-u_1),\ldots,w_M(x_{oM}-u_M),p_1(y_{o1}-v_1),\ldots,p_N(y_{oN}-v_N))\|_h}{\|(w_1x_{o1},\ldots,w_Mx_{oM},p_1y_{o1},\ldots,p_Ny_{oN})\|_q} : (u,v)\in\partial^S(T)\right\}. \quad (9.16)$$

The way of computing the above measure in the context of DEA, under VRS, is through mixed-integer programming. Specifically,

$$TI_{WSHölder(G)}(x_o, y_o; h) = \min_{s^-,s^+,\pi,\lambda,\gamma,a,b,d} \frac{\left(\sum_{m=1}^{M}\left|w_m s_m^-\right|^h + \sum_{n=1}^{N}\left|p_n s_n^+\right|^h\right)^{1/h}}{\|(w_1x_{o1},\ldots,w_Mx_{oM},p_1y_{o1},\ldots,p_Ny_{oN})\|_q}$$

$s.t.$

$$s_m^- = x_{om} - \sum_{j\in E}\lambda_j x_{jm}, \quad m = 1,\ldots,M \quad (9.17.1)$$

$$s_n^+ = y_{on} - \sum_{j\in E}\lambda_j y_{jn}, \quad n = 1,\ldots,N \quad (9.17.2)$$

$$\sum_{j\in E}\lambda_j = 1, \quad (9.17.3)$$

$$-\sum_{m=1}^{M}a_m x_{jm} + \sum_{n=1}^{N}b_n y_{jn} + \pi + d_j = 0, \quad j\in E \quad (9.17.4)$$

$$d_j \le K\gamma_j, \quad j\in E \quad (9.17.5)$$

$$\lambda_j \le 1-\gamma_j, \quad j\in E \quad (9.17.6)$$

$$\lambda_j \ge 0, \quad j\in E \quad (9.17.7)$$

$$d_j \ge 0, \quad j\in E \quad (9.17.8)$$

$$a_m \ge 1, \quad m = 1,\ldots,M \quad (9.17.9)$$

$$b_n \ge 1, \quad n = 1,\ldots,N \quad (9.17.10)$$

$$s_m^- \mathit{free} \quad (9.17.11)$$

$$s_n^+ \mathit{free} \quad (9.17.12)$$

$$\pi \ \mathit{free} \quad (9.17.13)$$

$$\gamma_j \in \{0,1\}, \quad j\in E \quad (9.17.14)$$

where E is the set of extreme efficient units and K is a strictly positive big number.

Model (9.17) is, in general, nonlinear, except for the two polyhedral norms $h = 1$ and $h = \infty$, where the unit sphere related to the norm is a convex polyhedron (see, for example, Fig. 9.1). In these cases, we could incorporate $\|(w_1x_{o1},\ldots, w_Mx_{oM}, p_1y_{o1},\ldots, p_Ny_{oN})\|_q = 1$ to the set of constraints of the model (9.17) and, additionally, apply the change of variables $|z| = u + v$, $z = u - v$, $u \geq 0$ and $v \geq 0$. As for the new constraint $\|(w_1x_{o1},\ldots, w_Mx_{oM}, p_1y_{o1},\ldots, p_Ny_{oN})\|_q = 1$, for the case $h = \infty$, we have $\|(w_1x_{o1}, \ldots, w_Mx_{oM}, p_1y_{o1}, \ldots, p_Ny_{oN})\|_1 = \sum_{m=1}^{M} w_mx_{om} + \sum_{n=1}^{N} p_ny_{on} = 1$, which is clearly linear. For the case $h = 1$, we have $\|(w_1x_{o1},\ldots, w_Mx_{oM}, p_1y_{o1},\ldots, p_Ny_{oN})\|_\infty = \max\{|w_1x_{o1}|,\ldots, |p_Ny_{oN}|\} = \max\{w_1x_{o1},\ldots, p_Ny_{oN}\} = 1$, which can be equivalently implemented in a linear way as $w_mx_{om} + r_m = 1$, $r_m \leq Mb_m^-$, $r_m \geq 0$, $b_m^- \in \{0, 1\}$, $m = 1, \ldots, M$, $p_ny_{on} + f_n = 1$, $f_n \leq Mb_n^+$, $f_n \geq 0$, $b_n^+ \in \{0, 1\}$, $n = 1, \ldots, N$, and $\sum_{m=1}^{M} b_m^- + \sum_{n=1}^{N} b_n^+ \leq M + N - 1$, where K is a strictly positive big number. In this way, we would obtain a mixed-integer linear program. Notice also that (9.17.5)–(9.17.6) could be modeled as the complementarity condition $d_j\lambda_j = 0$, which may be implemented as a special ordered set (SOS) in usual optimizers.

Regarding its relation with $\Pi I_h(x_o, y_o, w, p)$, the next proposition states that $TI_{WSHölder}(x_o, y_o; h)$ is a lower bound of $N\Pi I_h(x_o, y_o, \tilde{w}, \tilde{p})$.

Proposition 9.5 $N\Pi I_h(x_o, y_o, \tilde{w}, \tilde{p}) \geq TI_{WSHölder(G)}(x_o, y_o; h)$ for any $h = 1, \ldots, \infty$.

Proof Given that the vector $(x^\Pi, y^\Pi) \in \partial^S(T)$, we have that $N\Pi I_h(x_o, y_o, \tilde{w}, \tilde{p}) \geq TI_{WSHölder(G)}(x_o, y_o; h)$ by (9.16). ■.

The above result establishes an inequality relationship between profit inefficiency and technical inefficiency in the context of Pareto-Koopmans efficiency for the Hölder distance functions. From Proposition 9.5, it is possible to decompose $N\Pi I_h(x_o, y_o, \tilde{w}, \tilde{p})$ into $TI_{WSHölder(G)}(x_o, y_o; h)$ plus a residual term corresponding to the Hölder allocative measure of profit inefficiency:

$$\underbrace{N\Pi I_h(x_o, y_o, \tilde{w}, \tilde{p})}_{\text{(Normalized) Profit Inefficiency}} = \underbrace{TI_{WSHölder(G)}(x_o, y_o; h)}_{\text{Technical Inefficiency}} + AI_h(x_o, y_o, \tilde{w}, \tilde{p}). \tag{9.18}$$

Now, we theoretically show that the term that we denote as AI really measures allocative inefficiency. To do that, let us assume that (x^*, y^*) is an optimal solution of the optimization model in (9.16) such that $(x^*, y^*) = (x^\Pi, y^\Pi)$, i.e., (x^*, y^*) coincides with the production plan of the firm-maximizing profit and, therefore, the "technical" benchmark is really free of market price inefficiency. Then, by (9.15) and (9.16), we have necessarily that $N\Pi I_h(x_o, y_o, \tilde{w}, p) = TI_{WSHölder(G)}(x_o, y_o; h)$ and, consequently, the term AI equals zero in (9.18), as would be expected if AI truly measures allocative inefficiency. This shows that the profit decomposition based on the weighted strongly Hölder graph measure of technical inefficiency satisfies the essential property discussed in Sect. 2.4.5 of Chap. 2.

Additionally, if we multiply each component that appears in (9.18) by the factor $\|(w_1x_{o1}, \ldots, w_Mx_{oM}, p_1y_{o1}, \ldots, p_Ny_{oN})\|_q$, then each one of them will be expressed in monetary terms, what it is interesting for comparison proposes among different decomposing alternatives.

9.4 The Input-Oriented Hölder Distance Functions and the Decomposition of Cost Inefficiency

Although the oriented versions of the Hölder distance functions have been clearly less utilized in the literature than the graph general version, it can be also interesting to show the main results related to the cost and revenue functions. In particular, in this section, we focus our attention on the input-oriented Hölder distance functions and the existing duality with the cost function.

Briec and Lesourd (1999) defined the input-oriented weakly efficient Hölder distance function, also called input metric distance function, for DMU$_o$ with vector of inputs and outputs (x_o, y_o), as follows:

$$TI_{WH\ddot{o}lder(I)}(x_o, y_o; h) = \inf_v \left\{ \|x_o - v\|_h : v \in \partial^W(L(y_o)) \right\} \quad (9.19)$$

The optimization model that appears in (9.19) minimizes the (mathematical) distance from x_o to the weakly efficient frontier of the input production set $L(y_o)$, and in this sense, it represents the Hölder input measure of technical inefficiency. Hereinafter, as in the graph case, we will use the word *weakly* in order to distinguish this notion from one where $\partial^W(L(y_o))$ is substituted with $\partial^S(L(y_o))$ in its definition.

As far as computation is concerned, as we aforementioned in the text, the Hölder distance functions in the case of piece-wise linear technologies can be easily implemented through linear programming only for the polyhedral metrics, i.e., $h = 1$ and $h = \infty$. For the remaining metrics, the computation is not so easy. Specifically, for $h = 1$, $TI_{WH\ddot{o}lder(I)}(x_o, y_o; 1)$ is calculated as the minimum of the values $TI_{DDF(G)}\left(x_o, y_o; \left(0, \ldots, 1_{(m')}, \ldots 0\right)\right)$, $m' = 1, \ldots, M$, where these values are determined through model (9.3) and $\left(0, \ldots, 1_{(m')}, \ldots 0\right)$ is a vector with $M + N$ components where all components are zero except for the m'-th input. Consequently, the computation of $TI_{WH\ddot{o}lder(I)}(x_o, y_o; 1)$ depends on the calculation of M input-oriented directional distance functions.

For $h = \infty$, the optimization program to be solved would be the following directional distance function, where the reference vector is $g = (1_M, 0_N)$:

$$TI_{DDF(G)}(x_o, y_o; 1_M, 0_N) = \underset{\beta,\lambda}{max} \ \beta$$
$$s.t.$$
$$\sum_{j=1}^{J} \lambda_j x_{jm} \leq x_{om} - \beta, \qquad m = 1, \ldots, M$$
$$\sum_{j=1}^{J} \lambda_j y_{jn} \geq y_{on}, \qquad n = 1, \ldots, N \tag{9.20}$$
$$\sum_{j=1}^{J} \lambda_j = 1,$$
$$\lambda_j \geq 0, \qquad j = 1, \ldots, J$$
$$\beta \geq 0$$

Another interesting case is that related to $h = 2$, where the Euclidean norm is applied. Following similar arguments than in the case of the graph version, the Euclidean distance from a point x_o to the weakly efficient frontier of $L(y_o)$ can be calculated through a bi-level linear program:

$$TI_{WH\ddot{o}lder(I)}(x_o, y_o; 2) = \underset{x,\lambda,\beta,\gamma}{\min} \sqrt{\sum_{m=1}^{M} (x_{om} - x_m)^2} \tag{9.21.0}$$
$$s.t.$$
$$\sum_{j=1}^{J} \lambda_j x_{jm} \leq x_{jm}, \qquad m = 1, \ldots, M \tag{9.21.1}$$
$$\sum_{j=1}^{J} \lambda_j y_{jn} \geq y_{on}, \qquad n = 1, \ldots, N \tag{9.21.2}$$
$$\sum_{j=1}^{J} \lambda_j = 1, \tag{9.21.3}$$
$$\beta = 0, \tag{9.21.4}$$
$$\underset{\beta,\gamma}{\max} \ \beta \tag{9.21.5}$$
$$s.t. \ \sum_{j=1}^{J} \gamma_j x_{jm} \leq x_m - \beta, \qquad m = 1, \ldots, M \tag{9.21.6}$$
$$\sum_{j=1}^{J} \gamma_j y_{jn} \geq y_{on}, \qquad n = 1, \ldots, N \tag{9.21.7}$$
$$\sum_{j=1}^{J} \gamma_j = 1, \tag{9.21.8}$$
$$\lambda_j, \gamma_j \geq 0, \qquad j = 1, \ldots, J \tag{9.21.9}$$
$$x_m \geq 0, \qquad m = 1, \ldots, M \tag{9.21.10}$$

Model (9.21) seeks the point $x \in L(y_o)$ that minimizes the Euclidean distance from x_o, thanks to the objective function and the constraints (9.21.1)–(9.21.3). However, not every point in $L(y_o)$ is feasible in model (9.21). Constraints (9.21.4)–(9.21.8) ensure that $x \in \partial^W(L(y_o))$.

Finally, a way to solve (9.21) consists of transforming the bi-level linear program into a traditional single-level optimization program. It is possible by resorting to the Karush-Kuhn-Tucker conditions of the linear program that appears as a constraint in model (9.21). In this way, we should substitute the linear program (9.21.5)–(9.21.8) by the following set of constraints:

$$\sum_{j=1}^{J} \gamma_j x_{jm} = x_m - \beta - s_m^x, \quad m = 1, \ldots, M \tag{9.22.1}$$

$$\sum_{j=1}^{J} \gamma_j y_{jn} = y_{on} + s_n^y, \quad n = 1, \ldots, N \tag{9.22.2}$$

$$\sum_{j=1}^{J} \gamma_j = 1, \tag{9.22.3}$$

$$\sum_{m=1}^{M} v_m = 1, \tag{9.22.4}$$

$$\sum_{m=1}^{M} v_m x_{jm} - \sum_{n=1}^{N} \mu_n y_{jn} + \psi - \tau_j = 1, \quad j = 1, \ldots, J \tag{9.22.5}$$

$$\tau_j \gamma_j = 0, \quad j = 1, \ldots, J \tag{9.22.6}$$

$$v_m s_m^x = 0, \quad m = 1, \ldots, M \tag{9.22.7}$$

$$\mu_n s_n^y = 0, \quad n = 1, \ldots, N \tag{9.22.8}$$

$$\gamma_j, \tau_j \geq 0, \quad j = 1, \ldots, J \tag{9.22.9}$$

$$v_m, s_m^x \geq 0, \quad m = 1, \ldots, M \tag{9.22.10}$$

$$\mu_n, s_n^y \geq 0, \quad n = 1, \ldots, N \tag{9.22.11}$$

The constraints (9.22.6)–(9.22.8) are complementarity constraints that can be implemented in any solver through special ordered sets (SOS). Moreover, the square root in the objective function in (9.21) may be deleted. Therefore, the final model to be solved is a quadratic programming problem with SOS conditions.

Now, we turn on the duality results between the cost function and the input-oriented weakly efficient Hölder distance functions. The origin of these results is Briec and Lesourd (1999).

Proposition 9.6. [Briec & Lesourd, 1999] Let $x_o \in L(y_o)$ and let ℓ_q be the dual norm of ℓ_h with $1/h + 1/q = 1$. Then,

$$TI_{WH\ddot{o}lder(I)}(x_o, y_o; h) = \inf_{d \geq 0} \left\{ \sum_{m=1}^{M} d_m x_{om} - C(d, y_o) : \|d\|_q \geq 1 \right\}. \tag{9.23}$$

However, given a market input price vector w, Proposition 9.6 can be used to derive a first relationship between the cost function and the input-oriented weakly efficient Hölder distance functions that depends on the units of measurement of prices. In order to get a similar one but satisfying units invariance, it is enough to include a normalizing factor in the formulation, as the following proposition states:

Proposition 9.7 Let $x_o \in L(y_o)$ and let ℓ_q be the dual norm of ℓ_h with $1/h + 1/q = 1$. Let also $w \in R^M_{++}$. Then,

$$\frac{\sum_{m=1}^{M} w_m x_{om} - C(w, y_o)}{\|w\|_q} \geq TI_{WHölder(I)}(x_o, y_o; h). \tag{9.24}$$

Proof The proof is very similar to Proposition 9.2. ■.

Thanks to the inequality (9.24), we are able to establish the decomposition of the Hölder cost inefficiency measure in the following terms:

$$NCI_{WHölder(I)}(x_o, y_o, \tilde{w}; h) = \underbrace{\frac{\sum_{m=1}^{M} w_m x_{om} - C(w, y_o)}{\|w\|_q}}_{\text{(Normalized) Cost Inefficiency}} = \underbrace{TI_{WHölder(I)}(x_o, y_o; h)}_{\text{Input Technnical Inefficiency}} + AI_{WHölder(I)}(x_o, y_o, \tilde{w}; h) \tag{9.25}$$

where the last term represents the Hölder allocative measure of cost inefficiency. The terms in (9.25) can be defined in monetary units by multiplying each one by $\|w\|_q$.

From the definition of the input-oriented weakly efficient Hölder distance functions, it is easy to define a version that satisfies units invariance with respect to the units of measurement of inputs. So, we introduce the input-oriented weighted weakly efficient Hölder distance function as follows:

$$TI_{WWHölder(I)}(x_o, y_o; h) = \inf_u \left\{ \left\| \left(\frac{x_{o1} - u_1}{x_{o1}}, \ldots, \frac{x_{oM} - u_M}{x_{oM}} \right) \right\|_h : u \in \partial^W(L(y_o)) \right\}. \tag{9.26}$$

To determine the value of $TI_{WWHölder(I)}(x_o, y_o; h)$ for $h = 1, 2, \infty$ is enough to follow the same steps described in Sect. 9.2.

Next, we state that it is possible to establish an inequality like in Proposition 9.7 but with respect to the input-oriented weighted weakly efficient Hölder distance function.

Proposition 9.8 Let $x_o \in L(y_o)$ such that $x_o \in R^M_{++}$. Let ℓ_q be the dual norm of ℓ_h with $1/h + 1/q = 1$. Let $w \in R^M_{++}$. Then,

$$\frac{\sum_{m=1}^{M} w_m x_{om} - C(w, y_o)}{\left\|(w_1 x_{o1}, \ldots, w_M x_{oM})\right\|_q} \geq TI_{WWH\ddot{o}lder(I)}(x_o, y_o; h). \tag{9.27}$$

Proof The proof is very similar to Proposition 9.4. ■.

Again, the Hölder cost inefficiency measure may be calculated and decomposed from Proposition 9.8 as follows:

$$NCI_{WWH\ddot{o}lder(G)}(x_o, y_o, \tilde{w}; h) = \underbrace{\frac{\sum_{m=1}^{M} w_m x_{om} - C(w, y_o)}{\left\|(w_1 x_{o1}, \ldots, w_M x_{oM})\right\|_q}}_{\text{Cost Inefficiency}} = \underbrace{TI_{WWH\ddot{o}lder(I)}(x_o, y_o; h)}_{\text{Input Technical Inefficiency}} + AI_{WH\ddot{o}lder(I)}(x_o, y_o, \tilde{w}; h). \tag{9.28}$$

The left-hand side in (9.28) is a normalized measure of cost inefficiency, where the normalization is, in particular, the mathematical norm of the vector of the cost of each input. On the other hand, the right-hand side represents the sum of technical inefficiency in the input side and allocative inefficiency. Moreover, the terms in (9.28) may be expressed in monetary units by multiplying each one by $\|(w_1 x_{o1}, \ldots, w_M x_{oM})\|_q$.

So far, in this section, we were working with the notion of technical efficiency linked to Farrell and Debreu. Now, we want to deal with the concept of Pareto-Koopmans efficiency. Few papers have considered this context for oriented measures when a Hölder norm is taken as tool for determining technical inefficiency. One of them is Aparicio et al. (2017c).

Now, we need to define the input-oriented strongly efficient Hölder distance function as follows:

$$TI_{SH\ddot{o}lder(I)}(x_o, y_o; h) = \inf_{v} \left\{ \|x_o - v\|_h : v \in \partial^S(L(y_o)) \right\} \tag{9.29}$$

Next, we adapt the results of Aparicio et al. (2020a) for the input-oriented version (9.29). We first define cost inefficiency for the unit (x_o, y_o) as a measure that explicitly considers the distance in the input space between x_o and the benchmark where minimum cost is achieved x^C:

$$NCI_h(x_o, y_o, \tilde{w}) = \frac{\left(\sum_{m=1}^{M} \left| w_m \left(x_{om} - x_m^C \right) \right|^h \right)^{1/h}}{\left\| (w_1 x_{o1}, \ldots, w_M x_{oM}) \right\|_q} \tag{9.30}$$

To decompose the above Hölder cost inefficiency measure is necessary to introduce a weighted version of the input-oriented strongly efficient Hölder distance function where, additionally, the market prices are present:

$$TI_{WSHölder(I)}(x_o, y_o; h) = \min_u \left\{ \frac{\left\| (w_1(x_{o1} - u_1), \ldots, w_M(x_{oM} - u_M)) \right\|_h}{\left\| (w_1 x_{o1}, \ldots, w_M x_{oM}) \right\|_q} : u \in \partial^S(L(y_o)) \right\}. \tag{9.31}$$

The way of computing the above measure in the context of DEA, under VRS, is through the following bi-level program (see Aparicio et al. 2020a):

$$TI_{WSHölder(I)}(x_o, y_o; h) = \min_{s^-, s^+, \lambda, \gamma, x} \frac{\left(\sum_{m=1}^{M} \left| w_m s_m^- \right|^h \right)^{1/h}}{\left\| (w_1 x_{o1}, \ldots, w_M x_{oM}) \right\|_q}$$

s.t.

$$\sum_{j=1}^{J} \lambda_j x_{jm} \leq x_m, \qquad m = 1, \ldots, M \tag{9.32.1}$$

$$\sum_{j=1}^{J} \lambda_j y_{jn} \geq y_{on}, \qquad n = 1, \ldots, N \tag{9.32.2}$$

$$\sum_{j=1}^{J} \lambda_j = 1, \tag{9.32.3}$$

$$\sum_{m=1}^{M} s_m^- + \sum_{n=1}^{N} s_n^+ = 0, \tag{9.32.4}$$

$$\max_{\substack{s_1^-, \ldots, s_M^- \\ s_1^+, \ldots, s_N^+ \\ \gamma_1, \ldots, \gamma_J}} \sum_{m=1}^{M} s_m^- + \sum_{n=1}^{N} s_n^+ \tag{9.32.5}$$

$$\text{s.t.} \sum_{j=1}^{J} \gamma_j x_{jm} = x_m - s_m^-, \qquad m = 1, \ldots, M \tag{9.32.6}$$

$$\sum_{j=1}^{J} \gamma_j y_{jn} = y_{on} + s_n^+, \qquad n = 1, \ldots, N \tag{9.32.7}$$

$$\sum_{j=1}^{J} \gamma_j = 1, \tag{9.32.8}$$

$$\lambda_j, \gamma_j \geq 0, \qquad j = 1, \ldots, J \tag{9.32.9}$$

$$x_m \geq 0, \qquad m = 1, \ldots, M \tag{9.32.10}$$

$$s_m^-, s_n^+ \geq 0, \qquad \forall m, n \tag{9.32.11}$$

The objective function in (9.32) is clearly nonlinear except for the two polyhedral norms, i.e., $h = 1$ and $h = \infty$. In these cases, we could incorporate $\|(w_1 x_{o1}, \ldots, w_M x_{oM})\|_q = 1$ to the set of constraints of the model (9.32). For the case $h = \infty$, we have $\|(w_1 x_{o1}, \ldots, w_M x_{oM})\|_1 = \sum_{m=1}^{M} w_m x_{om} = 1$, which is clearly linear. For the case $h = 1$, we have $\|(w_1 x_{o1}, \ldots, w_M x_{oM})\|_\infty = \max\{|w_1 x_{o1}|, \ldots, |w_M x_{oM}|\} = \max\{w_1 x_{o1}, \ldots, w_M x_{oM}\} = 1$, which can be equivalently implemented in a linear way as $w_m x_{om} + r_m = 1$, $r_m \leq K b_m$, $r_m \geq 0$, $b_m \in \{0, 1\}$, $m = 1, \ldots, M$, and $\sum_{m=1}^{M} b_m \leq M - 1$, where K is a strictly positive big number. Additionally, we will have to apply the change of variables $|z| = u + v$, $z = u - v$, $u \geq 0$, and $v \geq 0$ for the objective function. In this way, we would obtain a bi-level liner program. Regarding the way of solving this type of optimization model, the usual trick consists of transforming (9.32) into a single-level program. To do that, we could substitute the second-level program by its corresponding Karush-Kuhn-Tucker conditions:

$$
\begin{aligned}
&\sum_{j=1}^{J} \gamma_j x_{jm} = x_m - s_m^-, && m = 1, \ldots, M \\
&\sum_{j=1}^{J} \gamma_j y_{jn} = y_{on} + s_n^+, && n = 1, \ldots, N \\
&\sum_{j=1}^{J} \gamma_j = 1, && \\
&\nu_m \geq 1, && m = 1, \ldots, M \\
&\mu_n \geq 1, && n = 1, \ldots, N \\
&\sum_{m=1}^{M} \nu_m x_{jm} - \sum_{n=1}^{N} \mu_n y_{jn} + \psi - \tau_j = 1, && j = 1, \ldots, J \\
&\tau_j \gamma_j = 0, && j = 1, \ldots, J \\
&\nu_m s_m^- = 0, && m = 1, \ldots, M \\
&\mu_n s_n^+ = 0, && n = 1, \ldots, N \\
&\gamma_j, \tau_j \geq 0, && j = 1, \ldots, J \\
&\nu_m, s_m^- \geq 0, && m = 1, \ldots, M \\
&\mu_n, s_n^+ \geq 0, && n = 1, \ldots, N
\end{aligned}
\tag{9.33}
$$

Regarding its relation with $NCI_h(x_o, y_o, \tilde{w})$, the next proposition states that $TI_{WSHölder(I)}(x_o, y_o; h)$ is a lower bound of $NCI_h(x_o, y_o, \tilde{w})$.

Proposition 9.9 $NCI_h(x_o, y_o, \tilde{w}) \geq TI_{WSHölder(I)}(x_o, y_o; h)$ for any $h = 1, \ldots, \infty$.

Proof Follow the proof of Proposition 9.5. ■.

Proposition 9.9 states an inequality relationship between cost inefficiency and technical inefficiency in the context of Pareto-Koopmans efficiency for the input-oriented Hölder distance functions. From Proposition 9.9, it is possible to decompose the Hölder cost inefficiency measure $CI_h(x_o, y_o, w)$ into technical inefficiency and the residual Hölder allocative measure of cost inefficiency:

$$\underbrace{NCI_h(x_o, y_o, \tilde{w})}_{\text{(Normalized) Cost Inefficiency}} = \underbrace{TI_{WSH\ddot{o}lder(I)}(x_o, y_o; h)}_{\text{Input Technical Inefficiency}} + AI_h(x_o, y_o, w). \tag{9.34}$$

The terms in (9.34) can be defined in monetary units by multiplying each one by $\|(w_1 x_{o1}, \ldots, w_M x_{oM})\|_q$.

9.5 The Output-Oriented Hölder Distance Functions and the Decomposition of Revenue Inefficiency

Once we have introduced the main results associated with the Hölder distance functions and overall efficiency in the contexts of graph measures and input-oriented efficiency measurement, we extend them to the output-oriented framework. Accordingly, next, we directly show the particularization of the results of the input-oriented Hölder distance functions to the case of considering their output-oriented counterpart.

The output-oriented weakly efficient Hölder distance function for DMU$_o$ with vector of inputs and outputs (x_o, y_o) may be defined as follows:

$$TI_{WH\ddot{o}lder(O)}(x_o, y_o; h) = \inf_u \left\{ \|u - y_o\|_h : u \in \partial^W(P(x_o)) \right\} \tag{9.35}$$

Regarding computation, for $h = 1$, $TI_{WH\ddot{o}lder(O)}(x_o, y_o; 1)$ is calculated as the minimum of the values $TI_{DDF(G)}\left(x_o, y_o; \left(0, \ldots, 1_{(n')}, \ldots 0\right)\right)$, $n' = 1, \ldots, N$, where these values are determined through model (9.4) and $\left(0, \ldots, 1_{(m')}, \ldots 0\right)$ is a vector with $M + N$ components where all components are zero except for the n'-th input. For $h = \infty$, the optimization program to be solved would be the following directional distance function, where the reference vector is $g = (0_M, 1_N)$:

$$TI_{DDF(G)}(x_o, y_o; 0_M, 1_N) = \max_{\beta,\lambda} \ \beta$$
$$\begin{aligned} & s.t. \\ & \sum_{j=1}^{J} \lambda_j x_{jm} \leq x_{om}, \qquad m = 1, \ldots, M \\ & \sum_{j=1}^{J} \lambda_j y_{jn} \geq y_{on} + \beta, \qquad n = 1, \ldots, N \\ & \sum_{j=1}^{J} \lambda_j = 1, \\ & \lambda_j \geq 0, \qquad j = 1, \ldots, J \\ & \beta \geq 0 \end{aligned} \tag{9.36}$$

For the Euclidean metric, this distance from a point y_o to the weakly efficient frontier of $P(x_o)$ may be calculated through the following bi-level linear program:

$$TI_{WHölder(O)}(x_o, y_o; 2) = \min_{y,\beta,\lambda,\gamma} \sqrt{\sum_{n=1}^{N} (y_n - y_{on})^2} \tag{9.37.0}$$

$$s.t.$$

$$\sum_{j=1}^{J} \lambda_j x_{jm} \leq x_{om}, \qquad m = 1, \ldots, M \tag{9.37.1}$$

$$\sum_{j=1}^{J} \lambda_j y_{jn} \geq y_n, \qquad n = 1, \ldots, N \tag{9.37.2}$$

$$\sum_{j=1}^{J} \lambda_j = 1, \tag{9.37.3}$$

$$\beta = 0, \tag{9.37.4}$$

$$\max_{\beta,\gamma} \ \beta \tag{9.37.5}$$

$$s.t. \ \sum_{j=1}^{J} \gamma_j x_{jm} \leq x_{om}, \qquad m = 1, \ldots, M \tag{9.37.6}$$

$$\sum_{j=1}^{J} \gamma_j y_{jn} \geq y_n + \beta, \qquad n = 1, \ldots, N \tag{9.37.7}$$

$$\sum_{j=1}^{J} \gamma_j = 1, \tag{9.37.8}$$

$$\lambda_j, \gamma_j \geq 0, \qquad j = 1, \ldots, J \tag{9.37.9}$$

$$y_n \geq 0, \qquad n = 1, \ldots, N \tag{9.37.10}$$

To solve (9.37), we transform the bi-level linear program into a single-level optimization program. It is possible by resorting to the Karush-Kuhn-Tucker conditions of the second-level program that appears as a constraint in model (9.37). In particular, we should substitute that linear program by the following set of constraints:

$$\sum_{j=1}^{J}\gamma_j x_{jm} = x_{om} - s_m^-, \quad m = 1, \ldots, M \quad (9.38.1)$$

$$\sum_{j=1}^{J}\gamma_j y_{jn} = y_{on} + \beta + s_n^+, \quad n = 1, \ldots, N \quad (9.38.2)$$

$$\sum_{j=1}^{J}\gamma_j = 1, \quad (9.38.3)$$

$$\sum_{n=1}^{N}\mu_n = 1, \quad (9.38.4)$$

$$\sum_{m=1}^{M}\nu_m x_{jm} - \sum_{n=1}^{N}\mu_n y_{jn} + \psi - \tau_j = 1, \quad j = 1, \ldots, J \quad (9.38.5)$$

$$\tau_j\gamma_j = 0, \quad j = 1, \ldots, J \quad (9.38.6)$$

$$\nu_m s_m^- = 0, \quad m = 1, \ldots, M \quad (9.38.7)$$

$$\mu_n s_n^+ = 0, \quad n = 1, \ldots, N \quad (9.38.8)$$

$$\gamma_j, \tau_j \geq 0, \quad j = 1, \ldots, J \quad (9.38.9)$$

$$\nu_m, s_m^- \geq 0, \quad m = 1, \ldots, M \quad (9.38.10)$$

$$\mu_n, s_n^+ \geq 0, \quad n = 1, \ldots, N \quad (9.38.11)$$

Now, we show the main result relating the revenue function to the output-oriented weakly efficient Hölder distance functions.

Proposition 9.9 Let $y_o \in P(x_o)$ and let ℓ_q be the dual norm of ℓ_h with $1/h + 1/q = 1$. Let also $p \in R_{++}^N$. Then,

$$\frac{R(p, x_o) - \sum_{n=1}^{N} p_n y_{on}}{\|p\|_q} \geq TI_{WHölder(O)}(x_o, y_o; h). \quad (9.39)$$

Proof The proof is very similar to Proposition 9.2. ■.

From the above proposition, we are able to define the Hölder revenue inefficiency measure and its decomposition into the technical inefficiency component and the residual Hölder allocative measure of revenue inefficiency:

$$NRI_{WH\ddot{o}lder(O)}(x_o, y_o, \tilde{p}; h) = \underbrace{\frac{R(p, x_o) - \sum_{n=1}^{N} p_n y_{on}}{\|p\|_q}}_{\text{(Normalized) Revenue Inefficiency}} = \underbrace{TI_{WH\ddot{o}lder(O)}(x_o, y_o; h)}_{\text{Output Technical Inefficiency}} + AI_{WH\ddot{o}lder(O)}(x_o, y_o, \tilde{p}; h). \tag{9.40}$$

Additionally, the terms in (9.40) may be expressed in monetary units by multiplying each one by $\|p\|_q$.

Now, we introduce the output-oriented weighted weakly efficient Hölder distance function as follows:

$$TI_{WWH\ddot{o}lder(O)}(x_o, y_o; h) = \inf_u \left\{ \left\| \left(\frac{u_1 - y_{o1}}{y_{o1}}, \ldots, \frac{u_N - y_{oN}}{y_{oN}} \right) \right\|_h : u \in \partial^W(P(x_o)) \right\}. \tag{9.41}$$

To determine the value of $TI_{WWH\ddot{o}lder(O)}(x_o, y_o; h)$ for $h = 1, 2, \infty$ is enough to follow the same steps described in Sect. 9.2.

Next, we state that it is possible to establish an inequality like in Proposition 9.10 but with respect to the output-oriented weighted weakly efficient Hölder distance function.

Proposition 9.11 Let $y_o \in P(x_o)$ such that $y_o \in R^N_{++}$. Let ℓ_q be the dual norm of ℓ_h. with $1/h + 1/q = 1$. Let $p \in R^N_{++}$. Then,

$$\frac{R(p, x_o) - \sum_{n=1}^{N} p_n y_{on}}{\|(p_1 y_{o1}, \ldots, p_N y_{oN})\|_q} \geq TI_{WWH\ddot{o}lder(O)}(x_o, y_o; h). \tag{9.42}$$

Proof The proof is very similar to Proposition 9.4. ∎.

Then, the corresponding Hölder allocative measure of revenue inefficiency can be defined and decomposed as follows:

$$\begin{aligned}NRI_{WWHölder(O)}(x_o, y_o, \tilde{p}; h) &= \underbrace{\frac{R(p, x_o) - \sum_{n=1}^{N} p_n y_{on}}{\|(p_1 y_{o1}, \ldots, p_N y_{oN})\|_q}}_{\text{(Normalized) Revenue Inefficiency}} \\ &= \underbrace{TI_{WWHölder(O)}(x_o, y_o; h)}_{\text{Output Technical Inefficiency}} \\ &\quad + AI_{WWHölder(O)}(x_o, y_o, \tilde{p}; h). \end{aligned} \tag{9.43}$$

Again, both revenue inefficiency and its components may be gauged in monetary units by multiplying each term by $\|(p_1 y_{o1}, \ldots, p_N y_{oN})\|_q$.

Now, we need to define the output-oriented strongly efficient Hölder distance function as follows:

$$TI_{SHölder(O)}(x_o, y_o; h) = \inf_u \left\{ \|u - y_o\|_h : u \in \partial^S(P(x_o)) \right\} \tag{9.44}$$

Next, we introduce the definition of the Hölder revenue inefficiency measure in the context of dealing with the Pareto-Koopmans notions of technical efficiency:

$$NRI_h(x_o, y_o, \tilde{p}) = \frac{\left(\sum_{n=1}^{N} \left| p_n \left(y_n^R - y_{on} \right) \right|^h \right)^{1/h}}{\|(p_1 y_{o1}, \ldots, p_N y_{oN})\|_q} \tag{9.45}$$

To decompose in a suitable way the above measure of revenue inefficiency is necessary to introduce a weighted version of the output-oriented strongly efficient Hölder distance function where, additionally, the output market prices are present in the following definition:

$$TI_{WSHölder(O)}(x_o, y_o; h) = \min_u \left\{ \frac{\|(p_1(u_1 - y_{o1}), \ldots, p_N(u_N - y_{oN}))\|_h}{\|(p_1 y_{o1}, \ldots, p_N y_{oN})\|_q} : u \in \partial^S(P(x_o)) \right\}. \tag{9.46}$$

The way of computing the above measure in the context of DEA is through the following bi-level program:

$$TI_{WSHölder(O)}(x_o, y_o; h) = \min_{y, s^-, s^+, \lambda, \gamma} \frac{\left(\sum_{n=1}^{N} \left|p_n s_n^+\right|^h\right)^{1/h}}{\|(p_1 y_{o1}, \ldots, p_N y_{oN})\|_q} \tag{9.47.0}$$

$$s.t. \sum_{j=1}^{J} \lambda_j x_{jm} \leq x_{om}, \qquad m = 1, \ldots, M \tag{9.47.1}$$

$$\sum_{j=1}^{J} \lambda_j y_{jn} \geq y_n, \qquad n = 1, \ldots, N \tag{9.47.2}$$

$$\sum_{j=1}^{J} \lambda_j = 1, \tag{9.47.3}$$

$$\sum_{m=1}^{M} s_m^- + \sum_{n=1}^{N} s_n^+ = 0, \tag{9.47.4}$$

$$\max_{s^-, s^+, \gamma} \sum_{m=1}^{M} s_m^- + \sum_{n=1}^{N} s_n^+ \tag{9.47.5}$$

$$s.t. \sum_{j=1}^{J} \gamma_j x_{jm} = x_{om} - s_m^-, \qquad m = 1, \ldots, M \tag{9.47.6}$$

$$\sum_{j=1}^{J} \gamma_j y_{jn} = y_n + s_n^+, \qquad n = 1, \ldots, N \tag{9.47.7}$$

$$\sum_{j=1}^{J} \gamma_j = 1, \tag{9.47.8}$$

$$\lambda_j, \gamma_j \geq 0, \qquad j = 1, \ldots, J \tag{9.47.9}$$

$$y_n \geq 0, \qquad n = 1, \ldots, N \tag{9.47.10}$$

$$s_m^-, s_n^+ \geq 0, \qquad \forall m, n \tag{9.47.11}$$

The objective function in (9.47) is clearly nonlinear except for the two polyhedral norms, i.e., $h = 1$ and $h = \infty$. In these cases, we could incorporate $\|(p_1 y_{o1}, \ldots, p_N y_{oN})\|_q = 1$ to the set of constraints of the model (9.47). For the case $h = \infty$, we have $\|(p_1 y_{o1}, \ldots, p_N y_{oN})\|_q = \sum_{n=1}^{N} p_n y_{on} = 1$, which is clearly linear. For the case $h = 1$, we have $\|(p_1 y_{o1}, \ldots, p_N y_{oN})\|_\infty = \max\{|p_1 y_{o1}|, \ldots, |p_N y_{oN}|\} = \max\{p_1 y_{o1}, \ldots, p_N y_{oN}\} = 1$, which can be equivalently implemented in a linear way as $p_n y_{no} + f_n = 1$, $f_n \leq K b_n$, $f_n \geq 0$, $b_n \in \{0, 1\}$, $n = 1, \ldots, N$, and $\sum_{n=1}^{N} b_n \leq N - 1$, where K is a strictly positive big number. Additionally, we will have to apply the change of variables $|z| = u + v$, $z = u - v$, $u \geq 0$, and $v \geq 0$ for the objective function. In this way, we would obtain a bi-level liner program. Finally, we will have to substitute the second-level optimization program by its Karush-Kuhn-Tucker conditions:

$$
\begin{array}{ll}
\sum_{j=1}^{J} \gamma_j x_{jm} = x_{om} - s_m^-, & m = 1, \ldots, M \\
\sum_{j=1}^{J} \gamma_j y_{jn} = y_n + s_n^+, & n = 1, \ldots, N \\
\sum_{j=1}^{J} \gamma_j = 1, & \\
v_m \geq 1, & m = 1, \ldots, M \\
\mu_n \geq 1, & n = 1, \ldots, N \\
\sum_{m=1}^{M} v_m x_{jm} - \sum_{n=1}^{N} \mu_n y_{jn} + \psi - \tau_j = 1, & j = 1, \ldots, J \\
\tau_j \gamma_j = 0, & j = 1, \ldots, J \\
v_m s_m^- = 0, & m = 1, \ldots, M \\
\mu_n s_n^+ = 0, & n = 1, \ldots, N \\
\gamma_j, \tau_j \geq 0, & j = 1, \ldots, J \\
v_m, s_m^- \geq 0, & m = 1, \ldots, M \\
\mu_n, s_n^+ \geq 0, & n = 1, \ldots, N
\end{array}
\tag{9.48}
$$

As for its relation with $NRI_h(x_o, y_o, \tilde{p})$, the next proposition states that $TI_{WSHölder(O)}(x_o, y_o; h)$ is always a lower bound of $NRI_h(x_o, y_o, \tilde{p})$.

Proposition 9.12 $NRI_h(x_o, y_o, \tilde{p}) \geq TI_{WSHölder(O)}(x_o, y_o; h)$ for any $h = 1, \ldots, \infty$.

Proof It is like Proposition 9.5. ■.

From Proposition 9.12, it is possible to decompose the Hölder revenue inefficiency measure $NRI_h(x_o, y_o, \tilde{p})$ into its corresponding technical inefficiency and residual Hölder allocative measure of revenue inefficiency:

$$
\underbrace{NRI_h(x_o, y_o, \tilde{p})}_{\text{(Normalized) Revenue Inefficiency}} = \underbrace{TI_{WSHölder(O)}(x_o, y_o; h)}_{\text{Output Technical Inefficiency}} + AI_h(x_o, y_o, \tilde{p}). \tag{9.49}
$$

Finally, $NRI_h(x_o, y_o, \tilde{p})$, $TI_{WSHölder(O)}(x_o, y_o; h)$, and $AI_h(x_o, y_o, \tilde{p})$ may be expressed in monetary units if we multiply each one by $\|(p_1 y_{o1}, \ldots, p_N y_{oN})\|_q$.

9.6 Empirical Illustration of the Hölder Profit, Cost, and Revenue Inefficiency Models

In this section, we illustrate the calculation of the three economic inefficiency measures and their decomposition based on their corresponding weakly efficient Hölder distance functions and using the example data presented in Sect. 2.6 of Chap. 2. Table 9.1 replicates the data.

Given the different Hölder norms that are available when measuring economic inefficiency, we illustrate the different models choosing alternative options. For this purpose, we rely on the ℓ_1 norm to decompose cost inefficiency, on the ℓ_∞ norm to decompose revenue inefficiency, and on the Euclidean norm ℓ_2 to decompose profit inefficiency. The following functions, included in the "Benchmarking Economic Efficiency" package for the Julia language, solve these three norms in all economic inefficiency models in both their unweighted and weighted versions. For the weighted versions, as remarked in the previous sections, the efficiency measures satisfy the units invariance property. Specifically, the functions that compute these measures, as well as their decompositions into technical and allocative inefficiencies, are the following:

```
deaprofitholder(X, Y, W, P, l=2, weight=true, names=FIRMS)
```

```
deacostholder(X, Y, W, l=2, weight=true, names=FIRMS)
```

```
dearevenueholder(X, Y, P, l=2, weight=true, names=FIRMS)
```

The above syntax includes "`l=2`" and "`weight=true`" indicating that the Euclidian norm ℓ_2 and the weighted version of the efficiency measures have been selected. These two options may be replaced with the aforementioned metrics ℓ_1 and ℓ_∞, in

Table 9.1 Example data illustrating the economic inefficiency models

	Model							
			Input orientation			Output orientation		
	Graph profit model		Cost model			Revenue model		
Firm	x	y	x_1	x_2	y	x	y_1	y_2
A	2	1	2	2	1	1	7	7
B	4	5	1	4	1	1	4	8
C	8	8	4	1	1	1	8	4
D	12	9	4	3	1	1	3	5
E	6	3	5	5	1	1	3	3
F	14	7	6	1	1	1	8	2
G	14	9	2	5	1	1	6	4
H	9.412	2.353	1.6	8	1	1	1.5	5
Prices	$w = 1$	$p = 2$	$w_1 = 1$	$w_2 = 1$			$p_1 = 1$	$p_2 = 1$

Table 9.2 Directional vectors and weights corresponding to Hölder norms

Norm	Unweighted*	Weighted "weight=true"
"l=1"	$g_x = \left(0, \ldots, 1_{(m')}, \ldots 0\right), m' = 1, \ldots, M$ $g_y = \left(0, \ldots, 1_{(n')}, \ldots 0\right), n' = 1, \ldots, N$	$g_x = \left(0, \ldots, x_{(om')}, \ldots 0\right), m' = 1, \ldots, M$ $g_y = \left(0, \ldots, y_{(on')}, \ldots 0\right), n' = 1, \ldots, N$
"l=Inf"	$g = (g_x, g_y) = (1_M, 1_N)$	$g = (g_x, g_y) = (x_o, y_o)$
"l=2"	$(1_M, 1_N)$	$((1/x_o)^2, (1/y_o)^2)$

Notes: *Unweighted results are obtained by default when omitting "weight=true" from the syntax

their weighted and unweighted versions. From a computational perspective, while the technical inefficiencies associated with ℓ_1 and ℓ_∞ can be computed using linear programming techniques, this is not the case for the Euclidean norm that requires quadratic optimization methods linked to the use of special ordered sets (SOS)—see model (9.6) with constraints (9.7). To solve these models, the "Benchmarking Economic Efficiency" package resorts to the Gurobi Optimizer (Gurobi, 2021), which requires adding it to Julia. This can be accomplished under a free license for academic use only or a paid commercial version. The optimizer can be downloaded from the company's website (https://www.gurobi.com/).[2]

The alternative norms imply that different directional vectors are used to calculate the weakly technical inefficiencies corresponding to ℓ_1 and ℓ_∞ and normalizing the different economic inefficiencies. Table 9.2 summarizes the vectors of each directional distance function in their unweighted and weighted versions for DMU o when evaluating profit inefficiency using the graph model. On its part, the weighted version of the weakly technical inefficiency based on the ℓ_2 norm requires assigning specific factors. In particular, the weighted version $TI_{WWHölder}(x_o, y_o; 2)$ includes the square of the inverse of the observed quantities as weights in the objective function of (9.6) including the constraints in (9.7): $\min \sum_{m=1}^{M} \left(\frac{1}{x_{om}}\right)^2 (x_{om} - x_m)^2 + \sum_{n=1}^{N} \left(\frac{1}{y_{on}}\right)^2 (y_n - y_{on})^2$, as shown in Table 9.2. Note that the unweighted versions are the default option in these functions, as calculating the weighted models requires the inclusion of the option ("weight=true"). Regarding the cost and revenue inefficiency models and their technical inefficiency counterparts, the directional vectors and weights use only the input or output dimension required for each orientation.

[2] A free academic license can be obtained from https://www.gurobi.com/downloads/end-user-license-agreement-academic/. Once registered, it is possible to download it from https://www.gurobi.com/downloads/gurobi-optimizer-eula/. Upon installation, it is possible to add the package "Gurobi.jl" to Julia by running the following commands: "using Pkg," "Pkg.add("Gurobi")," and "Pkg.build("Gurobi")."

Table 9.3 Implementation of the ℓ_2 Hölder profit inefficiency model using BEE for Julia

In[]:	`using DataEnvelopmentAnalysis`
	`using BenchmarkingEconomicEfficiency`
	
	`X = [2; 4; 8; 12; 6; 14; 14; 9.412];`
	`Y = [1; 5; 8; 9; 3; 7; 9; 2.353];`
	`W = [1; 1; 1; 1; 1; 1; 1; 1];`
	`P = [2; 2; 2; 2; 2; 2; 2; 2];`
	`FIRMS = ["A", "B", "C", "D", "E", "F", "G", "H"];`
	
	`deaprofitholder(X, Y, W, P, l=2, weight=true, optimizer = DEAOptimizer(Gurobi.Optimizer), names=FIRMS)`

Out[]:	`Profit Hölder L2 DEA Model`
	`DMUs = 8; Inputs = 1; Outputs = 1`
	`Returns to Scale = VRS`
	`Weighted (weakly) Hölder distance function`

	Profit	Technical	Allocative
A	2.828	0.0	2.828
B	0.186	0.0	0.186
C	0.0	0.0	0.0
D	0.092	0.0	0.092
E	0.943	0.485	0.458
F	0.404	0.286	0.118
G	0.175	0.0	0.175
H	1.207	0.710	0.497

9.6.1 The ℓ_2 Hölder Profit Inefficiency Model

We rely on the open (web-based) Jupyter notebook interface to illustrate our economic models. Nevertheless, they can be implemented in any integrated development environment (IDE) of preference.[3] To calculate the weighted Hölder profit inefficiency model (9.13) under the ℓ_2 norm, enter the following code in the "`In[]:`" panel, and run it. The corresponding results are shown in the "`Out[]:`" panel in Table 9.3.

We can learn about the reference benchmarks for each firm using the "peersmatrix" function with the corresponding economic or technical model. For the economic model, executing "`peersmatrix(deaprofitholder(X, Y, W, P, l=2, weight=true, optimizer = DEAOptimizer(Gurobi.Optimizer), names=FIRMS))`" identifies firm C as the reference benchmark-maximizing profit for the rest of the firms (see Fig. 9.2).

[3] We refer the reader to Sect. 2.6.1 in Chap. 2 for the installation of the "Benchmarking Economic Efficiency" Julia package. All Jupyter notebooks implementing the different economic models in this book can be downloaded from the reference site: http://www.benchmarkingeconomicefficiency.com

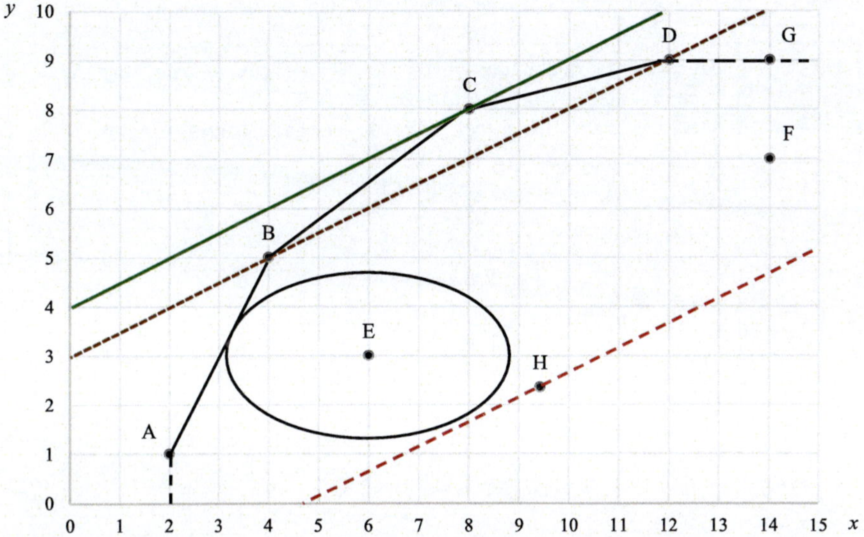

Fig. 9.2 Example of the ℓ_2 Hölder profit inefficiency model using BEE for Julia

Table 9.4 Implementation of the ℓ_2 Hölder graph inefficiency measure using BEE for Julia

In[]:

```
deaholder(X, Y, l = 2, weight = true, orient = :Graph, rts
= :VRS, optimizer = DEAOptimizer(Gurobi.Optimizer), names
= FIRMS)
```

Out[]:

```
Hölder L2 DEA Model
DMUs = 8; Inputs = 1; Outputs = 1
Orientation = Graph; Returns to Scale = VRS
Weighted (weakly) Hölder distance function
```

	efficiency	slackX1	slackY1
A	0.0	0.0	0.0
B	0.0	0.0	0.0
C	0.0	0.0	0.0
D	0.0	0.0	0.0
E	0.485	0.0	0.0
F	0.286	2.0	0.0
G	0.0	0.0	0.0
H	0.710	0.0	0.0

As for the underlying weighted (weakly) Hölder (graph) technical efficiency model, we can obtain all the information running the corresponding function, as shown in Table 9.4. In these results, the value of the technical inefficiency and the optimal slacks are obtained by solving (9.6) with the constraints in (9.7), which yields a zero value in the input slack for firm G. As opposed to other additive

Table 9.5 Reference peers of the ℓ_2 Hölder graph inefficiency measure using BEE for Julia

In[]:	`peersmatrix(deaholder(X, Y, l = 2, weight = true, orient = :Graph, rts = :VRS, optimizer = DEAOptimizer(Gurobi.Optimizer), names = FIRMS))`
Out[]:	see below

```
1.0    .      .    .    .    .    .    .
 .    1.0     .    .    .    .    .    .
 .     .     1.0   .    .    .    .    .
 .     .      .   1.0   .    .    .    .
0.412 0.588   .    .    .    .    .    .
 .     .      .   1.0   .    .    .    .
 .     .      .    .    .    .   1.0   .
0.610 0.390   .    .    .    .    .    .
```

measures, for weakly efficient firms, this method does not rely on the additive model to obtain the value of the slacks in a second stage, which would produce an input slack of two units.

It is also of interest to identify the reference benchmarks of the ℓ_2 Hölder graph distance function. Once again, these benchmarks can be recovered through the "peersmatrix" function; i.e., "`peersmatrix(deaholder(X, Y, l = 2, weight = = true, orient = :Graph, rts = :VRS, optimizer = DEAOptimizer (Gurobi.Optimizer), names = FIRMS))`". The output results shown in Table 9.5 ("`Out[]:`") identify firms A, B, C, D, and G as those conforming the weakly efficient production possibility set, i.e., those with unit values in the main diagonal of the square ($J \times J$) matrix containing their own intensity variables λ (note the matrix syntax in "`In[]:`") .

Figure 9.2 illustrates the results for the weakly Hölder profit inefficiency model. There, for firm E, we identify that its normalized profit inefficiency with respect to firm C, according to (9.13), is equal to $N\Pi I_{WWH\ddot{o}lder}(x^E, y^E, \tilde{w}, \tilde{p}; 2) = 0.943 = (8-0)/\sqrt{(2 \times 3)^2 + (1 \times 6)^2}$, which can be decomposed into the weighted Hölder distance function representing technical inefficiency and whose value is $TI_{WWH\ddot{o}lder}(x^E, y^E; 2) = 0.485$, and allocative inefficiency $AI_{WWH\ddot{o}lder}(x^E, y^E, \tilde{w}, \tilde{p}; 2) = 0.458 = 0.943–0.485$. Note that for this example and contrary to the cost and revenue inefficiency examples that follow, none of the firms identifies the same economic and technological benchmark, i.e., firm C.

9.6.2 The ℓ_1 Hölder Cost Inefficiency Model

We now solve the example for the weakly Hölder cost inefficiency model using the norm ℓ_1 as option. We consider the weighted version that searches for the minimum distance to the weakly efficient frontier among the set of directions represented by the individually observed input quantities: $g_x = \left(0, \ldots, x_{(om')}, \ldots 0\right)$, $m' = 1, \ldots, M$. To calculate this model, type the code included in the "`In[]:`" panel in the notebook, and execute it. The corresponding results are shown in the "`Out[]:`" panel of Table 9.6.

As before, we can learn about the reference benchmarks using the "peersmatrix" function with the corresponding economic or technical model. For the cost model, we run "`peersmatrix(deacostholder(X, Y, W, l=1, weight=true, names=FIRMS))`". In this case, firm A is identified as the only firm-minimizing cost (see Fig. 9.3).

As for the corresponding ℓ_1 weakly Hölder (input-oriented) technical inefficiency model, we obtain all the information running the corresponding function, as shown in Table 9.7. For inefficient firms, the function returns the input dimension that minimizes the (weighted) distance to the weakly efficient frontier, which in this case is the first input except for firm F (for efficient firms, the first input is displayed by default). Note that despite the input orientation, this function returns the slack values for both inputs and outputs.

Table 9.6 Implementation of the ℓ_1 Hölder cost inefficiency model using BEE for Julia

In[]:

```
using DataEnvelopmentAnalysis
using BenchmarkingEconomicEfficiency

X = [2 2; 1 4; 4 1; 4 3; 5 5; 6 1; 2 5; 1.6 8];
Y = [1; 1; 1; 1; 1; 1; 1; 1];
W = [1 1; 1 1; 1 1; 1 1; 1 1; 1 1; 1 1; 1 1];
FIRMS = ["A", "B", "C", "D", "E", "F", "G", "H"];

deacostholder(X, Y, W, l=1, weight=true, names=FIRMS)
```

Out[]:

```
Cost Hölder L1 DEA Model
DMUs = 8; Inputs = 2; Outputs = 1
Orientation = Input; Returns to Scale = VRS
Weighted (weakly) Hölder distance function
```

	Cost	Technical	Allocative
A	0.0	0.0	0.0
B	0.25	0.0	0.25
C	0.25	0.0	0.25
D	0.75	0.625	0.125
E	1.2	0.8	0.4
F	0.5	0.0	0.5
G	0.6	0.5	0.1
H	0.7	0.375	0.325

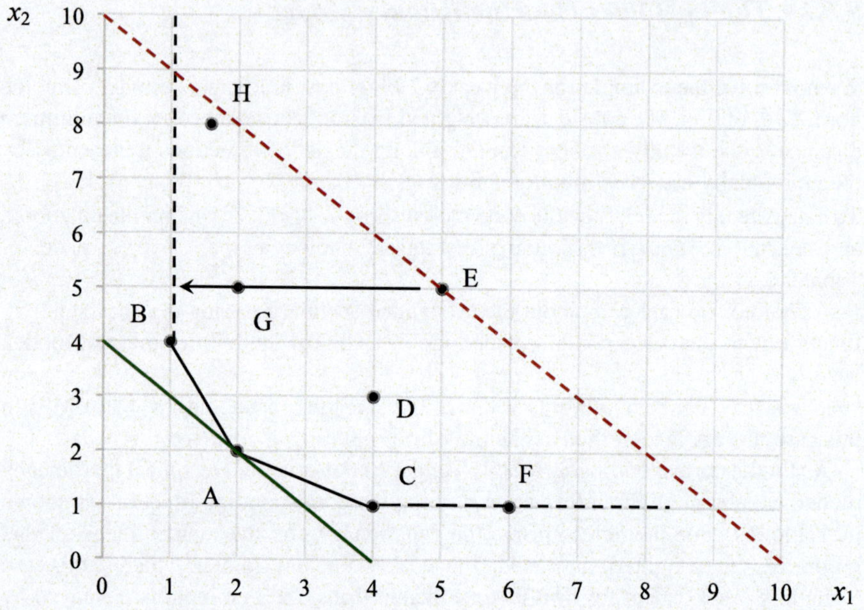

Fig. 9.3 Example of the ℓ_1 weakly Hölder cost inefficiency model using BEE for Julia

Table 9.7 Implementation of the ℓ_1 Hölder input inefficiency measure using BEE for Julia

In[]:

```
deaholder(X, Y, orient = :Input, rts = :VRS, l = 1, weight
= true, names = FIRMS)
```

Out[]:

```
Hölder L1 DEA Model
DMUs = 8; Inputs = 2; Outputs = 1
Orientation = Input; Returns to Scale = VRS
Weighted (weakly) Hölder distance function
```

	efficiency	minimum	slackX1	slackX2	slackY1
A	0.0	X1	0.0	0.0	0.0
B	0.0	X1	0.0	0.0	0.0
C	0.0	X1	0.0	0.0	0.0
D	0.625	X1	0.0	0.0	0.0
E	0.8	X1	0.0	1.0	0.0
F	0.0	X2	2.0	0.0	0.0
G	0.5	X1	0.0	1.0	0.0
H	0.375	X1	0.0	4.0	0.0

Table 9.8 Reference peers of the ℓ_1 Hölder input inefficiency measure using BEE for Julia

In[]:

```
peersmatrix(deaholder(X, Y, orient = :Input, rts = :VRS, l
= 1, weight = true, names = FIRMS))
```

Out[]:

```
1.0   .    .    .    .    .    .    .
 .   1.0   .    .    .    .    .    .
 .    .   1.0   .    .    .    .    .
0.5  0.5   .    .    .    .    .    .
 .   1.0   .    .    .    .    .    .
 .    .   1.0   .    .    .    .    .
 .   1.0   .    .    .    .    .    .
 .   1.0   .    .    .    .    .    .
```

Again the reference benchmarks of the technical model can be recovered using the "peers" function, i.e., "`peersmatrix(deaholder(X, Y, orient = :Input, rts = :VRS, l = 1, weight = true, names = FIRMS))`." The output shown in Table 9.8 identifies firms A, B, and C as those conforming the production frontier (see "`Out[]:`").

Figure 9.3 illustrates the results for the weakly Hölder cost inefficiency model under the ℓ_1 norm. There, for firm E, we learn that its normalized cost efficiency with respect to firm A, according with (9.28), is equal to $NCI_{WHölder(I)}(x_E, y_E, \tilde{w}; 1) = 1.2 = (10\text{–}4)/5$, which can be decomposed into the Hölder distance function, whose value is $TI_{WWHölder(I)}(x_E, y_E; 1) = 0.8$, and the residual allocative inefficiency $AI_{WHölder(I)}(x_E, y_E, \tilde{w}; 1) = 0.4 = 1.2\text{–}0.8$. Note that for all technically inefficient firms, their economic and technical reference peers are different. For example, for firm E, while its cost-efficient peer is firm A, firm B represents its technological benchmark. The same pair of reference benchmarks is observed for firms G and H, but not for firm F whose technological benchmark is firm C. Consequently, all firms are allocative-inefficient, with $AI_{WHölder(I)}(x_o, y_o, \tilde{w}; 1) > 0$.

9.6.3 The ℓ_∞ Hölder Revenue Inefficiency Model

We now illustrate the revenue inefficiency model based on output-oriented weakly Hölder distance function under the ℓ_∞ norm. We consider the weighted version of the model corresponding to a directional vector whose elements are the observed output quantities: $g = (g_x, g_y) = (0_M, y_o)$. To calculate the model, we type the code presented in "`In[]:`" (Table 9.9). The corresponding results are shown in the "`Out[]:`" panel.

Table 9.9 Implementation of the ℓ_∞ Hölder revenue inefficiency model using BEE for Julia

In[]:

```
using DataEnvelopmentAnalysis
using BenchmarkingEconomicEfficiency

X = [1; 1; 1; 1; 1; 1; 1; 1];
Y = [7 7; 4 8; 8 4; 3 5; 3 3; 8 2; 6 4; 1.5 5];
P = [1 1; 1 1; 1 1; 1 1; 1 1; 1 1; 1 1; 1 1];
FIRMS = ["A", "B", "C", "D", "E", "F", "G", "H"];

dearevenueholder(X, Y, P, l=Inf, weight=true, names=FIRMS)
```

Out[]:

```
Revenue Hölder LInf DEA Model
DMUs = 8; Inputs = 1; Outputs = 2
Orientation = Output; Returns to Scale = VRS
Weighted (weakly) Hölder distance function
```

	Revenue	Technical	Allocative
A	0.0	0.0	0.0
B	0.167	0.0	0.167
C	0.167	0.0	0.167
D	0.75	0.556	0.194
E	1.333	1.333	0.0
F	0.4	0.0	0.4
G	0.4	0.273	0.127
H	1.153	0.6	0.554

To know the reference set for the evaluation of economic and technical inefficiency, we rely on the "peersmatrix" function with the corresponding model. For the revenue model, we execute "`peersmatrix(dearevenueholder(X, Y, P, l=Inf, weight=true, names=FIRMS))`". The output identifies firm A as the benchmark-maximizing revenue for the rest of the firms (see Fig. 9.4).

As for the associated ℓ_∞ Hölder distance function, corresponding to the output-oriented measure, it is possible to identify its value and slacks running the code shown in Table 9.10. Again, it returns the slack values for both inputs and outputs.

Again the reference benchmarks of the technical inefficiency model can be recovered using the "peersmatrix" function, i.e., "`peersmatrix(deaholder(X, Y, orient = :Output, rts = :VRS, l = Inf, weight = true, names = FIRMS))`". The output shown in Table 9.11 identifies firms A, B, and C as those defining the strongly efficient production possibility set ("`Out[]:`")—while firm F defines the weakly efficient frontier as shown by its null efficiency score and positive slack value in Table 9.10.[4]

[4] Table 9.11 reports the optimal values of the lambda multipliers λ_j, obtained when solving program (9.36) with $g = (g_x, g_y) = (0_M, y_o)$. For firm F, there are two optimal solutions with $\beta = 0$: $\lambda_C = 1$ and $\lambda_F = 1$. In the first case, shown in Table 9.11, the output constraint is satisfied as an inequality, while in the second case, it is satisfied as an equality.

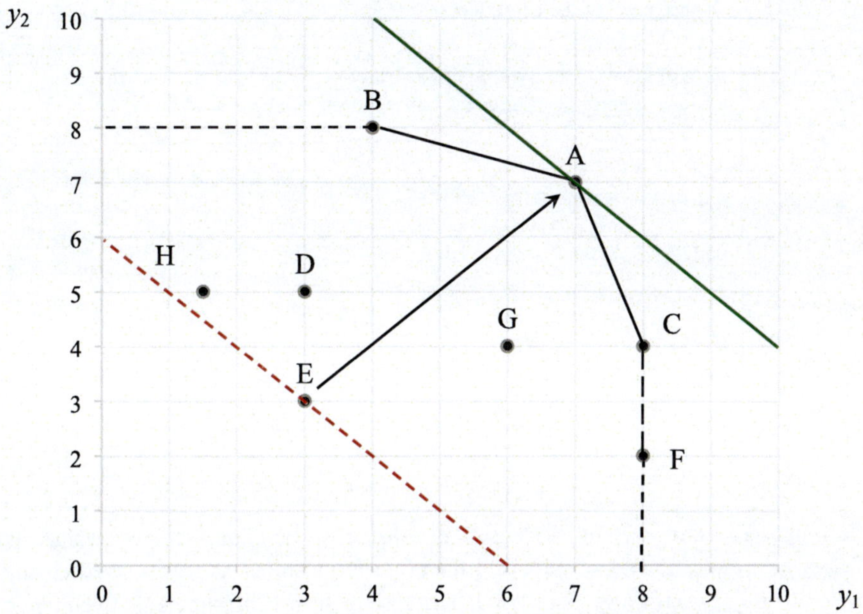

Fig. 9.4 Example of the ℓ_∞ Hölder revenue inefficiency model using BEE for Julia

Table 9.10 Implementation of the ℓ_∞ Hölder output inefficiency measure using BEE for Julia

In[]:

```
deaholder(X, Y, orient = :Output, rts = :VRS, l = Inf,
weight = true, names = FIRMS)
```

Out[]:

```
Hölder LInf DEA Model
DMUs = 8; Inputs = 1; Outputs = 2
Orientation = Output; Returns to Scale = VRS
Weighted (weakly) Hölder distance function
```

	efficiency	slackX1	slackY1	slackY2
A	0.0	0.0	0.0	0.0
B	0.0	0.0	0.0	0.0
C	0.0	0.0	0.0	0.0
D	0.556	0.0	0.0	0.0
E	1.333	0.0	0.0	0.0
F	0.0	0.0	0.0	2.0
G	0.273	0.0	0.0	0.0
H	0.6	0.0	1.6	0.0

Figure 9.4 illustrates the results for the weakly Hölder revenue inefficiency model. There, for firm E, we see that for the ℓ_∞ norm, normalized economic inefficiency with respect to firm A, as defined in (9.43), is equal to $NRI_{WHölder(O)}(x_A, y_A, \tilde{p}; \infty)$=1.333 = (14–6)/(3 + 3). Revenue inefficiency can be

Table 9.11 Reference peers of the ℓ_∞ Hölder output inefficiency measure using BEE for Julia

In[]:	`convert(Matrix, peers(deaholder(X, Y, l = Inf, weight = true, orient = :Output, rts = :VRS, names = FIRMS)))`
Out[]:	see below

```
1.0    .      .      .   .   .   .   .
 .     1.0    .      .   .   .   .   .
 .      .     1.0    .   .   .   .   .
0.222  0.778  .      .   .   .   .   .
1.0     .     .      .   .   .   .   .
 .      .     1.0    .   .   .   .   .
0.363   .     0.637  .   .   .   .   .
 .     1.0    .      .   .   .   .   .
```

decomposed into the weakly Hölder distance function, whose value is $TI_{WWHölder(O)}(x_A, y_A; \infty) = 1.333$, and therefore the residual allocative inefficiency is null, $AI_{WHölder(O)}(x_A, y_A, \tilde{p}; \infty) = 0$. The case of firm E illustrates that economic efficiency models under the ℓ_∞ norm satisfy the essential property presented in Sect. 2.4.5 of Chap. 2. This is because under this particular metric, the Hölder distance function coincides with the directional distance function, which complies with this property, as discussed in the previous chapter. In any case, the Hölder distance functions meet the essential property in general, as was pointed out in the text. This is in sharp contrast to other definitions and decompositions of economic efficiency based on alternative additive distance functions, for instance, the case of the weighted additive distance function (WADF) presented in Chap. 6.

9.6.4 *An Application to the Taiwanese Banking Industry*

As in previous chapters, we now calculate profit inefficiency using the dataset of 31 Taiwanese banks observed in 2010 (see Juo et al. (2015)). A brief presentation of the data, including descriptive statistics, can be found in Sect. 2.5.2 of Chap. 2. In this dataset, individual firm prices for each input and output are observed. We adopt the standard approach in the literature and determine maximum profit for each firm under evaluation using its own prices as reference. The variation of prices makes the results specific for each firm, and therefore bilateral comparisons of profit inefficiency are price-dependent. For instance, it is possible that a technically efficient firm is profit-inefficient under its own prices by not demanding the optimal input and output mix (allocative inefficiency), yet it may maximize profit under other firm's prices, serving as reference target. Of course, the opposite situation can be observed.

Table 9.12 Decomposition of profit inefficiency based on the ℓ_∞ Hölder distance function

Bank	Economic inefficiency, eq. (9.13)			Slacks, eqs. (9.6) and (9.7)				
	Profit Ineff. $N\Pi I_{WWH\ddot{o}lder}(x_o, y_o, w, p; 2)$	Technical Ineff. $TI_{WWH\ddot{o}lder}(x_o, y_o; 2)$	Allocative Ineff. $AI_{WWH\ddot{o}lder}(x_o, y_o, \tilde{w}, \tilde{p}; 2)$	Funds (x_1) s_1^-	Labor (x_2) s_2^-	Ph. Capital (x_3) s_3^-	Investments (y_1) s_1^+	Loans (y_2) s_2^+
1	0.000	0.000	0.000	0.0	0.0	0.0	0.0	0.0
2	0.116	0.000	0.116	0.0	0.0	0.0	0.0	0.0
3	0.302	0.000	0.302	0.0	0.0	0.0	0.0	0.0
4	3.237	0.279	2.959	0.0	328.7	198.1	1,908.9	0.0
5	0.000	0.000	0.000	0.0	0.0	0.0	0.0	0.0
6	0.139	0.000	0.139	0.0	0.0	0.0	0.0	0.0
7	0.216	0.000	0.216	0.0	0.0	0.0	0.0	0.0
8	0.240	0.043	0.197	0.0	999.1	4,294.7	0.0	0.0
9	0.400	0.048	0.351	0.0	2,054.3	9,296.1	0.0	0.0
10	0.000	0.000	0.000	0.0	0.0	0.0	0.0	0.0
11	1.324	0.239	1.085	0.0	2,489.7	12,087.4	0.0	0.0
12	1.383	0.109	1.275	0.0	0.0	3,393.5	0.0	0.0
13	36.337	0.406	35.932	0.0	2,246.4	5,438.7	10,587.2	0.0
14	0.484	0.000	0.484	0.0	0.0	0.0	0.0	0.0
15	0.666	0.117	0.549	0.0	470.2	0.0	0.0	62,380.9
16	55.761	0.725	55.036	0.0	1,422.1	5,413.3	3,910.9	0.0
17	1.282	0.139	1.143	0.0	3,497.6	9,826.0	0.0	0.0
18	1.336	0.115	1.221	0.0	1,846.8	0.0	0.0	0.0
19	4.856	0.414	4.441	0.0	973.1	2,633.0	0.0	0.0
20	2.917	0.135	2.782	105,132.0	1,223.7	0.0	8,364.3	0.0
21	0.621	0.000	0.621	0.0	0.0	0.0	0.0	0.0
22	7.928	0.294	7.633	0.0	1,157.6	6,888.6	15,024.6	0.0
23	14.392	0.480	13.912	0.0	868.7	6,113.5	8,924.2	0.0
24	0.340	0.024	0.315	0.0	1,634.2	1,821.4	0.0	0.0
25	2.952	0.228	2.724	0.0	871.8	0.0	30,073.7	0.0
26	1.424	0.000	1.424	0.0	0.0	0.0	0.0	0.0
27	7.948	0.502	7.446	0.0	526.2	650.8	5,178.0	0.0
28	10.722	0.400	10.322	52,372.8	779.4	0.0	6,252.1	0.0
29	1.755	0.000	1.755	0.0	0.0	0.0	0.0	0.0
30	0.463	0.088	0.374	0.0	1,253.0	0.0	0.0	0.0
31	6.902	0.226	6.677	0.0	1,940.4	2,602.1	26,397.2	0.0
Average	5.369	0.162	5.207	5,080.8	857.5	2,279.3	3,762.0	2,012.3
Median	1.324	0.109	1.143	0.0	779.4	0.0	0.0	0.0
Maximum	55.761	0.725	55.036	105,132.0	3,497.6	12,087.4	30,073.7	62,380.9
Minimum	0.000	0.000	0.000	0.0	0.0	0.0	0.0	0.0
Std. Dev.	11.686	0.192	11.538	20,813.0	928.3	3,460.2	7,604.3	11,203.9

For the implementation of the weakly Hölder profit inefficiency, we choose the weighted ℓ_2 norm that uses the square of the inverse of the observed quantities of inputs and outputs as norms—see Table 9.2. Table 9.12 presents the values of profit inefficiency in the second column, including its descriptive statistics at the bottom. In this model, profit inefficiency is normalized by the Euclidean norm $\|(w_{o1}x_{o1}, \ldots, w_{oM}x_{oM}, p_{o1}y_{o1}, \ldots, p_{oN}y_{oN})\|_q$, i.e., the denominator in (9.13) with $q = 2$ and including the prices considered for each firm. Three banks are profit-efficient under their own prices (no. 1, no. 5, and no. 10), with $\Pi I_{WWHölder}(x_o, y_o, w, p; 2) = 0$ and constituting the most frequent benchmarks for the remaining banks. From a technical perspective, as in any of the chapters included in this book, 11 banks are efficient, while the remaining 20 banks are both technical- and allocative-inefficient. Technical and allocative inefficiencies are reported in the third and fourth columns of Table 9.12. In this case, average normalized profit inefficiency equals 5.369, while average technical and allocative inefficiencies are 0.162 and 5.207, respectively. Therefore, most of the normalized profit loss is due to allocative inefficiency, whose share in the total economic inefficiency is 97%, while that corresponding to technical inefficiency is 3%.

In the last five columns of Table 9.12, we present the optimal slacks obtained when solving eq. (9.6) with the restrictions presented in (9.7). On the one hand, looking at the three inputs we observe that the largest average slack amount corresponds to financial funds (x_1), whose value is 5,080.8 million TWD, while the smallest slack is observed for labor (x_2), with an average of 857.5 employees. On the other hand, financial investments (y_1) present the largest slack in the output dimension, with a value of 3,762.0 million TWD. The slack in unrealized loans (y_2), while still large at 2,012.3 million TWD, corresponds to a single bank (#15). Finally, it is worth mentioning that in this real dataset, the violation of the so-called essential property was not detected.

9.7 Summary and Conclusions

This chapter revises the main contributions in the literature that tries to measure and decompose overall inefficiency through a mathematical metric. In particular, we first showed how to measure technical inefficiency in the most general case, allowing the modification of inputs and outputs at the same time, by means of the notion of Hölder distance functions. We considered two definitions of this measure, depending on the selected reference set for comparison: the weakly efficient frontier or the strongly efficient frontier. Secondly, we showed the main relationships that can be established between the profit function and the Hölder distance functions. Moreover, we also showed how to decompose this measure into technical and allocative inefficiency components. Additionally, we provided the mathematical models necessary to implement all the calculations resorting to traditional optimizers. In some cases, we formulated the models as bi-level linear programs. Afterwards, we particularized the general results to the case of input-oriented and output-oriented contexts.

An interesting point from the point of view of the decomposition of economic inefficiency is that the Hölder distance functions satisfy the so-called essential property but they do not fulfill the extended version of that property (see Chap. 2 for a description of both properties). At this respect, the "residual" term that appears in the decomposition can be actually interpreted as price inefficiency, which is crucial for empirical applications. However, the allocative inefficiency assigned to an interior point is not equivalent to the allocative inefficiency linked to the corresponding technical projection point, which can seem odd.

A challenge associated with the Hölder distance functions is augmenting the number of real applications where this measure is used. Despite these types of mathematical metrics which are very usual in physics, chemistry, and all sciences in general, their frequency of appearance in microeconomics for measuring overall and technical efficiency is very low. It is probably the consequence of the difficulty of their computation in practice. Nevertheless, we have shown that both the polyhedral metrics and the Euclidean distance can be implemented in usual solvers in an easy way. Additionally, we provided a software for calculating all these measures. Accordingly, we believe that we are helping to encourage researchers to apply these tools more often in practice.

Chapter 10
The Loss Distance Function: Economic Inefficiency Decompositions

10.1 Introduction

From the beginning of DEA as a well-defined multi-output-multi-input tool for measuring efficiency, a huge number of technical efficiency measures have been introduced in the literature. Each of them implements a different way of gauging the "distance" from a firm in the interior of the technology to its efficient frontier (radially, hyperbolically, through additive slacks, following a reference directional vector, etc.). Probably, the existence of a wide range of different measures was the cause of encouraging certain researchers to introduce general frameworks that encompass all or most or the DEA technical efficiency measures.

Chronologically speaking, the first attempt to introduce a common structure for DEA models was the paper by Yu et al. (1996a), which was later utilized for finding the supporting hyperplanes of the DEA polyhedral production possibility set in Yu et al. (1996b) and for analyzing the properties of the K-cones in Wei and Yu (1997). Yu et al. (1996a) introduced a generalized DEA model with three binary parameters to give a unification of different radial measures. Following Yu et al. (1996a), Wei et al. (2008) extended that approach resorting to bi-objective optimization and allowing equiproportionally increasing outputs and decreasing inputs in a simultaneous way. Another line of research for generalizing the DEA models is that introduced by Yun et al. (2004), who resorted to the augmented Chebyshev scalarizing function for encompassing the CCR model (Charnes et al., 1978), the BCC model (Banker et al., 1984) and even the radial models under the FDH approach (Deprins et al., 1984). On the other hand, Kleine (2004) formulated a general DEA model employing scalarizing functions known from multi-criteria decision-making, which fundamentally aggregates input and output slacks. Kleine's approach encompasses a wide list of traditional DEA technical efficiency measures. However, it does not include the well-known enhanced Russell graph (ERG) measure (Pastor et al., 1999) presented in Chap. 7, also known as slacks-based

J. T. Pastor et al., *Benchmarking Economic Efficiency*, International Series in Operations Research & Management Science 315,
https://doi.org/10.1007/978-3-030-84397-7_10

measure (SBM) (Tone, 2001). It was Pastor et al. (2012) who, for the first time, introduced a common general framework for the most popular DEA measures, including the SBM.

To get the desired general framework in the DEA context, Pastor et al. (2012) introduced the notion of loss distance function, inspired by Debreu (1951). Basically, the loss distance function measures the "distance" from the evaluated firm to the efficient DEA frontier using a set of normalization constraints for the input and output shadow prices. The loss distance function can generate a multitude of technical (in)efficiency measures simply by changing the normalization constraints. In the case of resorting to linear normalization constrains, then most of the traditional DEA measures can be obtained from the general structure. For example, the loss distance function encompasses the Hölder metric distance functions, the directional distance functions, Shephard's input and output distance functions, the weighted additive models, and the ERG=SBM measure, as aforementioned. Additionally, other new measures of technical efficiency could be derived by resorting to different sets of normalization constraints, even nonlinear ones.

The seminal ideas of the loss distance function come from Debreu (1951)—see Sect. 2.1 in Chap. 2. Debreu (1951) introduced the well-known *coefficient of resource utilization*, which has been interpreted as a "radial" efficiency measure in the context of production. Debreu derived this measure from the less known "dead loss" function, which characterizes the monetary value of the inefficiencies (the distance from the firm in the interior of the technology to the efficient frontier) and which is to be minimized as any inefficiency. In particular, the minimization problem proposed by Debreu was

$$\underset{z,p_z}{Min}\left\{\sum p_{zt}(z_{ot}-z_t)\right\}, \tag{10.1}$$

where z_o is a vector representing the actual allocation of resources and z is a vector belonging to the set of optimal allocations, while p_z is the shadow price vector associated with z. For Debreu, the optimal value of (10.1) allows identifying a lower bound of the economic loss due to being inefficient. However, to solve this optimization problem, Debreu noted that the shadow prices are affected by an arbitrary positive scalar. It means that the magnitude of the loss can be driven to zero by appropriately scaling all components of vector p_z. To prevent this possibility, Debreu suggested to introduce a deflator, reformulating (10.1) as

$$\underset{z,p_z}{Min}\left\{\sum p_{zt}(z_{ot}-z_t)\Big/\sum p_{zt}z_t\right\}, \tag{10.2}$$

which is mathematically equivalent (regarding the optimal solution) to the following one:

$$\underset{z,p_z}{Max}\left\{\sum p_{zt}z_t / \sum p_{zt}z_{ot}\right\}. \tag{10.3}$$

In this way, Debreu was able to prove that an optimal solution to the above maximization problem is always $z^* = \gamma z_o$, where the scalar γ $(0 < \gamma \leq 1)$ is his famous coefficient of resource utilization. Note also that solving (10.3) is equivalent to solving (10.4),

$$\underset{z,p_z}{Max}\left\{\sum p_{zt}z_t : \sum p_{zt}z_{ot} = 1\right\}, \tag{10.4}$$

where we are using a normalization constraint defined over the shadow prices.

It is worth to mention that Debreu studied an economic system consisting of two activities, production and consumption, and allowing for three sources of economic loss: underemployment of resources, inefficiency in production, and imperfection of the economic organization. Pastor et al. (2012) simplified matters by studying the production activity of an economic system having one source of loss, which linked to the technical inefficiency of production units.

The loss distance function, in a production context, utilizes the minimization of the loss function introduced by Debreu to evaluate the technical efficiency of any producer, assuming that the optimal producers have shadow prices affected by a positive scalar unless a normalization scheme is introduced. The proposal by Pastor et al. (2012) consists of using different normalization conditions to eliminate the arbitrary multiplicative factor drawback presented in the Debreu problem, instead of resorting to a unique possibility: that introduced by Debreu and associated with the radial models in DEA.

From the point of view of economic inefficiency measurement, the loss distance function also permits establishing a general dual correspondence with respect to the profit function, in such a way that most of the previous dual relations proposed in the literature are special cases of this general result. In this respect, the main results were already published in Aparicio et al. (2016b). In this chapter, we will briefly revise these results and particularize them to the input- and output-oriented contexts. Additionally, we will relate the loss distance function with the traditional Russell Graph measure, a result that is new in some sense, thanks to the recent contribution by Halická and Trnovská (2021).

The remaining of this paper unfolds as follows: In Sect. 10.2, we introduce the loss distance function and provide the main duality results regarding the profit function. In Sect. 10.3, we discuss the case of the input-oriented loss distance function and its relationship with the cost function. In Sect. 10.4, we study the output-oriented case. Section 10.5 concludes.

10.2 The Graph Loss Distance Function and the Decomposition of Profit Inefficiency

In this section, we introduce the notion of loss distance function and show its main properties. As for duality, we state the main relationship between the loss distance function and the profit function. Specifically, it is shown that under appropriate normalization conditions defined over the shadow input and output prices, the loss distance function encompasses a wide set of distance functions and technical efficiency measures in DEA. Additionally, we show that most previous dual connections appearing in the literature are special cases of the general dual correspondence between the loss distance function and the profit function.

We start with the definition of the most important notion in this chapter: the loss distance function. Now, we are ready to introduce the concept of the loss distance function, which is measured with respect to a given normalization set denoted by *NS*.

Definition 10.1 Let $(x, y) \in R_+^{M+N}$ be an input-output vector and let $NS \subset R_+^{M+N}$. The loss distance function $TI_L : R_+^{M+N} \times 2^{R_+^{M+N}} \to [-\infty, +\infty]$ is defined by

$$TI_L(x, y; NS) = \inf_{\overline{x}, \overline{y}, \overline{w}, \overline{p}} \left\{ \sum_{m=1}^{M} \overline{w}_m(x_m - \overline{x}_m) + \sum_{n=1}^{N} \overline{p}_n(\overline{y}_n - y_n) : (\overline{x}, \overline{y}) \in \partial^W(T), (\overline{w}, \overline{p}) \in Q_{(\overline{x}, \overline{y})} \cap NS \right\}, \tag{10.5}$$

where $Q_{(\overline{x},\overline{y})} = \{(v, u) \in R_+^{M+N} : (v, u) \text{ is a shadow price vector of } (\overline{x}, \overline{y})\}$. Expression (10.5) can be considered as the loss distance function graph measure of technical inefficiency. *NS* is the "normalization" set, which is defined over the shadow price space. Later, we will specify this normalization set in several examples, illustrating its usefulness. In particular, we will show that if one defines *NS* in certain way, then one gets a certain technical inefficiency measure.

For convenience, we may rewrite the loss distance function as follows:

$$TI_L(x, y; NS) = \inf_{\overline{x}, \overline{y}, \overline{w}, \overline{p}} \left\{ \sum_{m=1}^{M} \overline{w}_m(x_m - \overline{x}_m) + \sum_{n=1}^{N} \overline{p}_n(\overline{y}_n - y_n) : (\overline{w}, \overline{p}) \in NS, (\overline{x}, \overline{y}) \in D_{(\overline{w}, \overline{p})} \right\} \tag{10.6}$$

where $D_{(\overline{w},\overline{p})} = \left\{ (x, y) \in T : \sum_{n=1}^{N} \overline{p}_n y_n - \sum_{m=1}^{M} \overline{w}_m x_m = \Pi(\overline{w}, \overline{p}) \right\}$. In this second way of expressing the loss function, we are using $D_{(\overline{w},\overline{p})}$, which is the set of feasible input-output vectors that have $(\overline{w}, \overline{p})$ as shadow prices. Formulations (10.5) and (10.6) are equivalent.

In order to have a suitable definition that considers all possible scenarios, it is necessary to take into account the following situation: if $NS = \emptyset$ or if, in general, the optimization programs in (10.5) and (10.6) are infeasible, then we must set $TI_L(x, y; NS) = +\infty$. Additionally, the loss distance function presents the same arbitrary multiplicative scalar problem that Debreu (1951) pointed out with respect to (10.1). One of the goals of *NS* is to eliminate this weakness.

In words, $TI_L(x, y; NS)$ in (10.5) may be seen as the distance from (x, y) to the weakly efficient frontier of the technology *T* but calculated in terms of the normalization set defined over the shadow price vectors. To obtain a distance with economic meaning, the loss distance function evaluates the value of the vector $(x_1 - \overline{x}_1, \ldots, x_M - \overline{x}_M, \overline{y}_1 - y_1, \ldots, \overline{y}_N - y_N)$ by the shadow prices $(\overline{w}, \overline{p})$ associated with $(\overline{x}, \overline{y}) \in \partial^W(T)$. In economic terms, the loss distance function is the monetary value sacrificed by the firm due to technical inefficiency.

Some interesting questions are as follows: How the normalization set should be? And what properties it should satisfy? The key property that it needs to meet is one associated with avoiding the arbitrary multiplicative scalar problem on the shadow prices. A way of satisfying this property consists of defining a closed *NS* such that $(0_M, 0_N) \notin NS$ (C1). Another additional regularity condition, which will be invoked in the results related to the loss distance function, is one linked to having at least a "representative" of each ray that belongs to R_+^{M+N}. Mathematically speaking, this condition can be expressed as (C2) $\forall (v, u) \in R_+^{M+N}$, $(v, u) \neq (0_M, 0_N)$, $\exists k > 0$ such that $k \cdot (v, u) \in NS$.

The notion of loss distance function is general in the sense that it does not specify the way in which the technology is defined or estimated in practice. In the case of assuming the usual postulates of Data Envelopment Analysis, Pastor et al. (2012) showed how to calculate the loss distance function through an optimization program. Both the objective function and the constraints are linear except the normalization set, which could be defined by linear and/or nonlinear constraints. The optimization program to be solved would be the following one:

$$
\begin{aligned}
TI_L(x, y; NS) = \min_{\substack{\alpha, u_1, \ldots, u_N \\ v_1, \ldots, v_M}} \quad & \alpha - \left(\sum_{n=1}^{N} u_n y_n - \sum_{m=1}^{M} v_m x_m \right) \\
\text{s.t.} \quad & \alpha \geq \sum_{n=1}^{N} u_n y_{jn} - \sum_{m=1}^{M} v_m x_{jm}, \qquad j = 1, \ldots, J, \\
& (v, u) \in NS, \\
& v_m, u_n \geq 0, \qquad \forall m, n
\end{aligned}
\tag{10.7}
$$

where the decision variable α may be interpreted as (shadow) profit at optimum.

As Pastor et al. (2012) proved, varying the normalization set, one gets most of the DEA technical efficiency measures. This means that most of the technical efficiency measures in DEA share the same structure. Table 10.1 shows the list of well-known efficiency measures that are obtained from specific linear normalization conditions.

Table 10.1 Different normalization sets and their corresponding DEA technical inefficiency measures

Normalization condition	Technical inefficiency
$\sum_{m=1}^{M} v_m g_m^- + \sum_{n=1}^{N} u_n g_n^+ = 1$	DDF
$\sum_{m=1}^{M} v_m + \sum_{n=1}^{N} u_n = 1$	ℓ_∞-Hölder distance function
$\sum_{m=1}^{M} v_m g_{x_m} = 1, \sum_{n=1}^{N} u_n g_{y_n} = 1$	MDDF (see next chapter)
$v_m \geq \rho_m^-, m = 1, \ldots, M$ $u_n \geq \rho_n^+, n = 1, \ldots, N$	Weighted additive
$v_m \geq \frac{1}{Mx_m}, m = 1, \ldots, M$ $u_n \geq \frac{1}{Ny_n}\left(1 + \sum_{n=1}^{N} u_n y_n - \sum_{m=1}^{M} v_m x_m - \alpha\right), n = 1, \ldots, N$	ERG = SBM

Recently, Halická and Trnovská (2021) have shown that even the loss distance function can be generalized by introducing a penalizing function at the objective function. In particular, these authors work with a penalizing function and normalization set in such a way that the "general" loss distance function encompasses the traditional nonlinear graph Russell measure. The program to be solved is as follows:

$$
\begin{aligned}
\min_{\substack{\alpha, u_1, \ldots, u_N \\ v_1, \ldots, v_M \\ t_1, \ldots, t_N}} \quad & \alpha - \left(\sum_{n=1}^{N} u_n y_n - \sum_{m=1}^{M} v_m x_m \right) + \frac{1}{M+N} \sum_{n=1}^{N} F(t_n) \\
s.t. \quad & \alpha \geq \sum_{n=1}^{N} u_n y_{jn} - \sum_{m=1}^{M} v_m x_{jm}, & j = 1, \ldots, J, \\
& v_m \geq \frac{1}{(M+N)x_m}, & m = 1, \ldots, M \\
& u_n \geq \frac{1}{M+N} \frac{t_n}{y_n}, & n = 1, \ldots, N \\
& v_m, u_n \geq 0, & \forall m, n
\end{aligned}
\tag{10.8}
$$

where $F(t_n) = (1 - \sqrt{t_n})^2$.

This more general expression of the loss distance function gives rise to a new line of research for generating new nonlinear technical efficiency measures under a DEA framework.

Additionally, we have already commented the notion derived from Definition 10.1, which is more general than that associated with a measure of technical inefficiency. For us, a distance function in production theory must satisfy several postulates. First, in the case of evaluating an observed firm or, in general, a firm belonging to the technology, then the value of the distance function should be interpreted as a technical inefficiency measure. Second, the value of the distance function should characterize whether the unit under evaluation belongs to the technology or not, i.e., the representation property. Third, the distance function should present a dual relationship with respect to some support function (e.g., profit, cost, revenue functions).

The loss distance function, by definition, trivially satisfies the first point above. We next show that the value of the loss distance function is also able to signal if a firm is in or out the technology, i.e., it satisfies the representation property.

Proposition 10.1 Let $(x, y) \in R_+^{M+N}$, and let NS be a nonempty subset of R_+^{M+N} that satisfies C1 and C2. Then, $(x, y) \in T$ if and only if $TI_L(x, y; NS) \geq 0$.

Proof On the one hand, if $(x, y) \in T$, then $\sum_{n=1}^{N} \overline{p}_n y_n - \sum_{m=1}^{M} \overline{w}_m x_m \leq \Pi(\overline{w}, \overline{p})$ $\forall(\overline{w}, \overline{p}) \in R_+^{M+N}$. This is equivalent to $\left(\sum_{n=1}^{N} \overline{p}_n \overline{y}_n - \sum_{m=1}^{M} \overline{w}_m \overline{x}_m\right) - \left(\sum_{n=1}^{N} \overline{p}_n y_n - \sum_{m=1}^{M} \overline{w}_m x_m\right) \geq 0$, $\forall(\overline{w}, \overline{p}) \in R_+^{M+N}$ and $\forall(\overline{x}, \overline{y}) \in D_{(\overline{w}, \overline{p})}$. Therefore, $\sum_{m=1}^{M} \overline{w}_m (x_m - \overline{x}_m) + \sum_{n=1}^{N} \overline{p}_n (\overline{y}_n - y_n) \geq 0$, $\forall(\overline{w}, \overline{p}) \in R_+^{M+N}$ and $\forall(\overline{x}, \overline{y}) \in D_{(\overline{w}, \overline{p})}$. Therefore, by (10.6), $TI_L(x, y; NS) \geq 0$. On the other hand, if $(x, y) \notin T$, then $\exists(v, u) \in R_+^{M+N} \backslash \{(0_M, 0_N)\}$ such that $\sum_{n=1}^{N} u_n y_n - \sum_{m=1}^{M} v_m x_m > \Pi(v, u)$ and $\exists(x', y') \in D_{(v, u)}$. By C2, $\exists k > 0$ such that $k \cdot (v, u) \in NS$, and consequently, $k \cdot (v, u) \in Q_{(x', y')}$. Therefore, $\sum_{m=1}^{M} k v_m (x_m - \overline{x}_m) + \sum_{n=1}^{N} k u_n (\overline{y}_n - y_n) = k\left[\left(\sum_{n=1}^{N} u_n y'_n - \sum_{m=1}^{M} v_m x'_m\right) - \left(\sum_{n=1}^{N} u_n y_n - \sum_{m=1}^{M} v_m x_m\right)\right] = k \cdot \left[\Pi(v, u) - \left(\sum_{n=1}^{N} u_n y_n - \sum_{m=1}^{M} v_m x_m\right)\right] < 0$. Finally, by the definition of the loss distance function as an infimum, we have that $TI_L(x, y; NS) < 0$. ■

Regarding the third condition that distance functions should meet, we next show that the loss distance function can be recovered from the information of the profit function. The result is very ease to be proved, thanks to the definition of the loss distance function.

Theorem 10.1 Let NS be a nonempty subset of R_+^{M+N}. Then,

$$TI_L(x, y; NS) = \inf_{(v, u) \in R_+^{M+N}} \left\{ \Pi(v, u) - \left(\sum_{n=1}^{N} u_n y_n - \sum_{m=1}^{M} v_m x_m \right) : (v, u) \in NS \right\}. \tag{10.9}$$

Proof If $(\bar{x},\bar{y}) \in D_{(v,u)}$, then $\sum_{m=1}^{M} v_m(x_m - \bar{x}_m) + \sum_{n=1}^{N} u_n(\bar{y}_n - y_n) = \left(\sum_{n=1}^{N} u_n\bar{y}_n - \sum_{m=1}^{M} v_m\bar{x}_m\right) - \left(\sum_{n=1}^{N} u_n y_n - \sum_{m=1}^{M} v_m x_m\right) = \Pi(v,u) - \left(\sum_{n=1}^{N} u_n y_n - \sum_{m=1}^{M} v_m x_m\right)$. By (10.6), $TI_L(x,y;NS) = \inf_{\bar{x},\bar{y},\bar{w},\bar{p}} \left\{\sum_{m=1}^{M} \bar{w}_m(x_m - \bar{x}_m) + \sum_{n=1}^{N} \bar{p}_n (\bar{y}_n - y_n) : (\bar{w},\bar{p}) \in NS, (\bar{x},\bar{y}) \in D_{(\bar{w},\bar{p})}\right\} = \inf_{(v,u)\in R_+^{M+N}} \left\{\Pi(v,u) - \left(\sum_{n=1}^{N} u_n y_n - \sum_{m=1}^{M} v_m x_m\right) : (v,u) \in NS\right\}$.

■

Theorem 10.1 implies that it is possible to recover the loss distance function from the information of the profit function and the set *NS*, defined on the shadow prices. Notice that this theorem holds independently of whether the set *NS* satisfies C1 and C2, or not.

Now, if one exploits condition C2, given a vector of input and output market prices $(w,p) \in R_{++}^{M+N}$, there exists $k > 0$ such that $k(w,p) \in NS$. Thus, by Theorem 10.1, $TI_L(x,y;NS) \leq \Pi(k(w,p)) - \left(\sum_{n=1}^{N} kp_n y_n - \sum_{m=1}^{M} kw_m x_m\right)$ since $k(w,p)$ is a feasible solution of the optimization model that appears in the above theorem. Additionally, by the homogeneity of degree +1 of the profit function, we get $TI_L(x,y;NS) \leq k\Pi((w,p)) - k\left(\sum_{n=1}^{N} p_n y_n - \sum_{m=1}^{M} w_m x_m\right)$, which, finally, implies

$$k\left[\Pi(w,p) - \left(\sum_{n=1}^{N} p_n y_n - \sum_{m=1}^{M} w_m x_m\right)\right] \geq TI_L(x,y;NS), \tag{10.10}$$

which is the general expression from which we can define specific loss DF profit inefficiency measures. Now, let us illustrate through an example that expression (10.10) contains most of the Fenchel-Mahler inequalities shown in this book. In particular, we will show how to derive the dual relationship between the directional distance function and (normalized) profit inefficiency.

From Table 10.1, we know that $NS_{DDF} = \left\{(v,u) \in R_+^{M+N} : \sum_{m=1}^{M} v_m g_{x_m} + \sum_{n=1}^{N} u_n g_{y_n} = 1\right\}$ is the normalization set that causes the loss distance function to collapse to the directional distance function, i.e., $TI_L(x,y;NS_{DDF}) = TI_{DDF}(x,y;g_x,g_y)$. On the other hand, given a vector of input and output market prices (w,p), $k = \frac{1}{\sum_{m=1}^{M} w_m g_{x_m} + \sum_{n=1}^{N} p_n g_{y_n}}$ is a scalar such that $k(w,p)$ always belongs to NS_{DDF}. This means that C2 holds and, therefore, we can apply inequality (10.10):

Table 10.2 Different values for k and their corresponding DEA technical inefficiency measures

Technical inefficiency	k
DDF	$\left(\sum_{m=1}^{M} v_m g_{x_m} + \sum_{n=1}^{N} u_n g_{y_n}\right)^{-1}$
ℓ_∞-Hölder distance function	$\left(\sum_{m=1}^{M} v_m + \sum_{n=1}^{N} u_n\right)^{-1}$
MDDF	$\left(\min\left\{\sum_{m=1}^{M} v_m g_{x_m}, \sum_{n=1}^{N} u_n g_{y_n}\right\}\right)^{-1}$
Weighted additive	$\left(\min\left\{\frac{v_1}{\rho_1^-}, \ldots, \frac{v_M}{\rho_M^-}, \frac{u_1}{\rho_1^+}, \ldots, \frac{u_N}{\rho_N^+}\right\}\right)^{-1}$

$$\frac{\Pi(w,p) - \left(\sum_{n=1}^{N} p_n y_n - \sum_{m=1}^{M} w_m x_m\right)}{\sum_{m=1}^{M} w_m g_{x_m} + \sum_{n=1}^{N} p_n g_{y_n}} \geq TI_L(x, y; NS_{DDF})$$
$$= TI_{DDF}\left(x, y; g_x, g_y\right). \tag{10.11}$$

This expression coincides with the well-known inequality derived by Chambers et al. (1998) for the directional distance function.

Next, we show the expressions that the scalar k takes associated with each technical efficiency measure in Table 10.2. The case of the ERG = SBM is special and, consequently, not considered here since in the normalization constraints that yield the corresponding *NS* appears the term $\left(1 - \left(\alpha - \left(\sum_{n=1}^{N} u_n y_n - \sum_{m=1}^{M} v_m x_m\right)\right)\right)$, where α is present, something that does not happen in the remaining cases. Remember that α can be interpreted as shadow profit at optimum. Nevertheless, we show in this book a way of deriving two dual inequalities with respect to the profit function and the ERG = SBM in Chapter 7.

Finally, it is worth mentioning that following Farrell's tradition, the general inequality in (10.10) could be transformed into an equality by adding a term with meaning of allocative or price inefficiency, i.e., a loss DF allocative measure of profit inefficiency, as long as the essential properties are satisfied (see Chapter 2).

10.3 The Input-Oriented Loss Distance Function and the Decomposition of Cost Inefficiency

In Aparicio and Pastor (2011), one may find the introduction of the notion of the loss distance function under the context where the output mix and input market prices are fixed, and each firm faces the problem of minimizing its production cost. In particular, Aparicio and Pastor (2011) introduce the concept of loss (or general) input distance function as follows:

Definition 10.2 Let $(x, y) \in R_+^{M+N}$ be an input-output vector and let $NS_I \subset R_+^M$. The loss input distance function $TI_{L(I)} : R_+^M \times 2^{R_+^M} \to [-\infty, +\infty]$ is defined as

$$TI_{L(I)}(x, y; NS_I) = \inf_{\bar{x}, \bar{w}} \left\{ \sum_{m=1}^{M} \overline{w}_m (x_m - \bar{x}_m) : \bar{x} \in \partial^W(L(y)), \overline{w} \in Q_{\bar{x}} \cap NS_I \right\}, \tag{10.12}$$

where $Q_{\bar{x}} = \{v \in R_+^M : v \text{ is a shadow price vector of } \bar{x}\}$. Expression (10.12) can be regarded as the loss distance function input measure of technical inefficiency. NS_I, as before, is the normalization set, but, in this case, it is defined over the input shadow price space.

The loss input distance function may be interpreted as a measure of the distance from $x \in R_+^M$ to the weakly efficient frontier of the set $L(y)$, which would be expressed in input quantities. To get a distance with an economic meaning, the loss input distance function values these quantities through the (shadow) prices of the corresponding benchmark firm at the frontier. In economics terms, the loss input distance function represents the monetary value sacrificed due to technical inefficiency. Thus, the loss input distance function could be interpreted as an opportunity cost.

Of course, it is necessary to establish some properties for the normalization set in order to avoid the arbitrary multiplicative scalar problem on the shadow input prices, as happened in general in the graph case. In the same way, NS_I must be a closed set such that $0_M \notin NS_I$ (C1). And additionally, $\forall v \in R_+^M$, $v \neq 0_M$, $\exists k > 0$ such that $kv \in NS_I$ (C2).

Although the loss input distance function could be used regardless how technology is defined, in the particular case of assuming the usual postulates of DEA, $TI_{L(I)}(x, y; NS_I)$ could be calculated through an optimization program where both the objective function and the constraints are linear except for the case of the normalization constrains that define NS_I. These normalization conditions could be linear or nonlinear. The optimization program to be solved would be the following one:

$$\begin{aligned} TI_{L(I)}(x, y; NS_I) = \min_{\substack{\alpha, u_1, \ldots, u_N \\ v_1, \ldots, v_M}} \quad & \alpha - \left(\sum_{n=1}^{N} u_n y_n - \sum_{m=1}^{M} v_m x_m \right) \\ s.t. \quad & \alpha \geq \sum_{n=1}^{N} u_n y_{jn} - \sum_{m=1}^{M} v_m x_{jm}, \quad j = 1, \ldots, J. \\ & v \in NS_I, \\ & v_m, u_n \geq 0, \quad \forall m, n \end{aligned} \tag{10.13}$$

Table 10.3 Different normalization sets and their corresponding input-oriented DEA technical efficiency measures

Normalization condition	Technical efficiency
$\sum_{m=1}^{M} v_m x_m = 1$	Input Shephard
$\sum_{m=1}^{M} v_m g_{x_m} = 1$	Input-oriented DDF
$\sum_{m=1}^{M} v_m = 1$	Input-oriented ℓ_∞-Hölder distance function
$v_m \geq \rho_m^-, m = 1, \ldots, M$	Input-oriented weighted additive
$v_m \geq \frac{1}{Mx_m}, m = 1, \ldots, M$	Input Russell

Depending on the constraints that we use for defining the normalization set, we get a different input-oriented technical efficiency measure. Table 10.3 shows the list of well-known efficiency measures that are generated from linear normalization conditions.

On the other hand, the sign of the loss input distance function allows us to determine whether an input vector belongs or not to the input set $L(y)$.

Proposition 10.2 Let $(x, y) \in R_+^{M+N}$, and let NS_I be a nonempty subset of R_+^M that satisfies C1 and C2. Then, $x \in L(y)$ if and only if $TI_{L(I)}(x, y; NS_I) \geq 0$.

Proof The proof is like the proof of Proposition 10.1. ■

In the same way of the loss distance function in the graph context, the loss input distance function may also be recovered from the information of a support function. In this case, we are referring to the cost function.

Theorem 10.2 Let NS_I be a nonempty subset of R_+^M. Then,

$$TI_{L(I)}(x, y; NS_I) = \inf_{v \in R_+^M} \left\{ \sum_{m=1}^{M} v_m x_m - C(v, y) : v \in NS_I \right\}. \tag{10.14}$$

Proof The proof is similar to the proof of Theorem 10.1. ■

Invoking C2 and given a vector of input market prices $w \in R_{++}^M$, there exists $k > 0$ such that $kw \in NS_I$. Therefore, by Theorem 10.2, $TI_{L(I)}(x, y; NS_I) \leq \sum_{m=1}^{M} kw_m x_m - C(kw, y)$ since kw is a feasible solution of the optimization model in Theorem 10.2. Additionally, by the homogeneity of degree +1 of the cost function, we have $TI_{L(I)}(x, y; NS_I) \leq k \sum_{m=1}^{M} w_m x_m - kC(w, y)$, which, finally, implies

Table 10.4 Different values for k and their corresponding DEA input-oriented technical inefficiency measures

Technical efficiency	k
Input Shephard	$\left(\sum_{m=1}^{M} v_m x_m\right)^{-1}$
Input-oriented DDF	$\left(\sum_{m=1}^{M} v_m g_{x_m}\right)^{-1}$
Input-oriented ℓ_∞-Hölder distance function	$\left(\sum_{m=1}^{M} v_m\right)^{-1}$
Input-oriented weighted additive	$\left(\min\left\{\frac{v_1}{\rho_1^-}, \ldots, \frac{v_M}{\rho_M^-}\right\}\right)^{-1}$
Input Russell	$(\min\{Mx_1v_1, \ldots, Mx_Mv_M\})^{-1}$

$$k\left[\sum_{m=1}^{M} w_m x_m - C(w,y)\right] \geq TI_{L(I)}(x,y;NS_I), \tag{10.15}$$

which is the general expression that allows defining a specific loss distance function cost inefficiency measure. Next, we show through an example that expression (10.15) contains most of the Fenchel-Mahler inequalities shown in this book in the input-oriented framework. Our example will consist in deriving the dual relationship that exists between the input-oriented weighted additive model and cost function.

From Table 10.3, if we define $NS_{A(I)} = \left\{v \in R_+^M : v_m \geq \rho_m^-, m = 1, \ldots, M\right\}$, we get $TI_{L(I)}(x,y;NS_{A(I)}) = TI_{A(I)}(x,y;\rho^-)$. Note that $v_m \geq \rho_m^-, m = 1, \ldots, M$ is equivalent to $\min\left\{\frac{v_1}{\rho_1^-}, \ldots, \frac{v_M}{\rho_M^-}\right\} \geq 1$. Consequently, given a vector of input market prices w, $k = \frac{1}{\min\left\{\frac{w_1}{\rho_1^-}, \ldots, \frac{w_M}{\rho_M^-}\right\}}$ is a scalar such that $kw \in NS_{A(I)}$. This implies that C2 holds and, therefore, we are ready to invoke inequality (10.15):

$$\frac{\sum_{m=1}^{M} w_m x_m - C(w,y)}{\min\left\{\frac{w_1}{\rho_1^-}, \ldots, \frac{w_M}{\rho_M^-}\right\}} \geq TI_{L(I)}\left(x,y;NS_{A(I)}\right) = TI_{A(I)}\left(x,y;\rho^-\right). \tag{10.16}$$

This expression coincides with the inequality derived by Cooper et al. (2011) for the weighted additive model in DEA.

Table 10.4 shows the expressions that the scalar k takes related to each input-oriented technical efficiency measure in Table 10.3.

Finally, the general inequality in (10.15) may be transformed into an equality by adding a term with meaning of allocative inefficiency, i.e., loss distance function allocative measure of cost inefficiency. This decomposition can be determined if and only if the essential properties are satisfied (see Chapter 2).

10.4 The Output-Oriented Loss Distance Function and the Decomposition of Revenue Inefficiency

In this section, we show the definition of the loss output distance function and its main results regarding the decomposition of overall efficiency. In this case, each firm faces the problem of maximizing revenue given a fixed input vector and an output market price vector.

We start this section with the definition of the loss output distance function.

Definition 10.3 Let $(x, y) \in R_+^{M+N}$ be an input-output vector and let $NS_O \subset R_+^N$. The loss output distance function $TI_{L(O)} : R_+^N \times 2^{R_+^N} \to [-\infty, +\infty]$ is defined by

$$TI_{L(O)}(x, y; NS_O) = \inf_{\bar{y}, \bar{p}} \left\{ \sum_{n=1}^{N} \bar{p}_n (\bar{y}_n - y_n) : \bar{y} \in \partial^W(P(x)), \bar{p} \in Q_{\bar{y}} \cap NS_O \right\}, \tag{10.17}$$

where $Q_{\bar{y}} = \{u \in R_+^N : u \text{ is a shadow price vector of } \bar{y}\}$. Expression (10.17) can be regarded as the loss distance function output measure of technical inefficiency. NS_O is defined over the output shadow price space and also needs that C1 and C2 hold.

In the case of assuming a DEA technology, the loss output distance function should be computed as follows:

$$\begin{aligned} TI_{L(O)}(x, y; NS_O) = \min_{\substack{\alpha, u_1, \ldots, u_N \\ v_1, \ldots, v_M}} \quad & \alpha - \left(\sum_{n=1}^{N} u_n y_n - \sum_{m=1}^{M} v_m x_m \right) \\ s.t. \quad & \alpha \geq \sum_{n=1}^{N} u_n y_{nj} - \sum_{m=1}^{M} v_m x_{mj}, \qquad j = 1, \ldots, J \\ & u \in NS_O, \\ & v_m, u_n \geq 0, \qquad \forall m, n \end{aligned} \tag{10.18}$$

If we vary the normalization conditions that define NS_O, we obtain different well-known output-oriented technical efficiency measure of the DEA literature. Table 10.5 shows the list of these measures when the normalization conditions are linear.

As in the case of the graph and input-oriented loss distance functions, the loss output distance function is able to characterize the belonging to $P(x)$.

Proposition 10.3 Let $(x, y) \in R_+^{M+N}$ and let NS_O be a nonempty subset of R_+^N that satisfies C1 and C2. Then, $y \in P(x)$ if and only if $TI_{L(O)}(x, y; NS_O) \geq 0$.

Table 10.5 Different normalization sets and their corresponding output-oriented DEA technical efficiency measures

Normalization condition	Technical efficiency
$\sum_{n=1}^{N} u_n y_n = 1$	Output Shephard
$\sum_{n=1}^{N} u_n g_{y_n} = 1$	Output-oriented DDF
$\sum_{n=1}^{N} u_n = 1$	Output-oriented ℓ_∞-Hölder distance function
$u_n \geq \rho_n^+, n = 1, \ldots, N$	Output-oriented weighted additive
$u_n \geq \frac{1}{Ny_n}, n = 1, \ldots, N$	Output Russell

Proof See Proposition 10.1. ■

The following result allows decomposing revenue inefficiency into technical inefficiency and allocative inefficiency:

Theorem 10.3 Let NS_O be a nonempty subset of R_+^N. Then,

$$TI_{L(O)}(x, y; NS_O) = \inf_{u \in R_+^N} \left\{ R(u, x) - \sum_{n=1}^{N} u_n y_n : u \in NS_O \right\}. \tag{10.19}$$

Proof See Theorem 10.1. ■

To decompose revenue inefficiency into its usual drivers, let $p \in R_{++}^N$ be an output market price vector. By C2, there exists $k > 0$ such that $kp \in NS_O$. Applying Theorem 10.3, $TI_{L(O)}(x, y; NS_O) \leq R(kp, x) - \sum_{n=1}^{N} kp_n y_n$. Moreover, by the homogeneity of degree +1 of the revenue function, we have $TI_{L(O)}(x, y; NS_O) \leq k\left[R(p, x) - \sum_{n=1}^{N} p_n y_n\right]$, which, finally, implies

$$k\left[R(p, x) - \sum_{n=1}^{N} p_n y_n\right] \geq TI_{L(O)}(x, y; NS_O), \tag{10.20}$$

which is the general expression that allows defining a specific loss distance function revenue inefficiency measure. The inequality (10.20) encompasses most of the Fenchel-Mahler inequalities shown in this book for output-oriented efficiency measures. We next show, as an example, that (10.20) is able to yield the inequality associated with the output-oriented Russell measures.

Table 10.6 Different values for k and their corresponding DEA output-oriented technical efficiency measures

Technical efficiency	k
Output Shephard	$\left(\sum_{n=1}^{N} u_n y_n\right)^{-1}$
Output-oriented DDF	$\left(\sum_{n=1}^{N} u_n g_{y_n}\right)^{-1}$
Output-oriented ℓ_∞-Hölder distance function	$\left(\sum_{n=1}^{N} u_n\right)^{-1}$
Output-oriented weighted additive	$\left(\min\left\{\frac{u_1}{\rho_1^+}, \ldots, \frac{u_N}{\rho_N^+}\right\}\right)^{-1}$
Output Russell	$(\min\{Nu_1p_1, \ldots, Nu_Np_N\})^{-1}$

From Table 10.5, if we define $NS_{R(O)} = \left\{u \in R_+^N : u_n \geq \frac{1}{Ny_n}, n = 1, \ldots, N\right\}$, we obtain $TI_{L(O)}(x, y; NS_{R(O)}) = TI_{R(O)}(x, y)$. Note that $u_n \geq \frac{1}{Ny_n}, n = 1, \ldots, N$ is equivalent to $\min\{Nu_1p_1, \ldots, Nu_Np_N\} \geq 1$. So, given a vector of output market prices p, $k = \frac{1}{\min\{Nu_1p_1, \ldots, Nu_Np_N\}}$ is a scalar such that $kp \in NS_{R(O)}$. Therefore, we found the scalar k that appeared in condition C2. Finally, invoking Theorem 10.3,

$$\frac{R(p, x) - \sum_{n=1}^{N} u_n y_n}{\min\{Nu_1p_1, \ldots, Nu_Np_N\}} \geq TI_{L(O)}\left(x, y; NS_{R(O)}\right) = TI_{R(O)}(x, y). \tag{10.21}$$

This expression coincides with the inequality derived by Aparicio et al. (2015a) for the output-oriented Russell measure in Data Envelopment Analysis.

Table 10.6 shows the expressions that the scalar k takes associated with most of the famous output-oriented technical efficiency measure in DEA.

The final allocative or price term corresponding to the loss distance function allocative measure of revenue inefficiency can be obtained from (10.21) by closing the inequality, if and only if the decomposition satisfies the essential properties (see Chapter 2).

10.5 Summary and Conclusions

This chapter was devoted to introducing the notion of loss distance function, as a general distance function, which encompasses most of the well-known distance functions and technical efficiency measures in the DEA literature. To do that, we recovered the seminal idea of Debreu (1951) of evaluating the loss in the context of the production theory for measuring inefficiency. The loss distance function generalizes the radial measures, the directional distance function, the weighted additive model, the Russell measures, and, even, the enhanced Russell graph measure or slacks-based measure. Additionally, we proved a general duality relation between the profit function and the loss distance function. And the same was stated for the cost and revenue functions regarding the loss input and output distance functions, respectively.

From a practical viewpoint, the loss distance function can be useful for generating new technical efficiency measures, by considering different normalization conditions. Generating new measures relying on the loss distance function is convenient, because it allows to have a direct characterization of the technology and a dual relationship with a support function. In particular, this last point could be of interest for generating economic (in)efficiency measures and their corresponding decompositions into technical and allocative components.

Finally, an interesting avenue for further research could be working with the most general loss distance function that can be defined from the model by Halická and Trnovská (2021), where a penalizing function has been introduced to the original definition of the loss distance function. Another stimulating line of research could be analyzing what normalization conditions lead to a decomposition of economic efficiency that verifies the essential properties.

Chapter 11
The Modified Directional Distance Function (MDDF): Economic Inefficiency Decompositions

11.1 Introduction

As we showed in Chap. 8, by duality, the directional distance function (DDF) is related to a measure of profit inefficiency that is calculated as the normalized deviation between optimal and actual profit at market prices. However, in the most usual case where the selected directional vector corresponds to the observed values in inputs and outputs of the evaluated firm, the associated normalization coincides with the sum of its actual revenue and the actual cost (see expression (8.10)). Although some authors have interpreted this normalization quantity as an indication of the "size" of the firm (see Leleu & Briec, 2009), it is clear that it has no obvious economic meaning from a managerial point of view since this quantity is not present in day-to-day manager's control panel for decision-making.

To overcome this drawback of the DDF, Aparicio et al. (2013a) modified the standard directional distance function in such a way that the new measure allows outputs to expand and inputs to contract by different proportions, something that contrasts with the original version of the DDF. This results in a modified DDF that generalizes the original one while retaining most of its properties. The new measure also presents a dual relationship with the profit function but with a sensible interpretation as the lost profit on (average) outlay, which can be additionally decomposed into technical and allocative inefficiency components.

In the present chapter, we review the main properties and dual relationship of the modified directional distance function (MDDF), a new graph measure of technical inefficiency that is directly related to the DDF. In particular, we are interested in showing that the MDDF provides a lower bound on the lost profit on average cost. The used normalization is different than that associated with the traditional DDF and yields a measure of technical efficiency that is a component of profit economic inefficiency measured by the lost profit on *dollar spent* (cost) rather than on *the sum of dollars earned and dollars spent* (revenue plus cost). In line with the rest of this

J. T. Pastor et al., *Benchmarking Economic Efficiency*, International Series in Operations Research & Management Science 315,
https://doi.org/10.1007/978-3-030-84397-7_11

book, we will show how to operationalize the measure in a Data Envelopment Analysis context.

The rest of the chapter is organized as follows: Sect. 11.2 introduces the modified directional distance function in the framework of DEA. Section 11.3 relates the MDDF to the "lost profit on average cost" through duality. Section 11.4 provides a numerical example. In Sect. 11.5, we show the main conclusions.

11.2 The Modified Directional Distance Function

In this section, we introduce the modified directional distance function as in Aparicio et al. (2013a) both in general terms and under the vision of Data Envelopment Analysis.

Recall first the formulation of the standard directional distance function (DDF) under variable returns to scale as presented in Chap. 8:

$$TI_{DDF(G)}\left(x_o, y_o; g_x, g_y\right) = \sup\left\{\beta : \left(x_o - \beta g_x, y_o + \beta g_y\right) \in T\right\}. \tag{11.1}$$

In a DEA context, (11.1) would be operationalized as follows:

$$\begin{aligned} TI_{DDF(G)}\left(x_o, y_o; g_x, g_y\right) = & \max_{\beta, \lambda_1, \dots, \lambda_J} \beta \\ s.t. & \\ \sum_{j=1}^{J} \lambda_j x_{jm} \leq x_{om} - \beta g_{x_m}, & \quad m = 1, \dots, M \\ \sum_{j=1}^{J} \lambda_j y_{jn} \geq y_{on} + \beta g_{y_n}, & \quad n = 1, \dots, N \\ \sum_{j=1}^{J} \lambda_j = 1, & \\ \lambda_j \geq 0, & \quad j = 1, \dots, J \\ \beta free. & \end{aligned} \tag{11.2}$$

The optimal value of (11.2), β^*, times the directional vector $g = \left(g_x, g_y\right) \in \mathbb{R}_+^M \times \mathbb{R}_+^N \backslash \{0_{M+N}\}$, represents the amounts in which the observed input quantities must be reduced and the observed output quantities must be increased to reach the production frontier. If, for instance, the researcher selects $(g_x, g_y) = (x_o, y_o)$, the corresponding projection on the weakly efficient frontier becomes $((1 - \beta^*)x_o, (1 + \beta^*)y_o)$. Under this choice, β^* is known as the proportional DDF due to its interpretation. Let us assume that $\beta^* = 0.25$. This means that the input mix should be scaled down by 25%, whereas the output mix should be scaled up by 25% for the evaluated firm to reach the frontier of the technology. In this way, it is easy to see that the DDF includes both input and output inefficiencies.

Although more flexible than the input-oriented and output-oriented radial measures, the DDF has some limitations. One of them is related to the interpretation of the normalized economic inefficiency considering input and output market prices, when the researcher looks at the duality between the profit function and the directional distance functions. As we showed in Chap. 8, expression (8.11), the corresponding Fenchel-Mahler inequality was presented by Chambers et al. (1998):

$$\frac{\Pi(w,p) - \left(\sum_{n=1}^{N} p_n y_{on} - \sum_{m=1}^{M} w_m x_{om}\right)}{\sum_{n=1}^{N} p_n g_y + \sum_{m=1}^{M} w_m g_x} \geq TI_{DDF(G)}\left(x_o, y_o; g_x, g_y\right). \tag{11.3}$$

The numerator in (11.3) is the difference between the maximum attainable profit and the firm's actual profit. In other words, the numerator is the lost profit due to inefficiency. For $(g_x, g_y) = (x_o, y_o)$, the most usual selection of the reference vector in practice, the denominator in (11.3) is the sum of the actual revenue and the actual cost of the firm—we further consider this case in the next section. Consequently, the LHS in (11.3) is not the standard ratio used as an economic index of the performance of a firm in order to evaluate the level of lost profit. Indeed, this expression has no obvious economic meaning. By implication, the profit inefficiency measure related to the DDF has no intuitive interpretation from a managerial point of view. Zofío et al. (2013) introduce a profit inefficiency model that projects the firms under evaluation to the maximizing profit benchmark by endogenizing the directional vector, $(g_x, g_y) = \left(g_x^*, g_y^*\right)$, while normalizing it so the denominator in (11.3) is equal to one: $\sum_{n=1}^{N} p_n g_{y_n}^* + \sum_{m=1}^{M} w_m g_{x_m}^* = 1$—see Petersen (2018) for a recent study on endogenous directional vectors and economic efficiency measurement based on the work by the previous authors. Only in this particular case model (11.3) has a direct interpretation in terms of monetary loss due to economic inefficiency. Otherwise, the absence of a meaningful interpretation is a weakness of the directional distance functions that must be solved.

In Aparicio et al. (2013a), the focus is on decreasing inputs and increasing outputs simultaneously, as the DDF, but using a different coefficient for inputs and outputs instead of the same "beta" for all dimensions/variables. We show the basic model for the MDDF under variable returns to scale and a production possibility set estimated by Data Envelopment Analysis:

$$
\begin{aligned}
& TI_{MDDF(G)}\left(x_o, y_o; g_x, g_y\right) = \max_{\beta_x, \beta_y, \lambda_1, \ldots, \lambda_J} \quad \beta_x + \beta_y \\
& s.t. \\
& \sum_{j=1}^{J} \lambda_j x_{jm} \leq x_{om} - \beta_x g_{x_m}, \qquad m = 1, \ldots, M \\
& \sum_{j=1}^{J} \lambda_j y_{jn} \geq y_{on} + \beta_y g_{y_n}, \qquad n = 1, \ldots, N \\
& \sum_{j=1}^{J} \lambda_j = 1, \\
& \lambda_j \geq 0, \qquad j = 1, \ldots, J \\
& \beta_x, \beta_y \geq 0
\end{aligned}
\quad , \tag{11.4}
$$

where $\left(g_x, g_y\right) \in R_{++}^{M+N}$. Expression (11.4) corresponds to the modified DDF graph measure of technical inefficiency.

In the simple case of producing only one output from the consumption of only one input, the MDDF coincides with the weighted additive model presented in Chap. 6. To see that result, it is enough to define the change of variables $s_1^- = \beta_x g_{x_1}$ and $s_1^+ = \beta_y g_{y_1}$. In this way, the objective function to be maximized would be $\frac{s_1^-}{g_{x_1}} + \frac{s_1^+}{g_{y_1}}$. However, it is worth emphasizing that, for the general case, the MDDF does not coincide with the weighted additive model.

The general formulation of the MDDF corresponds to the following expression:

$$
TI_{MDDF(G)}\left(x_o, y_o; g_x, g_y\right) = \max \left\{\beta_x + \beta_y : \left(x_o - \beta_x g_x, y_o + \beta_y g_y\right) \in T, \ \beta_x, \beta_y \geq 0\right\}. \tag{11.5}
$$

Contrary to the traditional DDF, the choice of the observed input and output quantities as reference vector, $(g_x, g_y) = (x_o, y_o)$, allows different rates of output expansion, β_y, and input contraction, β_y, allowing a flexibility that the former model cannot offer:

$$
\begin{aligned}
& TI_{MDDF(G)}\left(x_o, y_o; g_x, g_y\right) = \max_{\beta_x, \beta_y, \lambda_1, \ldots, \lambda_J} \quad \beta_x + \beta_y \\
& s.t. \\
& \sum_{j=1}^{J} \lambda_j x_{jm} \leq (1 - \beta_x) x_{om}, \qquad m = 1, \ldots, M \\
& \sum_{j=1}^{J} \lambda_j y_{jn} \geq \left(1 + \beta_y\right) y_{on}, \qquad n = 1, \ldots, N \\
& \sum_{j=1}^{J} \lambda_j = 1, \\
& \lambda_j \geq 0, \qquad j = 1, \ldots, J \\
& \beta_x, \beta_y \geq 0
\end{aligned}
\tag{11.6}
$$

Regarding the traditional DDF, it is well-known that any vector $\left(g_x, g_y\right) \in R_+^{M+N}$ with $(g_x, g_y) \neq (0_M, 0_N)$ could be used for measuring technical inefficiency. The same can be applied for the MDDF, since the reference vector (g_x, g_y) is arbitrarily chosen by the researchers. Nevertheless, they usually select it to be the observed input-output vector, which is in the spirit of the original Farrell measures and Shephard's distance functions and results in the proportionality interpretation of the MDDF. Moreover, as shown in what follows, when $(g_x, g_y) = (x_o, y_o)$, we obtain a desirable dual relationship with the profit function.

11.3 Duality and the Decomposition of the Lost Profit on Outlay

In the private sector, besides having information on the input and output quantities of the firms, it is normal to observe market prices. In these sectors or industries, the measurement of profit inefficiency is a must and, knowing the drivers of this value, traditionally technical inefficiency and allocative inefficiency, is particularly important. As we remarked, profit inefficiency compares the observed profit of the firm with respect to the maximum attainable profit at the given market prices. As for the decomposition, technical inefficiency captures how close the firm is to the frontier of the production possibility set. Under the Farrell tradition, allocative inefficiency is the remaining profit inefficiency (the residual) once the unit being evaluated has achieved technical efficiency, implying that additional improvements can be accomplished by reallocating input demands and output supplies along the efficient frontier (i.e., achieving the optimal mix across inputs and outputs that maximizes profit).

Regarding the measurement and decomposition of the profit inefficiency, the most popular approach is that related to the directional distance function (Chambers et al., 1998). Although from a technological perspective the DDF nests Shephard's input and output distance functions (or Farrell's efficiency measures), this does not extend to economic efficiency and, specifically, as shown by Aparicio et al. (2017b), to allocative efficiency. By duality, the directional distance function is associated with the profit function through a particular normalization condition on market prices: the sum of the value of the directional vector (see the denominator of the ratio in (11.3)). Particularly, if we consider the usual reference vector $\left(g_x, g_y\right) = \left(x_o, y_o\right)$, then we get

$$\frac{\Pi(w,p) - \Pi_o}{R_o + C_o} \geq TI_{DDF(G)}\left(x_o, y_o; x_o, y_o\right), \tag{11.7}$$

where Π_o, R_o, and C_o are, respectively, the firm's actual profit, revenue, and cost at market prices (w, p). Note, however, that, in this case, the profit inefficiency measure, the left-hand side in inequality (11.7), presents some problems with respect to its economic interpretation. The sum of the actual revenue and cost of the firm cannot be recognized as a financial figure that managers examine. Unfortunately, this is the normalization that is derived from duality in a natural way in the case of the DDF and the profit function. The necessity of considering a normalization condition goes back to Nerlove (1965). Nerlove (1965, p. 94) highlighted that the quantity $\Pi(w,p) - \Pi_o$ may not be a suitable economic measure because it is homogeneous of degree one in prices. This means that we obtain a different value if we work with dollars or if we work with euros (i.e., it is unit-dependent). Consequently, it is necessary to consider a normalization factor (a deflator) as a way of overcoming this weakness. As we pointed out, one solution to this problem was proposed by Chambers et al. (1998) through the DDF. Regrettably, the fundamental drawback of this option is the lack of easy interpretability of the measure from the perspective of the firm's management.

In view of the preceding discussion, it seems appropriate to propose a suitable normalization condition for the term $\Pi(w,p) - \Pi_o$. Appropriate means that it has to satisfy several required properties and also that the normalized profit inefficiency measure should make economic sense. The approach by Aparicio et al. (2013a) allows deriving such type of association in a natural way by applying duality, as we show next.

First of all, in order to explain the main contribution of Aparicio et al. (2013a) regarding duality, we need to show the dual linear program of (11.6):

$$\begin{aligned}
&\min_{\substack{\alpha_o, u_{o1}, \ldots, u_{oN} \\ v_{o1}, \ldots, v_{oM}}} \quad \alpha_o - \sum_{n=1}^{N} u_{on} y_{on} + \sum_{m=1}^{M} v_{om} x_{om} \\
&s.t. \\
&\alpha_o - \sum_{n=1}^{N} u_{on} y_{jn} + \sum_{m=1}^{M} v_{om} x_{jm} \geq 0, \qquad j = 1, \ldots, J \\
&\sum_{m=1}^{M} v_{om} x_{om} \geq 1, \\
&\sum_{n=1}^{N} u_{on} y_{on} \geq 1, \\
&u_{on} \geq 0, \qquad n = 1, \ldots, N \\
&v_{om} \geq 0, \qquad m = 1, \ldots, M \\
&\alpha_o \text{ free.}
\end{aligned} \tag{11.8}$$

By duality in linear programming, $TI_{MDDF(G)}(x_o, y_o; x_o, y_o)$ equals the optimal value of program (11.8). Moreover, another interesting result states that if $(u_o^*, v_o^*, \alpha_o^*)$ is an optimal solution of (11.8), then $\alpha_o^* = \Pi(v_o^*, u_o^*)$. It means that u_o^* and v_o^* may be interpreted as input and output shadow prices, respectively, and α_o^* as their corresponding shadow profit. This result is very easy to be proven. Let $(u_o^*, v_o^*, \alpha_o^*)$ be an optimal solution of (11.8). Then, $(u_o^*, v_o^*, \Pi(v_o^*, u_o^*))$ is a feasible solution of (11.8) since, by definition of profit function, $\Pi(v_o^*, u_o^*) \geq \sum_{n=1}^{N} u_{on}^* y_{jn} - \sum_{m=1}^{M} v_{om}^* x_{jm}$, $j = 1, \ldots, J$. Let us assume that $\alpha_o^* > \Pi(v_o^*, u_o^*)$. Then, $\Pi(v_o^*, u_o^*) - \sum_{n=1}^{N} u_{on}^* y_{jn} + \sum_{m=1}^{M} v_{om}^* x_{jm} < \alpha_o^* - \sum_{n=1}^{N} u_{on}^* y_{jn} + \sum_{m=1}^{M} v_{om}^* x_{jm}$, which would be a contradiction with the fact that $(u_o^*, v_o^*, \alpha_o^*)$ is an optimal solution of (11.8). So, $\alpha_o^* \leq \Pi(v_o^*, u_o^*)$. Under VRS in DEA, maximal profit is always achieved at an extreme efficient unit. It is due to the fact that the DEA technology is a polyhedron defined from its corners. Therefore, $\Pi(v_o^*, u_o^*) = \max_{j=1,\ldots,J}\left\{\sum_{n=1}^{N} u_{on}^* y_{jn} - \sum_{m=1}^{M} v_{om}^* x_{jm}\right\}$. Note that, by the feasibility of $(u_o^*, v_o^*, \alpha_o^*)$, we have that $\alpha_o^* \geq \sum_{n=1}^{N} u_{on}^* y_{jn} - \sum_{m=1}^{M} v_{om}^* x_{jm}$, $j = 1, \ldots, J$, which implies that $\alpha_o^* \geq \max_{j=1,\ldots,J}\left\{\sum_{n=1}^{N} u_{on}^* y_{jn} - \sum_{m=1}^{M} v_{om}^* x_{jm}\right\} = \Pi(v_o^*, u_o^*)$. Finally, we have $\alpha_o^* = \Pi(v_o^*, u_o^*)$. This result is the key for the proof of the next proposition.

Proposition 11.1 Let $x_o > 0_M$ and $y_o > 0_N$. Then,

$$
\begin{aligned}
TI_{MDDF(G)}(x_o, y_o; x_o, y_o) = \; & \min_{\substack{u_{o1},\ldots,u_{oN} \\ v_{o1},\ldots,v_{oM}}} \frac{\Pi(v_o, u_o) - \left(\sum_{n=1}^{N} u_{on} y_{on} - \sum_{m=1}^{M} v_{om} x_{on}\right)}{\min\left\{\sum_{m=1}^{M} v_{om} x_{om}, \sum_{n=1}^{N} u_n y_{on}\right\}} \\
& s.t. \\
& \sum_{m=1}^{M} v_{om} > 0, \\
& \sum_{n=1}^{N} u_{on} > 0, \\
& v_{om} \geq 0, \qquad m = 1, \ldots, M \\
& u_{on} \geq 0, \qquad n = 1, \ldots, N
\end{aligned}
\tag{11.9}
$$

Proof Given that $\alpha_o^* = \Pi(v_o^*, u_o^*)$ and that the profit function contains all the information on the technology (in particular, $\Pi(v_o, u_o) \geq \sum_{n=1}^{N} u_{on} y_{jn} - \sum_{m=1}^{M} v_{om} x_{jm}$, $j = 1, \ldots, J$), we can equivalently rewrite model (11.8) as

$$\begin{aligned}
&\underset{\substack{u_{o1},\ldots,u_{oN}\\ v_{o1},\ldots,v_{oM}}}{Min} \quad \Pi(v_o,u_o)-\sum_{n=1}^{N}u_{on}y_{on}+\sum_{m=1}^{M}v_{om}x_{om}\\
&s.t.\\
&\sum_{m=1}^{M}v_{om}x_{om}\geq 1,\\
&\sum_{n=1}^{N}u_{on}y_{on}\geq 1,\\
&u_{on}\geq 0, \qquad\qquad n=1,\ldots,N\\
&v_{om}\geq 0, \qquad\qquad m=1,\ldots,M
\end{aligned} \tag{11.10}$$

Finally, since $\min\left\{\sum_{m=1}^{M}v_{om}x_{om},\sum_{n=1}^{N}u_{on}y_{on}\right\}=1$ implies that $\sum_{m=1}^{M}v_{om}x_{om}\geq 1$ and $\sum_{n=1}^{N}u_{on}y_{on}\geq 1$, and exploiting that the objective function in model (11.10) is homogeneous of degree +1, we get the equivalence between (11.10) and (11.9). ■

Next, we get the key result regarding the Fenchel-Mahler inequality that allows us to define and decompose the economic inefficiency measure associated with this model, i.e., the modified DDF profit inefficiency measure. It states that the lost profit on outlay of the firm can be lower bounded by the modified DDF.

Proposition 11.2 Let $x_o > 0_M$, $y_o > 0_N$ and $\Pi_o \geq 0$. Then,

$$\frac{\Pi(w,p)-\Pi_o}{C_o}\geq TI_{MDDF(G)}(x_o,y_o;x_o,y_o). \tag{11.11}$$

Proof On the one hand, by hypothesis, $\Pi_o \geq 0$, which implies that $\min\left\{\sum_{m=1}^{M}w_m x_{om},\sum_{n=1}^{N}p_n y_{on}\right\}=\sum_{m=1}^{M}w_m x_{om}=C_o$. On the other hand, we are in conditions to apply Proposition 11.1 because the vector (w,p) is trivially a feasible solution of model (11.9). Thus, we get $\frac{\Pi(w,p)-\Pi_o}{C_o}\geq TI_{MDDF}(x_o,y_o;x_o,y_o)$. ■

The expression $(\Pi(w,p)-\Pi_o)/C_o$ provides a measure of the profit lost by not operating in an economic efficient way. This term represents the normalized deviation between optimal profit and actual profit for the assessed unit at market prices (w,p). Unlike the traditional DDF discussed in Chap. 8 and even other measures, for example, the model based on the weighted additive distance function (WADF) (Chap. 6), where the normalization used does not have a clear interpretation, in this case the normalization factor corresponds the actual cost of the firm. It means that the overall inefficiency measure proposed by Aparicio et al. (2013a) is really associated with the lost return on outlay (see Ray, 2004, pp. 233–234). Nevertheless, the lost return on outlay was related to an input-oriented measure in Ray (2004), neglecting the technical inefficiencies due to the output side. In the case of Aparicio et al. (2013a, b), they resort to a graph technical measure, the modified directional distance function, which simultaneously considers input contractions and output expansions.

In the Farrell (1957) tradition, we define the modified DDF allocative measure of profit inefficiency (*AI*) as the residual derived from closing the inequality in Proposition 11.2, providing us with the decomposition of the lost profit on costs into technical and allocative terms:

$$N\Pi I_{MDDF(G)}(x_o, y_o, \widetilde{w}, \widetilde{p}) = \underbrace{\frac{\Pi(w,p) - \Pi_o}{C_o}}_{\text{(Normalized) Profit Inefficiency}} = \underbrace{TI_{MDDF(G)}(x_o, y_o; x_o, y_o)}_{\text{Technical Inefficiency}} + \underbrace{AI_{MDDF(G)}(x_o, y_o, \widetilde{w}, \widetilde{p})}_{\text{Allocative Inefficiency}}. \tag{11.12}$$

The measure $(\Pi(w,p) - \Pi_o)/C_o$ meets a list of interesting properties from the point of view of index numbers. The lost profit on outlay is homogeneous of degree zero in prices and quantities, which means that it is independent of the units of measurement. Moreover, the lost profit on costs is also well-defined for non-positive profit. Additionally, the measure is non-negative with nil inefficiency when it takes value zero. Certainly, the measure satisfies the condition that it is zero if and only if the evaluated firm coincides with that one maximizing profit. So, the lost profit on outlay satisfies the property of indication. Additionally, it is worth mentioning that profit, technical, and allocative inefficiency in (11.12) would express in monetary units if each term is multiplied by C_o. Last, as explicitly stated in Proposition 11.2, the above results are based on the condition that firms do not incur in losses. This is based on the assumption that although firms with negative profits may be observed in the short run, this situation is untenable in the long term, and therefore economic efficiency analyses resting on the "lost return on outlay" measure, which excludes from the evaluation observations with negative returns, can be seen as a valid assessment of performance for viable firms. Related to this problem that was not addressed by Aparicio et al. (2013a) and for the sake of completeness, we extend their analysis to the case of failing firms exhibiting negative profits, i.e., the condition $\Pi_o < 0$, which is opposite to that invoked in Proposition 11.2. In this case, actual revenue is lower than observed cost for the assessed unit. What can be done in this specific situation? We answer this particular question in the next proposition.

Proposition 11.3 Let $x_o > 0_M$, $y_o > 0_N$, and $\Pi_o < 0$. Then,

$$\frac{\Pi(w,p) - \Pi_o}{R_o} \geq TI_{MDDF(G)}(x_o, y_o; x_o, y_o). \tag{11.13}$$

Proof The proof is identical to that of Proposition 11.2 but considering that $\min\left\{\sum_{m=1}^{M} w_m x_{om}, \sum_{n=1}^{N} p_n y_{on}\right\} = \sum_{n=1}^{N} p_n y_{on} = R_o$. ■

The overall measure of (negative) economic inefficiency in (11.13), $(\Pi(w, p) - \Pi_o)/R_o$, shifts the normalization to actual revenue, yielding lost profit per each dollar earned, which is a ratio that continues to have a meaningful economic interpretation. Additionally, it inherits the same good properties of the lost profit on outlay and can de decomposed, by analogy, into a term capturing technical inefficiency, the MDDF, and a component measuring allocative inefficiency:

$$N\Pi I'_{MDDF(G)}(x_o, y_o, \widetilde{w}, \widetilde{p}) = \underbrace{\frac{\Pi(w,p) - \Pi_o}{R_o}}_{\text{(Normalized) Profit Inefficiency}} = \underbrace{TI_{MDDF(G)}(x_o, y_o; x_o, y_o)}_{\text{Technical Inefficiency}} + \underbrace{AI'_{MDDF(G)}(x_o, y_o, \widetilde{w}, \widetilde{p})}_{\text{Allocative Inefficiency}}. \tag{11.14}$$

Note that $AI'_{MDDF(G)}(x_o, y_o, \widetilde{w}, \widetilde{p})$ in expression (11.14) does not have to coincide with $AI_{MDDF(G)}(x_o, y_o, \widetilde{w}, \widetilde{p})$ in expression (11.12). Therefore, although this result completes the analysis of profit inefficiency based on the modified DDF, we acknowledge that the measures obtained for firms presenting either positive and negative profits are not comparable. The reason is that the normalizations not only are unit-specific—i.e., observed cost C_o in (11.12) and observed revenue R_o in (11.14)—but also differ on the nature of the normalizing economic function, either cost or revenue. While the first drawback is common to all profit inefficiency measures whose normalizations depend on the input and output quantities, for example, as in the standard model based on the directional distance function (11.7) where the "economic size" of the firm depends on the its cost and revenue, $R_o + C_o$, the second drawback is specific to the modified DDF. Additionally, in (11.14), if each term is multiplied by R_o, one gets profit, technical, and allocative inefficiency indicators expressed in monetary units.

Finally, it is worth mentioning that the modified directional distance function collapses to the standard directional distance function when they are input- or output-oriented. So, the duality results that are valid for the "oriented" traditional DDF apply to the case of the "oriented" MDDF.

11.4 Empirical Illustration of the Modified DDF Profit Inefficiency Model

In this section, we illustrate the calculation of the profit inefficiency, normalized by either cost or revenue, and its decomposition based on the modified DDF. Since the MDDF model coincides with its directional distance function precursors in the case of the partial input and output orientations, both the cost and revenue inefficiency decompositions are equivalent to those already presented in Chap. 8 for the case of the traditional DDF. Therefore, here we present only the calculation of profit inefficiency using the data in Table 11.1, which are commented in Sect. 2.6 of Chap. 2.

The package function computing the measure of profit inefficiency based on expressions (11.12) and (11.14) is "`deaprofitmddf(X, Y, W, P, Gx = :Observed, Gy = :Observed, names=FIRMS)`".

We rely on the open (web-based) Jupyter notebook interface to illustrate the profit inefficiency model. However, it can be implemented in any integrated development environment (IDE) of preference.[1] To calculate the profit inefficiency measure and its technical and allocative components, type the following code in the "`In[]:`" panel, and run it. The corresponding results are shown in the "`Out[]:`" panel in Table 11.2.

We can learn about the reference peers for each firm using the "peersmatrix" function with the corresponding economic or technical model. For the profit model, executing "`peersmatrix(deaprofitmddf(X, Y, W, P, Gx = :Observed, Gy = :Observed, names = FIRMS))`" identifies firm C as the reference benchmark-maximizing profit for the rest of the firms (see Fig. 11.1).

Table 11.1 Example data illustrating the profit inefficiency model

	Model	
	Graph profit model	
Firm	x	y
A	2	1
B	4	5
C	8	8
D	12	9
E	6	3
F	14	7
G	14	9
H	9.412	2.353
Prices	$w = 1$	$p = 2$

[1] We refer the reader to Sect. 2.6.1 in Chap. 2 for the installation of the "Benchmarking Economic Efficiency" Julia package. All Jupyter notebooks implementing the different economic models in this book can be downloaded from the reference site: http://www.benchmarkingeconomicefficiency.com

Table 11.2 Implementation of the modified DDF profit inefficiency model using BEE for Julia

In[]:

```
using DataEnvelopmentAnalysis
using BenchmarkingEconomicEfficiency

X = [2; 4; 8; 12; 6; 14; 14; 9.412];
Y = [1; 5; 8; 9; 3; 7; 9; 2.353];
W = [1; 1; 1; 1; 1; 1; 1; 1];
P = [2; 2; 2; 2; 2; 2; 2; 2];
FIRMS = ["A", "B", "C", "D", "E", "F", "G", "H"];

deaprofitmddf(X, Y, W, P, Gx = :Observed, Gy = :Observed,
names = FIRMS)
```

Out[]:

```
Profit Modified DDF DEA Model
DMUs = 8; Inputs = 1; Outputs = 1
Returns to Scale = VRS
Gx = Observed; Gy = Observed
```

	Profit	Technical	Allocative
A	4.0	0.0	4.0
B	0.5	0.0	0.5
C	0.0	0.0	0.0
D	0.167	0.0	0.167
E	1.333	1.167	0.167
F	0.571	0.571	0.0
G	0.286	0.143	0.143
H	2.700	2.550	0.150

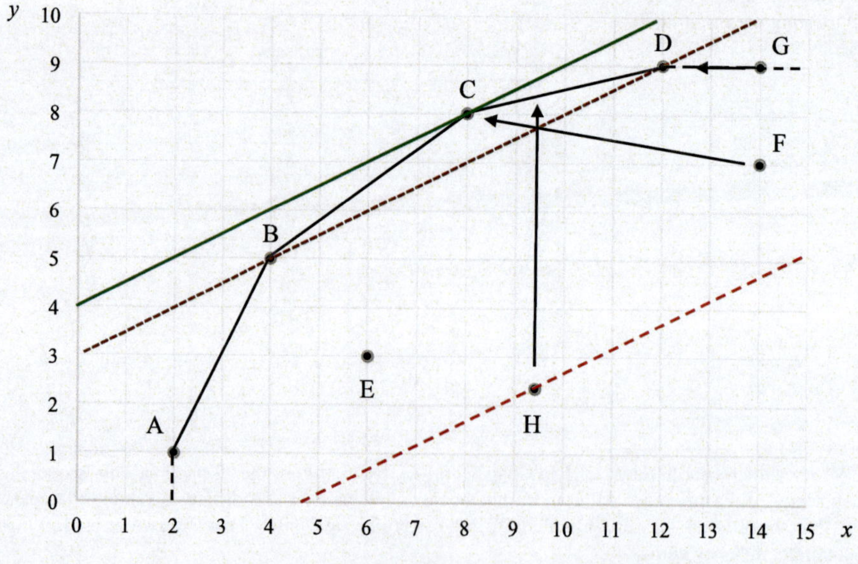

Fig. 11.1 Example of the MDDF profit inefficiency model using BEE for Julia

Table 11.3 Implementation of the modified DDF graph inefficiency measure using BEE for Julia

In[]:
```
deamddf(X, Y, rts = :VRS, Gx = :Observed, Gy= :Observed,
names = FIRMS)
```

Out[]:
```
Modified DDF DEA Model
DMUs = 8; Inputs = 1; Outputs = 1
Returns to Scale = VRS
Gx = Observed; Gy = Observed
```

	efficiency	βx	βy	slackX1	slackY1
A	0.0	0.0	0.0	0.0	0.0
B	0.0	0.0	0.0	0.0	0.0
C	0.0	0.0	0.0	0.0	0.0
D	0.0	0.0	0.0	0.0	0.0
E	1.167	0.0	1.167	0.0	0.0
F	0.571	0.429	0.143	0.0	0.0
G	0.143	0.143	0.0	0.0	0.0
H	2.550	0.0	2.550	0.0	0.0

Table 11.4 Implementation of the modified DDF graph efficiency measure using BEE for Julia

In[]:
```
peersmatrix(deamddf(X, Y, rts = :VRS, Gx = :Observed, Gy =
:Observed, names = FIRMS))
```

Out[]:

1.0	.	.	.	.	.	.	.
.	1.0	.	.	.	.	.	.
.	.	1.0	.	.	.	.	.
.	.	.	1.0	.	.	.	.
.	0.5	0.5	.	.	.	.	.
.	.	1.0	.	.	.	.	.
.	.	.	1.0	.	.	.	.
.	.	0.647	0.353	.	.	.	.

As for the underlying graph technical efficiency model corresponding to the modified DDF (11.4), we can obtain all the information running the corresponding function, as shown in Table 11.3.

Besides the technical inefficiency scores, the results window reports the values of the input and output coefficients, β_x and β_y, constituting the objective function of (11.4). From this program, we confirm that in this single input-single output example, the values of the input and output slacks, s_{om}^- and s_{on}^+, are zero, and therefore the technical projections belong to the strongly efficient frontier. Nevertheless, for higher dimensions, the values can be positive. It is also of interest to identify the reference benchmarks of the modified DDF graph measure of technical efficiency (11.4). We make use once again of the "peersmatrix" function, i.e., "`peersmatrix (deamddf(X, Y, rts = :VRS, Gx = :Observed, Gy = :Observed, names = FIRMS))`". The output results shown in Table 11.4 ("`In[]:`") identify firms A, B, C, and D as those conforming the strongly efficient production possibility set i.e., those with unit values in the main diagonal of the square ($J \times J$) matrix containing their own intensity variables λ.

Figure 11.1 illustrates the results of the modified DDF profit inefficiency model. There, we focus on firms F, G, and H that, respectively, present null, positive, and negative profits. Hence, the first two are evaluated according to expression (11.12) while the last one according to expression (11.14). All firms are evaluated against firm C that is the common economic benchmark. In the case of firm G, profit inefficiency is equal to 0.286 = (8 − 4)/14. Profit inefficiency can be decomposed into the modified DDF measure of technical inefficiency and the residual allocative inefficiency. As for technical inefficiency, this value is equal to $TI_{MDDF(G)}(x_G, y_G) = 0.143 = \beta_x + \beta_y = 0.143 + 0$, and therefore input inefficiency drives the technical projection towards firm D. The difference between the normalized profit inefficiency and technical inefficiency yields 0.143 as allocative inefficiency: 0.143 = 0.286 − 0.143. As for firm F with null profit, its profit inefficiency is 0.571 = (8 − 0)/14, which can be decomposed into technical inefficiency, $TI_{MDDF(G)}(x_F, y_F) = 0.571 = \beta_x + \beta_y = 0.429 + 0.143$, and the residual allocative inefficiency, which in this case is equal to zero because profit and technical inefficiencies are equal. We note that in this example the essential property discussed in Sect. 2.4.5 of Chap. 2 is verified since allocative inefficiency for firm F, having the same profit and technological benchmark (firm C), is null. Finally, as for firm H, whose profit inefficiency is normalized by its revenue, we obtain a value of 2.7 = (8 − (−4.706))/4.706. This firm is projected in the output dimension and shows a technical inefficiency score of $TI_{MDDF(G)}(x_H, y_H) = 2.55 = \beta_x + \beta_y = 0 + 2.55$. Consequently, allocative efficiency is equal to 0.15 = 2.7 − 2.55.

11.4.1 An Application to the Taiwanese Banking Industry

We conclude this empirical section solving the economic decomposition of profit inefficiency based upon the modified DDF, with the directional vector corresponding to the observed inputs and outputs of the assessed DMU, for the panel of 31 Taiwanese banks observed in 2010 (see Juo et al. (2015)). A brief presentation of the data, including descriptive statistics, can be found in Sect. 2.6.2 of Chap. 2. We remark that we are using these data only as an example, and therefore do not aim at analyzing the economic results of the Taiwanese banking industry or any individual bank. The data set includes individual prices for each firm. Here we follow the standard approach that finds the maximum profit for the firm under evaluation using its observed prices. Hence, a firm can be profit-inefficient under its own prices yet maximize profit under other firm's prices, serving as reference peer (and vice versa).

Table 11.5 presents the values of the profit inefficiency in the second column, including its descriptive statistics at the bottom. Out of the 31 banks, 22 present a positive profit $\Pi_o > 0$, and therefore its economic inefficiency is evaluated according

Table 11.5 Decomposition of profit inefficiency based on the Modified Directional Distance Function (MDDF)

Bank	Economic inefficiency, eqs. (11.12) and (11.14)			Technical Ineff., eq. (11.4)		Slacks				
	Profit Ineff. $N\Pi I_{MDDF(G)}$	Technical Ineff. $TI_{MDDF(G)}$	Allocative Ineff. $AI_{MDDF(G)}$	Inputs β_x	Outputs β_y	Funds (x_1) s_1^-	Labor (x_2) s_2^-	Ph. Capital (x_3) s_3^-	Investments (y_1) s_1^+	Loans (y_2) s_2^+
1	0.000	0.000	0.000	0.000	0.000	0.0	0.0	0.0	0.0	0.0
2	0.597	0.000	0.597	0.000	0.000	0.0	0.0	0.0	0.0	0.0
3	1.100	0.000	1.100	0.000	0.000	0.0	0.0	0.0	0.0	0.0
4	9.751	0.362	9.389	0.000	0.362	0.0	210.0	0.0	7,113.7	0.0
5	0.000	0.000	0.000	0.000	0.000	0.0	0.0	0.0	0.0	0.0
6	0.343	0.000	0.343	0.000	0.000	0.0	0.0	0.0	0.0	0.0
7	0.716	0.000	0.716	0.000	0.000	0.0	0.0	0.0	0.0	0.0
8	0.714	0.056	0.658	0.056	0.000	0.0	711.5	3,446.0	0.0	0.0
9	1.331	0.065	1.266	0.065	0.000	0.0	1,740.6	8,277.1	0.0	0.0
10	0.000	0.000	0.000	0.000	0.000	0.0	0.0	0.0	0.0	0.0
11	4.074	0.384	3.690	0.000	0.384	0.0	1,551.4	9,045.5	0.0	0.0
12	4.710	0.113	4.596	0.113	0.000	0.0	0.0	1,876.2	0.0	0.0
13	113.884	0.691	113.193	0.000	0.691	0.0	1,951.9	4,260.5	12,936.6	0.0
14	1.884	0.000	1.884	0.000	0.000	0.0	0.0	0.0	0.0	0.0
15	2.062	0.158	1.904	0.158	0.000	0.0	0.0	2,448.5	0.0	0.0
16	319.036	1.244	317.792	0.000	1.244	0.0	1,225.8	4,627.6	9,770.8	0.0
17	5.603	0.194	5.409	0.000	0.194	0.0	3,122.8	8,994.7	0.0	0.0
18	7.644	0.144	7.500	0.144	0.000	0.0	1,464.3	0.0	0.0	0.0
19	26.780	0.628	26.152	0.000	0.628	0.0	747.7	1,952.1	0.0	0.0
20	8.754	0.194	8.560	0.000	0.194	80,613.5	1,148.0	0.0	7,617.6	0.0
21	2.421	0.000	2.421	0.000	0.000	0.0	0.0	0.0	0.0	0.0
22	24.295	0.436	23.859	0.000	0.436	0.0	1,017.0	6,326.2	18,303.6	0.0
23	625.176	0.746	624.430	0.000	0.746	0.0	708.9	5,474.0	13,701.7	0.0
24	1.011	0.033	0.978	0.033	0.000	0.0	1,507.8	1,557.5	0.0	0.0
25	12.005	0.295	11.710	0.000	0.295	0.0	740.8	0.0	39,044.5	0.0
26	3.765	0.000	3.765	0.000	0.000	0.0	0.0	0.0	0.0	0.0
27	27.986	0.731	27.254	0.000	0.731	0.0	409.1	182.1	7,639.0	0.0
28	36.742	0.638	36.104	0.000	0.638	10,850.5	651.1	0.0	12,956.4	0.0
29	7.822	0.000	7.822	0.000	0.000	0.0	0.0	0.1	0.0	0.0
30	1.621	0.111	1.510	0.000	0.111	0.0	1,042.4	0.0	0.0	0.0
31	25.817	0.347	25.471	0.000	0.347	0.0	1,717.2	1,708.9	29,414.5	0.0
Average	41.214	0.244	40.970	0.018	0.226	2,950.5	699.0	1,941.2	5,112.9	0.0
Median	4.074	0.113	3.765	0.000	0.000	0.0	651.1	0.0	0.0	0.0
Maximum	625.176	1.244	624.430	0.158	1.244	80,613.5	3,122.8	9,045.5	39,044.5	0.0
Minimum	0.000	0.000	0.000	0.000	0.000	0.0	0.0	0.0	0.0	0.0
Std. Dev.	123.503	0.311	123.308	0.043	0.321	14,544.6	794.0	2,912.9	9,486.4	0.0

to (11.12) using observed cost to normalize the difference between maximum profit and observed profit. The remaining 9 incur in losses, $\Pi_o < 0$, and therefore their profit inefficiency is normalized by observed revenue, corresponding to expression (11.14). These latter firms are shaded in gray in Table 11.5. In this empirical application, we highlight that observed cost and observed revenue depend on unit-specific prices and quantities. This means that the industry does not face exogenously determined market prices, but they differ across firms. Three banks are profit-efficient given their observed prices (no. 1, no. 5, and no. 10), representing the most frequent benchmarks for the remaining banks. From a technical perspective, 11 banks are efficient, while the remaining 20 banks are both technical- and allocative-inefficient. Technical and allocative inefficiencies are reported in the third and fourth columns of Table 11.5. In this case, average normalized profit inefficiency equals 41.214, while average technical and allocative inefficiencies are 0.244 and 40.970, respectively. Consequently, most of the normalized profit loss is attributed to allocative inefficiency, whose proportion is 99.4% versus that corresponding to technical inefficiency, 0.6%. The specific parameters β_x and β_y associated with the modified directional distance function (11.4) are reported in the fifth and sixth columns of Table 11.5. Interestingly, in this empirical application, none of the inefficient banks exhibit inefficiencies in both dimensions. Out of the 20 technically inefficient banks, 6 are inefficient in the input dimension, $\beta_x > 0$, and the remaining 14 in the output dimension, $\beta_y > 0$. The higher frequency and mean of β_y show that output inefficiency is larger and more relevant when reaching the production frontier.

Finally, in the last columns of Table 11.5, we present the values of the individual slacks for the three inputs and two outputs. These slacks are obtained after solving Eq. (11.4) for β_x^* and β_y^* and afterwards solving the standard additive model in a second stage for the efficient projections of the firms on the strongly efficient frontier. Looking at the three inputs, we observe that the largest slack inefficiency corresponds by large to financial funds (x_1), whose average slack is 2,950.5 million TWD, followed by physical capital (x_3) and labor (x_2), whose average slacks are 1,941.2 million TWD and 699 employees, respectively. On the output side, financial investments (y_1) exhibit the largest inefficiency with an average slack equal to 5,112.9 million TWD, while there is no inefficiency in the form of unrealized loans (y_2). It is worth mentioning that, in this real dataset, the violation of the so-called essential property was not detected. However, under the context of producing only one output from only one input, the MDDF coincides with the weighted additive model, which suffers the violation of the essential property. Consequently, the modified directional distance function also fails the satisfaction of this property linked to a consistent decomposition of the profit inefficiency. This also means that the MDDF does not satisfy the extended version of the essential property either (see Chap. 2).

11.5 Summary and Conclusions

The directional distance function (DDF) is one of the most important measures in efficiency analysis when the measurement and decomposition of profit inefficiency of a firm is one of the research objectives. This gauge function is interesting due to the satisfaction of multiple properties. From the point of view of economic efficiency, the DDF allows decomposing profit inefficiency in an additive way satisfying the essential property of the decomposition of overall efficiency. Specifically, if the projection benchmark onto the frontier, following the prefixed directional vector, coincides with the feasible point that maximizes profit, then the allocative inefficiency term is always zero. However, the validity of the measure for providing a suitable economic efficiency index is also linked to the satisfaction of other conditions, for example, from the viewpoint of interpretability of the index. In this sense, the DDF is problematic since the most popular way of defining the directional vector is associated with the use of the actual input and output vector of the evaluated firm, which implies that the deflator term used by the profit inefficiency index equals the sum of cost and revenue. This deflator is not a financial figure usually examined by the managers. Accordingly, it was interesting to introduce some modifications of the directional distance function to overcome this weakness. One of them has been reviewed in this chapter: the so-called modified directional distance function (MDDF).

In contrast to the original DDF, the MDDF uses a different coefficient for decreasing inputs and increasing outputs. This distinction has implications with respect to the formulation followed by the (normalized) profit inefficiency index, determined by duality from the MDDF approach. The normalization utilized by the MDDF changes, depending on the sign of the actual profit of the evaluated firm. In the case of non-negative observed profit, profit inefficiency is defined as the lost profit on the outlay (cost) of the firm. In the case of strictly negative actual profit, the profit inefficiency under the MDDF approach is the lost profit on the revenue of the firm. In both scenarios, the profit inefficiency may be decomposed into technical inefficiency, i.e., the MDDF measure, and allocative inefficiency, retrieved as a residual. However, the decomposition linked to the MDDF approach does not meet the essential property. When we are analyzing a database, this means that we could find units that are really allocatively efficient but present a value strictly positive in the component associated with price inefficiency in the decomposition.

Chapter 12
The Reverse Directional Distance Function (RDDF): Economic Inefficiency Decompositions

12.1 Introduction

The reverse directional distance function, henceforth *RDDF*, is a relatively recent concept introduced by Pastor et al. (2016). It is an apparently simple idea and, at the same time, a fruitful one. Let us start considering an efficiency measure (*EM*) and a finite sample of firms to be analyzed, F_J.[1] As we have shown throughout most of the previous chapters, by solving a mathematical program for each firm of the sample, we obtain two relevant outcomes: the maximum of its objective function,[2] which usually corresponds to the technical (in)efficiency associated with the mentioned firm, and a point that belongs to the technological frontier and corresponds to the technical-efficient projection of the firm. Consequently, the efficiency measure (EM) we are going to consider assigns an inefficiency score as well as a single projection to each firm being rated. These are the two conditions required for introducing the *RDDF*. Let us denote as EM^S any efficiency measure that generates a single inefficiency projection together with its inefficiency score for each inefficient firm—denoted by superscript *S*. This condition is satisfied by all the additive measures presented in Part II of the book, except for the *modified DDF*-related efficiency measures introduced by Aparicio et al. (2013a). The *modified DDF* assigns two different scores to the input and output dimensions: β_x^* and β_y^*, respectively—see expression (11.5) of the previous chapter. Given a directional vector $g = (g_x, g_y)$, observed outputs are increased by the amount $\beta_y^* g_y$, while observed inputs are reduced by the amount $\beta_x^* g_x$. We will also show in section 12.6 how to define the RDDF for these types of functions. Moreover, several multiplicative measures presented in Part I fail to satisfy this condition, calculating instead two inefficiency scores, one related to inputs and the other one to outputs.

[1] J is a natural number that indicates the number of firms belonging to set F_J.

[2] Most programs maximize to identify a frontier projection, in which case the program is linear.

J. T. Pastor et al., *Benchmarking Economic Efficiency*, International Series in Operations Research & Management Science 315,
https://doi.org/10.1007/978-3-030-84397-7_12

The most prominent example is the hyperbolic (graph) measure (Färe et al., 1985), which calculates an efficiency score φ^* measuring the proportion in which the inputs can be reduced, while its inverse corresponds to the proportional expansion of the outputs under CRS. It represents a particular case of the generalized distance function introduced by Chavas and Cox (1999) (see expression (4.4) in Chap. 4).

Each time we consider an EM^S, we can define a specific *DDF* that generates, for each firm of the considered sample, the same two EM^S outcomes—a single inefficiency score and a single frontier projection. We call it the *RDDF* associated with $\left(EM^S, F_J, \widehat{F}_J\right)$, where $\widehat{F}_J$ represents the set of single projections of the finite sample of firms.[3] As we will show in Sect. 12.2, to define the *RDDF* associated with $\left(EM^S, F_J, \widehat{F}_J\right)$, we only need to determine, for each firm of F_J, the corresponding directional vector. In our exposition, we are going to distinguish between graph and oriented EM^Ss, since they will generate RDDFs of the same type, which means that the corresponding directional vectors will also be graph or oriented.

A particular and relevant case is associated with the two—oriented—Shephard's distance functions discussed in Chap. 3, representing the first known connection between the multiplicative world, to which the last-mentioned radial measures belong, and the additive world, to which their associated *RDDFs* belong.[4] Moreover, any newly proposed efficiency measure in the literature, satisfying the required inefficiency score uniqueness, can be transformed immediately into its associated *RDDF*, that is, into an equivalent directional distance function, provided the set of projections $\widehat{F}_J$ has been calculated. Through this transformation, the already known and the still unknown efficiency measures satisfying the mentioned condition inherit all the relevant properties associated with a DDF, already presented in Chap. 8.

At this point, it is interesting to distinguish between EM^S and EM^M, where EM^M denotes the set of all the efficiency measures that yield a single inefficiency score but generate more than one projection for at least one of the *J*-inefficient firms. While each single-valued EM^S generates a unique sample of inefficiency scores with their associated single projections and, consequently, a unique *RDDF*, each EM^M generates multiple benchmark samples with the same inefficiency score for each inefficient firm and, consequently, a potential big number of different *RDDFs*. When considering an EM^M, sometimes we are able to decide which sample of benchmarks is the most convenient one for achieving some additional objective or secondary goal, e.g., in terms of the decomposition of economic inefficiency into its technical

[3] The set of projections has the same number of elements as the considered sample of firms. The efficiency measure may be able to identify more than one projection for certain firms of the sample, but in order to define a specific *RDDF*, we need to select a single projection for each firm.

[4] The relation between Shephard's input distance functions and their corresponding directional distance function was established back in 1996, when the related notion of benefit function was introduced in the efficiency and productivity field by Chambers, Chung, and Färe (1996) (see Chap. 8). Shephard's distance functions are the inverse of the corresponding radial DEA-oriented measures, introduced by Charnes et al. (1978).

and allocative terms.[5] In those cases, we are reducing the original EM^M to an associated single-valued efficiency measure over the considered sample of firms, which implies that the corresponding *RDDF* is unique. In any case, we need to introduce a procedure for revealing if a certain efficiency measure over the sample of firms being rated generates single projections or not. In practice, not only the efficiency measure plays a relevant role but also the sample of firms being rated (see the Examples in Chap. 7).

Generally speaking, the efficiency measures that are based on slacks are likely to generate multiple projections, at least for some inefficient firms. This includes almost all the efficiency measures revised in Part II of the book, Chaps. 5 to 11. Notable exceptions are two well-known families of distance functions, *the DDFs* and *the Hölder distance functions*, revised in Chaps. 8 and 9, as well as *the modified DDF* in Chap. 11. What is clear is that each EM^M applied to a certain sample of firms yields as many associated *RDDF*s as the product of the number of projections of each firm of the sample.[6] This number may be large, thereby recommending the design of strategies suitable for identifying the most convenient set of benchmark projections. The most widely used strategy solves just two programs for each inefficient firm: first identifying an initial projection and afterwards a possible second projection that improves the first one in a given (desired) direction. Usually, the mathematical program that identifies the first projection of a certain inefficient firm calculates also its technical inefficiency. The second program tries to identify a second projection, which outperforms the first one according to some additional criterion and, at the same time, generates the same technical inefficiency.[7] Again, this task is not difficult to implement for achieving sensible economic inefficiency decompositions, as we have already shown in previous chapters when evaluating economic inefficiency.

The $EM^{I/O}$ measures, where the superscript *I/O* stands for input and output, i.e., representing evaluations in both the input *and* output dimensions, constitute a family of graph efficiency measures that may be additive or multiplicative in nature. Each of these measures generates two oriented inefficiency scores that are unique and a single projection for each firm, and, consequently, they cannot be directly related to a *DDF*. However, any of them can be related to a *bidirectional distance function*

[5]For instance, in Chap. 7, where the $ERG = SBM$ has been studied, we have shown three numerical examples—graph, input-oriented, and output-oriented—where multiple projections were initially obtained for at least one unit. However, we managed there to select the "best" projection for each firm in order to achieve the corresponding economic inefficiency decomposition. These are examples that show how the $ERG = SBM$, a typical EM^M measure, was reduced in each case to a single-valued efficiency measure, something that is a must for defining the corresponding *RDDF*.

[6]For example, let us imagine a sample of 30 firms, where half of them have a single benchmark projection and the other half have two projections. Then the number of different *RDDFs* that can be associated with the considered efficiency measure and to the mentioned sample of firms is $1^{15} \times 2^{15} = 32.768$.

[7]The fact that we have identified a second projection for certain firms does not exclude the possibility of additional ones.

(*BDF*), a new family of efficiency measures that we are going to introduce in Sect. 12.6, inspired by the *modified DF* of Aparicio et al. (2013) (see Chap. 11). Therefore, we can introduce the notion of a *reverse BDF*, associated with an $EM^{I/O}$, similar to the *RDDF* associated with an EM^S. To close the circle, we are going to show how to associate an *RDDF* with a *BDF*, which means that, at the end, we will be able to express an $EM^{I/O}$, which by definition satisfies the two mentioned conditions, as an *RDDF*. Moreover, there is a one-to-one relationship between the *BDF* and its associated *RDDF*, which means that the *two* $EM^{I/O}$*-oriented inefficiency scores* associated with each firm give rise to a unique *RDDF* inefficiency score, and conversely: for each firm, we will be able to recover the two oriented inefficiency scores associated with the original $EM^{I/O}$ based on the single inefficiency score associated with its *RDDF*. Therefore, we are able to identify, in two steps, an *RDDF* that transforms any $EM^{I/O}$—satisfying the two mentioned regularity conditions—into a *DDF* with the same projection for each firm and with a unique inefficiency score, and vice versa.

This chapter develops as follows: Section 12.2 defines the *RDDF* for any efficiency measure EM^S over a finite sample of firms. Section 12.3 compares the two profit inefficiency decompositions based on a graph EM^S and its associated *RDDF*. Sections 12.4 and 12.5 extend the methodology of the previous sections for comparing, in connection with oriented EM^S*s*, the corresponding cost inefficiency decompositions and the revenue inefficiency decompositions. Section 12.6 considers the family of graph efficiency measures $EM^{I/O}$ and introduces the notion of a BDF, showing how to associate with each of them a *RDDF*. Section 12.7 illustrates the different efficiency measures relaying on the software "Benchmarking Economic Efficiency" accompanying this book. Finally, Sect. 12.8 presents the conclusions.

12.2 The Reverse Directional Distance Function $RDDF\left(EM^S, F_J, \widehat{F}_J\right)$ Associated with the Efficiency Measure Triad $\left(EM^S, F_J, \widehat{F}_J\right)$

In the introduction, we have already explained the idea of defining a directional distance function (*DDF*), based on the functioning of an alternative efficiency measure. Our initial idea is to consider any efficiency measure EM^S whose functioning is similar to a *DDF*, which means that for evaluating any firm (x_j, y_j) of a finite sample F_J, the reference measure must identify, as any *DDF* does, a single frontier projection $\left(\widehat{x}_j, \widehat{y}_j\right)$ as well as a unique technical inefficiency score $TI_{EM^S}\left(x_j, y_j\right)$. As it is well known, for applying any *DDF* to a finite sample F_J, we need to know the elements that characterize a *DDF*, that is, each directional vector associated with each firm. Once each directional vector $\left(g_{x_j}, g_{y_j}\right)$ is known, it is easy to identify its single frontier projection as well as its unique technical inefficiency (see program (8.8) and its dual (8.9) in Chap. 8). When considering, for each firm, the two mentioned outcomes of a certain EM^S, we are facing the reverse situation: we know the two outcomes of a certain *DDF*, but we do not know its directional vector. This is the reason for calling it the reverse directional distance function (*RDDF*) associated with EM^S.

In what follows, we need to identify the profile of any efficiency measure whose outcomes can be obtained by means of a *RDDF*. Let us start by formally introducing the family of efficiency measures EM^S.

Definition 12.1
Any efficiency measure that generates a unique projection for each firm as well as a unique efficiency or inefficiency score is called an EM^Smeasure.

There are easy and well-known rules for transforming an efficiency score into an inefficiency score. In the multiplicative world, many measures have been created as efficiency measures, such as the first two oriented *DEA* measures proposed by Charnes et al. (1978), known as the oriented *CCR* models that are intimately related to the corresponding oriented Farrell measures (see Färe et al., 1985). Since then, many other efficiency multiplicative measures have been proposed, either as efficiency or inefficiency measures. An example of an additive inefficiency measure is the *WADF* discussed in Chap. 6, which directly offers the inefficiency scores needed for defining the corresponding *RDDF*. Therefore, we are concerned with measures that deliver efficiency or inefficiency scores, but what matters is to know the corresponding inefficiency scores. Moreover, we need to identify a single projection for each inefficient firm. These are the two requirements for deriving, in each case, the corresponding *RDDF*.

Let us start with the standard radial input-oriented efficiency model under any returns to scale as presented in program (3.23) of Chap. 3, whose efficiency score, denoted as θ^*, belongs to the interval $]0, 1]$ and generates an inefficiency score $\beta^* = 1 - \theta^*$, which belongs to the interval $[0, 1[$. For instance, $\theta^* = 1$ corresponds either to a strongly efficient firm or to a weakly efficient firm, with at least one input that cannot be reduced within *T*, and, therefore, its input radial inefficiency equals $\beta^* = 0$. On the other hand, recalling the radial output-oriented efficiency score presented in program (3.25) of Chap. 3, $\xi^* = 1/\phi^*$ belongs to the interval $[1, +\infty[$, while its associated inefficiency score, $\beta^* = 1/\phi^* - 1$, belongs to the interval $[0, +\infty[$.[8] Again, the inefficiency associated with an efficient firm is $\beta^* = 0$ which corresponds to $\phi^* = 1$. Basically, any oriented multiplicative efficiency measure has the same behavior as the corresponding *CCR* models. What can be somehow more surprising is that the graph multiplicative measures have been designed for getting efficiency scores which satisfy that they belong to the interval $]0, 1]$ or, alternatively, to $[1, +\infty[$. For instance, the $ERG = SBM$ of Chap. 7 was devised so that their efficiency scores belong to the interval $]0, 1]$, which means their associated inefficiency scores belong to the interval $[0, 1[$. However, if we consider the inverse of the

[8] In turn, ϕ^* is the technical efficiency measure defined in expression (2.7) of Chap. 2, coinciding with Shephard's output distance function: expression (3.8) of Chap. 3.

ERG = *SBM*, automatically their efficiency scores belong to $[1, +\infty[$, and, consequently, their corresponding inefficiency scores belong to $[0, +\infty[$.[9]

For associating with any EM^S a reverse directional distance function (*RDDF*), we need to carefully specify a finite sample of firms to be rated, F_J, and to identify, for each firm, its single non-negative EM^Stechnical inefficiency score as well as its single frontier projection. To this end, let us start precising the notion of *a triad* associated with any EM^S efficiency measure.

Definition 12.2
Given an EM^Sefficiency measure and a finite sample of firms F_J, we define the triad $\left(EM^S, F_J, \widehat{F}_J\right)$, where $\widehat{F}_J$is the finite set of single EM^Sprojections associated with F_J.

Examples of efficiency measures exist that are always single-valued for any sample of firms. Earlier on, the most popular ones were *the radial oriented measures* presented in Chap. 3, being nowadays the family of *DDFs* (see Chap. 8). Sometimes, multivalued efficiency measures can be classified as single-valued not over all but over certain samples of firms. The Last assertion is based on the fact that a multivalued efficiency measure cannot generate more than one projection for certain firms. For instance, a trivial case is when the sample of firms only contains efficient points. In that case, any efficiency measure is classified as an EM^S over this sample. However, it is not difficult to find non-trivial cases as the next numerical example shows.

Example 12.1
The *ERG* = *SBM*, introduced in Chap. 7, is well known for being a multivalued function. Let us consider the set of nine firms in the one input-one output space of Example 7.1: A = (3,5), B = (6,10), C = (12,12), D = (3,2), E = (9,10), F = (10,5), G = (12,2), H = (12,8), and I = (24,4). The first three are strongly efficient firms and the last six inefficient, under a *VRS* technology—as illustrated in Fig. 7.1. Moreover, we showed there that the last three inefficient firms had at least two projections, while the rest of the units had only a single projection (see the mentioned example). As a consequence, the *ERG* = *SBM*, when the sample of firms is reduced and contains only the first six mentioned units, is *a single-valued function*. Hence, if we consider $F_J = \{\text{A} = (3,5), \text{B} = (6,10), \text{C} = (12,12), \text{D} = (3,2), \text{E} = (9,10), \text{F} = (10,5)\}$, and $\widehat{F}_J$ as the set of their ERG = SBM projections, the triad $\left(ERG = SBM, F_J, \widehat{F}_J\right)$ satisfies that each firm has a single projection, which is crucial for defining its *RDDF*.

Moreover, we can even resort to efficiency measures with multiple projections and restrict them to get a single projection for each of the firms of the sample to be analyzed, by selecting a single projection for each firm. For instance, going back to

[9]This duality also appears reflected when measuring productivity through multiplicative measures, giving rise to the input or output Malmquist indexes.

Example 7.1, we can consider $\overline{F}_{\overline{J}}$ as the sample of all the nine original firms and $\widehat{\overline{F}}_{\overline{J}}$ as the sample of their single projections as calculated in the mentioned example. Let us point out, in relation to the said example, that we have not included in Table 7.1 the initial projections obtained for the non-efficient units F = (10,5), G = (12,2), H = (12,8), and I = (24,4). Instead, we were able to obtain "better" projections from the point of view of the Nerlovian profit inefficiency decomposition, generating lower allocative values.

We are now ready to pursue the primary objective of this section and, following the ideas of Pastor et al. (2016), introduce the reverse directional distance function. Intuitively, the *RDDF* associated with the inefficiency measure EM^S is simply a *DDF* that reproduces the functioning of EM^S over the sample of firms F_J, i.e., it assigns to each of the considered firms the same projection and the same inefficiency score as EM^S. Each time we change one or more projections of $\widehat{F}_J$ resorting to the same efficiency measure, the inefficiency scores will not change, but since the projections have changed, a different *RDDF* will be generated. Hence, the definition of the associated *RDDF* depends on $EM^S$and on the two sets F_J and $\widehat{F}_J$. Let us start considering a graph efficiency measure, $EM^S(G)$, and let us formulate the conditions that the triad $\left(EM^S(G), F_J, \widehat{F}_J\right)$ must satisfy to define its *RDDF*.

Definition 12.3

Conditions on EM^S, F_J, and $\widehat{F}_J$ to define its *RDDF*. To define the *RDDF* associated with a certain graph measure and a certain sample of firms, we need to know the next three elements, the $EM^S(G)$ graph measure, the finite sample of firms, F_J, the technical $EM^S(G)$ inefficiency for each firm of F_J, and the single $EM^S(G)$ projection for each of the mentioned firms, which conform the projection set $\widehat{F}_J$.[10] These three elements define the one-to-one triad $\left(EM^S(G), F_J, \widehat{F}_J\right)$ that give rise to the corresponding *RDDF*.

According to the last definition, only the one-to-one triads are able to generate the corresponding *RDDF*. Let us now formalize the *RDDF* concept. As already mentioned, $F_J = \left\{\left(x_j, y_j\right) \in \mathbb{R}_+^{M+N}, j \in J\right\}$ represents the finite sample of firms to be rated, and $EM^S(G)$ is the graph efficiency measure that allows us to calculate, for each firm $(x_j, y_j) \in F_J$, its single technical inefficiency $TI_{EM^S(G)}\left(x_j, y_j\right)$and its single projection $\left(\widehat{x}_j, \widehat{y}_j\right) \in \widehat{F}_J$.[11] The subset of firms of F_J for which $TI_{EM^S(G)}\left(x_j, y_j\right) > 0$ corresponds to the $EM^S(G)$-inefficient firms, while the rest of the firms satisfying $TI_{EM^S(G)}\left(x_j, y_j\right) = 0$ are known as the $EM^S(G)$-non-inefficient firms and belong to

[10] It should be clear that the number of projections in $\widehat{F}_J$is equal to the number of firms in F_J, since there is a one-to-one correspondence that relates each firm with its projection.

[11] Usually, to obtain the technical inefficiency and the frontier projection of each firm, a specific linear program must be maximized. This condition excludes all the minimizing techniques developed for finding the shortest distance between a firm and its projection, based on integer linear programs, started by Aparicio et al. (2007).

the technological frontier. Since $TI_{EM^S(G)}(x_j, y_j) > 0$ if, and only if, $(\widehat{x}_j, \widehat{y}_j) \neq (x_j, y_j)$, the last inequality also characterizes the subset of F_J that groups all the $EM^S(G)$-inefficient firms. Consequently, its complementary subset in F_J is also characterized by the equality $(\widehat{x}_j, \widehat{y}_j) = (x_j, y_j)$.

One final point is worth mentioning. Each time we resort to a graph measure $EM^S(G)$ that is strong efficient, the difference $(x_j - \widehat{x}_j, \widehat{y}_j - y_j)$ between a point $(x_j, y_j) \in F_J$ and its projection $(\widehat{x}_j, \widehat{y}_j)$ can occasionally have all its input or output components at level 0, which, as we will see, may give rise to an *RDDF* that is not a graph but a mixed *DDF*,[12] since the directional vector associated with each $(x_j, y_j) \in F_J$ can be graph, input-oriented, or output-oriented.

Definition 12.4

The graph or mixed $RDDF\left(EM^S(G), F_J, \widehat{F}_J\right)$. The graph—or mixed—reverse directional distance function (*RDDF*) associated with the triad $\left(EM^S(G), F_J, \widehat{F}_J\right)$ is defined as a *DDF* that associates to each firm $(x_j, y_j) \in F_J$ with the same projection as $EM^S(G)$, $(\widehat{x}_j, \widehat{y}_j) \in \widehat{F}_J$, and whose technical inefficiency β_j^* satisfies $\beta_j^* = TI_{EM^S(G)}(x_j, y_j)$.

According to Definition 12.4, the way to define the corresponding *RDDF* is simply to identify the appropriate directional vector for each firm. Prior to showing how it works for the graph technical efficiency measure $EM^S(G)$, let us decompose F_J into two disjoint subsets.

Definition 12.5

The measure $EM^S(G)$ splits the sample of firms F_J into two disjoint subsets: $F_O = \left\{(x_j, y_j) \in F_J : TI_{EM^S(G)}(x_j, y_j) = 0\right\}$ and $F_{J\sim O} = \{(x_j, y_j) \in F_J : TI_{EM^S}\ (G) \times (x_j, y_j) > 0\}$.

We can now propose the following proposition:

Proposition 12.1 The directional vectors for $RDDF\left(EM^S(G), F_J, \widehat{F}_J\right)$. Assuming that $EM^S(G)$ is a graph measure, the expression of the directional vector of the graph or mixed *RDDF* for firm $(x_j, y_j) \in F_J$ depends on the location of (x_j, y_j) with respect to the technological frontier, giving rise to two mutually exclusive possibilities related with its technical inefficiency:

1. If $(x_j, y_j) \in F_{J\sim O}$, define $\left(-g_{x_j}, g_{y_j}\right) = \left(\frac{-(x_j - \widehat{x}_j)}{TI_{EM^S(G)}(x_j, y_j)}, \frac{\widehat{y}_j - y_j}{TI_{EM^S(G)}(x_j, y_j)}\right), j \in F_{J\sim O}$, and $\beta_j^* = TI_{EM^S(G)}(x_j, y_j) > 0$.

[12]The notion of a *mixed DDF* was introduced in Chap. 8.

2. In case $(x_j, y_j) \in F_O$, define $\beta_j^* = TI_{EM^S(G)}(x_j, y_j) = 0$ and $\left(-g_{x_j}, g_{y_j}\right) = =$ $\left(-\overrightarrow{k}_{jM}, \overrightarrow{k}_{jN}\right) \in \mathbb{R}_{++}^{M+N}$, where $\overrightarrow{k}_{jM} \in \mathbb{R}_{++}^{M}$ is a constant vector where all its M components are equal to the fix positive number[13] $k_j > 0$ and similarly $\overrightarrow{k}_{jN} \in \mathbb{R}_{++}^{N}$ is a constant vector with all its N components equal to the same $k_j > 0$. Moreover, the quantity units attached to the components of the directional vector are the same as the corresponding to the components of $(x_j, y_j) \in F_O$.

Proof The proof is easy and it is only necessary to verify that the proposed expressions satisfy the corresponding equalities. Let us prove separately the two cases:

1. Assuming $TI_{EM^S(G)}(x_j, y_j) > 0$ and considering the decomposition of the projection $(\widehat{x}_j, \widehat{y}_j)$ for firm (x_j, y_j) as the sum $(\widehat{x}_j, \widehat{y}_j) = (x_j, y_j) + (\widehat{x}_j - x_j, \widehat{y}_j - y_j)$, it is straightforward to verify that $(\widehat{x}_j, \widehat{y}_j) = (x_j, y_j) + (\widehat{x}_j - x_j, \widehat{y}_j - y_j) = (x_j, y_j) +$ $+ TI_{EM^S(G)}(x_j, y_j)\left(\frac{-(x_j - \widehat{x}_j)}{TI_{EM^S(G)}(x_j, y_j)}, \frac{\widehat{y}_j - y_j}{TI_{EM^S(G)}(x_j, y_j)}\right) = (x_j, y_j) + \beta_j^*\left(-g_{x_j}, g_{y_j}\right)$.
   In other words, for any firm $(x_j, y_j) \in F_{J \sim O}$, the *DDF* with the proposed directional vector achieves the same benchmark as the original graph efficiency measure $EM^S(G)$, as well as the same positive technical inefficiency value$\beta_j^* = TI_{EM^S(G)}(x_j, y_j) > 0$. As already mentioned, the formal expression of $\left(g_{x_j}, g_{y_j}\right)$ does not exclude the possibility that some of their components are equal to 0 or even that all their input or all their output components are equal to 0, being always $\left(-g_{x_j}, g_{y_j}\right) \neq 0_{M+N}$.
2. In this case, according to Definition 12.4, $\beta_j^* = TI_{EM^S(G)}(x_j, y_j) = 0$. Consequently, $(\widehat{x}_j, \widehat{y}_j) = (x_j, y_j) + \beta_j^*\left(-g_{x_j}, g_{y_j}\right) = (x_j, y_j) + 0 \cdot \left(-g_{x_j}, g_{y_j}\right) =$ (x_j, y_j), which means that any numerical vector assigned to $\left(-g_{x_j}, g_{y_j}\right)$ does satisfy the last chain of equalities, and, in particular, the proposed vector $\left(-g_{x_j}, g_{y_j}\right) = \left(-\overrightarrow{k}_M, \overrightarrow{k}_N\right) \in \mathbb{R}_{++}^{M+N}$, whose numerical components are the same fixed constant satisfying the enounced condition relative to their units of measurement. □.

[13] Each time we define an *RDDF*, we must fix the value of the positive number k which guarantees that the mentioned *RDDF* is unique.

Corollary 12.1.1 The $RDDF\left(EM^S(G), F_J, \widehat{F}_J\right)$ associated with $\left(EM^S(G), F_J, \widehat{F}_J\right)$ is unique.

Proof $\left(EM^S(G), F_J, \widehat{F}_J\right)$ completely determines the single inefficiency score $TI_{EM^S(G)}\left(x_j, y_j\right)$ assigned to each firm $(x_j, y_j) \in F_J$ and, according to Proposition 12.1, the corresponding inefficiency associated with its *RDDF*, $\beta_j^* = TI_{EM^S(G)}\left(x_j, y_j\right)$. Additionally, the same proposition assigns to each firm $(x_j, y_j) \in F_{J \sim O}$ a single directional vector, $\left(\frac{-(x_j - \widehat{x}_j)}{TI_{EM^S(G)}\left(x_j, y_j\right)}, \frac{\widehat{y}_j - y_j}{TI_{EM^S(G)}\left(x_j, y_j\right)}\right)$, whose expression depends on the firm itself, on its $TI_{EM^S(G)}\left(x_j, y_j\right)$, and on its single EM^Sprojection $\left(\widehat{x}_j, \widehat{y}_j\right)$. Finally, for each firm $(x_j, y_j) \in F_O$ for which $\beta_j^* = TI_{EM^S(G)}\left(x_j, y_j\right) = 0$, last proposition assigns a single graph directional vector with all its components equal to the fixed number $k > 0$, with the same units of measurement as any firm. □.

Notes

1. Proposition 12.1 shows that if the sample has at least one inefficient firm $(x_j, y_j) \in F_{J \sim O}$, a requirement that is usually satisfied by real datasets and by our numerical examples and empirical application, the corresponding directional vector of the *RDDF* associated with this firm depends on $TI_{EM^S(G)}\left(x_j, y_j\right)$, on $\left(\widehat{x}_j, \widehat{y}_j\right)$, and on the firm itself. In other words, the *RDDF* depends on $\left(EM^S(G), F_J, \widehat{F}_J\right)$.
2. Since any graph multivalued efficiency measure $EM^M(G)$ generates at least two different $\widehat{F}_J$s, we can generate at least two *RDDFs* associated with $EM^M(G)$. In this way, we have reduced the original $EM^M(G)$ to a $EM^S(G)$, which allows us to identify its associated single $RDDF\left(EM^S(G), F_J, \widehat{F}_J\right)$. Also, $EM^M(G)$ generates at least two $EM^S(G)$, $EM^{S1}(G)$ and $EM^{S2}(G)$, which in turn give rise to their corresponding *RDDFs*, in practice and based on some additional criterion, we should be able to end up selecting a unique $\widehat{F}_J$ or, equivalently, a unique $EM^S(G)$ that gives rise to a unique *RDDF*.
3. When $\beta_j^* = TI_{EM^S(G)}\left(x_j, y_j\right) = 0$, we have fixed the corresponding directional vector for each firm $(x_j, y_j) \in F_O$ to $\left(-g_{x_j}, g_{y_j}\right) = \left(-\overrightarrow{k}_{jM}, \overrightarrow{k}_{jN}\right) \in \mathbb{R}_{++}^{M+N}$, where $k_j > 0$ is a constant. In each case, we have the flexibility to set the value of k_j, the easiest choice being to take $k_j = 1$ for all j. This flexibility allows us to compare the normalized profit inefficiency decomposition associated with a certain efficiency measure $EM^S(G)$ with that corresponding to its *RDDF*. In fact, in the next section, we will use this possibility for comparing Tables 12.2 and 12.3.

Let us consider in what follows the input-oriented and output-oriented efficiency measures. They must satisfy similar requirements as graph efficiency measures in order to define their associated *input RDDF* or *output RDDF*. Based on Proposition 12.1, let us now show how to identify, for any $EM^S(I)$ or $EM^S(O)$ measure, the corresponding *RDDF* by defining, through next Corollaries 12.1.2 and 12.1.3, the appropriate directional vector for each firm. The corresponding proofs are completely similar to the graph case and are therefore left to the reader.

Corollary 12.1.2 The directional vectors for $RDDF\left(EM^S(I), F_J, \widehat{F}_J\right)$. The expression of the directional vector associated with firm $(x_j, y_j) \in F_J$ necessary to define the input-oriented $RDDF\left(EM^S(I), F_J, \widehat{F}_J\right)$, assuming that each firm gives rise to a single technical inefficiency score and a single projection, depends on the value of $TI_{EM^S(I)}(x_j, y_j)$, as well as on its single projection $(\widehat{x}_j, \widehat{y}_j) \in \widehat{F}_J$, giving rise to the following two mutually exclusive possibilities:

1. If $TI_{EM^S(I)}(x_j, y_j) > 0$, define $\left(-g_{x_j}, g_{y_j}\right) = \left(\frac{-(x_j - \widehat{x}_j)}{TI_{EM^S(I)}(x_j, y_j)}, 0_N\right)$, where the quantity units of 0_N are the same as those associated with the outputs of the firms.
2. Alternatively, if $TI_{EM^S(I)}(x_j, y_j) = 0$, define $\left(-g_{x_j}, 0_N\right) = \left(-\vec{k}_M, 0_N\right) \in \mathbb{R}_+^{M+N}$, where k is a positive fixed number and where the associated quantity units of the input *DV* are the same quantity units attached to (x_j, y_j).

Corollary 12.1.3 The directional vectors for $RDDF\left(EM^S(O), F_J, \widehat{F}_J\right)$. Similarly, the expression of the directional vector corresponding to the output-oriented $RDDF\left(EM^S(O), F_J, \widehat{F}_J\right)$ is defined as follows:

1. If $TI_{EM^S(O)}(x_j, y_j) > 0$, define $\left(-g_{x_j}, g_{y_j}\right) = \left(0_M, \frac{\widehat{y}_j - y_j}{TI_{EM^S(O)}(x_j, y_j)}\right)$, where the quantity units of 0_M are the same as those associated with the inputs of the firms.
2. Alternatively, if $TI_{EM^S(O)}(x_j, y_j) = 0$, define $\left(-g_{x_j}, g_{y_j}\right) = \left(0_M, \vec{k}_N\right) \in \mathbb{R}_+^{M+N}$, where k is a positive fixed number and where the associated quantity units of the output DV are the same quantity units attached to (x_j, y_j).

The next corollary is similar to Corollary 12.1.1 and establishes the uniqueness of the RDDF for each of the two oriented cases. Its proof is left to the reader.

Corollary 12.1.4 The input-oriented $RDDF\left(EM^S(I), F_J, \widehat{F}_J\right)$ associated with $\left(EM^S(I), F_J, \widehat{F}_J\right)$ and the output-oriented $RDDF\left(EM^S(O), F_J, \widehat{F}_J\right)$ associated with $\left(EM^S(O), F_J, \widehat{F}_J\right)$ are both unique.

Notes

Exactly the same three notes that appear after Proposition 12.1 for a graph measure are valid for any oriented technical measure, after the corresponding adjustments.

Example 12.2 Let us consider the reduced version of Example 7.1 mentioned before in Example 12.1, comprising the six firms A = (3,5), B = (6,10), C = (12,12), D = (3,2), E = (9,10), and F = (10,5), in the one input-one output space. Their technical inefficiency scores and their *ERG* = *SBM* unique projections appear listed in columns 2 and 3 of Table 12.1. The three first units are strongly efficient and we decided to set for them $k_j = 1$ (see in the following Table 12.1 rows 2, 3, and 4).

It is easy to verify that the corresponding graph *RDDF* obtains the same projection and the same technical inefficiency as the *ERG* = *SBM* for each of the firms of the considered sample (compare Columns 2 and 3 of Table 12.1 with the same columns of Table 7.1 in Chap. 7). For instance, the first efficient firm, A = (3,5), is its own projection and the attached technical inefficiency is equal to 0. Hence, A = (3,5) = (3,5) + 0 × (−1,1), which is the corresponding *RDDF* equality for firm (3,5). Let us now consider the last firm, F = (10,5); its *ERG* = *SBM* projection is B = (6,10), while its technical inefficiency is 7/10. The two values obtained that define its graph directional vector are 40/7 and 50/7, and the next equality holds for its *RDDF*: B=$(6, 10) = (10, 5)$ + 7/10(−40/7, 50/7) = = $(10, 5)$ + $(-4, 5)$.A final case worth mentioning is that of firm D (3,2): although *ERG* = *SBM* is a graph measure, it identifies as benchmark for D the efficient firm A, which means that the corresponding input slack equals 0 while the output slack equals 3. Hence, the associated *RDDF* vector, which is equal to $\left(g_{x_D}, g_{y_D}\right)$ =(0,5), is obviously an output-oriented directional vector. Something similar occurs with the remaining firm E = (9,10), but in this case, the associated *RDDF* vector is equal to $\left(g_{x_E}, g_{y_E}\right)$=(9,0), which is clearly an input-oriented directional vector. This constitutes an easy example showing that the *RDDF* associated with the triad $\left(EM^S(G), F_J, \widehat{F}_J\right)$ can either be a *graph* − *RDDF* or a *mixed* − *RDDF*, as pointed out before.

In this section, we have been able to express any inefficiency measure associated with a finite sample of firms as a specific *DDF*, provided the measure generates a single inefficiency score and a single projection for each firm. As we will show in the next three sections, we can take advantage of the good properties of the *DDFs* when dealing with the aforementioned measures. More precisely, Sect. 12.3 revises the profit inefficiency decomposition of a certain graph inefficiency measure and compares it with the decomposition associated with its *RDDF*.

Table 12.1 The *RDDF* associated with the ERG = SBM

Firm	TI	Proj.	$g_{x_j} = \left\{ \begin{array}{ll} k_j = 1 & , eff. \\ \dfrac{(x_j - \widehat{x}_j)}{TI_{EM^U(G)}(x_j, y_j)} & , non - eff. \end{array} \right\}$	$g_{y_j} = \left\{ \begin{array}{ll} k_j = 1 & , eff. \\ \dfrac{\widehat{y}_j - y_j}{TI_{EM^U(G)}(x_j, y_j)} & , non - eff. \end{array} \right\}$
(1)	(2)	(3)	(4)	(5)
A = (3,5), eff.	0	(3,5)	1	1
B = (6,10), eff.	0	(6,10)	1	1
C = (12,12), eff.	0	(12,12)	1	1
D = (3,2)	3/5	(3,5)	0	$\frac{5-2}{3/5} = 5$
E = (9,10)	1/3	(6,10)	$\frac{(9-6)}{1/3} = 9$	0
F = (10,5)	7/10	(6,10)	$\frac{(10-6)}{7/10} = \frac{40}{7}$	$\frac{10-5}{7/10} = \frac{50}{7}$

Table 12.2 Profit inefficiency decompositions for $ERG = SBM$, $(p, w) = (2, 1)$

Firm	First projection	TI	ΠI	NF	$T\Pi I = TI \times NF$	$A\Pi I = \Pi I - T\Pi I$	ΠI/NF	AI=$A\Pi I$/NF
(1)	(2)	(3)	(4)	(5)	(6) = (3) × (5)	(7) = (4)-(6)	(8) = (4)/(5)	(9) = (7)/(5)
A = (3,5), eff.	(3,5)	0	7	**3**	0	**7**	7/3	7/3
B = (6,10), eff.	(6,10)	0	0	**6**	0	**0**	0	**0**
C = (12,12), eff.	(12,12)	0	2	**12**	0	**2**	1/6	1/6
D = (3,2)	(3,5)	3/5	13	**15/2**	9/2	**17/2**	26/15	17/15
E = (9,10)	(6,10)	1/3	3	**9**	3	**0**	1/3	**0**
F = (10,5)	(3,5)	7/10	14	**10**	7	**7**	14/10	7/10
G = (12,2)	(3,5)	9/10	22	**10**	9	**13**	22/10	13/10
H = (12,8)	(24/5,8)	3/5	10	**12**	36/5	**14/5**	5/6	7/30
I = (24,4)	(6,10)	9/10	30	**20**	18	**12**	3/2	3/5

Table 12.3 Profit inefficiency decompositions for the *RDDF*, $(p, w) = (2, 1)$ (associated with Table 12.2)

Firm	First projection	TI	Π*I*	NF	*T*Π*I* = *TI* × *NF*	*A*Π*I* = Π*I* − *T*Π*I*	Π*I*/NF	AI=*A*Π*I*/NF
(1)	(2)	(3)	(4)	(5)	(6) = (3) × (5)	(7) = (4)-(6)	(8) = (4)/(5)	(9) = (7)/(5)
A = (3,5), eff.	(3,5)	0	7	**3**	0	**7**	7/3	7/3
B = (6,10), eff.	(6,10)	0	0	**6**	0	**0**	0	**0**
C = (12,12), eff.	(12,12)	0	2	**12**	0	**2**	1/6	1/6
D = (3,2)	(3,5)	3/5	13	**10**	6	**7**	13/10	7/10
E = (9,10)	(6,10)	1/3	3	**9**	3	**0**	1/3	**0**
F = (10,5)	(3,5)	7/10	14	**10**	7	**7**	14/10	7/10
G = (12,2)	(3,5)	9/10	22	**50/3**	15	**7**	66/50	21/50
H = (12,8)	(24/5,8)	3/5	10	**12**	36/5	**14/5**	5/6	7/30
I = (24,4)	(6,10)	9/10	30	**100/3**	30	**0**	9/10	**0**

12.3 Improving the Profit Inefficiency Decomposition of the Graph Efficiency Measure $\left(EM^S(G), F_J, \widehat{F}_J\right)$ Resorting to Its *RDDF*

It is well established that different graph efficiency measures $EM^S(G)$ may satisfy different properties, not only as an efficiency measure but also with respect to their respective normalized profit inefficiency decompositions, since each of them is associated with different Fenchel-Mahler inequalities. Let us reveal these differences by means of two numerical examples that show the behavior of the graph $ERG = SBM$ in relation to its associated *RDDF*. Since, in two chapters of this book, we acknowledge the excellent behavior of the *DDF* profit inefficiency decomposition,[14] we can expect to find some differences in favor of the *RDDF*. In some sense, the decomposition associated with the *RDDF* should be better than the decomposition associated with the $ERG = SBM$. We have chosen the graph $ERG = SBM$ because it is a multivalued function, offering us the possibility of defining different *RDDFs* associated with different sets of projections. Additionally, it is the only known DEA efficiency measure that is able to generate different profit inefficiency decompositions resorting to the traditional Fenchel-Mahler inequality when considering different projections (see Chap. 7). In other words, the normalization factor for each firm depends on the associated projection. Curiously enough, this special behavior does not hold for the input-oriented $ERG = SBM$ nor for its output-oriented version. Our first example is based on a slightly modified version of Example 7.1 presented in Chap. 7.

Example 12.3 Let us consider the sample of nine firms in the one input-one output space of Example 7.1, already considered in Example 12.1. The nine firms are A = (3,5), B = (6,10), C = (12,12), D = (3,2), E = (9,10), F = (10,5), G = (12,2), H = (12,8), and I = (24,4), the first three being strongly efficient firms and the last six inefficient. This example differs from example 7.1 in the projection assigned to firms F = (10,5), G = (12,2), and H = (12,8), the only three firms of this sample that obtain more than one benchmark projection. Figure 12.1 illustrates the dataset, omitting the last unit for graphical convenience. In this example, we maintain the projections initially obtained for these three firms, namely, (3,5), (3,5), and (24/5,8) (see Chap. 7). We also maintain the market prices $(p, w) = (2, 1)$, which generate the same profit inefficiency value for each firm as in Example 7.1 and obviously the corresponding technical inefficiency values.[15]

[14] The reader can check out in Chap. 8 or 13 the desirable properties of the profit inefficiency decomposition based on the *DDF*.

[15] Strictly speaking, the market prices should be written as $(p, w) = \left(2_{\$/Q_O}, 1_{\$/Q_I}\right)$, where $\$/Q_O$ denotes monetary unit divided by quantity unit of output and similarly for input.

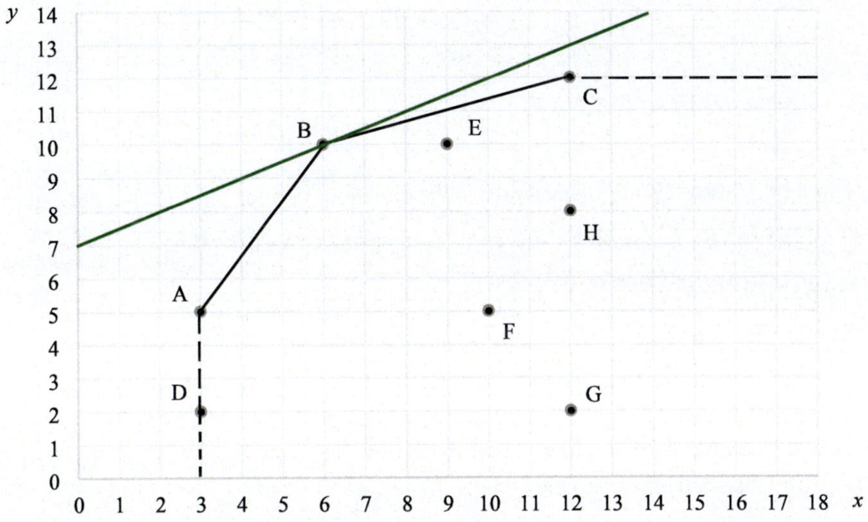

Fig. 12.1 Example of the $ERG = SBM$ profit inefficiency decomposition, $(p, w) = (2, 1)$

Table 12.2 is parallel to Table 7.1 but differs in rows 7, 8, and 9, associated with the three firms with multiple projections—only columns 1, 3, and 4 remain unchanged. The new normalization factors (NF) for the three firms with a new projection are calculated as usual,$NF(x_j, y_j) = \min\{2y_j, x_j\} \times \left(1 + \frac{s_j^{+*}}{y_j}\right)$ (see Chap. 7). Since for these three inefficient firms their new normalization factors, 9, 10, and 10, are smaller than in Table 7.1, 20, 20, and 15, the technical profit inefficiencies are also smaller in column 6, and with profit inefficiencies proving the same, the corresponding allocative profit inefficiencies are larger in column 7. Columns 4, 6, and 7 correspond to the profit inefficiency decomposition, while columns 8, 3, and 9 correspond to the normalized profit inefficiency decomposition (see Chap. 8). Lastly, we have deliberately presented the normalization factors of column 5 in bold. They are deeply related to the Fenchel-Mahler inequality associated with the $ERG = SBM$ measure, and they are going to change for the inefficient firms in the Table 12.3, related to their *RDDF*. Since the values in column 7 are essential for revising an interesting property, we have highlighted them in bold in both tables. Moreover, only the rows of column 9 that are equal to 0 are relevant for later checking another interesting property. We have also highlighted the corresponding zeros in bold.

Now, we are going to introduce the underlying expressions corresponding to the profit inefficiency measure together with its normalized profit decomposition associated with the reverse directional distance function. From Chap. 8, we know how to gauge and decompose profit inefficiency through the directional distance function (based on the *DDF* profit inefficiency measure):

$$\Pi I_{RDDF\left(EM^S(G),F_J,\widehat{F}_J\right)}(x_o, y_o, \widetilde{w}, \widetilde{p}) = \frac{\Pi I(x_o, y_o, w, p)}{\left(p \cdot g_{y_o} + w \cdot g_{x_o}\right)} = \\ = RDDF\left(EM^S(G), F_J, \widehat{F}_J\right) + AI_{RDDF\left(EM^S(G),F_J,\widehat{F}_J\right)}(x_o, y_o, \widetilde{w}, \widetilde{p}), \tag{12.1}$$

where $(\widetilde{w}, \widetilde{p})$ denotes normalized prices, the directional vector $\left(g_{x_o}, g_{y_o}\right)$ is defined as in Proposition 12.1, and $AI_{RDDF\left(EM^S(G),F_J,\widehat{F}_J\right)}(x_o,y_o,\widetilde{w},\widetilde{p}) := \Pi I_{RDDF\left(EM^S(G),F_J,\widehat{F}_J\right)}(x_o,y_o,\widetilde{w},\widetilde{p}) RDDF\left(EM^S(G),F_J,\widehat{F}_J\right)$, where $AI_{RDDF\left(EM^S(G),F_J,\widehat{F}_J\right)}(x_o,y_o,\widetilde{w},\widetilde{p})$ denotes the reverse *DDF* allocative measure of profit inefficiency and $RDDF\left(EM^S(G),F_J,\widehat{F}_J\right)$ denotes the reverse directional graph distance function measure of technical inefficiency. Note also that it is always possible to work in monetary terms by multiplying the left-hand side and right-hand side of expression (12.1) by the normalization factor $\left(p \cdot g_{y_o} + w \cdot g_{x_o}\right)$.

Let us next consider Table 12.3, which corresponds to the *RDDF* associated with the measure and the firms of the previous table. As shown above, the normalization factor associated with any graph *DDF* for the profit inefficiency decomposition is equal to the interior product of the price vector times the corresponding directional vector: $p \cdot g_y + w \cdot g_x$. For the *RDDF*, we consider the specific directional vector associated with any inefficient firm, as introduced in Proposition 12.1, $\left(g_{x_j}, g_{y_j}\right) = \left(\frac{x_j - \widehat{x}_j}{TI_{EM}(x_j, y_j)}, \frac{\widehat{y}_j - y_j}{TI_{EM}(x_j, y_j)}\right)$, as well as the vector of *k*s for any efficient firm (see Note 3 following Proposition 12.1). In order to compare Tables 12.2 and 12.3, we decide to assign, in Table 12.3 and for each of the three first efficient firms, the appropriate values of k_1, k_2, k_3, so that the corresponding normalization factors take the same value as in Table 12.2.[16] It is easy to check that the values we have considered are $k_1 = 1$for firm A = (3,5), $k_2 = 2$ for firm B = (6,10), and $k_3 = 4$ for the third efficient firm C = (12,12). Our recommendation is to select positive *k* values as simple and small as possible. This is the way to compare efficient units on an equal footing between both tables. We can appreciate that the normalization factor values for the inefficient units are greater or equal in Table 12.3 than in Table 12.2. This means that the corresponding normalized profit inefficiencies are smaller or equal and, with the technical inefficiency remaining the same in both tables, the derived allocative inefficiency will be also smaller or equal in the second table.

[16] This strategy has also been used in Chap. 13, in a rather different context, for comparing the traditional profit inefficiency decomposition with the general direct decomposition approach, based both on the same technical efficiency measure.

In other words, the Fenchel-Mahler inequality associated with the *RDDF* is tighter than that corresponding to *ERG* = *SBM*. Moreover, we also detect that the allocative inefficiency associated with the *RDDF* (see column 9) satisfies the essential property (see Sect. 2.4.5 of Chap. 2), which means that all the firms whose projection is a profit-maximizing firm obtain an allocative inefficiency equal to 0. In this case, the only profit-maximizing firm is B = (6, 10), and the only two inefficient firms whose projection is the mentioned firm are E = (9,10) and I = (24,4). The reader can verify that this property does not hold in Table 12.2 corresponding to the *ERG* = *SBM*. And finally, the allocative profit inefficiency in Table 12.3, reported in column 7, does not satisfy the extended essential property, which means that its value for any inefficient firm is the same as the corresponding value of its projection. For verifying it, we only need to calculate the allocative profit inefficiency associated with point (24/5,8). Let us point out that it corresponds to an efficient firm, whose technical inefficiency is equal to 0. Consequently, its allocative profit inefficiency must be equal to its profit inefficiency. Since we are working with a VRS technology and this point is a convex combination of firm A = (3,5) and B = (6,10), we can solve the linear equation $(24/5, 8) = \lambda(3, 5) + (1 - \lambda)(6, 10)$ getting $\lambda = 2/5$. Hence, its associated profit inefficiency is $\frac{2}{5} \times 7 + \frac{3}{5} \times 0 = \frac{14}{5}$, which is exactly the allocative profit inefficiency value of firm H = (12,8). The profit inefficiency, in column 4, is decomposed as the sum of the technical profit inefficiency and the allocative profit inefficiency, in columns 6 and 7 of both tables. In the last two tables, the first two mentioned terms are those related through an inequality by the corresponding Fenchel-Mahler inequality, which justifies that the third term is obtained as a residual. These three terms are directly comparable between firms. On the other hand, the three terms associated with the normalized profit inefficiency decomposition (see columns 4, 3, and 9 in both tables) cannot be compared between firms unless all the normalization factors are the same. This fact explains why the values of the allocative inefficiency, which appears in the last column of both tables, are distorted in comparison to the corresponding values of the allocative profit inefficiency, located in column 7 of both tables. Summarizing the profit inefficiency decompositions associated with the *RDDF* is more reliable than that corresponding original *ERG* = *SBM*, and, additionally, the *RDDF* satisfies two interesting properties that the *ERG* = *SBM* fails to verify.

We propose the reader to repeat the last comparison between the normalized profit inefficiency decompositions associated with the *ERG* = *SBM* measure and with its *RDDF* just for the three firms F, G, and H but using as alternative common projection the profit-maximizing firm B = (6,10). Table 12.4 shows the new results of this exercise.

For final comments, in column 5, the normalization factors generated by the *ERG* = *SBM* measure for each of the three considered firms are equal or smaller than the corresponding *RDDF*. Therefore, the technical profit inefficiency, in column 6, has the same behavior. Consequently, the allocative profit inefficiency, in column 7, which is equal to the profit inefficiency minus the technical profit inefficiency, is bigger for *ERG* = *SBM* than for RDDF. Finally, the allocative inefficiency, reported

Table 12.4 New results for firms F, G, and H of Table 12.3 with new projections

Firm	First projection	TI	ΠI	NF	TΠI	AΠI	ΠI/NF	AI=AΠI/NF
(1)	(2)	(3)	(4)	(5)	(6) = (3) × (5)	(7) = (4)-(6)	(8) = (4)/(5)	(9) = (7)/(5)
ERG = SBM	**ERG = SBM**			**ERG = SBM**		**ERG = SBM**		**ERG = SBM**
F = (10,5)	**(6,10)**	7/10	14	**20**	14	**0**	14/20	**0**
G = (12,2)	**(6,10)**	9/10	22	**20**	18	**4**	22/20	**4/20 = 1/5**
H = (12,8)	**(6,10)**	3/5	10	**15**	9	**1**	10/15	**1/15**
RDDF	**RDDF**			**RDDF**		**RDDF**		**RDDF**
F = (10,5)	**(6,10)**	7/10	14	**20**	14	**0**	14/20	**0**
G = (12,2)	**(6,10)**	9/10	22	**220/9**	22	**0**	9/10	**0**
H = (12,8)	**(6,10)**	3/5	10	**50/3**	10	**0**	3/5	**0**

in the last column, which is the difference of the normalized profit inefficiency in column 8 minus the technical inefficiency of column 3 is equal to 0 for the *RDDF* and bigger for the *ERG* = *SBM*. Once more, we can appreciate that the *RDDF* satisfies the essential property for these three firms, while the *ERG* = *SBM* measure does not.

Example 12.4 We may also ask what would happen if we tried to find the best projection for each firm with multiple projections, i.e., the one that gives rise to the best profit inefficiency decomposition, which corresponds to the projection that achieves the greatest possible normalization factor (see Chap. 13). Since beforehand we do not know which firm has—or has not—multiple benchmark projections, we need to solve a specific linear program for each inefficient firm, precisely the one that appears in Chap. 7 as program (7.12). The associated Table 12.5 is a copy of Table 7.1, reproduced below to facilitate the comparison with the following Table 12.6.

In comparison to Table 12.2, three inefficient firms—F, G, and H—have improved their projections (see rows 7, 8, and 9). Comparing the corresponding normalization factors for these three firms, the former values of 10, 10, and 12 in Table 12.2 have increased to the current values 20, 20, and 15 in Table 12.5 (see column 5 in both tables). As a direct consequence, their corresponding technical profit inefficiencies, reported in columns 6, have increased significantly, and with the same profit inefficiency, their allocative profit inefficiencies (see columns 7) have experimented a significant reduction from 7, 13, and 14/5 to 0, 4, and 1. Their allocative inefficiencies have experienced an even larger reduction, moving from the initial values of 7/10, 21/50, and 7/30 to 0, 2/10, and 1/15 (see corresponding column 9). However, in Table 12.5 the *ERG* = *SBM* does not satisfy the essential property for its allocative inefficiency nor the extended essential property for its allocative profit inefficiency.

Table 12.6 corresponds to the *RDDF* associated with the new *ERG* = *SBM* projections considered in Table 12.3. Just as before, the comparison of Tables 12.5 and 12.6 shows that the profit allocative inefficiency and the allocative inefficiency associated with the inefficient units have experimented a notable reduction. Moreover, the allocative inefficiency in Table 12.6 (see column 9) satisfies the essential property, while the allocative profit inefficiency (see column 7) satisfies the extended essential property, something that did not happen in Table 12.5.

As a summary, each pair of Tables 12.2–12.3 and 12.5–12.6 presents different profit inefficiency and normalized profit inefficiency decompositions, as could be expected after observing that the *ERG* = *SBM* projections for three inefficient firms in Table 12.6 generate new and bigger normalization factors.

Moreover, in both cases, the results associated with the *RDDF* satisfy two properties relative to their allocative components that the results associated with the *ERG* = *SBM* do not satisfy. We have been able to improve the profit inefficiency decomposition associated with the *ERG* = *SBM* resorting to its *RDDF* in two cases, associated with a different set of projections. Moreover, assuming that we are dealing with an inefficiency measure for evaluating a finite sample of firms that

Table 12.5 Profit inefficiency decompositions for $ERG = SBM$ based on the best projections, $(p, w) = (2, 1)$. (Reproduction of Table 7.1)

Firm	Best projection	TI	ΠI	NF	$T\Pi I = TI \times NF$	$A\Pi I = \Pi I - T\Pi I$	ΠI/NF	AI=$A\Pi I$/NF
(1)	(2)	(3)	(4)	(5)	(6) = (3) × (5)	(7) = (4)-(6)	(8) = (4)/(5)	(9) = (7)/(5)
A = (3,5), eff.	(3,5)	0	7	**3**	0	**7**	7/3	7/3
B = (6,10), eff.	(6,10)	0	0	**6**	0	**0**	0	**0**
C = (12,12), eff.	(12,12)	0	2	**12**	0	**2**	1/6	1/6
D = (3,2)	(3,5)	3/5	13	**15/2**	9/2	**17/2**	26/15	17/5
E = (9,10)	(6,10)	1/3	3	**9**	3	**0**	1/3	**0**
F = (10,5)	(6,10)	7/10	14	**20**	14	**0**	7/10	**0**
G = (12,2)	(6,10)	9/10	22	**20**	18	**4**	11/10	2/10
H = (12,8)	(6,10)	3/5	10	**15**	9	**1**	2/3	1/15
I = (24,4)	(6,10)	9/10	30	**20**	18	**12**	3/2	3/5

Table 12.6 Profit inefficiency decompositions for the *RDDF* based on the best projections,$(p, w) = (2, 1)$ (associated with Table 12.5)

Firm	Best projection	TI	ΠI	NF	$T\Pi I = TI \times NF$	$A\Pi I = \Pi I - T\Pi I$	ΠI/NF	AI=AΠI/NF
(1)	(2)	(3)	(4)	(5)	(6) = (3) × (5)	(7) = (4)-(6)	(8) = (4)/(5)	(9) = (7)/(5)
A = (3,5), eff.	(3,5)	0	7	**3**	0	**7**	7/3	7/3
B = (6,10), eff.	(6,10)	0	0	**6**	0	**0**	0	**0**
C = (12,12), eff.	(12,12)	0	2	**12**	0	**2**	1/6	1/6
D = (3,2)	(3,5)	3/5	13	**10**	6	**7**	13/10	7/10
E = (9,10)	(6,10)	1/3	3	**9**	3	**0**	1/3	**0**
F = (10,5)	(6,10)	7/10	14	**20**	14	**0**	7/10	**0**
G = (12,2)	(6,10)	9/10	22	**220/9**	22	**0**	9/10	**0**
H = (12,8)	(6,10)	3/5	10	**50/3**	10	**0**	3/5	**0**
I = (24,4)	(6,10)	9/10	30	**100/3**	30	**0**	9/10	**0**

have an associated *RDDF*, we have shown that resorting to the *RDDF* is useful for measuring more precisely the allocative inefficiency associated with the used inefficiency measure.

12.4 Improving the Cost Inefficiency Decomposition of $\left(EM^S(I), F_J, \widehat{F}_J\right)$ Resorting to Its $RDDF\left(EM^S(I), F_J, \widehat{F}_J\right)$

In the preceding section using numerical examples we have already shown the difference between using the first projection found and searching for the "best" projection for determining the "best" profit inefficiency decomposition, taking the *ERG* = *SBM* measure for calculating the technical inefficiency. We have to say that it constitutes a rather atypical case. As far as we know, it is the only case where a change in the projections induces a change in the corresponding normalization factors. In other words, usually the normalization factor is independent of the projection used, in the event there is more than one. Consequently, both for the input- and the output-oriented cases and for any other graph efficiency measures, we only need to calculate a single projection for each inefficient firm.[17]

Example 12.5 Let us consider the input-oriented *ERG* = *SBM*, denoted as *ERG* = *SBM(I)*.[18] As explained above, there is no need to search for a second projection because all the alternative projections give rise to the same normalization factor for each inefficient firm and, consequently, to the same cost inefficiency decompositions.[19] Hence, we will just consider one example associated with the aforementioned input-oriented measure, that exactly correspond to Table 7.2 and Fig. 7.2 in Chap. 7, and here to Table 12.7, where $w = (2, 1)$ is the vector of market costs. Just to remind the reader, we are considering a sample of firms with two inputs and a constant output, which is omitted from the tables.

Some comments are appropriate here. The first four firms are efficient, and the first two are also cost-minimizing firms (see their cost inefficiency values in Column 4). Consequently, the values of the two components of the cost inefficiency decomposition for A = (2, 10) and B = (4, 6) must be 0, as well as the values of the two

[17]It is straightforward to prove that when the normalization factor does not change, the corresponding normalized profit inefficiency decompositions are independent of the projections used.

[18]As is well known, the *ERG* = *SBM(I)*is exactly the same measure as the input-oriented Russell measure (see Chap. 7). Moreover, its associated *RDDF* is denoted as *RDDF(I)*.

[19]This means that for any firm, we must solve a single program. In fact, the different terms we are going to calculate depend only on the firm being considered and on its technical inefficiency, which is the same for alternative optimal projections.

Table 12.7 Results based on the $ERG = SBM(I)$, $w = (2, 1)$. (Reproduction of Table 7.2)

Firm	Project.RM(I)	$TI_{EM(I)}$	CI	NF	TCI=NFxTI	ACI=CI-TCI	NCI=CI/NF	AI = ACI/NF
(1)	(2)	(3)	(4)	(5)	(6) = (3) × (5)	(7) = (4)-(6)	(8) = (4)/(5)	(9) = (7)/(5)
A = (2,10)	(2,10)	0	0	**8**	0	**0**	0	**0**
B = (4,6)	(4,6)	0	0	**12**	0	**0**	0	**0**
C = (6,3)	(6,3)	0	15-14 = 1	**6**	0	**1**	1/6	1/6
D = (8,2)	(8,2)	0	4	**4**	0	**4**	1	1
E = (10,2)	(8,2)	1/10	8	**4**	2/5	**38/5**	8/4 = 2	19/10
F = (12,6)	(6,3)	1/2	16	**12**	6	**10**	16/12 = 4/3	5/6
G = (16,12)	(6,3)	11/16	30	**24**	33/2	**27/2**	30/24 = 5/4	9/16
H = (8,12)	(4,6)	1/2	14	**24**	12	**2**	7/12	1/12
I = (6,16)	(2,10)	25/48	14	**24**	25/2	**3/2**	7/12	1/16

components of their normalized cost inefficiency decomposition. The last two inefficient firms are the only ones projected onto these two differentiated points, while the last column shows that they have a positive allocative inefficiency, meaning that the essential property is not fulfilled. Something similar happens with the allocative cost inefficiency, listed in column 7, that fails to satisfy the extended essential property: none of the five inefficient points shows an allocative cost inefficiency equal to its efficient projection. Moreover, the normalization factors take different values, and therefore, the normalized cost inefficiencies cannot always be compared between firms.

Regarding the expressions corresponding to the cost inefficiency measure and its decomposition when the reverse directional distance function is used, we highlight that it mirrors the definitions corresponding to cost inefficiency associated with the input-oriented directional distance function in Chap. 8 (based on the *DDF* cost inefficiency measure):

$$\begin{aligned} NCI_{RDDF\left(EM^S(I),F_J,\widehat{F}_J\right)}(x_o,y_o,\widetilde{w}) &= \frac{CI(x_o,y_o,w)}{w\cdot g_{x_0}} = \\ = RDDF\left(EM^S(I),F_J,\widehat{F}_J\right) &+ AI_{RDDF\left(EM^S(I),F_J,\widehat{F}_J\right)}(x_o,y_o,\widetilde{w}), \end{aligned} \tag{12.2}$$

where $\widetilde{w}$ denotes normalized prices, the directional vector $\left(g_{x_0},0_N\right)$ is defined as in Corollary 12.1.2, and $AI_{RDDF\left(EM^S(I),F_J,\widehat{F}_J\right)}(x_o,y_o,\widetilde{w}) := CI_{RDDF\left(EM^S(I),F_J,\widehat{F}_J\right)}(x_o,y_o,\widetilde{w})$ - $RDDF\left(EM^S(I),F_J,\widehat{F}_J\right)$, where $AI_{RDDF\left(EM^S(I),F_J,\widehat{F}_J\right)}(x_o,y_o,\widetilde{w})$ denotes the reverse *DDF* allocative measure of cost inefficiency and $RDDF\left(EM^S(I),F_J,\widehat{F}_J\right)$ denotes the reverse directional input distance function of technical inefficiency. Additionally, it is always possible to work in monetary terms by multiplying the left-hand side and right-hand side of expression (12.2) by the normalization factor $\left(w\cdot g_{x_0}\right)$.

Let us now focus on the input-oriented *RDDF* and elaborate the corresponding table with the two cost inefficiency decompositions. According to Corollary 12.1.2, the directional vector of the *RDDF(I)* associated with any inefficient unit (x_j, y_j) and with its projection $\left(\widehat{x}_j,\widehat{y}_j\right)$ has the expression $\left(g_{x_j},g_{y_j}\right) = \left(\frac{x_j-\widehat{x}_j}{TI_{EM(I)}\left(x_j,y_j\right)},0_N\right)$.

We start fixing the values of the directional input vector for each of the four efficient firms, so that their normalization factors are exactly the same as in the preceding table. To give one example, since the normalization factor for the first efficient firm A = (2,10) is equal to $(w_1,w_2)\cdot(k_1,k_1) = 2k_1 + k_1 = 3k_1$ in Table 12.8, but, according to Table 12.7, it must be equal to 8, the only possibility is to define k_1 = 8/3.The comparison of the last two tables shows a more regular behavior of Table 12.8. In fact, looking at column 7, we see that the allocative cost inefficiency of each input-inefficient firm takes the same value as their respective projections, something that does not happen in Table 12.7. Besides satisfying last property, known as the extended essential property, the allocative inefficiency also satisfies

Table 12.8 Results based on the associated *RDDF(I)*, $w = (2, 1)$. (Reproduction of Table 8.3)

Firms	First projection	TI	CI	NF	TCI=NFxTI	ACI=CI-TCI	CI/NF	AI = ACI/NF
(1)	(2)	(3)	(4)	(5)	(6) = (3) × (5)	(7) = (4)-(6)	(8) = (4)/(5)	(9) = (7)/(5)
A = (2,10)	(2,10)	0	0	**8**	0	**0**	0	**0**
B = (4,6)	(4,6)	0	0	**12**	0	**0**	0	**0**
C = (6,3)	(6,3)	0	1	**6**	0	**1**	1/6	1/6
D = (8,2)	(8,2)	0	4	**4**	0	**4**	1	1
E = (10,2)	(8,2)	1/10	8	**40**	4	**4**	1/5	1/10
F = (12,6)	(6,3)	1/2	16	**30**	15	**1**	8/15	1/30
G = (16,12)	(6,3)	11/16	30	**464/11**	29	**1**	165/232	11/464
H = (8,12)	(4,6)	1/2	14	**28**	14	**0**	1/2	**0**
I = (6,16)	(2,10)	25/48	14	**672/25**	14	**0**	175/336	**0**

the essential property: the inefficient firms whose projection is a cost-minimizing benchmark, in this case any of the two first listed firms, have the same allocative inefficiency value as its projection, i.e., 0 (see last column 9 of Table 12.8).

12.5 Improving the Revenue Inefficiency Decomposition of $\left(EM^S(O), F_J, \widehat{F}_J\right)$ Resorting to Its $RDDF\left(EM^S(O), F_J, \widehat{F}_J\right)$

In this section, we will revise the revenue inefficiency decompositions associated with an output-oriented efficiency measure and compare it with its associated output *RDDF*. The treatment and the results that we are going to obtain mirror the input-oriented case of the previous section. As already explained at the beginning of Sect. 12.4, we just need to consider the first projection—obtained by means of any output-oriented efficiency measure—for each inefficient firm, simply because the normalizing factor associated with each firm of the considered sample is independent of their benchmarks.[20] In other words, the table we are going to present associated with the first calculated projection obtained through the considered efficiency measure will be the same for any possible benchmark, in the event that we are using an output-oriented efficiency measure that generates multiple projections.

Example 12.6 As we did in the two preceding sections, we are going to again consider the *output-oriented ERG-SBM* measure, denoted as$ERG = SBM(O)$, with the same sample of nine firms considered in Chap. 7. Table 12.9 is a reproduction of Table 7.3. Just to remind the reader, all firms have the same single input value and two output values that identify them. For a graphical display of their relative positions with respect to the VRS frontier, see Fig. 7.3.

Firms D = (2,1) and F = (4,2) have multiple projections, namely, all convex linear combination of firms A = (4,8) and B = (8,6), which are both revenue-maximizing firms, with a revenue inefficiency (*RI*) equal to 0. Let us develop the table associated with its *RDDF*, which appears below as Table 12.10. But before doing that, let us introduce the expressions for measuring and decomposing revenue inefficiency under the reverse directional distance function (see Chap. 8 for revising the expressions corresponding to the directional distance function, based on the *DDF* revenue inefficiency measure):

[20] As aforementioned, when dealing with output-oriented measures, the only known measure with multiple projections that can generate normalization factors that depend on the alternative projection considered is the *graph ERG = SBM*.

Table 12.9 Results based on the $ERG = SBM(O)$, $p = (1, 2)$

Firm	Project	TI	RI	NF	TRI=NF×TI	ARI = RI-TRI	RI/NF	AI = ARI/NF
(1)	(2)	(3)	(4)	(5)	(6) = (3) × (5)	(7) = (4)-(6)	(8) = (4)/(5)	(9) = (7)/(5)
A = (4,8)	(4,8)	0	0	**8**	0	**0**	0	**0**
B = (8,6)	(8,6)	0	0	**16**	0	**0**	0	**0**
C = (12,2)	(12, 2)	0	4	**8**	0	**4**	1/2	1/2
D = (2,1)	(8,6)	4/5	16	**4**	16/5	**64/5**	4	16/5
E = (2,4)	(8,6)	7/11	10	**4**	28/11	**82/11**	5/2	41/22
F = (4,2)	(8,6)	3/5	12	**8**	24/5	**36/5**	3/2	9/10
G = (4,6)	(8,6)	1/5	4	**8**	8/5	**12/5**	1/2	3/10
H = (6,4)	(8,6)	5/17	6	**12**	60/17	**42/17**	1/2	7/34
I = (10,2)	(10,4)	1/3	6	**8**	8/3	**10/3**	3/4	5/12

$$NRI_{RDDF\left(EM^S(O),F_J,\widehat{F}_J\right)}(x_o, y_o, \widetilde{p}) = \frac{RI(x_o, y_o, p)}{p \cdot g_{y_0}} =$$
$$= RDDF\left(EM^S(O), F_J, \widehat{F}_J\right) + AI_{RDDF\left(EM^S(O),F_J,\widehat{F}_J\right)}(x_o, y_o, \widetilde{p}), \tag{12.3}$$

where $\widetilde{p}$ denotes normalized prices, the directional vector $\left(0_M, g_{y_0}\right)$ is defined as in Corollary 12.1.3, and $AI_{RDDF\left(EM^S(O),F_J,\widehat{F}_J\right)}(x_o, y_o, \widetilde{p}) := RI_{RDDF\left(EM^S(O),F_J,\widehat{F}_J\right)}(x_o, y_o, \widetilde{p})$ - $RDDF\left(EM^S(O), F_J, \widehat{F}_J\right)$, where $AI_{RDDF\left(EM^S(O),F_J,\widehat{F}_J\right)}(x_o, y_o, \widetilde{p})$ denotes the reverse *DDF* allocative measure of revenue inefficiency and $RDDF\left(EM^S(O), F_J, \widehat{F}_J\right)$ denotes the reverse directional output distance function of technical inefficiency. Moreover, we could work with the revenue inefficiency and its components in monetary terms by multiplying the left-hand side and right-hand side of expression (12.3) by the normalization factor $\left(p \cdot g_{y_0}\right)$.

The three initial efficient firms, A, B, and C, maintain all their row values since we can maintain their original normalization factors by choosing the appropriate k_1, k_2, and k_3 values. For instance, for firm A, its normalization factor in Table 12.9 equals 8, which means that the normalization factor of its *RDDF*, which is equal to $p_1 \cdot k_1 + p_2 \cdot k_1 = 3k_1$, must satisfy $3k_1 = 8$, which means that $k_1 = 8/3$. Moreover, the first four columns are identical. We need to start calculating the corresponding normalization factors for the inefficient units associated with a *DDF*, which, as already explained in Chap. 8, are equal to $p_1 g_{y1}$ + $p_2 g_{y2}$. For the particular case of an *RDDF* and according to Corollary 12.1.2, we know that for any inefficient firm (y_{j1}, y_{j2}) the corresponding directional vector is $\left(g_{y_{j1}}, g_{y_{j2}}\right) ==$

Table 12.10 Results based on the associated *RDDF(O)*, $p = (1, 2)$

Firm	Project	TI	RI	NF	TRI=NF×TI	ARI = RI-TRI	RI/NF	AI = ARI/NF
(1)	(2)	(3)	(4)	(5)	(6) = (3) × (5)	(7) = (4)-(6)	(8) = (4)/(5)	(9) = (7)/(5)
A = (4,8)	(4,8)	0	0	**8**	0	**0**	0	**0**
B = (8,6)	(8,6)	0	0	**16**	0	**0**	0	**0**
C = (12,2)	(12, 2)	0	4	**8**	0	**4**	1/2	**1/2**
D = (2,1)	(8,6)	4/5	16	**20**	16	**0**	4/5	**0**
E = (2,4)	(8,6)	7/11	10	**110/7**	10	**0**	7/11	**0**
F = (4,2)	(8,6)	3/5	12	**20**	12	**0**	3/5	**0**
G = (4,6)	(8,6)	1/5*	4	**20***	4	**0**	1/5	**0**
H = (6,4)	(8,6)	5/17	6	**102/5**	6	**0**	5/17	**0**
I = (10,2)	(10,4)	1/3	6	**12***	4	**2**	1/2	**1/6***

$\left(\frac{\widehat{y}_{j1}-y_{j1}}{TI_{EM}(x_j,y_j)}, \frac{\widehat{y}_{j2}-y_{j2}}{TI_{EM}(x_j,y_j)}\right)$. For instance, for firm D (2,1), its directional vector is $\left(\frac{\widehat{y}_{j1}-y_{j1}}{TI_{EM}(x_j,y_j)}, \frac{\widehat{y}_{j2}-y_{j2}}{TI_{EM}(x_j,y_j)}\right) = \left(\frac{8-2}{\frac{4}{5}}, \frac{6-1}{\frac{4}{5}}\right) = \left(\frac{30}{4}, \frac{25}{4}\right)$, and its normalization factor is $\frac{30}{4} + 2\frac{25}{4} = \frac{80}{4} = 20$. The rest of column 4 for the five remaining inefficient units are calculated similarly. Comparing the last two tables, we reach the same conclusions for the graph case and for the input-oriented case. While the allocative revenue inefficiency, in column 7 of Table 12.10, satisfies the extended essential property, the same column in the preceding table does not; and while the allocative inefficiency, in column 9 of Table 12.10, satisfies the essential property, the same column in the preceding table does not. Hence, the associated *RDDF* also provides a better decomposition than the corresponding output-oriented $ERG = SBM(O)$.

12.6 Introducing the Bidirectional Distance Functions $\left(BDF, F_J, \widehat{F}_J\right)$: Deriving for Each $\left(BDF^S, F_J, \widehat{F}_J\right)$ Its Reverse Directional Distance Function $RDDF\left(BDF^S, F_J, \widehat{F}_J\right)$

We are now going to introduce the bidirectional distance function $\left(BDF, F_J, \widehat{F}_J\right)$, which assigns to each firm belonging to a finite sample of firms F_J two—input and output—directional vectors that are used for calculating the optimal values of two input- and output-oriented technical inefficiency scores, which in turn identify at least one frontier projection for each firm (x_o, y_o). The next Example 12.7 shows that a *BDF* may have multiple projections for one or more firms, in which case we denote it as BDF^M. As for the rest of efficiency measures, in order to define the corresponding *RDDF*, we need to identify for each firm of the finite sample F_J a single pair of oriented inefficiency scores that give rise to a single benchmark. There are also *BDFs* that generate a single projection for each firm, and we refer to them as BDF^S. Any BDF^M generates at least two BDF^S, which happens when only one firm of F_J has only two possible projections and the rest of the firms have a single benchmark.[21] We end up selecting one of them, based on some economic criterion, and after identifying "the best" BDF^S, we are ready to define its $RDDF\left(BDF^S, F_J, \widehat{F}_J\right)$, which requires the need to derive a single *DV* for each firm related to its two previous oriented *DVs*. The next section will reveal the relevance of selecting a single BDF^S in order to define its corresponding $RDDF\left(BDF^S, F_J, \widehat{F}_J\right)$.

[21] Example 12.7 shows an "extreme" BDF^M, where a firm has an unlimited number of projections.

12.6.1 The Bidirectional Distance Function $\left(BDF, F_J, \widehat{F}_J\right)$

The bidirectional distance function (*BDF*), inspired on Aparicio et al's (2013a, b) modified directional distance function (*MDDF*) (discussed in Chap. 11, program 11.4), is defined as follows[22]:

$$
\begin{aligned}
&\overleftrightarrow{D}\left(x_o, y_o; g_{x_o}, g_{y_o}\right) = \max_{\beta_{x_o}, \beta_{y_o}, \lambda} \quad \beta_{x_o} + \beta_{y_o} \\
&s.t. \\
&\sum_{j=1}^{J} \lambda_j x_{jm} \leq x_{om} - \beta_{x_o} g_{x_o}, \quad m = 1, \ldots, M \\
&\sum_{j=1}^{J} \lambda_j y_{jn} \geq y_{on} + \beta_{y_o} g_{y_o}, \quad n = 1, \ldots, N \qquad (12.4) \\
&\sum_{j=1}^{J} \lambda_j = 1, \\
&\lambda_j \geq 0, \quad j = 1, \ldots, J \\
&\beta_{x_o}, \beta_{y_o} \geq 0, \; g_{x_o} \geq 0_M, g_{y_o} \geq 0_N.
\end{aligned}
$$

Besides the general condition included in model (12.4) that specifies that both the input and the output directional vector cannot be equal to 0_M or to 0_N, the additional *conditions* that the *directional vector associated with any inefficient firm must satisfy are the following*:

Additional Conditions Let us calculate the best lower bound for each input and the best upper bound for each output over the considered sample of firms: $\underline{x}_{jm} = \min\left\{x_{jm} : \left(x_j, y_j\right) \in F\right\}, m = 1, \ldots, M$, $\overline{y}_{jn} = \max\left\{y_{jn} : \left(x_j, y_j\right) \in F\right\}, n = 1, \ldots, N$. Let us now consider the subset of inefficient firms, $F_I = \{(x_j, y_j) \in J : (x_j, y_j) \notin \partial(T)\}$, which is a strict subset of F. For each of this inefficient firms $(x_j, y_j) \in F_I$, its associated directional vector must satisfy the next conditions: for any input m such that $x_{jm} = \underline{x}_{jm}$, the corresponding input directional vector component is necessarily

[22]The original definition is slightly modified by adding that the two oriented directional vectors must be non-negative and have at least one positive component each. As these restrictions are normally met in empirical applications, in the software package "Benchmarking Economic Efficiency" accompanying this book, we rely on the *modified DDF* when calculating the *reverse DDF* associated with this model; i.e., the projections used to recover the directional vectors and calculate the *reverse DDF* correspond to program (11.6). In the software, we implement two standard choices of directional vectors, namely, the observed quantities, $\left(g_{x_j}, g_{y_j}\right) = \left(x_j, y_j\right)$, and the unitary directional vector, $\left(g_{x_j}, g_{y_j}\right) = (1_M, 1_N)$. Both satisfy our slightly modified definition and are ready to be used for generating *BDFs*.

$g_{x_{jm}} = 0$; and, similarly, for any output n that satisfies that $y_{jn} = \overline{y}_{jn}$, the corresponding output directional vector component is necessarily $g_{y_{jn}} = 0$.

These additional conditions, for $m \geq 2$ and $n \geq 2$, guarantee in many cases that the two input and output efficiency scores associated with each inefficient firm are both positive.[23] For instance, for $m = 2$ and for a certain inefficient firm with inputs x_{j1}, x_{j2}, if $x_{j1} = \underline{x}_{j1}$, we should expect that $x_{j2} > \underline{x}_{j2}$, unless we are dealing with a "Leontief-type" frontier. The introduced conditions guarantee that the inputs or outputs that have the minimum possible values in a VRS production possibility set do not interfere with the remaining inputs or outputs in order to find the maximum input and output efficiency scores. We expect, for any inefficient units, that both oriented scores are positive, which justifies the new introduced term *bidirectional distance function (BDF)*.

Linear program (12.6) is clearly not a DDF since instead of delivering a single inefficiency score it delivers two, an input inefficiency score $\beta^*_{x_o}$ and an output inefficiency score $\beta^*_{y_o}$, whose values may be different or equal. Hence, any *BDF* can be classified as a graph measure although for certain firms $\beta^*_{x_o}$ or $\beta^*_{y_o}$, or both, can be equal to 0. If both are 0, the firm being rated is a frontier firm, which may belong to the strong efficient frontier or not. If at least one oriented inefficiency score is positive, the corresponding firm is a non-efficient firm. Hence, the *BDF* projection of any inefficient firm can follow three different paths: input-oriented, output-oriented, or graph. The presence of two oriented inefficiency scores suggests the name bidirectional distance function (*BDF*) and recommends avoiding the classification of any *BDF* as a graph or an oriented measure, as it may be a combination of both. According to Chap. 8, when a *DDF* deals, at the same time, with oriented and graph directional vectors, we call it a mixed *DDF*. Hence, we can expect that a *BDF* also ends up being a mixed *BDF*.

Since the input-oriented directional vector and the output-oriented directional vector work separately, a BDF may have multiple projections for a given firm, as the next simple example shows.

Example 12.7 Let us consider in the one input-one output space the next four firms: A = (2,6), B = (4,8), C = (6,10), and D = (6,6). The first three firms belong to the VRS-efficient frontier defined by the segment [(2,6), (6,10)]. The last firm D = (6,6) is clearly inefficient and dominated by any of the efficient firm. Let us assign to the *BDF* of thc inefficient firm the two oriented directional vectors $\left(g_{x_D}, 0\right) = (1, 0)$, $\left(0, g_{y_D}\right) = (0, 1)$. The next three optimal solutions satisfying $\beta^*_{x_D} + \beta^*_{y_D} = 4$ project firm D = (6,6) onto each of the three efficient firms: $\beta^*_{x_D} = 4, \beta^*_{y_D} = 0$, onto A = (2,6), $\beta^*_{x_D} = 2, \beta^*_{y_D} = 2$ onto B = (4,8), and $\beta^*_{x_D} = 0, \beta^*_{y_D} = 4$ onto C = (6,10).

[23] However, Example 12.7 shows that the mentioned condition may fail when $m = 1$ and $n = 1$, although it identifies a bunch of possible projections and most of them identify two non-zero inefficiency scores.

Additionally, it is easy to show that any point of the segment that constitutes the efficient frontier can emerge as the projection of D = (6,6), since the mentioned firm can always be represented as a convex linear combination of the two extreme points. In fact, any point of the mentioned segment can be written as $\lambda(2,6) + (1-\lambda)(6,10) = (2\lambda + 6 - 6\lambda, 6\lambda + 10 - 10\lambda) = (6,6) + (-4\lambda, 4 - 4\lambda)$, $\lambda \in [0,1]$, which shows that it is certainly a projection of firm D = (6,6) obtained by setting $\beta^*_{x_D} = 4\lambda, \beta^*_{y_D} = 4(1-\lambda)$,[24] since $(-4\lambda, 4-4\lambda) = 4\lambda(-1,0) + (4-4\lambda)(0,1)$. For instance, for $\lambda = \frac{1}{4}$, we get $\beta^*_{x_D} = 4\frac{1}{4} = 1, \beta^*_{y_D} = 4\left(1 - \frac{1}{4}\right) = 3$ and a as new projection point $(6,6) + 1\,(-1,0) + 3(0,1) = (6-1, 6+3) = (5,9) \in [(2,6),(6,10)]$. We conclude that the *BDF* considered is an extreme BDF^M.

The last numerical example shows clearly that the set of projections $\widehat{F}_J$ matters, and justifies why in the title of this section the *RDDF* associated with a BDF has been defined over the triad $\left(BDF^S, F_J, \widehat{F}_J\right)$. Moreover, the last example also shows that we may have many possible projections for each firm and that basically each of these benchmarks may generate a different $\left(BDF^S, F_J, \widehat{F}_J\right)$. Each of these $\left(BDF^S, F_J, \widehat{F}_J\right)$ gives rise to a different $RDDF\left(BDF^S, F_J, \widehat{F}_J\right)$, whose directional vectors can be input-oriented, output-oriented, or graph.[25]

12.6.2 *Defining the RDDF Associated with a Bidirectional Distance Function* $\left(BDF^S, F_J, \widehat{F}_J\right)$

As explained in the previous subsection, we must be aware that any BDF^S projects each firm of F_J into a single firm of $\widehat{F}_J$ according to the optimal values of its two oriented inefficiency scores, giving rise to four types of firms. Type 1 corresponds to all the non-inefficient firms,[26] while the next three types correspond to inefficient firms. Here are the characteristics of the four types, classified as mentioned above:

1. Type 1 non-inefficient firms: any firm (x_o, y_o) that obtains two zero oriented inefficiency scores, $\beta^*_{x_o} = 0, \beta^*_{y_o} = 0$.
2. Type 2 input inefficient firms: any firm (x_o, y_o) that obtains only the input-oriented inefficiency score different from 0, $\beta^*_{x_o} > 0, \beta^*_{y_o} = 0$.
3. Type 3 output inefficient firms: any firm (x_o, y_o) that obtains only the output-oriented inefficiency score different from 0, $\beta^*_{x_o} = 0, \beta^*_{y_o} > 0$.

[24] These new family of bidirectional vectors also satisfy the equality $\beta^*_{x_o} + \beta^*_{y_o} = 4$.

[25] These types of *RDDFs or DDFs* were baptized in Chap. 8 as *mixed DDFs*.

[26] These non-inefficient firms are surely frontier firms, including the efficient firms. But there can be other frontier firms belonging to type 2 or type 3.

4. Type 4 graph inefficient firms: any firm (x_o, y_o) that obtains the two oriented inefficiency scores different from 0, $\beta^*_{x_o} > 0, \beta^*_{y_o} > 0$.

This classification of each firm according to its projection allows us to define the associated $RDDF\left(BDF^S, F_J, \widehat{F}_J\right)$ for types 1, 2, and 3 firms, since it is straightforward to identify the corresponding *RDDF* directional vector for each firm (x_o, y_o), denoted as $\left(\widetilde{g}_{x_o}, \widetilde{g}_{y_o}\right)$, in terms of the two oriented directional vectors of the *BDF*, as well as its new *RDDF* inefficiency score, β^*_o. Type 4 will be studied later.

Definition 12.6

The $RDDF\left(BDF^S, F_J, \widehat{F}_J\right)$ directional vector $\left(\widetilde{g}_{x_o}, \widetilde{g}_{y_o}\right)$ associated with firm (x_o, y_o) and its *RDDF* unique inefficiency score β^*_o are defined as follows in each of the three first cases:

1. If $\beta^*_{x_o} = 0, \beta^*_{y_o} = 0$, take $\left(\widetilde{g}_{x_o}, \widetilde{g}_{y_o}\right) = \left(g_{x_o}, 0_N\right) + \left(0_M, g_{y_o}\right)$, that is, the sum of the two oriented directional vectors of BDF, and set $\beta^*_o = 0$.
2. If $\beta^*_{x_o} > 0, \beta^*_{y_o} = 0$, take $\left(\widetilde{g}_{x_o}, \widetilde{g}_{y_o}\right) = \left(g_{x_o}, 0_N\right)$, and set $\beta^*_o = \beta^*_{x_o} > 0$.
3. If$\beta^*_{x_o} = 0, \beta^*_{y_o} > 0$, take $\left(\widetilde{g}_{x_o}, \widetilde{g}_{y_o}\right) = \left(0_M, g_{y_o}\right)$, and set $\beta^*_o = \beta^*_{y_o} > 0$.

Type 4 inefficient firms for which $\beta^*_{x_o} > 0, \beta^*_{y_o} > 0$ require a more elaborated solution for defining their associated $RDDF\left(BDF^S, F_J, \widehat{F}_J\right)$. We need to find a unique inefficiency score $\widetilde{\beta}^*_o > 0$ as well as a unique directional vector $\left(\widetilde{g}_{x_o}, \widetilde{g}_{y_o}\right)$ that satisfies that the projection of (x_o, y_o) obtained by means of the BDF, $(\widehat{x}_o, \widehat{y}_o) = (x_o, y_o) + \beta^*_{x_o}\left(g_{x_o}, 0_N\right) + \beta^*_{y_o}\left(0_M, g_{y_o}\right)$, can alternatively be expressed as $(x_o, y_o) + \widetilde{\beta}^*_o\left(\widetilde{g}_{x_o}, \widetilde{g}_{y_o}\right)$. Hence, we need to define both $\left(\widetilde{g}_{x_o}, \widetilde{g}_{y_o}\right)$ and $\widetilde{\beta}^*_o > 0$ attached to the RDDF such that $\beta^*_{xo}\left(g_{x_o}, 0_N\right) + \beta^*_{y_o}\left(0_M, g_{y_o}\right) = \widetilde{\beta}^*_o\left(\widetilde{g}_{x_o}, \widetilde{g}_{y_o}\right)$. There are many mathematical possibilities, and we are going to propose just a single, easy-to-remember, solution.

Proposition 12.2

Assuming that the two oriented inefficiency scores of a given $\left(BDF^S, F_J, \widehat{F}_J\right)$ for the inefficient firm (x_o, y_o) satisfy $\beta^*_{x_o} > 0, \beta^*_{y_o} > 0$ and that their two oriented directional vectors $\left(g_{x_o}, 0_N\right)$ and $\left(0_M, g_{y_o}\right)$ necessarily satisfy $g_{x_o} \neq 0_M$ and $g_{y_o} \neq 0_N$, define the *RDDF* efficiency score as $\widetilde{\beta}^*_o = \beta^*_{x_o} + \beta^*_{y_o}$ and the *RDDF* directional vector as $\left(\widetilde{g}_{x_o}, \widetilde{g}_{y_o}\right) = \left(\frac{\beta^*_{x_o}}{\beta^*_{x_o}+\beta^*_{y_o}} g_{x_o}, \frac{\beta^*_{y_o}}{\beta^*_{x_o}+\beta^*_{y_o}} g_{y_o}\right)$. Then, the next equality holds: $\beta^*_{x_o}\left(g_{x_o}, 0_N\right) + \beta^*_{y_o}\left(0_M, g_{y_o}\right) = \widetilde{\beta}^*_o\left(\widetilde{g}_{x_o}, \widetilde{g}_{y_o}\right)$.

Proof The proof is an easy algebraic exercise around the last equality. Its left-hand side term is equal to $\left(\beta^*_{x_o} g_{x_o}, \beta^*_{y_o} g_{y_o}\right)$, while its right-hand side term is, according to the two defined terms, equal to $\widetilde{\beta}^*_o\left(\widetilde{g}_{x_o}, \widetilde{g}_{y_o}\right) = \left(\beta^*_{x_o} + \beta^*_{y_o}\right)\left(\widetilde{g}_{x_o}, \widetilde{g}_{y_o}\right) = \left(\beta^*_{x_o} + \beta^*_{y_o}\right)\left(\frac{\beta^*_{x_o}}{\beta^*_{x_o}+\beta^*_{y_o}} g_{x_o}, \frac{\beta^*_{y_o}}{\beta^*_{x_o}+\beta^*_{y_o}} g_{y_o}\right) = \left(\beta^*_{x_o} g_{x_o}, \beta^*_{y_o} g_{y_o}\right)$, which means that the desired equality holds. □.

Note

The former equality guarantees that the benchmark projection $(\widehat{x}_o, \widehat{y}_o)$ of (x_o, y_o) obtained by means of the considered $\left(BDF^S, F_J, \widehat{F}_J\right)$ is equal to the projection obtained by the associated $RDDF\left(BDF^S, F_J, \widehat{F}_J\right)$, that is, $(\widehat{x}_o, \widehat{y}_o) = (x_o, y_o) + \left(\beta^*_{x_o} g_{x_o}, \beta^*_{y_o} g_{y_o}\right) = (x_o, y_o) + \widetilde{\beta}^*_o\left(\widetilde{g}_{x_o}, \widetilde{g}_{y_o}\right)$.

Example 12.8

Let us go back to our previous numerical example and remember that the first three different projections of firm D = (6,6) by means of the BDF^M with bidirectional vectors $(-1, 0)$, $(0, 1)$ were A = (2,6) with$\beta^*_{x_D} = 4, \beta^*_{y_D} = 0$, B = (4,8) with $\beta^*_{x_D} = 2, \beta^*_{y_D} = 2$, and C = (6,10) with$\beta^*_{x_D} = 0, \beta^*_{y_D} = 4$. In the first case, according to Definition 12.6, the first associated $RDDF\left(BDF^{S1}, F_J, \widehat{F}^1_J\right)$ projects D = (6,6) onto A = (2,6), with $\widetilde{\beta}^*_D\left(\widetilde{g}_{x_D}, \widetilde{g}_{y_D}\right) = 4(-1, 0)$; in the second case, according to Proposition 12.2, the second associated $RDDF\left(BDF^{S2}, F_J, \widehat{F}^2_J\right)$ projects D = (6,6) onto B = (4,8), with $\widetilde{\beta}^*_D\left(\widetilde{g}_{x_D}, \widetilde{g}_{y_D}\right) = \left(\beta^*_{xo} + \beta^*_{y0}\right)\left(\frac{\beta^*_{xo}}{\beta^*_{xo}+\beta^*_{yo}} g_{xo}, \frac{\beta^*_{yo}}{\beta^*_{xo}+\beta^*_{yo}} g_{yo}\right) = (2 + 2) \times \left(\frac{2}{2+2}(-1, 0), \frac{2}{2+2}(0, 1)\right) = 2(-1, 1)$; and in the last case, the third associated $RDDF\left(BDF^{S3}, F_J, \widehat{F}^3_J\right)$ projects D = (6,6) onto C = (6,10), with $\widetilde{\beta}^*_D\left(\widetilde{g}_{x_D}, \widetilde{g}_{y_D}\right) = 4(0, 1)$.

12.7 Empirical Illustration of the RDDF Profit, Cost, and Revenue Inefficiency Models

In this section, we illustrate the calculation of the three economic inefficiency measures, profit, revenue, and cost, and their decomposition based on the reverse directional distance functions $RDDF\left(EM^S, F_J, \widehat{F}_J\right)$ and $RDDF\left(BDF^S, F_J, \widehat{F}_J\right)$. We rely on the data presented in Sect. 2.5 of Chap. 2, corresponding to simple examples and a real dataset on Taiwanese banks. Table 12.11 replicates the data for the examples.

Table 12.11 Example data illustrating the economic inefficiency models

	Model							
			Input orientation			Output orientation		
	Graph profit model		Cost model			Revenue model		
Firm	x	y	x_1	x_2	y	x	y_1	y_2
A	2	1	2	2	1	1	7	7
B	4	5	1	4	1	1	4	8
C	8	8	4	1	1	1	8	4
D	12	9	4	3	1	1	3	5
E	6	3	5	5	1	1	3	3
F	14	7	6	1	1	1	8	2
G	14	9	2	5	1	1	6	4
H	9.412	2.353	1.6	8	1	1	1.5	5
Prices	$w = 1$	$p = 2$	$w_1 = 1$	$w_2 = 1$			$p_1 = 1$	$p_2 = 1$

As remarked upon in previous sections, although any efficiency measure can eventually be expressed in terms of the reverse directional distance function,[27] the package "Benchmarking Economic Efficiency" implements the models considered in this chapter. Specifically, to illustrate the case of the $RDDF\left(EM^S, F_J, \widehat{F}_J\right)$, we choose the $ERG = SBM$ technical inefficiency measure discussed in Chap. 7, while for the case of the reverse directional distance function concerning BDF^S, the bidirectional distance function introduced in Sect. 12.6, $RDDF\left(BDF^S, F_J, \widehat{F}_J\right)$, we choose the modified directional distance function (*MDDF*) presented in Chap. 11. Following Definition 12.4 and for the sample of firms F_J, the $RDDF\left(EM^S(G), F_J, \widehat{F}_J\right)$ function first identifies the single benchmarks on the production frontier $\widehat{F}_J$ using the $ERG = SBM$ measure, recovers the corresponding directional vectors according to Proposition 12.1, and then, as shown in Sect. 12.3, expression (12.1), decomposes profit inefficiency into its technical and allocative components.

For the cost and revenue inefficiency models, we follow equivalent processes, adapting the measures to their corresponding input and output dimensions, and recover the directional vectors through Corollaries 12.1.2 and 12.1.3. From the perspective of these partial orientations, the input and output technical inefficiency measures are calculated by resorting to the Russell efficiency measures. The reason is that the $ERG = SBM$ generalized these latter measures to a graph representation of the technology, where inputs and outputs are simultaneously increased and reduced, respectively. Consequently, $ERG = SBM(I)$ and $ERG = SBM(O)$ measures are numerically related to their Russell counterparts under these partial orientations. Afterwards, cost and revenue inefficiencies are decomposed according to (12.2) and (12.3).

[27] Provided we have selected a single projection for each firm of our sample

The following functions compute the economic inefficiency models based on the reverse directional distance function, along with their decompositions into technical and allocative inefficiencies:

```
deaprofitrddf(X, Y, W, P, :ERG, names = FIRMS)
```

```
deacostrddf(X, Y, W, :ERG, names = FIRMS)
```

```
dearevenuerddf(X, Y, P, :ERG, names = FIRMS)
```

The above syntax includes "`ERG`" indicating that the associated efficiency measure is the $ERG = SBM$. As already explained, the input- and output-oriented $ERG = SBM$ efficiency measures are related to the oriented Russell efficiency measures discussed in Chap. 6. For this reason, the above functions call the Russell measures when evaluating the technical inefficiencies in the input and output orientations corresponding to the cost and revenue efficiency models.

The reverse model can be calculated also using the bidirectional distance function, BDF^S (see program (12.4)). This function is equivalent in practice to the modified directional distance function (*MDDF*) already implemented in Chap. 11. To use this model, one needs to replace the above syntax "`ERG`" with "`MDDF`." We illustrate this possibility using the dataset on Taiwanese banks in Sect. 12.7.4.

Finally, all decompositions can be recovered in monetary terms by including the option "`true`" in the above syntax, e.g., `deaprofitrddf`. For each firm, this option multiplies the economic inefficiency by the corresponding normalization factor, as well as its technical and (residual) allocative components. Clearly, one of the properties of economic inefficiency indices is that of units' independence or commensurability (see property (P6) in Sect. 2.3.5 of Chap. 2), so the efficiency values are not expressed in specific currencies. Nevertheless, from a managerial perspective, it may be relevant to know the profit loss in real values (i.e., dollar, euro, etc.) for actual decision-making. The option "`ERG`" offers the possibility of "translating" the technical and allocative inefficiencies to monetary terms.

12.7.1 The RDDF (ERG = SBM) Profit Inefficiency Model

We rely on the open (web-based) Jupyter notebook interface to illustrate the economic models. Nevertheless, they can be implemented in any integrated development environment (IDE) of preference.[28] To calculate profit inefficiency using the reverse directional distance function associated with the $ERG = SBM$ technical

[28] We refer the reader to Sect. 2.6.1 in Chap. 2 for the installation of the "Benchmarking Economic Efficiency" Julia package. All Jupyter notebooks implementing the different economic models in this book can be downloaded from the reference site: http://www.benchmarkingeconomicefficiency.com

Table 12.12 Implementation of the *RDDF (ERG = SBM)* profit inefficiency model using BEE for Julia

In[]:
```
using DataEnvelopmentAnalysis
using BenchmarkingEconomicEfficiency

X = [2; 4; 8; 12; 6; 14; 14; 9.412];
Y = [1; 5; 8; 9; 3; 7; 9; 2.353];
W = [1; 1; 1; 1; 1; 1; 1; 1];
P = [2; 2; 2; 2; 2; 2; 2; 2];
FIRMS = ["A";"B";"C";"D";"E";"F";"G";"H"];

deaprofitrddf(X, Y, W, P, :ERG, names = FIRMS)
```

Out[]:
```
Profit Reverse DDF DEA Model
DMUs = 8; Inputs = 1; Outputs = 1
Returns to Scale = VRS
Associated efficiency measure = ERG
```

	Profit	Technical	Allocative
A	4.0	0.0	4.0
B	0.5	0.0	0.5
C	0.0	0.0	0.0
D	0.167	0.0	0.167
E	0.8	0.6	0.2
F	0.571	0.524	0.048
G	0.286	0.143	0.143
H	0.949	0.8	0.149

inefficiency measure (12.1), enter the following code in the "`In[]:`" window, and run it. The corresponding results are shown in the "`Out[]:`" window of Table 12.12.

We can learn about the reference benchmarks for each firm using the "peersmatrix" function with the corresponding economic or technical model. For the economic model, executing "`peersmatrix(deaprofitrddf (X, Y, W, P, :ERG, names = FIRMS))`" identifies firm C as the reference benchmark that maximizes profit for the rest of the firms (see Fig. 12.2).

As for the underlying reverse technical inefficiency model, we can obtain the information running the corresponding function, as shown in Table 12.13. In these results, the value of the technical inefficiency corresponds to Definition 12.4 and is calculated according to Proposition 12.1.

Recall that to determine this inefficiency measure, the projections obtained by solving the $ERG = SBM$ model are used to calculate the directional vectors and, ultimately, the value of the RDDF itself. We refer the reader to Tables 7.6 and 7.7 of Chap. 7, presenting the example for the profit inefficiency model based on the $ERG = SBM$ measure. These tables report the initial $ERG = SBM$ technical efficiency scores and the set of peers $\widehat{F}_J$ that are used to recover each directional vector $\left(-g_{x_j}, g_{y_j}\right)$. In particular, the reverse technical inefficiency

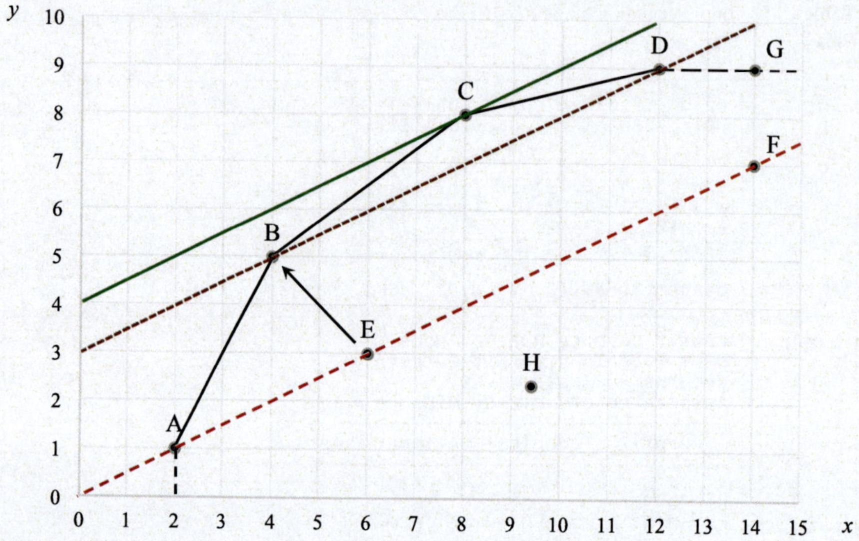

Fig. 12.2 Example of the *RDDF (ERG = SBM)* profit inefficiency model using BEE for Julia

Table 12.13 Implementation of the *RDDF (ERG = SBM)* graph inefficiency measure using BEE for Julia

In[]:	`dearddf(X, Y, :ERG, rts = :VRS, names = FIRMS)`
Out[]:	see below

```
Reverse DDF DEA Model
DMUs = 8; Inputs = 1; Outputs = 1
Orientation = Graph; Returns to Scale = VRS
Associated efficiency measure = ERG
─────────────
   efficiency
─────────────
A  0.0
B  0.0
C  0.0
D  0.0
E  0.6
F  0.524
G  0.143
H  0.8
─────────────
```

$RDDF\left(ERG = SBM, F_J, \widehat{F}_J\right)$ is equal to $TI_{ERG\ =\ SBM(G)}(x_o, y_o) = 1 - TE_{ERG\ =\ SBM(G)}(x_o, y_o)$. This last value, $TE_{ERG\ =\ SBM(G)}(x_o, y_o)$, is reported in Table 7.6, while its associated reference peers, which are obtained through the corresponding syntax "`peersmatrix(deaerg(X, Y, rts = :VRS, names = FIRMS))`," are shown in Table 7.7. Indeed, if we solve for the benchmarks of the reverse directional distance function associated with the ERG = SBM measure, we obtain the same information that

Table 12.14 Reference peers of the *RDDF (ERG = SBM)* graph inefficiency measure using BEE for Julia

In[]:	`peersmatrix(dearddf(X, Y, :ERG, rts = :VRS, names = FIRMS))`

Out[]:	<pre>1.0 . . . .
	 . 1.0 . . . . . .
	 . . 1.0 . . . . .
	 . . . 1.0 . . . .
	 . 1.0 . . . . . .
	 . 0.333 0.667 . . . . .
	 . . . 1.0 . . . .
	 . 1.0 . . . . . .</pre>

the one returned by the above function; i.e., the results in Table 12.14 obtained through "`peersmatrix(dearddf(X, Y, :ERG, rts = :VRS, names = FIRMS))`", coincide with those of Table 7.7. These results, shown in the "`Out[]:`" window, identify firms A, B, C, and D as those conforming the strongly efficient production possibility set, i.e., those with unit values in the main diagonal of the square ($J \times J$) matrix containing their own intensity variables λ (note the matrix syntax in "`In[]:`").

Figure 12.2 illustrates the results for the reverse directional distance function. There, for firm E, we identify that its normalized profit inefficiency with respect to firm C, according to (12.1), is equal to $N\Pi I_{RDDF\left(EM^S(G),F_J,\widehat{F}_J\right)}(x_E, y_E, \widetilde{w}, \widetilde{p}) = 0.8$, which can be decomposed into the reverse directional distance function representing technical inefficiency, whose value is $TI_{RDDF\left(EM^S(G),F_J,\widehat{F}_J\right)} = 0.6$, and allocative inefficiency $AI_{RDDF\left(EM^S(G),F_J,\widehat{F}_J\right)}(x_E, y_E, \widetilde{w}, \widetilde{p}) = 0.2 = 0.8\text{-}0.6$. Note that for this example and contrary to the cost and revenue inefficiency examples that follow, none of the firms identifies the same optimal economic and technological benchmark, i.e., firm C. Therefore, we cannot exemplify that the reverse directional distance function satisfies the essential property (D1) introduced in Sect. 2.4.5 of Chap. 2. However, it is possible to show that it does not comply with the extended essential property (D2), since the allocative efficiency of firm E differs from that of its technological benchmark B, i.e., $AI_{RDDF\left(EM^S(G),F_J,\widehat{F}_J\right)}(x_E, y_E, \widetilde{w}, \widetilde{p}) \neq AI_{RDDF\left(EM^S(G),F_J,\widehat{F}_J\right)}(x_B, y_B, \widetilde{w}, \widetilde{p})$.

12.7.2 *The RDDF (Russell) Cost Inefficiency Model*

We now solve the example for the reverse *DDF* cost inefficiency model considering the Russell technical inefficiency measure presented in Chap. 5. This is the reference model for the $ERG = SBM$ measure when a partial orientation is chosen for the economic analysis; i.e., the input-oriented measure $ERG = SBM(I)$ is equivalent to the Russell input-oriented measure, as examined in Chap. 7. The reason is that the $ERG = SBM$ model was aimed at generalizing the oriented Russell measures and, therefore, the latter constitute particular cases of the former. To calculate this model, type the code included in the "`In[]:`" panel in the notebook, and execute it. The corresponding results are shown in the "`Out[]:`" panel of Table 12.15.

We can learn about the benchmarks minimizing cost by running the "peers" function with the corresponding model. In this case, executing "`peersmatrix(deacostrddf(X, Y, W, :ERG, rts = :VRS, names = FIRMS))`" identifies firm A as the optimal firm in this example (see Fig. 12.3).

As for the underlying reverse technical inefficiency model, we can obtain the information running the corresponding function, as shown in Table 12.16. Again, the value of the technical inefficiency corresponds to Definition 12.4 and is calculated according to Corollary 12.1.2.

In this case, the projections obtained by solving the Russell efficiency model are used to calculate the directional vectors and, afterwards, the value of the $RDDF$. The technical efficiency measure $TE_{RM(I)}(x_o, y_o)$ and their associated projections can be consulted in Tables 5.6 and 5.7 of Chap. 5. We note that the value of the reverse technical inefficiency $RDDF\left(RM(I), F_J, \widehat{F}_J\right)$ is equal to $TI_{RM(I)}(x_o, y_o) = 1 - TE_{RM(I)}(x_o, y_o)$, while the set of peers that are used to recover the directional

Table 12.15 Implementation of the *RDDF* (Russell) cost inefficiency model using BEE for Julia

In[]:

```
using DataEnvelopmentAnalysis
using BenchmarkingEconomicEfficiency

X = [2 2; 1 4; 4 1; 4 3; 5 5; 6 1; 2 5; 1.6 8];
Y = [1; 1; 1; 1; 1; 1; 1; 1];
W = [1 1; 1 1; 1 1; 1 1; 1 1; 1 1; 1 1; 1 1];
FIRMS = ["A"; "B"; "C"; "D"; "E"; "F"; "G"; "H"];

deacostrddf(X, Y, W, :ERG, rts = :VRS, names = FIRMS)
```

Out[]:

```
Cost Reverse DDF DEA Model
DMUs = 8; Inputs = 2; Outputs = 1
Returns to Scale = VRS
Associated efficiency measure = ERG
```

	Cost	Technical	Allocative
A	0.0	0.0	0.0
B	0.5	0.0	0.5
C	0.5	0.0	0.5
D	0.417	0.417	0.0
E	0.6	0.6	0.0
F	0.25	0.167	0.083
G	0.525	0.35	0.175
H	0.533	0.438	0.095

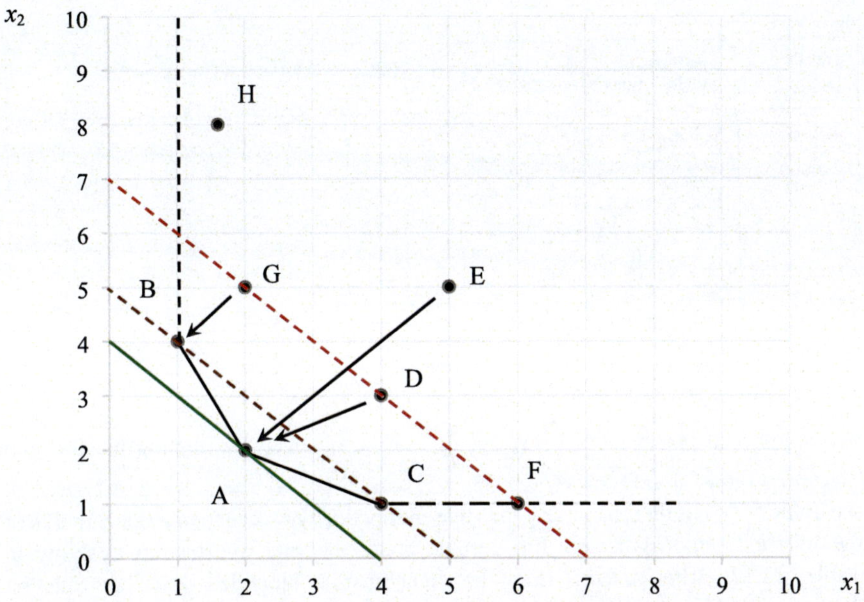

Fig. 12.3 Example of the *RDDF* (Russell) cost inefficiency model using BEE for Julia

Table 12.16 Implementation of the *RDDF* (Russell) input inefficiency measure using BEE for Julia

In[]:	`dearddf(X, Y, :ERG, orient = :Input, rts = :VRS, names = FIRMS)`
Out[]:	see below

```
Reverse DDF DEA Model
DMUs = 8; Inputs = 2; Outputs = 1
Orientation = Input; Returns to Scale = VRS
Associated efficiency measure = ERG
   efficiency
A     0.0
B     0.0
C     0.0
D     0.417
E     0.6
F     0.167
G     0.35
H     0.438
```

Table 12.17 Reference peers of the *RDDF* (Russell) input inefficiency measure using BEE for Julia

`In[]:`	`peersmatrix(dearddf(X, Y, :ERG, orient = :Input, rts = :VRS, names = FIRMS))`
`Out[]:`	see below

```
In[]:   peersmatrix(dearddf(X, Y, :ERG, orient = :Input, rts =
        :VRS, names = FIRMS))

Out[]:  1.0   .    .    .    .    .    .    .
         .   1.0   .    .    .    .    .    .
         .    .   1.0   .    .    .    .    .
        1.0   .    .    .    .    .    .    .
        1.0   .    .    .    .    .    .    .
         .    .   1.0   .    .    .    .    .
         .   1.0   .    .    .    .    .    .
         .   1.0   .    .    .    .    .    .
```

vector for each observation, $\left(-g_{x_o}, g_{y_o}\right)$, can be obtained by running the function "`peersmatrix(dearussell(X, Y, orient = :Input, rts = :VRS, names = FIRMS))`", see Table 5.7). If rather than using the Russell function we solve for the benchmarks of the reverse directional distance function, we obtain the same information, as shown in Table 12.17. This means that the benchmarks identified by the function "`peersmatrix(dearddf(X,Y, :ERG, orient = :Input; rts = :VRS, names = FIRMS))`" are those of Table 5.7. The results in the window "`Out[]:`" identify firms A, B, and C as those conforming the strongly efficient production possibility set in this case, i.e., those with unit values in the main diagonal of the square (J × J) matrix containing their own intensity variables λ (note also the matrix syntax in "`In[]:`").

Figure 12.3 illustrates the results for the reverse directional distance function model under the input-oriented Russell measure. There, for firm G, we learn that its normalized cost efficiency with respect to firm A, as stated by (12.2), is equal to $NCI_{RDDF\left(RM(I),F_J,\widehat{F}_J\right)}(x_G, y_G, \widetilde{w}) = 0.6$, which can be decomposed into technical inefficiency, whose value is $RDDF\left(RM(I), F_J, \widehat{F}_J\right) = 0.35$, and residual allocative inefficiency $AI_{RDDF\left(RM(I),F_J,\widehat{F}_J\right)}(x_G, y_G, \widetilde{w}) = 0.175 = 0.525\text{-}0.35$. Note that for the technically inefficient firms D and E, whose economic and technical peer is firm A minimizing cost, their allocative inefficiency is zero, thereby satisfying in both cases the essential property (D1) presented in Sect. 2.4.5 of Chap. 2. This is in contrast to the decomposition of cost inefficiency directly based on the Russell measure rather than the RDDF. As shown in Sect. 5.5.2, the allocative efficiency of firm D is positive, $AI_{RM(I)}(x_D, y_D, \widetilde{w}) = 0.083$, despite being technically projected to firm A, failing to meet the essential property. This example shows the advantage of using the indirect approach offered by the RDDF to decompose cost inefficiency in a meaningful way. Nevertheless, as in the profit case, we can show that it fails to satisfy the extended essential property (D2) since the allocative inefficiency of firm G is different from that of its technological benchmark B.

12.7.3 The RDDF (Russell) Revenue Inefficiency Model

We now solve the example for the reverse *DDF* revenue inefficiency model considering the output-oriented version of the Russell technical inefficiency. As in the cost example, the Russell model is the reference for the *ERG* = *SBM (O)* measure when a partial orientation is chosen for the economic analysis. To calculate the revenue inefficiency score and its decomposition into technical and allocative terms according to (12.3), run the code included in the "`In[]:`" window of the notebook. The corresponding results are shown in the "`Out[]:`" panel of Table 12.18.

To determine the reference set for the evaluation of economic and technical inefficiency, we use the "peersmatrix" function with the corresponding model. For the revenue model, we execute "`peersmatrix(dearevenuerddf (X, Y, P, :ERG, names=FIRMS))`". The output identifies firm A as the benchmark-maximizing revenue for the rest of the firms (see Fig. 12.4).

Regarding the underlying reverse technical inefficiency model, we can run the corresponding function, as shown in Table 12.19. As before, the value of the technical inefficiency corresponds to Definition 12.4 and is calculated according to Corollary 12.1.2.

The projections obtained from the Russell output-oriented model are used to calculate the directional vectors and, afterwards, the value of the *RDDF*. The

Table 12.18 Implementation of the *RDDF* (Russell) revenue inefficiency model using BEE for Julia

In[]:

```
using DataEnvelopmentAnalysis
using BenchmarkingEconomicEfficiency

X = [1; 1; 1; 1; 1; 1; 1; 1];
Y = [7 7; 4 8; 8 4; 3 5; 3 3; 8 2; 6 4; 1.5 5];
P = [1 1; 1 1; 1 1; 1 1; 1 1; 1 1; 1 1; 1 1];
FIRMS = ["A"; "B"; "C"; "D"; "E"; "F"; "G"; "H"];

dearevenuerddf(X, Y, P, :ERG,  names = FIRMS)
```

Out[]:

```
Revenue Reverse DDF DEA Model
DMUs = 8; Inputs = 1; Outputs = 2
Returns to Scale = VRS
Associated efficiency measure = ERG
─────────────────────────────────────
     Revenue  Technical  Allocative
─────────────────────────────────────
A    0.0      0.0        0.0
B    0.25     0.0        0.25
C    0.25     0.0        0.25
D    0.464    0.464      0.0
E    0.571    0.571      0.0
F    0.667    0.333      0.333
G    0.314    0.314      0.0
H    0.818    0.673      0.145
─────────────────────────────────────
```

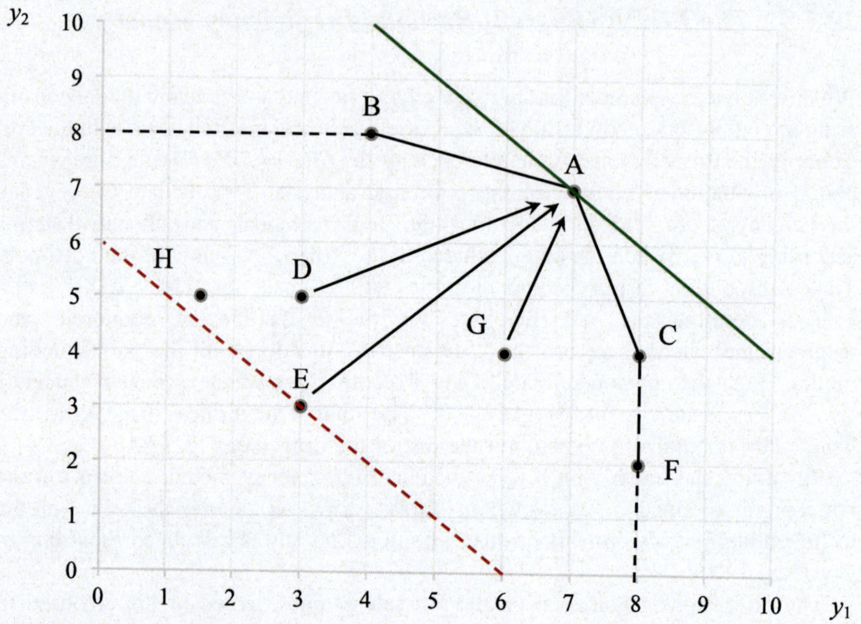

Fig. 12.4 Example of the *RDDF* (Russell) revenue inefficiency model using BEE for Julia

technical efficiency measure $TE_{RM(O)}(x_o, y_o)$ along with their projections can be consulted in Tables 5.9 and 5.10 of Chap. 5. Now the value of the reverse technical inefficiency $RDDF\left(RM(O), F_J, \widehat{F}_J\right)$ is equal to $1 - 1/TE_{RM(O)}(x_o, y_o)$, while the set of peers used to recover the directional vectors $\left(-g_{x_o}, g_{y_o}\right)$ can be obtained by running the function "`peersmatrix(dearddf(X, Y, :ERG, orient = :Input; rts =:VRS, names = FIRMS))`" (see Table 12.19). These results do not differ from those obtained for the underlying Russell measure, obtained through "`peersmatrix(dearussell(X, Y, orient =:Output, rts = :VRS, names = FIRMS))`", and therefore Table 5.7 is the same as Table 12.20. The results in "`Out[]:`" identify firms A, B, and C as those conforming the strongly efficient production possibility set.

Figure 12.4 illustrates the results for the RDDF revenue inefficiency model. The normalized cost efficiency of firm E with respect to firm A, according to (12.3), is equal to $NRI_{RDDF\left(RM(O), F_J, \widehat{F}_J\right)}(x_E, y_E, \widetilde{p}) = 0.571$. All revenue inefficiency is due to technical inefficiency because $RDDF\left(RM(O), F_J, \widehat{F}_J\right) = 0.571$, and therefore there is no allocative inefficiency: $AI_{RDDF\left(RM(O), F_J, \widehat{F}_J\right)}(x_E, y_E, \widetilde{p}) = 0$. Note that the technically inefficient firms D and G, whose economic and technical peer is also firm A maximizing revenue, are allocative-efficient. This shows once again that the RDDF complies with the essential property (D1; see Sect. 2.4.5 of Chap. 2), thereby

Table 12.19 Implementation of *RDDF* (Russell) output inefficiency measure using BEE for Julia

In[]:
```
dearddf(X, Y, :ERG, orient = :Output, rts = :VRS, names =
FIRMS)
```

Out[]:
```
Reverse DDF DEA Model
DMUs = 8; Inputs = 2; Outputs = 1
Orientation = Output; Returns to Scale = VRS
Associated efficiency measure = ERG
─────────────────
   efficiency
─────────────────
A      0.0
B      0.0
C      0.0
D      0.464
E      0.571
F      0.333
G      0.314
H      0.673
─────────────────
```

Table 12.20 Reference peers of the *RDDF* (Russell) output inefficiency measure using BEE for Julia

In[]:
```
peersmatrix(dearddf(X, Y, :ERG, orient = :Input; rts =
:VRS, names = FIRMS))
```

Out[]:
```
1.0    .     .     .  .  .  .  .
 .    1.0    .     .  .  .  .  .
 .     .    1.0    .  .  .  .  .
1.0    .     .     .  .  .  .  .
1.0    .     .     .  .  .  .  .
 .     .    1.0    .  .  .  .  .
1.0    .     .     .  .  .  .  .
0.333  .    0.667  .  .  .  .  .
```

improving the revenue inefficiency model directly based on the Russell measure, for which firms D and G were allocative-inefficient despite being projected to firm A. For example, as reported in Sect. 5.5.3, the allocative inefficiency of firm G under the Russell model is positive, $AI_{RM(O)}(x_G, y_G, \tilde{p})$=0.042, thereby failing to meet the essential property. Again, this example stresses the advantage of using the indirect approach offered by the RDDF to decompose cost inefficiency in a meaningful way. Despite this advantage, once again, we remark that the extended essential property is not satisfied, e.g., the allocative efficiency of firm F is different from that of its projection C.

12.7.4 An Application to the Taiwanese Banking Industry

Following previous chapters, we now calculate profit inefficiency using the dataset of 31 Taiwanese banks observed in 2010 (see Juo et al. (2015)). A brief presentation of the data, including descriptive statistics, can be found in Sect. 2.5.2 of Chap. 2. In this dataset, individual firm prices for each input and output are observed. These are unit prices obtained by dividing individual costs and revenues by their corresponding quantities; i.e., prices are not directly observed. We adopt the standard approach in the literature and determine maximum profit for each firm under evaluation using its own prices as reference. The variation of prices makes the results specific for each firm, and therefore bilateral comparisons of profit inefficiency are price-dependent.

We calculate and decompose profit inefficiency based on the reverse directional distance function $RDDF\left(BDF, F_J, \widehat{F}_J\right)$ relying on the modified directional distance function (MDDF) already implemented in Chap. 11. The reason is that the bidirectional distance function presented in program (12.4) is computationally equivalent to the modified directional distance function (11.4) when the directional vectors $\left(g_{x_o}, g_{y_o}\right)$ are strictly positive. Since this condition is met when solving for the $RDDF\left(BDF, F_J, \widehat{F}_J\right)$ according to Definition 12.5 and Proposition 12.2, the following function allows calculating the corresponding profit inefficiency: "`deaprofitrddf(X, Y, W, P, :MDDF, Gx = :Observed, Gy = :Observed, names=FIRMS)`". In this case, the choice of directional vectors equals the quantities of the unit under evaluation, $\left(g_{x_o}, g_{y_o}\right) = (x_o, y_o)$.[29]

The function solves the modified directional distance function, recovers the directional vectors necessary to calculate the reverse directional distance function, and then calculates and decomposes profit inefficiency following expression (12.1). For this reason, in Table 12.21 presenting the results, the values of the technical inefficiencies, reported in the third column, coincide with those of Table 11.4 of Chap. 11. Also, in the fifth and sixth columns, we replicate the values of the input and output technical inefficiencies $\left(\beta_x^*,\ \beta_y^*\right)$, corresponding to programs (11.4) and (12.4). Regarding the profit inefficiency values, these are shown in the second column. As in the models presented in previous chapters, three banks are profit-efficient under their own prices (no.1, no.5, and no.10), with $N\Pi I_{RDDF\left(EM^S(G), F_J, \widehat{F}_J\right)}(x_o, y_o, \widetilde{w}, \widetilde{p}) = 0$, constituting the most frequent benchmarks for the remaining banks. A total of 11 banks are efficient once again.

---

[29] Just as the $ERG = SBM\ (I)$ and $ERG = SBM\ (O)$ collapse to their corresponding input and output Russell technical inefficiency measures presented in Chap. 5, the partially orientated *MDFF* collapses to its input and output directional distance functions, as presented in Chap. 8. This is relevant for the calculation and decomposition of cost and revenue inefficiencies using the *MDDF* model.

Table 12.21 Decomposition of profit inefficiency based on the reverse directional distance function, $RDDF\left(BDF, F_J, \widehat{F}_J\right)$

Bank	Economic inefficiency, eq. (12.1)			Technical Ineff., eq. (12.4)		Slacks				
	Profit Ineff. $N\Pi I_{RDDF(BDF,F_J,\hat{F}_J)}$	Technical Ineff. $RDDF\left(BDF,F_J,\hat{F}_J\right)$	Allocative Ineff. $AI_{RDDF(BDF,F_J,\hat{F}_J)}$	Inputs β_x	Outputs β_y	Funds (x_1) s_1^-	Labor (x_2) s_2^-	Ph. Capital (x_3) s_3^-	Investments (y_1) s_1^+	Loans (y_2) s_2^+
1	0.000	0.000	0.000	0.000	0.000	0.0	0.0	0.0	0.0	0.0
2	0.597	0.000	0.597	0.000	0.000	0.0	0.0	0.0	0.0	0.0
3	1.100	0.000	1.100	0.000	0.000	0.0	0.0	0.0	0.0	0.0
4	3.403	0.362	3.041	0.000	0.362	0.0	210.0	0.0	7,113.7	0.0
5	0.000	0.000	0.000	0.000	0.000	0.0	0.0	0.0	0.0	0.0
6	0.343	0.000	0.343	0.000	0.000	0.0	0.0	0.0	0.0	0.0
7	0.716	0.000	0.716	0.000	0.000	0.0	0.0	0.0	0.0	0.0
8	0.262	0.056	0.206	0.056	0.000	0.0	711.5	3,446.0	0.0	0.0
9	0.453	0.065	0.388	0.065	0.000	0.0	1,740.6	8,277.1	0.0	0.0
10	0.000	0.000	0.000	0.000	0.000	0.0	0.0	0.0	0.0	0.0
11	1.236	0.384	0.852	0.000	0.384	0.0	1,551.4	9,045.5	0.0	0.0
12	1.663	0.113	1.549	0.113	0.000	0.0	0.0	1,876.2	0.0	0.0
13	30.760	0.691	30.069	0.000	0.691	0.0	1,951.9	4,260.5	12,936.6	0.0
14	1.884	0.000	1.884	0.000	0.000	0.0	0.0	0.0	0.0	0.0
15	0.703	0.158	0.545	0.158	0.000	0.0	0.0	2,448.5	0.0	0.0
16	59.603	1.244	58.359	0.000	1.244	0.0	1,225.8	4,627.6	9,770.8	0.0
17	1.261	0.194	1.067	0.000	0.194	0.0	3,122.8	8,994.7	0.0	0.0
18	1.342	0.144	1.198	0.144	0.000	0.0	1,464.3	0.0	0.0	0.0
19	5.324	0.628	4.696	0.000	0.628	0.0	747.7	1,952.1	0.0	0.0
20	3.058	0.194	2.864	0.000	0.194	80,613.5	1,148.0	0.0	7,617.6	0.0
21	2.421	0.000	2.421	0.000	0.000	0.0	0.0	0.0	0.0	0.0
22	8.852	0.436	8.416	0.000	0.436	0.0	1,017.0	6,326.2	18,303.6	0.0
23	16.382	0.746	15.636	0.000	0.746	0.0	708.9	5,474.0	13,701.7	0.0
24	0.399	0.033	0.366	0.033	0.000	0.0	1,507.8	1,557.5	0.0	0.0
25	3.152	0.295	2.857	0.000	0.295	0.0	740.8	0.0	39,044.5	0.0
26	3.765	0.000	3.765	0.000	0.000	0.0	0.0	0.0	0.0	0.0
27	8.932	0.731	8.201	0.000	0.731	0.0	409.1	182.1	7,639.0	0.0
28	11.749	0.638	11.111	0.000	0.638	10,850.5	651.1	0.0	12,956.4	0.0
29	7.822	0.000	7.822	0.000	0.000	0.0	0.0	0.1	0.0	0.0
30	0.425	0.111	0.314	0.000	0.111	0.0	1,042.4	0.0	0.0	0.0
31	6.955	0.347	6.608	0.000	0.347	0.0	1,717.2	1,708.9	29,414.5	0.0
Average	5.954	0.244	5.709	0.018	0.226	2,950.5	699.0	1,941.2	5,112.9	0.0
Median	1.663	0.113	1.549	0.000	0.000	0.0	651.1	0.0	0.0	0.0
Maximum	59.603	1.244	58.359	0.158	1.244	80,613.5	3,122.8	9,045.5	39,044.5	0.0
Minimum	0.000	0.000	0.000	0.000	0.000	0.0	0.0	0.0	0.0	0.0
Std. Dev.	11.787	0.311	11.533	0.043	0.321	14,544.6	794.0	2,912.9	9,486.4	0.0

We remark that following Definition 12.5 and Proposition 12.2, the results for technically efficient firms are identical to those of the underlying technical model; i.e., profit, technical, and allocative inefficiencies are equal to those calculated in Chap. 11 for the *MDDF*. The reason is that the same normalization factors are used, resulting in equal results. However, this is not the case for the technically inefficient firms, whose inefficiency values differ because their normalization factors are those associated with the reverse directional distance function: $p \cdot \widetilde{g}_y + w \cdot \widetilde{g}_x$. We stress that the reverse directional distance function makes the numerical results fully comparable, besides the advantage of ensuring that the essential property is verified.

Comparing the results in Tables 11.4 and 12.21, we observe that for the technically inefficient firms, all inefficiencies in the decomposition directly based on the *MDDF* model (Chap. 11) are always larger or equal than those of the current indirect *RDDF* model. In this latter case, the average normalized profit inefficiency amounts 5.954, representing just 14.4%, of the average efficiency observed in the direct *MDDF* model, which is equal to 41.214. Since average technical inefficiencies are equal in both models, 0.244, the difference between profit inefficiencies is accommodated by the allocative inefficiency terms: 5.709 and 40.970, respectively. These differences translate into the relative shares of the technical and allocative inefficiencies in the overall profit inefficiency, whose proportions are 4.1% and 0.6% for the technical inefficiencies and 95.9% and 99.4% for allocative inefficiencies. Hence, although the numerical values change dramatically, their relative proportions remain similar. As previously remarked, the individual parameters β_x and β_y associated with the *MDDF* models (11.4) and (12.4) are reported in the fifth and sixth columns of Table 12.21. We highlight once again that none of the inefficient banks exhibit inefficiencies in both dimensions. Out of the 20 technically inefficient banks, 6 are inefficient in the input dimension, $\beta_x > 0$, while the remaining 14 are inefficient in the output dimension, $\beta_y > 0$. The higher frequency and mean of β_y show that output inefficiency is larger and more relevant when reaching the production frontier.

Finally, in the last columns of Table 12.21, we replicate the values of the individual slacks for the three inputs and two outputs. These slacks are obtained after solving program (12.4) for β_x^* and β_y^*. Then, for the efficient projections, a standard additive model is solved in a second stage to search for the efficient projections on the strongly efficient frontier. We do not comment on the numerical values of the slacks because they are reviewed in Chap. 11.

12.8 Summary and Conclusions

In this chapter, when analyzing the economic efficiency of a finite sample of firms, we have started by defining a family of efficiency measures that satisfy two characteristics: for each firm, the measure identifies a single projection and calculates a single inefficiency score. We refer to this type of measures as EM^S. This family includes oriented as well as graph efficiency measures. Based on the previous work of Pastor et al. (2016), we have been able to associate with each of these measures a reverse directional distance function (*RDDF*) that reproduces its functioning. After comparing the profit inefficiency, the cost inefficiency, and the revenue inefficiency of three different EM^S measures with their respective *RDDF*s, we have concluded that the latter better satisfy the properties than the former.

We have also been able to apply the notion of reverse directional distance function to a new defined family of graph efficiency measures that generate, for each firm of a finite sample, two oriented inefficiency scores. This refers to the so-called bidirectional distance function (*BDF*). As in previous chapters, we have shown how to solve and implement these models using the software "Benchmarking Economic Efficiency" using as underlying measures the $ERG = SBM$ and the modified directional distance function (*MDDF*). While the reverse technical efficiencies are equal or numerically related to these measures, profit and allocative inefficiencies differ with the reverse *DDF* approach. The advantage of the new approach is that it complies with the essential property, thereby solving the inconsistencies shown by the direct approaches.

Part III
New Approaches to Decompose Economic Efficiency

Chapter 13
A Unifying Framework for Decomposing Economic Inefficiency: The General Direct Approach and the Reverse Approaches

13.1 Introduction

The usual and well-established methods, explained and used in most of the previous chapters, for deriving a specific overall economic inefficiency decomposition associated with a given technical efficiency measure (multiplicative or additive), which we refer to as *the traditional approaches*, rely on the same "modus operandi"; i.e., they are based on dual relationships where allocative efficiency plays a fundamental role. Allocative inefficiency is obtained as the residual from a Fenchel-Mahler *inequality* that shows that the normalized economic inefficiency for a specific firm is greater or equal to its technical inefficiency.[1] Accounting for allocative efficiency allows the closure of the inequality and enables a decomposition of economic efficiency considering technical and price (allocative) criteria, with the value of allocative efficiency clearly depending upon the chosen technical efficiency measure. Researchers have been using these traditional methods for at least half a century, and we take stock of the existing contributions and current state of the art in the previous chapters.

In what follows we are going to introduce a new method, baptized as the *general direct approach* (Pastor et al., 2021b), characterized by the following distinguishing feature: it establishes a *general economic efficiency decomposition* valid for *any* technical efficiency measure (*EM*) by considering the same single *equality* each time. For any firm (x, y) and for an already selected *EM*, we just need to know two pieces of information, *its technical inefficiency* $TI_{EM}(x, y)$ and *its* associated *frontier projection* $(\widehat{x}_{EM}, \widehat{y}_{EM})$. Now let us be more precise by focusing on profit maximization, which results in an additive decomposition of *in*efficiencies. *Profit inefficiency* is defined as the difference between maximum profit and observed profit,

[1] See, in this respect, Figs. 2.6, 2.7, and 2.9 in Chap. 2 for cost, revenue, and profit functions, based on the ideas of Farrell (1957).

J. T. Pastor et al., *Benchmarking Economic Efficiency*, International Series in Operations Research & Management Science 315,
https://doi.org/10.1007/978-3-030-84397-7_13

$\Pi I(x, y, w, p) = \Pi(w, p) - (p \cdot y - w \cdot x)$, as explained in expression (2.25) of Chap. 2. The novelty of the proposal is that it breaks up profit inefficiency into the sum of two components. For a specific firm, denoted by $(x_o, y_o) \in \mathbb{R}_+^{M+N}$, $x_o \neq 0_M, y_o \neq 0_N$, the first component is the interior product of two vectors, the optimal slack vector $(x_o - \widehat{x}_{oEM}, \widehat{y}_{oEM} - y_o)$ and the market price vector (w, p), while the second component corresponds to the profit inefficiency at the projection $(\widehat{x}_{oEM}, \widehat{y}_{oEM})$. Both components have the intuitive technical and allocative interpretations. Needless to say, all three terms are expressed in monetary units. Moreover, the first derived component can be rewritten as the product of a certain normalizing factor, $NF_{EM}(x_o, y_o)$, times technical inefficiency $TI_{EM}(x_o, y_o)$. By dividing the three terms of the *equality* by the mentioned factor, we obtain a *general normalized profit inefficiency decomposition* that, as mentioned aforehand, can be calculated for any efficiency measure. Additionally, by resorting to a single equality, *we avoid the possibility of overestimating allocative inefficiency*, something that may happen when using inequalities, as the traditional approaches sometimes do, failing in some cases to satisfy the essential property introduced in Sect. 2.4.5 of Chap. 2. In what follows, we will first revise profit inefficiency, followed by cost and revenue inefficiency. In order to appreciate the numerical differences of the new direct approach with respect to the traditional approaches, we are going to develop, in each case, a simple numerical example.

The *general direct approach*, providing a unifying framework for decomposing economic inefficiency, follows similar steps to the traditional approach but is much easier to develop and implement. After selecting a specific efficiency measure (*EM*), e.g., the weighted additive distance function (see Chap. 6), the enhanced Russell distance function (Chap. 7), or the directional distance function (Chap. 8), we obtain the necessary information for its decomposition by solving, for each evaluated firm, the corresponding mathematical program, quite often linear. On the other hand, the traditional approach associated with the selected *EM* proves more demanding, not only requiring the need to solve the last-mentioned program in order to know the values of $TI_{EM}(x_o, y_o)$ as well as the *projection* $(\widehat{x}_{oEM}, \widehat{y}_{oEM})$ but also requiring the prior establishment of an *inequality relating economic inefficiency with technical inefficiency*, which can be more or less costly for each efficiency measure.[2] Both proposals end up decomposing economic inefficiency, after normalizing it, into the sum of a technical and an allocative component, but the *direct approach* is more general and reliable, proving easier to implement. It is *general* because it can be applied to any efficiency measure, *easier to implement* because it does not require searching for Fenchel-Mahler inequalities (although the underlying duality holds), and *more reliable* because working with equalities instead of inequalities avoids the possibility of overestimating the allocative inefficiency (i.e., failing to satisfy the essential property presented in Sect. 2.4.5 of Chap. 2). If we are dealing with an efficiency measure that generates a single projection for each firm, then both the traditional and general direct methods are well defined. Otherwise, the

[2]For a fairly complicated case, revise the case of the graph Russell measure developed in Chap. 7.

aforementioned efficiency measure may generate more than one projection for inefficient firms, in which case both methods need to select "the best projection" as well as to follow the same strategy, although proposing two different profit inefficiency decompositions. Worthy of mention is that the directional distance function discussed in Chap. 8 is, as far as we know, the only known efficiency measure whose traditional approach offers exactly the same decomposition as our new direct approach. This connects with Chap. 12, where we show how to express any single-projection efficiency measure in terms of a directional distance function.

Since the initial *basic equality of the general direct approach* only requires the knowledge of a certain projection for each firm, the possibility of applying it for covering different objectives exists. For instance, we may search for projections that are better suited to meet market optimality (e.g., profit maximization) than those obtained by means of the general direct approach combined with a certain efficiency measure. This is precisely the aim of the *two new reverse approaches* of Pastor et al. (2021b, c). While standard approaches start from a technical inefficiency measure and then recover allocative inefficiency as a residual, the new reverse approaches focus first on the allocative performance of firms. *They identify, for each firm, a certain projection*, the profit inefficiency of which is smaller than that corresponding to the evaluated firm, *without resorting to any efficiency measure*. The way to reach the projection is what differentiates the general direct approach and any of the two new reverse approaches. In our first proposal, identified as the *standard reverse (SR) approach*, the reduction in allocative inefficiency is achieved by searching for an appropriate *classical projection*, $(\widehat{x}_{oSR}, \widehat{y}_{oSR})$, which is obtained through a specific linear program. By classical projection, we understand that the *SR projection* $(\widehat{x}_{oSR}, \widehat{y}_{oSR})$ of firm (x_o, y_o) satisfies that $\widehat{x}_{oSR} \leq x_o, \widehat{y}_{oSR} \geq y_o$. Consequently, in the standard reverse approach, the *associated technical inefficiency* is considered as a multiplicative part of a residual and requires its own definition. The *associated inefficiency measure* developed for this purpose has interesting properties. Firstly, it satisfies *the essential property* (see Chap. 2). Secondly, it gives rise to a unique normalization factor for which the *normalized profit inefficiency decomposition* satisfies *the comparison property*, i.e., the three terms of the mentioned decomposition are comparable between firms. And finally, it satisfies also the extended essential property. In our second proposal, identified as the *flexible reverse (FR) approach*, the reduction in allocative efficiency is also obtained through a specific linear program, but now the projection has more degrees of freedom, since the L_1-path that connects each firm with its projection has *unrestricted in sign slacks*. Therefore, the flexible approach may yield larger *allocative reductions* than the standard one, at the expense of defining a technical inefficiency measure for which the associated projections do not satisfy the usual convention that $\widehat{x}_{oEM} \leq x_o, \widehat{y}_{oEM} \geq y_o$. On the other hand, the general direct approach must be slightly modified, giving rise to the generalized direct approach that allows us to consider unrestricted in sign slacks. These come to play a dual role depending on whether efficient or inefficient firms are being projected.

It is worthwhile making a final comment. In the reverse approaches, by focusing first on solving allocative inefficiency, the associated technical inefficiency values are larger, i.e., it implies *a longer path* between a specific firm and its projection on the production frontier. In real-life problems, we always bear in mind that the movement of a company towards its projection can be planned as a finite sequence of small movements over consecutive periods of time. If the firms being evaluated belong to the same organization, it can arouse far more interest to take advantage of the market conditions, reducing as much as possible the allocative inefficiency of each firm when moving from (x_o, y_o) to $(\widehat{x}_{oSR}, \widehat{y}_{oSR})$—e.g., so as to maximize profits—as opposed to being concerned with the length of the path, i.e., the technical performance of the firm only.[3] However, if the production unit has alternative projections with the same allocative reduction in inefficiency, we always recommend selecting the one that gives rise to the shortest path.

As usual and after revising the traditional approaches and introducing the new general direct approach and the two reverse approaches for decomposing profit inefficiency dealing with graph efficiency measures, we will subsequently introduce the cost inefficiency and the revenue inefficiency decompositions based on input-oriented and output-oriented measures, respectively, relying on the same four types of approaches.

13.2 Decomposing Profit Inefficiency

13.2.1 The Traditional Approach Based on a Specific Graph Efficiency Measure

The traditional approach for decomposing economic efficiency corresponds to those investigated in previous chapters, each one based on the corresponding technical efficiency measures. For example, to decompose profit inefficiency for firm (x_o, y_o), the traditional approach resorts to a particular efficiency measure (*EM*) that calculates not only its frontier projection $(\widehat{x}_{oEM}, \widehat{y}_{oEM})$ but also its technical inefficiency $TI_{EM}(x_o, y_o)$.[4] After showing for each *EM* that profit inefficiency is always greater or equal than technical inefficiency times a certain normalizing factor,[5] in all the preceding chapters dealing with non-multiplicative efficiency measures, we have

[3] In this respect, see the illustrative paper of Zofío et al. (2013).

[4] In most cases, the mathematical program used is linear or linearizable.

[5] This "normalizing factor," which is expressed in the same monetary units as the corresponding profit inefficiency, was suggested by economist Marc Nerlove (1965), in order to avoid the dependence of profit inefficiency on proportional price changes. In fact, the normalized profit inefficiencies associated with the different efficiency measures we have been dealing with are pure numbers, derived from the corresponding profit inefficiencies but always independent of proportional price changes.

presented a specific normalized profit inefficiency decomposition as the sum of technical inefficiency and a residual term identified as allocative inefficiency.[6]

To provide a first well-behaved example, let us consider the graph weighted additive distance function of Chap. 6. Reproducing its normalized profit inefficiency decomposition $N\Pi I(x_o, y_o, \rho^-, \rho^+, \widetilde{w}, \widetilde{p})$ in expression (6.7), we have

$$\begin{aligned} N\Pi I_{WA(G)}(x_o, y_o, \rho^-, \rho^+, \widetilde{w}, \widetilde{p}) &= \underbrace{\frac{\Pi(w,p) - (p \cdot y_o - w \cdot x_o)}{\min\left\{\frac{w_1}{\rho_1^-}, \ldots, \frac{w_M}{\rho_M^-}, \frac{p_1}{\rho_1^+}, \ldots, \frac{p_N}{\rho_N^+}\right\}}}_{\text{Normalized Profit Inefficiency}} = \\ &= \underbrace{TI_{WA(G)}(x_o, y_o, \rho^-, \rho^+)}_{\text{Technical Inefficiency}} + \underbrace{AI_{WA(G)}(x_o, y_o, \rho^-, \rho^+, \widetilde{w}, \widetilde{p})}_{\text{Allocative Inefficiency}}, \end{aligned} \tag{13.1}$$

where $\Pi(w, p)$ is maximum profit (see Sect. 2.3.4 in Chap. 2), $(p \cdot y_o - w \cdot x_o)$ is the observed profit of the unit under evaluation (x_o, y_o), ρ^-, ρ^+ are positive weights associated with inputs and outputs, and $\min\left\{\frac{w_1}{\rho_1^-}, \ldots, \frac{w_M}{\rho_M^-}, \frac{p_1}{\rho_1^+}, \ldots, \frac{p_N}{\rho_N^+}\right\}$ is the normalizing factor, written as $NF_{WA(G)}(x_o, y_o, w, p)$. This inefficiency measure has a nice behavior simply because *the normalizing factor* is independent of the production unit being analyzed and, consequently, *is always the same factor for any firm under evaluation*. Consequently, the three terms in the last equality are comparable between firms, and we say that *the normalized decomposition satisfies the comparison property*. This is obviously true for the technical inefficiency associated, in this case, to a specific weighted additive model; it is also true for the left-hand side term because their respective numerators are directly comparable and the denominator is the same for all the firms; and finally, it is true for the last term, the allocative inefficiency, because it has been calculated as a residual. Let us formally define the last-mentioned property, which can be applied to any type of normalized profit inefficiency decomposition.

Definition 13.1 A normalized profit inefficiency decomposition satisfies *the comparison property* if, and only if, the normalizing factor is the same for all the firms.

Unfortunately, the comparison property is unlikely to be achieved. For instance, even when dealing with measures that have relevant properties, such as the directional distance functions (*DDFs*), we find that its largest subset, integrated by the *DDFs* that resort to firm-specific directional vectors, does not satisfy the last property. For instance, a good example is the *proportional DDF* presented in Sect. 8.2.1 of Chap. 8, where the directional vector consists of the observed input and output amounts of the firm under evaluation.

[6]The mentioned inequality is a typical Fenchel-Mahler inequality, derived by resorting to duality results—see each of the preceding chapters devoted to different non-multiplicative efficiency measures, including distance functions, to understand how different the normalization factors are.

Generally speaking, with respect to the traditional approaches, relating normalized profit inefficiency with technical inefficiency through an inequality can be misleading because we may be overestimating allocative inefficiency. The latter situation emerges in a decomposition of economic efficiency which resorts to technical efficiency measures that do not satisfy the essential property, as discussed in Sect. 2.4.5 of Chap. 2. For this reason, we propose in what follows an alternative proposal that, based on equalities, presents several advantages over the traditional approaches.

13.2.2 The General Direct Approach Based on a Specific Graph Measure

Let us start developing *a general direct decomposition of profit inefficiency*, which instead of considering one or more inequalities uses a single equality (see Pastor et al. 2021a). Let us characterize the variable returns to scale (VRS) DEA technology through the following set (see Sect. 2.5.1 in Chap. 2):

$$T = \left\{ (x, y) \colon \sum_{j=1}^{J} \lambda_j x_{jm} \leq x_m, \;\; m = 1, \ldots, M; \;\; \sum_{j=1}^{J} \lambda_j y_{jn} \geq y_n, \;\; n = 1, \ldots, N; \right.$$
$$\left. \sum_{j=1}^{J} \lambda_j = 1, \;\; \lambda_j \geq 0, \;\; j = 1, \ldots, J \right\}. \tag{13.2}$$

We assume that market prices are known for inputs and outputs, as given through the positive vector $(w, p) \in \mathbb{R}_{++}^{M+N}$. We also consider the *maximum profit value* $\Pi(w, p)$ reached by one, or more, economic efficient firm(s) belonging to (13.2). From an empirical perspective, recalling program (2.71) in Sect. 2.5.3 of Chap. 2, maximum profit for a sample of firms is calculated by solving the following DEA linear program:[7]

[7] It is possible that multiple solutions may exist for piecewise linear technologies such as (13.2). This situation arises if several firms maximize profit. We consider this possibility later on in the chapter.

$$\begin{aligned} \Pi(w,p) = \max_{x,y,\lambda} \quad & \sum_{n=1}^{N} p_m y_m - \sum_{m=1}^{M} w_m x_m \\ \text{s.t.} \quad & \sum_{j=1}^{J} \lambda_j x_{jm} \leq x_m, \quad m = 1, \ldots, M, \\ & \sum_{j=1}^{J} \lambda_j y_{jn} \geq y_n, \quad n = 1, \ldots, N, \\ & \sum_{j=1}^{J} \lambda_j = 1, \\ & \lambda \geq 0. \end{aligned} \tag{13.3}$$

Since the profit associated with firm (x_o, y_o) is $(p \cdot y_o - w \cdot x_o)$, it is now possible to define the *profit inefficiency of firm* (x_o, y_o), $\Pi I(x_o, y_o, w, p)$, as the difference between maximum profit and observed profit: $(\Pi(w,p) - (p \cdot y_o - w \cdot x_o))$; i.e., see the numerator of expression (13.1). In our *general direct approach*, we commence with the traditional approach by selecting a particular *graph efficiency measure EM*(G),[8] obtaining its technical inefficiency $TI_{EM}(x_o, y_o)$ and its projection $(\widehat{x}_{oEM}, \widehat{y}_{oEM})$.[9] Our direct method is based on the relation between the profit inefficiencies at (x_o, y_o) and at $(\widehat{x}_{oEM}, \widehat{y}_{oEM})$,[10] which can be formalized through a single equality. We know that these two firms satisfy $\widehat{x}_{oEM} \leq x_o$ and $\widehat{y}_{oEM} \geq y_o$ and that they are also connected by means of an L_1-path, the components of which are the so-called optimal slacks $\left(s_{oEM}^{-*}, s_{oEM}^{+*}\right) \in \mathbb{R}_+^{M+N}$, defined as

[8] In what follows, we write *EM* instead of *EM(G)*, since we will denote oriented measures by *EM(I)* and *EM(O)*.

[9] When evaluating profit, a graph measure is the first choice in preference to any oriented measure because it provides more degrees of freedom in relation to the nonzero input and output slack values. The projection $(\widehat{x}_{oEM}, \widehat{y}_{oEM})$ of any firm (x_o, y_o), obtained by means of the specific *graph efficiency measure (EM)*, is always a frontier point. There are two types of frontier points: Firstly, the strongly efficient points that cannot be reduced for any of the inputs or augmented for any of the outputs without leaving the production possibility set *T* and, secondly, the weakly efficient points, which are not Pareto-Koopmans efficient, by admitting a reduction in some inputs or an expansion in some outputs within *T*. For instance, the variable returns to scale (*VRS*) proportional *DDF* generates projections that can be weakly efficient or strongly efficient, depending on the geometrical location with respect to the efficient frontier of the firm being rated. Only the efficiency measures that are known as strong efficiency measures, such as the ERG = SBM, guarantee that all the projections belong to the strongly efficient subset of the technology, $\partial^S(T)$. See the indication property (E1) in Sect. 2.2 of Chap. 2.

[10] If (x_o, y_o) is an efficient point, then $(\widehat{x}_{oEM}, \widehat{y}_{oEM}) = (x_o, y_o)$. The last equality can also be valid for certain weakly efficient firms and may depend on the efficiency measure used. In any case, the new profit decomposition we develop is valid for any firm.

$$\left(s_{oEM}^{-*}, s_{oEM}^{+*}\right) = \left(x_o - \widehat{x}_{oEM}, \widehat{y}_{oEM} - y_o\right). \tag{13.4}$$

Equivalently, we can write $\left(\widehat{x}_{oEM}, \widehat{y}_{oEM}\right) = (x_o, y_o) + \left(-s_{oEM}^{-*}, s_{oEM}^{+*}\right)$, and being profit-additive in nature, we obtain

$$p \cdot \widehat{y}_{oEM} - w \cdot \widehat{x}_{oEM} = (p \cdot y_o - w \cdot x_o) + \left(p \cdot s_{oEM}^{+*} + w \cdot s_{oEM}^{-*}\right). \tag{13.5}$$

Similarly, by writing the profit inefficiency at $\left(\widehat{x}_{oEM}, \widehat{y}_{oEM}\right)$ and decomposing it with the help of (13.4), we attain the desired relationship:

$$(\Pi(w,p) - (p \cdot \widehat{y}_{oEM} - w \cdot \widehat{x}_{oEM})) = \Pi(w,p) - \left(p \cdot \left(y_o + s_{oEM}^{+*}\right) - w \cdot \left(x_o - s_{oEM}^{-*}\right)\right) =$$
$$(\Pi(w,p) - (p \cdot y_o - w \cdot x_o)) - \left(p \cdot s_{oEM}^{+*} + w \cdot s_{oEM}^{-*}\right).$$

The last equality shows that the first expression is equal to the difference of the two last expressions. By transposing last expression, we isolate the profit inefficiency at (x_o, y_o) and show that it is equal to the sum of the slack expression plus the profit inefficiency at $\left(\widehat{x}_{oEM}, \widehat{y}_{oEM}\right)$, which constitutes our *first basic equality*:

$$\Pi I(x_o, y_o, w, p) = (\Pi(w,p) - (p \cdot y_o - w \cdot x_o)) = \left(p \cdot s_{oEM}^{+*} + w \cdot s_{oEM}^{-*}\right) +$$
$$+ (\Pi(w,p) - (p \cdot \widehat{y}_{oEM} - w \cdot \widehat{x}_{oEM})) = \left(p \cdot s_{oEM}^{+*} + w \cdot s_{oEM}^{-*}\right) + \Pi I\left(\widehat{x}_{oEM}, \widehat{y}_{oEM}, w, p\right). \tag{13.6}$$

The first term and the last two terms in (13.6) are non-negative and expressed in the same monetary units (e.g., dollars ($)). The first right-hand side term, representing the profit loss due to the technological gap between the firm and its *EM* projection, i.e., what we term *technological profit gap*,[11] is intuitively related, at least for measures based on slacks to $TI_{EM}(x_o, y_o)$, the technical inefficiency at point (x_o, y_o). In fact, we are going to decompose it below as the product of $TI_{EM}(x_o, y_o)$ and a certain factor.

Equality (13.6) constitutes the first step for developing our *general direct method*, which is *general* because it maintains the same structure regardless of the graph technical efficiency measure used. In fact, after using it for evaluating the technical inefficiency at point (x_o, y_o), we obtain as relevant by-products the projection $\left(\widehat{x}_{oEM}, \widehat{y}_{oEM}\right)$ and the optimal slack values, according to (13.4). To write down equality (13.6), we only need to add to the former information three profit values which are easy to calculate: *the maximum profit* $\Pi(w,p)$ and *the profits* at firms (x_o, y_o) and $\left(\widehat{x}_{oEM}, \widehat{y}_{oEM}\right)$.[12]

---

[11] Note that it is verified that $((p \cdot \widehat{y}_{oEM} - w \cdot \widehat{x}_{oEM}) - (py_o - wx_o)) = (p \cdot (\widehat{y}_{oEM} - y_o) - w \cdot (\widehat{x}_{oEM} - x_o)) = \left(p \cdot s_{oEM}^{+*} + w \cdot s_{oEM}^{-*}\right)$, where the last equality follows from $(\widehat{x}_{oEM} - x_o) = -s_{oEM}^{-*} \leq 0$. We may also refer to the technological profit gap as *the technological gap at market prices*.

[12] When the projection does not belong to the initial sample of firms, we call it a point, which we know is a convex linear combination of firms.

In order to relate the first right-hand side term in equality (13.6) with the technical inefficiency $TI_{EM}(x_o, y_o)$, we need to distinguish two subsets of firms. The first one corresponds to all the firms that satisfy $TI_{EM}(x_o, y_o) > 0$,[13] while the second one encompasses the rest of the firms for which $TI_{EM}(x_o, y_o) = 0$.[14] For a firm in the first subset, we decompose the *optimal slack term* as a product, multiplying and dividing it by the same number, precisely $TI_{EM}(x_o, y_o)$, obtaining the next equality:

$$0 < \left(ps^{+*}_{oEM} + ws^{-*}_{oEM}\right) = \left(\frac{ps^{+*}_{oEM} + ws^{-*}_{oEM}}{TI_{EM}(x_o, y_o)}\right) \times TI_{EM}(x_o, y_o). \tag{13.7}$$

For all the firms of the first subset, the next proposition holds.

Proposition 13.1 *$TI_{EM}(x_o, y_o) > 0$, if, and only if $(x_o, y_o) \neq (\widehat{x}_{oEM}, \widehat{y}_{oEM})$.*

Proof Let us start assuming that we have identified a single projection for each firm of our sample.[15] The *reverse DDF*, presented in Chap. 12, establishes that any efficiency measure (*EM*) can be formulated as a *DDF* that, for each firm, has exactly the same technical inefficiency value as *EM*. Hence, $0 < TI_{EM}(x_o, y_o) = TI_{RDDF(G)}(x_o, y_o)$. Since *RDDF* is a true *DDF*, the last equality shows that the Euclidean distance from (x_o, y_o) to its projection, which is equal to $TI_{RDDF(G)}(x_o, y_o)$ times the Euclidean length of the corresponding directional vector, is greater than 0. Therefore, $(x_o, y_o) \neq (\widehat{x}_{oEM}, \widehat{y}_{oEM})$. The converse statement is trivial by simply applying the above reasoning in reverse.□

Proposition 13.1 can also be formulated alternatively in three ways, as the next corollary shows.

Corollary 13.1.1 Proposition 13.1 can alternatively be formulated as

1. $TI_{EM}(x_o, y_o) > 0$ *if, and only if* $\left(s^{-*}_{oEM}, s^{+*}_{oEM}\right) \neq 0_{M+N}$.
2. $TI_{EM}(x_o, y_o) = 0$, *if, and only if* $\left(s^{-*}_{oEM}, s^{+*}_{oEM}\right) = 0_{M+N}$.

Proof The proof is left to the reader.

Corollary 13.1 states that if $TI_{EM}(x_o, y_o) > 0$, then $\left(s^{-*}_{oEM}, s^{+*}_{oEM}\right) \neq 0_{M+N}$, which in turn implies that $p \cdot s^{+*}_{oEM} + w \cdot s^{-*}_{oEM} > 0_{\$}$, and vice versa. Summarizing, the first right-hand term of (13.6) can be rewritten as

[13] This subset includes all the inefficient units and, depending on the efficiency measure used, may represent some or all of the weakly efficient firms.

[14] The second one certainly includes all the efficient units and all or some of the weakly efficient firms.

[15] Our general direct approach also deals with efficiency measures that give rise to multiple projections but requires selecting one of them in order to propose the corresponding normalized profit inefficiency decomposition, as we explain later on.

$$\left(p \cdot s_{oEM}^{+*} + w \cdot s_{oEM}^{-*}\right) = \left(\frac{p \cdot s_{oEM}^{+*} + w \cdot s_{oEM}^{-*}}{TI_{EM}(x_o, y_o)}\right) TI_{EM}(x_o, y_o), (x_o, y_o) \neq (\widehat{x}_{oEM}, \widehat{y}_{oEM}). \tag{13.8}$$

Let us now assume that $TI_{EM}(x_o, y_o) = 0$, which implies that $\left(s_{oEM}^{-*}, s_{oEM}^{+*}\right) = 0_{M+N}$ (see last corollary) and consequently

$$\left(ps_{oEM}^{+*} + ws_{oEM}^{-*}\right) = 0_{\$}, (x_o, y_o) = (\widehat{x}_{oEM}, \widehat{y}_{oEM}). \tag{13.9}$$

Combining (13.8) and (13.9) with (13.6), we obtain two *new profit inefficiency decomposition equalities*, (13.10) and (13.11), associated with each firm of the two complementary subsets already considered.

For any firm (x_o, y_o) for which $TI_{EM}(x_o, y_o) > 0$, *its profit inefficiency*, being a positive number expressed in monetary units,[16] *is decomposed as the sum of two terms*, also expressed in the same monetary units, with a positive first term expressed as the product of its technical inefficiency times the factor that appears in (13.8)[17] and a second term representing the profit inefficiency at its projection $(\widehat{x}_{oEM}, \widehat{y}_{oEM})$, which is a non-negative number:[18]

$$(\Pi(w,p) - (p \cdot y_o - w \cdot x_o)) = \left(\frac{p \cdot s_{oEM}^{+*} + w \cdot s_{oEM}^{-*}}{TI_{EM}(x_o, y_o)}\right) \times TI_{EM}(x_o, y_o) + (\Pi(w,p) - (p \cdot \widehat{y}_{oEM} - w \cdot \widehat{x}_{oEM})) \tag{13.10}$$

For any firm (x_o, y_o) for which $TI_{EM}(x_o, y_o) = 0$ (13.8) holds and the equality reduces to

$$(\Pi(w,p) - (p \cdot y_o - w \cdot x_o)) = 0_{\$} + (\Pi(w,p) - (p \cdot \widehat{y}_{oEM} - w \cdot \widehat{x}_{oEM})). \tag{13.11}$$

In both cases, the aforementioned first term of the right-hand side clearly corresponds to the part of the profit inefficiency associated with the technical inefficiency of (x_o, y_o), and therefore, we call it the *technical profit inefficiency at firm* (x_o, y_o).[19] As a consequence, the second term, which is the difference between the *profit inefficiency at* (x_o, y_o) and the *technical profit inefficiency at* (x_o, y_o), can be named as the *allocative profit inefficiency at* (x_o, y_o), which, as already shown, corresponds

[16] Since $TI_{EM}(x_o, y_o) > 0$, (x_o, y_o) cannot maximize profit.

[17] This factor is usually named as the *normalization factor*, as we make clear later on.

[18] The second right-hand side term is $0_{\$}$ if, and only if, the projection is a profit-maximizing point.

[19] A second geometrical intuitive justification is provided by the fact that the first right-hand side term is the difference between the *profit inefficiency at firm* (x_o, y_o) and the *profit inefficiency at* $(\widehat{x}_{oEM}, \widehat{y}_{oEM})$.

to the *profit inefficiency at* $(\widehat{x}_{oEM}, \widehat{y}_{oEM})$.[20] Hence, we can rewrite jointly expressions (13.10) and (13.11) as follows:

$$\begin{aligned} \Pi I(x_o, y_o, w, p) &= T\Pi I_{EM}(x_o, y_o, w, p) + A\Pi I_{EM}(x_o, y_o, w, p), \\ T\Pi I_{EM}(x_o, y_o, w, p) &\geq 0 \end{aligned} \quad (13.12)$$

In relation to (13.12), we face the next three extreme possibilities:

1. $\Pi I(x_o, y_o, w, p) = 0_\$$, which signals that (x_o, y_o) is a profit-maximizing firm. In this case, the firm is necessarily an efficient production plan that belongs to the strongly efficient frontier $\partial^S(T) = \{(x, y) \in T : (x', -y') \leq (x, -y), (x', y') \neq (x, y) \Rightarrow (x', y') \notin T\}$ —see expression (2.2) in Chap. 2. Moreover, its two components also satisfy that $T\Pi I_{EM}(x_o, y_o, w, p) = 0_\$ = A\Pi I_{EM}(x_o, y_o, w, p)$.
2. $T\Pi I_{EM}(x_o, y_o, w, p) = 0_\$$ and $\Pi I(x_o, y_o, w, p) > 0_\$$, which means that $(x_o, y_o) = (\widehat{x}_{oEM}, \widehat{y}_{oEM})$ is a frontier firm. Obviously, all the profit inefficiency is allocative, i.e.,$\Pi I(x_o, y_o, w, p) = A\Pi I_{EM}(x_o, y_o, w, p)$.
3. $A\Pi I_{EM}(x_o, y_o, w, p) = 0_\$$ and $\Pi I(x_o, y_o, w, p) > 0_\$$, which means that the projection $(\widehat{x}_{oEM}, \widehat{y}_{oEM})$ is a profit-maximizing firm.[21] In other words, all the profit inefficiency is technical, i.e.,$\Pi I(x_o, y_o, w, p) = T\Pi I_{EM}(x_o, y_o, w, p)$.

In all the remaining non-extreme possibilities, our new proposed profit inefficiency decomposition at (x_o, y_o) has the advantage that it identifies clearly which part of it is generated by the fact that firm (x_o, y_o) is technically inefficient and which part of it is generated by the profit inefficiency of its projection $(\widehat{x}_{oEM}, \widehat{y}_{oEM})$ when it is not a profit-maximizing benchmark, identified as its profit allocative component. As a summary, profit inefficiency of firm (x_o, y_o) is decomposed into two parts. The first one, the technical profit inefficiency, is nonzero whenever $(x_o, y_o) \neq (\widehat{x}_{oEM}, \widehat{y}_{oEM})$ or, equivalently, when $TI_{EM}(x_o, y_o) > 0$, while the second one, the allocative profit inefficiency, is nonzero whenever $(\widehat{x}_{oEM}, \widehat{y}_{oEM})$ is not a profit-maximizing point.

Uniqueness of the General Direct Profit Decomposition Approach

To achieve *a unique general direct profit decomposition approach*, we must distinguish two disjoint subsets of graph efficiency measures:

1. *The case of efficiency measures with single projections.*

In this case, our general profit decomposition approach is well defined since, for each firm, we obtain a *unique general direct profit decomposition.* This is the case, for example, for any *DDF* measure.

[20] The intuitive geometrical interpretation of the profit allocative term has its roots in the seminal work of Farrell (1957).

[21] The projection always satisfies that $TI_{EM}(\widehat{x}_{oEM}, \widehat{y}_{oEM}) = 0$.

2. *The case of efficiency measures with multiple projections.*

In this case, our general profit decomposition approach is not well defined, since, for each firm with more than one projection, we can obtain as many profit decompositions as different projections are available. Hence, we need to establish a criterion to select the most favorable one. It is clear that the most interesting projection is the one that minimizes profit inefficiency, according to (13.6), or, equivalently, the profit gain when moving from the mentioned firm to its projection is maximized (see (13.5)). In case of ties, we can resort to the second criterion: identify the projection that is L_1-closer to the firm, i.e., the projection that requires less effort in modifying inputs and outputs to reach the projection.

Example 13.1
Let us consider the ERG = SBM measure and Example 7.1 in Chap. 7—illustrated in Fig. 7.1. We are only going to consider the two efficient firms A = (3,5) and B = (6,10) and the inefficient firm F = (10,5). We further initially consider the same price vector $(p, w) = (2, 1)$—see Fig. 13.1. The profit associated with each efficient firm is, in the same order, \$7 and \$14, and it is shown in the mentioned example that (6,10) is the only profit-maximizing firm. The ERG = SBM projects (10,5) on any of the two given efficient firms, with an associated common $TI_{ERG=SBM(G)}(10, 5) = \frac{7}{10}$. As calculated in the mentioned example, $\Pi I(10, 5) = 14 - (2 \cdot 5 - 1 \cdot 10) = 14 - 0 = \$14$, the *profit inefficiency gap* with respect to (6,10) is $2 \cdot 5 + 1 \cdot 4 = \$14$ which means that the *profit allocative inefficiency* equals 0, as expected since (6,10) is a profit-maximizing firm. Moreover, when the projection is (3,5), the profit inefficiency gap is $2 \cdot 0 + 1 \cdot 7 = \$7$, equal to the *profit allocative inefficiency*. Hence, for price vector

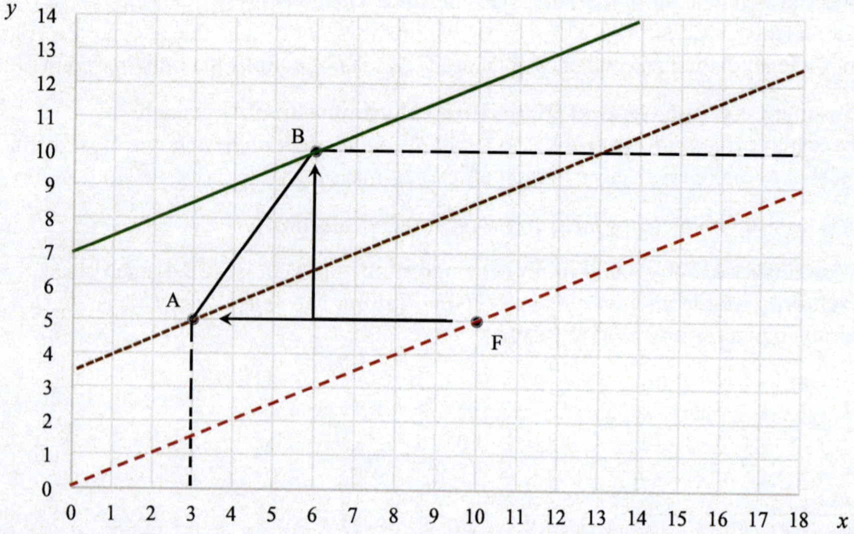

Fig. 13.1 Example of the general direct approach for profit inefficiency decomposition, $(p, w) = (2, 1)$

(2,1), it is clear that the single projection that we have to select is firm B = (6,10). Finally, let us imagine that a new price vector is being considered that has both efficient points as profit-maximizing points. Hence, in order to decide which is the "best" projection, we apply our second criterion that compares both L_1-distances from F to A and B and selects the shortest one. In this case, since $L_1(F,A) = 7$ and $L_1(F,B) = 9$, we prefer firm A = (3,5) as projection of firm F.

The last example is also valid for *revising the functioning of the traditional approach* associated with the same efficiency measure ERG = SBM.

Example 13.2
Considering again the same three firms, A = (3,5), B = (6,10), and F = (10,5), and the same efficiency measure, we get the same technical inefficiency for F, $\frac{7}{10}$, and the possibility of considering either A or B as its projection. According to Example 7.1, the normalization factor for projection A = (3,5) is equal to $\min\{p \cdot y_o, w \cdot x_0\} \times \left(1 + \frac{s_o^{+*}}{y_o}\right) = \min\{2 \cdot 5, 1 \cdot 10\}\left(1 + \frac{5-5}{10}\right) = \$9$, while for the alternative projection B = (6,10) the $NF = \min\{2 \cdot 5, 1 \cdot 10\}\left(1 + \frac{10-5}{10}\right) = 9 \cdot \frac{3}{2} = \$\frac{27}{2}$. The traditional *normalized profit inefficiency decomposition* taking A as the projection gives rise, multiplying by *NF*, to the next *profit inefficiency decomposition*, knowing that $\Pi I(10,5) = \$14$ (see Example 13.1): $\Pi I_A(10,5) = \$14 = NF_A \cdot TI + NF_A.AI_A = 9 \cdot \frac{7}{10} + 9 \cdot AI_A$ or $AI_A = \frac{14}{9} - \frac{7}{10} = \frac{140-63}{90} = \$\frac{77}{90}$. Similarly, for B, we get $\Pi I_B(10,5) = \$14 = NF_B \cdot TI + NF_B.AI_B = \frac{27}{2} \cdot \frac{7}{10} + \frac{27}{2} \cdot AI_B$ and, consequently, $AI_B = \frac{2}{27}\left(14 - \frac{27}{2} \cdot \frac{7}{10}\right) = \frac{28}{27} - \frac{7}{10} = \frac{280-189}{270} = \$\frac{91}{270}$. Since $AI_A = \frac{77}{90} = \$\frac{231}{270}$ is larger than $AI_B = \$\frac{91}{270}$, the traditional approach would also prefer firm B = (6,10) as the best projection. In this example, we also observe that the allocative inefficiency of the traditional approach clearly overestimates the allocative inefficiency of our new general direct approach.

The Normalized Profit Inefficiency Decomposition
We are now ready to propose a *general direct decomposition of the normalized profit inefficiency*, which is derived from *the general direct decomposition of the profit inefficiency* as given by equalities (13.10) and (13.11). For non-efficient firms with more than one projection, we propose selecting the projection that generates the lowest allocative profit inefficiency (see Example 13.2). All we have left to do is to define a *normalization factor* for firms that satisfy $TI_{EM}(x_o, y_o) = 0$ or, equivalently, $(x_o, y_o) = (\widehat{x}_{oEM}, \widehat{y}_{oEM})$ which implies $\left(ps_{oEM}^{+*} + ws_{oEM}^{-*}\right) = 0_\$$.[22] According to (13.11), we can assign any positive numerical value k_o to the normalization factor associated with (x_o, y_o), without forgetting that it must be expressed in the same monetary units as the market prices, that is, $k_{o\$}$.[23] Our proposal follows:

---

[22] See Corollary 13.1.

[23] Clearly $k_{o\$} \cdot TI_{EM}(x_o, y_o) = k_{o\$} \cdot 0 = 0_\$$, with k_o being any positive number. We prefer to fix the value of k_o for each firm (x_o, y_o) when it can be determinant for achieving some desirable property, such as the comparison property, or when we want to compare different decomposition approaches, as described in the next subsection.

$$NF_{EM}^{GD}(x_o, y_o, w, p) = \left\{ \begin{array}{l} \dfrac{(p \cdot s_{EM}^{+*} + w \cdot s_{EM}^{-*})}{TI_{EM}(x_o, y_o)}, (x_o, y_o) \neq (\widehat{x}_{oEM}, \widehat{y}_{oEM}) \\ k_{o\$}, k_o > 0 \quad , (x_o, y_o) = (\widehat{x}_{oEM}, \widehat{y}_{oEM}) \end{array} \right\}. \quad (13.13)$$

According to (13.13), our new *general direct approach associated with any graph measure* has the flexibility of assigning an undetermined normalization factor, $k_{o\$}$, to any frontier firm (x_o, y_o) that is projected onto itself, $(\widehat{x}_{oEM}, \widehat{y}_{oEM}) = (x_o, y_o)$. However, to propose a satisfactory decomposition, let us make some specific suggestions.

Four Options for Assigning Normalization Factor Values to $k_{o\$}$
When using the general direct profit decomposition approach, the problem to be solved is to assign a normalizing factor to the frontier firms (x_o, y_o) satisfying $TI_{EM}(x_o, y_o) = 0$ or, equivalently, to firms satisfying $(\widehat{x}_{oEM}, \widehat{y}_{oEM}) = (x_o, y_o)$. The first three options deal with a single graph efficiency measure and with the mentioned profit decomposition approach, while the fourth option also deals with a single graph efficiency measure but with two different profit decomposition approaches that we would like to compare.

Option 1. The frontier firm (x_o, y_o) is only the projection of itself. In this case, we assign to it a normalization factor equal to 1. This decision guarantees that the allocative inefficiencies are comparable between frontier firms with this particularity.

Option 2. Let us now assume that the frontier firm (x_o, y_o) is also the projection of just another inefficient firm, $(x_j, y_j) \neq (x_o, y_o)$ and $(\widehat{x}_{jEM}, \widehat{y}_{jEM}) = (x_o, y_o)$. Since (x_j, y_j) has its own normalization factor, we propose to assign it to (x_o, y_o). This hardly ever occurs, but in the case that (x_o, y_o) is the projection of two or more inefficient firms and all of them have the same normalization factor, we would make the same decision.

Option 3. In general, let us assume that the frontier firm (x_o, y_o) is the projection of two or more inefficient firms. In this case, we propose to assign to it the normalization factor of the inefficient firm that is L_1-closer to (x_o, y_o).[24]

Option 4. In case we are comparing the traditional approach with the general direct approach for a certain graph efficiency measure, our fourth option is to assign the value of the normalization factor of the traditional approach to the firms that are projected onto themselves (see, for example, Example 13.3).

First of all, let us point out that we have deliberately omitted in the definition of the normalization factor its dependence from the projection through the optimal slacks, which is justified whenever the projection is unique. However, we should not forget this dependency, which will appear later when comparing the traditional and the general direct approaches. Since the general direct normalization factor, $NF_{EM}^{GD}(x_o, y_o, w, p)$, is always positive, we can derive the same equality from

[24] This proposal guarantees that at least the closest inefficient firm has the same allocative inefficiency as its projection.

(13.10) and (13.11), achieving the *normalized profit inefficiency decomposition for the general direct approach*:

$$\frac{(\Pi(w,p)-(p\cdot y_o-w\cdot x_o))}{NF_{EM}^{GD}(x_o,y_o,w,p)}=TI_{EM}(x_o,y_o)+\frac{(\Pi(w,p)-(p\cdot \widehat{y}_o-w\cdot \widehat{x}_o))}{NF_{EM}^{GD}(x_o,y_o,w,p)}. \tag{13.14}$$

Realizing that the two fractions of (13.14) have exactly the same structure, we may consider the next equivalent expression for the last decomposition:

$$N\Pi I_{EM}(x_o,y_o,\widetilde{w},\widetilde{p})=TI_{EM}(x_o,y_o)+N\Pi I_{EM}(\widehat{x}_{oEM},\widehat{y}_{oEM},\widetilde{w},\widetilde{p}). \tag{13.15}$$

Equality (13.15) shows that, generally speaking, *allocative inefficiency* obtained traditionally as a residual term when working with inequalities *is obtained directly* through the new proposed approach as a second term when working with equalities. Moreover and as already noted above, it provides a *new general geometrical and intuitive interpretation of allocative inefficiency*:

$$AI_{EM}(x_o,y_o,\widetilde{w},\widetilde{p})=A\Pi I_{EM}(x_o,y_o,\widetilde{w},\widetilde{p})=N\Pi I_{EM}(\widehat{x}_{oEM},\widehat{y}_{oEM},\widetilde{w},\widetilde{p}). \tag{13.16}$$

In other words, *the allocative inefficiency associated with firm* (x_o, y_o) *is equal to the normalized profit inefficiency of the projection* $(\widehat{x}_{oEM},\widehat{y}_{oEM})$.

Our *general direct normalized profit inefficiency decomposition* based on a single equality (see (13.14) or (13.15)) is valid for any efficiency measure and, consequently, assumes that we need to start deciding on what efficiency measure to use. This decision implies that for each production firm (x_o, y_o), we start determining the technical inefficiency, $TI_{EM}(x_o, y_o)$, as well as its projection $(\widehat{x}_{oEM},\widehat{y}_{oEM})$. These two elements are all we need for completing proposal (13.15), our *general direct normalized profit inefficiency decomposition*. The latter's most relevant feature is that it offers a general unified approach with a clear geometrical interpretation.

From now on, when defining or considering a new efficiency measure, if wishing to use a profit inefficiency decomposition, there is no need to resort to duality tools, in order to find the specific Fenchel-Mahler inequality relating profit inefficiency with technical inefficiency, with the added concern that the obtained inequality, based on mathematical programming, may not be rigorous enough, allowing in certain cases, an inaccurate overestimation of the allocative inefficiency. Instead, we consider equality (13.14) associated with *the general direct approach*, in order to obtain, for each firm under scrutiny, its normalized general direct profit inefficiency decomposition. Our new proposal is a reliable method because the exclusive use of equalities guarantees that allocative inefficiency can never be wrongly estimated, being directly related to the used projection. It is also a more flexible method because in (13.13) we can choose the different k_o values for the different production firms (x_o, y_o) that satisfy $(x_o,y_o)=(\widehat{x}_{oEM},\widehat{y}_{oEM})$. Moreover and as already explained, it is easy to apply, and finally, it provides a unifying framework, since (13.14) is defined for any current or future efficiency measure.

One final question deserves consideration:

Do the traditional and the general direct approach guarantee the uniqueness of the corresponding profit inefficiency decompositions?

We anticipate the need to distinguish two alternative possibilities, determined by the *EM* considered and for which in both cases the answer is affirmative. The first case is when *EM* is a single-projection function, i.e., when each firm gets a single *EM* projection. The second case is when *EM* is a multi-projection function, which means that at least one firm obtains multiple *EM* projections.

First case: Each firm gets a single projection. In this case, there are no alternative options, and, consequently, the obtained profit inefficiency decompositions in any of the two approaches are unique.

Second case: At least one firm gets more than one projection, and all the projections have the same technical inefficiency. In order to ensure *the unicity property*, we need to introduce an additional criterion for choosing among the alternative projections, whenever the normalizing factor depends on them. For *the traditional approaches*, we have found *only one efficiency measure*, the *ERG* = *SBM*. According to Aparicio et al. (2017a), the normalizing factor in this case is equal to $\min\left\{,\frac{w_1}{\rho_1^-},\ldots,\frac{w_M}{\rho_M^-},\frac{p_1}{\rho_1^+},\ldots\frac{p_N}{\rho_N^+}\right\}\cdot\left(1+\frac{1}{N}\sum_{n=1}^{N}\frac{s_{on}^{+*}}{y_{on}}\right)$, which clearly depends on the output slacks that connect the inefficient firm (x_o, y_o) with its frontier projection $(\widehat{x}_{oEM}, \widehat{y}_{oEM})$. Since the technical inefficiency is constant, we propose the next criterion: *select the projection that minimizes the allocative inefficiency* or, equivalently, *that generates the biggest normalizing factor* (see the two first examples in this chapter).[25] For *the general direct approach*, there are a few more cases, such as the weighted additive model. For this second approach, we use exactly the same criteria in order to preserve the uniqueness of the decompositions. Our next example, based on the *ERG* = *SBM*, shows numerical results for both approaches applied to the same sample of firms.

13.2.3 *Profit Inefficiency Decompositions Based on a Traditional Approach and on the General Direct Approach: A Comparison, a Numerical Example, and Some Properties of the Direct Approach*

When dealing with graph efficiency measures, we have differentiated between the traditional approaches and the general direct approach. In Sect. 13.1, we have already pointed out that each traditional approach associated with a certain graph

[25] As explained in Chap. 7, it corresponds also to the projection with the highest profit.

measure needs to search for a specific Fenchel-Mahler inequality that shows that profit inefficiency is greater than or equal to technical inefficiency times a certain positive normalizing factor. Hence, each graph measure requires finding a specific inequality, and this is the reason for talking about *the traditional approaches* in plural. On the other hand, in Sect. 13.2, we have introduced *the general direct approach* of Pastor et al. (2021a) *that resorts to a single equality*, decomposing profit inefficiency into two terms with exactly the same structure for any graph efficiency measure. For each firm being analyzed, the first term is related to the L_1-path that connects the mentioned firm and its frontier projection, and the second term of the decomposition is always the profit inefficiency of its projection. Hence, the *general direct approach* is based on the same decomposition for any graph measure, and this is the reason why we talk about the general direct approach in singular.

Let us now consider a specific graph efficiency measure (*EM*). For each firm under evaluation (x_o, y_o), both approaches, the traditional and the general direct approach, need to know its technical inefficiency $TI_{EM}(x_o, y_o)$ and associated projection $(\widehat{x}_{oEM}, \widehat{y}_{oEM})$. In the traditional approach, the only economic inefficiency that has been decomposed so far is its *normalized profit inefficiency*, that is, its profit inefficiency divided by the corresponding normalizing factor, which is greater than or equal to its *technical inefficiency*. Subsequently, the *allocative inefficiency at* (x_o, y_o) is retrieved as a residual by subtracting the *technical inefficiency at* (x_o, y_o) from the *normalized profit inefficiency at* (x_o, y_o). Hence, in the traditional approach associated with a given *EM*, the *normalized profit inefficiency* associated with a given firm is decomposed as the sum of its *technical inefficiency* and its *allocative inefficiency*, requiring previous knowledge of the Fenchel-Mahler inequality associated with the *EM* and relating the first two concepts.

On the other hand, the *general direct approach* starts differently, decomposing the *profit inefficiency at firm* (x_o, y_o) as the sum of two terms, which we have identified as the *technological profit gap at* (x_o, y_o), which is exactly the sum of the products of each input and output slacks by their respective market prices, and the *allocative profit inefficiency at firm* (x_o, y_o), which is exactly the *profit inefficiency at its projection* $(\widehat{x}_{oEM}, \widehat{y}_{oEM})$. In a second step, the general direct approach breaks up the *technological profit gap*, called *the technical profit inefficiency at* (x_o, y_o) (*TΠI*), as the product of $TI_{EM}(x_o, y_o)$ times a certain factor, expressed in monetary units and called *normalization factor*, which leads to the corresponding *normalized profit inefficiency decomposition* associated with *the general direct approach*. To finish the argument and in order to compare both approaches, we only need to propose a *profit inefficiency decomposition for the traditional approach*. Starting with the *normalized profit inefficiency decomposition at firm* (x_o, y_o) of any traditional approach and proceeding backwards, we observe that the *profit inefficiency at* (x_o, y_o), which is equal to the *normalized profit inefficiency multiplied by the normalizing factor*, can be decomposed as *the technical inefficiency multiplied by the normalizing factor* plus the *allocative inefficiency multiplied also by the same normalizing factor*. Hence, for the traditional approach based on the efficiency measure (*EM*), the corresponding *profit inefficiency decomposition* consists of two components that are also related to technical inefficiency and to allocative inefficiency, $\Pi I_{EM}^{TR}(x_o, y_o, , \widetilde{w}, \widetilde{p}) = T\Pi I_{EM}^{TR}(x_o, y_o, , \widetilde{w}, \widetilde{p}) + A\Pi I_{EM}^{TR}(x_o, y_o, , \widetilde{w}, \widetilde{p})$, but that are in principle different to the corresponding components of the general direct approach. Being more precise, the two components, *the technical profit inefficiency* and *the allocative profit inefficiency*, associated with *the traditional approach* are defined as

$$T\Pi I_{EM}^{TR}(x_o, y_o, , \widetilde{w}, \widetilde{p}) = NF_{EM}^{TR}(x_o, y_o, , \widetilde{w}, \widetilde{p}) \times TI_{EM}(x_o, y_o),$$
$$A\Pi I_{EM}^{TR}(x_o, y_o, , \widetilde{w}, \widetilde{p}) = \Pi I_{EM}^{TR}(x_o, y_o, , \widetilde{w}, \widetilde{p}) - T\Pi I_{EM}^{TR}(x_o, y_o, , \widetilde{w}, \widetilde{p}).$$

Prior to showing a comparison based on a numerical example, let us summarize the basic steps required in the two mentioned approaches.

13.2.3.1 Comparison: Traditional Approach Versus General Direct Approach

We assume that both approaches are based on the same efficiency measure $\overline{EM}$.

Traditional Approach

First Step: Select $\overline{EM}$; *calculate for each* (x_o, y_o) *its projection*, $(\widehat{x}_{o\overline{EM}}, \widehat{y}_{o\overline{EM}})$, its *technical inefficiency*, $TI_{\overline{EM}}(x_o, y_o)$, and its *profit inefficiency* $\Pi I(x_o, y_o, w, p)$.

Second Step: Through duality, as shown in previous chapters, find for $\overline{EM}$ *a Fenchel-Mahler inequality with a positive normalizing factor that satisfies* $\Pi I_{\overline{EM}}^{TR}(x_o,y_o,w,p) \geq NF_{\overline{EM}}^{TR}(x_o,y_o,w,p) \cdot TI_{\overline{EM}}(x_o,y_o)$ *for all* (x_o,y_o). *When* (x_o,y_o) *has multiple projections, and the traditional normalization factor is not unique, select the factor associated with the projection that provides the highest profit. Based on the last inequality,* retrieve $A\Pi I_{\overline{EM}}^{TR}(x_o,y_o,\widetilde{w},\widetilde{p})$ *as a residual, and formulate* the profit inefficiency decomposition $\Pi I_{\overline{EM}}^{TR}(x_o,y_o,w,p) = NF_{\overline{EM}}^{TR}(x_o,y_o,w,p) \cdot TI_{\overline{EM}}(x_o,y_o) + A\Pi I_{\overline{EM}}^{TR}(x_o,y_o,w,p)$.

Third Step: Retrieve $AI_{\overline{EM}}^{TR}(x_o, y_o, \widetilde{w}, \widetilde{p})$ *as a residual, and get the normalized profit inefficiency decomposition:* $\frac{\Pi I(x_o, y_o, w, p)}{NF_{\overline{EM}}^{TR}(x_o, y_o, w, p)} = TI_{\overline{EM}}(x_o, y_o) + AI_{\overline{EM}}^{TR}(x_o, y_o, \widetilde{w}, \widetilde{p})$.□

General Direct Approach

First Step: The same as for any traditional approach.

Second Step: Leave out $TI_{\overline{EM}}(x_o, y_o)$. *For* $\overline{EM}$, *calculate* $\Pi I(\widehat{x}_{o\overline{EM}}, \widehat{y}_{o\overline{EM}}, w, p)$, *and deduce* $\left(p \cdot s_{o\overline{EM}}^{+*} + w \cdot s_{o\overline{EM}}^{-*}\right)$. *In case one or more firms have multiple projections, select for each of these firms a projection with the highest profit. After calculating* $\left(p \cdot s_{o\overline{EM}}^{+*} + w \cdot s_{o\overline{EM}}^{-*}\right)$, obtain the *next general direct profit inefficiency decomposition*, $\Pi I(x_o, y_o, w, p) = \left(p \cdot s_{o\overline{EM}}^{+*} + w \cdot s_{o\overline{EM}}^{-*}\right) + \Pi I_{EM}(\widehat{x}_{o\overline{EM}}, \widehat{y}_{o\overline{EM}}, w, p)$.

Third Step: Recover $TI_{\overline{EM}}(x_o, y_o)$, *and based on* $\left(p \cdot s^{+*}_{o\overline{EM}} + w \cdot s^{-*}_{o\overline{EM}}\right)$, *obtain* $NF^{GD}_{\overline{EM}}(x_o, y_o, w, p) > 0_\$$.[26] *Divide each term of the profit inefficiency decomposition by the normalizing factor, and obtain the corresponding normalized general direct profit inefficiency decomposition*:

$$N\Pi I^{GD}_{\overline{EM}}(x_o, y_o, \widetilde{w}, \widetilde{p}) = \frac{\Pi I(x_o, y_o, w, p)}{NF^{GD}_{\overline{EM}}(x_o, y_o, w, p)} = TI_{\overline{EM}}(x_o, y_o) + \frac{\Pi I(\widehat{x}_o, \widehat{y}_o, w, p)}{NF^{GD}_{\overline{EM}}(x_o, y_o, w, p)} = \\ = TI_{\overline{EM}}(x_o, y_o) + AI^{GD}_{\overline{EM}}(x_o, y_o, \widetilde{w}, \widetilde{p}). \tag{13.17}$$

Let us start developing a numerical example for comparing both approaches by resorting to the well-known efficiency measure *ERG* = *SBM* (see Chap. 7). We are going to consider a simple example with only one input and one output, so that the firms under scrutiny can be easily visualized, as well as their slack inefficiencies and their profit inefficiencies.

Example 13.3
Let us now consider the next "one input-one output example" with nine firms: A = (3,5), B = (6,10), C = (9,11), D = (12,12), E = (3,2), F = (10,5), G = (12,2), H = (12,11), and I = (16,12). Under VRS, we get that the first four firms are strongly efficient, firms E and I are weakly efficient, and the other three firms are inefficient. Moreover, there are only two efficient facets: the segment connecting firms A = (3, 5) and B = (6, 10) and the segment connecting firms B = (6, 10) and D= (12, 12), to which firm C = (9, 11) belongs. Let us further assume that the vector of prices (per unit) is $(p, w) = (6, 1)$. Hence, at each efficient firm, A = (3,5), B = (6,10), C = (9,11), and D = (12,12), the profit is equal to \$30–\$3 = \$27, \$60–\$6 = \$54, \$66–\$9 = \$57, and \$72–\$12 = \$60, which means that the only profit-maximizing firm is D = (12,12). Figure 13.2 illustrates the example, including the maximum isoprofit green line located at its top.

Let us resort to the *ERG* = *SBM* technical inefficiency (see Chap. 7), which is equal to $\dfrac{\frac{s^*_o}{x_o} + \frac{s^{+*}_o}{y_o}}{1 + \frac{s^{+*}_o}{y_o}}$. The technical inefficiency can be checked directly by looking at the optimal slacks. Our first profit inefficiency decomposition analysis corresponds to *the traditional approach* and *appears in* Table 13.1.

Prior to analyzing it, let us remind the reader that following Aparicio et al. (2017a), we have shown in Chap. 7 the best—or more tightened—normalizing factor associated with the *ERG* = *SBM* with its corresponding Fenchel-Mahler inequality. The mentioned factor, *NF*, for firm (x_o, y_o) and for the one input-one

[26]For each firm that is projected onto itself, select the fourth option described before.

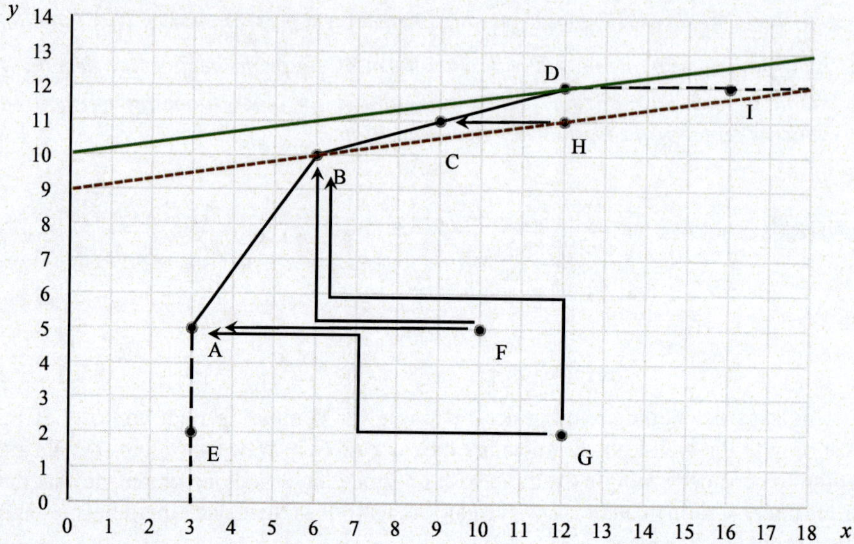

Fig. 13.2 Example of the traditional and general approaches for decomposing profit inefficiency, $(p, w) = (6, 1)$

output case, is equal to $\left(1 + \frac{s_o^{+*}}{y_o}\right) \cdot \min\{p \cdot y_o, w \cdot x_o\}$. The choice of this factor is tied to the selection of *the best projection* for each inefficient firm. In a profit-maximizing context, we should prefer the one that has the highest profit. In our example, there are just two inefficient firms, F = (10,5) and G = (12,2), with multiple optimal projections. Both firms can be projected to either firm A = (3,5) or firm B = (6,10). Since we have just calculated the profit for all the efficient firms, we know that the profits of A = (3,5) and B = (6,10) are \$27 and \$54, respectively. Consequently, the best projection for both firms is B = (6,10). After making this choice, we are ready to calculate the aforementioned normalizing factor.

Table 13.1 is organized as follows: the first column lists the firms of our sample, starting with the efficient ones in bold type. The next three columns, the *best projection*, *the technical inefficiency (TI)*, and *the profit inefficiency (ΠI)*, correspond to the three items calculated in the first step of *the traditional approach*. Next column 5 shows the obtained *normalization factors* (*NF*) according to the above expression. The two next columns have been added in order to compare them with the corresponding columns of the following Table 13.2 and reports on the two components of the *profit inefficiency decomposition* in monetary terms.[27] The first one, the *technical profit inefficiency (TΠI)* is obtained directly by multiplying the technical inefficiency by the normalizing factor, and the second one, the *allocative profit inefficiency (AΠI)* is retrieved as a residual, $A\Pi I = \Pi I - T\Pi I$. The two last

[27]The traditional approaches do not usually consider this type of decomposition.

Table 13.1 Results based on the traditional best decomposition of Aparicio et al. (2017a), $(p,w) = (6,1)$

Firm	$ERG = SBM\ projection$	TI	ΠI	NF	$T\Pi I = TI \times NF$	$A\Pi I = \Pi I - T\Pi I$	$N\Pi I = \Pi I/NF$	$AI = N\Pi I - TI$
(1)	(2)	(3)	(4)	(5)	(6) = (3) × (5)	(7) = (4)–(6)	(8) = (4)/(5)	(9) = (8)–(3)
A = (3,5)	(3,5)	0	33	3	0	33	11	11
B = (6,10)	(6,10)	0	6	6	0	6	1	1
C = (9,11)	(9,11)	0	3	9	0	3	1/3	1/3
D = (12,12)	(12,12)	0	0	12	0	0	0	0
E = (3,2)	(3,5)	3/5	51	15/2	9/2	93/2	34/5	31/5*
F = (10,5)	(6,10)	7/10	40	20	14	26	2	13/10*
G = (12,2)	(6,10)	9/10	60	60	54	6	1	1/10
H = (12,11)	(9,11)	1/4	6	12	3	3	1/2	1/4
I = (16,12)	(12,12)	1/4	4	16	4	0	1/4	0

columns, with the addition of the third column, give the normalized profit inefficiency decomposition based on the traditional approach for each firm, where the last column, reporting the *allocative inefficiency (AI)*, is also retrieved as a residual, $AI = N\Pi I - TI$.

Let us now apply our *general direct decomposition* to the same sample of firms, summarizing the results in Table 13.2. We maintain the ordering of the columns to ease the comparison between Tables 13.1 and 13.2. Each column is devoted to the same concept in the two tables, but to calculate them, we proceed differently, starting with column 5. We can appreciate that the first four columns in both tables are equal, with the second and the third columns dependent on the efficiency measure used, while the fourth column depends on market prices. The rest of the columns are different. In fact, if the normalization factors reported in column 5 were the same for each firm in both tables, then the results would be equal. But they are not. However, both columns 5 are rather similar. Besides the values of the normalization factors for the efficient firms that we have copied from the first to the second table, according to option 2 introduced below former expression (13.13), three out of the remaining five inefficient firms have exactly the same normalization factor in both tables. Curiously enough, all the subsequent columns show the same behavior, simply because the concepts they deal with are all derived from columns 3, 4, and 5. Hence, only the rows of firms E = (3,2) and F = (10,5) are different in the two tables, from column 5 to column 9. If we compare the data of the last column between tables for these two firms, we see that *the allocative inefficiency values* in Table 13.1 are greater than in the table below, $31/5 = 6.2 > 11/10 = 1.1$ and $13/10 = 1.3 > 21/170 \simeq 0.1$, indicating a considerable overestimation in the traditional approach with respect to the new general direct approach. These values have been marked with an "*" in the last column of both tables.

In Table 13.2, we can verify that each of the inefficient firms now exhibit the same allocative profit inefficiency value as its respective projections (see column 7), which is a consequence of equality (13.10) and corresponds to our geometrical intuition, and which does not happen in Table 13.1, with the firms E = (3,2) and F = (10,5) proving the exceptions once again. This is a strong reason for recommending the evaluation of the profit inefficiency decomposition in monetary values, as we have done in the two last tables (although at the cost of not being units' independent, i.e., failing to satisfy the commensurability property (P6) presented in Sect. 2.3.5 of Chap. 2). In contrast, we see in Table 13.2 that allocative inefficiencies are not directly comparable, the reason being that the corresponding normalization factors are different. However, the only firms that can be compared through the last column are those that obtain an *allocative inefficiency value equal to* 0, which correspond precisely to the two firms that are projected to the only profit-maximizing firm D. According to Sect. 2.4.5 in Chap. 2, we say that the corresponding *efficiency measure satisfies the essential property for the considered sample of firms*. Therefore, in this particular example, the $ERG = SBM$ satisfies the essential property both with the traditional approach and with the general direct approach. However, in Chap. 2, we have shown that, in general, very few efficiency measures always satisfy

Table 13.2 Results based on the general direct decomposition, $(p,w) = (6,1)$

Firm	*ERG* = *SBM projection*	*TI*	Π*I*	*NF*	*T*Π*I* = *TI* × *NF*	*A*Π*I*= Π*I* -*T*Π*I*	Π*I*/*NF*	*AI* = *A*Π*I* /*NF*
(1)	(2)	(3)	(4)	(5)	(6) = (3) × (5)	(7) = (4)–(6)	(8) = (4)/(5)	(9) = (7)/(5)
A = (3,5)	(3,5)	0	33	3!	0	33	11	11
B = (6,10)	(6,10)	0	6	6!	0	6	1	1
C = (9,11)	(9,11)	0	3	9!	0	3	1/3	1/3
D = (12,12)	(12,12)	0	0	12!	0	0	0	0
E = (3,2)	(3,5)	3/5	51	30	18	33	17/10	11/10*
F = (10,5)	(6,10)	7/10	40	340/7	34	6	14/17	21/170*
G = (12,2)	(6,10)	9/10	60	60	54	6	1	1/10
H = (12,11)	(9,11)	1/4	6	12	3	3	½	1/4
I = (16,12)	(12,12)	1/4	4	16	4	0	1/4	0

the essential property when resorting to the traditional normalized profit inefficiency decomposition based on duality. The $ERG = SBM$ is not among them.

Fortunately, the general direct approach has a better behavior than the traditional approach with respect to *the essential property*. In what follows, we are going to prove that the essential property is always satisfied by the normalized general direct profit inefficiency decomposition by means of next proposition.

Proposition 13.2 The normalized general direct profit inefficiency decomposition always satisfies the essential property, regardless of the graph efficiency measure used.

Proof According to (13.17), the normalized general direct profit inefficiency decomposition identifies the allocative inefficiency associated with any firm (x_o, y_o) as $\frac{\left(\Pi(w,p)-\left(p\cdot\widehat{y}_{oEM}-w\cdot\widehat{x}_{oEM}\right)\right)}{NF^{GD}_{EM}(x_o,y_o,w,p)}$. Similarly, the same decomposition delivers the allocative inefficiency associated with its projection, $\frac{\left(\Pi(w,p)-\left(p\cdot\widehat{y}_{oEM}-w\cdot\widehat{x}_{oEM}\right)\right)}{NF^{GD}_{EM}\left(\widehat{x}_{oEM},\widehat{y}_{oEM},w,p\right)}$. The essential property establishes that whenever the allocative inefficiency of $\left(\widehat{x}_{oEM},\widehat{y}_{oEM}\right)$ is 0, then the allocative inefficiency of (x_o, y_o) must also be 0. But $\frac{\left(\Pi(w,p)-\left(p\cdot\widehat{y}_{oEM}-w\cdot\widehat{x}_{oEM}\right)\right)}{NF^{GD}_{EM}\left(\widehat{x}_{oEM},\widehat{y}_{oEM},w,p\right)} = 0$ if, and only if, its numerator is equal to 0. Since the allocative inefficiency of (x_o, y_o) has exactly the same numerator, the proof is done.□

Based again on the two last expressions corresponding to the allocative inefficiency associated with (x_o, y_o) and $\left(\widehat{x}_{oEM},\widehat{y}_{oEM}\right)$, it is easy to establish a necessary and sufficient condition that guarantees that the normalized general direct profit inefficiency decomposition satisfies *the extended essential property*, introduced in Chap. 2. The proof is left to the reader.

Proposition 13.3
The normalized general direct profit inefficiency decomposition satisfies *the extended essential property* if and only if the normalizing factor associated with (x_o, y_o) is equal to the normalizing factor associated with its projection $\left(\widehat{x}_{oEM},\widehat{y}_{oEM}\right)$, regardless of the graph efficiency measure used.

The last proposition is very demanding. For instance, it requires that all the inefficient firms that have the same projection must also have the same normalizing factor. The next corollary establishes a sufficient—and restrictive—condition that guarantees the satisfaction of the *extended essential property*. Its proof is also straightforward.

Corollary 13.3.1
The normalized general direct profit inefficiency decomposition satisfies *the extended essential* property provided the next condition holds: any firm of the sample being considered whose technical inefficiency is equal to 0 can only be the projection of itself or the projection of itself and a single inefficient firm.

Note

In the first case, we assign to it a normalizing factor equal to 1, and in the second case, its normalizing factor is defined as the normalizing factor of the unique inefficient firm (x_o, y_o) that is projected onto it. The second case corresponds to former option 3 for assigning a normalizing factor to each frontier firm.

It is difficult for the traditional approaches to satisfy the *extended essential* property. For instance, Table 13.1 shows that $ERG = SBM$ does not satisfy it. As far as we know, only the *DDFs* satisfy this property, under certain hypotheses, as explained again in the next subsection.

Considering Tables 13.1 and 13.2 again, we would like to compare the non-normalized allocative terms listed in column 7. As already mentioned, there are only two firms that obtain different values in both tables: E = (3,2) and F = (10,5). In both cases, the value in Table 13.1 is greater than the value in Table 13.2: 93/2 > 33, and 26 > 6. It signals that, for these two firms, the Fenchel-Mahler inequality used is overestimating its allocative component.

The improvement of our general direct decomposition over the traditional ones is that we use a single equality exclusively in order to relate profit inefficiency with technical inefficiency for each firm (x_o, y_o). Moreover, our equality identifies two additive components of profit inefficiency, the technical profit inefficiency component and the allocative profit inefficiency component (see (13.10), (13.11), and (13.12)). The first component offers directly the normalization factor that can be different for each firm (see (13.13)), and dividing the last equality, we get the normalized profit inefficiency decomposition as the sum of technical inefficiency and allocative inefficiency (see (13.14)). As already pointed out, the *allocative profit inefficiency component* of (x_o, y_o) is exactly the *profit inefficiency of its projection* $(\widehat{x}_o, \widehat{y}_o)$ (see (13.10) and (13.11)), which guarantees that *all the firms that have the same projection get the same allocative profit inefficiency*. The latter corresponds with the intuitive geometrical ideas of Farrell (1957), represented in Fig. 13.1 by the parallel lines passing through firm D and through firms B and H.

As we have seen in our last example, the last intuitive property is not satisfied by the traditional approach considered. Summarizing, any traditional approach can be replaced by the general direct approach for performing a profit inefficiency decomposition as well as the corresponding normalized profit inefficiency decomposition, without resorting to the underlying Fenchel-Mahler inequality. Moreover, our recently developed approach is ready to be used for decomposing the profit inefficiency of any new efficiency measure that can be proposed in the future, without the need to derive a new Fenchel-Mahler inequality.

13.2.4 The Exceptional Case of the Directional Graph Distance Function

Interestingly, we are going to show that for any graph DDF (also called the directional graph distance function), its normalized profit inefficiency decomposition derived resorting to the traditional approach is exactly the same as the one derived with our general direct decomposition. In other words, in this case, the Fenchel-Mahler inequality associated with the DDF is strict enough to guarantee that the allocative inefficiency is correctly estimated. As far as we know, it is the only graph inefficiency measure that satisfies this property, and, consequently, we tag it as an *exceptional case*. Moreover, *the general direct approach*, even though it does not depend on any Fenchel-Mahler inequality, can also be interpreted as *an extension* of the well-known *graph DDF profit inefficiency decomposition to any other graph-oriented efficiency measure*, provided the efficiency measure assigns a single projection to each firm.[28] As aforementioned, if the inefficiency measure we are considering does not generate multiple projections, then *the normalized profit inefficiency decomposition associated with the general direct approach is unique*, which is the case of the *graph DDF*.

We have already pointed out in Example 13.3 when comparing Tables 13.1 and 13.2 the relevance of the normalization factor. In what follows, we are going to show that the usual normalization factor of the traditional approach for any directional graph distance function is coincident with the normalization factor of the direct approach. In other words, both decompositions are the same. In the traditional approach applied to any *graph DDF*, it is well known that its normalizing factor $NF_{DDF(G)}(g_x, g_y, w, p)$ is equal to $p \cdot g_y + w \cdot g_x$ (see Chambers et al., 1998).[29] If we multiply and divide by $TI_{DDF(G)}(x_o, y_o) = \beta^* > 0$, we get $NF_{DDF(G)}(g_x, g_y, w, p) = (p \cdot g_y + w \cdot g_x) = \frac{\beta^*(p \cdot g_y + w \cdot g_x)}{\beta^*} = \frac{p \cdot (\beta^* g_y) + w \cdot (\beta^* g_x)}{\beta^*} = \frac{p \cdot s^{+*}_{DDF} + w \cdot s^{-*}_{DDF}}{TI_{DDF(G)}(x, y)}$, which is exactly our general normalizing factor as given in (13.13), when $\beta^* > 0$. In the case $\beta^* = 0$, we know that the traditional approach proposes the same normalizing factor $p \cdot g_y + w \cdot g_x$, that we assume as the value of $k_{o\$}$ according to option 2 introduced beforehand.

One particular case is worth mentioning. Let us assume that *the directional vector used is common to all firms*, for example, *the fixed vector* (g_x, g_y), independent of any firm (x_j, y_j), $j \in J$. It is obvious that all the firms would have the same normalizing factor $(p \cdot g_y + w \cdot g_x)$. The consequence is that if we go back to (13.14), where the normalized profit inefficiency is decomposed, we obtain the next equality which is valid for *any* firm (x_j, y_j), $j \in J$, and for any *directional graph distance function that resorts to a constant DV*:

[28] This connects with Chap. 12 devoted to the *Reverse DDF*, which assigns a specific *graph DDF* to any *graph efficiency measure*, satisfying the requirement expressed above. Hence, the *reverse DDF* constitutes the bridge between the graph efficiency measure that does not satisfy the essential property and the *graph DDF* that complies with it.

[29] Strictly speaking we should have written the normalization factor as $NF_{DDF(G)}(x, y, g_x, g_y, w, p)$, but considering the general notation introduced in Sect. 13.2.3.1, we prefer to write a reduced expression. The same applies to the expression $TI_{DDF(G)}(x, y)$.

$$\frac{(\Pi(w,p) - (p \cdot y_j - w \cdot x_j))}{(p \cdot g_y + w \cdot g_x)} = \beta_o^* + \frac{(\Pi(w,p) - (p \cdot \widehat{y}_j - w \cdot \widehat{x}_j))}{(p \cdot g_y + w \cdot g_x)}, \forall j.$$

The result, in this particular case, is that *the three expressions in the last equality are comparable* between firms: *the normalized profit inefficiency of* (x_j, y_j) *has the same denominator across all the firms*, which means that it is a true and comparable representation of the normalized profit inefficiency for each firm (x_j, y_j); for the same reason, the allocative inefficiency is comparable, since it corresponds, according to (13.16), to the normalized profit inefficiency of its projection, which is also a firm of our finite sample; and finally the technical inefficiency can be retrieved as a residual of the last two comparable numbers and is therefore also comparable. When this happens, we say that *the normalized profit inefficiency decomposition satisfies the comparison property*, as already defined in Sect. 13.2.1. Hence, *the last considered DDF, based on a constant graph DV, satisfies the comparison property.* Moreover, the use of a constant graph DV, common to all firms, ensures that both *the essential and the extended essential properties* are satisfied.

The requirement that (g_x, g_y) *is a fixed common vector for all firms* is too demanding and can be weakened. In fact, *we have introduced a new technique in Sect. 8.7 in Chap. 8, which solves the last-mentioned problem* by modifying the different *DVs* while maintaining the three mentioned properties.[30]

13.2.5 The Graph Reverse Approaches for Profit Decompositions

It may happen that, in practice, a certain hierarchical organization that rules a set of production branches is more interested, when trying to reduce the profit inefficiency of each branch, in minimizing, in the first place, its allocative inefficiency. As pointed out by Bogetoft and Hougaard (2003):

> *There are many possible rationales for slack.*[31] *Measured technical inefficiency can be part of the (fringe) compensation paid to stake holders, e.g., the employees, the owners, the local community etc., and it may actually be the cheapest way to provide such compensation. Inefficiency can also contribute to incentives. For example, the firm can pay its employees more than their opportunity costs in order to make them work efficiently out of fear of the harsh penalty associated with a dismissal for poor performance. It can create loyal employees and thereby reduce costly turnovers in the labour force.*

[30] It is quite obvious that two *DDF inefficiency scores* are *comparable* as long as the corresponding *DVs* give rise to the same *profit*, i.e., $wg_{x_j} + pg_{y_j} = k$, for all j.

[31] "Slack" means the technical inefficiency detected in any of the inputs and outputs of a firm.

Hence, technical inefficiency does not necessarily mean losses. Bogetoft et al. (2006) added two more arguments for adopting what they called *the reverse approach*. First, the focus of microeconomics is more on the interaction of firms over market—which means reducing allocative inefficiency—than on the production processes inside the firms. It could be easier to motivate not only employees but also stakeholders for recognizing that *doing the right things according to the market conditions is the first goal of an organization*. In what follows, we are going to propose two graph reverse approaches, inspired on the philosophy of the reverse approach of Bogetoft et al. (2006) but with different degrees of freedom. Both will be developed resorting to the general direct approach of Sect. 13.2.2.

First, we are going to develop *the standard reverse approach* (*SR approach*), proposed by Pastor et al. (2021b). Basically, for any firm being analyzed, the SR approach starts identifying a projection that is as "close" as possible to a profit-maximizing firm or, equivalently, a projection whose profit inefficiency is as small as possible.[32] Therefore, the SR approach no longer starts by evaluating the technical inefficiency of the firm based on a certain previously selected efficiency measure, which corresponds to the traditional and general direct approaches, but it goes the other way around and begins to reduce allocative inefficiency as an easier way to *accommodate our production firms to existing market conditions*. This first step is achieved by identifying for each non-efficient firm a proper classical projection, that is, a projection that Pareto dominates the mentioned firm. However, since our final goal is to achieve the corresponding profit inefficiency decomposition, *the SR approach* needs to further consider a specific second step in order to measure the technical inefficiency component of the mentioned decomposition. This measurement is relatively standard since, as already said, *the SR approach* resorts to a classical projection.

Our second reverse approach, called the *flexible reverse approach* (*FR approach*), follows Pastor et al. (2021c) and is more iconoclastic as well as more ambitious. It also follows the philosophy of the general direct approach for obtaining the corresponding normalized profit inefficiency decomposition, but it is radically different from the *SR approach*. Basically, it starts allowing freedom of movement for any efficient firm within the production possibility set, identifying as the best projection any profit-maximizing firm, which reduces its allocative inefficiency as much as possible. Meanwhile, any non-efficient firm requires a previous classical movement towards the strong efficient frontier to identify its technical inefficiency in a particular way, its efficient projection being treated later similar to any of the efficient firms. Non-efficient firms also meet the basic objective of the *FR approach*, as they maximize their respective allocative inefficiencies. In case more than one final projection meets our basic objective, we introduce a second criterion, namely, the reduction of the L_1-distance between the firm under study and its final projection. The basic difficulty with *the flexible reverse approach* is to define an appropriate technical

[32] When using the general direct approach as we do, to search for a projection with a reduced profit inefficiency is equivalent to getting a reduced allocative profit inefficiency.

inefficiency measure that has nothing to do with any of the technical inefficiency measures designed and used previously, since, as already said, its objective is to reach an efficient projection that offers as much allocative inefficiency as possible.

13.2.5.1 The Standard Reverse Approach and Its Profit Inefficiency Decomposition

The *SR approach*, design for being implemented in a DEA framework, assumes that the projection $(\widehat{x}_{oSR}, \widehat{y}_{oSR})$ of firm (x_o, y_o), capable of minimizing the allocative profit inefficiency of the mentioned firm, satisfies $(-x_o, y_o) \leq (-\widehat{x}_{oSR}, \widehat{y}_{oSR})$ (see footnote 3). More precisely, this means that both the input slacks $s^-_{oSR} = (x_o - \widehat{x}_{oSR})$ and the output slacks $s^+_{oSR} = (\widehat{y}_{oSR} - y_o)$ must be non-negative or, in other words, that the way for reducing first the allocative profit inefficiency searching for an appropriate projection shows the same features—reducing inputs and increasing outputs—as the well-known traditional and direct procedures for determining in the first place its technical projection. Besides this similarity, the procedure is completely different. Since we know that a *profit-maximizing firm* belongs to the efficient frontier and our aim is to obtain for each firm (x_o, y_o) a projection $(\widehat{x}_{oSR}, \widehat{y}_{oSR})$ that is as close as possible to it, Pastor et al. (2021c) decided to resort to a nonstandard weighted additive model knowing that it always identifies technical efficient projections that belong to the Pareto-Koopmans efficient frontier.[33] Being more precise, the first objective of the *SR approach* for any non-efficient firm is to *minimize* the allocative profit inefficiency, $A\Pi I(x_o, y_o) = (\Pi(w, p) - (p \cdot \widehat{y}_{oSR} - w \cdot \widehat{x}_{oSR}))$ resorting to our general direct approach (13.12).[34] Since the technical inefficiency associated with any efficient firm is 0, this first objective only affects non-efficient firms.[35]

Let us first solve the problem for a non-efficient firm, which means that $(x_o, y_o) \neq (\widehat{x}_{oSR}, \widehat{y}_{oSR})$. In this case, the relation between the firm (x_o, y_o) and its future efficient projection is coincident with the former equality (13.5) as long as we make the corresponding adjustments in their subindexes, which gives rise to the next equality: $(p \cdot \widehat{y}_{oSR} - w \cdot \widehat{x}_{oSR}) = (p \cdot y_o - w \cdot x_o) + \left(p \cdot s^{+*}_{oSR} + w \cdot s^{-*}_{oSR}\right)$. Consequently, *the linear programming model* to be solved *for minimizing the allocative profit inefficiency* as much as possible, incorporating the restrictions imposed on the slacks *by the SR*

[33]The reader must be aware that when using a VRS DEA piecewise linear frontier, many profit-maximizing points may exist, for instance, all the points that belong to a certain frontier facet. In the following section dealing with the flexible reverse approach, we account for this possibility and introduce a mathematical program that finds the closest L_1 projection of the firm under evaluation to the profit-maximizing benchmarks.

[34]When we talk about (13.12), we mean to resort to the corresponding equality for decomposing profit inefficiency but adapted to the new situation, where the new projection $(\widehat{x}_{oSR}, \widehat{y}_{oSR})$ is in general different from the old one $(\widehat{x}_{oEM}, \widehat{y}_{oEM})$, obtained through a certain efficiency measure (*EM*). Let us also observe that minimizing the allocative profit inefficiency is equivalent to minimizing the allocative inefficiency.

[35]Based on the general direct approach, it is obvious that minimizing the allocative profit inefficiency of any firm is equivalent to maximizing the profit of its frontier projection.

approach, is introduced below as model (13.19). It is a *nonstandard* weighted additive model due to its peculiar objective function, expressed in monetary units; i.e., the weights depend on prices rather than quantities which would ensure that the inefficiency measure is units' invariant. Our primary interest in its optimal value $\left(p \cdot s_{oSR}^{+*} + w \cdot s_{oSR}^{-*}\right)$ is simply that, adding to it the fixed value $(p \cdot y_o - w \cdot x_o)$, we obtain $\left(p \cdot \widehat{y}_{oSR} - w \cdot \widehat{x}_{oSR}\right)$, which in turn can be subtracted from $\Pi(w,p)$ in order to know how relatively small our actual allocative component is. Obviously, if $\left(p \cdot \widehat{y}_{oSR} - w \cdot \widehat{x}_{oSR}\right)$ equals $\Pi(w,p)$, our obtained projection is a profit-maximizing firm which corresponds to the lowest "allocative" result we can obtain. In any case, since the general direct approach decomposes the profit inefficiency of (x_o, y_o), which is a fixed monetary value into the sum of $\left(p \cdot s_{oSR}^{+*} + w \cdot s_{oSR}^{-*}\right)$ and the profit inefficiency of its projection, it is clear that maximizing the first addend is equivalent to minimizing the second. Hence, we solve the next linear program:

$$
\begin{aligned}
\max_{s_{oSR}^{-}, s_{oSR}^{+}, \lambda} \quad & p \cdot s_{oSR}^{+} + w \cdot s_{oSR}^{-} \\
s.t. \quad & \\
& \sum_{j=1}^{J} \lambda_j x_{jm} + s_{oSRm}^{-} = x_{om}, \qquad m = 1, \ldots, M \\
& \sum_{j=1}^{J} \lambda_j y_{jr} - s_{oSRn}^{+} = y_{on}, \qquad n = 1, \ldots, N \\
& \sum_{j=1}^{J} \lambda_j = 1, \\
& s_{oSR}^{-} = \left(s_{oSR1}^{-}, \ldots, s_{oSRM}^{-}\right) \geq 0_M, \\
& s_{oSR}^{+} = \left(s_{oSR1}^{+}, \ldots, s_{oSRN}^{+}\right) \geq 0_N, \\
& \lambda = (\lambda_1, \ldots, \lambda_J) \geq 0_J.
\end{aligned}
\tag{13.19}
$$

In case $\left(p \cdot s_{oSR}^{+*} + w \cdot s_{oSR}^{-*}\right) > 0_{\$}$, we know that all the slacks cannot be equal to 0, or equivalently, we can measure somehow the associated technical inefficiency, as we will show in the next subsection. Before accomplishing this task, let us summarize the profit decomposition we have achieved by means of the *SR approach*:

$$
(\Pi(w,p) - (p \cdot y_o - w \cdot x_o)) = \left(p \cdot s_{oSR}^{+*} + w \cdot s_{oSR}^{-*}\right) + \left(\Pi(w,p) - \left(p \cdot \widehat{y}_{oSR} - w \cdot \widehat{x}_{oSR}\right)\right). \tag{13.20}
$$

It is formally the same decomposition obtained in our general direct approach (see (13.6)), but it differs in how the projection is obtained, which, generally speaking, will give rise to a rather different decomposition. The *SR approach* does not resort to any known efficiency measure; instead it identifies a projection for any non-efficient firm that maximizes the technological profit gap or, equivalently, that minimizes the profit allocative inefficiency of (x_o, y_o) in (13.20).

The last equality corresponds to the *profit inefficiency decomposition of the SR approach* for any *non-efficient firm*. For any *efficient firm*, (13.20) is also valid, considering that model (13.19) gets an optimal objective function value $\left(p \cdot s_{oSR}^{+*} + w \cdot s_{oSR}^{-*}\right) = 0$ for this subset of firms.[36] Therefore, for any efficient firm, equality (13.20) is reduced to

$$(\Pi(w,p) - (p \cdot y_o - w \cdot x_o)) = (\Pi(w,p) - (p \cdot \widehat{y}_{oSR} - w \cdot \widehat{x}_{oSR})),$$
$$\text{for} \quad (x_o, y_o) = (\widehat{x}_{oSR}, \widehat{y}_{oSR}). \tag{13.21}$$

Let us call the attention of the reader that in order *to derive a normalized profit inefficiency decomposition for the SR approach*, we need to measure the technical inefficiency associated with the identified projections. At this point, we again follow Pastor et al. (2021b) when considering the same proposed efficiency measure that fulfills this task (see next subsection).

The last result shows that, for technically efficient firms, the considered SR approach is unable to reduce their allocative inefficiencies, bringing up the paper by Zofío et al. (2013), the title of which is illustrative enough: "The directional profit efficiency measure: on why profit inefficiency is either technical or allocative."[37] In this respect, Pastor et al. (2021c) have introduced the so-called flexible reverse approach that is able to reduce the profit inefficiency decomposition to a single term, because the allocative component is always reduced to 0. We are going to introduce it later on. Next, let us introduce a specific inefficiency measure for the SR approach that will allow us to first derive the SR technical inefficiency for each firm and then generate the corresponding SR normalized profit inefficiency decomposition.

13.2.5.2 Deriving a Specific Inefficiency Measure for the SR Approach

Based on Pastor et al. (2021b), we are going to develop the definition of *a new strong inefficiency measure related to the SR approach* that gives rise to a technical inefficiency score for each firm being rated satisfying the usual properties. Linear model (13.19) gives us an optimal non-negative objective function value for each firm of our sample, which means that we have exactly J optimal output slack values and the same amount of optimal input slack values. Let us assume that our sample of firms contains at least one inefficient firm, which means that any upper bound for the optimal values of model (13.19) is positive. Consider now the tightest upper bound for the optimal values of the mentioned model associated with all the firms of our finite sample:

[36] The nature of model (13.19) classifies the units directly as efficient or non-efficient.

[37] The mentioned article refers to the DDFs, while our approach here is based on the additive slack model.

$$U_{SR} = \max\left\{p \cdot s_{jSR}^{+*} + w \cdot s_{jSR}^{-*}, j \in J\right\} > 0_{\$}. \tag{13.23}$$

The monetary value of this upper bound is achieved at least in one of the considered inefficient firms of our sample. The next inequality is straightforward:

$$U_{SR} \geq \left(p \cdot s_{jSR}^{+*} + w \cdot s_{jSR}^{-*}\right), \forall j \in J. \tag{13.24}$$

Now we are ready to define the *standard technical inefficiency measure* $TI_{SR}(x_o, y_o)$ associated with the *SR approach.*

Definition 13.2 The *standard reverse technical inefficiency measure* $TI_{SR}(x_o, y_o)$ for any firm of our finite sample is defined as

$$TI_{SR}(x_o, y_o) := \left(\frac{p}{U_{SR}} \cdot s_{oSR}^{+*} + \frac{w}{U_{SR}} \cdot s_{oSR}^{-*}\right). \tag{13.25}$$

The last expression is based on the optimal solution of model (13.19) obtained for each firm (x_o, y_o) and on its natural considered upper bound. The new introduced technical inefficiency measure $TI_{SR}(x_o, y_o)$ satisfies four basic properties, first introduced by Cooper et al. (1999) for measuring technical efficiency (*TE*). For this type of measures, the next equality holds: $TE = 1 - TI$. Since in this context we are not interested in *TE*, we are going to enunciate the four properties for $TI_{SR}(x_o, y_o)$.

Proposition 13.4 *The SR technical inefficiency measure satisfies the next four properties*:

P1. $0 \leq TI_{SR}(x_o, y_o) \leq 1$.
P2. $TI_{SR}(x_o, y_o) = 0$ if, and only if, (x_o, y_o) is an efficient firm.
P3. $TI_{SR}(x_o, y_o)$ is a strongly monotonic inefficiency measure.
P4. $TI_{SR}(x_o, y_o)$ is invariant to the units of measurement of inputs and outputs.

Proof

P1. Is a direct consequence of Definition 13.2. The definition of the upper bound guarantees that at least one firm has its technical inefficiency equal to 1.

P2 and P3. After knowing the value of the upper bound $U_{SR} > 0_{\$}$, we can formally consider a slightly modified version of model (13.19), substituting its objective function with expression (13.25), which, according to P4, is a typical weighted additive model that, according to Chap. 6, satisfies both properties.

P4. The technical inefficiency value (13.25) of (x_o, y_o), $\left(\frac{p}{U_{SR}} \cdot s_{oSR}^{+*} + \frac{w}{U_{SR}} \cdot s_{oSR}^{-*}\right)$, shows clearly that the units of measurement of the weight associated with each output and each input are *price per unit of quantity*[38] in the numerator and the

[38] Each output and each input has its own quantity measure.

value of $U_{SR} > 0_\$$ in the denominator that jointly[39] give rise to *the inverse of* a *unit of quantity*, which, after multiplying by the corresponding slack expressed in the same *unit of quantity*, gives rise to the sum of pure numbers, which are independent of the units of measurement of inputs and outputs, this concluding the proof. □

Resorting to the new defined technical inefficiency measure (see (13.25)), it is straightforward to obtain the new *normalized SR profit inefficiency decomposition* just by considering equalities (13.20) and (13.21), as shown in the next subsection.

13.2.5.3 The SR Approach and Its Normalized Profit Inefficiency

So far, we have introduced a specific slack-based model, (13.19), which identifies for each firm (x_o, y_o) an efficient projection $(\widehat{x}_{oSR}, \widehat{y}_{oSR})$ that minimizes its allocative profit inefficiency $(\Pi(w,p) - (p \cdot \widehat{y}_{oSR} - w \cdot \widehat{x}_{oSR}))$ or, as we have shown above, that maximizes the objective function of model (13.19), $\left(p \cdot s^{+}_{oSR} + w \cdot s^{-}_{oSR}\right)$. Interestingly enough, its optimal solution $\left(p \cdot s^{+*}_{oSR} + w \cdot s^{-*}_{oSR}\right)$, the so-called technological profit gap, has been transformed into an inefficiency measure, as expression (13.25) certifies, just by introducing an appropriate change in the objective function of model (13.19) so as to get rid of its units of measurement and guaranteeing, at the same time, that the obtained technical inefficiency belongs to the interval [0, 1] and satisfies the properties listed above. Moreover, the new defined *SR technical inefficiency* is useful because it is closely related to the mentioned gap of the profit inefficiency decomposition, as given by equality (13.20).[40] Therefore, (13.20) can be rewritten as follows:

$$
\begin{aligned}
&(\Pi(w,p) - (p \cdot y_o - w \cdot x_o)) = \left(p \cdot s^{+*}_{oSR} + w \cdot s^{-*}_{oSR}\right) + (\Pi(w,p) - (p \cdot \widehat{y}_{oSR} - w \cdot \widehat{x}_{oSR})) = \\
&= U_{SR}\left(\frac{p}{U_{SR}} \cdot s^{+*}_{oSR} + \frac{w}{U_{SR}} \cdot s^{-*}_{oSR}\right) + (\Pi(w,p) - (p \cdot \widehat{y}_{oSR} - w \cdot \widehat{x}_{oSR})) = \\
&= U_{SR} \times TI_{SR}(x_o, y_o) + (\Pi(w,p) - (p \cdot \widehat{y}_{oSR} - w \cdot \widehat{x}_{oSR})).
\end{aligned}
$$

Hence, taking U_{SR} as a common *normalizing factor* expressed in monetary units, which we denote in what follows as $NF_{SR\$}$, we get the next normalized profit decomposition, corresponding to the so-called Nerlovian inefficiency:

---

[39] For instance, the units of measurement of each component of p, the output prices in the numerator, are $\left(\frac{\$}{q_1^+}, \ldots, \frac{\$}{q_N^+}\right)$, while in the denominator the corresponding products have as units $\frac{\$}{q_n^+} \times q_n^+ = \$, n = 1, \ldots, N$. Hence, its output ratios have as units $\left(\frac{\$}{q_n^+}/\$\right) = \frac{1}{q_n^+}, n = 1, \ldots, N$.

[40] Equality (13.21) is subsumed by expression (13.20) since it corresponds to the particular case when $\left(p \cdot s^{+*}_{oRA} + w \cdot s^{-*}_{oRA}\right) = 0_\$$, that is, when we are considering any efficient firm.

$$\frac{(\Pi(w,p) - (p \cdot y_o - w \cdot x_o))}{NF_{SR\$}} = TI_{SR}(x_o, y_o) + \frac{(\Pi(w,p) - (p \cdot \widehat{y}_{oSR} - w \cdot \widehat{x}_{oSR}))}{NF_{SR\$}},$$
$$NF_{SR\$} = U_{SR}. \tag{13.26}$$

It is worth pointing out two facts. First, last expression is valid for any firm (x_o, y_o) of our sample. And second, the normalizing factor, as already mentioned above, is the same for all the observations. This means that the last decomposition satisfies *the comparison property*—as formulated in Sect. 13.1—and, consequently, the three terms of (13.26) are comparable between firms. It also satisfies two other relevant properties that are not easy to achieve when considering technical inefficiencies associated with efficiency measures (see Sect 2.4.5 of Chap. 2): *the essential property* and *the extended essential property*. The latter one states that the allocative inefficiency of any firm must be equal to the allocative inefficiency of its efficient projection. According to (13.26), the allocative inefficiency associated with firm $(x_o,\ y_o)$, $\frac{(\Pi(w,p) - (p \cdot \widehat{y}_{oSR} - w \cdot \widehat{x}_{oSR}))}{NF_{SR\$}}$, corresponds clearly to the Nerlovian inefficiency of its efficient projection $(\widehat{x}_{oSR}, \widehat{y}_{oSR})$, which in turn is equal to its own allocative inefficiency, and we conclude that the *Nerlovian SR profit inefficiency decomposition* fulfills *the extended essential property*. In particular, efficient points that are profit maximizers have a zero allocative inefficiency, and the same happens for any inefficient firm that is projected onto any of them. The last statement is also expressed by saying that *the Nerlovian SR profit inefficiency decomposition* fulfills *the essential property*.

As a summary, *the Nerlovian SR profit inefficiency decomposition* fulfills *a relevant condition* and three interesting properties. First, it determines a *classical efficient projection*–outputs are increased and inputs are reduced to identify the projection for each firm–and, at the same time, this is the novelty; *the allocative inefficiency is reduced as much as possible*. Second, *the new associated SR inefficiency measure generates a normalization factor that is the same for all firms*, and, consequently, *the corresponding Nerlovian SR profit inefficiency decomposition* allows the direct comparison between firms of its three terms, i.e., it *satisfies the comparison property*. And third, *it satisfies the extended essential property*, and, consequently, *it also satisfies the essential property*, something that, as already pointed out before, is not easy to achieve.

13.2.5.4 Numerical Example for the SR Approach

Let us consider again the numerical example of Sect. 13.2.4 that we have used for illustrating the functioning of the general direct approach. As we have shown, *the SR approach* does not resort to any of the well-established technical efficiency measures simply because its first action is to reduce the allocative profit inefficiency of any firm by identifying its *best efficient classical projection* through model (13.19). Its second action, with the objective of obtaining a profit inefficiency decomposition, is to measure the technical inefficiency associated with the already identified projection, which requires *the design of a completely new technical inefficiency measure*, i.e., expression (13.25). The results obtained fulfill our research goal, resulting in a manageable *standard reverse approach* that satisfies three interesting properties, as already mentioned at the end of the previous subsection.

Example 13.4
Table 13.3 shows the relevant information of both the profit decomposition and the normalized profit decomposition associated with our *SR approach*. It incorporates the data of any of the two preceding tables, dispensing with a useless column, the one reporting the normalizing factor. Instead, we have one new row at the end, where we show the new and unique normalizing factor. Since we maintain the same market prices, $(p, w) = (6, 1)$, as in the preceding tables, it is clear that again the only profit-maximizing firm is D = (12,12), with $\Pi(w, p) = \$60$. Since we are resorting to the SR approach, which calculates the two components of the normalized profit inefficiency decomposition just the opposite way to the direct approach, Table 13.3 presents a different ordering of its columns in comparison to any of the two previous tables.

Let us revise each of the columns of new Table 13.3, and compare them with the two previous tables. Column 1, where the list of *nine firms* under study appears, and column 3, where the *profit inefficiency* of each firm is recorded, are the only ones that match columns 1 and 4 of the two previous tables. Column 2 reports *the efficient projection* of each firm according to the *SR approach* and shows large differences with respect to the same column of the two previous tables for most inefficient firms. As can be expected, the two terms of the profit inefficiency decomposition, the *technical profit inefficiency* and the *allocative profit inefficiency*, listed, respectively, in columns 4 and 5, are also different from the two previous tables for most inefficient firms. The first component, *TΠI*, is directly obtained by solving model (13.19) for each non-efficient firm. Their maximum value, 60, appears as ***NF*** in the last row of the same column. The second component, *AΠI*, in column 5, is retrieved from columns 3 and 4 as a residual. We can appreciate that each inefficient firm gets the same allocative profit inefficiency value as its efficient firm projection, with the exception of firm F whose projection is not a firm but the next convex combination of efficient firms: (2/3)C+(1/3)D. Hence, its *AΠI* must be equal to (2/3)3 + (1/3)0 = 2 (see column 5). Column 6 reports the *technical inefficiency* (*TI*), which is obtained by dividing technical profit inefficiency, in column 3, by 60, the value of the fix normalization factor of its last row. Column 7 is the *normalized profit inefficiency* obtained by dividing each value of the third column by the normalization factor. And, finally, column 8, the *allocative inefficiency*, corresponds to the difference of columns 7 and 6. Here we can appreciate one of the properties mentioned before:

Table 13.3 Results based on *the SR approach*, $(p, w) = (6,1)$

Firm	*SR project.*	$\Pi I_\$$	$T\Pi I_\$ = \left(p \cdot s_{oRA}^{+*} + w \cdot s_{oRA}^{-*}\right)_\$$	$A\Pi I_\$$	$TI = \frac{T\Pi I_\$}{NF_{SR\$}}$	$N\Pi I = \frac{\Pi I_\$}{NF_{SR\$}}$	$AI = \frac{\Pi I_\$}{NF_{SR\$}} - TI$
(1)	(2)	(3)	(4)	(5) = (3) – (4)	(6)	(7)	(8) = (7) – (6)
A = (3,5)	(3,5)	33	(6,1)·(0,0) = 0	33	0	33/60	33/60
B = (6,10)	(6,10)	6	(6,1)·(0,0) = 0	6	0	6/60	6/60
C = (9,11)	(9,11)	3	(6,1)·(0,0) = 0	3	0	3/60	3/60
D = (12,12)	(12,12)	0	(6,1)·(0,0) = 0	0	0	0	0
E = (3,2)	(3,5)	51	(6,1)·(3,0) = 18	33	18/60	51/60	33/60
F = (10,5)	(10,34/3)	40	(6,1)·(19/3,0) = 38	2	38/60	40/60	2/60
G = (12,2)	(12,12)	60	(6,1)·(10,0) = 60	0	60/60	60/60	0
H = (12,11)	(12,12)	6	(6,1)·(1,0) = 6	0	6/60	6/60	0
I = (16,12)	(12,12)	4	(6,1)·(0,4) = 4	0	4/60	4/60	0
–	–	–	$NF_{SR\$} = 60$	–	–	–	–

the allocative inefficiency of any non-efficient firm and of its projection is the same.[41] This is precisely *the extended essential property*.

As a final comment, if we compare Table 13.3 with Table 13.2; that is, *if we compare the SR approach with the general direct approach*, we appreciate that only three firms have changed their projection and all three reach the profit-maximizing peer. There are obvious differences with respect to the technical inefficiency, which in all but one firm are smaller in Table 13.3 and obviously in the normalizing factor. Finally, the allocative inefficiency is *much smaller in the SR approach* than in the direct approach.

13.2.5.5 The Graph Flexible Reverse Approach and Its Profit Inefficiency Decomposition

The next *flexible reverse profit approach* (*FR approach*), also proposed by Pastor et al. (2021c), is the most permissive reverse approach one can think of. It is inspired by Zofio et al. (2013) and translates the original ideas based on directional distance functions to slack-based measures. We are going to show how the *FR approach* works, being able to guarantee that the final projection of any firm is a profit-maximizing firm or, equivalently, its allocative inefficiency equals 0. However, we need to study separately the projection of any firm belonging to the subset of efficient firms from the rest of the firms that obviously belong to the subset of non-efficient firms.[42] If we represent, as usual, the finite set of firms as $F = \{(x_j, y_j), j \in J\}$, the non-empty subset of efficient firms will be denoted as $F_E := \left\{ \left(x_{j_E}, y_{j_E} \right), j_E \in J_E \right\}$, while the non-empty subset of non-efficient firms is identified as $F_N := \left\{ \left(x_{j_N}, y_{j_N} \right), \right.$ $\left. j_N \in J_N \right\}$, where $F_E \cup F_N = F$ and $F_E \cap F_N = \varnothing$.[43] The reason for considering these two subgroups of firms is that the corresponding *FR projections*, despite being obtained in a similar way, lead to completely different interpretations. While the profit inefficiency decomposition associated with any firm is straightforward, we need to define first *the generalized direct approach* that is basically a general direct approach that, for the first time, allows the presence of unrestricted in sign input and output slacks.

---

[41]The only firm that cannot be directly tested in our Table is (10,5) because its projection does not belong to our sample of firms but does belong to the efficient facet defined by the firms B = (6,10) and D = (12,12). In this case, the convex combination that relates the benchmark (10,34/3) with the two mentioned firms is (10,34/3) = 1/3(6,10) + 2/3(12,12), which allows us to express the allocative inefficiency of the mentioned benchmark as a convex combinations of the two considered firms. We leave this exercise to the reader.

[42]The subset of non-efficient firms includes both *the inefficient firms and* the firms that belong to the frontier but are not efficient, also called *weakly efficient firms*.

[43]The relation between the set of firms E and N can equivalently be expressed resorting to the corresponding subindexes J_E and J_N.

Case 1: The Subset of Efficient Firms $F_E \subset \partial^S(T)$

Our goal is to project any efficient firm $\left(x_{j_E}, y_{j_E}\right) \in F_E$ onto a profit-maximizing firm $(x^{\Pi}, y^{\Pi}) \in F_E$. Defining the unrestricted in sign slacks that correspond to the L_1-path that connects the efficient firm with its projection as $\left(u^-_{j_E FR}, u^+_{j_E FR}\right) \in \mathbb{R}^{M+N}$, the next equality holds:

$$\left(u^-_{j_E FR}, u^+_{j_E FR}\right) = \left(x_{j_E} - x^{\Pi}, y^{\Pi} - y_{j_E}\right), \tag{13.27}$$

It may happen that the efficient firm $\left(x_{j_E}, y_{j_E}\right) \in F_E$ is itself a profit-maximizing firm, which corresponds to the trivial case in which the firm is its own benchmark and all the slacks are zero. In any other case, since both firms are Pareto-efficient, the slacks that connect both firms must be unrestricted in sign, as the next proposition shows in a general setting.

Proposition 13.5 *Let us consider the efficient firm (x_o, y_o) and its projection $(\widehat{x}_o, \widehat{y}_o)$ that is also an efficient firm, with $(x_o, y_o) \neq (\widehat{x}_o, \widehat{y}_o)$. Let us further consider the corresponding vector of slacks $\left(u_o^-, u_o^+\right) = (x_o - \widehat{x}_o, \widehat{y}_o - y_o)$. Then at least one of the slacks must be strictly negative and another must be strictly positive.*

Proof Since $(x_o, y_o) \neq (\widehat{x}_o, \widehat{y}_o)$, let us first assume that all the slacks are non-negative with at least one strictly positive, and let us deduce a contradiction. In this case, equality (13.27) shows that efficient firm $(\widehat{x}_o, \widehat{y}_o)$ would dominate efficient firm (x_o, y_o), since $x_o - \widehat{x}_o = u_o^- \geq 0_M$ and $\widehat{y}_o - y_o = u_o^+ \geq 0_N$ implies $x_o \geq \widehat{x}_o$ and $\widehat{y}_o \geq y_o$, which is a contradiction since the two firms considered are efficient, and the desired conclusion holds. The only alternative assumption that requires to be proved is to consider that all the slacks are non-positive with at least one strictly negative. The corresponding proof is very similar, and we leave it to the reader. The conclusion of the two reasonings is that at least one of the slacks must be strictly negative and another one strictly positive. □

Let us introduce the *generalized direct profit decomposition approach* that constitutes a generalization of the *general direct approach* as it accepts non-negative and negative input and output slacks. Let us assume, in the most general case, that

$$\left(u_o^-, u_o^+\right) = (x_o - \widehat{x}_o, \widehat{y}_o - y_o),$$

being (x_o, y_o) any firm of the production possibility set; $(\widehat{x}_o, \widehat{y}_o)$ its strong efficient projection, obtained through a particular inefficiency model; and $\left(u_o^-, u_o^+\right) \in \mathbb{R}^{M+N}$. The last equality is a generalization of (13.27) and formally equal to (13.4). Consequently, (13.5) and (13.6) are also satisfied, which gives rise to the next proposition whose proof is left to the reader.

Proposition 13.6 *The generalized direct profit decomposition approach satisfies*

$$\Pi I(x_o, y_o, w, p) = (\Pi(w,p) - (py_o - wx_o)) = \left(p \cdot u_o^+ + w \cdot u_o^-\right) + (\Pi(w,p)) - (p \cdot \widehat{y}_o - w \cdot \widehat{x}_o) = = \left(p \cdot u_o^+ + w \cdot u_o^-\right) + \Pi I(\widehat{x}_o, \widehat{y}_o, w, p),$$

where $\left(u_o^-, u_o^+\right) = (x_o - \widehat{x}_o, \widehat{y}_o - y_o)$ *are unrestricted in sign slacks and the considered firm is efficient.*

While formally the generalized direct approach is similar to the general direct approach, the fact that slacks can take not only non-negative but also negative values is decisive for its subsequent interpretation that differentiates both approaches. Now let us go back to solve Case 1, where the nonprofit-maximizing efficient firm $\left(x_{j_E}, y_{j_E}\right) \in F_E$ is projected onto the profit-maximizing firm $(x^\Pi, y^\Pi) \in F_E$, with $\left(u^-_{j_EFR}, u^+_{j_EFR}\right) \in \mathbb{R}^{M+N}$ the slacks that connect both firms. According to last proposition, $\Pi I\left(x_{j_E}, y_{j_E}, w, p\right) = \left(p \cdot u^-_{j_EFR} + w \cdot u^-_{j_EFR}\right) + \Pi I(x^\Pi, y^\Pi, w, p) = \left(p \cdot u^-_{j_EFR} + w \cdot u^-_{j_EFR}\right)$, which allows us to draw three conclusions:

1. Since $\Pi I(x^\Pi, y^\Pi, w, p) = 0_\$$, the profit-maximizing projection plays no role in the last chain of equalities from a numerical perspective.
2. Since $\left(x_{j_E}, y_{j_E}\right)$ is efficient and $\Pi I\left(x_{j_E}, y_{j_E}, w, p\right) = \left(p \cdot u^-_{j_EFR} + w \cdot u^-_{j_EFR}\right)$, the last term can only be interpreted as an allocative profit inefficiency term, since it corresponds to the profit inefficiency of an efficient firm. For the first time, a term based on slacks is interpreted as an allocative component. In particular, if $\left(x_{j_E}, y_{j_E}\right)$ is a profit-maximizing firm, also its own allocative component is equal to $0_\$$.
3. One of the characteristics that distinguish the generalized direct approach from the general direct approach is linked to the subset of efficient firms. The interpretation of the market value of the new slacks is no longer linked to the technical component and, consequently, it appears linked to the allocative component.

Case 2: The Subset of Firms that Do Not Belong to $\partial^S(T)$

In this case, the interpretation of the corresponding *generalized direct profit decomposition* is just the opposite coinciding in this case with that of the general direct approach. Hence, our strategy is the same as before, but the result is not. We directly project the considered firm $\left(x_{j_N}, y_{j_N}\right)$ onto a profit-maximizing firm $(x^\Pi, y^\Pi) \in F_E$. According to the last proposition, it holds $\Pi I\left(x_{j_N}, y_{j_N}, w, p\right) =$

$\left(p \cdot u^{+}_{j_N FR} + w \cdot u^{-}_{j_N FR}\right) + \Pi I(x^{\Pi}, y^{\Pi}, w, p) = \left(p \cdot u^{+}_{j_N FR} + w \cdot u^{-}_{j_N FR}\right)$, which allows drawing the following conclusions:

1. Since $\Pi I(x^{\Pi}, y^{\Pi}, w, p) = 0_{\$}$, the profit-maximizing projection plays no role in the last chain of equalities from a numerical perspective.
2. Since $\left(x_{j_N}, y_{j_N}\right)$ is non-efficient and $\Pi I\left(x_{j_N}, y_{j_N}, w, p\right) = \left(p \cdot u^{+}_{j_N FR} + w \cdot u^{-}_{j_N FR}\right)$, the last term can only be interpreted as a technological profit inefficiency term since, as already said, the allocative profit inefficiency term associated with a profit-maximizing firm is always equal to $0_{\$}$. Hence, the term based on slacks is interpreted as a technological component, despite the fact that some individual slacks can be positive or negative.

From an empirical perspective, it is possible that several efficient firms maximize profit, and therefore, from a production perspective, it is adequate to find the closest benchmark. We can resort to a mathematical program that directly finds the profit-maximizing point that is the L_1-closest to each firm being analyzed. Otherwise, we would need to resort to several spreadsheet calculations, first identifying all the efficient profit-maximizing firms, then calculating the L_1-distances from each firm in our sample to each one of these benchmarks, and finally identifying the one that is closest to each firm. To this end and for each firm of our sample $(x_o, y_o) \in F$, let us reformulate the set of unrestricted in sign input and output slacks, $\left(u^{-}_{oFR}, u^{+}_{oFR}\right) \in \mathbb{R}^{M+N}$, in terms of couples of non-negative input and output slacks:

$$u^{-}_{oFR} = s^{-}_{oFR} - t^{-}_{oFR}, u^{+}_{oFR} = s^{+}_{oFR} - t^{+}_{oFR}, s^{-}_{oFR} \geq 0_M, t^{-}_{oFR} \geq 0_M, s^{+}_{oFR} \geq 0_N, t^{+}_{oFR} \geq 0_N.$$

This corresponds to a typical decomposition first introduced in goal programming by Charnes et al. (1955). According to the last definition, it should be clear that the absolute value of each unrestricted in sign slack variable can be formulated as follows: $\left|u^{-}_{moFR}\right| = s^{-}_{moFR} + t^{-}_{moFR}, m = 1, \ldots, M,$ $\left|u^{+}_{noFR}\right| = s^{+}_{noFR} + t^{+}_{noFR}, n = 1, \ldots, N$. Consequently, the next linear program finds the *FR projection* for each firm $(x_o, y_o) \in F$ that is L_1-closest to a profit-maximizing benchmark:

$$\begin{aligned}
\min_{s^-_{oSR}, t^-_{oSR}, s^+_{oSR}, t^+_{oSR}, \lambda} \quad & \sum_{m=1}^{M} \left(s^-_{oFRm} + t^-_{oFRm}\right) + \sum_{n=1}^{N} \left(s^+_{oFRn} + t^+_{oFRn}\right) \\
s.t. \quad & p \cdot \left(y_o + \left(s^+_{oFR} - t^+_{oFR}\right)\right) \\
& \quad -w \cdot \left(x_o - \left(s^-_{oFR} - t^-_{oFR}\right)\right) = \Pi(p, w), \\
& \sum_{j=1}^{J} \lambda_j x_{jm} + \left(s^-_{oFRm} - t^-_{oFRm}\right) = x_{om}, \qquad m = 1, \ldots, M \\
& \sum_{j=1}^{J} \lambda_j y_{jn} - \left(s^+_{oFRn} - t^+_{oFRn}\right) = y_{on}, \qquad n = 1, \ldots, N \\
& \sum_{j=1}^{J} \lambda_j = 1, \\
& s^-_{oFR} \geq 0_M, t^-_{oFR} \geq 0_M, s^+_{oFR} \geq 0_N, t^+_{oFR} \geq 0_N, \\
& \lambda = (\lambda_1, \ldots, \lambda_J) \geq 0_J.
\end{aligned} \tag{13.28}$$

Let us point out that although the proposed decomposition of the absolute value of each of the original input and output slacks is not unique, the solution of the last linear program is. For instance, if we assume that the input slack first component satisfies $u^-_{1oFR} = -1$, we can take $s^-_{oFR1} = 0, t^-_{oFR1} = 1$, but also $s^-_{oFR1} = 1, t^-_{oFR1} = 2$, or, in general, $s^-_{oFR1} = q, t^-_{oFR1} = q + 1$, where q is any positive number. The same happens with any of the rest of unrestricted in sign slacks. Fortunately, since the objective function of (13.28) minimizes the sum of all the pairs of an s-slack and the associated t-slack, we are sure that the optimal value of each of the mentioned slacks will take the minimum possible values. For example, if the shortest path that connects firm (x_o, y_o) with its closest profit-maximizing projection $\left(x_o - \left(s^-_{oFR} - t^-_{oFR}\right), y_o + \left(s^+_{oFR} - t^+_{oFR}\right)\right)$ has an optimal $u^{-*}_{oFR1} = s^{-*}_{oFR1} - t^{-*}_{oFR1}$ equal to -1, we are sure that last program will deliver as the first component of its optimal solution $s^{-*}_{oFR1} = 0, t^{-*}_{oFR1} = 1$.

Finally, *the generalized direct profit decomposition approach* combined with *the FR profit approach* gives rise to the next pair of equalities:

$$\begin{aligned}
\Pi I_{FR}\left(x_{j_E}, y_{j_E}, w, p\right) &= 0_\$ + \left(p \cdot u^+_{j_E FR} + w \cdot u^-_{j_E FR}\right), \left(x_{j_E}, y_{j_E}\right) \in F_E, \\
\Pi I_{FR}\left(x_{j_N}, y_{j_N}, w, p\right) &= \left(p \cdot u^+_{j_N FR} + w \cdot u^-_{j_N FR}\right) + 0_\$, \left(x_{j_N}, y_{j_N}\right) \in F_N.
\end{aligned} \tag{13.29}$$

It shows the two dual generalized direct FR profit inefficiency decompositions associated with efficient and non-efficient firms: while for any efficient firm all the profit inefficiency is allocative profit inefficiency, for any non-efficient firm, all the profit inefficiency is technological profit inefficiency. Therefore, the associated free slacks play the opposite role in each of the two cases.

In the next subsection, we are going to define a *measure of technical inefficiency* associated with *the FR profit approach* to obtain the corresponding *Nerlovian profit inefficiency decomposition* for each firm.

13.2.5.6 Deriving a Specific Inefficiency Measure for the FR Profit Approach

As usual, to derive *the normalized profit inefficiency* of each firm associated with *the FR profit approach*, we need to obtain a technical inefficiency measure associated with the optimal slacks obtained for each firm through linear program (13.28). Based on (13.29), let us start considering the technological profit inefficiency for each firm:

$$T\Pi I_{FR}(x_j, y_j) = \left\{ \begin{array}{ll} 0_\$, & (x_j, y_j) \in F_E \\ \left(p \cdot u^+_{j_N FR} + w \cdot u^-_{j_N FR}\right), & (x_j, y_j) \in F_N \end{array} \right\}.$$

For the non-empty subset of non-efficient firms, it holds that $\Pi I_{FR}(x_{j_N}, y_{j_N}, wp) = \left(p \cdot u^+_{j_N FR} + w \cdot u^-_{j_N FR}\right)$, and knowing that any non-efficient firm cannot be a profit maximizer, we deduce that $\left(p \cdot u^+_{j_N FR} + w \cdot u^-_{j_N FR}\right) > 0_\$$. Let us consider the next maximum value:

$$U_{FR} = \max\left\{\left(p \cdot u^+_{j_N FR} + w \cdot u^-_{j_N FR}\right), (x_j, y_j) \in F_N\right\} > 0_\$. \tag{13.30}$$

The next definition is straightforward:

Definition 13.3
The technical inefficiency associated with any firm is defined as

$$TI_{FR}(x_j, y_j) = \frac{T\Pi I_{FR}(x_j, y_j)}{U_{FR}}, (x_j, y_j) \in F. \tag{13.31}$$

The novelty of this new technical inefficiency definition is that the slacks involved are unrestricted in sign. However, we are going to show that it is a true technical inefficiency measure, since it satisfies the four basic properties first required for traditional efficiency measures by Cooper et al. (1999).

Proposition 13.7
The SR technical inefficiency measure satisfies the next four properties:

P1. $0 \leq TI_{FR}(x_j, y_j) \leq 1$, $(x_j, y_j) \in F$.
P2. $TI_{FR}(x_j, y_j) = 0$ *if, and only if,* $(x_o, y_o) \in F_E$.
P3. $TI_{FR}(x_j, y_j)$ *is a strongly monotonic inefficiency measure.*
P4. $TI_{FR}(x_j, y_j)$ *is invariant to the units of measurement of inputs and outputs.*

Proof

P1. Is a direct consequence of Definition 13.3. The definition of the upper bound guarantees that at least one firm has its technical inefficiency equal to 1.

P2 and P3. P2 holds thanks to the above definition of $T\Pi I_{FR}(x_j, y_j)$ and the closely related definition of $TI_{FR}(x_j, y_j)$ (see (13.31)).

For proving P3, it is sufficient to consider any non-efficient firm, which we label as *first firm*, that identifies a specific L_1-path towards its strong frontier projection and compare it with another different non-efficient firm, which we label as *second firm*, that belongs to the considered path. Let us prove P3 by showing that the length of the path that connects the second firm with its own projection is strictly smaller than the length of the path associated with the first firm. Since the two firms considered are different, the second firm will have a strictly shorter sub-path to reach the first firm projection than the path associated with the first firm. Since the first firm path has at most $M + N$ nonzero slacks, the two firms can differ in any of the mentioned slacks, being the first restriction associated with the existence of a sub-path for the second firm that the sign of the nonzero slacks associated with inputs or outputs of the second firm must be the same as the corresponding to the first firm and the second one that the existence of first firm slacks equal to 0 implies that the corresponding slacks for the second firm must also be 0. In any case, there exists a sub-path that projects the second firm towards the projection of the first firm, which shows that the first firm projection is a feasible projection for the second firm. Since program (13.28) minimizes the length of the path that connects the second firm with its optimal projection, the aforementioned length must be less than or equal to the length of the sub-path towards the first firm projection, which in turn is strictly shorter than the length of the path associated with the first firm, which concludes the proof of P3.

P4. The technical inefficiency value, $TI_{FR}\left(x_j, y_j\right) = \frac{T\Pi I_{FR}\left(x_j, y_j\right)}{U_{FR}}$, $\left(x_j, y_j\right) \in F$, shows clearly that the units of measurement of $T\Pi I_{FR}(x_j, y_j)$ are monetary units, just the same as the units of the denominator, and consequently, that $TI_{FR}(x_j, y_j)$ is a pure number for any firm, which concludes the proof. □

Resorting to (13.31), the new defined technical inefficiency measure, it is straightforward to obtain the new *normalized FR profit inefficiency decomposition*, just by considering equalities in (13.29), corresponding to the *FR profit inefficiency decomposition*, as shown in the next subsection.

13.2.5.7 The FR Approach and Its Normalized Profit Inefficiency

By dividing the FR profit inefficiency decomposition by $U_{FR} > 0_{\$}$, as reported in (13.29) and based on the generalized direct approach, we obtain the next normalized profit inefficiency decomposition:

$$N\Pi I_{FR}\left(x_{j_E}, y_{j_E}, \widetilde{w}, \widetilde{p}\right) = \frac{\Pi I_{FR}\left(x_{j_E}, y_{j_E}, w, p\right)}{U_{FR}} = 0 + \frac{\left(p \cdot u^{-}_{j_E FR} + w \cdot u^{-}_{j_E FR}\right)}{U_{FR}},$$
$$\left(x_{j_E}, y_{j_E}\right) \in F_E,$$
$$N\Pi I_{FR}\left(x_{j_N}, y_{j_N}, \widetilde{w}, \widetilde{p}\right) = \frac{\Pi I_{FR}\left(x_{j_N}, y_{j_N}, w, p\right)}{U_{FR}} = \frac{\left(p \cdot u^{+}_{j_N FR} + w \cdot u^{-}_{j_N FR}\right)}{U_{FR}} + 0,$$
$$\left(x_{j_N}, y_{j_N}\right) \in F_N. \tag{13.33}$$

As usual, the *FR Nerlovian - or normalized - profit inefficiency* is decomposed as the sum of two terms: first, the *technical inefficiency* of the firm being analyzed and, second, its *allocative inefficiency*. The first term is 0, in case (x_o, y_o) is efficient (see the first chain of equalities in (13.33)), or positive if it is not (see the second chain of equalities). The second term works the other way around: it is positive and corresponds to the allocative inefficiency of firm $\left(x_{j_E}, y_{j_E}\right)$ (see the first row) or equals 0 and corresponds to the FR profit inefficiency associated with the profit-maximizing projection of non-efficient firm $\left(x_{j_N}, y_{j_N}\right)$ (see the second row).

Let us finally revise which *properties* are satisfied by the *FR profit approach*. Since the normalizing factor is unique, *it satisfies the comparison property*. On the other hand, since the Nerlovian profit inefficiency of any efficient firm is equal to its own allocative inefficiency and the allocative inefficiency of any non-efficient firm is the profit inefficiency of its closest profit- maximizing projection, we conclude that both *the essential property* and *the extended essential property* are also satisfied.

13.2.5.8 Numerical Example for the FR Profit Approach

Example 13.5
Let us consider again the same numerical example used for the *SR profit approach* (see Table 13.3). Our new Table 13.4 maintains the same columns as the previous one, but its rows are grouped into two parts. Specifically, the first-row headers correspond to the subset of four efficient firms, A, B, C, and D, listed below it, while the sixth-row headers correspond to the subset of five inefficient firms, E, F, G, H, and I, listed below it. We highlight in the first row headers of column 4 the absence of any technology movement associated with the efficient units and in the fifth row headers of column 6 the absence of any allocative movement associated with the non-efficient units. These two facts clearly differentiate the *FR profit approach* in Table 13.4 from the *SR profit approach* in Table 13.3. Comparing columns 2 of both tables, we can clearly appreciate that six out of nine firms obtain a different *FR projection* from their former *SR projection*. Therefore, only the three rows analyzing the three inefficient firms G, H, and I, which obtain the same final

Table 13.4 Results based on *the FR approach*, $(p, w) = (6,1)$

Efficient firms	*FR Profit Maximizing Projection*	$\Pi I_{\$}$	$T\Pi I_{\$} = 0_{\$}$ *Absence of technology movement*	$A\Pi I_{\$} = \Pi I_{\$}$ *(of each efficient firm)*	$TI = 0$	$\frac{\Pi I_{\$}}{NF_{\$}}$	$AI = \frac{A\Pi I_{\$}}{NF_{\$}}$
A = (3,5)	(12,12)	33	(6,1)·(0,0) = 0	33	0	33/60	33/60
B = (6,10)	(12,12)	6	(6,1)·(0,0) = 0	6	0	6/60	6/60
C = (9,11)	(12,12)	3	(6,1)·(0,0) = 0	3	0	3/60	3/60
D = (12,12)	(12,12)	0	(6,1)·(0,0) = 0	0	0	0	0
Non-efficient firms	*FR Profit Maximizing Projection*	$\Pi I_{\$}$	$T\Pi I_{\$} = \left(p \cdot s_{oRA}^{+*} + w \cdot s_{oRA}^{-*}\right)_{\$}$ *(of each non-efficient firm)*	$A\Pi I_{\$} = 0_{\$}$ *Absence of allocative movement*	$TI = \frac{T\Pi I_{\$}}{NF_{\$}}$	$\frac{\Pi I_{\$}}{NF_{\$}}$	$AI = \frac{A\Pi I_{\$}}{NF_{\$}}$
E = (3,2)	(12,12)	51	(6,1)·(10,-9) = 51	0	51/60	51/60	0
F = (10,5)	(12,12)	40	(6,1)·(7,-2) = 40	0	40/60	40/60	0
G = (12,2)	(12,12)	60	(6,1)·(10,0) = 60	0	1	60/60	0
H = (12,11)	(12,12)	6	(6,1)·(1,0) = 6	0	6/60	6/60	0
I = (16,12)	(12,12)	4	(6,1)·(0,4) = 4	0	4/60	4/60	0
–	–	–	$NF_{\$} = 60$	–	–	–	–

projection in both approaches, are equal in both tables, despite the fact that both normalization factors take the same value in both tables. Solving program (13.28) all firms obtain the same *FR projection*, D = (12,12), as shown in column 2 of our new table, simply because the profit-maximizing point is unique in this example. Two conclusions are at hand. First, while both the *FR profit approach* and the *SR profit approach* aim at minimizing allocative inefficiency, their projections on the efficient frontier are quite different, because the latter allows for slack adjustments that are unrestricted in sign, while the former implies that movements within the production possibility can be attained only by reducing inputs and increasing outputs. And second, our new reverse approach offers comparable Nerlovian inefficiencies, reported in the last three columns and satisfies the essential and the extended essential property (see the last column).

To close this subsection and in order to show how model (13.28) works, let us consider as a new vector of market prices $(p, w) = (3,1)$. Now the profit-maximizing points is the facet whose extreme firms are B and D. Since each firm selects as *FR projection* its closest profit-maximizing point, the reader can verify that the new closest projections are *proj(A)* = *D*, *proj(B)* = *B*, *proj(C)* = *C*, *proj(D)* = *D*, *proj (E)* = *B*, *proj(F)* $= \frac{1}{3}(6, 10) + \frac{2}{3}(12, 12) = \left(10, 11\frac{1}{3}\right)$, *proj(G)* = *D*, *proj(H)* = *D*, and *proj(I)* = *D*. Consequently, two efficient firms, B and D, and two inefficient firms, E and F, have changed their projections. We leave to the reader the exercise of elaborating the corresponding table for these new market prices, as well as deducing the optimal unrestricted in sign slack values associated with model (13.28).

13.3 Decomposing Cost Inefficiency

13.3.1 The Traditional Approaches Based on Input-Oriented Efficiency Measures

In this section, we are going to deal exclusively with input-oriented measures. As usual, we want to analyze a finite sample of firms and are interested only in reducing inputs keeping the level of outputs. Hence, for analyzing firm (x_o, y_o), we no longer consider the whole production possibility set under variable returns to scale, T, but focus on the subset consisting of all the observations that produce y_o as its output vector, known as *the input set* $L(y_o) := \{x : (x, y_o) \in T\}$—see Sect 2.2 of Chap. 2. This subset has its own frontier, which is obviously a subset of $\partial^W(T)$, and, as usual, we need to select a certain input-oriented efficiency measure, $EM(I)$, for evaluating $TI_{EM(I)}(x_o, y_o)$, the technical inefficiency of the firm under scrutiny, and for identifying its frontier projection $\left(\widehat{x}_{oEM(I)}, y_o\right)$.

Let us assume, as usual, that T is generated by a finite sample of production firms $(x_j, y_j), j \in J$ according to (13.2). Given market input prices $w > 0_M$, the *minimum cost for points* (x, y_o) *satisfying* $x \in L(y_o)$, denoted as $C(y_o, w)$, is obtained by solving the next linear program:

$$
\begin{aligned}
C(y_o, w) = \quad & \min_{x,\lambda} \sum_{m=1}^{M} w_m x_m \\
& s.t. \\
& \sum_{j=1}^{J} \lambda_j x_{mj} \leq x_m, \quad m = 1, \ldots, M, \\
& \sum_{j=1}^{J} \lambda_j y_{nj} \geq y_{no}, \quad n = 1, \ldots, N, \\
& \sum_{j=1}^{J} \lambda_j = 1, \\
& \lambda_j \geq 0, \quad j = 1, \ldots, J, \\
& x_m \geq 0, \quad m = 1, \ldots, M.
\end{aligned}
\tag{13.34}
$$

Any optimal solution of the last program, (x^*, y_o) is a *cost-minimizing point.*[44] For any firm (x_o, y_o), its *cost inefficiency* is defined as $CI(x_o, y_o, w) = w \cdot x_o - C(y_o, w) \geq 0$ (see expression (2.18) in Sect. 2.3 of Chap. 2), that is, the difference between the input costs at (x_o, y_o), $w \cdot x_o$, and the minimum cost in $L(y_o)$, $C(y_o, w)$. For defining the inequality that *the traditional approach* associates with a certain input-oriented efficiency measure, $EM(I)$, we need to resort to duality results which end up by obtaining a Fenchel-Mahler inequality, valid for any firm (x_o, y_o), that establishes that its cost inefficiency $CI(x_o, y_o, w)$, which is expressed in monetary units, is greater or equal than *the product of a certain positive factor*, also expressed in monetary units, times its technical inefficiency $TI_{EM(I)}(x_o, y_o)$. In the last inequality, the factor mentioned is called the *normalization factor*. By dividing the mentioned inequality by this factor, we obtain a final inequality that relates the *normalized cost inefficiency*, $CI(x_o, y_o, \widetilde{w})$, which is a pure number, with its *technical inefficiency* $TI_{EM(I)}(x_o, y_o)$, which is also a pure number. Finally, the mentioned inequality is transformed into an equality, by adding to the technical inefficiency a second term that is retrieved as a residual, known as the *allocative inefficiency* $AI_{EM(I)}(x_o, y_o, \widetilde{w})$. Since each $EM(I)$ requires deducing a specific inequality, as can be observed in the preceding chapters, we are going to talk about *the traditional approaches*, each one associated with a specific input-oriented efficiency measure and each generating *a different normalized cost inefficiency decomposition for* (x_o, y_o), since *the normalizing factor* and *the technical inefficiency* are almost always different for each $EM(I)$.

To give a single example, let us consider *the input-oriented weighted additive distance function*, *WADF(I)*, of Chap. 6. Recalling its *normalized cost inefficiency decomposition*, identified as (6.19) in the mentioned chapter, we have

$$\begin{aligned} CI_{WADF(I)}(x_o, y_o, \widetilde{w}) &= \underbrace{\frac{\sum_{m=1}^{M} w_m x_{mo} - C(y_o, w)}{\min\left\{w_1/\rho_1^-, \ldots, w_M/\rho_M^-\right\}}}_{\text{Cost Inefficiency}} \\ &= \underbrace{TI_{WADF(I)}(x_o, y_o, \rho^-)}_{\text{Technical Inefficiency}} + AI_{WADF(I)}(x_o, y_o, \rho^-, \widetilde{w}), \end{aligned}$$

where ρ^- are the input weights and $\min\left\{\frac{w_1}{\rho_1^-}, \ldots, \frac{w_M}{\rho_M^-}\right\}$ is the normalizing factor, which we denote as $NF_{WADF(I)}(x_o, y_o, w)$. This efficiency measure has a nice

[44] Strictly speaking, the optimal solution of program (13.34) is point $\left(\sum_{j=1}^{J} \lambda_j^* x_j, \sum_{j=1}^{J} \lambda_j^* y_j\right)$. But since its input side is able to generate its output side, it is also able to generate a diminished output side as y_o. Within a DEA framework, even in the low-dimensional two input-one output space, we can find multiple optimal solutions, depending on the relative position of the hyperplane $w_1x_1 + w_2x_2 = C(y_o, (w_1, w_2))$ with respect to the polyhedral frontier of the input set within the plane $y = y_o$.

behavior because the normalizing factor is unique and independent of the production firm being analyzed and, therefore, applies to all firms. As a consequence, *the three terms in the last equality are comparable* between firms, a quality that has been already baptized, in the preceding section, as *the comparison property*. Comparison on an equal footing is obviously true for the technical inefficiency, associated, in this case, with a specific weighted additive model; it is also true for the left-hand side term because their respective numerators are directly comparable and the denominator is the same for all firms; and finally, it is true for the last term, the allocative inefficiency, being a residual of the two other terms. Hence, the key for achieving the comparison property between traditional normalized cost inefficiency decompositions is to obtain *the same normalization factor* for all the firms of the sample. Later on, we will also verify that this condition is a sufficient condition for achieving the extended essential property, provided that we resort to the general direct approach.

13.3.2 The General Direct Approach Based on a Specific Input-Oriented Efficiency Measure

The reasoning is similar to the one previously developed in connection with the profit function and is also based on Pastor et al. (2021a). Therefore, we will try to be as concise as possible since the underlying philosophy has been previously exposed for the profit case in Sect. 13.2.2. Our *general direct approach* establishes a *general single equality valid for any efficiency measure*, in contrast with any of the traditional approaches that need to develop a specific Fenchel-Mahler inequality each time. Initially, the general direct approach, when applied to firm (x_o, y_o), only requires knowing its projection.[45] The *general direct approach* can obviously be applied when the mentioned projection $\left(\widehat{x}_{oEM(I)}, y_o\right)$ is obtained through any *input-oriented efficiency measure* $EM(I)$. In this case, it starts by obtaining a *general direct cost inefficiency decomposition* and ends up deducing *a general direct normalized cost inefficiency decomposition*, which requires the additional knowledge of the technical inefficiency $TI_{EM(I)}(x_o, y_o)$, as we indicate as follows.

The optimal input slacks that connect (x_o, y_o) with its $EM(I)$ projection satisfy $\left(s^{-*}_{oEM(I)}, 0_N\right) = (x_o, y_o) - \left(\widehat{x}_{oEM(I)}, y_o\right) \geq 0_{M+N}$ or, focusing on the input components,

$$\widehat{x}_{oEM(I)} = x_o - s^{-*}_{oEM(I)} \geq 0_M. \tag{13.35}$$

Obviously, $s^{-*}_{oEM} = 0_M$ is equivalent to $\left(\widehat{x}_{oEM(I)}, y_o\right) = (x_o, y_o)$ which signals that (x_o, y_o) is a frontier firm of $L(y_o)$. Since, by definition, *the cost inefficiency at the projection* is equal to $w\widehat{x}_{oEM(I)} - C(y_o, w) \geq 0$, we can decompose it as follows:

[45] Since the initial information needed is only the projection of the firm being rated, the general direct approach for decomposing cost inefficiency has the potential of being applied in quite different settings, as we will show later on when introducing the reverse approaches.

$$w \cdot \widehat{x}_{oEM(I)} - C(y_o, w) = w \cdot \left(x_o - s^{-*}_{oEM(I)}\right) - C(y_o, w)$$
$$= (w \cdot x_o - C(y_o, w)) - w \cdot s^{-*}_{oEM(I)}.$$

Finally, by transposing the last term, we obtain our *first basic equality*:[46]

$$w \cdot x_o - C(y_o, w) = w \cdot s^{-*}_{oEM(I)} + \left(w \cdot \widehat{x}_{oEM(I)} - C(y_o, w)\right) \tag{13.36}$$

Equality (13.36) tells us that the cost inefficiency at (x_o, y_o), $CI(x_o, y_o, w)$ is equal to the cost of the input slacks that connect (x_o, y_o) with its projection, $w \cdot s^{-*}_{oEM(I)}$, which we refer to as the *technological cost gap*, plus the cost inefficiency at its projection $CI\left(\widehat{x}_{oEM(I)}, y_o, w\right)$. Shortly, $CI(x_o, y_o, w) = w \cdot s^{-*}_{oEM(I)} + CI\left(\widehat{x}_{oEM(I)}, y_o, w\right)$. Hence, (13.36) constitutes *the general direct cost inefficiency decomposition.*

In case the first right-hand side term of (13.36) is equal to $0_\$$, it is obvious that $\widehat{x}_{oEM(I)} = x_o$, which implies that $TI_{EM(I)}(x_o, y_o) = 0$, and we can rewrite $w \cdot s^{-*}_{oEM(I)} = 0_\$$ as $k_{o\$} \cdot 0$, with $k_{o\$}$ being any positive constant expressed in monetary units.[47] Otherwise, $w \cdot s^{-*}_{oEM(I)} > 0_\$$, which implies that $\widehat{x}_{oEM(I)} \neq x_o$, in which case $TI_{EM(I)}(x_o, y_o) > 0$, and we can decompose $w \cdot s^{-*}_{oEM(I)}$ as the product $\left(\frac{w \cdot s^{-*}_{oEM(I)}}{TI_{EM(I)}(x_o, y_o)}\right) \times TI_{EM(I)}(x_o, y_o) > 0$. Hence, *the normalization factor* $NF^{GD}_{EM(I)}(x_o, y_o, w)$ attached to the technical inefficiency has been identified and can be formulated as follows[48]:

$$NF^{GD}_{EM(I)}(x_o, y_o, w) = \left\{ \begin{array}{ll} \dfrac{w \cdot s^{-*}_{oEM(I)}}{TI_{EM(I)}(x_o, y_o)} > 0_\$, & (x_o, y_o) \neq \left(\widehat{x}_{oEM(I)}, y_o\right) \\ k_{o\$}, k_o > 0 & , (x_o, y_o) = \left(\widehat{x}_{oEM(I)}, y_o\right) \end{array} \right\}. \tag{13.37}$$

Consequently, we can rewrite (13.36) as the next equality

$$w \cdot x_o - C(y_o, w) = NF^{GD}_{EM(I)}(x_o, y_o, w) \times TI_{EM(I)}(x_o, y_o)$$
$$+ \left(w \cdot \widehat{x}_{oEM(I)} - C(y_o, w)\right), \tag{13.38}$$

which shows the *general direct cost inefficiency decomposition at* (x_o, y_o) *as the sum of* a first cost inefficiency term related to technical inefficiency and a second cost inefficiency term associated with its input projection $\left(\widehat{x}_{oEM(I)}, y_o\right)$. We refer to each of these two components as *technical cost inefficiency and allocative cost inefficiency*. Moreover, dividing by the normalizing factor, which is, for each firm, a

[46] All the terms of (13.36) are expressed in monetary units, e.g., in dollars ($).

[47] In principle, we can fix $k_{o\$} = 1_\$$ for all firms with $TI_{EM(I)}(x_o, y_o) = 0$ or consider other possibilities as shown in Example 13.2.

[48] The firms that satisfy $(x_o, y_o) = (\widehat{x}_o, y_o)$ are called the non-inefficient firms.

positive number expressed in monetary units, we obtain the desired *general direct normalized cost inefficiency decomposition for firm* (x_o, y_o), which, is a pure number, as *the sum of its technical inefficiency and its allocative inefficiency*:

$$\frac{(w \cdot x_o - C(y_o, w))}{NF^{GD}_{EM(I)}(x_o, y_o, w)} = TI_{EM(I)}(x_o, y_o) + \frac{(w \cdot \widehat{x}_{oEM} - C(y_o, w))}{NF^{GD}_{EM(I)}(x_o, y_o, w)}. \tag{13.39}$$

This last decomposition implies several well-known and intuitive facts:

1. If (x_o, y_o) is a cost-minimizing firm, i.e., $(w \cdot x_o - C(y_o, w)) = 0_\$$, then the three terms of (13.39), the normalized cost inefficiency, the technical inefficiency, and the allocative inefficiency, must all be 0.
2. If the technical inefficiency is 0, then (x_o, y_o) is a frontier firm, and all the normalized cost inefficiency corresponds to allocative inefficiency.
3. And last, if the allocative inefficiency is 0, then all the normalized cost inefficiency is technical.

Depending on the nature of *EM*(*I*), we may obtain only strong efficient points as projections—e.g., the weighted additive distance function (*WADF*), discussed in Chap. 6. This is relevant from the perspective of Pareto-Koopmans efficiency because, in that case, the *technical inefficiency* accounts for all types of input inefficiencies (radial and non-radial).

We have considered the *uniqueness* of the two general direct *profit* inefficiency decompositions at the end of Sect. 13.2.2 (see the paragraph just above Example 13.1). With minor adaptations, similar criteria are valid for the *cost inefficiency decompositions*. In case the used measure identifies only a *single projection for each firm* being rated, the *traditional approach* and the *general direct approach decompositions* are *unique and may be different*.

Just as we did for the profit inefficiency decomposition, there are four basic options for assigning the value of the normalizing factor (see (13.37)), with three of them devoted to the frontier firms and the fourth one to facilitate the comparison between any traditional decomposition cost approach and the new general direct cost approach.

Four Options for Assigning Normalization Factor Values to $k_{o\$}$

As mentioned previously, let us consider first how to assign, when using the general direct profit decomposition approach associated with a certain input-oriented efficiency measure, a normalizing factor to any frontier firm (x, y_o) satisfying $TI_{EM(I)}(x, y_o) = 0$ or, equivalently, satisfying $(\widehat{x}_{oEM}, y_o) = (x_o, y_o)$. Here are the three options:

Option 1. The frontier firm (x, y_o) is only the projection of itself. In this case, we assign to it a normalization factor equal to 1. This decision guarantees that the allocative inefficiencies are comparable between frontier firms with this particularity.

Option 2. Suppose now that the frontier firm (x, y_o) is also the projection of just another inefficient firm, $(x_j, y_o) \neq (x, y_o)$ and $(\widehat{x}_{jEM(I)}, y_o) = (x, y_o)$. Since (x_j, y_o)

has its own normalization factor, we propose to assign it to (x, y_o). It happens quite seldom, but in case (x, y_o) is the projection of two or more inefficient firms and all of them have the same normalization factor, we make the same decision.

Option 3. In general, let us assume that the frontier firm (x, y_o) is the projection of two or more inefficient firms. In this case, we propose to assign to it the normalization factor of the inefficient firm that is L_1-closer to (x_o, y_o).[49]

Option 4. For a certain input-oriented efficiency measure, our fourth option when comparing the traditional approach with the general direct approach is to assign the value of the normalization factors of the traditional approach to the firms that are projected onto themselves (see, for example, Example 13.6).

Doubts on what option to select arise when the chosen input inefficiency measure identifies more than one projection for at least one of the inefficient firms being analyzed. Anytime that we face this possibility, which depends on the inefficiency measure we are using, we must check if any non-efficient firm of the sample being analyzed effectively gets more than one projection.[50] In those cases, we need to establish a secondary criterion for selecting *the most appropriate projection.*[51] In fact, this task is not only necessary for guaranteeing that the *general direct approach* ends up with a *unique cost inefficiency decomposition* and a *unique normalized cost inefficiency decomposition* but also for seeking *the best cost projection*, i.e., the projection that achieves the lowest cost inefficiency among the possible projections.[52] The same consideration is valid *for any input-oriented traditional approach*, although it is quite unusual in the specialized literature to deal with more than one technical optimal projection, probably because most of the usual input-oriented measures only deliver single projections.

Let us briefly develop the last idea. In the case of multiple projections for any single non-efficient firm, there is one easy criterion for deciding which projection to choose. We start by identifying from among the subset of all the non-efficient firms of our sample those that have more than one projection. The mentioned criteria must be applied to any firm with at least two projections. Focusing first on our *general direct cost inefficiency decomposition*, $w \cdot x_o - C(y_o, w) = w \cdot \overline{s}^{-*}_{oEM(I)} + \left(w \cdot \widehat{x}_{oEM(I)} - C(y_o, w)\right)$, the value of the left-hand side is constant because it depends exclusively on the firm being rated and on the input costs, while the technological gap as well as the cost inefficiency associated with the projection, on the right-hand side, can vary for two alternative optimal projections. Hence, considering the last equality, if we

[49]This proposal guarantees that at least the closest inefficient firm has the same allocative inefficiency as its projection.

[50]The *ERG* = *SBM*, presented in Chap. 7, is likely to generate multiple solutions. See the mentioned chapter where we explain how to calculate them.

[51]Alternative projections have a common feature: all of them have associated the same valued technical inefficiency.

[52]The best cost projection means the projection that has the lowest cost inefficiency among the alternative projections. We just need to calculate one of these projections.

select the optimal projection with *the largest technological cost gap* $w \cdot s^{-*}_{oEM(I)} > 0_{\$}$, we will *pick up the projection that has the smallest cost inefficiency,* which is precisely the projection that is "closer" to a cost-minimizing benchmark. This strategy gives rise to a *general direct normalized cost inefficiency decomposition,* whose *normalizing factor is as large as possible,* because the *technical inefficiency* associated with all the alternative projections is the same and whose associated *allocative inefficiency* (i.e., that of the best projection) is, consequently, the smallest. Summing up, in case one or more non-efficient firms obtain multiple projections, we propose to *achieve* the *uniqueness of the cost decompositions* associated with the general direct approach by *identifying, in each case, a projection with the smallest possible cost.*[53]

13.3.3 Cost Inefficiency Decomposition Based on the Traditional and on the General Direct Approach: A Comparison, a Numerical Example, and Some Properties of the Direct Approach

Let us start by establishing the comparison between both approaches, assuming that both use the same efficiency measure for determining the technical inefficiency of each firm.

Comparison

Basically, in order to implement each of the two approaches, we need to take three consecutive steps. The first steps are just the same, but the second ones are completely different. The third steps are almost the same if the efficiency measure of choice identifies a single projection for each firm (e.g., in case of the directional distance function discussed in Chap. 8). Otherwise, the mentioned step is simpler in the traditional approach and more complex in the general direct approach, with the characteristic that the last one is able to get a lower allocative inefficiency for the firms with multiple projections. In conclusion, when multiple projections are detected, the new considered approach selects the "best" one, while the traditional one does not depend on the characteristics of the projection and always offers the same decompositions.

Traditional Approach

First Step: Select $\overline{EM(I)}$*; calculate for each* (x_o, y_o), $\left(\widehat{x}_{o\overline{EM(I)}}, y_o\right)$, $TI_{\overline{EM(I)}}(x_o, y_o)$ *and its cost inefficiency* $CI(x_o, y_o, w)$.

Second Step: For $\overline{EM(I)}$*, find a Fenchel-Mahler inequality that provides a normalizing factor satisfying* $CI(x_o, y_o, w) \geq NF^{TR}_{\overline{EM(I)}}(x_o, y_o, w) \cdot TI_{\overline{EM(I)}}(x_o, y_o)$ *for all*

[53] In case two or more projections lead to the same smallest cost inefficiency, we can select any of them or consider a second criterion, as suggested before for the case of profit inefficiency.

(x_o, y_o). *Since the normalizing factor is unique to any of the known input inefficiency measures, the last inequality is unique to any firm as well. Based on the last inequality*, retrieve $ACI^{TR}_{\overline{EM(I)}}(x_o, y_o, \widetilde{w})$ *as a residual, and formulate* the cost inefficiency decomposition $CI(x_o, y_o, w) = NF^{TR}_{\overline{EM(I)}}(x_o, y_o, w) \cdot TI_{\overline{EM(I)}}(x_o, y_o) + ACI^{TR}_{\overline{EM(I)}}(x_o, y_o, \widetilde{w})$.

Third Step: Dividing *all the terms of the last equality by the normalizing factor, formulate* the normalized cost inefficiency decomposition: $\frac{CI(x_o, y_o, w)}{NF^{TR}_{\overline{EM(I)}}(x_o, y_o, w)} = TI_{\overline{EM(I)}}(x_o, y_o) + AI^{TR}_{\overline{EM(I)}}(x_o, y_o, \widetilde{w})$.

General Direct Approach

First Step: The same as for the traditional approach.

Second Step: Leave out $TI_{\overline{EM(I)}}(x_o, y_o)$. *For* $\overline{EM(I)}$, *calculate* $CI\left(\widehat{x}_{o\overline{EM(I)}}, y_o, w\right)$. *In case one or more firms have multiple projections, select for each of these firms the projection with the lowest cost. After calculating* $w \cdot s^{-*}_{o\overline{EM(I)}}$, obtain the *cost inefficiency decomposition,* $CI(x_o, y_o, w) = w \cdot s^{-*}_{o\overline{EM(I)}} + CI_{EM}\left(\widehat{x}_{o\overline{EM(I)}}, y_o, w\right)$.

Third Step: Recover $TI_{\overline{EM(I)}}(x_o, y_o)$. Obtain *first* the normalizing factor $NF^{GD}_{\overline{EM(I)}}(x_o, y_o, w)$ *dividing* $w \cdot s^{-*}_{o\overline{EM(I)}}$ *by* $TI_{\overline{EM(I)}}(x_o, y_o)$ *and, after, the corresponding* cost inefficiency decomposition for each firm *dividing all the terms of the cost inefficiency decomposition by the normalizing factor:*[54]

$$CI^{GD}_{\overline{EM(I)}}(x_o, y_o, \widetilde{w}) = \frac{CI(x_o, y_o, w)}{NF^{GD}_{\overline{EM(I)}}(x_o, y_o, w)} = TI_{\overline{EM(I)}}(x_o, y_o) + \frac{CI\left(\widehat{x}_{o\overline{EM(I)}}, y_o, w\right)}{NF^{GD}_{\overline{EM(I)}}(x_o, y_o, w)} = . \\ = TI_{\overline{EM(I)}}(x_o, y_o) + AI^{GD}_{\overline{EM}}(x_o, y_o, \widetilde{w}) \quad (13.40)$$

Example 13.6

Let as start reminding the reader that the input-oriented Russell measure of our next example, which is likely to produce multiple projections, has been studied in Chap. 5.[55] Let us now consider the next "two input-one output example" with nine firms, where all firms have the same output value y_o. This decision simplifies our calculus, because $L(y_o)$ and $C(y_o, w)$ are a common subset and a common value for all the firms of this example. Hence, since we are going to use an input-oriented measure, *it is sufficient to consider for each firm its two inputs*. Here is the sample of nine firms: A = (2,10), B = (4,6), C = (6,3), D = (8,2), E = (10,2), F = (12,6),

[54]For each firm that is projected onto itself, select one of the three options described before.

[55]This input-oriented measure is a particular case of the $ERG = SBM$, defined by Pastor et al. (1999) for a graph- input or output- representation of the technology.

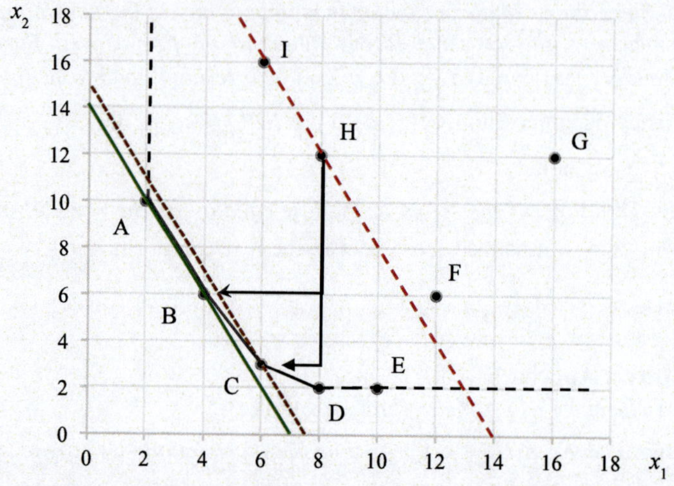

Fig. 13.3 Example of the traditional and general approaches to decompose cost inefficiency, $w = (2, 1)$

G = (16,12), H = (8,12), and I = (6,16). Figure 13.3 illustrates the example, including the minimum isocost line in green. Under VRS, we get that the first four firms are strongly efficient, while the last five firms are inefficient.[56]

Graphically, we appreciate that the strong efficient frontier has three facets, respectively defined by the pair of firms {A,B} = {(2,10),(4,6)}, {B,C} = {(4,6),(6,3)}, and {C,D} = {(6,3),(2,10)}. We will see later on that the rest of the firms are inefficient, only one of them, firm E = (10,2), proving weakly efficient. Let us further assume that the market input costs (per firm) are $w = (w_1, w_2) = (2, 1)$. Hence, at each efficient firm, A = (2,10), B = (4,6), C = (6,3), and D = (8,2), the cost is equal to 4 + 10 = \$14, \$14, \$15, and \$18, which means that the two *cost-minimizing efficient firms* are A = (2,10) and B = (4,6), and consequently, all the firms belonging to their facet are also cost-minimizing benchmarks. The technical inefficiency for firm (x_o, y_o) is equal to $\frac{1}{2}\left(\frac{s_{o1}^{-*}}{x_{o1}} + \frac{s_{o2}^{-*}}{x_{o2}}\right)$, and the general normalizing factor, according to Aparicio et al. (2015a) (see expression (5.21) in Chap. 5), is equal to $M \cdot \min\{x_{o1}w_1, \ldots, x_{oM}w_M\}$, which simplifies, when dealing with two inputs, to $2 \cdot \min\{x_{o1}w_1, x_{o2}w_2\}$.[57] Let us analyze Table 13.5, indicating that two of our inefficient firms get a couple of alternative projections, which means that the input Russell technical inefficiency associated with each inefficient firm is the same

[56] Since the measure we are using is a strong efficient measure, in order to classify the efficiency of firms, we can rely on the—simplest—additive model or, alternatively, draw a picture in the two-input plane to see geometrically the position of the firms (see Fig. 13.3).

[57] Let us point out that the normalizing factor of the traditional approach for this particular efficiency measure does only depend on the input components of the firm being rated and on market prices, which shows that in case of multiple projections any of them will give rise to the same normalized cost decomposition.

Table 13.5 Results based on the traditional decomposition of Aparicio et al. (2015a) (Chap. 5), $w = (2, 1)$

Firm	*Project. RM(I)*	$TI_{EM(I)}$	*CI*	*NF*	$TCI = NF \times TI$	$ACI = CI - TCI$	*CI/NF*	$AI = ACI/NF$
(1)	(2)	(3)	(4)	(5)	(6) = (5) × (3)	(7) = (4) – (6)	(8) = (4)/(5)	(9) = (7)/(5)
A = (2,10)	(2,10)	0	0	8	0	0	0	0
B = (4,6)	(4,6)	0	0	12	0	0	0	0
C = (6,3)	(6,3)	0	15–14 = 1	6	0	1	1/6	1/6
D = (8,2)	(8,2)	0	4	4	0	4	1	1
E = (10,2)	(8,2)	1/10	8	4	2/5	38/5	8/4 = 2	19/10
F = (12,6)	(6,3)	1/2	16	12	6	10	16/12 = 4/3	5/6
G = (16,12)	(6,3)	11/16	30	24	33/2	27/2	30/24 = 5/4	27/48
H = (8,12)	(4,6)	1/2	14	24	12	2	7/12	1/12
I = (6,16)	(2,10)	25/48	14	24	25/2	3/2	7/12	1/16

for its two projections. Firm F = (12,6) has the option to choose between efficient firms D = (8,2) and C = (6,3), while firm H = (8,12) has C = (6,3) and B = (4,6) as possible peers. In both cases, their input Russell inefficiency scores are equal to ½. Although any of the two projections in the two cases will give rise to the same decompositions when using the traditional approach, we have selected the "best" projection for both approaches in order to compare them. As already explained before, for the general direct approach, the *best projection* means the one that has the lowest cost. Hence, looking back at the cost associated with each efficient firm calculated before, we conclude that we should prefer firm C = (6,3) as projection for F = (12,6), while for firm H = (8,12), our best choice is firm B = (4,6), which is a cost-minimizing firm; the corresponding isocost lines for B = (4,6), C = (6,3), and H = (8,12), are shown in Fig. 13.2. Let us consider Table 13.5 again and add some comments.

Some particularities are worth mentioning. All the projections correspond to strong efficient firms. The last two inefficient firms whose projection corresponds to the two cost-minimizing firms do not achieve an allocative inefficiency equal to 0 (see the last column). Hence, the input-oriented Russell measure combined with the traditional approach does not satisfy the *essential property* introduced in Sect. 2.4.5 of Chap. 2. Neither does it satisfy the *comparison property*, because the normalization factors are different. From the point of view of the cost inefficiency, we appreciate a certain regularity between columns 3 and 4 of Table 13.5: a larger technical inefficiency almost corresponds to a greater cost inefficiency. It can be better explained looking at the *cost inefficiency decomposition*, where its technical part is much larger than its allocative part, at least for the last four firms. One final comment, assume for a moment that we choose as a projection of firm F = (12,6) the other possibility, firm D = (8,2). If we revise in Table 13.5 the row associated with F = (12,6), with the exception of the second column, the rest of the data will not vary: the technical inefficiency, in column 3, is exactly the same, by definition. The cost inefficiency, in column 4, is the same because it depends only on firm F = (12,6) and on the minimum cost, independent of the projection used. The normalization factor, in the next column, only depends on the firm and on the costs (see its expression above). And, finally, the rest of the columns, being derived from the former five, only depend on the firm being rated and on its technical inefficiency, and not on its projection. *The uniqueness of the traditional approach for this particular efficiency measure*, which does not depend on the projection chosen, explains this last outcome.

Let us now apply our *general direct decomposition* to the same data, summarizing the results in the following Table 13.6. Now the normalizing factor for each inefficient firm is equal to $\frac{w \cdot s_{oEM}^{-*}}{TI_{EM(I)}(x_o, y_o)}$. For the remaining four firms at the top of Table 13.6, we have the option of deciding which normalization factor to use. As we did before, we choose the same factors as those corresponding to Table 13.5, which corresponds to our second proposed option.

Let us analyze Table 13.6, which resorts to our general direct decomposition method, in relation to Table 13.5, based on the traditional approach and, particularly,

Table 13.6 Results based on the general direct decomposition, $w = (2, 1)$

Firm	*Project. RM(I)*	$TI_{EM(I)}$	*CI*	$NF = TCI/TI$	$TCI = ws^{-*}$	$ACI = CI - TCI$	*CI/NF*	$AI = ACI/NF$
(1)	(2)	(3)	(4)	(5)	(6)	(7) = (4) – (6)	(8) = (4)/(5)	(9) = (7)/(5)
A = (2,10)	(2,10)	0	0	*8*	0	0	0	0
B = (4,6)	(4,6)	0	0	*12*	0	0	0	0
C = (6,3)	(6,3)	0	1	*6*	0	1	1/6	1/6
D = (8,2)	(8,2)	0	18 – 14 = 4	*4*	0	4	1	1
E = (10,2)	(8,2)	1/10	8	40	4	4	8/40 = 1/5	1/10
F = (12,6)	(6,3)	1/2	16	30	15	1	16/30 = 8/15	1/30
G = (16,12)	(6,3)	11/16	30	464/11	29	1	330/464 = 165/232	11/464
H = (8,12)	(4,6)	1/2	14	28	14	0	14/28	0
I = (6,16)	(2,10)	25/48	14	672/25	14	0	14(25/672) = 25/48	0

on the normalization factor derived in Chap. 6 for the input-oriented Russell measure. As can be seen, the first four columns are the same in both tables. Columns 5 and 6 are reversed in Table 13.5 and Table 13.6, because in Table 13.5 we *first* obtain *the normalization factor* based on the corresponding inequality and, subsequently, *the technical cost inefficiency* as the *product* of the mentioned *factor* and the *technical inefficiency*, while in Table 13.6 it is the other way around: the *technical cost inefficiency* is one of the components of the cost inefficiency decomposition (see equality (13.36)), and dividing it by the *technical inefficiency*, we derive the corresponding *normalization factor*. We confirm that by using the general direct approach, *each of the inefficient firms always exhibits the same allocative cost inefficiency value as the cost inefficiency of their respective projections* (see column 7 of Table 13.6), whereas this does not happen with the traditional approach (see the same column of Table 13.5). Moreover, coming back to Table 13.6 and observing that the normalizing factors in column 5 are all different, the *allocative inefficiency*, reported in column 9, will not have the last-mentioned property of column 7, with the only exception of the firms that get a 0 value, precisely the last two firms of Table 13.6. When this happens, we say that the *essential property* is fulfilled, i.e., as in Table 13.6 but not in Table 13.5. If we compare the data of the last column between tables, we see that the allocative inefficiency values in Table 13.5 are greater than in Table 13.6 for most firms. In fact, the allocative inefficiencies of the five last firms are much bigger in the preceding table than in the last one, indicating the overestimation associated with the traditional approach for technical inefficiency measures yielding multiple projections.

As a conclusion, we realize that cost inefficiency for input-oriented measures has a parallel behavior with respect to profit inefficiency for graph measures. For instance, the essential property introduced in Chap. 2 for the normalized profit inefficiency decomposition in connection with certain traditional approaches can be extended to the cost inefficiency decomposition of the general direct approach *for any technical inefficiency measure*. Let us now briefly analyze the general direct approach for input-oriented measures.

Properties of the General Direct Approach for Input-Oriented Measures

Definition 13.4 The *general direct cost inefficiency decomposition* associated with a certain *approach* satisfies the *extended essential property* when each firm has the same allocative cost inefficiency as its projection.

Proposition 13.8

1. *Any cost inefficiency decomposition that satisfies the extended essential property also satisfies the essential property.*
2. *The general direct approach always satisfies the extended essential property.*

Proof The proof is similar to Proposition 13.3 and is left to the reader.

As a summary of the findings derived from our last numerical example, where we have confronted the traditional approach versus the general direct approach resorting, in both cases, to the input-oriented Russell measure, we can conclude that as opposed to what happens with the general direct approach, it is not easy for the traditional approach to satisfy the extended essential property. As far as we know, only the input-oriented directional distance functions satisfy this property, as shown in the next subsection.

13.3.4 The Exceptional Case of the Directional Input Distance Function

Parallel to what we have shown for any graph DDF in Sect. 13.2.4, here we emphasize that for *any input-oriented DDF* (also called directional input distance function), the *normalized cost inefficiency decomposition derived resorting to the traditional approach is exactly the same as the one derived with the general direct decomposition*. As far as we know, it is the only input-oriented inefficiency measure that satisfies this property and, consequently, we tag it as an *exceptional case*. Moreover, *the general direct approach*, despite the fact that it does not depend on any Fenchel-Mahler inequality, can also be interpreted as *an extension* of the well-known *input-oriented DDF cost inefficiency decomposition* to *any* other *input-oriented efficiency measure*.[58] As already mentioned, if the inefficiency measure we are considering does not generate multiple projections, then *the normalized profit inefficiency decomposition associated with the general direct approach is unique*, which is valid for any *input-oriented DDF*.

Since our *general direct normalization factor* proposed in (13.37) admits any value for firms which satisfy $(x_o, y_o) = (\widehat{x}_o, \widehat{y}_o)$, we just need to show that both factors are the same when $(x_o, y_o) \neq (\widehat{x}_o, \widehat{y}_o)$. In that case, it is well known that $NF^{TR}_{DDF(I)}(x_o, y_o) = w \cdot g_{x_o}$ (see Chambers et al., 1998). If we multiply and divide this last equality by $TI_{DDF(I)}(x_o, y_o) = \beta^*_o > 0$, we get

$$NF^{TR}_{DDF(I)}(x_o, y_o) = w \cdot g_{x_o} = \frac{\beta^*_o (w \cdot g_{x_o})}{\beta^*_o} = \frac{w \cdot (\beta^*_o g_{x_o})}{\beta^*_o} = \frac{w \cdot s^{-*}_{oDDF(I)}}{TI_{DDF(I)}(x_o, y_o)},$$

which is exactly our general normalizing factor as given by (13.37).

We can immediately derive two implications for any input-oriented DDF related to the two properties we are considering. First, since our general direct approach satisfies the *essential property*, so does the traditional approach for *any input-oriented DDF*. Second, according to Proposition 13.4, any input-oriented DDF also satisfies the *extended essential property*. And third, in case *all the normalizing factors are equal*, the general direct approach guarantees that all the normalized cost inefficiency components are comparable, which corresponds to *the comparison property*. In fact, considering again (13.39), where the normalized cost inefficiency

[58] This connects with Chap. 12 devoted to the *reverse DDF*, which assigns a specific input-oriented DDF to any input-oriented efficiency measure, provided the efficiency measure assigns a single projection to each firm.

is decomposed, we get the next equality which is valid for any firm (x_o, y_o) and *any input-oriented DDF* with a constant normalization factor for all firms:

$$\frac{(w \cdot x_o - C(y_o, w))}{w \cdot g_x} = TI_{DDF(I)}(x_o, y_o) + \frac{(w \cdot \widehat{x}_{oEM} - C(y_o, w))}{w \cdot g_x}.$$

Under the assumption made, *the three expressions in the last equality are comparable* between firms: the normalized profit inefficiency has the same denominator across all the firms, which means that is a true and comparable representation of cost inefficiency across all firms in the sample; the technical inefficiency has been directly obtained through an efficiency measure and, consequently, is also comparable; and last, the allocative inefficiency is also a true and comparable representation of profit inefficiency at each projection $(\widehat{x}_o, \widehat{y}_o)$. In other words and as said before, *any input-oriented DDF with a fixed normalization factor satisfies the comparison property*.

It is obvious that if all the units have the same directional vector, g_x, then they will also have the same normalization factor, $w \cdot g_x$. But what really matters is to have the same normalization factor, a condition that can be fulfilled without having the same directional vector. Let us explore this possibility when dealing with a low number of inputs. When dealing with a single input, the only possibility for having the same normalization factor across firms is that the directional vector is constant. But when dealing with two or more inputs, the options grow. For instance, with two dimensions, what is required is that the corresponding normalization factor, $w \cdot g_x = w_1 g_{x1} + w_2 g_{x2}$, is constant across firms. Since the interior product of two vectors is equal to the product of their L_2-lengths times the cosine of the angle defined by the two vectors and the vector $w = (w_1, w_2)$ is fixed, there are two possible choices for g_x, being the only exception when g_x has exactly the same direction as w. For instance, in case $w_1 = w_2 = 1_\$$, any pair of vectors that are symmetric with respect to w, such as $\left(\frac{1}{2}, \frac{\sqrt{3}}{2}\right)$ and $\left(\frac{\sqrt{3}}{2}, \frac{1}{2}\right)$, give rise to the same normalization factor. In three input dimensions, if we consider the cost vector $w = (w_1, w_2, w_3) \in \mathbb{R}^3_{++}$ and the hyperplane that has $w = (w_1, w_2, w_3)$ as its directional vector and contains its endpoint, we can imagine a circle inside that hyperplane centered in the mention endpoint. Any vector with start point at the origin of the coordinates and with endpoint belonging to the considered circle has the same value of its inner product with the cost vector, provided that the coordinates of the endpoint are non-negative. A spatial intuition is provided if we think that the cost vector corresponds to an umbrella handle and that the points of the circle are the endpoints of the umbrella rods. Any case, even with just three inputs, we can obtain a nonfinite number of directional vectors for our DDF all of which satisfy that $w \cdot g_x = k_\$$; that is, all the firms have the same normalization factor. Obviously, the possibility of selecting different directional vectors that give rise to the same $w \cdot g_x$ increases with the number of inputs. In conclusion, from the point of view of the comparison property and in connection with input-oriented DDFs, the choice of a fixed directional vector is not the only option, because there are many others. Obviously, it is the easiest option, but also the most restrictive one.

13.3.5 The Input-Oriented Reverse Approaches for Cost Decompositions

Let us first introduce *the standard reverse cost approach* (*SR cost approach*), following Pastor et al. (2021b). Basically, for any firm being analyzed, the *SR cost approach* starts identifying a *classical projection*[59] that is as "close" as possible to a cost-minimizing firm or, equivalently, a projection whose cost inefficiency is as small as possible.[60] Therefore, the *SR cost approach* does no longer start by evaluating the input technical inefficiency of the firm based on a certain previously selected input-oriented efficiency measure corresponding to the traditional approach, but it goes the other way around and begins to *reduce allocative inefficiency* as an easier way to *accommodate our production firms to existing cost conditions*. This first goal is achieved by considering the *general direct cost inefficiency decomposition*, introduced previously, that decomposes the cost inefficiency of each firm as the sum of two non-negative terms, which we refer to as *the technology cost gap* and the *allocative cost gap*. The *technology cost gap* only requires knowledge on the input slacks that connect the considered firm with its frontier projection and, at the same time, that guarantee that the first aforementioned goal is achieved. These input slacks are obtained through a specific new linear program. However, since we also want to deduce the corresponding *Nerlovian cost inefficiency decomposition*, *the SR cost approach* needs to measure the *input technical inefficiency*, related to the technology cost gap. This measurement is relatively standard since, as already said, *the SR cost approach* resorts to a classical projection.

Our second input reverse approach, called the *flexible reverse cost approach* (*FR cost approach*), inspired in Pastor et al. (2021c), is more iconoclastic as well as more ambitious than the previous one. It also resorts to the *general direct cost inefficiency decomposition* for obtaining the corresponding *FR cost decomposition* but is radically different from the *SR cost decomposition*. Basically, it allows freedom of movement for any efficient firm within the production possibility set identifying as the best projection any profit-maximizing firm, which reduces its allocative inefficiency as much as possible. Meanwhile, any non-efficient firm may also require a free movement towards the strong efficient frontier in order to identify its input technical inefficiency in a particular way, with its efficient projection also proving to be a cost-minimizing firm. In case more than one final projection meets our basic objective, we introduce as a second criterion the reduction of the L_1-distance between the firm under study and its final projection. The main difficulty with *the FR cost approach* is to define an appropriate technical inefficiency measure that has nothing to do with any of the technical inefficiency measures designed and used previously, since its objective is to reach as an efficient projection any cost-minimizing firm.

[59] *A classical projection of a firm* means a projection that belongs to the efficient frontier which is obtained by nonincreasing the input and by nonreducing the output values of the mentioned firm.

[60] When using the general direct approach as we do, seeking a projection with the lowest possible cost inefficiency, equates to obtaining the least allocative cost inefficiency of the projection.

13.3.5.1 The Standard Reverse Cost Approach and Its Cost Inefficiency Decomposition

Since our aim now is to start reducing, as much as possible, the allocative cost inefficiency of the benchmark on the frontier, meaning that our new projections should be as "close" as possible to a cost-minimizing firm, we have to discard the idea of resorting to the *traditional or classical approaches*, because they just select a certain input inefficiency measure and, based on it, identify for each firm a projection and its technical inefficiency. That is, any traditional approach is not concerned with the cost inefficiency of each of the projections. The new standard reverse approach we propose has the advantage that it identifies directly the "best" projection without considering any other alternative projections.

For input-oriented models, the *SR approach* uses the same philosophy introduced and explained before for graph models in Sect. 13.2.5.1, based on the corresponding general direct approach. Now our aim is to start identifying, for each firm (x_o, y_o) of our finite sample, *a projection* $\left(\widehat{x}_{oSR(I)}, y_o\right)$, with $\widehat{x}_{oSR(I)} \leq x_o$, such that *its cost inefficiency is as small as possible*. The general direct approach shows that the cost inefficiency of $\left(\widehat{x}_{oSR(I)}, y_o\right)$ is equal to the allocative cost inefficiency of (x_o, y_o) and is expressed as $w \cdot \widehat{x}_{oSR(I)} - C(y_o, w)$ (see expression (13.36)). But minimizing last expression, being $C(y_o, w)$ a constant, is equivalent to minimizing $w \cdot \widehat{x}_{oSR(I)}$. Since $w \cdot \widehat{x}_{oSR(I)} = w \cdot \left(x_o - s^-_{oSR(I)}\right)$ and $w \cdot x_o$ is also a constant and can be ignored, we end up finally maximizing $w \cdot s^-_{oSR(I)}$. The linear program for achieving this objective is the next one:

$$
\begin{aligned}
&\max_{s^-_{oSR},\lambda} \quad w \cdot s^-_{oSR} \\
&s.t. \\
&\qquad \sum_{j=1}^{J} \lambda_j x_{jm} + s^-_{oSRm} = x_{om}, \qquad && m = 1, \ldots, M, \\
&\qquad \sum_{j=1}^{J} \lambda_j y_{jr} \geq y_{on}, && n = 1, \ldots, N, \\
&\qquad \sum_{j=1}^{J} \lambda_j = 1, \\
&\qquad s^-_{oSR} = \left(s^-_{oSR1}, \ldots, s^-_{oSRM}\right) \geq 0_M, \\
&\qquad \lambda = (\lambda_1, \ldots, \lambda_J) \geq 0_J.
\end{aligned}
\tag{13.41}
$$

This input-oriented weighted additive model is peculiar because its objective function is expressed in monetary units. If we subtract its optimal value from $w \cdot x_o$, we obtain $w \cdot \widehat{x}^*_{oSR}$ that can be compared to $C(y_o, w)$ for evaluating how close the cost of the identified projection is from the minimum cost. It may happen that the optimal objective function value equals $0_\$$, which means that $s_{oSR}^{-*} = 0_M$. In this case, the firm being evaluated is a frontier point that satisfies $(x_o, y_o) = (\widehat{x}_{oSR}, y_o)$, whose allocative cost inefficiency cannot be reduced at all. The rest of the firms get a $w \cdot s_{oSR}^{-*} > 0_\$$, which means that their allocative cost inefficiency can be reduced as much as $w \cdot s_{oSR}^{-*}$ when moving from (x_o, y_o) to $\left(\widehat{x}_{oSR}^{*}, y_o\right)$. As mentioned before, equality (13.36) also represents the *cost inefficiency decomposition for the SR approach.* With our next objective aimed at deriving a *normalized cost inefficiency decomposition for the SR approach*, we need to generate a technical inefficiency measure associated with it, which is accomplished next.

13.3.5.2 The Technical Inefficiency Measure Associated with the Input Standard Reverse Approach

We have introduced in Sect. 13.2.5.2 the standard reverse approach for decomposing profit inefficiency giving priority to reduce, as much as possible, the corresponding allocative profit inefficiency or, equivalently, to increase as much as possible its technological cost gap. In the previous subsection we followed the same procedure, this time reducing as much as possible the allocative cost inefficiency, after having identified the *projection* for each firm through model (13.41).[61] Hence, we are going to derive a *technical inefficiency* for each firm based on the mentioned projection, resorting to the equality associated with *the general direct approach.* We have already identified a cost-weighted L_1-path that connects each firm with its projection. As usual, our aim is to decompose it as the product of a technical inefficiency score times a certain factor, which we refer to as the *normalizing factor.* Based on them and on the already considered *general direct cost inefficiency decomposition*, we will be able to finally derive the corresponding *normalized cost inefficiency decomposition.* Just to remind the readers, since these decompositions resort exclusively to equalities, they do not need to consider any inequality based on duality results.

We continue following Pastor et al. (2021c) and need to consider, for all the firms (x_o, y_o) being rated, the introduction of a big enough denominator for each technological cost gap that guarantees that the corresponding ratio is always upper bounded by 1. This set of ratios will constitute the technical inefficiency scores associated with the firms being analyzed after verifying that they satisfy several properties.

Linear model (13.41) produces, for each firm, the corresponding optimal input slacks. Let us denote by $U_{SR(I)}$ the monetary quantity obtained by taking the maximum of the optimal value of model (13.41) associated with each firm of our sample,

[61] The projection, according to footnote 1, is $\left(\sum_{j=1}^{J} \lambda_j^* x_{mj}, y_o\right) \in L(y_o)$.

$$U_{SR(I)} = \max\left\{w \cdot s^{-*}_{jSR(I)}, \forall j \in J\right\}. \tag{13.42}$$

It is clear that the value delivered by $U_{SR(I)}$ satisfies

$$U_{SR(I)} \geq w \cdot s^{-*}_{jSR(I)}, \forall j \in J. \tag{13.43}$$

Assuming the presence of at least one inefficient firm, (x_o, y_o), for which $w \cdot s^{-*}_{oSR(I)} > 0_\$$, inequality (13.43) guarantees that $U_{SR(I)} > 0_\$$, which is crucial for defining a *new technical inefficiency measure* $TI_{SR(I)}(x_o, y_o)$, obtained by means of the next definition.

Definition 13.5 *Assuming that our sample of firms contains at least one inefficient firm, let us define the technical inefficiency measure associated with the SR cost approach for each firm* (x_o, y_o) *as*

$$TI_{SR(I)}(x_o, y_o) \equiv \frac{w \cdot s^{-*}_{oSR(I)}}{U_{SR(I)}} \tag{13.44}$$

The way to calculate $TI_{SR(I)}(x_o, y_o)$ for any of the firms of the original sample is to solve (13.41) for all the firms and then derive the maximal price value to be used as denominator, finally calculating the corresponding *technical inefficiency score* for any observation as given by (13.44) according to (13.42), $TI_{SR(I)}(x_o, y_o) \equiv \frac{w \cdot s^{-*}_{oSR(I)}}{U_{SR(I)}}$.

Equality (13.44) belongs to the family of weighted additive models, as defined by Lovell and Pastor (1995) and is discussed in Chap. 6. In fact, the technical inefficiency expression shows that the m coefficients of the vector of optimal input slacks, $\frac{w_m}{U_{SR(I)}}, m = 1, \ldots, M$, are ratios whose dimensions are *costs per unit of quantity* in the numerator and *costs* in the denominator that jointly give rise to $(quantity)^{-1}$, which, after multiplying by the corresponding slack expressed as a *quantity*, gives rise to the sum of pure numbers, the latter being independent of the measurement units of inputs, a property that is required for any well-defined inefficiency measure (see P4 below). Moreover, the new introduced technical inefficiency measure, $TI_{SR(I)}(x_o, y_o)$, satisfies the next properties[62]:

Properties of the Standard Technical Input-Oriented Inefficiency Measure
P1. $0 \leq TI_{SR(I)}(x_o, y_o) \leq 1$.
P2. $TI_{SR(I)}(x_o, y_o) = 0$ if, and only if, (x_o, y_o) is an input-efficient firm.
P3. $TI_{SR(I)}(x_o, y_o)$ is a strong monotonic inefficiency measure.
P4. $TI_{SR(I)}(x_o, y_o)$ is invariant to the units of measurement of inputs and outputs.

---

[62] The proofs are a consequence of model (13.44) being a weighted additive inefficiency model. The list of four properties listed above are similar to the list of properties first published by Cooper et al. (1999) for certifying a well-defined efficiency measure (see also Sect. 2.2 in Chap. 2). In our case, the associated efficiency measure $EM_{SR}(x_o, y_o)$ would be equal to $1 - TI_{SR}(x_o, y_o)$.

Let us go to the next subsection and discuss the behavior of the two cost inefficiency decompositions associated with the SR approach.

13.3.5.3 The Input-Oriented Standard Reverse Approach and Its Normalized Cost Inefficiency Decomposition

The technological cost gap for each non-efficient firm (x_o, y_o) obtained through the linear model (13.41) allows us to write down *the general direct cost inefficiency decomposition* associated with the mentioned firm for *the standard reverse cost approach* as follows:

$$w \cdot x_o - C(y_o, w) = w \cdot \overline{s}^{-*}_{oSR(I)} + \left(w \cdot \widehat{x}^{*}_{oSR(I)} - C(y_o, w) \right). \tag{13.45}$$

Moreover, by relating the technological cost gap with the technical inefficiency, we obtain the next *normalization factor* associated with *the input-oriented SR approach*,
$w \cdot \overline{s}^{-*}_{oSR(I)} = U_{SR(I)} \left(\frac{w \cdot \overline{s}^{-*}_{oSR(I)}}{U_{SR(I)}} \right)$ and, consequently, $NF_{SR(I)}(x_o, y_o, w) = U_{SR(I)} > 0_{\$}$.

Finally, the *normalized cost inefficiency decomposition* associated with the *input-oriented SR approach* and to any non-efficient unit (x_o, y_o) is obtained, as usual, by dividing each term of the cost inefficiency decomposition by the normalization factor:

$$\frac{(w \cdot x_o - C(y_o, w))}{U_{SR(I)}} = TI_{SR(I)}(x_o, y_o) + \frac{\left(w \cdot \widehat{x}^{*}_{oSR(I)} - C(y_o, w) \right)}{U_{SR(I)}}. \tag{13.46}$$

For the efficient units, since $(x_o, y_o) = \left(\widehat{x}^{*}_{oSR(I)}, y_o \right)$, $TI_{SR(I)}(x_o, y_o) = 0$ according to the last model. Therefore, for any of these units the normalizing factor can take any positive value expressed in monetary units, $k_{o\$}$, $k > 0$, and, in particular, we can assign the value $U_{SR(I)} > 0_{\$}$ to it, which finally causes all the firms in our sample to obtain the same normalization factor.

Some final comments are at hand. With the decomposition of cost inefficiency associated with the SR approach reflecting the same structure as that corresponding to the general direct approach, we are sure that it satisfies the *extended essential property*, as well as the *essential property*. Moreover, since the normalizing factor is the same across all the firms, the normalized cost inefficiency decomposition of the SR approach also satisfies the *comparison property*.

13.3.5.4 Numerical Example for the Input-Oriented Standard Reverse Approach Cost Decompositions

Example 13.7

Let us go back to Sect. 13.3.3 and consider the example reported in Table 13.6, which uses the general direct approach combined with the input-oriented Russell measure. The key difference between new Table 13.7 and the two preceding tables is that we do not need to resort anymore to an external efficiency measure in order to establish the technical inefficiency of a firm, because the new method designs a specific inefficiency measure after having identified first the projection of any non-efficient firm (see (13.43)). Let us consider the same input costs as in Table 13.6, $w = (2,1)$.

With respect to Table 13.6, in Table 13.7, we have deleted only former column 5, presenting the different normalization factors, and have reordered the rest of the columns to accommodate the natural ordering of our new proposed *SR cost approach*. The last added row is almost empty. Column 1 is exactly the same as in Table 13.6, while column 2, reporting the projection of each firm, maintains the same values in its first five rows and in the last one. Considering that the first four rows correspond to efficient firms that are not able to change their projections, we conclude that all the firms that have the opportunity to improve the said projections have done it with the exceptions of E = (10,2) and of I = (6,16). What happens is that the previous projections of firms E and I were already those corresponding to the SR approach. Column 3 corresponds to the *cost inefficiency* associated with each of the firms and is exactly the same as column 4 of the preceding table. New column 4 corresponds to the *technical cost inefficiency*, also known as the *technological cost gap* of each of the nine firms. Curiously enough, the technological cost gaps are fairly similar to the ones shown in column 6 of Table 13.6, although the projections are not. Moreover, we have added a row at the bottom of Table 13.7 to include the value of the unique normalization factor, which appears precisely at the bottom of column 4 because, in the *SR approach*, it is closely related to the *technological cost gaps*. The rest of the last row is empty. Column 5 is devoted to the second component of the cost inefficiency decomposition, the *allocative cost inefficiency*. In comparison with the corresponding column of the previous table, column 7, we see that *the SR approach* has been able to improve the value of this component for firms F = (12,6) and G = (16,12). The last three columns of Table 13.7 are devoted to the decomposition of the normalized cost inefficiency. Column 6 is obtained by dividing each value of column 3 by the unique normalization factor obtaining the *normalized cost inefficiency*. Column 7, which reports the *technical inefficiency* associated with each firm, is derived similarly as its previous column but taking the values of column 4 which correspond to the *technical cost inefficiency*. The influence of the normalization factor is remarkable not only in column 6, when comparing both tables, but even more in the last column reporting *the allocative inefficiency*, which is lower in Table 13.7 for the five firms that obtained a positive value in previous table. Clearly, the objective of reducing the allocative inefficiency

Table 13.7 Results based on the standard reverse approach cost decompositions, $w = (2,1)$

Firm	*SR(I) project.*	*CI*	$TCI = w\bar{s}^{-*}$	$ACI = CI - TCI$	$NCI = CI/NF$	$TI_{SR(I)} = TCI/NF$	*AI*
(1)	(2)	(3)	(4)	(5) = (3) – (4)	(6)	(7)	(8) = (6) – (7)
A = (2,10)	(2,10)	0	0	0	0	0	0
B = (4,6)	(4,6)	0	0	0	0	0	0
C = (6,3)	(6,3)	1	0	1	1/30	0	1/30
D = (8,2)	(8,2)	4	0	4	4/30	0	4/30
E = (10,2)	(8,2)	8	(2,1)(2,0) = 4	8–4 = 4	8/30	4/30	4/30
F = (12,6)	(4,6)	16	(2,1)(8,0) = 16	16–16 = 0	16/30	16/30	0
G = (16,12)	(2,10)	30	(2,1)(14,2) = 30	30–30 = 0	30/30	30/30	0
H = (8,12)	(2,10)	14	(2,1)(6,2) = 14	14–14 = 0	14/30	14/30	0
I = (6,16)	(2,10)	14	(2,1)(4,6) = 14	14–14 = 0	14/30	14/30	0
–	–	–	$U_{SRC} = NF_\$ = 30_\$$	–	–	–	–

by means of the *SR cost approach* has been achieved in the last table in comparison to the previous one. If we go further back and take a look at Table 13.5, which reports the results of the traditional decomposition based on the same inefficiency measure mentioned before, we see that none of the inefficient firms obtain a zero allocative inefficiency. Moreover, the allocative inefficiency associated with the mentioned firms is much higher than in Table 13.6 and substantially higher with respect to the SR approach of the last table. Let us conclude reviewing the properties satisfied by the new standard reverse cost approach. Since our *SR cost approach* is also based on the general direct approach for input-oriented measures, we appreciate also that *the allocative cost inefficiency* is always the same for any inefficient firm as for its projection. Hence, it satisfies the *extended essential property* and, consequently, the *essential property*. Moreover, since in this case the normalizing factor is the same for all firms, we can also conclude that the *normalized cost inefficiency decomposition* also satisfies the *comparison property*.

13.3.5.5 The Flexible Reverse Approach for Cost Inefficiency Decompositions

The philosophy of this approach is the same as the one explained previously for profit in Sect. 13.2.5.5. Hence, the difference between this *FR cost approach* and the *FR profit approach* is that now only the *input slacks will be considered*. Also, instead of considering the general direct FR cost approach designed for non-negative slacks, we will turn to the *generalized direct FR cost approach* that allows non-negative and negative slacks, as we did previously for the profit case.

The next *input flexible reverse approach* (*input FR approach*), proposed by Pastor et al. (2021c), is the most demanding reverse approach one can think of and extends the already explained *standard reverse approach* in an unconventional way. It is inspired in Zofio et al. (2013) and translates the original ideas based on directional distance functions to slack-based measures. We are going to show how the *input FR approach* is able to guarantee that *the final projection of any firm is a cost-minimizing firm* or, equivalently, the allocative inefficiency of the final projection is always equal to zero. As usual, we are considering a finite sample of firms $F = \{(x_j, y_j), j \in J\}$ that generates a *VRS* production possibility set T. Likewise, for each specific firm (x_o, y_o), the associated input production possibility set $L(y_o) := \{(x, y_o) \in T\}$. The mentioned firm either belongs to the strong efficient frontier of $L(y_o)$, $\partial^S L(y_o)$, or not. Let us revise both cases.

Case 1: (x_o, y_o) Belongs to $\partial^S L(y_o)$

Let us start considering that firm $(x_o, y_o) \in \partial^S L(y_o)$, which means that none of its inputs can be reduced without leaving $L(y_o)$. In other words, the technical projection of (x_o, y_o) is itself, which implies that the corresponding input technological price gap equals $0_\$$. Let us consider that the fixed vector of market input prices, $w > 0_M$, allows us to identify at least one firm (x^C, y_o) that satisfies $w \cdot x^C \le w \cdot x, \forall\, x : (x, y_o) \in L(y_o)$. In other words, (x^C, y_o) is a cost-minimizing firm. In case (x_o, y_o) is itself a cost-minimizing firm, then $w \cdot x_o = w \cdot x^C$, or, equivalently, $CI(x_o, y_o, w) = w \cdot x_o - w \cdot x^C = 0_\$$, and we select (x_o, y_o) as *FR projection* of itself. Resorting to *the general direct approach*, we obtain the next *cost inefficiency FR decomposition* for *the cost-minimizing* frontier *firm* (x_o, y_o):

$$CI_{FR(I)}(x_o, y_o, w) = TCI_{FR(I)}(x_o, y_o, w) + ACI_{FR(I)}(x_o, y_o, w) = 0_\$ + 0_\$. \quad (13.47)$$

In this first case, we consider as projection of any cost-minimizing firm the firm itself, which is obviously the closest cost-minimizing efficient projection.

Alternatively, if (x_o, y_o) belongs to $\partial^S L(y_o)$ but $CI(x_o, y_o, w) = w \cdot x_o - w \cdot x^C > 0_\$$, the general direct approach projects again (x_o, y_o) onto itself, providing the next *cost inefficiency FR decomposition* for *the non-cost-minimizing frontier firm* (x_o, y_o):

$$\begin{aligned} CI_{FR(I)}(x_o, y_o, w) &= TCI_{FR(I)}(x_o, y_o, w) + ACI_{FR(I)}(x_o, y_o, w) \\ &= 0_\$ + ACI_{FR(I)}(x_o, y_o, w) > 0_\$. \end{aligned} \quad (13.48)$$

The last equality shows that being $ACI_{FR(I)}(x_o, y_o, w) = CI_{FR(I)}(x_o, y_o, w)$, all cost inefficiency of (x_o, y_o) is allocative. In this second case, we proceed next to identify the efficient cost-minimizing benchmark (x^C, y_o) of the firm under evaluation (x_o, y_o). This requires extending *the general direct approach* to consider this final cost-efficient projection generating, as in the profit case, *the generalized FR direct approach for cost inefficiency decomposition*. With both efficient firms (x_o, y_o) and (x^C, y_o) proving technically efficient, the analysis focuses solely on the allocative component of cost inefficiency. Moreover, since we are willing to relate any firm belonging to the strongly efficient frontier of $L(y_o)$ with a certain cost-minimizing firm also belonging to the same frontier, we are therefore relating two Pareto-efficient points on the said frontier. The next proposition shows that the input slacks that connect x_o with x^C are unrestricted in sign. Its proof mirrors that of former Proposition 13.5 and is left to the reader.

Proposition 13.9 *Let us assume that (x_o, y_o) is any strong efficient firm of $L(y_o)$ and that (x^C, y_o) is any cost-minimizing firm. Then the input slack vector $u^-_{oFR(I)} \in \mathbb{R}^M$ that connects the input components of both firms, $x^C_o = x_o - u^-_{oFR(I)}$, must have at least one positive component and at least one negative component. Moreover, any cost-minimizing firm can be used as a final projection.*

Note. We would like to call the attention of the reader on how the strong efficient firm (x_o, y_o) is related with its cost-minimizing projection (x^C, y_o). Formally the relation is the same as for the *general direct approach*, although with two distinguishing features: the slacks are unrestricted in sign, and the decomposition is *exclusively* based on the *allocative cost inefficiency* component.

Let us show how it works. Since $x^C_o = x_o - u^-_{oFR(I)}$, with $u^-_{oFR(I)} \in \mathbb{R}^M$, it is easy to establish, according to (13.48), the following result:

$$\begin{aligned} CI_{FR(I)}(x_o, y_o, w) &= TCI_{FR(I)}(x_o, y_o, w) ACI_{FR(I)}(x_o, y_o, w) \\ &= 0_\$ + w \cdot u^-_{oFR(I)}, \end{aligned} \tag{13.49}$$

which corresponds to the *new FR cost decomposition approach for strongly efficient firms. It has no technological cost inefficiency*, which is equal to $0_\$$ and does not appear in (13.49). In fact, its first equality $CI_{FR(I)}(x_o, y_o, w) = ACI_{FR(I)}(x_o, y_o, w)$ excludes the technological cost inefficiency term. The second equality corresponds to the projection of (x_o, y_o) onto the cost-minimizing firm (x^C, y_o), whose allocative inefficiency according to (13.47) is $0_\$$, showing that *the allocative cost inefficiency of* (x_o, y_o) *is equal to* $w \cdot u^-_{oFR(I)}$; i.e., the cost of the unrestricted in sign input slacks that connect the two aforementioned efficient points. In the event that we have more than one cost-minimizing firm, we are interested in decomposing the cost inefficiency of any efficient firm by choosing the closest possible cost-minimizing projection, for which it is enough to resort to the model (13.51) presented below. This guarantees the least allocative cost inefficiency for the efficient firm considered.

Case 2: (x_o, y_o) Does Not Belong to $\partial^S L(y_o)$

Since the firms we are considering now do not belong to $\partial^S L(y_o)$, it is obvious that their technical inefficiency is positive, no matter what inefficiency measure we consider or design for measuring it. Moreover and following the seminal paper by Zofio et al. (2013), we can decide to directly project the input-inefficient firm (x_o, y_o) towards a cost-minimizing firm (x^C, y_o), which is also a frontier firm. In this case, we show that the corresponding *FR cost inefficiency decomposition, based* also *on the generalized direct FR approach*, classifies *the entire cost inefficiency* associated with (x_o, y_o) as *technical cost inefficiency*, since the cost inefficiency of the cost-minimizing benchmark (x^C, y_o) is equal to $0_\$$ (see (13.47)). Similar to Case 1, the relation between firm (x_o, y_o) and its projection (x^C, y_o) verifies that $x^C_o = x_o - u^-_{oFR(I)}$, with $u^-_{oFR(I)} \in \mathbb{R}^M$, which means that some of the input slacks can be negative and others positive, although there may also exist some input-inefficient firms whose associated slacks are all non-negative, as we are going to show below through an example. In this case, the generalized direct approach gives the next *FR cost inefficiency decomposition*:

$$\begin{aligned} CI_{FR(I)}(x_o, y_o, w) &= TCI_{FR(I)}(x_o, y_o, w) + ACI_{FR(I)}(x_o, y_o, w) \\ &= w \cdot u^-_{oFR(I)} + 0_\$. \end{aligned} \tag{13.50}$$

Now we appreciate that the cost of the input slacks that connect each input-inefficient firm with its cost-minimizing projection corresponds to the technical cost inefficiency, while the allocative cost inefficiency equals $0_\$$, i.e., that of its benchmark projection (x^C, y_o). Since (x_o, y_o) is an input-inefficient firm and can therefore not be a cost-minimizing firm, we are sure that $CI_{FR(I)}(x_o, y_o, w) > 0_\$$, which implies, according to (13.50), that $w \cdot u^-_{oFR(I)} + CI_{FR(I)}(x^C, y_o, w) = w \cdot u^-_{oFR(I)} > 0_\$$. Mathematically this result may be surprising, since the slacks are unrestricted in sign, although in economic terms the result is perfectly acceptable. In summary, the flexible reverse cost inefficiency decomposition also exhibits a dual behavior with respect to the subsets of efficient firms and non-efficient firms, as shown by equalities (13.49) and (13.50).

In order to derive, in both cases, the corresponding *Nerlovian FR cost inefficiency decomposition*, we need to develop a new technical inefficiency measure related to the technical cost inefficiency expression. We develop this measure in the following section. However, before doing so, we consider the possibility that several efficient firms minimize cost and, therefore, from a production perspective, it is adequate to find the closest benchmark. We can resort to a mathematical program that directly finds the minimum cost benchmark that is the L_1-closest to each firm being analyzed. Following the methodology leading to program (13.28) in the profit case, let us reformulate for each firm of our sample, $(x_o, y_o) \in F$, the set of unrestricted in sign input slacks, $u_{oFR}^{-} \in \mathbb{R}^M$, in terms of a couple of non-negative input slacks:

$$u_{oFR}^{-} = s_{oFR}^{-} - t_{oFR}^{-}, \quad s_{oFR}^{-} \geq 0_M, t_{oFR}^{-} \geq 0_M.$$

According to the last definition, it should be clear that the absolute value of each unrestricted in sign slack variable can be formulated as follows: $\left|u_{moFR}^{-}\right| = s_{moFR}^{-} + t_{moFR}^{-}, m = 1, \ldots, M$. Consequently, the next linear program finds the *FR projection* for each firm $(x_o, y_o) \in F$ that is L_1-closer to a cost-minimizing benchmark:

$$\begin{aligned}
\min_{s_{oSR}^{-}, t_{oSR}^{-}, \lambda} \quad & \sum_{m=1}^{M} \left(s_{oFRm}^{-} + t_{oFRm}^{-}\right) \\
s.t. \quad & w \cdot \left(x_o - \left(s_{oFR}^{-} - t_{oFR}^{-}\right)\right) = C(y_o, w), \\
& \sum_{j=1}^{J} \lambda_j x_{jm} + \left(s_{omFR}^{-} - t_{omFR}^{-}\right) = x_{om}, \qquad m = 1, \ldots, M \\
& \sum_{j=1}^{J} \lambda_j y_{jn} \geq y_{on}, \qquad n = 1, \ldots, N \\
& \sum_{j=1}^{J} \lambda_j = 1, \\
& s_{oFR}^{-} \geq 0_M, t_{oFR}^{-} \geq 0_M, \\
& \lambda = (\lambda_1, \ldots, \lambda_J) \geq 0_J.
\end{aligned} \tag{13.51}$$

Let us point out once again that although the proposed decomposition of the absolute value of each of the input slacks unrestricted in sign is not unique, the solution of the last linear program is. The same happens with any of the remaining unrestricted in sign slacks. Again, since the objective function of (13.51) minimizes the sum of all the pairs of an s-slack and the associated t-slack, we are sure that the optimal value of each of the aforementioned slacks will take the minimum possible value.

13.3.5.6 The Technical Inefficiency Measure Associated with the Input Flexible Reverse Approach

Let us consider the finite sample of firms under scrutiny belonging to $L(y_o)$, which we denote as $F(y_o) = \{(x_j, y_o), j \in J\}$. Then let us further think about the two disjoint subsets of $F(y_o)$, $F_E(y_o)$ and $F_N(y_o)$, that obviously satisfy the next equality $F(y_o) = F_E(y_o) \cup F_N(y_o)$. It should be clear that $F_E(y_o) = \{(x_j, y_o) \in \partial^S L(y_o), j \in J\}$, while $F_N(y_o) = \{(x_j, y_o) \notin \partial^S L(y_o), j \in J\}$. The first subset corresponds exactly with Case 1 firms, whose technical cost-inefficient component is always equal to $0_\$$. The second one parallels Case 2 firms that, according to (13.50), have an allocative cost inefficiency component always equal to $0_\$$. Moreover, for each firm $(x_j, y_o) \in F_N(y_o)$, its technical cost inefficiency component equals $w \cdot u^-_{jFR(I)} > 0_\$$. Let us define as $U_{FR(I)}$ the maximum of all these technical cost-inefficient components:

$$U_{FR(I)} = \max\left\{w \cdot u^-_{jFR(I)}, (x_j, y_j) \in F_N(y_o); 0_\$, (x_j, y_j) \in F_E(y_o)\right\}. \quad (13.52)$$

Assuming that $F_N(y_o)$ is non-empty, we deduce that $U_{FR(I)} > 0_\$$. The next definition is straightforward:

Definition 13.6
The technical inefficiency associated with any firm of $F(y_o)$ is defined as

$$TI_{FR(I)}(x_j, y_o) = \frac{TCI_{FR(I)}(x_j, y_o)}{U_{FR(I)}}, (x_j, y_o) \in F(y_o). \quad (13.53)$$

The novelty of this new technical inefficiency definition is that some of the input slacks involved can be negative. However, we are going to show that it is a true technical inefficiency measure, since it satisfies the four basic properties first required for traditional efficiency measures by Cooper et al. (1999).

Proposition 13.10
The FR(I) technical inefficiency measure defined above satisfies the next four properties:

P1. $0 \leq TI_{FR(I)}(x_j, y_o) \leq 1$, $(x_j, y_o) \in F(y_o)$.
P2. $TI_{FR(I)}(x_j, y_o) = 0$ *if, and only if,* $(x_j, y_o) \in F_E(y_o)$.
P3. $TI_{FR(I)}(x_j, y_o)$ *is a strongly monotonic inefficiency measure.*
P4. $TI_{FR(I)}(x_j, y_o)$ *is invariant to the units of measurement of inputs and outputs.*

Proof

P1. Is a direct consequence of Definition 13.6 based on (13.52). The definition of the upper bound $U_{FR(I)}$ guarantees that at least one input-inefficient firm has its technical inefficiency equal to 1.

P2 and P3. P2 holds as a consequence of the values of $TCI_{FR}(x_j, y_o)$ and the closely related values of $TI_{FR(I)}(x_j, y_o)$ for $(x_j, y_o) \in F_E(y_o)$.

For proving P3, it is sufficient to consider any input-inefficient firm, which we label as *first firm*, that identifies a specific L_1-input path towards its strong frontier projection and compare it with any other different input-inefficient firm, which we label as *second firm*, that must belong to the considered input path. Let us prove P3 by showing that the length of the path that connects the second firm with its own projection is strictly smaller than the length of the input path associated with the first firm. Since the two firms considered are different, the second firm will have a strictly shorter input sub-path to reach the first firm projection than the input path associated with the first firm. Since the first firm path has at most M nonzero input slacks, the two firms can differ in any of the mentioned slacks and satisfy necessarily the next two conditions: the first one establishes that the existence of an input sub-path for the second firm implies that the sign of the nonzero slacks associated with inputs of the second firm must be the same as that corresponding to the first firm. The second condition establishes that if any first firm input slack is equal to zero, then the same input slack for the second firm must also be zero. In any case, there exists a sub-path that projects the second firm towards the projection of the first firm, which shows that the first firm projection is a feasible projection for the second firm. Since we have adopted as a secondary criterion that each input-inefficient firm selects the cost-minimizing firm that is closer to it, the length of the path that connects the second firm with its optimal projection must be less than or equal to the length of the sub-path toward the first firm projection, which in turn is strictly shorter than the length of the path associated with the first firm, and the proof is done.

P4. The technical inefficiency value, $TI_{FR(I)}\left(x_j, y_o\right) = \frac{TCI_{FR(I)}\left(x_j, y_o\right)}{U_{FR(I)}}, \left(x_j, y_o\right) \in F\left(y_o\right)$, shows clearly that the units of measurement of $TCI_{FR(I)}(x_j, y_o)$ are monetary units, just the same as the units of the denominator, $U_{FR(I)}$, which shows that $TI_{FR(I)}(x_j, y_o)$ is a pure number for any firm, which concludes the proof. □

Resorting to (13.53), the new defined technical inefficiency measure, it is straightforward to obtain the new *normalized FR cost inefficiency decomposition*, just by considering equalities (13.49) and (13.50) corresponding to the *FR cost inefficiency decomposition*, as shown in the next subsection.

13.3.5.7 The Input-Oriented Flexible Reverse Approach and Its Nerlovian Cost Inefficiency Decomposition

Equalities (13.49) and (13.50) show the *FR cost inefficiency decomposition* for firms (x_j, y_o) of each of the two disjoint subsets of $F(y_o) = F_E(y_o) \cup F_N(y_o)$. We can summarize both decompositions as follows:

$$CI_{FR(I)}(x_j, y_o, w) = \left\{ \begin{array}{ll} 0_\$ + ACI(x_j, y_o) = 0_\$ + w \cdot u^-_{oFR(I)}, & (x_j, y_o) \in F_E(y_o) \\ TCI(x_j, y_o) + 0_\$ = w \cdot u^-_{oFR(I)} + 0_\$, & (x_j, y_o) \in F_N(y_o) \end{array} \right\}. \tag{13.54}$$

We would like to highlight, once more, the difference of the above cost inefficiency decomposition associated with $(x_j, y_o) \in F(y_o)$: if the mentioned firm is strongly efficient in $L(y_o)$, the upper equality applies, which means that all the cost inefficiency is allocative cost inefficiency, that can be calculated in terms of the unrestricted in sign input slacks that connect (x_j, y_o) with any cost-minimizing strong efficient firm. For these efficient firms, the general direct approach is no longer valid, and we resort instead to *the direct allocative decomposition approach* introduced before. In terms of cons, for any input-inefficient firm (x_j, y_o), the *general direct decomposition approach* still works assuming that slacks can also be negative, and the lower equality of (13.54) applies, which means that all the cost inefficiency is technical cost inefficiency, calculated in the same way, i.e., identifying the slacks that connect (x_j, y_o) with any cost-minimizing firm. In the latter case, the input slacks can be unrestricted in sign or non-negative, while in the former one the input slacks are always unrestricted in sign, with at least one negative and one positive input slack (13.54) shows the dual behavior of the flexible reverse cost inefficiency decomposition with respect to the two subsets of efficient and non-efficient firms. The same is true for the corresponding normalized version, see (13.55) below.

The preceding subsection provides us with a true technical inefficiency measure (see (13.53)) that can be introduced in (13.54) so as to get the desired Nerlovian FR cost inefficiency decomposition. Based on (13.53), all we need to do is to rewrite $TCI(x_j, y_o)$ as the product $TI_{FR(I)}(x_j, y_o)U_{FR(I)}$ and, with $U_{FR(I)} > 0_\$$, to divide (13.54) by $U_{FR(I)}$ in order to obtain the next *Nerlovian FR cost inefficiency decomposition*:

$$NCI_{FR(I)}(x_j, y_o, w) = \left\{ \begin{array}{ll} 0 + \dfrac{ACI(x_j, y_o)}{U_{FR(I)}} = 0_\$ + \dfrac{w \cdot u^-_{oFR(I)}}{U_{FR(I)}}, & (x_j, y_o) \in F_E(y_o) \\ \dfrac{TCI(x_j, y_o)}{U_{FR(I)}} + 0_\$ = \dfrac{w \cdot u^-_{oFR(I)}}{U_{FR(I)}} + 0_\$, & (x_j, y_o) \in F_N(y_o) \end{array} \right\}. \tag{13.55}$$

Just by dividing each term of (13.54) by *the normalization factor* $NF_\$ = U_{FR(I)} > 0_\$$, we obtain the corresponding *Nerlovian FR cost inefficiency decomposition*, which *is decomposed as the sum of* a first term which corresponds to *the technical inefficiency of the firm* and a second term that corresponds to *its allocative inefficiency*. Moreover, since the normalizing factor is expressed in monetary units and takes the same value for all firms, we conclude that the obtained *Nerlovian FR cost decomposition satisfies* the *comparable property* between firms. However, *their allocative terms do not satisfy* the *essential property* as a consequence of the *FR cost decomposition approach* expression associated with the subset of efficient firms. This is one of the main differences between the *SR cost approach* and the *FR cost approach*.

13.3.5.8 A Numerical Example for the Input-Oriented Flexible Reverse Approach

Example 13.8
Let us consider again the same data as in previous Examples 13.6 and 13.7. Our aim is to set up a new table for the *input-oriented FR approach* and to compare the new results with the former ones associated with the *input-oriented SR approach* and presented in previous Table 13.7. Since there are only *two cost-minimizing efficient firms*, A = (2,10) and B = (4,6), with $C(y_o, w) = \$14$, the remaining seven firms can select any of these two firms as their final projection. Resorting to program (13.51), we select *the L_1-closest projection* for each firm, which are reported in the second column of the new Table 13.8. For instance, the L_1-distance from firm C = (6,3) to A = (2,10) is (4 + 7) =11, while its distance to B = (4,6) is (2 + 3) = 5. Hence, in new Table 13.8 appears B = (4,6) as projection of C = (6,3). There are three firms, C, D, and E, that have changed their former *SR projections*, C, D, and D (see previous Table 13.7), obtaining as new *FR projections*, the same cost-minimizing firm B (see column 2 of Table 13.8).
First of all, let us explain how Table 13.8 is constructed. The first column contains the nine firms to be analyzed, the first four being the efficient units, written in bold characters. Only the two inputs of each firm appear in column 1 since all the firms have the same positive output. Column 2 shows the L_1-closest cost-minimizing projection for each firm. Column 3 shows the cost inefficiency associated with each firm, showing that only A and B are cost-minimizing firms. Since the market cost vector is the same in Tables 13.7 and 13.8, both columns 3 are also the same. According to (13.54), columns 4 and 5 report the two terms of the corresponding cost inefficiency decomposition, the technical cost inefficiency and the allocative

Table 13.8 Results based on *the FR cost approach*, w = (2,1)

Efficient firms	*FR Cost Minimiz. projection*	$CI_\$$	$TCI_\$ = 0_\$$	$ACI_\$ = w \cdot u^-_{j_E FR(I)}$	$NCI = \frac{CI_\$}{NF_\$}$	$TI = \frac{TCI_\$}{NF_\$}$	$AI = \frac{ACI_\$}{NF_\$}$
(1)	(2)	(3)	(4)	(5) = (3)-(4)	(6)	(7)	(8)=(6)-(7)
A=(2,10)	(2,10)	0	0	0	0	0	0
B=(4,6)	(4,6)	0	0	0	0	0	0
C=(6,3)	(4,6)	1	0	1	1/30	0	1/30
D=(8,2)	(4,6)	4	0	4	4/30	0	4/30
Non-efficient firms	*FR Cost Minimiz. Projection*	$CI_\$$	$TCI_\$ = w \cdot u^-_{j_N FR(I)}$	$ACI_\$ = 0_\$$	$NCI = \frac{CI_\$}{NF_\$}$	$TI = \frac{TCI_\$}{NF_\$}$	$AI = \frac{ACI_\$}{NF_\$}$
E=(10,2)	(4,6)	8	8	0	8/30	8/30	0
F=(12,6)	(4,6)	16	16	0	16/30	16/30	0
G=(16,12)	(2,10)	30	30	0	30/30	30/30	0
H=(8,12)	(2,10)	14	14	0	14/30	14/30	0
I=(6,16)	(2,10)	14	14	0	14/30	14/30	0
—	—	—	$NF_\$ = 30_\$$	—	—	—	—

cost inefficiency, showing the expected dual functioning: while for the first efficient firms the values of their *TCIs* are equal to $0_\$$ in column 4, for the last five inefficient firms, the values of their *TCIs* are equal to their *CI values* in Column 3. Moreover, the inverse relationship holds for *ACI* reported in column 5, where the corresponding *ACI* = *CI* values appear for the efficient units and a value equal to $0_\$$ associated with the last five inefficient firms. This dual behavior recommends separating the firms in Table 13.12 into two subgroups: the efficient ones, which appear in rows 3 to 6, and the non-efficient ones, in rows 8 to 12. At the bottom of column 4, the value of the common normalization factor $NF = 30$ is reported which, in this particular case, takes the same value as in Table 13.7 for the *SR cost approach*. Consequently, being the cost inefficiency the same in both tables as well as the normalization factor, the same happens with the normalized cost inefficiency, see Column 6 in both tables. The last two columns, where the technical inefficiency and the allocative inefficiency are reported, are exactly the same in both tables with the only exception of inefficient firm E, whose SR projection was point D = (8,2) and whose actual FR projection is cost-minimizing firm B = (4,6). The fact that the remaining three inefficient firms obtain the same projection in both tables shows that their associated technical inefficiency reported in the last table, which is equal to $\frac{w \cdot u^-_{oFR(I)}}{NF_\$}$, $NF_\$ = U_{FR(I)}$, is related in all cases to non-negative input slacks.

13.4 Decomposing Revenue Inefficiency

13.4.1 The Traditional Approaches Based on Output-Oriented Efficiency Measures

In this section, we are going to deal exclusively with output-oriented efficiency measures. The structure of this section is the same as those of the two preceding sections. Here, we are interested in expanding outputs while keeping the same level of inputs. Therefore, for analyzing firm (x_o, y_o), instead of considering T, i.e., the whole production possibility set under variable returns to scale, we consider the *output set* $P(x_o) := \{y : (x_o, y) \in T\}$, whose frontier is a subset of $\partial^W(T)$—see Sect. 2.2. of Chap. 2. A relevant component of the revenue inefficiency decomposition for firm (x_o, y_o) is its technical inefficiency, obtained by means of a previously selected output-oriented efficiency measure *EM*(*O*), which also identifies its frontier projection $\left(x_o, \widehat{y}_{oEM(O)}\right)$. Depending on the nature of *EM*(*O*), two issues are relevant. First, we want to know if all the projections are strongly efficient, in which case they satisfy the indication property (E1a) presented in Sect. 2.3 of Chap. 2, by accounting for all types of inefficiencies. Second, we would like to know if *EM*(*O*) is able to generate, at least for one firm, multiple projections, in which case we need to identify the most convenient one, so as to get a unique revenue inefficiency decomposition when applying the new method to be introduced.

Let us assume that T is generated by a finite sample of production firms (x_j, y_j), $j \in J$. Given market output prices $p > 0_N$, the *maximum revenue* $R(x_o, p)$ *for points*

(x_o, y) *satisfying* $y \in P(x_o)$ is obtained as the optimal solution of the next linear program:[63]

$$
\begin{aligned}
R(x_o, p) = \quad & \max_{y,\lambda} \sum_{n=1}^{N} p_n y_n \\
s.t. \quad & \\
& \sum_{j=1}^{J} \lambda_j x_{jm} \leq x_{om}, \quad m = 1, \ldots, M, \\
& \sum_{j=1}^{J} \lambda_j y_{jn} \geq y_n, \quad n = 1, \ldots, N, \\
& \sum_{j=1}^{J} \lambda_j = 1, \\
& \lambda_j \geq 0, \quad j = 1, \ldots, J, \\
& y_n \geq 0, \quad n = 1, \ldots, N.
\end{aligned}
\tag{13.56}
$$

Any optimal solution of the last program (x_o, y^*) is a *revenue-maximizing point.*[64] For any firm (x_o, y_o), its *revenue inefficiency* is defined as $RI(x_o, y_o, p) = R(x_o, p) - p \cdot y_o \geq 0$ (see expression (2.21) in Sect. 2.3 of Chap. 2). What the traditional approach associated with a certain $EM(O)$ does is to relate $RI(x_o, y_o, p)$ with a specific technical inefficiency measure $TI_{EM(O)}(x_o, y_o)$ through a certain inequality derived resorting to duality methods, which results in a *Fenchel-Mahler type inequality*. In the mentioned inequality, the technical inefficiency, which is a pure number, appears multiplied by a certain positive factor, called *normalizing factor*, and expressed in monetary units. By dividing the mentioned inequality by the normalizing factor, we obtain a final inequality that relates the *normalized revenue inefficiency*, $NRI_{EM}(x_o, y_o, \widetilde{p})$, with its technical inefficiency $TI_{EM(O)}(x_o, y_o)$. Once the mentioned inequality has been obtained, $NRI_{EM}(x_o, y_o, \widetilde{p})$ is decomposed as the sum of two terms, $TI_{EM(O)}(x_o, y_o) + AI_{EM(O)}(x_o, y_o, \widetilde{p})$, the second one being retrieved as a residual and named *allocative inefficiency*.

By resorting to the initial inequality, we are also able to consider a first *revenue inefficiency decomposition*, which has as its first component the product of the normalizing factor times the technical inefficiency which we denote as *technical*

[63]Let us observe that any optimal solution of (13.56) may not belong to $P(x_o)$, simply because the optimal inputs $\sum_{j=1}^{J} \lambda_j^* x_j$ are less than x_o. In that case, the point $\left(x_o, \sum_{j=1}^{J} \lambda_j^* y_j\right)$ that obviously belongs to T also belongs to $P(x_o)$ and is also a revenue-maximizing point.

[64]Even in the low-dimensional one input-two output space, we can find multiple optimal solutions, depending on the relative position of the hyperplane $p_1 y_1 + p_2 y_2 = R(x_o, (p_1, p_2))$ with respect to the polyhedral frontier of the output set.

revenue inefficiency and as its second component, which is retrieved as a residual, the so-called allocative revenue inefficiency.[65]

To offer a first well-behaved example, let us now consider the output-oriented weighted additive distance function of Chap. 6. Reproducing its normalized profit inefficiency decomposition, identified as (6.25) in the mentioned chapter, we have

$$NRI_{WADF(O)}(x_o, y_o, \widetilde{p}) = \underbrace{\frac{R(x_o, p) - \sum_{n=1}^{N} p_n y_{on}}{\min\left\{p_1/\rho_1^+, \ldots, p_N/\rho_N^+\right\}}}_{\text{(Normalized) Revenue Inefficiency}} = \underbrace{TI_{WADF(O)}(x_o, y_o, \rho^+)}_{\text{Technical Inefficiency}} + AI_{WADF(O)}(x_o, y_o, \rho^+, \widetilde{p}) \tag{6.25}$$

The weights associated with outputs by the corresponding distance function are ρ^+, and $\min\left\{\frac{p_1}{\rho_1^+}, \ldots, \frac{p_N}{\rho_N^+}\right\}$ is the normalizing factor. This efficiency measure has a nice behavior because the normalizing factor is independent of the production firm being analyzed and, consequently, is unique and constant across firms. Therefore, the three terms in the last equality are comparable between firms, something that has been baptized as *the comparison property*.

13.4.2 The General Direct Approach Based on Output-Oriented Efficiency Measures

The reasoning, based on Pastor et al. (2021a), mirrors what has already been developed in the two previous sections. Our *output-oriented general revenue inefficiency decomposition* resorts to a *unique single equality*,[66] valid for any efficiency measure, in contrast to any of the traditional approaches that need to develop a specific inequality each time. Initially, the decomposition requires only knowledge of the firm being rated (x_o, y_o) and its output projection obtained through the selected output-oriented efficiency measure $\left(x_o, \widehat{y}_{oEM(O)}\right)$. The optimal output slacks that connect (x_o, y_o) with its projection satisfy $\left(0_M, s_{oEM(O)}^{+*}\right) = \left(x_o, \widehat{y}_{oEM(O)}\right) - (x_o, y_o) \geq 0_{M+N}$ or, focusing on its output components,

[65]This decomposition has not even been previously considered due to the strong influence of Nerlove's precise definition of economic inefficiency (Nerlove, 1965), which was assumed and disseminated by Chambers et al. (1998) in his seminal paper on directional distance functions.

[66]In case the efficiency measure used gives rise to multiple equivalent projections at least for one firm of our finite sample, the method has to be refined in order to preserve the uniqueness of the decomposition.

$$s^{+*}_{oEM(O)} = \widehat{y}_{oEM(O)} - y_o \geq 0_N. \tag{13.57}$$

Obviously, $s^{+*}_{oEM} = 0_N$ is equivalent to $\left(\widehat{x}_{oEM(O)}, y_o\right) = (x_o, y_o)$ which signals that (x_o, y_o) is a frontier firm. Since, by definition, *the revenue inefficiency at the projection*, $RI\left(x_o, \widehat{y}_{oEM(O)}, p\right)$ is equal to $R(x_o, p) - p \cdot \widehat{y}_{oEM(O)}$, we can decompose it as follows:

$$\begin{aligned} R(x_o, p) - p \cdot \widehat{y}_{oEM(O)} &= R(x_o, p) - p \cdot \left(y_o + s^{+*}_{oEM(O)}\right) \\ &= (R(x_o, p) - p \cdot y_o) - p \cdot s^{+*}_{oEM(O)}. \end{aligned}$$

Transposing the last term, we get our *first basic equality*:

$$R(x_o, p) - p \cdot y_o = p \cdot s^{+*}_{oEM(O)} + \left(R(x_o, p) - p \cdot \widehat{y}_{oEM(O)}\right). \tag{13.58}$$

This equality shows that the revenue inefficiency at (x_o, y_o), $RI(x_o, y_o, p)$ is equal to the value of the output slacks that connect (x_o, y_o) with its projection $\left(\widehat{x}_{oEM(O)}, y_o\right)$, $p \cdot s^{+*}_{oEM(O)}$, quantifying the revenue loss due to technical inefficiency, which we term *technological revenue gap*, plus the revenue inefficiency at its projection $RI\left(x_o, \widehat{y}_{oEM(O)}, p\right)$. Briefly,

$$RI(x_o, y_o, p) = p \cdot s^{+*}_{oEM(O)} + RI\left(x_o, \widehat{y}_{oEM(O)}, p\right).$$

In case, the first right-hand side term of (13.58) is positive, it is obvious that $(x_o, y_o) \neq \left(x_o, \widehat{y}_{oEM(O)}\right)$ or, equivalently, that $TI_{EM(O)}(x_o, y_o) > 0$, in which case we can multiply and divide the mentioned term by the technical inefficiency giving rise to the next equality: $p \cdot s^{+*}_{oEM(O)} = \left(\frac{p \cdot s^{+*}_{oEM(O)}}{TI_{EM(O)}(x_o, y_o)}\right) \times TI_{EM(O)}(x_o, y_o) > 0$. The factor that multiplies the technical inefficiency has the characteristics of *a normalizing factor* because it is positive and expressed in monetary units. Alternatively, if $(x_o, y_o) = \left(x_o, \widehat{y}_{oEM(O)}\right)$, necessarily $TI_{EM(O)}(x_o, y_o) = 0$, or, equivalently, $p \cdot s^{+*}_{oEM(O)} = 0_\$$, which allows us to set forth the general expression for the associated *normalizing factor*:[67]

[67] k_o represents any positive real number that we need to fix for those firms satisfying $(x_o, y_o) = \left(x_o, \widehat{y}_{oEM(O)}\right)$.

$$NF^{GD}_{EM(O)}(x_o, y_o, p) = \begin{Bmatrix} \dfrac{p \cdot s^{+*}_{oEM(O)}}{TI_{EM(O)}(x_o, y_o)}, (x_o, y_o) \neq \left(x_o, \widehat{y}_{oEM(O)}\right) \\ k_{o\$}, k_o > 0 \quad , (x_o, y_o) = \left(x_o, \widehat{y}_{oEM(O)}\right) \end{Bmatrix}. \tag{13.59}$$

Consequently, we can rewrite (13.58) as the next equality:

$$RI(x_o, y_o, p) = NF^{GD}_{EM(O)}(x_o, y_o, p) \cdot TI_{EM(O)}(x_o, y_o) + RI\left(x_o, \widehat{y}_{oEM(O)}, p\right), \tag{13.60}$$

which shows that *revenue inefficiency at* (x_o, y_o) *decomposes into the sum of* a first revenue inefficiency term related to technical inefficiency and a second revenue inefficiency term related to the output projection $(\widehat{x}_{oEM}, y_o)$. We refer to each of these two components as *technical revenue inefficiency and allocative revenue inefficiency*. Moreover, dividing by the normalizing factor, which is always a positive number expressed in monetary units, we obtain the desired *normalized revenue inefficiency decomposition* as *the sum of technical inefficiency and allocative inefficiency*:

$$\frac{(R(x_o, p) - p \cdot y_o)}{NF^{GD}_{EM(O)}(x_o, y_o, p)} = TI_{EM(O)}(x_o, y_o) + \frac{\left(R(x_o, p) - p \cdot \widehat{y}_{oEM(O)}\right)}{NF^{GD}_{EM(O)}(x_o, y_o, p)}. \tag{13.61}$$

This last decomposition, where the three terms are non-negative dimensionless numbers, satisfies the next three well-known and intuitive statements:

1. If (x_o, y_o) is a revenue-maximizing point, i.e., $R(x_o, p) - p \cdot y_o = 0_\$$, then its technical and allocative inefficiencies must be 0.
2. If technical inefficiency equals 0, then normalized revenue inefficiency is equal to allocative inefficiency.
3. And last, if allocative inefficiency equals 0, then all normalized revenue inefficiency is technical.

13.4.3 Revenue Inefficiency Decomposition Based on the Traditional and on the General Direct Approach: A Comparison, a Numerical Example, and Some Properties of the Direct Approach

Let us start by establishing the comparison between both approaches, something that is only possible if we assume that both use the same output-oriented efficiency measure for determining the same technical inefficiency of each firm.

Comparison

Output-Oriented Traditional Approach

First Step: Select $\overline{EM(O)}$. *Calculate for each* (x_o, y_o), $\left(x_o, \widehat{y}_{o\overline{EM(O)}}\right)$, $TI_{\overline{EM(O)}}(x_o, y_o)$, *and* $RI(x_o, y_o, p)$.

Second Step: For $\overline{EM(O)}$, find a Fenchel-Mahler inequality *that provides a normalizing factor satisfying* $RI(x_o, y_o, p) \geq NF^{TR}_{\overline{EM(O)}}(x_o, y_o) \cdot TI_{\overline{EM(O)}}(x_o, y_o)$ *for all* (x_o, y_o). *Since the normalizing factor is unique to any of the known output inefficiency measures, the last inequality is unique to any firm as well. Based on the last inequality, retrieve* $ARI^{TR}_{\overline{EM(O)}}(x_o, y_o, p)$ *as a residual, and formulate* the revenue inefficiency decomposition $NRI(x_o, y_o, p) = \left(NF^{TR}_{\overline{EM(O)}}(x_o, y_o, p) \cdot TI_{\overline{EM(O)}}(x_o, y_o)\right) + ARI^{TR}_{\overline{EM(O)}}(x_o, y_o, p)$.

Third Step: Dividing all the terms of the last equality by the normalizing factor, formulate the normalized revenue inefficiency decomposition $NRI^{TR}_{\overline{EM(O)}}(x_o, y_o, \widetilde{p}) = \frac{RI(x_o, y_o, p)}{NF^{TR}_{\overline{EM(O)}}(x_o, y_o, p)} = TI_{\overline{EM(O)}}(x_o, y_o) + AI^{TR}_{\overline{EM(O)}}(x_o, y_o, \widetilde{p})$.

Output-Oriented General Direct Approach

First Step: The same as for the traditional approach.

Second Step: Leave out $TI_{\overline{EM(O)}}(x_o, y_o)$. *For* $\overline{EM(O)}$, *calculate* $RI\left(x_o, \widehat{y}_{oEM(O)}, p\right)$. *In case one or more firms have multiple projections, select for each of these firms a projection with the highest revenue inefficiency. Derive* $p \cdot s^{+*}_{o\overline{EM(O)}}$ *as a residual, and obtain the revenue inefficiency decomposition,* $RI(x_o, y_o, p) = p \cdot s^{+*}_{o\overline{EM(O)}} + RI\left(x_o, \widehat{y}_{o\overline{EM(O)}}, p\right)$.

Third Step: Recover $TI_{\overline{EM(O)}}(x_o, y_o)$, *and calculate* $NF^{GD}_{\overline{EM(O)}}(x_o, y_o, p)$ *dividing* $p \cdot s^{+*}_{o\overline{EM(O)}}$ *by* $TI_{\overline{EM(O)}}(x_o, y_o)$; *thereafter, divide each term of the last decomposition by* $NF^{GD}_{\overline{EM(O)}}(x_o, y_o, p)$, *and generate the next normalized inefficiency decomposition*:

$$NRI^{GD}_{\overline{EM(O)}}(x_o, y_o, \widetilde{p}) = \frac{RI(x_o, y, p)}{NF^{GD}_{\overline{EM(O)}}(x_o, y_o, p)} = TI_{\overline{EM(O)}}(x_o, y_o) + \frac{RI\left(x_o, \widehat{y}_{oEM(O)}, p\right)}{NF^{GD}_{\overline{EM(O)}}(x_o, y_o, p)} = \\ = TI_{\overline{EM(O)}}(x_o, y_o) + AI^{GD}_{\overline{EM(O)}}(x_o, y_o, \widetilde{p}). \tag{13.62}$$

Just as we did for the profit and the cost inefficiency decompositions, there are three basic options for assigning the value of the normalizing factor (see (13.59)), for firms that identify themselves as benchmarks. Let us briefly expose them.

Three Options for Assigning Normalization Factor Values to $k_{o\$}$

1. First option: let us assume that any frontier firm (x_o, y_o) satisfying $(x_o, y_o) = \left(x_o, \widehat{y}_{oEM(O)}\right)$ is also the output projection of just one other firm, $(x_o, y_o) = \left(x_o, \widehat{y}_{jEM(O)}\right)$, $(x_o, y_j) \neq (x_o, y_o)$. It is obvious that (x_o, y_j) has its own fixed normalization factor equal to $\frac{p \cdot s^{+*}_{jEM(O)}}{TI_{EM(O)}\left(x_o, y_j\right)} > 0$, and our proposal is to assign it to (x_o, y_o).
2. In case we are comparing, for a certain output efficiency measure, the traditional approach with the general direct approach, our second option is to assign to the firms that are projected onto themselves the value of the normalization factor of the traditional approach. See, for instance, next Example 13.9.
3. In the rest of the cases, we assign to any frontier firm satisfying $(x_o, \widehat{y}_{oEM}) = (x_o, y_o)$ the minimum of the normalization factors associated with the rest of the firms. This decision is based on our empirical experience when applying the traditional approach to different efficiency measures.

Doubts may arise when the chosen efficiency measure identifies more than one projection for at least one of the analyzed inefficient firms. Anytime we face this situation, which depends on the efficiency measure we are using, we must check if any non-efficient firm of the sample being analyzed effectively obtains more than one projection.[68] Each time we resort to an efficiency measure that may generate alternative technical projections, we need to establish a criterion for selecting *the most appropriate projection.*[69] In fact, this task is not only necessary to ensure that the *general direct approach* ends up with a *unique revenue inefficiency decomposition* and a *unique normalized revenue inefficiency decomposition* but also when seeking *the best revenue projection*, i.e., the projection that achieves the highest revenue among the possible projections.[70] The same consideration is valid *for any output-oriented traditional approach*, although it is quite unusual in the specialized literature to deal with more than one technical optimal projection, probably because most of the frequently used output-oriented measures only deliver single projections.

Let us introduce an easy criterion for selecting from among the alternative optimal projections. We start by identifying among the subset of all the non-efficient firms of our sample which of them have more than one projection. Focusing first on our *general direct revenue inefficiency decomposition*,

[68] The $ERG = SBM$, presented in Chap. 7, is likely to generate multiple solutions. See the already mentioned chapter where we present the DEA program that allows its calculation.

[69] Alternative projections have a common feature: all of them have associated the same technical inefficiency.

[70] The best revenue projection means the projection that hast the lowest revenue inefficiency among the alternative projections. We just need to calculate one of these projections.

$RI(x_o, y_o, p) = NF_{EM(O)}(x_o, y_o) \cdot TI_{EM(O)}(x_o, y_o) + RI\left(x_o, \hat{y}_{oEM(O)}, p\right)$, the value of the left-hand side is constant because it depends exclusively on the firm being rated and on the output prices, while the technological gap as well as the revenue inefficiency associated with the projection, on the right-hand side, can vary for two alternative optimal projections. Hence, considering the last equality, if we select the optimal projection with *the largest technological revenue gap* $p \cdot s^{+*}_{\overline{oEM(O)}}$, we will *pick up the projection that has the smallest revenue inefficiency*, which is precisely the projection that is "closer" to a revenue-maximizing point. This strategy gives rise to a *general direct normalized revenue inefficiency decomposition*, whose *normalizing factor is as big as possible*, due to the fact that the *technical inefficiency* is the same for all the alternative projections, and whose *allocative inefficiency* is, consequently, as small as possible. Hence, in case one or more non-efficient firms obtain more than one projection, we propose *achieving* the *uniqueness of the revenue decompositions* associated with the general direct approach by *identifying, in each case, a projection with the smallest possible revenue inefficiency*,[71] which is equivalent to saying with *the maximum possible revenue.*

Example 13.9

Let us rely once again on *the output-oriented ERG = SBM* presented in Chap. 7 to illustrate the new general direct approach.[72] We consider the next "one input-two output example" with nine firms, where all the inputs take the same value, let's say x_o. Hence, $P(x_o)$ and $R(x_o, p)$ are a common subset and a common value for all the firms of this example. Moreover, since we are going to use an output-oriented measure, it is sufficient to consider for each firm its two outputs. Here are the output values for all the firms of our finite sample: A = (4,8), B = (8,6), C = (12,2), D = (2,1), E = (2,4), F = (4,2), G = (4,6), H = (6,4), and I = (10,2). Next, Fig. 13.4 illustrates the example, including the maximum isorevenue line as well as that line associated with firm F. Under variable returns to scale, we obtain that the first three firms are strongly efficient, while the last six firms are inefficient.[73] Graphically, we appreciate that the strong efficient frontier has two facets, respectively, defined by the pair of firms {(4,8), (8,6)} and {(8,6), (12,2)}. Let us further assume that the market output prices are $p = (p_1, p_2) = (1, 2)$. Hence, at each efficient firm, A = (4,8), B = (8,6), and C = (12,2), the revenue is equal to 20, 20, and 16, which means that the two *revenue-maximizing efficient firms* are A = (4,8) and B = (8,6); consequently, all the points that belong to this facet are also revenue-maximizing points. The *output-oriented ERG = SBM* technical inefficiency for firm (x_o, y_o) is equal to $\frac{1}{2}\left(\frac{s^{+*}_{o1}}{y_{o1}} + \frac{s^{+*}_{o2}}{y_{o2}}\right)$, and the corresponding normalizing factor, according

[71] In case two or more projections lead to the same smallest revenue inefficiency, we can select any of them, since both give rise to the same decomposition. However, we may consider a second proximity criterion, as we have suggested in the profit case.

[72] This output-oriented measure overlaps with the output-oriented Russell measure, as shown in Pastor et al. (1999).

[73] Since the measure we are using is a strongly efficient measure, we can use the additive model to identify the efficient firms.

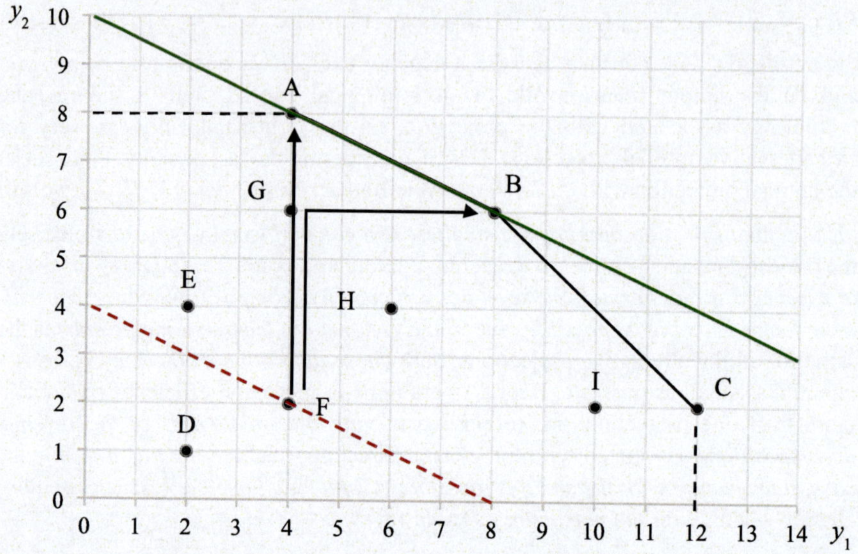

Fig. 13.4 Example of the traditional and general approaches to decompose revenue inefficiency, $p = (1, 2)$

to Aparicio et al. (2015a) (see Chap. 5) is equal to $M \cdot \min\{p_1 y_{o1}, \ldots, p_N y_{oN}\}$, which simplifies in our case to $2 \cdot \min\{y_{o1}, 2y_{o2}\}$. Before revising the results reported in Table 3.9, corresponding to the traditional approach, and comparing it with Table 3.10, elaborated according to the *general direct approach*, let us remind the reader that the Russell output-oriented measure *may produce multiple projections*. In our case, two of our inefficient firms obtain a couple of alternative projections, which means that the technical inefficiency associated with each inefficient firm is the same for its two projections.

Firms D = (2,1) and F = (4,2) have the same double option between efficient firms A = (4,8) and B = (8,6), as shown by the projecting lines for the latter. The choice is initially easy because we are involved in a revenue-maximizing process: we should take as a projection the one that has the maximum revenue, but in this particular case, both projections are revenue-maximizing firms. Considering that the actual production plan of each firm is the most similar to B = (8,6), we decide to select it as the projection of both firms.[74] Let us consider the following Table 13.9 on page 583 and make some comments on it.

[74]Since the normalizing factor in the traditional approach is independent of the projection, we can choose any of them for the two mentioned firms with double projections. Moreover, for the general direct approach, in this case, the same conclusion is valid, since both possible benchmarks are revenue-maximizing firms. Hence, the uniqueness of the revenue inefficiency decompositions is guaranteed in this case for both approaches, being independent of the assigned projection. We add an asterisk to the projection of each of these two units in Table 13.9 to indicate that a second projection is possible.

First of all, let us comment that the projection of the last firm, I = (10,2), is the convex combination of two of the efficient firms, $\frac{1}{2}(8,6)+\frac{1}{2}(12,2)$. We will use it very soon when analyzing its allocative inefficiency. The first two columns of Table 13.9 are devoted, as usual, to identifying each firm and its output-oriented $ERG = SBM$ projection. The next three columns report the items integrating the Fenchel-Mahler inequality: column 3 reports the output-oriented $ERG = SBM$ technical efficiency scores, column 4 the revenue inefficiency, while column 5 the normalization factor. With respect to *the revenue inefficiency decomposition*, we have to consider columns 4, 6, and 7. Column 6, *the technical revenue inefficiency*, is just the product of columns 3 and 5, which is easy to obtain. Moreover, column 7, *the allocative revenue inefficiency*, is retrieved as a residual from columns 4 and 6. It is curious that all the firms that have the same projection do not obtain the same value in column 7.[75] The third column, together with the two last columns, reports the values of *the normalized revenue inefficiency decomposition*. The story is similar to that explained for the non-normalized decomposition, and, obviously, the five firms of the sample that have an allocative revenue inefficiency equal to $0_{\$}$ obtain the same numerical value, 0, for *the allocative inefficiency*. *The essential property* is not met–e.g., for firms E = (2,4) and H = (6,4)–nor is *the comparison property*, just because the normalizing factors are different. However, *the revenue inefficiency decomposition* always allows classifying firms in terms of their efficiency status. At the firm level, the first two efficient firms are revenue maximizers, with their three normalized components at level 0. The third efficient firm, C = (12,2), has obviously 0 as technical inefficiency, which means that its normalized revenue inefficiency, 1/2, is all allocative. Moreover, the first five inefficient firms have all the same projection, firm B = (8,6). Three of them show an allocative inefficiency equal to 0, similar to their common projection, but the other two have nonzero allocative values. However, the last firm exhibits in this respect a better behavior. The same convex combination that applies for locating it in the facet determined by B= (8,6) and C = (12,2) is useful for relating their allocative inefficiencies: $\frac{1}{4}=\frac{1}{2}\times 0+\frac{1}{2}\times\frac{1}{2}$. We can see clearly in column 4 that there are three highly *revenue-inefficient firms*, with values in the interval [10,16], and another three moderately inefficient firms, with values in the interval [4,6]. On the other hand, the *technical revenue inefficiencies* are quite similar to the revenue inefficiencies but follow a slightly different pattern, with just two highly inefficient firms with values in the interval [12,16], and another four moderately inefficient ones, with values in the range [4,7]. Therefore, the *allocative revenue inefficiency* is mostly equal to 0 and for the remaining four firms presents moderate values in the range [1,4].

Let us now move on to Table 13.10 on page 585, corresponding to the *general direct approach*, where the columns appear in the same order as in Table 13.9. The four initial columns are inherited from Table 13.9. The fifth column, which corresponds to the normalizing factor, is elaborated according to the sixth column, whose definition changes with respect to the preceding table. In fact the technical revenue

[75]This property is always satisfied by the general direct approach, as we show below.

Table 13.9 Results based on the traditional decomposition of Aparicio et al. (2015a), $p = (1, 2)$

Firm	*Project.* $ERG = SBM(O)$	$TI_{EM(O)}$	RI	NF	$TRI = NF \times TI$	$ARI = RI - TRI$	$NRI = RI/NF$	AI
(1)	(2)	(3)	(4)	(5)	(6) = (5) × (3)	(7) = (4) – (6)	(8) = (4)/(5)	(9) = (8) – (3)
A = (4,8)	(4,8)	0	0	8	0	0	0	0
B = (8,6)	(8,6)	0	0	16	0	0	0	0
C = (12,2)	(12, 2)	0	20 – 16 = 4	8	0	4	1/2	1/2
D = (2,1)	(8,6)*	4	16	4	16	0	4	0
E = (2,4)	(8,6)	7/4	10	4	7	3	5/2	3/4
F = (4,2)	(8,6)*	3/2	12	8	12	0	3/2	0
G = (4,6)	(8,6)	1/2	4	8	4	0	1/2	0
H = (6,4)	(8,6)	5/12	6	12	5	1	1/2	1/12
I = (10,2)	(10,4)	1/2	6	8	4	2	3/4	1/4

Table 13.10 Results based on the general direct approach, $p = (1, 2)$

Firm	Project. $ERG = SBM(O)$	$TI_{EM(O)}$	RI	NF	$TRI = ps^{+*}$	$ARI = RI - TRI$	$NRI = RI/NF$	AI
(1)	(2)	(3)	(4)	(5)	(6)	(7) = (4) – (6)	(8) = (4)/(5)	(9) = (8) – (3)
A = (4,8)	(4,8)	0	0	8	0	0	0	0
B = (8,6)	(8,6)	0	0	16	0	0	0	0
C = (12,2)	(12, 2)	0	4	8	0	4	1/2	1/2
D = (2,1)	(8,6)	4	16	4	16	0	4	0
E = (2,4)	(8,6)	7/4	10	40/7	10	0	7/4	0
F = (4,2)	(8,6)	3/2	12	8	12	0	3/2	0
G = (4,6)	(8,6)	1/2	4	8	4	0	1/2	0
H = (6,4)	(8,6)	5/12	6	72/5	6	0	5/12	0
I = (10,2)	(10,4)	1/2	6	8	4	2	3/4	1/4

inefficiency corresponds now to the *priced technological gap*, $p \cdot s^{+*}_{oEM(O)}$ (see (13.58)), which can be calculated as $p \cdot s^{+*}_{oEM(O)} = p \cdot \left(\widehat{y}_{oEM(O)} - y_o\right) = \left(\widehat{y}_{o1EM(O)} - y_{o1}\right) + 2 \cdot \left(\widehat{y}_{o2EM(O)} - y_{o2}\right)$. Column 6 of Table 13.10 clearly shows that the general direct approach delivers a positively priced technological gap only for the inefficient firms, as expected. All the firms with a projection of B = (8,6) have an allocative revenue inefficiency equal to 0, the same as their projection. Now the *essential property* is satisfied, something that can also be observed in column 9, where AI is listed. The distributions of revenue inefficiency and of its first component, technical revenue inefficiency, are almost identical (see columns 4 and 6), which signals that the other component, the allocative revenue inefficiency, is 0 in most cases. Exactly the same analysis is valid for the normalized revenue inefficiency decomposition. Only two inefficient firms, E = (2,4) and H = (6,4), show different figures in both tables. In our opinion, *we gain coherence regarding the relation between each firm and its benchmark* when resorting to the general direct approach in comparison to the traditional one, and, additionally, we find that two more firms have null allocative inefficiency. In fact, for firms E and H, the traditional approach overestimates their allocative inefficiency. Finally, *the extended essential property* is also satisfied, since in column 7 each firm shows the same allocative revenue inefficiency as its projection, including the last firm I = (10,2), since its projection is the point $\frac{1}{2}(12, 2) + \frac{1}{2}(8, 6)$, with ARI= $\frac{1}{2}4 + \frac{1}{2}0 = 2$.

13.4.4 *The Exceptional Case of the Directional Output Distance Function*

We are going to show, for the particular case of any output-oriented *DDF* (also called directional output distance function), that the two normalized revenue inefficiency decompositions obtained by the two considered alternative approaches are identical. Since both approaches share the same technical inefficiency, $TI_{DDF(O)}(x_o, y_o) = \beta^*_o$, it is sufficient to prove that the two normalization factors are equal. It is well known that, in the traditional approach, the normalization factor corresponding to an output-oriented *DDF* is equal to $NF^{TR}_{DDF(O)}(x_o, y_o) = p \cdot g_{y_o}$. The *technical revenue inefficiency* in the traditional approach is equal to $NF^{TR}_{DDF(O)}(x_o, y_o) \cdot TI_{DDF(O)}(x_o, y_o) = \left(p \cdot g_{y_o}\right)\beta^*_o = p \cdot \left(\beta^*_o g_{y_o}\right)$, while in the general direct approach we have $p \cdot \left(\beta^*_o g_{y_o}\right) = p \cdot s^{+*}_{oDDF(O)} = NF^{GD}_{DDF(O)}(x_o, y_o) \cdot TI_{DDF(O)}(x_o, y_o)$, which proves that $NF^{TR}_{DDF(O)}(x_o, y_o) = NF^{GD}_{DDF(O)}(x_o, y_o)$, the desired result.

We left to the reader the argument that, as a consequence of the last result, the normalized revenue inefficiency decomposition of any output-oriented *DDF* satisfies the *essential property* and in case all the normalization factors $p \cdot g_{y_o}$ are equal, also the *comparison property*. Moreover, the revenue inefficiency decomposition satisfies the *extended essential property*, as any general direct decomposition does.

13.4.5 The Output-Oriented Reverse Approaches for Revenue Decompositions

The two output-oriented reverse approaches start out by reducing allocative inefficiency first, which means that they search for projections located as close as possible to any revenue-maximizing firm.[76] Therefore, we must discard the idea of resorting either to the *output-oriented traditional approaches* or to the recent *output-oriented general direct approach* because both begin identifying a frontier benchmark for each firm through a certain output-oriented technical inefficiency measure, without being concerned in the first place about the revenue inefficiencies of its benchmarks. For any inefficient firm, any "technical" movement toward the frontier will identify a projection whose revenue inefficiency is better than the revenue inefficiency of the firm, but we do not know in advance the amount of this improvement. We expect that the two next reverse approaches, namely, the *standard* and *flexible* reverse approaches, will be able to identify as benchmarks a set of frontier points that have smaller revenue inefficiencies. We are also confident that the second reverse approach will achieve better improvements than the first one since, as we are going to show, it has more freedom when moving toward the frontier projections.

The reverse approaches are a new way of reducing revenue inefficiencies searching for appropriate benchmarks or, equivalently, of increasing revenues from the beginning onward. Instead of reducing first, for each firm, the inefficiency associated with its technical component, the idea set out by Pastor et al. (2021b, c) is to reduce first its allocative component, with the objective of identifying, for each firm, a frontier projection whose revenue is as close as possible to the maximum revenue. The latter thereby improves the usual technical projection, which is the same for the traditional approach and for the general direct approach (provided that both resort to the same efficiency measure). As occurring before for the profit and cost cases, the reverse strategy is materialized by resorting either to *the standard reverse approach* or to *the flexible reverse approach*. The first one allows only increments in outputs while maintaining the inputs fixed, while the second one allows increments or reductions in outputs without modifying the input side. The first one is called *classical*, in the sense that its output movements follow traditional efficiency analysis, which presents as a positive characteristic the fact that it is relatively easy to derive an appropriate technical inefficiency measure associated with it. The second one is *iconoclastic*, because it allows any output movements, bearing the advantage of offering better projections with greater revenue improvements. In fact, it offers the largest possible allocative inefficiency reduction for any firm of the sample, since we are going to prove that it always ends up selecting as benchmark a revenue-maximizing firm. Its disadvantage is that deriving a reasonable technical inefficiency measure is apparently more difficult since the usual Pareto-Koopmans dominance between firms does not longer hold. Moreover, the scope of

[76] See subsection 13.2.5 for an interesting introduction to the two reverse approaches in the case of profit, which also applies to the cases of cost and revenue.

the flexible reverse approach is wider, allowing a better projection for any nonprofit-maximizing firm, while the standard reverse approach is only able to obtain a better projection for the subset of non-efficient firms.

Finally, only the standard reverse approach resorts to the general direct decomposition for deriving the appropriate technical inefficiency measures at a second stage. For its part, the flexible reverse approach requires a generalized direct approach that considers the existence of slacks of any sign with a new and surprising dual interpretation.

13.4.5.1 The Standard Reverse Approach for Revenue Inefficiency Decompositions

As already explained above, the aim of the output standard reverse approach, abbreviated to *output SR approach*, is to identify, for each non-efficient firm (x_o, y_o) of our finite sample, a projection $\left(x_o, \widehat{y}_{oSR(O)}\right)$, with $\widehat{y}_{oSR(O)} \geq y_o$, such that its revenue inefficiency is as small as possible. *The revenue inefficiency of* $\left(x_o, \widehat{y}_{oSR(O)}\right)$, previously identified as the *allocative revenue inefficiency* of (x_o, y_o) by the *output general direct approach*, is expressed as $RI\left(x_o, \widehat{y}_{oSR(O)}, p\right) = \left(R(x_o, p) - p \cdot \widehat{y}_{oSR(O)}\right)$. Since $R(x_o, p)$ is a constant, minimizing the last expression is equivalent to maximizing $p \cdot \widehat{y}_{oSR(O)}$. And, finally, given that $p \cdot \widehat{y}_{oSR(O)} = p \cdot y_o + p \cdot s^{+*}_{oSR(O)}$, where $p \cdot y_o$ is also a constant, we end up maximizing $p \cdot s^{+*}_{oSR(O)}$ to reach our goal. The linear program for achieving this objective is the next one:

$$
\begin{aligned}
\max_{s^{+*}_{oSR(O)}, \lambda} \quad & p \cdot s^{+*}_{oSR(O)} \\
s.t. \quad & \\
& \sum_{j=1}^{J} \lambda_j x_{jm} \leq x_{om}, && m = 1, \ldots, M, \\
& \sum_{j=1}^{J} \lambda_j y_{jn} + s^{+*}_{onSR(O)} = y_{on}, && n = 1, \ldots, N, \\
& \sum_{j=1}^{J} \lambda_j = 1, \\
& s^{+*}_{oSR(O)} = \left(s^{+}_{o1SR(O)}, \ldots, s^{+}_{oNSR(O)}\right) \geq 0_N, \\
& \lambda = (\lambda_1, \ldots, \lambda_J) \geq 0_J.
\end{aligned}
\tag{13.63}
$$

This model is a peculiar output-oriented weighted additive model because its objective function is expressed in monetary units. If we add its optimal value to

$p \cdot y_o$, we obtain $p \cdot \widehat{y}^*_{oSR(O)}$,[77] which can be compared to the maximal revenue value $R(x_o, p)$ to assess the size of the projection revenues. It may happen that the optimal objective function value equals $0_\$$, which means that $s^{+*}_{oSR(O)} = 0_N$. In this case, the firm being evaluated is a frontier point that satisfies $(x_o, y_o) = \left(x_o, \widehat{y}^*_{oSR}\right)$, whose allocative revenue inefficiency cannot be reduced at all, at least by trying to increase outputs in the classical way. The firms for which $(x_o, y_o) \neq \left(x_o, \widehat{y}^*_{oSR}\right)$ obtain a $p \cdot s^{+*}_{oSR(O)} > 0$, which means that their allocative revenue inefficiency can be increased as much as $p \cdot s^{+*}_{oSR(O)}$ when moving from (x_o, y_o) to $\left(x_o, \widehat{y}^*_{oSR}\right)$. As mentioned before, the next *first basic equality* also represents the *revenue inefficiency decomposition for the SR approach*:

$$R(x_o, p) - p \cdot y_o = p \cdot s^{+*}_{oSR(O)} + \left(R(x_o, p) - p \cdot \widehat{y}^*_{oSR(O)}\right). \tag{13.64}$$

The last equality is formally the same as the equality associated with the general direct approach (see (13.58)).[78] However, there is a noticeable difference: now $p \cdot s^{+*}_{oSR(O)}$ is obtained by means of linear program (13.63) that determines the corresponding projection, while in the general direct approach $p \cdot s^{+*}_{oEM(O)}$ was achieved by solving a different program associated with the technical efficiency measure $EM(O)$, determining in most cases a different projection.

With our next objective being to derive a *normalized revenue inefficiency decomposition for the output SR approach*, we need to generate a technical inefficiency measure associated with it, which is accomplished next.

13.4.5.2 The Technical Inefficiency Measure Associated with the Output Standard Reverse Approach

Once the projection for each non-efficient firm has been obtained according to the philosophy of the *output SR approach* exposed in the previous subsection, we can easily obtain the value of the *priced technological gap*, which enables us to propose through equality (13.64) the *revenue inefficiency decomposition for each firm*. To obtain the *normalized profit inefficiency decomposition*, we need to go one step further by learning how to measure the corresponding output-oriented technical inefficiency. Since the first stage of this process has been performed without resorting to any output-oriented efficiency measure, it seems quite clear that we have to devise *a specific output-oriented technical inefficiency measure* that is compatible with the already calculated *priced technological gaps* as well as with the already obtained *SR projections*. Based on (13.64), this is a sensible way for

[77] When the projection is derived based on the optimal slacks obtained through model (13.63), we add an asterisk to its outputs.

[78] This is the reason for maintaining the same terminology in the SR approach.

deriving the corresponding *normalized revenue inefficiency decomposition* associated with the *output SR approach.*

Let us start by defining a *technical inefficiency score* for each firm based on the mentioned projections. We have already identified a price-weighted L_1-path that connects each firm with its benchmark projection. As usual, our aim is to decompose it as the product of a technical inefficiency score times a certain factor, which we will identify later as the *normalizing factor.* Based on these and on the already defined *revenue inefficiency decomposition,* we will be able to finally derive the corresponding *normalized revenue inefficiency decomposition.* Just to remind the readers once more, since these decompositions resort exclusively to equalities, we do not need to consider any inequality based on duality results.

We continue following Pastor et al. (2021b) and need to consider, for all the firms (x_o, y_o) being rated, the introduction of a big enough denominator for the calculated priced technological gaps that guarantees that the corresponding ratios are always upper bounded by 1.

Linear model (13.63) produces, for each firm, the corresponding optimal output slacks. Let us denote as $\overline{s}^{+}_{SR(O)}$ the vector obtained by taking the maximum of the optimal slacks associated with each output over the sample of firms:

$$\overline{s}^{+}_{nSR(O)} = \max\left\{s^{+*}_{njSR(O)}, j \in J\right\}, n = 1, \ldots, N. \tag{13.65}$$

It is clear that the economic value delivered by the vector $\overline{s}^{+}_{SR(O)}$ satisfies

$$p \cdot \overline{s}^{+}_{SR(O)} \geq p \cdot s^{+*}_{jSR(O)}, \forall j \in J. \tag{13.66}$$

Assuming the presence of at least one inefficient firm for which $p \cdot s^{+*}_{SR(O)} > 0_{\$}$, the last proposition guarantees that $p \cdot \overline{s}^{+}_{SR(O)} > 0$, which is crucial for defining a *new technical inefficiency measure* $TI_{SR(O)}(x_o, y_o)$, obtained by solving the next linear program, closely related to model (13.63).

Definition 13.7

$$\begin{aligned} TI_{SR(O)}(x_o, y_o) \equiv \max_{s^{+*}_{oSR(O)}, \lambda} \; & \frac{p \cdot s^{+*}_{oSR(O)}}{p \cdot \overline{s}^{+}_{SR(O)}} \\ s.t. \; & \text{restrictions of model (13.60).} \end{aligned} \tag{13.67}$$

The easiest way to calculate $TI_{SR(O)}(x_o, y_o)$ for any of the firms of the original sample is to solve (13.63) for all the non-efficient firms, getting all the $p \cdot s^{+*}_{oSR(O)}$ values, to then obtain the value of the denominator, and to calculate finally the corresponding *technical inefficiency score* for any non-efficient observation (x_o, y_o), $TI_{SR(O)}(x_o, y_o) = \frac{p \cdot s^{+*}_{oSR(O)}}{p \cdot \overline{s}^{+}_{SR}}$.

Model (13.67) belongs to the family of weighted additive models, as defined by Lovell and Pastor (1995) and explained in Chap. 7. In fact, the expression of the technical inefficiency shows that the coefficients of the vector of optimal output slacks, $\frac{p_n}{p \cdot s^{+}_{SR(O)}}, n = 1, \ldots, N$, are ratios whose dimensions are *price per unit of quantity* in the numerator and *price* in the denominator that jointly give rise to $(quantity)^{-1}$, which, after multiplying by the corresponding slack expressed as a *quantity*, gives rise to the sum of pure numbers, which are independent of the units of measurement of outputs, something that is compulsory for any well-defined inefficiency measure (see P4 below). Moreover, the new introduced technical inefficiency measure, $TI_{SR(O)}(x_o, y_o)$, satisfies the next properties:[79]

Properties of the Standard Technical Output-Oriented Inefficiency Measure
P1. $0 \leq TI_{SR(O)}(x_o, y_o) \leq 1$.[80]
P2. $TI_{SR(O)}(x_o, y_o) = 0$ if, and only if, (x_o, y_o) is an output-efficient firm.[81]
P3. $TI_{SR(O)}(x_o, y_o)$ is a strong monotonic inefficiency measure in $P(x_o)$.
P4. $TI_{SR(O)}(x_o, y_o)$ is invariant to the units of measurement of outputs.

In Sect. 13.3.5.2, we have already studied the obtained input-oriented technical inefficiency and have concluded that, due to its definition as a true weighted additive model, it corresponds to a standard inefficiency measure. Here the situation is similar, and the reasoning is the same, concluding that we are facing a true output-oriented inefficiency measure. Resorting to it, we can easily obtain the *normalized revenue inefficiency* decomposition for the *output SR approach* as we show in the next subsection.

13.4.5.3 The Output-Oriented Standard Reverse Approach and Its Normalized Revenue Inefficiency Decomposition

Based on (13.64) and (13.67), it is straightforward to write down the *normalized inefficiency decomposition* for the standard reverse approach:

$$\frac{(R(x_o, p) - p \cdot y_o)}{NF_{SR(O)}(x_o, y_o)} = TI_{SR(O)}(x_o, y_o) + \frac{\left(R(x_o, p) - p \cdot \widehat{y}_{osSR(O)}\right)}{NF_{SR(O)}(x_o, y_o)}, \tag{13.68}$$

[79] The proofs are a consequence of model (13.67) being a weighted additive inefficiency model. The list of four properties listed above is similar to those published by Cooper et al. (1999) for sanctioning a well-defined efficiency measure (see also Sect. 2.2 in Chap. 2). In our case, the associated efficiency measure $EM_{SR(O)}(x_o, y_o)$ would be equal to$(1 - TI_{SR(O)}(x_o, y_o))$.

[80] We can expect almost always a strict second inequality as a consequence of the definition of the common denominator.

[81] An output-efficient firm is a firm for which none of its outputs can be increased without leaving $P(x_o)$.

where $NF_{SR(O)}(x_o, y_o) = p \cdot \overline{s}^{+}_{SR(O)} > 0_{\$}$ and $TI_{SR(O)}(x_o, y_o) =$

$$\begin{cases} \dfrac{p \cdot s^{+*}_{oSR(O)}}{p \cdot \overline{s}^{+}_{SR(O)}}, (x_o, y_o) \neq \left(x_o, \widehat{y}_{oSR(O)}\right) \\ 0 \quad , (x_o, y_o) = \left(x_o, \widehat{y}_{oSR(O)}\right) \end{cases}.$$

This definition has the advantage of keeping the same normalization factor for all the firms, which guarantees that the *comparison property* will be satisfied.

13.4.5.4 Numerical Example for the Output-Oriented Standard Reverse Approach

Example 13.10
Let us go back to Example 13.9 considered in Sect. 13.4.3. The real difference between the following table and the previous Table 13.10 of the mentioned example is that we do not start from a certain output-oriented efficiency measure for determining the projection of any firm. In fact, the *output SR approach* starts identifying the projection of each non-efficient firm that most improves its revenues by means of linear program (13.63). This is enough for achieving the corresponding *revenue inefficiency decomposition* based on the general direct approach. In a second stage, the *SR approach* allows the introduction of an *appropriate technical inefficiency measure*, as well as its associated *normalizing factor*, that provides us with the corresponding *normalized revenue inefficiency decomposition.* Let us consider Table 13.10, associated with *the general direct approach* and with a specific inefficiency measure, *ERG* = *SBM*, and let us indicate why Table 13.11 has a

Table 13.11 Results based on the standard reverse approach, $p = (1, 2)$

Firm	*SR(O)* projection	*RI*	$TRI = ps^{+*}$	*ARI* = *RI* − *TRI*	*NF*	$TI_{SR(O)} =$ *TRI/NF*	*NRI* = *RI/NF*	*AI*
(1)	(2)	(3)	(4)	(5) = (3) − (4)	(6)	(7)	(8)	(9)
A = (4,8)	(4,8)	0	0	0	16	0	0	0
B = (8,6)	(8,6)	0	0	0	16	0	0	0
C = (12,2)	(12,2)	4	0	4	16	0	1/4	1/4
D = (2,1)	(8,6)	16	16 = 6+10	0	16	16/16 = 1	1	0
E = (2,4)	(8,6)	10	10 = 6+4	0	16	10/16 = 5/8	5/8	0
F = (4,2)	(8,6)	12	12 = 4+8	0	16	12/16 = 3/4	3/4	0
G = (4,6)	(8,6)	4	4 = 4+0	0	16	4/16 = 1/4	1/4	0
H = (6,4)	(8,6)	6	6 = 2+4	0	16	6/16 = 3/4	3/4	0
I = (10,2)	(10,4)	6	4 = 0+4	2	16	4/16 = 1/4	3/8	1/8
–	–	–	*NF* = 6+10 = *16*	–	–	–	–	–

different ordering of its columns. We have also added a last row to our new table for displaying the fixed denominator needed for defining the new technical inefficiency measure. This fixed denominator is the *common normalizing factor*. The first two columns in Table 13.11 are a copy of the corresponding columns in Table 13.10, which means that the benchmarks obtained through model (13.63) are exactly the same as those of the preceding table, something that is highly infrequent. As a consequence, columns 4 and 5 of Table 13.11, showing the two components of the *revenue inefficiency decomposition*, are the same as columns 6 and 7 of the previous table. Since the fixed normalizing factor is new and based on the maximum slack values, the rest of the columns are different. The technical inefficiency values of the inefficient firms are completely different from Table 13.10, as well as the values of the *normalized revenue inefficiencies* listed in both tables in column 8. However, *the allocative inefficiencies* in both tables differ only for the third and last unit, maintaining the same proportion because both models exhibit the same *allocative revenue inefficiency*. We can also appreciate that the *output SR approach* satisfies the *essential property* as well as the *extended essential property*. Moreover, the *comparison property* is also valid. As a final comment, let us underline that, on this occasion, the *output-oriented SR approach* has been very effective in its effort to *reduce the allocative inefficiency* since all the units but two have achieved a zero value.

13.4.5.5 The Flexible Reverse Approach for Revenue Inefficiency Decomposition

The notable difference between the *output FR approach* and the *output SR approach* is the nature of the output slacks required for reaching the corresponding efficient projection. While in the *SR revenue approach* the slacks are necessarily non-negative, in *the FR revenue approach* they are unrestricted in sign, which means that the range of possible projections is as broad as possible. Basically, we are going to achieve similar results as in the two previous sections devoted to the flexible reverse approach for profit and cost. We leave the proofs of the proposition and the corollary that we will be proposing below to the reader, since they are akin to the preceding case devoted to cost inefficiency. Once again, the FR revenue approach does not agree with the general direct approach, so we must consider *the FR revenue generalized direct approach* that assumes that the new slacks have a dual behavior depending on the type of firm being projected.

The next *output flexible reverse approach* (*output FR approach*), recently proposed by Pastor et al. (2021c), is the most demanding reverse approach one can think of and follows a different philosophy to the already explained *standard reverse approach*. Inspired by Zofio et al.'s (2013) innovative proposal, *the FR revenue approach* mirrors *the FR cost approach* previously presented, identifying as the final projection of any firm a *revenue-maximizing firm* instead of a cost-minimizing firm. In other words, the final *FR revenue projection* has its revenue inefficiency equal to $0_\$$, which implies that its allocative component is also $0_\$$. As usual, we are considering a finite sample of firms $F = \{(x_j, y_j), j \in J\}$ under a *VRS* production possibility set *T*. In the output-oriented approach, for each specific firm (x_o, y_o), we consider the associated output production possibility set $P(x_o) := \{(x_o, y) \in T\}$. The aforementioned firm either belongs to the strong efficient frontier of $P(x_o)$, $\partial^S P(x_o)$, or not. Let us expose both cases separately.

Case 1: (x_o, y_o) Belongs to $\partial^S P(x_o)$

We are assuming that firm $(x_o, y_o) \in \partial^S P(x_o)$, which means that none of its outputs can be increased without leaving $P(x_o)$. Consequently, any technical projection of (x_o, y_o) is itself, which means that the corresponding technological revenue gap equals $0_\$$. Let us consider that the fixed vector of market output prices, $p > 0_N$, allows us to identify at least one firm (x_o, y^R) that satisfies $p \cdot y^R \geq p \cdot y, \forall y : (x_o, y) \in P(x_o)$. In other words, (x_o, y^R) is a revenue-maximizing firm. In case (x_o, y_o) is itself a revenue-maximizing firm, then $p \cdot y_o = p \cdot y^R$, or, equivalently, $RI(x_o, y_o, w) = p \cdot y^R - p \cdot y_o = 0_\$$, and we select (x_o, y_o) as the *FR projection* of itself. Resorting to *the general direct approach*, we obtain the next *FR revenue inefficiency decomposition* for *the revenue-maximizing* frontier *firm* (x_o, y_o):

$$RI_{FR(O)}(x_o, y_o, p) = TRI_{FR(O)}(x_o, y_o, p) + ARI_{FR(O)}(x_o, y_o, p) = 0_\$ + 0_\$. \quad (13.69)$$

Alternatively, if $(x_o, y_o) \in \partial^S P(x_o)$ but $RI(x_o, y_o, w) = p \cdot y^R - p \cdot y_o > 0_\$$, the general direct approach projects (x_o, y_o) again onto itself, providing the next *FR revenue inefficiency decomposition for* the non-revenue-maximizing firm (x_o, y_o):

$$\begin{aligned} RI_{FR(O)}(x_o, y_o, p) &= TRI_{FR(O)}(x_o, y_o, p) + ARI_{FR(O)}(x_o, y_o, p) \\ &= 0_\$ + ARI_{FR(O)}(x_o, y_o, p) > 0_\$. \end{aligned} \quad (13.70)$$

The last equality shows that $ARI_{FR(O)}(x_o, y_o, p) = RI_{FR(O)}(x_o, y_o, p)$, i.e., for any non-revenue-maximizing efficient firm, all revenue inefficiency is allocative. We have not finished our task yet, since our objective is to project (x_o, y_o) towards a revenue-maximizing benchmark. As we did for the profit and the cost decompositions, let us consider that we project (x_o, y_o) to its reference benchmark firm-maximizing revenue (x_o, y^R). As both (x_o, y_o) and (x_o, y^R) are technically efficient, we are dealing exclusively with allocative inefficiency. Moreover, since both firms belong to the strong efficient frontier of $P(x_o)$, we are relating two Pareto-efficient points of the same frontier. The next proposition shows that the input slacks that connect y_o with y^R are unrestricted in sign. Its proof, similar to the corresponding proofs of Propositions 13.4 and 13.8, is left to the reader.

Proposition 13.11

Let us assume that (x_o, y_o) is any strong efficient firm of $P(x_o)$ and that (x_o, y^R) is any revenue-maximizing firm. Then the output slack vector $u^+_{oFR(O)} \in \mathbb{R}^N$ that connects the output components of both firms, $y^R = y_o + u^+_{oFR(O)}$, must have at least one *positive component and at least one negative component. Moreover, any cost-minimizing firm can be used as a final projection.*

Note We would like to call the attention of the reader on how the strong efficient firm (x_o, y_o) is related with its revenue-maximizing projection (x_o, y^R): formally the relation is the same as for the *general direct approach*, although with two distinguished features—the slacks are unrestricted in sign, and the decomposition is *exclusively* based on *allocative cost inefficiencies*. Therefore, we call it, as already said before, *the generalized direct FR revenue decomposition approach.*

Based on (13.70) and on the definition of the output slack vector that connects (x_o, y_o) with (x_o, y^R), it is straightforward to write the last decomposition as follows: $0_\$ < RI_{FR(O)}(x_o, y_o, p) = ARI_{FR(O)}(x_o, y_o, p) = p \cdot y^R - p \cdot y_o = p \cdot u^+_{oFR(O)}$. It is noteworthy that the last decomposition is the same for any revenue-maximizing projection, the reason being that $p \cdot u^+_{oFR(O)}$ is always equal to $ARI_{FR(O)}(x_o, y_o, p) > 0_\$$. Combining (13.70) with the last result, we finally achieve *the generalized direct FR revenue decomposition approach for the subset of efficient firms:*

$$\begin{aligned} RI_{FR(O)}(x_o, y_o, p) &= TRI_{FR(O)}(x_o, y_o, p) + ARI_{FR(O)}(x_o, y_o, p) \\ &= 0_\$ + p \cdot u^+_{oFR(O)}. \end{aligned} \tag{13.71}$$

Case 2: (x_o, y_o) Does Not Belong to $\partial^S P(x_o)$

Following once again Zofío et al. (2013), let us formalize the relation between any non-efficient firm (x_o, y_o) of $P(x_o)$ and its revenue-maximizing projection (x_o, y^R). It is clear that the output technical inefficiency of (x_o, y_o) is positive. Prior to measuring it, let us develop the associated *generalized direct FR revenue decomposition*, which basically needs to know the relation between the output-inefficient firm (x_o, y_o) and its projection (x_o, y^R). In *Case 2*, the relation is similar but different from *Case 1*, since defining $u^+_{oFR(O)} := y^R - y_o \in \mathbb{R}^N$ allows, if necessary, for some of the output slacks to be negative. Considering the revenue inefficiency of (x_o, y_o), $RI_{FR(O)}(x_o, y_o, p) = p \cdot y^R - p \cdot y_o$, the calculated output technical inefficiency slacks, $u^+_{oFR(O)}$, and knowing that its allocative inefficiency, corresponding to that of its economic benchmark (x_o, y^R), is zero, then $ARI_{FR(O)}(x_o, y_o, p) = ARI_{FR(O)}(x_o, y^R, p) = 0_\$$ (see (13.69)), with the next chain of equalities being straightforward to obtain:

$$\begin{aligned} RI_{FR(O)}(x_o, y_o, p) &= TRI_{FR(O)}(x_o, y_o, p) + ARI_{FR(O)}(x_o, y_o, p) \\ &= p \cdot u^+_{oFR(O)} + 0_\$. \end{aligned} \tag{13.72}$$

Case 2 obtains precisely the opposite decomposition to *Case 1*: all the revenue inefficiency is technical revenue inefficiency, $p \cdot u^+_{oFR(O)}$, which means that the allocative revenue inefficiency is $0_\$$.

In order to derive, in both cases, the corresponding *Nerlovian FR revenue inefficiency decomposition*, we need to develop *a new technical inefficiency measure* related to the technical revenue inefficiency expression in (13.72). We undertake this question in the following section. However, before doing so, we deal with the possibility that, as in the profit and cost cases, several efficient firms maximize profit, and therefore, we are interested in finding the closest benchmark which requires the minimum changes in the output quantities to resolve all the revenue inefficiency. We resort to the same mathematical program that directly finds the revenue-maximizing benchmark, that is, the L_1-closest to each firm being analyzed. To this end and for each firm of our sample $(x_o, y_o) \in F$, let us reformulate the set of unrestricted in sign output slacks, $u^+_{oFR(O)} \in \mathbb{R}^N$, in terms of a couple of non-negative output slacks:

$$u^+_{oFR(O)} = s^+_{oFR(O)} - t^+_{oFR(O)}, s^+_{oFR(O)} \geq 0_N, t^+_{oFR(O)} \geq 0_N.$$

Given this last definition, the absolute value of each unrestricted in sign slack variable can be formulated as follows, $\left|u^+_{noFR}\right| = s^+_{noFR} + t^+_{noFR}, n = 1, \ldots, N$ and, consequently, the following linear program finds the *FR projection* for each firm $(x_o, y_o) \in F$ that is L_1-closer to a revenue-maximizing benchmark.

$$\begin{aligned}
&\min_{s^+_{oSR}, t^+_{oSR}, \lambda} && \sum_{n=1}^{N} \left(s^+_{oFRn} + t^+_{oFRn}\right) && \\
&s.t. && p \cdot \left(y_o + \left(s^+_{oFR} - t^+_{oFR}\right)\right) = R(x_o, p), && \\
& && \sum_{j=1}^{J} \lambda_j x_{jm} \leq x_{om}, && m = 1, \ldots, M \\
& && \sum_{j=1}^{J} \lambda_j y_{jn} - \left(s^+_{onFR} - t^+_{onFR}\right) = y_{on}, && n = 1, \ldots, N \\
& && \sum_{j=1}^{J} \lambda_j = 1, && \\
& && s^+_{oFR} \geq 0_N, t^+_{oFR} \geq 0_N, && \\
& && \lambda = (\lambda_1, \ldots, \lambda_J) \geq 0_J. &&
\end{aligned} \tag{13.73}$$

As before, we note that although the proposed decomposition of the absolute value of each of the output slacks unrestricted in sign is not unique, the solution of the last linear program is. Since the objective function of (13.73) minimizes the sum of all the pairs of an s-slack and the associated t-slack, we are sure that the optimal value of each of the aforementioned slacks will take the minimum possible values.

13.4.5.6 The Technical Inefficiency Measure Associated with the Output Flexible Reverse Approach

Let us consider the finite sample of firms under scrutiny belonging to $P(x_o)$, which we denote as $F(x_o) = \{(x_o, y_j), j \in J\}$. Let us further consider the two disjoint subsets of $F(x_o)$, $F_E(x_o)$ and $F_N(x_o)$, which obviously satisfy the next equality $F(x_o) = F_E(x_o) \cup F_N(x_o)$. It should be clear that $F_E(x_o) = \{(x_o, y_j) \in \partial^S P(x_o), j \in J\}$, while $F_N(x_o) = \{(x_o, y_j) \notin \partial^S P(x_o), j \in J\}$. The first subset corresponds exactly with *Case 1* firms, whose technical revenue-inefficient component is always equal to $0_\$$, and the second one with *Case 2* firms that, according to (13.72), have a positive technical revenue inefficiency component. For each firm $(x_o, y_j) \in F_N(x_o)$, we have shown that the mentioned component equals $p \cdot u^+_{oFR(O)} > 0_\$$. Let us define $U_{FR(O)}$ as the maximum of all this technical revenue-inefficient components:

$$U_{FR(O)} = \max\left\{p \cdot u^+_{oFR(O)} > 0_\$,\ (x_o, y_j) \in F_N(x_o); 0_\$,\ (x_0, y_j) \in F_E(y_o)\right\}. \tag{13.74}$$

Assuming that $F_N(x_o)$ is non-empty, we deduce that $U_{FR(O)} > 0_\$$. The next definition is straightforward.

Definition 13.8
The technical inefficiency associated with any firm of $F(x_o)$ is defined as

$$TI_{FR(O)}(x_o, y_j) = \frac{TRI_{FR(O)}(x_o, y_j)}{U_{FR(O)}},\ (x_o, y_j) \in F(x_o). \tag{13.75}$$

The novelty of this technical inefficiency definition is that some of the output slacks involved can be negative. However, we are going to show that it is a true technical inefficiency measure, since it satisfies the four basic properties first required for the traditional efficiency measures by Cooper et al. (1999).

Proposition 13.12
The technical inefficiency measure defined above through (13.75) satisfies the next four properties:

P1. $0 \le TI_{FR(O)}(x_o, y_j) \le 1$, $(x_o, y_j) \in F(x_o)$.
P2. $TI_{FR(O)}(x_o, y_j) = 0$ *if, and only if,* $(x_0, y_j) \in F_E(x_o)$.
P3. $TI_{FR(O)}(x_o, y_j)$ *is a strongly monotonic inefficiency measure.*
P4. $TI_{FR(O)}(x_o, y_j)$ *is invariant to the units of measurement of inputs and outputs.*

Proof

P1. Is a direct consequence of Definition 13.8. Moreover, the definition of the upper bound $U_{FR(O)}$ guarantees that at least one input-inefficient firm has its technical inefficiency equal to 1.

P2. P2 holds as a consequence of the values of $TRI_{FR(O)}(x_o, y_j)$ for $(x_0, y_j) \in F_E(x_o)$.

P3. For proving P3, it is sufficient to consider any output-inefficient firm, which we label as *first firm*, that identifies a specific L_1-output path towards its strong frontier projection and compare it with any other different output-inefficient firm, which we label as *second firm*, that must belong to the considered output path. Let us prove P3 by showing that the length of the path that connects the second firm with its own output projection is strictly smaller than the length of the output path associated with the first firm. Since the two firms considered are different, the second firm will have a strictly shorter output sub-path for reaching the first firm projection compared to the output path associated with the first firm. Since the first firm path has at most N nonzero output slacks, the two firms can differ for any of the aforementioned slacks and necessarily satisfy the next two conditions: the first one establishes that the existence of an output sub-path for the second firm implies that the sign of the nonzero slacks associated with outputs of the second firm must be the same as those corresponding to the first firm. The second condition establishes that if any first firm output slack is equal to 0, then the same output slack for the second firm must also be 0. In any case, there exists a sub-path that projects the second firm towards the projection of the first firm, which shows that the first firm projection is a feasible projection for the second firm. Since we have adopted as a secondary criterion that each output-inefficient firm selects the revenue-maximizing firm that is closer to it, the length of the path that connects the second firm with its optimal projection must be less than or equal to the length of the sub-path towards the first firm projection, which in turn is strictly shorter than the length of the path associated with the first firm. Hence, the proof is done.

P4. The technical inefficiency value, $TI_{FR(O)}\left(x_o, y_j\right) = \frac{TRI_{FR(O)}\left(x_o, y_j\right)}{U_{FR(O)}}$, $\left(x_o, y_j\right) \in F\left(x_o\right)$, shows clearly that the units of measurement of $TRI_{FR(O)}(x_o, y_j)$ are monetary units, just the same as the units of the denominator, $U_{FR(O)}$, which shows that $TI_{FR(O)}(x_o, y_j)$ is a pure number for any firm.

This concludes the proof. □

Resorting to (13.75), the new defined technical inefficiency measure, it is straightforward to obtain the new *normalized FR revenue inefficiency decomposition*, just by considering equalities (13.71) and (13.72) corresponding to the *FR revenue inefficiency decomposition* for *Cases 1 and 2*, as shown in the next subsection.

13.4.5.7 The Output-Oriented Flexible Reverse Approach and Its Nerlovian FR Revenue Inefficiency Decomposition

Equalities (13.71) and (13.72) show the *FR revenue inefficiency decomposition* for the firms (x_o, y_j) of each of the two disjoint subsets of $F(x_o) = F_E(x_o) \cup F_N(x_o)$. We can summarize both decompositions as follows:

$$RI_{FR(O)}(x_j, y_o, p) = \left\{ \begin{array}{ll} 0_\$ + ARI(x_o, y_j) = 0_\$ + p \cdot u^+_{oFR(O)}, & (x_o, y_j) \in F_E(x_o) \\ TRI(x_o, y_j) + 0_\$ = p \cdot u^+_{oFR(O)} + 0_\$, & (x_o, y_j) \in F_N(x_o) \end{array} \right\}. \tag{13.76}$$

We would like to highlight, once more, the defining characteristic of the above revenue inefficiency decomposition associated with $(x_o, y_j) \in F(x_o)$: if the mentioned firm is strongly efficient in $P(x_o)$, the upper equality applies, which means that all the revenue inefficiency is allocative revenue inefficiency, that can be calculated in terms of the unrestricted in sign output slacks that connect $(x_o, y_j) \in F_E(x_o)$ with any revenue-maximizing efficient firm. For these efficient firms, the general direct approach is no longer valid, and we resort instead to *the generalized direct FR decomposition approach* introduced before. In terms of cons, for any output-inefficient firm $(x_o, y_j) \in F_N(x_o)$, the *generalized direct FR decomposition approach* still works assuming that slacks can also be negative, and the lower equality of (13.76) applies, which means that all the revenue inefficiency is technical revenue inefficiency, calculated in the same way, i.e., identifying the output slacks that connect (x_o, y_j) with any revenue-minimizing firm. In the latter case, the output slacks can be unrestricted in sign or non-negative, while in the former one the output slacks are always unrestricted in sign, with at least one negative and one positive output slack.

The preceding subsection provides us with a true technical inefficiency measure (see (13.75)) that can be introduced in (13.76) so as to get the desired *Nerlovian FR revenue inefficiency decomposition*. All we have to do is to rewrite $TRI(x_o, y_j)$ as the product $U_{FR(O)}TI_{FR(O)}(x_o, y_j)$ and divide the two expressions of (13.76) by $U_{FR(O)}$ obtaining the next *Nerlovian FR revenue inefficiency decomposition*:

$$NRI_{FR(O)}(x_j, y_o, \widetilde{p}) = \left\{ \begin{array}{ll} 0 + \dfrac{ARI(x_o, y_j)}{U_{FR(O)}} = 0 + \dfrac{p \cdot u^+_{oFR(O)}}{U_{FR(O)}}, & (x_o, y_j) \in F_E(x_o) \\ \dfrac{TRI(x_o, y_j)}{U_{FR(O)}} + 0 = TI_{FR(O)}(x_o, y_j) + 0, & (x_o, y_j) \in F_{OI}(x_o) \end{array} \right\}. \tag{13.77}$$

By simply dividing each term of (13.76) by *the normalization factor* $NF_\$ = U_{FR(O)} > 0_\$$, we have been able to obtain the corresponding *Nerlovian FR revenue inefficiency decomposition*, which *is decomposed as the sum of* a first term which corresponds to *the technical inefficiency of the firm* and a second term that corresponds to *its allocative inefficiency*. Moreover, since the normalizing factor is expressed in monetary units and takes the same value for all firms, we conclude that the obtained *Nerlovian FR revenue decomposition satisfies* the *comparison property* between firms. However, *their allocative terms do not satisfy* the *essential property* as a consequence of the *general direct decomposition approach* no longer being valid, which has been the reason for defining a new *generalized FR direct decomposition approach*. It constitutes one of the remarkable differences between the *SR revenue approach* and the *FR revenue approach.*

13.4.5.8 A Numerical Example for the Output-Oriented Flexible Reverse Approach

Example 13.11

Let us elaborate for the *revenue FR approach* a new table, Table 13.12, resorting to the same constant input and two output datasets of the nine firms considered in Table 13.11, where *the revenue SR approach decomposition* was presented. We will also consider the same vector of market output prices, $p = (1,2)$, for which the only revenue-maximizing firms are the two first efficient firms, A = (4,8) and B = (8,6); i.e., $R(x_o, p) = \$20$. Obviously these two firms are projected onto themselves, resulting in a null revenue inefficiency. The same happened in Table 13.11. Consequently, the rows associated with A and B are equal in both tables since their revenue inefficiency decomposition has its two additive terms equal to $0_\$$ in both cases. The rest of the seven firms experiment a significant change in their projections in comparison to the SR approach.

Let us start searching for the projection of efficient firm C = (12,2). Initially we can project it either onto A or onto B. However, searching for the closest projection

Table 13.12 Results based on the *flexible reverse revenue approach*, $p = (1,2)$

Efficient firms	*FR Revenue Maximiz. Projection*	$RI_\$$	$TRI_\$ = 0_\$$	$ARI_\$ = p \cdot u^{+}_{j_E FR(O)}$	$NRI = \frac{RI_\$}{NF_\$}$	$TI = \frac{TRI_\$}{NF_\$}$	$AI = \frac{ARI_\$}{NF_\$}$
(1)	(2)	(3)	(4)	(5)=(3)-(4)	(6)	(7)	(8)=(6)-(7)
A=(4,8)	(4,8)	0	0	0	0	0	0
B=(8,6)	(8,6)	0	0	0	0	0	0
C=(12,2)	(8,6)	4	0	4	0	1/4	2/8
Non-efficient firms	*FR Revenue Maximiz. Projection*	$RI_\$$	$TRI_\$ = p \cdot u^{+}_{j_N FR(O)}$	$ARI_\$ = 0_\$$	$\frac{RI_\$}{NF_\$}$	$TI = \frac{TRI_\$}{NF_\$}$	$AI = \frac{ARI_\$}{NF_\$}$
D=(2,1)	(4,8)	16	16	0	16/16=1	1	0
E=(2,4)	(4,8)	10	10	0	10/16=5/8	5/8	0
F=(4,2)	(4,8)	12	12	0	12/16=6/8	6/8	0
G=(4,6)	(4,8)	4	4	0	4/16=2/8	2/8	0
H=(6,4)	(8,6)	6	6	0	6/16=3/8	3/8	0
I=(10,2)	(8,6)	6	6	0	6/16=3/8	3/8	0
—	—	—	$NF_\$= 16$	—	—	—	—

according to program (13.73), we find that the closest revenue-maximizing firm is B = (8,6), with a L_1-*distance* equal to (4 + 4) = 8 (the distance to A = (4,8) is equal to (8 + 6) = 14). In both cases, according to Proposition 13.10, the output slacks associated with the first and second outputs are for the first case negative and for the second case positive, although for calculating the distance we must always consider the absolute value of each slack. Let us now revise the first output-inefficient unit D = (2,1). Its L_1-*distance* from A = (4,8) is (2 + 7) = 9 while from B = (8,6) is (6 + 5) = 11, which means that A is its closest projection. In this case, both sets of output slacks are positive. The reader can verify that the same occurs with the inefficient firms E, F and G, with all three having firm A as their closest projection. H has firm B as its closest projection, with a distance equal to (2 + 2) = 4 that is shorter than its distance to A, (2 + 4) = 6. The last firm, I = (10,2), has a negative output slack, the first one in either of the projections. Its closest projection is also firm B. Hence, the first four inefficient firms have changed their projections in comparison to the SR approach as well as the last one (see Table 13.11). However, for this sample of firms, the FR revenue approach and the SR revenue approach, despite displaying rather different projections, give rise to exactly the same decomposition except for the case of the last firm I: while in the SR revenue approach both the technical and allocative revenue inefficiency components were positive, in the FR approach, all revenue inefficiency is technical. This is because in the latter approach it is directly projected to the revenue-maximizing benchmark represented by firm B while in the former approach, restricting all the output slacks to be positive, results in a projection to the strongly efficient firm (10,4)—namely, a linear combination of firms B and C.

13.5 Empirical Illustration of the General Direct Approach to Decompose Economic Inefficiency

In this section, we illustrate the calculation of the three economic inefficiency measures and their decomposition resorting to the general direct approach and considering the *ERG* = *SBM* as the reference technical inefficiency measure—see Chap. 7. We rely on the data presented in Sect. 2.5 of Chap. 2, corresponding to three simple examples, and on the real dataset for Taiwanese banks. Table 13.13 replicates the data for the examples.

For each economic inefficiency model, the package "Benchmarking Economic Efficiency" implements the decompositions associated with the *general direct approach* (GDA), both in monetary and normalized terms. As shown in Sect. 13.2.2, the latter model divides economic inefficiency expressed in monetary terms, as well as its technical and allocative components, by the normalization factor corresponding to the chosen technical inefficiency model—in this case, the *ERG* = *SBM*—thereby resulting in terms that comply with the desirable units' independence (commensurability property, P6), as discussed in Sect. 2.3.5 of

Table 13.13 Example data illustrating the economic efficiency models

	Model							
	Graph profit model		Input orientation Cost model			Output orientation Revenue model		
Firm	x	y	x_1	x_2	y	x	y_1	y_2
A	2	1	2	2	1	1	7	7
B	4	5	1	4	1	1	4	8
C	8	8	4	1	1	1	8	4
D	12	9	4	3	1	1	3	5
E	6	3	5	5	1	1	3	3
F	14	7	6	1	1	1	8	2
G	14	9	2	5	1	1	6	4
H	9.412	2.353	1.6	8	1	1	1.5	5
Prices	$w = 1$	$p = 2$	$w_1 = 1$	$w_2 = 1$			$p_1 = 1$	$p_2 = 1$

Chap. 2. However, as we show in the following examples, the extended essential property (D2) of the economic decompositions (see Sect. 2.4.5 of Chap. 2), by which the allocative efficiency of the inefficient firms is equal to that of their projections, is not verified.

The following functions compute the *normalized* economic inefficiencies corresponding to the general direct approach, along with their decompositions into technical and allocative terms:

```
deaprofitgda(X, Y, W, P, :ERG, names = FIRMS)
deacostgda(X, Y, W, :ERG, names = FIRMS)
dearevenuegda(X, Y, P, :ERG, names = FIRMS)
```

The above syntax includes "`:ERG`" indicating that the associated efficiency measure is ERG = SBM. As already explained in previous chapters, the input- and output-oriented ERG = SBM efficiency measures are equivalent to the oriented versions of the Russell efficiency measure discussed in Chap. 5. The reason is that the ERG = SBM model was proposed as a generalization of the Russell measures to the graph (input-output) space and, therefore, the latter can be considered as particular cases of the former. For this reason, the above functions call the Russell measures when evaluating the technical inefficiencies in the input and output orientations associated with the cost and revenue efficiency models.

Finally, relying on the general direct approach, the decomposition of economic inefficiency in monetary terms can be obtained by including the option "`monetary = true`" in the above syntax, e.g., `deaprofitgda(X, Y, W, P, :ERG, monetary = true, names=FIRMS)`. The possibility of expressing economic efficiency in monetary terms proves useful from a managerial perspective by enabling the quantification of the profit loss and its sources in real values (i.e., dollars, euros, etc.). In this regard, the option "`monetary = true`" offers the possibility of recovering the technical and allocative inefficiencies in monetary terms. Clearly, the decompositions of economic inefficiency in monetary values are unit-dependent, failing to satisfy the commensurability property (P6) but in turn satisfy the extended essential property (D2).

13.5.1 The General Direct Approach (ERG = SBM) to Decompose Profit Inefficiency

We rely on the open (web-based) Jupyter notebook interface to illustrate the economic models. Nevertheless, they can be implemented in any integrated development environment (IDE) of preference.[82] To calculate profit inefficiency using the general direct approach associated with the ERG = SBM technical inefficiency measure (expression (13.17)), enter the following code in the "`Out[]:`" window, and run it. The corresponding results are shown in the "`In[]:`" window of Table 13.14.

Table 13.14 Implementation of the GDA (ERG = SBM) profit inefficiency model using BEE for Julia

In[]:

```
using DataEnvelopmentAnalysis
using BenchmarkingEconomicEfficiency

X = [2; 4; 8; 12; 6; 14; 14; 9.412];
Y = [1; 5; 8; 9; 3; 7; 9; 2.353];
W = [1; 1; 1; 1; 1; 1; 1; 1];
P = [2; 2; 2; 2; 2; 2; 2; 2];
FIRMS = ["A";"B";"C";"D";"E";"F";"G";"H"];

deaprofitgda(X, Y, W, P, :ERG, names = FIRMS)
```

Out[]:

```
General Direct Approach Profit DEA Model
DMUs = 8; Inputs = 1; Outputs = 1
Returns to Scale = VRS
Associated efficiency measure = ERG
```

	Profit	Technical	Allocative
A	4.0	0.0	4.0
B	0.5	0.0	0.5
C	0.0	0.0	0.0
D	0.167	0.0	0.167
E	0.8	0.6	0.2
F	0.571	0.524	0.048
G	0.286	0.143	0.143
H	0.949	0.8	0.149

[82] We refer the reader to Sect. 2.6.1 in Chap. 2 for the installation of the "Benchmarking Economic Efficiency" Julia package. All Jupyter notebooks implementing the different economic models in this book can be downloaded from the reference site: http://www.benchmarkingeconomicefficiency.com

Contrary to the examples of the previous sections, for this common example of profit inefficiency solved in each chapter of the book, the results for the normalized direct approach coincide with those reported in Table 7.5, reporting the decomposition of profit inefficiency based on the traditional ERG = SBM measure. The only exception is firm H. The reason why they do not differ for the rest of the firms is that the traditional and generalized approaches happen to yield the same normalization factors, $NF_{EM}^{TR}(x_o, y_o, w, p) = NF_{EM}^{GD}(x_o, y_o, w, p)$, while none of the inefficient firms identifies multiple technological benchmarks, among which select the "best" one, i.e., that one exhibiting the highest profit or, alternatively, minimizing allocative profit inefficiency. When comparing the results of the new general direct approach to those of the reversed directional distance function, calculated again under the $ERG = SBM$ measure and presented in Table 12.12, we observe that in this case they are equal for all firms.

We can learn about the reference benchmarks for each firm using the "peersmatrix" function with the corresponding economic or technical model. For the economic model, executing "`peersmatrix(deaprofitgda(X, Y, W, P, :ERG, names=FIRMS))`" identifies firm C as the reference benchmark that maximizes profit for the rest of the firms (see Fig. 13.5 below).

Recall that the technical inefficiency in the general direct approach corresponds to the chosen technical inefficiency measure, which in this case is $TI_{ERG\,=\,SBM(G)}(x_o, y_o) = 1 - TE_{ERG\,=\,SBM(G)}(x_o, y_o)$. This last value, $TE_{ERG\,=\,SBM(G)}(x_o, y_o)$, is reported in Table 7.6 of Chap. 7. For convenience, we replicate this table in Table 13.15,

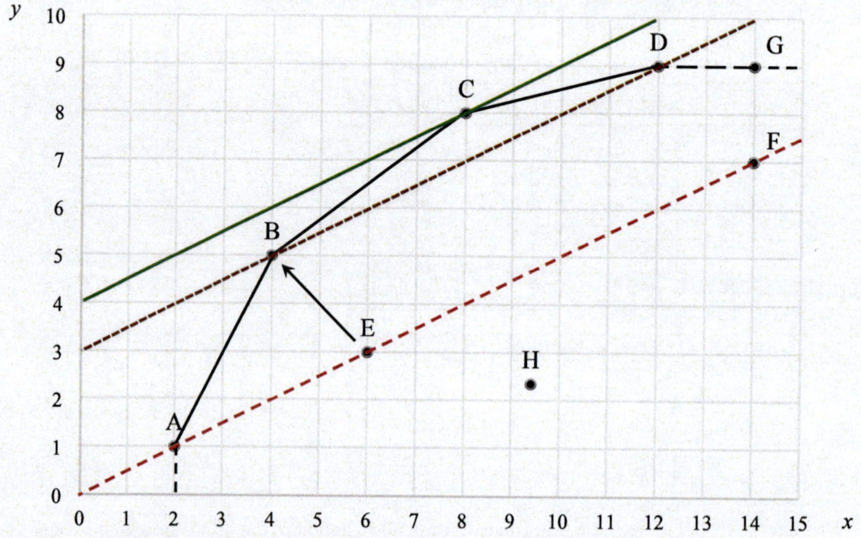

Fig. 13.5 Example of the GDA (ERG = SBM) profit inefficiency model using BEE for Julia

Table 13.15 Implementation of the GDA (ERG = SBM) inefficiency using BEE for Julia

In[]:
```
deaerg(X, Y, rts  = :VRS, names = FIRMS)
```

Out[]:
```
Enhanced Russell Graph Slack Based Measure DEA Model
DMUs = 8; Inputs = 1; Outputs = 1
Orientation = Input; Returns to Scale = VRS
```

	efficiency	beta	slackX1	slackY1
A	1.0	1.0	0.0	0.0
B	1.0	1.0	0.0	0.0
C	1.0	1.0	0.0	0.0
D	1.0	1.0	0.0	0.0
E	0.4	0.6	2.0	2.0
F	0.476	1.0	7.333	0.0
G	0.857	1.0	2.0	0.0
H	0.2	0.471	5.412	2.647

presenting all the information corresponding to the underlying ERG = SBM measure.

The projections obtained by solving the ERG = SBM efficiency model are used to calculate the *technological profit gap* $\left(p \cdot s^{+*}_{oEM} + w \cdot s^{-*}_{oEM}\right)$, then recover the normalization factor $NF^{GD}_{EM}(x_o, y_o, w, p)$ according to (13.13), and from there calculate the normalized profit inefficiency decomposition shown in Table 13.14.

Figure 13.5 illustrates the results for the generalized direct approach. There, for firm E, we identify that its normalized profit inefficiency with respect to firm C, according to (13.17), is equal to $N\Pi I(x_E, y_E, \widetilde{w}, \widetilde{p}) = 0.8$, which can be decomposed into the ERG = SBM technical inefficiency measure, whose value is $TI_{EM}(x_E, y_E) = TI_{ERG\,=\,SBM(G)}(x_E, y_E) = 0.6 = 1\text{–}0.4 = 1 - TE_{ERG\,=\,SBM(G)}(x_E, y_E)$ and allocative inefficiency $AI_{EM}(x_E, y_E, \widetilde{w}, \widetilde{p}) = AI^{GD}_{ERG=SBM(G)}(x_E, y_E, \widetilde{w}, \widetilde{p}) = 0.2$. In this example, firm E is projected to firm B. We observe that, as anticipated, the extended essential property is not satisfied because the allocative inefficiencies of the technically inefficient firms may be different from those of their benchmarks, i.e., $AI^{GD}_{ERG=SBM(G)}(x_E, y_E, \widetilde{w}, \widetilde{p}) \neq AI^{GD}_{ERG=SBM(G)}(x_B, y_B, \widetilde{w}, \widetilde{p})$. On the contrary, if we include the option "`monetary = true`" in the function, thereby running the following syntax, "`deaprofitgda(X, Y, W, P, :ERG, monetary = true, names=FIRMS)`", the allocative inefficiencies would be equal and easily interpretable in monetary values but would be denominated in a particular currency.

13.5.2 The General Direct Approach (Russell) to Decompose Cost Inefficiency

We now solve the example for the normalized general direct approach and decompose cost inefficiency considering the Russell input technical inefficiency measure presented in Chap. 5. This is the reference model for the ERG = SBM measure when a partial orientation is chosen for the economic analysis. Following expression (13.40), to calculate this model, type the code included in the "`Out[]:`" window of the notebook, and execute it. The corresponding results are shown in the "`In[]:`" window of Table 13.16.

On this occasion, the above results differ from those obtained in Chap. 5 for the cost inefficiency model based on the Russell input measure, representing the traditional approach in this example. Specifically, if we compare Table 13.16 to Table 5.5, we observe that the normalized profit inefficiency is different for the inefficient firms D, F, G, and H. This difference emerges from the disparity in the normalization factors associated with both approaches: $NF_{EM}^{TR}(x_o, y_o, w) \neq NF_{EM}^{GD}(x_o, y_o, w)$. On the contrary, we note in passing that the obtained results do not differ from those of the reverse directional distance function presented in Table 12.15 of the preceding chapter.

We gain knowledge about the benchmark-minimizing cost by running the "peersmatrix" function with the corresponding model. In this case, executing

Table 13.16 Implementation of the GDA (Russell) cost inefficiency model using BEE for Julia

In[]:

```
using DataEnvelopmentAnalysis
using BenchmarkingEconomicEfficiency

X = [2 2; 1 4; 4 1; 4 3; 5 5; 6 1; 2 5; 1.6 8];
Y = [1; 1; 1; 1; 1; 1; 1; 1];
W = [1 1; 1 1; 1 1; 1 1; 1 1; 1 1; 1 1; 1 1];
FIRMS = ["A"; "B"; "C"; "D"; "E"; "F"; "G"; "H"];

deacostgda(X, Y, W, :ERG, names = FIRMS)
```

Out[]:

```
General Direct Approach Cost DEA Model
DMUs = 8; Inputs = 2; Outputs = 1
Orientation = Input; Returns to Scale = VRS
Associated efficiency measure = ERG
```

	Cost	Technical	Allocative
A	0.0	0.0	0.0
B	0.5	0.0	0.5
C	0.5	0.0	0.5
D	0.417	0.417	0.0
E	0.6	0.6	0.0
F	0.25	0.167	0.083
G	0.525	0.35	0.175
H	0.533	0.438	0.095

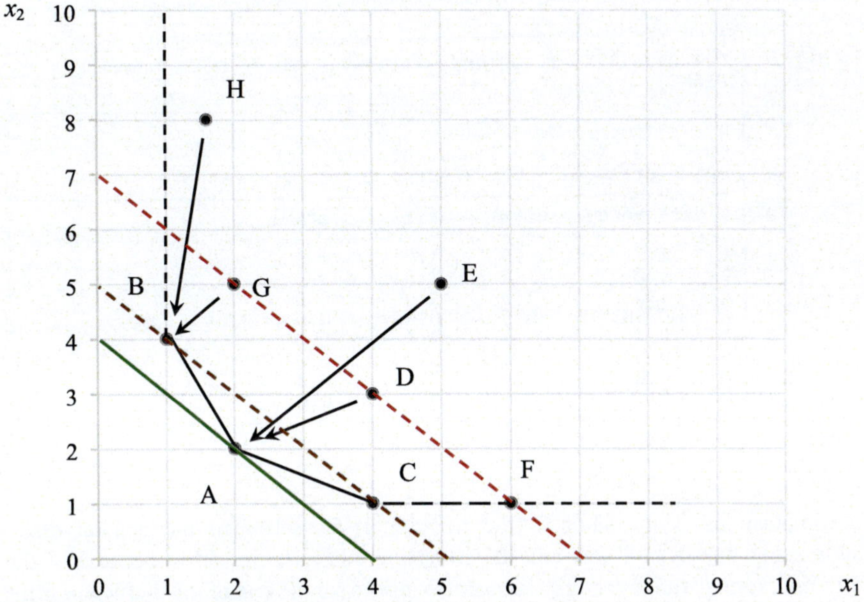

Fig. 13.6 Example of the GDA (Russell) cost inefficiency model using BEE for Julia

"`peersmatrix(deacostgda(X, Y, W, :ERG, rts = :VRS, names = FIRMS))`" identifies firm A as the cost-minimizing benchmark in this example (see Fig. 13.6).

As for the underlying technical efficiency model, we can obtain the information running the corresponding function. In this case, the function "`deacostgda(X, Y, W, :ERG, rts = :VRS, names = FIRMS)`" internally solves the Russell input measure corresponding to program (5.11) in Chap. 5 and calculates the inefficiency presented in Table 13.16 as $TI_{RM(I)}(x_o, y_o) = 1 - TE_{RM(I)}(x_o, y_o)$. We replicate in what follows the technical efficiency scores $TE_{RM(I)}(x_o, y_o)$ shown in Table 5.6, which are obtained by running the code presented in the "`In:`" window (i.e., the "`dearussell`" function presented in Sect. 5.5.2 of Chap. 5). Note that this function returns zero-valued slacks for both inputs and outputs (Table 13.17).

In this case, the projections obtained by solving the Russell efficiency model are used to calculate the *technological cost gap*, $w \cdot s^{-*}_{oEM(I)}$, and from there recover the normalization factor $NF^{GD}_{EM(I)}(x_o, y_o, w)$ according to (13.37), which ultimately allows us to calculate the cost inefficiency decomposition presented in Table 13.16.

Next, Fig. 13.6 illustrates the results for the general direct approach considering the input-oriented Russell model as technical efficiency. Here, for firm H, we see that its normalized cost efficiency with respect to firm A, as stated by (13.40), is equal to $CI^{GD}_{\overline{EM(I)}}(x_H, y_H, \widetilde{w}) = 0.533$, which can be decomposed into technical and allocative inefficiency with respective values of $TI_{\overline{EM(I)}}(x_H, y_H) = TI_{RM(I)}(x_H, y_H) = 0.438$ and $AI^{GD}_{\overline{EM}}(x_H, y_H, \widetilde{w}) = 0.095$. Although the technical inefficiency component of both

Table 13.17 Implementation of the GDA (Russell) input inefficiency using BEE for Julia

In[]:

```
dearussell(X, Y, orient = :Input, rts  = :VRS, names =
FIRMS)
```

Out[]:

```
Russell DEA Model
DMUs = 8; Inputs = 2; Outputs = 1
Orientation = Input; Returns to Scale = VRS

    efficiency   effX1    effX2   slackY1

A   1.0          1.0      1.0     0.0
B   1.0          1.0      1.0     0.0
C   1.0          1.0      1.0     0.0
D   0.583        0.5      0.667   0.0
E   0.4          0.4      0.4     0.0
F   0.833        0.667    1.0     0.0
G   0.65         0.5      0.8     0.0
H   0.562        0.625    0.5     0.0
```

decompositions is the same in the traditional (Russell) and the general direct approaches, the overall cost and the allocative inefficiencies differ because of the different normalization factors. The same happens for the rest of the inefficient firms whose decompositions differ from those of Chap. 5, except for firm E, which has the same normalization factor in both approaches, meaning that both methods are equivalent.

Relevant in the discussion of this example is that, as opposed to the traditional approach, we show that the general direct approach satisfies the extended essential property. Both inefficient firms D and E are projected to the cost-minimizing benchmark A and therefore, in order to comply with the essential property (D1, see Sect. 2.4.5 of Chap. 2), their allocative inefficiency should be equal to zero. This is the case for the normalized general direct approach, but not the traditional approach based on the Russell measure, where firm D has a positive allocative inefficiency equal to $AI_{RM(I)}(x_{\mathrm{D}}, y_{\mathrm{D}}, \widetilde{w}) = 0.83$—see Table 5.5 in Chap. 5. However, we observe that the normalized direct approach fails to satisfy the extended essential property (D2). In particular, firms G and H, having B as the reference technological benchmark, exhibit allocative inefficiencies different from that of their projection: $AI^{GD}_{RM(I)}(x_{\mathrm{B}}, y_{\mathrm{B}}, \widetilde{w}) = 0.5$. Using the option "`monetary = true`" results in the satisfaction of the property, but it would make the decomposition dependent on a specific currency.

13.5.3 *The General Direct Approach (Russell) to Decompose Revenue Inefficiency*

We now illustrate how to decompose revenue inefficiency based on the general direct approach and considering the output-oriented Russell measure as technical inefficiency. As in the cost example, the Russell measure is the reference for the

Table 13.18 Implementation of the GDA (Russell) revenue inefficiency model using BEE for Julia

In[]:

```
using DataEnvelopmentAnalysis
using BenchmarkingEconomicEfficiency

X = [1; 1; 1; 1; 1; 1; 1; 1];
Y = [7 7; 4 8; 8 4; 3 5; 3 3; 8 2; 6 4; 1.5 5];
P = [1 1; 1 1; 1 1; 1 1; 1 1; 1 1; 1 1; 1 1];
FIRMS = ["A"; "B"; "C"; "D"; "E"; "F"; "G"; "H"];

dearevenuegda(X, Y, P, :ERG, names=FIRMS)
```

Out[]:

```
General Direct Approach Revenue DEA Model
DMUs = 8; Inputs = 1; Outputs = 2
Orientation = Output; Returns to Scale = VRS
Associated efficiency measure = ERG
```

	Revenue	Technical	Allocative
A	0.0	0.0	0.0
B	0.25	0.0	0.25
C	0.25	0.0	0.25
D	0.867	0.867	0.0
E	1.333	1.333	0.0
F	1.0	0.5	0.5
G	0.458	0.458	0.0
H	2.5	2.056	0.444

ERG = *SBM (O)* model when a partial orientation is chosen for economic analyses. To calculate revenue inefficiency and its decomposition into technical and allocative terms based on (13.62), run the code included in the "`In[]:`" window. The corresponding results are shown in the "`Out[]:`" panel of Table 13.18.

To determine the reference set for the evaluation of economic and technical inefficiency, we use the "peersmatrix" function with the corresponding model. For the revenue model, we execute "`peersmatrix(dearevenuegda(X, Y, P, :ERG, names = FIRMS))`". The output identifies firm A as the benchmark-maximizing revenue for the rest of the firms (see Fig. 13.7).

Regarding the underlying reverse technical inefficiency model, the function "`dearevenuegda`" resorts to the Russell function presented in Sect. 5.5.3 of Chap. 5. In particular, it solves program (5.23) and calculates the inefficiency presented in Table 13.18 as $TI_{RM(O)}(x_o, y_o) = 1 - TE_{RM(O)}(x_o, y_o)$; i.e., once again, technical inefficiencies are the same for the traditional and general direct approaches. We replicate in what follows the technical efficiency scores $TE_{RM(O)}(x_o, y_o)$ reported in Table 5.9 of Chap. 5, which are obtained by running the code presented in the "`In[]:`" window (Table 13.19).

In this case, the projections obtained by solving the Russell efficiency model are used to calculate the *technological revenue gap*, $p \cdot s^{-*}_{oEM(I)}$, and from there recover the normalization factor $NF^{GD}_{EM(O)}(x_o, y_o, p)$ according to (13.59), which ultimately

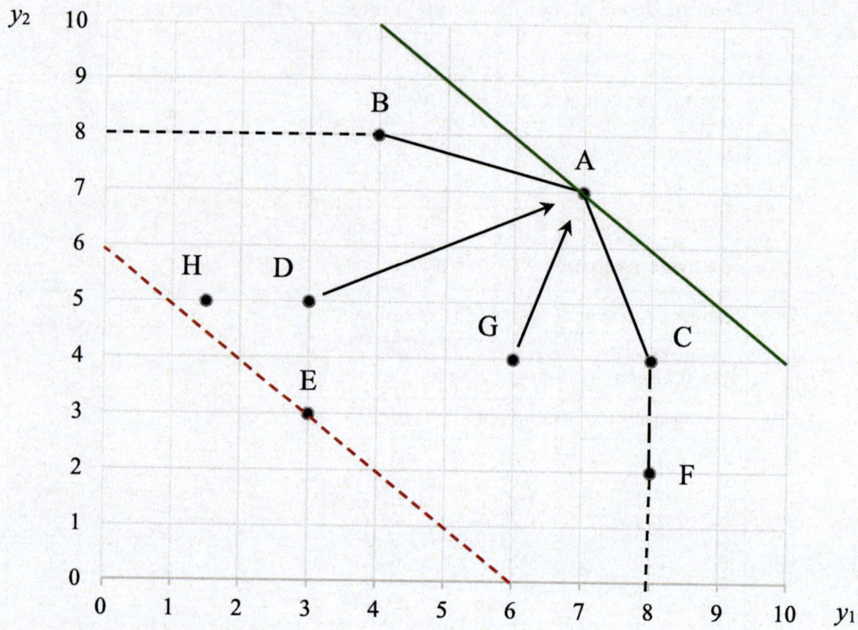

Fig. 13.7 Example of the GDA (Russell) revenue inefficiency model using BEE for Julia

allows us to calculate the revenue inefficiency decomposition presented in Table 13.18.

In this example, only the inefficiency results of firms D and G differ slightly from those of the traditional (Russell) model reported in Table 5.8 of Chap. 5. Specifically, these firms now exhibit null allocative inefficiencies, and therefore their cost inefficiencies are equal to the value of their technical inefficiencies: $TI_{RM(O)}(x_D, y_D) = 0.867$ and $TI_{RM(O)}(x_G, y_G) = 0.458$. This is an expected outcome since the general direct approach satisfies the essential property (D1) presented in Sect. 2.4.5 of Chap. 2, while the traditional Russell approach fails to verify it. Indeed, firms D and G, being projected to the revenue-maximizing firm A, should exhibit a zero-valued allocative inefficiency, as they do in the general direct approach. The reason for this difference emerges once again from the disparity in the normalization factors associated with both approaches: $NF_{\overline{EM}}^{TR}(x_o, y_o, p) \neq NF_{\overline{EM}}^{GD}(x_o, y_o, p)$. We also note that the results obtained also differ from those of the reverse directional distance function presented in Table 12.17 of the previous chapter. In this case, none of the inefficient firms present the same revenue inefficiencies, neither technical nor allocative components.

Figure 13.7 illustrates the results for the general direct model based on the Russell output measure. Besides illustrating that it satisfies the essential property through

Table 13.19 Implementation of the GDA (Russell) output inefficiency using BEE for Julia

In[]:
```
dearussell(X, Y, orient = :Output, rts  = :VRS, names =
FIRMS)
```

Out[]:
```
Russell DEA Model
DMUs = 8; Inputs = 1; Outputs = 2
Orientation = Output; Returns to Scale = VRS
```

	efficiency	effY1	effY2	slackX1
A	1.0	1.0	1.0	0.0
B	1.0	1.0	1.0	0.0
C	1.0	1.0	1.0	0.0
D	1.867	2.333	1.4	0.0
E	2.333	2.333	2.333	0.0
F	1.5	1.0	2.0	0.0
G	1.458	1.167	1.75	0.0
H	3.056	5.111	1.0	0.0

firms D and G, as commented above, we also observe though firm F that the extended essential property (D2) is not verified since its allocative inefficiency is different from that of its benchmark, firm B. Again, the option "`monetary = true`" would result in the satisfaction of the property, at the expense of being dependent on the local currency.

13.5.4 An Application: Taiwanese Banking Industry

Following previous chapters, we now calculate profit inefficiency using the dataset of 31 Taiwanese banks observed in 2010 (see Juo et al., 2015). A brief presentation of the data, including descriptive statistics, can be found in Sect. 2.5.2 of Chap. 2. In this dataset, individual firm prices for each input and output are observed. These are unit prices obtained by dividing individual costs and revenues by their corresponding quantities, i.e., prices are not directly observed. We adopt the standard approach in the literature and determine maximum profit for each firm under evaluation and use its own prices as reference. The variation of prices makes the results specific for each firm, and therefore bilateral comparisons of profit inefficiency are price-dependent.

We calculate and decompose profit inefficiency based on the general direct approach and selecting the *ERG* = *SBM(G)* as the technical efficiency measure—see Chap. 7. As presented in the three-step process introduced in Sect. 13.2.3, once the benchmark projections on the frontier have been identified, it is possible to calculate the technological profit gap, $\left(p \cdot s^{+*}_{\overline{oEM}} + w \cdot s^{-*}_{\overline{oEM}}\right)$, which, along with the profit inefficiency of the projections $\Pi I\left(\widehat{x}_{\overline{oEM}}, \widehat{y}_{\overline{oEM}}, w, p\right)$, yields the following general direct profit inefficiency decomposition in monetary terms: $\Pi I(x_o, y_o, w, p)$

$= \left(p \cdot s^{+*}_{o\overline{EM}} + w \cdot s^{-*}_{o\overline{EM}}\right) + \Pi I_{EM}\left(\widehat{x}_{o\overline{EM}}, \widehat{y}_{o\overline{EM}}, w, p\right)$. Finally, in order to obtain the normalized version of the decomposition, we calculate the normalization factor $NF^{GD}_{EM}(x_o, y_o, w, p)$ as stated in (13.13) and divide each term of the monetary decomposition by it. This yields $N\Pi I^{GD}_{EM}(x_o, y_o, \widetilde{w}, \widetilde{p})$, which can be decomposed following expression (13.17). Note that in the normalizing factor, each firm's specific prices w_{om} and p_{om} are considered.

Table 13.20 presents the results of solving the latter normalized model. Regarding the profit inefficiency values, these are shown in the second column. As for the rest of the models presented in previous chapters, three banks are profit-efficient under their own prices (no. 1, no. 5, and no. 10), with $N\Pi I^{GD}_{EM}(x_o, y_o, \widetilde{w}, \widetilde{p}) = 0$, constituting the most frequent benchmarks for the remaining banks. A total of 11 banks are technically efficient once again: $TI_{\overline{EM}}(x_o, y_o) = 0$. The technical efficiency values, $TE_{\overline{EM}}(x_o, y_o)$, and the optimal β^* scores and input and output slacks coincide with those reported in Table 7.8 of Chap. 7, since the underlying technical efficiency measure is the $ERG = SBM$. In this model, average normalized profit inefficiency equals 2.862, while average technical and allocative inefficiencies are 0.418 and 2.444, respectively. Consequently, most of the normalized profit loss is attributable to allocative inefficiency, whose proportion is 85.4%, compared to 14.6% for technical inefficiency. A description of the magnitude and relative importance of the input and output slacks can be consulted in Sect. 7.6.1 of Chap. 7.

Rather than solving the normalized version of the general direct approach, we rely on its initial monetary definition, which shows the value of the inefficiencies denominated in the currency used by the firms in their accounting records. This is achieved by running the profit function with the option "`monetary = true`." Table 13.21 reports the values of the profit, technical, and allocative inefficiencies in million TWDs. In the fifth column, we have the value of the profit loss due to technical inefficiencies in the input and output dimensions, termed the *technological profit gap*. The extra costs and foregone revenues are shown in the last five tables, where the input and output slacks of Table 13.20 are multiplied by their respective prices (Table 13.21).

13.6 Summary and Conclusions

In this chapter, we have introduced a recent methodology for decomposing economic inefficiency developed by Pastor et al. (2021a, b, c). The first three sections of the chapter are devoted to profit, cost, and revenue inefficiencies, in this order. As we comment in what follows, the new *general direct approach* has several advantages over the traditional ones, presented in the previous chapters of this book. The new approach resorts to a single equality that gives rise to *the economic inefficiency decomposition* associated with a given firm (x_o, y_o) calculated as the sum of two components. This implies that we do not need to resort to Fenchel Mahler

Table 13.20 Normalized general direct approach decomposition of profit inefficiency based on the $ERG = SGM\ (G)$

Bank	Economic inefficiency, eq. (13.17)			Technical Efficiency, eqs. (7.5) and (7.4).						
	Profit Ineff. $N\Pi I_{\overline{EM}}^{GD}(x_o, y_o, \tilde{w}, \tilde{p})$	Technical Ineff. $TI_{\overline{EM}}(x_o, y_o)$	Allocative Ineff. $AI_{\overline{EM}}^{GD}(x_o, y_o, \tilde{w}, \tilde{p})$	Technical Eff. $TE(x_o, y_o)$	Beta β	Funds (x_1) s_1^-	Labor (x_2) s_2^-	Ph. Capital (x_3) s_3^-	Investments (y_1) s_1^+	Loans (y_2) s_2^+
1	0.000	0.000	0.000	1.000	1.000	0.0	0.0	0.0	0.0	0.0
2	0.300	0.000	0.300	1.000	1.000	0.0	0.0	0.0	0.0	0.0
3	0.550	0.000	0.550	1.000	1.000	0.0	0.0	0.0	0.0	0.0
4	2.729	0.783	1.946	0.217	0.222	1,680.2	0.0	129.2	117,345.0	0.0
5	0.000	0.000	0.000	1.000	1.000	0.0	0.0	0.0	0.0	0.0
6	0.712	0.000	0.712	1.000	1.000	0.0	0.0	0.0	0.0	0.0
7	0.565	0.000	0.565	1.000	1.000	0.0	0.0	0.0	0.0	0.0
8	0.293	0.208	0.086	0.792	1.000	62,264.6	1,594.1	8,968.7	0.0	0.0
9	0.535	0.364	0.171	0.636	0.887	0.0	2,071.2	12,530.9	65,394.4	0.0
10	0.000	0.000	0.000	1.000	1.000	0.0	0.0	0.0	0.0	0.0
11	1.009	0.593	0.416	0.407	0.669	262,932.0	2,101.0	16,042.7	160,570.0	0.0
12	2.060	0.257	1.802	0.743	0.977	84,708.6	0.0	5,833.0	10,933.0	0.0
13	3.498	0.934	2.564	0.066	0.109	28,607.9	1,123.7	5,671.8	225,670.0	0.0
14	0.942	0.000	0.942	1.000	1.000	0.0	0.0	0.0	0.0	0.0
15	0.690	0.217	0.473	0.783	1.000	150,628.0	681.6	4,857.9	0.0	0.0
16	9.693	0.988	8.705	0.012	0.029	32,486.0	1,118.0	4,943.0	112,761.0	2,104.0
17	1.175	0.532	0.643	0.468	0.798	56,043.9	3,130.1	11,485.8	102,533.0	0.0
18	1.537	0.416	1.121	0.584	0.718	0.0	1,395.0	402.8	86,299.5	0.0
19	2.868	0.813	2.056	0.187	0.265	13,184.2	339.9	2,457.0	148,341.0	0.0
20	4.015	0.735	3.279	0.265	0.306	58,873.3	401.0	0.0	143,014.0	0.0
21	1.210	0.000	1.210	1.000	1.000	0.0	0.0	0.0	0.0	0.0
22	6.140	0.959	5.181	0.041	0.063	0.0	515.9	6,735.0	165,582.0	0.0
23	7.839	0.981	6.858	0.019	0.030	10,089.7	324.0	5,854.6	149,088.0	0.0
24	0.612	0.279	0.333	0.721	0.830	0.0	1,277.0	1,983.4	64,649.4	0.0
25	7.242	0.877	6.365	0.123	0.130	0.0	0.0	481.7	194,898.0	0.0
26	4.773	0.000	4.773	1.000	1.000	0.0	0.0	0.0	0.0	0.0
27	13.561	0.959	12.602	0.041	0.046	1,955.9	109.7	286.0	128,784.0	0.0
28	7.020	0.942	6.078	0.058	0.077	29,993.2	504.4	0.0	89,301.6	0.0
29	3.911	0.000	3.911	1.000	1.000	0.0	0.0	0.0	0.0	0.0
30	0.536	0.227	0.310	0.773	0.920	67,084.9	1,172.7	1,349.8	46,597.5	0.0
31	2.711	0.906	1.805	0.094	0.119	0.0	636.8	3,081.9	258,025.0	0.0
Average	2.862	0.418	2.444	0.582	0.651	27,759.1	596.6	3,003.1	73,218.9	67.9
Median	1.210	0.279	1.121	0.721	0.887	0.0	324.0	402.8	64,649.4	0.0
Maximum	13.561	0.988	12.602	1.000	1.000	262,932.0	3,130.1	16,042.7	258,025.0	2,104.0
Minimum	0.000	0.000	0.000	0.012	0.029	0.0	0.0	0.0	0.0	0.0
Std. Dev.	3.308	0.398	3.036	0.398	0.408	55,722.5	801.2	4,331.4	78,937.9	377.9

Table 13.21 General direct approach decomposition of profit inefficiency based on the ERG = SGM (G) (monetary values)

Bank	Economic inefficiency, eq. (13.12)				Valued slacks				
	Profit Ineff. $\Pi I(x_o, y_o, w, p)$	Technical Ineff. $T\Pi I_{EM}(x_o, y_o, w, p)$	Allocative Ineff. $A\Pi I_{EM}(x_o, y_o, w, p)$	Profit tech. gap $p \cdot s^{+*}_{oEM} + w \cdot s^{-*}_{oEM}$	Funds (x_1) $w_{1o}s^-_{1oEM}$	Labor (x_2) $w_{2o}s^-_{2oEM}$	Ph. Capital (x_3) $w_{3o}s^-_{3oEM}$	Investments (y_1) $p_{1o}s^+_{1oEM}$	Loans (y_2) $p_{2o}s^+_{2oEM}$
1	0.0	0.0	0.0	0.0	0.0	0.0	0.0	0.0	0.0
2	5,023.7	0.0	5,023.7	0.0	0.0	0.0	0.0	0.0	0.0
3	5,712.8	0.0	5,712.8	0.0	0.0	0.0	0.0	0.0	0.0
4	10,063.1	2,887.4	7,175.7	2,887.4	9.2	0.0	32.3	2,846.0	0.0
5	0.0	0.0	0.0	0.0	0.0	0.0	0.0	0.0	0.0
6	5,303.2	0.0	5,303.2	0.0	0.0	0.0	0.0	0.0	0.0
7	5,664.1	0.0	5,664.1	0.0	0.0	0.0	0.0	0.0	0.0
8	5,996.7	4,247.0	1,749.7	4,247.0	327.9	2,120.9	1,798.3	0.0	0.0
9	8,575.6	5,832.1	2,743.5	5,832.1	0.0	2,728.9	2,122.7	980.5	0.0
10	0.0	0.0	0.0	0.0	0.0	0.0	0.0	0.0	0.0
11	27,079.6	15,912.3	11,167.3	15,912.3	1,294.9	2,556.5	4,714.8	7,346.1	0.0
12	11,718.2	1,464.5	10,253.6	1,464.5	365.2	0.0	997.2	102.2	0.0
13	267,854.0	71,488.2	196,366.0	71,488.2	227.8	805.6	1,769.0	68,685.8	0.0
14	3,229.2	0.0	3,229.2	0.0	0.0	0.0	0.0	0.0	0.0
15	10,102.3	3,179.2	6,923.1	3,179.2	788.0	655.4	1,735.8	0.0	0.0
16	312,974.0	31,902.3	281,072.0	31,902.2	290.4	1,266.0	1,491.2	28,710.1	144.5
17	20,584.6	9,319.4	11,265.2	9,319.4	277.5	3,231.5	3,839.7	1,970.7	0.0
18	9,960.2	2,695.7	7,264.6	2,695.6	0.0	1,398.0	273.8	1,023.8	0.0
19	17,139.2	4,855.1	12,284.1	4,855.1	72.5	303.7	921.8	3,557.1	0.0
20	16,544.6	3,030.3	13,514.3	3,030.3	373.0	360.0	0.0	2,297.3	0.0
21	19,556.8	0.0	19,556.8	0.0	0.0	0.0	0.0	0.0	0.0
22	36,540.2	5,706.4	30,833.8	5,706.4	0.0	454.5	612.5	4,639.4	0.0
23	46,263.0	5,791.9	40,471.1	5,791.9	70.7	280.3	585.0	4,855.9	0.0
24	6,428.9	2,933.5	3,495.4	2,933.5	0.0	1,724.0	415.8	793.6	0.0
25	18,187.5	2,201.7	15,985.8	2,201.7	0.0	0.0	149.1	2,052.6	0.0
26	2,763.9	0.0	2,763.9	0.0	0.0	0.0	0.0	0.0	0.0
27	20,401.6	1,442.3	18,959.3	1,442.3	13.5	112.1	78.8	1,237.9	0.0
28	26,821.9	3,600.4	23,221.5	3,600.4	201.5	437.5	0.0	2,961.5	0.0
29	2,792.6	0.0	2,792.6	0.0	0.0	0.0	0.0	0.0	0.0
30	7,615.2	3,218.1	4,397.1	3,218.1	336.5	1,522.6	558.4	800.6	0.0
31	57,210.8	19,126.9	38,083.9	19,126.9	0.0	549.9	1,006.0	17,571.0	0.0
Average	31,874.4	6,478.5	25,395.9	6,478.5	150.0	661.5	745.2	4,917.2	4.7
Median	10,063.1	2,887.4	7,175.7	2,887.4	0.0	280.3	149.1	800.6	0.0
Maximum	312,974.0	71,488.2	281,072.0	71,488.2	1,294.9	3,231.5	4,714.8	68,685.8	144.5
Minimum	0.0	0.0	0.0	0.0	0.0	0.0	0.0	0.0	0.0
Std. Dev.	70,549.7	13,845.2	58,927.0	13,845.2	280.4	936.2	1,155.1	13,226.2	26.0

inequalities to decompose economic inefficiency. The two components can be obtained knowing, in addition to the market prices, just the projection on the frontier of (x_o, y_o), which we denote as $(\widehat{x}_o, \widehat{y}_o)$. Any firm and its projection are related through the corresponding set of slacks. For instance, if we resort to a graph efficiency measure for decomposing profit inefficiency and identified the projection of firm (x_o, y_o), then the associated slacks can be easily calculated: $s_o^- = x_o - \widehat{x}_o, s_o^+ = \widehat{y}_o - y_o, s_o^- \geq 0_M, s_o^+ \geq 0_N$, where some or all of their values are positive. If a partial orientation is chosen to analyze cost (or revenue) inefficiency, then only some or all input slacks (or some or all output slacks) are positive. We have also shown that *the economic inefficiency at* (x_o, y_o) *is equal* to the sum of *the economic inefficiency at* $(\widehat{x}_o, \widehat{y}_o)$ and a term called *profit (cost or revenue) technological gap*, which is the sum of the product of each slack by its market price. These three non-negative terms are all expressed in the same monetary units, and some or all of them can be zero. This provides a brand new *general direct decomposition of economic inefficiency* as the sum of a *technical economic inefficiency*, corresponding to the *price technological gap*, and an *allocative economic inefficiency*, corresponding to *the economic inefficiency at* $(\widehat{x}_o, \widehat{y}_o)$.

Once the *general direct economic inefficiency decomposition* has been obtained for each firm, we can directly derive the corresponding *general direct normalized economic inefficiency decomposition*. Almost always we resort to an *efficiency measure* to obtain the mentioned projection for each firm, which means that we already know *its associated technical inefficiency*. All that is left to accomplish the normalized decomposition is to split *the price technological gap of each firm* as *the product of the technical inefficiency times a* certain *normalization factor*, which must be positive and expressed in monetary units. Dividing the three terms by the mentioned factor, which can be specific to each firm, we obtain the normalized economic inefficiency decomposition of each firm, which decomposes the *normalized economic inefficiency*, or *Nerlovian inefficiency*, as *the sum of* the *technical inefficiency plus* the *allocative inefficiency*.

The advantages of the general direct approach over traditional approaches are quadruple. It is *general*, which means that we can use the same single equality for obtaining the decomposition when considering the projection and the technical inefficiency of any of the already known efficiency measures or even of any new efficiency measure that can be created in the future. It is *easier to implement* than the traditional approaches because we do not need to search for any Fenchel-Mahler inequality based on duality. It is *more reliable*, since resorting to an equality guarantees that the allocative inefficiency will not be overestimated, something that cannot be guaranteed when resorting to inequalities. And finally, it has a normalized version that is independent of the monetary units considered. Moreover, the general direct approach satisfies both the essential property (D1) and the extended essential property (D2) presented in Sect. 2.4.5 of Chap. 2. Comparing the new approach to the traditional ones, there is only one distinguished case where *the two approaches are coincident*: when considering as an inefficiency measure any *directional distance function*.

Finally, the general direct approach is well suited for identifying projections that take advantage of the market conditions and do not need to start by resorting to any efficiency measure. We have presented two models, identified as *the general direct standard reverse approach* and *the generalized direct flexible reverse approach*. The first stage of both approaches consists of identifying an efficient projection that gives rise to the smallest allocative inefficiency or, equivalently, a projection whose economic inefficiency is the lowest possible. *The standard reverse approach assumes the classical way of projecting* firms towards the benchmark frontier, relying on the criterion of Pareto-Koopmans dominance and is based on the general direct approach. On the contrary, *the flexible reverse approach* allows freedom of movement inside the production possibility set, which means that the slacks can take any unrestricted value. For this reason, the flexible reverse approach does not fit well with the general direct approach, so it requires a more pliant definition, which we have called the generalized direct approach. The latter admits that slacks have a dual function depending on the firm being considered, appearing related to the technological component or, alternatively, to the allocative component. Obviously, the flexible model can be expected to be more conclusive in its results. As we have shown in the chapter, for any firm, it always identifies a projection with the best economic inefficiency. The second stage in both reverse approaches is to define an appropriate technical inefficiency measure that allows obtaining the corresponding normalized economic inefficiency decomposition. In this sense, the standard reverse approach is closer to the classic models than the flexible one, because the corresponding technical inefficiency abides by the concept of Pareto-Koopmans dominance. However, both the SR approach and the FR approach always give rise to a single normalization factor valid for all firms, which offers nice properties to the corresponding normalized economic inefficiency decomposition, such as the *comparison property* or the aforementioned *essential* and *extended essential properties*.

Chapter 14
A Final Overview: Economic Efficiency Models and Properties

14.1 Introduction

The canonical model of perfect competition, resulting in social welfare maximization, assumes all kinds of technical and allocative inefficiencies away. In equilibrium, economic theory establishes that in contestable markets, competition forces draw firms towards profit maximization (Vickers, 1995). This in turn requires that, on one hand, firms exploit the existing technology at its full, so there are not engineering failures in the production of goods and services, while, on the other hand, optimal input and output amounts are, respectively, demanded and supplied according to their relative market prices. In any neoclassical microeconomics textbook, right after discussing production theory and cost minimization (normally in separate chapters), the chapter on profit maximization and competitive supply describes the adjustment processes towards short-run and, through entrants and exiters, long-run equilibria. This process is related to the evolutionary notion of competitive selection. However, it is self-evident that, at one moment in time, the forces behind the stylized postulates of competitive markets are far from being observed in real life, failing to discipline suboptimal behavior, and ensuring that inefficient firms are driven out of the industry. The mounting evidence published in the general media and academic journals confirm that economic inefficiency originating from technical and allocative inefficiencies is pervasive across markets. Economics rationalize this reality by doing away with the postulates of perfect competition and entering market failures, most notably the existence of imperfect conditions associated with market power, differentiated products, or imperfect information, which result in firms being price setters rather than price takers. All these factors would allow inefficient firms to survive in the market, even if they are not economically efficient, either in technological or allocative terms.

As the number of theoretical models, empirical investigations, and case studies increases, this book is generally concerned with the measurement and decomposition

J. T. Pastor et al., *Benchmarking Economic Efficiency*, International Series in Operations Research & Management Science 315,
https://doi.org/10.1007/978-3-030-84397-7_14

of economic inefficiency of the firms competing within an industry. We assume that firms are rational agents operating in imperfectly competitive output and input markets, where the level of effective competition leaves room for technical and allocative inefficiencies. As in the extant literature, in the theoretical models, we assume for simplicity that prices are exogenously given and common to all firms, implying that firms produce and demand relatively homogenous goods and services. Empirically, however, it is frequent that they operate under different prices, as in the dataset of financial institutions that we use to illustrate the different models.

As motivated in the introduction, economic efficiency analysis is relevant not only for managers of individual firms, who can learn from their benchmarks to improve their own performance, but also to other stakeholders such as government agencies responsible for regulating essential industries or antitrust authorities supervising the existence of effective competition levels. In this respect, the measurement of economic efficiency could be seen as a way of characterizing or testing the degree of competition in a market. If the value of economic inefficiency is relatively low in the industry, this would imply that competition forces are at work, which would correlate with the existence of a large number of firms and products largely homogenous and the existence of low barriers to entry. Contrarily, if the value of economic inefficiency is large and pervasive across firms, then one could explore if high levels of market concentration and market power exist, whether goods and services are differentiated across the product space or geographically, and if there are large barriers to entry, e.g., high start-up costs, regulatory hurdles, or other obstacles preventing the entrance of new competitors.

We study the economic performance of firms from four different but complementary economic functions: cost, revenue, profitability, and profit. From an applied perspective, the choice for a specific approach depends on the industry characteristics and the restrictions that firms face, most particularly the relative discretion that managers have over output production and input usage. This sets the stage for the economic objective of the firm that, in an unconstrained input and output setting, is assumed to maximize either profitability or profit, both of which can be related to cost minimization and revenue maximization. In case outputs levels are exogenously given, a cost minimization approach must be considered, while the opposite takes place when inputs are not under the discretion of managers, leading to a revenue-maximizing approach.

Once a given objective is chosen, one must approach the technical (primal) dimension of the problem from a backward perspective to determine the optimal representation of the technology in the first place. For profitability and profit maximization, the technology is represented by technical efficiency measures that simultaneously take into consideration the input and output dimensions, i.e., graph measures. Alternatively, if the economic (dual) problem of the firm is cost minimization, then an input orientation is necessary. Finally, if what concerns the study is revenue maximization, an output orientation should be chosen. The different chapters of this book cover all three possibilities by considering the graph, input, and output definitions of the alternative technical efficiency measures, as well as the economic decompositions that they define for each orientation and based on the corresponding economic function. This enables the decomposition of economic efficiency in a way that is consistent with economic (duality) theory. Indeed, given that the technical efficiency measures capture the economic loss due to production inefficiencies, the remaining difference between observed cost, revenue, profitability or profit, and the optimally observed benchmark—whatever the approach—can be attributed to allocative inefficiency, i.e., the inability to demand and supply the optimal amount of inputs and outputs given their market prices.

This book shows that although the research question is fairly simple, the multiplicity of modeling choices may be overwhelming. This is because once an economic efficiency model has been selected (e.g., cost efficiency), there is not a unique way of decomposing it into technological and allocative sources. In the first stage, researchers may choose between a multiplicative and an additive setting. On a second stage, the characterization of the production technology can be done resorting to different distance functions or, more generally, technical efficiency measures. Although these choices are primarily driven by standard practice in most applications, showing a path dependency from the seminal contributions in the literature, the truth is that, under close scrutiny, not enough justification is normally given in empirical research for the choice of model, based on the priors or conditions of the research question and industry at hand. We argue that this "one-size-fits-all" rule by which the most popular models can be applied to all applications is both inadequate and, more importantly, nowadays unnecessary, given the current choice of complete and flexible characterizations of the production technology. This book intends to bring order to this situation and to provide specific guidance for practitioners when settling for a specific economic efficiency model and the underlying characterization of the technology that is consistent with duality principles.

14.2 Multiplicative or Additive Decompositions of Economic (In)efficiency

Economic efficiency can be defined and decomposed in a multiplicative or additive way, and this book is organized following this distinction. Profitability (or return-to-dollar) efficiency is defined multiplicatively as revenue divided by cost, while profit defines as revenue minus cost. Cost and revenue can be defined both ways, depending on the efficiency measure that is chosen for the decomposition. Interestingly, while business economics has traditionally assumed that firms are profit maximizers, the early definitions and decomposition of economic efficiency were based on the multiplicative definition of either cost or revenue efficiencies proposed by Farrell (1957). This is because a natural dual for the profit function that would allow its additive decomposition would not be available until Chambers et al. (1998) reinterpreted Luenberger's (1992a, b) shortage function as the well-known directional distance function. In the book, we adopt a historical approach to present the alternative economic efficiency definitions and therefore, after presenting the basic concepts, terminology, and empirical tools, devote the first part of the book to the multiplicative approach. As previously mentioned, the multiplicative approach is not restricted to the partially oriented cost and revenue approaches, as this line of research has been complemented with the concept of profitability efficiency, defined as the ratio of revenue to cost, which following Zofío and Prieto (2006) can be decomposed into a technical efficiency term represented by the generalized distance function introduced by Chavas and Cox (1999) and allocative efficiency.

Subsequently, the second part of the book is devoted to the additive approach where much progress has been made in the last years with the introduction of a wide range of duality results based on several additive efficiency measures or distance functions. A distance function behaves as a technical efficiency measure when an observation belonging to the reference technology is evaluated, with a meaning of "distance" from a firm to the boundary of the production possibility set. In this respect, there has been so much research in this area, including ourselves, that we devote most of the chapters to different additive characterizations of the production technology. There are many refinements of the oriented Russell measures introduced by Färe and Lovell (1978) or the additive model introduced by Charnes et al. (1985), for example, the enhanced Russell graph measure by Pastor et al. (1999), also known as the slacks-based measure (Tone, 2001), whose duality with the profit function has been recently introduced by Halická and Trnovská (2018). Initial progress was made through the so-called directional distance function, whose definition and duality are due to Chambers et al. (1998). This in turn was rendered more flexible by Aparicio et al. (2013a, b), who allow for different proportions between and within input reductions and output expansions. Also, Pastor et al. (2016) proposed the transformation of any technical inefficiency model into the directional distance function through their reverse directional distance function methodology. In a different strand of literature, numerous economic inefficiency models belonging to the family of the weighted additive distance function have been proposed, for which Aparicio et al. (2016a, b) introduce general duality results. This model encompasses previous measures like the normalized weighted additive model (see Lovell & Pastor, 1995), the measure of inefficiency proportions (MIP), the range-adjusted measure (RAM) of inefficiency (see Cooper et al., 1999), and the bounded adjusted measure (BAM) of inefficiency presented by Cooper et al. (2011). Also, general duality results based on the Hölder norms, following the work by Briec (1998), have been extended by Aparicio et al. (2017a, b). Finally, in the third part of the book, we also propose alternative approaches that do not rely on duality theory when decomposing economic inefficiency, such as the general direct approach by Pastor et al. (2021a).

14.3 On the Choice of Economic (In)efficiency Models

All this literature shows the myriad of possibilities that researchers have at their disposal when measuring and decomposing economic inefficiency. So, a natural question is which economic (in)efficiency model should be used? First, one needs to choose the economic approach, cost, revenue, profitability, or profit. As already mentioned, this decision is based on the market conditions faced by the firm, managers' discretionality over input and output adjustments, and subsequent economic behavior. Then, one must decide for the multiplicative or additive approach and, afterwards, the type of distance function or efficiency measure that best represents technical (in)efficiency. Choosing the multiplicative approach provides results that can be expressed in percentage terms of the best performance, whose values can be readily comparable across firms. For cost and revenue efficiency analyses, there exist additive counterparts that can be interpreted in proportional terms. These correspond to the family of inefficiency measures based on the directional distance function (i.e., the DDF, the modified DDF, and the reverse DDF) when the directional vector is equal to the observed input or output quantities. However, as shown by Aparicio et al. (2017a, b), a numerical relationship between the technical and allocative components of the multiplicative approach based on Shepard's distance functions and their counterparts in the additive approach based on the oriented directional distance functions cannot be established. If one is interested in profitability analysis, then a multiplicative approach based on duality must be followed. There is no natural additive counterpart to profitability efficiency, just as there is no natural multiplicative counterpart to profit inefficiency.

14.4 Decompositions of Economic (In)efficiency of the Taiwanese Banking Industry

Table 14.1 summarizes the descriptive statistics of the results obtained for the sample of Taiwanese banks studied throughout the book using the multiplicative decomposition of cost and revenue efficiency, which relies on the input and output distance functions (Chap. 3), and of profitability efficiency, considering the generalized distance function (Chap. 4). The cost, revenue, and profitability values are not comparable as they address different dimensions of the economic performance of firms. Moreover, the underlying technological characteristics of these models are different, since cost and revenue efficiency measurement do not require that firms produce at the optimal scale, i.e., increasing or decreasing returns may exist at the economic benchmarks, while profitability efficiency requires scale efficiency, i.e., firms maximizing profitability exhibit constant returns to scale. Thanks to the profitability analysis, we learn that scale inefficiency is quite pervasive across financial institutions and even larger than technical efficiency with respect to the variable returns to scale frontier.

Regarding profit inefficiency, because the obtention of a duality relationship between the profit function and a particular technical inefficiency measure requires some form of explicit normalization, which differs across models, this prevents the numerical comparison of the inefficiency scores across firms for the different models. Table 14.2 reports the descriptive statistics of profit inefficiency and its

Table 14.1 Multiplicative decompositions of cost, revenue, and profitability efficiency of Taiwanese banks

	Oriented models (input or output dimensions) (Chap. 3)						Graph model (input and output dimensions) (Chap. 4)				
	Cost efficiency			Revenue efficiency			Profitability efficiency				
	CE	$TE_{R(I)}$	$AE_{R(I)}$	RE	$TE_{R(O)}$	$AE_{R(O)}$	ΓE	TE_G^{CRS}	TE_G^{VRS}	SE_G	AE
Average	0.672	0.799	0.815	0.737	0.845	0.840	0.362	0.578	0.827	0.677	0.827
Median	0.704	0.887	0.841	0.859	0.900	0.947	0.385	0.578	0.895	0.667	0.895
Maximum	1.000	1.000	1.000	1.000	1.000	1.000	1.000	1.000	1.000	1.000	1.000
Minimum	0.127	0.228	0.559	0.104	0.446	0.176	0.048	0.195	0.354	0.375	0.354
Std. dev.	0.270	0.232	0.149	0.275	0.169	0.222	0.173	0.254	0.192	0.196	0.192

Notes: Generalized distance function: $\alpha = 0.5$

Table 14.2 Additive decomposition of profit inefficiency of Taiwanese banks

	Measure							
	Russell IM (Chap. 5)	Weighted additive DF (Chap. 6)	Enhanced Russell graph IM (Chap. 7)	Directional DF (Chap. 8)	Hölder DF (Chap. 9)	Modified DDF (Chap. 11)	Reverse DDF (Chap. 12)	General direct IM (Chap. 13)
	Profit inefficiency: $\Pi I(x, y, \widetilde{w}, \widetilde{p})$							
Average	18.927	4,518,402.4	3.357	2.885	5.369	41.214	5.954	2.862
Median	1.121	1,844,604.0	2.105	0.639	1.324	4.074	1.663	1.210
Maximum	146.250	35,007,191.0	15.719	31.301	55.761	625.176	59.603	13.561
Minimum	0.000	0.0	0.000	0.000	0.000	0.000	0.000	0.000
Std. dev.	40.803	8,288,407.2	3.743	6.302	11.686	123.503	11.787	3.308
	Technical inefficiency: $TI_{EM(G)}(x, y)$							
Average	0.229	110,508.7	0.418	0.111	0.162	0.244	0.244	0.418
Median	0.154	112,051.2	0.279	0.056	0.109	0.113	0.113	0.279
Maximum	0.701	478,809.8	0.988	0.520	0.725	1.244	1.244	0.988
Minimum	0.000	0.0	0.000	0.000	0.000	0.000	0.000	0.000
Std. dev.	0.225	109,534.7	0.398	0.137	0.192	0.311	0.311	0.398
	Allocative inefficiency: $AI_{EM(G)}(x, y, \widetilde{w}, \widetilde{p})$							
Average	18.698	4,407,893.7	2.938	2.774	5.207	40.970	5.709	2.444
Median	0.805	1,724,445.2	1.573	0.547	1.143	3.765	1.549	1.121
Maximum	145.549	34,844,867.0	14.760	30.781	55.036	624.430	58.359	12.602
Minimum	0.000	0.0	0.000	0.000	0.000	0.000	0.000	0.000
Std. dev.	40.638	8,241,475.5	3.457	6.193	11.538	123.308	11.533	3.036

Notes: Specific models: Weighted additive distance function (WADF), with weights $(\rho^-, \rho^+) = (1,\ 1)$; directional distance function (DDF), with directional vector $(g_x, g_y) = (x_o, y_o)$; Hölder DF, solved for the weighted ℓ_2 norm; reverse DDF (RDDF), under the ERG=SBM technical inefficiency model; generalized direct approach (GDA), under the modified DDF technical inefficiency model decomposition for the sample of Taiwanese banks. A discussion of each model can be found in the empirical section of the corresponding chapter—see the notes to Table 14.2. Depending on the models being compared, the numerical differences may amount to several orders of magnitude, which shows the difficulty of interpreting the additive results when addressing a managerial audience. But then even within the same category of models, there are literally an infinite number of possibilities. For example, the flexibility offered by the generalized distance function when setting the bearing parameter α, or the directional distance functions when choosing the directional vector $g = (g_x, g_y)$, allows to choose any orientation when projecting the firms to the production frontier. For the latter model, this affects the value of the economic inefficiency through the normalization factor of the profit inefficiency model. The same happens when profit inefficiency is measured relying on the weighted additive model, given the numerous options available to weight the input and output slacks, with these weights appearing, once again, in the normalization factor. In summary, one relevant conclusion from this book is that there are as many decompositions of economic efficiency as technical (in)efficiency measures exist. The reason is that any decomposition depends on the magnitude of its technical component and the normalization factor.

Regarding the results of the additive models reported in Table 14.2, a common feature of this approach is that allocative inefficiency is by far the main source of profit inefficiency, regardless the model. This is in sharp contrast to the results of the multiplicative models in Table 14.1, where allocative efficiency is higher than technical efficiency in the cost and profitability approaches. Regarding profit and allocative inefficiencies, an additional difficulty comes from the fact that in many studies, input and output prices vary across observations, as in the financial dataset that we consider in this book to illustrate the different models. Therefore, the economic benchmarks depend on individual quantities and individual prices. Even if in the theoretical models we assume the existence of common prices, we show how to implement them using a dataset that includes different prices because the accompanying "Benchmarking Economic Efficiency" software is programmed to accommodate this reality.

A solution to the difficulty of interpreting the numerical results of the different models would be to express economic efficiency in monetary values, i.e., without normalizing the difference between maximum profit and observed profit. This approach would be preferred by managers, but it makes the profit efficiency dependent on the measurement units, a key property of the economic efficiency measure that was considered, among others, by Farrell (1957) and Nerlove (1965). An additional drawback is that the technical inefficiency component is also expressed in monetary terms, and therefore its value depends on both quantities and prices. Duality theory, allowing a consistent decomposition of economic inefficiency which is units invariant, implies a normalization of economic efficiency through specific normalizing factors, which in turn results in the diversity of values reported in Tables 14.1 and 14.2. A roundabout is the general direct approach presented in the previous chapter, which does not relay on duality results while relating a monetary-valued profit inefficiency with the technical efficiency of an underlying model.

The relevance of the general direct approach is twofold. First and according to Pastor et al. (2021b), it allows to check if any of the previously known economic decompositions underestimate the value of the allocative inefficiency by not satisfying the essential properties. And second, it makes possible, for the first time, the introduction of the standard reverse approach (see Pastor et al., 2021c) and of the flexible reverse approach (see Pastor et al., 2021d). Both reverse approaches start searching for an efficient projection for each firm that minimizes its allocative inefficiency. The standard approach allows only traditional movement towards the frontier (input reductions and output expansions), while the flexible approach allows any type of movements and is, therefore, more effective. Moreover, in both cases, a new—and different—technical inefficiency measure has been introduced based on the price technological gap that satisfies the usual properties.

14.5 Properties of the Economic Efficiency Models

The problem of choosing a particular decomposition does depend not only on the interpretability of results but also on the desirable properties that the (in)efficiency measure satisfies, along with those of its technical and allocative components. This is especially important in the context of Data Envelopment Analysis, where there is not a measure of goodness of fit (e.g., as R^2), which makes it necessary to use other alternative criteria when selecting an efficiency or inefficiency measure. One possibility is invoking an axiomatic perspective, satisfying a list of sensible tests or properties. In the second chapter of the book, we have discussed at length the different properties that the technical and economic efficiency should satisfy to correctly quantify and represent technical and allocative (in)efficiencies.

Regarding the technical component, the literature on efficiency measurement is plenty of contributions devoted to introducing and discussing the set of properties that a technical efficiency measure should satisfy from a technological perspective (see, for example, Färe & Lovell, 1978; Pastor et al., 1999; Russell & Schworm, 2018). In this regard, over the years, a consensus has emerged in the literature about the properties or tests that technical (in)efficiency measures should pass from an axiomatic perspective. Some of the most relevant properties that are identified as natural requirements for an efficiency measure are indication, monotonicity, homogeneity, units' invariance, and translation invariance, among others. Complying with these properties is also critical to the analysis of economic efficiency. To the extent that allocative efficiency is calculated as a residual, the (mis)measurement of technical efficiency (e.g., complying with the Indication property related to Pareto-Koopmans efficiency) is key to a consistent decomposition of overall efficiency. Concerning the desirable properties that an economic efficiency measure should satisfy, various researchers have adopted, explicitly or implicitly, a number of axioms for the profit inefficiency measure, e.g., Asmild et al. (2007), Kuosmanen et al. (2010), Cooper et al. (2011), and, more recently, Färe et al. (2019). Several of these desirable properties in relation to profit inefficiency are the following: the measure should take non-negative values, indication, and homogeneity of degree zero in prices and quantities. Equivalent counterparts can be stated for the additive cost and revenue inefficiency decompositions.

While the extant literature has clearly established the properties that technical and economic efficiency measures must satisfy, this is not the case for the decomposition of economic efficiency itself, which extends to the allocative efficiency term. To the best of our knowledge, no authors have discussed the properties that the decomposition of an economic efficiency index or indicator into technical and allocative components should meet (see Aparicio et al., 2021). The main reason for this situation seems to be that the residual nature of the allocative component does not merit its individual consideration. In this regard, we highlight two properties that we term essential because their satisfaction implies that a meaningful and consistent decomposition of economic efficiency can be performed (see Sect. 2.4.5 of Chap. 2). Hence, we contend that any reasonable decomposition of economic (in)efficiency should satisfy them, becoming the yardstick to judge the appropriateness of each proposal. The most important one is related to the scenario where the technical efficiency measure directly projects the assessed unit onto the point that is optimal from an economical perspective, depending on the objective considered (cost minimization, revenue maximization, profitability maximization, or profit maximization). In that case, there is no room for price inefficiency. Consequently, the corresponding allocative term in the decomposition should be one for the multiplicative approach or zero for the additive approach. A refinement of that property is one that establishes that the value of the allocative (in)efficiency component for a firm under evaluation should always coincide with that of its technological benchmark at the production frontier. Throughout the book, we have shown that only a few of measures satisfy both requirements, which are key for a correct interpretation of the technical and allocative terms of the decomposition.

Table 14.3 summarizes the set of most relevant properties satisfied by each decomposition of cost, revenue, profitability, and profit inefficiency based on a specific technical inefficiency measure. It follows the proposed list of properties presented in the second chapter for technical efficiency measures (Sect. 2.2.4), overall economic efficiency measures (2.3.5), and their associated allocative efficiency measures (2.4.5). Throughout the book, we have discussed at length the different properties concerning the technical efficiency measures associated with the multiplicative approach and the inefficiency measures associated with the additive approach. The most relevant is the indication property, establishing if the efficient measures complies the notion of Pareto-Koopmans efficiency. In case it does not, the technical efficiency would be overvalued and, correspondingly, allocative efficiency undervalued. In general, there is a trade-off between the satisfaction of this property, which is not verified by the multiplicative measures and the family of additive directional distance functions (DDF and modified DDF), but is met by the technical inefficiency measures based on slacks, and the essential and refined essential properties, which are satisfied by the former but not the later. The two-step reversed DDF was designed so it would comply with the indication property by defining the DDF to a reference benchmark on the production frontier that is previously identified

Table 14.3 Properties of economic efficiency decompositions: technical, economic, and allocative

		Multiplicative models		Additive models							
	Economic model	Oriented models: cost and revenue eff.	Graph model: profitability efficiency								
		Measure									
	Property	Farrell/ Shephard DFs (Chap. 3)	Generalized DF (Chap. 4)	Russell IM (Chap. 5)	Weighted additive DF (Chap. 6)	Enhanced Russell graph IM (Chap. 7)	Directional DF (Chap. 8)	Hölder DF (Chap. 9)	Modified DDF (Chap. 11)	Reverse DDF (Chap. 12)	General direct IM (Chap. 13)
Technical eff. properties (Sect. 2.2.4)	E1. Indication[(1)]	✗	✗	✓	✓	✓	✗	✗	✗	✓	✓
	E2. Monotonicity[(2)]	✓	✓	✓	✓	✓	✓	✓	✓	✓	✓
	E3. Homogeneity	✓	✓[(3)]	✗	✗	✗	✗[(4)]	✗	✗	✗	✗
	E4. Commensurab.[(5)]	✓	✓	✓	✓[(6)]	✗	✗[(7)]	✗[(8)]	✗[(9)]	✗[(10)]	✗
	E5. Translation inv.[(11)]	✓[(12)]	✗	✓	✓	✗	✓[(13)]	✓	✓	✗	✗
Economic eff. properties (Sect. 2.3.5)	P1. Boundness	✓	✓	✓	✓	✓	✓	✓	✓	✓	✓
	P2. Indication	✓	✓	✓	✓	✓	✓	✓	✓	✓	✓
	P3. Price homog.	✓	✓	✓	✓	✓	✓	✓	✓	✓	✓
	P4. Quant. homog.	✓	✓	✓	✓	✓	✓	✓	✓	✓	✓
	P5.Commensurab.[(14)]	✓	✓	✓	✓	✓	✓	✓	✓	✓	✗
Allocative eff. properties (Sect. 2.4.5)	D1. Essentiality	✓	✓	✗	✗	✗	✓	✓	✗	✓	✓
	D2. Refined essent.	✓	✓	✗	✗	✗	✓[(15)]	✗	✗[(15)]	✓[(15)]	✓

Notes: [(1)]Pareto-Koopmans efficiency. [(2)]Weak monotonicity. [(3)]Satisfies almost homogeneity. [(4)]Satisfies translation property. [(5)]Units invariance. [(6)]Yes for weights different from one. [(7)]Yes for the proportional DDF with $(g_x, g_y) = (x_o, y_o)$. [(8)]Yes for weighted norms. [(9)]Yes for the proportional MDDF with $(g_x, g_y) = (x_o, y_o)$. [(11)]For variable returns to scale. [(12)]For the input orientation, it is translation invariant for output, and vice versa. [(13)]Yes, under specific condition for the directional vector (Aparicio et al., 2015a, b). [(14)]Units invariance. [(15)]Yes when the normalization factor is the same for all firms: $p \cdot g_y + w \cdot g_x$

through an additive measure and therefore complies with the indication property. In this case, it starts out from benchmarks located on the strongly efficient production frontier. One problem is that there may exist multiple optimal benchmarks, which requires the introduction of a secondary goal like choosing the projection that minimizes allocative inefficiency. The reverse DDF satisfies the indication property and enjoys the good behavior of the DDF regarding the satisfaction of the essential property. However, it does not comply with the refined essential property because the normalization factor is not common to all firms. In principle, it is possible to correct this by adjusting the normalization factor, but this requires one additional step. In a sense, the reverse DDF "inherits" the good properties of the technical efficiency measure satisfying the indication property from which it departs and then fulfills the first essentiality criterion for the allocative efficiency term. The general direct approach follows a similar path but does not rely on duality to decompose overall profit efficiency. Nevertheless, although it satisfies the essential properties, it is not units' invariant, which nevertheless is easier to interpret in monetary terms. In this respect, the general direct approach is easier to implement and is flexible enough to accommodate any inefficiency measure satisfying the indication property.

Among the decompositions based on duality, considering interpretation easiness, the existing trade-offs among properties, but prioritizing the essential properties introduced in this book, we favor the use of the multiplicative model for the cost, revenue, and profitability efficiency analysis—in the latter case the multiplicative approach is the only option. On the one hand, regarding their numerical interpretation, they measure the gap in percentage terms from observed cost, revenue, or profitability to the optimal benchmark. Also, while they do not comply with the indication property, they satisfy the two essential properties. In the case of profit inefficiency, we tend to favor the directional distance function with the same directional vector for all firms. This makes the numeral value of profit efficiency readily comparable across firms, while it can be easily transformed in monetary values multiplying it by the common normalization factor. Also, it is rather flexible by accommodating alternative values for the common directional vector, which can be endogenized. Finally, it also satisfies all essential properties. The only drawback, once again, is that it fails to satisfy the indication property. The reverse DDF is a valid alternative that satisfies all properties, at the cost of requiring several steps for its computation.

We conclude mentioning additional models of production efficiency that can benefit from our research on economic efficiency. These models can be extended to accommodate the different measures of technical and allocative efficiency that we study, for example, those concerned with the evaluation of economic efficiency in environmental models differentiating between desirable and undesirable outputs. Recently, Aparicio et al. (2020a, b) introduced a model that maximizes the difference between the private revenues associated with desirable outputs with market value and the social cost caused by their undesirable by-products. In this model, leading firms are those that not only bring profits to their shareholders but do so in a sustainable way, thereby reducing the social cost of their environmental footprint. A second example concerns the extension of the cross-sectional models studied here to multiple periods, thereby relating the changes in economic efficiency to productivity. In these approaches, considering the multiplicative approach represented by the generalized distance function, cost (or revenue) change can be decomposed into multiplicative indices and additive indicators measuring technological change, efficiency change, and price change (see Balk and Zofío (2020)). Similarly, profitability change can be multiplicatively related to the Malmquist indices (Zofío and Prieto, 2006), while in the additive approach and using the directional distance function, profit change can be related to the so-called Luenberger indicators (Juo et al., 2015, Balk, 2018). Both environmental economic efficiency and economic efficiency change through time could be measured and decomposed considering the different models presented in the book.

Bibliography

Aczél, J. (1966). *Lectures on functional equations and their applications*. Academic Press.

Aigner, D., Lovell, C. K., & Schmidt, P. (1977). Formulation and estimation of stochastic frontier production functions models. *International Economic Review, 17*, 377–396.

Ali, A. I., & Seiford, L. M. (1993). Computational accuracy and infinitesimals in data envelopment analysis. *Infor, 31*(4), 290–297.

Ali, A. I., Lerme, C. S., & Seiford, L. M. (1995). Components of efficiency evaluation in data envelopment analysis. *European Journal of Operational Research, 80*, 462–473.

Álvarez, I. C., Barbero, J., & Zofío, J.L. (2020). A data envelopment analysis toolbox for MATLAB. Forthcoming in the *Journal of Statistical Software*. http://www.deatoolbox.com/.

Amirteimoori, A., & Kordrostami, S. (2010). A Euclidean distance-based measure of efficiency in data envelopment analysis. *Optimization, 59*, 985–996.

Andersen, P., & Petersen, N. C. (1993). A procedure for ranking efficient units in data envelopment analysis. *Management Science, 39*(10), 1261–1264.

Ando, K., Kai, A., Maeda, Y., & Sekitani, K. (2012). Least distance based inefficiency measures on the Pareto-efficient frontier in DEA. *Journal of the Operations Research Society of Japan, 55*, 73–91.

Ando, K., Minamide, M., & Sekitani, K. (2017). Monotonicity of minimum distance inefficiency measures for data envelopment analysis. *European Journal of Operational Research, 260*(1), 232–243.

Aparicio, J. (2016). A survey on measuring efficiency through the determination of the least distance in data envelopment analysis. *Journal of Centrum Cathedra, 9*(2), 143–167.

Aparicio, J., & Pastor, J. T. (2011). A general input distance function based on opportunity costs. *Advances in Decision Sciences, 2011*, 505241, 11 p.

Aparicio, J., Pastor, J. T. & Ray, S. C. (2013). An overall measure of technical inefficiency at the firm and at the industry level: The 'lost profit on outlay'. European Journal of Operational Research, 226, 154–162.

Aparicio, J., & Pastor, J. T. (2014a). On how to properly calculate the Euclidean distance-based measure in DEA. *Optimization, 63*(3), 421–432.

Aparicio, J., & Pastor, J. T. (2014b). Closest targets and strong monotonicity on the strongly efficient frontier in DEA. *Omega, 44*, 51–57.

Aparicio, J., & Zofío, J. L. (2017). Revisiting the decomposition of cost efficiency for non-homothetic technologies: A directional distance function approach. *Journal of Productivity Analysis, 48*(2), 133–146.

Aparicio, J., & Zofío, J. L. (2020a). Economic cross-efficiency. *Omega, 100*, 102374.

J. T. Pastor et al., *Benchmarking Economic Efficiency*, International Series in Operations Research & Management Science 315,
https://doi.org/10.1007/978-3-030-84397-7

Aparicio, J., & Zofío, J. L. (2020b). New definitions of economic cross-efficiency. In J. Aparicio, C. A., Knox Lovell, J. T. , Pastor, J. T., & J. Zhu (Eds.) *Advances in efficiency and productivity II* (International Series in Operations Research & Management Science, pp. 11–32). New York: Springer.

Aparicio, J., Ruiz, J. L., & Sirvent, I. (2007). Closest targets and minimum distance to the Pareto-efficient frontier in DEA. *Journal of Productivity Analysis, 28*(3), 209–218.

Aparicio, J., Pastor, J. T., & Ray, S. C. (2013a). An overall measure of technical inefficiency at the firm and at the industry level: The 'lost profit on outlay'. *European Journal of Operational Research, 226*(1), 154–162.

Aparicio, J., Borras, F., Pastor, J. T., & Vidal, F. (2013b). Accounting for slacks to measure and decompose revenue efficiency in the Spanish designation of origin wines with DEA. *European Journal of Operational Research, 231*(2), 443–451.

Aparicio, J., Mahlberg, B., Pastor, J. T., & Sahoo, B. K. (2014). Decomposing technical inefficiency using the principle of least action. *European Journal of Operational Research, 239*(3), 776–785.

Aparicio, J., Borras, F., Pastor, J. T., & Vidal, F. (2015a). Measuring and decomposing firm′ s revenue and cost efficiency: The Russell measures revisited. *International Journal of Production Economics, 165*, 19–28.

Aparicio, J., Pastor, J. T., & Zofio, J. L. (2015b). How to properly decompose economic efficiency using technical and allocative criteria with non-homothetic DEA technologies. *European Journal of Operational Research, 240*(3), 882–891.

Aparicio, J., Pastor, J. T., & Vidal, F. (2016a). The weighted additive distance function. *European Journal of Operational Research, 254*(1), 338–346.

Aparicio, J., Borras, F., Pastor, J. T., & Zofío, J. L. (2016b). Loss distance functions and profit function: General duality results. In *Advances in efficiency and productivity* (pp. 71–96). Springer.

Aparicio, J., Ortiz, L., & Pastor, J. T. (2017a). Measuring and decomposing profit inefficiency through the slacks-based measure. *European Journal of Operational Research, 260*(2), 650–654.

Aparicio, J., Pastor, J. T., & Zofio, J. L. (2017b). Can Farrell's allocative efficiency be generalized by the directional distance function approach? *European Journal of Operational Research, 257*(1), 345–351.

Aparicio, J., Cordero, J. M., & Pastor, J. T. (2017c). The determination of the least distance to the strongly efficient frontier in data envelopment analysis oriented models: Modelling and computational aspects. *Omega, 71*, 1–10.

Aparicio, J., Ortiz, L., & Pastor, J. T. (2018). Design and implementation of a shiny interactive web application by RStudio for estimating data envelopment analysis efficiency measures. *Boletin de Estadística e Investigación Operativa, 34*(1), 25–50. https://deaumh.shinyapps.io/DEASHINY/

Aparicio, J., Pastor, J. T., Sainz-Pardo, J. L., & Vidal, F. (2020). Estimating and decomposing overall inefficiency by determining the least distance to the strongly efficient frontier in data envelopment analysis. *Operational Research, 20*, 747–770.

Aparicio, J., Kapelko, M., & Zofío, J. L. (2020). The measurement of environmental economic inefficiency with pollution-generating technologies. *Resource and Energy Economics, 62*, 101185.

Aparicio, J., Pastor, J. T., & Zofío, J. L. (2021) *Decomposing economic efficiency: An essential property, ERIM report series research in management ERS-2021-001-LIS*. Erasmus Research Institute of Management (ERIM), Erasmus University Rotterdam, The Netherlands.

Asmild, M., & Pastor, J. T. (2010). Slack free MEA and RDM with comprehensive efficiency measures. *Omega, 38*, 475–483.

Asmild, M., Paradi, J. C., Reese, D. N., & Tam, F. (2007). Measuring overall efficiency and effectiveness using DEA. *European Journal of Operational Research, 178*(1), 305–321.

Atkinson, S. E., & Tsionas, M. G. (2016). Directional distance functions: Optimal endogenous directions. *Journal of Econometrics, 190*(2), 301–314.

Baek, C., & Lee, J. (2009). The relevance of DEA benchmarking information and the least-distance measure. *Mathematical and Computer Modelling, 49*, 265–275.

Balk, B. M. (1998). *Industrial price, quantity, and productivity indices: The micro-economic theory and an application*. Kluwer Academic Publishers.

Balk, B. M. (2003). The residual: On monitoring and benchmarking firms, industries, and economies with respect to productivity. *Journal of Productivity Analysis, 20*(1), 5–47.

Balk, B. M. (2008). *Price and quantity index numbers: Models for measuring aggregate change and difference*. Cambridge University Press.

Balk, B. M. (2018). Profit-oriented productivity change: A comment. *Omega, 78*, 176–178.

Balk, B. M., & Zofío, J. L. (2018). *The many decompositions of Total factor productivity change. ERIM report series research in management*, no. ERS-2018-003-LIS. Erasmus Research Institute of Management, Erasmus University, Rotterdam. Available from http://hdl.handle.net/1765/104721.

Balk, B. M., & Zofío, J. L. (2020). Symmetric decompositions of cost variation. Forthcoming in the *European Journal of Operational Research.*

Balk, B. M., Färe, R., Grosskopf, S., & Margaritis, D. (2008). Exact relations between Luenberger productivity indicators and Malmquist productivity indexes. *Economic Theory, 35*(1), 187–190.

Balk, B. M., De Koster, M. B. M., Kaps, C., & Zofío, J. L. (2021). An evaluation of cross-efficiency methods: With an application to warehouse performance. *Applied Mathematics and Computation, 406*, 126261.

Banker, R. D., & Thrall, R. M. (1992). Estimation of returns to scale using data envelopment analysis. *European Journal of Operational Research, 62*(1), 74–84.

Banker, R. D., Charnes, A., & Cooper, W. W. (1984). Some models for estimating technical and scale inefficiencies in data envelopment analysis. *Management Science, 30*(9), 1078–1092.

Beattie, B. R., Taylor, C. R., & Watts, M. J. (2009). *The economics of production* (2nd ed.). Krieger Publishing.

Bezanson, J., Edelman, A., Karpinski, S., & Shah, V. B. (2017). Julia: A fresh approach to numerical computing. *SIAM Review, 59*(1), 65–98.

Blackorby, C., & Diewert, W. E. (1979). Expenditure functions, local duality, and second order approximations. *Econometrica, 47*(3), 579–602.

Bogetoft, P., & Hougaard, J. L. (1999). Efficiency evaluations based on potential (nonproportional). Improvements. *Journal of Productivity Analysis, 12*(3), 233–247.

Bogetoft, P., & Hougaard, J. L. (2003). Rational inefficiency. *Journal of Productivity Analysis, 20*, 243–271.

Bogetoft, P., & Otto, L. (2011). *Benchmarking with DEA, SFA, and R*. Springer.

Bogetoft, P., Färe, R., & Obel, B. (2006). Allocative efficiency of technically inefficient production units. *European Journal of Operational Research, 168*(2), 450–462.

Bol, G. (1986). On technical efficiency measures. *Journal of Economic Theory, 38*, 380–385.

Boles, J. N. (1967). Efficiency squared-efficient computation of efficiency indexes. In *Western farm economic association, proceedings 1966* (pp. 137–142). Pullman.

Boles, J. N. (1971, February). *The 1130 Farrell efficiency system-multiple products, multiple factors*. Giannini Foundation of Agricultural Economics.

Boussemart, J. P., Briec, W., Kerstens, K., & Poutineau, J. C. (2003). Luenberger and Malmquist productivity indices: Theoretical comparisons and empirical illustration. *Bulletin of Economic Research, 55*(4), 391–405.

Boussemart, J.-P., Briec, W., Peypoch, N., & Tavéra, C. (2009). α-Returns to scale in multi-output technologies. *European Journal of Operational Research, 197*(1), 332–339.

Briec, W. (1997). A graph-type extension of Farrell technical efficiency measure. *Journal of Productivity Analysis, 8*(1), 95–110.

Briec, W. (1998). Hölder distance function and measurement of technical efficiency. *Journal of Productivity Analysis, 11*, 111–131.

Briec, W., & Leleu, H. (2003). Dual representations of non-parametric technologies and measurement of technical efficiency. *Journal of Productivity Analysis, 20*, 71–96.

Briec, W., & Lemaire, B. (1999). Technical efficiency and distance to a reverse convex set. *European Journal of Operational Research, 114*, 178–187.

Briec, W., & Lesourd, J. B. (1999). Metric distance function and profit: Some duality results. *Journal of Optimization Theory and Applications, 101*(1), 15–33.

Briec, W., Kerstens, K., & Peypoch, N. (2012). Exact relations between four definitions of productivity indices a indicators. *Bulleting of Economic Research, 64*(2), 265–274.

Briec, W., Kerstens, K., & Van de Woestyne, I. (2021) Nonconvexity in production and cost. Functions: An exploratory and selective review. Forthcoming in *Annals of Operations Research*.

Camanho, A. S., & Dyson, R. G. (2008). A generalisation of the Farrell cost efficiency measure applicable to non-fully competitive settings. *Omega, 36*, 147–162.

Caves, D. W., Christensen, L. R., & Diewert, W. E. (1982). The economic theory of index numbers and the measurement of input, output, and productivity. *Econometrica, 50*, 1393–1414.

Chambers, R. G. (1988). *Applied production analysis: A dual approach*. Cambridge University Press.

Chambers, R. G., & Mitchell, T. (2001). Homotheticity and non-radial changes. *Journal of Productivity Analysis, 15*(1), 31–39.

Chambers, R. G., & Pope, R. D. (1996). Aggregate productivity measures. *American Journal of Agricultural Economics, 78*(5), 1360–1365.

Chambers, R. G., Chung, Y., & Färe, R. (1996, August). Benefit and distance functions. *Journal of Economic Theory, 70*(2), 407–419.

Chambers, R. G., Färe, R., & Grosskopf, S. (1996b). Productivity growth in APEC countries. *Pacific Economic Review, 1*(3), 181–190.

Chambers, R. G., Chung, Y., & Färe, R. (1998, August). Profit, directional distance functions, and Nerlovian efficiency. *Journal of Optimization Theory and Applications, 98*(2), 351–364.

Charnes, A., & Cooper, W. W. (1962). Programming with linear fractional functionals. *Naval Research Logistics Quarterly, 9*(3–4), 181–186.

Charnes, A., Cooper, W. W., & Ferguson, R. (1955). Optimal estimation of executive compensation by linear programming. *Management Science, 1*, 138–151.

Charnes, A., Cooper, W. W., & Rhodes, E. (1978). Measuring the efficiency of decision making units. *European Journal of Operational Research, 2*, 429–444.

Charnes, A., Cooper, W. W., Golany, B., Seiford, L. M., & Stutz, J. (1985). Foundations of data envelopment analysis for Pareto-Koopmans efficient empirical production functions. *Journal of Econometrics, 30*(1–2), 91–107.

Charnes, A., Rousseau, J. J., & Semple, J. H. (1996). Sensitivity and stability of efficiency classifications in data envelopment analysis. *Journal of Productivity Analysis, 7*(1), 5–18.

Chavas, J.-P., & Cox, T. L. (1999, October). A generalized distance function and the analysis of production efficiency. *Southern Economic Journal, 66*(2), 294–318.

Cherchye, L., & Van Puyenbroeck, T. (2001). A comment on multi-stage DEA methodology. *Operations Research Letters, 28*, 93–98.

Cherchye, L., Kuosmanen, T., & Post, T. (2000). What is the economic meaning of FDH? A reply to Thrall. *Journal of Productivity Analysis, 13*(3), 259–263.

Cherchye, L., De Rock, B., & Walheer, B. (2015). Multi-output efficiency with good and bad outputs. *European Journal of Operational Research, 240*, 872–881.

Choi, Y., Zhang, N., & Zhou, P. (2012). Efficiency and abatement costs of energy-related CO2 emissions in China: A slacks-based efficiency measure. *Applied Energy, 98*, 198–208.

Chung, Y. (1996). *Directional distance functions and undesirable outputs*. Ph.D. dissertation, Southern Illinois University at Carbondale.

Coelli, T. (1998). A multi-stage methodology for the solution of orientated DEA models. *Operations Research Letters, 23*(3–5), 143–149.

Colson, B., Marcotte, P., & Savard, G. (2007). An overview of Bilevel optimization. *Annals of Operations Research, 153*(1), 235–256.

Cook, W. D., & Hababou, M. (2001). Sales performance measurement in bank branches. *Omega, 29*(4), 299–307.

Cooper, W. W., & Pastor, J. T. (1995). *Global efficiency measurement in DEA*. Working paper. Depto. de Estadística e Investigación Operativa, Universidad de Alicante, Alicante, Spain.

Cooper, W. W., Park, K. S., & Pastor, J. T. (1999). RAM: A range adjusted measure of inefficiency for use with additive models, and relations to others models and measures in DEA. *Journal of Productivity Analysis, 11*, 5–42.

Cooper, W., Seiford, L., & Tone, K. (2007). *Data envelopment analysis. A comprehensive text with models, applications, references and DEA-software* (2nd ed.). Kluwer.

Cooper, W. W., Pastor, J. T., Borras, F., Aparicio, J., & Pastor, D. (2011a). BAM: A bounded adjusted measure of efficiency for use with bounded additive models. *Journal of Productivity Analysis, 35*(2), 85–94.

Cooper, W. W., Pastor, J. T., Aparicio, J., & Borras, F. (2011b). Decomposing profit inefficiency in DEA through the weighted additive model. *European Journal of Operational Research, 212*(2), 411–416.

Cuesta, R. A., & Zofío, J. L. (2005). Hyperbolic efficiency and parametric distance functions: With application to Spanish savings banks. *Journal of Productivity Analysis, 24*(1), 31–48.

Cuesta, R. A., Lovell, C. A. K., & Zofío, J. L. (2009). Environmental efficiency measurement with Translog distance functions. *Ecological Economics, 68*, 2232–2242.

Dakpo, K. H., Jeanneaux, P., & Latruffe, L. (2016). Modelling pollution-generating technologies in performance benchmarking: Recent developments, limits and future prospects in the nonparametric framework. *European Journal of Operational Research, 250*(2), 347–359.

Daraio, C., Kerstens, K., Nepomuceno, T., & Sickles, R. C. (2019). Productivity and efficiency analysis software: An exploratory bibliographical survey of the options. *Journal of Economic Surveys, 33*, 85–100.

Daraio, C., & Simar, L. (2007). *Advanced robust and nonparametric methods in efficiency analysis*. Springer.

Debreu, G. (1951, July). The coefficient of resource utilization. *Econometrica, 19*(3), 273–292.

Deprins, D., Simar, L., & Tulkens, H. (1984). Measuring labor inefficiency in post offices. In M. Marchand, P. Pestieau, & H. Tulkens (Eds.), *The performance of public enterprises: Concepts and measurements* (pp. 243–267). North-Holland.

Diewert, W. E. (1971). An application of the Shephard duality theorem: A generalized Leontief production function. *Journal of Political Economy, 79*(3), 481–507.

Diewert, W. E. (1974). Applications of duality theory. In M. Intriligator & D. A. Kendrick (Eds.), *Frontiers of quantitative economics* (Vol. II, pp. 106–206). North-Holland.

Diewert, W. E. (2005). Index number theory using differences rather than ratios. *The American Journal of Economics and Sociology, 64*(1), 311–360.

Diewert, W. E. (2014). Decompositions of profitability change using cost functions. *Journal of Econometrics, 183*(1), 58–66.

Dmitruk, V., & Koshevoy, G. A. (1991). On the existence of a technical efficiency criterion. *Journal of Economic Theory, 55*, 121–144.

Dunning, I., Huchette, J., & Lubin, M. (2017). JuMP: A Modeling language for mathematical optimization. *SIAM Review, 59*(2), 295–320.

Econometric Software Inc. (2014). *LIMDEP 11*. Plainview. http://www.limdep.com/.

Emrouznejad, A., & Cabanda, E. (Eds.). (2014). *Managing service productivity: Using frontier efficiency methodologies and multicriteria decision making for improving service performance*. Springer.

Färe, R. (1988). *Fundamentals of production theory*. Springer.

Färe, R., & Grosskopf, S. (1996). *Intertemporal production Frontiers: With dynamic DEA*. Kluwer Academic Publishers.

Färe, R., & Grosskopf, S. (2000). Theory and application of directional distance functions. *Journal of Productivity Analysis, 13*, 93–103.

Färe, R., & Lovell, C. K. (1978). Measuring the technical efficiency of production. *Journal of Economic Theory, 19*(1), 150–162.

Färe, R., & Primont, D. (1995). *Multi-output production and duality: Theory and applications*. Kluwer Academic Publishers.

Färe, R., Grosskopf, S., & Lovell, C. A. K. (1985). *The measurement of efficiency of production*. Kluwer-Nijhoff.

Färe, R., Grosskopf, S., Lovell, C. A., & Pasurka, C. (1989). Multilateral productivity comparisons when some outputs are undesirable: A nonparametric approach. *The Review of Economics and Statistics, 71*(1), 90–98.

Färe, R., Grosskopf, S., & Lovell, C. A. K. (1994). *Production frontiers*. Cambridge University Press.

Färe, R., Grosskopf, S., & Zaim, O. (2002). Hyperbolic efficiency and return to dollar. *European Journal of Operational Research, 136*, 671–679.

Färe, R., Grosskopf, S., & Zelenyuk, V. (2007). Finding common ground: Efficiency indices. In *Aggregation, efficiency, and measurement* (pp. 83–95). Springer.

Färe, R., Margaritis, D., Rouse, P., & Roshdi, I. (2016). Estimating the hyperbolic distance function: A directional distance function approach. *European Journal of Operational Research, 254*, 312–319.

Färe, R., He, X., Li, S., & Zelenyuk, V. (2019). A unifying framework for Farrell profit efficiency measurement. *Operations Research, 67*(1), 183–197.

Farrell, M. J. (1957). The measurement of productive efficiency. *Journal of Royal Statistical Society, Series A, 120*(III), 253–290.

Farrell, M. J., & Fieldhouse, M. (1962). Estimating efficient production functions under increasing returns to scale. *Journal of the Royal Statistical Society: Series A (General), 125*(2), 252–267.

Fenchel, W. (1949). On conjugate convex functions. *Canadian Journal of Mathematics, 1*(1), 73–77.

Førsund, F. R., & Sarafoglou, N. (2002). On the origins of data envelopment analysis. *Journal of Productivity Analysis, 17*(1–2), 23–40.

Fox, K. (2018). The ET interview: Professor W. Erwin Diewert. *Econometric Theory, 34*, 509–542.

Frei, F. X., & Harker, P. T. (1999). Projections onto efficient frontiers: Theoretical and computational extensions to DEA. *Journal of Productivity Analysis, 11*, 275–300.

Fried, H. O., Knox Lovell, C. A., & Schmidt, S. S. (2008). *The measurement of productive efficiency and productivity growth*. Oxford University Press.

Fukuyama, H., & Weber, W. L. (2009). A directional slacks-based measure of technical inefficiency. *Socio-Economic Planning Sciences, 43*(4), 274–287.

Fukuyama, H., Maeda, Y., Sekitani, K., & Shi, J. (2014a). Input-output substitutability and strongly monotonic p-norm least-distance DEA measures. *European Journal of Operational Research, 237*, 997–1007.

Fukuyama, H., Masaki, H., Sekitani, K., & Shi, J. (2014b). Distance optimization approach to ratio-form efficiency measures in data envelopment analysis. *Journal of Productivity Analysis, 42*, 175–186.

Fukuyama, H., Hougaard, J. L., Sekitani, K., & Shi, J. (2016). Efficiency measurement with a non-convex free disposal hull technology. *Journal of the Operational Research Society, 67*(1), 9–19.

Georgescu-Roegen, N. (1951). The aggregate linear production function and its application to von Neumann's economic model. In T. Koopmans (Ed.), *Activity analysis of production and allocation* (pp. 116–131). Wiley, New York.

Gonzalez, E., & Alvarez, A. (2001). From efficiency measurement to efficiency improvement: The choice of a relevant benchmark. *European Journal of Operational Research, 133*, 512–520.

Greene, W. (2008). The econometric approach to efficiency analysis. In H. Fried, C. A. Lovell, & S. S. Schmidt (Eds.), *The measurement of productive efficiency and productivity growth*. Oxford University Press.

Grifell-Tatjé, E., & Knox Lovell, C. A. (2015). *Productivity accounting: The economics of business performance*. Cambridge University Press.

Grifell-Tatjé, E., Lovell, C. A. K., & Pastor, J. T. (1998). A Quasi-Malmquist productivity index. *Journal of Productivity Analysis, 10*, 7–20.

Grosskopf, S. (1986). The role of the reference technology in measuring productive efficiency. *The Economic Journal, 96*(382), 499–513.

Gurobi. (2021). *Gurobi optimizer reference manual: Version 9.1*. Gurobi Optimization.

Hailu, A., & Veeman, T. S. (2001). Non-parametric productivity analysis with undesirable outputs: An application to the Canadian pulp and paper industry. *American Journal of Agricultural Economics, 83*, 605–616.

Halická, M., & Trnovská, M. (2018). The Russell measure model: Computational aspects, duality, and profit efficiency. *European Journal of Operational Research, 268*(1), 386–397.

Halická, M., & Trnovská, M. (2019). Duality and profit efficiency for the hyperbolic measure model. *European Journal of Operational Research, 278*(2), 410–421.

Halická, M., & Trnovská, M. (2021). A unified approach to non-radial graph models in data envelopment analysis: Common features, geometry, and duality. *European Journal of Operational Research, 289*(2), 611–627.

Jiménez-Sáez, F., Zabala-Iturriagagoitia, J. M., Zofío, J. L., & Castro-Martinez, E. (2011). Evaluating research efficiency within National R&D Programs. *Research Policy, 40*, 230–241.

Jiménez-Sáez, F., Zabala-Iturriagagoitia, J. M., & Zofío, J. L. (2013). Who leads research productivity growth? Guidelines for R&D policy-makers. *Scientometrics, 94*, 273–303.

Johnson, A. L., & Kuosmanen, T. (2015). An introduction to CNLS and StoNED methods for efficiency analysis: Economic insights and computational aspects. In Ray, S. C., Kumbhakar, S. & Dua, P. (eds.), Benchmarking for Performance Evaluation, Springer, New Delhi, 117–186.

Johnson, A. L., & McGinnis, L. F. (2009). The hyperbolic-oriented efficiency measure as a remedy to infeasibility of super efficiency models. *Journal of the Operational Research Society, 60*(11), 1511–1517.

Juo, J.-C., Fu, T.-T., Yu, M.-M., & Lin, Y.-H. (2015). Profit-oriented productivity change. *Omega, 57*, 176–187.

Kendrick, J. W. (1984). *Improving company productivity: Handbook with case studies*. Johns Hopkins University Press.

Kleine, A. (2004). A general model framework for DEA. *Omega, 32*(1), 17–23.

Koopmans, T. C. (1951). An analysis of production as an efficient combination of activities. In T. C. Koopmans (Ed.), *Activity analysis of production and allocation, Cowles Commission for research in economics, monograph N° 13*. Wiley.

Kopp, R. J. (1981). Measuring the technical efficiency of production: A comment. *Journal of Economic Theory, 25*(3), 450–452.

Kopp, R. J., & Diewert, W. E. (1982). The decomposition of frontier cost function deviations into measures of technical and allocative efficiency. *Journal of Econometrics, 19*, 319–331.

Kousmanen, T. (2013). Duality theory of non-convex technologies. *Journal of Productivity Analysis, 20*, 273–304.

Kumbhakar, S. C., & Dua, P. (Eds.). *Benchmarking for performance evaluation: A production frontier approach*. Springer.

Kumbhakar, S. C., & Lovell, C. A. (2000). *Stochastic frontier analysis*. Cambridge University Press.

Kumbhakar, S. C., Orea, L., Rodríguez-Álvarez, A., & Tsionas, M. G. (2007). Do we have to estimate an input or an output distance function? An application of the mixture approach to European Railways. *Journal of Productivity Analysis, 27*(2), 87–100.

Kumbhakar, S. C., Hung-Jen, W., & Horncastle, A. P. (2015). *A practitioner's guide to stochastic frontier analysis using Stata*. Cambridge University Press.

Kuosmanen, T. (2003). Duality theory of non-convex technologies. *Journal of Productivity Analysis, 20*, 273–304.

Kuosmanen, T., Kortelainen, M., Sipiläinen, T., & Cherchye, L. (2010). Firm and industry level profit efficiency analysis using absolute and uniform shadow prices. *European Journal of Operational Research, 202*(2), 584–594.

Lau, L. J. (1972). Profit functions of technologies with multiple inputs and outputs. *Review of Economics and Statistics, 54*, 281–289.

Leleu, H., & Briec, W. (2009). A DEA estimation of a lower bound for firms' allocative efficiency without information on Price data. *International Journal of Production Economics, 121*, 203–211.

Lovell, C. A. K., & Pastor, J. T. (1995). Units invariant and translation invariant DEA models. *Operations Research Letters, 18*, 147–151.

Lovell, C. K., Pastor, J. T., & Turner, J. A. (1995). Measuring macroeconomic performance in the OECD: A comparison of European and non-European countries. *European Journal of Operational Research, 87*(3), 507–518.

Lozano, S., & Villa, G. (2005). Determining a sequence of targets in DEA. *Journal of Operational Research Society, 56*, 1439–1447.

Luenberger, D. G. (1992a). Benefit functions and duality. *Journal of Mathematical Economics, 21*, 461–481.

Luenberger, D. G. (1992b). New optimality principles for economic efficiency and equilibrium. *Journal of Optimization Theory and Applications, 75*, 221–264.

Madden, P. (1986). *Concavity and optimization in microeconomics*. Blackwell Publishers.

Mahler, K. (1939). Ein übertragungsprinzip für konvexe körper. *Časopis pro pěstování matematiky a fysiky, 68*(3), 93–102.

Malmquist, S. (1953). Index numbers and indifference surfaces. *Trabajos de Estadística, 4*(1), 209–242.

Mangasarian, O. L. (1994). *Nonlinear programming* (Vol. 10 of Classics in applied mathematics). SIAM.

Mangasarian, O. L. (1999). Arbitrary-norm separating plane. *Operations Research Letters, 24*, 15–23.

McFadden, D. (1978). Cost, revenue, and profit functions. In M. Fuss & D. McFadden (Eds.), *Production economics: A dual approach to theory and applications*. North-Holland.

Minkowski, M. (1911). Zur physiologie der Sehsphäre. *Pflüger's Archiv für die gesamte Physiologie des Menschen und der Tiere, 141*(4), 171–327.

MirHassani, S. A., & Alirezaee, M. (2005). An efficient approach for computing non-Archimedean ε in DEA based on integrated models. *Applied Mathematics and Computation, 166*(2), 449–456.

Morrison, C. J. (1993). *A microeconomic approach to the measurement of economic performance: Productivity growth, capacity utilization, and related performance indicators*. Springer.

Nerlove, M. (1965). *Estimation and identification of Cobb-Douglas production functions*. Rand McNally.

O'Donnell, C. J. (2008). *An aggregate quantity-price framework for measuring and decomposing productivity and profitability change*. Centre for Efficiency and Productivity Analysis Working Papers WP07/2008. University of Queensland, Queensland.

O'Donnell, C. J. (2012). An aggregate quantity framework for measuring and decomposing productivity change. *Journal of Productivity Analysis, 38*, 255–272.

Parmeter, C. F., & Kumbhakar, S. C. (2014). Efficiency analysis: A primer on recent advances. *Foundations and Trends in Econometrics, 7*(3–4), 191–385.

Pastor, J. T. (1996). Translation invariance in DEA: A generalization. *Annals of Operations Research, 66*(2), 91–102.

Pastor, J. T., & Aparicio, J. (2010). Distance functions and efficiency measurement. *Indian Economic Review, 45*(2), 193–231.

Pastor, J. T., Ruiz, J. L., & Sirvent, I. (1999). An enhanced DEA Russell graph efficiency measure. *European Journal of Operational Research, 115*(3), 596–607.

Pastor, J. T., Lovell, C. K., & Aparicio, J. (2012). Families of linear efficiency programs based on Debreu's loss function. *Journal of Productivity Analysis, 38*(2), 109–120.

Pastor, J. T., Aparicio, J., Alcaraz, J., Vidal, F., & Pastor, D. (2015). An enhanced BAM for unbounded or partially bounded CRS additive models. *Omega, 56*, 16–24.

Pastor, J. T., Aparicio, J., Alcaraz, J., Vidal, F., & Pastor, D. (2016). The reverse directional distance function. In *Advances in efficiency and productivity* (pp. 15–57). Springer.

Pastor, J. T., Lovell, C. A. K., & Aparicio, J. (2020). Defining a new graph inefficiency measure for the proportional directional distance function and introducing a new Malmquist productivity index. *European Journal of Operational Research, 281*(1), 222–230.

Pastor, J. T., Zofío, J. L., Aparicio, J., & Pastor, D. (2021a). *A new general direct approach for decomposing economic inefficiency*. Working paper. Erasmus Research Institute of Management (ERIM), Erasmus University Rotterdam, The Netherlands.

Pastor, J. T., Aparicio, J., Zofío, J. L., & Borrás, F. (2021b). *The standard reverse approach for decomposing economic inefficiency considering market conditions*. Working paper. Erasmus Research Institute of Management (ERIM), Erasmus University Rotterdam, The Netherlands.

Pastor, J. T., Zofío, J. L., Aparicio, J., & Alcaraz, J. (2021c). *The flexible reverse approach for decomposing economic inefficiency considering market conditions*. Working paper. Erasmus Research Institute of Management (ERIM), Erasmus University Rotterdam, The Netherlands.

Petersen, N. C. (2018). Directional distance functions in DEA with optimal endogenous directions. *Operations Research, 66*(4), 1068–1085.

Petersen, N. C. (2020). Units of measurement and directional distance functions with optimal endogenous directions in data envelopment analysis. *European Journal of Operational Research, 282*(2), 712–728.

Podinovski, V. V. (2015). DEA models with production trade-offs and weight restrictions. In J. Zhu (Ed.), *Data envelopment analysis: A handbook of models and methods* (pp. 105–144). Springer.

Portela, M. C. A. S., & Thanassoulis, E. (2014). Economic efficiency when prices are not fixed: Disentangling quantity and price efficiency. *Omega, 47*, 36–44.

Portela, M. C. A. S., Castro, P., & Thanassoulis, E. (2003). Finding closest targets in non-oriented DEA models: The case of convex and non-convex technologies. *Journal of Productivity Analysis, 19*, 251–269.

Portela, M. S., Thanassoulis, E., & Simpson, G. (2004). Negative data in DEA: A directional distance approach applied to bank branches. *Journal of the Operational Research Society, 55* (10), 1111–1121.

Prieto, A. M., & Zofio, J. L. (2001). Evaluating effectiveness in public provision of infrastructure and equipment: The case of Spanish municipalities. *Journal of Productivity Analysis, 15*(1), 41–58.

Ray, S. C. (2004). *Data envelopment analysis. Theory and techniques for economics and operations research*. Cambridge University Press.

Rockafellar, R. T. (1972). *Convex analysis second printing*. Princeton University Press.

Ruiz, J. L., & Sirvent, I. (2011). A DEA approach to derive individual lower and upper bounds for the technical and allocative components of the overall profit efficiency. *Journal of the Operational Research Society, 62*(11), 1907–1916.

Russell, R. R. (1985). Measures of technical efficiency. *Journal of Economic Theory, 35*(1), 109–126.

Russell, R. R. (1988). On the axiomatic approach to the measurement of technical efficiency. In *Measurement in economics* (pp. 207–217). Physica.

Russell, R. R., & Schworm, W. (2009). Axiomatic foundations of efficiency measurement on data-generated technologies. *Journal of Productivity Analysis, 31*, 77–86.

Russell, R. R., & Schworm, W. (2011). Properties of inefficiency indexes on <input, output> space. *Journal of Productivity Analysis, 36*, 143–156.

Russell, R. R., & Schworm, W. (2018). Technological inefficiency indexes: A binary taxonomy and a generic theorem. *Journal of Productivity Analysis, 49*, 17–23.

Sealey, C. W., Jr., & Lindley, J. T. (1977). Inputs, outputs, and a theory of production and cost at depository financial institutions. *The Journal of Finance, 32*(4), 1251–1266.

Seiford, L. M., & Zhu, J. (2002). Modeling undesirable factors in efficiency evaluation. *European Journal of Operational Research, 142*(1), 16–20.

Ševčovič, D., Halická, M., & Brunovský, P. (2001). DEA analysis for a large structured bank branch network. *Central European Journal of Operations Research, 9*(4), 329–343.

Sexton, T. R., Silkman, R. H., & Hogan, A. J. (1986). Data envelopment analysis: Critique and extension. In R. H. Silkman (Ed.), *New directions for program evaluation*. Jossey-Bass.

Sharp, J. A., Meng, W., & Liu, W. (2007). A modified slacks-based measure model for data envelopment analysis with 'natural' negative outputs and inputs. *Journal of the Operational Research Society, 58*, 1672–1677.

Sheel, H. (2000). *EMS: Efficiency measurement system user's manual*. University of Dortmund.

Shephard, R. W. (1953). *Cost and production functions*. Princeton University Press.

Shephard, R. W. (1970). *Theory of cost and production functions*. Princeton University Press.

Sherman, H., & Zhu, J. (2006). *Service productivity management: Improving service productivity using data envelopment analysis (DEA)*. Springer.

Simar, L., & Wilson, P. W. (2007). Estimation and inference in two-stage, semi-parametric models of production processes. *Journal of Econometrics, 136*(1), 31–64.

Smith, I. G. (1973). *The measurement of productivity: A systems approach in the context of Productivity agreements*. Gower Press.

Sueyoshi, T., & Sekitani, K. (2007a). Computational strategy for Russell measure in DEA: Second-order cone programming. *European Journal of Operational Research, 180*(1), 459–471.

Sueyoshi, T., & Sekitani, K. (2007b). Measurement of returns to scale using a non-radial DEA model: A range-adjusted measure approach. *European Journal of Operational Research, 176* (3), 1918–1946.

Suzuki, S., Nijkamp, P., Rietveld, P., & Pels, E. (2010). A distance friction minimization approach in data envelopment analysis: A comparative study on airport efficiency. *European Journal of Operational Research, 207*(2), 1104–1115.

ten Raa, T. (2008). Debreu's coefficient of resource utilization, the Solow residual, and TFP: The connection by Leontief preferences. *Journal of Productivity Analysis, 30*, 191–199.

Thompson, R. G., Singleton, F. D., Thrall, R. M., & Smith, B. A. (1986). Comparative site evaluations for locating a high-energy physics lab in Texas. *Interfaces, 16*, 35–49.

Thrall, R. M. (1999). What is the economic meaning of FDH? *Journal of Productivity Analysis, 11* (3), 243–250.

Tone, K. (2001). A slacks-based measure of efficiency in data envelopment analysis. *European Journal of Operational Research, 130*(3), 498–509.

Tone, K. (2004). Malmquist productivity index. In *Handbook on data envelopment analysis* (pp. 203–227). Springer.

Tone, K., & Tsutsui, M. (2009). Network DEA: A slacks-based measure approach. *European Journal of Operational Research, 197*(1), 243–252.

Tone, K., & Tsutsui, M. (2010). Dynamic DEA: A slacks-based measure approach. *Omega, 38* (3–4), 145–156.

Tone, K., & Tsutsui, M. (2014). Dynamic DEA with network structure: A slacks-based measure approach. *Omega, 42*(1), 124–131.

Tone, K., Chang, T. S., & Wu, C. H. (2020). Handling negative data in slacks-based measure data envelopment analysis models. *European Journal of Operational Research, 282*(3), 926–935.

Vickers, J. (1995). *Entry and competitive selection*. Working paper. Institute of Economics and Statistics, Oxford University.

Wächter, A., & Biegler, L. T. (2006). On the implementation of a primal-dual interior point filter line search algorithm for large-scale nonlinear programming. *Mathematical Programming, 106*, 25–57.

Wang, K., Xian, Y., Lee, C. Y., Wei, Y. M., & Huang, Z. (2019). On selecting directions for directional distance functions in a non-parametric framework: A review. *Annals of Operations Research, 278*(1), 43–76.

Wei, Q., & Yu, G. (1997). Analyzing properties of K-cones in the generalized data envelopment analysis model. *Journal of Econometrics, 80*(1), 63–84.

Wei, Q., Yan, H., & Xiong, L. (2008). A bi-objective generalized data envelopment analysis model and point-to-set mapping projection. *European Journal of Operational Research, 190*(3), 855–876.

Wheelock, D. C., & Wilson, P. W. (2009). Robust nonparametric quantile estimation of efficiency and productivity change in U.S. commercial banking, 1985-2004. *Journal of Business and Economic Statistics, 27*(3), 354–368.

Wilson, P. W. (2008). FEAR: A software package for frontier efficiency analysis with R. *Socio-Economic Planning Sciences, 42*(4), 247–254.

Yu, M. M., & Lee, B. C. Y. (2009). Efficiency and effectiveness of service business: Evidence from international tourist hotels in Taiwan. *Tourism Management, 30*(4), 571–580.

Yu, G., Wei, Q., & Brockett, P. (1996a). A generalized data envelopment analysis model: A unification and extension of existing methods for efficiency analysis of decision making units. *Annals of Operations Research, 66*(1), 47–89.

Yu, G., Wei, Q., Brockett, P., & Zhou, L. (1996b). Construction of all DEA efficient surfaces of the production possibility set under the generalized data envelopment analysis model. *European Journal of Operational Research, 95*(3), 491–510.

Yun, Y. B., Nakayama, H., & Tanino, T. (2004). A generalized model for data envelopment analysis. *European Journal of Operational Research, 157*(1), 87–105.

Zaim, O., & Taskin, F. (2000). Environmental efficiency in carbon dioxide emissions in the OECD: A non-parametric approach. *Journal of Environmental Management, 58*(2), 95–107.

Zhu, J. (2014). Models for evaluating supply chains and network structures. In J. Zhu (Ed.), *Quantitative models for performance evaluation and benchmarking data envelopment analysis with spreadsheets* (3rd ed., pp. 311–344). Springer.

Zieschang, K. D. (1984). An extended Farrell technical efficiency measure. *Journal of Economic Theory, 33*(2), 387–396.

Zofio, J. L., & Knox Lovell, C. A. (2001). Graph efficiency and productivity measures: An application to US agriculture. *Applied Economics, 33*(11), 1433–1442.

Zofio, J. L., & Prieto, A. M. (2001). Environmental efficiency and regulatory standards: The case of CO2 emissions from OECD industries. *Resource and Energy Economics, 23*(1), 63–83.

Zofio, J. L., & Prieto, A. M. (2006). Return to dollar, generalized distance function and the fisher productivity index. *Spanish Economic Review, 8*(2), 113–138.

Zofio, J. L., Pastor, J. T., & Aparicio, J. (2013). The directional profit efficiency measure: On why profit inefficiency is either technical or allocative. *Journal of Productivity Analysis, 40*(3), 257–266.

Author Index

J. T. Pastor et al., *Benchmarking Economic Efficiency*, International Series in Operations Research & Management Science 315,
https://doi.org/10.1007/978-3-030-84397-7

Subject Index

J. T. Pastor et al., *Benchmarking Economic Efficiency*, International Series in Operations Research & Management Science 315,
https://doi.org/10.1007/978-3-030-84397-7

M

N

P

S

T